PRESENT

AT THE

CREATION

"Had I been present at the creation I would have given some useful hints for the better ordering of the universe."

—Alphonso X, the Learned,
1252–84, King of Spain

PRESENT

AT THE

CREATION

My Years in the State Department

DEAN ACHESON

W. W. NORTON & COMPANY
New York • London

For information about permission to reproduce selections from this
book, write to Permissions, W. W. Norton & Company, Inc.,
500 Fifth Avenue, New York, NY 10110

Maps by R. D. Palacios from the book *The Korean War,*
copyright © 1967 by Matthew B. Ridgway
Doubleday & Company, New York.

Library of Congress Catalog Card No. 69–14692

ISBN 978-0-393-30412-1 pbk.

W. W. Norton & Company, Inc., 500 Fifth Avenue, New York, N.Y. 10110
www.wwnorton.com

W. W. Norton & Company Ltd., 15 Carlisle Street, London W1D 3BS

TO HARRY S. TRUMAN

"The captain with the mighty heart"

CONTENTS

PART TWO: ACTION BEGINS

Under Secretary of State, August 1945–June 1947

PART THREE: YEARS OF RESPONSIBILITY
Secretary of State, 1949–1953
Section A. Decisions Were Made Fast in 1949

Section B. *Problems Came Faster in 1950*

Section C. *1951: Year of Troubles and Progress*

Section D. *1952: Success and Failure at the End*

PART FOUR: EPILOGUE

Retrospection in Tranquillity

APPENDICES

Photographs may be found following page 414

ACKNOWLEDGMENTS

WITHOUT THE indefatigable and scholarly help of three assistants who have been with me every step of the way through this book, the effort would have been beyond me. Mrs. Marina S. Finkelstein, now Editor of Publications of the Harvard Center for International Affairs, and Miss Corinne Lyman, at present on the faculty of Ohio Wesleyan University, took over the scholarly examination of innumerable documents that fell from me during twelve busy years like autumn leaves, fitting the account of an individual life into greater surrounding action and tracing the influence and reaction of each on the other. They thus laid the foundation for my work and then rendered equal assistance by reviewing it and holding me to what Honor Tracy's Irish priest might have called the straight and narrow path between truth and error.

Miss Barbara Evans has played once more in this our sixth book together her familiar role as the custodian of my papers, my memory, and my conscience. From the first deciphering of an exotic calligraphy to the last grooming of the proof, she has pursued the serpent of error like a female St. Patrick. My gratitude to these three invaluable colleagues is great indeed.

For all of us the correction of errant memory has been greatly aided by the kindness of former Secretary of State Dean Rusk and Dr. William Franklin, Director of the Historical Office of the Department of State. Assistance on matters too numerous to list was rendered also by Dr. Arthur Kogan, Donald J. Simon, and Wilmer P. Sparrow, all of the Department of State, and by their helpful and resourceful staffs. To all we are deeply grateful.

Due to the forethought and kindness of the late Dr. Robert Oppenheimer, Director of the Institute for Advanced Study at Princeton, a group of my colleagues in the State Department met at the Institute with him and me every other month during 1953 and 1954 to record our recollections of how the major foreign policies of President Truman's Administration came into being and our appraisal of the considerations that affected them and us. This group included Dean Rusk, W. Averell Harriman, Herbert Feis, Edward W. Barrett, Paul H. Nitze, Adrian S. Fisher, Joseph E. Johnson, George W. Perkins, and George C. McGhee, and (to stimulate and cross-examine us) McGeorge Bundy, then Dean of the Faculty of Arts and Sciences at Harvard, Dr. Edward M. Earle of the Institute, and Professors George A. Graham and Harold Sprout of Princeton University. These seminars added to the account of those times the essential factors of causation that the bare official record so rarely reveals.

APOLOGIA PRO LIBRE HOC

"Pen, ink and paper," John Adams confided to his diary in 1770, "and a sitting posture are great helps to attention and thinking."[1] I shall need them all in writing this book, which only five years ago I forswore. Why, I was then asked, "stop with the experiences of Morning and Noon? Why not go on to Afternoon, the time of larger events?" Because "detachment and objectivity" would become suspect. "The element of self-justification could not be excluded." It was all very simple, reasonable, and probably the right decision.

Yet I do go on. Why? Because I have changed my mind. The experiences of the years since I wrote have brought the country, and particularly its young people, to a mood of depression, disillusion, and withdrawal from the effort to affect the world around us. Today detachment and objectivity seem to me less important than to tell a tale of large conceptions, great achievements, and some failures, the product of enormous will and effort. Its hero is the American people, led by two men of rare quality, President Truman and General Marshall, served by lieutenants of whom I had the great good fortune to be one. The enormity of the task before all of them, after the wars in Europe and Asia ended in 1945, only slowly revealed itself. As it did so, it began to appear as just a bit less formidable than that described in the first chapter of Genesis. That was to create a world out of chaos; ours, to create half a world, a free half, out of the same material without blowing the whole to pieces in the process. The wonder of it is how much was done.

In the epigraph Alphonso X, King of Spain, is quoted to the effect that if he had been present at the creation he would have given some useful hints for the better ordering of the universe. In a sense the postwar years were a period of creation, for the ordering of which I shared with others some responsibility. Moreover, the state of the world in those years and almost all that happened during them was wholly novel within the experience of those who had to deal with it. "History," writes C. V. Wedgwood in her biography of William the Silent, "is lived forwards but it is written in retrospect. We know the end before we consider the beginning and we can never wholly recapture what it was to know the beginning only."[2] In a way, this volume is an attempt to do just that; for those who acted this drama did not know, nor do any of us yet know, the end.

DEAN ACHESON

I

YEARS OF LEARNING

Assistant Secretary of State, 1941–1945

1. ENLISTMENT FOR THE WAR TO COME

IN SEPTEMBER 1939, soon after war broke out in Europe, a bitter debate engulfed the United States. One side, led by an organization called the America First Committee, proclaimed traditional isolationist views. The other, which I joined, rallied around the Committee to Defend America by Aiding the Allies, founded by the salty editor of the *Emporia* (Kansas) *Gazette,* William Allen White. Soon I was involved in more than debate, helping to bring about the destroyer-bases agreement between this country and Britain and to write speeches in the White House for the 1940 campaign. All of this, which has been told in detail elsewhere,[1] led, in December 1940, to an invitation from Secretary of State Cordell Hull to leave my growing and pleasant law practice to join his Department as Assistant Secretary of State for Economic Affairs.

At that time I was forty-seven years old, in the middle of middle age, as Duff Cooper has defined the years from thirty to sixty. Neither the proffered office nor a return to the Roosevelt Administration held much appeal for me. I was no stranger to the latter. In 1933 I had served in it as Under Secretary of the Treasury—more accurately, as Acting Secretary due to Secretary Woodin's fatal illness—for six months until a spectacular row with the President and my resignation took me back to private life. Although the years that followed had brought reconciliation and generous attempts by the President to lure me back to public service, I had declined them.[2] My attitude toward the President was one of admiration without affection.†

However, the wars in Europe and Asia were fast moving, as I saw it, toward disaster for the United States as well as the allies. The President and a good part of the government and the country seemed to me to be paralyzed between apprehension and action. Without illusions, I resigned from a partnership to which I was deeply attached and on February 2, 1941, reported for duty as Assistant Secretary of State.

THE WORLD AROUND US

The period covered by this book—1941 through 1952—was one of great obscurity to those who lived through it. Not only was the future clouded, a common enough situation, but the present was equally clouded. We all had far more than the familiar difficulty of determining the capabilities and intentions of those who inhabit this planet with us. The significance of events was shrouded in ambiguity. We groped after interpretations of them, sometimes reversed lines of action based on earlier views, and hesitated long before grasping what now seems obvious. The period was marked by the disappearance of world powers and empires, or their reduction to medium-sized states, and from this wreckage emerged a multiplicity of states, most of them new, all of them largely undeveloped politically and economically. Overshadowing all loomed two dangers to all—the Soviet Union's new-found power and expansive imperialism, and the development of nuclear weapons.

Moreover, the real nature of the European and Asian wars in the midst of which we found ourselves was obscured both to us in the State Department and to our fellow citizens. Our very name for the cataclysm—the Second World War—showed incomprehension. It was not until after we had left office that that percipient observer, Desmond Donnelly, M.P., suggested a beginning of comprehension of the intrinsic nature of the whole period from 1914 to 1945 by his term, the "European Civil War."[3]

The European Civil War • In the hundred years from Waterloo to Mons so gradually did the power of Germany grow—that combination of population, resources, technology, and will—that, like the growth of a child, those close to it were hardly aware of its extent. Nor were they fully conscious of technological changes that affected the relative power of Germany and Russia. In 1814 the combined power of all Europe was barely able to stop the French bid for hegemony. A century later it was thought—erroneously, as it proved—that the combined power of Europe could stop the German bid. By 1917 it was clear that this could not be done; the United States intervened to prevent German domination of Europe.†

Hitler tried again from 1939 to 1945. Two German bids for dominance in Europe constituted a thirty-year death struggle, with a truce in the middle. The great empires of Europe destroyed one another and, in doing so, the European-dominated world of the nineteenth century. This book begins four years before the end of the European Civil War. By that time the Ottoman and Austro-Hungarian empires had disappeared altogether. The czarist empire had been replaced by the beleaguered, ruthless, powerful, and revolutionary Soviet dictatorship. France was defeated, disorganized, and occupied; her colonies in Asia were occupied by Japan, and in Africa were precariously held by Vichy. Britain, fighting gallantly, had bled near to death. Germany had lost her non-European colonies and possessions. She had, however, organized Europe as had not been done even by Napoleon. Hitler's will reigned from eastern Poland and Bessarabia to the Pyrenees and the Atlantic.

The Asian Civil War • Fair objection may be raised to Mr. Donnelly's phrase, the European Civil War, for ignoring the Asian Civil War, into which the United States was also drawn. The nineteenth century, which had seen such great development in Europe and America, produced the opposite result in China. There the impact of the West, and especially of its obstreperous offspring, Japan, disintegrated four millennia of civilization and the governmental system that had so well served this vast area and population. Finally the territorial integrity of the state itself dissolved.

Catholic missionaries had come to China from Europe as early as the six-teenth century, and the two areas were known to one another; but it was not until the eighteenth century that merchants followed in any number—the first American ship arrived toward the end of the century—and that Chinese art, architecture, and thought, as well as Chinese products imported by the East India companies, played a large and fashionable part in both Europe and America. At first the merchants were confined to Canton and to the "factories" there. The trials and frustrations of European attempts to negotiate with Chinese authorities are graphically told in Maurice Collis' book, *Foreign Mud*[4] (the Chinese name for opium), an account of Lord Napier's negotiations at Canton in the 1830s.

Soon the "barbarians" from the West and from Japan, finding the Celestial Empire too resistant to penetration through negotiation, resorted to five wars in a century to obtain their treaty ports, settlements, concessions, capitulations, and spheres of influence. New ideas, brought to China by hosts of returning students and through busy financial and industrial centers like Shanghai and Hong Kong, undermined the old ways and old loyalties. On the death of the Empress Dowager in 1911, the tottering Manchu Empire collapsed at the push of revolution. Five more years of effort by Yuan Shih-kai to hold China together as a republic collapsed with his death in 1916. After four thousand years the greatest agglomeration of territory and people ever governed by man dissolved into a geographical expression ready for some new master or masters to conquer in whole or in parts, as opportunity offered.

The Japanese stood ready to seize such an opportunity while others were busy elsewhere. After their military defeat of Russia in the Far East in 1904 they succeeded to Russian interests in southern Manchuria and Korea, annexing the latter five years later. Further opportunity came during the opening phase of the European Civil War to seize the Shantung Peninsula from the Germans. Then the United States made a major mistake. Charles Evans Hughes was a gifted man, but his reputation as a Justice and Chief Justice of the United States Supreme Court is likely to be rated higher than as a Secretary of State. At the Washington Conference of 1921, in his eagerness to terminate the Anglo-Japanese alliance, he agreed to a limitation of naval armaments and to prohibitions against fortifying Pacific islands, which gave the Japanese military supremacy in the northwestern Pacific.†

They were not long in taking advantage of it. The Chinese state, as already noted, had disintegrated into a series of areas kaleidoscopically changing, merging, and separating again as the fortunes of various warlords rose and fell. Under the surface of this near anarchy two principles of organization were struggling for mastery—nationalism and communism. In 1923 they merged. Mikhail Borodin arrived in Canton from Moscow to help Sun Yat-sen put together an instrument—the Communist-Nationalist Kuomintang—for the creation of a modern, independent China free of foreign interference, except possibly Russian. Initially the movement met with swift success, as its forces moved north, taking over foreign-owned property and driving out its owners. Then the leaders fell out. In 1927 the Nationalists, led by Chiang Kai-shek, turned, in a bitter blood purge, against their erstwhile Communist comrades, who after some years of fighting found refuge, after their "long march," in north-central China. The Nationalists went on to Peking and declared themselves the government of China.

For the Japanese, however, the moment had come to stop this movement toward national reunification before it got out of hand. In 1931 and 1932 they occupied all of Manchuria, organizing it into a separate, Japanese-protected state. An attack on Shanghai in 1932 caused fulminations in the League of Nations, investigations, and resolutions. Disregarding these, the Japanese march into north and central China continued in 1934 and 1935. In the next two years it moved into south China. By 1938 the Nationalists had been driven into the southwest, and the Communists into the northwest, of China proper. Then a stalemate of sorts set in. Each of the three combatants wanted, and occasionally attempted, to injure the other two. However, the Chinese Nationalists and Communists lacked the capability to do so, and the Japanese, worried by growing American hostility to the Japanese co-prosperity sphere in Asia, their name for the conquest of China and domination of East Asia, hesitated to commit themselves fully.

AMERICAN ATTITUDES TOWARD THE OUTSIDE WORLD

The nature of the world around us in 1941 was one thing; American notions about it were quite another. Two contrary and equally unrealistic ideas about it competed for the national mind, both springing from our earlier history. From the American phases of the European wars of the eighteenth century— the dominant memory of the founders of this country—came the doctrine promulgated in the Farewell Address, in 1941 called isolationism. From the experience of the long period of world peace and economic development in the nineteenth century following the settlement of Vienna and the British Navy's support of the Monroe Doctrine, came the dream of universal law and internationally enforced peace, embodied and embalmed in the League of Nations and resurrected in the United Nations.

The Eighteenth-Century Experience • With all respect, General Washington took too narrow a view of the American phases of the European wars of the eighteenth century when he thought of them as resulting from mere dynastic rivalries of no concern to people beginning to think of themselves as "Americans." But he had a good excuse, for at the time both Europeans and Americans thought of these wars and named them in this way. The War of the Grand Alliance was known here as King William's War, the War of the Spanish Succession as Queen Anne's War, and the War of the Austrian Succession as King George's War; only the Seven Years' War was called the French and Indian War. General Washington in his Farewell Address bade his fellow countrymen to avoid entanglement with Europe.

The wars of the eighteenth century sprang from causes deeper than dynastic rivalries. For a century and a quarter French power—whether directed by the Bourbon monarchy, the French republic, or the Bonapartist empire—drove with immense vitality for hegemony in Europe, North America, the West Indies, the Middle East, and South Asia. It was present and aggressive in North America, determined to keep the English settlements pinned between the Atlantic and the eastern slopes of the Alleghenies. The long struggle ended only at Waterloo.†

The Nineteenth-Century Experience • The statesmanship of Metternich, Castlereagh, and Talleyrand brought about the settlement of the wars with France. Begun at Vienna and finished at Paris, it permitted a century of international peace and of greater technological and economic development than in the whole period since the invention of the sail and wheel. But it was Canning who made it not only possible but inevitable that General Washington's advice should be followed. By putting the sanction of the British fleet behind the Monroe Doctrine, he made sure that the scattered and divided nine million Americans, with their center of population a few miles west of their capital city—as raw and unestablished as their state—could attack the enormous task of occupying an unexplored continent free from interference from Europe's hundred and ninety million, or any part of them.

Thus in the Europe-oriented-and-dominated world of the nineteenth century the western hemisphere became out of bounds for colonial expansion. But not for investment. Europe, after a few years of doubt, stood ready to invest in the American gamble. Throughout the century the flood of "foreign aid" grew and grew until in the half century preceding 1914 Western Europe, led by Great Britain, "had invested abroad almost as much as the entire national wealth of Great Britain. . . . If the same proportion of American resources were devoted to foreign investment as Britain devoted . . . in 1913, the flow of investment would require to be thirty times as great. The entire Marshall Plan would have to be carried out twice a year."[5]

Economically the globe was indeed "one world." The great empires of Europe, through their colonies and spheres of influence, spread authority, order, and respect for the obligation of contract almost everywhere; and where their writs did not run, their frigates and gunboats navigated. Methods were rough, division of benefits was unfair, and freedom was not rated high among the priorities; but people, goods, and ideas moved around the world with less restraint than ever before and, perhaps, ever again. Tennyson's "Locksley Hall" (1842) contains a nineteenth-century forecast of a United Nations.†

American Notions About China • Throughout the nineteenth century, and even later, the attitude of Americans toward China had been ambivalent. Their government described the American aim as the "Open Door" policy: the door to trade should be open—the very thing the Chinese authorities did not want—and the opportunities for trade should be equal. It opposed private entrances to spheres of influence. When the Boxers rose against all foreigners, whom the Empress Dowager had condemned to wholesale death, the United States joined in the military expedition for their suppression. After the uprisings, the victorious allies exacted reparations from China for the damage done to them, but the United States set aside its share of the indemnities for the education of Chinese students.

The U.S. clipper ships that were racing to the Orient, as intent upon the profits of the China trade as any, also carried missionaries to educate the minds and heal the bodies as well as save the souls of the heathen Chinese. Hardly a town in our land was without its society to collect funds and clothing for Chinese missions, to worry about those who labored in distant, dangerous, and exotic vineyards of the Lord, and to hear the missionaries' inspiring reports.

Thus was nourished the love portion of the love-hate complex that was to infuse so much emotion into our later China policy. Also out of this background came, much later, a notion of President Roosevelt's which seemed quixotic to Churchill and Stalin: that China, with our help and under our tutelage, would rise from its ashes to the position of a great power and play a beneficent role after the war in bringing stability to Asia.

Ideas of the world around us such as I have described could hardly have been relevant to the steep rush into world war toward which both the government I joined and the people it served were soon to experience. My story deals with how both adjusted themselves to harsh reality.

2. THE "OLD" STATE DEPARTMENT

In FEBRUARY 1941 the Department over which the Secretary of State presided was less than a quarter of its present size, made up at home and abroad of twelve hundred officers and twenty-nine hundred other American employees. With the Bureau of the Budget it shared the old State, War, and Navy Building on Pennsylvania Avenue, across West Executive Avenue from the White House, and had bureaus scattered all over town. "Old State," a well-known Washington architect has maintained, was built from the same basic plan as the Treasury on the other side of the White House, although it was erected half a century later and thus, in accordance with the architectural style of the period, has pillared porticoes and a mansard roof instead of the classic simplicity of the Treasury. Only a few years ago it was regarded as a horror. Now Congress has appropriated a staggering sum to restore the much-cut-up interior, which houses the Executive Office of the President, to the spacious dignity it had when, after the Civil War, it was built to accommodate three whole departments of government. It is to be preserved as a "national monument." Congress does not entertain the same sentiment about those who have inhabited it.

THE SECRETARY OF STATE

Cordell Hull was a handsome man. He looked like a statesman in the classic American tradition—the tradition of the great Virginia dynasty, of Henry Clay, of Daniel Webster (but much handsomer, more like Warren Harding). His well-structured face was sad and thoughtful, his speech slow and gentle, except when he was aroused, as over the duplicity of the Japanese emissaries at the time of Pearl Harbor. Suspicious by nature, he brooded over what he thought were slights and grievances, which more forthright handling might have set straight. His brooding led, in accordance with Tennessee-mountain tradition, to feuds. His hatreds were implacable—not hot hatreds, but long cold ones. In no hurry to "get" his enemy, "get" him he usually did.

Mr. Hull's feuds grew out of his relations with President Franklin Roosevelt. The natures of the two men being what they were, their relations were bound to have been difficult. The Secretary—slow, circuitous, cautious—concentrated on a central political purpose, the freeing of international trade from tariff and other restrictions as the prerequisite to peace and economic development. With almost fanatical single-mindedness he devoted himself to getting legislative authority, and then acting upon it, to negotiate "mutually beneficial reciprocal trade agreements to reduce tariffs" on a basis of equal application to all nations, a thoroughly Jeffersonian policy. These often-enunciated words, due to a speech impediment, emerged as the "wecipwocal twade agweement pwogam to weduce tawiffs."

Mr. Hull's amazing success with this important undertaking, a reversal of a hundred years of American policy, was due both to his stubborn persistence and to his great authority in the House of Representatives and the Senate, in each of which he had served. It is all the more remarkable that, unlike almost all the New Deal economic legislation once regarded as radical, the executive power to negotiate trade agreements has not been permanently incorporated in American legislation, but only extended from time to time for short periods with alternating contractions and expansions of scope.

While the Secretary had concentrated on external trade in the prewar administration, the President's interest was absorbed by the effects of the Great Depression on the internal economy. Neither man—in common with most of his fellow citizens—was aware of the catastrophe building up in Europe and Asia, which would dwarf the preoccupations of both. When, later on, the President's quicker perception awakened to it, he got little help from the Secretary and turned elsewhere for it. At the outset, however, economic problems strained their relations.

The strains began with the debacle of the London Economic Conference of July 1933, torpedoed by the President with the Secretary on the bridge. Looking back on that unhappy episode, it seems to have been caused primarily by divided counsel within the Administration and sloppy preparation, which obscured for both the President and the Secretary the relation between the foreign and domestic issues involved and the essential connection between foreign trade policy and international monetary arrangements. Eleven years later, in 1944—the last year of Mr. Hull's long tenure—these issues had been resolved, and brilliant results were achieved at the International Monetary Conference at Bretton Woods. Ironically, this conference was presided over by the Secretary's arch rival for the President's favor, Secretary of the Treasury Henry Morgenthau.

In 1933 Mr. Hull did not fix blame for the disaster upon the ineptness of a new and disorderly administration, nor would loyalty permit him to place it upon the President. However, a satisfactory villain was at hand. Raymond Moley, a professor of economics at Columbia University and a member of Governor Roosevelt's campaign "brain trust," had been made an Assistant Secretary of State. The appointment would not have been made over the Secretary's objection, but he accepted and resented it. Years later he wrote: "Mr. Roosevelt, without much ceremony, appointed Raymond Moley as one of my Assistant Secretaries of State. . . . I . . . concluded that Mr. Roosevelt was placing him in this position, not to render regular service as Assistant Secretary of State, but to continue to stay close around the President. . . . In any event, I was not at all enthusiastic about this sort of appointment, and I grew less enthusiastic until the London Economic Conference was over and Moley retired from the State Department."[1]

Mr. Moley's flamboyant part in the collapse of the conference humiliated

Mr. Hull. Before long, other duties were found for Mr. Moley, and he returned, disgruntled, to Columbia. Mr. Hull cut a notch in his rifle stock.

Trouble, however, continued. The President chose to raise prices as the principal method of stimulating American agriculture and industry. To accomplish this he set about depreciating the dollar by monetary devices. This campaign conflicted sharply with Mr. Hull's principal aim, the freeing and stimulation of international trade. If American prices were artificially raised, they would attract foreign goods, which would defeat the price rise. Accordingly, these goods must be excluded. The Agricultural Adjustment Act, the brain child of Secretary of Agriculture Henry Wallace, gave the President power to do so should he find that imports threatened to imperil domestic prices. Where foreign markets were of great importance, as they were to farm products, such men as George N. Peek, former Administrator of the Agricultural Adjustment Administration, advocated bilateral, practically barter, deals with selected nations, a deathblow to the most-favored-nation principle. Mr. Hull was constantly fighting the President's favorites for the very life of his basic policy.

More and more the President turned to other, more energetic, more imaginative, more sympathetic collaborators—General Hugh Johnson, "Old Ironpants" of the NRA; Henry Wallace and Rexford G. Tugwell for agriculture and housing; Harry Hopkins and Harold Ickes to create employment; Morgenthau and Jesse Jones to rehabilitate finance; Frances Perkins to do the same for labor. Except for the secretaries for the armed services, whom the President dealt with directly as Commander in Chief, the Secretary of State—the senior Cabinet officer—became one of the least influential members at the White House. It was neither the first nor the last time this has happened. It is never good for the United States.

A HOUSE DIVIDED AGAINST ITSELF

Even in his own field and in his own Department the Secretary's influence and authority were diluted. His first Under Secretary, William Phillips, a great gentleman and an experienced diplomat but not a strong administrator, resigned in 1937 to become Ambassador to Italy. Mr. Hull has told us that he regretted this because he knew that it would "open Pandora's box." But, again, as in the case of Moley's appointment, he did nothing about the succession and remained passive, leaving the decision to the President. Two assistant secretaries —Sumner Welles and R. Walton Moore—were vying for Phillips' place. Welles had been an Assistant Secretary since the beginning of the Administration, except for a few months as Ambassador to Cuba, during which his activities produced a regime that gave way to the Grau San Martin-Batista dictatorship after three weeks. Welles had close family relations with the President and had gone to the same school; with Mr. Hull he was stiff and formal. Walton Moore, with the same southern legal and political background as the Secretary's, had served with him in Congress; they were easy and companionable together.

Mr. Hull, believing that the President favored Welles, would make no recommendation. The President, believing that Mr. Hull favored Moore, took no action. Finally the two assistant secretaries worked out a compromise. Welles would be Under Secretary and Moore would become Counselor, an office which had been allowed to lapse. The Secretary and the President accepted the compromise. But, as in the case of Moley, it was a mistake. Increasingly, Welles worked directly with the President, naturally enough in view of their close relationship and of Welles's incisive mind and decisive nature. He grasped ideas quickly and got things done. More and more he took over liaison with the White House on international political matters. Mr. Hull rankled under what he believed to be Welles's disloyalty and the President's neglect. The Department became divided into Welles men, who looked to the Under Secretary, particularly in the Latin American field, and Hull men, who sought guidance from the chief. This unhealthy situation blew up in August 1943, when, as Mr. Hull relates it, he asked the President to remove Welles and the President complied.[2] Meanwhile it poisoned the Department.

My own relations with Welles were good throughout this period. He had been in the class ahead of me at boarding school, and we met again during my brief time in the Treasury. His manner was formal to the point of stiffness. His voice, pitched much lower than would seem natural, though it had been so since he was a boy, lent a suggestion of pomposity. Once, when a remark of my wife's made him laugh, he quickly caught himself and said, "Pardon me. You amused me." Out of the office he could be a charming host and an appreciative guest. Perhaps his greatest recommendation to me was the devoted friendship of his classmate, Charles P. Curtis of Boston, one of the most original minds and delightful of companions. Welles was not an easy man to know, but I respected and liked him.

MY COLLEAGUES

My fellow assistant secretaries were a mixed bag. The senior of them was Breckinridge Long, formerly of Missouri but in 1941 the owner of one of Maryland's most beautiful colonial houses, Montpelier, near Laurel. Like Mr. Hull, he was a gentleman of the old school—spare, courteous, and soft-spoken. As his house and his wife Christine's distinguished collection of silverware indicated, he was well off. Thoroughbreds graced the pastures surrounding Montpelier; destined for the track, their promise always seemed to exceed their performance. Genial and popular at the Metropolitan and Alibi clubs, Breck Long took life easily and enjoyed it.

In Missouri he had been a staunch Wilson Democrat, during the war serving for a while under Lansing as Assistant Secretary of State. Then, when Wilson's health and fortunes were hopelessly broken, Breck with courage above and beyond the call of duty fought two elections for the Senate against the Missouri machine of Wilson's arch enemy, Senator James A. Reed, one of them against the old "irreconcilable" opponent of the League of Nations himself. But those times, which I have called "the desert years of the human spirit," were as bitter for Democrats in Missouri as they were elsewhere, as another Missourian, Harry S. Truman, was also learning.

In 1933 a new President recalled the old soldier from the wilderness and sent him off as Ambassador to Italy. Long began with admiration for Mussolini, which earned him enemies at home, but, earlier than most of his critics, he saw the drift of affairs and coming dangers in Europe. At that point illness retired him to private life for three years. In September 1939, as the war he foresaw broke out, he returned to the State Department at Mr. Hull's call.

It was pretty plain that Long was Mr. Hull's principal confidant and emissary. In his diary he describes playing the part of sympathetic friend, as Mr. Hull

launched into the White House attitude and treatment of the Department and encroachment in Foreign Affairs; criticized the appointment of Winant [as Ambassador to Great Britain] as being entirely unacquainted with the operations of Foreign Affairs, though a "fine young man" . . . ; then for relying on Hopkins and some others for advice as to policy; . . . and then Mrs. Roosevelt for encouraging persons to strike, as she is reported to have done yesterday.

He was in a sombre mood and very communicative—and it seems to be my fate to receive confidences of Secretaries of State in disagreement with their Presidents— but this is child's play compared to the Lansing situation.[3]

I do not recall him taking part in Mr. Hull's speech-writing or Sunday-morning conferences. This may be failure of memory, but I put his absence down to good judgment, of which Breckinridge Long had plenty.

A month after I came to the Department, Howland Shaw was appointed Assistant Secretary in Charge of Administration, a job which should be undertaken only by a saint or a fool. Shaw was no fool, and had many saintly qualities as well as some hard common sense. He needed all of these, for the House and Senate subcommittees in charge of appropriations, their chairmen, and the Comptroller General's office make this job a perfect hell. Like an ill-tempered chatelaine of a medieval manor, her keys hanging from her belt, Congress parsimoniously and suspiciously doles out supplies for the shortest time, each item meticulously weighed and measured, each request at first harshly denied. Almost simultaneously yesterday's accounting goes on amid screamed accusation and denunciation of every purpose of policy.

Howland and I had been at school together for a while. He had gone into the Foreign Service, principally in the Near East. It had not been the layman's idea of a diplomatic environment. His experience there began when Mustapha Kemal, later called Ataturk, a man of extraordinary stature, was defying the armed forces of the allies and the centuries-old customs and lethargy of the Turks to make a new and modern nation. One of Shaw's dispatches describes a scene early one morning in the square of the then mud village of Ankara, high on the Anatolian plain, during Kemal's suppression of a Kurdish revolt:

"Each man was hung from a tripod and had on a sort of white smock with a placard pinned to him on which was scrawled his name and some account of his crime. There were groups of spectators in front of each tripod and others, intent I suppose upon a more careful inspection, were seated upon the steps of nearby houses. Children were scurrying about and nobody seemed particularly concerned. It was a sight like any other."[4]

Shaw, a bachelor and a most eligible one, seemed to be a likely prospect for that most sought-after necessity of the Washington dinner party, an unattached man. But he resolutely refused to go out. A converted Catholic, he threw himself with great devotion into the work of the National Catholic Welfare Conference and, over the years, became a recognized authority on juvenile delinquency. This point of view he brought to the decision of a group of cases that came before him, Adolph Berle, and me as members of the Foreign Service Board. A Foreign Service officer, wishing to marry a foreign national, had to seek permission from us and file, along with his request for it, an undated resignation. Whether this was a test of serious intention or to relieve us from direct heart breaking was unclear. Our approaches to the problem were diverse. Shaw leaned toward the litmus test of home leave and a change of post. Berle saw the dangers to security. I was inclined to favor Anglo-Saxons and Latin Americans as readily convertible, disfavor Europeans—except Italians—and to be inquisitive about the how, when, and why of the romance. On the whole, we were not stern judges.

In another situation, however, it was necessary to be—where officers abroad sold their dollar salary and allowance checks on the black market. The temptation to do so was great, since the official exchange rate often bore little relation to the actual value of the local currency. If a Foreign Service inspector could turn up these deals, they must be pretty generally known in the mission and in the community. The advertisement of potential venality in an embassy could open the way to a host of troubles. If—as once occurred—the politically appointed ambassador, beyond our reach, condoned these dealings because "everybody else did it," we found it no excuse for his staff. We could and did report the facts to the Secretary, who had his own method of bringing about a transfer of the chief of mission to a country with a stronger currency.

Among the duties of the Foreign Service Board was the recommendation of promotions and retirements. To read and discuss efficiency reports gives one interesting insights into both the writer and subject, and, when continued over four years in a service of less than a thousand people, half of whom one had also met, a pretty good knowledge of the group. Of course, not all officers in the Department then—or, indeed, now—were in the Foreign Service; in 1941 more were under civil service and could not be assigned to duty abroad. These, too, one came to know and appraise.

Howland Shaw retired in 1944, when Mr. Hull did so, and devoted himself to welfare work. He was a lonely man. Nothing described this side of him more movingly than the last line of his obituary in the *Washington Post* after his death in August 1965. It read simply, "He had no survivors."

I have mentioned Adolph Berle. The fact that we disliked one another is too well known to attempt to disguise. Its causes are irrelevant—and useless to discuss, for, as Horace observed, *de gustibus non est disputandum*. At any rate, for four years, until he became Ambassador to Brazil, we maintained a wary coexistence on the second floor of Old State, separated by the offices of the Secretary and Under Secretary, who side by side managed to do the same thing.

THE LOCATION OF BUREAUCRATIC POWER

An understanding of the ancient and, to outsiders, mysterious organization, as it was to me when I joined it, requires a look at its work and at those who did it. The prewar State Department was closer to its nineteenth-century predecessors in both what it did and how the work was done than to the department I was later to command. Between the two a great world change and General Marshall had intervened.

As the preceding chapter has indicated, the impingement in the nineteenth century of what the Supreme Court has called "the vast external realm" upon American interests occurred rarely, and usually only when wars between foreign nations interfered with our commerce or when foreign nations intervened in our hemisphere, as the French did in Mexico and the British in Venezuela. For the most part the prewar Department was concerned with treaties of commerce or navigation or, during the Bryan period, of arbitration, while the general run of business involved extricating Americans from trouble abroad or helping them engage in commercial ventures from which others wished to exclude them. Most revealing is the utter triviality of the correspondence between President Harrison and Secretary of State James G. Blaine, from 1889 to 1892.[5] In the infancy of the telephone and the typewriter, they wrote to each other in longhand almost every day, largely about appointments and minute points of draftsmanship in the Bering Sea seal fisheries treaty.

As a result, most matters that concerned the Department arose from specific incidents or problems and then evolved into policies, rather than beginning as matters of broad decision and ending in specific action. In this way the departmental division having jurisdiction to deal with the incident became the basic instrument for the formulation and execution of policy. Having a supposed monopoly of knowledge of the subject matter, it advised the Secretary on the action, if any, to be taken in the case at hand—thus becoming a formulator of policy—and, after the Secretary's decision, had charge of transmitting instructions to the field.

Bureaucratic power had come to rest in the division chiefs and the advisers, political, legal, and economic. To the traditional four geographic divisions—American Republics, European, Near Eastern, Far Eastern—and the Legal Adviser, had been added, after the First World War, the Passport and Visa divisions, with almost absolute power to decide who might leave and enter the country. Mr. Stimson had created the Economic Adviser, and Mr. Hull the Commercial Treaties and Agreements Division and the Division of Special Research, the latter to concern itself with world organization for peace.

The heads of all these divisions, like barons in a feudal system weakened at the top by mutual suspicion and jealousy between king and prince, were constantly at odds, if not at war. Their frontiers, delimited in some cases by geography and in others by function, were vague and overlapping. Obscurity in lines of command of the assistant secretaries permitted the division chiefs to circumvent them at will and go directly to the Secretary or Under Secretary. In such a situation it is not surprising that the table of organization, so-called, for the Department of State was not the source of authority. In reality, authority fell to him—or to her, in the case of the Queendom of Passports ruled over by Mrs. Ruth Shipley—who could take and hold it. For the most part the barons were knowledgeable people performing in a way that the times had completely outdated, a fact of which they were quite unaware. Townsend Hoopes, later to be Under Secretary of the Air Force, has put his finger on what was the basic weakness of the Department at the time of which I write: "Our difficulty is that, as a nation of short-term pragmatists accustomed to dealing with the future only when it has become the present, we find it hard to regard future trends as serious realities. We have not achieved the capacity to treat as real and urgent—as demanding action today—problems which appear in critical dimension only at some future date. Yet failure to achieve this new habit of mind is likely to prove fatal."[6] In this weakness, however, the division chiefs were not unique. The President and his Administration had come to power contemporaneously with Hitler but, as mentioned earlier, had remained curiously insensitive to the significance of developments in Europe and Asia during their nearly ten years in office. Intense in his concentration on the domestic depression and social and economic reforms, the President failed to see the aggressive intentions and power to back them developing in Germany and Japan and left foreign affairs to the moralistic, pacifist, and laissez faire preachments of the State Department and the isolationist sentiments of the Congress and the country. Awakened by Dunkirk, he found Germany in control of Europe and Japan in control of east China. The position of the United States had undergone a drastic change; the purposes and capabilities of the State Department had not.

Within a year of my arrival in the Department, American military forces would be actively engaged in all four of the geographic areas and our representatives would be organizing economic supply and warfare all over the globe. However, the Department had no ideas, plans, or methods for collecting the information or dealing with the problems that this situation presented. With some brilliant exceptions, the bureaucracy was unequipped for appraisals of capability based on quantitative and technical judgments and of intentions by painstaking and exhaustive collection and correlation of intelligence. Only Herbert Feis, the Economic Adviser, foreseeing trouble, was at work on the stockpiling of strategic materials.

MY SEARCH FOR A FUNCTION

My inherited quarters consisted of two large, high-ceilinged rooms in the southwest corner of Old State, adjoining Mr. Hull's office. A corridor between the rooms had been enclosed to provide space of sorts for secretaries. Together we stifled under the full blast of the summer sun aided by its reflection from the roof of the portico just below the corridor window and unabated by any such newfangled contrivance as air conditioning. We stifled all winter, too, through equal inability to control the government's heating system. The other room housed my assistants—Donald Hiss, who had been a law clerk for Justice Holmes; Adrian Fisher, who joined us after service with Justices Brandeis and Frankfurter; Edward G. Miller of New York, later an Assistant Secretary of State under me; Jacques Reinstein; and Robert Carr. My secretary, Miss Barbara Evans, who had come—and happily still remains—with me, presided in between. That corner lives in memory as a crowded, busy, hot, noisy, and—gradually—embattled place. Outside our door a messenger dozing in a wooden swivel chair awakened occasionally to escort papers on their supposed appointed round of the Department, followed by other baying messengers pursuing fugitive documents. Barbara Evans devised a system for logging papers in and out of our corner that greatly increased our defensive position and was used by others in their search for lost papers.

I soon discovered that the greater part of a day in Old State was devoted to meetings. Where the boundaries of jurisdiction were fuzzy or overlapping, meetings became inevitable. Most questions affected a number of functional and geographic divisions. Who called a meeting and who attended, both matters of prestige, depended on early claim and persistent support of it. These meetings gave the illusion of action, but often frustrated it by attempting to reconcile the irreconcilable. What was most often needed was not compromise but decision.

My official duties were summed up in the *Department of State Bulletin* by a misleading platitude: "coordination of commercial and economic questions with questions of major policy." In fact, however, they had no such sweep since responsibility for a lot of this coordination lay elsewhere in the Department. For instance, among Berle's assignments was "coordination of financial questions with questions of major policy" and, as I have pointed out, Feis had long concerned himself with stockpiling foreign materials for war production and other supply problems.

The fine print of the departmental order stated more revealingly: "General supervision of the following units of the Department of State, including, except as otherwise provided, the signing of correspondence with respect to the work thereof: Division of Commercial Treaties and Agreements; Division of Controls; Treaty Division; Division of Commercial Affairs; and the Editor of Treaties."[7]

The war had reduced to a bare minimum the usual activities of the divisions under my supervision, except for the Division of Controls, which dealt with the issuance of export licenses. As may be imagined, its business had boomed. Although paper work and committee meetings continued in the other divisions, the work did not amount to much. Discussion of a trade agreement with Ecuador dragged along. A desultory argument with Haiti debated whether her proposed arrangements with the Dominican Republic violated the most-favored-nation principle. Talks opened with Iceland that over the next four years were to teach me more about sheepskins than I wanted to know; the United States came to own more of these than Abraham ever dreamed of. Discussions with India of a "treaty of establishment, commerce, navigation and consular rights" were abruptly terminated by a significant message from the Indian Agency General that it was felt "wiser, in view of the changed situation in India, to defer the conclusion of the negotiations until conditions are more settled."[8] They were destined to become less settled before they were more settled.

In accepting Mr. Hull's invitation to enlist, I had a much clearer idea of what I wanted to do than he had of what he wanted me to do. Ever since the invasion of Poland, all through the "phony war," I had thought and said that the United States was deeply involved in the struggles going on in both Europe and Asia. The German assault on France, the disaster in Dunkirk, and the Battle of Britain all urged action in our own interest before, as Colonel Stimson kept saying, it might be too late. Both Mr. Hull and the President knew of my activity before I came to the State Department. They also knew me and, surely, had not asked me into the Department to perform the largely nonexistent duties defined in the *Bulletin.*

Whose idea it was to appoint me I learned only recently. When Mr. Hull issued the invitation, he gave the impression that it was his. Felix Frankfurter believed that FDR took the initiative. Looking through Breckinridge Long's *War Diary,* I came across a notation under the date of January 3, 1941, that Mr. Hull had shown him a chit signed "F.D.R." saying "that he wanted Dean Acheson to fill the vacancy Grady left."[9] Digging up this little fact buried for a quarter of a century gave me real pleasure. For a long time I had belonged to the dubious few whom FDR had fired. Now I had the distinction of joining the even fewer he had ever taken back. At any rate, I did not come back to dream in a somnolent office. Plainly plenty of work was waiting to be done. The question was: Would the State Department do it? I proposed to have a shot at finding out.

The handiest entrance for me to the field of action was through supervision of the Division of Controls. The State Department had gotten into the licensing of exports through the Neutrality Acts of the 1930s, a product of the Nye Committee's investigation and belief that wars came from the munition makers' desire to sell their wares. So their export was forbidden, save as the Department in charge of our foreign relations under the President might find in the national interest. When, however, in July 1940, Congress broadened the executive authority to control export of anything essential to our national defense, the President took the first step toward diminishing, if not virtually eliminating, the Department's function in this field.

"While the control of exports is primarily a national-defense matter," his press statement of July 2, 1940, read, "the Department of State provides the machinery for the actual issue of licenses under which any controlled items are released for export." By an accompanying "military order," he designated "Lieutenant Colonel Russell L. Maxwell, U.S. Army, Administrator of Export Control to administer the provisions of the said section under the direction and supervision of the President as Commander-in-Chief of the Army and Navy of the United States."[10]

It was, of course, artful in the election year 1940 to represent the extension of export controls as a mere prudent measure for husbanding militarily essential goods and to minimize its foreign policy aspects, but it soon became apparent that it was far from the truth. Within the month the export of aviation gasoline was restricted to the western hemisphere. The Japanese reaction was immediate: "As a country whose import of American aviation gasoline is of immense volume, Japan would bear the brunt of the virtual embargo. The resultant impression would be that Japan had been singled out for and subjected to discriminatory treatment. . . . The Government of Japan wishes to protest against the policy of the Government of the United States."[11]

On September 30, 1940, the same limitations were placed on the exportation of "all iron and steel scrap of every kind and description, classified and unclassified." This time export to Great Britain was exempted from the order. Again the response was immediate.

In view of the fact that Japan has been for some years the principal buyer of American iron and steel scrap, the announcement . . . cannot fail to be regarded as directed against Japan, and, as such, to be an unfriendly act.

The Japanese Government protests . . . .

*   *   *

. . . In view of the high feeling in Japan it is apprehended that, in the event of continuation by the United States Government of the present attitude toward Japan in matters of trade restriction, especially if it leads to the imposition of further measures of curtailment, future relations between Japan and the United States will be unpredictable.

These were strong words in days when nations still addressed one another with the restraint of diplomatic usage and before shoes were used to beat desks for emphasis. Again in December similar restrictions and exceptions were applied to all iron and steel—ores, pig iron, alloys, and both semifinished and finished products. Once more the Japanese protested "against this fresh measure of discrimination."

A few more categories were added to the list in the late winter and spring after I joined the Department, and there the matter hung fire until well into the summer. Discussion went on in Mr. Hull's Sunday-morning staff meetings.† The issue was over the embargo or drastic reduction of petroleum exports other than the already embargoed aviation gasoline. The aim was to limit Japanese military action in East and Southeast Asia; the danger, provoking Japan to seize or intimidate the Dutch East Indies—a great source of petroleum —or to move against us. The soldiers were quoted as favoring delay while we rearmed and increased our potential threat, and the civilian secretaries as being inclined to a bolder course. The argument for it was that no rational Japanese could believe that an attack on us could result in anything but disaster for his country. Of course, no one even dimly foresaw the initial success of an attack. A Japanese move against the Indies, it was thought, involved too great a risk with our fleet in the Pacific and possibly a futile one if the Dutch oil wells and refineries were put out of business.

Discussion suffered from two weaknesses. The Japanese military leaders were not rational regarding their interests and purposes, which an oil embargo would threaten. Furthermore, our discussions were not analytical or quantitatively precise, but rambling and argumentative. Mr. Hull had the mind of a debater rather than of a judge. He thought orally and aurally, stating all sides of a question and settling on the one that appealed to him as most convincing. He was helped in deciding what he thought by hearing what he said. Although the words had not been thought of, I was a "hawk" and each Sunday, wholly without result, battled the "doves" in the seminar.

3. THE YEAR WE HELD OUR BREATH

AGONY OF IRRESOLUTION

ARTHUR SCHLESINGER, JR., has written of President Roosevelt that the "more serious complaint against him was his weakness for postponement." So it seemed to me in 1941. Schlesinger adds: "Yet his caution was always within an assumption of constant advance."[1] This, also, is true; but the advance in 1941 was agonizingly slow while hazards mounted and even preparations lagged. Certainly the man down the line cannot grasp all the factors that the Commander in Chief must weigh, but he is not called upon to do so. His is not the duty to lead. Over the years I have been impressed by how often political leaders have misjudged the people's willingness to follow a strong lead. The repeal of prohibition was a cause looking for a leader until Dwight Morrow showed the way. Colonel Stimson tells us that on April 22, 1941, he cautioned the President "on the necessity of his taking the lead and that without a lead on his part it was useless to expect the people would voluntarily take the initiative in letting him know whether or not they would follow him if he did take the lead."[2]

Two other friends in the Cabinet, Henry Morgenthau and Harold Ickes, took the same view, and constantly presssed for such action as lay immediately within our power to impede the axis, to aid its victims, and to prepare ourselves for the inevitable hostilities which Colonel Stimson predicted. Yet it was easy enough to see why the President delayed involvement. He still remembered the storm in 1937 over his Chicago speech proposing to "quarantine" the dictators. In the 1940 campaign he had gone far to promise the voters that their sons would not be sent abroad to fight foreign wars. Our military posture was weak and our armament industry, despite the "arsenal of democracy" speech in December 1940, largely nonexistent. Controversy still raged between the America Firsters and the William Allen White Committee to Defend America by Aiding the Allies. The draft was unpopular. Many in the army were chalking up the motto, "O.H.I.O."—"over the hill in October," when under existing law the draftees' term of service would end. Before this, the House on August 12 extended the draft law by the slim margin of one vote. Walter Lippmann a few days earlier had entitled his column, "The Case for a Smaller Army."

Looking back, one can hardly doubt that by the spring of 1941 the American people were ready for a stronger lead toward intervention.[3] But President Roosevelt was not looking back. His crystal ball of the future was very clouded. General Marshall used to say that the rarest gift the gods ever give to man is the capacity for decision. At the top there are no easy choices. All are between evils, the consequences of which are hard to judge. Unfortunately, the capacity to decide does not descend in pentecostal fashion upon every occupant of the White House. But if President Roosevelt lacked decisiveness in the degree his successor possessed it, he had a sense of direction in which he constantly advanced. It seemed to those in the government whose views I shared that our most useful function was to increase, so far as we could, the rate of that advance. This effort was to have a wholly unexpected result.

INSTRUMENTS OF DECISION

The two most beckoning salients at the time for a Washington warrior were those of economic warfare and economic aid. Economic warfare was then very much in favor and fashion due to the efforts of two young people at the British Embassy, Miss Mary Craig McGeachy, a Canadian, and Noel Hall, an English don serving as British Minister for War Trade. One gathered that their activities were more stirring than James Bond's of a later day and their ministry potent enough to strangle Hitler's Europe. Everyone in Washington "wanted in" on economic warfare, and soon nearly everyone had a share. By the end of July 1941 an Economic Defense Board under the chairmanship of Vice President Henry Wallace included representatives of State, Treasury, War, Navy, and Commerce (which, through Secretary Jesse Jones, included the Reconstruction Finance Corporation). At first the board was nothing more than an interdepartmental committee where differences were aired and rarely composed. When Mr. Hull tired of it, I represented State. Later, Henry Wallace appointed Milo Perkins as Executive Director, acquired staff, powers, and money, and went to work in earnest. But that long story of internecine warfare with State must wait.

Meanwhile, two other potent instruments for helping friends and harming foes were being forged—furnishing supplies to our friends by lend-lease and withholding them from foes by financial freezing orders. Both came out of the Treasury. Henry Morgenthau was the most dynamic character in Washington; he had passion. His description of the kind of man he wanted hired was: "Does he want to lick this fellow Hitler . . . , that is what I want to know. . . . Does [he] hate Hitler's guts."[4] Henry did.

Early in January, when I was still in private practice, Morgenthau called me in to work with his General Counsel, Edward H. Foley, Jr., on the lend-lease bill about to go to Congress and numbered—to confuse the opposition—H.R. 1776. Hardly were we established in our corner rooms in the State Department when in March I was asked to draft the first lend-lease agreements. The British agreement raised most of the problems with which we would become familiar over the years to come. It dragged on for interminable months, but brought me two more cherished friendships—one with the British Ambassador, Edward Halifax, the other with Maynard Keynes—and ever-increasing involvement with allied supply problems. I will come back to it after turning to foreign funds control, which touched off the big event of 1941.

To begin with, this subject should not have been a concern of mine. The "coordination of financial questions with questions of major policy" was by departmental ukase within Adolph Berle's jurisdiction. Again it was Henry Morgenthau who got me involved. "There was no one at the State Department," he said at the time, "with whom he could talk candidly except for Dean Acheson."[5] There was no one at all with whom I could talk—sympathetically. From top to bottom our Department, except for our corner of it, was against Henry Morgenthau's campaign to apply freezing controls to axis countries and their victims.

Freezing controls stemmed from the Trading with the Enemy Act of 1917. Under it the President could forbid whole categories of transactions that he found beneficial to any enemy. These might range from withdrawing or transferring funds from a bank to buying or selling anything or issuing any document relating to any of these transactions. An order could block them all unless specifically permitted by license. In some instances general licenses permitted whole categories of acts; in others, specific licenses might be required for each separate transaction. The authority to issue these orders was a powerful weapon.

Throughout 1940 Morgenthau pressed to have freezing controls extended to Germany and Italy, but the President and the Secretary of State refused to move. The policy remained one of protecting the victims of aggression against the theft of their American assets by freezing them, but permitting the aggressors free use of theirs. The State Department and the White House, worrying from different points of view, saw anything more as unneutral, as, indeed, it would have been.

In February 1941, returning to the battle, Morgenthau again made no headway. In April I urged him to have another try at moving Mr. Hull, but found him reluctant. By June, Hitler's virtual conquest of all Europe had undermined Mr. Hull's position; and on the fourteenth the President, without dissent in his Cabinet, extended freezing controls to all countries on the continent of Europe. Since my own views and those of the Department now happily coincided, so far as Europe was concerned, I became the Department's representative on the State-Treasury-Justice policy committee (known as the Foreign Funds Committee) with Edward Foley of Treasury and Francis Shea of Justice.

THE BATTLE OVER POLICY TOWARD JAPAN

The committee could now concentrate its attention on the control of Japanese assets. The Secretary continued to be opposed, but Welles and some others were sympathetic although watchful of the White House. Secretary Ickes gave strong support from his key post of Petroleum Administrator. Morgenthau, while in favor, did not lead as he had in the case of Europe. Leadership ultimately came from the President.

To the principal antagonists over policy toward Japan, Secretaries Hull and Ickes, the issue was tightening the limited embargo on oil. In late June and during July the views of all participants were shaken by Hitler's attack on the Soviet Union. Would Japan move north against Siberia as Hitler urged or south against Indochina and Indonesia, where raw materials beckoned? On July 2 the Japanese Government called up a million men; on the twenty-fifth it announced a protectorate over Indochina.

Meanwhile, the United States hesitated on the brink of action. When it did act on the twenty-sixth, it is by no means clear who intended to do what. Mr. Hull, tired and ill, had gone off to White Sulphur Springs. On the seventeenth he telephoned Welles but, finding him out, talked with me. It was a crucial talk. We should find out, he said, what the Japanese Government had in mind, whether it was "going to stay hooked up with Hitler's program of conquest." If so, we should put obstacles in its way by helping Chinese and French-Indochinese resistance, if there was any, and by economic restrictions on Japan. He wanted what he described as "a general tightening up, but always short of becoming involved in war with Japan." He thought that the main Japanese thrust would be southward into Southeast Asia and the East Indies. At this point Welles came in, took over the phone, and was told the same thing. We agreed that Mr. Hull was making progress.

The next day Welles attended a Cabinet meeting and reported the probable and imminent Japanese move into Indochina. When Morgenthau asked the President what he would do in response to it, the President reiterated his opposition to an embargo on oil as likely to drive the Japanese on to Indonesia. Welles suggested freezing Japanese assets and the President seemed to agree.

Welles's suggestion was, of course, far from clear. It could have been an alternative to an embargo or regarded as the same thing, depending on how it was administered. Similarly, it could or could not be within Mr. Hull's telephoned prescription for action. Its very ambiguity could well have made it the sort of response to the Japanese that would appeal to both FDR and his Secretary, giving the appearance of action without carrying specific or irrevocable commitment. In today's jargon, it would seem to "preserve all the options."

Welles told Stanley Hornbeck, Adviser on Political Relations, and me to prepare the freezing order, the idea being to restrict exports of petroleum products to "normal quantities and low-octane grades." The drafting devolved upon my small group and our Treasury friends. By July 21 we had prepared a simple freezing order, merely adding Japan and China, aggressor and victim, to the general order promulgated a month earlier, and a proposed policy paper strictly limiting exports of oil, cotton, and other goods to be paid for by equivalent imports of silk. On instruction, we informed the British of the proposed action, asking what that government might do. They expected it to "tighten controls."

At a Cabinet meeting on the twenty-third the President, brushing aside objections, authorized the freezing order as soon as complementary action could be worked out with the British and the Dutch East Indies and our military commanders could be alerted.[6] The policy paper was put aside, since the President and Welles agreed that we should feel our way along in administering the order until we got a sense of Japanese reaction to it.

The Dutch bravely (for they were, or thought they were, in the most exposed position) acted with us. In the light of our new orders, I would have to report to the British a more vague and cautious policy than I had outlined two days before. The opportunity came when the British Minister, Neville Butler, and Noel Hall came in on July 23 to tell me how stalwart the British were prepared to be. They had recommended to the dominions, the Netherlands Government, and the Free French that they follow the British in freezing Japanese and Chinese assets. The British export policy would probably duplicate ours, as I had forecast it, permitting only such exports as were needed to pay for strategic materials from Japan. The new instructions from above required me to reverse engines at this point. I had, I said, perhaps given the wrong impression. We looked forward to reaching that result but not in one step. We would first observe the effect of the freezing order and act in the light of developments, keeping the British informed and giving them ample notice of intended action. This they thought would provide opportunity for consultation with us and the dominions. A near fumble due to a faulty pass had been recovered.[7]

On July 25, the day before issuance of the freezing order, the White House released a statement of the President "speaking informally" to the Volunteer Participation Committee, volunteers for civilian-defense activities. FDR was at his best, making policy clearer than truth itself. He spoke of the "apparent anomaly" of curtailing domestic consumption of gasoline while thousands of tons of it were being sent from the West Coast to Japan "and we are helping Japan in what looks like an act of aggression."

All right. Now the answer is a very simple one. There is a world war going on, and has been for some time—nearly two years. One of our efforts, from the very beginning, was to prevent the spread of that world war in certain areas where it hadn't started. One of those areas is a place called the Pacific Ocean—one of the largest areas of the earth. There happened to be a place in the South Pacific where we had to get a lot of things . . . .

. . . So it was essential for Great Britain [too] that we try to keep the peace down there in the South Pacific.

All right. And now here is a nation called Japan. Whether they had at that time aggressive purposes to enlarge their empire southward, they didn't have any oil of their own up in the north. Now, if we cut the oil off, they probably would have gone down to the Dutch East Indies a year ago, and you would have had war.

Therefore, there was—you might call—a method in letting this oil go to Japan, with the hope—and it has worked for two years—of keeping war out of the South Pacific for our own good, for the good of the defense of Great Britain, and the freedom of the seas.

You people can help to enlighten the average citizen who wouldn't hear of that, or doesn't read the papers carefully, or listen to the radio carefully—to understand what some of these apparent anomalies mean.[8]

Whatever help the Volunteer Participation Committee may have received, the Foreign Funds Committee was not enlightened on administering the President's policy of no policy. Therefore, when Foley, Shea, and I met with the press on July 26, we were understandably reticent. The press interpreted this as meaning that the order was a paper tiger and portended no substantial change in flow of oil to Japan. Like everyone else, they were wrong: it portended a great change. Their error came from looking in the wrong direction. The change was to come from a wholly unforeseen cause—the action of the Japanese themselves. At this time three Japanese ships were approaching San Francisco. Orders from Japan halted them outside our territorial waters and directed them to discharge their passengers there and return to Japan. Two did so; the third, the *Tatuta Maru,* lacked sufficient bunkers for the return journey and came in on assurances that bunkers would be licensed. Once she was in, private parties filed a law suit (called a libel in admiralty) against her, which would keep her in unless a bond took her place. A bond would require a license. Thus the *Tatuta Maru,* like the USS *Maine* and Jenkins' ear, became the instrument of great events. Through the *Tatuta Maru* the Japanese tested the freezing order.

The first policy guide to our committee came in a late-July talk I had with Welles. The happiest solution with respect to Japanese trade, he told me, would be for the Foreign Funds Committee to take no action on Japanese applications. We immediately took three positions to discourage applications. First, we would not issue advisory opinions; specific applications must be made to apply specific funds to payment for specific purposes. Second, we were averse to licensing blocked funds when we believed that secret funds in the United States or Latin America were available. Third, we would prefer to have exports paid for with funds earned by imports. In any event, each transaction must be carefully considered on its individual merits. To our surprise and pleasure, these proposals met with unanimous support for the first time within our government.

It also mystified our allies, whose representatives, as well as the Japanese, constantly sought enlightenment. The Governor General of the Indies stated his perplexity: while our export policy appeared to contemplate licenses for certain quantities and grades of petroleum, under freezing control means of payment did not seem to be available. What was the policy? Might he have a "clear statement"? After careful coordination with Messrs. Hull, Hornbeck, and Maxwell M. Hamilton, Chief of the Division of Far Eastern Affairs, I wrote out a statement which had their approval, asked Baron (Pim) van Boetzelaer, the Netherlands Counselor, to call, and read it to him on September 22. Pim van Boetzelaer was and is a cherished friend and, had he not been so experienced a diplomatist and able to interpret language intended to cloak ideas, would have been entitled to a more candid answer. But the situation was still too delicate for complete candor and the ultimate truth too unformed for statement.

The fact was, I told him, that no shipment of petroleum products had gone to Japan since the freezing order. Although three export licenses for small amounts had been granted some time ago, no action had been taken to move them, because the Japanese refused to turn in hidden cash as payment and no satisfactory alternative had been agreed upon. Our government expected to continue in the same way, with the same results. Should anything occur to warrant reconsideration of this policy, we would discuss it with the Netherlands. The inarticulate major premise was that whether or not we had a policy, we had a state of affairs; the conclusion, that until further notice it would continue. I stressed Mr. Hull's wish that this information be held as closely as possible and that nothing be said ascribing any particular policy to the United States Government.[9]

A few days later the same statement was read to Noel Hall of the British Embassy. United States policy was then set, though not stated.

The indefatigable Sadao Iguchi, Counselor of the Japanese Embassy, got a more dusty answer from me and the Treasury. Two more Japanese ships, tankers without bunkers, had entered West Coast ports. The *Tatuta Maru* had discharged her cargo and was no longer held by the libel. After some bickering she had been given bunkers and a ballast cargo of asphalt and sent home. Talk went on about paying for an oil cargo for the tankers. The use of frozen funds was rejected. Replenishment of the Yokohama Specie Bank's account with its funds in Latin America was found impracticable because bank examiners were engaged in a lengthy examination of its condition. We had no desire to delay the tankers; bunkers would be made available and payment excepted from usual policy. They went home without cargo. On August 5 Japan announced withdrawal of its merchant marine from the American trade. The use of funds for purposes other than exports ran into a variety of difficulties, such as the refusal of reciprocity in Japan and the fact that other funds were available. On November 22 I reported to Mr. Hull that the freezing controls had brought a great stillness over trade and financial relations between Japan on one side and the United States, the British Commonwealth, and Netherlands Indies on the other.[10] Stillness had only two weeks more to last.

LEND-LEASE

If our corner in Old State had seemed quiet in February, it was no longer so in July. Not only were we deep in foreign funds control, but in the intervening months had become more and more involved in lend-lease arrangements with the British. In late June we acquired another client when Hitler attacked the Soviet Union.

As soon as the bill authorizing lend-lease was passed, the President decided that he would administer operations through Harry Hopkins as his deputy and with a Cabinet Advisory Committee of Cordell Hull, Henry Morgenthau, Henry Stimson (War), and Frank Knox (Navy), a typical Roosevelt prescription for confusion. Without money, the authority granted by Congress was empty. Plans for an appropriation began amid hurt feelings, annoyance with the British, and the usual confusion in policy. Morgenthau, who had carried the burden of the battle, resented the introduction of Hopkins and the Advisory Committee and complained about the British foot-dragging in the sale of their American securities to pay what they could on war purchases. This had been promised to Congress as evidence of Britain's good faith and need. The President wanted a lend-lease agreement with the British, based on the conception not of a loan of money but of goods, as soon as possible.

The President's ideas about the lend-lease agreement were not intended, so I believed, to be taken literally. If the parentage of lend-lease had been stated in the language of the *Thoroughbred Stud Book,* it would have been "by Political Necessity out of Poetic License." The idea of returning, after the war, billions of dollars' worth of goods was only a little less absurd than paying billions of dollars which the British would have to earn by selling goods and services. Arms and ships in existence at the end of the war could be returned if we wanted a disarmed ally, but the likelihood was all the other way. After Dunkirk, Churchill in one of his exuberant moods had declared, "Give us the tools and we will finish the job." That was an exaggeration, of course; Britain could not finish the job. But the hire-purchase of the tools, as the British would have put it, was their use in the common task and the promise of such later cooperation as one nation may honorably give another.

Both treasuries were slow in understanding this. Henry Morgenthau was a brave man in the critical days of 1941, not because he was one of those rare creatures who do not know fear—he was naturally timid, nervous, and apprehensive of Congress and of what he called "going out on a limb"—but because he overcame his fears. However, he did not want to go farther than immediate necessity demanded. My ideas, he thought, would prejudice the appropriation. This difference in approach persisted to the war's end. When, as always happens, the original Cabinet committee descended to what arrogant subordinates called the "working level"—Harry White (Treasury), John J. McCloy (War), and myself (State)—the battle continued over the level of British gold and dollar reserves which might be accumulated under lend-lease. McCloy and I would accuse the Treasury of envisaging a victory where both enemies and allies were prostrate—enemies by military action, allies by bankruptcy. We finally worked the British reserves up from rock bottom to double the Treasury's minimum, until, like Sisyphus, our labors were undone when President Truman made what he called his greatest mistake: in August 1945, upon the advice of Foreign Economic Administrator Leo Crowley and Under Secretary of State Joseph Grew, he terminated lend-lease. However, I am far ahead of my story.

In March 1941 the dispute over a British agreement was shelved for the moment by the necessity of getting an appropriation sufficient to begin operations. The congressional hearings and the bill passed without casualties. But more delay awaited us. Harry Hopkins was slow in getting started, baffled by the intricacy of financial and procurement problems, and hampered by fending off almost daily exhaustion of British reserves and by assembling a staff. Some time went by before an able and energetic group under the direction of Oscar Cox got these problems sorted out, an organization established, and lend-lease under way. On August 28 Hopkins turned its administration over to Edward R. Stettinius, Jr., retaining only an unofficial supervisory role.

Meanwhile, during this period of lend-lease's gestation, my own labors centered about the British agreement and discussions with our new client, the Soviet Union. In May the President prodded Mr. Hull to press on with a temporary agreement with the British dealing with the broad principles involved. The latter charged me with responsibility for a draft. A large group in the Department produced a crop of ideas, which a smaller group—Herbert Feis, the Economic Adviser; Harry Hawkins, Chief of the Division of Commercial Treaties and Agreements; John Hickerson, Assistant Chief of the European Division; and I—winnowed over with Mr. Hull. By mid-July we had a draft.

Earlier in the month John Maynard Keynes, then in Washington as a representative of Mr. Churchill on lend-lease matters, called on me. Keynes was not only one of the most delightful and engaging men I have ever known but also, in a true sense of the word, one of the most brilliant. His many-faceted and highly polished mind sparkled and danced with light. But not all felt his charm; to some he appeared arrogant. His call might have given me that impression, but it did not. He had come, he said, at the President's request to inform me of a talk he and Lord Halifax had had with the President about a temporary lend-lease agreement, so that we might get on with drafting. They had ranged over some not unfamiliar ideas, which he recounted. Within a few days he gave me a draft he had already prepared. As I noted at the time, it was "wholly impossible," providing "merely that lend-lease aid should be extended; that the British should return what was practicable for them to return; that no obligation should be created; and that they would be glad to talk about other matters."[11] Keynes did not appear to think it unusual that I should receive instructions from the President via the British Embassy. I was sure that FDR, as well as I, got some amusement from the idea too.

By the end of July our draft had been approved by the Secretary and the President and given to Keynes for discussion. It provoked plenty. The draft was simple and amazingly liberal. The United States would furnish the British with such defense articles, services, and information as the President authorized. The British would contribute to our defense what they were able to. (This provision proved immensely helpful when our great army was assembled in England for the invasion of Europe.) The British would not transfer to others anything furnished by us without our consent; they would protect and compensate American patent owners; they would return articles in existence at the end of the war if we asked for them. What they might furnish us would be taken into account in any final settlement. So far—with adequate explanations—there was no problem. Then followed Article VII, which precipitated six months of discussion.

Twenty years of painful experience with the war debts of 1914–18 had dictated an admirable opening provision. The terms of a final lend-lease settlement should "be such as not to burden commerce between the two countries but to promote mutually advantageous economic relations between them and the betterment of world-wide economic relations." So far so good; here was a blow struck for the Hull liberal commercial policies open to all. Then came the apple of discord. In addition to promoting good, the final settlement should prohibit evil, or what Mr. Hull thought was evil. It should "provide against discrimination in either the United States or the United Kingdom against the importation of any product originating in the other country."[12] This, too, was the purest essence of Hull doctrine and boded ill for imperial preference tariffs set up in Great Britain as the reaction of the Ottawa agreements of 1932 against the infamous United States tariff act of 1930.

When Keynes had read this, he asked whether the paragraph referred to imperial preferences and exchange and trade controls as practiced between the wars. I said that it did, upon which he burst into a speech such as only he could make. The British could not "make such a commitment in good faith"; "it would require an imperial conference"; "it saddled upon the future an ironclad formula from the Nineteenth Century"; "it contemplated the . . . hopeless task of returning to a gold standard"; and so on.

I pointed out the paragraph did not ask for unilateral promises from the British, nor did it by any word or phrase seek to impose rigid or unworkable formulas upon the future. No man was less likely than the President to want this. Keynes's statements seemed to me "extreme and unjustified." Then, as coldly as I could—which I have been told is fairly cold—I added that "the purpose of Article VII was to provide a commitment, which it should not be hard for the British to give, that, after the emergency was over and after they had received vast aid from this country, they would not regard themselves free to take any measures they chose against the trade of this country but would work out in cooperation with this country measures which would eliminate discrimination and would provide for mutually fair and advantageous relations."[13]

At this he cooled off and spoke wisely about a postwar problem that he foresaw far more clearly than I did—our great capacity to export, the world's need for our goods, and the problems of payment. He mentioned the division of opinion in England about postwar trade between the free traders, the advocates of a managed economy, and a group who leaned toward imperial policies. At the end he thought us agreed on broad policies but in need of more clarification.

The next day, clearly unhappy about our talk, he wrote me from New York on his way home. I should not think because of his "caviling at the word 'discrimination' that the excellence and magnanimity of the first part of the Article VII and of the document as a whole had gone overlooked." He would do what he could to interpret the President's mind. Lord Halifax was due in London soon and would help. We must not expect an early reply. Then, in his own inimitable style, he went on:

My so strong reaction against the word "discrimination" is the result of my feeling so passionately that our hands must be free to make something new and better of the postwar world; not that I want to discriminate in the old bad sense of that word—on the contrary, quite the opposite.

But the word calls up, and must call up—for that is what it means strictly interpreted—all the old lumber, most-favored-nation clause and the rest which was a notorious failure and made such a hash of the old world. We know also that won't work. It is the clutch of the dead, or at least the moribund, hand. If it was accepted it would be cover behind which all the unconstructive and truly reactionary people of both our countries would shelter. We must be free to work out new and better arrangements which will win in substance and not in shadow what the President and you and others really want. As I know you won't dispute this, we shall be able to work something out. Meanwhile forgive my vehemence which has deep causes in my hopes for the future. This is my subject. I know, or partly know, what I want. I know, and clearly know, what I fear.[14]

In August and September we were diverted from the problems of Article VII by the tense days of the Japanese freezing order and by the thorny and recurring difficulties arising from the use of lend-lease materials, or similar materials of British origin, in British export trade. In late September Ambassador John G. Winant pressed Foreign Minister Eden for a response to our July draft. This was stimulated by my appearance before a House committee hearing our request for a supplemental appropriation of just under six billion dollars for lend-lease. The committee had asked what we had done toward agreeing on "the terms and conditions upon which any such foreign government receives any aid." It received with remarkable patience my verbose report that we were working on it. Action was imperative. Eden promised that Halifax would return with an answer.

He returned without it, due to disagreements within the Cabinet. A few weeks later he asked me to call, and on October 17, 1941, showed me a document.[15] He did not want to present it formally but in the most informal manner and as a highly tentative suggestion. A glance was enough to show that the insertion of some slippery words and phrases had robbed of all meaning our prohibition of discrimination against the importation of American goods into Britain. Instead, their proposed settlement would commit the two countries "each working *within the limits* of *their* governing economic conditions [an escape clause large enough for a Sherman tank] . . . to securing *as part of a general plan* [that is, British obligations in return for lend-lease to be conditioned upon, say, Latin America's accepting the same] the *progressive* attainment of a *balanced* international economy, [here were two Humpty Dumpty words which could mean whatever one wished them to mean] the avoidance of harmful discriminations, [harmful discriminations, I said to Halifax, are always the other fellow's discriminations, never one's own] and generally the economic objectives" of the Atlantic Charter of the preceding August. The countries would begin to talk ways and means in the near future.

Hawkins, who was with me, and I did our best to assure Lord Halifax that our draft if accepted would not itself repeal tariff legislation; it was an agreement to work together to bring about the elimination of discriminatory legislation. But we did not seem to lessen his worries. Feis feared that we might stir up a crisis among the Commonwealth countries over the Ottawa preferences. This seemed to me highly unlikely. Australia and New Zealand were far too concerned in enlisting our protection to quarrel with us over postwar tariffs. Mr. Hull concurred and advised the President, who promptly agreed, that the British draft was wholly inadequate.

In fairness to Maynard Keynes it would be wrong to leave the impression that he had inspired the haggling over details of draftsmanship to gain some narrow advantage for Britain. He was, I think, genuinely doubtful about our ability to see clearly or far into the postwar world or to control by international arrangements, however cunningly devised, forces that might be let loose there. He was distrustful of supposedly self-operating mechanisms. For instance, if alive today, he would not be as surprised as many are at the use to which General de Gaulle put the Common Market—that is, as an exclusionary device to direct European trade in the interest of France and against that of the United States, Britain, and other countries. In this Mr. Hull, for different reasons, might be in agreement. Similarly, Keynes would, I suggest, point out that some of the rigidities built into the Bretton Woods agreements by the Morgenthau-White doctrines have increased our difficulty in correcting present shortcomings in the Bretton Woods system that contribute to our much-discussed balance-of-payments troubles. These matters would come up again three years later, in the summer of 1944.

At the time, however, I was not disturbed by such far-reaching thoughts or doubts. In November, drawing in representatives of lend-lease and of economic warfare, we obtained the President's and Mr. Hull's approval of a new draft. It used some of the British language to broaden the conception of a postwar economic settlement but kept the obligations clear. On December 2 Herbert Feis and I presented it to Lord Halifax, explaining that it represented the careful and deliberate conclusions of the whole government as approved by the President.[16]

After the highly acceptable beginning that the final settlement should not burden commerce but should better it, we put in a new provision about how to better it. This was to be done by an agreement between the two countries, open to all others sympathetic with the ideas, "directed to the expansion, by appropriate international and domestic measures, of production, employment, and the exchange and consumption of goods." In other words, both countries would agree on measures to bring about an expanding economy. We would invite all to join us who would. In the setting of this aim—the increase of production, employment, trade, and consumption—all forms of discrimination were to be eliminated and tariffs and other trade barriers reduced. We accepted British references to the Atlantic Charter and early discussion of procedures.

Here, we explained to Lord Halifax and Redvers Opie, we had tried to dispel British fears that we were seeking to impose on them either unilateral obligations or the moribund hand of the nineteenth century. We were embracing the Keynesian ideas of an expanding economy. If it needed to be managed, let us do it together and not separately.

Mr. Hull cabled Ambassador Winant to urge speedy acceptance upon the Prime Minister. Lord Halifax made the same recommendation. Then began two months of blindman's buff. Winant found Churchill absorbed in the loss of HMS *Prince of Wales* and HMS *Repulse* off Malaya and his coming trip to Washington, and was referred to the Chancellor of the Exchequer. He in turn passed the matter back to Halifax to be taken up with Churchill when he arrived in Washington. Mr. Hull urged FDR to do the same. The great man came and went, but no one in either capital seemed able to find out what had happened. In January I asked Mr. Hull, as a matter of great urgency, since more appropriations hearings were coming up, to find out. He told me to do it myself; on January 29 I did so.

The President told me that on several occasions during Churchill's visit he (FDR) had brought up the lend-lease agreement but that the Prime Minister showed a strong desire to postpone discussions and to have them go through someone else. The President had not insisted further in view of the pressure of other matters. He now wanted a speedy conclusion of the matter. In response to my report that the British constantly asked whether Article VII and the State Department's view of its importance and urgency really represented the President's ideas, he said most emphatically that they did and that I should say so. My memorandum to him ended with two numbered recommendations: (1) that we make another effort to get the British to accept our latest draft, and (2) if the British continued to object to the reference to "discrimination," we drop the whole article and merely say that the parties would promptly discuss the whole matter anew. This would leave us as well as the British free to adopt any attitudes which we might wish. The President took my memorandum and wrote at the end of it: "I strongly hope the British will accept (1)—because (2) leaves them in a much more difficult future economic situation. FDR"

Finally, when I pointed out that hearings on the next year's appropriations bill were only a week away and that four months ago we had told Congress we were hopeful of an early agreement with the British, he said that we should make clear that the delay was not on our side. The next day I reported all this to Halifax, as instructed, showing him the President's note and saying that the Department would no longer assume responsibility for delay. From then on it would be clear that the British had only themselves to blame. He agreed to do all he could, adding sadly that the Cabinet clung stubbornly to the belief that the mere signing of the agreement itself abrogated imperial preferential tariffs.

I had hoped that this was the end, but the lion had one more roar in it. On February 6, 1942, the Cabinet met and, as reported by Eden to Winant, confirmed Halifax's worst fears. They were unwilling, he said, "to barter Empire preference in exchange for . . . planes, tanks, guns, goods, et cetera, because of the political repercussion that they believed would result."[17] We must agree that "discrimination" as used in Article VII did not apply to special arrangements between members of the same commonwealth or federation such as the British Commonwealth or the United States of America. When Halifax presented this view to Feis and me the next day, we turned it down flat and told him we saw no use in further discussion. He did not dissent.

We reported the stalemate to Welles and the President. Winant spent the weekend with the Prime Minister and talked Article VII and imperial preferences. Then Hopkins came to see me with the draft of a telegram from "FDR to a former Naval Person." We worked it over; Welles thought the result an improvement, and the President fired it off. He was not, he said, asking for any advance commitments on Empire preference. He wanted to make it clear that nothing was excluded from conversations before we sat down at the table.[18]

If this did not illumine the subject, as Professor Whitehead said of a lecture by Lord Russell on higher mathematics, it did not deepen the surrounding darkness. At any rate, it worked. The British signed.

I have gone into this episode at greater length than its inherent importance warrants because it illustrates a problem that was to occur later in attempts to win British cooperation in broad postwar plans. The qualities which produce the dogged, unbeatable courage of the British, personified at the time in Winston Churchill, can appear in other settings as stubbornness bordering on stupidity.

These qualities, so admirable in the war, lost the British great opportunities in the 1950s.

HELP TO RUSSIA

Hitler's attack on the Soviet Union brought a reversal of policy easier to make in theory than in practice. Before June 22 it had been one of coolness to the point of hostility, but not so hostile as "to drive Stalin further into the arms of Hitler"—whatever that then-popular cliché meant. It furnished little guidance on whether to grant or deny a specific export license. The safest course had been to stall them all. As late as June 14 the Soviet Union had been added to the list of countries subject to the freezing order, and had protested.

Constantine A. Oumansky, the Soviet Ambassador, belonged to the new school of offensive Soviet diplomats. They never learned the manners of the old Russian Foreign Office, as had Chicherin, Litvinov, and Maisky. The new men cultivated boorishness as a method of showing their contempt for the capitalist world, with which they wished minimum contact. Vishinsky was a natural blackguard, but cultivated and amusing; Gromyko's gaucheness was relieved by a grim, sardonic humor. Oumansky had no redeeming qualities. To frustrate him with icy politeness had given me considerable pleasure. So it was difficult to reverse course and, as policy cleared, to begin helping instead of hindering Russian procurement in the United States. When Oumansky was killed in a plane crash of suspicious cause on his way to a post as Ambassador to Mexico, we felt no sense of loss.

The first lend-lease agreement with the Russians throws some light on our general expectations of the course of events. It took the form of an exchange of letters between the President and Stalin by which we agreed to furnish aid up to a billion dollars which the Russians would repay without interest over a ten-year period beginning five years after the war's end.[19]

In order to get needed goods moving to the Soviet Union, Welles established a small group under me, directed first by Charles Curtis and later by another friend, Charles Bunn, a lawyer from Minneapolis. We were wholly inadequate in prestige and knowledge in dealing with the new wartime bureaucracy of Washington and the armed services and the British supply missions, which through membership on the joint boards had wormed their way into the very allocation procedure itself. Our clients, too, were clumsy and difficult. Not daring to depart in the smallest particular from their instructions, they had no flexibility, no feel for the possible. By the end of the year, admitting defeat, I was glad to give up the struggle and become a member of the President's Soviet Protocol Committee, which Harry Hopkins gathered together to hear orders from the White House about what must go to the Soviet Union.

SUNDAY, DECEMBER 7

On Sunday, December 7, Archie and Ada MacLeish drove out to our Maryland farm north of Washington to get some exercise by clearing up fallen timber in our woods and to share a picnic lunch. He was then Librarian of Congress and head of the "Office of Facts and Figures," FDR's ingenious name for our foreign propaganda bureau. The MacLeishes had to get back to town for an afternoon appointment and left us soon after lunch. In a few minutes Archie was running down the hill from the house shouting, "The Japanese have attacked Pearl Harbor. Turn on your car radio." Then he was gone.

We soon followed him, listening to reports of unbelievable disaster as we drove. I dropped off at the Department. On the second floor south little groups stood about the corridor, talking almost in whispers, doing nothing. Mr. Hull was shut up with a few intimates, still, it was reported, in a towering rage. The Japanese Ambassador, Admiral Kichisaburo Nomura, and their special ambassador, Saburo Kurusu, had left him only a couple of hours before. Each group added its bit of gossip. Mr. Hull had reportedly castigated the departing envoys in native Tennesseean as "scoundrels and piss-ants." War had or had not been declared. Germany would or would not join Japan. The axis plan was or was not to involve us in the Pacific leaving the European partners a free hand to finish the European war first; and so on. Our Petroleum Adviser, Max Thornburg, reported having seen terrifying telegraphed photographs of our shattered fleet. When no one seemed to have any use or orders for us, the groups dissolved and we went home.

Although, happily, we did not know it, that Sunday afternoon's experience was an augury of the Department's coming role in the war years.

4. RETROSPECT

SOME TIME WENT BY before I discovered how little I had been taken into the confidence of the government I served. This was to continue throughout my time as Assistant Secretary. I have no complaint; there was nothing personal about it. The economic side was simply "below stairs" in Old State and, for the most part, kept to its useful but humbler tasks and role. For instance, I knew nothing about an atomic weapon until the bombs were exploded over Hiroshima and Nagasaki—although later I was to know a good deal. Similarly, I knew little, as we tightened the economic blockade of Japan, of the tension it was producing there, nothing of the Japanese messages we were reading or what they portended, and nothing of the agony of indecision that gripped the Administration as Japanese military forces moved southward in Indochina toward southern Siam and Singapore. Even if I had, it is doubtful whether it would have changed my views: first, because those in the Cabinet with whom I most agreed—Colonel Stimson, Harry Hopkins, and later the President—did not change theirs; and, second, because even the most cautious, including Mr. Hull, were unwilling to back down from positions taken. Only retreat would have affected events.

I suggested earlier that everyone in the Department—and in the government generally—misread Japanese intentions. This misreading was not of what the Japanese military government proposed to do in Asia, not of the hostility our embargo would excite, but of the incredibly high risks General Tojo would assume to accomplish his ends. No one in Washington realized that he and his regime regarded the conquest of Asia not as the accomplishment of an ambition but as the survival of a regime. It was a life-and-death matter to them. They were absolutely unwilling to continue in what they regarded as Japan's precarious position surrounded by great and hostile powers—the United States, the Soviet Union, and a possibly revived and restored China. This is what Ambassador Kurusu meant on December 2 when, in Mr. Welles's words, the Ambassador said to him that "the Japanese people believe that economic measures are a much more effective weapon of war than military measures; that . . . they are being placed under severe pressure by the United States to yield to the American position; and that it is preferable to fight rather than to yield to pressure."[1]

The day before, at the meeting of the Privy Council which decided on war, General Tojo had described the consequences of submission: "The United States, however, has not shown any sign of concession from its past position. . . . Should Japan submit to her demands, not only would Japan's prestige be entirely destroyed and the solution of the China Affair rendered impossible, but Japan's existence itself would be endangered. It is now clear that Japan's claims

cannot be attained through diplomatic measures."[2] To General Tojo and the
Privy Council Japan's existence meant existence in the larger sense envisaged
by her "claims" in the "China Affair." To him the issue was fight or surrender.
He no less than Winston Churchill rejected all "reasonable" odds in making
that decision.

However faulty American knowledge of Japanese military psychology and
her judgment of Japan's intentions may have been, Japanese judgment was far
worse. The one course the American people and government could not and
would not tolerate was an attack on American territory and the American fleet.
The result was bound to be war. This, of course, Tokyo expected. The consequences of war, in view of the vastly preponderant strength of the United States
and the temper of our people, were almost certain to be disastrous to Japan.
A far wiser and safer course for General Tojo's government, and one within the
scope of his policies and premises, would have been a move to obtain the oil of
Indonesia by pressure on the Dutch and, if necessary, their removal through a
Japanese-instigated-and-supported Indonesian revolution. In Washington the
Cabinet and the Army and Navy were all divided about how to respond to an
expected move south. Observation and decoded messages reported large troop
movements in that direction. Opinion polls reported doubt as to whether Congress or the people would support war to protect foreign colonial possessions in
the South Pacific, and certainly any support would not be unanimous. The
armed forces were far from ready and said so. If Singapore and Malaya were
left alone, would the British take on a new war? Could they be effective if they
did?

Indeed, the move south was Japan's central purpose and real objective,
and the Pearl Harbor attack a diversion to protect it.

No greater folly can be imagined, despite the promised support of a German declaration of war. That, too, was colossal folly on Hitler's part. Already
in great trouble before Moscow, his best chance to extricate himself from his
Russian mistake and still play for hegemony in Europe lay in directing American power to the Asian battle. To betray Japan presented him with no problem.
Nevertheless, after four days for thought, on December 11 he declared war
against the United States. At last our enemies, with parallel stupidity, resolved
our dilemmas, clarified our doubts and uncertainties, and united our people for
the long, hard course that the national interest required. Those of us who had
been holding our breath while the future of the world hung in balance could
breathe once more. Our enemies had identified themselves and their purposes.
Our immediate military task was clear; what should be our longer-range political aims and purposes, what were our major difficulties and dangers, remained
shrouded in obscurity.

Two aspects of the attack on Pearl Harbor are often confused: the tactical
military surprise and the strategic political surprise. A government should, of
course, be prepared for both. The former should be much easier to guard
against than the latter. I am not competent to discuss our unpreparedness at
Pearl Harbor and in any event, Roberta Wohlstetter's superb book, *Pearl Harbor*,[3] makes it unnecessary. The political problem of where among a wide range

of choices an enemy will strike is a different matter. The high command, civil and military, had no doubt in 1941 that an attack—Mr. Hull called it "some deviltry"—was coming. Several spots on Siamese, Malayan, British, and Dutch territory seemed more likely to be struck than any on ours. Of all points, our bastion at Pearl Harbor did not seem a likely target. Nine years later, in June 1950, Korea did not seem the most likely trouble point. In 1941 Ambassador Grew in Tokyo took notable exception to the prevailing opinion; he believed that Pearl Harbor was not only a possible but the probable target. Whether or not the government was negligent in not being prepared for an attack on Pearl Harbor, it was not stupid in not expecting it to fall there. The thesis that the President offered the fleet for sacrifice to bring on a war seems to me utterly preposterous.

If the Army and Navy were unprepared for war, the State Department was no less so. It never did seem to find its place. As I shall relate later, the Secretary's ebbing energy was drained off into that legacy of the nineteenth century, the United Nations; many of us spent inordinate time in bureaucratic warfare either for survival—as it seemed then—or to preserve prerogatives—as it seems now; others did *ad hoc* jobs in aid of economic warfare and raw-material supply—and did them with professional skill—or, in aid of military operations, such as dealings with the Free French, the antifascist Italians, or the future occupation zones in a defeated Germany, without noticeable brilliance; still others were caught up in preparatory conferences to deal with such postwar problems as food, agriculture, relief, and monetary arrangements. Few made any contribution to the conduct of the war or to the achievement of political purposes through war. *Silent leges inter arma.* Diplomacy, it seems, was here as silent as law. Yet there was room for something a little more modern and percipient than FDR's adoption of General Grant's "unconditional surrender" or Henry Morgenthau's conception of Germany as a group of agrarian states. In justice to my colleagues, I must plead as guilty as any of escaping into immediate busywork to keep from the far harder task of peering into a dim future, which, of course, should be one of a diplomatist's main duties.

As I look back upon the period to which I now turn, my memory (perhaps an unfair or incomplete one) is of a department without direction, composed of a lot of busy people working hard and usefully but as a whole not functioning as a foreign office. It did not chart a course to be furthered by the success of our arms, or to aid or guide our arms. Rather it seems to have been adrift, carried hither and yon by the currents of war or pushed about by collisions with more purposeful craft.

5. ECONOMIC WARFARE AT HOME

ON MONDAY MORNING, December 8, Washington awoke, a capital at war. The indecisions, hesitations, and doubts of the past year, the pretenses and fumblings, were gone. Argument over, the country and its capital turned to what Americans like and do best, action. In a few months half a continent and a hundred and thirty million people were transformed into the greatest military power the world had seen. Amid this burst of energy the State Department stood breathless and bewildered like an old lady at a busy intersection during rush hour. All around it vigorous, effective people were purposefully on their way to do jobs that needed doing. Nowhere was this more true than in making and executing plans for economic dealings with friends, enemies, and neutrals all over the world. The object was to corner all useful materials for our side and preclude the enemy from getting them. These were not operations for which State Department officers were trained or fitted, though they reeked of foreign policy.

As we entered the war, these functions, as already suggested, were scattered all over Washington and all over the Department of State. It was inevitable, even in a disorderly administration, that they should be drawn together; it was also important that the State Department should not be cut off from making a contribution to the foreign policy aspects of these decisions and their execution. The British from their experience had made this clear to us, but we had not had their training in Cabinet coordination. Our vigorous Cabinet men—Morgenthau, Jesse Jones, Henry Wallace—were empire builders, impatient with what seemed to them State Department fussiness and diplomatic obstruction. The result of the conflict of these forces was altogether predictable: more and more the State Department fought desperately for a shrinking place. In this battle it fell to me to champion State—hazardous work, as I nearly got shot by my own side when the Secretary and Breck Long interpreted the struggle as one between radicals and conservatives, classifying me among the former. However, I can say with Abbé Sieyès, when asked what he did during the French Revolution: "I survived."

HENRY WALLACE'S GREAT INVASION

For us in State the Washington war began before we enlisted in the international one, and began with a minor victory to be followed by a crushing defeat. For some time axis subversion in Latin America had been carried on by persons of German, Italian, or Japanese ancestry, some still nationals of those countries, others claiming citizenship within the western hemisphere. A group under Nelson Rockefeller, Coordinator of Commercial and Cultural Relations Between the American Republics (a title itself in derogation of the State Department's role), had been at work on a list of these people. A presidential order of July 17, 1941, authorized the Secretary of State to publish such a list and keep it current. Persons listed were to be treated under the freezing orders, as were citizens of Germany or Italy. A Division of World Trade Intelligence was created within the State Department with John S. Dickey (later President of Dartmouth), who had prepared the list, as its chief. Henceforth he and I worked together and formed one of the most cherished friendships of my life.

This small step forward was soon offset by a large one backward. I have already described the innocuous first move, the establishment of the Administrator of Export Control, described as "primarily a national defense matter," under which State would provide the machinery for the actual issue of licenses. The Administrator was a genial and pleasant man, Colonel—in a few months, Brigadier General—Russell Maxwell, known affectionately and disrespectfully as Slapsie-Maxie. Export control was not to be his life work. He had little experience in framing policies for trade with two areas of great importance to the Department, Latin America and the European neutrals. We in the Department, therefore, devised a simple and effective method by which we wrote for the Administrator his orders to us determining which export licenses should be granted or denied, and he permitted us broad latitude in interpreting our handiwork. We appeared to have contained the first assault.

At first sight the second assault seemed more dangerous but to seasoned bureaucratic infighters it bore all the earmarks of futility and early demise. Under the chairmanship of Vice President Henry Wallace, most of the Cabinet (State, Treasury, War, Navy, Justice, Agriculture, and Commerce), collectively known as the Board of Economic Warfare—originally christened the Economic Defense Board—were to advise the President on the entire range of international economic, financial, patent, and communication fields, coordinate work of the various departments in these fields, and develop integrated plans for the war and postwar periods. Administration of various activities relating to economic defense, under policies formulated by the board, was, however, to remain with the departments and agencies then charged with it.

While the franchise of the board seemed to absorb all international aspects of economic policy and action, an old inhabitant of the bureaucratic jungle like Mr. Hull knew that Cabinet boards and committees were paper tigers. They made a fine show in a parade but soon dissolved in the rain. Cabinet officers are too busy and too suspicious of one another to join a raid against a colleague. At first the board furnished Mr. Hull with just another grievance against the President over his conduct of foreign affairs. After attending a few meetings, the Secretary of State deputized me "to explain his absence" and substitute for him.

Henry Wallace soon confounded all expectations about the board by a gross departure from the rules of bureaucratic warfare. He introduced into a harmless committee of busy men an executive director in the person of one of the most able, adroit, and energetic administrators whom the war had brought to Washington. Milo Perkins was Wallace's own importation out of the Southwest into the Agricultural Adjustment Administration. A fighter, imaginative, armed with funds so abundantly available to war agencies, Perkins soon had a large organization and began to act through his own people. Though cast in the role of opponents, he and I soon became warm friends, which we continue to be. Breckinridge Long thought we were both dangerous radicals because we were friends of Felix Frankfurter. Today we are both regarded as far to the right.

In the spring of 1942 under Perkins' skillful management the Board of Economic Warfare took a "great leap forward." A new presidential order hit us a stunning and unexpected blow.[1] Arthur Krock wrote with relish in *The New York Times* of the unforgettable "anguish of Sumner Welles when felled by this sudden blow to the solar plexus" and the "moments when it seemed that . . . Assistant Secretary of State Acheson would never stop vibrating."[2]

The order took from Jesse Jones and the Reconstruction Finance Corporation and gave to the board the power and funds to buy abroad materials for production, civilian economy, or denial to the enemy; made it the State Department's adviser on lend-lease agreements; and gave it authority to arrange for reciprocal aid from foreign countries, to "represent the United States Government in dealing with the economic warfare agencies" of allied countries, and to send abroad "technical, engineering, and economic representatives responsible to the Board as the Board may deem necessary." The last three of these grants of authority were direct encroachments upon the most ancient of the State Department's roles and prerogatives—to conduct for the President negotiations with foreign nations and the representation of this country abroad. Before the Second World War the Department had carried on a long and largely successful struggle to transfer into the Foreign Service persons theretofore serving abroad as representatives of other departments—Treasury, Agriculture, Commerce, and (later) Labor. The order of April 13 was a painful, bitter, and humiliating defeat.

Mr. Hull was away when the blow fell. Welles's protests at the White House had been unavailing. The old gentleman, thoroughly aroused, mounted a strong counterattack, which left the President an avenue of retreat—that his assent to the order had been obtained without knowledge that the State Department was unaware of what was going on. If he had known that, said the President, he would never have signed the order. Weeks of meetings and drafting at the White House brought forth a mouse, called a "Clarification and Interpretation."[3] A more inappropriate description can hardly be imagined. Both the title and the document must have greatly amused its author.

In the succeeding months the decline of the State Department was as liberally paved with the slippery phrases of this document as the descent to hell is with good intentions. The document, like Solomon, proposed to divide the baby of economic foreign policy; unlike Solomon, however, the document did divide it.

In the making of decisions, the board was admonished to recognize the primary responsibility and position, under the President, of the Secretary of State "in the formulation and conduct of our foreign policy and our relations with foreign nations." On the other hand, "in matters of business judgment concerned with . . . procurement of materials . . . the Department will recognize the primary responsibility and position of the Board." However, in many cases a decision might involve both matters of foreign policy and business judgment in varying degrees, in which case no clear-cut separation was possible. So the Secretary of State and the Chairman of the board should "reach a joint decision, in matters of sufficient importance obtaining direction from the President. . . . In short, for the effective exercise of the functions both of the Board and the Department, it [was] essential that from the inception of any project there be complete exchange of information, mutual consultation and mutual confidence," none of which existed or was likely to exist.

In the field all negotiations were to be authorized or conducted by State with the board participating in procurement discussions and being kept informed of lend-lease discussions. The chief of diplomatic mission in each country would be in charge and would coordinate everyone's activities. If, alas, he failed to do so, an appeal lay to the Secretary and the Chairman, two men who rarely met and thoroughly disliked each other. A committee in the Department would clear all proposals to send people abroad on official business—Welles, the Chairman, and Shaw for administrative matters, I for "the economic aspects."

With this spoonful of soothing syrup Mr. Hull and his cohorts had to be content. In the contest between Henry Wallace and Jesse Jones the round clearly went to Wallace.

THE PRESIDENT BROADENS THE BATTLE ROYAL

The successful allied landings in North Africa on November 8–10, 1942, ushered in a winter of discontent for the beleaguered State Department. With the end of the fighting, civilians from both the British and American governments converged on Algiers to represent their various ministries and agencies in the first exciting adventure of occupying conquered territory. There was, of course, some doubt whether the territory—that is, the French part of it—was conquered or liberated, and, if the latter, who should represent the "liberatee." The Washington battle over who should "coordinate" the civilians was quite as sharp.

The British had no trouble. In their simple and direct way they sent out a Cabinet minister of commanding force and character, a former Guards officer, and everyone fell into disciplined order. But we had no one at home or abroad among the civilians who had, in a phrase that Harold Macmillan once used to me, "the stuff of command in him." Both within the Department and between agencies we fell into bickering. Into this explosive situation the President tossed a lighted firecracker. On November 21 the White House announced that Governor Herbert H. Lehman of New York would resign shortly to become associated with the Department of State as Director of Foreign Relief and Rehabilitation Operations.[4] He would organize American participation in assistance to "victims of war in areas reoccupied by the forces of the United Nations." This was all that was needed to make the next round of the battle of Washington an enthralling spectacle. Governor Lehman might be slow but he looked like a heavyweight.

Even before the Governor's appointment the preliminary fights had begun in the Department. This time trouble came from the political sector. As civilians on government missions began entering their spheres of influence, the chiefs of geographic divisions became restless. They also had internal problems since, while Wallace Murray's barony covered the Near East and Africa, Ray Atherton was responsible for dealing with the two European nations that with us had become involved in North Africa. As the center of interest moved eastward, Murray's claims grew but, for the moment and in the common defense against economic upstarts, he accorded Atherton primacy. Ray went with his troubles to Breck Long, who diagnosed them as a struggle for power among "the radical boys." Wallace and Perkins, he thought, were backing Berle, "Frankfurter and his crew, acting through Acheson." Mr. Hull, he believed, wanted Atherton, who hesitated on the brink of involvement.[5]

In true conspiratorial style Long poured out his story to the President's secretary, Marvin McIntyre, insisting that he (Long) should "not appear in it at all."[6] The upshot of the whole sorry matter was another letter from the President to the Secretary putting him in charge of all nonmilitary matters affecting the interests of the United States as a result of the occupation of territories in Europe and North Africa. Mr. Hull on November 25 assigned this authority to the Division of European Affairs. The order created in the division an Office of Foreign Territories. Paul Appleby, the Under Secretary of Agriculture (upon whom Wallace, Perkins, and I had agreed as the man to handle this work before the row started), was put in charge of the office. All other divisions and officers were to continue their prior responsibilities except as the order "shall supersede the provisions of any existing Order"![7]

The old geographic divisions and their officers had no experience or knowledge of conducting an operation where men, machines, and materials were used to an end. Their experience and training had been in discussion and reporting. The Office of Foreign Territories failed lamentably. Appleby, who could run the wheat-acreage-allocation plan, or the Bureau of Marketing, or supervise the Farm Credit Administration, could not understand the Division of European Affairs, and vice versa. In less than two months he resigned and returned to the more congenial environment of the Department of Agriculture.

Meanwhile, I had turned to a new set of problems presented by Governor Lehman and the relief and rehabilitation of occupied and liberated territory. The Governor gave me my first exposure to high state officials. FDR did not count since to him the Governorship had been a mere passing phase; Herbert Lehman had been Governor of our then most populous state for a decade (1933–42). I soon concluded that the training ground of future presidents would not be in the Governorship of the states. Later, Lehman was a useful member of the United States Senate, but the simplest executive task was beyond him. This he soon demonstrated.

We began with trouble in getting his role, the new Office of Foreign Territories, and my work straightened out. Both Mr. Hull and Breck Long were persuaded that I would be a malign and dangerous influence. I was already rumored, as head of the Frankfurter contingent, to "have appropriated" the Governor, and Long urged the Secretary to get Lehman out of the State Department and "set him up as an independent agency under the President."[8] Instead, he remained to confound confusion.

The original presidential announcement on November 21 appointing Lehman seemed to have been already limited by the order of November 25, and as the Governor probed deeper he found further reasons for unhappiness. Even the negotiation of a United Nations relief agency was to remain in the Secretary's province, with me as his deputy. In March of 1943 he was knocking at the White House door to find out what he was supposed to do. The answer granted broad authority with one generous hand while the other, more parsimonious one, took it away.[9] He was to plan, coordinate, and arrange for our government's part in the "relief of victims of war in areas liberated from Axis control"—a pretty broad grant of authority—but he was expected to use the "facilities of the various government departments, agencies, and officials which [were] equipped to assist in this field" and might issue to them such directives as he deemed necessary. Finally, his operations were to "be subject to the approval of the U.S. military commander in the area" (who was already doing what the Governor was now being told to do); in general foreign policy, to the directives of the Secretary of State; to agreements made in each area with our allies; and to a United Nations organization when created. In short, the Governor was to be a coordinator among coordinators, administrators, and warriors. With this hunting license he went off on a visit to London, announcing "that he did not intend to carry on negotiations for a joint United Nations approach to the relief and rehabilitation problem, since such negotiations will be conducted here [Washington] by the Secretary of State."[10] To those negotiations we shall return after we have followed civil economic warfare to its denouement toward the end of the year.

THE BUDGET BUREAU CONFOUNDS CONFUSION

Among the roles of the Budget Bureau was that of constant critic and improver of administration in the federal executive branch. In my day this work had fallen to the products of graduate schools of civil administration. Their ideas, some of which I have just recounted, seemed to me theoretical nonsense. They were about to produce a masterpiece. The President gave them their opportunity by directing them to bring some order out of the confusion reigning in the direction and execution of foreign economic policy in liberated areas. On June 3, 1943, the completed work went to the Secretary of State with a "Dear Cordell" letter.[11] Younger readers may never have heard of the cartoonist Rube Goldberg, famous a generation ago, whose forte was drawing bizarre and infinitely complicated devices for doing the most simple acts like picking up a shoe or putting the cat out. The new proposal would have ranked among his best.

The letter pointed the broad scheme: the Governor would distribute goods and provide technical advice and services for all civilian purposes; lend-lease would obtain and pay for most of these when acquired in the United States; the Board of Economic Warfare would undertake foreign purchases, industrial development, and economic intelligence; and the Treasury would be responsible for exchange rates, monetary control, and fiscal matters. All of these activities would be "coordinated" by an Assistant Secretary of State—alas, myself—and area directors. The area directors should have "ample authority to act 'on the spot,' " subject to the orders of the military commander. The Assistant Secretary should act within policies laid down by two committees composed of himself and representatives of six departments and agencies.

I shall not go further. The reader is weary. Anyone experienced in Washington could have told the Budget reorganizers that Cabinet officers and heads of agencies cannot be coordinated by a junior official, especially one whose authority is so hedged about by intra- and interdepartmental committees as was done in this case. If the Vice President could not do it, an Assistant Secretary clearly could not. In any event, the scheme was superseded in three months.

Within a week of the signing of this order, Henry Wallace and Jesse Jones tried the President's patience too far. Just when the landings on Sicily were imminent and Stalin was threatening and bullying for a second front against Germany, Wallace began and Jones enthusiastically joined in a childish brawl over the Board of Economic Warfare's program of purchasing foreign strategic materials. The President boiled over. On July 15, acting on the advice of James F. Byrnes, the "Assistant President," he abolished the BEW and took away all Jones's powers relating to foreign purchases. All the powers of both were given, in September 1943, to a new agency under the President, the Office of Economic Warfare, headed by a newcomer to the field, Leo Crowley, hitherto the Alien Property Custodian. The contestants were thus narrowed for the final bout.

In the meantime I had been attempting to persuade Mr. Hull that it was not enough to have the President recite the litany that in foreign policy he was Allah and Cordell Hull was his prophet who would "coordinate" the faithful. The prophet needed also a sword for the unbelievers. On July 10 Mr. Hull sent the President a memorandum that I had prepared for him with the approval of my colleagues Howland Shaw, Green Hackworth, Ray Atherton, Thomas Finletter (then serving as assistant to Governor Lehman), and Herbert Feis. The covering note described it as a statement of his views on a subject "you and I have frequently discussed [i.e.,] the relationship that should exist between State and other agencies engaged in activities abroad." Nothing came of it at the time; however, the relationship portrayed is not far from that which existed in fact in the last six years of President Truman's administration.

On the day after Wallace and Jones had made their exit and Crowley his entrance, Feis and I were summoned to James F. Byrnes's office in the White House, the Office of War Mobilization, along with representatives of the Budget, Governor Lehman, Lend-Lease, and Leo Crowley himself, to discuss Mr. Hull's request that Byrnes make a strong statement concerning the primacy of

State in foreign affairs. The representatives of the other agencies present said that everything was working well. I argued that, although the principle of State's primacy in foreign policy was accepted, the recent executive order of June 3 had created so much doubt about what was foreign policy as to make it very difficult for the Department to get people to carry on its work and in specific cases to get acceptance of its rulings from other agencies. In many cases they went ahead with their own plans, talking to foreign representatives without informing the Department. The result was that the Department had responsibility without authority. Some clear statement of procedure was necessary. Mr. Byrnes refused to issue any further general instructions but announced that the Department was to determine foreign policy and that it had the last word. This left us where we were. At the end of the meeting Crowley sensibly observed to me that further discussion would not get anywhere and that the proper course for the Department was vigorously to fight out difficulties as they arose in connection with specific issues.

PEACE THROUGH HUMAN SACRIFICE

For some time rumors of a personal nature about Welles had been circulating in Washington, assiduously furthered by his malign enemy, William Christian Bullitt, a singularly ironic middle name. Mr. Hull fretted the President about what he termed Welles's "disloyalty" to him. They agreed that Welles should resign as Under Secretary and be offered a mission to Moscow, which he saw fit not to accept.[12] Mr. Byrnes believed that this vacancy in the State Department would make possible a remedy for the confusion in the duplication of our economic activities overseas, regarding which he had been overwhelmed with complaints from the armed forces and the State Department.[13] On September 25 Welles's resignation and the nomination of his successor, Edward R. Stettinius, Jr., were announced by the White House. On the same day it also announced the creation of the Foreign Economic Administration, at the head of which, appropriately enough, was the man who had not lost his own in the shuffle, Leo Crowley. To his inheritance from Wallace and Jones he added Lend-Lease from Stettinius, Relief from Governor Lehman, and Coordination from me. "One of the best administrators in or out of government," the President said of him; he would need to be.

The Governor had to be satisfied with appointment as "Special Assistant to the President for the purpose of perfecting the plans for the meeting of representatives of the United Nations on November 9" to set up the United Nations relief organization.[14] "Perfecting" was a particularly artful choice of terms. For some time I had been making and would continue to make all these arrangements, even drafting and negotiating the agreement. When the meeting convened I would be made its chairman.

Mr. Hull was more than appeased by the sacrifice of Welles and by the close liaison between State and FEA "to assure conformity of our foreign economic operations to our national foreign policy," which was promised in October and announced in November.

The FEA was the last battle in the civil war within the Roosevelt Administration over the control of economic policy and operations abroad. However, the struggle is an endless one to which there is no definite answer, certainly not in the form of drawing-board diagrams. "Stettinius," wrote Robert E. Sherwood, "at Roosevelt's direction, made a determined effort to reorganize the State Department and bring it up to date. He drew up an enormous and impressive chart with myriad boxes in orderly array. But he found out that this rearrangement could produce no real change in the character of the State Department as long as the occupants of the boxes . . . remained the same; and they did remain the same."[15] Sherwood was on the track of the truth, but he went astray in believing that the important boxes were those that housed the "divisional chiefs," the "career men." The ones that Stettinius and Mr. Hull occupied are far more important. Strong men can accomplish a lot even with poor organization, but weakness at the top cannot be overcome by the best. On the larger scale the final determinant is what kind of man occupies the box labeled "President" and what sort of relations he has with his chief Secretary.

One often reads of Franklin Roosevelt that he liked organizational confusion which permitted him to keep power in his own hands by playing off his colleagues one against the other. This, I think, is nonsense. Such is a policy of weakness, and Roosevelt was not a weak man. Furthermore, it did not keep power in his own hands; it merely hindered the creation of effective power by anyone. Roosevelt had no trouble in commanding Colonel Stimson, General Marshall, and Admiral King, far stronger men than Wallace, Jones, Lehman, or Hull. He understood military organization. On the other hand, he was tone deaf to the subtler nuances of civil governmental organization. This was messed up in his administration for the simplest of reasons: he did not know any better.

The moral of this long tale of administrative bungling is not that it prevented our economic policies abroad from effectively helping our military effort and weakening our enemies (we shall turn to the positive side in the next chapter), but to illustrate concretely and precisely that government is an art, perhaps the most difficult of the arts. It cannot be learned from a textbook. No pamphlet of instructions comes with the Presidency.

One must add, too, that the FEA did improve the environment for our work. The reduction of competition lessened tensions. So, also, did a concomitant element of Leo Crowley's nature. He understood very well Talleyrand's admonition, "Above all, no zeal."

6. ECONOMIC WARFARE ABROAD:

DEADLOCK

THE AIM OF economic warfare is to cut the enemy's supplies, information, and funds from foreign territory and prevent his communication with it. The European Civil War developed economic warfare far beyond the old blockade tactic used prior to 1914, which was merely the naval interdiction of a coast. Economic warfare rested upon control of the seas but also used control of communication, commerce, and finance. Intercontinental mails were routed through control points, read, and stopped when desired; telephone, telegraph, and wireless communications were dealt with in the same way. Through the navicert system and allied control over bunkers and ships' stores, a ship could not move without allied permission. International legal ideas about the rights of neutrals, neutral trade, and the freedom of the seas became irrelevant to immovable ships. The blacklist and freezing controls stopped leaks through the blockade to the enemy by reaching enemy sympathizers' own assets, not merely shipments.

Another aim of economic warfare was to control overland trade between neutrals and the enemy within the continent he dominated. In doing so, it posed hard problems in dealing with both the foreign neutral and our own people. When neutrals feared an enemy such as Germany, as all European neutrals did in the early years of the war, and yet needed goods from Germany, the greater pressures were for German trade. But neutrals also needed materials from outside Europe, especially food and oil. Here lay the basis for urging them to sell to the allies and withhold from Germany. The extent to which they would do so would clearly depend on the fortunes of war.

At home the public, almost to a man, regarded arrangements to supply the neutrals as traitorous connivance at trading with the enemy. Neutrals were judged to be enemy sympathizers. General Franco's government in Spain, in particular, was denounced as no better than a Nazi ally of Hitler. Oil to Spain might go into a German submarine, despite Franco's promises, and be used to sink our ships. The possibility could not be denied. Then, too, trade with neutrals seemed unfair to our friends in occupied Europe. Under the harsh rule of German military government, they were treated by our economic-warfare policies as enemies. Twenty-five years before, the Commission for the Relief of Belgium had fed and clothed the inhabitants of that unhappy occupied country. But in the 1940s no similar differentiation was made between the enemy and his defeated victims. We waged economic war on foes and friends within their grasp alike, spreading deprivation with evenhanded harshness. Why, then, asked many, were we so solicitous about enemy-aiding neutrals?

Some high officials were strongly of this opinion. One was Robert Patterson, Under Secretary of War, "Old Thorough," as Colonel Stimson used to call him in Oliver Cromwell's phrase. All Patterson's opinions were strongly, even passionately, held. He disposed of the whole matter of neutral trade with Germany by announcing emphatically and upon the highest authority, "He that is not with me is against me!" I first met General Eisenhower when Feis and I, urging Stimson to moderate Patterson's belief that his general principle should decide all concrete cases, were sent to the Army's Chief of Operations. Eisenhower understood the problem and very quickly got our discussions on a more pragmatic basis.

Sometimes passionate objection to the trade held by enthusiasts in the ranks caused grave breaches of discipline. On one occasion, when Churchill was staying at the White House, its occupants were embarrassed and annoyed by publication in a column by a violently anti-Franco correspondent of excerpts from the Prime Minister's notes to the President. Churchill, as I recall it, was urging some concession to Spain in return for a benefit to Britain. He was bitterly attacked as appeasing Franco. The usual stir to find the perpetrator of the leak had about ended in the usual failure, when, on studying the column and the Churchill papers, I saw that the excerpts were taken not from one paper but from two. The number who had seen both papers might be more limited than those who had seen only one. This proved to be true. Those who had seen both and knew the columnist as well would be even more limited. In a short time the FBI had the culprit, a well-meaning but overzealous assistant to Stettinius. He resigned, went into the Army, and made an excellent record in the Pacific theater.

On another occasion meager shipments to French North Africa under the so-called Murphy-Weygand agreement were held up for months in 1942 at the Treasury, where ideological positions were strongly held, despite the fact that under the agreement we had twelve vice consuls in North Africa who were furnishing information vital to the landing planned for the autumn.

However, the difficulties inherent in the supply-purchase arrangements with European neutrals lay not so much in rejection by unsophisticated minds as in the fact that at the outset we were constructing economic policies out of differing opinions as to the emphasis to be given to imponderables outside the field of economics. A chart of allied reverses and successes in the field and in attempting to reduce neutral trade with Germany would have shown the same curves. Neutral response to attempted pressure followed their appraisal of the course of our arms.

In 1941 and the first half of 1942 allied military prospects gave no leverage to economic warfare. The German sweep into Russia and allied disasters at Pearl Harbor and in Southeast Asia left few counterpressures to German demands on the neutrals. Rommel driving east through North Africa and the German conquest of the Balkans and Greece as far south as Crete seemed to threaten the British with another disaster in Egypt. I well remember the gloom in the White House offices when Mr. Churchill, a visitor upstairs, got word of the fall of Tobruk. There seemed no end to bad news. Of necessity we bore in silence Franco's insults and predictions of allied defeat, as well as the flood of goods moving to Germany across Europe and the Baltic.

But the news did improve in the last quarter of 1942. Eisenhower and Montgomery struck Rommel from west and east in North Africa and crushed him the next spring. Success continued into the summer with the conquest of Sicily, the early promise of the landings in Italy, and the mounting Russian counteroffensive on the eastern front. But there things hung for a year as the fighting gradually simmered down in preparation for the great pushes of 1944.

All this was reflected on the economic front. The strategy, tactics, and guerrilla fighting of those campaigns do not belong in this book; they have been described admirably elsewhere.[1] My own part in them took the form of negotiating with the neutrals during the periods of crisis when, after months of deadlock between allied demands and neutral concessions, the nerves and tempers of both had been set on edge. A description of the stalemate on Swedish, Swiss, and Iberian fronts will give the setting.

DEADLOCK IN SWEDEN

When we entered the war, the limits of trade between the United States and Sweden were those of the Anglo-Swedish agreement of 1939. But we had other interests in Sweden than her trade with Germany. One of our greatest military needs was for trained pilots for the Air Force. Invested in them was the precious element of time. If they were hit over Germany or escaped from German prisoner-of-war camps, pilots made, where possible, for Sweden or Switzerland. There they would be interned, but, if a neutral government wished to be cooperative, there were ways of flying the pilots at night by mosquito planes to Britain and thus back to service. Again, both Sweden and Switzerland, surrounded as they were by axis military forces, permitted, as sparingly as they dared, German military rail movements across their territory. These movements could be restricted by "repairing" roadbeds and tunnels. A willingness to be cooperative was invaluable and could be lost by policies that the neutral believed to be harsh beyond reason.

So, also, the delivery of industrial diamonds (so vital to proximity and other fuses) from Switzerland to Germany was much simpler than to allied territory. The latter required more than cooperation by the Swiss, often complicity in illegality or indifference to it. Here, again, a harsh attitude on our part could beget a similar one on the other side. Finally, both Swedes and Swiss are among the most independent-minded, not to say stubborn, people in the world. All these considerations made negotiation with them difficult and delicate.

The autumn of 1942, before the allied successes in North Africa, was a troublesome and tense time. The flow of supplies, particularly of petroleum, from the United States to Sweden had practically stopped. So low were their stocks, the Swedish Government bitterly complained, that their navy and air force were practically inoperable in case of aggression. In some Washington quarters doubt was expressed whether Sweden had the will to resist aggression. In October my friend Erik Boheman, then Secretary General of the Swedish Foreign Office (later, when I was Secretary of State, the Swedish Ambassador in Washington), came over to confer with us. Fourteen years before as young men we had been friends in Stockholm, when I had spent several months there preparing an international-law case for his government.[2] He was, and is, a most intelligent and delightful companion. But in 1942 friendship could not solve our problems. At most it could smooth the path of discussion with courtesy and some mutual understanding.

It was Boheman's first visit to the United States. He found it, and especially its wartime government, almost incomprehensible. He was to negotiate with a committee, so he was told, of which I was the chairman, though he would never see the committee together. "It was generally considered," he has recorded, "that we [Swedes] were, perhaps, worth some pity but had no liberty of action and were forced to submit to every whim from Hitler's side. If oil was sent to Sweden, one could equally well send it directly to the Germans. Our will and determination to defend ourselves was not believed in. . . . All in all I played my record for between eighty and a hundred people. The lack of knowledge and the misconceptions with regard to Sweden were in most cases monumental and I became very hoarse. I soon found that communication between different departments was to a great extent lacking and that different departments had widely different views. What a difference from the British administration at that time."[3]

After endless negotiation, largely among ourselves, we got the President's approval to release two Swedish tankers for their air force and navy needs and to resume shipments of some other essential supplies. But it was not for another ten months that any real progress toward agreement seemed to be possible. Even that proved illusory.

Success of our arms enhanced negotiating power, as recorded in an agreement of September 23, 1943. In return for United States agreement to continue the "basic rations" provided in 1939, Sweden would (1) refuse further credits to Germany and associated or occupied countries; (2) reduce 1943 exports to these areas by at least fourteen per cent by value below those of 1942, with further reductions in 1944, and prohibit, as of July 1, 1943, all exports of arms, munitions, and means of transport; (3) reduce export of various ores and relate them to imports from Germany of coal and coke; (4) impose conditions against re-export on all exports to neutrals; and (5) establish a system in Sweden to satisfy the United States and United Kingdom legations regarding use of United States and United Kingdom imports. In addition, the Swedish Government unilaterally announced the end of German troop traffic across Sweden on October 1, 1943, and the end of all transit of German military goods, including petroleum, on October 15.

This agreement by its terms promised allied gain; the Swedes failed to live up to it. While the negotiators haggled, the spectacular advance of armies in Italy and Russia had slowed to a halt. By interpretations more ingenious than ingenuous the Swedish Foreign Office attempted to explain away iron-ore exports to Germany not only above those for 1942 but above the limits set in 1939. Even more exasperating, the Swedish company SKF increased exports of all ball bearings and their parts far beyond the 1942 level, despite governmental promises to the contrary and very considerable British preclusive buying. This Swedish action, counteracting as it did the risks and losses incurred in bombing the ball-bearing plants at Schweinfurt, enraged American opinion. Investigation disclosed that to accommodate British buying intended to limit German purchases, SKF had built a new factory.

Attempts to obtain redress from the Swedish Government failed. State and the Foreign Economic Administration agreed to increase pressure on the Swedish Government by a direct assault on SKF, vulnerable through its substantial interests in the United States to threats of blacklisting and freezing. By April of 1944 discussion seemed to be stalemated.

DEADLOCK IN SWITZERLAND

If the Swedes were stubborn, the Swiss were the cube of stubbornness. In June 1941 the British gave up argument and placed a total embargo on all goods "capable of benefiting the enemy's war effort," while continuing, however, the existing rations of foodstuffs and fodder. Long months of talks in London between American and British negotiators and the Swiss finally produced an outline of possible agreement in December. But German pressure resulted in Swiss refusal to meet allied demands for reduction of Swiss arms and ammunition going to Germany, and nothing came of it.

Our successes in North Africa in 1943 registered slowly on the Swiss mind. They gave greater weight to the more immediate German presence on their borders, allowing the Nazis further clearing arrangements in return for promised coal deliveries. In mid-August, however, the allies thought that concessions were in the offing. They agreed to open half the foodstuff quotas which had been closed off in May in return for Swiss reduction in the arms traffic to Germany. Almost at once they learned the shocking truth that, instead of reducing exports to Germany in the second quarter of 1943, the Swiss had actually increased them over the first quarter by from fifty to a hundred per cent. They also withheld the figures from the British and ourselves until after the agreement was made. Winfield Riefler, our Economic Minister in London, described this Swiss performance, moderately, as a "flagrant violation of good faith."[4] In the remainder of 1943, while the allied advance was stalled at the Gustav line, Swiss trade with Germany increased further. After months of stubborn argument, we and the British threatened postwar retaliation and cancellation of all import permits, and began to place individual Swiss firms engaged in important German trade on the blacklists, threatening to extend the practice to all firms in the trade. The Swiss wavered at year's end sufficiently to warrant a *modus vivendi* with them pending further talks.[5]

When discussion was renewed in February, the Swiss were if possible less malleable. Their chief negotiator, Professor Paul Keller, said that his journey across Europe to London brought home to him Switzerland's plight, entirely surrounded as she was by German forces. "To Switzerland's great dismay the power situation had not yet changed to the degree hoped for by Switzerland, and . . . the Swiss were therefore unable to be as tough with the Germans as they would in their own interests wish to be." They would like to begin the talks "with the questions of credits to Germany and the delisting" of blacklisted companies.[6] We had no intention of agreeing to either. In Switzerland, as in Sweden in the spring of 1944, the eve of great events found us in deadlock. In both places the central issues revolved around Germany's most essential need, steel, and around the neutrals' illusion regarding the true power situation.

DEADLOCK IN THE IBERIAN PENINSULA

The most elusive political imponderable to confuse economic warfare calculations was the danger of a German-Spanish attack on Gibraltar. Hitler had wrung a promise from Franco at the Hendaye meeting in September 1940 to join in this, but had failed to pin him to a date. The plan called for its completion and exclusion of the British from the western Mediterranean and North Africa before Hitler started his great gamble against Russia. Franco continued to wriggle free, trading insults to the United States in place of fixed dates to fight Britain, moved to this as much by fear of his ally as of his enemy. But this conduct diminished to the vanishing point Washington's appetite for a trade agreement with Franco. The British seemed led toward an agreement by the belief that Franco would betray his ally to the limit of safety.

Hitler's target date for the attack on Gibraltar was early February 1941.[7] That particular crisis passed when he turned his attention to the eastern Mediterranean. But the British Foreign Office never lost its obsessive fear that the danger would recur. As we shall see, the British thwarted all our efforts to use to the utmost our considerable powers to limit Franco's help to Germany.

Dr. Salazar's policy for Portugal was one of classical legal neutrality. Under the circumstances this policy both favored and was of great importance to Germany. Ninety-five per cent of Europe's production of wolfram, a tungsten ore essential in making steel armor plate, comes from the peninsula. A free market in wolfram would have run up the price to the benefit of our larger purse. It would also, as Dr. Salazar was fully aware, produce inflation disastrous to his years of highly successful work in stabilizing and developing the Portuguese economy.

Consequently he attempted to fix a moderate price and eliminate competition between the belligerents by allocating ore and the ownership of producing mines to the two sides. We grumbled and protested that Germany had been favored. Perhaps so; but I doubt whether the favor more than reflected Dr. Salazar's computation of the relative danger of German and allied military pressure on him. German troops in Spain would be as uncomfortable for Portugal as had been Napoleon's a century and a quarter earlier.

In Spain no basis existed for confidence in negotiation. Franco's purposes were hostile, his officials' statements mendacious, and their statistics falsified. Thus with no confidence in the facts, there could be no confidence in a bargain. This supply program fell into a pattern. For two years or more the process began by cutting off supplies, principally petroleum, as a sort of rough rectification of fraudulent figures. As stocks sank to the point of exhaustion, cries of anguish would begin in Madrid, be taken up by the U.S. Ambassador to Spain, Carlton J. H. Hayes, and by London, echoed by our Petroleum Adviser, Max Thornburg, and Ray Atherton, and be derided by most of the American government and press. When it reached a crescendo after a few months, Feis would lose faith in his own judgment, and a tanker or two would be released amid a chorus of vituperation. It was not an ideal system but about as good a one as circumstances permitted. It probably kept Spanish stocks low enough to prevent much leakage to German uses.

What we got for our supplies in the way of reducing Spanish help to Germany was also problematical. We could find no firm basis for calculation. Competitive purchases raised the price of wolfram to fantastic heights, yet the Germans were furnished with pesetas to buy. The more we bought, the more there was to buy. The situation was ideally designed to spur the imagination and daring of Walton Butterworth, a most able Foreign Service officer in charge of operations in the peninsula. In Butterworth's New Orleans ancestry, proper and respectable beyond question, must have lurked a pirate, for his methods had about them a verve and dash, a touch of the black flag and the black market, admirably suited to economic or other warfare in the Spanish Main. Some reports hint at bribery, smuggling, flooding mines, hijacking, black-market purchases, and tying up transportation.[8] However this may be, Butterworth's procedures were well devised for security of communication and favorable answers to his proposals. He would get off a telegram from Lisbon and then arrive by Pan American Clipper in Washington to "hand process" it (in the barbarism of the time) to the highest authorities. Then, drafting an affirmative answer to his own proposal, he would bring it to me for signature. I cannot recall that any of these maneuvers ever shocked the moral sensibilities of this son of a bishop. Perhaps Franco had made them impervious to shock.

One of these flights landed Butterworth in serious trouble and might have been his last. The sturdy old clipper crashed on the Tagus, breaking apart. Half of it floated. Butterworth, once a member of the Princeton swimming team, helped some survivors in the sinking tail to reach the floating section and then swam about for an hour or more until help came. When rescued he was still holding his brief case with its secret documents. This devotion to duty he passed over with the observation that the brief case also provided a gratifying degree of buoyancy.

By March of 1944 the quarrel with Spain over trade with Germany had come to a peak. So had tempers in Washington, London, and Madrid. To make matters worse, the allies had fallen out. In Washington all concerned, for once wholly in agreement, had demanded from Spain as the price of further supplies from us an embargo on wolfram to Germany and a drastic reduction in production to prevent smuggling. U.S. Ambassador Hayes in Madrid reported British

Ambassador Sir Samuel Hoare (of the Hoare-Laval agreement to scuttle Ethiopia) to the effect "that Washington's conditions . . . are thoroughly unacceptable to British Government and that after discussion by War Council Churchill had telegraphed a personal plea to the President."[9] It was not clear which side Hayes had decided to be on now that the chips were down. The next day General Francisco Gómez Jordana, the Spanish Foreign Minister, aware that his opponents were divided, rejected our demand for an embargo.

A BLOW TO BREAK THE DEADLOCK

Thus it was that at the same time on all the neutral fronts the same crisis flowered on the same central issue with pretty much the same division of forces. It also happened that at just this time luck brought me a rare opportunity to strike a blow by a mightier arm than mine. I have long been the advocate of the heretical view that, whatever political scientists might say, policy in this country is made, as often as not, by the necessity of finding something to say for an important figure committed to speak without a prearranged subject. April 9, 1944, was such an occasion; Secretary of State Cordell Hull, the important person.

Leo Pasvolsky was Mr. Hull's principal speech writer. Or, one might say, he wrote Mr. Hull's principal speech; for, whatever the occasion or title, the speech was apt to turn into a dissertation on the benefits of unhampered international trade and the true road to it through agreements reducing tariffs. When a speech impended, we would all be summoned to Mr. Hull's overheated office and given copies of Leo's draft. Presiding at his large desk, Mr. Hull would put on his black-rimmed pince-nez with its black ribbon and announce, "We will now go over the speech pawagwaph by pawagwaph." This, of course, made impossible any discussion of the theme or its appropriateness or treatment, and reduced the exercise to one of verbal and grammatical criticism. The result could hardly be called "variations on a theme," since the same collaborators tended to insist on their usual amendments, so that the document would soon take on the well-remembered form.

I submitted to this routine, if not docilely, at least with resignation, until this fateful day in April 1944 when, on receiving the usual slip, I threw it in the wastebasket and went on with the problems presented by the European neutrals. The next morning the same thing happened. Then the Secretary's messenger summoned me to the presence. Mr. Hull looked pained.

"Are you refusing to come to my speech meeting?" he asked. I explained that I was and why it was a waste of time to go through the form of editing Leo's liturgy. He seemed surprised and with hardly more than a trace of sarcasm said: "I suppose you think that you could write a better speech." I said one could certainly try.

He suggested that I do so and gave me the existing draft. I had long waited for an opportunity to push economic warfare a stage farther ahead. My friend John Dickey, then working on the blacklist, joined the effort. Enough of the old could be left to enlist departmental support, but a new "lead" should be added to capture worldwide attention. This "lead" would warn the European neutrals that their last clear chance to join the winning side with credit would soon be gone.

A night of work produced a draft. Acceptance of a few amendments won support from important division chiefs. Mr. Hull, surprised at the speed with which his suggestion had been taken up, hesitated over accepting its forthright position. I suggested sending the draft to the President for guidance from him, well aware that his support was vital in view of Mr. Churchill's intervention in the Spanish phase of the battle. This was done. Back it came with some editing in the President's own hand and a scribbled note that "Cordell" should by all means make it and that it would rank among his best. So encouraged, he did.

The speech plunged into the current struggle to move the neutrals.[10] With the fall of France in 1940, the Secretary said, we had started on the long hard road of mobilizing our great natural resources, productive power, and reserves of manpower to defend ourselves and to strengthen those who were resisting aggression.

Since that major decision of foreign policy, we and our allies had moved far toward attaining a strength that could leave no doubt of the outcome. This growth of strength entailed consequences in our relations with the neutral nations.

In the two years following Pearl Harbor, while mustering our strength, our attitude toward neutral nations and their relations toward our enemies had been conditioned by the fact that our power was limited. They and we were continually forced to accept compromises we certainly would not have chosen. That period, the Secretary continued, was rapidly drawing to a close. In now asking these neutral nations not to prolong the war by sending aid to the enemy, we were not asking them to risk destruction.

We could no longer acquiesce in neutrals' drawing upon the resources of the allied world when they at the same time contributed to the strength of its enemies and theirs. We had scrupulously respected their sovereignty and not coerced any nation to join us in the fight. We now pointed out to them that it was no longer necessary for them to purchase protection against aggression by furnishing aid to our enemy—whether by permitting official German agents to carry on within neutral borders their activities of espionage against the allies, or by sending to Germany the essential ingredients of the steel that killed our soldiers, or by permitting highly skilled workers and factories to supply products that could no longer issue from the smoking ruins of German factories. We asked them only, but with insistence, to cease aiding our enemy.

The meaning of the speech came through to the neutrals loud and clear. "You may be sure," cabled our negotiators with Switzerland, "that the Swisss are profoundly aware of the address of the Secretary of State and the recent action of the Turkish Government [in suspending shipments of chrome to Germany] which have been given wide and favorable publicity here."[11] The usual protests were made, especially in Sweden, against the indignity of negotiating under pressure, but negotiate they did. Moreover, Mr. Hull, having tasted blood, liked it. "Your oral remarks to be made when you deliver the ball-bearing note," he cabled our Minister in Stockholm, "should be couched in the strongest possible language making full use of those sections of my speech of April 9 which refer to our intention to make every effort to reduce neutral aid to the enemy. Our intentions in this respect are firm, are backed by developing public opinion in the United States, and are of the utmost importance for military reasons. . . . You should inform the Swedish Foreign Minister that this matter is receiving my personal attention." The next day he instructed the Minister that despite his "recommendation that the threat clause be eliminated from the ball-bearing note . . . [he felt] constrained to retain the clause."[12] Washington was on the march, with the old Tennesseean enjoying his unusual position in the van.

7. ECONOMIC WARFARE ABROAD:
DEADLOCK ENDS

THE SWEDES AND SWISS GIVE WAY

THE TACTIC OF sending Stanton Griffis† as special negotiator to both threaten and entice SKF proved successful. It offered cover behind which the Swedish Government might retreat and made easier both threat and compensation. Griffis was tough and competent, as stubborn as the Swedes, and impervious to entreaties from the British to move *"molliter et molle manu."*† After two months of hard bargaining, and two days after the first Normandy landing, he cabled Washington: "With great assistance from your cable of instructions from Washington . . . and undoubted help from General Eisenhower, we have substantially closed deal with SKF well within the limit of your instructions."[1]

SKF, which during the discussions had suspended shipments to Germany, undertook to restrict them in 1944 to one-quarter of their contract commitments. The United States maintained its demand for total embargo and retained freedom to impose sanctions at any time. The Swedish Government moved with more deliberate dignity. In August a joint note from Stettinius and Eden again urged Sweden to end all trade with Germany, but this was not done until the end of December. Meanwhile propitiating morsels were thrown to the wolves: in August the Bothnian transit route to Finland was closed and insurance canceled on Swedish ships entering German ports; in September all Baltic ports were closed to German ships; later, rail traffic to and from Narvik was interrupted by "repairs" to the roadbed.

Negotiations with the Swiss moved at their glacial rate. We took advantage of the uncertainty the military situation had created in communication with Switzerland to suspend shipments. Even Mr. Hull entered the fray, saying to the Swiss Minister that "neutral aid to the enemy in order primarily to gratify some businessmen . . . presented a most serious question to this country . . . that one of these days the stand of some of the Swiss businessmen in question would be uncovered as in these cases of certain people in Sweden, resulting in inevitable friction between our countries."[2]

At length, in August, the Swiss put a ceiling on exports to Germany. When we pressed them to end transit of enemy goods across their country, their reply concluded with a delightful and typical Swiss statement of policy: "It goes without saying that the war as it nears the Alps changes aspect of the transit problem and has a bearing upon its solution. For this reason the federal authorities keep this problem under constant and careful watch. They have thus been able to observe that traffic in both directions has in general decreased and not increased since spring. In the spirit of true neutrality which guides them they will see to it that it follows the trend circumstances demand."[3]

On October 1 the Swiss prohibited the export to Germany of all arms, munitions, and military supplies. At the end of the month they closed the Simplon routes to transit traffic, though not the Gotthard.

Thus painfully we inched along through 1944.

Finally, in April 1945, the Swiss surrendered—only a month before General Jodl did.

SPAIN CRACKED LAST

As for Spain, economic warfare there ended in a flare-up of tempers between allies in Washington and London. We had demanded a total embargo on wolfram to Germany as the price for any oil whatever. Spanish tanks were nearly dry. Jordana threatened to end all restrictions on German trade unless oil shipments were resumed. Under presidential orders and with mutinous murmurs, we joined in a British proposal to resume oil supplies if wolfram shipments ceased until July and thereafter did not exceed three hundred tons in the next six months. Franco insisted on some additional shipments before July.

On April 11 I celebrated my fifty-first birthday with an attempt to stiffen the British through Lord Halifax.[4] The main thrust of argument was the vast harm a further reward to Spanish stubbornness could do in the pending crises with Sweden, Switzerland, Portugal, and Turkey. In answer to his question as to what new points our ambassadors could make in Madrid, I pointed out that in a short time our main concern would be with supplies for our friends in liberated Europe. We would have little sympathy with the needs of hostile neutrals who had aided the enemy until his last gasp. The Spanish would do well to think that over.

Lord Halifax repeated the familiar arguments, referred to Samuel Hoare's greater familiarity with the Spanish situation, and asked whether we would agree to the British-endorsed Spanish position rather than have negotiations collapse. Thoroughly exasperated with this guaranteed road to defeat, I said so and urged that we give the Spanish evidence of determination and unity by having both.

Mr. Hull backed me up by going over the same ground with Halifax and shrewdly adding that if the British had special reasons for propitiating Spain which we did not share it "would seem . . . entirely logical and practicable for the British to sponsor the oil shipments which would be a counterpart to the arrangements they might wish to make with regard to the shipment to Germany of wolfram and other commodities which are involved in the military situation." A further contribution by Hoare to ill will and to our mutual dislike of each other was passed on by Hayes:

"[Hoare] was disturbed and indignant. He said the telegram [reporting my conversation with Halifax] was a very bad distortion. . . . It omitted Halifax's 'telling' arguments with which Halifax reported Acheson had been impressed. Hoare especially resented the implication that he had not backed me up, and maintained that he had supported my efforts all along. . . . Hoare said that what he objected to most . . . was . . . the indefinite postponement of a greatly desired settlement merely for the sake of the insignificant amount of 60 tons of wolfram." To Hayes's credit he did not let this latter remark pass without remarking that "if the amount was insignificant to us as Hoare stated it must also seem insignificant to Spain in comparison with its increasingly urgent need for petroleum and other commodities."

Here I interrupt the narrative for a reflection, suggested by the reports of the two participants in the conversation between Lord Halifax and myself. I have never yet read a memorandum of conversation in which the writer came off second best. As evidence they should be received with caution. For this reason, and to save time, in later years I usually had an officer present to write the memorandum. Most ambassadors brought one for the same purpose. Sometimes this defeated the strong diplomatic interest in confidential relations. I have often had requests for confidential discussions with no third parties present; sometimes an ambassador wishes to make observations unheard by his own staff.

On April 21 the President, replying to another appeal from Churchill, urged him to stand firm in demanding no further wolfram shipments to Germany until July "in the hope and belief that shipments thereafter in the second half of the year in the amounts agreed to will not be practicable." He stressed also the adverse effect of concessions upon other negotiations. But the "former Naval Person" could be as stubbornly set on retreat as upon standing fast. His reply to the President, as Mr. Hull reported it in a cable to Ambassador Hayes, stated that he "would assume the whole responsibility for settlement himself. This would involve British sponsorship of shipments of oil to Spain. [Thus Churchill outbluffed Hull.] It is obvious that should this procedure eventuate it would be necessary for me to release to the press a statement which would of necessity indicate clearly a break in the Anglo-American united front which is so essential in the conduct of the general war effort. Such a result would be regrettable." Mr. Hull reluctantly authorized Hayes to go along with the British Ambassador in reaching a settlement with the Spanish Government.

All of us resented bitterly the British refusal to cooperate in the best opportunity economic warfare had had to make a telling contribution. Mr. Hull summed up our resentment in a cable to Hayes: "I in no way wish to detract from the results you have obtained as a result of these very trying negotiations with the Spanish. The American public well knows that we have been holding out for total and permanent embargo. Because of our insistent position we have whittled down the Spanish in spite of an absence of wholehearted British support. Had we had full British support I am convinced we could have obtained our objective. . . . Without detracting from what you have accomplished I feel I must let our people know that it was at British insistence that we accepted on a basis less than the one we sought. . . . I propose to release our statement at 8 P.M. tonight."

In Madrid the settlement ended in a "My dear Mr. Minister and Friend" exchange of letters. Our attitude could have been expressed in an adaptation of the old song at the time of the Philippine insurrection—"He may be a friend of Ambassador Hayes, but he ain't no friend of mine."

In reviewing these long-forgotten arguments of twenty years and more ago, I am surprised at the apparent sincerity with which, until almost the end of the war, the neutrals and British alike voiced fear of German occupation to justify trade with the enemy. In April 1944 Boheman spoke of "the iniquity of our [U.S.] pressure . . . [upon] a small neutral country in such a perilous position as Sweden to compliance with demands which if granted would put Sweden on brink of ruin and in a position where the United States would not be able to give any assistance."[5] Later he "emphasized the grave responsibility on the part of the Government for the protection of the independence of the country and the lives of the Swedish people; that Sweden had no intention or desire to undergo the unnameable horrors of a German occupation."[6] In January Swiss Minister Charles Bruggmann complained to H. Freeman (Doc) Matthews, Chief of the Division of European Affairs, that "as an act of final desperation the Germans might be tempted to invade Switzerland purely for 'vengeance.' " Matthews asked him how many divisions the Swiss had, and Bruggmann replied, "Fifty, well-armed and well-equipped. [Matthews] said [he] did not see where Germany was going to find fifty-plus Divisions available at this stage of the war for a diversion into Switzerland."[7] Again, as late as the end of December the Counselor of the British Embassy urged me to agree to "token" shipments of ball bearings to Germany for fear that the Germans might close the port of Gothenburg. I replied that we had already accepted this risk and saw no reason for modifying that decision. The Germans made no attempt to close the port.[8]

Whether this proves that fears or arguments or both continue long after the basis for either has disappeared, it is interesting evidence of the persistence of habit in thought and judgment. More than this, the role played by Mr. Churchill in deflecting our economic pressure was my first experience of what was to recur often in the next decade—that is, of a relatively weak ally by determined, sometimes reckless, decisions changing and even preventing action by a much stronger one charged with ultimate responsibility. General de Gaulle was to demonstrate this; so was Syngman Rhee in Korea. In fact, almost all recipients of our economic or military aid have shown us how useless threats to stop aid are in trying to pressure the recipients to use it for its intended purpose. After the war was over I was to learn other and more drastic limitations upon the exercise of power.

CONCLUSIONS ABOUT ECONOMIC WARFARE
AND OTHER MATTERS

Is it possible to draw conclusions about the contribution to the war of all the money and manpower invested in the economic warfare effort? Restricting the question to effort in Europe, I would venture with some confidence the following opinions:

It was worth doing.

The procurement of materials for our own war production was useful and important.

The denial of materials for enemy war production was much less successful and important. Until the latter part of 1944 it was marginal everywhere. From then on it was more successful in Sweden than elsewhere.

A good case can be made for the argument that economic measures resulted in stopping important exports for military needs from Sweden to Germany about six months before military measures would have done so. Exports from Switzerland and the Iberian Peninsula probably moved in minimum necessary quantities until military measures stopped them.

However, such economic measures as raising prices and preclusive buying reduced all other exports from all neutral sources to the injury of the enemy.

Not all the arts of diplomacy are learned solely in its practice. There are other exercise yards. In the long struggle over the problem of oil shipments in the Spanish trade agreements a good deal of blood was spilled in Washington. The press as a whole was anti-appeasement-of-Franco and not too discriminating in the Washington targets for its saturation bombing. The State Department was one of them, although the old lady was shaking her umbrella as threateningly as anyone. Of course, degrees of belligerency existed within our building. In the year or so since the struggle over oil to Japan, my wife and I and Harold and Jane Ickes became close friends. He knew that I was sound on the Spanish issues but suspected that appeasers lurked within the State Department. Indeed, it seemed more than likely that some of the bombs dropped on us had been manufactured in the Interior Department's Petroleum Administration. Dealing with Ickes required some little knowledge of the man.

The Ickes place, Headwaters Farm, twenty miles into Maryland due north of the White House, was only two miles from our beloved Harewood. We were able to spend the summers of short gasoline rationing at Harewood due solely to Harold Ickes' kindness in motoring me back and forth to work.

The "Old Curmudgeon"—a title that secretly pleased him—delighted in controversy. I used to tell him that, as Norman Hapgood had said of Felix Frankfurter, he liked nothing better than to win an argument, and by unfair means if possible. Only some dramatic gesture could deflect him from a debate that might become embarrassing. One day driving home he began to warm up on a favorite subject, the shortcomings of my two superiors, Messrs. Hull and Welles. I pointed out that this discussion was as distasteful to me as a parallel one about him would be for his assistant secretaries. But on he went. As we approached a traffic light, I asked Carl, his chauffeur, to pull over to the curb, as I was getting out.

"How will you get home?" Harold Ickes asked. I replied that it was time I learned how to thumb a ride.

"I believe you're just damned fool enough to do it," he went on. "Sit down and I'll shut up." I relaxed and he shifted the debate to safer ground.

So when Mr. Hull, during the oil-to-Spain controversy, received a letter from his Cabinet colleague bitterly attacking our Petroleum Adviser, Max Thornburg, I intervened. The letter, copies of which had been sent to the President, Vice President, and others, charged that Thornburg, one of the officers principally concerned with the Spanish oil problem, was improperly influenced by connections in the oil industry. It was true that Thornburg, like Churchill, was in favor of a more liberal oil allowance to Spain than were most of the rest of us, but he was no more moved to judgment by improper influences than Churchill was. While Harold Ickes' charges were quite unfounded, the source of the argument *ad hominem* was not obscure. The Petroleum Adviser to Ickes had been a rival officer in the same company with Thornburg. Their opinions of one another were not laudatory, and this was not the first spat they had had. Since the oil controversy provided enough inflammable material without added charges of this nature, I asked Mr. Hull to allow me to handle the matter and he, glad to be rid of the whole disagreeable business, assented.

Max Thornburg agreed to my plan. I telephoned Harold Ickes, told him that Mr. Hull had demanded an investigation of his charges, and said that one would be held that afternoon, with witnesses to be sworn and their testimony reported.

"Investigation!" he roared. "Before whom?"

"Before you," I said.

"What in hell is going on?" he demanded. "Are you crazy?" I explained that I was not; that, although it was well known that he was a curmudgeon, I was betting that he was an honest curmudgeon and would be willing to hear and decide upon the evidence my contention that he was mistaken about Thornburg. As the enormity and, at the same time, the humor of my effrontery sank in, he murmured, "Well, I'll be damned," and set an hour to receive us.

We went through with the judicial farce: witnesses sworn by a court reporter, testimony taken stenographically, and cross-examination offered to the Solicitor of Interior—now an eminent justice. The substance of the charges was disproved. No improper interest in conflict with Thornburg's duty had influenced his advice. Ickes agreed to this and was about to dismiss us when I pointed out that the retraction, like the charges, should be in writing and go to the same people. He agreed to this, also, and called a secretary and dictated an ungrudging letter saying that on further investigation he found that he had been mistaken and withdrew what he had said. A copy was given to the reporter.

We had risen to leave when in an audible *sotto voce* Harold added, as a postscript, "Anyway, I still think he's a so-and-so."

"Mr. Thornburg," I said, "resume the stand. Do you know the ordinary and usual meaning of the term Secretary Ickes has just used?"

"Oh my lord," Harold shouted, "skip it. I withdraw that, too. Now get out of here and let me do some work."

"Good-bye," I said, as we filed out. "I'll see you at six o'clock." And I did.

8. PREPARATION FOR AN UNKNOWN WORLD

THE ESTABLISHMENT ORGANIZES[1]

AFTER AN abortive start in 1940, Mr. Hull and his chief lieutenant, Leo Pasvolsky, laid out in the next year a plan and organization for a massive inquiry into the problems of the postwar world. A network of committees was charged with encyclopedic projects of research. They met faithfully. The record shows—a record that later President Truman directed me to have compiled and published[2]—that the economic work was divided between two committees of overlapping membership, of which Berle was chairman of one and I of the other. The combined committees met twenty-six times under Berle's chairmanship and fourteen times under mine. Yet I cannot remember one of these meetings. Neither can I recall any other meetings. Paging through the printed report, the whole effort, except for two results, seems to have been a singularly sterile one, uninspired by gifts either of insight or prophecy. One of these results was the foundation work for the United Nations Charter; the other, which laid an even broader foundation, the education of Senator Arthur Vandenberg to understanding that beyond the borders of the United States existed a "vast external realm," which could and would affect profoundly our interests and our destiny.

However, some preparations for the future went on outside the Hull-Pasvolsky establishment. These centered principally on planning for the surrender and occupation of Germany through the tripartite Commission for Europe; convening international conferences to deal with food, agriculture, relief, and rehabilitation; and making international monetary and financial arrangements.

With the first of these I had nothing whatever to do, either in the first phase when the political terms of surrender, zones of occupation, and the like were determined, in the later work for the Quebec conference where the conception of Germany as a group of agricultural states appeared, or finally in preparation for the Potsdam meeting in 1945. My part lay wholly in the work of the international conferences of 1943 and 1944.

EVENTS INTRUDE

Hardly settled in the State Department, I found that I had inherited a correspondence with an old friend of my Treasury days,[3] Sir Frederick Leith-Ross, then Director General of the British Ministry of Economic Warfare. He and my predecessor, Henry Grady, had been corresponding on what was called "the surplus problem," or how to deal with such staples of world trade as wheat, cotton, wool, and coffee, the markets for which had been disrupted by the war and which had not yet been taken over for purchase and distribution by the combined United States–United Kingdom boards. Grady and Leith-Ross had not gotten far, but far enough to have identified, as one of the aspects of the problem, the future restocking and supplying of Europe once it had been freed from German occupation. This Leith-Ross mentioned to me almost casually in February 1941, suggesting that "relief of destitute areas" might "appropriately be handled by private charitable organisations." As yet none of us had any conception of the dimensions of the problems about to engulf us.

Maynard Keynes's visit to Washington in the early summer of 1941 made possible long talks with him, which opened up the far-reaching complexities of the field into which Leith-Ross and I had—at least on my part—innocently entered. These complexities ranged far beyond those of international commodity agreements and raised again most of the questions brought out by our contemporaneous discussion of Article VII of the lend-lease agreement. They were inextricably entwined with the issues of commercial and monetary policy of an expanding and open world economy. As June merged into July, I became convinced that the postwar relief problem must be separated from this congeries of economic problems. The European governments-in-exile pushed the British Government toward the same conclusion.

These exiles fretted restlessly in London, wanting to do something for their distressed fellow countrymen, finding little to be done, and worrying about the result of their inactivity upon opinion at home. More and more they wanted to buy supplies for postwar use, fearing to be caught unprepared by an early liberation yet not wishing to upset military purchasing for a long war.

In July messages crossed between London and Washington. One came from Eden telling us of his plans for an early-autumn meeting of the exiled governments to consider plans for the supply of food and raw materials to Europe after liberation. Another was from me to Leith-Ross, telling him of my talks with Keynes and agreeing with two suggestions of his—to postpone tackling the longer-range complexities of the commodities problem in favor of the more immediate need of planning postwar relief, and to begin by inviting the exiled governments to prepare a list of, say, their first six months' requirements after liberation to be put together with other needs for planning purposes. Thus seeds planted in London and Washington, probably in both places by Keynes, sprouted simultaneously.

In late September the meeting authorized joint studies under Leith-Ross's chairmanship and with the aid of a bureau of British civil servants under his direction. An American "observer" would keep us informed. Leith-Ross wrote me that he would come to Washington to talk with us about the next steps. There seemed plenty of time for that. Then urgency came from unexpected quarters—from the Russians and from the governments-in-exile.

In January 1942 the Russians tossed into the London arena the first suggestion of an internationally controlled, manned, and operated relief organization with many of the Russian features with which later we were to become familiar. Ambassador Winant asked for our views. While we were assembling these, Noel Hall reported cables from Leith-Ross which told us that the Dutch and Norwegians had quietly sent missions to South America to begin buying for postwar use on their own. Apparently allies large and small had become suspicious of Britons bearing gifts over which they appeared determined to retain control. Two practical considerations determined policy—one, to suppress rebellion where we could; two, General Forrest's famous formula: "If you can't lick 'em, join 'em." We dealt with both simultaneously, and the dealing fell to me.

May was the month of movement and decision. The Russian proposal had received wide study in the Department. It proposed to build up the Inter-Allied Committee for Postwar Requirements into an international organization with powers. The membership should be Australia, Belgium, Canada, Czechoslovakia, Free France, Great Britain, Greece, India, Luxembourg, the Netherlands, New Zealand, Norway, Poland, the Soviet Union, South Africa, and Yugoslavia. The absence of the United States was later rectified.

All countries should be "on the basis of equality," and all decisions of the committee should be by unanimous vote of the representatives, ratified by unanimous endorsement of the governments.

The committee should have a secretariat of four or five—representatives of Great Britain and the Soviet Union, and two or three delegates representing all the others. It should have two commissions of experts, one on food and raw materials, the other on transport.

The tasks of the committee should be: (1) to prepare food- and raw-material-requirement estimates of "countries occupied and robbed by Hitlerite Germany and her European accomplices"; (2) to estimate food and raw-material resources of member countries, the United States, and others which could be used to meet requirements; (3) to allocate resources among the various countries; (4) to find means of purchasing these resources "by the countries which experienced especially severe suffering from Hitler's aggression"; (5) to study prices and control of prices of foods and raw materials to combat speculation, but not to buy or sell these commodities.

It was immediately clear that this plan had grave defects and risked serious distortion and dislocation of postwar arrangements. It gave preference to the needs of invaded European countries over those of other belligerent, neutral, or enemy countries (the last contrary to Article 4 of the Atlantic Charter†), both in Europe and Asia and in other continents. Its scope extended beyond relief and threatened to invade economic and commercial policy. The position of the Soviet Union and its negative power of veto would give it a dominant position where its political and economic policies might well be at variance with those of Western nations.

The best procedure seemed to be to declare our agreement "in principle" with both British and Soviet ideas and then make principle specific by putting forward our own proposal. This we did in a long telegram to London on May 7. Before going into it, I must discuss the sterner measures taken to suppress trouble elsewhere.

In April the British and we made an effort to restrain the Dutch and Norwegians from making purchases on their own for postwar relief supplies by appealing to the better angels of their nature. We were about to lay a comprehensive postwar arrangement before them; to anticipate it by individual purchases only confused both the conduct of war supply and the arrangement of orderly postwar relief. Their entrance on the scene now would also inflate prices and create preferences. We urged them to desist. The result was to bring the Yugoslavs and Greeks into the act also. In both Washington and London the Norwegians put on a major offensive, protesting through their Prime Minister and their Foreign Minister, Trygve Lie (later the first Secretary General of the United Nations), against the restrictions imposed upon them. Then they proceeded to act. The British and we concerted plans and acted, too, with instantaneous effect.

On July 1 an irate Norwegian Ambassador, Wilhelm Morgenstierne, my old friend of twenty years before when we were colleagues in an arbitration at The Hague, stormed into the Department in articulate protest, saying that the Chief Cable Censor had held up cables attempting to establish credits in South America for a Norwegian shipping and supply mission. The battle was sharp and spirited. When the smoke cleared, the Norwegians had agreed in exchange for these credits to postpone further purchases until some joint solution of the relief problem could be worked out, to open no further credits in Latin America without prior consultation with us, and to sell for the common war effort all existing or future purchases not needed for the Norwegian merchant marine or armed forces. Later this arrangement was extended to the other governments-in-exile.

We had made clear that our position against individual preparation for relief had more than pure reason to support it and was accompanied by an offer of collective preparation for a common effort.

The next order of business was to get our own house in order. This involved putting some one person in charge of the relief discussions and getting the President's approval of the program. As in the case of the freezing operation, on paper policy direction was under Berle, while I had in fact been carrying the ball. Leith-Ross was expected by the end of June. Decisions were urgently needed. When Leith-Ross arrived, Mr. Hull informed him that I was to be in charge and authorized me to discuss with him and the Russian and Chinese ambassadors a draft relief agreement. The next year was devoted to that discussion, which gradually extended to representatives of other foreign powers and of our own House and Senate. In these months I was initiated into two arts in which in later years I attained some proficiency—one the art of chairmanship, the other that of congressional relations.

THE FOUR WISE MEN

From January to June a group of four worked out a draft agreement, starting with our governmental paper. Our group was a congenial one, often escaping from the confines of an uninspiring agenda to speculate about the world which was to be. Tall and gaunt Lord Halifax, the British Ambassador in Washington, an English aristocrat reminiscent of the second quarter of the nineteenth century, might have been Lord Melbourne, mentor of the young Victoria, if he had been a bit handsomer, lighter, and more amusing. His manner, courteous and apparently hesitating, avoided obstinacy by circuitous restatement of the same position so that it kept reappearing as a new one.

Maxim Litvinov, an old bolshevik but an old-school Russian as well, also understood the forms and uses of courtesy, as some of the new types in the Soviet establishment did not. Roly-poly, short, and voluble, he presented an amusing antithesis to Lord Halifax, never bothering to cloak stubbornness, but making his points clearly and courteously. Mme. Litvinov, a pleasant English-woman and a painting companion of my wife, turned up often by the fall of protocol cards as my dinner partner. I recall that she often sought comfort at dinner by escaping the confinement of her evening slippers. Occasionally one would wander off and my longer legs would be needed to retrieve it. Once a slipper strayed too far, so that when the guests rose from the table I had to dive to find it.

The Chinese Ambassador, Wei Tao-ming, had recently taken over his post and the UNRRA discussions from Ambassador Hu Shih, a distinguished Chinese scholar who had undertaken to diminish my vast ignorance of Confucian and Buddhist thought. From him I learned that the Chinese mind, like my own, was baffled by the mysticism of most religious teaching and found itself more at home with ethical and philosophic concepts. This was why, he thought, Buddhism had made so little headway in China, which had few, if any, great religious leaders.

Before we began—our first meeting took place on January 11, 1943—my own ideas of the postwar problem had grown from the time when Leith-Ross suggested, and I agreed, that private philanthropic organizations could play a large part in it. We were all thinking then of the task as a "restocking" operation, building up supplies of food and raw materials, soup kitchens, and inventories. Meanwhile bombing and obsolescence had pointed to a larger problem, and the word "rehabilitation" was added to "relief." The occupied countries must not merely be fed, they must be helped to be self-supporting. We were still four years away from grasping the true dimensions of the problem, solemnly reassuring one another that international finance, investment, and reconstruction were something wholly different and not at all pressing. "I have assumed," cabled Winant, "that the relief organization was to be concerned only with relief. . . . I note, however, that the word 'rehabilitation' is added to relief in the new draft of the relief agreement. I would be interested to know the definition given the word in this context."

A good question it was, but never answered. To us the word had no definition; rather it was a propitiation by ignorance of the unknown. UNRRA would have done its work and passed away before we were to know what "rehabilitation" really required from us, and General Marshall was to outline the task at Harvard.

The interesting developments in this story for the first three quarters of 1943 were the emergence of Russian attitudes, of which we were to become increasingly and painfully aware as time went on, and the development of executive-congressional interplay, which was to make so vast a difference in the position of the United States after the second phase of the European Civil War from its confusion after the first. The development of UNRRA played a special part in this.

At our first meeting Litvinov uncovered the classic Soviet positions toward international institutions. Nothing might be done within any country without that country's consent and except through its agencies; decisions by UNRRA must be unanimous; an Executive Committee consisting of China, the Soviet Union, Great Britain, and the United States, also acting unanimously, should be the supreme power when the full membership was not in session; actions of the Director General must be subject to constant review and approval or rejection by the Executive Committee, which might also dismiss him; regional committees must have broad powers over action within their regions; and the Soviet Union and Great Britain must be permanent members of the Committee for Europe. One can recognize the now familiar pattern by which the Soviet Union has sought in the quarter century since the war to protect itself from foreign penetration and to insure its power to negate any international action uncongenial to Soviet designs. We were present, so to speak, at the creation of the pattern.

On the whole, the three of us did rather better with the USSR in our negotiation than many of our successors have done since, not due, I hasten to add, to our skill but to the Soviet desire for relief assistance. Litvinov was adamant on the first point, that nothing should be done in any given country except with that country's consent and as it chose. In vain we argued that this must be the case in any country with an established government such as the Soviet Union, but that his provision would lead to confusion and delay in many areas in Europe where contending groups might be struggling for power. Relief, we said with righteous fervor, must be kept free from politics. The idea amused Litvinov. In the Soviet Union nothing was free from politics. His amendment appeared in the next draft circulated on March 25, 1943.[4]

On the second point—the demand for unanimity—we won, perhaps for the last time in any such negotiations. I suggested avoiding any fixed rule for voting; sometimes, perhaps normally, a majority should control; sometimes, a larger proportion; on occasion, unanimity might be necessary because of the very nature of the question. These situations should be spelled out. When I pulled a rather long bow by foreseeing trouble from a stubborn individual blocking action though not instructed to do so, Litvinov found the situation beyond his imagination.[5] Not until the final draft of September 1943 was this troublesome question solved by the adoption of majority rule, except in case of three actions by the Executive Committee: the nomination and removal of the Director General and the recommendation to the membership of common action outside the relief field.

This solution neatly checkmated the Soviet attempt to make the Director General a mere creature of the Executive Committee and brought us to the composition of that body. Here Wei, Litvinov, and I were united against Lord Halifax, who wanted to add three more and suggested Canada, Brazil, and a European country. This we were sure would open Pandora's box. British persistence suggested that a commitment had been made to Canada. A call on me by Lester B. Pearson, then Minister Counselor of the Canadian Legation and later Prime Minister, confirmed the idea. Membership on the Executive Committee was important to Canada, he said, because his country would be a large supplier of relief. I suggested chairmanship of the Committee on Supplies as more appropriate. He was interested but doubtful and must confer with Ottawa.

Ottawa raised the matter to the plane of high principle upon which the Department of External Affairs prefers to rest Canada's more mundane interests. There were "great practical difficulties in creating effective international agencies that are properly representative. . . . These difficulties are a challenge to statesmanship [in this case, apparently, to American statesmanship]; they must be faced and on their solution depends in large measure the possibility of enduring peace. No lasting international system can be based on . . . a few large Powers' . . . denial of the democratic principle. . . . It would . . . be unreal."[6] Canadian membership on the executive committee of UNRRA seemed a small price to pay for all this and heaven too.

Yet the Canadians settled for less—a secret deal that a Canadian should be chairman of the Committee on Supplies and sit with the Executive Committee whenever it discussed supplies. Thus did statesmanship meet the challenge.

Thus, also, it met the challenge of Litvinov's demand for a Soviet Deputy Director General and membership on the Committee of Europe, when these were supported by similar claims from China. We raised the Sino-Soviet claims to the level of a general principle, which, although not insuring a lasting peace or the democratic principle, was very real. "It would be natural and desirable," I reported to my three colleagues, "that in the appointment of Deputy Directors General nationals of [Executive Committee] countries would be included in their number. When Deputies are assigned responsibilities and duties in connection with the Administration's work in the European region and in the Far Eastern region, it is anticipated that among their number would be" Soviet and Chinese deputies respectively.[7] They heartily agreed that such results would, indeed, be natural, desirable, and to be anticipated.

By the first of June our group had cleared its hurdles and was prepared to submit its work to the critical appraisal of "the United Nations." The organization was a simple one. The members, present and future signers of the United Nations declaration, formed the council, which should meet twice a year. A Central Committee exercised its powers in between times. A Director General was to handle operations. All power to give or not to give, or to distribute in other ways, was retained by the member states. President Roosevelt explained the situation to the "congressional leaders" (none of whom were on either the Foreign Affairs or the Foreign Relations Committee), who showed little interest, and then published the agreement for information and discussion. We expected about as much comment as a Red Cross drive evokes, and could not have been more wrong.

The Vandenberg Saga · Without warning a hurricane struck. The word is used advisedly to describe a severe cyclonic disturbance caused by hot air revolving counterclockwise (in fact, it turned the clock back about four months). Its center was filled with a large mass of cumulonimbus cloud, often called Arthur Vandenberg, producing heavy word fall. Senator Vandenberg, for whom I came to have great respect and considerable affection, had the rare capacity for instant indignation, often before he understood an issue, or even that there was one. Furthermore, he was just emerging from his isolationist chrysalis and had not yet learned to manage his new wings. So he fired off letters to Mr. Hull and to Senator Charles McNary and Representative Joseph Martin, the congressional minority leaders who had apparently remained calm after exposure to the UNRRA draft agreement.[8] In the letters he asked the Secretary whether the draft would be submitted to Congress for approval and the congressmen whether they had agreed to the contrary. The latter replied—as well they might —that they had never agreed to bypass the Congress. This fed the hot flame of Senator Vandenberg's indignation, which huffed and puffed around the Senate press gallery. There hounds scented a controversy, which is to journalism what a fox is to fox hunting. Soon the whole pack, kenneled too long by war-induced unanimity, was in full cry.

   Then we in the State Department, misled by Pope's aphorism, "He's armed without that's innocent within," made a bad mistake. We should have answered Senator Vandenberg that of course everything would and must be submitted to the Congress since American participation would be wholly dependent upon Congress to both authorize and appropriate the funds with which to do so. Instead, we had drafted for Mr. Hull a short, technical reply saying, "It has been decided, after consultation with the majority and minority leaders of both houses of Congress, that the United States participation in the establishment of this United Nations' administration should be through an executive agreement." To Vandenberg, and to the whole isolationist press, this meant the opposite of the truth and that the Congress was to be bypassed—and especially the Senate, where Vandenberg immediately introduced a resolution to inquire whether the agreement "partakes of the nature of a treaty and should be submitted to the Senate for ratification."[9]

   An ecstatic phrase in the draft, by which "each member government pledge[d] its full support to the Administration, within the limits of available resources and subject to the requirements of its constitutional procedure," aroused the anti-New Dealer in Vandenberg to rotund hyperbole. The draft, he wrote, "pledged our total resources to whatever illimitable scheme for relief and rehabilitation all around the world our New Deal crystal gazers might desire to pursue . . . [with] no interference with this world-wide prospectus as it might be conceived by Roosevelt, Lehman, Hopkins and Co., until that long last moment when Congress would be confronted with a 'fait accompli.' "[10]

Our mistake, however, was greater than a mere maladroit response to Vandenberg's letter—and we never made it again. In fact, Mr. Hull was already insuring that it should not blight the United Nations Charter as it had the Covenant of the League. We had failed to bring the Congress into participation in the great endeavor. In extenuation, I can only plead that it no more occurred to me that Congress would feel left out of organizing a relief organization than in not being included in a Washington Community Chest drive. One learns in time that the right to be indignant at either inclusion or exclusion—at either "putting Congress on the spot" or "bypassing" it—is a congressional prerogative, highly prized.

Senator Connally of Texas, Chairman of the Committee on Foreign Relations, was alert to Vandenberg's penchant for stealing the limelight. A slow starter in this meeting, he had to count on a thunderous finish. So he put himself on the subcommittee to conduct what a newspaperman called "a first showdown as to where President Roosevelt's treaty-making power leaves off and that of the Senate begins."[11] When Mr. Hull and I made our pilgrimage to do penance at Canossa on Capitol Hill, we found two angry popes waiting for a bewildered monarch with no sense of guilt. But Mr. Hull had a sense of outrage. He left that meeting swearing never to return, as President Washington had left the Senate chamber when during his first and only visit there to ask its advice he had been treated like a pickpocket. It fell to me to pick up the pieces. This was not hard to do. Time, some judicious eating of crow, and many sessions explaining to Arthur Vandenberg and Theodore Green of Rhode Island what the problem had been, and why we had handled it as we had, finally converted them to strong partisans of UNRRA and the procedure we had originally designed. We changed the semantics and no longer talked of executive agreements but of an authorizing act of Congress (after, however, the agreement had been signed and the first council meeting held). We also changed the unfortunate "pledges full support" phrase to a more sober "insofar as its appropriate constitutional bodies shall authorize." This is about the only change in the draft I can identify as flowing from the congressional teapot in which the whole tempest blew itself out.

Vandenberg, however, clung to the belief that he had wrung vast changes from us, for the storm he had started threatened to engulf him. He was accused by his erstwhile isolationist friends of selling out. All his dramatic arts were needed to make his efforts appear truly Herculean. As he later wrote, if he could "force a highly reluctant Administration to submit the UNRRA agreement to Congress . . . as I have already forced it to substantially rewrite the text—I shall consider it a major one-man victory." Far from a "surrender," his was a " 'triumph' of constitutional procedure." But it was still a near thing, as he saw it; he was unable really to "believe that the President will sanction the State Department's wholesale surrender."[12] However, he did; and we went ahead as planned, all of us happy in the result and some of us wiser in method.

9. THE INTERNATIONAL
CONFERENCE STAGE

I INTERRUPT the relief story to recount a brief excursion into another international planning effort for the future. In February 1943 my colleague Emilio (Pete) Collado, an economist, and I were summoned to the Under Secretary's office. The President, Welles told us, had decided to call a United Nations conference as soon as the preparatory work could be rushed through. Speed was important. The subject would be food and agriculture. The place was to be the Homestead Hotel in Hot Springs, Virginia, recently vacated by the interned Japanese diplomatic and consular corps. The high wire fence that had been put around it for security purposes was to remain and would continue to be guarded by military police. The press were to be excluded. He wished to reproduce as nearly as he could the conditions of seclusion and quiet that had so contributed to his confidential discussion with Mr. Churchill during the Atlantic Conference in Placentia Bay, Newfoundland, eighteen months before.

When this seemed to complete Welles's instructions, I asked what the President wanted done about food and agriculture. He replied brusquely, "That, my dear Dean, is for you and Pete to work out." Further questioning elicited only that the President regarded food and agriculture as perhaps man's most fundamental concern and a good place to begin postwar planning. With that we were sent off to begin our own planning.

Inquiry over the years has thrown no light on where the idea for this conference originated. Some have suggested Mrs. Roosevelt or Henry Wallace, or both, as the source, but admittedly this is pure speculation. We found no cell championing the idea as one usually does when a proposal is planted. Most shared Keynes's disappointment that, after all the high economic aspirations of the lend-lease discussions, the first two conferences planned should have been on such bread-and-butter subjects as those chosen. Since my own interest in the field and my knowledge of it were less than meager, I embraced the theory that the mark of a good administrator was his willingness to delegate.

Collado and I got a group together under Dr. Howard Tolley, Chief of the Bureau of Agricultural Economics of the Department of Agriculture, and Roy Stinebower from State, who in a remarkably short time prepared an agenda and a set of working papers for the conference and later functioned as its secretariat. A delegation was selected consisting of Marvin Jones of Texas, Judge of the

U.S. Court of Claims and assistant to the Director of Economic Stabilization, as chairman; Paul H. Appleby, Under Secretary of Agriculture; Will L. Clayton, Assistant Secretary of Commerce; Dr. Thomas Parran, Surgeon General of the Public Health Service; Murray D. Lincoln, Executive Secretary of the Ohio Farm Bureau Federation; and Miss Josephine Schain. Having contributed to this excellent start, I retired—or thought I had retired—from further responsibility for the project.

Trouble started on April 10 when the State Department released a revised notice of conference plans postponing the opening date until May 18. The notice stated that the Homestead would be "for the exclusive use [of] the Conference sessions and for the accommodation of the official delegations" and "anticipated that the Conference will be as informal as possible," adding that "plans are being made for opening and closing plenary sessions to which press and radio representatives will be accredited."[1] Alerted by this ominous language, *The New York Times* probed further and reported on April 11 that aside from the opening and closing meetings the press would have no occasion to go to the hotel at all and that Michael J. McDermott, the Department's press officer, would dispense information from an office in Hot Springs. Uproar spread like a prairie fire. On April 13 and 14 Representative Fred Bradley and Senator Homer Ferguson, both of Michigan, introduced condemnatory resolutions. Representative Joseph Martin, Minority Leader, called for an open conference with congressional participation.

On April 20 at the White House Judge Jones tried to turn away wrath with humor (such as it was). He thought the press were "making a mountain out of a mole hill" and referred to the President's press conference of March 19: "The President was asked whether newspapermen would be permitted to cover the food conference when it occurred. The President replied facetiously that he hoped not, and his reply was greeted with laughter. This reply indicates the humor in which the President replied to the question."[2] Perhaps so; but Judge Jones was not the most perceptive man I have known, nor did his expressed belief that all could be worked out satisfactorily carry conviction. At any rate, all was not worked out satisfactorily.

On May 15 the conference began to assemble. The first arrivals were Mike McDermott and a group of newspapermen. They were followed that night by military police from Fort Jay, who barred, with the aid of side arms and the fence, all access to the hotel. Temporary press headquarters were set up in the casino about fifty feet from the hotel, from which a siege was mounted. Meanwhile the press maintained heavy artillery fire on the Administration ("Is this what we are fighting for?"), while feeble placatory statements came back. The press would be invited to receptions and they could talk with delegates on the golf course and tennis courts.

Then came the delegates to the conference and their staffs, escorted into the beleaguered fortress by military police. Beyond the fence lay enemy country. The delegates felt cooped in. Since the only secret within a hundred miles was what they were there for and no one seemed to know the answer to that, they could see no purpose in the elaborate security. Mutinous murmurs emanated from the besieged. The conference was getting a bad press.

The President made his final contribution to confusion. The press, he said, at his conference on May 18, might just as well ask to sit at Cabinet meetings or attend secret conferences in his office, or even to watch him take his bath, as to attend the FAO meetings.[3]

Mr. Hull had little interest in the conference, which he considered a mere side show to the greater performance which he was planning, but he saw the whole subject of postwar planning being endangered by the President's controversy with the press. Favoring peace at any price, he asked me to go to Hot Springs and help McDermott and Judge Jones find a peaceful solution. I pointed out that the trouble lay in the White House, not in Hot Springs. The President had what he used to call his "Dutch" up and nothing could be done until he got it down again. The trouble in Hot Springs could be solved if he and Mr. Byrnes would persuade the President to leave it alone.

A mob scene awaited me at the main entrance before reaching the military police. For once the press wanted to talk rather than question. Soon I became the interviewer and in no time was overladen with messages, requests, demands, and threats. Revolution was well advanced. Once inside, my State Department colleagues convinced me that rebellion there was at the same stage.

For a few hours I shuttled back and forth between the lines, bearing suggestions and countersuggestions. Both sides agreed that peace was desirable and had to be achieved imperceptibly and without claims of victory or defeat. Receptions could be given often and long; delegates might invite members of the press to dine after meeting hours; the press might have a convenient room in the hotel equipped with telephones without too stringent hours for use. By the end of the day a cease-fire was agreed on, subject to good behavior on both sides. I was free to go back to Washington and my own troubles with the Senate. At Hot Springs tensions eased as nothing of much account happened at the conference and press interest and attendance dwindled.

One lesson, however, was well learned. If and when an UNRRA conference might be called, we could do without military police, and the press could see or hear anything they chose. When, a few months later at Atlantic City, the Russians, citing the precedent of Hot Springs, suggested excluding the press, as chairman I found ways of burying the proposal.

The first of the receptions at Hot Springs, a Russian one complete with vodka and caviar, produced a memorable incident. The pleasant and friendly head of the British delegation, Richard Law, later Lord Coleraine, a son of Bonar Law, occupied one of the grander suites assigned to VIPs, which were located at the end of each floor of the wings radiating out from the public rooms of the Homestead. Having done his bare duty by the increasingly noisy reception, Law left it for a night's rest. As he later reported his adventure, sleep at length ended in a nightmare in which he could see a great hairy gorilla stealthily approaching his own recumbent form. With a terror-stricken shout, he sat up to see the gorilla scoop up his clothes from the floor and take off naked down the corridor. The next day he received more vodka and caviar and an apology from his Russian colleague, who had an identical suite above or below him.

UNRRA LAUNCHED

Domestic criticism of the relief agreement was soon matched by voices from overseas. As might have been expected, our foreign friends centered their fire on the four-member executive committee, called the Central Committee. With the Dutch leading, they blazed away at big-power domination as the negation of the democratic principle. In a relief organization the negation seemed to me understandable, but only the Russians, Chinese, and (rather feebly) the British agreed with me. In a meeting with them on July 21 I stated the three courses open to us—to stand firm, to modify the powers of the committee, or to enlarge its membership. The least harmful seemed to be the second.[4]

We had perhaps justified criticism in giving the Central Committee the authority to exercise all the powers of the full council between the sessions of the latter. As the Dutch pointed out, this included the power to reverse decisions of the supposed governing body. A strategic retreat appeared indicated.

We retreated with dignity and logic. The committee's power was restricted to making "policy decisions of an emergency nature" between council sessions. These were to be communicated at once to the membership and be open to reconsideration at any later session of the larger body.[5] To discourage further discussion, the Department announced United States willingness to sign the document and go forward with the first council meeting immediately. November 9 at the White House was suggested for the ceremony, and November 10 at the Claridge Hotel in Atlantic City, New Jersey, for the beginning of the meeting.[6] The President designated me to represent the United States on the council and more than adequately equipped me with advisers, liaison officers, and two excellent assistants, Kermit Roosevelt, Jr., and Edward G. Miller, Jr., secretary of the delegation.

Forty-four of us met with the President in the East Room of the White House on November 9 and watched him and each of the others sign the revised agreement. This, he told us, was a "historic occasion" and he garnished it with some oratory, not of the first quality. ("The sufferings of the little men and women who have been ground under the Axis heel can be relieved only if we utilize the production of *all* the world to balance the want of *all* the world"[7]— a rather more grandiose scheme than we had undertaken.) Then he sent us off to Atlantic City.

There we met for three weeks, though nothing we accomplished should have taken so long. For one thing, the Russians coming by way of the Pacific were late and not much could be done until they arrived. For another, instantaneous translation had not yet been devised. And, finally, a good deal of maneuvering and politicking was necessary to sort out committee memberships and the scope and method of operations and of contribution. I was elected chairman of the council meeting, and Governor Lehman the Director General of the relief administration (UNRRA). The membership of that first meeting contained many able and delightful men. I already knew the French representative, one of the greatest of Frenchmen, Jean Monnet. We had been friends for many years. Happily in those weeks we had opportunities for long talks on the famous boardwalk along the winter ocean. Monnet gave me fascinating glimpses into General de Gaulle, who was as yet only a controversial mystery to me, and into Monnet's own pragmatic view of Europe's need to escape its historic parochialism.

Jan Masaryk was a charming, gay (and, later, tragic) figure who made even the dullest subject entertaining. John (Jay) Llewellin (later Lord Llewellin), British Minister of Food, on the surface a perfect embodiment of John Bull, lubricated long night conferences with excellent Scotch to the undoing of our secretary's minutes. Two junior assistants of his became my lifelong friends: John Maud (now Lord Redcliffe-Maud), who presently is Master of University College, Oxford, and Oliver (later Lord) Franks, who is now Master of Worcester College, Oxford, and was then the official head of the Ministry of Supply and later became British Ambassador to the United States while I was Secretary of State. I first met Paul-Henri Spaak of Belgium at Atlantic City, as well as Kyriakos Varvaressos, the Governor of the Bank of Greece and former Minister of Finance. We became warm friends. The same was true of Sir Girja Bajpai, Agent General of India in Washington. As always, Sir Owen Dixon, the Australian Minister in Washington, was a wise and sympathetic counselor. Later he became Chief Justice of Australia's High Court. Felix Frankfurter used to say that Sir Owen was the most distinguished judge in the English-speaking world, and when Frankfurter conceded him the palm, none could dispute it.

Perhaps my deepest gratitude, as well as warm affection, was inspired by the Cuban delegate, López Castro. He came to my aid, at considerable risk to himself, when I needed a friend.

It came about in this way. On November 15 I introduced what became known as the American plan for financing relief, although it was the outgrowth of talks among Richard Law, Maynard Keynes, Governor Lehman, Harry White of the Treasury, and myself. The plan called for a single subscription from countries that had not been invaded of one per cent of their national income, to be paid as needed, a small part in foreign exchange, the rest in goods or domestic funds. Countries which could purchase their supplies were to do so, and those which received funds from UNRRA might be required to pay local currency to be used for relief purposes. Administrative expenses were to be contributed separately. After a good deal of talk the plan went through, but to the Latin Americans an organization in which they were exclusively on the giving side was a novel and not altogether welcome experience. This attitude found expression in a thoroughgoing, if not dilatory, criticism of the plan. At length López Castro, prodded by Eddie Miller, suggested an evangelical meeting in my sitting room during which, after giving the brethren spirituous sustenance, I should recall them to their Christian duty.

When the time came, I did my part but the response seemed all too slow. López Castro took the floor with more direct and forceful language. His colleagues, he said, reminded him of a familiar scene at a great fiesta. He pictured the square in front of the cathedral packed with people and banners, the choir and clergy leading the crowd within in a devout *te deum*. But when the collection was taken up, some members of the congregation began slipping out the side doors. The time had come to pay up. Cuba would begin by pledging its one per cent. The others came along. López Castro had turned the tide.

Until the Russian delegation arrived, Litvinov's second in command, Andrei Gromyko, who had succeeded him as Ambassador, filled in but was not instructed on many matters of substance. Gromyko's sobriquet "Old Stone Face," belied a dry, sardonic humor when he chose to turn it on. It accurately described an impenetrable mask, which may well have contributed to his amazing and unique record of survival amid the changes and chances of life in Russia from 1909 to the present. When the delegation arrived, its head, a young man perhaps in his thirties, took over. Vasili Alexeevich Sergeev, People's Vice Commissar for Foreign Trade, was a different type. Affable, the son of a steel worker, and educated as an engineer, he was a product of the new regime. His English was excellent, his manner confident but cautious, since he was venturing for the first time outside the Soviet Union and was on his guard, undoubtedly accentuated by the presence among his delegation of members of the secret police. Relations with him became easier than with Gromyko as we felt one another out, but I rarely saw him alone and never had the sense of rapport that I felt with so many of the other men present. In fact, in years of dealing with Russian Communists I never felt this with any of them. Nor do I know any of my colleagues who did.

The principal task and partial achievement of the meeting at Atlantic City was educational—to talk things out and get some realistic consensus on what the relief administration could do and should try to do, its scope and limits, its methods of financing, and its appropriate clients and methods of dealing with them. To most of those present the problems were new and the proposed solutions unfamiliar. All of us were dealing with conditions as yet unimagined, but the main task of guidance fell to the British and ourselves, who had done more exploration than the others. Looking over the long-forgotten resolutions of the council, I am impressed with their sensible approach. They were not formal recitations and were not written as laws but as explanatory papers to guide administrators, recipients, and givers of relief as to what to expect, what to do, and how to go about it. A memorandum of mine written before the conference gave the general principle: "UNRRA should do those things which will not be done without it and avoid what can be done with existing means. The problems will be so great and the demands so many that UNRRA should adopt something in the nature of an international Jeffersonian principle of doing the least which is necessary to accomplish the result—which is another way of saying that it should center its attention upon the essential problems which cannot be solved without it."

As far as the Russians were concerned, the organization existed to give prizes for fighting Hitler. From our first meeting with Litvinov until they nearly wrecked the organization in 1945 by demanding practically its entire fund, their view was that those who fought hardest were entitled to most even though in fact there were few nations better able to provide and pay for their own relief.

These conflicting points of view made for sharp arguments. Few of them were settled—in the sense of ended—at Atlantic City. They remained with us for a long time, but the issues were clarified.

One of the first problems, discussed before, during, and after Atlantic City, was the proper relation of UNRRA to the military authorities. In the course of the long debate the parties almost completely swapped positions. The reliefers, at first, were eager to tread on the armies' heels, and the soldiers, not unnaturally, chafed over the proposed intrusion of civilians. Later my friends in the War Department, John J. McCloy and General John Hilldring, would insist that the Army could not "get into the relief business," that its responsibility to a civilian population was to furnish what was necessary "to prevent disease and unrest in the wake of battle." I would point to the inescapable fact that only the Army could command the necessary shipping, supplies, and people to do the minimum and that with a constantly advancing battle its "wake" continued to be an active zone of operations.

When relief was needed in an area such as Greece, where our forces had responsibility for supply but not operations, the question arose as to who would protect the supplies and their distribution against local disorder. Hilldring's view that the local citizenry could choose between fighting and eating earned him the title of "No Forcible Feeding" Hilldring. One learned by hard experience that general principles do not resolve concrete problems and that things are rarely what they seem. At Atlantic City a foundation was laid for this process of operation by trial and success or error in North Africa.

A FORECAST OF THE DIVISION OF POLAND

Just before the council meeting ended, an incident occurred that cast a long shadow into the future. Sergeev came to me with a request to show a film of, as he described it, "the fighting on the eastern front," just received from Russia. This promised to give some idea of the devastation "in the wake of battle" with which we were planning to deal. I saw no objection and announced an evening showing for the whole conference and staff. To my chagrin, the film turned out to be a propaganda picture of triumphant Russian occupation of parts of Poland with the population embracing not only the troops but—so the dubbed-in commentary explained—the Communist doctrines they carried with them. My error in not investigating the film before arranging for its showing was underlined by the Polish Ambassador's angry protest as we left the hall. I promised to consider what could be done.

Jan Ciechanowski, an accomplished diplomat and a charming gentleman, had already taken a distrustful view of UNRRA. In July he had called on me twice in distress because of remarks the President and Governor Lehman had made to the Polish Prime Minister, General Igor Sikorski, which, as the Ambassador had understood and translated them, referred to "food as a weapon" in the sense that relief supplies would be used to influence European countries after their liberation. Mr. Hull reported this to the President, who replied in some heat that "the impression which the Polish Ambassador received is of course utterly contrary to the fact. In my talk with General Sikorski and the Ambassador I spoke of food as a weapon in the actual war."[8] In the same month the Polish Government had protested against the powers of the four-member Central Committee.[9] The Ambassador now saw his fears strengthened by the ominous implication of the Russian film, apparently shown under my sponsorship.

When we discussed it, Jay Llewellin and I saw nothing to be done beyond making clear that we had been taken as much by surprise as anyone and regretted the showing. He proposed that then and there we call on Ambassador Ciechanowski, express our regret, and, taking him by the hand, proclaim our friendship. When I doubted the effectiveness of this procedure with someone who had just heard the future of his country imperiled, Llewellin asked whether I had a better plan. I had none, so we adopted his.

The first phase of UNRRA ended in a glow of cordiality, which gave comforting assurance that two lessons had been learned in the School of Hard Knocks. McDermott's assistant press officer, Lincoln White, who had gone with us to Atlantic City, wrote me a warm letter expressing the appreciation of the press for the arrangements made for them and the efforts to keep them fully informed. When the President asked for legislation to authorize and appropriate funds for UNRRA, the process was painless and swift. Senator Vandenberg told the Senate Committee on Foreign Relations, "I think it also ought to be said that the State Department was amazingly cooperative, almost without precedent." Representative John Vorys, Republican of Ohio, echoed the sentiment before the House committee.[10]

10. THE BRETTON WOODS AGREEMENTS

AGRICULTURE AND RELIEF were simple matters compared to international monetary arrangements. The period of gestation of the latter about doubled that of elephants. Conceived in May 1941 in the lend-lease talks with Maynard Keynes, the agreements were brought forth in July 1944. For nearly two years the and Harry Dexter White for us, exchanged drafts and ideas. From time to time treasuries of the two countries, with Maynard Keynes leading for the British State and other agencies participated in a subsidiary way, our interest being directed chiefly to commercial policy and commodity agreements. At first during this period Berle, Feis, and I each played a small part; gradually the other two dropped out.

By the spring of 1943 the White draft of an international monetary fund, with Keynesian amendments, cleared with Parliament and congressional committees, was distributed for study and further discussion in Washington. Nineteen of the governments sent experts to meet in June and make a report. An Anglo-American group in the autumn added sections on commercial policy, commodity agreements, cartels, and employment. The work of both groups emerged in the spring of 1944 as a "Joint Statement of Technical Experts on the Establishment of an International Monetary Fund." Meanwhile, the Treasury also conferred with congressional committees and then published a draft outline of a proposed International Bank for Reconstruction and Development. In May the State Department issued invitations to forty-odd governments to meet on July 1 at Bretton Woods, New Hampshire, "for the purpose of formulating proposals of a definite character for an international monetary fund and possibly a bank for reconstruction and development."[1]

Henry Morgenthau deserves the same high praise that has been given Mr. Hull regarding the United Nations Charter for the patience and thoroughness with which he prepared with Congress, foreign governments, and the public these intricate and most important agreements. They could not have been put through without his special quality of leadership. The field, especially of the Monetary Fund, was so technical that it necessitated picking a highly qualified lieutenant to do the technical work and backing him to the hilt. The field of monetary arrangements itself evoked very little popular and no congressional interest. Here Morgenthau's capacity for almost obsessive concentration on the matter in hand became of great importance. Harry White, so far as I could observe, served Secretary Morgenthau with complete loyalty and great skill. In later years it was charged that he had Communist sympathies. I have often been so outraged by Harry White's capacity for rudeness in discussion that the charges made against him would have seemed mild compared to expressions I have used, but he could be equally pleasant and amusing, as I well remember from an evening when we joined the Keyneses for dinner at the Whites'. I have often differed, sometimes violently, with his policies, but they were usually policies that I knew were strongly favored by his chief. He died suddenly in 1948, and time has mellowed for me the harsher side of his nature. I say to his restless spirit with kindliness, *"Requiescat in pace."*

By the time invitations to the conference went out, I had been left without competitors as State's representative in the enterprise. Bretton Woods had been chosen both for the beneficent climate of the White Mountains and the availability there of a summer hotel of adequate size and condition. However, having been closed for three years, it presented problems of staffing and operation in wartime that had not been fully considered. Having at least recognized them, I did not stay in the hotel myself but in a comfortable inn at nearby Crawford Notch. The transportation problem was solved by appropriate attention to the military police assigned to guard our privacy and well-being.

Henry Morgenthau put me on the delegation despite an argument I had with him over its selection. He wished to include in it the ranking majority and minority members of the Banking and Currency committees of the two houses.† However, Senator Charles Tobey of New Hampshire, the ranking Republican on the Senate committee, was reputed to be an extreme isolationist, and Morgenthau wanted to bypass him in favor of the next Republican. To have been pointedly excluded from a conference held in his own state when he was running for re-election would have been an insult Senator Tobey could not have overlooked. The sacred rights of seniority would have ranged his colleagues on his side and an enterprise that needed all the congressional support it could get would have been launched with a bitter partisan row. This, I told Morgenthau, could prove its death warrant; I might be a novice in international monetary arrangements, but I was a professional in senatorial ones. Reluctantly, he backed away from this folly and Tobey became one of the most effective supporters in the Congress of the international bank and fund. He also became a devoted and loyal friend to me.

While we were battling the disorganization during the opening weekend at Bretton Woods, Senator Tobey came to me with a request. The Fourth of July and the need for an address at the conference were hard upon us. So was the Republican primary in New Hampshire, where he faced opposition. If he could make the Independence Day address, he would receive most gratifying publicity throughout the state. With the help of Fred Vinson it was arranged, and our relations were forever cemented.

The evening of our arrival at Bretton Woods, unknown to me, proved to be the five-hundredth anniversary of the concordat between King's College, Cambridge, and New College, Oxford. Maynard Keynes, a devoted Kingsman, had arranged a celebration into which he poured his exuberant enthusiasm. Overcoming the near anarchy in the kitchen and wine cellar, he had organized a dinner for seven or eight representing the two colleges as well as Yale University, with which King's had a special relation, originating when a Kingsman, Charles Seymour, became President of Yale. H. H. Kung, the Chinese Finance Minister, who had recently received an honorary degree from the university, Oscar Cox, and I represented Yale. In private Keynes disrespectfully referred to His Excellency as "the old Mandarin" and in public delighted in asking his views on the most complicated monetary problems. But "H.H.," who had married a sister of Mme. Sun Yat-sen and Mme. Chiang Kai-shek, was quite able to hold his own in any company. He did so that evening, when Keynes was at his most charming and brilliant on the subject of the contribution of universities to civilization.

For nearly four weeks the work of the conference went on all day and often far into the night. Keynes thought that the pressure was "quite unbelievable," though by our standards it did not seem unusual. After attending some night sessions, contrary to his doctor's orders, he suffered a heart attack and forswore them. An effort to keep Keynes's illness quiet proved unsuccessful and led to the usual investigations of who leaked the story to the press. It appeared that on the evening of his attack an alarmed Lady Keynes, looking for someone to fetch a doctor, found a most helpful young man who, of course, turned out to have been a newspaper correspondent.

The chief work and arguments of the conference concerned the International Monetary Fund, where the State Department's interest in maintaining the freedom of trade from legal or monetary restraints was watched over by Pete Collado and Leo Pasvolsky. Under the monetary conditions existing at the end of the war, what Mr. Hull had always opposed as impediments to trade were seen by the Treasury as discriminations against the United States and just as vigorously opposed. My own duties and interest centered in the work of Committee II on the international bank, to which under Keynes's chairmanship I had been assigned and put in charge of drafting the bank's charter. Years later George Woods, then President of the bank, expressed his gratitude for its flexibility and broad powers. As contrasted with the fund, whose charter was largely dictated by monetary experts and narrowly hedged about, the bank management could do anything it wanted to. This restrictiveness of the fund document, mistakenly attributed by Keynes to the lawyers, was what he had in mind when he said in the final plenary session of July 22: "I wish that [the lawyers] had not covered so large a part of our birth certificate with such very detailed provisions for our burial service, hymns and lessons and all."

Keynes did not like lawyers. He thought the United States "a lawyer-ridden land" and believed that "the *Mayflower,* when she sailed from Plymouth, must have been entirely filled with lawyers." However, he paid our little band at Bretton Woods a handsome compliment for approaching his ideal lawyer: "I want him [a lawyer] to tell me how to do what *I* think sensible, and, above all, to devise means by which it will be lawful for me to go on being sensible in unforeseen conditions some years hence. . . . Too often lawyers are men who turn poetry into prose and prose into jargon. Not so our lawyers here in Bretton Woods. On the contrary, they have turned our jargon into prose and our prose into poetry. And only too often they have had to do our thinking for us."[2]

In our discussions of the bank in Committee II we ran into three substantive issues, which in the end were worked out by private negotiation. The first of these grew out of the competing claims for loans of war-torn and undeveloped areas. Keynes and I favored equitable consideration of both, the criteria being the need for and efficacy of the project rather than the cause of it. White disagreed. The solid weight of the Latin American delegations threw the decision our way. More difficult was the desire of all delegations, led by the Russians closely followed by the Latin Americans, for much lower subscriptions to the capital of the bank than to that of the fund. The reason, of course, was that drawings upon the fund were related to subscriptions and quotas, while borrowings from the bank would be unrelated to ownership of the capital stock. However, a general failure to subscribe would mean either no bank or one financed largely by the United States. Henry Morgenthau put a great effort into getting the Soviet Union to raise its subscription to the bank to the level of its quota in the fund. He was able to announce the achievement of this goal at the final plenary session. It was, however, a short-lived success, since the Soviet Union did not ratify either agreement.

Eddie Miller and I had more enduring success with the American republics. This involved many and long discussions with the principal delegations, followed by meetings with the whole group. One problem was to find a place spacious but private enough for so large and so confidential a meeting. My so-called office was clearly not that, as a more or less enclosed corner of the ballroom, now the plenary-session hall, had been turned over to me. It had once been a bar and still had the curtain that had been pulled across at closing time. Into this small spot of happier memories Miss Evans moved her typewriter and used the sink designed for washing glasses as a filing cabinet. She soon adopted other officeless waifs, including a spaniel, which frequently added its comments to the debates in progress on the other side of the curtain. We found other places to meet with our Latin American friends, who soon succumbed to Eddie's charm and persuasiveness in Spanish, Portuguese, and English.

The third issue was solved by changing our minds. The British had wanted the bank's lending power to be limited to the amount of its capital and surplus, while we had advocated a high ratio of loans to assets. However, our commercial-banker member, Ned Brown, pointed out to us that we would be defeating our own purposes in taking this view. The bank's bonds could not, at least initially, be sold without some guarantee by the United States Government, and our proposed original position would have required an open-ended commitment from the United States. We hastily joined the British in their position.

Toward the end of July the Bretton Woods conference ended amid mutual congratulations and we returned from our White Mountain resort to the muggy heat of a Washington August, intensified by the even more sultry stickiness of a negotiation with the Russians.

LEND-LEASE NEGOTIATIONS WITH MOSCOW

Our original lend-lease arrangement with the Soviet Union at the time of Hitler's attack in the summer of 1941 provided for one billion dollars of supplies to be repaid within ten years after the war. This optimistic agreement had long since been outdated both in the amount furnished and in the conception of settlement. The Soviet Union had suffered grievously under Hitler's attack. The Administration thought that the time had come for new discussions about the future, and the Soviet delegation to Bretton Woods had stayed over for the purpose. Fortified by representatives of the Foreign Economic Administration and the Treasury, I was designated to conduct them, and did so in the almost unbearable heat of our southwest-corner room in Old State.

The surrounding circumstances were no more propitious than the weather. Poland was in the midst of the agonizing uprising of General Bor's forces in Warsaw against the Germans, signaled by the Russians just across the Vistula, who then waited before crossing it until the Germans had destroyed the insurgents and much of the population of Warsaw. Messages flew from Roosevelt and Churchill to an unmoved Stalin. Feelings ran high. Even the heat of our room could not warm the chill between allies into cordiality. Since our discussions were quite fruitless, I shall not bother with them.[3] Moscow knew that in the last bitter struggle with a desperate Hitler we could not and would not interrupt the flow of supplies to the Russian divisions that kept so many Germans busy in the east while we had all we could handle in the west. The President decided to adjourn the discussions.

For me the importance of these negotiations was the lesson they taught me under Averell Harriman's coaching. We began with generous proposals submitted before the discussions started; broadly speaking, they provided for writing off materials consumed or destroyed during the war, returning ships and similar surviving loans, and paying on easy terms for goods they wanted to keep. For days the meetings went on with exactly the same points, often in the same words, made by each side. Attempts to vary proposals, to feel out the other side for signs of flexibility, brought only the same stolid and verbose replies from the Russians. Then I remembered the sound advice Averell Harriman had given me sometime earlier, when he was home from Moscow: not to ignore a fundamental fact of Communist negotiating procedure—that no Soviet representative would ever report home what an opponent *said*. To do so would give the impression that he had been impressed or was weak or lacked zeal in carrying out his instructions. Furthermore, unfriendly NKVD men on the delegation could use any willingness to compromise against him. He could report only what he said, how well, and with what telling effect.

The way to make progress toward some conclusion—even one that no agreement was possible—was to recess the meetings for a day or two, signaling an important consultation, and then to present a paper with some modification of position toward the ultimate acceptable one. This should be followed by another recess to give the Soviet delegation an opportunity to communicate with Moscow. The paper would be communicated, since not to do so would be a grave fault. On getting a reply the Soviet negotiator would ask for a resumption of discussion. Each such exchange must be played for a while to indicate the serious consideration being given to it. One could soon decide whether movement was only circular or toward an agreement. We soon determined that in our case it was purely circular.

Ending negotiations if they were getting nowhere was as difficult as conducting them. It was like playing Old Maid: no one wanted to be left with the queen of spades, the onus of having broken them off. The exit from them was an indefinite adjournment.

Direct dealings by a Western embassy with the Soviet Foreign Office have been described by Sir William Hayter, formerly the British Ambassador in Moscow and later Warden of New College, Oxford, as like dealing with an old-fashioned penny slot machine: one rarely got out of it what one wanted, but one got something. One could "sometimes expedite the process by shaking the machine," but it was "useless to *talk* to it."[4]

For us in State, however, this frustrating Russian interlude was soon forgotten amid the greater events then impending.

11. A CHANGE OF SECRETARIES
AND OF JOBS

ON SEPTEMBER 30, 1944, Mr. Hull, a very ill man, confided to his friend, Assistant Secretary Breckinridge Long, that within a day he would see the President and tell him "that while he would not resign before election that he would leave immediately after that." "It was a sombre conversation," Long notes in his diary. "He was tired of intrigue . . . tired of being by-passed . . . tired of being relied upon in public and ignored in private . . . tired of fighting battles which were not appreciated . . . tired of making speeches and holding press interviews—tired of talking and tired of service. . . . The end of a long career is at hand—ending not in satisfaction, as it should, but in bitterness."[1] Long was sworn to secrecy, but his diary was not. To read Mr. Hull's own account of his feelings at the time[2] in the light of Long's is a warning to memoir writers.

About the middle of October, being summoned to Under Secretary Stettinius' office, I found Long and Joseph C. Grew, then acting as Special Assistant to the Secretary, already there. They told me something of the nature of Mr. Hull's illness and that he was to move from his apartment where he had been for a week or two to Bethesda Naval Hospital, and showed me a proposed press statement. This not only stated that the Secretary was going into the hospital, but it would have raised serious doubt that he would ever come out. It seemed a dubious contribution to the political campaign. They agreed to substitute an innocuous announcement of a proposed rest and medical checkup.

Mr. Hull's resignation was announced on November 27. At once I wrote him and within a day had a note from him, courteous, reserved, and formal:

Dear Mr. Acheson: *November 30, 1944*

I wish to express my warmest thanks for the kind and generous message contained in your letter of November twenty-eighth. I deeply appreciate what you say. At the same time I want you to know that I am grateful for the very splendid cooperation and assistance you invariably gave me as one of my principal associates in the Department. I shall always remain greatly indebted to you.

With every good wish to you and your family for a full measure of success and happiness in the future, and with kindest personal regards.   Sincerely yours,

Cordell Hull

Curiously, it was only after Mr. Hull's retirement that a real friendship developed between us, which continued until his death. The copy of his memoirs he sent me was inscribed "with warmest friendship," a considerable departure from his formal style. Throughout the years when illness confined him alternately to the hospital or his apartment I visited him as regularly as duties permitted. We had long gossips, usually about the past. Sometimes he reviewed grievances, as he had with Long—and they still rankled; sometimes he took obvious pleasure in arguing that few of his positive acts had been mistakes. It is equally possible, though I did not point it out, to make mistakes by inaction. On other visits, but less often, he would want to know what was going on, the news behind the news. Other callers reported that he enjoyed these visits. He touched me deeply in December 1950 when I was about to go to Europe while under heavy attack in Congress. Word came to me that Mr. Hull had come to wish me good luck and bon voyage, but could not leave his car, which was in the Department's basement garage. I went down to see him and found quite a reception going on as word had spread of the old gentleman's presence. He told me that there were times when friends might be useful and that he wanted to be publicly counted among mine. In the Tennessee mountains, where feuds were serious, friendships were also.

Hard on the heels of Mr. Hull's resignation came the nomination of the Under Secretary, Edward R. Stettinius, Jr., to succeed him. This led to speculation in the press that the President would be—or, perhaps, would continue to be—as they expressed it, "his own Secretary of State," a most misleading phrase. The President cannot be Secretary of State; it is inherently impossible in the nature of both positions. What he can do, and often has done with unhappy results, is to prevent anyone else from being Secretary of State. The office can be filled; some person can perform its ceremonial duties—and, perhaps, a little more; but the function of a foreign office and of its head is simply not performed by anyone.

President Roosevelt's virtual exclusion of Secretary Hull from high-policy decisions during the war had more far-reaching effects than its contribution to the estrangement of the two men. It led directly to the theoretical and unreal nature of the State Department's—and, hence, the Government's—thinking on postwar problems. Largely detached from the practicalities of current problems and power relationships, the Department under Mr. Hull became absorbed in platonic planning of a utopia, in a sort of mechanistic idealism. Perhaps, given the nature of the current problems, of the two men, and of the tendency to accept dichotomy between foreign and military policy, this would have occurred in any event. But it accentuated the isolation of the Secretary and the Department in a land of dreams.

BRAVE NEW WORLD

Before arriving in Washington at the age of thirty-eight, Stettinius had gone far with comparatively modest equipment. Enthusiastic, good-natured, and with prematurely white hair, an engaging smile, and a gift for public relations, he had been Vice President of General Motors and Chairman of the Board of United States Steel. Two types of businessmen come to Washington. One is the product of a staff, is lost without it, and usually finds Washington a graveyard; the other is his own staff and relies on his own ability and drive. Stettinius was unique in that he belonged to the first group but did not find Washington a graveyard, even though he became Secretary of State. He was confirmed immediately and with only Senator Langer of North Dakota dissenting.

Shortly afterward Joe Grew came to me. A serious interview clearly lay ahead, for Joe had the solemn and portentous look of an eminent physician about to impart grim news. The Secretary, he said (how quickly attendants adopt the new titles of their master!)—the Secretary was about to make extensive changes to further departmental efficiency. My three colleagues were leaving—Long and Shaw for private life, Berle to become Ambassador to Brazil. The "moving finger," having written, moved on, leaving my own position obscure. Grew himself was to be Under Secretary, and Will Clayton was to be Assistant Secretary for Economic Affairs, the position which I was still occupying. Julius Holmes would be in charge of administration and Archibald MacLeish of public and cultural affairs, a new post not altogether clearly defined. Supervision of the geographic divisions was to be divided between two assistant secretaries: Nelson A. Rockefeller, formerly Coordinator of Inter-American Affairs, would supervise our relations with the American republics, and James C. Dunn, formerly Director of the Office of European Affairs, those with all other states.

There was one post left. Clearly the choice, if I was to have one, could only be between this, whatever it might be, and resignation. The Secretary, Grew continued, was pleased to offer me the field of "congressional relations and international conferences."

The offer carried with it the distinct impression that it was expected to be declined, but my mind did not need the speed and competence of a computer to veto that conclusion. Surely better opportunities to leave the Department could be managed than during a general housecleaning. Furthermore, relations between the Congress and the Department were bound to be active as the end of the war approached. The management of such matters as the Bretton Woods agreements, the United Nations Charter already being negotiated by Stettinius, another renewal of the Trade Agreements Act, a treaty with Mexico on the uses of international waters, and all the inevitable agreements, treaties, and legislation growing out of the war could provide a strong position from which to influence policy. The Department had always listened to an oracle who prophesied what Congress would or would not tolerate, particularly if the oracle could do anything to effectuate his prophecies. What the reference to international conferences added was not clear. Probably it was intended as garnishment to a position that might otherwise seem meager. At most it might refer to the arrangements with local authorities and others necessary to house, protect, and operate a conference, which were handled by the Division of International Conferences. With solemnity and fervor equal to his own, I told Grew that my desire was to serve where duty called and accepted the offer, to preclude its reconsideration.

Our first view of the Stettinius style came with the hearings before the

Senate committee on the confirmation of what he called "the team which the President and I have chosen to assist me in directing the Department of State."[3] He and his acolytes—referred to by the press as Snow White and the seven dwarfs—appeared before the committee en masse. Stettinius had suggested to me that I appear with them and offer myself for examination, a proposal I flatly rejected. Already holding office and being under no obligation to assume the sacrificial role of an appointee to a new one, I did not propose to begin my task of dealing with Congress with so naïve a performance as volunteering for the abattoir.

The proceedings opened with a sketch by Stettinius of his reorganized department and of the several qualifications of the team, including myself, for our new posts. Then he called upon each to make a statement. Joe Grew began with a declaration of faith, including "I believe in Mr. Stettinius. . . . He is 'the man who gets things done.' "[4] The committee was well disposed and inclined to recommend confirmation and call it a day. But the eager, amateurish innocence of the whole performance evoked senatorial humor, and senatorial humor contains a sadistic element. A little fun was necessary to lighten all this solemnity. With Jimmie Dunn it took the form of getting this able, delightful, and basically shy man thoroughly rattled; with Archie MacLeish, to ask him as the future propounder of the mysteries of foreign policy to expound some selected lines of his own verse. Archie wisely chose safety over valor and retreated behind Browning's defense that when the lines were written he and God both understood them, but that at the moment the latter alone could recall what they meant.

When the Senate had given its advice and consent, an oath-taking ceremony was arranged in the large conference room at Old State adjoining the Secretary's office. It resembled a mass baptism. Stettinius, snow-capped and episcopal, flanked by the protocol officer holding a Bible, received the line of initiates. Grouped near them were their wives, garbed in fur and identified by one or more orchids. The room was filled with spectators and photographers; flashbulbs popped. Each candidate in turn laid left hand on the Bible and, raising his right, swore to defend the Constitution of the United States without mental reservation or purpose of evasion. Each then kissed his wife, showing undoubtedly that his latest promise had not diminished an earlier one.

The company moved across the hall to the diplomatic reception room from which the beautiful and delicate Madison desk had been removed to make more room for moving-picture cameras. There Stettinius introduced each recruit, who stepped before a microphone and briefly elaborated upon his oath of allegiance. As the last turned back, a thought obviously struck the Secretary. "And now," he said, "last, but by no means least, we have a member of the team who took his oath of office four years ago, Assistant Secretary Dean Acheson." I can only describe what followed in biblical terms. As I was pushed before the microphone, an evil spirit entered into me. I heard what seemed to be my voice say:

> These little pigs went to market
> But this little pig stayed home.

Stettinius was not amused.

The festivities, however, were not over. All the Department had been invited to Constitution Hall to view the new team in the flesh. Walking over there, a friend in the Foreign Service observed to me that he had not seen such organized spontaneous fervor since Ed Stettinius had been head cheerleader at the University of Virginia, adding that he hoped the performance of Ed's team would be better than that of the university's in those earlier days. Supported by a few other officers, the novitiates sat in a crescent on the stage. The scarlet-coated Marine Band played. Again the Secretary introduced the team, and on their behalf Joe Grew pledged loyalty to the chief. We rose for the national anthem and returned to our desks, rededicated men and women. The brave new leadership in the Department was already in sight of its end.

ORGANIZING FOR MY NEW JOB

My change of jobs carried with it a change of habitat. The old southwest-corner rooms were to know us no longer, and were swept out to make space for the new Secretary's expanded staff. Whoever chose its stenographic component had a good eye and a partiality for redheads. Our new quarters looked out on the west entrance to the White House and its elm-shaded lawn. They promised, at least, to be cooler in the summer, though we were not to stay through a whole one. The first task was to think about what the job should be and how to organize to do it. Precedent posed no problems. Breck Long, who handled congressional matters out of his hat and on a purely personal basis, had an assistant, unique and invaluable, whom I pre-empted at once. Felton Johnston of Mississippi (known as Skeeter for reasons never explained to me) had come to Washington to work his way through college by means of a job in the capital obtained for him by Senator Pat Harrison of his own state.

Most of my own colleagues of the past four years were scattered. Adrian Fisher and Edwin McElwain were navigating bombers over Germany. Donald Hiss and Eugene Rostow (later Dean of the Yale Law School and Under Secretary of State for Political Affairs) had gone off to a stint in Algeria and then to the hospital. Recuperation from a collapsed lung took Donald into private practice, and a successful spinal operation led Gene to a noncombat commission in the Army. But Eddie Miller was within call and some new talent was available. But, first, the conception.

What the Department needed was the advice, the practical guidance, and the operational help of a first-class law firm organized within the old gray building. The office of the Legal Adviser had never done anything of this sort. In the days I am writing of, it dealt largely with claims by or against the United States on account of its own or its citizens' wrongs, suffered or inflicted, treaty drafting, and the legal dialectics of an international imbroglio. None of its ordnance was later than the eighteenth century, except possibly some Civil War cannon used to support the blockade of southern ports. The Legal Adviser's office in 1944 dealt largely with ancient law, not with the new products that the Department would soon be ordering from the temperamental management of the law factory on Capitol Hill. Though new, they would nonetheless be laws. In true

Rooseveltian style, we would create a new agency to draw their specifications and see them through to production.

Our new agency would have somewhat more than the duties and functions of "house counsel" to a large business corporation. To begin with, we must establish intimate contact with the powers that regulated us and know their minds before they had been collectively made up. At that time the Committee on Foreign Relations held a commanding position in the Senate, with reservations when an issue involved either tariffs or appropriations. Its prestige resulted not so much from tradition as from the individual weight carried by its members, though the two factors interacted. The committee's jurisdiction and powers attracted men of substance and authority, while the membership of such men enhanced the prestige of the committee. In the House, and especially when tariffs and appropriations were involved, the Committee on Foreign Affairs was less prestigious. Here tradition from the days when foreign affairs dealt largely with treaty making (which excluded the House) had played a part. The prize committees began with Ways and Means and Appropriations. In the House, therefore, to influence the membership on matters of foreign policy, it was indispensable to have the help of the Speaker and the Majority Leader in support of the Committee on Foreign Affairs.

After establishing contact with our principal committees, the next step would be to make clear to all members of Congress that for action from the Department they must look to our group. If we were to be held responsible for guiding legislation, we must develop the political equivalent of patronage. No one looked to the Department of State in the appointment of postmasters, marshals, collectors of customs or internal revenue, or in drawing up contracts for ships, planes, or camps. What small assets we had must be husbanded and made much of. At the cost of considerable internal friction we established the practice that, no matter how an inquiry or request from Congress came into the Department, our office should answer it. Frank Merkling, a genius at this, would get off an acknowledgment the day a congressional inquiry was received and then follow it with a series of progress reports to the inquirer until the final answer could be given or action reported. To the member of Congress the Department seemed like a pack of beagles in frenzied pursuit of the information or action he wanted, and he knew who whipped in the hounds. The service was not great but it nourished a sense of obligation or, at least, a friendly attitude.

The nature of the times created other opportunities to show the importance of good relations with us. During the war all foreign travel was controlled by the military, who, except where their own interests were concerned, asked the views of the State Department on most congressional requests. These became more common when, in expanding areas, fighting ended and occupation began. Again our office arranged to transmit the answers, thus radiating an aura of power. Again, as the allied armies moved deeper into Europe, congressmen and senators felt the urge to speak on the great issues of building a peaceful world. Our group could and did emulate the public letter writers in an Asian bazaar, furnishing both political literacy and themes. In return we hoped, with some justification, for sympathetic action on bills the Department favored.

On occasion the situation could be more complicated, as when an able freshman congressman from a protectionist state hesitated to support renewal of the Reciprocal Trade Agreements Act for fear of punishment in the next election. We suggested that he build up a strong enough individual reputation to support a degree of independence. John Dickey, who was working with us on the renewal, had done some academic work on a proposal to amend the Constitution by having treaties ratified by a majority vote in both houses instead of by a two-thirds vote of the Senate alone. Peace treaties being a subject of lively interest, a proposal for House participation would give pleasure there, bring the new member into favorable notice, and give him publicity at home. The project went off as planned; the young man was invited to speak before his own and other state legislatures; the trade bill gained a vote; and the public welfare was served.

In order to interest and inform more members of the House committee about foreign affairs, we encouraged the creation of regional subcommittees to study particular areas in depth. This, in time, developed the countervailing hazard of congressional travel with its burden upon embassy staffs and its dangers of utterances or conduct not calculated to enhance an idol much worshiped in this country, the American image. But the travel is worth its vexations. Since Ulysses' day it has been an instrument of education, and, as for the American image, we shall be better off to be thought of as we are—with warts and all, in Oliver Cromwell's honest phrase—than as some advertising man's prettified conception of how he would like other people to picture us.

Our hardest work, of course, consisted of the legislative program for the congressional session. Each partner in our firm was assigned certain bills or treaties. As senior partner, I planned and helped on all the work. The man in charge was responsible for drafting, sponsorship in Congress—often a delicate matter—and marshaling testimony and outside support for the legislation. He drew heavily on the division of the Department involved—often more than one —for help and witnesses. Skeeter Johnston was like an army scout in Indian territory—spying out the land and identifying friends, enemies, those open to recruitment, and problems in general. From his guidance the rest of us would begin to tramp the corridors of the Senate and House office buildings, carrying the gospel to converted and pagan alike; neither liked to be taken for granted. Often someone who had to go on record against us could be induced to do it in the least harmful way. For instance, in the House a vote cast against us on a roll call, when Johnston's constantly revised list of votes assured us of a safe margin, would do no harm, while teller or voice votes could be chancy, with members drifting in and out of the chamber. A friendly enemy might be content to make his record and let it go at that. On one occasion, when a member was causing confusion and harassment during the marking up of a bill in committee, we got her to desist from her gleeful wickedness by the promise of a powerful speech against the bill when it came up for final vote in the House. We duly wrote it and all parties profited.

Our "law firm," though small, was highly competent. Its thoroughness in preparation left no contingencies uncovered. Edward Miller came with me from the economic work. John Ferguson, another lawyer out of New York but with an Oklahoma origin, which was highly satisfactory for congressional purposes even if somewhat unbelievable, joined us from the Foreign Economic Administration. Our last recruit, Herbert Marks, was to pilot me into a weird and nightmare land as yet undreamed of—the world of the atom. Together, after talks within the Department, we planned a legislative program for the first half or more of 1945. Program planning was not only novel in the Department but involved rather more than merely writing down what needed to be done. First of all, we wanted to begin with a success, and then to assign major legislation to each house, so that different hearing and committee work could go on simultaneously; and we wanted to start the most time-consuming legislation first and yet begin with what was ready. Department convenience had to be reconciled with the larger Administration needs and desires. Finally, each chairman, and later each committee, had to be consulted and won over to accepting our calendar as a convenience in planning their own work. In time it was all done.

12. CHIEF LOBBYIST FOR STATE

WE LAID OUT A busy schedule for the first session of the Seventy-ninth Congress. The Senate Committee on Foreign Relations would start with the Mexican Water Treaty, while on the House side the Ways and Means Committee would take up the renewal of the Reciprocal Trade Agreements Act, and the Banking and Currency Committee an act authorizing participation in the Bretton Woods International Monetary Fund and Development Bank. With these well started on their legislative course, we would feed into the Senate the United Nations Charter (not yet negotiated) and two tax treaties, and, into the House, bills authorizing continuation and enlargement of the authority and funds of the Export-Import Bank (which I had fathered in 1933) and our participation in the Food and Agriculture Organization. This work would keep us all busy until after midsummer.

One reason for leading off with the Mexican Water Treaty was to broaden and popularize the idea that foreign policy should be nonpartisan, outside of politics. If the opposition were brought into the formulation of policy—so the doctrine ran—they would be guilty of a foul in attacking it later on. Mr. Hull had put forward the idea in 1934 in the most political of all areas of foreign policy—tariff making—but it had not flourished. He revived it in his talks with selected members of Congress during 1943 and 1944 about a world organization to enforce peace and, in the campaign autumn of 1944, by his arrangement with Dewey through Dulles that the war should be kept out of election issues. On a minor scale we had succeeded in taking postwar relief—UNRRA—out of the political arena.

THE THEORY OF NONPARTISAN FOREIGN POLICY

We now wanted to go further. Plainly, no effective postwar foreign policy could emerge from political controversy. The idea of a nonpolitical foreign policy was the holy water sprinkled on a political necessity. The perhaps apocryphal sign in the Wild West saloon—"Don't Shoot the Piano Player"—was the basic idea of nonpolitical foreign policy. Foreign policy has no lobby, no vested interest to support it, and no constituents. It must be built on a broad conception of the national interest, which lacks the attraction and support that can be generated by, say, a tax reduction, a tariff increase, or an agricultural subsidy. The Constitution makes the President the piano player of foreign policy, but unless his immunity from assault with intent to kill is extended to members of either party who work with him in the legislative branch, no consistent foreign policy is possible under the separation of powers. The doctrine, of course, aids the Administration, but its immediate beneficiaries are in the Congress.

This beneficent attitude has its limitations. As Senator Vandenberg would often wryly point out, it did not bring him Democratic support on election day. In his more reflective comments he was quite aware that "common action does not mean that we cease to be 'Republicans' or 'Democrats' at home." It meant that in foreign policy cooperation could be purchased at the price of "consultation and mutual decision from start to finish."[1] This was not Senator Robert Taft's view. "The purpose of an opposition," he said, "is to oppose"; and oppose he did, from start to finish.

By virtue of intelligence, convictions, and force of character, Senators Vandenberg, Taft, and Eugene Millikin of Colorado exerted the greatest influence on Republican policy in the Senate. By tacit understanding, Vandenberg took the lead in foreign affairs and the others led in fiscal and domestic matters. Where the currents crossed, as in tariff and trade policies, the sea was always rough. Gene Millikin insisted that he was the most honest of the triumvirs, adducing as proof that although all three were bald, he let a shining pate proclaim the fact, while the other two, in a vain effort to mislead onlookers in the Senate gallery, brushed hair from the side of their heads over their arid crowns.

The notion that cooperation in a nonpartisan foreign policy could be purchased by consultation is too broad. "Historically," wrote Vandenberg, "this [nonpartisanship] has not been the case in China, Palestine or Japan."[2] He attributed the exceptions to lack of consultation, a plausible but disingenuous explanation. There was endless consultation. The true explanation was wholly understandable Republican unwillingness to take on the responsibility for what looked like thoroughly messy and probably losing ventures. It is interesting to note that Vandenberg mentioned Japan as one of the countries outside the nonpartisan-policy sphere in August 1948. Three years later greatly improved prospects and the appointment of a Republican, John Foster Dulles, to conduct the negotiations leading to the Japanese peace treaty brought the treaty within the nonpartisan-policy area and led to its overwhelming ratification by the Senate in the midst of the presidential election campaign of 1952. The possibility of this happy result did not escape President Truman in his consideration of the Dulles appointment.

In short, the doctrine and practice of nonpartisanship in foreign policy is a very practical political expedient, designed to moderate asperities inherent in our constitutional system. "The doctrine of the separation of powers," Justice Brandeis has explained, "was adopted by the Convention of 1787, not to promote efficiency but to preclude the exercise of arbitrary power. The purpose was, not to avoid friction, but, by means of the inevitable friction incident to the distribution of the governmental powers among three departments, to save the people from autocracy."[3] Today, in the determination of our policies toward "the vast external realm" with all its complexities and dangers, there is a superabundance of friction to save the people from the autocratic imposition of courses of action. The purpose of nonpartisanship is to ease the difficulties in the way of maintaining continuity and predictability in action. To borrow a phrase of Woodrow Wilson's, it is the essential "oil of government."

THE PRACTICE OF NONPARTISAN FOREIGN POLICY

The nonpartisan oil of government lubricated the machinery of legislation through the leadership. In the Seventy-ninth Congress this operated in the Senate out of the Secretary of the Senate's office, and in the House out of Speaker Rayburn's "Board of Education" room in the basement of the Capitol. Here "Mister Sam" presided at a large desk over a select company ensconced in overstuffed sofas and chairs and refreshed from an immense refrigerator. The Secretary of the Senate's quarters, west of the Senate chamber, were equally secluded from public view and inquiry, approached from a dead-end corridor and through a busy document-and-record office. A long narrow room lined with chairs along two sides ended with Leslie Biffle's desk. A door to the left of it led into his private dining room, served from the Senate restaurant. Here the power structure of the Senate met and decided what, at first, appeared to be largely matters of procedure—what should be taken up, when, how long it should be discussed, when voted on, and so forth. But with experience, and recalling Justice Holmes's dictum that "legal progress is secreted in the interstices of legal procedure," one came to realize that legislative achievement was secreted in the interstices of these procedural decisions and the attitude of the Senate hierarchy that they embodied.

At the committee stage, nonpartisan foreign policy was a *sine qua non*. There we worked with Tom Connally and Arthur Vandenberg in the Senate and their equally colorful counterparts in the House, Sol Bloom of New York and "Doc" Eaton, once the pastor of John D. Rockefeller's Baptist church in Cleveland and later of the Madison Avenue Church in New York, and in 1945 representative of the Fifth New Jersey district and senior minority member of the Foreign Affairs Committee. With adequate "consultation and mutual decision" they could bring most of their colleagues through the marking-up and committee-report stages of the legislative process. But this only launched the vessel with a fair wind. The hazards of the cruel sea lay ahead. If the bill happened to deal with trade agreements, Senators Taft and Millikin would deny it a fair wind in the Finance Committee, and in the Ways and Means Committee of the House going was heavy on both sides to begin with. On the floor of both chambers any foreign affairs legislation needed strong support. This was arranged in Les Biffle's dining room and in the "Board of Education."

In the former the gay, genial Majority Leader, Alben Barkley of Kentucky, presided while Biffle, the silent, smooth, friendly Secretary of the Senate, the most knowledgeable operator on the Hill, acted as chief of staff. Solemn, courteous, and kindly Walter George of Georgia, the Nestor of the gathering, usually put the seal on a decision by his pronouncement at the end of a rambling discussion over "bourbon and branch water" or lunch. Barkley and Biffle invited those who might be especially wanted, and others wandered in more or less regularly from the Senate floor at about noon. Sometimes Biffle, I, or one of the senators gave a luncheon. Membership in the group was bipartisan though heavily weighted on the Democratic side. Vandenberg, Robert M. LaFollette, Jr., of Wisconsin, and Wallace H. White, Jr., of Maine were always welcome. Membership seemed to emerge from personality—congeniality, good humor, willingness to compromise and get on with the Senate's business, and general friendliness to the Administration, in varying degrees. Some who had many or all of these qualities I never saw there—for instance, Mr. Truman either before or after he became Vice President, doubtless because he was too occupied with more specific interests. In other instances absence might be due to the angularity of nature or sharpness of tongue, which often made Tom Connally an uncomfortable colleague. The habitués included Ernest W. McFarland and Carl Hayden of Arizona, George L. Radcliffe and sometimes Millard E. Tydings of Maryland, Burton K. Wheeler of Montana, Theodore Francis Green of Rhode Island, Carl A. Hatch of New Mexico, Burnet R. Maybank of South Carolina, Lister Hill of Alabama, and Scott W. Lucas of Illinois. The effectiveness of decisions by this group came not from its sheer power to put them through the Senate but from its knowledge of how to put them through and the willingness to put its knowledge to use.

In the House, leadership was more compact and authoritarian—the Speaker; the Majority Leader, John W. McCormack of Massachusetts; the Majority Whip, Robert Ramspeck of Georgia; and the Chairman of the Rules Committee, Adolph J. Sabath of Illinois. In the Rules Committee resided the all-important power of determining when and under what procedural conditions a bill might come before the House. After a preliminary talk with the Speaker, and then with the rest of the leadership, the time would be ripe for a slightly larger group to meet in "Board of Education" to set the stage. Sam Rayburn, a man of few words (once asked about General Eisenhower's qualifications for the Presidency, he is said to have replied, "Good man; wrong job"), was a loyal and true friend. Earlier a small service had earned me McCormack's favor. Mrs. McCormack had been awarded a papal decoration, but under war conditions difficulty arose in getting it from Rome to Washington. A little negotiation succeeded in its being brought over in the diplomatic pouch of Myron C. Taylor, President Roosevelt's Personal Representative at the Vatican. Bob Ramspeck, a most courteous and helpful gentleman, never failed us. Sabath I left entirely to the Speaker; he was not amenable to any persuasions of mine.

The leadership in both houses helped those who helped themselves. Self-help included not only the basic committee work, the hearings, and work with the committee staffs on their reports but the initial canvassing of members' voting predilections. Here one needed both strong feet and patience. At this time and later, as Sam Rayburn would tell our weaker successors, day after day Will Clayton and I would take corridor after corridor of the House office building— Will on one side and I on the other—calling at every office, making our sales talk, and keeping a record of the responses we got for Skeeter Johnston's always-current voting lists. Our weapons were reason and eloquence. The leadership worked on the waverers' hope of favors or fear of penalties to come. It also divided the labor of debate, allotting, according to skills and with an authority that we could not command, exposition and guerrilla warfare against the opposition.

REFLECTIONS ABOUT CONGRESS

All through this book runs the thread of my multifarious relations with the Congress, sometimes tumultuous, sometimes calmly cooperative, sometimes framed in the adversary ritual of committee hearings. To make specific episodes more understandable, I have pulled together here a few reflections of a broader character on the nature of the institution, its actual role in our scheme of government as against the constitutional theory of it, and my actual relations with its members, much warped through the myth popularized by press and commentators.[4]

Long ago Henry Adams pointed out that the chief concern of the Secretary of State—the world beyond our boundaries—was to most members of the Congress only a troublesome intrusion into their chief interest—the internal affairs of the country, and especially of the particular parts of it they represented.

Two aspects of this basic fact should be stressed. First, the principal consequence of foreign impact upon particular districts is trouble; rarely is it, or is it seen to be, beneficial. Second, the legislative branch is designed with a constitutional purpose of making each legislator the representative of a specific and limited area. Reapportionment does not affect this fact. The President is the only elected official with a national constituency. Senators, since their direct popular election, are the ambassadors of states, concerned with their parochial interest. The focus and representation of members of the House of Representatives are even more narrowly circumscribed. Almost every time they legislate they affect foreign interests, but this concerns them only indirectly and seemingly distantly, for the familiar aspects of foreign affairs are war, relief, and trade; and trade more often appears as a threat of foreign competition than as potential markets for American goods. Even producers of commodities historically dependent on export matters, like wheat and cotton, have long been conscious of surplus problems and the increasing foreign production of these staples.

For the most part, then, the Secretary of State comes to Congress bearing word of troubles about which Congress does not want to hear. Furthermore, the members of the legislative branch not only represent narrower constituencies and interests than does the President and those he has chosen to aid him in dealing with the broadest national and international affairs, but largely they share the narrower interests and attitudes which they represent. That this should be so is wholly natural and proper, since under our system they must be residents of the state, in the case of the Senate, and of the district, in the case of the House. Those who live long enough among their constituents to win confidence, support, and the responsibility of representing them are pretty likely to share prevalent views. To say this invites criticism, but it is a simple and obvious fact.

The result is a built-in difference in the point of departure between the legislative and executive branches when problems of foreign policy are considered. Furthermore, the wide difference in their duties creates differences in the time that each can and must allot to foreign affairs and the amount of recent intelligence and deeper background that each has available. This is no different from the relation between a parent and a physician in considering a medical problem of a member of the family; each brings something different and important to the discussion.

What the executive brings is initiative, proposal for action; what the legislature brings is criticism, limitation, modification, or veto. In foreign affairs the tendency toward this division of function has always existed; since the second quarter of this century it has become true of nearly all domestic as well as foreign policy. Once it was thought that Congress would press forward with popular initiatives and the President could hold back with more conservative caution. To aid him he was given a negative veto in each house equal to a third of the total. However, today both the complexity and urgency of matters calling for action and the difference in the nature of the constituencies have made the President the active and innovative initiator and the legislators the more conservative restrainers. They are powerfully armed to perform this role by the complicated annual procedures with which they have surrounded and often whittled down such policies, for instance, as foreign aid, requiring four committee hearings a year accompanying an authorizing act of Congress and an appropriation.

The most publicized weapon of Congress—and one which as often as not proves frustrating to those who employ it—is the investigation. One cannot improve upon Woodrow Wilson's comment upon it: "Congress stands almost helplessly outside of the departments. Even the special, irksome, ungracious investigations which it from time to time institutes . . . do not afford it more than a glimpse of the inside of a small province of federal administration. . . . It can violently disturb, but it cannot often fathom, the waters of the sea in which the bigger fish of the civil service swim and feed. Its dragnet stirs without cleansing the bottom."[5]

These experiences induce an attitude of exasperated frustration in many members of Congress, which may be expressed in the kind of sulky opposition that characterized the last two years of relations between the Senate Committee on Foreign Relations and the Johnson Administration, or the destruction that flowed from Congressman John J. Rooney, of the Appropriations Committee, when he acquired a distaste for the State Department's cultural relations program, which doubtless his Brooklyn district shares, or Senator Allen Ellender's hostility to foreign aid, which his constituents in Louisiana would probably agree was "pouring good money down a rat hole."

To bridge these and other gaps in values and understanding required hours of tramping the halls of the House and Senate office buildings, innumerable gatherings and individual meetings, social occasions of all sorts at which all the arts of enlightenment and persuasion were employed. My years as Assistant Secretary were generously given over to these efforts and brought me a large and pleasant acquaintance and some warm friendships at both ends of the Capitol. The much-publicized political attacks on me in 1950 and 1951 were accompanied in only a few cases by personal animosity. For instance, Senator William F. Knowland, who later criticized and opposed me strongly, in private always remained most courteous and friendly.

In making our calls, particularly in the Senate, we learned to bear the irrelevant with more than patience as it ate up precious time. Those who assert that I do not suffer fools gladly—and I have seen that view in print—do me less than justice for these anguishing hours. Despite current folklore, one could and did learn to suffer, if not gladly, at least patiently when, as often happened, doing so paid dividends. This recalls a story that Sir Robert Menzies, the former Prime Minister of Australia, has told on himself. At a party victory celebration a particularly crashing and somewhat inebriated bore, poking his grubby finger in Menzies' shirtfront, announced, "The trouble with you, Bob, is you don't suffer fools gladly."

"What," asked Sir Robert coldly, "do you think I am doing now?"

WE TAKE OUR CASE TO THE PEOPLE

During this period not all work was with the Congress. Two friends, Archibald MacLeish and his assistant, John Dickey, were engaged in an attempt to humanize and bring closer to our fellow citizens the work of the State Department. To some extent I was drawn into this estimable but not wholly successful effort. Its most spectacular failure occurred when, between the Yalta and San Francisco conferences, our energetic Secretary went to Chapultepec, Mexico, with a large staff to reorganize the inter-American system. My friends' idea was to dramatize the far-flung work of the Department by a conversation between its officers thousands of miles apart—the Secretary and his party in Mexico City bringing us in Washington up to date on the conference, while we filled him in on events at home. The American people would be "bugged in" on this homey chat between their shirt-sleeved diplomats at work.

MacLeish, Will Clayton, and I, with John Dickey and others who were managing the program, were assembled in a studio in Washington; the Secretary and his followers, in another in Mexico City. Our clocks were allegedly attuned. The zero hour was counted off backward as it is when rockets are blasted off at Cape Kennedy. When the countdown ended, the director pointed his finger at Archie. But science let us down. As Archie began his introduction, we heard the voice of the Secretary of State in Mexico City saying emphatically, "Shut up, you fellows. We will be on the air in thirty seconds." With this, considerable chatter diminished, but hell broke loose. For some reason unknown to me the clocks were never coordinated, nor was the script. We remained thirty seconds ahead of Mexico City. Some stations, I am told, cut out Washington; others cut out Mexico City; some left them both on; some cut them both off. The result, to put it mildly, was chaotic. When the horror finally ended and we were all being driven home, Dickey seemed to be having hysterics. Finally able to speak, he gasped out that if MacLeish were unsuccessful in his effort to sell the State Department to the American people, he certainly would have a buyer in Barnum and Bailey's circus.

THE FOURTH TERM BEGINS

As we worked at our small tasks, great events were impending—an era and a war were coming to their ends. Because of the war, so it was said, the inauguration on January 20 was a small affair held on the south portico of the White House. I sent off a brief description of it to our son, then the communications officer of a destroyer escort in the Western Pacific.

We have entered upon the Fourth Term. Alice and I were invited, with a considerable number of our fellow citizens, to stand in the cold behind the White House to witness the very brief ceremonies. They had a most complicated arrangement of roping off various spaces. Apparently it gives great satisfaction to the human spirit to be enclosed, if only by a rope and out-of-doors in a small area, seeing other citizens enclosed in a different area. There seemed to be little or no choice since the portico could be seen perfectly well from any one of the enclosures and all the words were bellowed forth by loud speakers. However, the congressmen being by themselves felt superior to the officials, who were by themselves and in turn felt superior to the congressmen and various other groups. On the portico were the Justices and their wives, and the Cabinet members and their wives, and a large number of Roosevelt daughters-in-law, present and past, with their various offspring.

I was interested to see how fundamental to the American nature is the "yoo-hoo" spirit. The Cabinet ladies grouped around the rail of the portico were having a marvelous time waving to various lesser fry standing out on the grass. Everybody "yoo-hooed" to somebody else. This gave the ladies on the portico a definite feeling of condescension and in turn raised the spirits of some creatures standing in the mud to be thus singled out for attention. All in all we had a considerable amount to entertain us and to philosophize about while we were waiting.

The proceedings were opened and closed, quite appropriately, by prayer—opened by Bishop Dun of the Episcopalian communion and closed by Bishop Ryan of the Church of Rome. I was interested to observe that Bishop Dun took a more detached view of the situation than did his Catholic brother. He avoided arraigning the Lord in any intimate way with present hostilities, but merely asked that they should end with the triumph of the right ideas, it being implied that those ideas were ours. However, Bishop Ryan left nothing to chance and made it quite clear that he wanted the Lord on our side.

Henry Wallace then swore in the new Vice President. He did this in loud, ringing, and impressive tones. This was favorably commented upon. The Chief Justice then swore in the President, who delivered a very short inaugural of not more than five minutes. As you know, I do not like speeches very much and the chief impression that I got of this one was that the only two persons quoted were Endicott Peabody and Emerson. After this we all left the premises to return at five o'clock to be received by Mrs. Roosevelt and Mrs. Truman in rather close quarters. In this manner the Fourth Term was inaugurated.

A few days before the inauguration I met with President Roosevelt for the last time. Leo Pasvolsky, Alger Hiss, and I went with Stettinius to brief the

President for the forthcoming meeting at Yalta on Russian claims to multiple votes in the General Assembly of the proposed United Nations. The Russian argument was that since various British Commonwealth countries would vote in the United Nations, an equal number of Soviet republics should be admitted and vote also.

We were all shocked by the President's appearance. Thin, gaunt, with sunken and darkly circled eyes, only the jaunty cigarette holder and his light-hearted brushing aside of difficulties recalled the FDR of former days. I reported that the Russian position would cause trouble on the Hill. He would deal with it, he said, by claiming a vote for each of the forty-eight states and work it out from there.† We wished him well as he gave us a farewell handshake.

Aside from the distant glimpse at the inauguration, I saw him only once again. It was in the chamber of the House of Representatives on his return from Yalta. If possible, he looked even worse. Contrary to his usual custom of walking down the aisle in his iron braces, steadied by the arm of an aide, and standing as he spoke, he was wheeled into the well of the House. He asked "pardon . . . for the unusual posture of sitting down during the presentation of what I wish to say, but I know you will realize it makes it a lot easier for me in not having to carry about 10 pounds of steel around on the bottom of my legs and also because of the fact I have just completed a 14,000-mile trip."⁶ The voice had lost its timbre. It was an invalid's voice.

THE END OF AN ERA

Thursday, April 12, 1945, opened as the rainy, dismal beginning of my fifty-third year. Dusk came early toward the end of the afternoon. Mr. Karsh, the famous Canadian photographer, had arranged his camera, screens, and lights at one end of my State Department office, lowering the blinds to shut out what was left of the fading daylight. The room was dark with bright light focused on my chair. The door from Barbara Evans' office opened. "The President," she said, "is dead." She knew nothing more than that the press room had this flash from Warm Springs, Georgia, where he had been resting. I walked to the window and raised the blind. The White House flag was at half-mast. We went on with the photographing.

During the next days a dazed sensation developed. No one at home, on the street, in the Department, had much to say. From our windows we watched the flag-covered coffin carried from the caisson into the White House, then out again to lie in state in the rotunda of the Capitol. Day and night the radio played dim, funereal music. "Large crowds," I wrote at the time, "came and stood in front of the White House. There was nothing to see and I am sure that they did not expect to see anything. They merely stood in a lost sort of way." One felt as though the city had vanished, leaving its inhabitants to wander about bewildered, looking for a familiar landmark. The dominant emotion was not sorrow so much as apprehension on discovering oneself alone and lost. Something which had filled all lives was gone. The familiar had given way to an ominous unknown.

13. SUCCESS, DISENCHANTMENT,
AND RESIGNATION

"The new President has done an excellent job," I wrote to our son on April 30, 1945. "It so happened that two days before the President's death, I had a long meeting with Mr. Truman and for the first time got a definite impression. It was a very good impression. He is straight-forward, decisive, simple, entirely honest. He, of course, has the limitations upon his judgment and wisdom that the limitations of his experience produce, but I think that he will learn fast and will inspire confidence. It seems to me a blessing that he is the President and not Henry Wallace. I am afraid that we would have been plunged into bitter partisan rowing under Henry Wallace. I listened to him testify the other day on our trade agreements bill and got, in a few minutes, a complete demonstration of how his weak points completely destroy his strong ones. He was well informed and gave excellent testimony. However, on two or three occasions hostile questions made him quite lose his temper, whereupon he made some ill-considered remarks and the whole hearing turned into a brawl."

The meeting with Mr. Truman—the only one I recall before he became President—took place when I went to him for help and received, instead, consolation.

Senator Pat McCarran of Nevada, Chairman of the subcommittee of the Senate Committee on Appropriations, before which was pending the Department's appropriation for the fiscal year beginning July 1, 1945, had summoned me to learn of his and Mrs. McCarran's wish to attend the forthcoming United Nations conference in San Francisco with official status and as guests of the United States Government. The Senator was not a person who in the eighteenth century would have been termed a man of sensibility. When I pointed out that the delegation had been completed and the long list of senators with equal or better claims who shared his desire to attend the conference, he observed that surely I would be ingenious enough to overcome these obstacles, especially after careful consideration of the alternative. That was, already, only too clear to me. An appeal to Senator McKellar, chairman of the full committee, to promise review and repair of any damage which refusal might bring upon our appropriation was answered, quite reasonably, by his observation that the committee could never get through its work if it undertook minute revision of subcommittee action, especially when it had resulted in cuts of departmental requests.

Then it was that I asked to see the Vice President. He received me in his office in the Capitol and listened sympathetically, and with proper expressions of outrage, as I poured out my woes. His colorful outline of what, in my place, he would say to his former colleague from Nevada struck a stout blow for righteousness. When I explained the consequences and asked who in the Senate, or from the House in the conference committee (to adjust differences between them), would restore a truncated appropriation, the color faded. In the end both of us concluded that under the circumstances exposure of the Senator to an international conference of such lofty purpose might soften his isolationism and, hence, prove in the public interest. We parted with warm expressions of mutual regard, and the Senator went to San Francisco.

A few days after Mr. Truman assumed the Presidency, his first and I think, at that time, only personally selected assistant, Matthew Connelly, asked me to meet him in the Cabinet Room of the White House just across the street from my office. The west-wing offices were in confusion as movers boxed President Roosevelt's papers. Connelly had two or three men with him, among them an amusing Mississippian and friend of Mr. Truman's, George Allen, at the time manager of the Willard Hotel. George Allen had come to Washington to seek the fortune that he found there. His rise is recounted in his book, *Presidents Who Have Known Me.*[1] President Truman used to recall that when in introducing Allen to the President's mother he added, "Mr. Allen never saw a Republican until he was twenty-four," that grand old lady, many of whose qualities her son inherited, observed, "He didn't miss much."

The group in the Cabinet Room had a problem, Connelly said, and the President, remembering me and my proximity, thought I might give a lead. Neither the President nor I can remember what the problem was. I was, however, taken through the office of his secretary, Rose Conway, to discuss it with him. He was cordial, simple, and gracious, as he was so often when I saw him thereafter. In a few minutes the problem, whatever it was, was put in the proper channels for solution.

After that the calls across the street continued, particularly when statements of one sort or another were being drafted. Soon my own business on the Hill brought me over to confer with his congressional liaison people and others as his office staff developed. They often took me in to talk with "the Boss." During those first weeks of the Truman Administration the executive office in the White House operated most informally.

From then until the President went to Potsdam on July 7 I was frequently at the White House, especially from the middle of May on, when I worked with the President on his speech closing the San Francisco United Nations conference. Indeed, our daughter, Mary Bundy, contributed from her sick bed at Saranac Lake an excellent and apt quotation from Edmund Burke, which survived in the speech-writing tournament until nearly the semifinals.

Also in May the President called me in for discussions and dinner and luncheon with the Regent of Iraq on a matter that seemed to involve congressional action. "He is a dapper little man, dark, slim, a slight mustache," I wrote. "He might be a dentist in Eldora, Iowa. But he isn't. And so we had a good dinner and came home early." At a later meeting he said that he had great sympathy for President Truman, since he himself had never expected to be a ruler.

As he told me, one day his brother was killed in an automobile accident, and the next day he had a kingdom on his hands in the midst of all the trouble and intrigue of the early part of the war.

The Regent paid us another visit later on with the young King when I was Secretary. We all gained very considerable respect for him and were saddened and shocked by his tragic and brutal death at the hands of the Baghdad mob in the revolution of 1958.

In May rumor reached me that Fred Vinson would sound me out about succeeding Leo Crowley as Administrator of the Foreign Economic Administration, which he did on June 3. The proposal had no appeal to me, since I must soon return to the practice of law. Saying so, I agreed to think it over. A week later we resumed our talk in Vinson's White House office. My recommendation was to add the duties of the Administrator's office to Will Clayton's existing duties as Assistant Secretary of State. He could have his assistant, Willard Thorp, actually run the FEA, while the elimination of friction by combining the offices and the additional powers would greatly strengthen Will's position within the government and abroad.

Vinson was impressed by the suggestion, which was a truly sensible one. Had it been adopted, it would have prevented the harm that flowed from the ill-considered ending of all lend-lease hardly more than sixty days later upon Japan's surrender. Vinson asked me what I would do should the President insist on my taking over the post. I replied that I would do my best to convince him of the wisdom of the Clayton appointment, and, if I failed, accede to his request. The next day the White House operator tried for hours to get me, calling everywhere except where I told her I would be at definite times. "My curiosity," I wrote Mary, "is almost too much, but superstition prevents my calling to find out what it is all about. If I do, it will turn out to be something that I don't want to have catch up with me." The proposal was never mentioned to me again, although rumors kept appearing in the press that I would be drafted.

BACK TO LOBBYING

From mid-May, for two and a half months, our legislative calendar demanded my attention for its most nerve-racking stage—that of voting in the committees and on the floor of both houses. The Mexican Water Treaty had been approved in April. All the other bills had now reached the point where months of preparatory labor would be put to the acid test of the yeas and nays. The first to come up was the Trade Agreement Renewal Bill in the House. Paragraphs from my letters to our daughter carry something of the tension of dispatches from the front in hard-fought battles.

DA to MAB   *May 16*
    We had a great victory in the Ways and Means Committee on our Trade Agreements Bill. We were licked a week ago, but today won a favorable report 14 to 11— all Republicans and one Democrat against us. It now looks as though we should have the same result, or about it, on Bretton Woods. The Republicans are playing rather stupid politics, I think.

DA to MAB   *May 22*

The House got started on the Trade Agreements debate today. I listened for four hours. A dreary and wholly unrealistic debate. Few of the claimed virtues of the bill were really true and none of the fancied dangers. The true facts lay in a different field from that where the shells from both sides were landing.

At lunch at the Capitol I was asked to sit at a table with Jessie Sumner of Illinois, the worst of the rabble rousing isolationists of *Chicago Tribune* fame. We got along famously. She is a grand old girl and reminded me of the madam in *Cannery Row,* sort of low, humorous and human. We became great friends and are going to lunch again. I often wonder whether I have any principles at all. It's a confusing world.

DA to MAB   *May 25*

I have had a day of frenzied lobbying on the Hill. We are in real trouble and may or may not come through tomorrow. We are trying to get a letter from the President in which he lays his political head on the block with ours. It will be interesting to see if he signs it.

DA to MAB   *May 26*

We have had a great day and a great victory. The Trade Agreements Bill came on for voting on amendments and final passage in the House today. We won by a final majority of 86. But this does not tell the true story. It was very close on the critical amendments which would have killed the bill. Our toughest one was an amendment to strike out the additional authority given the President to reduce tariffs.

We won that by a majority of only 23. The Democratic majority in the House is 51. This took weeks of work, ending with a letter which I got the President to sign this morning—having written it last night. I gave it secretly to the Speaker, Sam Rayburn, who used it with great dramatic effect today. This stopped the Old Guard just short of victory.

From then on we gained strength. The last real test gave us a majority of 31. Then the Republican ranks broke and we licked them by 86 on the final vote at about 6:30.

We all went down to the Speaker's room, drank some whiskey, and called Mr. Hull. No one thought to call the President, who had done a great job for us.

The House Committee vote on Bretton Woods was pretty good too. 23–3 for it. I think we shall put that through the House with a bang. The Senate will give us trouble on both bills.

This life is amusing but not calculated to engage or extend all those faculties which when used to the full give one the sense of the good life. But the good life is very hard and takes much courage and much character.

DA to MAB   *June 7*

My poor aching feet! The badge of a statesman lobbying on Capitol Hill. I was at it from nine A.M. to five P.M. in an attempt (a) to get the Trade Agreements Bill ready for a [Senate Finance] Committee vote tomorrow morning, and (b) to express appreciation to the Banking and Currency Committee of the House over Bretton Woods.

That bill had a smash hit success today. It was approved by 345 to 18. Only a declaration of war gets a vote like that, and six weeks ago we were defeated in that Committee—that is, we would have been if the vote had been taken then.

Some of the success came from the panic of the Republicans over their absurd performances on Trade Agreements. They simply couldn't afford to be against every international measure, so they flocked to a man to vote for Bretton Woods. The 18 against are almost a roster of absolute isolationists—all are within the daily circulation of the *Chicago Tribune*.

Tonight we think that we have a majority of one on the Finance Committee for the Trade Agreements Bill. It is very close. Every Republican is against us again. On the floor of the Senate we think we are all right if we can get our boys back. They will travel at the wrong times.

This is a low life but a merry one.

DA to MAB   *June 8*

Today we had a disappointment. Senator Walsh and Senator LaFollette promised to vote with us in the Finance Committee on Trade Agreements. That would give us a majority of one. On the critical vote Walsh moved over to the other side, which gave them a majority of one. So we have our bill reported with its heart out. We can, we think, put it back again. But it was rather a sad day for us, particularly after yesterday's great success.

DA to MAB   *June 15*

We did not get a vote on Trade Agreements today, but we shall on Monday. It still looks as though we shall win. I talked with old Mr. Hull twice today and gave him reports from the front. He was much pleased.

DA to MAB   *June 19*

Today we had a great victory in the Senate—a vote of 47 to 33 to restore the House bill [on trade agreements] in its original form. This was our most severe test, as we saw it, and I think we have won hands down.

DA to MAB   *June 20*

Our job is done. Finally after what seemed like a millennium of talk the Senate passed our Trade Agreements Act today by a vote of 54 to 21. It was a fine result and one quite unexpected by any of the higher ups in the Senate when we began. They told us that it could not be done. Now I can only hope that the Department can use the Act to some good purpose.

Our next job is to get Bretton Woods out of the lotus-eaters' hands and on the floor of the Senate. Then this San Francisco treaty, and I shall be through!

DA to MAB   *June 21*

I had a fine lunch today in the office of the Secretary of the Senate with Senators and House members. A real Texas ham was offered and whiskey. I am getting to be a real politician.

DA to MAB   *June 25*

I had hoped to give this note to Alice so that you could get one from me tomorrow, but I nearly missed her and made her miss her train. Senator Barkley gave a lunch for Clayton, [Charles P.] Taft and me at the Secretary of the Senate's private room. We were late in starting; and what with speeches from everybody, it got to be 2:45 before I could get out of the Capitol. Your poor mama was a bit nervous. However, a good time was had by all and we all expressed the highest regard and sentiments for each other. That is good Senatorial behavior. . . . I find it harder and harder to settle down to hard and sustained application to work. This business of talking to everyone and attending meetings all day is a shiftless way of conducting oneself.

DA to MAB   *July 14*

Yesterday the Senate Committee on Foreign Relations reported out the Charter 20 to 0. It will come up on the floor July 23rd. Bretton Woods comes up on Monday. The House yesterday passed our Export-Import Bank bill with only 6 dissenting votes. We hope to get that through the Senate before it adjourns. So far so good. A pretty fair record.

DA to MAB   *July 19*

Today another chapter closed. The Senate approved Bretton Woods 61 to 16.

We shall have a day or so of frantic effort to get the rest of our legislative program through. Tax treaties with the UK, the Food and Agriculture Organization, the Export-Import Bank. And then the [UN] Charter, which I have always thought was the easiest of all. When it is over, I shall be glad to take a bit of a rest. It has been a rather long grind and, I think, a rather successful one.

DA to MAB   *July 20*

We have a law a day these days. Yesterday Bretton Woods (today the House agreed to the Senate amendments); today the Export-Import Bank Bill; tomorrow the Food and Agriculture Organization Act and two tax treaties. This, with the Charter, winds up our program for the season. It has been a big job.

DA to MAB   *July 22*

The Food and Agriculture Bill was passed on Saturday. The Charter comes up Monday.

DA to MAB   *July 28*

We are, I hope, on the last day of the Charter debate. I have taken a chance which has annoyed some of the Senators. I got a letter from the President to Senator McKellar, the President Pro Tempore of the Senate, saying that he proposes to take subsequent steps under the Charter by statute which requires a majority of both houses rather than by treaty. This may make a flurry and hold things up, but I think not. Rather it will take advantage of all the popular steam behind the Charter to settle the fight our way.

The United States Senate on July 28, 1945, at 5:14 P.M. approved the Charter of the United Nations by a vote of 89 to 2. This completed my legislative labors as Assistant Secretary of State.

However, the record of the eventful summer of 1945 must go on to include the goings and comings in official Washington (my own in both directions) and the end of the Great War. The first day of changes came on Wednesday, May 23. Francis Biddle was replaced as Attorney General by Assistant Attorney General Tom Clark of Texas; Claude Wickard, Secretary of Agriculture, by "a nice congressman from New Mexico, Clinton Anderson, whom I know and like —a clear gain"; and Miss Perkins, Secretary of Labor, by a former Senator and Judge, Lewis Schwellenbach. The next day I had a talk with Francis Biddle, of which I made a note, who told me that "Steve Early [a presidential secretary] called him up last Monday and said that the President wanted his resignation. Francis replied that a Cabinet Officer might expect to hear that from the President himself. Whereupon the President sent for him and told him the same. Francis says that Harold Ickes will be the next to go. . . . He expects that Ed Stettinius will survive until the San Francisco Charter is well on its way through the Senate. . . . He told me that he had explained to HST that FDR wanted to appoint me Solicitor General and who the other candidates were. It was Francis' belief that the Administration would appoint a political figure. [This the President did when he named J. Howard McGrath on September 28 to be Solicitor General.] This I said was all right with me as I did not want to be Solicitor anyway, since I had my eye on August or earlier with Mary."

On June 27 Francis Biddle's prediction about Stettinius came true.

DA to MAB   *June 27*

Today has been an eventful one. Ed Stettinius has resigned. The gossip is that Byrnes will succeed him. . . . Archie [MacLeish] says that Ed forced the issue by insisting that he could not go on in this vague way. He must be in or out. And the answer was out.

It will mean other changes, too. Archie and I will be gone soon.

DA to MAB   *June 28*

Today has been a day of rumors and little work. Archie came for advice as to whether he should resign before Monday, because it was said that Byrnes would be appointed and fire him and Rockefeller. I dissuaded him. One should not hurry mounting the tumbril.

It is said that we shall all be fired except Clayton and Grew.

It is said that Grew will certainly be fired.

It is said that I will be made Secretary—Under Secretary—Administrator of F.E.A.—Solicitor General—President of the Bretton Woods Bank, etc.

I say that I shall resign as of the end of this session, rest and then go to the Union Trust Building again [my old law firm].

Make your own bets.

News Item

Last night about 11:30 John Dickey and I were walking home passing the Penna. Ave. side of the Treasury. We were talking of Ed's resignation. On the street, passing us, was a police derrick truck towing a limousine. Suddenly its license plate hit us like a land mine—Government 120, the Secretary of State's car. We stopped for a moment speechless. Then John said, "Well, they certainly do things thoroughly."

This morning I asked about it and found that last night as usual Ed's chauffeur, Rudolph Warren, delivered the car at the government garage door. A man came to take it, turned it around and disappeared in a cloud of dust. It took the police four hours to find it. Some lad!

DA to MAB   *July 3*

Today we acquired our new Secretary. We all repaired to the White House where we encountered a noble company of the country's political great—Senators, Congressmen, office holders and would-be such. The press was too great for the

President's office so we all moved out to the garden behind the west wing of the White House. There the oath was administered by Chief Justice Whaley of the Court of Claims, a symbolic performance, and the speeches made.

The most important item in the speech to us was that we were asked to stay at our posts until the poor old Department was reorganized again and the Secretary returned from the Big Three meeting. I shall tell him that, of course, I shall stay until then; but then I must go.

In fact, the next day I tried to get the new Secretary to fix some date when, at least for planning purposes, I could look forward to release from official duties. But he did not wish to discuss the matter until his return from Europe.

FIRST ENCOUNTER WITH THE UNITED NATIONS

When President Truman replaced Mr. Stettinius as Secretary of State with Mr. Byrnes, he announced that the former Secretary would become our representative at the site of the United Nations when its organization had been established.

Before Mr. Byrnes left for Europe, Mr. Stettinius' staff sent to the President, who sent it on to the Secretary, a draft proposal for establishing the position of United States Representative at the United Nations as they wished it. Not unnaturally, these men were interested in exalting this position, even though it might be at the expense of the Secretary of State. The staff paper gave its occupant a seat in the Cabinet and, in general, seemed to equate his position with that of the Secretary of State. Mr. Byrnes, in view of Mr. Stettinius' somewhat ruffled feelings at being summarily replaced, was not inclined to make an issue of it, but I persuaded him that he must do so. The whole integrity of his position was at stake as well as an infinity of trouble over who would be the President's chief adviser and secretary on foreign policy. Mr. Byrnes was able to block the move without a public row; and the Act of Congress creating the post as later passed set it up as another ambassadorial post reporting through and instructed by the Secretary of State. Eight years later the earlier proposal was revived to exalt the position for former Senator Henry Cabot Lodge, one of General Eisenhower's chief backers for the Presidency. It has been a source of trouble for secretaries of state ever since. But at least three secretaries were spared this embarrassment.

Although I had nothing to do with the planning of the United Nations Charter or the negotiations at Dumbarton Oaks in Washington or the conference in San Francisco that led to its adoption, the management of the hearings before the Senate Committee on Foreign Relations regarding its ratification fell within my field of responsibility. I did my duty faithfully and successfully but always believed that the Charter was impracticable. Moreover, its presentation to the American people as almost holy writ and with the evangelical enthusiasm of a major advertising campaign seemed to me to raise popular hopes which could only lead to bitter disappointment. In Chapter 1 I briefly recalled the nineteenth-century faith in the perfectibility of man and the advent of universal peace and law. This faith was dying in Europe, as "Locksley Hall Sixty Years

After" sadly recalls, when it crossed the Atlantic to inspire American idealists, and none more than Woodrow Wilson.

As applied to foreign affairs, Americans—as Sir Harold Nicolson pointed out in his brilliant Chichele lectures at Oxford in 1953—distilled from this idealistic belief a number of subsidiary faiths that added up to a grand fallacy. They began with the idea that one could—and should— apply to external affairs the institutions and practices of legislative procedure in liberal democracies. This was regarded as preferable to diplomacy (almost by definition tricky and insincere) because it reached through a façade to The People. Furthermore, diplomacy was thought to be an instrument of power, the great corrupter of man, which was almost synonymous with force and violence. Among peace-loving peoples—and all others should be or had been suppressed—violence could and would be superseded by reason. What was reasonable and right would be determined by majority vote; and just as the equality of man led to one man one vote, so the doctrine of the "sovereign equality of states" led to one state one vote.

Thus to the true believer, of whom Arthur Vandenberg was to become one of the most vociferous, the General Assembly appeared as the Town Meeting of the World. Unfortunately, the proliferation of states and the perverse ingenuity of man (to which, as we shall see, I was to make a not inconsiderable contribution) have minimized the more modest role of the United Nations as an aid to diplomacy, which Dag Hammarskjold saw as its true role.† Instead it has become a possible instrument of interference in the affairs of weak white nations, as Rhodesia is experiencing as I write.

When later the United Nations was looking for a site, I believed that it should be in Europe and favored Geneva or Copenhagen, but pressure grew for its headquarters to be in the United States. President Truman's offer of the beautiful Presidio site on the shore of the Pacific at the Golden Gate seemed a perfect one, establishing its home in the city of its birth. The misplaced generosity of the Rockefeller family, however, placed it in a crowded center of conflicting races and nationalities.

THE WAR ENDS AND I RESIGN

When the President and the Secretary went to Potsdam on July 7 for a month, most of us in the Department were left in a fog of rumor and ignorance about the war in the Pacific. Events were moving to a crisis of some sort. Troops and supplies bound westward betokened, we assumed, an invasion of Japan on the model of General Eisenhower's operation in Europe. Committees within the Department and between the Department and War and Navy discussed postsurrender policies toward Japan. Sitting with them because of the obvious necessity at some point of bringing in congressional leaders, I was soon engaged in a sharp difference of opinion with Joe Grew regarding the future of the Emperor of Japan. Grew argued for his retention as the main stabilizing factor in Japan; I argued that he should be removed because he was a weak leader who had yielded to the military demand for war and who could not be relied upon.

Grew's view fortunately prevailed. I very shortly came to see that I was quite wrong.

The proclamation issued on July 26[2] by the heads of governments of the United States, the United Kingdom, and China—the Soviet Union was not at this time at war with Japan—disturbed me greatly. It would, I feared, lose us the opportunity for complete victory over Japan without avoiding the losses which had been predicted. Regarded not as an ultimatum but as an invitation to negotiate, it would lead us into a trap both at home and in Japan. The ruling military and economic groups in Japan would stay in control, and the war would end inconclusively. I thought all these things because, of course, neither I nor the rest of the world knew what the authors of the proclamation were talking about. After defining clear and harsh terms for the surrender of Japan, they issued what was intended to be an ultimatum before the use of the atomic weapon. But this was not referred to and was, of course, then profoundly secret. The last paragraph of the proclamation now gives the clue: "We call upon the government of Japan to proclaim now the unconditional surrender of all Japanese armed forces, and to provide proper and adequate assurances of their good faith in such action. The alternative for Japan is prompt and utter destruction."

The destruction of Hiroshima came on August 6, of Nagasaki on August 9. The meaning of that last paragraph was plain to all. What was not known was that those two bombs comprised our whole stock. But that, if known, would only have raised a question of time.

On the evening of the sixth I wrote: "The news of the atomic bomb is the most frightening yet. If we can't work out some sort of organization of great powers, we shall be gone geese for fair. It makes the prospect of Ed Stettinius as our representative on the UN even more fantastic than ever."

AN ATTEMPTED JAIL BREAK

The President and Mr. Byrnes returned from the Potsdam Conference on August 7, 1945. They were deep in a series of almost continuous meetings with military and political leaders regarding negotiations for the surrender of Japan, carried on through the Swiss. It was both impossible and absurd to try to see either one of them to discuss my personal affairs at such a time. Trivial as they were amid the great events impending, they were not trivial to me. I had no part in the discussions of the Japanese surrender. If I stood aside, it was quite possible that weeks might go by before either the President or the Secretary had the opportunity to release me from service in a war that was already over. Some matter, now forgotten, took me into Mr. Byrnes's office on August 8. Before leaving, I handed him a letter to the President resigning my office and asked Mr. Byrnes's kindness in presenting it with a recommendation that it be accepted.

My dear Mr. President: *August 8, 1945*
    I herewith submit my resignation as Assistant Secretary of State.
    The work for which I stayed on at the time of the reorganization of the Depart-

ment has been finished, and, after four and one-half years of public service, some attention to my own affairs is long overdue.

For the unfailing kindness and support which you have given me I am deeply grateful, as well as for the opportunity to have served the country in these eventful years.

May I assure you of every wish for your continued success in the leadership which you are giving to us all.   Very respectfully,

Dean Acheson

The next day I got from his office the long-awaited reply.

Dear Mr. Acheson: *August 9, 1945*

I have your letter of resignation as Assistant Secretary of State.

The Secretary of State advised me of your conversation with him and of the personal reasons which you believe make it imperative that you should at this time leave the public service. With reluctance I accept your resignation.

You refer to having served for more than four years. I am aware of that fact and I am aware, too, of the fine character of the service you have rendered during that period. You have served at great personal sacrifice but you have the satisfaction of knowing that you have made a substantial contribution to your government in time of war.

Since you feel that you now should return to your profession, I want you to know that you have my best wishes for your success and happiness.

Sincerely yours,

Harry Truman

That evening Eugene Meyer, the publisher of the *Washington Post,* was having a small, stag dinner. Of the guests I remember clearly Fred Vinson, the Secretary of the Treasury, and Wayne Coy, an assistant editor of the *Post* and former Assistant Director of the Budget. A vague recollection that Harry Hopkins was there persists. There were perhaps one or two others. All of us were full of the surrender of Japan. I mentioned that this had brought to me my release and that I was off after another day for a rest and return to private life. Fred Vinson and Wayne Coy, both of whom had become warm friends, protested vigorously, but I assured them that the die was cast.

After dinner the company sat out on the high terrace looking down from the top of the 16th Street hill over the lights of the city. Vinson and Coy began to talk about the State Department, the jumbled personnel made up in part of aging veterans of Mr. Hull's tenure, some wartime volunteers, and a sprinkling of Ed Stettinius' public relations assistants. They spoke of its organization, which resembled that with which General Winfield Scott began the Civil War. I contributed some comments and a few almost elemental suggestions. Having been through the same conversation so many times over the past four years, it had little interest for me, and my mind was occupied with the new future which was to begin tomorrow.

The next day we packed up and went to New York. The following morning at the crack of dawn a train began its wandering over most of New York

State, bringing us in early evening to Saranac Lake, where the first of several anticipatory celebrations of Japan's surrender was being touched off. Our daughter, looking radiant and well on the way to recovery, was awaiting us in her bedroom. Our dear friend, Ray Atherton, then Ambassador to Canada, was driving down from Ottawa to dine with us, spend a day or two with Mary, and then take us on to Ottawa. After a first round of embraces, Mary remembered to tell us that Secretary Byrnes had been trying all day to get me on the telephone.

II

ACTION BEGINS

Under Secretary of State
August 1945–June 1947

14. A NEW JOB AND WIDENING RESPONSIBILITIES

No PREMONITORY PRICKLE warned me of trouble lurking in the Secretary of State's call. Doubtless some loose end needed tying up. There was no hurry about it.

When some hours later that evening Secretary Byrnes came on the telephone, he told me cheerily that the acceptance of my resignation had been an error due to the confusion and pressure of the moment and that, on the contrary, he and the President wished me to come back as Under Secretary of State. This amazed me then as much as it still does today. My appointment, Mr. Byrnes suggested, was not the only replacement under consideration. Although both dumbfounded and appreciative, I clung to my decision to return to private life, but Mr. Byrnes would have none of it. It was, he said, too complicated and serious a matter to be decided in a telephone conversation. He would send an Army plane for me and we would talk it out thoroughly in Washington. The next day, August 12, was our daughter's and my wife's joint birthday. The surrender of Japan was in the final stage of discussion through the Swiss Foreign Office. Combining these private and public exigencies, I got Mr. Byrnes to postpone our confrontation for a few days. My wife suggested that in the interval I assume for one day that I had accepted Mr. Byrnes's proposal and for the next that I had declined it, and see which made me feel worse. The experiment did not help. Both assumptions depressed me.

On Tuesday, August 14, at six o'clock in the evening, the Swiss Chargé d'Affaires brought word to the Secretary of State of Japan's surrender. The next day I flew back to Washington in the Army plane and my wife motored to Ottawa to stay at the embassy with the Athertons until I could join her.

On the afternoon of the fifteenth I had a rambling talk with Mr. Byrnes. Will Clayton had agreed to stay on in his post. Benjamin V. Cohen would become Counselor. This post had been a source of trouble with the Under Secretary when it was last occupied by Judge Walton Moore, but Ben Cohen's nature and our long friendship gave assurance that it would not be so with me. To my deep regret Archie MacLeish's resignation had been tendered and accepted. Nelson Rockefeller's would be. Jimmie Dunn would stay on but would be abroad while the European treaties were being negotiated. I tried to get a commitment to keep Julius Holmes in charge of administration, but could get nothing definite. Mr. Byrnes spoke of his former law partner, Donald Russell of South Carolina (later named as the Secretary's choice); a man who knew nothing of the Department did not seem promising in this post. When I spoke of the importance of properly amalgamating the new wartime agencies dealing with intelligence and information into the Department, Mr. Byrnes gave me a Budget Bureau plan of reorganization to read overnight. When we parted, I was still free and uncommitted. The reorganization plan was full of Budget Bureau nonsense about coordination and weak on lines of command, but the parts on the intelligence and information units were sound.

During the night I came to a decision in the curious way one does. One moment one is still pushed about by doubts and hopes and, in the next, clear. In so far as the process was rational, I was pretty sure that the experience would be a frustrating one; but I would never know unless I tried it, so try it I would. The frustrations were all that I expected them to be, but for reasons impossible to foresee at the time, the decision was one of the most fortunate of my life. Again I was to learn how vast a part luck plays in our lives.

The next morning Mr. Byrnes and I talked again briefly. He told me that he had approached Walter Lippmann to take on the post Archie MacLeish had vacated, but that Lippmann had refused on the ground that his role as commentator would be destroyed if he became involved in the active conduct of affairs. Mr. Byrnes asked me what I would think of Spruille Braden for the Latin American post. I did not know Braden but said that I had heard well of him.

Then I signed on as mate of the good ship "Jimmie Byrnes" and the Army flew me to Ottawa for my holiday. All the business of resigning and coming back again was too much for the administrative end of the State Department, so it simply ignored the polite exchange of letters between the President and me. On the official record I went happily along as Assistant Secretary until I took over my new post. It made bookkeeping so much easier.

The mystery of the sudden decision to recall me still remains. I did not feel free to cross-examine the Secretary of State, and the only written reference to it which I have from him is not enlightening. It is written on the flyleaf of his book, *Speaking Frankly,* which he kindly gave me.

I could make the trips described on a preceding page only because I was confident that in my absence the Department was ably administered by the Under-Secretary Dean Acheson. During the war he rendered patriotic service. In July 1945, he had earned the right to return to his profession, but at my request agreed to remain as Under Secretary. He did it to serve his country, but at the same time he rendered me a great service. His loyal friendship always will be appreciated by me.

Dec. 1st 1947   James F. Byrnes

It is quite probable that in the busy days of July and August, after Mr. Byrnes's appointment, neither he nor the President had time to think about staffing the State Department. Both left immediately for the Potsdam Conference and then were overwhelmed by the events leading to the surrender of Japan. Undoubtedly Fred Vinson and Wayne Coy, who had had occasion in the past to consider the organization of the Department, spoke to them both about my departure as soon as they learned of it and stressed the need for a successor to Mr. Grew. This seems the most plausible explanation of how and why my escape from government service was frustrated at the very moment when I thought myself free. At any rate, the whole course of my life was completely changed.

My own about-face on the decision to return to private life apparently baffled our daughter Jane (Mrs. Dudley Brown) as much as it did me. She suggested an answer to the puzzle:

JAB to DA *September* 1945

Heaven knows where you are now. I have given up trying to keep up with your movements and career. The last development has inspired me to write:

I'm Just a Guy Who Can't Say "No"
(With apologies to Celeste Holm)

I'm just a guy who can't say, "No!"
    I'm in a terrible jam.
I always say, "Okay, I'll bite."
    Just when I ought to say, "Scram!"

When a Sec. begins to plead with me,
    I'm sure I should say, "Hell, no!"
But when they intercede with me,
    Somehow I say, "Let's go!"

I'm just a fool when people beg.
I seem made for a saint.
I ain't got no restraint!
How can I be what I ain't?
I can't say no!

Suppose they say no other will do;
    They gotta have you some maw?
What'ja gonna do when they talk like that?
    Practice law?

For a while I said, and thought it true,
    I'm a weary and broke old man.
When they said you're the fella to make
    the world new,
I wonder—Perhaps, I am!

Whether or not this shot hit the bull's eye, I cannot say that in reversing myself and going back to the Department I was not aware of the difficulties and dangers which awaited the second in command in that place at that time. Not fully aware, to be sure, but acutely conscious that I was entering Indian country. Trouble did not even await our return to Washington.

THE END OF LEND-LEASE

While we were vacationing in Canada and Will Clayton was absent in England discussing British economic problems for the coming year, an action was taken in Washington that had most far-reaching and harmful consequences. If either Clayton or I had been there, I cannot believe it would have been taken.

The action, announced by President Truman on August 21, directed the Foreign Economic Administration to discontinue all lend-lease operations and notify foreign governments accordingly.[1] The decision, made two days earlier as a result of a recommendation by Joseph Grew, Under Secretary of State, and Leo Crowley, Foreign Economic Administrator, was arrived at without adequate consideration of its consequences, doubtless without an understanding of them, by those involved. Indeed, in later years President Truman said to me that he had come to think of this action as a grave mistake. Not for two years more was the American Government to understand the full seriousness of even the situation in Europe. In Britain there was no such delay. Mr. Attlee and Mr. Churchill saw Britain in a "very serious financial position" and as the recipient of "very grave disquieting news."[2] Will Clayton saw Britain facing disaster, and the Secretary of the Treasury immediately recommended a group to deal with the impending crisis in Britain.

At the time, Mr. Truman said to the press in explanation, "The reason is that the bill passed by Congress defined Lend-Lease as a weapon of war, and after we ceased to be at war it is no longer necessary."[3] This statement was untrue and the decision disastrous. Made even before the surrender of Japan had been signed on board the USS *Missouri,* when millions of our own and our allies' troops still had to disarm our enemies and occupy their territory and to stabilize as yet unplumbed situations in Europe, Asia, the Middle East, and Africa, it knocked the financial bottom out of the whole allied military position. While lend-lease could not have been made the vehicle for postwar foreign aid, a decision to end it five days after the white flag was run up in Tokyo was unnecessary and wrong. This is not said in criticism of a new and inexperienced President confronted with thoroughly bad advice from supposedly responsible officials—in this case, what Edmund Burke called "the irresistible operation of feeble councils"—but to mark the point from which he began almost immediately to grow.

On Monday, August 27, I took the oath of office as Under Secretary of State—and was to remain in it under two secretaries until July 1, 1947, a period of six hundred and seventy-two days. During a little more than a third of that time I acted as Secretary of State during my chiefs' many and often protracted absences. The appointment, Congress being absent, was a "recess appointment," which meant that the nomination would have to be submitted to the Senate for confirmation when Congress reassembled. This situation offers the appointee an opportunity to supply senators with grounds for criticizing him. I was not slow to seize it.

DA to MAB   *August 29*

I have been here three days. . . . The bloom is off the peach. Everyone has said how wonderful I am. The power and the glory are over.

My sunburn is fading. My smile is more rubbery. I am looking forward with dread and fascination to Monday when I am left in charge to sink or swim without any idea of what we are trying to do. [Mr. Byrnes was in London at the Council of Foreign Ministers from September 4 to October 8.]

DA to MAB   *September 13*

Here we are snowed under, exhausted, and getting more so. There are three of us at the head of the Department instead of eight. The place is disorganized, the morale low, and no one has the authority to take the steps which have to be taken. So we struggle on as best we can . . . .

DA to MAB   *September 18*

Sometimes I wish that I could speak with a little more freedom [a wish I was to fulfill the next day]. The President has been very kind and backed me up at all times. I like him a great deal.

INTRODUCTION TO ATOMIC ENERGY

At a Cabinet luncheon on September 18, 1945, the President discussed briefly the need for determining an approach to the international discussion of atomic energy. The Cabinet meeting on Friday, September 21, would be Colonel Stimson's last. The President proposed to devote it to this subject and to center it upon a memorandum by Colonel Stimson. This memorandum was misunderstood at the time and has been since, partly because the accompanying letter[4] referred to "sharing the atomic bomb with Russia," and this put off many in the Cabinet. The memorandum, however, was addressed to the much narrower question of how to approach discussion with the Russians on the questions raised by our development of the bomb. The crucial sentences were:

> Those relations may be perhaps irretrievably embittered by the way in which we approach the solution of the bomb with Russia. For if we fail to approach them now and merely continue to negotiate with them, having this weapon rather ostentatiously on our hip, their suspicions and their distrust of our purposes and motives will increase. . . .
>
> I emphasize perhaps beyond all other considerations the importance of taking this action with Russia as a proposal of the United States—backed by Great Britain but peculiarly the proposal of the United States. Action of any international group of nations, including many small nations who have not demonstrated their potential power or responsibility in this war would not, in my opinion, be taken seriously by the Soviets.[5]

The discussion was unworthy of the subject. No one had had a chance to prepare for its complexities. Asked as Acting Secretary of State to lead off after Colonel Stimson's statement, I agreed that we should take the initiative with the USSR, being assured of British backing, before going into any larger group. I did this partly out of deference and respect for Colonel Stimson and also because our Government had previously sought a nucleus of agreement on all post-war problems before plunging into the intricacies of United Nations discussions. As earlier chapters have shown, every subject had been approached in this way, from lend-lease principles through UNRRA and Bretton Woods to the United Nations Charter. It seemed fundamental common sense.

Fred Vinson, Tom Clark, and Clinton Anderson opposed Colonel Stimson's proposal partly on the ground that we should not "share the bomb." The Colonel had not proposed that we should. What he had proposed was discussing with Russia a sharing of basic scientific data, excluding information on the industrial processes used to manufacture atomic weapons. Others, as I wrote my daughter, "expressed more or less agreement with Colonel Stimson. Henry Wallace soared into abstractions, trailing clouds of aphorisms as he went." The discussion got nowhere, but distorted accounts of it to the effect that the President was contemplating sharing the bomb were leaked to the press, putting the Congress into an uproar. The President met with senatorial leaders. Prime Minister Attlee urged a tripartite conference with Mackenzie King. A message to Congress was gotten under way.

During the morning before the Cabinet luncheon I had had a meeting with the President on atomic energy legislation. For some weeks George L. Harrison, Governor of the Federal Reserve Bank of New York, and John J. McCloy, who had been collaborating with Colonel Stimson on atomic energy matters, had been urging Mr. Byrnes and me—since I would soon take over from him in his absence—to support with the President the May-Johnson bill on domestic control. Mr. Byrnes had agreed to this before his departure. However, I had become impressed by the complications that might arise if the Administration went too far with domestic legislation before formulating any approach to international problems. I asked Herbert S. Marks, who had been with me since I had taken over liaison with Congress in 1944, to give me a "talking brief" on the matter for my meeting with the President. We had already seen Colonel Stimson's memorandum, so that Marks's brief stressed the necessary information the President would want to determine his position on that proposal and, if he approved it, on problems of timing the overtures with domestic legislation, on consultation with legislators, and on harmonizing the substance of national and international proposals. After our discussion the President asked for a memorandum on the international aspects.

Meanwhile Senator Vandenberg went to work on the Hill in an attempt to head off jurisdictional battles in both houses of Congress over atomic legislation. This he proposed to do by establishing a special Senate-House Joint Committee on Atomic Energy. On September 20 the President decided that his message to Congress should deal with both national and international control. My memorandum on various aspects of the latter, for which he had asked, went off to him on the twenty-fifth. It was deeply influenced by Colonel Stimson's paper. Its conclusion—the premises being stated—was that a policy of scientific secrecy would be futile and dangerous and that the real issues involved the methods and conditions that should govern interchange of scientific knowledge and the international controls that should be sought to prevent a race toward mutual destruction. Its recommendations were that the United States approach the Soviet Union, after discussion with the British, to attempt to work out a program of mutual exchange of scientific information and collaboration in the development of atomic power to proceed gradually and upon condition that weapons development should be renounced with adequate opportunity for inspection; and that in due course the plan be opened to other nations. Concurrently with these discussions, of which Congress should be fully informed, the Congress should proceed with consideration of domestic legislation to be recommended by the President and later with requests for congressional action on any agreements that might result from these discussions.

The President, after generally approving these recommendations, set me, Judge Samuel Rosenman, his Counsel, and the Pentagon to work on a draft message. Not forgetting the Secretary, absent in London, I cleared it with Benjamin V. Cohen on his behalf over the telecon, a secure and secret telegraphic device. Under instruction I also informed the British Government through Lord Halifax on October 1. The President sought the opinion of Speaker Rayburn and Senate Majority Leader Barkley and was reassured that the addition of the international proposal would help rather than hurt the message. The message itself, after stating the reasons for international collaboration set forth in the memorandum, proposed "to initiate discussions, first with our associates in this discovery, Great Britain and Canada, and then with other nations, in an effort to effect agreement on the conditions under which cooperation might replace rivalry in the field of atomic power."[6] The full text of the international portion will be found in the Notes.

By all the careful clearance of this message, I hoped that the road had been kept open for discussion with Britain and the Soviet Union before getting into larger and more formal conferences. But it was not to be. Secretary Byrnes, returning from London with painful memories of Molotov's obstructive tactics, had no stomach for taking on another thorny subject with the Russians, an attitude fully shared by his colleagues, Secretaries Robert Patterson and James Forrestal. A month later in the discussions of atomic energy control with Attlee and Mackenzie King, in which I played no part, we agreed to the course that Colonel Stimson had specifically disapproved—to begin international discussions in a large group of nations that included many small ones of no demonstrated power or responsibility. But I doubt whether a contrary decision would have changed the result. The evidence is now strong—including the urgent Soviet collecting of German nuclear scientists and missile experts—that probably by this time, and certainly a very short time later, Stalin had given top priority to the development of a nuclear weapon. It seems most unlikely that even if given complete control of method and means Colonel Stimson could have persuaded Stalin to have forgone a Soviet nuclear-armament system.

A BRUSH WITH SENATORS

At the time of my appointment as Under Secretary, General Douglas MacArthur, Supreme Commander Allied Powers in Tokyo, sent me a warm message of congratulation and an invitation to view the situation in Japan at first hand. I replied appreciatively, hoping that I might be able to do so. There seemed little chance, however, for in those days under secretaries did not travel, but minded the store.

On September 17 General MacArthur announced that the occupation force in Japan would be reduced to two hundred thousand men within six months. Asked about this by the press on the eighteenth, the President said that General MacArthur had not consulted him. He was glad to see that the General would not need as many troops as he had originally estimated. Thirty days earlier it had been five hundred thousand, which had been reduced to four hundred thousand, and then cut in half.[7]

The next day, September 19, I was asked whether I had been disturbed by the General's statements and if I had any comment on the occupation. The number of troops required, I said, was a purely military matter with which the State Department was not properly concerned. I then added, and authorized direct quotation:

The important thing is that the policy in regard to Japan is the same policy which has always been held by this Government and is still held so far as I know, and I think I know. In carrying out that policy, the occupation forces are the instruments of policy and not the determinants of policy and the policy is and has been that the surrender of Japan will be carried out; that Japan will be put in a position where it can not renew aggressive warfare; that the present economic and social system in Japan which makes for a will to war will be changed so that that will to war will not continue; and that whatever it takes to carry this out will be used to carry it out.[8]

That same day the President sent my nomination to the Senate. Senators Kenneth Wherry of Nebraska and A. B. (Happy) Chandler of Kentucky delayed action on it, Wherry insisting that I had "blighted the name" of General MacArthur, and Chandler that I had insulted the General. Senator Wherry sent me a long questionnaire concerning policies and authority in Japan, including my own views on both. I replied with relevant documents. The White House released the "U.S. Initial Post Surrender Policy for Japan" and a statement defining General MacArthur's authority.

Thus the stage was set for a Senate debate on Monday, September 24, supposedly on my confirmation but in reality on General MacArthur's position and authority in relation to the position and authority of the President of the United States. It was angry and bitter. Senator Taft observed that he intended to vote against Senator Wherry's motion to recommit the nomination, as he thought I was qualified to be Under Secretary of State. In view of his belief that the policies of the United States were made by the President and not by under secretaries, he did not believe "that the disagreement with Mr. Acheson's policies as expressed in the controversy, so-called, with General MacArthur [was] any ground for refusing to confirm this nomination"—this, in spite of his earlier statement that what I had said at my press conference was "one of the most extraordinary statements on policy I have ever heard." Senators Barkley and Connally defended me stoutly. On the motion to recommit the nomination, Senator Wherry got eleven senators to join him.† The roll-call vote to confirm was 69 in favor to 1, Senator Wherry, opposed.[9] When I told this to our care-taker at Harewood, our farm at Sandy Spring in Montgomery County, Mary-land, he said cheerfully, "Hardly worthwhile for the other fella to run!" If we could have seen into the future, we might have recognized this skirmish as the beginning of a struggle leading to the relief of General MacArthur from his command on April 11, 1951.

A CONGERIES OF TASKS

Despite this time-consuming and absurd flurry, the five weeks during which I was "Acting" for Mr. Byrnes were constructive ones. On September 13 financial talks began with the British to find an alternative to lend-lease. I was a member of the United States Group and participated in its decision. So far as meetings of the combined groups were concerned, I contented myself with sup-porting Will Clayton, who carried the laboring oar for the Department. Having represented our Government in similar talks a year earlier, I found the ground to be covered familiar.

During this time the Department received new facilities with which to dis-charge enlarged responsibilities. At the end of August the President had trans-ferred to us the foreign functions, facilities, and personnel of the Office of War Information, and in mid-September William Benton arrived to supervise their incorporation into the Department. Later in the month the Research and Analy-sis Branch and the Presentation Branch of the Office of Strategic Services also came to us. Colonel Alfred McCormack was appointed Special Assistant to the Secretary in charge of research and intelligence. The Department muffed both of these opportunities. The latter, research and intelligence, died almost at once as the result of gross stupidity, discussed in the next chapter. When, therefore, in 1947 the Central Intelligence Agency was proposed as part of the armed services unification bill, the State Department had abdicated not only leadership in this field but any serious position. Information and public affairs had a better chance and were well served by several devoted assistant secretaries. Eventually they succumbed to the fate of so many operating agencies with which the State Department has had a go, including economic warfare, lend-lease, foreign aid, and technical assistance.

In all these cases, either the Department was not imaginative enough to see its opportunity or administratively competent enough to seize it, or the effort became entangled in red tape and stifled by bureaucratic elephantiasis, or con-flict with enemies in Congress absorbed all the Department's energies. Then, in the stock market phrase, the new function was "spun off" to live a sort of blood-less life of administration without policy, like the French bureaucracy between Bonaparte and de Gaulle. At about the same time we also received for liquida-tion a portion of the estate of that problem agency, the Foreign Economic Ad-ministration. None mourned its death.

In the week of September 24, the Department and Secretary Ickes brought to conclusion two matters on which I had been working for some time. One con-cerned an international petroleum agreement; the other, conservation of natural resources in the subsoil and on the sea bed of the continental shelf and of the fishery resources contiguous to our coasts.[10] These were matters of considerable importance.

It was no small triumph for State and Interior to collaborate successfully. The petroleum agreement was with Great Britain and laid the basis for jointly sponsoring and preparing for an "international [petroleum] agreement among all countries interested in the petroleum trade, whether as producers or consumers," the purpose of which would be to seek the orderly development of this trade in the interest of all parties to it. Already signs of the trouble soon to break out in the Middle East were manifest. Many conflicting interests needed reconciliation, including those between the producing companies and the governments of producing nations; between producing areas—such as the Persian Gulf, the East Indies, and South America—and the United States; between orderly development, including conservation, and unrestricted competition; between producers and consumers; and between commercial and security interests. Unfortunately, our efforts were too little and too late. They came to nothing, and were engulfed by the turmoil of European economic crisis, Middle Eastern nationalism and nationalization, and the distractions of the cold war. Some such agreement should come about, if this limited natural resource is to be wisely used.

In the conservation effort, more immediately practicable because it was within our own national capacity, we were successful. In proclamations that the departments submitted to him, the President specifically declared the character of the waters involved as "high seas" and that the right to their free and unimpeded navigation was in no way affected by the proposed regulations. In the case of subsoil development, and of fisheries which had been or might be developed by Americans alone, the United States would establish conservation zones where it would regulate and control drilling and fishing. Where fisheries had been or might be developed jointly with commercial interests in other nations, the regulation and control should be by agreements with the other nations concerned. Happily it fell to me, as Acting Secretary, to attest the President's signature on the proclamations, the results of so much patient work.

Finally, the President began another stage of a long effort to complete the seaway and power development on the St. Lawrence River in his October 3 message to Congress asking for the necessary legislation. Weeks of preparatory work in my former role had gone into cultivating the legislative soil, but it remained reluctant. Interests fearing competition from seaports on the Great Lakes—railroads, labor, Atlantic ports—were too strong. For nearly ten years the struggle went on, until on May 13, 1954—more than a year after we had left office—a bill was passed.

15. TROUBLE IN HIGH PLACES

WHEN THE SECRETARY returned to Washington early in October, my pumpkin coach vanished and I found myself back in the kitchen. Meanwhile an instrument had been forged, the "nine-thirty meeting," which gave me some measure of control over or, at least, a knowledge of what was going on in the Department. The meeting in my office was a short one, no more than half an hour, attended by the chief operating officers. With the Secretary's approval I continued it after his return, since he, with a lawyer's impatience of routine, did not wish to take it over. The meeting kept changing its form and losing its utility through growth; only continuous pruning saved it. The most useful period in its history came later, after General Marshall created the Central Secretariat, which served his office and mine and through which we kept track of everything coming in or going out of the Department, and the progress, or lack of it, being made on each matter. Its chief was also kept informed by General Marshall and me of all policy decisions in which we took part in high places. His discretion was our security. With his collaboration the nine-thirty meeting brought the work of the Department under the direction of a chief executive officer. The purpose of the meeting was not to devise policy. That was done elsewhere. Still less was it to discuss and exchange information. It was to assign responsibility for new matters as they arose; to follow and guide work in progress; to assign additional help when needed; to reassign when necessary; and, when ready for action, to present proposals to the President for necessary decisions, authority, and means. The meeting became an administrative method of the greatest importance, but required the sternest discipline. It also gave me an excellent insight into my colleagues.

Parkinson's Law applies to meetings as well as to organizations. Attendance at our meetings soon became a status symbol. Feelings had to be hurt, and were. People invited in for a special matter wanted to stay and had to be ejected. The enemy of its purpose was irrelevancy to that purpose, and irrelevancy mounts with numbers. Finally, to preserve the life and sanity of the secretary of the meeting, we had a large meeting once a week chiefly for morale purposes. Other meetings were, of course, held on specific subjects, and I shall return to them later. Proliferation of meetings, as I have suggested earlier, is an inevitable product of weak leadership and administration in the Department. When it is run by meetings, committees, or soviets, it isn't run at all.

STRANGE INTERLUDE

A song of many years ago proclaimed the somber sentiment that "into each life some rain must fall." Some was about to fall in mine. The Department had committed me as substitute for my busy superior to a speech in mid-November in New York at a rally sponsored by the National Council of Soviet-American Friendship. The drafting of the speech was in hand, and I would be supported by messages extolling our ally from the President, Secretary of War Robert Patterson, Admiral Ernest King, and other sound men. We did not know in 1945 as much about what to expect of such a rally as we do now, but I do remember being vaguely apprehensive as I traveled to New York because it was being held in Madison Square Garden. That did not suggest the study group on Soviet-American relations for which my speech seemed designed. It had a mildly hopeful, though neutral, tone, produced by blending a past of historical friendship and helpfulness during the stress of the American Revolution and the Civil War with present ideological differences. Apprehension became acute when I got to the Garden. Our information had been gravely defective.

The vast place was packed and vociferous. In its center an elevated boxing ring had been erected with a runway going up to it from a curtained enclosure in which I met my fellow performers: Corliss Lamont, president of the Council, a son of Thomas W. Lamont, Chairman of the Board of J. P. Morgan & Company; Joseph E. Davies, who had been Ambassador to Moscow and written an enthusiastic account entitled *Mission to Moscow;* Paul Robeson, the great Negro bass who later became a Soviet citizen; and, to top the list, the Very Reverend Hewlett Johnson, the "Red" Dean of Canterbury Cathedral. On the floor below the prize ring an orchestra played incendiary music. It stopped. Accompanied by a roll of drums and a comparative hush, Ambassador Davies mounted the ramp and the podium. He would, his voice blared through powerful amplifiers, announce the speakers of the evening as they came to the platform. Each did so to a roll of drums, as aristocrats did to Madame Guillotine in the Place de la Révolution or as King Charles I approached the block through the window of his Palace of Whitehall. Paul Robeson and Dean Johnson were clearly the favorites. Indeed, the "Red" Dean received a tumultuous ovation, as he sashayed around the ring like a skater, in the long black coat and gaiters of an English prelate, his hands clasped above his head in a prize fighter's salute. Corliss Lamont opened with a brief welcome. Then Paul Robeson's magnificent voice began the low rumble of "Ole Man River," that moving song of the oppressed and hopeless. It did not end in hopelessness and resignation as the river just kept on rolling along, however, but in a swelling protest, ending on that magnificent high note of defiance produced by a great voice magnified by all the power of science. The crowd went wild.

In time it quieted down enough to be stirred up again by the Dean's rabble-rousing, which even his Oxford accent could not dampen. The speech became an antiphony, the Dean shouting the rhetorical questions, the crowd roaring back the responses. After an ovation, as much for themselves as the speaker, or for him as one of themselves, my hour had come. I felt like a bartender announcing that the last drink before closing time would be cambric tea. Fortunately mine was a short speech, but between me and the end of it was a paragraph of my own devising—one of the few. It followed an acknowledgment of the Soviet Union's reasonableness in desiring friendly governments along her borders. Then this: "But it seems equally clear to us that the interest in security must take into account and respect other basic interests of nations and men, such as the interest of other peoples to choose the general surroundings of their own lives and of all men to be secure in their persons. We believe that that adjustment of interests should take place short of the point where persuasion and firmness become coercion, where a knock on the door at night strikes terror into men and women."[1]

I hurried on, trying to outrun the pursuing boos and catcalls, tossing to these wolves a quotation from Molotov and one from Stalin. But I had shown my colors; those who took their red straight, without a chaser of white and blue, were not mollified. When I finished, protest drowned out even polite applause. At the end of the ramp a policeman touched me on the arm. "Come," he said, "I can show you a quiet way to your car." Nothing could have been more welcome, except possibly the quiet scotch waiting for me at the friend's house where I was staying.

Some years later, during what has come to be known as the "McCarthy period," my presence at the Madison Square meeting was adduced as evidence of sympathy for communism. This seemed to me to add a companion thought to Lincoln's conclusion of the impossibility of fooling all the people all the time, the difficulty of pleasing any of the people any of the time.

AN ATOMIC CONFERENCE AT THE SUMMIT

Meanwhile, November 10 to 16 were busy days in Washington. Prime Ministers Attlee of Great Britain and Mackenzie King of Canada had come to discuss with President Truman international aspects of atomic energy. These discussions were carried on with secrecy in a very small circle in which I was not included. My old friend Ben Cohen, who had been brought into the Department as its Counselor, and Vannevar Bush worked with Mr. Byrnes on this matter. To insure privacy the crucial discussion was held, as I recall, on the Secretary of the Navy's yacht, *Sequoia*. If I was consulted at all about the discussions, I have forgotten it.

These meetings resulted on November 15 in an Agreed Declaration by the three heads of government in which they favored the availability and free interchange of the "fruits of scientific research," but not "of detailed information concerning the practical industrial application of atomic energy" or of its "military exploitation." This must await, they declared, "effective, reciprocal, and enforceable safeguards acceptable to all nations. . . . A Commission should be set up under the United Nations Organization to prepare recommendations for submission to the Organization"; its work "should proceed by separate stages, the successful completion of each one of which will develop the necessary confidence of the world before the next stage is undertaken."[2] Thus, a series of leaks and pressures, and responses to both, had brought the Administration to the opposite pole from Colonel Stimson's position. But Colonel Stimson had been quite right. Although I was far from realizing it at the time, I was destined to be one of the principal instruments in proving Colonel Stimson's point.

UNRRA AND THE BRITISH LOAN

Meanwhile Will Clayton and I were busy with the supply and financial problems of our allies. On November 13 the President asked Congress for one and a third billion dollars for our share of the second year of UNRRA's operations. Clayton and I bore the burden of testimony for the Government before the House Foreign Affairs Committee. One of the methods by which the Congress keeps a tight rein on the executive is by authorizing appropriations for such endeavors as UNRRA, foreign aid, and lend-lease for only one year at a time. Since a point of order will lie against any appropriation not authorized by law, two legislative acts each year, requiring four hearings before four separate committees, are necessary to keep each activity going. The substantive committee of each house—say Foreign Relations and Foreign Affairs—must authorize an appropriation; the Appropriations Committee of each must recommend the amount to be appropriated. Depending on the end of Pennsylvania Avenue from which one views the procedure, it is either needed insurance against executive extravagance or congressional usurpation and harassment. As might be expected, I strongly hold the latter view, especially about the annual authorization, which seems to me the product of committee jealousy at its most picayune.

At about that time our Division of Chinese Affairs issued a statement that takes a high place in the category of "famous last words." It noted that our forces in China were assisting the Chinese Government in effecting the surrender, disarming, and repatriation of Japanese troops in China—approximately two million men—and then concluded: "The activities of our armed forces in the Far East, including the transport of Chinese troops, are being carried out solely for the purposes indicated above. It is neither our purpose nor our desire to become involved in the internal affairs of China."[3] In a month we were involved over our heads.

Early in December the combined British and American groups completed an immense schedule of invaluable work on a loan to Britain, a settlement of lend-lease and reciprocal lend-lease accounts, the disposition of surplus American property in Britain, settlement of mutual damage and other claims, and a comprehensive agreement on proposals for expansion of world trade and employment, including the creation of an International Trade Organization. On any standard of scope or excellence, it was an impressive achievement of international collaboration. As chief contributors, it is enough to single out three men, all of whom are now dead—Maynard Keynes, Harry White, and Will Clayton.

Alas! Good as was the work of those months and those men, it still lacked that little more of imagination, daring, and luck essential to success. The lack was chiefly on our side. The loan—three and three-quarters billion dollars—was too small; we still vastly underestimated the extent of British and European economic and financial exhaustion. The brave new world of expanding trade and employment we envisioned was to run into a block in the Republican Eightieth Congress. As helpful as Vandenberg proved to be in the areas within his sphere of influence, it did not extend to trade matters. In that area the most powerful Republican senators, Millikin of Colorado and Taft, were not seeing visions or dreaming dreams. The Marshall Plan would prove to be acceptable if Vandenberg approved, but lowering protective tariffs had gone far enough, and from the Imperial Box thumbs were turned down on the International Trade Organization and its purposes. But all that was still in the future. Flushed with success, we turned confidently to new problems, to be met by a vicious line squall out of smiling skies.

INTRODUCTION TO CHINA AND GENERAL MARSHALL

Patrick J. Hurley, the former Oklahoma cowboy who struck it rich, Secretary of War under Hoover, a Major General wounded in action by the Japanese, was at the moment U.S. Ambassador to China, home for consultation. Trouble moved with him like a cloud of flies around a steer. Handsome, vain, and reckless, he boasted of lethal speed on the draw in the old days in the West and gave ample evidence of seeking equally simplistic answers to complicated problems in this present mission. His complaints were vocal but unclear. They began with charges that Foreign Service officers in China had been undercutting him and United States policy in China and ended with an attack on the Department generally, and presumably the Secretary, for not making its policy clear to the public. Throughout his charges ran the demagogic note of the impending epoch, that those who differed with him were "soft on communism."

I had had my own troubles with Hurley in 1944 when, after being invalided out of active military service, he was attached to the Middle East Supply Center. Then, as this time, he had returned to Washington breathing charges about the misuse of lend-lease goods, chiefly that they were being distributed in Iran by the British. This was correct, since British forces held southern Iran and the exigencies of war prevented the presence of Americans. When that factor was eliminated by victory in North Africa, Americans handled lend-lease to Iran. Another charge deplored Russian and British imperialism and urged that the United States disassociate itself from and supplant this by bringing the message of democracy. Hurley's memorandum was sent to Mr. Hull for comment and by him to various of us for reply. I was, perhaps, too brusque with Hurley's proposal to bring democracy to occupied Iran, describing it in the phrase of one of my assistants as "messianic globaloney" which might await the end of the war against Hitler and Mussolini in which we and our criticized allies were cooperating. The phrase leaked to Hurley. I continued the story before the Senate Committee on Foreign Relations:

> . . . a few weeks after that General Hurley, who was on his way back from the Middle East, came to my office and asked for a meeting on the subject. We had a meeting of several officers of the Department, including a young assistant of mine. The meeting progressed amicably for a while, and then General Hurley referred with some heat to a phrase used in my memorandum to the Secretary. He attributed this phrase to the young assistant, who was present. I pointed out to the General that how I conducted the internal affairs of my office was not of any concern outside of the office, and that all memoranda which bore my name were my responsibility, and this one in particular was. The General brushed that aside as a somewhat quixotic attitude on my part, and continued to attack the assistant.
>
> The matter became heated. Temperature rose, and with it the voices of the contestants, until finally the General asked my assistant why he was not in uniform, fighting with the forces of this country.
>
> That seemed to me a particularly undesirable and unfortunate observation, because the young man not only had tried very hard to get in the Army, but he had been in the Army and had been discharged because he had a serious ailment of the back, for which he was then preparing for a major operation. He shortly afterward had that operation and was laid up for the better part of a year.
>
> I intervened in the debate at this point and drew the General's attention to the undesirability of his remark. The general temperature seemed to cool a bit. We got everyone seated and withdrew appeals which had been made to trial by combat, and finally we worked out an agreement by which the General withdrew this unhappy remark and I apologized to the General for any observations in my memorandum which he might regard as personally offensive.
>
> That seemed to solve the matter and we went on and had a very amicable discussion, and I never heard of the thing from that day until it was printed in Mr. Pearson's newspaper column on May 20th, and I never heard of it again until the General brought it up in his testimony.
>
> We have met several times. We have had several discussions of the subject of lend-lease supplies, and I had not realized that I was supposed to have wrecked any policy. . . .
>
> The idea expressed by the General that I am in favor of monopoly and imperialism and against democracy is utterly fantastic. No action of mine, no word of mine, has ever furnished any basis whatever for such a statement.[4]

Such was the man who now charged other officers of the Department with wrecking other policies on the other side of the globe. Secretary Byrnes dealt with him tactfully and soothingly, as only he could do, and had, so he thought, on the morning of November 27, persuaded Hurley to go back to China. By lunch time at the White House, he discovered the extent of his illusion. There the President and Cabinet were informed that at the National Press Club Hurley had launched a passionate attack not only upon the Department but upon the Administration, charging a lack of any clear policy regarding China. His resignation, he said, was on Mr. Byrnes's desk. That afternoon the President telephoned General Marshall, who was planning to retire from active service for a long rest, and asked him to go to China as his personal representative with the rank of ambassador. Typically, the General answered that he would serve any-where in any capacity that the President wished. The same day the White House announced both resignation and appointment.

Although Hurley's nature was not one to excite sympathy, his frustration later became the frustration of us all. The Administration had a policy and pro-ceeded to define it clearly. It was to do all we could to restore a "strong, united, and democratic China," without intervening in the Chinese civil war but by reconciling the warring factions. Pending that time we would continue to recog-nize Chiang Kai-shek's Nationalist Government and "cooperate with it in in-ternational affairs and specifically in eliminating Japanese influence from China."[5] General Hurley had long proclaimed these dual purposes as his. They were fully shared throughout the Administration, the Congress, and the coun-try. However, few if any of us, including Hurley, myself, the Secretary, General Marshall, and the President, realized that these admirable aims were mutually exclusive and separately unachievable. How and when this realization came we shall leave until later chapters.

RIFT BETWEEN PRESIDENT AND SECRETARY OF STATE

Even before General Marshall set out for China, Secretary Byrnes flew to Moscow for a meeting with Molotov and Bevin to discuss five important mat-ters: the procedure for arriving at peace treaties with European enemy states, excepting Germany; Balkan problems; Chinese pacification; Japanese occupa-tion; and international control of atomic energy. Procedures were agreed upon for the first, fourth, and last of these, which proved successful in the first and fourth and failed in the last. Agreements reached on the second and third points brought nothing but bitter disappointment. They taught us, however, that So-viet diplomatic method was to bargain hard, accept all concessions in the other side's sphere, and nullify all apparently granted in their own.

However, the principal result of the Moscow conference of 1945 was the rift it opened between the President and the Secretary of State. Mr. Byrnes in-tensely disliked large retinues. He traveled light, taking to Moscow hardly more than a half dozen officers and counting on the embassy for essential ser-vices. The communications he sent back were few and terse. The manner of his departure left disquiet behind him. The instructions that he had had worked out for himself on atomic energy were somewhat more liberal in seeking collabora-tion from the Soviet Union than the terms of the Agreed Declaration of Novem-ber 15. General Groves and Secretary Forrestal expressed uneasiness. Before leaving Washington on December 12 for Moscow, the Secretary discussed his plans with several members of the Committee on Foreign Relations and the Special Committee on Atomic Energy and the uneasiness grew. Two days after his departure the Special Committee met with the President, who had me pres-ent. They wanted new and stricter instructions issued. Instead, the President merely had me report the discussion to the Secretary, who replied that he would stay within the terms of the Declaration. The President had me reassure Byrnes that the congressional flurry had not disturbed him, adding that he would be glad to consider any proposals the Russians might have. Very little information came out of Moscow.

On December 27 the President was in Independence. A coded message began to come in to us from Moscow announcing the end of the Council of Ministers and their conclusions. Before we had its full text, press summaries were in the papers and on the air. Vandenberg, misreading one section, was up in arms. The President was annoyed by the failure to make any progress with the Russians on Balkan matters. By the time the President and I had got Vandenberg reassured and calmed, it was my unhappy duty to ruffle the President's temper still further. Mr. Byrnes had cabled me the date of his arrival in Washington and asked me to arrange a time that evening when he could make a report to the nation over all radio networks. This was not in accordance with etiquette, nor was it wise in view of the President's state of mind. Both required that he report first to the President, get straightened away there, and then make his speech with the President's blessing. Despite knowing that Mr. Byrnes might take exception to my doing so, I suggested to the President that it would be more convenient for all concerned, including the networks, if Mr. Byrnes spoke the day after his return. The President agreeing, we arranged it this way.

Driving from the airfield to the Department with the Secretary, I broke to him gently the President's displeasure. He was disbelieving, impatient, and irritated that Mr. Truman had sailed down the Potomac on the *Williamsburg,* leaving word for him to follow. Tired from his long flight, he had had enough traveling for that day. Afterward both men gave me accounts of their meeting. The President's report was even more vivid than the one published in his memoirs, and included the memorandum which he reports having written out and read.[6] In it he insisted that the concomitant of his giving scope to the Secretary was the Secretary's keeping him fully informed. Mr. Byrnes's account could not have been more different. To him the discussion was informative on his side and pleasant on the President's. They parted with affectionate mutual good wishes for the new year. Mr. Byrnes thought me an imaginer of trouble where none existed.

Both impressions were quite possibly entirely genuine. On most occasions Mr. Truman's report of his bark vastly exaggerated it. When thoroughly aroused by what he construed as a discourtesy to Mrs. Truman or his daughter, he could lose his temper and lash out viciously. But Mr. Truman is a kindly and courteous man. However spicy his political comments may be, his private talk is most considerate of others' feelings. I have never heard him say, or heard of him saying, a harsh, bitter, or sarcastic word to anyone, whatever the offense or failure. Mr. Byrnes is not sensitive or lacking in confidence. A vigorous extrovert, accustomed to the lusty exchanges of South Carolina politics, where by ancient tradition all opponents debate together in every county, he would not take as personal criticism Mr. Truman's desire to be kept more fully informed.

Furthermore, Mr. Byrnes maintained toward Mr. Truman—at least so the President thought—the attitude of the leader of the Senate to a freshman senator. To this was added the bitter experience of the vice-presidential nomination in 1944. I mention it only because it is relevant to what happened later. In the early summer of 1944 many Democratic leaders, including Mr. Byrnes and Mr. Truman, but not Robert Hannegan, believed that FDR wanted Byrnes rather than Wallace as the vice-presidential candidate in the coming campaign. Accordingly, at Mr. Byrnes's request, Senator Truman agreed to nominate him at the Chicago convention. However, at the convention Hannegan argued strongly that the Senator's information was wrong and that FDR wanted neither Wallace nor Byrnes on the ticket with him, but Truman. Then he got the President on the telephone as he was about to board the *Baltimore* to meet Admiral Nimitz and General MacArthur at Pearl Harbor. Explaining Truman's belief and purpose, Hannegan turned the receiver so all could hear the President confirm Hannegan.[7] Deeply embarrassed, Truman was reluctant to accept even the President's request, which involved going back on a promise to a friend. At length convinced, he went to Byrnes, told him the story, and asked to be released. Although bitterly disappointed and angry at Hannegan's part in his rejection, Byrnes remained on friendly terms with Truman. This is the story as written by Mr. Truman and told to me before that. He added that Byrnes could hardly help but wonder how determined his resistance had been to the wiles of the anti-Byrnes cabal, and that in offering Byrnes the chief Cabinet post on the way back from the Roosevelt funeral he was not only recognizing and using great ability but compensating in part for what Byrnes believed to have been a gross injustice at the hands of the late President.

The whole unhappy episode impressed me deeply with the reciprocal nature of the President–Secretary of State relationship. If, as pointed out earlier, the President cannot be his own Secretary of State, it is equally true that the Secretary cannot be his own President. However much freedom he may properly be given for operation and maneuver, he cannot be given or take over the ultimate presidential responsibility. To discharge that, the President must be kept fully informed far enough in advance of the need for decision to make choice possible. On his future trips Mr. Byrnes took with him fully instructed communications officers to keep the Department, and through it the White House, advised.

When four years later my own secretarial travels began, I put these lessons to use. The staff was fully equipped to report. Officers attended all meetings for this purpose or received immediate reports from me on private ones. A detailed cable went off every day to the Department with a shorter summary for the President's use if his time was short or to show senators and others. He also received personal—"for his eyes only"—estimates of the situation, dictated by me, containing appraisals of people, of obstacles ahead and methods of avoiding them, and of opportunities for initiatives, as well as requests for suggestions if any occurred to him. He often said that these made him feel present at the scene and participating. We received frequent helpful and encouraging replies from him. The Department, fully informed also, could and did play its part in furnishing us with material and advice.

Another point about traveling secretaries of state is worth mentioning here—the degree to which they divest themselves of their office while away except as it pertains to their mission. General Marshall was meticulous that when the door to his aircraft closed, the command passed. He even on occasions asked for instructions when a wholly novel and unexpected point arose. Mr. Byrnes was inclined occasionally, as when in 1946 Tito's planes downed two Army transport C-47s, to give us instructions while he was away from Washington. This is workable, but eventually commands have to issue from Washington. The Marshall procedure seemed tidier to me when the time came.

16. WASHINGTON AGENT FOR THE MARSHALL MISSION: PHASE ONE

THE SITUATION AS WE SAW IT

EVEN BEFORE Ambassador Hurley's dramatic exit had made Chinese affairs a main concern of the State Department's high command, the recalcitrance of events in China in refusing to conform to any preconceived pattern had made them a principal concern of mine. The immediate occasion was a paper that came to me on November 15, 1945, on its way from the Joint Chiefs of Staff to Secretary Byrnes. Both the paper, which asked whether and when United States Marines should be withdrawn from China, and the State Department's comments upon it seemed to me inadequate as a basis of judgment. Accordingly, I asked John Carter Vincent, Director of the Office of Far Eastern Affairs, to prepare a more comprehensive analysis and alternative recommendations. On the nineteenth he gave me a memorandum. It suggested four possible courses of action:

1. To withdraw the Marines from north China. (This was the course recommended by General Wedemeyer, Commanding General in China.)

2. To leave the Marines in China without changing their mission. (There seemed to be a dispute between General Wedemeyer and the Joint Chiefs as to what this mission was. The former thought it was to facilitate the takeover of China south of the Great Wall by Nationalist troops from the Japanese, which had not yet been completed.)

3. To leave the Marines in China and enlarge their mission to provide assistance to the Nationalist Government in stabilizing conditions in north China and Manchuria. (It was not clear what "stabilizing conditions" meant or what force would be required.)

4. To leave the Marines in China with the mission of providing a more effective and speedy surrender and repatriation of the Japanese.

The Marines had been sent to north China to seize and hold certain port areas and airfields to assist the surrender and repatriation of Japanese forces and the transport of Chinese Nationalist forces to key areas where they could assume responsibility for the surrender. An estimated one million Japanese troops remained in north China, of whom about a third had not been disarmed. Many were still located at inland points. Also about one hundred sixty thousand Nationalist troops and an estimated four hundred fifty thousand Communist troops were in north China. The Joint Chiefs believed that the Japanese troops could not be repatriated without the presence and aid of the Marines, and that if political agreement between the factions in China had not been reached by the time of withdrawing the Marines, any Japanese troops remaining in China would be employed in the resulting Chinese civil war. Alternatively, the Soviet Union might obtrusively enter the scene. It was not a reassuring picture.

This paper and one by the armed services were discussed by the Secretaries of State, War, and Navy at a meeting on November 27 just before Ambassador Hurley's resignation burst upon the astonished capital. As I contemplated the papers and listened to the discussion, certain conclusions seemed to emerge inevitably from the facts. Toward the end of the meeting I stated them to clarify the discussion for the Cabinet officers. They were:

1. The Marines must be kept in China.

2. We must prepare to move other Chinese Nationalist armies north and support them. (Presumably, though not stated, this could include movement to Manchuria as well as to north China.)

3. In areas now held by Japanese troops and which might later be disputed by Nationalist and Communist forces we should seek to arrange a truce.

4. We should continue to support the efforts somewhat desultorily conducted by Nationalists and Communists to bring about a political settlement under Chiang Kai-shek and including the Communist areas and forces in a unified China state and Chinese army. (The Joint Chiefs doubted Chiang Kai-shek's capability to reunify China, and especially Manchuria, by military means.)

This summary was well received by the Cabinet group. Although a duality of policy is clearly apparent in it—the military support of Chiang Kai-shek against the Communists while sponsoring an attempt to work out a political agreement between them—it was not so clear to us at the time. As we shall see, in our talks about his instructions General Marshall worried from time to time that they might require a prestidigitator's skill to execute. But only later did we understand that we were, in effect, seeking the reconciliation of irreconcilable factions. The people's democracy of Mao would not willingly accept the dominance of Chiang Kai-shek nor a democratic China friendly to the United States, while the Nationalist Government could not impose its dominance on the Communists without the military intervention of the United States (if it could even with it) due to the ineptitude of the Kuomintang. That the policy adopted is now seen to have been doomed carries no implication that any other would not have been equally doomed. Hindsight does not carry comfort, like a St. Bernard to an exhausted traveler.

A WORD ABOUT GENERAL MARSHALL

The moment General Marshall entered a room everyone in it felt his presence. It was a striking and communicated force. His figure conveyed intensity, which his voice, low, staccato, and incisive, reinforced. It compelled respect. It spread a sense of authority and of calm. There was no military glamour about him and nothing of the martinet.

With General Marshall self-control came, as I suppose it always comes, from self-discipline. He was, in a phrase that has quite gone out of use, in command of himself. He could make himself go to bed and go to sleep on the eve of D Day because his work was done and he must be fresh for the decisions of the day to come. He could put aside the supreme command in Europe in favor of General Eisenhower because his plain duty was to stay in the Pentagon dealing with that vast complex of forces that, harnessed, meant victory.

My first meeting of any length with General Marshall left an abiding memory of his self-command. It was during the war. We had both gone to Hot Springs, Virginia, to address meetings of the Business Advisory Council of the Department of Commerce. At the time both Mrs. Marshall and the General's close colleague and friend, Field Marshal Sir John Dill, were seriously ill. But the General, having made the engagement, kept it, and was to fly back to Washington after he spoke. During dinner a note was brought to him informing him of the death of Sir John Dill. He spoke unhurriedly for an hour on the military situation, giving, with maps, an appreciation of the problems and possibilities on all fronts and the resources necessary to exploit them. After another hour to answer questions, all of which he did without involving security either by way of excuse for not answering or by indiscretion in answering, he went to his plane.

Never was I more conscious of how richly endowed was General Marshall than when, years ago, we talked through several long evenings about the considerations that led him to favor Operation Overlord (the invasion of Hitler's Europe across the Channel from England) over Mr. Churchill's plan to seek a junction with the Russians farther to the east by striking at the "soft underbelly of Europe" in the eastern Mediterranean.

What impressed me was the wide scope of the factors he had weighed. They went far beyond the purely military considerations and the usual political ones. He thought of the vast amount of shipping involved in shifting the allied army, its supplies and base, from England two thousand miles or more eastward, of the delay of perhaps a year in the final move on Japan, of a million additional casualties. He was aware of President Roosevelt's obviously deteriorating health, of the possible coincidence of the congressional election of 1946 with a crisis of the war in the Far East, and of the mutual and interacting effect of these momentous developments.

All elements of the problem were held, as it were, in solution in his mind until it was ready to precipitate a decision. This is the essence and the method —or rather the art—of judgment in its highest form. Not merely military judgment, but judgment in great affairs of state, which requires both mastery of precise information and apprehension of imponderables.

It is not by chance that the man who possessed this capacity served his country not as soldier-President—we have had many of these—but as General of the Army and Chief of Staff throughout the war, as Ambassador, Secretary of State, and Secretary of Defense. Here truly was a Man for All Seasons, a man who understood the relevancy to military decision and action of considerations transcending those of the service in which he had been trained, or even those thought only a few years ago to have been comprised within the whole field of military interest.

WE DRAFT THE GENERAL'S INSTRUCTIONS

At the time of his selection to go to China, General Marshall was appearing before the Senate's Pearl Harbor investigating committee. He requested specific written instructions governing his proposed mission to China. Mr. Byrnes turned to me and John Carter Vincent, already immersed in China policy, and shortly afterward read to General Marshall our memorandum outline of instructions. General Marshall did not approve it. It seemed to him to be susceptible of serious misunderstanding and that it was not definite enough to serve as a basis for a directive to General Wedemeyer, to give Chiang Kaishek an understanding of the number of troops available to him, or to inform the American public. He therefore tried his own hand at a draft with the help of Generals Thomas T. Handy, Deputy Chief of Staff, U.S. Army, John E. Hull, and Louis A. Craig. The draft of the four generals increased clarity and definiteness at the expense of one of the conflicting elements of policy. Vincent sought to restore a balance by amending the Marshall redraft to preclude the transport of Nationalist Government troops by the United States into areas, such as north China, when their introduction would prejudice the objectives of the military truce and the political negotiations. Secretary Byrnes and I supported Vincent's point and forwarded to General Marshall an amended version of the four generals' draft containing it.

General Hull complained to General Marshall that the amendment put a basic contradiction in the policy. Here he erred; the contradiction was there all the time. The real issue was what to do. General Hull was in favor of transporting the Nationalist armies north and taking over from the Japanese before attempting to negotiate a military truce and political settlement. The State Department officers believed that to do this would prejudice the attempt and perhaps precipitate civil war.

On Sunday, December 9, Secretary Byrnes and General Marshall met in Old State, with General Hull, Vincent, and myself present, to discuss the generals' draft with State's amendments. Mr. Byrnes made a strong statement in support of it; General Hull reiterated his worries about a basic contradiction in the statement of policy. In the meantime a message from Generals MacArthur and Wedemeyer and Admiral Raymond A. Spruance (Commander in Chief Pacific) to the Joint Chiefs opened an escape from direct confrontation in execution of policy between the diplomatists and the military. The Far East commanders approved the basic decision to move more Chinese armies north and to repatriate the Japanese troops, but suggested that its execution be left in General Marshall's hands in negotiating a compromise agreement between the major opposing groups in order to promote a unified, democratic China.

The upshot of the meeting was agreement upon General Marshall's draft as amended and giving to him discretion to determine when Chinese troops might be moved to north China consistently with the purposes of his mission. This was set forth in a memorandum from Secretary Byrnes to the War Department dated December 9, 1945, and approved by the President.

At this meeting and at two subsequent meetings with the President, General Marshall asked for specific agreement on how he should exercise his discretion to move Nationalist troops into north China in the event that negotiations for national unity broke down through the Generalissimo's failure to make reasonable concessions. On December 9 Mr. Byrnes replied that General Marshall should inform Chiang Kai-shek that no assistance to move the troops would be provided and that we would be forced to deal directly with the Communists in repatriating the Japanese from north China. At a meeting on December 11 with the President, Secretary Byrnes, and Admiral Leahy (at which I was not present), General Marshall raised the question again, apparently dissatisfied with Secretary Byrnes's earlier reply. He favored supporting the Generalissimo and moving the troops. The President and Secretary agreed.

At this meeting the President also went over and approved the statement of policy and the memorandum to the War Department. A letter from the President to General Marshall to which the other documents would be attached was not yet completed. This I brought to him when General Marshall and I (Secretary Byrnes having gone to Moscow) met with him on December 14. He inquired whether the papers before us had been approved by all concerned. Told that they had been, he signed the letter and handed it and the enclosures to General Marshall.† General Marshall then said that he would like (possibly for emphasis, possibly because I, now Acting Secretary, had not been present on December 11) to go over once again his instructions in the event of failure of the negotiations. He repeated them as recorded here, and again the President concurred and asked whether anything further could be done to facilitate his mission.

The General said that he would need what was known in the Army as a rear echelon, a person left behind with right of access at any time to the Commander in Chief, in this case the President, through whom General Marshall would communicate. This man would bear personal responsibility for immediate reply and for action upon his requests, with authority to call on the President himself for help, if necessary, to get action. The General would want an Army officer detailed to handle incoming and outgoing messages through Army channels, which would be used exclusively as they were the only reliable facilities in China. This officer would deliver the messages to the rear echelon personally, not through a secretary, and would receive the answers. General Marshall wanted personal, not institutional, responsibility. He was no stranger to Washington bureaucracy.

When the President agreed and asked whom he would select, the General said that he would like to have me charged with this duty. I asked that my assuming it be cleared with Secretary Byrnes, pointing out that I would necessarily have to act out of channels and, probably, annoy a good many people in fulfilling this assignment. My intuition was entirely correct. The relationships established in those few minutes greatly affected my life. They were also to create most confusing and difficult conflicts of loyalties. The beginning of these was not far distant.

We walked across the street to my office. The General asked whether I knew a suitable officer with whom I could work happily on his communications. I did. General John Hilldring, Chief of G-5, military government, on the Army staff, had an able aide, Colonel James A. Davis, a lawyer in civil life from Cedar Rapids, Iowa. He had earned my respect by outmaneuvering us several times in the past. I mentioned him, adding for its stimulating effect that General Hilldring would probably not let him go. Hilldring had been saved by General Marshall from retirement when he had a heart attack while commanding a division and been put into a Pentagon job. He had a drill-field voice. We used to tell him not to bother with the telephone, just to open his Pentagon window and speak naturally. I got him on the telephone. General Marshall's end of the conversation went something like this:

"Hilldring? General Marshall speaking. Do you have a Colonel James Davis? Very well. Have him detached and assigned to duty with Acheson at the State Department." A dull crackling came from the receiver. "Did you say something, Hilldring? Tomorrow morning will do."

After waiting a discreet period, Hilldring called me back. The receiver crackled again as a colorful description of my character as seen from G-5 came over the wire. Jim Davis proved as capable as I thought he would be and later received from General Marshall an oak leaf cluster on his military medal. General Hilldring became my colleague as Assistant Secretary of State for Occupied Areas in April 1946 and served until September 1947.

MONTHS OF HOPE

General Marshall's mission to China went on throughout the whole year 1946. It falls into three periods. From the beginning until April 18, when the General returned to China after a brief visit to the United States, were months of hope. Then hope was succeeded by reluctant and growing pessimism, until in October China plunged into a long civil war that led, finally, to the collapse of the Nationalist Government. The last two months saw the liquidation and withdrawal of the mission. It is not my purpose to detail its history but to view it from the point of view of its Washington agent, destined to inherit the consequences of its failure.

By the beginning of January we had Colonel Davis and a small staff installed in the State Department to provide liaison with the Pentagon in communicating with the General. I had also arranged to have W. Walton Butterworth, then Counselor of Embassy in Madrid and my old friend from the days of economic warfare in the Iberian Peninsula, ordered to China to run the embassy there. Minister Walter Robertson assisted General Marshall at Executive Headquarters (the joint Nationalist-Communist-American organization supervising the armistice). Butterworth's Far Eastern experience had been only as a vice consul in Singapore in 1929–31, but he was one of our most able and resourceful officers and I counted on him to supply what the General would also need on his staff: energy and imagination to deal with wholly novel situations. Thus began five years of intensive experience in Chinese affairs, entailing painful, even near disastrous, consequences for this friend and colleague. That they did not impair our friendship is a measure of his generosity.

In the first few weeks after his arrival in China, General Marshall achieved a personal dominance of the situation and produced an apparent movement toward compromise, which raised our hopes. In part this came from cautious maneuvering by both Chinese sides while appraising the extent and significance of the new American intervention through our most imposing citizen. Neither side wished to cast the first stone. Each found in the truncated statement of policy that the White House made public on December 15, 1945 (as the General later reported) "justification for its attitude."

We have already described the strength of the three military forces in north China when General Marshall arrived—the Nationalists, the Communists, and the Japanese. The Communists were demanding a cease-fire and end of the reinforcement of Nationalist strength in north China. The Nationalists' precondition was that the Communists cease cutting Nationalist communications. On the political side, also, the General found another fundamental cleavage between the viewpoints of the Kuomintang and the Communist Party. The former contended that the integration of the Communist forces into a national army should precede the establishment of a coalition government, while the Communists were equally insistent that a coalition government in which they had a substantial voice should precede the integration of the forces. Again, while the two parties had agreed that constitutional questions not already settled between them should go to a Political Consultative Conference (PCC), each side wanted to hold the conference when it was ahead militarily.

General Marshall's strategy was to concentrate first on a cease-fire as essential to the solution of other problems and a psychological prelude to opening the Political Consultative Conference, and then to tie solutions of other problems together in a comprehensive package that both parties would prefer to returning to war. This rested on the premise that a compromise could be devised which both would trade for their chances of total victory. This proved to be an illusion, but not at first. In January it seemed full of promise. A Committee of Three, with General Marshall presiding and Generals Chang Shun and Chou En-lai (whose ability much impressed the General) representing the Nationalists and Communists respectively, recommended the terms of a cease-fire and permissible movements of troops, which Chiang and Mao proclaimed on January 10. An elaborate organization policed it, headed by three commissioners, with Walter Robertson presiding and an operations section headed by Colonel Henry A. Byroade, USA, with a hundred and twenty-five American members and a hundred and seventy from each of the two Chinese sides. In a short time the fighting stopped in north China. Problems proved less malleable in Manchuria.

On the political side progress was equally promising. The Political Consultative Conference met from January 10 to 31 and reached agreement on directives in five areas: government organization, a program for peaceful national reconstruction, military problems, the National Assembly, and revision of the 1936 draft constitution. The last held the seeds of future trouble. The Kuomintang believed that PCC principles, which represented the views of the Chinese liberals as well as the Communists, were too liberal and opened the way for capture of the government by the Communists; it wished to retain a maximum of power in a minimum number of hands, General Marshall reported. He was encouraged, reporting at the beginning of February:

Affairs are progressing rather favorably. The Political Consultative Conference did their job well and included enough of the details of the interim constitution I had most confidentially given the Generalissimo to provide a fairly definite basis for a democratic coalition government. . . .

As to the nationalization of the armies . . . prospects are favorable for a solution to this most difficult of all the problems.

I am getting lined up to expedite the formation of the coalition government. . . . If agreement [is reached on these two matters] then I will be ready to propose . . . discussions in the U.S. regarding financial loans.

The "Basis for Military Reorganization and for the Integration of the Communist Forces into the National Army" was signed by the two Chinese sides on February 25, 1946. General Marshall had played a major role in the negotiation of this important agreement. The new army was to consist of sixty divisions, of which fifty were to be Nationalist Government divisions and ten Communist, mixed together in several armies. All other units on both sides should be demobilized. The armies would be stationed in certain numerical strengths in various parts of China. Manchuria should have fifteen divisions, of which fourteen should be Nationalist; in northwest China, all should be Nationalist. When the Communists dragged their feet in executing the agreement because—so the General thought—of the shabby comparison of their troops beside the American-equipped-and-trained Nationalists, he offered similar equipment and training for the elements of their ten divisions when selected and assigned. But the trouble lay deeper. Agreement to execute the Basic Plan under the Executive Headquarters was reached on February 27 and signed March 16, but the Communists refused to designate the ten divisions until full and public agreement was reached on the implementation of the PCC resolutions. The Central Committee of the Kuomintang, meeting March 1 to 17, was intended to do so; and General Marshall left for Washington March 11 to arrange the financial credits, hopeful that both interim government and army integration were well on their way to acceptance.

But, alas, neither was to occur. Indications soon appeared that that "approval had been hedged by reservations and that irreconcilable elements within the Kuomintang were endeavoring to sabotage the PCC program," whereupon the Communist Party and the Democratic League refused to nominate members to the State Council (of the interim government), and the Communists also refused to approve the PCC resolutions. General Marshall later concluded that "no real settlement of governmental and constitutional questions in China could be reached so long as the Manchuria problem remained unsolved."[1] Perhaps we might add today, or vice versa. We shall return to that problem after a brief look at the Washington scene.

While General Marshall was having successes in China, we of the rear echelon were getting together tools and information for him. At the time both he and we thought that the command of economic resources would be invaluable in his bargaining. The President, in his December 15, 1945, letter to General Marshall, had written: "In your conversations with Chiang Kai-shek and other Chinese leaders you are authorized to speak with the utmost frankness. Particularly, you may state, in connection with the Chinese desire for credits . . . that a China disunited and torn by civil strife could not be considered realistically as a proper place for American assistance along the lines enumerated."[2] But, as we were soon to learn in Europe, it was easier to offer credits than to find the funds, with lend-lease ending, demobilization in full swing, Congress cutting appropriations, and the domestic economy calling for goods of every sort. Even with the President's full support, the obstacles in the way of a seeker-for-funds-and-goods for China were formidable. First, the National Advisory Council established by the Bretton Woods legislation had to give its approval to foreign credits, with Secretary of the Treasury Vinson, its chairman, and the Treasury bureaucracy, its staff, both bent on achieving a balanced budget. The Export-Import Bank took a skeptical view of the Nationalist Government's probity and competence in managing borrowed funds. The Nationalists' existing resources available for stabilization and expenditure were not crystal clear, nor were the activities of their host of missions, agents, and lobbyists working for a five-hundred-sixty-million-dollar credit toward a three-year program of reconstruction amounting to about two billion dollars. UNRRA reportedly had under consideration five hundred million dollars in materials for delivery by March 1947. Those in charge of property disposal in the Pacific as yet hardly knew what they had available. Lastly, to discover what and how much China in its existing state of disorganization could absorb was perhaps the most difficult problem of all.

Skeptics could, and did, ask who, in a contest for supreme control in China, where the winner took all, would be influenced to do what by this carrot of economic and financial aid. Hardly the Communists, who could well doubt that, if they won, the United States would finance them. More and more the Kuomintang evinced the conviction that pursuit of a united and democratic China meant that they would lose all. That their own policy of seeking a military decision would lead to the same result did not weaken this conviction. By the time General Marshall returned to Washington in March 1946 he was able to assemble an imposing—or, at least, respectable—bundle of carrots consisting of the revival of lend-lease to cover equipment and supplies, if agreed before June 30, 1946; cotton credits of thirty million dollars; credits for transportation and telecommunications; Export-Import Bank credit of five hundred million dollars (though hedged about by the need for approval of specific projects, and progress toward internal stability); and arrangements for acquiring surplus property such as river boats and for settling wartime accounts. Finally, the United States share of UNRRA goods delivered to China through 1947 would amount to approximately four hundred seventy-five million dollars. All of this had been preceded by orders under presidential authority to stop all civilian agencies and the Army and Navy departments from negotiating with the Chinese and centering all authority to do so in General Marshall. During this period the Chinese authorities in Washington were about as difficult to deal with as the Russians had been during the war. They examined all of every gift horse's teeth, and gave it a thorough checkup as well.

17. THE ACHESON-LILIENTHAL REPORT

HARDLY HAD Secretary Byrnes caught his breath after the Moscow conference when he was off again on January 7, 1946, to London for the first meeting of the General Assembly of the United Nations. Again the command passed to me and with it a collection of tasks and troubles great and small. They revealed that my relations with the President and the Secretary of State were to be more complicated than even the first three months had suggested. My first trouble was a small one, a social *faux pas,* which came close to worsening our already deteriorating relations with the Russians.

A SOCIAL FAUX PAS †

In January the President decided that the annual diplomatic dinner at the White House, discontinued during the war, should be reinstated. Stanley Woodward, Chief of Protocol, brought me the word and a problem caused by the population explosion of nation-states. If following past practice all the chiefs of mission, their deputies, and the wives of both were invited together with the essential official Americans and wives, the dinner would swamp the White House. How could the number be divided and yet avoid the impression of first- and second-class affairs? Like a good staff officer, Woodward was ready with a suggested solution of his own problem: to number the missions in their alphabetical order and invite the odd numbers for one date and the even numbers for another. It seemed a brilliant idea and immediately found favor at the White House. Alas, we overlooked an elemental precaution—careful scrutiny of the resulting lists.

On the afternoon before the first dinner Woodward was informed by a female voice with fragmentary command of English that the Soviet Ambassador and his Counselor had unfortunately been taken ill and regretted that they would be unable to dine with the President. To be sure that we were not the victims of a practical joke, we put through a call to Ambassador Nicolai V. Novikov, which found him apparently gay and cheerful in New York. However, inquiries about his health and plans for the evening brought confirmation of poor health in the Soviet Embassy. Woodward went off to rearrange the seating.

No cloud darkened the dinner. It was the Trumans' first state affair, conducted with a dignity that I found agreeable after the bonhommie of FDR. The

President made no comment on the absence of the Russians. Our colleagues in the Eastern European Office, however, soon found the cause of the trouble. Our odd-and-even selection had invited to the same dinner the envoys of the USSR and Lithuania, whose country, along with Latvia and Estonia, had been swallowed by the Soviet Union though they are still recognized by us as independent states. Doubtless poor Novikov had only received instructions at the last moment. So when we were sent for next morning by the President, Woodward and I were prepared for a good wigging for sloppy work.

We were not, however, prepared to be directed to tell the Soviet Ambassador that he was no longer welcome here, since he had been inexcusably rude to Mrs. Truman. We threw ourselves into the breach, explaining Novikov's dilemma, proclaiming our own ineptitude, warning of the serious consequences of such a step and the dismay of even our best friends abroad. The President remained adamant. Matt Connelly came in and handed him the telephone, saying, "Mrs. Truman." He listened for a while, and then said, "I'm talking with him now. He agrees with you." After listening again, he handed the receiver to me. I must not, Mrs. Truman said, let the President go through with his plan. I agreed in the objective, but asked for operating instructions. Mrs. Truman thought delay while the President's temper cooled the best procedure. She added that if he went ahead his critics would have a field day. This gave me an idea. While she talked I murmured in horror pretending to repeat phrases that she never uttered, such as ". . . above himself . . . delusions of grandeur . . . too big for his britches . . ."

The President took the receiver away from me. "All right, all right," he said. "When you gang up on me I know I'm licked. Let's forget all about it." He hung up the receiver, already smiling, and picked up an old-fashioned gold-filigree photograph frame, opened it, and handed me a photograph of a young woman in the costume of my youth.

"I guess you think I'm an old fool," he said, "and I probably am. Look on the back," he added. There was written, "Dear Harry, May this photograph bring you safely home again from France—Bess." It was dated 1917.

As we went out he called after us, "Tell Old Novocaine we didn't miss him!"

STALIN'S SPEECH AND KENNAN'S REPORT

Evidence had been accumulating that Stalin was steering foreign policy of the Soviet Union on an ominous course. On February 9, 1946, before a vast "election" audience in Moscow, he stated with brutal clarity the Soviet Union's postwar policy.[1] Finding the causes of the late war in the necessities of capitalist-imperialist monopoly and the same forces still in control abroad, he concluded that no peaceful international order was possible. The Soviet Union must, therefore, be capable of guarding against any eventuality. The basic materials of national defense—iron and steel—must be trebled, and coal and oil, the sources of energy, doubled. Consumer goods, so desperately needed in

Russia, must wait on rearmament. This grim news depressed even the ebullient spirits of the Secretary of State. They were soon to be depressed even further.

In response to a request for elucidation of this startling speech, George F. Kennan, then Chargé d'Affaires in Moscow, cabled a long and truly remarkable dispatch. It had a deep effect on thinking within the Government, although Government response with action still needed a year's proof of Soviet intentions as seen by Kennan. He found "at the bottom of the Kremlin's neurotic view of world affairs" centuries of a Russian fear of physical, and a tyranny's fear of political, insecurity. To the Government, whether czarist or bolshevik, penetration by the Western world was its greatest danger. Marxism "with its basic altruism of purpose" furnished them with justification for their "fear of [the] outside world. . . . In the name of Marxism they sacrificed every single ethical value in their methods and tactics. Today they cannot dispense with it. It is [the] fig leaf of their moral and intellectual respectability."

Kennan predicted that Soviet policy would be to use every means to infiltrate, divide, and weaken the West. Means would include the foreign communist parties, diplomacy, international organizations—blocking what they did not like, starting false trails to divert—probing weak spots by every means. To seek a *modus vivendi* with Moscow would prove chimerical, a process leading not to an end but only to political warfare. His recommendations—to be of good heart, to look to our own social and economic health, to present a good face to the world, all of which the Government was trying to do—were of no help; his historical analysis might or might not have been sound, but his predictions and warnings could not have been better.[2] We responded to them slowly.

INTERNATIONAL CONTROL OF ATOMIC ENERGY

My principal task and concern during my chief's absence was an assignment that he had given me a few minutes before boarding his plane for London. Typically, we had had no prior discussion of it or of the policy decision upon which it was based and which was contrary to that which I had recommended to the President in September. In my schizophrenic official life what had seemed policy in the autumn was a hallucination in the winter. Instead of beginning our exploration of international control of atomic energy by consultation with the British and Russians before going into a larger body, we had been committed in November to starting off in a United Nations commission. However, my present assignment was not when or how to start, but what to start with.

The Secretary reached me in my bed at home, where I had been laid low by influenza, to tell me of my appointment as chairman of a committee to draft a plan for the international control of atomic energy. Protests that I knew nothing about the subject were waved aside with the cheering answer that other members of the committee knew a lot. They were to be Dr. Vannevar Bush, President of the Carnegie Institution and former Director of the Office of

Scientific Research and Development; Dr. James B. Conant, President of Harvard; General Leslie R. Groves, Commandant of the Manhattan Project, which built the Hiroshima and Nagasaki bombs; and John J. McCloy, former Assistant Secretary of War under Colonel Stimson—a strong group.

The committee obviously could not remain in continuous session to do the necessary preparatory work, nor did its members have sufficient technical and engineering knowledge of all phases of nuclear development. Here my brilliant and imaginative assistant, Herbert Marks, came to the rescue, suggesting that we supplement the committee with a Board of Consultants. His first nominee, David E. Lilienthal, Chairman of the Tennessee Valley Authority, helped us with the selection of the others—Chester I. Barnard, President of the New Jersey Bell Telephone Company; Dr. J. Robert Oppenheimer, formerly Director of the Los Alamos Atomic Laboratory but at that time back at the University of California at Berkeley; Dr. Charles A. Thomas, Vice President of Monsanto Chemical Company; and Harry A. Winne, Vice President of General Electric Company. Their function, as I reported it, was to ascertain and report the facts concerning atomic energy that were relevant to the problem of safeguards and controls, including inspection, and to give an appraisal of that problem and of the potential of other nations in the field of atomic energy as compared with the United States. The committee approved the idea of the Board of Consultants and its membership.

The two groups worked closely and harmoniously together. My own contribution was principally in bringing this about and maintaining it. The strength of our report would lie not only in its substance but its unanimity. In a field so esoteric, the united recommendation of a group so qualified would carry great authority. We had among us some whose individuality of thought and opinion was not easily blended, but blending was of the essence; it fell largely to David Lilienthal, Herbert Marks, and me. The consultants led by Lilienthal and Oppenheimer met and worked almost continuously with Herbert Marks and with Dr. Bush's assistant, Carroll L. Wilson—and intermittently with me—until they had a paper to submit to the full group. It held four plenary, all-day meetings on March 7, 8, 16, and 17 at Dumbarton Oaks, the beautiful mansion that Mr. and Mrs. Robert Woods Bliss restored to house their Byzantine collection and later gave to Harvard University. We began by reading the paper aloud and ended by either approving, amending, or directing a reworking of each section. The main idea to come out of the committee was that there should be a proposal, even if in very general terms, as to how one got through a transitional stage into international control. Why not add a section at the end of the report, I suggested, that would provide one? To this we turned our main attention. Reviewing the minutes of these meetings, two points I made seem worth recalling. We should not, as one member suggested, use the effort for international control of atomic energy to attempt to open up Russian society, or expect an agreement to do away with Soviet-American tensions or the posssibility of war. We should insist that in exchange for submitting to control, vivid danger signals would be provided to show whether and when that control was being evaded.

All the participants would, I think, agree that the most stimulating and creative mind among us was Robert Oppenheimer's. On this task he was also at his most constructive and accommodating. Robert could be argumentative, sharp, and, on occasion, pedantic, but no such problem intruded here.

When later I achieved a wholly undeserved reputation for expertise in nuclear matters, no one knew better than Robert Oppenheimer how fraudulent this was. At the beginning of our work he came to stay with us and after dinner each evening would lecture McCloy and me with the aid of a borrowed blackboard on which he drew little figures representing electrons, neutrons, and protons, bombarding one another, chasing one another about, dividing and generally carrying on in unpredictable ways. Our bewildered questions seemed to distress him. At last he put down the chalk in gentle despair, saying, "It's hopeless! I really think you two believe neutrons and electrons *are* little men!" We admitted nothing.

In such a group of strong-minded men with very fixed views in this field, unanimous agreement at times seemed impossible; yet at our last meeting we were about to reach it when a dispute arose over the drafting of a critical paragraph. At first I thought the problem a mere choice of words, but soon to my dismay a series of compromises appeared to be coming unstuck. At this point Herbert Marks's invaluable secretary, Miss Anne Wilson (now Mrs. Herbert Marks), made a brilliant contribution. She whispered in my ear, "Recess the meeting for coffee." I did so. She brought coffee, doughnuts, and cheerful conversation. I collected Conant, Oppenheimer, Lilienthal, and Groves and gave them a new form of words, suggested that they change them as they wished, and, when the committee came to order, introduce their joint solution. Anne circulated, keeping the rest happy until our quartet had solved the problem. This they did to our satisfaction.

A letter from the committee to the Secretary of State transmitting and joining in the consultants' report I drafted myself while my colleagues went out for lunch. Into it went peripheral and cautionary views of the committee members, thus making them heard without breaking the continuity and thought of the report. This compromise satisfied all my colleagues.

The report became known as the Acheson-Lilienthal report after the chairmen of the committee and the board, but, as I have said, it was the work of the whole group, to which each made valuable contributions. Although a series of closely connected proposals, which revealed the broad-minded internationalism of American policy, its basic conception was stated simply by Dr. Bush and me over the radio after its publication:

In plain words, the Report sets up a plan under which no nation would make atomic bombs or the materials for them. All dangerous activities would be carried on—not merely inspected—by a live, functioning international Authority with a real purpose in the world and capable of attracting competent personnel. This monopoly of the dangerous activities by an international Authority would still leave a large and tremendously productive field of *safe* activities open to individual nations, their industries and universities. . . .

. . . the extremely favored position with regard to atomic devices, which the United States enjoys at present, is *only temporary. It will not last.* We must use that advantage now to promote international security and to carry out our policy of building a lasting peace through international agreement.[3]

Presenting the report to Mr. Byrnes on the Sunday evening on which it was finished, I urged him to release it as soon as the President approved. The public at home and abroad should be allowed to read the document itself and not a distorted version made out of rumors and leaks. In agreeing, he told me that he would recommend to the President that Bernard M. Baruch be appointed, as he has somewhat unflatteringly put it, "for the task of translating the various proposals stimulated by the Acheson-Lilienthal report into a workable plan."[4]

I protested, distrusting Mr. Baruch's translation and dissenting from Mr. Byrnes's—and the generally held—view that this so-called "adviser of Presidents" was a wise man. My own experience led me to believe that his reputation was without foundation in fact and entirely self-propagated. Mr. Baruch was undoubtedly a money maker through shrewd stock market speculations, as he himself has claimed.[5] He made equally shrewd political use of his fortune, rarely squandering it on large party contributions, but dispensing it judiciously—and often nonpartisanly—in small individual contributions to senatorial and congressional primary or election campaigns. This practice multiplied his admirers in the Congress while his gifted friend, Herbert Bayard Swope, polished his public "image." My plea was useless. Mr. Byrnes, like his successor, General Marshall, had fallen victim to Mr. Baruch's spell.

After submission of the report to the Secretary, I performed my duty to the Senate-House Joint Committee on Atomic Energy, chaired by Senator McMahon, by explaining and giving it to them also. This occurred at an executive hearing on March 25. To no one's surprise, an account of the report appeared in the afternoon newspapers. When the Department released the full text three days later, the press gave it extensive publicity intensified by the discussion it received in public and private groups. This was neither surprising nor undesired, since one purpose of the exercise was governmental and public education in the actual problems involved in the international control of this radical new force so glibly talked about and so little understood. To Mr. Baruch this was a source of annoyance, he said to me a little later, as the report rapidly began to be regarded as official policy without any approval by the Secretary or the President.

However it soon ceased to be. On April 10 Mr. Byrnes wrote to me that while he had agreed to a suggestion originating with the committee that with the filing of the report it be discharged, "Mr. Baruch, who has been appointed by the President to the [United Nations] Atomic Energy Commission, is very earnest in his request that I urge you and the gentlemen associated with you to continue to act in an advisory capacity on this subject." The committee was divided in its response to this proposal, but the consultants believed that to be of any use they would have to work full time, which they could not do. Moreover, they insisted on remaining free to express their own ideas, which they held so strongly. They all, however, agreed to meet with Mr. Baruch and his group—Herbert Swope, John Hancock, Ferdinand Eberstadt, Fred Searls, General Thomas F. Farrell, and Richard C. Tolman—at the Blair-Lee House on May 17 and 18.

These meetings made clear that others would not be profitable, but unhappily the release did not extend to me. Mr. Baruch enlarged upon some points of disagreement with the report, his principal one being the report's failure to recommend sanctions to be provided in the scheme of international control as punishments for violations of it. Mr. Byrnes has explained the Baruch view: "He [Mr. Baruch] insisted the plan should provide that, once the treaty was ratified, any government violating its treaty obligation and developing or using atomic energy for destructive purposes should be subjected to swift and sure punishment; and in case of violation no one of the permanent members of the Security Council should be permitted to veto punitive action by the council."[6]

This matter had been discussed at length by the committee. After careful analysis we had concluded that provisions for either "swift and sure," or "condign," punishment for violation of the treaty were very dangerous words that added nothing to a treaty and were almost certain to wreck any possibility of Russian acceptance of one. The Soviet Union was undoubtedly doing all in its power to develop nuclear weapons at the moment. (Just under four years later the Soviet Union exploded its first nuclear device.) If so, the "swift and sure punishment" provision could be interpreted in Moscow only as an attempt to turn the United Nations into an alliance to support a United States threat of war against the USSR unless it ceased its efforts, for only the United States could conceivably administer "swift and sure" punishment to the Soviet Union. This meant the certain defeat of the treaty by Soviet veto. On the other hand, if some other nation was charged with a violation (including possibly ourselves) what, if anything, could be done would depend upon what nation it was, its relation to either the Soviet Union or the United States, the circumstances, and whether these two nations were agreed or at odds (the latter seemed more likely) about what should be done.

Into these complexities intruded the problem of the veto. "Swift and sure punishment" for violation of the treaty, if realistically considered, seemed uncomfortably close to war, or certainly to sanctions that under the United Nations treaty were subject to the veto of permanent members of the Security Council. Did it seem likely that they would forgo it here? The only practicable safeguard in case of violations would be clear notice and warning that they were occurring. This would give other parties to the treaty knowledge that it was being breached and an opportunity to take such action, separately or collectively, for their own protection as might be possible. Provisions for paper police sanctions to be imposed by the same parties were only an illusion. These views were explained fully to Mr. Baruch.

Other proposals by the Baruch group seemed to the consultants to weaken their plan by moving away from the concept of the international authority as the sole performer of dangerous activities toward that of a regulation of their performance by others. At the end of the two days no meeting of minds had occurred. Mr. Baruch asked the consultants to summarize their recommendations in writing, which they did. Both they and the committee then dissolved as organized units and the members went their various ways. I, however, remained.

At the end of May Messrs. Baruch and Hancock had two meetings with Mr. Byrnes and me about their operating instructions, at which they stated their ideas for modifying the report and I explained it. The Secretary overruled two of their proposals—one for a preliminary raw-material survey, the other for expanding the UN Atomic Energy Commission's field of study and recommendation to include other weapons. Mr. Byrnes discussed the matter of "automatic sanctions" with the President, who approved Mr. Baruch's position. Instructed to prepare a draft instruction for Mr. Baruch on the basis of our recommendations as modified by decisions of the President and the Secretary, Herbert Marks and I did so. After several further versions back and forth, the President approved the policy.

Throughout this episode, as throughout the one related in the next chapter, relations between my chief and myself remained cordial and easy. But both experiences, occurring almost coincidentally, led me to review my position carefully and to attempt a precautionary measure, which—perhaps fortunately —did not come off, as the next chapter also relates. Relations with Mr. Baruch went on smoothly when in Mr. Byrnes's absence I had to obtain advice and assistance for him in his arduous negotiation, but I had no doubt that, as he himself made clear later, he deeply distrusted me. During the summer amusing evidence of this cropped up.

After a telephone conversation in August Mr. Baruch wrote to me as follows: ". . . before you came on the phone, a voice in your office said, 'Put on recorder one or four.'† I do not know whether there was any significance in this remark. What I should like to know is whether the conversations that pass between myself and your office are recorded, and if so, whether you would be good enough to send me a copy of the recordings."

I replied at once that I had no recording device in the office and had had no stenographic record taken. He could put his mind at ease about the privacy of our conversations.

Mr. Baruch proposed the U.S. plan with considerable fanfare. The UN Atomic Energy Commission discussed it for the rest of the year and in late December, with the USSR and Poland abstaining, voted 10 to 0 to recommend adoption of a comprehensive international system. Its report substantially adopted the American plan. There the matter died. Mr. Molotov rather neatly escaped a propaganda defeat by introducing in the General Assembly, and strongly urging, a plan for a general regulation and reduction of armaments.

18. THE DEPARTMENT MUFFS ITS
INTELLIGENCE ROLE

THE NATURE OF INTELLIGENCE

THE BATTLE WITHIN the Department over disposition of the research and intelligence units transferred from the Office of Strategic Services in October 1945 is worth recalling to catch the first warning of McCarthyism to come, and to understand the self-inflicted wounds which impaired the standing of the State Department within the Government. It brought out, too, the issue between the bureaucracy and myself over where decisions should be made and where command should lie. The attitude that presidents and secretaries may come and go but the Department goes on forever has led many presidents to distrust and dislike the Department of State.

Intelligence is information, a key to decision: "It deals with all the things which should be known in advance of initiating a course of action."[1] It is both a process and a product—the process of information collection, and the product "from the collection, evaluation, analysis, integration and interpretation of all available information."[2] Intelligence is of different types: counterintelligence attempts to frustrate hostile foreign intelligence operations; operational intelligence, to aid the conduct of a specific mission; strategic intelligence, to gather information regarding the capabilities, vulnerabilities, and intentions of foreign nations to aid foreign policy decision of the most vital importance and at the highest level. As Sherman Kent has written: "If foreign policy is the shield of the republic . . . then strategic intelligence is the thing that gets the shield to the right place at the right time."[3]

Prior to the Second World War the United States had the most rudimentary foreign intelligence service. The Department's technique of gathering information, I told the House Appropriations Committee, "differed only by reason of the typewriter and the telegraph from the techniques which John Quincy Adams was using in St. Petersburg and Benjamin Franklin was using in Paris." Referring to the Army's intelligence service up to the same time, General Eisenhower has recorded that there was "a shocking deficiency that impeded all constructive planning," and General Marshall that our foreign intelligence was "little more than what a military attaché could learn at a dinner, more or less, over the coffee cups."[4]

By the time of Pearl Harbor, techniques had improved but not that of picking out the "significant sounds" from the "background noises," as Roberta

Wohlstetter has brilliantly pointed out.[5] At that time all the information to anticipate the attack was available but not the organization and techniques to evaluate and disseminate it to the right places at the right time with the right orders.

In 1942 the Army and Navy combined their efforts into a Joint Intelligence Committee as a defensive alliance against Colonel William (Wild Bill) Donovan's OSS—also under their jurisdiction.† By the end of the war, he had twelve thousand people in all branches of his intelligence operation. A year before the State Department had eighteen persons specifically assigned to this work.[6] In 1943 Donovan's plea to the Chiefs of Staff for a centralized service was blocked in the Pentagon. The next year he carried an appeal to the White House, which invited the views of the Joint Chiefs. Their views leaked to the press, whereupon, amid charges of a Gestapo and so on, a general Donnybrook ensued. The State Department inherited with Research and Intelligence from OSS a major role in a civil war.

When President Truman turned his attention to this problem, one thing was clear to him—the hour for improvement had struck. He had before him a recommendation from Secretary Byrnes, shared by the Budget Bureau, that an intelligence agency should be responsible to the Secretary of State; Donovan's plea for a permanent centralized intelligence agency; and the armed services' view that "complete merger of the intelligence services of the State, War, and Navy departments is not considered feasible since each of these departments requires operating intelligence peculiar to itself" and their recommendation of a Central Intelligence Agency "to coordinate [that slippery word again] and, as far as practicable, unify all foreign intelligence activities and to synthesize . . ." etc., etc.[7] The President turned over both Colonel Donovan's intelligence facilities and the solution of the intelligence problem to the Secretary of State.†

PRIMACY IS OFFERED TO THE DEPARTMENT

"I particularly desire," the President wrote Mr. Byrnes, "that you take the lead in developing a comprehensive and coordinated foreign intelligence program for all Federal agencies concerned with that type of activity. This should be done through the creation of an Inter-departmental Group, heading up under the State Department, which should formulate plans for my approval." This order seemed plain enough. So did the plan of the Budget Bureau upon which the President was acting. This had been shown to Mr. Byrnes, by him to me, and agreed between us as our procedure when he had offered and I had accepted the Under Secretaryship. The plan provided that the Secretary of State should be the focal point for leadership in intelligence activities, which should be supervised by a civilian director—a State Department man—enabled to speak with authority by reason of heading a strong, unified intelligence organization within the State Department. To form this organization, the bureau recommended, and the President on September 20 ordered, the transfer of the Research and Intelligence personnel to State.

Colonel Alfred McCormack of Army Intelligence had already been designated by Secretary Byrnes, at my suggestion, as his Special Assistant for Research and Intelligence. On October 1, as Acting Secretary, I gave him the necessary instructions to carry out the President's order. These, as they stated, had already been cleared with the Secretary. Colonel McCormack had earned a high reputation during the war for his intelligence work in the Army. Before that, as a partner in one of New York's largest and best-known law firms, he stood at the forefront of the rising younger men at the bar. So far as organization within the Department was concerned, his orders directed him to survey the various parts of the OSS to determine what units and personnel the State Department should retain beyond the terminal date of January 1, to survey organizations within the Department engaged in intelligence work to decide what should be transferred to the intelligence group. The final step should be to "consolidate the units within OSS which we wish to retain and the units of the Department of State now participating in intelligence activities so that, by January 1, all intelligence activities within the Department will be under your [i.e., Colonel McCormack's] own control."

WE MEET OPPOSITION

At this point Colonel McCormack and I encountered heavy flak. It came from three sources: congressional opposition to professional intelligence work, civil disobedience in the State Department, and indecision in high places brought on by military opposition to both unification of the services and civilian control of intelligence.

The Congress struck the first blow. Clamoring to reduce appropriations made for the war, the House cut eight and a half billion dollars beyond the President's recommendation. This reduced the amount transferred to us for intelligence work by eleven and a half million dollars. What was left was not enough to finish the current fiscal year. Appearing before the Senate committee to ask for restoration of a small part of these funds, McCormack met, especially from the chairman, Senator Kenneth McKellar, a hostile and suspicious attitude toward the basic idea of a professional intelligence service. Colonel McCormack was heckled and sniped at, and the cut was sustained.[8] A supplemental budget estimate was prepared.

Meanwhile, in the State Department the geographic divisions were moving into solid opposition to intelligence work not in their organizations and under their control. "Among the conservative element of the department," writes an historian of this period, "which was also the regnant element, there was little or no comprehension of what intelligence was and no disposition to support an intelligence staff."[9] The Assistant Secretary for Administration, Donald Russell, was of the same opinion. He met McCormack's supplemental budget request to hold his organization together with the question "of whether the intelligence research of the Department should not be done on a decentralized basis (in the various functional and geographic offices) instead of on a centralized basis as contemplated in the budget estimate."[10]

On October 27 I called to my office the persons principally involved in this growing controversy in an effort to head it off. McCormack and I attempted to explain the nature of the work his organization proposed to do and its importance both within the Department and to the Department within the Government.

It soon became apparent that the opposition sprang from Spruille Braden and Loy Henderson, Chiefs of the Latin American and Near Eastern divisions, and Russell and his assistant, Joseph Panuch, from the administrative side. Braden was a bull of a man physically and with the temperament and tactics of one, dealing with the objects of his prejudices by blind charges, preceded by pawing up a good deal of dust. He did both here. Later, in 1954, stating his views to a Senate Subcommittee on "Interlocking Subversion," he described McCormack's staff as "alphabet men," inexperienced, who did their work badly and were not needed. "We . . . resisted this invasion of all these swarms of people . . . mostly collectivists and 'do-gooders' and what-nots." It was, he said, "a knockdown, dragout fight." At the meeting I called, he told the committee, he had thumbed through the directive to the intelligence group and come to an instantaneous decision: "I protest on this proposition because I have glanced through here and there is not one single item or function I can find in these pages which is not being fully and competently performed by the Office of American Republics Affairs. . . . This is a complete duplication. There is no need for it. It is an extravagance, an inefficiency, and I protest."

According to Braden, it was Russell's persuasiveness with his former law partner, Mr. Byrnes, that won the fight for the geographic divisions, but that was some weeks off. At this time the Secretary approved the request for a supplemental appropriation to complete the fiscal year ending June 30, 1946. I went to work on the House Appropriations Committee to get this money for the intelligence group and finally succeeded. Russell, meanwhile, set up a group within the Department to consider the proposal to break it up. This group voted nine to eight for a unified intelligence group. On January 5, 1946, before going off to Europe, Secretary Byrnes stated that he would decide the issue in February after his return. Meanwhile, each side prepared its briefs; and persons unknown then or now introduced a new "persuader" into the debate, one destined to be all too familiar, the "loyalty" theme.

THE HIGH COMMAND WAVERS

Before this broke, both the President and the Secretary retreated, leaving the position of the intelligence group in the State Department exposed. In September they had both favored a "leading" position for the Secretary and the Department. Colonel McCormack tried to persuade the services to accept this point of view.[11] Although they agreed with him in opposition to uniting all intelligence directly under the President, they objected also to a looser grouping of agencies under the supervision of the Secretary and his Director. Their persuasion led Mr. Byrnes to join them in an odd plan for a National Intelligence Authority and a Central Intelligence Group. The President accepted it in a directive of January 22, 1946, in which he changed his position by moving primacy in intelligence from the State Department to the Executive Office of the President. He further weakened his earlier stand by not giving the Director a strong staff under his own control.

The National Intelligence Authority, which was to formulate high policy, would consist of the Secretaries of State, War, Navy, and a presidential appointee. Admiral Leahy, the Director of the Central Intelligence Group, would sit with the others but not vote. The Group, which would get its staff and money from the State, War, and Navy departments, would do the planning, development, and coordination of all foreign intelligence work. How often these same dismal words and futile charts of organization had issued from the White House during the war to "clarify" various powers, functions, and responsibilities granted in the field of foreign economic activities. A good many of us had cut our teeth and throats with this sort of nonsense. From that experience we learned that no committee can govern and no man can administer without his own people, money, and authority.

On February 12 Secretary Byrnes heard argument and received memoranda from me, Colonel McCormack, and the geographic assistant secretaries, taking the issue under advisement. Two weeks later Russell gave him a memorandum proposing the "Russell Plan," whether by request or not I do not know. The plan called for transfer of the units doing work on specific areas— the bulk of the staff—to the geographic divisions; the rump of the organization would be renamed the Office of Intelligence Coordination and Liaison and deal with other intelligence agencies throughout the government. While the Secretary cogitated for a month, the "loyalty" issue broke from insinuation within the Department to attack from the Congress.

A PRE–MCCARTHY ATTACK

Representative Andrew Jackson May, Democrat, chairman of the House Committee on Military Affairs, was the chosen instrument for the attack. On March 14, May charged that persons with "strong Soviet leanings," who had been forced out of the War Department, were now to be found in State, and that he had complained strongly to Mr. Byrnes and had named names. The latter denied the basic charge and said his screening committee had found and removed only one person as suspect. Colonel McCormack, at the time engaged with testimony in support of his appropriation for the ensuing fiscal year before a House subcommittee, soon made public a letter denying May's charge and demanding to be heard.[12] May refused for lack of committee jurisdiction. McCormack demanded retraction, defending the persons—some twenty in all —brought over from military intelligence. The Appropriations Committee cut out his entire appropriation, although later restoring a part.

Panuch had been peddling the same charges, among others, against the people brought over from OSS, saying:

The underlying purposes of this merger, in my opinion, were:

1. To shift control over the formulation of foreign policy from the career Foreign Service officers of the Department to personnel of reliable [sic] ideological orientation. . . .

4. To shift the center of gravity in the process of United States foreign policy formulation from a national to an international orientation via the supranational United Nations Organization. . . .

Thus, in September and October of 1945 the State Department—theretofore a relatively small, but compact policy agency—became a huge, bloated organization with a confused mission, swamped with inexperienced, untrained—and what is worse, unscreened—personnel. . . .

. . . Their ideology was far to the left of the views held by the President and his Secretary of State.

The end of this ideology may fairly [sic] be described as a socialized America in a world commonwealth of Communist and Socialist states dedicated to peace through collective security, political, economic, and social reform; and the redistribution of national wealth on a global basis.

Such were the views of Mr. Russell's chief assistant. The only one of them which requires mention is that the people transferred were "unscreened." Somewhat over sixteen hundred persons were transferred. They were all carefully reviewed by Colonel McCormack and fifty per cent were retained.

SECRETARY BYRNES DECIDES AGAINST ME

On April 22 Secretary Byrnes issued orders putting the Russell recommendations into effect.[13] The next day he left Washington for a month. On the same day Colonel McCormack submitted his resignation to me, as Acting Secretary. My letter accepting it concluded:

May I add my own word. I know with what reluctance you gave up last fall your intention to return to private life in order to do this work in the Department. I know the untiring energy which you devoted to it. I know the effort which you have put into surmounting the difficulties which were inherent in the task. All of us who have worked with you are deeply grateful. When you joined us, you and I had only a slight acquaintance; I knew you chiefly through your work. As you leave, you take with you my increased admiration for that and a deep personal regard. I hope that the future holds opportunities for us to work together again and to happier outcomes.

I was under no illusion about the position in which Secretary Byrnes's decision had left me as well as my departing colleague, nor of the character and disposition of some of the remaining ones over whom I had theoretical command. Perhaps as revealing as any aspect of this sorry episode is a phrase used by Panuch in his 1953 testimony in which he stated that one of the purposes of the merger was "to shift control over the formulation of foreign policy from the career Foreign Service officers." This was, indeed, where too many of them believed that it rested. For five years the conviction had been growing upon me that what the Department needed most was a disciplinary innovation which would convince its members that in fact as well as in theory "control" and all that that implied and required resided in the Secretary of State as the President's chief secretary. However, that would have to await the arrival of General Marshall.

I DECIDE TO RESIGN

Mr. Byrnes returned from London at the end of January to spend three months with us. After that, except for two visits, he was gone again until after the middle of October. He was an individual operator using half a dozen close associates upon those problems that engaged his attention. For him the four or five thousand other people in the Department and any problems upon which he was not working personally hardly existed. It was not strange, then, that ideas of organization were not congenial to him and that "the reorganization to end all reorganizations," which he had promised in August, never materialized except for a welcome pay raise. What did materialize, as I mentioned earlier, was Assistant Secretary Russell's split up of the research and intelligence work, the consequent resignation of Alfred McCormack, and the weakening of the Department's capacity to maintain a global view of the offensive being mounted from Moscow.

On April 23, 1946, Mr. Byrnes was to go to Paris for two meetings of the Council of Foreign Ministers before the Paris Peace Conference to conclude treaties with Italy, Finland, Bulgaria, and Rumania, and then to the conference itself, which with two brief breaks would keep him there until October 17. In these circumstances my position seemed to have some elements of dangerous instability. As Acting Secretary I had, with the President's backing, ample scope and authority, except in matters of departmental organization. But as Under Secretary my position was far from clear, since many people could and did go to the Secretary for approval of action without informing me. In other words, lines of command were not clear. They had not been clear under Mr. Hull, either. This created trouble then and it could again. Furthermore, it seemed quite possible that further misunderstanding between my two superiors, similar to that which occurred at the end of December, might occur again. As the man in the middle, my position could be unenviable. Therefore, I wrote a letter of resignation to take effect at such time after the Secretary's return as might be convenient to him and to the President.†

I took the letter to the Secretary, explained that if he and the President should fall out I would like the record to show that my resignation was dated before the fracas, and asked him to put the letter on deposit in the White House. He was not only taken with the idea but the next day showed me a letter of his own emulating it. As I recall, it reported the doctor's finding of a heart murmur, nothing serious, but not to be neglected indefinitely. It asked for relief after completion of the satellite peace treaties. The upshot of the matter was that he filed his letter and did not file mine. In due course, this produced quite a different result from that which I had in mind for myself in writing my letter or from that which the Secretary had in mind for himself when he wrote his.

19. THE QUEBEC AGREEMENT

DURING THE WINTER OF 1945–46 I learned about a matter that was to disturb me for some years to come, for with knowledge came the belief that our Government, having made an agreement from which it had gained immeasurably, was not keeping its word and performing its obligations. Like all great issues it was not simple. Grave consequences might follow upon keeping our word, but the idea of not keeping it was repulsive to me. The analogy of a nation to a person is not sound in all matters of moral conduct; in this case, however, it seemed to me pretty close. Even in *realpolitik* a reputation for probity carries its own pragmatic rewards.

When we entered the war, British scientific development was ahead of ours in some important areas, notably the electronics of naval warfare and the field of nuclear physics. To obtain the greatest security and benefit of all the material resources and scientific talent of our ally and ourselves in the development of a nuclear weapon seemed to dictate pooling them in our country and under our direction. Full agreement on doing so was not reached until the Quebec agreement of August 1943. Earlier in the war, even before we ourselves became belligerents, informal exchanges of information on weapons research and development had been carried out, including some interchange on atomic matters. General Leslie Groves was placed in charge of the "Manhattan District" in September 1942, when we were making ready our major establishments at Oak Ridge, Hanford, and in the New Mexico desert. General Groves was not a scientist, but he was a most capable administrator of this great scientific project. As Robert Oppenheimer said of him, "he had a fatal weakness for good men."

He also had reservations about full exchange of information regarding what was becoming an increasingly American effort. Secretary Stimson sought guidance from President Roosevelt, who decided that, pending a talk with Mr. Churchill, no more information should be shared than was necessary for the conduct of the project. The British protested but the President confirmed a recommendation of "interchange of information only to the extent that it can be used now by the recipient."[1]

This was how matters stood when the agreement between the United Kingdom and the United States governing their collaboration in the development of "tube alloys," the British code name, was written down by the two heads of government at their August 1943 meeting in Quebec. Like so much of the writing emanating from their meetings, it was not a careful lawyers' document, but rather a memorandum of what they had agreed on so far as they had discussed the matter. It recited the decision to pool in the United States brains and resources to insure their most provident use and to speed the project, with the result that a far larger part of the expense had fallen on the United States. It was agreed that the parties would never use "this agency" against each other, nor would they use it against third parties without each other's consent, nor communicate any information about tube alloys except by mutual consent. Britain disclaimed any "post-war advantages of an industrial or commercial character" beyond what might be considered by the President of the United States to be "fair and just and in accordance with the welfare of the world."[2] The agreement provided for a Combined Policy Committee of three American officials, two British, and a Canadian, which should agree from time to time on the program of work to be carried on, allocate materials, plant, and apparatus in limited supply, and settle questions arising under the agreement. Complete interchange of all information and ideas on all sections of the project should take place among the Policy Committee members and their advisers and on scientific research and development between those engaged in the same sections of the field. Interchange regarding design, construction, and operations of large-scale plants should be regulated by *ad hoc* agreements in the interest of the earliest completion of the project and approved by the Policy Committee.

The strict construction placed by American officials on the meaning of the agreement was spelled out for President Truman at the time of his November 1945 talks with Prime Minister Attlee. But the basic ambiguity surrounding the commitments, which was to give me so much discomfort, is underlined by another agreement of Churchill and Roosevelt in September 1944 that "full collaboration" between the two governments "in developing Tube Alloys for military and commercial purposes should continue after the defeat of Japan unless and until terminated by joint agreement."[3] Three months earlier the two had established a Combined Development Trust, administered by six persons appointed and removable by the Combined Policy Committee and charged with acquiring, developing, and holding as the agent of the Policy Committee uranium and thorium supplies originating outside the jurisdiction of the two governments and the Commonwealth (i.e., at that time chiefly in the Belgian Congo). Its operations were to be financed equally by the two governments.

When the new President and Prime Minister met in November 1945 they agreed that there should be "full and effective cooperation in the field of atomic energy between the United States, the United Kingdom and Canada," that the Combined Policy Committee and the Combined Development Trust should be continued, and that the former should recommend arrangements to achieve this purpose.[4]

So far as I can recall, my first knowledge of these highly secret and important affairs came shortly before Mr. Byrnes took me to a meeting of the Combined Policy Committee on February 15, 1946, called principally to recast the Quebec agreement. We had before us proposals drafted by a subcommittee consisting of General Groves, Roger Makins of the British Foreign Office, and

Lester B. Pearson. One of these proposals we were later to wish most fervently that we had put into effect at the earliest opportunity, as it would have changed the second article of the Quebec agreement to provide that atomic weapons should not be used against third parties without prior consultation between the two governments rather than "without each other's consent." However, the amendments were a "package," as the phrase goes, and some of them caused considerable concern, not least to their co-author, General Groves, who until the Atomic Energy Act of 1946 remained in charge for the Army of all our Government's operations in the atomic field.

The General, therefore, threw a monkey wrench into the negotiating machinery. He pointed out to Secretary Byrnes, who raised the objection in the meeting, that although the heads of government had directed the preparation of the amendments, the United Nations Charter, which took effect October 24, 1945, required the registration of all international agreements with the United Nations. Lord Halifax strongly opposed delay but Mr. Byrnes, who saw the propaganda advantage to the Russians in bringing to light active Anglo-American-Canadian agreements on atomic energy when we three were the proponents of international control, remained hesitant. He must discuss this problem with the President.

What particularly bothered General Groves were two changes in prior practice. One would alter the allocation to the United States of all ores obtained by both countries, as had been done during the war, in favor of an even division of ore on the ground that each country paid for half and should receive half. The other matter was the British request for technical information needed to build a large-scale atomic plant in the United Kingdom. The General argued that an even division of ore would soon bring our operations to a halt. We had used our only two atomic weapons and needed to make more, while the British could not yet use any ore. He also saw an atomic plant in England as far too vulnerable to Russian attack. If built at all, it should be built in Canada. The honeymoon of Anglo-American relations existing during the war was clearly coming to an end, and some of the commitments of the marriage seemed to be causing pain to one of the spouses.

A correspondence between President Truman and Prime Minister Attlee failed to resolve the issue of technical help in building the atomic plant. The President's view was that the exchange of information contemplated in the agreements related only to basic scientific research and that to enlarge the area while both the Atomic Energy Act of 1946 and international control through the United Nations were still pending would be a serious mistake. The Prime Minister argued that help on the plant had never been ruled out but retained as a possibility and that equitably it was justified by British help to us in the development of radar and jet engines.

When the raw-materials issue became deadlocked in the Combined Policy Committee, I was drawn into an attempt to work out an agreement, with Dr. Bush and General Groves as my colleagues working with Roger Makins and Sir James Chadwick on the British side. After much discussion the British representatives offered to recommend to London that the one hundred per cent allocation to the United States of all material going through the Combined Development Trust should continue through March 31, 1946, with the United Kingdom getting fifty per cent for the rest of the year without prejudice to different allocations in subsequent years. We recommended this solution to the Combined Policy Committee as one that would permit the United States to maintain its scheduled operations for the remainder of the year. The Secretary of War and the President approved on July 10, 1946.

By the time the President's correspondence with the Prime Minister had run down and the new allocation of raw materials had been made, the UN Atomic Energy Commission was convening for discussions that would focus on the American proposal for international control of atomic energy, and the Congress in August would greatly change the situation by its domestic control act. Neither the British Government nor ours believed the hour propitious for embarking on further discussions to amend the Quebec agreement. This still remained highly classified as top secret and became increasingly a source of acute embarrassment.

Indeed, so closely was knowledge of the Quebec agreement held that Secretary of Defense Forrestal did not know of it until some time after I did.[5] What disturbed me when I did learn of it was the problem presented in our relations with Congress. The Administration had for some time been discussing with Congress, in considerable detail and apparently in complete candor, all aspects of both national and international control of nuclear energy and weapons, without mentioning the existence of so relevant and important a matter as this agreement. The somewhat incredible truth was that very few knew about it (due, in part, to so many changes in high office), and those who did thought of it as a temporary wartime agreement to be superseded by broader arrangements currently and constantly discussed.

The immediate problem seemed to be how to purge ourselves of an imputation of bad faith, a problem I was eager to have decided by my superiors and betters, the President and the Secretary of State. They, however, operating on the principle that the bearer of bad news should do something about it, sent me to the Capitol to begin by making a disclosure to Senator Vandenberg, share with him his first moments of anguish, and bear his recriminations. Since I was innocent myself, I could, at least, urge that while we at the other end of the avenue might be fools, we were not knaves. No competitors for the honor of this mission appearing, I performed it. Senator Vandenberg had with him his colleague on the Foreign Relations and Joint Atomic Energy committees, Senator Bourke Hickenlooper, Republican of Iowa. Senator Vandenberg later described the agreement I disclosed as "astounding" and "unthinkable."[6] It was thinkable enough, however, to permit a considerable flow of words of a highly unfavorable nature from both senators. My role was to bear them submissively and patiently until a reduction in the temperature of the conversation returned the whole subject to the realm of the thinkable. When we had jointly thought about it for a while, the agreement appeared less unusual as a wartime agreement between allies engaged in the joint development of this horrendous weapon. Nor was it immediately clear that the best interests of either or both countries would be served by cutting off all relations between them on atomic matters. Doubtless the Quebec agreement needed modification in the light of the rapidly, and not too favorably, developing situation, but just what modification would require some thought and discussion with our British colleagues.

Later negotiations, resulting in the so-called *modus vivendi* of 1948, were carried on by my successor, Robert Lovett. These relieved the extreme apprehension of the senators but left the British with a sense of having been ungenerously, if not unfairly, treated. When I returned to office in 1949, the problem of our relations with the British on nuclear matters was still unresolved. Tackling it again, I found my views out of sympathy with the more extreme nationalist ones prevailing in the Congress and in some parts of the executive branch. I was not proud of the resulting governmental attitude. But all this belongs to later chapters.

20. THE PUZZLE OF PALESTINE

ALMOST IMMEDIATELY UPON becoming President, Mr. Truman with the best will in the world tackled that immensely difficult international puzzle—a homeland in Palestine for the Jews. Inevitably I was sucked in after him. The fate of the Jewish victims of Hitlerism was a "matter of deep personal concern" to him and as President he "undertook to do something about it." The Balfour Declaration, promising the Jews the opportunity to re-establish a homeland in Palestine, had always seemed to him "to go hand in hand with the noble policies of Woodrow Wilson, especially the principle of self-determination."[1] From many years of talk with him I know that this represented a deep conviction, in large part implanted by his close friend and former partner, Eddie Jacobson, a passionate Zionist.

Both Prime Minister Attlee and Ernest Bevin, in the heat of their annoyance with Mr. Truman, charged that his support of Jewish immigration into Palestine was inspired by domestic political opportunism. This was not true despite the confirming observations of some of his associates, such as Bob Hannegan, Jim Forrestal, and James Byrnes, collected by Mr. Attlee in his memoirs.[2] Mr. Truman held deep-seated convictions on many subjects, among them, for instance, a dislike of Franco and Catholic obscurantism in Spain.

I did not share the President's views on the Palestine solution to the pressing and desperate plight of great numbers of displaced Jews in Eastern Europe, for whom the British and American commanders in Germany were temporarily attempting to provide. The number that could be absorbed by Arab Palestine without creating a grave political problem would be inadequate, and to transform the country into a Jewish state capable of receiving a million or more immigrants would vastly exacerbate the political problem and imperil not only American but all Western interests in the Near East. From Justice Brandeis, whom I revered, and from Felix Frankfurter, my intimate friend, I had learned to understand, but not to share, the mystical emotion of the Jews to return to Palestine and end the Diaspora. In urging Zionism as an American governmental policy they had allowed, so I thought, their emotion to obscure the totality of American interests. Zionism was the only topic that Felix and I had by mutual consent excluded from our far-ranging daily talks.

By the time I took up my duties as Under Secretary in September 1945 it was clear that the President himself was directing policy on Palestine. I detected no inclination on the part of Secretary Byrnes to project himself into this issue, but rather a tendency to leave supervision of the Department's work on it more and more to me. Despite my own views, I did my best loyally to see that the President's wishes were understood and carried out, taking at this time more of an administrative than an advisory role. The officers of the Office of Near Eastern and African Affairs, who under the instruction of President Roosevelt and Secretary Stettinius had been following a neutral role on the Palestine issue, faithfully adapted themselves to President Truman's different approach. Later on, some ardent Zionist sympathizers attacked the head of the Near Eastern Office, Loy Henderson, for obstructing the President's policy. This was untrue and grossly unfair to this entirely loyal and competent officer.

At the time of which I am writing, President Truman's views centered exclusively upon two points: first, immediate immigration into Palestine of one hundred thousand displaced Jews from Eastern Europe; second, the determination to assume no political or military responsibility for this decision. To accomplish the former would require Britain, the mandatory state, to change its policy, which restricted immigration into Palestine to fifteen hundred per month. The President wrote Mr. Churchill of his desire to discuss this at their prospective meeting at Potsdam. When the time came, Mr. Attlee had succeeded Mr. Churchill as Prime Minister and was not prepared. While waiting for him to get prepared, the President responded to the Egyptian and other Arab prime ministers that he wished "to renew the assurances which your Government has previously received to the effect that . . . no decision should be taken regarding the basic situation in Palestine without full consultation with both Arabs and Jews." Regarding this, the President later observed, "To assure the Arabs that they would be consulted was by no means inconsistent with my generally sympathetic attitude toward Jewish aspirations."[3] The Arabs may be forgiven for believing that this did not exactly state the inconsistency as they saw it.

At the end of August the President sent by Secretary Byrnes, who was going to London, another appeal to the British Prime Minister to open up Jewish immigration into Palestine. Mr. Attlee returned a dilatory reply asking for more time and no action "in the interval." At the same time Mr. Henderson gave Mr. Byrnes some observations, the wisdom of which has been amply borne out by subsequent events. He pointed out the grave complications involved in either horn of the Palestine dilemma—in moving toward Palestine either as an Arab state with a Jewish minority or as a Jewish state with an Arab minority. Therefore, he urged, while there was still time before the dilemma became too painful, we should attempt to get British, Soviet, United States, and, if possible, French agreement upon a solution and then consult the Jews and Arabs before putting the plan into effect. Otherwise one or more of the powers might lay responsibility for what might be done upon the others and encourage either Jews or Arabs or both to agitate or possibly fight against it. There is no record that this advice ever reached the President or that it would have worked if attempted, but it was surely a shrewd sighting of troubles to come and worth careful thought.

The President's thoughts, however, were quite different. He has told us that he entirely separated the long-range problem from the short-range one.

"My basic approach was that the long-range fate of Palestine was the kind of problem we had the U.N. for. For the immediate future, however, some aid was needed for the Jews in Europe."[4] This idea that the United Nations was and should be something different from its members and could assume responsibility without power has been a curiously persistent one.

Such was the situation when I assumed my new duties and, in my superior's absence, found myself on the Palestine tightrope, balancing precariously. Both Jewish and Arab leaders called on me to ask what was going on. Current press gossip and speculation had made the Jewish leaders more relaxed and optimistic than the Arabs. I told the former that these important questions were receiving the President's personal attention and that I was not authorized to say more. The President's assurance about consultation should be enough. Knowing that they would be in touch with David Niles, the President's assistant for minority groups, who would be more communicative than I, what I said seemed adequate.

The Arab group were more specific. On October 3, 1945, the Egyptian Minister spoke of their disquiet over reports that the President was pressing the British for a hundred thousand Jewish immigrants into Palestine, which he found hard to believe in view of President Roosevelt's clear commitment about consultation. They would appreciate assurance from me that United States policy toward Palestine had not been changed and that our Government intended to adhere strictly to its undertaking about consultation. What conversations had taken place between Messrs. Attlee and Byrnes I did not know, nor did I wish to elaborate on the President's views on the scope and significance of consultation. I told them, therefore, that during the brief time I had been in office I had not familiarized myself with the Palestine situation, and that the Secretary would be back in a few days and would be informed at once of their request. When Secretary Byrnes returned, I told him of the request and he urged the President to release for publication President Roosevelt's letter to King Ibn Saud written just before FDR's death and to reaffirm his predecessor's statements of neutrality and friendship for the Arabs. On October 18, 1945, the President authorized the former but not the latter. When the Syrian Minister, not to be outdone, asked our agreement to publish FDR's letter to the President of Syria, I decided that we had published enough of these all-too-fulsome documents and told Henderson to reassure him in a more austere manner.

THE ANGLO-AMERICAN COMMITTEE OF INQUIRY

Prime Minister Attlee, who had been doing some cogitating about the President's letter, decided understandably to move us from our position of private exhorter to a publicly responsible partner in Palestine affairs. Accordingly, he proposed an Anglo-American committee of inquiry. During Attlee's visit in November to discuss the international control of nuclear energy, Mr. Byrnes and the President ironed out with him some differences between the

British and ourselves in our approach to the Palestine inquiry. I did not complain about my exclusion from both these discussions. The Palestine committee was to examine the needs of displaced Jews in Eastern Europe and the number that could be received in Palestine under "prevailing political, economic and social conditions." It was also to recommend provisional and permanent solutions for Palestine. Loy Henderson had warned against giving any one of the European states the enviable opportunity to incite the Arabs and Jews to hostility against a plan proposed by less than all of the major powers. We were about to give the Russians just that priceless opportunity.

I must mention the committee's membership and report because of the controversy that grew out of it with me in the storm center. Judge Joseph C. Hutcheson of the U.S. Fifth Circuit Court of Appeals, a fiery Texan and friend of the President, was American chairman, flanked by Dr. Frank Aydelotte, former President of Swarthmore College; Frank W. Buxton, editor of the *Boston Herald;* William Phillips, former Under Secretary of State; James G. McDonald, former League of Nations High Commissioner for Refugees; and Bartley C. Crum, a California lawyer. The committee reported to the two governments on April 22, 1946. Being then in charge, I received a telegram from Averell Harriman, our Ambassador in London, asking on behalf of the British Government that we release the whole report at one time, so that it might be considered as a whole (which we did on May 1, 1946), rather than releasing only the conclusions or some of them apart from the whole.

The President, however, as perhaps the British feared, latched onto one of the recommendations of this report, that a hundred thousand certificates should be issued for early emigration to Palestine.[5] The recommendations were interdependent. Government in Palestine was to be based on the principles that (1) Jew should not dominate Arab, nor Arab Jew; (2) the state should be neither Jewish nor Arab; (3) it should protect and preserve the interests of all in the holy places of the Christian, Moslem, and Jewish faiths. The mandate should become a trust to work for the conditions referred to. Standards should be equalized, bringing Arab up to Jewish. Immigration should continue to be facilitated after the first one hundred thousand, and land-policy restrictions eased. Economic development, education, and domestic tranquillity were to be fostered.

Unfortunately, the only significant omissions were how these goals, so unanimously desired, were to be achieved. President Truman at once approved the recommendations on immigration and easing the land-acquisition restriction. He reserved judgment on the long-range proposals. On the same day Mr. Attlee told Commons that the report must be considered as a whole and means found for carrying it out as a whole. The United Kingdom could not do this until it found out to what extent the United States "would be prepared to share the . . . additional military and financial responsibilities."[6] The one hundred thousand immigrants could not be admitted until the illegal armies had been disbanded and the Jewish Agency for the Development of Palestine (an outgrowth of the Zionist Congress in Zurich in 1929) resumed cooperation in suppressing terrorism. The United States and the United Kingdom were farther apart than ever.

Mr. Attlee was annoyed by Mr. Truman's taking the plum out of the pudding, and President Truman by what some of his advisers thought was Mr. Attlee's stalling on the central issue of immigration. With Mr. Byrnes away at the Paris Peace Conference, I was again called from sidelines into the thick of the fray. John Hilldring, Assistant Secretary of State in Charge of Occupied Territories, bombarded me with complaints about British stalling on the refugees while the situation in Germany and Austria deteriorated. The Near East Division answered that the British would not issue the hundred thousand certificates to relieve our problem in Europe until we took some share in their responsibility in Palestine, and it also reminded me of our promise to consult with the Arabs and Jews. The press bombarded me for a statement. I replied that it was too early.

The problem before me was clear but not simple: to bring Mr. Truman closer to Mr. Attlee's position that the report should be considered as a whole, and Mr. Attlee closer to President Truman's desire to get on with the issuance of some, at least, of the hundred thousand certificates. Since neither of these gentlemen was of a yielding disposition, the odds were against the success of the effort. The best method seemed a proposal to Mr. Attlee to hold consultations with the Arabs and Jews within two weeks on the basis of the Anglo-American report, and, in view of the urgency of the immigration matter, to complete consultations "at the earliest possible moment." On May 6, 1946, I went to the President with a telegram along these lines, which he kept for further thought after listening to me. Two days later he sent the telegram and received a prompt reply from Mr. Attlee asking for a delay in our consultation.

Although we consented, the Arabs did not. Ministers of five countries— Egypt, Iraq, Lebanon, Saudi Arabia, and Syria—called on me in a body on May 10 to complain of the "painful impression in the Arab world" made by the report and urge us to restore tranquillity by repudiating it. I promised them consultation before action was taken. After another long talk with the President, we prepared a letter and memorandum of consultation, which with similar documents by the British were submitted to the Jewish Agency and the Arab Higher Committee, other official organizations, and the Arab governments on May 20. Toward the end of June the Jewish Agency replied equivocally, complaining that immigration of one hundred thousand Jews was to follow agreement upon the whole Palestine question. The Arabs unanimously and flatly rejected the whole report and denied the right of the United States to intervene. On June 12 Mr. Bevin made ill feeling unanimous by stating to the Bournemouth meeting of the Labour Party, "I hope it will not be misunderstood in America if I say, with the purest of motives, that [U.S. policy toward Jewish immigration into Palestine] was because they did not want too many of them in New York."[7] Both Bevin and his motives were clearly understood in America. He added that His Majesty's Government was not prepared to put another division in Palestine to help the immigration of a hundred thousand Jews from Europe.

Once again I gratefully resumed my seat on the sidelines when my chief briefly returned to Washington. Henderson had wisely advised that if the Administration wanted substantial Jewish immigration it must do more than urge; planning with the British was necessary regarding who should go, how they should be chosen, how transported, how housed on arrival, temporarily and permanently, how this should be financed, and how public order was to be maintained. Mr. Byrnes proposed to send Treasury and War Department officials to London as aides to Harriman in discussing these pressing problems. Attlee also wanted to move the Americans from fluent advice to immersion in the tough details of this problem. He sent a list of over forty specific questions calling for specific answers. The President decided to appoint a Cabinet committee of State, Treasury, and War, with alternates, to help him formulate and execute policy regarding Palestine, negotiate with the British, and keep in touch with private organizations.

THE CABINET COMMITTEE

In the latter part of June an outburst of violence erupted in Palestine. Explosions, pitched battles in Haifa, curfews, "roundups," and arrests became endemic. On June 28 the Prime Minister informed the President that the High Commissioner had been authorized to take stern military action to cope with the situation. This he did by arresting the Zionist leaders. President Truman announced that the United States Government was prepared to assume technical and financial responsibility for transporting a hundred thousand Jews to Palestine. The Prime Minister, left with the military responsibility and the dam about to burst, urged speedy resumption of talks. The President had the Cabinet Alternates flown to London in his own plane. This group consisted of Henry F. Grady, a former Assistant Secretary of State, a strong personality; Goldthwaite Dorr, a New York lawyer temporarily serving in the War Department; and Herbert Gaston, a former Assistant Secretary of the Treasury. The Alternates pressed hard for immediate admission of the one hundred thousand.

Shortly after they arrived, the King David Hotel in Jerusalem, which housed the Secretariat of the mandatory government and part of the British Army GHQ, was blown up on July 22 with casualties of forty-one killed and forty-three injured. The secret Jewish organization, Irgun Zvai Leumi, claimed responsibility. Three days later the plan of the British-American conferees in London was leaked to the press. The plan provided for a Jewish and an Arab province in a federal Palestine, the provinces with powers largely limited to local matters. A strong federal government under the control of the mandatory state would have direct authority in Jerusalem, Bethlehem, and the Negev and jurisdiction over such matters as defense, foreign affairs, taxation, courts, post office, and—very importantly—immigration. The admission of the hundred thousand immigrants was made dependent upon acceptance of the federalization plan and American economic aid was recommended for all the Arab states, with fifty million dollars specifically for the Palestinian Arabs.

ONCE MORE UNTO THE BREACH

It needed only a few days over the end of July and beginning of August for Jews, Arabs, and Senators Wagner and Taft (and a few days later nine more senators and representatives) to reject the plan—now known as the Morrison-Grady Plan—for Herbert Morrison, Lord President of His Majesty's Council, to announce it in Parliament, and for President Truman to order the Cabinet Committee Alternates home. Mr. Byrnes, who had been in touch from Paris with Grady, Bevin, and Attlee and had tried to launch the report with a fair wind, had had his fill of Palestine. The President summoned me once more to the stricken field.

It was, indeed, a stricken field. Attlee had deftly exchanged the United States for Britain as the most disliked power in the Middle East. Furthermore, the center of battle interest was moving from Israeli-British fighting in Palestine to civil war along the Potomac. Staff members of the Cabinet Committee were attacking the chairman; the American members of the Anglo-American Committee of Inquiry were attacking the Cabinet Committee; the President informed the British that he could not support its report; and Mr. Churchill advised the House of Commons to give up the mandate if the United States would not help. In this situation a meeting of the American members of both committees was called to reconcile their views, with me as chairman. The Archangel Gabriel would have declined the assignment, but he had more latitude than under secretaries of state. Like the Light Brigade, "Theirs not to reason why—theirs but to do or die!" Often both.

I pass over the meeting quickly. Judge Hutcheson demanded to know why his committee had been summoned. I replied, to hear their views on the Morrison-Grady report. This answer was a mistake, as he and his colleagues gave them with passion and at length. As they saw it, the report proposed a ghetto in attenuated form, a sellout—"very pretty, even grandiose—but a sellout, nevertheless." In Billy Phillips' more restrained diplomatic vocabulary, the plan was "entirely unacceptable"; he was not aware, he said, that the United States had become "the tail to the British kite." To prove their case to the hilt, Judge Hutcheson asked that the meeting continue through the next day, necessitating a postponement of the President's meeting with them. I notified him that my effort to reconcile the Americans had been no more successful than the earlier attempt to reconcile the Arabs and Jews. Palestine was not a subject that lent itself to adjustment of views.

The Judge declared that the report violated the Cabinet Committee's instruction first by nullifying and not carrying out his own committee's earlier recommendations, and, secondly, by violating the League of Nations mandate by its recommendations for cantonization and restriction of movement in Palestine. Furthermore, he argued, the President had no power—for legal reasons—

to agree to a change in the mandate without the advice and consent of the Senate. Due to pride in its own report, I felt, the Hutcheson group had gone too far. The Morrison-Grady report had in it the makings of a compromise; indeed, later on the Jewish Agency suggested some helpful amendments, and the United Nations Special Committee report of August 31, 1947, shows its influence. For a while the President contemplated modifying the report, but the dog had been given a bad name and for the time being was of no use.

THE YOM KIPPUR STATEMENT: OCTOBER 4, 1946

At this juncture my efforts and energy were diverted to coping with a crisis more immediately menacing than Palestine—Yugoslavia's downing of American planes. The President turned his to an unsuccessful plea for congressional liberalization of our own immigration laws, "authorizing the entry into the United States of a fixed number of these [displaced] persons, including Jews." We joined forces again at Yom Kippur in a move which, as one now looks back, seems to have been of doubtful wisdom. At the time I did not think so, and agreeing with the President that the situation called for restatement of his views, helped him prepare them. The statement was attacked then and has been since as a blatant play for the Jewish vote in Illinois, Ohio, Pennsylvania, and New York in the congressional elections only a month away and an attempt to anticipate an expected similar play by Governor Dewey. Plainly it could be so interpreted, but I do not believe that it had any such purpose.

When President Truman engaged in a political maneuver, he never disguised his undiluted pleasure in it. His "nonpolitical" political trips and speeches, his calling the Eightieth Congress into special session in the pre-election summer of 1948, his occasional political appointments, some of which I opposed and in some of which I cooperated—all of these were frankly put forward to us as political and discussed as such. He would extol to the voters such actions of his administration as he thought were right and should commend themselves to them. But he never took or refused to take a step in our foreign relations to benefit his or his party's fortunes. This he would have regarded as false to the great office that he venerated and held in sacred trust.

About the Yom Kippur statement the President was very serious. For a year he had urged immigration to relieve the Jewish refugees in Europe and satisfy their yearning to go to Palestine, yet the possibility seemed dimmer than in 1945. Dissension at home had been added to strain between Britain and America, conflict between Arab and Jew, and terrorism in the Holy Land. A conference convened by the British in London between more moderate Arabs and Jews had broken down. The Day of Atonement seemed to come on a particularly dark day in Jewish history. The President chose it as a fitting occasion to announce that he would continue his efforts for the immigration of the one hundred thousand into Palestine and the liberalization of immigration into the United States. He also said that some plan for Palestine based upon partition between Arabs and Jews "would command the support of public opinion in the United States."[8]

Among those who called to tell me that the statement had been a mistake was G. E. Hopkins, Associate Secretary of the Division of Foreign Missions of the Methodist Church. When I asked whether this judgment would apply to its effect on the displaced-persons camps in Europe, he thought not. While the British prepared for their London conference and Secretary Byrnes was in New York for a foreign ministers' conference and meetings of the UN General Assembly, the Palestine issue marked time and I found myself dealing with foreign probes to locate, if possible, our exact position, which the foreign observer might be excused—not knowing the President's position as well as some of us did—for regarding as ambivalent. President Truman continued to be concerned almost exclusively with the immigration of the one hundred thousand Jews. Others saw this as depending upon the ultimate fate of Palestine, which the President, in turn, regarded as a separate question to be decided by a slightly mystical entity, the United Nations. Hence the baffling and circular nature of all the talks.

The chief inquirers about our position at this time were the British Ambassador and two princely visitors from Saudi Arabia. The two princes differed in manner and appearance, but not at all in their views about Zionism and Jewish immigration. His Royal Highness, Amir Faisal, the present King but at that time Minister of Foreign Affairs, came to Washington in mid-December, preceding his brother, Crown Prince Saud, by a month. The Amir, striking in white burnoose and golden circlet, which heightened his swarthy complexion, with black, pointed beard and mustache topped by a thin hooked nose and piercing dark eyes, gave a sinister impression, relieved from time to time by a shy smile. Hollywood would have cast him as a dark and mysterious shiek. But his manner, like his brother's, was composed and dignified, hands hidden in flowing sleeves and voice solemn and never excited. He spoke of the high regard his father, King Ibn Saud, had for the late President, whom he had met on a destroyer in the Red Sea when the President was returning from Yalta shortly before his death. The King was still, as he had been then, deeply concerned about Zionist plans for Palestine, which would not make for peace in the Near East.

As he talked with President Truman, it seemed to me that their minds crossed but did not meet. The Amir was concerned with conditions in the Near East, the President with the condition of the displaced Jews in Europe. Neither really grasped the depth of the other's concern; indeed, each rather believed the other's was exaggerated. The conversation ended in platitudes, which were seized upon as agreement. I found it a disturbing conversation. The Amir impressed me as a man who could be an implacable enemy and who should be taken very seriously.

The Crown Prince, on the other hand, was a much more enigmatic figure, larger, heavier, less finely chiseled both in body and mind, bafflingly shrouded behind dark glasses protecting weak eyes. The President's meeting with him, which both Secretary Byrnes and I attended, for the most part dealt with matters irrelevant to the Palestine issue. On that it was singularly unproductive, since the views of Crown Prince and President were diametrically opposite, the one wishing immigration to cease altogether, the other to increase it greatly. My abiding memory of the meeting is of the Crown Prince's immobility throughout its hour-and-a-half duration. His feet remained close together on the floor, his hands motionless in his sleeves. This so impressed me that, when the boredom of presiding over public meetings would overcome me, I used to practice immobility. It requires immense self-control. The temptation to pull an ear or rub the nose can become agonizing, but less so than listening to speeches.

Lord Inverchapel, the British Ambassador, was an agreeable companion but unsatisfactory as a diplomatic colleague. Unquestionably eccentric, he liked to appear even more eccentric than he was, producing an ultimate impression odd enough to be puzzling. He also professed strong Zionist sympathies, certainly not shared by Attlee or Bevin. This deepened the conversational puzzle of knowing what he meant, whose views he was representing, and how what one said in reply appeared in his telegrams to London. Our talks began in November and went on until February, when the crisis over British withdrawal from Greece again briefly interrupted my responsibility for Palestine matters. At first the Ambassador's inquiries were at large; later on, they were directed toward learning whether the impending change of Secretary of State from Mr. Byrnes to General Marshall might involve a change in policy.

Bevin, so the Ambassador told me in late November, had made clear to Jewish leaders in New York that if he could not get a permanent solution to the Palestine problem within a short time, Britain would give up the mandate to the United Nations, after first offering it to the United States. His hearers had been aghast, protesting that this would produce disaster, and had urged partition, though not personally favoring it, as preferable. Bevin had replied that Attlee and Churchill had already agreed to give up the mandate and that the decision would be made. In any case, he added, the mandatory state could not decide on partition without the approval of the United Nations, where it would be defeated. Rabbi Abba H. Silver was reported as believing that if both Britain and the United States would approve the proposal it could be passed. If their agreement could be assured, he thought that the assembled Jewish organizations could also be brought to approve it at the Zionist congress to be held in Basle in December. Bevin thought well of the idea. What Lord Inverchapel wanted to know was whether he would be justified in encouraging Bevin to believe that the United States would support partition.

The supposed facts from which this inquiry sprang rested so exclusively on His Lordship's hearsay evidence that prudence in reply seemed indicated. Why, I asked, did Mr. Bevin not ask this question of Mr. Byrnes, who was staying in the same hotel with him in New York? So important a matter would warrant Mr. Byrnes coming to Washington for a talk with the President or instructing me to consult him. Lord Inverchapel thought that Bevin would probably do this the following week after the Cabinet had considered a paper Bevin had laid before it. What was wanted now was my preliminary reading. I obliged with caution. In his October 4 statement, I said, the President had not advocated partition as a solution, but rather had stated that a solution based on partition would, in his judgment, command the support of American public opinion. The version advanced by the Morrison-Grady report had not commanded it. However, the gap between its version and that suggested by the Jewish Agency did not seem unbridgeable. Therefore, if such a bridge could be found, I believed the President would be willing to recommend it to the Congress. This seemed all that Lord Inverchapel's effort deserved.

He tried me out again on January 21, 1947, the day General Marshall assumed his duties as Secretary of State. The British Government, he said, reading from a paper, was about to begin a conference with Arab and Jewish leaders in London. It did not expect agreement. It might be that one solution would be "acquiesced in," however grudgingly, with the minimum of opposition. That would be the solution the British Government would seek. It would undoubtedly have to resort to the United Nations and would want to know the United States' attitude to the solutions before shaping the outcome toward one. The alternatives were: (1) outright partition; (2) cantonization—federalization (Morrison-Grady); (3) surrender of the mandate to the United Nations. In a discussion with Bevin, Byrnes had urged the first solution (partition) but Bevin could not free himself from some doubt about our attitude. Would we support, and with what vigor, such a solution in the General Assembly? Would any other seem to us preferable?

I replied that I was not authorized to speak for the United States Government but would report his questions to General Marshall, who would reply promptly. My own impressions, for what they were worth, were not novel. A solution based on partition would be the easiest to support, both because of domestic opinion and because the opposition in Palestine was more likely to be vocal than physical. The United States Government could not participate in carrying out a solution by force. Since partition seemed the best hope, it should be explored fully both to gain acceptance and to reduce opposition. The responsibility for decision rested with the British Government. The London conference seemed to me to offer the last chance for peaceful solution. One factor seemed to me essential to any solution: immigration of the hundred thousand Jews now waiting in the European camps. Arab opposition seemed primarily based on the belief that it would produce a Jewish majority in Palestine. Since the Arabs already had a large majority and a higher birth rate, a controlled immigration would not have this result. The essential aim should be a solution with the maximum possibility of being put into effect, not the one theoretically or dialectically most advantageous.

Lord Inverchapel then asked me about his other two suggestions—the Morrison-Grady Plan and the idea of turning the mandate over to the United Nations. The difficulty with the first, I said, had already been demonstrated— the almost universal opposition to it. Perhaps a combination of the two might be explored, a modified Morrison-Grady Plan for a limited time with reserved power in the United Nations to make the ultimate decisions. A mere surrender of the mandate, I feared, would be a confession that no solution was possible and an invitation to civil war.

Since this was the first policy matter to be taken up with the new Secretary of State, I submitted to him a memorandum of my conversation with Lord Inverchapel, with a note that the Ambassador wished an answer during the week, a suggestion that the Secretary discuss the matter with the President, and the recommendation that I be instructed to confirm the personal views already expressed. Within the week the Ambassador also received from me a memorandum along these lines.

BEVIN THROWS IN THE TOWEL

The day on which Lord Inverchapel received this memorandum saw the opening in London of the second phase of the London conference, again without Jewish participation. The United States Government played no part in it. After two weeks Mr. Bevin informed General Marshall that it was a failure and that on February 14, 1947, the British Government would refer "the whole problem to the United Nations." The Secretary assured him, "I am . . . most anxious not to embarrass you in your delicate and difficult task." The day following this sobering announcement I talked with Sir John Balfour, British Minister (the President, the Secretary, and the Ambassador all being away), urging him that instead of maintaining, as his government proposed to do, the present immigration rate of fifteen hundred a month, it should double the rate. This was on the theory that one might as well be hanged for a sheep as a lamb, with the additional argument that the increase would hardly excite the Arabs more than they were but might lead them to be less satisfied with the status quo of stalemate. A talk I had had with Rabbi Silver disclosed a subdued and rather frightened mood, which might be helpful.

In informing Henderson of this talk, I added that if the British were going to withdraw from leadership in the United Nations on the subject as well as from responsibility in Palestine, I did not see how we could safely avoid assuming some leadership. Whatever the United Nations might propose, we would be asked to finance it. It was to our interest, therefore, that the United Nations proposal should be as sensible as possible. Hitherto we had favored a solution based on partition. Did this policy carry too great a weight of foreign opposition from all quarters to be possible in the United Nations? We must avoid being committed to any discussion with the British, which would surely leak and cause domestic repercussions with us, before getting our own ideas as crystallized and accepted within the Government as possible. "I am aware," I concluded, "that this only poses but does not answer the sixty-four-dollar question, but I have come to the end of my ideas for the morning."

RESPONSIBILITY PASSES TO THE UN

On February 21, 1947, before General Marshall left Washington to speak at Princeton and then to go to Southern Pines, North Carolina, for the weekend, he sent a telegram to Bevin reminding him that "the transfer of the vexatious problem to the United Nations unfortunately does not render it any less complicated or difficult." Returning to President Truman's preoccupation, he asked whether, without markedly disturbing the situation while the United Nations considered it, immigration might be increased appreciably, adding "but the British must decide." After he had left town, Bevin turned the tables of responsibility by informing us that within a month the British would withdraw from responsibility for Greece, leaving to us the task of restoring that unhappy country to security and stability. Three days later in the House of Commons Bevin attacked American policy in Palestine and was cheered. For the next month, as related in Chapters 24 and 25, I was pretty busy on problems of Greece and Turkey and had little time for Palestinian matters. Then General Marshall's departure for Moscow turned them over to me once more.

Lord Inverchapel wanted ideas about how the United Nations should be organized to consider the problem. Obviously the whole General Assembly, with about sixty members, could not hope to understand the problem or come to any sensible conclusions without collected and organized information. Two questions arose: Who should collect and arrange the material so as to avoid charges of prejudice and attempts to slant it toward a particular conclusion? Who should initially appraise it and make recommendations to the Assembly? He asked for our considered opinion in writing. After discussion and guidance from the President, who brought shrewd judgment to the matter, we recommended a small neutral group to work with the UN Secretariat for the first task, and, for the second, an *ad hoc* committee with broad terms of reference and composed of neutral nations that had taken no stand in the matter, nine or ten in number, and excluding all the larger powers. We also recommended that the agenda of a special session of the General Assembly, if called, should contain no other business than the appointment of the special committee, a view opposed to the Arabs' desire that it should also terminate the British mandate.

On April 2 the British asked the Secretary General to "summon, as soon as possible, a special session of the General Assembly for the purpose of constituting and instructing a special committee to prepare for the consideration" of the problem of Palestine and its future government at the next regular session of the General Assembly. The special session met from April 28 to May 15, setting up the committee as requested and as recommended. General Marshall recorded that this action was "very satisfactory and afforded ground for hope that a practicable solution may be presented to the General Assembly in September."

By mid-June he had changed his opinion. "An agreed settlement no longer appears possible," he wrote to Ambassador Warren Austin at the United Nations. Every solution would meet with strong opposition. "A certain degree of force may be required [for] any solution." The whole situation must be reviewed "to make certain that any solution ... can be defended before the world both now and in the future." My own days as Under Secretary were running out, with my resignation accepted to take effect at midyear. My last recorded view, brought out by pressure from the Jewish Agency to state an American policy and press for increased immigration, was just the opposite. I thought it unwise to apply pressure of any sort to the Special Committee and impair the complete neutrality of its approach.

In retrospect, the importance of impartiality was probably restricted to the deliberations of the General Assembly. It did not help the report of the Special Committee made on August 31 in the eyes of either Jews or Arabs in Palestine. In fact, by mid-July more than forty-five hundred illegal immigrants detained at Haifa were returned to Europe. By the year's end fighting was general throughout Palestine. By that time I no longer had any responsibility.

21. TROUBLE BREWS IN WASHINGTON

THE SUMMER OF 1946 was a time of almost uninterrupted troubles both in Washington and abroad. In Washington those that involved me included both small, often amusing ones, and larger troubles in which the element of amusement was wholly lacking.

TROUBLE FROM A COMMENCEMENT SPEECH

In June our daughter-in-law was being graduated with honors from Bryn Mawr College. We were proud of her and her achievement, performed while her husband was serving most actively in the Pacific naval theater of war. I was pleased to be asked to speak at her commencement exercises. In an attempt to introduce a little spice into the annual surfeit of June banalities, I touched on one aim of education—to develop an independent critical spirit. This I now see is one of the most subversive of doctrines. Certainly to one of my hearers I chose an infuriating illustration. The Star Chamber, I said, a room in Westminster Palace with a ceiling decoration of stars, had gotten a bad name from the Puritans since there the King's counselors reinforced by judges sat by statute to try offenders too powerful for the law courts. Meetings on other subjects sometimes took place in secret and the council also undertook to license printing presses and their uses. To characterize a proceeding today as a "star chamber" one was to apply a highly pejorative epithet. Yet what came to be called the Court of Star Chamber was one of the principal instruments by which the Tudors ended the Wars of the Roses and guided England out of the Middle Ages into a modern centralized state.

This was too much for Fulton Oursler, then senior editor of the *Reader's Digest*. He immediately protested to me in person on the spot and by letters to the President and the Secretary of State. He reported my speech in hair-raising terms, concluding, "I suggest that such views are treasonable to the philosophy of American government and that no man holding such views deserves public office." They were signed, "Yours for the Constitution."

Alas, he was unfamiliar with the workings of bureaucracy. The letter to the President was referred to the State Department for reply. In Mr. Byrnes's absence it was referred to me. For the same reason his letter to the Secretary of State came along with it. I took particular pleasure, writing on behalf of my superiors, in being excessively patient and polite, regretting that I had disturbed him and attributing this to my failure to make myself clear rather than to the content of my thought. The same views contained in testimony before a Senate committee, which I enclosed, had failed to produce shock. I cited learned authorities in support of my point. I was saddened that he should doubt my loyalty to the First Amendment to the Constitution, concluding:

I have sworn many times to defend that document against all enemies, foreign and domestic . . . [and] gone to some trouble and inconvenience to carry out my oath. So while I see much to be said for your view that I should not hold public office —though for different reasons than those you give—I cannot share your opinion that my views are treasonable to the philosophy of American Government.

Let's put it down to a difficulty in communication.

RESTLESSNESS IN THE CABINET

The months since April 1945 had brought me into continuous and close relations with President Truman. My regard and affection for him had grown steadily. In the summer those members of the Cabinet who had private dining rooms in their departments—principally the Secretaries of the Treasury and Defense and the Attorney General—began a friendly practice of inviting their colleagues in a body to luncheon, about once a week. Very shortly the talk turned to official matters and, with the campaign of 1946 carrying ominous overtones of popular discontent over high taxes and price controls, to politics. Jim Forrestal had been reading—or, perhaps, misreading—Walter Bagehot on the British cabinet system and talked with us about the desirability of the Cabinet's taking greater corporate responsibility. Bagehot's writing was of much earlier cabinet practices in Britain than those that currently prevailed. In 1946 the relation of the Prime Minister to his Cabinet—except for its lack of formality—was closer to that of the President to his than to Bagehot's description of mid-nineteenth-century practice.

At any rate, the idea appeared to be taking hold that at our luncheons we should discuss broad governmental policies in preparation for more orderly, serious, and effective discussions than usually took place in the somewhat haphazard weekly Cabinet meetings. This filled me with forebodings. Of all those present I was probably the only one who had been living in Washington during President Wilson's illness when Secretary Lansing, after weeks of silence from the White House, called the Cabinet together to consider some pressing matters of Government business. When President Wilson learned of it, Lansing received a note of summary dismissal. Our meetings, like his, were convened in all innocence and complete loyalty to the President, but it did not require much imagination to foresee what bad blood could be produced if news of these meetings leaked to the press, as most things do in Washington. It seemed clear to me that the meetings should end and that the ending should come from a friendly suggestion of the President before and not after any sinister purposes should be attached to them.

After the third or fourth of these luncheons I asked James E. Webb, then Director of the Budget and later my Under Secretary of State, who had been asked to join us, to drive back to the office with me, and I put my worries to him. He thoroughly agreed. We changed our destination to the White House, where the President was able to receive us immediately and privately. He saw at once both the innocence and the indiscretion of the lunches and said that he would handle the matter in a relaxed way at the next Cabinet meeting.

This he did to perfection. Opening the meeting, he said that he wanted us to see one another socially as well as officially and to develop the warmest of friendships and loyalties. The Cabinet as a group should not meet out of his presence or take up Government business except with him and as his advisers. Other courses would lead to misconceptions, speculation, and harmful gossip. He then went on to other business. The luncheons ended without embarrassment to anyone.

TROUBLE FROM A LADY

During these months another small incident, intended to have only temporary consequences, produced an institution that has not always been beneficial. On one of his short visits to Washington during the summer Secretary Byrnes told me that our distinguished and much-beloved colleague, Will Clayton, Assistant Secretary for Economic Affairs, had asked to be permitted to resign and return to private life. After some discreet inquiries I reported to Mr. Byrnes that, in my judgment, this request did not represent Will Clayton's wish in any respect. He loved the tremendous challenge of his post and the problems he faced. What was wrong was Mrs. Clayton's sense of injustice because Will bore the title of Assistant Secretary, while I, whom he had once superseded, carried a higher one. Why not, I suggested, try out the soothing effect on "Miss Sue's" ruffled feelings of a proposal that Will be made Under Secretary of State for Economic Affairs. This must be done carefully, for if proposed to Will Clayton by the Secretary himself, he would turn it down at once, great gentleman that he was, as an encroachment on my position. I assured the Secretary that nothing could impair the harmony with which Will Clayton and I worked together; I asked only to be allowed to handle the matter myself. He agreed.

I went to the Clayton house one late afternoon for a private chat, which I had no doubt "Miss Sue" would overhear. Will and I sat on the terrace behind the house as the sun went down. Disclosing no knowledge of his proposed departure, I said that Mr. Byrnes and I had concluded that his heavy burden would be eased in the bureaucratic in-fighting, and abroad too, by the addition of some rank to his own prestige. Another star had helped even Generals Eisenhower and Marshall. He should be made an Under Secretary of State, which would help me also. A voice from the window above us said solemnly, "That is a very sensible idea, Will Clayton. You should accept it." Neither of us acknowledged the existence of this voice offstage, but went on with our conversation. In due course, Will agreed and I took my leave.

We had no trouble with Congress, which readily gave the temporary authority for the additional position. When Will Clayton did retire in 1947, his office was allowed to lapse. When it was revived for Douglas Dillon in 1958, it performed a useful purpose in giving prestige to the economic function. But later, when it became merely a second Under Secretaryship, often called Under Secretary for Political Affairs, as it is while I write, it is a fifth wheel, an embarrassment, and should be abolished. The offices men create live after them, the good is oft interred with their purpose.

MR. MOLOTOV PAYS US A VISIT

On November 6, 1946, Mr. Byrnes telephoned me from New York to tell me that Molotov was coming to Washington for the celebration of the Russian "October" (old-style calendar) Revolution, when the bolsheviks took over in Petrograd. He asked me to meet Molotov, ease his day in Washington, and not allow any incident, however trivial, to add to Mr. Byrnes's problems at the United Nations or the Council of Foreign Ministers.

A letter to our daughter, Mary, gives an account of the day.

I explained to Solomon Bostic [chauffeur to the Under Secretary] that the old car, which Eddie Miller always called the Atchison, Topeka and Santa Fe, had to be shined as never before as we were going to bring Mr. Molotov up from the train in it.

We arrived at the railroad station to find more guards, both Russian and American, than I had seen for some time. The Soviet Ambassador discussed whether I should have the honor of driving him and Mr. Molotov in my car but came to no decision, because the Ambassador had no idea what Mr. Molotov might want to do and no intention of committing himself.

When the train came in we were at the bottom of the car steps to welcome the great man, and for me to extend President Truman's assurances of his pleasure in looking forward to their meeting. This was not true, but it had the desired effect. It was my first experience with the interpreter, Pavlov, an extraordinary fellow. He did not wait for one party to a conversation to finish before translating, but talked along in the opposite language from that of the speaker, two or three words behind him. The result was good because the conversation remained current, but at first gave me the feeling that I was actually speaking Russian.

When Mr. Molotov decided that he would ride with me, he and the Ambassador, the interpreter, and I got into the car. This was most fortunate, as his own car—brand-new and shiny—burst into flames as soon as the chauffeur stepped on the starter. The trouble appeared to be faulty ignition, but of course it gave all the appearances of a first-class plot. We went roaring out of the station with, to Bostic's delight, an escort of motorcycle police, all blowing whistles, sirens, and with great backfiring of motors. For once in his life, Bostic had the joy of driving as fast as he liked through Washington with all traffic stopped.

As we tore along the streets, Mr. Molotov after one or two tentative starts asked why it was that he never saw me at conferences. I told him that the only answer I could give to that was an answer which Mr. Hull had given to me when I asked him the same question several years ago. I said that Mr. Hull had told me that he would give two reasons. I could choose either the one which I thought was the truer or the one that pleased me most. He said one reason might be that I was so valuable in Washington that I could not be spared for other work. The second might be that if he ever let me out of his sight he would not have the slightest idea what I might do. Mr. Molotov was considerably entertained by this and said that he presumed unquestionably that the first explanation was the correct one but if, by any chance, the second one was right, he would like to be there to see the result. He then said to the Ambassador, according to the interpreter, "The Secretary has the jolly spirit."

By the time we got to the Embassy we were old friends. He asked when he could call on me. I suggested at twenty minutes before we both would call on the President at 4:00. I received him in the Secretary's office and we engaged in chitchat until it was time to go to see the President.

Being determined that this would take place in style, instead of walking the thirty or forty feet across the street, we all got in cars, Bostic again officiating, and drove out to Pennsylvania Avenue and back in to the White House offices.

After the interview with the President, Mr. Molotov got back into his car and I went to call on him at the great reception. The doorman told me that I was the one thousandth person to be recorded on his counting device. When I asked to pay my respects to Mr. Molotov, the Ambassador assigned a naval officer to take me to him. After a long walk through rooms jammed with people, the naval officer knocked on a closed door as we used to do at speakeasies on Fifty-Second Street. It was opened a crack, a whispered conversation took place, and I was ushered into a large room with a table heaped with every sort of food, wine, whisky, and vodka, with only Mr. Molotov, the interpreter, former Ambassador Joseph E. Davies and former Chairman of the Council of Economic Advisers Leon Henderson and his wife to enjoy it all. When after another chat I was let out, Averell Harriman was let in. Apparently very few indeed went through that portal.

Stanley Woodward said that it was unnecessary for me to go to the train to say goodby. But I told him of the old woman who was seen by one of her daughters putting on black underclothing to attend a funeral. When she was asked why, she said, "Child, when I moans, I moans."

So at 9:00 o'clock off we went. Mr. Molotov, sitting alone in the compartment of a car filled with thirty guards and attendants, was overwhelmed at the distinguished courtesy paid to him, as apparently were the Russian occupants of the car. As I left him, they all stood up in two long rows, bowing to me as I passed between them.

Thus Mr. Molotov departed.

BULL IN A GOOD-NEIGHBOR SHOP

Disillusion with my colleague Spruille Braden, well advanced by the end of the battle over intelligence, was completed by participation in his frustrating battle with Colonel Juan Perón, the President and "strong man" of Argentina. Not that I did not join the crusade willingly enough. Perón was a fascist and a dictator detested by all good men—except Argentinians. But I had still to learn the hard way what Woodrow Wilson's experience with Huerta in Mexico should have taught me—that dictators, in Latin America or elsewhere, are not overthrown by withholding recognition and dollars or even by harsh verbal disapproval. In fact, such treatment may well make them national heroes. Perón learned to run against Braden—"Perón o Braden!"—as successfully as Mayor Thompson of Chicago used to run against King George VI.

For some time before Braden came along, our policy toward Argentina had alternated between a harsh and a soft line. Few of our good neighbors were any more enthusiastic than we had been about breaking with Germany or

Japan. Argentina lagged behind the rest in doing so and in checking our enemies' economic and political influence. Mr. Hull, thoroughly exasperated, adopted a harsh line. After Colonel Perón's putsch in March 1944, relations grew worse. In August we froze Argentine assets, restricted exports to that country, and after October forbade American ships to enter Argentine ports. Argentina was also excluded from the Chapultepec Conference and the same policy had been proposed for the United Nations Conference at San Francisco, but Nelson Rockefeller and Stettinius switched to a soft line and let Argentina attend and become an original member. Taking advantage of Perón's brief exile, we rescinded sanctions on April 4, and on April 19 recognized the Argentine Government. Yet at the same time Stettinius chose as Ambassador to Argentina Spruille Braden, who was strongly opposed to Juan Perón and in his speeches and press conferences in Argentina was highly critical of Argentina's government, while Stettinius in Washington spoke of friendship, agreed to send arms there, and then changed his mind.

Coming into the Argentine imbroglio in September 1945, I immediately got into trouble. Braden and I met with Senators Vandenberg, Connally, Wallace White, and George to let them know that we had asked Brazil, the host government, to broach postponement of the conference to be convened in Rio de Janeiro in October, as agreed at Chapultepec. Its purpose was to negotiate an inter-American defense treaty. *Our* proposal was to do it through diplomatic channels instead, so as to exclude Argentina. The senators thoroughly disagreed with the postponement largely because they had not been consulted in advance,[1] as did the full committee when it met two days later. In its annoyance, it refused to consider Braden's confirmation. Since, however, a meeting of the Governing Board of the Pan American Union had been called for October 5 to consider postponement, there was nothing to be done.

In the meantime, I had announced our view to the press, explaining the illogicality of negotiating a defense treaty with Argentina, which had refused to honor obligations undertaken as recently as Chapultepec.[2] Our position was logical but unwise. The Governing Board reluctantly approved postponement. By these clumsy maneuvers, we had gotten ourselves at cross-purposes with the Senate and our Latin American friends. Even so, more was yet to come.

Perón, returning dramatically from a week's exile forced on him by his enemies, promptly announced his candidacy for the Presidency in the coming February elections. Shortly afterward, Secretary Byrnes strongly endorsed Uruguayan Foreign Minister Eduardo Rodríguez Larreta's proposal for collective intervention when an American nation denied its citizens their essential rights or defaulted on its international obligations. Nonintervention, the Minister said, should not be a "shield behind which crime may be perpetrated, law may be violated, agents and forces of the Axis may be sheltered, and binding obligations may be circumvented."[3] To most Latin Americans the proposal had an anti-Argentine purpose, and, even worse, was too reminiscent of Theodore Roosevelt's gloss on the Monroe Doctrine.† Mr. Byrnes was its sole supporter.

Two weeks before the Argentine election the Department made public under the guise of consulting the other American republics the famous Blue

Book,[4] prepared by Braden and his staff. This cited chapter and verse to show that Argentine governments had for years helped "the enemy," worked against hemisphere cooperation, engaged in subversion against its neighbors, and maintained a "vicious partnership" with totalitarian forces. In Latin America its reception was cool. Perón hastened to embrace the issue tendered—"Perón o Braden!"—and won the election handily.

In the Department we licked our wounds, while each side made cautious reconciliatory gestures, ours under the guidance of George Messersmith, an old Latin American hand who had become Ambassador in Buenos Aires. But our hearts were not in it. The situation was an ironic one. When the Department refuses, as it should, to be governed in its course toward another state by popular approval or disapproval of that state's internal policies, it is bitterly criticized for immoral or amoral behavior. On those occasions when it yields to what would be the popular attitude, if the public knew and cared enough to have an attitude, it is also—and rightly—criticized. These are occupational hazards. The sound rule would seem to be that if our interests are hurt enough by the acts of another state, internal or external, we should act to stop them, or make our protest fór the record.

In May the President sent to Congress, in anticipation of an inter-American defense agreement, a bill authorizing some of the acts which would be necessary to carry it out, such as assignment of training missions and transfer of weapons.[5] The eminently sensible purpose of such an effort was to anticipate and prevent the proliferation in Latin America of European training missions and of innumerable types of foreign equipment common in Latin America which both created dangerous influences and greatly impeded any effort toward common plans, operations, and supply. The danger cited was, of course, that dictators might use these arms against their own people; yet no one proposed the disarming of dictators. The proposal had strong military support. Despite this, when General von der Becke, former Chief of Staff of the Argentine Army, came to Washington in June 1946 and urgently wished to see me, I received him coolly, under the watchful eye of Spruille Braden, and "set forth the position of this Government in keeping with a statement made by Secretary Byrnes on April 8, 1946."[6] This reference did not warm the diplomatic atmosphere, since Mr. Byrnes had said: "The policy of non-intervention in internal affairs does not mean the approval of local tyranny. Our policy is intended to protect the right of our neighbors to develop their own freedom in their own way. It is not intended to give them free rein to plot against the freedom of others."[7]

When Mr. Byrnes came home in October, our Argentine policy was widely criticized as futile and disruptive of hemisphere relations, and blamed on Braden. Mr. Byrnes stoutly supported him and reaffirmed his own earlier statements. After that we drifted until General Marshall took over as Secretary of State. When, toward the end of my tenure, he was able to give attention to hemisphere matters, he found our policy, as he aptly put it, was "not all of one piece." Our mood alternated between the emphasis that Messersmith in Buenos Aires and the Defense Department in Washington gave to patching things up and Braden's determination to concede nothing to Perón. General Marshall was hearing from both Senators Vandenberg and Connally and from the Latin American embassies an increasing desire to get on with the conference at Rio de Janeiro. In this situation Messersmith moved to Mexico City, and the conflict between the two men continued in a new setting and over a new issue.

A shipment of prize bulls arrived in Mexico from some area infected with hoof-and-mouth disease. Under arrangements existing between Mexico and the United States which permitted importation of cattle from Mexico, Mexico had agreed not to receive imports from any infected area. In this case a Mexican request to quarantine the bulls on an island for a suitable period was refused by the Department of Agriculture as not safe. Messersmith combated the decision; Braden supported it. General Marshall directed that no concession be made. The bulls were landed and quarantined, with—it was charged—Messersmith's collusion, if not consent. To General Marshall this appeared to be direct disobedience. The facts immediately became clouded in dispute. I recommended to the General that, the situation and the relations between the two men, and between each of them and the Department, having become intolerable, I be permitted to deal with the problem by eliminating it—that is, by acting in his name to recall and retire Messersmith and to ask for Braden's resignation. Upon his agreement I did so, taking upon myself the onus of the decision and its communication to the two. While memory of the action remained in the Foreign Service, it had the powerful effect of transforming an instruction from the Department from an invitation to debate to an order to act. It was small recompense for all that General Marshall had done for me.

THE IMMOLATION OF MR. BYRNES

Hardly had Secretary Byrnes and his colleagues, Senators Connally and Vandenberg, weathered the crises of August 1946 precipitated by Stalin and Tito and recounted in the next chapter, than another burst on them from Washington. In this episode I had no part, being away in Canada on a much-needed vacation. As was suggested in Chapter 15, the President thought that at the Moscow conference of December 1945 Mr. Byrnes had compromised too far to reach agreement with Stalin. "I do not think," he had said, "we should play compromise any longer. . . . I'm tired of babying the Soviets."[8] Secretary Byrnes had followed his chief's policy all through the weary months of negotiating the Italian and Eastern European peace treaties at the Paris Peace Conference. On September 6, 1946, he made a speech expressing it in Stuttgart, Germany. A week later in Madison Square Garden, his Cabinet colleague, Secretary of Commerce Henry Wallace, replied in the manner of all critics of United States policy in Europe over the next twenty years.

The issues were posed as follows: Mr. Byrnes, regretting the Soviet refusal to consider his offer at Paris in April 1946 of a twenty-five-year treaty to maintain a peaceful Europe guaranteed against rearmament in Germany, called for the return of government and industry to a demilitarized and denazified Germany under supervision in which the United States would participate.[9] Secretary Wallace said that "getting tough" would get us nowhere: "The tougher we get, the tougher the Russians will get. . . . The real peace treaty we now need is between the United States and Russia." He appeared to envision each country having spheres of influence within which each would scrupulously remain in peaceful coexistence, they communizing in theirs, we democratizing in ours, both in the nicest possible way. "Under . . . peaceful competition the Russian world and the American world will gradually become more alike."[10]

Before delivering the address Henry Wallace had shown Mr. Truman the typescript of it, but the President had not read it then. It is possible that even by the time of his press conference, before the speech was made, he had not read it. At any rate, the following passage from the forthcoming Wallace speech was read to him at the press conference: "When President Truman read these words, he said that they represented the policy of this administration." To which the President replied, "That is correct." (The specific words in the speech to which Wallace referred, but which were not mentioned in the press conference question, were, "I am neither anti-Russian nor pro-Russian.") The conference continued:[11]

Q: My question is, does that apply just to that paragraph, or to the whole speech?
The President: I approved the whole speech. . . .
Q: Mr. President, do you regard Wallace's speech a departure from Byrnes's policy—
The President: I do not.
Q: —toward Russia?
The President: They are exactly in line.

The following day James Reston wrote in *The New York Times:*

Mr. Truman seems to be the only person in the capital who thinks that Mr. Wallace's proposals are "in line" with Mr. Truman's or Mr. Byrnes'. . . .
The truth seems to be less dramatic [than a change in policy]. The President has been preoccupied with domestic issues. Mr. Wallace sent him the speech, and under our usual casual Cabinet system Mr. Truman glanced at it hastily and evidently let it go without taking time to study the implications or how it would read here and abroad.[12]

To the men in Paris no such relaxed view was possible. The speech was bad enough in all conscience, but the President's approval—despite his belated lame explanation that he did not approve its content but only Wallace's making it—made it a land mine exploded under them. Nor did the President's additional sentence—"There has been no change in the established foreign policy of our Government"—help much, for Wallace responded by stating that he would speak again and released a letter of July 23, 1946, to the President even more critical of administration policy toward Russia than the speech had been. On September 18 Mr. Byrnes informed the President that his resignation, tendered in April, would have to take effect immediately unless the President could control Wallace. There could not be two secretaries of state.[13]

On September 19 the President and Wallace were closeted together for two and a half hours. When the Secretary of Commerce emerged, wreathed in smiles, he read from a penciled statement: "The President and the Secretary of Commerce had a most detailed and friendly discussion, after which the Secretary reached the conclusion he would make no public statements or speeches until the Foreign Ministers' conference in Paris is concluded." When a newspaperman asked whether he had everything "patched up," Mr. Wallace replied, "Everything's lovely."[14]

Mr. Byrnes, understandably concluding that the President's response to his earlier message had been somewhat less than adequate, sent a long, restrained, and admirable message, asking to be relieved of his responsibilities at once.[15] The next day the President asked for and received Henry Wallace's resignation.

Throughout this episode President Truman was naïve. This is not a serious indictment. In the first place he was still learning the awesome responsibilities of the President of the United States. It did not occur to him that Henry Wallace, a responsible and experienced high officer of government, should not make a speech he had carefully prepared. Pleased that his permission was asked, he readily gave it, without, as Reston wrote, worrying about the content of the speech. Years later he would order General MacArthur to withdraw a message that he had released but not yet delivered. Even after Mr. Byrnes's first message, he did not understand the deep damage that Wallace had done to foreign confidence in the United States. It seemed a personal quarrel that could be patched up. Secondly, he was not good in the fast back-and-forth of a press conference. President Truman's mind is not so quick as his tongue. As the transcript quoted above indicates, he could not wait for the end of a question before answering it. Not seeing where he was being led, he fell into traps. He thought FDR's apparent free-and-easy dialogue with the press was as easy and candid as it seemed, a profound illusion. This tendency was a constant danger to him and bugbear to his advisers. His press conferences and, even more, his early-morning walks followed by inquisitive reporters were a constant menace.

When I came out of the peace and quiet of the Canadian Rockies, where with Ambassador and Mrs. Atherton we had ridden north through Jasper Park to the Arctic Circle and back, and learned what had happened, my worst forebodings about trouble between my chiefs seemed justified. My journey back to Washington, knowing what I did about the President's action already taken on Mr. Byrnes's April resignation, was a worried one.

I had learned about that action through the correspondence between the President and General Marshall of which I was the intermediary. One day during the summer a passage in one of the General's cables from China was too obscure for me. I asked the President whether he wanted it clarified. He then told me of Mr. Byrnes's resignation of April—about which I already knew

—and added that during the summer he had explained the situation to General Eisenhower, who was about to leave for a tour of inspection in the Far East, and asked him to inquire of General Marshall whether he would be willing to take Mr. Byrnes's place when the time came for him to leave office. The reply had again been that General Marshall would serve in whatever capacity the President wished.† Never have I so regretted sharing a secret. When I asked whether the President had told Mr. Byrnes of this development, he said that he had not had a secure opportunity to do so, and that meanwhile unless the knowledge of it were restricted to the four who now knew of it, the usefulness of both Secretary Byrnes and General Marshall would be destroyed.

22. TROUBLE BREAKS IN EUROPE

The Eastern Mediterranean · Stalin's offensive against the United States and the West, announced in his speech of February 9, 1946, had begun in Poland in 1945 and would reach its crescendo in Korea and the "hate America" campaign of the early 1950s. This was the start of the "cold war," and was to condition the rest of my official life. The offensive was mounted on territory thought most favorable to the interior lines of the Soviets, where their military power was superior, and on political issues in international discussion, where stubborn and skillful opposition to American proposals could be successful with little cost. Geographically, therefore, the attack was concentrated along Russia's borders in Eastern Europe and the Middle East, where the Soviets' physical position was strongest and that of the United States weakest. Politically it centered against efforts to create a United Nations military force and the United States plan to put atomic energy under effective international control. Blocking tactics in the United Nations were made easy by Soviet possession of the veto. The creation of Soviet satellites succeeded only where the Red Army was present to reinforce it. When the attempt moved beyond the Soviet-occupied areas of Eastern Europe to West Germany, the Balkans, and the Middle East, the United States Government gave fair warning that, if necessary, it was prepared to meet Soviet force with American force, rather than with mere protests and resolutions in the United Nations. The first warning was given in August 1946 but Stalin continued to probe cautiously and to receive firm but cautious responses until June 1950, when, throwing off pretense, he made an attack in force through a satellite on the other side of the world in Korea. Here the American response was unequivocal.

Mr. Byrnes was finding the Council of Foreign Ministers meeting on peace treaties hard going. The most difficult snag proved to be the Italian-Yugoslav border in the Trieste area. In May it had turned into a prestige battle between the Russian and the Anglo-American positions, the former backing the Yugoslav claim to the whole eastern coast of the Adriatic, the latter supporting the retention by Italy of the northeastern littoral, which included the city of Trieste and the adjacent Italian-populated environs. The council had come to rest, without conviction or satisfaction to anyone, upon a recommendation to the peace conference, about to meet a month later, of a Free Territory of Trieste. Meanwhile, Anglo-American forces faced Yugoslav troops along the Morgan Line of zonal occupation, which bisected the former Italian province of

Venezia Giulia. On both sides of the line demonstrations in favor of hostile positions dangerously fired local passions. When the conference met in Paris, a Yugoslav coup in Trieste was freely predicted in the halls.

In this situation the already unhappy Secretary of State found himself enfiladed from three fields of fire. On August 7 the Soviet Government demanded that Turkey allow the USSR to participate in what it called the defense of the Straits, but which meant the occupation of Turkey. On August 9 the Yugoslavs forced down, and then on August 19 shot down, unarmed U.S. Army transport planes flying over Venezia Giulia. Simultaneously the Soviet Government, which had backed Yugoslavia and Bulgaria in border pressure on Greece to detach her northern provinces, opened an all-out drive in the United Nations against the Greek Government in support of an attempted Communist takeover in Athens by the National Liberation Front (EAM).

In Washington I had already been charged by the President to prepare with the Secretaries of War and Navy and the Chiefs of Staff recommendations for action to deal with the Russian move on the Straits. Secretary Byrnes telephoned me from Paris to work out with the President and the services fighter protection for Army transport aircraft flying over Venezia Giulia. Generals Eisenhower and Spaatz, however, turned down Mr. Byrnes's idea of using fighter escorts to convoy the slower C-47s in the narrow corridor along the Adriatic, recommending instead the use of armed fighter-bombers to do the transport work with orders to shoot if interfered with. The President approved.

In the Department we were taking another look at our rather reserved attitude toward the Greek Government, which had seemed to us a pretty weak reed in an area of British responsibility. In January I had already warned, when informing them of a twenty-five-million-dollar loan, that they would have to do much better in controlling their economy before we could advance any more money.[1] It might be that we would have no such choice.

On August 15 we went to the White House with our report on the Straits —Secretary of the Navy Forrestal, Under Secretary of War Kenneth Royall, and the Chiefs of Staff. Acting as spokesman, I sat at one end of a crescent around two sides of the President's desk with General Eisenhower, Chief of Staff of the Army, beside me. Our report expressed the seriousness of the Russian moves against Turkey and Greece, which aimed at the domination of the Balkans and the eastern Mediterranean. They should be resisted at all costs. Our note to the Russians should by its studied restraint impress the Russians that we meant every word of it. Where they had valid criticisms of the Treaty of Montreux, we should say so, but be adamant against any interference with exclusive Turkish defense of the Straits. We recommended making very plain to the Russians, Turks, British, and French that we were in deadly earnest. The USS *Missouri* was already at Istanbul, where it had been sent earlier with the ashes of a former Turkish Ambassador. We urged sending a powerful naval force, including the newly commissioned supercarrier *Franklin D. Roosevelt,* to join her. The President listened carefully, then told us to prepare the necessary notes and orders.

General Eisenhower asked me in a whisper whether I had made it sufficiently clear that the course we had recommended could lead to war. Before I could answer, the President asked whether the General had anything to add. I repeated his question to me. The President took from a drawer of his desk a large map of the Middle East and eastern Mediterranean and asked us to gather around behind him. He then gave us a brief lecture on the strategic importance of the area and the extent to which we must be prepared to go to keep it free from Soviet domination. When he finished, none of us doubted he understood fully all the implications of our recommendations.

The next day I sent him a note saying that, as he had instructed, I had informed Secretary Byrnes of our meeting and the President's views, in which the Secretary "heartily concurs." I proposed, therefore, to send off the notes right away. It came back with the notation, "Approved. Harry S. Truman," in the President's hand. Ambassador Edwin C. Wilson in Ankara was informed of the preparation of the notes, of their central theme—the preservation of Turkish sovereignty and of sole responsibility for defense of the Straits in Turkey—and was asked to urge that the Turkish reply to Moscow be "reasonable but firm." On August 19 I delivered our note to the Soviet Chargé d'Affaires, Fedor T. Orekhov,[2] and sent copies to Ankara, Paris, and London urging their agreement. Two days before I had briefed the press, stressing the seriousness of the situation, our decision to stand firm against any outside military interference with the defense of the Straits, and the undesirability of speculation upon possible developments.

On the day we delivered our note Tito's planes shot down the second American transport. We did not know at the time that its crew had been killed, and, therefore, demanded the release of both crews within forty-eight hours. The President ordered our troops along the Morgan Line augmented and the reinforcement of our air forces in northern Italy. As soon as the necessary naval forces could be assembled, they were moved into Greek waters. Tito quickly got the point and backed down. The offensive against Trieste and the Straits quieted. The Russian offensive moved to the northern border of Greece, the eastern provinces of Turkey, and northern Iran. The autumn would witness Soviet fire increasingly concentrated there.

Trouble Moves Eastward to Iran • Throughout 1946 demobilization in the United States went forward apace under the same strong pressures of public demand that voted in the November election for liquidation of other wartime inconveniences. Speaking in Boston in June, I voiced disquiet at the trend: "The slogans 'Bring the boys home!' and 'Don't be Santa Claus!' are not among our more gifted or thoughtful contributions to the creation of a free and tranquil world. This seems to me true for the simplest of all reasons, which is that the sensible way to strengthen a structure is not to weaken its most essential parts."[3]

The year 1946 was for the most part a year of learning that minds in the Kremlin worked very much as George F. Kennan had predicted they would. We reacted vigorously to the grosser forms of Communist probing, such as the downing of our planes in Venezia Giulia, but we were slower to see through the murkier methods by which Moscow was extending its control, always under the shadow of the Red Army. Henry Wallace had many followers in his doctrine that the Soviet Union was entitled to its spheres of influence. The Russians themselves greatly helped our education. In picking the Straits and Iran as points of pressure, they followed the route of invasion by barbarians against classical Greece and Rome and later of the czars to warm water. From Thermopylae to the Crimea the responses to pressure at these points had been traditional. If some Americans found their history rusty, neither the British nor the President did.

The Iranian crisis of 1945–46 revolved about two issues: whether the Soviet Union would withdraw its troops from northern Iran as it had agreed to do in 1942 and 1943, and whether it would succeed in creating out of the northern Iranian province of Azerbaijan an autonomous entity subject to Soviet control. In 1942 the Soviet Union and Great Britain had put troops into northern and southern Iran, respectively, to block a possible German move and to protect Iranian oil. Troops were to be withdrawn six months after the end of hostilities. In the Teheran Declaration of December 2, 1943, Roosevelt, Churchill, and Stalin had reaffirmed Iranian independence and integrity. In September 1945 Bevin and Molotov set the date of troop withdrawal as not later than March 2, 1946.

Meanwhile, the Soviet Government had been arming a separatist movement (the Tudeh Party) in Azerbaijan, and when it staged a revolt against the Shah in November 1945 refused to allow his troops access to the province to suppress it. The crisis was on, with the United States and Britain supporting Iran. It continued throughout the year in the Council of Foreign Ministers and the United Nations, where Gromyko walked out when the Security Council accepted jurisdiction. Bilateral discussions were carried on amid mutual suspicion. The date for troop withdrawal passed without action. In the spring tension increased through reports of reinforcement of Soviet forces in Azerbaijan. We addressed a public inquiry to Moscow.[4]

At this point, on March 24, Teheran and Moscow reached an agreement that seemed dubious. Russian troops would be withdrawn, while Iran would agree to a joint oil company and to arrangements which seemed to permit consolidation of the autonomous Azerbaijan regime. However, in the Near East things are not always what they seem. Russian troops withdrew in April, but the Majlis (Iranian parliament) repudiated the joint oil company. Tension grew again as the Tudeh Party demanded an election under its control. In October I had a series of visits from the Iranian Ambassador, Hussein Ala, as Mr. Byrnes was still away. The Ambasador, a good man, wanted the United States to take the initiative in reopening the Iranian case in the Security Council and in having it supervise elections in Azerbaijan. I said to him—with the President's and Secretary's approval—and asked our Ambassador to tell Qavam, the Prime Minister, that we could not act for but only in support of the Iranian Government. It must take the initiatives. Furthermore, it seemed a mistake to hold elections until Iranian authority was established in the province. Then United Nations observation could be useful. A little later, similarly authorized, we sent a favorable response to Qavam's request for our strong support should the Soviet Union object to Iranian troops entering Azerbaijan. When the troops arrived they were wildly welcomed, and the separatist regime collapsed. The troop movement, begun as a tentative feeler, ended in the reacquisition of the whole province.

With the crisis over, Ambassador George Allen cabled on December 17, 1946, that in the Iranian view the quick collapse of the Tudeh Party was due to the conviction of everyone—the Russians, the Iranians, and the Azerbaijanis— that the United States was not bluffing but solidly supporting Iranian sovereignty; as he put it, "Iran is no stronger than the UN and the UN, in the last analysis, is no stronger than the US."

Then to Greece and Turkey · Disappointed in its direct pressure on Iran, the Soviet Union turned with renewed vigor to the pressure it was putting on Greece and Turkey. Some background is necessary here, for with the months our involvement grew until inexorably events led on to President Truman's great decision of March 1947. However, when German forces were expelled from Greece in October 1944 that country was almost wholly an area of British responsibility. It had been so decided during the night of October 9–10, 1944, and recorded on the famous "half a sheet of paper" by Churchill and Stalin that assigned to Britain ninety per cent "of the say" in Greece with ten per cent to Russia in return for Russian predominance in other parts of the Balkans.[5] We did not much like this, but we had not been asked about it.

Under the Caserta agreement of September 26, 1944, between Minister Resident Harold Macmillan and the British Ambassador to Greece, Reginald Leeper, on one side, and Greek leaders Andreas Papandreou, Social Democrat, Napoleon Zervas, Nationalist, and General Stefanos Sarafis of the Communist National Army of Liberation, a government of national unity was created and installed in Athens less than a month later. All Greek forces, government and guerrilla, acknowledged the authority of this government and the military command of General Sir Henry Maitland Wilson as commander in chief and General Ronald McKenzie Scobie as commander in Greece. They would take no action except as ordered by the latter. General Scobie also commanded sixty thousand British troops in Greece.

Neither the agreement nor the government lasted much more than a month. When the government attempted to exert authority over the People's National Army of Liberation (ELAS), the Communists resisted and a general strike took place. Churchill instructed Scobie to act as though he were in a conquered city in which a rebellion was in progress. General Harold Alexander, who came to investigate, warned that military means alone would not solve the Greek problem. Churchill and Foreign Minister Eden flew to Athens. A regency was established under Archbishop Damaskinos and a "best men" government under General Nicholas Plastiras. The year 1945 saw two more governments, the spread of lawlessness, and crisis follow crisis.

Some light in Greek skies early in 1946 proved to be a false dawn. We granted an Export-Import Bank credit of twenty-five million dollars in January to support the economic program of my friend from early UNRRA talks, Kyriakos Varvaressos, governor of the Bank of Greece and Minister without Portfolio, by far the best man in the Greek Government. Elections held at the end of March under the observation of an international group containing six hundred Americans were declared by it to be "essentially free and fair." As a result, Constantine Tsaldaris, Royalist, became Prime Minister. He was a weak, pleasant, but silly man, obsessed by the idea, of which he talked incessantly, of solving Greek problems by obtaining from the peace conference, then meeting in Paris, cession of territory in the north and rivaling Venizelos, who at Versailles obtained Crete for Greece. He also asked us for six billion dollars in economic aid. Mr. Byrnes and I struggled without much success to focus his interest on more possible and essential achievements. In September a plebiscite returned a seventy per cent vote in favor of the return of King George II, who was not much more help than Tsaldaris.

We had the good fortune at this time, and through the war, of having a sympathetic, wise, and first-rate Ambassador to Greece, Lincoln MacVeagh. His reports drew an increasingly gloomy and serious picture of the Greek predicament. Communist bands were forming in the north, which could and did move back and forth across the Albanian and Yugoslav borders, gaining help and recruits from both countries. Greek economic affairs were becoming steadily more and more chaotic and irresponsible. We began to talk less about what we would not do, and more of what they must do, less about our aid and more about positive steps by which they could increase their own income. In October both Mr. Byrnes and I proposed an economic mission to make comprehensive recommendations on their whole economic situation. Paul Porter, former Administrator of the Office of Price Administration, would head it. It was Paul who described his mission as one to convince the Greeks that they should, in the words (wholly apocryphal) of Old Hickory to his men at the Battle of New Orleans, "Elevate them guns a little lower!"

The State-War-Navy Coordinating Committee prepared a specific and alarming paper on the strategic considerations involved, which Secretary Byrnes approved. Ambassador MacVeagh cabled in December that the Soviet Union wanted complete control of Greece and would interfere with all positive steps by the Greeks to save themselves.

Against this background the Porter mission set out for Greece in December, while Henderson and I listened for two hours to Tsaldaris discuss a list of Greek demands given to Mr. Byrnes. When he became eloquent on Greek claims to northern Epirus, I quite lost patience with him and told him what sort of statesmanship it was that frittered away its time and energy on territorial claims, when not only northern Greece but all Greece was headed hell-for-leather toward total destruction. Whether it stopped him, at least it saved me from the necessity of listening to any more of these dissertations.

Turkey, like Greece, was also being subjected to a softening-up process. On June 7, 1945, Soviet Foreign Minister Molotov informed the Turkish Ambassador to the Soviet Union of a Soviet claim to the Kars-Ardahan regions of eastern Turkey. These regions, of over six and a half thousand square miles and a population of three hundred thousand people, border on the Georgian and Armenian Soviet republics. The republics immediately outdid Mr. Molotov: the Georgian republic, claiming twenty-five thousand square miles with a population of a million and a quarter in northeastern Turkey along the Black Sea; the Armenian republic, claiming about the same size area to the south of this, with some six hundred ninety thousand people. The Turkish Government replied that with or without the aid of the United Nations it would fight to retain its "present territory and sovereignty."

A RECEPTION COMMITTEE OF ONE

The election of 1946 fulfilled our worst forebodings. Toward the end of the campaigning Bob Hannegan had brought us cheerful reports.† But they did not cheer me. The attack on the Administration had been bitter, brutal, and —I feared—effective. And so it turned out. The Democrats lost control of Congress for the first time in sixteen years.

The President had gone to Independence to vote and was returning by train with Mrs. Truman and their daughter Margaret the next morning. It had for years been a Cabinet custom to meet President Roosevelt's private car on his return from happier elections and escort him to the White House. It never occurred to me that after defeat the President would be left to creep unnoticed back to the capital. So I met his train. To my surprise and horror, I was alone on the platform where his car was brought in, except for the station master and a reporter or two. What the President expected, I do not know. He took me with them back to the White House and kept me to meet with his immediate staff on plans and a statement. A suggestion was made that an extra session of the Senate be called, before control passed to the Republicans in January, to confirm a large number of accumulated nominations to such offices as postmaster and collector of internal revenue and of customs and thus raise the sagging morale of the party faithful. I objected strongly—and found an effective ally in Charles Ross, the Press Secretary—on the ground that so cynically partisan a response to the election would have a deplorable effect. It would be far better to acknowledge frankly that the will of the people had been constitutionally and clearly expressed and that the President would cooperate in every way with the new Congress that they had created. He agreed, and together we drafted a statement that was issued at his next press conference.

BATTENING DOWN THE HATCHES

After the November election Will Clayton and I as the President's emissaries sought out two of the masters of the new Republican Senate, Arthur Vandenberg, who would be chairman of the Foreign Relations Committee, and Eugene Millikin of the Finance Committee; our purpose—to avoid warfare where possible by compromise, and to save what we could of the trade-agreements program. We attached more immediate importance to the latter than it was to have. Immunity from threats of immediate repeal of the act, which probably could not have been carried over a veto but would have precipitated a long and wasteful fight, was purchased by voluntary acceptance of some restrictions on executive power to reduce tariffs. The senators also agreed not to impede the scheduled discussions at Geneva on a broad new international plan for tariffs and trade. All of us understood that the election of 1948, rather than any present skirmishing, would determine the shape of the future. The Republicans were happily confident of that.

To clear away another source of trouble with Congress, we made clear that UNRRA would be wound up at the end of the current year. Its council had so decided in 1945, but many were regretting this as the needs for relief, instead of declining, seemed due to rise. Indeed the Food and Agriculture Organization was predicting food shortages of famine proportions. But to both Congress and the Administration, internationally administered relief had been a failure. The staff obtainable had been weak and the leadership weaker. UNRRA supplies turned up all too frequently in black markets, but, far more serious, the bulk of them, from our point of view, went to the wrong places and were used for wrong purposes. Due to rules built into the charter of UNRRA, as described in Chapter 9, the great bulk of relief, largely supplied or paid for by the United States, went to Eastern Europe and was used by governments bitterly hostile to us to entrench themselves, contrary to agreements made at Yalta and in countless resolutions of the organization.

American relief should be concentrated, the President decided, in areas of need in which we had special responsibilities and interests. He specified Italy, Austria, Greece, Hungary (whose popularly elected government we supported), and Poland, asking for three hundred fifty million dollars for relief under American supervision. The Congress was slow to act. The request was soon overtaken, as were the Balkans and Europe as a whole, by a flood of disasters, capped by the terrible winter of 1946–47.

RUSSIAN INTENTIONS IN CHINA

SOON AFTER his arrival in China in December 1945, General Marshall tele-graphed Secretary Byrnes, then leaving Moscow for Washington, asking whether the difficulties that Generalissimo Chiang Kai-shek was reporting in his dealings with the Russians in Manchuria were similar to our own difficulties in Europe or whether Soviet policy in China was deliberately designed to block creation of an effective and unified China. This question, appearing to present a dichotomy, produced a misleading answer. Secretary Byrnes had the word from Stalin that Soviet troops were in Manchuria at the request of the Chinese Nationalist Government and believed their relation to China to be of the same nature as our relation to Europe. He also believed that Stalin would live up to his treaty with China and not impede our efforts for a unified China.

Kennan, giving his own estimate a week later from Moscow, saw far deeper into Stalin's aims in China, as he did in his already-reported appraisal of Soviet aims in Europe. The USSR sought predominant influence in China. It would attempt to attain it by "nonintervention" on the part of the Soviet Government, brazen intrigue on the part of the Communist Party, and ad-vocacy of a coalition government through which the Chinese Communist Party could hope to control or capture the government. The USSR was for the time being retaining its diplomatic mobility between support of Chinese Nationalist or Communist elements.

Kennan stated frankly that he did not know what the relationship be-tween Yenan and Moscow was. Quite prepared to believe that the Chinese Communist Party, like others, was subservient to Moscow, he still hesitated to accept it as established truth. Moscow-Yenan relations were most subtle and obscure. Yenan might enjoy a surprising degree of independence, since (1) the Chinese Communist Party had little reason to be grateful to the USSR—it had survived and grown not because of, but in spite of, Moscow; (2) the CCP had developed its own brand of Marxism and indigenous traditions; (3) the CCP was no fugitive band of conspirators—for ten years it had had a regime, army, and civil administration; and (4) the CCP had taken on nationalistic coloration. Yet Yenan had had no latitude for choice in its foreign relations. The net result, Kennan felt, had been that Moscow had disarmed considerable Western suspicion of Soviet political respectability, befogged issues for Chungking, taught Yenan not to take too much for granted, and placed itself in a position to capitalize on developments in China no matter what direction they took. Moscow's possibilities for making its influence effective in Yenan in decisive moments were enormous.

Brilliant as was this analysis, it failed as a prophecy. Moscow did not persuade, or try to persuade, Yenan to enter or capture a coalition government, a course much feared by the Kuomintang. For one thing, the Soviet Army was not in a position to play the role in China that it played in Eastern Europe; for another, Yenan was seeking a dominant not a satellite role. Chiang Kai-shek also wanted dominance in all China, including Manchuria, and believed he must gain it by military means. However, to achieve this end by this means was beyond his capabilities, as General Wedemeyer repeatedly warned. The United States would not, and in the light of domestic and foreign realities probably could not, have enabled him to achieve it. What brought about the total failure of the Marshall mission was not the independence, or lack of it, of Yenan from Moscow, as much as the death wish of the Kuomintang in taking on an offensive military campaign against the Communists for control of all China.

CHIANG'S MANCHURIAN BLUNDER

Trouble and mistakes began in Manchuria. Chiang Kai-shek had gambled in moving troops there to take over from the Russians. General Wedemeyer had advised the Nationalists to consolidate their position in south China before taking on the vast problems of north China and Manchuria. Fear of a divided China weighed against this wise advice, and the cease-fire agreement of January 10 gave the Nationalists the right to move into Manchuria. Molotov had agreed in the communiqué issued at the Moscow foreign ministers' conference in December 1945 that Russian troops would be withdrawn beginning February 1, 1946. The Generalissimo refused until March 27 to allow joint Executive Headquarters teams to enter Manchuria to police a cease-fire, fearing—so General Marshall reported—Soviet demands to be included in them and not wishing to recognize the Communist Party forces in Manchuria. Sporadic fighting broke out between the Chinese. February 1 came and went without Russian withdrawal. The Communists gained strength as they infiltrated forces into Manchuria and, with Russian collusion, took over surrendered Japanese weapons. The communication lines of the Nationalists became dangerously overextended. In the middle of March the Nationalists moved into Mukden when the Russians suddenly withdrew from that city; but a month later, on the day of General Marshall's return to China—April 18—the Communists captured Changchun, the capital of Manchuria, in flagrant violation of the cessation-of-hostilities agreement.

General Marshall on his return cabled sadly to the President that he found irreconcilables in the saddle and received the reproaches of Chiang for false conceptions of the dependability of the Communists, who, Chiang claimed, were in league with the Russians. On this Chiang was at least partly wrong.

The Soviet delay in withdrawing from Manchuria was not primarily to benefit the Chinese Communists, but to carry out their own systematic looting of the industrial equipment of Manchuria and its removal to the Soviet Union as "war booty." A Job's comforter, the President replied to General Marshall that Chiang must soon come to see that "his agreement to your proposals for achieving peace and unity cannot realistically be viewed as a self-denying relinquishment of Kuomintang power but . . . as a means of preserving for him and the liberal element in the Kuomintang a place and influence in the government of a united China which otherwise might only be secured, and this doubtfully, by all-out civil war." Issuing censure with an even hand, the President went on to say that "chances of unity would be greatly enhanced if . . . the opportunistic disregard for agreement which characterized [the Communist] recent move in Manchuria would cease." Candor requires me to add the last line of the message: "The Acting Secretary of State joins me in the foregoing views."

With the tired patience of Sisyphus, General Marshall began rolling his unwieldy stone uphill again. He worked hard to obtain agreement that the Communists would withdraw from Changchun, the Nationalists stop their advance upon it, and Executive Headquarters establish an advance section there. But on May 23 the Nationalist forces took the city, seriously compromising the good faith of General Marshall's position. Nevertheless, he obtained a truce to continue until the end of June. In the meantime the Committee of Three would attempt to terminate hostilities in Manchuria, re-establish communication between the Chinese factions on steps to a united China, and carry out the agreement of February 25 for the reorganization of the armed forces.

GENERAL MARSHALL'S INFLUENCE DECLINES

As the end of June approached, the General could report that hostilities had been pretty well brought under control and negotiations between the two sides resumed, although their positions seemed farther apart than ever. However, a new difficulty had developed, brought on by well-meant efforts in Washington to initiate measures for the aid of China. One was a proposal before Congress to establish a military advisory group to assist in the contemplated reorganization of the Chinese military forces. Another was an agreement, which had to be completed by the end of June, for carrying through lend-lease aid. These produced double trouble in China. Die-hard Kuomintang members, the General reported, used them to urge the Generalissimo to renew the war against the Communists, since American help would be forthcoming in any event. The Communists, reaching the same conclusion, used the proposed legislation as proof that concessions to the Nationalists in furtherance of unity were useless. Both sides attacked General Marshall, one for holding them back from victory, the other for selling them out by deceptive proposals designed to weaken them. "It would be helpful if government spokesmen in Washington seized a favorable occasion to explain the aims and development of American measures for aid to China," cabled the harassed General.

With the President's approval, I immediately issued a statement saying that press reports from China indicated the gravest misconceptions there of the preparations being made here to help carry out the agreements, some already reached in China, others under negotiation there to work out a plan and program for national unity. Illustrative descriptions of our efforts showed how they would fit into Chinese plans in several fields.

The General was grateful, but the negotiations begun in April, after sprouting hopefully, withered. The opening days of July found General Marshall in a rare period of discouragement. He was, he cabled me, "so closely engaged and so close to the trees" that he lacked perspective. He would appreciate a "frank and quite informal" appraisal of the situation as Vincent and I saw it. We sent a joint reply two days later, unhappily giving little comfort. The basic cause of trouble was plain enough—the total lack of any element of trust or confidence not only between the Kuomintang and the Communists but between both and the Chinese people. Only the extremists on both sides wanted war, but both sides feared the concessions which were necessary to compromise. Neither wished to incur responsibility for failure of the negotiations and the mission. Hence, negotiations had a degree of momentum; the soundest tactic was to keep them going. The Communists seemed unlikely to resume warfare since they were overextended militarily. The Kuomintang hotheads possessed the old warlord mentality that military success was evidenced by an extension of territorial control rather than by defeat of the enemy's forces. Yet such a policy would obviously overextend the Nationalists and concentrate their enemies to the advantage of the latter.

While, as we saw it, the General should strive to keep the talks going, he must face the possibility of a stalemate. In case of a stalemate without war, the General might do well to maintain contact but relax his efforts and reduce United States aid. This might bring a greater sense of responsibility and urgency to the Chinese. If war was resumed, we suggested maintaining relations with the government and considering a withdrawal of U.S. military forces from China and a cessation of material support. If the Soviet Union should support the Chinese Communists, a major reassessment of U.S. policy would be necessary.

Another task assigned to me at this time by General Marshall will illustrate the many-sided duties of his rear echelon. Although designated as the President's Special Representative in China, the General had, in fact, been performing all the duties of ambassador. In order to relieve himself of these duties and to take up a position more detached from the Government of China, General Marshall asked me to discuss with the President the appointment as ambassador of General Wedemeyer, whose experience commanding U.S. Forces, China Theater, had made him thoroughly familiar with the military and political problems with which General Marshall was dealing. The President and General Wedemeyer were willing to do whatever General Marshall wished, Wedemeyer asking only that Congress by special act preserve his military status for resumption later. One other matter bothered him. As a serving officer long off at the wars, he did not have the expensive civilian clothes expected of an ambassador. What was expected in China and what should he do about it? I had no idea, but as General Marshall's rear echelon some of his decisiveness had rubbed off on me. Left over from the war days, the Secretary of State had a "confidential fund" for which he was not accountable. I had never dealt in such secret financial affairs, but the time had come to begin.

"Equip yourself, General," I said, "with whatever clothes the Post Report recommends and send me the bill." General Hurley, who was quite a dresser, would have seen that the specifications were adequate. His successor was delighted to obey his first diplomatic instruction.

Now, however, we were notified of a reversal of position in China. For two months General Marshall had held up Wedemeyer's appointment due in part to anti-Marshall propaganda in China linking Wedemeyer with him. In early July the General cabled me that changed circumstances had impaired Wedemeyer's usefulness. He had decided on John Leighton Stuart, the President of Yenching University, the most respected foreigner in China, "whose standards of integrity and actions through the fifty years of his life out here have been a model of the best in the Western world." Walton Butterworth, the Minister-Counselor, would carry on the business of the embassy. With Dr. Stuart in high position, the General "could capitalize on his influence with the various political leaders, most all of whom he knows intimately." The negotiations were entering their last critical stage. "I would not have in mind his service longer than nine months." In the tragic event of open civil war he would be recalled for consultation.

Another cable asked me to proceed without delay with the President, whom General Marshall had not approached in order not to embarrass him in case Chiang had objected. The cable ended, "Please explain matters to General Wedemeyer." Such were the prestige of General Marshall and the veneration he inspired that all involved—the President, General Wedemeyer, the rear echelon, and the Senate—were eager and anxious to cooperate fully and cheerfully to carry out his recommendation.

"What," asked the former Ambassador Presumptive, "happens to the clothes?"

"They go to you," I answered, "with Happy Fourth of July wishes from your Uncle Sam."

HOPE FADES

In the next three months, one hope after another died. By October only the indomitable optimism of Vincent survived. "The chances are better than 50–50," a memorandum to me noted, "that the jig is not up . . . that the General will be successful in calling Chiang's hand." Ambassador Stuart was confirmed by the Senate on July 11. He took the occasion of presenting his credentials to have a long, frank talk with Chiang Kai-shek. He told the Generalissimo that he was losing public support; that there must be no more assassinations, no more suppression of newspapers, and a beginning of an end to "tutelage" by calling in session the steering committee of the Peoples Consultative Conference. But Chiang had already called the National Assembly to meet on November 12 and put through his own program. "The situation is critical," General Marshall wrote the President, "but through Dr. Stuart's great help we may be able to bring about an end to this confused and tragic mess . . . without violence and the danger of complete chaos." Chiang was counseling patience and citing a Chinese proverb that when the fruit is ripe it will drop into your hands. The President and I sent messages of encouragement and support.

By the end of July fighting had broken out again and was spreading rapidly quite beyond the power of Executive Headquarters to control. General Marshall believed that military aid to the Nationalists, originally justified under the plan for a unified Chinese army, had become wholly inconsistent with impartial efforts to suppress incipient civil war. He therefore called for and obtained immediate embargo of arms and munitions from the United States to China. This was to continue until May 1947. It had no ameliorating effect upon the actions of the contestants nor—as we shall see later—upon the outcome of the civil war.

After a full Cabinet review of the situation† (a Marine convoy en route from Tientsin to Peking had been ambushed by the Communists), the President proposed that he issue a public statement bringing up to date the policy statement of December 15, 1945, although not deviating from its basic principles. However, the General and the Ambassador demurred. A public statement, they thought, would strengthen Chiang's resistance to their current efforts for a cessation of hostilities and discussion of immediate creation of the State Council. They were working on a draft of a confidential message from the President to Chiang.

A proposal for discussion of the State Council in a Committee of Five, with Dr. Stuart in the chair and two members from each Chinese side, was accepted by the Generalissimo with five conditions, which the Communists rejected. It never met. The confidential message from President Truman went off on August 10. In it he noted his profound regret that General Marshall's efforts had proved unavailing, that the political situation in China was so rapidly declining as extremist elements on both sides obstructed the aspirations of the Chinese people. Increasingly in the United States, he wrote, people believed our policy must be re-examined as they learned of the assassination at Kunming of distinguished Chinese liberals, of the suppression of liberal views and freedom of the press, and of the resort to force and secret police instead of peaceful means to settle major social issues. If this deterioration could not be stopped, it would be necessary for him to redefine and explain the position of the United States to the people of America. The President earnestly hoped for some encouraging word from the Generalissimo.

He did not get it. Instead Chiang blandly and shortly placed the whole blame solely and squarely on the Communists. General Marshall had labored nobly. The Generalissimo was depending on the President's continued support in the realization of their common goal. Another presidential appeal at the end of the month was no more successful.

August closed with government military successes in Kiangsu. General

Marshall concluded that the Nationalists had decided on a policy of force and began turning over train convoys and bridge guards from the Marines to the Nationalists, refusing to continue this assistance. The area of hostilities grew. The Communists refused to have the Committee of Five meet to dicuss political issues until the Committee of Three had met and brought about a cease-fire. The Generalissimo insisted on the reverse procedure to test Communist good faith. Beneath these issues on tactics lay profound mutual distrust based on years of warfare, with the tilt of military advantage going to the Nationalists, which strengthened the Kuomintang extremists. Vincent and I discussed a message to General Marshall suggesting a "fish-or-cut-bait" ultimatum to the Communists and action in the various eventualities in which civil war might become general.

The Kuomintang chose this moment to throw a lighted firecracker into the General's powder keg. On October 2 he told me that he had learnd from T. V. Soong, Mme. Chiang Kai-shek's brother, via Ambassador Stuart that the Government wanted to capture Kalgan before a truce, although Chiang had previously agreed with him to leave the place alone. He also had received a letter from Chou En-lai saying that if operations against Kalgan were continued the Communist Party would be forced to accept this as a final break in negotiations and an abandonment by the Kuomintang of its announced policy for a peaceful settlement. General Marshall's cable continues in language so revealing of one facet of his character that I give it in full:

> I decided that a further participation by me in protracted negotiations or time-consuming message-carrying would inevitably be judged in effect as participation in negotiations which were a cloak to the continued conduct of a military campaign. I therefore sent a memorandum to the Generalissimo which concluded with this paragraph: "I will not refer to the circumstances connected with the ineffective negotiations since last March. I wish merely to state that unless a basis for agreement is found to terminate the fighting without further delays of proposals and counter-proposals, I will recommend to the President that I be recalled and that the US Government terminate its efforts of mediation. . . ."
>
> I am aware of the delicacy of the position my communication to the Generalissimo places the United States in its relationship to the situation in the Far East but I do not think our government can be a party to a course of questionable integrity in negotiations and I therefore felt that this fact must be made unmistakably clear to the Government.

"General Marshall," noted Vincent, "is obviously mad. He has virtually accused the Government leaders of duplicity, particularly with regard to the attack on Kalgan. . . . He clearly feels that his honor is at stake."

After a long talk with the President I cabled the General that the President's confidence in General Marshall's ability to do the job in China, if it were humanly possible, was unshaken. If he thought it desirable at this juncture for the President to call him home permanently or for consultation, he would do so. When this message became known to Chiang, he offered a ten-day truce in the Kalgan operation and agreed to meetings of the Committees of Three and Five, the latter to work out representation in the State Council and National

Assembly, the former to carry forward military reorganization. The Communists declined. On October 10 the Government captured Kalgan. The rest of the month produced a flurry of propaganda, all sides putting out a list of "points" stating their positions—the Government stated eight points, which General Marshall reported were "seemingly reasonable"; the Communists, three military and eight political points, which the General thought impugned his impartiality; a third-party effort found six points of difference between the two major sides and added three of their own. Utter confusion reigned. General Marshall believed further mediation to be futile. Ambassador Stuart agreed.

THE GENERAL PACKS UP

General Marshall's efforts ended with Chou En-lai's withdrawal to Yenan and his refusal to respond to the General's inquiry whether the Communists wished his mediation to continue. The Nationalist Government's military leaders, Marshall concluded, were in charge; they and the Kuomintang extremists believed that the Communists would not carry out any agreement and that coalition was impossible. They believed that the U.S. Government must support the Generalissimo whatever happened and wished to try for a military decision against the Communists, with or without U.S. military help, while the Russians were in no position to interfere. The Communists, he added, defeated themselves through their own suspicions. Ambassador Stuart believed that "every approach has been explored and every effort exhausted to induce the Communists to cooperate . . . but the complex of twenty years of intense hatred, suspicion and fear, aggravated by the difficulty of large-scale, voluntary, cooperative effort inherent in the Chinese tradition and by the techniques of Communist discipline has had its natural fruition." My own view was that each side, while willing to sign paper agreements, was determined to enlarge its controlled area by military maneuvers before serious discussion of a temporary or final government in China. Even that was probably too optimistic.

In November General Marshall and Admiral Charles M. Cooke, commanding the Seventh Fleet, wished to reduce, and soon remove, the Marines in north China before they became entangled in the looming civil war. The Navy Department in Washington dragged its feet. Finally, in exasperation, I went to the President, who issued a crisp instruction to Secretary Forrestal and Admiral Leahy that he wanted General Marshall's recommendations carried out explicitly and promptly. They were.

As the mission straggled to a discouraged and discouraging end in December, almost a year from its inception, it seemed to me that its whole conception and General Marshall's heroic efforts to achieve it were not understood at home, but, instead, had been obscured by criticism of details, the presence and mission of the Marines, the surplus-property sales, the proposed loans, the failure to aid the Nationalists in an attempt to defeat the Communists by arms. Would it not be helpful, I asked him, to prepare and submit to him a comprehensive paper for public information of what we had tried to do in the past year, what we had done and left undone, and why? It was not, he replied, a favorable moment for such a statement. He was developing his own ideas. At the month's end he gave them to us. As I read them now, they echo like the sad and forlorn blast of Roland's horn from Roncesvalles. He could, he believed, do much "to destroy the power of the reactionaries and bring a liberal element into control of the government by a frank statement" at the time of his return home. He could also "paint the Communist picture of misrepresentation and vicious propaganda . . . to weaken their position and give a little guidance to misinformed people. . . . Fortunately Dr. Stuart . . . will almost automatically continue to be sought by all sides and will increase in importance as time goes on. . . . It is quite clear to me that my usefulness will soon be at an end. . . . It is now going to be necessary for the Chinese, themselves, to do the things I endeavored to lead them into, but I believe I can strengthen the position and influence of the better elements by the procedure I have indicated."

The General was wrong on both counts—both as to the effect of his statement and as to Ambassador Stuart's future role, as Vincent commented in a note to me. "I am not at all sure," he wrote, "but that, with the return of General Marshall, we should go out of the negotiation business and see if the Chinese can't get together better without a 'middle man.' . . . [They] may endeavor with more earnestness of purpose to get together themselves." Vincent, too, was wrong. That the Chinese factions had no intention or desire to get together, I was now convinced. Both message and comment I passed on to Secretary Byrnes for reply. My role as rear echelon was becoming altogether too difficult.

The Secretary replied that he and the President heartily approved the General's proposed course. As for mediation by Stuart, that should await decision after General Marshall's return. "The President states," he concluded, "that as six months have elapsed since your last visit to talk with him he would appreciate it if at your earliest convenience you would return for consultation on China and other matters."

Colonel Marshall Carter, the liaison officer who had succeeded Colonel James Davis, sent his own message advising the General that according to the President the last two words in Secretary Byrnes's mesage related to "the project that the President has previously discussed with you." The General replied that he fully understood. "My answer is in affirmative if that continues to be his desire. My personal reaction is something else."

LAST SCENE

When Secretary Byrnes returned to Washington from a series of United Nations and foreign ministers' meetings in New York, he had been absent almost continuously for six months. Rumors were circulating that he had resigned and would shortly leave the Department. The President had never mentioned the matter to me, nor I to him, since he told me during the summer of General Eisenhower's mission and its result, but through General Marshall's messages I knew of his expectation of returning in January and taking over the State Department then. What, if anything, the President and the Secretary had said to each other since the crisis over Henry Wallace's speech in September I do not know. Mr. Byrnes has recorded: "A few days after my return [presumably a few days after the Council of Foreign Ministers meetings had adjourned in New York City on December 12, 1946] to Washington I called on President Truman to remind him that my letter of resignation, given to him in April, was to take effect upon the completion of the treaties. As this was now accomplished,† I hoped that he could release me. He said he hoped I had forgotten it. In a very friendly talk he gave several reasons why he felt I should remain."[1]

When Secretary Byrnes pressed his desire to resign, the President proposed General Marshall as his successor, but asked Mr. Byrnes to delay the announcement of the change for a few weeks to enable General Marshall to get a short and quiet rest. The exchange of letters dated December 16, 1946, and January 7, 1947, was made public due to a leak on January 7.[2] Meanwhile none of us in the Department were told anything. At last, on the evening of January 7, Mr. Byrnes and I met at the White House with our ladies for a reception of some sort. As we were walking up the stairs from the south entrance, rumor came like a prairie fire to meet us—"General Marshall will be Secretary of State." Mr. Byrnes left us, bounding up the stairs. When our more pedestrian progress brought us in sight of President and Mrs. Truman receiving, the Secretary of State was with them, radiant and gay, in animated conversation with host and guests. Thereafter, he never mentioned the subject to me. This whole episode is a thoroughly unhappy memory.

In three weeks General Marshall assumed command.

24. GENERAL MARSHALL TAKES OVER

NATURE DEALS A COLD HAND

IN EUROPE no one could remember such a winter as January 1947 ushered in. The one before had been bad enough, a winter of freezing drought. This was one of freezing blizzards. Since the surrender of Germany, the life of Europe as an organized industrial community had come well-nigh to a standstill and, with it, so had production and distribution of goods of every sort. Only in Britain and Russia did people have any confidence in government, or social or economic organization, or currencies. Elsewhere governments had been repudiated, or abolished by the conquerors; social classes were in bitter enmity, with resistance groups hunting out and executing, after drumhead trials, collaborators with the late enemy. The prewar economy had been taken over by Hitler and bombed out by the allies. Agricultural production was lower than at any time since the turn of the century, as the cities had little to exchange for produce of the country. Peasants produced only to nourish and clothe themselves.

Currency was worthless, the popular attitude toward it reflected by a remark made by Edward Playfair (later Sir Edward), who was then with His Majesty's Treasury, when the form of currency to be issued by the Anglo-American forces invading France in 1944 was being considered. There was much talk of who the issuer should be—Banque de France, République Française, or National Committee of Liberation. Playfair suggested that more thought be given to the obverse side. The Americans, he said, had had a good idea for their coins —"In God We Trust." He advanced a quotation from the Book of Job for the new invasion currency—"I know that my redeemer liveth." In Europe the people were not so sure.

Then came that awful winter. It is enough to say of it that perhaps its most crushing blows fell on Britain, our chief ally and collaborator, to whom we looked to take the lead in maintaining the eastern Mediterranean and sharing with us the burdens of occupation and defense of Europe. Week after week blizzards battered England, stopped production of fuel, transportation, electric power—until finally nearly all industry was shut down, as electricity was cut off from it and furnished for domestic use only for a few hours in the morning. Unemployment rose to over six million, rations were cut to below wartime levels, and the workless millions relegated to their freezing homes. British monetary reserves were running out.

THE STUFF OF COMMAND

In this situation General Marshall took the oath of office as Secretary of State on January 21, 1947. Five months later in presenting him with an honorary degree of Doctor of Laws at Harvard, Harvard President James B. Conant described him as "an American to whom freedom owes an enduring debt of gratitude, a soldier and statesman whose ability and character brook only one comparison in the history of this nation."

It was a gifted citation. No other American in our history can be imagined who could have taken over command from General Washington at Valley Forge. It was, indeed, an act of God that made him chief adviser to the President and head of the State Department in the no less critical winter of 1947.

The General and I walked across the street from the White House to my office, adjoining his new one.

"Will you stay?" he asked.

"Certainly," I answered, "as long as you need me, though before too long I ought to get back to my profession if I'm to have one."

"Would six months be too long?" he asked again. "That would get me started and give us time to find your successor." I agreed and we settled on June 30 as my retiring date. When asked what he expected of an Under Secretary, he said that he should be chief of staff and run the Department. Everything would come to the Secretary through the Under Secretary with his recommendation, unless the Under Secretary chose to decide the matter himself; everything from the Secretary would go, as his order, to the Department through the Under Secretary. There would be no other channel. He asked me why I was smiling. I replied that the incidence of heart attacks in the Department was due for a sharp increase, and that while the system could not work quite as he described it, we would try to approximate it. He sketched out the Central Secretariat to be installed and operated by Colonel Carlisle Humelsine from the Army General Staff. It would weld our offices into one and keep the unified office informed of all that was going on. From me he would expect complete and even brutal candor; he had no feelings, he said, "except those which I reserve for Mrs. Marshall." We were soon to test that broad statement.

Were there matters, he asked, awaiting decision? There were two in urgent need of it. One had been tearing the Department apart for six months for lack of it—whether we should move into the quarters built for the War Department before the war and abandoned for the Pentagon or attempt to stay where we were. Asked for the reasons for and against, I outlined them. For, the White House wanted our building for the countless branches of the Executive Office of the President; the building was hopelessly insecure for our cryptographic work; both buildings were too small, but the other had plenty of ground about it for expansion.

"Against?" he asked.

"Tradition."

"Move!" said the General. Orders were issued to move. I never mentioned it to him again, nor did anyone to me, because I would not listen.

The other matter was, of course, to reverse Mr. Byrnes's deplorable decision to split up the intelligence work among the geographic divisions. General Marshall understood what G-2 was in the Army Staff and needed no long explanation of what should be done. The necessary departmental order was, he directed, to be prepared at once. It went into effect on February 6, centering "the administration of all research and intelligence units, including the regional research divisions . . . in the Office of the Special Assistant to the Secretary of State."[1] Thus a year too late my recommendation to Secretary Byrnes was put into effect and his own unhappy action of the preceding April undone. A year too late, because in the meantime events had passed us by. Pressure had developed to strengthen the newly created National Intelligence Authority. This was done in July 1947 by the creation of the Central Intelligence Agency.[2] I had the gravest forebodings about this organization and warned the President that as set up neither he, the National Security Council, nor anyone else would be in a position to know what it was doing or to control it.

Discussion of the research and intelligence decision put me in mind of another reform long overdue. There was, I said, one related matter needing attention—the acceptance of a resignation. I added that we could go into the matter at length if he wished, but I had the impression that he wanted me to run the Department. He signed a letter of acceptance and Joseph Anthony Panuch left the Department of State. A new day had clearly dawned.

In addition to getting lines of command straight and clear, and setting up the Central Secretariat as an instrument of information and control, General Marshall created another institution—the Policy Planning Staff. He picked to head it George F. Kennan, the Foreign Service officer whose penetrating dispatches from Moscow in 1946 attracted so much attention among the higher officials in the Administration and who was currently lecturing at the War College. The General conceived the function of this group as being to look ahead, not into the distant future, but beyond the vision of the operating officers caught in the smoke and crises of current battle; far enough ahead to see the emerging form of things to come and outline what should be done to meet or anticipate them. In doing this the staff should also do something else—constantly reappraise what was being done. General Marshall was acutely aware that policies acquired their own momentum and went on after the reasons that inspired them had ceased.

These two tasks are extremely difficult to perform. Distraction lurks on two sides: on one, to be lured into operations; on the other, into encyclopedism, into the amassing of analyses of the problems of every area and country with the various contingencies that might arise and the courses of action that might be taken to meet them. Those who practice it seem to believe they are writing a "do-it-yourself" book of instructions for desk officers who would be enabled by looking up a country and a particular problem to find the answer. Under its first two chiefs, George Kennan and Paul Nitze, with whose work I am familiar, the staff was of inestimable value as the stimulator, and often deviser, of the most basic policies.

One of a Secretary of State's early duties is to be the luncheon guest of the National Press Club, make a speech, and answer questions. General Marshall chose to do this soon after assuming office. He read badly, much preferring to speak without a text, sometimes with a few notes when the subject was complicated, but usually after careful thought had fixed it well in his mind. His speeches delivered this way were excellent and, since during the war they were both entirely off the record and intended to give only broad perspectives, meticulous concern with words, sensibilities, and ordered plan was unnecessary. When the General discussed this particular speech with me, I pointed out that whatever the conventions of the press might be, the Secretary of State was never off the record, and that his speeches were never directed to swaying an audience to a specific result, like voting in an election, but to putting out ideas for thought at home and abroad. It was important, therefore, to say exactly what one meant to say, clearly—no more, no less. Substance was more important than manner of delivery—within, of course, reasonable limits. Curiously enough, I would have to learn my own lesson through the hard school of experience in a speech before the same audience three years later.

General Marshall was not convinced, but he did call in his military aide (a perquisite of a five-star general), Colonel Marshall Carter, Will Clayton, and one or two others, told us what he proposed to say, and appointed us a jury to attend the luncheon and report on whether he said what he had intended to say. He spoke well, received continuous applause, and returned well pleased with his performance. Having polled the jury on the ride back from the Press Club, I acted as foreman when we were called in to give our verdict that the informal method would not do; he should stick to the use of a text. As disappointed as a small boy, the General broke in to protest that the applause he had received showed that the audience liked the speech. Of course they did, I pointed out, since the General had followed the applause and given them what they liked, not what he had set out to give them. This was not the way to put out policy proposals. My fellow jurors supported me. Later on the stenographic transcript made the case even clearer; at the time he was inclined to argue with us. I reminded him that he had asked us for the ungarnished truth as we saw it —surely he was not now asking us to garnish it. He was not; sadly he agreed to the use of texts. Although his speeches will not rank with those of Demosthenes or Cicero as oratory, the change did not diminish their effect.

It may be noticed that I have thus far referred to the Secretary of State as General Marshall. I shall continue to do so. It was his own way of referring to himself. On picking up the telephone, he always said, "General Marshall speaking." All of those close to him, in and out of the Department, always so addressed him, including the President. Only a handful outside of his family— I can only recall Major General Frank R. McCoy—called him George. Perhaps those inveterate first-name users, President Roosevelt and Jim Forrestal, did, but certainly not even old associates such as Colonel Stimson or General Omar

Bradley. This was not because General Marshall had a trace of arrogance or stiffness popularly attributed to high military personages. Rationing his none-too-ebullient energy to meet the great demands upon it led to an aloofness, an ungregariousness, which was not ungraciousness. When a situation was of his own choosing, he had warmth and a strong social response. During a period when Mrs. Marshall was in the hospital he dined alone on several occasions with my wife and me. He would arrive at precisely seven o'clock, drink one bourbon and water, and, after dinner, sit with us until precisely nine o'clock. As a raconteur he excelled. These evenings we remember with delight.

Nor did General Marshall have what is generally thought of as a military type of mind. Perhaps no great soldiers have it. General Bradley does not. Both subjected themselves to the most severe self-discipline. They were both impatient with a type of nonsense particularly prevalent in the State Department known as "kicking the problem around." All of us who have worked with General Marshall have reported a recurring outburst of his: "Don't fight the problem, gentlemen. Solve it!" With him the time to be devoted to analysis of a problem, to balancing "on the one hand" against "on the other," was definitely limited. The discussion he wanted was about plans of action and must follow staff work.

Not long after General Marshall took over he told me one morning that his friend Bernard Baruch had said to him that there was a high officer in the Department whom the General could not trust. Baruch would say no more. What was at the bottom of it? I said that I was at the bottom of it, told of my disagreement with Mr. Baruch and his staff over the proposal for international control of atomic energy, and concluded that this had doubtless led them to label me as pro-Soviet and "soft on communism." General Marshall refused to believe it, and when I suggested asking Mr. Baruch, refused on the ground that it would appear disloyal to me. Not, I said, if he told Mr. Baruch that I had asked him to do so.

When I was proved to be right, the General gave me quite a lecture on not antagonizing people but managing them. Baruch was vain but could be useful if properly managed. His foibles could be sidetracked. For instance—the General warmed to his subject—in the rotunda of the War College were busts of the great captains of history—Alexander, Caesar, and so on. Stretching a point, General Marshall had gotten his old chief, General John J. Pershing, added to this hall of fame. Baruch wanted his bust included as the industrial organizer of victory in 1917–18. The General never allowed the matter to come to an issue, just kept delaying and postponing.

That evening I found waiting for me at home a handsome engraved invitation from the Commandant of the National War College to attend the unveiling of a bust of Mr. Bernard M. Baruch in the rotunda. General of the Army George C. Marshall, Secretary of State, would speak. The next morning I laid it on General Marshall's desk.

"Yes," he said solemnly, "I got one too."

"It seems to raise an interesting question," I observed, "as to who manages whom." He went on reading his papers.

THE DECISION TO HELP GREECE AND TURKEY

The situation in Greece, bad at the end of December, deteriorated rapidly during January and February 1947. All three of our scouts in Greece—Ambassador MacVeagh, Paul Porter, chief of the economic mission, and Mark Ethridge, who had been reporting to Mr. Byrnes on conditions in the Balkans—sent back increasingly alarming reports of imminent collapse due to mounting guerrilla activity, supplied and directed from the outside, economic chaos, and Greek governmental inability to meet the crisis. MacVeagh reported rumors of impending British troop withdrawals; Waldemar J. Gallman, Minister in London, that the British Cabinet had met to discuss Greece, and would be asking for help from the United States. All signs pointed to an impending move by the Communists to take over the country, which Loy Henderson discussed in a memorandum entitled "Crisis and Imminent Possibility of Collapse," which I edited and sent on to General Marshall. It urged that only a national coalition government and substantial aid could save Greece. Before leaving the next day —Friday, February 21, 1947—to speak at Princeton's bicentennial celebration, the General instructed me to prepare the necessary steps for sending economic and military aid.

Shortly after the General had gone, the British Ambassador's private secretary asked urgently that his chief might see the Secretary of State to deliver "a blue piece of paper," the trade name for a formal and important message from His Majesty's Government, which Lord Inverchapel had been instructed to deliver personally to General Marshall. The Ambassador and I were close friends. He told me that the note contained important information about a crisis in British aid to Greece. I explained that unless he went to Princeton or North Carolina he could not catch General Marshall until Monday morning; that if he did the General would turn the note over to me; and that if he sent his First Secretary over with a copy and presented the ribbon copy to the General on Monday, the letter and spirit of his orders would have been meticulously obeyed. He agreed.

Henderson shortly received not one but two documents. They were shockers. British aid to Greece and Turkey would end in six weeks. Henderson and Hickerson brought them to me. They were brief and all too clear. One described the state of the Greek economy and army, which we all knew. It estimated Greece's current foreign-exchange needs at from two hundred forty million to two hundred eighty million dollars and, in addition, substantial sums over several years. The other reported Turkey as stronger but still unable to handle the financing of both the modernization and maintenance of the large army that Russian pressure demanded and the economic development of Turkey, which since Kemal Ataturk's time had been its first priority. The British could no longer be of substantial help in either. His Majesty's Government devoutly hoped that we could assume the burden in both Greece and Turkey.

I instructed Henderson and Hickerson to get the European and Near Eastern Division people together that evening and assign tasks for preliminary reports the next day on (1) facts as seen by United States representatives; (2) funds and personnel currently available; (3) funds and personnel needed; (4) significance of an independent Greece and Turkey to Western Europe. They should also confer the next day with Admiral Forrest Sherman, Deputy Chief of Naval Operations, and General Lauris Norstad, Army Director of Plans and Operations, so that they might brief the Secretaries of Navy and War on military-aid needs and available supplies for a meeting with the Secretary on Monday morning. Then, by telephone, I explained to the President and General Marshall what had happened, what had been done, and asked for further orders. They had none.

Reports kept coming in to me on Saturday from various working groups. These were studied, discussed, and sent back for further development and documentation. On Sunday they were brought to my house in Georgetown for final review. They were in good shape. Henderson asked me whether we were still working on papers bearing on the making of a decision or the execution of one. I said the latter; under the circumstances there could be only one decision. At that we drank a martini or two toward the confusion of our enemies.

General Marshall found the early-morning hours, before the place got cluttered up, his most productive time. Then he read the papers that Colonel Marshall (Pat) Carter had arranged for him and noted instructions for me. On Monday, February 24, although I came in early, he had already read the British notes and our memoranda preparatory to his meeting with Lord Inverchapel at ten o'clock. As usual, probing the essential points, he wanted to know whether we were sure of our facts about Greek and Turkish financial weakness; how long British troops could be induced to stay in Greece; what military forces would replace them; how we proposed to get an effective governmental organization in Greece; what were our estimates of cost and over how long? The consequences of inaction were clear enough. Of the answer to the first question I was sure; to the others, the answers had to be tentative, subject to further work. As we ended, the General said that I must continue to take the principal responsibility in this matter. He would be going to Moscow for the foreign ministers' meeting in a little over a week and had a lot of preparatory work to do. It would be essential to have continuity of direction. He would do everything possible to get us started.

The meeting with Lord Inverchapel, which I did not attend, was brief, performing its essential function of convincing the Ambassador of the General's grasp of the situation and its critical importance. Later the General went off to a Cabinet luncheon at the White House, staying afterward for a discussion with the President, the Secretaries of War and Navy, Admiral Sherman, and General Norstad. At its end the service secretaries and officers resumed it with Henderson, Hickerson, and me in my office. We agreed that the President and his principal advisers seemed convinced that it was vital to the security of the United States for Greece and Turkey to be strengthened to preserve their national independence, that only the United States could do this, that funds and authority from Congress were necessary, and that State would prepare for concurrence by War and Navy specific recommendations for the President.

General Marshall approving, Henderson and his staff worked with me preparing the recommendations.

The next day, the three secretaries concurring, the President approved the paper for action. This moved us from consideration through decision by the Executive. The President set up a meeting for the following day to begin the all-important next step of consultation with the legislative branch, now controlled by the opposite political party. The actual planning had advanced only to the extent of a decision to send as soon as possible such funds and equipment as existing legislative authority permitted, to give Greece priority in assigning military aid, and to find out at once what British military help we could expect and for how long. A Pentagon proposal, voiced by General Eisenhower, to include in our request funds for other countries in need of bolstering was rejected because we already had more to deal with than the time available permitted.

When we convened the next morning in the White House to open the subject with our congressional masters, I knew we were met at Armageddon. We faced the "leaders of Congress"—all the majority and minority potentates except Senator Taft, an accidental omission to which Senator Vandenberg swiftly drew the President's attention.

My distinguished chief, most unusually and unhappily, flubbed his opening statement. In desperation I whispered to him a request to speak. This was my crisis. For a week I had nurtured it. These congressmen had no conception of what challenged them; it was my task to bring it home. Both my superiors, equally perturbed, gave me the floor. Never have I spoken under such a pressing sense that the issue was up to me alone. No time was left for measured appraisal. In the past eighteen months, I said, Soviet pressure on the Straits, on Iran, and on northern Greece had brought the Balkans to the point where a highly possible Soviet breakthrough might open three continents to Soviet penetration. Like apples in a barrel infected by one rotten one, the corruption of Greece would infect Iran and all to the east. It would also carry infection to Africa through Asia Minor and Egypt, and to Europe through Italy and France, already threatened by the strongest domestic Communist parties in Western Europe. The Soviet Union was playing one of the greatest gambles in history at minimal cost. It did not need to win all the possibilities. Even one or two offered immense gains. We and we alone were in a position to break up the play. These were the stakes that British withdrawal from the eastern Mediterranean offered to an eager and ruthless opponent.

A long silence followed. Then Arthur Vandenberg said solemnly, "Mr. President, if you will say that to the Congress and the country, I will support you and I believe that most of its members will do the same." Without much further talk the meeting broke up to convene again, enlarged, in a week to consider a more detailed program of action.

25. THE TRUMAN DOCTRINE

WITH THE President and both the executive and legislative leaders agreeing in principle to our assumption of responsibility in the eastern Mediterranean, we turned to the task of preparing a concrete program of operation and explaining it to the Congress and the country. Francis Russell, Director of the Office of Public Affairs, would take on the campaign of public information, and other assignments in the political and economic fields had to be made and meshed. Believing that everyone involved should understand the full crisis and its importance, I got them all together, told them what I had told the legislators and their response, gave them the President's and the Secretary's orders for urgent action and General Marshall's magnificent instruction about himself. On March 5 he was going to Moscow, where he would be when our whole program became public. We were to go forward, he instructed me, with utmost vigor and without regard to him and his meeting. Events had relegated that to secondary importance. The prime necessity was to save the pivotal position occupied by Greece and Turkey. Many years would go by before an officer commanding in a forward and exposed spot would call down his own artillery fire upon his own position to block an enemy advance. The spirit which inspired us all at the time has been well put by Joseph M. Jones of the Office of Public Affairs, who was both a participant in and the historian of all this effort: "All . . . were aware that a major turning point in American history was taking place. The convergence of massive historical trends upon that moment was so real as to be almost tangible, and it was plain that in that carrefour of time all those trends were being to some degree deflected."

Groups were appointed by Henderson, who was in charge, with Hickerson as his second, to draft the legislation, to organize and recruit the civilian group to exercise control and direction in Greece, to set up with the Pentagon the military training and advisory teams, to order supplies and weapons, and to procure shipping. Joseph Jones would prepare a draft of the President's message for the White House. Everyone knew that the State Department was facing its last clear chance to get a job done. The job of briefing the press I took on myself, talking on the evening of February 27 off the record and with the greatest frankness to a group of twenty men regularly assigned to the Department.

The next day with Lord Inverchapel I attempted to inject some flexibility into the British position. We were moving with incredible speed for so vast a country to assume a novel burden far from our shores. The British should not set such short and arbitrary deadlines, especially for the withdrawal of their troops. I quoted to him the Seabees' motto, "We do the difficult at once; the impossible takes a little longer." London agreed to keep the troops on for a while longer and to advance a little more cash for the Greek army provided our aid was moving smartly along.

All this time Greece was in the position of a semiconscious patient on the critical list whose relatives and physicians had been discussing whether his life could be saved. The hour had come for the patient to be heard from. On March 3, with the support of kind friends and their guidance of a feeble hand, the Greek Government wrote asking for the help—financial, economic, military, and administrative—which has already been mentioned. Of all this we kept General Marshall in Moscow fully informed, including a draft of the message to Congress that Joseph Jones had given to Clark Clifford, Counsel to the President. The General approved the message.

Like all presidential messages, this one stimulated controversy within the government. George Kennan thought it too strong, since it took the line I had taken with the legislative group, and feared that it might provoke the Soviet Union to aggressive action. Clark Clifford thought it too weak and added some points that I thought unwise. Using General Marshall's great prestige, I got Clark to withdraw his additions and recommend the message as the General had approved it. The President, back from a meeting with the Mexican President and a speech in Texas, met with me on March 7. Deciding that he had no alternative but to go ahead, and realizing that this was only a beginning, he approved a request for two hundred fifty million dollars for Greece and one hundred fifty million dollars for Turkey, and the message to Congress. We then moved into the Cabinet Room, where the President laid out the whole program, which got unanimous Cabinet support, and ordered a meeting with congressional leaders for March 10 and, depending on its outcome, a presidential appearance before Congress on March 12. I came back to the Department somewhat breathless. When President Truman had made a decision, he moved fast.

The large group of senators and congressmen who met in the President's office on March 10 gave us, despite Arthur Vandenberg's earlier assurance, a cool and silent reception. During the past three weeks the attitude of Congress toward Europe had been one of hardly suppressed skepticism. Its majority members had been elected after a campaign for economy and against the policies of President Truman. On the day (February 21) the British notes were given to me, and in ignorance of them, the President had asked Congress for three hundred fifty million dollars for relief, splitting both Republican and Democratic ranks. To add to the confusion, former President Hoover, who had returned from a tour of Europe to examine the food situation, urged Congress to "stop, look, and listen" before formulating a relief plan. He reported Europe to be on the verge of starvation, estimated its needs at a billion dollars, and, quite unrealistically, proposed that the British and we provide the funds equally on a loan basis. At this point the press brought news of the British notes and Congress dropped the whole matter until it could learn more, but not before the

Democratic Congressional Conference in a long and secret meeting—fully reported in the press—warned the Administration against supporting British policies in the Mediterranean or the Greek monarchy. The Senate on March 4 had voted to cut the President's budget for the next fiscal year by four and a half billion dollars, the House earlier having voted a cut of six billion. Finally, Senator Taft had expressed opposition to the President's request for an extension of the War Powers Act and the Selective Service Act.

Such was the situation when we met with the legislative leaders who shared with us the responsibilities of government. The meeting did not materially change it. In his matter-of-fact way the President laid out the need for action and the action proposed, calling on me for detail from time to time. Vandenberg reiterated his insistence that the President put the crisis before Congress in its broadest setting. No one else said very much. No commitments were made. The meeting could be called a success only in the sense referred to by a colleague of Lester B. Pearson, later Prime Minister of Canada, for whom he made an election speech some years ago. To Pearson's surprise, the colleague was enthusiastic about the speech, while Pearson thought the audience wholly unresponsive. "That's just it," replied the colleague happily. "Not a boo! Not a boo!"

Two days later the Cabinet in a body went to the chamber of the House of Representatives to hear the President deliver his message. After describing the military and political pressures being applied to Greece and Turkey, their state of exhaustion, the consequences to ourselves and the free world should they collapse, and the absence of any other source of help, he said:

I believe that it must be the policy of the United States to support free peoples who are resisting attempted subjugation by armed minorities or by outside pressures.

I believe that we must assist free peoples to work out their own destinies in their own way.

I believe that our help should be primarily through economic and financial aid which is essential to economic stability and orderly political processes.

The world is not static, and the *status quo* is not sacred. But we cannot allow changes in the *status quo* in violation of the Charter of the United Nations by such methods as coercion, or by such subterfuges as political infiltration. In helping free and independent nations to maintain their freedom, the United States will be giving effect to the principles of the Charter of the United Nations. . . .

Should we fail to aid Greece and Turkey in this fateful hour, the effect will be far-reaching to the West as well as to the East.

We must take immediate and resolute action.

I therefore ask the Congress to provide authority for assistance to Greece and Turkey in the amount of $400,000,000 for the period ending June 30, 1948. In requesting these funds I have taken into consideration the maximum amount of relief assistance which would be furnished to Greece out of the $350,000,000 which I recently requested that the Congress authorize for the prevention of starvation and suffering in countries devastated by the war.

In addition to funds, I ask the Congress to authorize the detail of American civilian and military personnel to Greece and Turkey, at the request of those countries, to assist in the tasks of reconstruction, and for the purpose of supervising the use of such financial and material assistance as may be furnished. I recommend that authority also be provided for the instruction and training of selected Greek and Turkish personnel.

Finally, I ask that the Congress provide authority which will permit the speediest and most effective use, in terms of needed commodities, supplies, and equipment, of such funds as may be authorized.[1]

When he finished, the President received a standing ovation from both parties. This was a tribute to a brave man rather than unanimous acceptance of his policy. As I cabled to General Marshall in Moscow, the response to the message was not one of opposition, but it "did disclose the inevitable pain and anguish of Congress in facing a difficult situation." For more than two months it would undergo the anguish of its labor pains before an "Act to Provide for Assistance to Greece and Turkey" would be delivered to the President for approval.

VANDENBERG AND THE LEGISLATION

Arthur Vandenberg's part in the enactment of this proposal into law was invaluable. He was born to lead a reluctant opposition into support of governmental proposals that he came to believe were in the national interest. A leader should be in advance of his followers, but not so far in advance as to be out of touch. It helps, also, if he can believe in his own little stratagems. One of Vandenberg's stratagems was to enact publicly his conversion to a proposal, his change of attitude, a kind of political transubstantiation. The method was to go through a period of public doubt and skepticism; then find a comparatively minor flaw in the proposal, pounce upon it, and make much of it; in due course propose a change, always the Vandenberg amendment. Then, and only then, could it be given to his followers as true doctrine worthy of all men to be received. He did this, as we have seen, with UNRRA. He did it now with the Greek-Turkish proposal. He would do it again with the Marshall Plan. Its strength lay in the genuineness of his belief in each step. He was not engaged in strategy; rather he was a prophet pointing out to more earthbound rulers the errors and spiritual failings of their ways.

Within a few days of the message, Senator Vandenberg had found, though he did not discover, his issue. The press and various organized groups charged us with "bypassing the United Nations." That ambivalent Jeremiah of the press, Walter Lippmann, although he had advocated unilateral action in Greek-Turkish aid, found us grievously at fault in not doing all the consulting with the United Nations we should have done. We should expiate our sin by "a full explanation and a willingness to consider objections."[2] This fortunate error was mine. The President had made minimal obeisance to the United Nations, but since time was so short had not been advised to go through the futility of appeal to an organization in which the Soviet Union would veto action and where in any event any help must come from the United States. If we had proposed it, Vandenberg's task would only have been harder. We had made, he penciled in his private papers, "a colossal blunder in ignoring the U.N."[3] He proposed to correct it and, as corrected, to adopt our fumbling efforts.

Like Mr. Jorrocks' foxes, I lustily cried *"Peccavi!"* and offered to make amends. But the Senator was going to make the amends and the amendments himself. These took two forms. First, Senators Vandenberg and Connally drafted introductory "whereas" paragraphs to the bill, setting forth that Greece and Turkey had asked help from the United States and the United Kingdom as the United Nations Food and Agriculture Organization had advised them to do; the United Nations, the introduction continued, had recognized the seriousness of the border trouble in northern Greece and "if the present emergency is met" could "assume full responsibility for this phase of the problem," but it could "not now . . . furnish to Greece and Turkey the financial and economic assistance which is immediately required" and which "will contribute to the freedom and independence of all members of the United Nations." Second, Vandenberg introduced a curious amendment to section five directing the President to withdraw all aid if requested to do so by a government of either country "representing a majority of the people," or if the President found that the purposes of the aid had been accomplished by any intergovernmental body or could not be accomplished or if the Security Council (the United States waiving its veto) or the General Assembly found that United Nations action had made the aid undesirable.

This, of course, was window dressing and must have seemed either silly or cynical or both in London, Paris, and Moscow. Nevertheless, it was a cheap price for Vandenberg's patronage and warmly welcomed by Warren Austin, our representative at the United Nations. He had succeeded Stettinius and, a former senator himself, could play legislative games with all the hyperbolic sincerity of Vandenberg himself. The amendment won over the bulk of doubters. Remaining objections—that the President's proposals put us on the road to imperialism, spheres of influence, and war, put forward by Senators Taft, Edwin C. Johnson, Democrat of Colorado, and Claude Pepper, Democrat of Florida, and that it was too "military," a favorite of some columnists and poll takers—soon received the kiss of death from Henry Wallace and a following from the extreme left and right. Public distrust of these views was accentuated when Wallace established a foreign base in England from which to attack the Administration, and Gromyko joined in from Moscow. We were fortunate in our enemies. Our friends were powerfully augmented on March 23 by Governor Thomas E. Dewey of New York.

Amid growing support for the policy, hearings in the House and Senate began and continued simultaneously from mid-March until the Senate committee unanimously reported its bill on April 23; the House committee, with only Representative Lawrence H. Smith of Wisconsin dissenting, reported its version on April 25. These hearings added to the heavy burden that had fallen on me since the last days of February. My colleague Will Clayton, who had been ill in Texas, came back to testify before going off again to Geneva for the meetings on trade and tariff policies. The world outside Greece and Turkey did not stand still. General Marshall needed constant material for the Moscow conference, which, as might be expected, was going badly. We were engaged in futile protests to Moscow and General V. P. Sviridov in Budapest over the ousting of the popularly elected Smallholders government. State trials were going on in Rumania and Bulgaria. On the home front an official of the Democratic National committee, Gael Sullivan, well intentioned but without judgment, proposed to his Republican opposite number that top members from both parties on both foreign committees endorse the purposes and methods of the Administration regarding the Greek-Turkish bill. Days went by before the dovecotes settled down after this assininity. Finally, the Republican members of the Senate asked for immediate answers, which we gave, to one hundred and ten questions on the bill and its implications.

It fell to me to lead off both the executive and public hearings before both committees.[4] I appeared frequently and at length. The questions principally directed at me grew out of the general statements in the President's message in response to Senator Vandenberg's repeated request that the problems of the two small countries be put in the setting of the larger confrontation between the Soviet Union and ourselves. They were sharpened by the cross-examiners' desire to embarrass a witness by pushing statements to what has been called a "dryly logical extreme." Would we advocate doing the same thing everywhere under all conceivable circumstances? Obviously we were not doing the same thing almost next door in Hungary, because the circumstances, particularly for effective action, were wholly different. The China specialists, notably Representative Walter Judd of Minnesota, pressed me on what we should do in China. We were doing a great deal under radically different circumstances. He thought not enough. Senator Connally, a good friend in a free-for-all, summed up the position helpfully:

Senator Connally: This is not a pattern out of a tailor's shop to fit everybody in the world and every nation in the world, because the conditions in no two nations are identical. Is that not true?

Mr. Acheson: Yes, sir; that is true, and whether there are requests, of course, will be left to the future, but whatever they are, they have to be judged, as you say, according to the circumstances of each specific case.[5]

At length, the weary weeks came to an end, and, as the event showed, not without having had a useful effect. The Greek-Turkish Aid Act passed the House by a vote of 287 to 107, and the Senate by 67 to 23. The President signed it on May 22.

The Department turned most effectively to administering the act. This fell largely to others. I faced another looming and even more menacing crisis about to engulf all Europe.

26. THE CRISIS BROADENS:
BIRTH OF THE MARSHALL PLAN

FIRST STIRRINGS

IT WILL BE RECALLED that when the State, War, and Navy departments were preparing material for the President on Greece and Turkey, General Eisenhower had suggested that the request to Congress should include funds for other countries resisting Communist penetration. We had feared that enlarging the proposal would complicate and delay it. Other needs were great, but the collapse of Greece, unless aid came, was only weeks away. By March 5, however, it was plain that we should get work started in the three departments on the suggestion and be ready to propose a much larger program in Europe as soon as we knew the facts. Accordingly I wrote the two service secretaries saying that Assistant Secretary of State Hilldring, the chairman of the State, War, and Navy Coordinating Committee, would get that group to work on the problem with the aid of Treasury, and urging the Secretaries to prod their people on. This they did. The work of the three departments would be put together by Colonel William A. Eddy, Chief of Research and Intelligence in State, Brigadier General George A. (Abe) Lincoln for War, and Rear Admiral E. T. Wooldridge, for Navy. They worked fast.

On the day these letters were written my colleague Will Clayton, ill and on a plane to Tucson for a short rest before going to Europe, penned an urgent memorandum on the same subject. He was deeply disturbed, he wrote, by the world situation and its implications for our country. Only immediate assertion of leadership by the United States could prevent war in the next decade. In every nation in the eastern hemisphere, and in some in the western, systematic campaigns were going on to destroy national integrity and independence. "Feeding on hunger, economic misery and frustration," he wrote, "these attacks have already been successful in some of the liberated countries." Prompt and effective aid for gravely threatened countries was essential to our own security. The President and the Secretary of State must shock the country into a realization of its peril by telling it the facts which daily poured in through our cables. He advocated a Council of National Defense of leading Cabinet officers and members of Congress and an emergency fund of five billion dollars.

In the interstices between appearances on Capitol Hill, meetings with the President, innumerable problems of organization, personnel, moving, and current work, I encouraged and harassed those assembling the facts. General

Marshall would want these in intelligible form to know in detail the nature, location, and extent of the evil to be cured. His cables showed full awareness of dangers, both in Moscow and in Europe, and little hope of any desire in Moscow to cooperate in alleviating them.

MY SPEECH IN MISSISSIPPI

At this point the President intervened to stimulate my personal involvement in the larger crisis. On April 7 he said he was going to ask a favor of me, one he especially hoped that I could grant. Some time ago he had promised two warm friends, Mr. and Mrs. William T. Wynne, of Greenville, Mississippi, that he would speak at a meeting of the Delta Council to be held at the Delta State Teachers College at the neighboring town of Cleveland on May 8. The afternoon before he was to attend a gala reception in Greenville. It was a long-standing date; the Wynnes had gone to a great deal of trouble and had their hearts set on the occasion, and they had been devastated on learning that he contemplated asking to be excused. However, the fatal illness of Senator Theodore (The Man) Bilbo of Mississippi and the bitter fight that had broken out over the succession would make the President's presence in the state a serious embarrassment to him. The Wynnes had agreed to forgive him if he would provide me (in the absence of General Marshall) to make an "important foreign policy" speech.

Of course I agreed, and added that I had in mind a speech which very much needed to be made, but which must be very carefully considered. We could not afford a false start. The President had been kept in touch with the increasingly gloomy prospects in Europe and in Moscow as seen by the Secretary of State. He knew Will Clayton's views and the work on which I had started the State, War, and Navy committee. We could no longer postpone attention to this situation. Even if Congress passed the three-hundred-fifty-million-dollar relief bill, it would be pitifully inadequate. By the end of the fiscal year we would have no funds for Europe except for Greece and Turkey. Events were outrunning preparation. What I wanted to do was not to put forward a solution or a plan, but to state the problem and the facts. To do this would, as Clayton had pointed out, shock the country—and both the Administration and the Congress—into facing a growing crisis. Did the President agree to this being done? To my doing it? I was an eager volunteer and the time was short. If the Delta Council wanted an "important foreign policy" speech, here was one.

The President's answer to both questions was yes. But I remembered Henry Wallace and thought that between agreement and delivery of the speech there should be more talks with President and Secretary. However, galloping events and the attitudes of General Marshall and Will Clayton, when they both returned from Europe, eliminated any doubt that the shocking problem should be presented as soon as we could be ready. Joseph Jones and Francis Russell were deputized to start on the speech, which I outlined to them, with authority to commandeer help from anyone working on the problem. The committees were well along with their tasks when General Marshall got back from Moscow on April 28. Both the State Department group and the State-War-Navy group had filed reports—the latter ninety-three pages long—bristling with grisly facts. The General brought his own cargo of bad news. He could report no progress in his discussions with the Soviet Union. As for Europe, he reported to the country over the radio:

. . . We were faced with immediate issues which vitally concerned the impoverished and suffering people of Europe who are crying for help, for coal, for food, and for most of the necessities of life, and the majority of whom are bitterly disposed towards the Germany that brought about this disastrous situation. . . .

. . . The recovery of Europe has been far slower than had been expected. Disintegrating forces are becoming evident. The patient is sinking while the doctors deliberate . . . action cannot await compromise through exhaustion.[1]

He immediately put the Policy Planning Staff to work on suggestions for a plan of action to deal with facts already known. It accomplished little more than reiteration that the crisis was immediate and desperate and called urgently for action. Not until a month later, when Clayton returned from Europe with a memorandum written on the plane, did a concrete outline for the Marshall Plan emerge.

Meanwhile my own speech, a speech to state the problem—"the prologue to the Marshall Plan," as the President was to call it—took form. On April 23 a first draft was produced. On May 1 my helpers came with me to an off-the-record luncheon with a group of League of Women Voters officers, where I gave it a "preliminary canter" to see how it would go. We thought it sound. It was finished on the sixth.

The Mississippi Valley south of Vicksburg contains one of the most lush and prosperous agricultural areas in the South. A drive through it showed me dairy cattle standing knee-deep in rich pastures and new strains of beef cattle adapted to hot weather; fields set aside for new crops to provide an escape from one-crop cotton culture; picturesque but ramshackle shanties giving way to neat, well-fenced farms and painted houses. This area is called the Delta. Once a year the Delta Council meets on the tree-shaded lawn of the Teachers College at Cleveland, bringing families and relatives with them to discuss their own area's interests and problems and to hear about the great world to which historically their products have gone. Those most immediately concerned listen to the speaker in the large gymnasium of the college. His words are carried to many more thousands on the surrounding lawn while they eat sandwiches, drink pop, and keep an eye on sleeping children. The scene is an easygoing, good-natured, shirt-sleeved, thoroughly American one—a far cry from the conventional setting for striped-pants diplomatic utterances; but the people in the gymnasium are serious.

Before leaving Washington, I had had luncheon, as I often did, with three British newsmen, Leonard Miall of the British Broadcasting Corporation, Malcolm Muggeridge of the *Daily Telegraph,* and René MacColl of the *Daily Express,* and explained to them, off the record, what I was doing, why I was doing it, and under what authority. Europe was beginning to wonder whether the military and political aspects of the struggle in southeast Europe had blinded the United States to the imminent collapse of Western Europe. It was of the greatest importance that European opinion, distracted by Henry Wallace's campaign, should be set right about this, and there was no better place to begin than London. Also, I was under no illusion as to the impact of an Under Secretary's remarks upon the American press and public. It would do no harm if whatever direct effect the speech might have could be reinforced by a returning wave of comment from abroad.

The speech[2] can be summarized as follows:

Europe and Asia were in a state of utter exhaustion and economic dislocation, resulting from (1) "planned, scientific destruction . . . carried out by both sides during the war"; (2) the fact that Germany and Japan, two of the greatest workshops of Europe and Asia, had not yet begun the process of reconstruction; and (3) the unprecedented natural disasters of the last two terrible winters.

The result had been that the world needed and should receive in 1947 exports from the United States—the only source—of sixteen billion dollars (four times our prewar exports), and could find imports to the United States with which to pay for them of only half that sum. The deficit would be made up by loans and grants from us and the remaining financial reserves of the stricken countries, leaving them bankrupt and hopeless. These means of meeting the deficit, after the current year, would no longer be available. We should therefore increase imports as much as possible to close the gap and find new methods of financing it.

In thinking about how to go about this, the speech continued, we must be acutely conscious of other facts of life. We could not greatly increase exports, since goods were urgently needed at home, too. Therefore we must export selectively to areas of special concern to us and our purposes.

Our objective was not relief, but to revive agriculture, industry, and trade so that stricken countries might be self-supporting. The countries of our immediate concern were those of the free world. The free areas of Europe and Asia could not function vigorously and healthily unless Germany and Japan could play a strong, productive role. General Marshall had concluded after weeks in Moscow that European recovery could not await "compromise through exhaustion" and must proceed without four-power agreement.

The conclusion, I said, was inescapable: new financing was needed from Congress in amounts and through methods beyond existing authorizations, and new powers also to allocate commodities and such services as shipping which might be in short supply. Finally, time was running out:

Not only do human beings and nations exist in narrow economic margins, but also human dignity, human freedom, and democratic institutions.

It is one of the principal aims of our foreign policy today to use our economic and financial resources to widen these margins. It is necessary if we are to preserve our own freedoms and our own democratic institutions. It is necessary for our national security. And it is our duty and our privilege as human beings.

I did not think at the time that my trumpet note from Cleveland, Mississippi, was the call to arms that would start the American people on one of the greatest and most honorable adventures in history. General Marshall sounded that a month later in Cambridge, Massachusetts. Perhaps it is not too much to say that it was reveille, which awoke them to the duties of that day of decision. At any rate the trumpet did not give an uncertain sound. On both sides of the Atlantic it stimulated a good deal of discussion, most of it encouraging to those preparing themselves for the battle. In one mind, however, it stirred disquiet. I had been discreet and vague about total amounts of money involved. Inferences could be drawn, but amounts, duration, and specific areas had purposefully been left undefined. Others, however, had not been so reticent. Henry Wallace, Harold Stassen, and, nearer to home, Ben Cohen, in a speech in San Francisco, mentioned large amounts. This disquieted Arthur Vandenberg, who communicated his worries to General Marshall. The General invited him and me to a quiet and very private talk in the seclusion of Blair House, across Pennsylvania Avenue from Old State. There, away from inquiring reporters, telephones, and efficient secretaries, we had a long and useful talk.

Vandenberg began, as he had with UNRRA and the Greek-Turkish proposal, by viewing with alarm. What were we up to? Where was all this to end, with even Alben Barkley talking about opening the Treasury to every country in the world? General Marshall let him run on for a few minutes to reduce his steam pressure, and then told the Senator that the Administration had no intention of asking any further appropriation at the present session of Congress. If he had to change his mind, it would be only a small amount to carry over until the next session. Vandenberg visibly relaxed. The General went on to say that we wanted, in the meantime, to share our researches and our problem with congressional leaders and later with public groups. The situation called for wide national agreement on one of the greatest problems our people had ever faced. Now as never before national unity depended upon a truly nonpartisan policy in the year of a presidential election. Who would carry out an agreed policy no one was bold enough to predict—Vandenberg still had hopes that he might be the man. The security of the country itself was the supreme consideration. At the end of the meeting conversion had been accomplished and a search for the Vandenberg brand had begun. It was to turn up about a month later.

I shall not attempt to trace the genesis of the Harvard speech. It has been well done by Joseph Jones[3] and will be further studied in Forrest Pogue's admirable biography of General Marshall. A few recollections will suffice.

CLAYTON'S SECOND MEMORANDUM

The first of these concerns the powerful effect of a second memorandum[4] of my colleague, Will Clayton, written on his flight home from Geneva, upon General Marshall's thinking and the framing of his proposal. The memorandum came to me on May 27 and went on at once to the General. Clayton began by stating what has been one of the main themes of this book: "It is now obvious that we have grossly underestimated the destruction to the European economy by the war." We could see the physical destruction but the effect of vast economic disruption and political, social, and psychological destruction from five years of Hitler's remaking of Europe into a war machine completely escaped us.

Europe was steadily deteriorating, the memorandum continued. "The political situation reflects the economic. . . . Millions of people in the cities are slowly starving." French grain acreage was twenty-five per cent under prewar and grain was fed to cattle. The peasant had nothing to buy with the deteriorating currency. The current annual balance-of-payments deficit of four areas alone—the United Kingdom, France, Italy, and the U.S.-U.K. zones of Germany—was five billion dollars for this subminimum standard of living.

To survive, Clayton wrote, Europe must have two and a half billion dollars annually of coal, bread grains, and shipping services until her own shipping and production should be rebuilt. Further study was unnecessary. The facts were well known. The problem was to organize our fiscal services and our own consumption so that enough could be made available out of our own vast production. This should be paid for out of taxes and "not by addition to debt."

According to the memorandum, Europe should have from us a grant of "6 or 7 billion dollars worth of goods a year for three years . . . principally of coal, food, cotton, tobacco, shipping services," largely in surplus. With this help, the International Bank should enable European reconstruction to get under way. (This calculation of the role of the Bank and Fund and the composition of the aid turned out to be unrealistic and erroneous.)

The three-year grant should be "based on a European plan which the principal European nations, headed by the UK, France and Italy, should work out." (Clayton also recommended a European economic federation in which he was nearly a decade ahead of the Treaty of Rome.)

Other nations might help with surplus food and raw materials, Clayton concluded, "but we must avoid getting into another UNRRA. *The United States must run this show.*"

When Clayton sent this memorandum to me, he asked that a meeting be arranged to discuss it with the General. This I did for the next day, giving him the memorandum to read. Meanwhile Kennan's study, requested by General Marshall, had come in. It was more cautious than Clayton's, dwelling more on difficulties and dangers—which were certainly there—than on the imperative need for action. It agreed that European countries must produce a plan for recovery but pointed out how difficult a task this would be with the Soviet Union in its present mood. When we met on May 28 we had both papers before us.

Will Clayton was one of the most powerful and persuasive advocates to whom I have listened. Both qualities came from his command of the subject and the depth of his conviction. What he said at the meeting added to his paper principally corroborative detail to illustrate the headlong disintegration of the highly complex industrial society of Europe, through the breakdown of interrelations between the industrial cities and the food-producing countryside. Millions of people would soon die, creating a chaos of bloodshed and disorder in doing so. To organize the great effort needed to prevent this disaster would take time, but it had to begin here and now. Surely the plan should be a European plan and come—or, at any rate, appear to come—from Europe. *But the United States must run the show.* And it must start running it now.

On this main point there was no debate. It would be folly, the General said, "to sit back and do nothing." His principal concern was whether any proposal we might make should be addressed to all Europe or to Western Europe only. We were agreed—Clayton, Cohen, Kennan, Bohlen, and myself—that the United States should not assume the responsibility of dividing Europe. I pointed out that Russian obstruction in developing a European plan could be overcome by not requiring her agreement; what might be fatal to congressional support would be Russian support and demands, as Henry Wallace had been advocating, of up to fifty per cent of the benefits. Kennan suggested that we might blandly treat the Soviet Union as, like ourselves, a donor of raw materials. The matter was left inconclusive. The General cautioned sternly against leaks. A hint of a new request for vast funds would cause immediate and adverse action; the manner of the first approach must be carefully considered. As one looks back on it, he left us with very little to leak.

His concern about congressional reaction was borne out a few hours later. Leslie Biffle, Secretary to the Minority, had invited me to lunch in his office with about a dozen senators. The talk there, as my memorandum to General Marshall reported, convinced me that some discussion with Congress in the near future was a necessity. With Brien McMahon of Connecticut taking the lead, they insisted that they should be told what the Administration had in mind, or, at least, what the problem was as we saw it. If we attempted to confront them with a *fait accompli,* they would refuse to vote grants or credits. I was urged to talk to the policy committee of the Democratic minority—which would have been a fatal mistake. I was convinced that the General should begin talks very soon about the great seriousness of the problems and, later on, make a speech about them, before suggesting any solutions.

GENERAL MARSHALL'S HARVARD SPEECH

The next day he mentioned to me a Harvard invitation to receive an honorary degree, which had been pending for a long time, said he would probably be asked to make a short speech, and asked whether this would be a good time to say something about Europe. I advised against it on the ground that commencement speeches were a ritual to be endured without hearing. Undeterred, he accepted the invitation and agreed to speak. Bohlen was asked to draft something from the Kennan and Clayton memoranda. A few days later Clayton and I saw the draft, contributed our own suggestions, and heard no more. The most difficult portions of the speech were, obviously, to whom should the proposal be addressed and what should the proposal be. Whether the General discussed the speech with the President and, if so, what they said,

I do not know. It is hard to believe that they did not discuss it. It will also surprise many that the Secretary of State went off to deliver so momentous a speech with an incomplete text and never informed the Department of its final form. I had to pry it out of Colonel Marshall Carter at almost the last moment over the telephone. We had the release ready not too long before General Marshall began to speak at midafternoon on June 5, but he knew that the attention paid to what he would say that day would not be affected by the techniques of publicity.

The speech was short, simple, and altogether brilliant in its statement of a purpose and a proposal adapted to the necessities of his position. A little more than half of the speech, just over a printed page, set forth the condition of Europe and the causes for it. This came straight from the two Clayton memoranda.

The statement of purpose was designed to win over the critics of the Truman Doctrine both at home and abroad, who deprecated its stress on the confrontation with the Soviet Union strategically and ideologically. Yet it did this without leaving doubt that along with real understanding of the problem went determined will to resolve it. Three notes composed this chord:

1. Our policy is directed not against any country or doctrine but against hunger, poverty, desperation, and chaos. Its purpose should be the revival of a working economy in the world so as to permit the emergence of political and social conditions in which free institutions can exist.

2. Such assistance, I am convinced, must not be on a piecemeal basis as various crises develop. Any assistance that this Government may render in the future should provide a cure rather than a mere palliative.

3. Any government that is willing to assist in the task of recovery will find full cooperation, I am sure, on the part of the United States Government. Any government which maneuvers to block the recovery of other countries cannot expect help from us. Furthermore, governments, political parties, or groups which seek to perpetuate human misery in order to profit therefrom politically or otherwise will encounter the opposition of the United States.[5]

If General Marshall believed, which I am sure he did not, that the American people would be moved to so great an effort as he contemplated by as Platonic a purpose as combating "hunger, poverty, desperation, and chaos," he was mistaken. But he was wholly right in stating this as the American *governmental* purpose. I have probably made as many speeches and answered as many questions about the Marshall Plan as any man alive, except possibly Paul Hoffman, and what citizens and the representatives in Congress alike always wanted to learn in the last analysis was how Marshall aid operated to block the extension of Soviet power and the acceptance of Communist economic and political organization and alignment. Columnists and commentators might play with bloodless words and conceptions like projectors of silent moving pictures, but the bulk of their fellow citizens were unimpressed.

It was in the formulation of the "proposal" that the genius of General Marshall's statement stands out. It comprised six sentences, only one of which concerned what this country might do:

It is already evident that, before the United States Government can proceed much further in its efforts to alleviate the situation and help start the European world on its way to recovery, there must be some agreement among the countries of Europe as to the requirements of the situation and the part those countries themselves will take in order to give proper effect to whatever action might be undertaken by this Government.

It would be neither fitting nor efficacious for this Government to undertake to draw up unilaterally a program designed to place Europe on its feet economically.

This is the business of the Europeans.

The initiative, I think, must come from Europe.

The program should be a joint one, agreed to by a number of, if not all, European nations.

The role of this country should consist of friendly aid in the drafting of a European program and of later support of such a program so far as it may be practical for us to do so.[6]

Surely no sensible man could object to a suggestion that if the Europeans, all or some of them, could get together on a plan of what was needed to get them out of the dreadful situation depicted and how they proposed to go about it, we would take a look at their plan and see what aid we might practically give. However, it was more than possible that an imaginative European could go far with such a start. I made sure that at least one should be given his chance. Getting hold of my British friends, Miall, MacColl, and Muggeridge, with whom a month before I had discussed the purpose of my Delta Council speech, I explained the full import of the Harvard one, asking that they cable or telephone the full text and have their editors send a copy to Ernest Bevin with my estimate of its importance. This they did while Miall broadcast the story to Britain from Washington.

Bevin was quick to seize the opportunity that General Marshall had offered him. Some years later Bevin told me that after reading the speech William Strang, then Permanent Under Secretary of the Foreign Office, suggested inquiring through the British Embassy in Washington what specifically the Secretary of State had in mind. Mr. Bevin vetoed the suggestion. He would not, he said, pry into what General Marshall was thinking about; what he had said was good enough for Bevin. He got in touch at once with Georges Bidault, Foreign Minister of France. In two weeks' time they met with Molotov in Paris to discuss how Europeans might devise a European recovery plan, its requirements, and the parts they would play in it. The tripartite aspect of the talks soon blew up. I have described the scene as Bevin told it to me: "It seems that Molotov has a bump on his forehead which swells when he is under emotional strain. The matter was being debated and Molotov had raised relatively minor questions or objections at various points, when a telegram was handed to him. He turned pale and the bump on his forehead swelled. After that, his attitude changed and he became much more harsh. . . . I suspect that Molotov must have thought that the instruction sent him was stupid; in any case, the withdrawal of the Russians made operations much more simple."[7]

On the next day, July 3, Bevin and Bidault issued a joint communiqué inviting twenty-two other European nations to send representatives to Paris to consider a recovery plan. (Czechoslovakia, which had at first agreed to attend, withdrew its acceptance after a visit to Moscow by Premier Gottwald and poor Jan Masaryk, the Foreign Secretary.) Once again General Marshall's judgment and his luck combined to produce the desired result.

I was to make one more official contribution to the Marshall Plan before my days in the Under Secretary's office in "New State" expired. Although members of Congress were now assured that they were not to be confronted by some sudden and unexpected demand, the conviction was growing that in time they would, if the Europeans should do their part, be confronted with a very sizable one. How could they participate in the preparation of some preliminary defenses? Arthur Vandenberg began to feel for a method. General Marshall in the Harvard speech had suggested that one part of this country's role might be "friendly aid in the drafting of a European program." On June 14 in *The New York Times* William S. White reported Vandenberg's idea of a nonpartisan commission at the highest level to advise coordination of our resources with foreign needs. I feared a tripartite monstrosity like the contemporaneous Hoover Commission on Administrative Reform appointed by the House, the Senate, and the President. It seemed to me of the greatest importance for the President to anticipate this move by appointing as soon as possible a committee of his own choosing, after consultation with leaders of Congress, and I asked General Marshall to urge the President to do so, which he did. Within an hour I would have a list of suggested committeemen representing all branches of American life.

After consultation with Clayton, Harriman—then Secretary of Commerce and the prospective chairman of our committee—and a few in the Department, we soon got together an eminent, knowledgeable, and representative committee. On the afternoon of June 22 everything, including a press release, was ready for the President when we met in his upstairs study in the White House with a nonpartisan group that included Senators Vandenberg, Connally, White, and Barkley, and Secretaries Marshall, Snyder, Clinton Anderson of Agriculture, and Julius A. Krug of Interior. I acted as recording secretary.

The President gave Vandenberg full credit for the suggestion, read off the committee members and their qualifications (which were impressive), and asked for suggestions. Vandenberg suggested former Senator Robert M. La-Follette, Jr., of Wisconsin, whom the President added to the list. After a pause, he told me to go out and release the appointment of the committee and the membership to the press. The group then went on to discuss a second group to assist Secretary Krug in a study of available raw-material and basic potential production of such necessities as coal and steel here and abroad, and another under chairman, Edwin G. Nourse of the Council of Economic Advisers, to study the effect of this amount of foreign aid on the economy of the United States. By the time the meeting broke up, the Harriman Committee was an established fact.

27. MUSTERED OUT

GENERAL MARSHALL went about choosing my successor as he did other decisions—no meetings, no lists of names, no papers on desired qualifications. He thought about the question and came to a conclusion. What would I think, he asked me, of Robert A. Lovett? He had been Assistant Secretary of War for Air during the war and had gone back to his banking business in New York. We had known each other since Yale days. He had all the necessary requirements of mind, character, and Washington experience. Most importantly, that experience included years of working with General Marshall under the severe pressures of wartime. He knew Europe well. I thought it an excellent idea.

Bob Lovett's nomination went to the Senate and came before the Foreign Relations Committee in May. I obtained permission from Senator Vandenberg to introduce my successor to the committee. Contrary to popular mythology, my relations with the committee then and later were most friendly. I told the senators of our long association and my high regard for him, of his distinguished record in two wars, as a young naval aviator in 1917–18 and as the civilian organizer of the great Army Air Corps in 1940–45, of his knowledge of the prewar economics of Europe and its postwar dislocations, of General Marshall's great confidence in him. Then, asking for the same kindness from the committee that it had always extended to me, I withdrew and left him on his own. It was no new experience for him and, of course, resulted in his unanimous confirmation on May 28.

This gave us time for a period and method of preparation that so far as I know is without parallel before or since—though why, it is hard to understand. For a month before he took over the Under Secretary's duties Lovett went through what might be called "on-job training." First he learned the organization and functioning of the Department and met its principal officers in the course of doing so. Then he sat beside me in my office or in the Secretary's, hearing all conversations, reading all papers, attending all meetings, and participating in all decisions. More and more I pushed him forward and withdrew myself. On Tuesday, July 1, 1947, he merely moved to the chair at the desk, thoroughly familiar with what was going across it.

Robert Lovett did a superlative job for the next eighteen months, during a substantial part of which he shouldered the added burdens of being Acting Secretary when General Marshall was absent in South America and in Paris at meetings of the United Nations attempting to deal with the blockade of Berlin.

During international tension in Europe and election tension at home he kept close and constructive relations with Senators Vandenberg and Connally and others in Congress. The Marshall Plan legislation and appropriation were passed; the Vandenberg Resolution, forerunner of NATO, voted; and the North Atlantic Treaty negotiations begun. Under great difficulties American leadership went forward without a moment of faltering. Among the important contributions to this remarkable achievement was Robert Lovett's. His relationship with Senator Vandenberg was indispensable to it.

TAKING THE SALUTE

Monday, June 30, 1947, was my last day as Under Secretary of State. Lovett was ready to take the oath of office and thoroughly familiar with current matters. The formalities of resignation had been attended to in May, leaving ample time for my successor's nomination and confirmation. I had also written the President a more personal note of farewell. His longhand response gives some sense of his warm humanity.

Dear Dean,   *May 6, 1947*
I am a damned sentimentalist. Your note touched me where I live. You are too kind to me but I like it and I am glad you are. You have been an arm for me to lean upon. As Marse Robert said when Stonewall lost his left arm at Chancellorsville, "General Jackson has lost his left arm, I have lost my right"—that's the way I feel when you leave State.
With you and our incomparable Secretary, the General, over there I don't have a worry in the world. He says you are a tower of strength to him. But the die is cast and I'll stand by it.
May you live long and prosper and may I always deserve your good will and friendship—you always have mine.   Sincerely, Harry S. Truman

My last appearance at the "nine-thirty meeting" started off the day. It went with the usual briskness. As it adjourned, Will Clayton said that there would be no farewells but they had ventured to have prepared a memento of our service together. I still use it daily—a thermos carafe for ice water on a silver tray with their signatures inscribed around the circumference—and I have their accompanying note before me as I write:

This gift comes to you with the admiration, affection ("free and unfettered"), and enduring friendship of the officers who have enjoyed and benefited from participation in that uniquely Achesonian organization, the Nine-Thirty Club—or Prayer Meeting.

With our very best wishes,

Chip Bohlen	John Hilldring
Will Clayton	Alger Hiss
Ben Cohen	Doc Matthews
Charlie Fahy	Jack Peurifoy
Ernie Gross	Dean Rusk
Loy Henderson	Willard Thorp
Jack Hickerson	John Carter Vincent

General Marshall asked me to go with him to the White House at noon, as the President wanted to discuss one last matter with us both before I left. Aside from that, only signing answers to the flood of letters which had followed the announcement of my resignation and farewells within the Department remained. From my chair in the President's office I could see through the double glass door into the rose garden. A group seemed to be assembling there. The conversation in the office was singularly purposeless. Suddenly in the group outside I caught sight of my wife. At that moment I was led out to join the company. The President announced that he was conferring on me the Medal of Merit, pinned the insignia on my lapel, and read the citation:

Mr. Acheson, as a private citizen in 1940, was among those who first saw clearly the Fascist threat to our national existence. He exerted his distinguished advocacy to rally his fellow citizens in favor of the delivery of American destroyers to beleaguered Britain.

As Assistant Secretary of State from February 1, 1941, to August 16, 1945, and as Under Secretary until today, he has been one of the architects of victory and of the struggle for peace.

In his relations with the Congress Mr. Acheson fostered a responsive relationship between the executive and legislative branches of the Government in the field of foreign affairs; and he brought to the councils of Government a long view and a genius for bold design typified by the Acheson-Lilienthal plan for international control of atomic energy.

The secret had been perfectly kept; I could not have been more surprised. After I had greeted kind friends who had assembled, the President carried me off to the Cabinet luncheon in the White House, where he put me on his right and gave me a pleasant opportunity to take leave of colleagues with whom I had served so closely for so much of the past two years.

That evening, after dining with General Marshall and a group of colleagues whom he had assembled and with their generous words still ringing in my ears, I was driven home to a private—or, at least, semiprivate—life.

THE HABIT-FORMING DRUG OF PUBLIC LIFE

After a six-and-a-half-year "hitch" in the Department under war and near-war conditions, I was tired. How tired, I realized only after the sustaining prop of responsibility was gone. Then came the lesson that before rest and rebuilding reserves can begin one must unwind and relax. The partners in the old law firm relieved concern about a visible means of support by asking me to rejoin them after this second desertion. They have always been kind and generous friends, not only receiving the prodigal but sending him off, first, for a long vacation. This began with a time at our farm and went on to a camping trip with the truest of friends, Ray and Maude Atherton, who were then presiding over our embassy in Ottawa. Our campsite must surely have been the most beautiful on earth—beside a lake nestled in the towering Canadian Rockies at Jasper Park. There the superintendent of the park and his delightful wife, Mr. and Mrs. James Wood, joined us for an idyllic holiday. All too soon we were back in Washington.

Readjustment from public to private life involves something of the anguish and unhappiness of a drug addict in his "withdrawal" period. That comes, I am told, from the protests of a system too long accustomed to overstimulation to its being withdrawn. Public life is not only a powerful stimulant but a habit-forming one. Moreover, it is an insidious and seductive drug, a kind of "happiness drug"—at least, sometimes. Henry Nevinson suggests why: "I have certainly found true joys springing up along the edges of many paths, but never for the seeking or 'according to plan.' Suddenly and unexpectedly they have appeared. . . . As to what those paths might be, I must go back to the old Greek definition of happiness as 'The exercise of vital powers along lines of excellence, in a life affording them scope.' "[1]

With all its tribulations—and there are many—no one should doubt that public life, especially on the national stage, offers scope for the exercise of vital powers, and along lines of excellence. Indeed, so great is the scope, so vast the tasks, so limitless the horizons, that vital powers are exercised far beyond what one had thought of as his strength. One seems to live in a world of problems and demands—intellectual, emotional, psychological, and, often, physical—larger than most men are ordinarily called upon to meet. Then suddenly this stops. The stimulation is gone, but the glands go on working for a time. This period of readjustment to shrinkage in the scope for action is not altogether an easy or a happy one. Its outstanding sensation is of the flatness of life; its immediate need, the acquisition or reacquisition of new values.

RETURN TO SEMIPRIVATE LIFE

For a lawyer returning to private practice, the test of scope as an ingredient of happiness can hardly lie in the importance of what he does, since little that will come his way will equal in importance matters that concerned him as a public servant, however his client may view the comparison. But the degree to which a matter may challenge and open the way for the exercise of his professional skills, imagination, and judgment is another matter. At least I found it true in reviving my interest in my profession, though the time given to me was unhappily too short to revive with it either legal reputation or competence.

Two professional matters chiefly occupied these brief months: one the argument in the Supreme Court of the United States of two cases for impecunious farmers and fishermen of Japanese descent, prosecuted under California statutes attempting to exclude them from their means of livelihood; the other the defense of one of the industrial giants of our time against an attempt by the federal government to terminate its relations with another giant. Each of these tasks called out the best my colleagues and I had to give. Despite this, it may not altogether surprise all of my readers to learn that our poor clients triumphed and our rich client met defeat.

The Citizens' Committee for the Marshall Plan • By midsummer 1947 an organization had been formed to gain popular and legislative support for the Marshall Plan. This was so uniquely and typically American that it deserves a bit more than passing notice. What made it so was, first, that it was privately organized and, second, that it supported a policy for which the Government was also seeking support. Many private organizations, in the United States and elsewhere, protest, sometimes against Government action, sometimes against social or economic disadvantages. But few organize privately to support Government, and fewer still to support policies or measures not directly beneficial to themselves or their group. Before the Citizens' Committee for the Marshall Plan, the last great effort of this sort had been the Committee to Defend America by Aiding the Allies in 1939 and 1940. When I described these endeavors to Robert Schuman as the European Defense Community was running into increasing trouble in France, he was convinced that similar efforts would be impossible in France.

Colonel Stimson lent his immense prestige as our honorary president, while former Secretary of War Robert Patterson and I took on operational responsibility. Harold Stein, later Director of the Woodrow Wilson School of Government at Princeton University, John Ferguson, my colleague in the Department, and a host of friends and associates manned our central offices. With the help of world affairs groups and others, branch committees were formed all over the country—no sizable place was overlooked—which raised money for local education, particularly of the local press. The central office supplied pamphlets, speakers, and newsletters and called for help with Congress at critical moments.

As one of the speakers supplied, I found myself by autumn performing a fairly rugged role. Beginning with a debate on the *Town Meeting of the Air* before a New York City audience in which Max Lerner and I took on Henry J. Taylor and Henry Hazlitt, I went to the West Coast for a series of meetings with organizing groups and speeches to audiences of diverse natures. Starting in San Francisco with a luncheon and speech with the World Affairs Council and a dinner and speech at the Commonwealth Club, interspersed with talks to press and civic groups, I spent another day with students and faculty members at Stanford University, and then moved on to Portland, Oregon, to speak at the Portland Foreign Affairs Council. Another overnight journey took me to Spokane, Washington, for a luncheon speech before a general conference of the Pacific Northwest Trade Association. Two nights and a day in the comparatively restful sanctuary of a train did something to prepare me for two days and a night in the company of a human tornado who was then Mayor of Minneapolis, Hubert Horatio Humphrey.

The Mayor was engaged in his successful campaign for the United States Senate. After speaking in Minneapolis Mr. Humphrey and I teamed up for a joint attack on Duluth during a truly remarkable evening. Busloads of miners and their families had driven into town from the Mesabi range. We first spoke to a large crowd of them in the armory, each of us for about half an hour—I on the Marshall Plan, Humphrey on Humphrey, with cross-assists. Then, returning to the hotel, a marathon of talk began. Payment of twenty-five cents entitled an adult, with accompanying young, to admission to the ballroom for forty-five minutes and one cup of coffee. When the room was comfortably full, the doors were shut and first Humphrey and then I, standing precariously on a chair, made a fifteen-minute speech. Then the ballroom was emptied, filled again, and the performance rerun.

This went on until the early hours of the morning. In time, we reversed the order of speaking, since the Mayor seemed to have more ideas than I, or less terminal capacity, or both. At any rate, the Marshall Plan's share of the evening was progressively diminishing. At last the speechmaking ended, but not for blessed rest. The stalwart remnant of the party adjourned to the only place in town still open, a lunchroom near the railway station, for the refreshment of scrambled eggs and dancing to the music of a jukebox in a spot cleared of tables. Clearly a weakling, I abandoned my more rugged friends in favor of a few hours of sleep before Humphrey drove us back to Minneapolis for one more speech—to the Twin Cities Committee on Foreign Relations—before wearily heading back to Washington.

For another four months the work went on. In January two such disparate bodies as a convention at Atlantic City of the National-American Wholesale Grocers' Association and the Committee on Foreign Affairs of the House of Representatives heard from me; in March the *Philadelphia Bulletin* Forum and in April the College Symposium on Foreign Policy of Oberlin College in Ohio. These long-forgotten meetings and speeches have no importance in themselves but are illustrative of the efforts of hundreds, perhaps thousands, of other speakers and workers who by their sweat and tears reached the minds, or at least the attention, of innumerable others—and all this effort eventually came back to affect the several hundred people in Washington who would write and enact the European Recovery Program into law.

A FALSE ALARM

On Sunday, April 4, 1948, the day after he had signed the Foreign Assistance Act of 1948, the President telephoned me at Harewood, our farm in Maryland where we were spending the weekend. Would I, he asked, consider returning to public life? He would shortly have to nominate an administrator provided for in the act and would like to nominate me. In the long conversation that resulted I argued that this would be a great mistake. Vandenberg and others had been worried throughout the congressional debate that the billions required for the recovery program might be used to influence the coming election. I knew that they would insist on a nonpolitical person to direct the program. My relations with both the President and General Marshall were so close that, while I would be regarded as honest, I could never be thought of as nonpartisan.

I reminded the President that the act just signed carried no money. It was merely an authorization to ask for some. To get money in adequate amounts would be hard enough under the most favorable conditions. It would be impossible if doubts and suspicions were aroused. Vandenberg must be wholly on the President's side in the coming arguments with the appropriations committees. My suggestion to the President was to consult with Vandenberg about the nomination, telling him quite frankly that he had thought of me and asking the Senator for his opinion. He would, I thought, dissent strongly and propose Paul Hoffman. Paul was a good man; the President would do well to accept him and, by doing so, irrevocably commit Vandenberg to the support of an adequately financed program. If I was wrong and the Senator accepted me, I would do it.

Reluctantly the President agreed to the consultation. Later he called me again to say that it went exactly according to my scenario. The appointment was an excellent and highly successful one.

THE FIRST HOOVER COMMISSION

The summer of 1947 also saw the creation by act of the Eightieth Congress of the Commission on the Organization of the Executive Branch of the United States Government. Its members were appointed in equal numbers by the Speaker of the House, the President Pro Tempore of the Senate, and the President of the United States, who appointed me a member and vice chairman, imposing on me the duty of seeing to it that the commission was not used in any way in the political campaign of 1948. This was an easy task, since no such attempt was made, and former President Hoover, who had been designated as chairman, would not have permitted it if one had been made. The commission did useful work. Equally interesting to me was the new impression it gave me of a former President whom I had never known.

After a year or more of firsthand association in a common task, Mr. Hoover was no longer the figure I had created from press and radio. He had humor, a sense and enjoyment of the bizarre and ridiculous; he could and did laugh, though he was more inclined to chuckle. He understood and practiced both satire and irony, as exemplified by his description of President Coolidge's expanding conception of fun during his summer vacations while President, or his classification of politicians by their attitude toward and practice of fishing —fly-fishing was one of his true joys. In controversy he was tough, though not mean, appreciating Leo Durocher's axiom that "nice guys come in last." He did not like to lose; but when he did, he did not sulk—long. Finally, when he asked for advice, he wanted it straight and did not get angry when it was not what he hoped for. One day he asked me why we spent so much time at our meetings in quarrels over procedure. Because, I said, he drove us too hard to be orderly and relevant; if he would let us wander a little first and then nip a leg or two like a sheep dog, we would move along. Barking got everyone nervous. The next day I saw him learning his lesson by doodling with the word "follow," writing in ever-diminishing letters within embellishments.

We had only one real collision, and my success in that instance led him to have the law changed when the Second Hoover Commission was created in the Eisenhower Administration. It was a disagreement over whether the commission's jurisdiction was limited to organization of the government for administering the laws as they stood, or whether it extended to changes in laws that the commission believed unwise. Foreseeing endless debates over New Deal legislation and the welfare state, I argued strongly for the narrower view and was supported by a majority of the commission. Mr. Hoover did not like losing this point at all; it took him some little time to warm up again. One of our last meetings occurred a year or two later, when, walking home from the United Nations buildings to the Waldorf Towers, where we were both living, I overtook him.

"Mr. President," I said from behind him, "it would greatly improve my financial and social standing if I might be seen walking with you."

"Anything I can do," he replied, "short of a loan."

In only two respects did the commission's recommendations bear directly on my future work, those on foreign affairs and what was then known as the National Military Establishment as set up by the act of 1947. This latter the commission characterized as "perilously close to the weakest type of department."[2] Its recommendations, based upon an experienced task force's report, have been largely enacted into law, and have transformed the weak "establishment"—a first faltering step toward unification of the military services under a sort of umpire without power of final decision—to a strong department headed by a Secretary whose powers are formidable when wielded by a strong man. In one respect only George Mead, James Pollock, James Rowe, Jr., and I wished our brethren to go farther than they were willing to go. Our disagreement was not nearly so great as they seemed to think it was.

Battle Over a Chief of Staff • They recommended the organization of the Joint Chiefs of Staff as it exists today, in the form of a committee of the chiefs of the services, who vote, presided over by a voteless chairman. The members of the committee are burdened by both staff and command duties, some of which require committee action. This organization is extremely difficult for civilian officers engaged in foreign affairs to work with. All too often it produces for those looking for military advice and guidance only oracular utterances. Since it is a committee and its views are the result of votes on formal papers prepared for it, it quite literally is like my favorite old lady who could not say what she thought until she heard what she said. Even on a tentative basis, it is hard for high officials to get military advice in our government. When one does get it, it is apt to be unresponsive to the problems bothering the civilian official.

Our proposal was only a step on the way to improving the situation. We recommended creation by Congress of the post of Chief of Staff for the Armed Services, the incumbent to be appointed by the President and confirmed by the Senate. He would have staff functions only, not command functions; the Secretary and President would decide the orders. He would preside over the meetings of the service chiefs and report their recommendations with his own. His post would carry the most senior rank in the services. He would have his own staff, designated by the Secretary. He would advise civilian policy makers on the military aspects of their problems, and be kept advised of national policy and problems.

To some extent the ability of officers who have served as chairmen of the Joint Chiefs of Staff has produced a part of what our proposal sought. But the prestige of form, rank, and authority to recommend, as well as the help of a staff, would accomplish even more.

The arguments of our brethren were antiquated ones. The "man on horseback" was one, though not since Napoleon had a major dictator held field rank, nor since Jackson had a general been a strong president. Hitler never rose above the rank of corporal. In the southern hemisphere the time when soldiers turn to political conspiracy is when they are colonels. The arguments for diffusing power among the services were once made for diffusing it within them. Secretary of War Elihu Root began the process of subordinating the chiefs of cavalry, infantry, and artillery to a chief of staff, and General Marshall, over great objection, completed it. The mild reform contained in our proposal after twenty years still awaits action.

Recommendation of One Service in State • The commission's report on organization for the conduct of foreign affairs was also a good one. Most of its recommendations were put into effect within a year or two. One, however, was not and this delay caused criticism of a different sort. Recommendation number 20 was: "The personnel in the permanent State Department establishment in Washington and the personnel of the Foreign Service above certain levels should be amalgamated over a short period of years into a single foreign affairs service obligated to serve at home or overseas and constituting a safeguarded career group administered separately from the general Civil Service."

Secretary Forrestal cautioned that this excellent recommendation, in which I heartily concurred, should "not be permitted to operate so as to destroy the morale or spirit of either group." The Hoover Commission understood this, as it indicated by stating that it "should be carried out *gradually* over a short period of years."[3] The reason for this was that those permanently employed in Washington who had never contemplated or desired a peripatetic life abroad needed time either to retire or move into the general Civil Service and find as congenial work as possible in other offices. On the other hand, the Foreign Service, whose roster fluctuated at a little over a thousand officers, regarded itself as an elite corps and faced with distaste the idea of being diluted to the extent necessary to do the work of those previously stationed permanently at home. These had increased in numbers by five hundred per cent since the beginning of the war. Those who recall the attitude of regular officers of the Army and Navy to reserve officers and "ninety-day wonders" of the 1941–45 war will not find Foreign Service officers unique. To maintain the morale of the Foreign Service, the process of recruitment required both time and painstaking methods to insure that the quality of the recruits should be high and that it should be recognized as being high.

My Later Attempt to Create One Service · In December 1949 the Secretary of State appointed James H. Rowe, Jr., of the Hoover Commission, Robert Ramspeck, chairman of the Civil Service Commission, and Ambassador William S. DeCourcy of the Foreign Service to advise him how to go about the task recommended by the commission. In the meantime cautious, perhaps too cautious, experimentation with methods was going on. The group made its report in August 1950. It endorsed the unified service recommended by the Hoover Commission, stated that it should be established by statute, pointed out what recruitment was possible without new legislation and urged more energetic action, set forth the requirements for a new personnel system and urged that a plan should be adopted as early as practicable, and discussed the difficult morale problem. "The transition to an integrated service will be difficult," wrote the commission.[4]

The Department took some of the steps recommended in this report but, as was stated in the order, did "not at this time go as far as the program recommended by the Committee."[5] It was already facing troubles enough at home to induce moderation in reorganizing its harassed staff. Since the first of the year Senator Joseph McCarthy, with help from various other internal-security investigations and loyalty boards, was keeping administrative officers busy and both Foreign Service officers and departmental staff thoroughly upset. It would seem understandable that the Secretary regarded a far-reaching and basic reorganization of the status of every person in the Department as General Grant might have regarded a similar proposal for the Army of the Potomac between the Wilderness and Appomattox.

Not so, however, a committee appointed by and reporting to Secretary Dulles in 1954, known as the Wriston Committee. This group found that its work had been done for it by the Hoover Commission in 1949 and the Rowe-Ramspeck-DeCourcy committee in 1950. But, it wrote reprovingly, "these reports did not result in any measurable action, and it is this Committee's considered judgment that, had proper and prompt steps been taken during those years, much valuable time would have been utilized in developing the Foreign Service along the lines this Report proposes."[6] This is undoubtedly true—had any Foreign Service remained to be developed and had the crises in Europe and Asia conveniently postponed themselves. It is, perhaps, significant that all eight members of this committee knew the prior Secretary of State, five had served with him, two were Foreign Service officers. Yet it is not recorded that any of them suggested to him or the Department what later seemed to them so palpable a failure of action.

They also found what would not seem strange after Secretary Dulles had put administration of the Department in the hands of Senator Henry Styles Bridges' assistant, Scott McLeod, and had opened the Foreign Service to the investigation of Senator McCarthy's coadjutors Cohn and Schine of malodorous memory. "The morale of that [the Foreign Service] today," they discovered, "stands in need of repair." They found, too, that the "causes of the decline are manifold and interacting. Perhaps the most serious single contributing cause has been the absence of strong administrative leadership within the Department of State and the Foreign Service." Another cause was "a disturbed feeling on the part of the Service itself that its work has not been fully understood by its countrymen." Before leaving the subject, however, the committee did not fail to note that "another factor has also been at work . . . namely, the Government's security program."

Upon this the committee took a forthright position:

The Department of State, in all its branches, accepts, of course, the need for a thoroughgoing security check of its ranks. The Committee has examined the actions taken by the Secretary of State to implement Executive Order 10450 and can report that the program has been drastic and thorough . . . has inevitably occasioned uncertainties, doubts, and fears which will be fully dissipated only when the process is completed during the coming summer. . . . Investigations of such sensitive character should be conducted with the professional impartiality associated in the public mind with the Federal Bureau of Investigation. . . . Among the things that must be protected for the Foreign Service is the tradition of frank and objective reporting that long has constituted one of the State Department's most enduring sources of strength.[7]

But enough. Mind you, the members of the committee were otherwise honorable men. Acting in a time of fear and hysteria they could not, perhaps, be expected to rise above standards set by a President of the United States and his Secretary of State. Nevertheless, it is difficult to disguise an attitude suggested by Douglas Southall Freeman when he wrote, "Acheson found it difficult to conceal his contempt for the contemptible."[8]

III

YEARS OF RESPONSIBILITY

Secretary of State, 1949–1953

Section A. Decisions Were Made Fast in 1949

28. RECALLED TO ACTIVE DUTY

TOWARD THE END OF November the President sent word asking me to call on him at Blair House. The White House, weakened for over a century or more by British arson and careless American remodeling, had been pronounced unsafe and was being completely rebuilt. Only the outside wall—for sentimental reasons—had been shored up and left standing. Informal talks between us to discuss the progress of the Hoover Commission and other matters were not uncommon. When I was shown into his minute office in the adjoining Blair-Lee House, which had been opened into the larger building, he asked me to sit down, adding with a grin, "You had better be sitting down when you hear what I have to say."

Then without stopping he went on, "I want you to come back and be Secretary of State. Will you?" To his amusement I was utterly speechless. After collecting my wits, I asked about General Marshall's health and desires, the President's requirements, other possibilities, and so on. The President spoke very simply and frankly. General Marshall, who was still in Walter Reed Hospital after having a kidney removed, would have to retire. He would stay in office until the end of the presidential term on January 20, 1949, which would complete to the day two full years as Secretary of State. The President had carefully considered all alternatives and told me why he had come to the conclusion he had. I asked him to believe me, knowing a good deal about the situation, in saying that I was not qualified to meet the demands of the office in that unprecedented time. The President replied that we must be quite sensible. What I said was doubtless true. He could say the same of himself. But the fact was that he was President and he did want me to be Secretary of State. So the question was whether I would do so or not. Before I could answer, he told me to go home, talk it over with my wife, and no one else, and call him in the morning. He would like to see, he added, whether for once a secret could be kept in the city of Washington.

My wife cheerfully agreeing, I told the President the next day that I would be at his service. So well was the secret kept that I received a useful lesson in modesty, for when speculation began about the General's continuation in office and his possible successors, I was by no means in the forefront. When the announcement came six weeks later, no one was more surprised than my partners and my associates on the Hoover Commission.

Before it was made, the President discussed with me the appointment of an Under Secretary, saying that Bob Lovett wished to retire, as I already knew, with General Marshall. Properly attaching great importance to having someone he knew and had confidence in to act in my place when I might be away, the President asked whether James E. Webb, the Director of the Budget, with whom we had both worked closely, would be agreeable to me. Webb, who later held the highly responsible position of Administrator of the National Aeronautics and Space Agency, was and is able and loyal. He knew more about administration than foreign policy, but the Department could use this ability. Also, it was of utmost importance to strengthen the President's confidence in the Department at all times. All presidents I have known have had uneasy doubts about the State Department. They extend to the White House staff, and in fact often originate there. They are strongest at the beginning of presidential terms, when the incumbent and his new associates in the White House believe that foreign affairs are simpler than they in fact are and that they can be confidently approached under the guidance of principles (liberal, conservative, idealistic, or moral) even without much knowledge or experience. Foreign Service officers seem to them cynical, unimaginative, and negative. These views are not held about the Department of Justice, or Agriculture, or the Treasury—except, as I ruefully remember, when I was the acting head of the last mentioned.

So I was glad to welcome the President's suggestion of Jim Webb as second in command. Although he was never, I think, altogether happy in the Department, he served faithfully and well for three years, accomplishing what both the President and I hoped for from him. I remain deeply grateful to him.

NOMINATION, HEARINGS, AND CONFIRMATION

On January 7, 1949, President Truman announced General Marshall's resignation as Secretary of State, my nomination to succeed him, and Jim Webb's as Under Secretary. The General's retirement inspired proper and sincere regret; the nominations, little surprise, some approval, and no great enthusiasm—all proper and understandable responses. Within a week hearings on the confirmation of the nominations began before the Senate Committee on Foreign Relations in the great Caucus Room of the Senate office building.

One of the themes of the hearings, though not yet strong enough to dominate them, had been building up under the incendiary guidance of the House Committee on Un-American Activities. This was the loyalty and Communist-subversion theme, which, within the year, had been given a most dramatic personal twist. In August 1948 charges of involvement in a Communist cell in Washington had been made before the committee by one Whittaker Chambers, an admitted former Communist turned anti, against a former State Department officer, then President of the Carnegie Endowment for International Peace. Alger Hiss had been recommended by the Chairman of the Carnegie Endowment Board, John Foster Dulles, who had been much impressed by his work on the United Nations Charter at both Dumbarton Oaks and San Francisco. His brilliance was unchallenged; opinions about his personality differed. I had known him since his graduation from Harvard Law School, when he became law clerk to Justice Holmes, but had had no close association with him until in 1946 his work in charge of United Nations liaison in the Department brought him under my supervision. His brother, Donald, however, had served as my assistant from 1941 to March 1944, and was, in 1949 as he is at the time of this writing, one of my partners in the practice of law. This is the first appearance of the Alger Hiss affair in this book. It is enough to say of it here that at the time of the hearings what had seemed in the beginning incredible and bizarre had moved into personal tragedy. It was destined to go on to something approaching national disaster, lending, as it did, support to a widespread attack throughout the country upon confidence in government itself.

Early in the hearing[1] Senator Connally, Chairman of the committee, asked me whether it was true that as "has been charged over the radio and in the press and by word of mouth that, while you were Assistant Secretary, Mr. Alger Hiss was your chief of staff or was your special assistant." I replied that, as a preliminary matter, I should like the committee to understand that my friendship was not easily given nor easily withdrawn. Donald Hiss had been my assistant when I was Assistant Secretary of State, had served me and the country with complete fidelity and loyalty, and at the time I was speaking was my partner in the practice of law "with everything that that relationship implies." Alger Hiss had been an officer of the Department most of the time I served there. We had become friends and remained friends. I did not wish in any way to detract from that statement in pointing out that he had never been my assistant and had never, except for the last few months of his service when I was Acting Secretary of State, reported to me.

From the time I came into the Department in 1941 to sometime in April or May 1946, I told the committee, Alger Hiss had worked first for Dr. Stanley Hornbeck in the Far Eastern Division and later for Dr. Leo Pasvolsky in a division preparing for and participating in the Dumbarton Oaks and San Francisco conferences on the United Nations and the Chapultepec conference in Mexico, and still later in the winter of 1945–46 he participated in the organizational meeting of the United Nations in London. None of this work came under my supervision. In April or May 1946 he was put in charge of a division having charge of our relations with the United Nations. He reported to Secretary Byrnes, or to me in the Secretary's absence, until he left the Department for the Carnegie Endowment around the end of the year.

From this general statement I went on to specific remarks of former Assistant Secretary of State Adolph Berle to the Un-American Activities Committee, of which the only portion worth mentioning here is that "in the fall of 1944 there was a difference of opinion in the State Department." He felt, Berle continued, "that the Russians were not going to be sympathetic and cooperative . . . and [he] was pressing for a pretty clean-cut show-down when our position was strongest. The opposite group in the State Department was largely the men in Mr. Acheson's group, of course, with Mr. Hiss as his principal assistant in the matter. . . . At that time Mr. Hiss did take what you would call today the pro-Russian point of view. That was a cause for worry." Berle concluded by saying that he "got trimmed in that fight and as a result went to Brazil." There he was Ambassador.

I pointed out to the committee once again that Alger Hiss had never been my assistant, that Donald Hiss had left my office in the preceding March, that from June to October I had been away at conferences almost continuously and had no assistant, that Berle and I were in Washington at the same time only from October 8 to November 1, when he left for an international air conference, returning only to leave for his ambassadorial post.

"Therefore," I concluded, "I want to point out that whoever had any controversy with Mr. Berle at this time [the fall of 1944], it was not I. Whoever assisted anyone in any controversy with Mr. Berle, it was not either one of the Hisses."

The rest of the hearing was taken up with answering various charges that I or my partners had in some vague and undefined way profited through my holding office. The one exception was a helpful, but not too successful, attempt by Senator Vandenberg to find some way of reassuring the committee that in future policy I could be counted on to be sound and sensible. He had told me what he intended to do, so that I had come armed with past utterances over quite a period.

However, I suggested, Senator Vandenberg's concern was with the worry, the regret so widely felt, that the President must lose the powerful help and support of General Marshall, the great figure of the whole war period. Nothing could change that situation; no one could take General Marshall's place. But one who had worked under him could do his best with what strength and ability were given to him to follow the General's example. President Truman's policies had been evolved with the help of two secretaries of state. I had served them both as their Under Secretary and knew something of the circumstances and problems the President's actions had been designed to meet and the need for steadiness and continuity. Before that I had served two other secretaries and learned something about the function of an adviser to his chief—to be frank, forthright, and vigorous in counsel; energetic and loyal in accepting decisions and carrying them out. This was the school in which I had been taught. It was not an easy one to equal.

In executive session the committee returned to the Chambers-Hiss controversy, trying to puzzle out some rational explanation. We tried the experiment of examining the conduct of both on the assumption that what Chambers had said was true, and then on the assumption that it was false. On neither assumption was their conduct explicable on any reasonable basis. Some parts of the puzzle seemed to be missing. The mystery remained, as it does today. We also discussed communism both as an economic and political doctrine and as an active force in national and international affairs. At the end of the session the committee took the unusual step of making public an "excerpt" from my testimony, in the authorship of which Senator Vandenberg had collaborated: "It is my view that communism as a doctrine is economically fatal to a free society and to human rights and fundamental freedom. Communism as an aggressive factor in world conquest is fatal to independent governments and to free peoples."[2]

On January 14, 1949, the committee voted unanimously to recommend confirmation. This the Senate did by a vote of 83 to 6. Senator Vandenberg spoke in support of confirmation, although his private view was that "Mr. Acheson would *not* have been my choice for Secretary of State,"[3] and he continued to worry that the nonpartisan collaboration that had become so intimate between him and General Marshall and Robert Lovett would diminish.

ON JANUARY 21, the day after President Truman's inauguration, I took the oath of office as the fifty-second Secretary of State of the United States. Chief Justice Vinson administered the oath in the President's office. The President had with him to provide bipartisan blessing the chairmen and ranking minority members of the Senate and House foreign committees, Senators Connally and Vandenberg and Representatives Bloom and Eaton. He had also thoughtfully invited a large group of family—his and mine—and friends from the Supreme Court, Cabinet, Congress, and the Department. The thought of General Marshall, still in the hospital, brought to mind a sentence from the First Book of Kings often quoted by another great predecessor, Colonel Stimson: "Let not him that girdeth on his harness boast himself as he that putteth it off." With this thought I went to the State Department to sit in General Marshall's chair.

One result of the President's desire to keep my appointment secret until only two weeks before I took office was to preclude any thorough advance briefing on the exact nature and state of the work in process—and of the problems, too. Those two weeks were pretty fully occupied with the hearings on confirmation and winding up my affairs at the law office. Once again my loyal and able secretary, Barbara Evans, packed up to move the few blocks to a wholly different life. Both Robert Lovett and Clark Clifford most helpfully gave me broad instruction in a few secret evening meetings in their homes, but for the most part not until taking office did I get down to essentials. For instance, my first knowledge of the famous Point Four Program, which I was to carry out, came on the platform in front of the Capitol listening to the President expound it in his inaugural address.

THE STATE OF THE DEPARTMENT

Before turning to the decisions which began to come fast after my return to the Department of State, it may be helpful to note briefly the state of the Department. That long-suffering institution did not escape the "reorganization" that every new Secretary imposes on it, even as he "girdeth on his harness." In this case, however, it had better credentials than most, coming as it did from recommendations of the Commission on the Organization of the Executive Branch of the Government. The President had asked for the necessary legislation in January and got it in Public Law 73 of May 26, 1949. This authorized, in addition to the Secretary and Under Secretary, ten Assistant Secretaries (two of whom might be designated as Deputy Under Secretaries), a Counselor with the rank of Assistant Secretary, and a Legal Adviser, all to be appointed by the President with the consent of the Senate. All laws granting authority to subordinate officers were repealed and all authority to direct personnel and the performance of duties and functions assigned to the Department was vested in the Secretary.

By the end of June with the new authority in hand—and being able to keep with us a bit over half of General Marshall's high command—our roster was:

Under Secretary of State	James E. Webb
Assistant Secretaries	
Designated as Deputy	
Under Secretaries	
For Administration	John E. Peurifoy
For Substance	Dean Rusk
In Charge of	
Inter-American Affairs	Edward G. Miller, Jr.
European Affairs	George W. Perkins
Far Eastern Affairs	W. Walton Butterworth
Near Eastern, South Asian,	
and African Affairs	George C. McGhee
United Nations Affairs	John D. Hickerson
Economic Affairs	Willard L. Thorp
Public Affairs	George V. Allen
Congressional Relations	Ernest Gross
Counselor	George F. Kennan
Legal Adviser	Adrian S. Fisher
Director, Policy Planning	George F. Kennan
Succeeded January 1, 1950, by	Paul H. Nitze
Ambassador at Large	Philip C. Jessup
Director, Executive Secretariat	Carlisle H. Humelsine
Special Assistant for Research	
and Intelligence	W. Park Armstrong
Special Assistant for Press	Michael J. McDermott
Chief of Protocol	Stanley Woodward

The structural and operating reorganization that took place in stages throughout 1949 was to get lines of command and responsibility clear and simple. The Deputy Under Secretary for Administration, John Peurifoy, had command over and responsibility through Webb to me for the whole administrative area, consisting of the Offices of Personnel (of every sort), Consular Affairs, Operating Facilities, and Management and Budget.

The Deputy Under Secretary of State for substantive matters, Dean Rusk, helped the Under Secretary on policy matters and served as chief liaison officer between State and Defense. The Hoover Commission's Task Force on Foreign Affairs had seen the need for effective assistance to the Under Secretary in shaping up important decisions and bringing together into clear-cut recommendations for action the views and knowledge of the two types of substantive work carried on by the geographic divisions and the functional divisions.

AN INDISPENSABLE AIDE

A vitally important step within the Department was the selection from among the young officers of a personal assistant for me—what the British call "private secretary to the Minister." I shall always be deeply grateful to Carl Humelsine for recommending a tall, good-looking Floridian, Lucius D. Battle, then serving on the Canadian desk, as meeting my requirements by being a bachelor, bright, pleasant, knowledgeable about the Department, energetic, and responsible. At our interview he confirmed Carl's good judgment. I made the job seem as horrendous as possible, particularly in two respects. First, his continued status as a bachelor was essential. We should be traveling, perhaps without much notice, working late, undependable about social engagements. My own family would be enough for us to worry about without adding one of his own. At the first twinge of a tender emotion he would be expected to draft his request for other duty. He assured me that he was heart-whole and fancy-free and expected to remain so. Rightly I was more impressed by the fact than by the prediction. Second, the job with me would probably blight his career, since his duty would involve standing between me and senior officers who would believe that seeing me instantly, whenever they wished, would be essential to the public welfare. He could well become the most unpopular man in the Department.

No better choice could have been made. Both my wife and I came to have the same regard and affection for Luke Battle that we had for our son. In time he did succumb to the tender emotion. Barbara Evans told me that he was depressed at the thought of ending our work together. In her view I had been putting on an act and should stop it. Inured to female domination by three diverse methods in the family, I agreed, with one attempt to save face—the young lady should obtain my consent *in loco parentis*. A message suitably altered brought about our meeting and my instant collapse. If Luke had to go away often and unexpectedly, she observed gently, she had gotten along without him for a good part of her life and could readjust to a quite familiar situation.

Toward the end of my tenure the Battles went off to a foreign post, and another officer, Jeffrey Kitchen—this time already provided with a most delightful wife—took over as my assistant. The same close relations were soon established as Jeff served me with equal devotion for the last six months or more of my term. The careers of both men suffered, for a time, from the bitterness which the McCarthy outrage provoked against those close to me. Happily, that passed and both went on to distinguished work and positions in the Department and later in private life.

As every administrator knows, good organization is a great help to those who can command, who know what they want to do, and who are prepared to do it. For those who approach decision with an attitude wavering between velleity and regret, it is irrelevant. The reorganization orders of 1949, along with General Marshall's innovations, greatly facilitated the supervision and control of the Department—the issuance, transmission, and execution of orders, and the location of responsibility for results. This was all one could expect of them.

THE STATE OF THE WORLD

While I had never been wholly out of touch with affairs, it was surprising to learn on coming back into close touch how much in a few spots and how little in so many the world of 1949 had changed from the one with which I had dealt during the two years after the end of formal warfare in 1945. Then, wherever one turned, what little was left of social, economic, and political stability seemed about to be submerged. The other world superpower appeared determined to push this process forward in the apparent belief that chaos was the stage preparatory to communism. When I returned to office the surrounding gloom had deepened, or remained impenetrable, in most areas, but in one at least, Western Europe, the Marshall Plan had brought the dawn of a revivification unparalleled in modern history. After a general survey, we shall return to this and another area where much had changed.

In Asia the effort to restore a Chinese society and state based upon an amalgamation of Chiang Kai-shek's Kuomintang and Mao Tse-tung's Communists had failed, and Chiang was in the last stages of collapse. I arrived just in time to have him collapse on me. In Korea our hope was the unpromising one that the United Nations might bring about the withdrawal of both Russian and United States troops from that divided country, to be followed by its unification. Both Washington and General MacArthur were agreed that the occupation of Japan was a rapidly diminishing asset, but no one had yet grasped the nettle of a peace treaty—what kind and how to get it. In both Indochina and Indonesia colonial rule was beyond the power of either France or the Netherlands. Both resisted our efforts to move them toward preparing for independence. The French fought to the end; the Dutch capitulated under pressure. In both cases independence was to bring results close to disaster. We had launched the Philippines into independent national life, with a pretty fair preparation and a sound fisc, but mismanagement and corruption were bidding fair to turn the effort into a shambles. The end of British rule in India and Pakistan had eliminated one problem, leaving age-old hostility between Hindu and Moslem in the midst of bitter poverty.

The British were in trouble and were headed for more in Iran and Egypt, while the French in Indochina and in North Africa had opened their veins and were bleeding to death. The future in the rest of Africa was still veiled in obscurity.

In that area of special American worry, the Good Neighborhood, there was plenty to worry about. Here Hispano-Indian culture—or lack of it—had been piling up its problems for centuries. An explosive population, stagnant economy, archaic society, primitive politics, massive ignorance, illiteracy, and poverty—all had contributed generously to the creation of many local crises, tending to merge into a continental one. Added to this was a further factor. The foreign investment that the whole continent needed as much as it needed population control caused an ambivalent response in Latin America. On the one hand, it promised escape from the peonage of centuries; on the other, it appeared to threaten United States exploitation—especially in the extractive industries—and the perpetuation of domestic control by the small, reactionary ruling class that had dominated Latin America since Columbus and the Conquistadores.

The Arab-Israeli Impasse · While I was out of Government service in 1947–48, a great deal had happened in the Middle Eastern confrontation between Arab and Jew. We left this problem in mid-June 1947, as my under-secretarial tenure was running out and Bevin had asked for a special session of the General Assembly of the United Nations to receive Britain's surrender of the Palestinian mandate and provide for future government in that area. Fighting between Jews and Arabs had become general throughout Palestine. While committees debated, divided, and reported, confusion had grown. The mandate, all were agreed, should be terminated in two years, during which Britain should maintain order. A majority had favored partition; a minority, a federal state. Arab delegates had walked out of the United Nations. On December 3, 1947, the British had announced that their responsibility would end on the following May 15. On May 14 the Republic of Israel had been proclaimed in Palestine and recognized the same day by President Truman on a de facto basis while his representative at the United Nations, Dr. Philip C. Jessup, was, under instructions, speaking in the General Assembly in favor of a temporary trusteeship.

Count Folke Bernadotte of Sweden, appointed UN mediator on May 20, 1948, had maintained an uneasy truce until his assassination in September. A few days later his report was made public, recommending modifications in the United Nations resolution of November 29, 1947. Fighting had broken out again in December 1948, during which Israeli forces swept into Egyptian territory until the acting mediator, Ralph Bunche, obtained a cease-fire in early January and called for negotiations on the Island of Rhodes. The Israelis held strong positions while their opponents suffered from the shock of military defeat and political disunity.

In this situation, ten days before I was to take office, Bevin approached Acting Secretary Lovett through the British Ambassador, Oliver Franks, seeking a joint Anglo-American position on Palestine—or, put more realistically, American help in escaping from the bind in which British treaties with Egypt and Jordan placed him. The Israeli drive deep into the Negev had produced urgent Arab calls upon him for British forces to hold Aqaba and British arms to strengthen the Arab Legion in Jordan. Here is where I came in, with all-too-vivid memories of the pains attendant upon efforts to coordinate Palestine problems with Bevin. On this occasion he was even more emotionally aroused than in the past. The same questions were involved as on successive future occasions—the fixing of boundaries, recognition of Israel, Israeli withdrawal from military gains, refugees.

Lovett had carried the President with him in a shrewd analysis for the British of their position. In effect, the British had proposed a retraction of the Israeli-held area, which would be surrounded by a circle of weak Arab states held together by foreign aid, given also to Israel, and the whole result disciplined and restrained by Anglo-American agreement. This, Lovett had insisted, was not a solution, since it would not be accepted in the Middle East or in the United States and would constitute a continuing invitation to Soviet intrigue and intervention in the area. While the United States would strongly favor any practicable steps to confine the dispute to the former mandated area, attempts at imposed settlements within it had lamentably failed whether made by Anglo-American initiative or by a UN-sponsored group of noninvolved states without large-power interference. Jews and Arabs had now, perhaps, been sobered by an experience of trial by combat and were due to attempt a negotiated settlement under Ralph Bunche's skilled guidance. The Lovett view was that this should not be prejudiced by Anglo-American interference.

A few days after the Lovett-Franks talks I took over command in the Department from Lovett and with it his appraisal of the Israeli-Arab situation. While Dr. Bunche's negotiations held a spark of hope, we gave them a free field and hearty support. When they failed, I pushed the same policy and effort in the successor forum, the Palestine Conciliation Commission of the United Nations. It too failed. Throughout 1949 and 1950, as will be told, the Department's efforts in every field to ameliorate this problem claimed my own time and attention. Unhappily, none of our efforts bore fruit or the promise of any. Conflict simmered down during my tenure, but flared up again later on. Having no desire to recall and inflict on the reader a long record of failure, this book will not detail the time and effort spent on Arab-Israeli conflict, the inherent difficulties of the problem (such as providing in these barren lands for large and growing populations), and the intractability of opposing attitudes and emotions.

Soon after taking office I asked Dr. Ralph Bunche, with the President's approval, to join us in the Department as Assistant Secretary of State for Near Eastern, South Asian, and African Affairs. In the most courteous manner he declined the invitation. All too much of his present duty, he said, had been taken up with these seemingly unsolvable problems. His most heartfelt wish was for relief from them, not deeper involvement. How often I was to remember and echo his wish!

United States Policy Toward Germany • Europe was almost unique in that the outlook there was not the general one of deterioration and gloom but a heightening of both hopes and fears. Four years of increasingly purposeful effort had brought the beginnings of recovery in Western Europe, but at the same time had intensified Soviet control of Eastern Europe and produced dangerous action farther west, of which the most ominous was the blockade of Berlin.

American ideas had changed greatly in the four years since the harsh occupation policy laid down in the April 1945 Joint Chiefs of Staff directive (JCS 1067) to General Eisenhower and his deputy for military government of the American zone, Major General Lucius D. Clay. This triune document had resulted from the uneasy blending of State, War, and Treasury (Morgenthau Plan) ideas. Its basic objectives were (1) to bring home to the Germans that they could not escape the suffering they had brought upon themselves; (2) to be firm, aloof, and discourage all fraternization; (3) to prevent Germany's ever becoming a threat to the peace—by eliminating nazism and militarism, apprehending and punishing war criminals, controlling Germany's capacity to make war, and preparing her for eventual democratic government; (4) to enforce reparations and restitution and the return of war prisoners; (5) to control German economy to achieve these objectives and prevent any higher standard of living than in neighboring nations. From the outset General Clay and his organization believed JCS 1067 to be unworkable.

Secretary Byrnes joined in this view as soon as Stalin's offensive against the West demonstrated the failure of the Potsdam program. Secretary Byrnes's speech in Stuttgart on September 6, 1946, mentioned in Chapter 21, marked a strong swing away from earlier policies. Germany, he said, should not be turned into an economic poorhouse; rather, we favored economic unification and, under proper safeguards, giving German people throughout Germany "primary responsibility for the running of their own affairs."[1] These ideas got another push in December when Byrnes and Bevin announced the economic union of the British and American zones. "Bizonia" went into effect on May 29, 1947, when the new administration was set up in Bonn, allowing Germans to run their own economy subject to a bipartite control office. The French, in one of their noncooperative moods, refused for the time being to join their zone with the others.

In the United States I made my Cleveland, Mississippi, speech on May 8, 1947, pointing out that the world would need in that year goods from the United States to the extent of sixteen billion dollars, for half of which no means of payment was discernible, and adding: "The fourth thing we must do in the present situation is to push ahead with the reconstruction of those two great workshops of Europe and Asia—Germany and Japan—upon which the ultimate recovery of the two continents so largely depends."[2] On June 5 General Marshall made his speech at Harvard. Within a month a new and more liberal directive issued from Washington (JCS 1779 of July 11, 1947), aimed at the attainment of a self-sustaining German economy at the earliest practicable date. A U.K.-U.S. bizonal agreement in August permitted industrial production in Germany at the 1936 rate, an increase of one-third. At this evidence of movement to a new policy toward our former enemy, France during late August showed cautious willingness to add its zone to the other two in pursuit of it. By November the three allies were able to present a solid front to the Russians at the London meeting of the Council of Foreign Ministers.

Crisis in Germany[3] · From then on events moved swiftly to crisis. Soviet action to divide Europe into hostile camps accelerated as Congress debated the European Recovery Program. By Communist coup in February 1948 Czechoslovakia was added to Soviet satellites. On March 17 the Western European allies signed the Brussels Defense Pact. Three days later the Soviet representative walked out of the Allied Control Council in Berlin, and on April 1 Soviet authorities imposed restrictions on allied (but not German) rail and road traffic between the western zones and Berlin. The allies responded with the "little airlift" to supply, at this time, only their troops in Berlin.

In the meantime a six-nation negotiating group—the three occupying West Germany and the three Benelux governments—went to work on plans to strengthen Germany against developing Russian pressure. Preliminary recommendations in late March, as the Foreign Assistance Act for 1948 became law, provided for economic coordination of the three zones for association in the European Recovery Program, and broad agreement that a federal form of government was best adapted to eventual German unity. Final recommendations, announced in June from London, covered political institutions for the West Germans with "the minimum requirements of occupation and control." To reassure the French, provision was made for the control of the Ruhr and the continuance of supreme allied authority.

The Blockade of Berlin · These recommendations and the much-needed currency reform for West Germany (though, at this time, not for Berlin, still regarded as under four-power control) triggered the final break with the Soviet Union in Germany. The calendar for June 1948 shows its precipitous course.

June   7 London recommendations announced.

June 11 Soviet Union stops rail traffic between Berlin and West for two days.

June 12 Soviets stop traffic on a highway bridge for "repairs."

June 16 Soviet representative leaves Kommandatura (four-power military control in Berlin).

June 18 Western powers announce currency reform in West Germany.

June 23 Soviet Union orders its own currency system for East Germany and all Berlin.

Western powers extend West German currency reform to West Berlin.

June 24 Soviet Union imposes full blockade on Berlin.

Western powers stop freight from combined zones to Soviet zone.

After a difficult and tense period in which General Clay's calm determination steadied our own government and held our allies together, the Western powers settled down to build up the airlift, tighten their own countermeasures against the Soviet Union, and fight the propaganda battle in the Paris sessions of the United Nations, which proved unable to ameliorate the situation. Soviet authorities, meanwhile, though belligerent in words, were careful to avoid physical interference with the airlift. The combined lift increased from seventy thousand tons in June and July 1948 to two hundred fifty thousand tons in May 1949.

General Clay and his Political Adviser, Ambassador Robert D. Murphy, believed and advised at the time that we should inform the Soviet authorities that on a specific date we would "move in an armed convoy which would be equipped with the engineering material to overcome the technical difficulties which the Soviet representatives appeared unable to solve. . . . In my [Clay's] view the chances of such a convoy being met by force with subsequent developments of hostilities were small. I was confident that it would get through to Berlin and that the highway blockade would be ended. . . . I shall always believe that the convoy would have reached Berlin."[4] The President is reported to have said that if the Joint Chiefs of Staff would approve this recommendation in writing, he would add his approval, too. However, neither they nor the Secretary of State nor the governments of Britain and France would approve. General Clay's confidence that an armed convoy on the ground would not be stopped was not based on belief that the Russians could not stop it but that they would not. "But," Murphy has written, "the National Security Council did not share our confidence that the Russians were bluffing." Clay, however, did not write that the Russians were bluffing, but that he believed that the "chances of such a convoy being met by force with subsequent developments of hostilities were small." President Truman reports asking him what "risks would be involved" if we tried armed road convoys and receiving the reply that "he thought the initial reaction of the Russians would be to set up road blocks. Our engineers would be able to clear such obstacles, provided there was no Russian interference, but the next step the Russians would take, General Clay thought, would be to meet the convoys with armed force." Indeed, when in April 1948 General Clay had tested a Russian order forbidding allied military trains to go to Berlin without Russian inspection, he had had a revealing experience. "The train," he tells us, "progressed some distance into the Soviet Zone but was finally shunted off the main line by electrical switching to a siding, where it remained for a few days until it withdrew rather ignominiously. *It was clear the Russians meant business.*" (Italics supplied.) The train crew would have been able to clear the obstacle by turning the switch, "provided there was no Russian interference." But since the Russians "meant business," there would have been interference. The question then would have been who would have shot first and what would have been the response to shooting. In April General Clay—I think wisely—did not attempt to find out.

Having had experience in counseling more than one President in problems about access to Berlin, it has never seemed wise to me to base our own action on a bluff or to assume that the Russians are doing so. Neither side wishes to be driven by miscalculation to general hostilities or humiliation. Therefore initial moves should not, if it is possible to avoid it, be equivocal— as a small ground probe would be—or reckless—as a massive one would be. So, although I was a mere observer in 1948, the choice of the airlift seemed to me the right one. It showed firm intention to insist upon a right, plain beyond question, and gave the Russians the choice of either not interfering or of initiating an air attack, which might have brought upon them a devastating response. To say, as Murphy has done, that the decision to use the "airlift was a surrender of our hard-won rights in Berlin,"[5] seems to me silly. One can as well say that to put one's hands up at the command of an armed bandit is to surrender one's hard-won right to keep them down. One regains it, as we have regained and are now enjoying our hard-won rights to Berlin.

30. AN EVENTFUL SPRING

THE EXPECTATION

THE LAST YEAR OF President Truman's first term and his inaugural address at the beginning of his second seemed to give a clear enough clue to my opening tasks. Mr. Lovett and Senator Vandenberg, working together, had produced a unique prologue to a major innovation in American foreign policy. Even more basic, however, than the Vandenberg Resolution in bringing about this innovation was the Communist *coup d'état* in Prague in February 1948. This capped the growing tension in Europe and underlined Europe's insecurity. Nowhere was this more clearly shown than in the pause in economic recovery after the first surge ahead accompanying the repair of physical damage and the replenishment of inventories. Real advance could not be expected until a sense of security made possible a repatriation of capital. This was the impetus that moved the Vandenberg Resolution, adopted on June 11, 1948, by a vote of 64 to 4. It informed the President that the sense of the Senate was that the United States Government should pursue:

Progressive development of regional and other collective arrangements for individual and collective self-defense in accordance with the purposes, principles, and provisions of the Charter [of the United Nations].

Association of the United States, by constitutional process, with such regional and other collective arrangements as are based on continuous and effective self-help and mutual aid, and as affect its national security.[1]

In his inaugural address the President laid down four major guidelines for his foreign policy. The first two—support of the United Nations and continuation of the economic recovery policy—he regarded as extensions of the major achievements of his first administration. The third—a strengthening of the free nations against aggression—was a political innovation based on the Vandenberg Resolution. It would, he said, be spelled out by "joint agreement designed to strengthen the security of the North Atlantic area" and "provide unmistakable proof of the joint determination of the free countries to resist armed attack from any quarter."

The fourth point made in the address was a plan to "embark on a bold new program for making the benefits of our scientific advances and industrial progress available for the improvement and growth of underdeveloped areas." The last two points, while by no means novel, required much breaking of new ground. On January 21 I started hopefully on both, turning to Assistant Secretary Willard Thorp for chief direction and organization of the "bold new program" and to John Hickerson and Robert Lovett to tell me what had happened regarding the treaty. The new treaty was to move much faster than the new program.

POINT FOUR

The State Department was slow in realizing the importance of Point Four and in getting a program in motion. Technological help for developing countries had for some time been a feature of the good-neighbor policy in the western hemisphere. The idea of expounding it on a worldwide basis originated with Clark Clifford, then Counsel to the President, who included it in a draft of the inaugural address sent to Acting Secretary Robert Lovett and Paul Nitze of the Policy Planning Staff. They were neither enthusiastic nor impressed with its utility. Nevertheless, it went into the inaugural address and became much talked about.

The President's language in presenting his fourth point tended to merge it with ideas of relief and longer-range development. He spoke of the suffering of half the people of the world from inadequate food, disease, and primitive and stagnant economic life, while "for the first time in history, humanity possesses the knowledge and skill to relieve the suffering of these people." The United States was pre-eminent in industrial and scientific techniques. Although our material resources available for foreign aid were limited, our resources for technical knowledge were inexhaustible. We should, he said, make them available to others. We should also foster capital investment in areas needing development.

The aim was to help free peoples through their own efforts to produce more food, clothing, housing, and power to lighten their burdens; the method, to "invite other countries to pool their technological resources in . . . cooperative enterprise . . . through the United Nations . . . with the cooperation of business, private capital, agriculture, and labor." However, "the old imperialism—exploitation for foreign profit—[had] no place in . . . the concepts of democratic fair dealing." Our allies in this enterprise were to be "the millions who hunger and thirst after righteousness."

Unfortunately, the hyperbole of the inaugural outran the provisions of the budget. Newspaper speculation helped raise expectations in undeveloped countries. The unpleasant task of deflating them fell to Assistant Secretary Thorp, when on February 25, 1949, he explained to the United Nations Economic and Social Council the program that we were prepared to support. The disappointment of his audience, general and bitter, was expressed by Dr. Charles Malik of Lebanon, who said that the lack among the poor nations was not technology but capital. He called for a large intergovernmental "Marshall Plan" by the developed countries. In this Dr. Malik was wrong. The success of the Marshall Plan came from its application to the most highly developed societies in the world, who could and did put to efficient use the capital made available to them.

Today, after twenty years of experience in aid, totaling billions of dollars from many nations directly and indirectly to undeveloped ones, the judgment is strong that capital loans in advance of technical and managerial competence are not only a waste but a disadvantage (through foreign exchange debts) to the borrowing country. Even surplus-food grants can cause cutback rather than development of food production at home and misallocation of resources. As one writer put it: "We [have] achieved whatever success we had through making the poor productive. The test for aid to poor nations is therefore whether it makes them capable of being productive. If it fails to do so, it is likely to make them even poorer in the—not so very—long run."[2]

After a slow start, our Technical Aid Program got under way, and in 1950, under the capable direction of Dr. Henry G. Bennett of Oklahoma Agricultural and Mechanical College, held out promise of approximating in a broader field the great benefit to agriculture that the Agricultural Extension Service had conferred in the United States. His untimely death in a plane crash in Iran the next year dimmed this prospect. Although the program continued to do a creditable job, it remained the Cinderella of the foreign aid family.

STRENGTHENING THE FREE NATIONS

Senator Vandenberg, the Vandenberg-Lovett-Marshall collaboration, and its product, the Vandenberg Resolution, made possible the North Atlantic Treaty. All too often the executive, having sweated through the compromises of a difficult negotiation, had laid the resulting treaty before a quite detached, uninformed, and unresponsive Senate in which a minority could reject the executive's agreement. On this occasion Senator Vandenberg took seriously and responsibly the word "advice" in the constitutional phrase giving the President power to enter into treaties "with the advice and consent of the Senate." By getting the Senate to give advice in advance of negotiation he got it to accept responsibility in advance of giving its consent to ratification. Equally important, he got the Senate to give good advice. Senators are a prolific source of advice, but most of it is bad. To accomplish so great an achievement requires serious and responsible leadership by the Chairman of the Foreign Relations Committee. Sporadic brilliance of an intellectual dilettante will not suffice. The man may be a prima donna, but he will need solid competence and power as well as temperament.

During the summer of 1948 Mr. Lovett met with the ambassadors of Canada and the Brussels Pact countries. They agreed on the need to go forward and on the general nature of the desired commitment. Discussions then broke off for work on drafts and the outcome of the American election.

Along with the treaty, the Department had been working with our allies on a number of other developments to strengthen Europe. A military assistance program would help them develop some military muscle. The Humphrey Committee report (its chairman, George Humphrey, was later General Eisenhower's Treasury Secretary) on reducing the dismantling of German factories for reparations (mostly to the Soviet Union) recommended that this punitive program be brought more in line with the European Recovery Plan. Trizonal unification and currency reform had brought a new era in German-allied relations to the verge of achievement, with a new government by Germans in the western zones and a new relation between it and allied authority. Finally, the Defense Establishment pressed for a shift of responsibilities for this relation from its own shoulders to those of the State Department. All these seemed to be the fields in which I would be working.

THE UNEXPECTED: ENDING THE BLOCKADE

Hardly had we started on an orderly plan of work when the disorderly and uncontrollable world around us took over and moved us into it in an unexpected way. In January, Kingsbury Smith, European General Manager of the International News Service (a Hearst organization), had filed with the Soviet Foreign Office four questions addressed to Stalin. This was common procedure. Sometimes questions were answered, if Stalin could see some advantage in doing so; more often they were ignored. Mr. Smith's, however, were answered within a few days, and the answers created a press sensation. On the day they appeared a small group discussed them with me in the Department and I took our conclusions to the President.

We judged the episode to be a cautious signal from Moscow. The significant fact was that in answering a question on ending the blockade, Stalin had not mentioned the stated Russian reason for it—the new West German currency. The signal, we thought, told us that Moscow was ready to raise the blockade for a price. The price would be too high if it required abandonment of tripartite plans for the allied zones of Germany, in which case the maneuver could be changed into a propaganda offensive against hard-won allied unity on German policy. I asked permission to signal back through a bland and relaxed press conference that we had gotten the message and then to follow this with a secret inquiry into just what Moscow was prepared to do. The President agreed, and agreed further that our purpose and operation should be kept as close and secret as his intention to nominate me to be Secretary had been.

The press conference took place on February 2,[3] on its regular day of the week, Wednesday, to rob it of any atmosphere of unusual significance. My remarks, though carefully thought out, were an "extemporaneous," patient examination of a press stunt built up out of all proportion to its intrinsic importance. No man of conscience, I said, should tamper with the world's hopes for peace by raising or lowering them as a move in any maneuver. In such an attitude we would examine what had been said.

I confessed myself puzzled by the first question Kingsbury Smith had put to Stalin—whether the Soviet Government would consider joining with the United States Government in declaring that neither had any intention of going to war with the other—and by Stalin's answer that "the Soviet Government would be prepared to consider the issuance of such a declaration." Both governments were already bound by the most explicit provisions of the United Nations treaty to "refrain . . . from the threat or use of force against" one another. Surely Stalin's willingness to consider saying it again was not news.

Then Stalin, when asked whether the Soviet Union would be willing to join with us in such measures as gradual disarmament to carry out such a declaration, had answered that "naturally" it would. "Now 'naturally,' " I said, meant " 'in the nature of things' " and the nature of things in the past three years would not have encouraged the expectation of much cooperation. Then I reviewed Russian obstruction in Europe since the war.

Would Stalin, he had next been asked by Mr. Smith, confer with President Truman about the declaration? His answer was ". . . there is no objection to a meeting." Clearly not. The President, I pointed out, had often invited Marshal Stalin to Washington but he would not come. Presidents Roosevelt and Truman had three times traveled halfway around the world to meet him. Was it worth doing again for so limited a purpose? We had repeatedly said that we could not discuss the affairs of others in their absence.

Finally we came to the only question Mr. Smith had asked relating to an issue between the Soviet Union and the allies: Would the USSR be willing to remove restrictions on traffic to Berlin if the United States, Britain, and France agreed not to establish a separate western German state pending a Council of Foreign Ministers meeting to discuss the German problem as a whole? Stalin answered that it would, upon acceptance by the allies of the condition stated in the question and upon their removing their counterrestrictions against traffic to the Soviet zone.

Stalin's second point, I said, raised no problem since the allies had "always stated that if the Soviet Government permits normal communications with and within Berlin their counter measures will, of course, be lifted." The important point, however, was that the very terms of the question made the answer unresponsive to the facts. The reasons given for the blockade had been technical transportation difficulties and the currency reform. At one time the question of postponing German governmental arrangements had been raised but had been abandoned by the Soviet Union as a condition to raising the blockade. The Western governments, I said, "have stressed, repeated again and again to the Soviet Union, that their agreements in regard to Western Germany do not in any sense preclude agreements on Germany as a whole . . . [and] are . . . purely provisional pending such agreement on Germany as a whole." For months, I continued, the "Western powers have tried patiently and persistently to solve the difficulties . . . put forward . . . as the reasons for the blockade," but Soviet authorities would not discuss them.

Then I signaled our message: "There are many ways in which a serious proposal by the Soviet Government . . . could be made. . . . I hope you [the press] will not take it amiss if I point out that if I on my part were seeking to give assurance of seriousness of purpose I would choose some other channel than the channel of a press interview."

This press conference aptly illustrates the difficulties faced by an open society in conducting diplomatic interchanges with a closed one through the press. Stalin need answer only such written questions as he chose to answer. He permitted no cross-examination. Whatever the correspondent cabled home went through a censor. The Secretary, however, spoke and was cross-examined *viva voce*. In this case I had two purposes—to play down Stalin's initiative in order to avoid premature hardening of the Russian position and to signal the Russians that if they wanted serious discussion they should use a more private channel. Continuation of a public one would be interpreted as an indication of propaganda purposes only. When I finished what I wanted to say for my purposes, able correspondents tried to push me further into saying what they wanted for their purposes, which unfortunately were incompatible with mine. They were entitled to try, but not to succeed.

What significance, they wanted to know, should be attached to Stalin's failure to mention the German-currency issue in his answers? If expressed, our view at the time would have been that it had quite possibly a good deal of significance, although it could have been a trap. The press could and would write their own ideas on the subject, but for me to disclose any of my own could only do harm. So I retreated behind the always reasonable refusal to speculate. The second question came more under the heading of having fun with the Secretary, trying to coax him onto the quicksand. Had my comment on the first question and answer been altogether ingenuous? Wasn't a joint declaration by the United States and the Soviet Union not to go to war with each other something different from the United Nations treaty? Suppose Kingsbury Smith had asked me that question—how would I have answered it? It was a good try, but irrelevant. Years later in response to a similar question, I recalled a politician from the Eastern Shore of Maryland who had got rid of a red-hot roast oyster in my partner's dining room with the ejaculation, "A damned fool would have swallowed that!" This time I merely refused to argue the merits of my remarks.

The Jessup-Malik Talks • A few days later we followed up on the press conference. Ambassador Jessup came to Washington from New York to talk with the Department's Counselor, Charles E. (Chip) Bohlen, and me rather than telephoning, telegraphing, or writing. We concluded that a highly secret, casual approach to the Russians could better be made by Jessup at the United Nations than through the embassy in Moscow or by the Deparment to the Russian Embassy. Fewer persons would be involved and those who were—Philip Jessup and Soviet Ambassador to the United Nations Jacob Malik—could act in purely personal and unofficial capacities. So it was agreed that Jessup when next he saw Malik should ask, as a matter of personal curiosity, whether the omission of any reference to the monetary reform in the Stalin answers was significant. An occasion to do so came as they walked into a Security Council meeting on February 15. Malik did not know the answer. Jessup suggested that if Malik learned anything about the matter, Jessup would be interested to know.

A month later Malik asked Jessup to call at his New York office, and told him that the omission was not accidental. The currency question was important, he said, but it could be discussed at a meeting of the Council of Foreign Ministers. Did that mean, asked Jessup, after the lifting of the blockade? Malik had not been asked to ask that question, he said, to which Jessup replied,

"Why don't you ask it now?" Less than a week later, on March 21, the answer came back that if a definite date for the foreign ministers' meetings could be set the blockade could be lifted before the meetings took place. It was now Malik's turn to ask a question. Would we hold up preparations for a West German government until after the meetings? As instructed, Jessup answered that we expected to continue preparations, but since they could not be completed for some time they would be of no moment—that is, if the Russians really wanted to get on with the Council of Foreign Ministers meetings. This caused a great deal of talk, but Jessup refused to waver from our simple logic.

The time had come to tell the British and French what was going on. Ernest Bevin and Robert Schuman were due in Washington in two weeks for the signing of the North Atlantic Treaty and important talks about Germany. The President, who had been kept closely in touch and was delighted at his Administration's ability to conduct a professional diplomatic maneuver, authorized Jessup to inform his British and French colleagues at the United Nations—Sir Eric Cadogan and Jean Michel Henri Chauvel, both experienced diplomats—of his private and personal explorations with Malik. Although the Quai d'Orsay's insecurity continued to be proverbial, its leaks were usually to the Russians. In this case these leaks might only give added assurance in Moscow of our seriousness as evidenced by our secrecy. The President also authorized me to continue to hold within our small group all knowledge of our feeler. Secrecy was of the utmost importance.

Meeting with Bevin and Schuman · Bevin and Schuman, neither of whom I had met before, arrived in Washington on March 31 and stayed a week. In that week began warm friendships, which grew through the all too few years left to both of them and, I believe, benefited far more than the individuals who shared them. Never were two men more different than these in appearance, temperament, and background. Bevin, short and stout, with broad nose and thick lips, looked more suited for the roles he had played earlier in life than for diplomacy. The child of a servant girl from western England and an unknown father, he had gone to work as a trucker after a few years of schooling. Moving on to a career as a labor leader and then to the top of the labor movement, on the way he organized the giant Transport and General Workers' Union and, with others, led the general strike of 1926. When Churchill became the hard-pressed wartime Prime Minister he drafted Bevin, whose steel he had felt from the government side in the general strike, into the War Cabinet for the heavy task of Minister of Labour. Bevin never became, like his two immediate successors, Herbert Morrison and Anthony Eden, "a House of Commons man"; he was more at home in the tougher atmosphere of the Trades Union Congress. When the Labour Party came to power in 1945, Bevin hoped for the Exchequer, but Attlee, husbanding his assets, chose Hugh Dalton and put Bevin in the Foreign Office.

Never has a Foreign Secretary been more beloved by his often formidable staff. Bevin knew his mind and his limitations. He could lead and learn at the same time, qualities much appreciated by a disciplined and professional Foreign Service. Soon he became absorbed in his work and often seemed to commune with the spirits of his predecessors with an informality that might have surprised them. One day he said to me, "Last night I was readin' some papers of old Salisbury. 'E had a lot of sense." He used to chuckle admiringly over "old Palmerston," too. George III, that much-painted monarch who gazed down from a panel behind Bevin's desk, might not have appreciated the Foreign Secretary's view that if the monarch had not been so stupid the United States might not have been so strong and, hence, so able to come to Britain's rescue in the war and after it.

Schuman, slender, stooped, bald, with long nose, surprised and shy eyes and smile, might have been a painter, musician, or scholar rather than a lawyer, member of parliament, former Premier of France who had put the Communists out of the Government. He had grown up and been educated for the law in Metz under German rule, was an intellectual, and broadly read in both French and German literature. His humor was quick, gentle, and ironic; Bevin's broad and hearty. The Quai d'Orsay did not give Schuman the support that Bevin got from the Foreign Office. It was deeply divided by strong personalities— Hervé Alphand, Maurice Couve de Murville, Alexandre Parodi, Maurice Schumann—and the victim of conspiratorial habits left over from the war and the resistance. This made for delays in negotiation with Schuman, who continually had to watch his flanks and rear and his communications with Paris.

Schuman's knowledge of English was always a source of amusement to me and often of confusion to him in our meetings. He spoke it haltingly and preferred to speak in French and use an interpreter. However, he could understand English if the words came through in recognizable sounds. Bevin's West Country speech, Morrison's cockney, and Anthony Eden's Eton-Oxford quite baffled him. However, to my embarassment he not only understood me but explained that this was due to my speaking slowly and clearly. One evening in New York we put his English to the test at Cole Porter's *Kiss Me Kate*. He recognized the plot of *The Taming of the Shrew* and loved the music, but the intrusion of the gangster theme threw him off the trail, as well it might.

Both Bevin and Schuman held firm political convictions growing out of the tragic experience of Europe in this century; both saw the menace of communism and of the imperialism of the Soviet state; both believed unshakably in the essential nexus of Western Europe and North America to maintain a balance of power and, with it, peace. Schuman, however, went further, and as a man of the border country between France and Germany, believed like Lincoln in reconciliation after strife and in unity.

My affection for both of these men became very great, but my relations with each developed differently. Bevin soon became "Ernie," while I became to him "me lad." Life with Ernie was gay and turbulent, for his temper could build up as suddenly as a summer storm, and could flash and thunder as noisily, then disappear as the sun broke through it. Schuman always remained "M. Schuman" or *"M. le Président"*—since a Premier was President of the Council of Ministers—while with me he always used formal address. Our terms of office almost coincided, his beginning in July 1948 and ending in January 1953.

Bevin came earlier to the Foreign Office, but resigned, and subsequently died, in 1950.

It was my good fortune during my time in office to work with colleagues from other countries who inspired both respect and affection—Sir Winston Churchill, Anthony Eden, later Lord Avon, and Oliver Franks, later Lord Franks, of Britain; Jean Monnet of France; Alcide de Gasperi of Italy; Dirk Stikker of the Netherlands; Halvard Lange of Norway; Konrad Adenauer of Germany; Lester Pearson and Hume Wrong of Canada; Sir Owen Dixon and Richard Casey of Australia; Antonio Espinosa de los Monteros of Mexico; Walther Moreira Salles of Brazil; Shigeru Yoshida of Japan. Since the best environment for diplomacy is found where mutual confidence between governments exists, relationships of respect and affection between the individuals who represent them furnish a vitally important aid to it.

Our first week with Bevin and Schuman in April 1949 was one of rarely equaled achievement. Its announced purpose was the final approval and signing of the North Atlantic Treaty. We three also agreed on our governments' positions for ending the Berlin blockade, on the Military Assistance Program operation, and on a plan for a German government in the western zones and its relations to the allied occupation authorities, which will be gone into later. First we went over in detail with Schuman and Bevin the Jessup-Malik talks and discussed whether, and if so how, to push the Russians farther. We all three saw the danger in allowing Stalin to edge his way into the incomplete and delicate negotiations among us regarding our relations among ourselves and with the Germans in our zones, which could lead to disunity among us and no progress in lifting the blockade. The greatest danger of disunity lay in any postponement of our tripartite preparations together and with the Germans. If the blockade was lifted and the Council of Foreign Ministers promptly convened, it would soon be apparent whether the Russians were serious about any plans for Germany as a whole acceptable to the three. My own view was that if the council meeting failed the blockade would not be reimposed. Stalin was lifting it because as a means to his end—allied withdrawal from Berlin—it had failed and was hurting him. He would not walk back into the trap.

We agreed that the Jessup-Malik exploration was the best method to pursue and that the support of the three ministers should now be thrown behind Jessup's position. He was given a short statement, which he read to Malik on April 5, to the effect that the three ministers understood that only two points were under discussion—simultaneously lifting the blockade and counterblockade, and fixing a date for a meeting of the Council of Foreign Ministers. They wished to be sure that these two points were not conditioned upon any other point. If this was clear, Jessup pointed out, no question of "postponement" of any preparations for a German government in the western zones arose. Malik insisted that the currency problem must appear on any agenda. Since it had been a matter of discussion for nearly a year, Jessup saw no problem.

While Malik was awaiting instructions from Moscow, the week with Schuman and Bevin saw almost prodigies of agreement on Germany (to which we shall return) and the signing of the North Atlantic Treaty. These events impressed Moscow that Western Europe, from which the Russians had withdrawn, was getting along well without them. Before the French and British ministers left Washington, we arranged that liaison among us on the blockade could be maintained through our representatives at the United Nations.

Here I should mention the emergence of a problem that at first was no bigger than a man's hand but was destined to grow: the uneasiness, even jealousy, that tripartite meetings of the occupying powers—Britain, France, and the United States—caused our other allies. We had problems that they did not share and that had to be dealt with. To obviate unnecessary travel we tried meeting before the general North Atlantic Treaty meetings. This produced murmurs that we were managing the agenda. When we postponed our tripartite business until after the meetings, we were pictured as favored guests who lingered after the party to discuss the other guests. To some extent the same criticism developed when the North Atlantic Treaty ministers met at the same time and place as the United Nations General Assembly. We reached the conclusion that in this age of the "common man" with its meeting-ridden diplomacy there was no escape from criticism of any sort of "exclusiveness." Our motto became Admiral Farragut's at Mobile Bay, "Damn the torpedoes! Go ahead!"

Agreement to Lift the Blockade · On April 10 the Russians were still trying to maneuver a cessation of preparations for a West German government. Malik told Jessup of Vishinsky's understanding that no such government would be established before or during the sessions of the Council of Foreign Ministers. Jessup had, of course, said nothing of the sort and made this clear.

The difficulty of multiparty diplomacy now appeared. The President approved a strong message to Malik in which the three ministers backed Jessup's position, but we could not get clearance from London. I urged upon Bevin the importance of pressing the Russians and, if necessary, taking some public action before they did. What we got was a leak out of London about the talks. This required an account of our own, which ended with this sentence: "If the present position of the Soviet Government is as stated in the Tass Agency release as published in the American press, the way appears clear for a lifting of the blockade and a meeting of the Council of Foreign Ministers." A few more weeks of jockeying among Washington, London, and Moscow were necessary to convince the Russians that there was no use delaying further.

While waiting for Vishinsky's unconditional agreement, we worked out with our allies important points of procedure. The ministers should meet in Paris on May 23, the blockade having been lifted not less than ten days before. Preliminary talks with British and French representatives on a joint position would begin on May 9 and be completed by the three ministers on May 21 and 22 in Paris. The agenda should not fix the order in which items must be discussed *and* disposed of; agreement would be reached on individual points only after discussion of all. Details of lifting restrictions would be reached locally after discussion with General Clay. After the blockade had been lifted we would apply to the United Nations to have this item dropped from the Security Council agenda.

On May 4 unconditional agreement was reached, and it was announced the next day in a four-power communiqué.[4] All restrictions imposed since March 1, 1948, would be removed on May 12, 1949. Eleven days afterward, on May 23, 1949, a meeting of the Council of Foreign Ministers would be convened in Paris to consider questions relating to Germany and problems arising out of the situation in Berlin, including also the question of currency in Berlin. The day was proclaimed a legal holiday and a day of rejoicing in Berlin. I paid grateful tribute to all those who through operation of the airlift had made this achievement possible. Great as it was, however, it had not solved the German problem. It put us, I warned, "again in the situation in which we were before the blockade was imposed." Whether a solution could be reached in Paris would depend upon Russian willingness not to retard the progress the Western powers had made in their efforts to make West Germany a peaceful and constructive member of the community of free nations in Europe.

My own view was that the airlift had been a success, but had not ended the Russian campaign. That would be continued at the foreign ministers' meetings. With the blockade a demonstrated failure, Stalin had raised it to carry on the war against a West German government by political means. Until the council session was over we could not judge the net effect of the attempt at coercion by the use of force and the threat to use more. I did not expect the Council of Foreign Ministers to accomplish more than uneasy *modus vivendi* with the Russians.

REFLECTIONS ON SOVIET DIPLOMACY

The history of the Berlin blockade is so typical a demonstration of Soviet political values and diplomatic method that it has been worth more than usual attention to detail. It shows the extreme sensitivity of Soviet authorities to developments in Germany and an almost equal lack of judgment in reacting to them. We were to see this again in 1952 when further steps would be taken by the West to move toward the end of the occupation and the association of Germany with NATO; again in 1955 when the actual admission of Germany was proposed; and once again in 1963 when closer association in nuclear planning was under consideration.

On all these occasions the same clumsy diplomacy resulted: an offer to abandon a long and bitterly held Soviet position was made on condition of allied abandonment of its proposed innovations. When this was firmly refused, the Soviet Union abandoned its own long-held position in the hope of dividing the allies or seducing the Germans. In 1952 this took the form of threats to Bonn if it should sign the 1952 agreements and offers if it should not; in 1955, of signing the long-delayed Austrian State Treaty and the reunification of Austria as an earnest of what Germany might get by declining to join NATO; in 1963, the nuclear-test ban as a means of staving off a multilateral force. What one may learn from these experiences is that the Soviet authorities are not moved to agreement by negotiation—that is, by a series of mutual concessions calculated to move parties desiring agreement closer to an acceptable one. Theirs is a more primitive form of political method. They cling stubbornly to a position, hoping to force an opponent to accept it. When and if action by the opponent demonstrates the Soviet position to be untenable, they hastily abandon it—after asking and having been refused an unwarranted price—and hastily take up a new position, which may or may not represent a move toward greater mutual stability.

Sir William Hayter has admirably summed up the Russian idea of negotiating:

Negotiation with the Russians does occur, from time to time, but it requires no particular skill. The Russians are not to be persuaded by eloquence or convinced by reasoned arguments. They rely on what Stalin used to call the proper basis of international policy, the calculation of forces. So no case, however skilfully deployed, however clearly demonstrated as irrefutable, will move them from doing what they have previously decided to do; the only way of changing their purpose is to demonstrate that they have no advantageous alternative, that what they want to do is not possible. Negotiations with the Russians are therefore very mechanical; and they are probably better conducted on paper than by word of mouth.[5]

31. THE NORTH ATLANTIC TREATY: AN OPEN COVENANT OPENLY ARRIVED AT

ON JANUARY 24, 1949, the President received me for the first of the two, and sometimes three, meetings that for the next four years we usually had alone each week. The two subjects discussed were the current ambassadorial negotiations on the North Atlantic Treaty text and his views about the Point Four (technical assistance) program. In the light of his guidance my first two press conferences took up these two subjects.

PROBLEMS OF NEGOTIATION

1. *The Press* · What I tried to do in the press conferences was give the men who covered the State Department a somewhat broader view of the purpose and significance of these great policy decisions than most of them had. With some distinguished exceptions, such as Paul Ward of the *Baltimore Sun* and John Hightower of the Associated Press, they were inclined to bring to the reporting of foreign affairs the same nose for controversial spot news that they had learned to look for on the City Hall and police-court beats. This did the country and their readers a disservice. In reporting news about the North Atlantic Treaty they tended to speculate on what countries might or might not be invited to sign it, what territory it might cover, what commitments might be made. None of these matters was ripe for decision. What I hoped to get them to discuss were the dangers the treaty was aimed to meet, how they could be met or avoided, the relation of the treaty to other measures contemplated—in other words, the place of the treaty in the developing strategy of the West. I made the same effort to enlighten reporting on the Point Four program.† What most of my hearers would have much preferred would have been comments on the attacks made on these measures by their opponents. That would be news!

2. *The Parties* · My education on past discussions about the treaty text was taken in hand by those of Mr. Lovett's assistants who had participated in them —Charles Bohlen, John Hickerson, Theodore Achilles, Dean Rusk, and Ernest Gross. When the sessions resumed in February, I found myself working with a group of ambassadors whom I had known well for so long that we were truly— and not spuriously—on a first-name basis. The original group was small— Oliver Franks of Britain, Hume Wrong of Canada, Henri Bonnet of France,

Eelco van Kleffens of the Netherlands, Robert Silvercruys of Belgium, and Minister Hugues Le Gallais of Luxembourg. Wilhelm Morgenstierne of Norway joined us on March 4. The Wrong-Acheson friendship went back over two generations. His father had been at the University of Toronto with mine, and Mrs. Wrong's father, Professor Hutton, had taught them both. Wilhelm Morgenstierne and I had first worked together twenty-eight years before; all the others had been colleagues of mine for many years. We talked easily and frankly. To preserve secrecy and the integrity of communications systems, reports of meetings were transmitted through our embassies to the various foreign offices.

3. The Congress · At our first meeting on February 8 I pointed out the unwisdom of our trying to move any faster with a text than I could move in my discussions with Senators Connally and Vandenberg, since agreement would mean little unless it carried senatorial opinion with it. In fact, I had already started with the senators on February 3 and had three more meetings with them during the month, and one with a group from the House Committee on Foreign Affairs. Three issues engaged both the ambassadors and the legislators: Should the treaty deal with more than military security? What nations should be signatories of it? What commitments should it contain? In general, the ambassadors wished to push further than the senators were prepared to follow. It was therefore most important to keep meetings with both groups moving along concurrently. I was like a circus performer riding two horses—for one to move ahead of the other would mean a nasty fall. Safety required use of the ambassadors to urge on the senators, and the senators to hold back the ambassadors.

The early drafts, the senators thought, went too far on all three issues. The first was the Canadian proposal of Article 2, which got us into cultural, economic, and social cooperation. The senators were strongly opposed. We had all just been through a punishing experience. On February 2 I had been before the Senate committee doing my best to support agreements that came out of the Bogotá Conference attended by General Marshall. The Senate would have none of them. The agreements announced sweeping alleged human rights to education, the good life, welfare, and so on, reminiscent of a good many UN resolutions but which to Senator George and others posed serious constitutional complications in federal-state relationships. Our senators saw Article 2 threatening our treaty with the same danger for no important benefit. I agreed, and proceeded to redraft the article toward the expression of desired goals. Even so defused, Article 2 has continued to bedevil NATO. Lester Pearson has continually urged the council to set up committees of "wise men" to find a use for it, which the "wise men" continually have failed to do.

4. New Members · Regarding membership, the original intention of the negotiating group (Belgium, Canada, France, Luxembourg, the Netherlands, the United Kingdom, and the United States) was to work out a text and then consider what other countries might be asked to join with us in signing it. Before the text was completed, however, other countries became interested and made inquiries. The first of these was Norway; soon afterward came two other Scandinavian countries, Denmark and Iceland, and then Italy from the Mediterranean. On February 7 Halvard Lange, the Norwegian Foreign Minister, arrived in Washington on a voyage of discovery. He came neither to apply for membership nor to ask for other help, but to learn what we were planning to do and to discuss Norway's problems. His visit set off a barrage of bluster and threats from Moscow that did not disturb him in the least. From our first meeting I found him a most delightful and impressive man. A member of the Norwegian resistance during the war, he had been caught—due to his own carelessness, he told me—and imprisoned under death sentence. For months he never knew whether footsteps approaching his cell were those of a guard bringing the inevitable vegetable soup and bread or a summons to face a firing squad. Eventually he was transferred to Dachau. This substitution, he said, of the grave risk of death for the near certainty of it was a change from hell to heaven. He emerged broken in health, but with his courage, high intelligence, and gift of humor unimpaired.

In Lange's view, experience had taught Norway that neutrality was an illusion. She must find security in association with others. Association in the United Nations, once so hopeful, had in recent years lost its promise. The Swedish proposal of a Scandinavian security treaty had much to be said for it, but Swedish insistence that its members must not seek other association would leave the group too weak to afford its members much protection. He asked both specific and general questions about our proposed treaty for the purpose of advising his Government upon his return. Would the territorial integrity of signatories be guaranteed? Would they have priority in military assistance over nonsignatories? The answer in both cases was no. The purpose was to establish a system of individual and collective self-defense against attack. No guarantees could be given, no system of priorities assigned. What Norway chose to do was for Norway to decide. We urged no course upon her people. If her Government wished to join the rest of us, the United States would support it. My clear impression was that both Lange and Wilhelm Morgenstierne, Norwegian Ambassador in Washington, favored that course, and that the lack of any pressure increased their desire to do so.

At the end of February the Norwegian Government made application to join. At once the French attempted to condition Norwegian membership upon acceptance of Italy also, Bonnet suggesting that "French public opinion" would not understand acceptance of Norway ahead of Italy. At the same time General de Gaulle, then in retirement, was reported as opposing both the North Atlantic Treaty, on the ground that it had been devised by the United States for its—not Europe's—security, and the Brussels Pact because it was meant to secure Britain, not Europe. The President and the two senators lost patience with this haggling. I reported to the ambassadors at our meeting on March 1 that our Government, while open-minded about Italy, was united in requesting that we accept Norway at that meeting. We would also agree to extend the treaty to cover Algeria. Norway was accepted. A few days later Wilhelm Morgenstierne joined our group. He was a solemn man, wholly lacking in humor, with an expression of having been weaned on Ibsen. In welcoming him I recalled a minister in my home town who welcomed new members of his church "to all our joys and all our sorrows," adding, "so far there haven't been many joys." I suggested that we were counting on Wilhelm to furnish joys for us.

Our next caller was Gustav Rasmussen, the Danish Foreign Minister. He brought irresistibly to mind a phrase in a letter from Abbé Bernard to Louis VII of France during the second crusade: "Like a sparrow with careful watchfulness, avoid the snares of the fowler." Rasmussen moved "like a sparrow with careful watchfulness"; he had to, dependent as he was on a coalition government at home and an unstable environment abroad. In the end he would probably do what the Norwegians did; and so he did. So did Foreign Minister Bjarni Benediktsson of Iceland.

5. *The Problem of Italy* · Italy presented a perplexing problem. She was most decidedly not a North Atlantic state in any geography. Both European and American military opinion held that Italy would make little military contribution to Western Europe's security against attack and might be a considerable drain on available military assets. Yet from a political point of view an unattached Italy was a source of danger. A former enemy state, without the connection with the United States such as Greece and Turkey had had since 1947 through our economic and military programs, without connections to Western Europe, except for the late, unlamented one made between Mussolini and Franco, Italy might suffer from an isolation complex and, with its large communist party, fall victim to seduction from the East. We had expressed these ideas to Bevin at the end of January, stressing the importance of strengthening Italian resistance to Russian domination and our intention to continue the supply of arms whether or not Italy became a party to the treaty. Although the senators were reluctant and Henri Bonnet's clumsy advocacy came near to defeating his purpose, we eventually joined in asking Italy to become an original signatory. The importance of Portugal, the possessor of the Azores, to Western European defense was clear enough. Here the difficulty was the other way around, in reconciling Dr. Salazar to an alliance from which Spain, because of strong objection from many members, was excluded. At length my close friend Pedro Pereira, the Portuguese Ambassador, was able to report that consultation between Portugal and Spain had convinced them that the North Atlantic Treaty was not incompatible with the nonaggression and friendship treaty between them.

On March 17 invitations went out from the eight states conferring in Washington to Italy, Denmark, Iceland, and Portugal to join them as original signatories of the treaty. Both before and after these invitations, representatives of Turkey had talked with me in considerable agitation over our failure to invite them, once the Atlantic character of the alliance had been breached by the invitation to Italy. No assurances, explanations, or other forms of words eased their painful sense of abandonment, soon shared in Greece. Their joint lamentations continued until, two years later, both countries were received into membership.

6. *The Issue of Automatic Involvement* • The most difficult issue both with the ambassadors and with the senators arose in the drafting of Article 5. The Vandenberg Resolution in broad generality supported "regional and other collective arrangements for individual and collective self-defense" and our "association" with such of them as might "affect [our] national security." Since individual and collective self-defense was expected to take place in Europe against Soviet (and possibly—as Henri Bonnet kept reminding us—German) attack, the Europeans were naturally the most fervent advocates of strong and unequivocal commitments for aid in case of attack. The British characteristically wished an opportunity to appraise an emergency before plunging in, and the Americans and Canadians were most wary of what came to be known as automatic involvement. All joined in the doubtful dogma that in two world wars Germany had picked off her victims one by one and that if her rulers had known from the start that such conduct would have brought in Britain and America (presumably at the start) neither war would have occurred. Therefore a collective-security agreement should make it clear to potential aggressors that to attack one member of the collectivity was to attack all. This was very resonant and rotund, but when one took pencil to draft, one was immediately reminded that "clear as day" must not mean "automatic involvement."

De Tocqueville has told us that in America every political question is soon transformed into a judicial one. Nowhere is this more true than in treaty making. According to the Constitution a treaty is the "supreme law of the land" and its provisions are drafted as if for the construction of a court, with our constitutional provisions not only in mind but often, as here, specifically preserved. So when Article 11 declared that "this Treaty shall be ratified *and its provisions carried out* by the Parties *in accordance with their respective constitutional processes,"* these words, insisted upon by the senators, meant to them that while the President by constitutional provision was Commander in Chief of the Army and Navy of the United States, the power to declare war was given to the Congress.† Against this background the negotiation of Article 5 became a contest between our allies, seeking to impale the Senate on the specific, and the senators, attempting to wriggle free. The struggle brought Vandenberg to an anguishing consciousness of his dilemma. He understood clearly that the more specifically the commitment was defined the more nearly the opposition might approach that one-third-plus-one of the senators present that could defeat it, while the more vaguely it was stated the less would it achieve his purpose. The dilemma seemed inherent in the Constitution: What was this sovereign— the United States of America—and how could it insure faith in promised future conduct? In reality, the problem was general and insoluble, lying in inescapable change of circumstances and of national leadership and in the weakness of words to bind, especially when the juice of continued purpose is squeezed out of them and their husks analyzed to a dryly logical extreme.

In our drafting we started out with two ideas familiar to the senators and previously approved. The idea of an attack on one considered as an attack on all came from the Treaty of Rio de Janeiro and the idea of allies jointly and severally taking measures to restore peace and security came from Article 51 of the United Nations Treaty, in both of which both Vandenberg and Connally had collaborated. To apply these ideas to Europe was new, but that hurdle had been passed in the Vandenberg Resolution. Then the question arose whether we should say that the action to be taken to restore peace and maintain security should be "such action as each deems necessary." It seemed to me clear that no power existed to force any other action upon any signatory, and that to appear to do so would only raise the outcry that General de Gaulle has since raised against transferring the sovereign power to declare war to some supranational organization. The senators, of course, agreed. The ambassadors believed this weakened the article.

However, they agreed that the net impact of the article would be strengthened if another phrase was added—such action as each deems necessary, *"including the use of armed force."* Logically the first clause included the second, but to leave no doubt that armed force was contemplated helped greatly.

A CAT AMONG THE PIGEONS

In our private talks Senator Connally was still worried about "automatic involvement," but Vandenberg argued strongly for "the concept of making our position clear as a preventive measure." At this point Senator Forrest C. Donnell, Republican of Missouri, set off a land mine under our discussions. It all came from an irresponsible senator reading the gossip of an irresponsible reporter. Senator Donnell was not my favorite senator. He combined the courtliness of Mr. Pickwick and the suavity of an experienced waiter with the manner of a prosecuting attorney in the movies—the gimlet eye, the piercing question. In administering the *coup de grâce* he would do it with a napkin over his arm and his ears sticking out perpendicularly like an alert elephant's. He read to the Senate a report from the *Kansas City Times* of a secret meeting between Lange of Norway and me at which I was said to have said that the treaty would contain "the strongest possible commitment to give prompt and effective aid if any one of the countries in the alliance is attacked, but only Congress can declare war. Military action, therefore, cannot be committed in advance. But in joining the Alliance, the American Government would subscribe to the principle that an attack on one member nation was an attack on all, and this would be interpreted as a moral commitment to fight."[1] Donnell, in protesting against any moral commitment to go to war, was in fact attacking the treaty language "including the use of armed force."

Vandenberg jumped to his feet, referred to the Rio treaty and the ideas that each signer must decide what action was required, that the whole matter was being worked out, that both world wars would have been prevented if the attitude of the United States had been made clear in advance. Tom Connally followed, asserting that there was no difference between a moral commitment and a legal one and the treaty would contain neither. William Knowland of California quite sensibly observed that the purpose was to make clear in advance our full commitment against aggression and any treaty which did not do that was useless. Cabot Lodge of Massachusetts said that what the signatories would do would be more important than the words they used; if they united to make themselves strong enough to resist aggression and did resist it, then they would have accomplished something. Connally, returning to the fray, spread total confusion by declaring that the Senate was quite as patriotic and able as the State Department to protect the United States, adding: "We cannot, however, be Sir Galahads, and every time we hear a gun fired plunge into war and take sides without knowing what we are doing and without knowing the issues involved. That is my attitude." Senator Donnell insisted that he was still not satisfied and did not want anything in the treaty "which constitutes 'the moral commitment to fight' referred to by the writer . . . [as] covered by Secretary Acheson." The next day Tom Connally in an effort to "clarify his position" stated that "we could not legally sign a treaty providing for automatic entrance into war," and gave his own version of a satisfactory Article 5.[2]

The press, having had a field day with the Senate, turned to the State Department and the White House to continue the fun. I opened my press conference[3] on February 16 with a statement that had been mimeographed for my questioners to prevent any possibility of misquotation. It pointed out that the treaty was still under negotiation; that there was no difference within the United States Government between the purposes stated in the Vandenberg Resolution, the President's inaugural address, and the unanimous report of the House Committee on Foreign Affairs on H.R. 6802 of the Eightieth Congress; that I was working in close consultation with senior members of the Senate committee; and that soon we hoped to have a draft treaty ready for discussion in all countries. In the meantime no further public discussion would be helpful. All efforts to draw me out failed. Similar efforts the following day with the President were equally unsuccessful. He adopted a procedure that we often used later in similar situations. My statement would lead off. When asked about the same subject the President would say merely that my statement had been made after consultation with him and that he had nothing to add to it. This smothered the fire.

AT LENGTH A TREATY EMERGES

I have reported this ridiculous episode at far greater length than its importance justifies because it illustrates the difficulty of negotiating when one is operating through an executive-legislative soviet. The tempest had the salutary result of convincing the negotiators that the time had come to conclude their work before it became impossible through what Brooks Adams described as the "degradation of the democratic dogma." On March 18, after much debate within the international and senatorial groups, we succeeded in releasing a treaty text for public discussion before final acceptance of it by governments (but, in reality, to force it). Never has a debutante been presented with more fanfare, appearing simultaneously in twelve capitals. In Washington I presented it with a detailed explanation of each paragraph at an early-morning press conference and again that evening in a radio address to the nation.[4]

On these two occasions I tried especially to give reality to the political commitment which as a nation it was proposed we make to our allies, and they to us. The confusion in people's minds was well brought out by a reporter's request to explain the "moral obligation as distinct from specific, written-out obligation to use armed force."

Decent people, I said, kept their contract obligations. If they could not, or if they differed over what they meant, then—and then only—they went to court. We were decent people, we could keep our promises, and our promises were written out and clear enough. They were to regard an attack on any of our allies as an attack on ourselves and to assist the victim ourselves and with the others, with force if necessary, to restore and maintain peace and security. Twice in twenty-five years there had been armed attacks in the area involved in this treaty and it was abundantly clear what measures had been necessary to restore peace and security. This did not mean that we would be automatically at war if one of our allies was attacked. We should and would act as a nation in accordance with our promises—not in repudiation of them—and, as a nation, "that decision will rest where the Constitution has placed it."

In press conference, speech, report to the President on the treaty, and testimony before the Senate committee I hammered away at this vital point, that the necessity of acting as a nation in the manner the Constitution provided did not mean either that in some undefined way the nation would act "automatically" or that legislators could act properly under "the law of the land"—in this case, the treaty—by going contrary to its provisions. No power but their own sense of right could force them to do their part in enabling the nation to keep its lawful promise, but that did not affect either the lawfulness or the meaning of the promise.

At the hearing before the Senate committee I applied this reasoning to Article 3 of the treaty, to the annoyance of the senators. This article bound the parties to develop their individual and collective capacity to resist armed attack by self-help and mutual assistance. If the treaty should be ratified, the United States, I said, was under obligation to do its part to assist others to develop a capacity to resist armed attack. A senator who opposed military assistance (as did Senator Taft) in any and all forms was, as part of the United States Government, repudiating that obligation. So far as I could prevent it, I would oppose attempting to win votes for the treaty by denigrating its commitments.

On the morning of March 19 a long telegram came in from President Truman, who had escaped from the Washington winter to the naval station at Key West, Florida, to clear up a bronchial trouble from which he often suffered. He and his party had listened to my speech; he was most generous in praise of it and, he said, approved every word. Another telegram gave his approval to my publishing his message if I wished to do so, which, of course, I did.[5] This was typical of the President's thoughtfulness in letting no opportunity pass to support and encourage me.

All the North Atlantic Treaty ministers met in Washington on April 2 to approve the draft treaty and arrange for its signature at a ceremony set for

April 4. Here President Truman again showed his consideration for me. I had told him that it would be appropriate and fitting for him to sign the treaty on behalf of the United States, but this he refused to do. He would attend the ceremony and stand beside me as I signed, but the treaty should bear my name. The meeting decided that before the signing each of the foreign ministers would make a statement. When I inquired about the languages they would use, so that appropriate interpreters would be present, Lester Pearson of Canada replied that he would speak "North American English with a French accent."

The signing ceremony was dignified and colorful, with the President and Vice President of the United States standing on either side of me as I signed the treaty. The Marine Band added a note of unexpected realism as we waited for the ceremony to begin by playing two songs from the currently popular musical play *Porgy and Bess*—"I've Got Plenty of Nothin' " and "It Ain't Necessarily So."

THE SENATE HEARINGS covered well-explored territory. Only two new ideas cropped up. Vandenberg asked me how the agreement of the United States to the accession of new signatories to the treaty would be expressed—that is, whether by the President alone or by the President acting by and with the advice and consent of the Senate. Fortunately we had thought of this point and I had asked the President to reflect upon our recommendation as it affected his prerogatives. After thinking the matter over, he gave me my answer. "I am authorized by the President of the United States," I said, "to say that in his judgment the accession of new members to this treaty creates in regard to each new member coming in in effect a new treaty between the United States and that nation, and that therefore the President would consider it necessary to ask for the advice and consent of the Senate before himself agreeing to the admission of a new member." To this Senator Vandenberg replied, "I do not know how you could make a more totally persuasive or righteous answer."[1]

A question from Senator Bourke Hickenlooper of Iowa evoked from me a less felicitous answer and a charge, later on, that I had misled the Senate. The question was whether under Article 3, which related to mutual assistance in developing capacity to resist armed attack, we were "going to be expected to send substantial numbers of troops over there as a more or less permanent contribution to the development of these countries' capacity to resist?"

"The answer to that question, Senator," I replied, "is a clear and absolute 'No.'" Even as a short-range prediction this answer was deplorably wrong. It was almost equally stupid. But it was not intended to deceive. This exchange occurred a year before the united command was thought of, at a time when our troops were regarded as occupation forces for Germany and not part of a defense force for Europe, which at that time was composed of Field Marshal Montgomery's Brussels Pact command. At the moment we had presented to Congress as fulfillment of our Article 3 obligation a Military Assistance Program consisting wholly of military hardware. I thought he was asking whether Article 3 would also obligate us to keep an army in Europe, and replied that it would not. When two years later in the "troops for Europe" debate Senator Hickenlooper threw this answer back at me, I could see that he had a point but was unwilling to cry *"Peccavi!"*

The debate in the Senate was long, often noisy and not a little ridiculous, and forecast some of our troubles in the next few years. Senators Connally and

Vandenberg led off on successive days to keep their press coverage undiluted. To Connally the treaty was "a flaming sign to any aggressor . . . — 'Do not enter,' " but it did not commit us to automatic involvement or an arms program. To Vandenberg it was a "warrant for . . . doom" for any aggressor; earlier he had hailed it as the "most important step in American foreign policy since the promulgation of the Monroe Doctrine."[2] Donnell spoke against it, asking whether Portugal was a democracy. Taft "with great regret" had to oppose it because he found it inseparably linked to the arms program. Ralph Flanders of Vermont came out for a strong United Nations and intensified propaganda, which wrung from William Langer of North Dakota the heartfelt ejaculation, "By God, absolutely unanswerable!" John Foster Dulles, appointed to the Senate on July 7 by Governor Dewey of New York to fill a vacancy, in a maiden speech a few days later supported the treaty and lashed out at "preposterous and dangerous interpretation[s]." This brought shouted and angry interruptions from Senator Taft. William Jenner of Indiana found the treaty shrouded in secrecy and wanted to know the whole truth, though about what remained vague. After ten days of such statesmanlike deliberation the vote was taken and the treaty approved by 82 to 13.[3]

TRIPARTITE AGREEMENT ON GERMANY

The formal signing of the North Atlantic Treaty made possible quiet meetings with Bevin and Schuman to begin another equally far-reaching move in Europe. Even before Stalin's answers to Kingsbury Smith's questions, developments in Germany had made a meeting of the Western occupying powers a necessity. The imminent possibility of the foreign ministers' meetings lent urgency to it. Our view in the Department was that the purpose of the Russian move was to stop or delay formation of a West German government, either as a condition to lifting the blockade or by dividing the Western powers on the subject during the council meetings. Therefore, agreement among the three powers on a plan was essential before we got into four-power talks. I found both Bevin and Schuman wholly agreed on this in our first meeting. Indeed, both thought the chances high that the Moscow move was a trap, Bevin even suggesting that it might be better to let things stay as they were in Berlin while we worked out an agreement on Germany and ratified the North Atlantic Treaty. Contributing to this view was an apprehension that a merely temporary lifting of the blockade might seriously disorganize the airlift. I believed that the spur of an approaching four-power meeting was the best inducement to agreement.

My first impression on going over the material prepared in London by British, French, and American "experts" in anticipation of the April meetings was one of despair. The papers were long, tremendously complex, and totally incomprehensible. Nearly two hundred questions had been "reserved" for decision by the ministers because of disagreement among the experts. The draft of the occupation statute was fifty pages long, almost all of it subject to dissents. The chances of the three ministers even understanding, to say nothing of disentangling, this mess seemed small. The uncharitable conclusion came to me that "experts" were expert because only they understood the makeshift complexities created as the zones began to operate together and rough divisions of function were made between German and occupation administrators. It was literally "unthinkable" to them to discard the whole substance of their expertise. But this had to be done.

Two weeks before the April meetings I did it, telling them to take their papers away and start over again. George Kennan had talked with Schuman in Paris and got from him the suggestion that we might find guidance in the simpler arrangements which had been followed in Austria, a liberated, not an enemy, country. This had the advantage of being sensible and of being attributable to Schuman. I asked for two papers, neither to exceed two or three pages. The first should be an occupation statute dealing with governmental powers to be turned over to German federal and Laender (state) governments to be exercised in accordance with a federal basic law and Laender constitutions that the Germans were drawing up, and with powers reserved to the three occupying nations. The other paper should state how, among themselves, the occupying states should exercise their reserved powers. These papers could be and must be as clear and simple as they were short, even though getting agreement, especially on the second, might be difficult. I told my Department colleagues to read the Constitution of the United States as a model of declaratory statement.

My first talks with Bevin and Schuman delighted me by their broad approach to European and German problems. Bevin told me of his hopes that arrangements under the Brussels treaty could include a cabinet for Western Europe. They must get used, he said, to dealing with matters of common concern and to reaching common judgments. He would like to see Germany brought in, and believed that the North Atlantic Treaty could give needed confidence in action of this kind. I agreed that the Council and Defense Committee proposed under the treaty should not "derogate from the effectiveness of Western Union." A year later, however, when Schuman moved, with the Coal and Steel Plan, to give real substance to the vague views that Bevin had voiced to me, the latter drew back. Unhappily, his health was then failing and his judgment with it. In April 1949 Schuman saw that the time had come in Germany to move from direct allied responsibility to maximum German responsibility under allied control and from military to civilian relations. These attitudes held high promise of an agreed plan for Germany, though there remained some rapids to shoot before we reached the calm of agreement.

Twenty years later what remains interesting in those talks is not what we agreed upon but how, through all the complexity and confusion, we found a path to agreement. The task was to fix on the broad line along which we wanted to move, and then by increasingly specific development find what was common ground and what was not. Disagreements could be dealt with last, and would then appear not as isolated points of principle but as items in an otherwise acceptable and workable scheme. We did not begin with papers, which so often divert readers to trivia, but with dialogue. To aid in it we had colleagues of high quality. With me were Philip Jessup and Robert Murphy, who had come back from Germany to head our German office. Bevin had Sir Oliver Franks, one of the most creative minds I have worked with, and Bevin's secretary, Roderick Barclay (later Sir Roderick). With Schuman were Couve de Murville, from the Foreign Office, and Ambassador Henri Bonnet.

I began by saying that our preliminary talks had left me with the impression that all of us wished to reduce the responsibilities for government in Germany that our occupation authorities had been carrying and increase the responsibilities of the Germans. Schuman in his earlier talks with Kennan had pointed to our experience in Austria as a guide. Such a plan would lighten our present task, since we could concentrate on what we wanted to reserve and how to exercise our reserved powers, leaving to the Germans how to manage all that was turned over to them. They were already at work on a federal basic law and constitutions for the Laender. Broadly speaking, what we would wish to reserve was supreme power to resume all authority, should that eventuality be necessary, but, more specifically, power to act directly in certain defined areas, such as disarmament, security, denazification, decartelization, foreign affairs, reparations, and so on. For the rest, the Germans should be free to govern themselves, subject to the power of the occupation to review and veto if they should wander outside their basic laws or run counter to occupation policy. All this met with approval and we undertook to begin broad drafts for discussion.

Resolving French Worries · Coming to our handling of reserved powers, I suggested that we might be preparing a model for the treatment of Germany as a whole, dim as that prospect might seem. We should keep to a minimum the power of one occupying government to paralyze action by the others or by the Germans and devise a system into which we would be willing to receive the Soviet zone and government. This proved to be a sobering and useful thought.

Letting these ideas simmer over the weekend, we came back to them on Monday after the treaty was signed, moving from dialogue to broad instructions for the ultimate drafters and still trying to avoid those meticulous pedants referred to by Mayor Fiorello La Guardia as "the semicolon boys." As anticipated, the occupation statute moved along without much trouble, but discussion of tripartite controls flushed some real problems, chiefly for the French. At the outset Bevin had fulminated that the power over financial matters which the United States claimed in the Trizonal Fusion Agreement went too far, giving the United States Military Governor a veto over state legislation and making him a tyrant over his colleagues. Proposed authority for the German Government to participate in European economic-recovery activities and to deal directly with the United States greatly eased this problem. But Schuman's worries were still acute, relating in one form or another to the extent to which France alone could block action upon which German, British, and American authorities were agreed.

One of our earliest agreements in principle had an important bearing upon this delicate and vital negotiation. We had decided that in all fields, even in those "reserved" to the occupying powers, decisions of German governing bodies would not require positive approval to be valid. They would be valid unless positively disapproved. This raised the question—disapproved by whom? Clearly, if all three occupying powers disapproved, the German action would be invalid. The same could be strongly argued if two disapproved. But it would require special provision to allow one to disapprove over the opposition of the other two. From the point of view of negotiating position, Schuman found himself at a disadvantage. It would not have bothered Vishinsky, but Schuman was an intellectually honest man and a very fair man. A solution was possible if we abandoned abstractions and began to analyze categories of specific issues that might arise from the point of view of France's special position and experience.

As we discussed we began to get imaginative and helpful ideas. One was to break down the conception of the occupying state into two separate realities: the individuals on the spot, and the government at home. The degree of involvement in an issue and the resulting stubbornness were different. So final decision should move from those scuffling at the front to the comparative calm and broader considerations affecting foreign offices. Then came the idea of the suspensive appeal and the possibility of different periods for different issues; in labor disputes a "cooling-off period" gave time for second thoughts and compromises. Again, the number of issues warranting a departure from majority rule on the spot ought to be rigorously cut down by the decent trust and comity among allies, for which I made an eloquent plea. Finally, I introduced an idea from American constitutional practice that proved helpful. A decision to repeal or amend a tripartite agreement would require tripartite agreement, but an action said by a dissenter to violate one could be only temporarily suspended.

At first, Schuman asked too much but, as I have said, he was eminently reasonable and fair. Also he followed the discussion remarkably closely, always speaking in French translated by Couve de Murville, but understanding most of the English. Final agreement, reached within a week of our first meeting, was completely realistic and workable. Allied controls would be in the hands of an Allied High Commission made up of three High Commissioners. Approval of amendments to the German federal constitution would require unanimous action and of requests for financial assistance from the United States approval by weighted voting, which in practice left the United States in control. Approval of all other matters required only a majority vote, with important qualifications. Where the proposed action would alter a tripartite agreement on specified matters of great importance to France an appeal would suspend action indefinitely, pending tripartite agreement. This gave a veto in a narrow section and raised the discussion to the intergovernmental level—a compromise by all three parties. In the case of other appeals suspension would continue, depending on the issue, from twenty-one to thirty days unless a majority voted to prolong it.

Within this same week seven important agreements were made about Germany, going beyond occupation matters to the Ruhr, reparations, state boundaries, the federal constitution, and our future policy to bring about the closest integration of the German people under a democratic federal state within the framework of a European association. The first week of April 1949 was one for which none of us ever needed to feel apologetic. The basic agreements were all made public within a month, before our representatives met in Paris to begin preparations for the meetings of the Council of Foreign Ministers scheduled to open May 23.

A PROGRESS REPORT TO THE NATION

Before plunging into these preparations myself, I took advantage of a meeting of the American Society of Newspaper Publishers on April 28 to broadcast a report to the nation not only on what we had just done but on our approach to the forthcoming talks with the Russians about Germany. Our recent agreements on West Germany did not mean, I said, that we had abandoned hope of a solution that would be applicable to Germany as a whole. It did mean that we were not prepared to wait indefinitely for four-power agreement before making a start on creating healthy and hopeful conditions in those parts of Germany where it could be done. We would do our best in the four-power discussions to help solve what was plainly one of the most crucial problems in world affairs. But certain principles we would not compromise:

The people of Western Germany may rest assured that this Government will agree to no general solution for Germany into which the basic safeguards and benefits of the existing Western German arrangements would not be absorbed. They may rest assured that until such a solution can be achieved, this Government will continue to lend vigorous support to the development of the Western German program.

The people of Europe may rest assured that this Government will agree to no arrangements concerning Germany which do not protect the security interests of the European community.

The people of the United States may rest assured that in any discussions relating to the future of Germany, this Government will have foremost in mind their deep desire for a peaceful and orderly solution of these weighty problems which have been the heart of so many of our difficulties in the postwar period.[4]

33. THE FOREIGN MINISTERS
MEET IN PARIS

ALL THE EFFORTS OF April—the conclusion of the North Atlantic Treaty and the agreements on a government for West Germany—had been preparatory to the meeting so clearly foreshadowed by Stalin's answers in February to Kingsbury Smith's questions. Even before April work had been going on in the Department, and between it and the Pentagon, which I had been discussing with the President in order to infuse his thoughts into its guidance.

OUR OBJECTIVE CLARIFIED

As our analysis of the German problem deepened, our conception of the principal objective changed. At first we had discussed the relative merits of placing primary importance either on the reunification of all Germany or on the unification and strengthening of West Germany. However, we soon came to believe that our chief concern should be the future of Europe, and that the reunification of Germany should not be regarded as the chief end in itself. It was plain that this would require the cooperation of the Soviet Union, which occupied a third of German territory. If reunification ranked first in importance, the price which might properly be paid for Soviet cooperation could be very high indeed. If, however, one attached first importance to the future of Europe and if the Soviet price for reunification of Germany imperiled or destroyed prospects for the future of Europe, then that price should not be paid.

The meeting of the Council of Foreign Ministers would probably disclose what price the Russians were demanding. European recovery was only at its beginning. It would not go far without both a sense of security and full German participation in the economic renaissance of Europe. A reunited Germany bought at the price of military insecurity in Europe, or milked by reparations, or paralyzed politically and economically by Soviet veto power or stultifying Soviet control over East German economy, would fatally prejudice the future of Europe. These ideas were embodied in a paper called "An Approach to the CFM," which was approved by the President and cabled to Bevin and Schuman as an indication of how our thoughts were running.

At the beginning of its work the Policy Planning Staff had been much interested in various plans by which Soviet and allied troops might be withdrawn from their respective zones to enclaves on the eastern and western borders of Germany. However, General Bradley, then Chairman of the Joint Chiefs of Staff and a worthy pupil of General Marshall, pointed out that the result of such an effort would be to back British and American forces into indefensible positions in port areas, while Russian forces would not be moved far enough eastward to make much difference. Interest in this approach waned. Other conclusions of our preparatory studies and my talks with the President were that the council meeting would probably not produce more than a *modus vivendi* on Berlin and an easing of the dangerous tension brought on by the open hostility of the blockade and our response. We could accept this without alarm, but we would like more. A good opportunity to get more should not be rejected on the theory that a better opportunity would surely come. Our reading of the future held no such assurance.

Our requirements for a "good opportunity" were severe but not impossible:

Any plan for four-power control over an all-German government must operate as automatically as possible, leaving no room for Russian opposition to stop the machinery. Russian assurances of good will and cooperation were worth nothing. Therefore, as in our tripartite agreement, the principle should be majority rule with a veto only as an exception from it in matters of truly basic importance to the security of one of the supervising powers.

The creation of an all-German government should be based on the reception of the eastern zone into the trizonal government already in process of creation. We could not set the clock back.

Discussion and settlement of the terms of union could be carried on by representatives of the East and West German regimes, provided that in properly supervised elections, in which all German parties might participate, East German representatives were given some real basis of popular representation, as in West Germany, and were not mere stooges of the Communist Party and hence of Moscow. A West German government could not be expected to negotiate with Moscow.

Another provision was that the eastern zone be freed of Russian reparation claims and that industrial enterprises partly or wholly owned by Soviet Government agencies be returned to private German interests. We did not propose to have Marshall Plan aid given to West Germany siphoned into Russia via East Germany.

We also put down as an objective to be sought in the council meetings obtaining some clear allied jurisdiction and exclusive control over the autobahn from the western zones to Berlin and much clearer rights than we had to a rail line also. The blockade and airlift had left us with a political stake in Berlin and moral obligation to its people, both of which we were ill equipped to sustain.

LITURGY AND TACTICS IN THE COUNCIL

From broad strategy we turned to tactics. The Council of Foreign Ministers over the years had developed a liturgy and tradition of its own. The ministers sat at a circular table covered by a green baize cloth. Each minister had three assistants with him at the table and others seated behind him. The sixteen people at the table completely filled it without crowding. The seating was rigidly formalistic. To the left of the French sat the British, then the Russians, and to their left the Americans. Speaking went in similar clockwise order. At the first meeting the host minister presided. The chairmanship moved each day to the left. Whether intended or not this arrangement gave both the laboring oar and the leadership to the American Secretary of State, since he always followed the Russian and set the tone for the next round. The meetings were unduly prolonged by two translations of each speech so that all three languages were covered. This was an excruciating bore except on those occasions when Vishinsky introduced a new gambit, which gave us plenty of time—usually far too much—to prepare our reply.

In the light of this procedure, opening tactics seemed to be pretty clear. We obviously wanted Vishinsky to disclose his hand as fully as possible as early as possible. This could best be done by Schuman opening the session with a welcome, a review of the unhappy past, and a plea for a brighter future. Bevin could then follow by goading the Russian. The Soviet Union had broken up four-power control of Germany, brought us perilously close to trouble of major proportions, and now insisted upon this meeting. Where did Vishinsky propose that we go from here?

With these ideas of strategy and tactics Jessup, Murphy, and Bohlen went to Paris to concert plans with British and French colleagues.

WE MOVE TO PARIS

On my last day in Washington, May 19, 1949, after a closed session with the Senate Committee on Foreign Relations, I urged that no one indulge extravagant hopes of our meeting. After reviewing earlier council failures to reach agreement with the Soviet Union, I concluded:

> It is not our intention, no matter how much we may desire agreement, to accept anything which would tend to undo what has been accomplished . . . toward the revival of health and strength for the free nations of the world. . . .
>
> There is perhaps nothing more important in the world today than the steadiness and consistency of the foreign policy of this Republic. Too much depends on the United States for us to indulge in the luxury of either undue pessimism or premature optimism. . . .
>
> It remains to be seen whether the present favorable developments have brought about a situation in which workable and effective agreements can be reached with the Soviet Union on the central problem of Germany. . . .
>
> I cannot, therefore, honestly state whether or not this new attempt will end in success.[1]

Whenever meetings took me abroad the President insisted that I travel in his own plane, the *Independence,* a most luxurious—for those days—DC-6 propeller plane. Only twice, when the *Independence* was away or in the shop, did we go in any other. My wife, Mr. and Mrs. John Foster Dulles, and a substantial staff had a comfortable overnight flight, which would now seem long. In Paris Ambassador and Mrs. David Bruce most hospitably took in the Achesons and Lucius Battle, from whom we were now inseparable. In the next three years, until David Bruce came back to Washington to be Under Secretary of State, we imposed unconscionably on the Bruces' kindness. It is no exaggeration to say that not since Benjamin Franklin had anyone been closer to or more understanding of the French situation than David Bruce. After 1953 he went on to a diplomatic career very probably unique in American history, adding to his service in Washington and Paris the representation of his country in Bonn and London.

Every morning a little party took the half-hour walk from the embassy residence on the Avenue d'Iéna to the Chancery at the Place de la Concorde. Besides myself, the party consisted of Ambassador Bruce (most of the time), Luke Battle, a French Sûreté officer, and one of my faithful and delightful security guards, either Frank Madden or Paul Cassidy (it was Paul who said, when I showed him the spot near the Place Royale where Henri IV was assassinated, "Gee, Mr. Secretary, there's a hell of a lot of history around here!"). Luke was nervous on these walks. He had been told that if I were killed, he had better not survive to tell how. One morning he edged over to me and said, "I don't want to alarm you, but a car is following us."

"Yes," interrupted the Sûreté officer, "it's mine."

Our advance party had done a good job of working out agreement with Quai d'Orsay and Foreign Office officials, but as Schuman, Bevin, and I went over it for two days, I had no conviction that it would withstand very heavy pressure from Vishinsky if Moscow had given him discretion for broad forays into our lines. Schuman's support of majority voting in four-power control of Germany would be weak. Bevin's support of the return of West German industry to German control would be the same. Both were nervous about advocating an armed German gendarmerie to maintain internal security, and yet this would be necessary if in all zones we wished occupation troops to withdraw as soon as possible from this controlling role.

The Paris meeting brought my introduction to Andrei Vishinsky, the Soviet Minister of Foreign Affairs. Short and slim, with quick, abrupt gestures and rapid speech, he gave an impression of nervous tension. His close-cropped gray mustache, mercilessly cold blue eyes, and sharply, if not finely, cut features set him apart from the stocky, peasant-faced Soviet officials and secret-police agents around him. Vishinsky had been born a Pole and educated for the law, entering the Communist faith as a menshevik, not a bolshevik. As public prosecutor during Stalin's bloody purges of the party, officialdom, and army in the 1930s, he had hounded former friends and colleagues to breakdown and death. Yet Vishinsky was never accepted into the hierarchy. He was an instrument, not a source of power. I was braced for a dangerous and adroit antagonist, but neither then nor later did I find him so. Instead he proved to be a long-winded and boring speaker, as so many Russians are. His debate held no surprises or subtleties; his instructions evidently left him little latitude.

THE SETTING OF THE CONFERENCE

The council meetings were held in the Palais Rose, so called because of what *The New York Times* described as the "acute sunburn" color of the marble pilasters set into its walls. Built by Count Boni de Castellane for his American bride, Anna Gould, the entrance hall and double marble staircase, on which the Garde Républicaine saluted the ministers with ruffles and flourishes on the opening day, embody its Edwardian elegance. My own office had been a bedroom suite, the original furnishings of which had given way to hotel sitting-room and office equipment, except that it lacked a filing cabinet. A bathtub with what appeared to be gold-plated fixtures served that purpose, although classified documents had to be returned each evening to the Chancery. Council meetings were held in the Grand Salon, upon the frescoed ceiling of which satyrs pursued nymphs through clouds without gaining on them even through the double translation of Vishinsky's longest speeches. French windows looked out on a garden. One day I got a smile out of Vishinsky by passing him a note drawing his attention to two pigeons building a nest and suggesting that they were Picasso's peace doves come to inspire him.

One of the memorable experiences of the Paris meetings was the afternoon drive from the Chancery, through the Place de la Concorde, then up the Champs Elysées, around the Arc de Triomphe to the Avenue Malakoff and the Palais Rose. The council meetings began in midafternoon (and continued late) so that there was plenty of time to get there, but a leisurely drive would have spoiled the fun for our French motorcycle escort. They seemed to be trying for a record and evolved an elaborate and thoroughly frightening system for achieving one. We would start off with six officers organized into three pairs like artillery horses, all with sirens shrieking. As we swung into the Champs Elysées, gathering speed, the first pair would sprint ahead to the first intersection, stopping across it on either side of the avenue to hold up traffic. Having done so, they would take off for the next intersection as our cavalcade approached. This led the more adventurous French drivers to attempt the crossing before we reached it. The second pair of officers would dash to intercept them, usually succeeding in stopping a car or two in the middle of the avenue. At this point strong men would avert their eyes as we plunged for a hole in the barricade, squeezed through and left two officers hopelessly entangled in the ensuing traffic jam. By the time we reached the Arc de Triomphe our escort was often reduced to two officers sedately riding forward of either front fender and trying to make up in noise for what they had lost in aggressive power. Smiling and well pleased, they would deliver us in the Palais court too early and nervously unstrung. The lost hounds always returned in time for the added hazards of the evening ride home.

THE MEETINGS BEGIN

In the first few minutes of the first day's meeting on May 23, Vishinsky caught us off guard by a proposal that we should now decide when we would take up, with China present, discussion of a peace treaty with Japan. He claimed that it had been decided at Potsdam by the four heads of government that the Council of Foreign Ministers, with China added, should be the forum in which a Japanese treaty would be worked out, and this decision was binding on us. What he wanted us to do then and there was to acknowledge this binding decision and to set a date for beginning work on the treaty. This was a frightening and impossible idea. Having gotten a German peace treaty hopelessly entangled in the council with its Soviet veto, Vishinsky now wanted to do the same with a Japanese treaty. I was not familiar with what, if anything, had been decided at Potsdam on this subject, but what Vishinsky now proposed simply could not be permitted to happen. If it had been, we would still have no Japanese treaty.

The tiresome process of double translation now proved to be of value. By some fast work we got hold of the Potsdam Declaration and had worked out a position by the time translations were completed. Potsdam, I said, gave the council as such no jurisdiction over Asian questions, only over European settlements. It did say that the four powers would consider how to go about a Japanese treaty and so they would, but not in the council, not until other members of the Far Eastern Council could be consulted, and not now. Schuman and Bevin took the cue, the latter stressing the particular necessity for him of Commonwealth consultation. After that we just refused to discuss the subject. Vishinsky had made a good try and failed.

It seemed to take the heart out of him for the day, for he made only token resistance to the agenda as presented by Schuman. The Russians in the past had attached importance amounting almost to mystique to the agenda, insisting that the council could not proceed from one item to another without reaching agreement on the item under discussion, a procedure that was eminently adaptable to blackmail, and distorting what had seemed to be merely clumsy English translation of agenda items into admissions and concessions. So great was the importance attached to the formulation of the agenda by Gromyko, Vishinsky's deputy, in preliminary conferences with Jessup and Bohlen in the same Palais Rose for a proposed session of the council in 1951 that after fifteen weeks no agenda was agreed upon and no council was held. In 1949 we dealt with the matter brutally. The agenda as put forward by Schuman was what we proposed to discuss; and when we found that, temporarily at least, the utility of discussing a subject had ended, we would pass on to the next. Even with that stern view, the spring 1949 session of the council went on for four weeks without reaching any agreement beyond maintaining the *modus vivendi* in Berlin.

A BLEAK EXCHANGE ABOUT GERMANY

The real business of the meeting began on May 24 with Vishinsky's presentation of the Soviet position on Germany. Though the discussion was conducted courteously and without polemics, the first week showed that the Russians had nothing to propose for Germany as a whole and sought only to recover the power to block progress in West Germany. One can trace the discussion from my daily cables to the President. Vishinsky led off with a plea to the Western powers to restore the Soviet Union (which had walked out) to the Allied Control Council for all Germany. Potsdam required it; it was a logical step following the tripartite agreement. On the next day we asked what the Soviet Union offered in return. There was no surplus in West German economy to be skimmed off for reparations. East Germany had a deficit economy. It had no vestige of free political institutions. What gain to the West could come from joint economic operation with the East under these conditions? I challenged him to discuss reparations and Soviet-held property in East Germany. His proposal, I said, was like asking a victim of paralysis who was three-quarters recovered to return to total paralysis. "Today's session," I cabled the President, "was completely sterile." Vishinsky was continuing to call for four-power control under the old system to perpetuate a split Germany with maximum East-West trade to Soviet advantage. We felt that Soviet intentions were sufficiently clear so that we could with confidence take positive initiative in the council.

This we did on the twenty-eighth, Bevin acting as our spokesman. We would extend the Bonn constitution to the whole country, making it one political and economic unity with one currency and free trade throughout. Reparations should end and Soviet-controlled stock companies (*Aktien Gesellschaften*) would end also. Elections would follow throughout Germany for a national federal government under four-power supervision everywhere and with all German parties, except Nazi ones, freely participating. Four-power supervision should act only on majority vote, except as specifically agreed otherwise. Vishinsky rejected this. Later he proposed that we receive a delegation from the Third Congress of the German people then meeting in Berlin. We declined and suggested that we go on to discuss Berlin.

On May 30 at the end of our first full week of discussion Schuman and I reviewed the situation after dinner at the Bruces. It seemed to us plain that Vishinsky had no proposals acceptable to us nor authority to accept, or even consider, any which we might make, consistent with the interests of Western Europe. The time had come to push on with the agenda in the hope of finding something, even though small, in our discussions of Berlin and Austria that would help ease our relations in either place. Perhaps I should have a brief talk with Vishinsky urging that we get on with the work, minimize the propaganda brawls, and find a way to end the council session without aggravating the situation. We decided to sound out Bevin. This we did, gaining his agreement and the valuable suggestion that we propose to Vishinsky an initial exploration of each subject in small meetings with minimum press briefing afterward. If any area for agreement existed this would permit us to find it before each attempted to place the blame for failure on the other side.

WE TRY PRIVATE MINISTERIAL MEETINGS

I saw Vishinsky in his room in the Palais Rose and gained his agreement. On June 3, after a final flurry of propaganda exchanges on our respective proposals for unifying Germany under four-power control, we turned without fuss to Berlin. I outlined our proposals in a secret session, described in a cable to the President as "the first businesslike session we have had so far," trying to inject some relaxed common sense into the discussion. A city was not a nation and it ought to be possible to let a unified municipal authority operate without four nations having to supervise everything down to and including street cleaning. The city charter and amendments to it would require approval, but other municipal decisions should stand unless within twenty-one days a majority of the Kommandatura (the four-power organization supervising the four zones of Berlin) disapproved. For a couple of days we went into details, including currency matters, and then heard Vishinsky's proposal, which, I cabled the President later, involved more extensive controls than before 1948. Under the Soviet plan "everything the Berliners might do except die required unanimous four-power permission." Soviet advisers made it plain to some of our delegation that the Russians would run no risk of having a German administration in Berlin adopt "anti-Soviet attitudes." When Vishinsky dined with us on June 4 every attempt to draw him out brought the reply that "the dinner was too good to be spoiled by business talk."

The tone of the discussions as well as their content declined. We were getting tired and exasperated. Bevin suggested that the council meet twice a day, in the morning as well as the afternoon. Vishinsky agreed but insisted on afternoon and evening meetings. Bevin said that the length of Vishinsky's speeches would put him to sleep in the evening, to which Vishinsky replied that something put Bevin to sleep in the afternoon. Bevin recommended the practice; it was restful and helped one through the meetings. The result of the evening meetings was a long day. Each of us had a meeting with our own delegation in the morning, then a tripartite meeting to go over the afternoon and evening programs. By the time the meetings were over and our cables sent, it was often two in the morning. As one of my colleagues remarked, "There must be an easier way of earning a living than this."

THE CONFERENCE FACES A CRISIS

By the end of the next week the situation in Berlin had become acute. By the Jessup-Malik agreement the council had been called upon condition of the mutual lifting of restrictions on traffic to Berlin and the eastern zone. But traffic was not flowing freely because of a railroad strike in Berlin. The railroad yards lay in East Berlin; the workers lived in West Berlin. The East German railway company paid them in eastmarks, which were worth little in West Berlin. With the support of the western commandants the railway workers struck; the Russians refused to attend any further meetings to work out this tangle. We had succeeded in blockading ourselves. The situation became serious when the Russians found an excuse to impose impediments to barge traffic. I proposed in our delegation to seek French and British agreement to a demand on Vishinsky that the four commandants find and report not later than the following Monday, June 13, a solution to all impediments to traffic with Berlin. After discussing this proposal and what sanction, if any, might follow Russian rejection of it, we agreed not to threaten anything—but, in fact, perhaps to terminate the council sessions. I said that I would not ask for a vote but would decide myself to go to Bevin and Schuman. Foster Dulles asked to be recorded in the minutes as opposing the idea.

The other ministers agreed and together we privately made the demand on Vishinsky. He wished to consider it overnight (obviously to get instructions). The next day at the beginning of the council meeting he rejected the proposal. This led to a rather heated discussion of whether in view of the failure of the New York agreements and of the council meetings there was any point in continuing the session. As we were about to recess the meeting, Vishinsky said that he had received new instructions from Moscow and would now accept our proposal. As he understood it, each government would instruct its own commandant. This *volte face* produced a good deal of amused comment. No one had seen any message brought to him during the meeting. The French press was full of quips about the invisible dove which had brought him the olive twig. The incident also had an amusing aftermath. When we got back to the Chancery after the meeting, Foster Dulles was waiting to see me. He had, he thought, been hasty in wishing to have recorded his dissent from our démarche; might it be deleted from the minutes? This was done.

On the tenth Bevin reported a hint from the *Pravda* correspondent to a Reuters man that a single managed currency for Berlin must be accepted before any accommodation there could be seriously discussed. Could a really secret meeting be managed, he asked, which would not appear in the Paris press? Vishinsky had invited Bevin to dinner that evening and he was anxious to make a try. We gave him our blessing. He tried and failed. So the next evening, it being my turn to dine at the Soviet Embassy, I tried my hand with a little, but not much more, success. After dinner I asked Vishinsky whether it would be abusing the privileges of a guest to discuss some business matters. With alacrity he pulled his chair over so that we might talk apart from our colleagues. Bevin, I said, had reported his conversation of the previous evening from which, as well as from the general tenor of our meetings, I concluded that no agreement would be possible on the underlying questions. But everyone expected some result from the council; let us try the small matters. Vishinsky agreed that it was clear to him, too, that we were not ready to settle the main questions.

I outlined four "small matters" and one larger one. It might prove possible to improve trade between the eastern and western zones. Trade improvement might extend farther into Eastern Europe. Vishinsky asked for clarification of what I meant. After explaining an idea of a general relaxing of trade restrictions, I picked up his idea of meetings of East and West Germans to discuss improvement of trade. Secondly, we might pick out some matters of Berlin city administration, nothing elaborate, and give authority to our representatives in Berlin to work out citywide cooperation. Thirdly, the French, British, and we ourselves wanted to improve our means of access to Berlin. The New York agreement did not go far enough and left too much room for minor officials on the spot to get us all involved in major friction. Fourth, we both needed an arrangement for continuing contact on German problems through a less cumbersome apparatus than the council. Finally, there was Austria. Its problems had been dragging on too long. These questions should, in all common sense, be settled before we broke up.

Perhaps, I concluded, the most useful thing the four ministers could do would be to meet absolutely alone after the scheduled meeting tomorrow, with only one interpreter, and discuss my suggestion. Vishinsky's immediate reaction indicated the nature of his personal problem. Would it not be possible, he asked, for each minister to have one adviser with him? I agreed, explaining that the purpose was to have very frank talk with no papers, nothing to accept or reject, no press briefing. If we could agree, we would work out a joint paper. If not, we would go back to plenary sessions and fight it out vigorously.

Vishinsky wanted to add to our list of topics procedures for a German peace treaty. I refused, saying that I was unprepared on the subject, had only recently come into office, and had never discussed the matter within our government. Privately, it seemed to me a silly idea to get involved in procedures for discussing a matter on the substance of which we were light-years apart. The council was to last ten days more. When it adjourned, our only agreements fell within the meager list I had outlined to Vishinsky.

THE CONFERENCE STRAGGLES TO AN END

The ten days alternated between secret meetings—or, more accurately, small meetings—in which we worked on our list of "small matters," and plenary sessions, where we ground out the propaganda. Vishinsky delighted in illuminating his arguments with "Russian" proverbs, including such expressions as "putting the horse behind the cart." Turning to our own folk past, I took to inventing American Indian proverbs. His demonstration one day that the military troop strength of the Western allies in Europe far exceeded the Russian struck me, I said, to use an old Indian expression, to be as full of propaganda as a dog is of fleas, though in this case it was all fleas and no dog. He conceded me that round. It was plain that on the only "small matter" of consequence, improvement of our access to Berlin, the Russians were unwilling to yield an inch, though on the Austrian treaty several small but sticky points were agreed on and sent back to the deputies for incorporation into the treaty. The other "small matters" padded out the communiqué but are not worth recalling here. Finally, and wearily, on June 20 we signed and released the communiqué, adjourned the council *sine die,* drank a last glass of champagne and parted about six o'clock hoping not to meet soon again.

Then a curious development occurred. About eight o'clock Vishinsky telephoned Schuman, then holding a press conference, and demanded that the council reconvene. We learned through French friends that Gromyko, Vishinsky's deputy, had telephoned him *en clair* from Moscow and told him in brutal language that the Austrian agreements were unsatisfactory and must be reopened. Bevin and I reached the Quai d'Orsay at the same time. As we got out of the creaking lift, Bevin, who had been dining well, asked (as I have told the story before):

"Do you know our labour song, 'The Red Flag?' " I had to confess ignorance. "The tune's the same as 'Maryland, My Maryland.' Y' know that, comin' from there. Let's sing 'em together, as a sign of solidarity, as we labour blokes say."

And so we did, robustly, arm-in-arm, walking through the sedate Second Empire anterooms, with the final bars at the very entrance of the meeting room. As a mark of solidarity it was impressive.

Vishinsky wanted a change, the significance of which he could not explain, in the wording of a financial clause of the Austrian agreement. "Bevin," as I have written, "congratulated him on a new record. Soviet agreements were fragile things but today's was the frailest yet. It had not even survived the day. However, he saw no reason to reconsider our adjournment, or change our words. Schuman and I briefly agreed. The meeting adjourned. By midnight the lights of Paris and then London disappeared behind us as the *Independence* gained altitude on her northerly course back to Washington."[2]

The President met us next day as we stepped out of the plane. "Well done!" he said. After hearing my report he gave out his own appraisal of the conference, beginning with a paragraph which reassured me that our system for communication had worked well. "The Secretary of State has given me daily reports, and now a final report, on the recently concluded session of the Council of Foreign Ministers." Thereupon, I met with the Senate and House foreign affairs committees on June 23 and 24 respectively.

Through a transcribed and released press conference,[3] I tried to explain to the country the significance of the council meeting as marking the changed positions of the United States and the Soviet Union in Europe over the past two years. In 1947 General Marshall had said that the great issue in Western Europe was whether or not it would recover and regain its strength. He had predicted that it would, the Soviet Union that it would not. Two years of intensive effort now showed General Marshall's prediction being fulfilled. The council meeting had been a clear indication of it, of a Soviet move from an offensive attitude in 1947 to a defensive one in 1949. They dared not relax in any degree such hold as they had on any part of Germany or Berlin. Since the essence of Western policy was to return responsibility in Germany to Germans, under a system that guaranteed the basic freedoms and contained the safeguards necessary for the security of Europe and the world, agreement between the two attitudes was not now possible. We wished to bring Germany into the life of a free and strong Europe as an equal. We would not retreat from our purpose. Its obvious and growing success was the most impressive fact in Europe. The Russians could not bring themselves to accept it.

34. SUMMER BRINGS DIFFICULT

DECISIONS

THE SUMMER OF 1949 brought difficult decisions, or, perhaps, decisions that brought difficulties. One was the decision to publish a White Paper on our relations with China; another, to ask Congress to authorize and finance an extensive military assistance program. Both were exremely unpopular.

THE CHINA WHITE PAPER

Hard upon our return from the Council of Foreign Ministers meetings I took a plunge that ranks high among those that have caused me immediate, unexpected, and acute trouble. The cause was the publication of the China White Paper, officially entitled *United States Relations with China with Special Reference to the Period 1944–1949*. Justice Felix Frankfurter used to say that intellectually I was a frustrated schoolteacher, persisting against overwhelming evidence to the contrary in the belief that the human mind could be moved by facts and reason. He attributed this idiosyncrasy to the influence of Justice Brandeis at a formative period in my life. In fact, Frankfurter had a good deal to do with it himself.

Early in the year, while talking with the President about congressional and press criticism of our policy in China, I suggested that much of it flowed from ignorance of the facts. General Marshall had been reluctant to present the full facts for fear of hurting further the Generalissimo's declining fortunes. It was now clear that the Nationalist regime on the mainland was on the verge of collapse and that American disengagement from support of it as such must follow. Let us, I urged, prepare a thorough account of our relations with China, centering on the past five years, and publish it when the collapse came. The President agreed, and a knowledgeable and professionally qualified group was put to work under W. Walton Butterworth, subsequently with Dr. Philip C. Jessup, then Ambassador at Large, as editor in chief. With a letter of transmittal the China White Paper was delivered to the President on July 29, 1949, and released a few days later. Since it was a long document—four hundred nine pages, extended by annexed documents to one thousand fifty-four pages—my letter of transmittal was also published separately, entitled *A Summary of American-Chinese Relations*. A short statement by the President underlined that his "primary purpose in having this frank and factual record released at this time is to ensure that our policy toward China, and the Far East as a whole, shall be based on informed and intelligent public opinion."[1] After twenty years the China White Paper still stands up well as a fair, accurate, and scholarly presentation and analysis of the facts. Attacks upon it—and there have been many—have not been sustained. Neither were my hopes in having the White Paper prepared. As a teacher shedding light, I was still destined to be frustrated, resembling more closely Arnold von Winkelried at the late-fourteenth-century battle of Sempach gathering the Austrian spears into his own bosom.

The conclusion of the summary was unpalatable to believers in American omnipotence, to whom every goal unattained is explicable only by incompetence or treason.

The unfortunate but inescapable fact is that the ominous result of the civil war in China was beyond the control of the government of the United States. Nothing that this country did or could have done within the reasonable limits of its capabilities could have changed that result; nothing that was left undone by this country has contributed to it. It was the product of internal Chinese forces, forces which this country tried to influence but could not. A decision was arrived at within China, if only a decision by default.

And now it is abundantly clear that we must face the situation as it exists in fact. We will not help the Chinese or ourselves by basing our policy on wishful thinking.[2]

At the same time I announced the appointment of Raymond Fosdick, former President of the Rockefeller Foundation, and Everett Case, President of Colgate University, to join with Ambassador Jessup in advising the Department. Our purposes toward China would remain what they had been, but we were confronted by a situation in which alternatives were very sharply limited.

The paper and announcement were greeted by a storm of abuse from very diverse groups in the Congress and the press. To explain the emotion that China policy could arouse we must go back over events that happened during General Marshall's service as Secretary of State, most of which occurred between my leaving and returning to office.

The Emotional Nature of the China Issue • Two fundamental and opposed political movements were active during this period. Through the medium of General Marshall and Senator Vandenberg a nonpartisan foreign policy was leading the United States into a new relationship with Europe. This involved the abandonment of a century and a half of traditional doctrine and acceptance of immense burdens and risks, the effects of which still defy calculation. At the same time the Republican Party, having captured the legislative branch in 1946, was moving to break sixteen years of Democratic dominance of the Government, which had come to be regarded with intense bitterness. The Republican leaders had not the slightest doubt that this would be the result of the election of 1948. Though without a shred of evidence to support the statement, I think it highly probable that General Marshall shared this view.

Partisan criticism had to find some outlet in foreign policy. China was made to order for the purpose, and the attack increasingly centered there.

Rationalization was at hand, too, in the charge that the Administration had failed to consult with Republicans on China policy. Consultation there had been aplenty,† though not to the extent which had been possible on Europe; but it led to nothing. No hopeful alternative policy was visible. Vandenberg himself was frank to admit this. "It is a very easy, simple matter," he said in the Senate, "to dissociate one's self from a policy. It is not quite so easy to assert what an alternative policy might have been. I concede that it is far easier to be critical than to be correct."[3] The China bloc had an alternative policy, which their more thoughtful colleagues and overwhelming American opinion repudiated—massive military aid without combat intervention in an attempt to defeat the Chinese Communists.[4] The Congress and—for the most part—the press recognized this for what it was: a political offensive and an attempt to embarrass provision of funds for the nonpartisan policy in Europe. In such a situation Vandenberg had no enthusiasm for consultation.

General Marshall, however, made concessions to Republican demands and attacks to ease Vandenberg's position and the progress of the European Recovery Program. On May 26, 1947, the embargo on shipment of munitions to China was lifted. From April to September, as the Marines withdrew from north China, they "abandoned" to the Nationalist forces sixty-five hundred tons of ammunition.[5] In July General Wedemeyer was sent on a fact-finding mission to China. In September John Carter Vincent was relieved as Chief of the Office of Far Eastern Affairs—being succeeded by Walton Butterworth —and sent to Switzerland as Minister, both to appease Republican critics and to remove him from the direct path of Republican vengeance. In 1948 the Administration agreed to a China Aid Act even larger than that finally enacted. In it the Congress provided two hundred seventy-five million dollars for economic aid and a hundred twenty-five million for special grants (military aid) to be used at the discretion of the Chinese Government, not the American.

In General Wedemeyer's report,† made to the President on September 19, 1947, the most striking recommendation was "that China request the United Nations to take immediate action to bring about a cessation of hostilities in Manchuria and request that Manchuria be placed under a Five-Power Guardianship [including the Soviet Union] or, failing that, under a Trusteeship in accordance with the United Nations Charter."[6] The reason given was that Manchuria was on the verge of being lost to the Communists. The President and General Marshall concluded at once that to publish this confidential report would have catastrophic consequences in China. They so informed the Generalissimo, who made no comment. The Administration found itself bitterly attacked for not publishing the report by those whose attack would have been even more bitter had it been published. The report also recommended continuing economic and military aid under strict conditions and urged sweeping reforms in China.

Meanwhile throughout 1947 and 1948 both the economic and military fortunes of the Nationalist Chinese continued an accelerating downward course to complete disaster. At the beginning of this period the Government had two million six hundred thousand men under arms; the Communists, one million one hundred thousand. The Government's superiority in rifles was variously estimated at from three or four to one. In addition to the aid given by U.S. Forces, China Theater, in redeploying the Chinese armies and repatriating the Japanese, by the Marines in north China and by the U.S. advisory groups, the United States provided from V-J Day through 1948 approximately a billion dollars in military aid and a similar amount in economic aid.[7]

This is not the place to go into the military campaigns of the civil war. The clearest account of the causes of Nationalist disaster has been given by Major General David Barr, Director of the United States Military Advisory Group to the Government of China.[8] Its first politico-military blunder, the General reported, was in concentrating its efforts after V-J Day on the military occupation of former Japanese-held areas and neglecting efficient administration. Moreover, the Chinese army was burdened with the unsound strategy of a militarily inept high command. Instead of being content with consolidating north China, it burdened the army with taking over Manchuria, a task beyond its logistic capabilities. Attempting to do too much with too little, it scattered its armies along thousands of miles of railroads, which, together with the cities through which they passed, had to be held, since the armies were supplied from central China. The armies degenerated from field armies with offensive spirit to garrison and lines-of-communication troops, developing the "wall psychology" of withdrawing into walled cities, assuming a purely defensive posture, and waiting for help that never came. Initiative passed to the Communists, who cut lines of communication and starved out the Nationalists. The latter, often without firing a shot, went over to the winning side with all their equipment. As the Communists grew stronger, attaining in 1948 a definite superiority, they took an even more offensive strategy. By the end of 1948 they had control of Manchuria and most of China north of the Yangtze.

General Barr reported on November 16 his conviction that

the military situation has deteriorated to the point where only the active participation of United States troops could effect a remedy. . . . No battle has been lost since my arrival due to lack of ammunition or equipment. Their military debacles in my opinion can all be attributed to the world's worst leadership and many other morale destroying factors that lead to a complete loss of will to fight. . . .

The Generalissimo has lost much of his political and popular support. It is unknown to what extent the nation would support his attempt to continue the present government in a new move. . . . For this reason unless all-out United States military assistance, including employment of United States Forces, which I certainly do not recommend, is given the government in its new location, I recommend that Jusmag [Joint U.S. Military Advisory Group] be withdrawn in accordance with present plans.[9]

On the day that I assumed my office Generalissimo Chiang Kai-shek resigned his, turning over the Presidency of the Republic to the Vice President, General Li Tsung-jen. Before doing so, however, he transferred China's foreign exchange and monetary reserves to Formosa and requested the United States to ship military equipment destined for China to Formosa. This left General Li without funds or a source of military equipment.

By direction of the President, the State Department asked for the advice of Major General David Barr about disposition of rifles and ammunition procured by the Army for the Chinese Government under the China Aid Act of 1948. General Barr advised holding them at Bangor, Washington, until the situation in China became clearer. The National Security Council, fearing that shipments would be likely to fall into Communist hands, advised the President to consult with congressional leaders, urging suspension pending clarification. He and I met with them on February 5 and found them opposed to doing so. A memorandum from the White House instructed me that in order not to discourage Chinese resistance to Communist aggression, military aid should not be suspended, but no effort should be made to expedite it. I was given the unenviable authority to "coordinate interpretation" of this instruction.

Two days later fifty-one Republican congressmen asked the President to appoint a commission to investigate and report on China. I volunteered to meet and reason with them. About half of them came to a meeting at which I furnished them with a weapon beyond their dreams. Asked to predict the course of events, I replied that when a great tree falls in the forest one cannot see the extent of the damage until the dust settles. In the next day's press our China policy was described as "wait until the dust settles." Quite futilely I attempted to explain that the phrase was not intended to describe a policy but my inability to see very far in this situation. Of course, any stick is good enough to beat a dog, but this was an example of my unhappy ability—if I may mix a metaphor—to coin a stick. The most famous was yet to come.

The next day Senator Pat McCarran of Nevada introduced the China bloc's proposal to provide a billion and a half dollars in loans for the Nationalist Government. Fifty senators, half of them Democrats, supported this bizarre idea in a letter to Senator Connally, Chairman of the Foreign Relations Committee. The last document in the White Paper is my memorandum to him of March 15, written with the full support of the President, rejecting the proposal *in toto.*† The Foreign Relations Committee strongly supported the Administration.

In mid-April the Communists served on General Li what amounted to a demand for surrender, threatening to cross the Yangtze—which General Wedemeyer had said could be defended with broomsticks by an army with the will to fight—unless Communist peace terms were accepted by April 20. The crossing began at midnight. "The ridiculously easy Communist crossing of the Yangtze," reported our embassy at Nanking, "was made possible by defections at key points, disagreements in the High Command, and the failure of the Air Force to give effective support."[10]

For a final appraisal of American help to the Chinese Government on the mainland we turn to a letter of Acting President Li to President Truman written on May 5, 1949. After referring to help given China during the war with Japan, he continued:

This policy of friendly assistance was continued when some years ago General George C. Marshall, under instructions from your good self, took up the difficult task of mediation in our conflict with the Chinese Communists, to which he devoted painstaking effort. All this work was unfortunately rendered fruitless by the lack of sincerity on the part of both the then Government and the Chinese Communists.

In spite of this, your country continued to extend its aid to our Government. It is regrettable that, owing to the failure of our then Government to make judicious use of this aid and to bring about appropriate political, economic and military reforms, your assistance has not produced the desired effect. To this failure is attributable the present predicament in which our country finds itself.[11]

It is not strange, looking back upon it, that the White Paper, documenting patiently and thoroughly the facts outlined here and in Chapters 16 and 23 and ending with the quotation just given from the Acting President of China, should have evoked bellows of pain and rage from the China bloc in Congress and the China lobby in the country, and enlisted the full efforts of their combined propaganda apparatus. Since, however, these did not affect the course of Administration policy or the strong support given it by the Foreign Relations Committee under Tom Connally's stalwart and loyal leadership, we shall pass on to other crowding developments of this eventful year.

THE MILITARY ASSISTANCE PROGRAM

The Nature of the Political Issue • The heat generated by the Military Assistance Program, which first obtained legislative authorization in 1949, came from subterranean fires far deeper than any issues contained in the legislation itself—desire for economy and a balanced budget at a low level, an unwillingness to face and accept the responsibilities of power, the China bloc's belief that our interest and funds were excessively concentrated in Europe, and, perhaps most of all, bitter resentment of the Republicans over the President's wholly unexpected victory in 1948. These were all present in the military aid controversy of 1949. They were all to grow in the next three years, until they at last reached the nearly nihilist proportions of a desire to destroy the very government the party wished to capture. Out of it sprang separate themes of distrust of the President and the State Department, the hysteria over Communists in government, education, and the church, and even a tinge of neo-xenophobic isolationism.

Discussion of a Military Aid Program, as of the North Atlantic Treaty, began early in 1948, motivated by fear in Europe of Stalin's increasingly minatory attitude. On March 17, 1948, five Western European states—Britain, France, and the Benelux countries—signed the Brussels Pact with American support and approval. In July decisions were made in Washington to have talks with these countries, some of which led to the North Atlantic Treaty and others to the Mutual Defense Assistance Program. Both, though separately developed, flowed from a common source. American officers, including a future Supreme Allied Commander, General Lyman L. Lemnitzer, were sent to Field Marshal Lord Montgomery's Western Union headquarters staff at Fontainebleau, where plans for defense of Western Europe were considered and lists of needed military equipment and supplies prepared. While this work went forward, the coup in Czechoslovakia and the blockade of Berlin exposed the shocking military weakness of Western Europe and the unpreparedness of the United States (we had at the time total ground reserves in the United States of two and a third divisions).[12]

From the earliest discussions both European defense planning and military assistance programs have been bedeviled by the conflict between the desirable and the attainable, or—putting it another way—by the attempt to clothe the attainable in respectable strategic theory. It was still going on three years later (as it is today), as we shall see in Chapter 65. At this time we did not have the vast number of strategists—military, semimilitary, and journalistic—who later did so much to confuse themselves and the rest of us.

The Nature of the Military Issue • The problem faced by the soldiers at Fontainebleau was a formidable one. The Soviet Union had present in Eastern Europe some thirty divisions. Facing them were three and a half American and two and a half British divisions scattered throughout Germany, performing occupation and police duty. The entire French establishment in Europe consisted of less than half a dozen ill-armed divisions. The Benelux countries could, perhaps, assemble as many more. The conception of a collective-security treaty in early 1948 was of a political commitment to go to war to aid any signatory allies attacked. It might also contain obligations on each and all to prepare the necessary forces and plans. In Washington and Europe the United States monopoly of nuclear weapons encouraged the hope that political commitment to fight would be enough to deter an attack upon or subversive overthrow of an allied state, but allied weakness in the face of the Russian-managed Communist takeover in Czechoslovakia and the blockade of Berlin gravely impaired confidence in this theory. The Russian nuclear explosion in 1949 and the attack on South Korea in June 1950 would destroy the myth that "making our intention clear" would provide security.

The soldiers properly began by considering what would be required to stop a Russian attack from overrunning Europe while American strength of all sorts was being brought to bear. The result was an impossible initial investment of between thirty and forty billion dollars and annual burdens far beyond practical capabilities. Paul Nitze of the Policy Planning Staff, after a tour of inquiry, suggested reversing the process and working backward from attainable figures to an appraisal of the military results they would produce. Accepting the principle that the first task of the European economies was recovery, the amounts available for defense could be fairly accurately judged. Amounts of United States aid varying between one and two billion dollars per annum were assumed. The result attainable would be a force in Europe that would preclude a quick victory by sudden marches, backed up by an American capability for punishing blows against an aggressor's home territory. This placed the emphasis on deterrence. Later in the year I described the effort as one to put a hard shell on the soft European community painfully exposed to predators. Even that was an exaggeration; it was only a start.

By the time the prime ministers met in Washington during April 1949 we were able to get a request from our allies for military aid on a basis which at least approached practicality. The Brussels group made a joint request; Denmark, Norway, and Italy separate ones. Original principles were simple and sensible. The Mutual Defense Assistance Program must not impede the European Recovery Program. Needs should be jointly considered and equipment jointly allocated. Forces should be developed on a coordinated and integrated basis to operate under a common strategic plan. Unnecessary duplication should be eliminated and maximum defense derived from available manpower, money, and materials. Agreement on these simple principles seemed to us adequate for a start on raising forces in Europe, a task that would take long enough to permit the development of strategic plans for their ultimate deployment and organization.

Vandenberg Leads a Revolt · Accordingly, within a few hours of signing the ratification of the North Atlantic Treaty on July 25, 1949, the President sent to Congress a request for military aid authorization in the amount of one billion four hundred million dollars, and with wide executive discretion regarding its use. Congress, particularly the Senate, was most unsympathetic. Senator Connally would later observe that the Military Assistance Program had been the most difficult major foreign policy legislation to enact since the Lend-Lease Act.[13] To be sure, trouble over military assistance had been forecast when I testified before the Senate committee on the North Atlantic Treaty in April and Senator Taft had voted against it because he foresaw an arms race ensuing. When now the arms bill itself came up, he returned to the fray with strengthened Republican cohorts and the formidable addition of Democratic Senators Byrd, George, and Russell on grounds of economy. Senator Vandenberg, going through the familiar gambit of opposing and obtaining amendment before he could support it, was also arrayed against us. Vandenberg hyperbole pointed to the horrendous fault of the dictatorial powers sought by the President. He wrote his wife: "It's almost unbelievable in its grant of unlimited power to the Chief Executive. It would permit the President to sell, lease or give away anything we've got at any time to any country in any way he wishes. It would virtually make him the number one war lord of the earth. In today's . . . Committee meeting, Walter George, Cabot Lodge, Bill Fulbright and Alex Wiley backed me up one hundred per cent. . . . The old bipartisan business is certainly 'out of the window' on this one. . . . So it's a pretty tight 'poker game' between Acheson and me."[14]

However, Senators Connally, Thomas of Utah, Lucas (the Majority Leader), Tydings, Green, and McMahon joined in introducing the bill. The fact that Vandenberg was now in the minority and Connally chairman of the committee, and very conscious of it as well as resentful of Vandenberg's recently acquired prestige as an "internationalist," made the "old bipartisan business" somewhat difficult to recapture.

On July 28 I opened the hearings before the House Committee on Foreign Affairs,[15] being supported in the next few days by Secretary of Defense Louis Johnson, General Bradley, General Marshall, and Ambassador Averell Harriman. We anticipated most of the objections that had been discussed publicly, and answered a rather steady stream of new ones from Republican members, largely centering on the desirability of postponing military assistance until strategic and organizational plans had been worked out and accepted by all the allies in the North Atlantic Treaty Council. These suggestions would have postponed a start on provision of the most elementary military formation until the Greek kalends. Few defections were apparent on the Democratic side.

On August 2, however, Louis Johnson and I attended an executive session of the combined Senate committees on foreign and military affairs, where we found that Arthur Vandenberg had stirred up such a revolution that, with the aid of important Democratic defections, at the moment he had the support of a majority of the two committees. With his usual dramatic flair the Senator has recorded his part in what he called "our telltale showdown on the arms program": "I bluntly laid the 'facts of life' before Secretary of State Acheson and Secretary of Defense Johnson. I gave 'em an ultimatum—write a new and reasonable bill or you will get no bill and it will be your fault! Both Committees backed me up—and at the end of a rather dramatic session, they went downtown to write a new bill."[16]

We Try a New Lure · In fact, we went downtown to see the President, who took the typically sensible position that he did not care about the section granting him powers, inserted to provide for unpredictable—and hence unlikely— developments, such as an Austrian peace treaty. What he wanted, and quickly, was the money. By August 5 we gave the Senate a new bill. Vandenberg metaphorically rubbed his hands. "The State Department," he wrote, "came up with a new bill today in re arms. They have totally surrendered on eighty per cent of my criticisms. The new bill is really pretty good. But it still has too much money." In fact, it authorized only ninety dollars less, but the total amount was divided into three categories: North Atlantic Treaty countries; Greece and Turkey; and Iran, Korea, and the Philippines. Vandenberg's concern over the President's broad powers to transfer was assuaged by forbidding any transfer out of U.S. military stocks if the Secretary of Defense after consultation with the Joint Chiefs of Staff should determine it detrimental to the national interest. Transfers of funds out of any category to other categories might not exceed in the aggregate five per cent of the amount out of which the transfer might be made. Generally speaking, the bill was shorter and its purposes more closely linked to the North Atlantic Treaty and other military purposes already authorized by Congress.

Senator Connally, who loyally took the laboring oar in getting the bill through the Senate and had not been overly pleased by the prominent position his colleague Vandenberg had taken in criticizing it, opened the hearings on August 8 with an attempt to give me a leg up in the new draft. As was well known, he said, it was a new edition of the earlier bill seeking to remove certain controversial points, and he added: "The Secretary of State rewrote the bill, and I want to pay him a high compliment on the magnificent job which he did in redrafting the measure. It elicited praise from some of those who had been opposing the original measure."[17]

In my statement,[18] in addition to explaining the limited purposes of the bill, I followed Senator Connally's cue by pointing out how it eliminated the major objections that had been advanced. It was not intended to put into effect a definitive plan for defending Europe against major attack. The immediate need for Atlantic security and world peace was to make plain that easy victory could not be gained by quick marches, and this could not brook delay. Vandenberg, however, now joined by John Foster Dulles, appointed to the Senate from New York to fill an unexpired term, returned to earlier demands for a mere interim measure to tide over until the North Atlantic Treaty Council had worked out a strategic plan which Congress could appraise. My rejection of so hesitant an approach with its possibilities of delay resulted in what the press called a "heated exchange," though the heat was largely forensic.

From then on for a month Washington enjoyed a ding-dong battle in which everyone, including the President, joined, where the advantage shifted from time to time as dramatically as at Gettysburg, and which proved that the Administration as well as the President could and would fight. Bipartisanship was not abandoned, but tempered by a little political bloodletting.

And Catch a Fish • The main engagement centered on the appropriation-authorization provisions. Here we had two groups of opponents: those who wanted to cut the amount authorized for economy reasons, led by Senators Byrd, George, and Russell and Representatives Richards and Vorys, and those who wanted to delay funds as much for ideological reasons as for economy, led by Vandenberg and Dulles. The two latter on August 15 made public their proposal to cut the treaty assistance authorization to one billion dollars (a cut of almost a hundred sixty-one million dollars) and insure that this amount would be available only to assist common defense plans made by the treaty council. To accomplish this a small amount would be authorized at once, more when the President approved the treaty defense plans, and five hundred million dollars authorized to be charged to the fiscal year ending June 30, 1951. This, as they put it, would give Congress "a second look" during the next session. The idea was wholly without merit, since it did not, as its proposers claimed, underline the supremacy of the council and its common-defense plan, which, in the absence of commander or staff, would exist only as provided by Washington. However, the tide of battle moved in such a sudden and unexpected direction that the Administration rose above ideology to the best compromise possible. This was to split our opponents and restore nonpartisanship by adopting Vandenberg's proposal.

On August 16 the House committee, having beaten back one attempt by Richards and another by Vorys to cut the bill drastically, sent it on to the House for action. There it met disaster. Richards and Vorys joined in offering an amendment on the floor to cut the appropriation in half. The House was in one of its berserk moods. In spite of Speaker Rayburn's deserting the rostrum and making an impassioned plea for the bill from the well of the House, the amendment carried 238 to 122. This blow was as surprising as it was stunning. On the twenty-second the President rallied our forces in a speech in Miami to the Veterans of Foreign Wars; the whips got to work; and the House awoke from its spree a trifle ashamed of such public irresponsibility.

The two Senate committees approved the Senate bill except for the big issue of the amount, which they passed over. August ended in a flurry of rumors, proposals, and counterproposals. During this time Washington was also racked by the Air Force debate over the B-36, the British monetary crisis, Yugoslav-Russian tension, the imminent arrival of Schuman and Bevin, and a hurricane in Florida. The congressional tempest was reduced to its true dimensions of one in a teapot. Happily, it was soon over. After Senators Connally and Knowland had exchanged high words over Chiang Kai-shek's appropriation of China's monetary reserves, we let it be known that if Congress chose to add seventy-five million dollars to the Military Assistance Program for the purposes and policies of the act "in the general area" of China, we would accept but not necessarily expend the sum. This was done. The two committees, first defeating Senator George's amendment to reduce the appropriation by more than two-thirds, approved it substantially as amended by Vandenberg. A hot fight had been expected in the Senate, but did not materialize. Connally opened the debate. Vandenberg acclaimed the bill as "bargain insurance for peace." Dulles joined in support. All attempts to reduce the amount were beaten down and on September 22 the Military Assistance Program passed the Senate by a vote of 55 to 24.

AN ILL WIND BLOWS SOME GOOD

At this time I was in New York attending the annual meeting of the General Assembly of the United Nations. Under Secretary James Webb telephoned to tell me that a most important matter had arisen requiring urgent action on which the President wanted my advice. The Air Force would fly Carlisle Humelsine, Director of the Executive Secretariat, to New York with some papers and an explanation of a matter that could not be discussed over the telephone. We arranged an hour for meeting at our apartment at the Waldorf. Carlisle soon arrived to tell me of the first Russian atomic explosion and to discuss what action the United States Government should take. First he explained to me how we knew what we knew, and then gave me the President's thoughts on the subject, which were for him to make a short and calm statement, a draft of which Carl had, and for me to accompany it with one relating current actions to the explosion. This statement Humelsine and I worked out together and gave out in New York on September 23.[19]

This action of the President in keeping me fully informed and in consulting with me even though we were separated was typical of his consideration and of the innate orderliness of his procedure as head of government. It made my discussion of the Russian atomic explosion with other delegates to the General Assembly infinitely more effective; it gave us in New York an assurance that we were in close touch with our own Government; and it enabled me to point out the urgent importance of the military assistance bill.

Once again the Russians had come to the aid of an imperiled nonpartisan foreign policy, binding its wounds and rallying the divided Congress into accepting the Senate version of the Mutual Defense Assistance Program. On October 6, 1949, the President signed the bill into law.

35. ANGLO-AMERICAN ATOMIC
COOPERATION REVIEWED

ONLY A FEW DAYS after my return to the Department in January 1949 the question of reviving Anglo-American atomic cooperation was raised again by a memorandum from the Department's Science Adviser, Gordon Arneson, telling me that Admiral Sir Henry Moore for the British Government had proposed to Secretary Forrestal a complete interchange of information on weapons. The initial Washington response the preceding autumn had been unfavorable, but no final answer had been given. A high-level meeting of State, Defense, and Atomic Energy Commission officials had been convened shortly before at Princeton to make a recommendation. The basic problem had substantially the same elements as it had had three years before. The group agreed that existing arrangements could no longer be kept secret and their revision would entail full public disclosure. This had led to the recommendation that the three agencies should develop a solution for the American members of the Combined Policy Committee to discuss with the British and Canadian members if approved by the President and the Congress.

Jim Webb and I thought this too important a matter to be handled in isolation from other foreign policy decisions. The forum for discussion should be the National Security Council. We were told that when the report of the Princeton meeting came back to the Atomic Energy Commission Lewis Strauss had voted against the commission's recommendation for broadened cooperation with the British and Canadians in the nuclear field. General Groves's opposition had already been made clear and I had had a foretaste of the attitude of Congress in my interview with Vandenberg and Hickenlooper informing them of how far we had gone during the war. So it was that, in spite of adequate warning of trouble to come and an already full schedule for that active winter and spring, leadership of a hazardous expeditionary force into enemy country was added to my duties.

OUR ADVICE TO THE PRESIDENT

The Special Committee of the National Security Council appointed by the President on February 10, with me as chairman, Secretary Forrestal, Sumner T. Pike, David E. Lilienthal, Acting Chairman of the Atomic Energy Commission, and Admiral Sidney W. Souers, invited to work with us General Eisenhower, then President of Columbia University; George F. Kennan and R. Gordon Arneson from State; William Webster and Kenneth D. Nichols from Defense; and Carroll L. Wilson and Joseph Volpe from the Atomic Energy Commission. The President gave the report of the Special Committee careful study, questioning many of those concerned with it, and on March 31 approved it.

The report recommended full cooperation on all atomic energy matters, including weapons. There should be freedom of action in national programs consistent with a due regard for strategic considerations. In line with this last requirement we thought that production plants, energy facilities, and stockpiles should be located to the "fullest extent practicable" in the United States or Canada; that the most effective use of joint resources, including raw materials and personnel, should be insured with major production in the United States and not more than ten per cent of the raw materials being allocated to the United Kingdom and Canada over the next five years; and that disclosure to other governments should be effectively coordinated. In addition, there should be coordination of both defense against attacks by atomic weapons and of bases for the delivery of atomic weapons. The Combined Policy Committee and Combined Development Trust would be continued under the terms of what should be a relatively long-term agreement.

The Special Committee also recommended that should the President approve the report and wish to discuss methods of going forward with its proposals, one or more preliminary meetings might be held at Blair House (where the President was then living) with the chairmen and ranking minority members of the Joint Committee on Atomic Energy and of the Senate Foreign Relations and House Foreign Affairs committees. Preliminary consideration of the problems involved and possible means of dealing with them would be useful preparation for sessions later with the full committees. Informal soundings might also be taken of British and Canadian opinion. In the congressional meetings we should consult on methods of obtaining congressional approval under the none-too-clear terms of the Atomic Energy Act of 1946.

As I look back on these proposals and the procedure for carrying them forward, I am amazed at their boldness and at our optimism—or, perhaps, foolhardiness—in believing that the operation could possibly succeed. The obvious need was for a high degree of discretion and secrecy among the participants and a fair wind from the press during the launching process. The nature of the opposition to any cooperation with any foreign nation in atomic matters and the growing popular fear of Communist penetration of government was such that the possibility of our having a fair hearing of our proposals was far too small. Worst of all, instigated by Senator Hickenlooper, the Joint Atomic Energy Committee was conducting an investigation of his charges of "incredible mismanagement" against Lilienthal and the Atomic Energy Commission.[1] This revealed more passion than substance in the charges, and in the hope that the former might cool off we postponed our effort so as to provide the opportunity.

However, it could not wait long—Lovett's *modus vivendi* would run out at the end of the year. This had provided that the whole output of the Belgian Congo raw materials for 1948–49 should go to the United States and, if this was not sufficient, then British stocks could be drawn upon to meet our needs. Our bargaining position worsened every day as British scientists and engineers mastered production problems without help from us. At the end of June the President approved our detailed procedural blueprint and at the beginning of July Louis Johnson and I consulted the Chairman of the Joint Committee, Senator Brien McMahon, on the auguries. In his view there could not have been a worse time. On the other hand, there was not much time, good or bad. Something had to be done in the next six months, if only to try for an extension of the *modus vivendi* and the existing allocation. So we crossed our Rubicon and with the President's concurrence decided to go ahead.

THE BLAIR HOUSE MEETING

On the evening of Thursday, July 14, Washington heat was broken by a violent and protracted thunderstorm. Inside Blair House—and dry—a considerable company convened duly noted by a congregation outside—and wet— of the press, doubtless tipped off by some of the more fortunate insiders. These consisted of the President and Vice President; Senators Connally, Vandenberg, McMahon, Hickenlooper, and Tydings; Speaker Sam Rayburn and Representatives Carl T. Durham and W. Sterling Cole; Secretary Louis Johnson; William Webster; General Eisenhower; David Lilienthal; Joseph Volpe; Gordon Arneson; and myself.

The President stated the problem about which he wanted the help and guidance of the assembled company, asking me to fill in the background. I added an account of the wartime pooling of effort, the postwar aloofness and the even division of raw materials, the imminent end of the *modus vivendi* and the need for some new arrangement, the developments since the war in the Soviet Union and Britain. Britain would have two reactors in operation within a year or so and her first bomb in less than four years without help or within two and a half years with help. David Lilienthal told of the Atomic Energy Commission's raw-material needs and the benefits that could flow both ways from a full exchange of information with the British.

The Defense representatives then took up the military aspects of the problem, General Eisenhower giving an admirable statement of the need for the fullest confidence between the British and ourselves in the event of another global war. Their advanced position would be a great advantage if allied with us and a great hazard to them if they were not. Our military fate and theirs were so interlocked that it made no sense to exclude one weapon—which they would soon have anyway—from the scope of our full partnership. The attempt to do so was already poisoning our relation of mutual trust and, if continued, could jeopardize our alliance.

I then read to the meeting the full text of our recommendation to the President regarding the objectives of a negotiation with the British. There could hardly have been a more full and timely disclosure to the leaders of Congress in an invitation to a bipartisan formulation of policy on a matter of outstanding importance. It is interesting to study the reaction of the congressional group, particularly of Vandenberg, the most articulate advocate of this procedure, toward this invitation, and the effect of the effort on the fate of the policy.

Vandenberg's opening attitude of histrionic opposition was his usual one —as I have pointed out before—to any proposal. It usually preceded embracing the proposal and making it his own with a Vandenberg amendment, which gave it saving grace; but not on this occasion. The United Kingdom, he argued, was much more dependent on us than we on her. We were constantly bailing her out and now proposed to do it again with our latest and most prized possession. The President patiently pointed out that the information we suggested giving was no more valuable to Britain than what we stood to get from her. Without any help from us, supporting voices volunteered, Britain was capable of producing atomic weapons. Moreover, we could prevent the waste of valuable raw material in clumsy production.

The answer to that, countered Vandenberg, was for us to become by agreement the sole producer of weapons and allocate some to Britain. I commented on the unrealistic nature of this proposal, which Vandenberg would see if he put himself in the position of a British Premier on the verge of producing his own atomic weapons and asked to give up the whole program and rely solely on the United States. Considering the on-again-off-again policy of the United States toward Britain since the Quebec agreement, a Prime Minister would be risking the continuance of his Government.

The Vice President, Speaker Rayburn, and Senator Connally spoke strongly in favor of the proposed negotiation before the *modus vivendi* expired. McMahon said that something should be done—but not what. Senator Vandenberg opposed the proposal, as he thought Britain should acknowledge our dominant position in the atomic field in view of our aid to her during and after the war and to avoid duplication of effort in the common defense; Senator Hickenlooper thought the proposal wrong on the grounds that it was contrary to the Atomic Energy Act of 1946 and that the raw-material situation was not serious enough to warrant giving away to the British our greatest heritage, particularly as he distrusted British security and feared the risk involved. The consensus was that a reversion to the *status quo ante* at the end of 1949 with the expiration of the *modus vivendi* would be most serious.

The meeting next took up the procedure to be followed and the form of any arrangement that might be made. A treaty, an agreement authorized by a joint resolution of Congress, or an executive agreement within the limits of the Atomic Energy Act of 1946 were all possibilities. I proposed meeting next with the full Joint Committee to get approval of our general position before any further step was taken. McMahon helpfully supported the view that informal discussions with the British and Canadians then be undertaken to discover what was possible before getting into a congressional wrangle about the precise form of arrangement. Any course was hazardous. All thought that if we could get congressional commitment to substance and move on to negotiations on this basis, leaving questions of form to be resolved later, we might avoid both a drumfire from Vandenberg and others that we were "bypassing Congress" and a civil war before we even started negotiations. In any event, we got some of both.

The hour was now growing late—ten-thirty—and the rain abating. The President dismissed us with an admonition to refrain from any comment to the reporters waiting outside. All questions were to be referred to his press officer, who was armed with innocuous replies. Alas! The press treated the official statement as only a spur to their sleuthing. Arthur Krock in *The New York Times* found the "melodramatic stage-setting" for the meeting the result of "naïveté and dormant imaginations." What was melodramatic about a meeting in the President's own house—rather than, perhaps, in the weekend camp in the Maryland hills—was not stated. The thunderstorm was not planned. Be that as it may, "the mysterious meeting" remained a mystery for only a matter of days until most congressional participants had given their versions and views. Senator McMahon reported to us that Vandenberg was much exercised over the Blair House meeting and had informed him that Senators Knowland and Millikin had presented their resignations from the Joint Atomic Energy Committee. McMahon had pointed out that this was a juvenile bit of stage-show. If they disapproved of the policy, the sensible course was to stay on the committee and oppose it. We were learning again—although we hardly needed to—what everyone in the executive branch since President Washington's day had learned, that to advise and consult with the Congress is next to impossible. One can learn its uninformed opinion or one can try to inform the opinion of a few key members by long, patient, secret talks, as Lovett had done with Vandenberg leading up to the Vandenberg Resolution of 1948; but to devise a joint approach to a complicated and delicate matter of foreign policy is not within the range of normally available time and people. Here the separation of powers really separates.

McMahon had offered to put off the meeting with the Joint Committee until the vote on ratification of the North Atlantic Treaty was out of the way. But given Vandenberg's vehemence in his talk with McMahon, I wanted to make sure the treaty did not get tied in with the atomic energy matter in a way probably harmful to both. So the meeting with the Joint Committee was arranged for the afternoon of July 20 on the home team's ground, Capitol Hill.

THE MEETING WITH THE JOINT COMMITTEE

We met, as *The New York Times* put it, "behind closed doors, and with window-blinds drawn," although none of us were under the illusion that security would be as tight as the room. Nearly the full committee attended: Senators McMahon, Connally, Vandenberg, Edwin Johnson of Colorado, Russell, Hickenlooper, and Knowland and Millikin (who had thought better of resigning), and Representatives Durham, Cole, Elston, Hinshaw, Holifield, and Jackson; Ernest Gross, Assistant Secretary for Congressional Relations, and Adrian Fisher, Legal Adviser, came with me. Secretary Johnson brought William Webster and General Eisenhower. The full Atomic Energy Commission appeared—Lilienthal, Pike, Smyth, Strauss, and Dean with Wilson and Volpe.

The meeting was a failure just short of a disaster. Vandenberg, Hickenlooper, Knowland, and Millikin attacked aggressively; our forces were shaken and I managed our side badly when the engagement became disorderly. The plan had been to repeat the points made at Blair House. But the Four Horsemen broke this up, disconcerting General Eisenhower with an attack on our whole position as a sellout to the British and a giveaway of invaluable secrets. These, in fact, the British had helped to develop, up to their final engineering features. Eisenhower had lost the fine evangelical fervor of the Blair House meeting, when he had portrayed the importance of Anglo-American solidarity, and retreated into a simple soldier unacquainted with complexities. Lilienthal's stout support was weakened when Strauss charged that he did not represent a unified commission since he (Strauss), who had been a minority of one, hoped to be joined by his two new colleagues, Gordon Dean and Henry Smyth.

Knowland, whose boiling point was low, blew up when I tried to get on with a more orderly procedure by stating what we proposed to do and how. The President, declared Knowland, should not even initiate talks with any government on atomic energy matters without first committing himself to obtaining the approval of Congress on the results, and unless the President conceded this publicly Knowland would denounce him in the Senate. I pointed out that the President was doing his best to consult the Congress on procedures and objectives. Other dissident senators asserted their "humiliation" at having to learn of the Blair House meeting through the newspapers. Apparently only a public address by the President to a joint session of Congress (or their inclusion in the meeting) would have met the proprieties. Senator Connally, voicing his disgust at his colleagues' behavior, left the meeting. Only Brien McMahon was reasonable and helpful throughout. The curtain fell on this disorderly performance when Louis Johnson neatly separated himself from me by suggesting that the Pentagon would have another look at the situation and, perhaps, have another suggestion to make.

The next day, after describing the shambles to the President, I asked for a few days to lick our wounds and investigate their depth before making a recommendation of what to do next. Louis Johnson and I made this on July 25: to accept a serious reverse and, in the language of military communiqués, "fall back and regroup." I asked to be authorized to say to the Joint Committee that the President believed, as he always had, that any action looking toward exchange of information regarding atomic energy to be successful should be preceded by agreement between the executive and legislative branches. This was what he had been seeking. He proposed to instruct me to endeavor to obtain from the British an extension of the present *modus vivendi*. He did not propose to make any other agreement at this time or to extend the areas of collaboration. I would in the course of my talks explore with the British and the Canadians the various problems discussed with the committee, not with a view to agreements or exchanges of information but to learn their attitudes and plans. We thought that this would cool off the hotheads in the Senate, get on with such controversial matters as the Military Assistance Program, and give us enough latitude to ease the atomic raw-materials situation and find out the problems of our allies for such future attention as might be possible.

The President agreed, and Johnson and I met again with the Joint Committee two days later. I made the statement, which Knowland said, as well he might, was a satisfactory *modus vivendi* between the legislative and executive branches. Hickenlooper still grumbled about my earlier statement, which he claimed had proposed illegal and unnecessary action. The committee wished the President to quiet the rumors they had started, which he did in a statement that reassured congressmen that he sought a "wide area of agreement between the executive and legislative branches," educated the public in the background of Anglo-American-Canadian cooperation, and announced that exploratory discussions on the basic questions would begin shortly.[2] His underlying purposes had not changed when I inquired in mid-August about my instructions. They were to go ahead with the talks with the British on the basis approved in March; when we knew more about what could and could not be done, we would chart a course through the congressional chambers and antechambers.

Under Secretary James Webb took over the negotiations with the British and Canadians, as I was overwhelmed with problems of military aid, NATO, German policy, and the devaluation of the pound sterling. On October 13, 1949, I reported again to the Joint Committee what had gone on in the tripartite discussions. Meanwhile an event of startling significance had taken place. The Russians had exploded an atomic device of their own and with it a good deal of the senatorial nonsense about our priceless secret heritage. The October meeting was much more sober and responsible than those in July. The Russians had anticipated all predictions by at least two years. I reported that an agreement was in sight on raw materials. For the present at least no shortage of materials confronted us even with the proposed accelerated program. Future relations, however, if collaboration was continued as authorized by the *modus vivendi,* would not be satisfactory. The definition of permissible and impermissible areas of exchange of information involved too much friction and uncertainty. The program would have to be scrapped altogether or considerably expanded. I was in favor of the latter, taking as a criterion the efficiency of the armament activities being carried on in the three countries, and also having in mind a sensible division of function and conservation of scarce materials.

This time there was neither shouting nor charges of selling out to the British. The Russians had been of some service in restoring our sense of reality. The committee approved our continuing the talks. Even Hickenlooper and Knowland conferred doubtful compliments on me for "keeping the faith." All this I reported to a pleased President. The press, referring to Hickenlooper as an "atomic isolationist,"[3] had anticipated that events would move us toward closer atomic relations with Britain and Canada. For the rest of the year the talks were reported as "jogging along comfortably." At its end the British made some far-reaching and sensible proposals, which agreed with our view that the main effort in atomic energy matters would be made in the United States with British scientists cooperating fully in the joint program. In particular, fabrication of atomic weapons would be concentrated on this side of the Atlantic with arrangements for a certain number to be allotted to the United Kingdom. Within this broad frame, differences still remained, but we were confident that they could be overcome.

Then a bomb exploded in London. A British scientist—Klaus Fuchs, who had been in this country working on the Manhattan Project during the war— was arrested on February 2, 1950, in England and charged with passing on to the Russians information he had acquired then and later. In due course, he was tried and convicted. Also in February, Senator McCarthy began his attacks on the State Department. The talks with the British and Canadians returned to square one, where there was a deep freezer from which they did not emerge in my time.

Ambassador Sir Oliver Franks and I by an exchange of letters in April agreed on an "interim allocation" of raw materials, a procedure that was continued by the two governments throughout President Truman's administration. A month later in London, invited to Ernest Bevin's apartment at No. 1 Carlton Gardens, I was surprised to find there Prime Minister Attlee, Lester B. Pearson of Canada, Roger Makins, and Patrick Gordon-Walker, Parliamentary Under Secretary of State for Commonwealth Relations. Attlee wanted to know whether there was any way of reviving the talks that had been interrupted by the Fuchs affair. The British Government must get on with their program, which had been held up while their proposals were being considered. I said regretfully that the effort I had tried so hard to pilot into safe waters had foundered and I doubted that it could be raised again. It was a casualty of the cold war. I would try but suspected it was beyond help.

From time to time efforts within the Administration to renew discussions ended with Louis Johnson's veto, apparently in the belief that amendment of the Atomic Energy Act of 1946 was required before anything else could be done. In fact, the only limitation we had accepted on the President's powers was that no final action, in whatever form deemed desirable, would be taken without congressional approval. This might carry with it amendment of the act. After Secretary Johnson left the Defense Department, there was a resurgence of interest in the idea of a joint program but in the end it came to nothing.

The British asked us in 1951 to test an atomic bomb for them. But even here we were held back by the need for congressional approval. So many restrictions had to be placed on the access of British scientists to the information to be gotten from the tests and on the mode of procedure that they had a change of heart and decided to test their own bomb, which they did in October 1952 in Australia.

36. DEVALUATION OF THE POUND

"THE BRITISH ARE COMING!"

IN JULY 1949 John Snyder, Secretary of the Treasury, met Douglas Abbott, the Canadian Finance Minister, in London. There both were informed by Sir Stafford Cripps, Chancellor of the Exchequer, that the British financial situation was precarious indeed. British monetary reserves of gold and dollars were low and getting lower, although Britain appeared to be enjoying an industrial boom with full employment and high prices. Indeed, this prosperity was, quite paradoxically, a cause of the trouble. Countries of what was called the sterling area deposited their reserves in London. Since pounds sterling were not freely convertible into hard currencies, principally dollars, these depositors, when they wished to make purchases, which they were eager to do for their own internal development, found it easier to make them in Britain or other countries of the sterling area. This situation, in effect, gave Britain a protected market at higher prices than would be competitive in the United States, so that she was paying her depositors with exports and using up her reserves to buy raw materials and food. This was almost a sure route to bankruptcy.

Sir Stafford wanted to talk about what should be done. John Snyder interpreted this as a euphemism for help and got out of the country as fast as possible, with the suggestion that talks be held in Washington at the time of the International Bank and Fund meeting in September. He flew back like a modern Paul Revere crying "The British are coming!" And come they did to create a situation of great complexity and embarrassment. Sometime before, it had been decided to take advantage of the presence of the finance ministers in Washington to get the foreign and defense ministers of North Atlantic Treaty countries there also so that a start could be made on treaty organization and plans in their diplomatic, military, and financial aspects. To all of these was added the unplanned influx of foreign diplomats coming to the United States for the fourth meeting of the General Assembly of the United Nations. In the midst of this considerable and busy international gathering, we now proposed to add Anglo-American-Canadian discussions of great delicacy and secrecy.

These talks began on September 7. On the day before, John Snyder and I spent an hour and a half in executive session with a nervous Senate Foreign Relations Committee, which feared that we might commit the United States to new obligations. Snyder, at any rate, had no intention of even considering this. When we came out of that meeting, he told the press that we had no plan for the coming meeting, though we were "hopefully determined to help promote the solution of Britain's external financial crisis." John and I had at the time different attitudes toward Britain's troubles. He was very wary about becoming involved in them, while to me it seemed both impossible and undesirable to avoid involvement. I saw them as part and parcel of larger problems that deeply concerned our interests and could be managed only under our leadership and with British association. This is perhaps as good a place as any for a digression that this observation suggests.

ANGLO-AMERICAN RELATIONS

The British Ambassador in Washington at this time was Sir Oliver Franks, one of the most able—and also most delightful—men it has ever been my good fortune to know and work with. His mind applied to any subject soon mastered it and he carried into each new field the same calm good judgment. Starting upon an academic career, he became professor of moral philosophy at Glasgow University, then moved to Oxford, where he was Master of Queens College. The war took him to a high position in the British Ministry of Supply, working at the heart of Britain's economic and production problems. I met him at that time in planning supplies for UNRRA's relief work. That others shared my admiration for this remarkable man is attested by Ernest Bevin's choice of him to head Britain's most important diplomatic post, his later service as President of Lloyds Bank in the City of London, and the fact, so well-supported rumor has it, that he was sought to head the Bank of England, the British Broadcasting Corporation, and *The Times* of London. He chose to return to his first choice, academic life, and became Provost of Worcester College, Oxford.

Not long after becoming Secretary of State, I made him an unorthodox proposal. On an experimental basis I suggested that we talk regularly, and in complete personal confidence, about any international problems we saw arising. Neither would report or quote the other unless, thinking that it would be useful in promoting action, he got the other's consent and agreement on the terms of a reporting memorandum or cable. The dangers and difficulties of such a relationship were obvious, but its usefulness proved to be so great that we continued it for four years. We met alone, usually at his residence or mine, at the end of the day before or after dinner. No one was informed even of the fact of the meeting. We discussed situations already emerging or likely to do so, the attitudes that various people in both countries would be likely to take, what courses of action were possible and their merits, the chief problems that could arise. If either thought that his department should be alerted to the other's apprehension and thoughts, we would work out an acceptable text setting out the problem and suggested approaches.

Later, comparing the relations between our governments during our time with those under our successors, we concluded that whereas we had thought of these relations and their management as a part of domestic affairs, they had regarded them as foreign affairs. The heart of the difference lay in the intimacy, the secrecy, and the complete confidence of Sir Oliver's and my relationship during the consultative period. Once a matter got into the flow of Foreign Office or departmental business, each organization had its special problem. With the Foreign Office it was the Commonwealth; with the Department, the Congress. Once either organization knew that even the most exploratory discussion was going on, the pressure for disclosure—consultation—was enormous for fear of the reproaches of senators and prime ministers if either learned of anything before the other. To inform either was to inform the press. From there on it was literally impossible to hear oneself think. For this reason, my relationship with Sir Oliver Franks was a great help and comfort to me.

FUTILE MEETINGS

One can readily imagine the quandary of Ernest Bevin and Sir Stafford Cripps when they arrived in Washington on September 5 with the secret authority of the British Government to take up with the International Monetary Fund the devaluation of the pound sterling from $4.03 to $2.80. They could not discuss this until it was done, and without knowledge of this central fact discussion of Britain's economic crisis was futile. Furthermore, discussion of currency matters had been excluded from the agenda of the American-British-Canadian meeting, since they fell within the jurisdiction of the Fund, about to convene in annual meeting.

The conferees, with Treasury Secretary Snyder presiding, consisted of Paul Hoffman, Administrator of the Economic Cooperation Administration, and myself for the United States; Bevin, Cripps, and Franks for Britain; and Lester Pearson, Minister of External Affairs, Douglas Abbott, Finance Minister, and Ambassador Hume Wrong for Canada. We all had too many staff assistants crowded around the walls of a too-small conference room in the new State Department building.

The first few days of the meeting were everything a conference should not be, and too many are—a complete waste of time with rising exasperation among the conferees. Hoffman announced that the European Recovery Program would be completed in 1952 and that the European countries should plan to have their balance-of-payments problems solved by then. The American delegation turned down a British request to waive Article 9 of the British-U.S. Loan Agreement of 1945–46, prohibiting discrimination against United States exports, in an effort to lessen the outflow of dollars. Then Paul Hoffman, who had an evangelical delivery and faith in salvation by exports, exhorted the British to forgo the easy markets of the sterling area, cut their costs—which obviously included wages and some of the welfare state—and earn dollars by exporting to the American market.

This was too much for Ernie Bevin, who won my admiration by departing from the scenario, much to his colleagues' confusion, and having a go at this economic ecumenicism. He had been interested, he said, for many years in British industry and several times he had heard free traders urge the British workers to make the sacrifices necessary to compete in the great American market. Every time, as soon as they made a little progress, the Congress set up a howl about cheap foreign labor and raised the tariff to new heights, the last time in 1930. He was not going home to flimflam the workers again. Mr. Hull had done a fine job, but imports during the Depression and the war had not been a big factor in the American market. Would we guarantee that if Europe sought to balance its payments by exports to the United States, Congress would let them come in? There was a good deal of sense in this and plenty of vigor. "Even the ranks of Tuscany could scarce forbear to cheer."

THE POINT FINALLY IS REACHED

However, this polemical exchange did convince the British that at least the principal American and Canadian representatives must be told what was going to happen. We were asked to meet with only ministers present, no ambassadors, staff, or note takers. This meant Cripps, Bevin, Pearson, Abbott, Snyder, Hoffman, and myself. When the door was shut, we were told of the forthcoming devaluation and pledged to secrecy, except that we Americans insisted, and the others agreed, that the President must also be told. The result was a nervous week, during which each of us worried that the news would leak and an accusing finger point at him. All went well and only French-British relations suffered when the devaluation was announced on Sunday, September 18, without prior notice to the French ministers who were present in Washington.

Once we knew the facts, our meeting got down to the business of improving the British economic position. A permanent Economic Council of the three countries was established; Sir Leslie Rowan, a senior Treasury man, was assigned to it; and sound resolutions were adopted.[1] But none of this amounted to very much due to an improvement in the economic atmosphere as quick and unexpected as the previous mild depression had been. In this situation the devaluation was more effective than any of us had thought it would be. The spring recession in this country had reduced our imports about twelve per cent in general, though twenty per cent from the Marshall Plan countries and nearly twice that in some raw-material-producing, sterling-area countries. This recession proved to be short-lived; our recovery and cheaper sterling prices increased our buying. This, when the Korean war started in the middle of the next year, created problems through its excesses.

Before recovery had started, however, we talked among ourselves about Britain's still-unsolved basic dilemma, a British politician's nightmare. This was to tell the workers and voters (and still hope to stay in office) that they must work harder and get paid less—for a time, at least—and, at the same time, tell the Commonwealth that their sterling deposits were really long-term investments and not available in cash or goods on demand. It seemed to us that, before the fundamental weakness of the British financial situation could be cured, there must be some refunding of the sterling balances and, with outside help, some reform of the British role as international banker and its incorporation in a larger and more inherently solvent arrangement. But this was something that one could not usefully discuss with the British except in time of crisis, and the recovery in 1950 ended that. The problem, however, still remains and darkens the entrance to the Common Market.

With Bevin and Schuman • An account of the next week or so is, perhaps, useful more to describe the environment in which a Secretary of State must do such thinking as he can rather than as a record of accomplishment. It was spent in almost continuous discussion with colleagues from abroad on the problems presented by almost every part of the world. First, starting on September 13, with Bevin and Schuman, sometimes separately and sometimes together as they preferred, the talk covered Europe, the Mediterranean, and the Far East. In Europe events had moved fast. On September 7 the Bundestag (the lower house) of the Federal Republic opened at Bonn. On the twelfth Theodor Heuss, a white-haired, kindly professor, had been elected President, and on the fifteenth Dr. Konrad Adenauer of the Christian Democratic Union, Chancellor of the Federal Republic. On the twenty-first civil government began in Germany with the proclamation of the Occupation Statute and the establishment of the Allied High Commission. The Bundestag on the very day it opened its session asked the occupying powers to re-examine their policy of dismantling German industry for reparations. As the supplier of materials for European recovery we were strongly in favor of the requested re-examination; the French opposed it; the British were in the middle, since at home they favored dismantling, while in Germany their zone, a highly industrialized area, was approaching the point where further dismantling would have to be done under military protection.

We met, therefore, on September 15 to discuss as our first business with the new German state an issue which bade fair to split us apart. We each took the position that might have been expected. Bevin worried aloud. The Americans, he said, luckily and quickly had finished their dismantling. The British had not, and were caught between one public opinion at home and an opposite one in Germany. Schuman urged us not to get excited by the Bundestag action and thereby let "the Germans dismantle Western solidarity." Bevin agreed on the importance of showing the Germans that the game of splitting the allies would not work. I argued that it would work, that dismantling and Marshall aid were obviously inconsistent, and that eventually we would and must yield on dismantling, but—if we followed his and Schuman's advice—only after having generated the maximum ill will. This would do vast harm to long-range solution of Franco-German enmity, which must be the aim of French leadership. Bevin pleaded for more time. After several repetitions of these views it was agreed to meet again in November in Paris and dispose of the issue then.

Austria came next on the agenda. Anticipating French and British emphasis on getting Russian troops out of Austria at almost any cost, we had had prepared some economic charts showing that a viable Austria could not be achieved if we yielded on any of our major positions. We had Sam Reber, our deputy on the Austrian treaty, present the Russian position, as the deputies had heard it, and his own view that even excessive concessions would not result in a treaty under existing circumstances. Hopes which had briefly risen during the spring meetings in Paris were now dead; but to leave nothing to chance, we agreed to ask Vishinsky for an informal meeting in New York to explore the possibilities.

When he met us on September 22 our fears were verified. He was at his worst, charging us with trying to inveigle him into an illegal meeting of the Council of Foreign Ministers. I went over a series of points that had been agreed in principle at Paris to be worked out in detail by the deputies and complained that the Russian deputy would either refuse to discuss a point or flatly repudiate the agreement. On some matters he had taken positions so unreasonable as to raise questions of good faith. Three futile meetings were held between September 26 and 29. Then Vishinsky broke them off until October 6 on the ground that he was too busy at the United Nations. The State Department advised me, and my colleagues, of its view that the Soviet Union wished to keep its troops in Austria due to troubles in Hungary and Rumania and was taking a more belligerent attitude as a result of its atomic explosion, the economic difficulties in the West, and the triumph of the Communists in China. In a private talk with Bevin and in another meeting with all of us on October 6, Vishinsky refused to yield an inch on any matter of substance. I reported this to the President, suggesting that the National Security Council review the serious questions presented and that congressional leaders be consulted early enough to participate in any decisions that might be necessary, but not at a time when public discussion might affect the imminent Austrian elections. He agreed, and discussions of an Austrian treaty hibernated until 1955, when the Soviet Union suddenly signed it as part of a campaign to prevent the German Federal Republic from joining the North Atlantic Alliance.

From Austria the talks with Bevin and Schuman touched briefly on Yugoslavia, agreeing that the interests of all three countries coincided in supporting Tito in his break with Stalin. "Tito may be a scoundrel," said Bevin, "but he's our scoundrel"—a view which Tito would not have shared on either count. Then we turned to the Far East, where Bevin was chiefly interested in China, Schuman in Indochina. Each discussed his special interest with me separately, and then together we discussed China.

Schuman trod warily in discussing Southeast Asia, and had no welcoming response to American interest. France, he said, at great expense was fighting the battle of all democratic peoples in Indochina. The United States could help by giving economic aid to the three "infant governments"—Vietnam, Laos, and Cambodia. They could not cope by themselves. The French were sponsoring their movement toward greater independence. French army and technical advisors were indispensable to the development of functioning and truly independent native governments. I said that I was glad to hear this. We believed that France could help more in preventing Communist domination by moving quickly to satisfy nationalist aspirations. Giving the three states established by the March 8 agreements—which will be discussed in Chapter 70—greater independence in foreign affairs (then administered by the French Ministry of Overseas Affairs) would encourage Asian governments to recognize and deal with them. But first the French Parliament must ratify these agreements. Schuman recognized these as valid points, but without noticeable enthusiasm.

He had little to say about China, but not so Bevin. He had listened restlessly during one meeting while I expounded the rather negative conclusions we had reached from our recent painful experiences. In brief, these were that Chiang Kai-shek and the Kuomintang were no longer an effective force on the mainland, where the Nationalist Government under Li Tsung-jen was about to collapse. No other leaders were apparent for the time being. Nor had friction yet developed between Mao and Stalin, though we believed that it would do so. Recognition seemed to us a futile gesture and would doubtless mean as little to the Chinese Communists as to us, while worrying other Asian states. The result indicated was to await a more propitious time for action of any sort that trouble in China or between China and Russia might bring. In the meantime, I hoped that the North Atlantic Treaty countries would concert their policies and that we would all impose controls on trade with Communist China.

Bevin would have to talk this over at home. Our interests in China, he thought, were divergent; the task was to reconcile our policies so far as possible. The United States Government was withdrawing; the United Kingdom, trying to hold on, to "keep a foot in the door and see what happens." The British were not in a hurry to recognize the Communists (this attitude soon changed), but they did have big commercial and trade interests in China and they intended "to hang on in Hong Kong and stay there." He feared that if the United States was too obdurate we would drive China into the arms of Russia. To which I added that they were there already. We agreed to keep on consulting.

With Other European Colleagues • Count Sforza of Italy and Foreign Ministers van Zeeland of Belgium and Dr. Caeiro da Matta of Portugal brought me matters of special concern to them but, after twenty years, no longer of any general interest. Then we all convened in the first session of the North Atlantic Council.

Count Sforza was a man of character and ability and had been a guest in my parents' house when, an exile from Mussolini's Italy, he had lectured at Wesleyan University. It could be said of him, as it has said of Balliol men, that he had a consciousness of effortless superiority. On one occasion he told me that his position of independence in Premier de Gasperi's cabinet was due to the fact that the other members were all Catholics. "But Count Sforza," I interjected, "you are a Catholic, too?"

"To be sure," he replied, "but the Sforzas were Catholics before there were popes." When I told this to another friend, an Italian Ambassador to the United States, he said, "Bah! He did not belong to those Sforzas at all."

Dr. Caeiro da Matta, a former professor of international law and a most courteous and delightful man, seemed to believe—perhaps due to his training —that his duty was done and his function performed when he had carefully and meticulously explained his point. How it was received did not seem to be of concern to him at all. He recalled to me a sentence at the beginning of Ann

Bridge's excellent book, *Peking Picnic*. "He was the sort of diplomat," she wrote, "who cabled home, 'Today I repeated to His Excellency what I had said to him last week.' "

At the first session of the NATO Council on September 17 we did not repeat lengthy sentiments expressed at the treaty's signing. I was elected the first chairman of the council. On the first of each succeeding year the chairmanship was to rotate in the alphabetical order, in English, of the signatory states. We then adopted a table of organization for the council: a Defense Committee; a Military Committee to sit permanently in Washington, with its executive agency, the Standing Group, consisting of military representatives of Britain, France, and the United States; and Regional Planning Groups for five regions of the North Atlantic area, together with the terms of reference of all these committees and groups. The council foresaw the need for means of dealing also with two other sets of problems relating to the defense of the area, questions of military production and supply, and economic and financial factors. It directed working groups to prepare recommendations for consideration at the second session of the council.

It is rather interesting to note that the organization then adopted was almost exactly the organization for executing the treaty which General de Gaulle would approve today—if one may be so bold as to hazard a prediction about the views of that unpredictable man. It was pre-integration organization, aimed to produce general plans for uncoordinated and separate action in the hope that in the event of trouble a plan and the forces to meet it would exist and would be adopted by a sort of spontaneous combustion. In less than a year it would be the French Govermnent which would take the lead in proclaiming this organization hopelessly inadequate and in pressing for a united command, forces in being and in position, and strategic plans for the use of all the weapons of the alliance. This produced NATO's integrated defense, that acme of deterrence that the General has done his best to destroy.

37. MORE MEETINGS AT HOME
AND ABROAD

THE FIRST HALF OF September had been busy enough with its incessant meetings to the accompaniment of the congressional guns of August, still booming away against the military assistance bill. Two major speeches in New York and the opening of the session of the General Assembly of the United Nations would make the second half no less so, against the even more ominous background of the more deadly Russian explosion.

Within two days, on September 19 and 21, I addressed both a Latin American gathering and the General Assembly of the United Nations. Both were ritualistic speeches. Every new Secretary of State must make a speech on Latin American affairs (mine was overdue) and every Secretary of State must each year participate in that utter futility, the "general debate," with which each session of the General Assembly wastes its opening weeks.

ON LATIN AMERICA "NOTHING NEW"

The first of these efforts was made in New York at a dinner of the Pan American Society of the United States.[1] I touched on all the familiar topics, within the conventional limitations of policy statements, leading off with the need for political stability and faith in democracy. Here the background of fact was grim. Perón's dictatorship then seemed established in Argentina with the support of the Army and the General Confederation of Labor. Military coups had recently been successful in Peru and Venezuela, and there had been a right-wing insurrection in Bolivia. The presidential election in Colombia would soon be held under "siege conditions," while plot and counterplot between the Nicaraguan and Dominican dictatorships and their armed exiles disturbed the Caribbean.

Under these conditions I pledged "our strongest efforts" to preserve the peace of the hemisphere, "in keeping with our international commitments." These commitments were to protect security, defend democracy, and refrain from intervention in the internal affairs of other American nations, a prescription, it might seem, for inaction (generally favored by the Good Neighbors) or sacrifice of one of our purposes or principles in pursuing others.

Regarding the recognition of governments which followed one another in the hemisphere, I repeated the familiar doctrine that recognition did not signify approval and should involve inter-American consultation and the application of accepted rules. (Schuman and Bevin might have pointed out that this was not altogether the same attitude we were taking toward recognition of the Communist regime in China.) Economic well-being, we had found, did not guarantee that democracy would flourish, but it helped. We therefore had aided and would continue to aid economic development among our neighbors. The Institute of Inter-American Affairs had, indeed, I said, "furnished the inspiration and the proving ground for the woild-wide program of technical cooperation envisaged in Point Four of President Truman's inaugural address." While these government-to-government efforts, enlarged and strengthened, would continue, they would be ineffective without strenuous self-help by the nations themselves in attacking endemic poverty and illiteracy and in creating an environment of fair treatment for foreign capital. This also was established doctrine. "If I have said nothing new tonight," I concluded, "it may well be because in a family of nations, as in families of individuals, we should expect nothing more sensational than growth."

UN PROBLEMS STILL REMAIN

The only interest remaining today in the speech to the General Assembly, a statement of United States policy on problems confronting the fourth General Assembly,[2] is that most of the problems still remain, some are decidedly worse, and on one the United Nations has given up entirely. The list began with Greece's internal trouble growing out of her historic difficulty in reconciling order with democracy and the involvement of her neighbors in that trouble. The identity of the nations involved has changed, but the trouble continues. On Palestine, the next problem area, I observed, perhaps somewhat prematurely, that "it is a source of considerable satisfaction that the period of active hostilities in that area has been brought to a close through the conclusion of armistice agreements between Israel and the several Arab states." The question of the disposition of the former Italian colonies, on which the signatories of the Italian peace treaty agreed to accept the recommendation of the General Assembly, was, after one failure, in due course answered by the Assembly's recommendation.

Turning to the problems of non-self-governing peoples, of which those of the people of Indonesia were in the forefront, I hopefully announced United States support to "those peoples who are working out their destinies in the spirit of the Charter of the United Nations to the end that they may achieve self-government or independence at the earliest practicable date." After twenty years' experience one would, perhaps, be less sure that independence was an end, rather than a beginning—as Indonesia was to demonstrate—of new troubles as tragic and bloody as any experienced in the past. Another group of problems noted were those involving, in the words of the Charter, "better standards of life in larger freedom." In the struggle against poverty, malnutrition, and disease the incredible fertility of the human species seems over the years to have submerged all our efforts. The search for security through the United Nations, through regional defense arrangements, and through attempts to regulate armaments seems even more baffling today than it was when it appeared to be the supreme problem of two decades ago. In fact, while I was regretting failure to persuade the Soviet Union to join in international control of atomic energy, the President was preparing to announce the Soviet atomic explosion, which made the nuclear problem even more intractable.

Fortunately, we see through a glass darkly. That made it easier to go back to Washington to struggle with all these problems against growing criticism of the executive's handling of our foreign relations. I was not detached enough at the time to realize that much of this criticism came from what wise men from Aeschylus to St. Paul have described as man's folly in kicking against the pricks.

RELATIONS WITH YUGOSLAVIA

Throughout my tenure as Secretary relations with Yugoslavia remained under my personal direction, because of the delicacy and difficulty of the relationship at both ends, Tito's and ours. The break between Stalin and Tito had occurred while I was absent from the Government. On June 28, 1948, growing resistance in Belgrade to dictatorship from Moscow had resulted in Yugoslavia's expulsion from the Cominform, the organization of Communist states, and a heavy Soviet barrage directed at Tito's deviationism. This happened during the blockade of Berlin and four days after the start of the airlift, when any trouble coming to Moscow was a boon to the Western allies. George Kennan's Policy Planning Staff immediately recognized the importance of this break within the Soviet monolith as the awakening of national independence and self-interest. Kennan counseled discreet and unostentatious support. Stalin was obviously determined to crush this rebellion by political, economic, and, if opportunity afforded, military measures. Our policy should be to thwart him without provoking him in the process.

To accomplish this policy meant overcoming or circumventing difficulties in Belgrade and Washington. Although Tito's challenge to Stalin's headship of international communism provided a strong inhibiting factor on Soviet actions in the international field and should be maintained, it would be bad politics and bad morals to represent him as an ally of the West. He was and would long remain a staunch Communist and the dictator of a police state. To represent him otherwise would injure both him and us. This honest attitude, however, raised difficulties in Congress, where Communists belonged to a genus without subordinate species. Two of my otherwise strong friends and supporters took this view and caused us some trouble, Congresswoman Edna Kelly (Democrat of Brooklyn), a member of the Foreign Affairs Committee who herself had Yugoslav antecedents, and Senator Tom Connally, Chairman of the Foreign Relations Committee. In the executive branch, however, the importance of supporting Tito was held unanimously in the field, the Department, and the White House.

Economic aid was inaugurated in the summer of 1949 with the granting of an export license to Yugoslavia for a steel-finishing mill and a twenty-million-dollar loan by the Export-Import Bank. In the autumn we gave success-ful political support in the United Nations to Yugoslavia's bid for a seat on the Security Council and to her approaches to the World Bank and to the Germans for development loans. At the end of the year the President appointed an ex-perienced career diplomat, George V. Allen, as Ambassador to Yugoslavia and authorized him to quote the President as saying that our support of the sov-ereign integrity of independent states applied as fully to Yugoslavia as to any other state. We also concerted with London steps to be taken in furnishing political and arms assistance should Stalin's growls develop into more articulate threats.

Nature took a hand in this drama by bringing on a severe drought in Yugoslavia during the summer of 1950. Edward Kardelj, their very capable Foreign Minister, came to Washington asking for extensive loans and grants. The drought had not only caused food shortages in the country but dried up exports that otherwise would have financed development projects. At the time we talked—October 19, 1950—we were having real trouble in Congress over military aid, China policy, and McCarthyism. I warned Kardelj that we could not take on a major Yugoslav financial program because of the ideological problems it would raise for him and us, but must muddle through with bits and pieces for the time being and such help as we could inspire in Europe. The result was not too bad. From the Marshall Plan authority (ECA) and Export-Import Bank we got together something over thirty million dollars for wheat and induced Congress to switch fifty million dollars previously appropriated for ECA to relief for Yugoslavia.

The collection of odds and ends went on until by August 1951 we had been able to give a hundred fifty million dollars in economic aid. Then Ambas-sador Popovic asked for arms, as the rumors of Soviet military intervention grew and tension increased. Military aid was difficult enough to get in all con-science, in view of the declarations of democratic faith and explanations of need that Congress had scattered like hurdles along the approaches. Popovic had been one of Tito's chief guerrilla lieutenants, an immense man who would be bad to meet in the dark on a mountain path. He was inaudible, whispering in some unidentifiable language. Since his interpreter read from a paper what Popovic was alleged to have said, I often wondered whether he had bothered to say it. What came out were the items and quantities of military equipment for which he asked and great reluctance to go far into such matters as existing stocks of these materials or any discussion of the type of campaign anticipated or where it might be conducted. This sort of thing was the lifeblood of Penta-gon bureaucrats. My view was that the Yugoslavs were wise to be reticent, that they knew best what they needed and would put it to good use if we could spare it—and that the last was the only real question. In the end we gave them about sixty million dollars in military items in 1951 and a little more the next years. It carried Tito through his troubles.

This excursion in aid to a Communist state nearly proved fatal to a good friend to our foreign policy in the Congress, James P. Richards of South Caro-lina, Chairman of the Committee on Foreign Affairs. Like many southern congressmen, Richards had built up seniority by his safe seat until he reached the top of the Democratic list on the committee and the chairmanship. In the process he had acquired an interest and competence in foreign affairs and had neglected his district's interest in the pork barrel. A young challenger in the primary in 1950 drew unfavorable comparison between Richards' record in obtaining federal buildings and works for the district and his zeal in helping some people called Yugoslavs, whose relation to South Carolina he challenged Mr. Richards to establish. Nor was this all; perhaps Mr. Richards would like to go further and explain who these people were and what sort of folks. The primary proved to be a close call for the chairman and a dampener upon his enthusiasm for the foreign field.

A VISIT FROM PANDIT NEHRU

Before keeping my date in Paris with Schuman and Bevin to discuss dismantling in Germany, another politico-social date faced us in Washington, a state visit by Prime Minister Nehru of India. He came in a prickly mood, annoyed by what he called "American intervention" in the Kashmir dispute. This grew out of the efforts of the United Nations Commission for India and Pakistan, of which the United States was a member, to arrange a truce in the hostilities between these two countries in Kashmir. Previous proposals having failed, the commission suggested the arbitration of certain issues by Admiral Chester W. Nimitz, who had been designated plebiscite administrator. President Truman wrote to both prime ministers urging agreement to the commission's suggestion. Nehru rejected it.

The great man arrived on October 11. The social protocol for state visits was and is a trial for the hardiest spirit, consisting of three large dinners (in addition to wreath-laying, speeches to Congress, etc.), given by the President for the Visitor at the White House; by the Secretary of State for the Visitor, in those days usually at Anderson House on Massachusetts Avenue; and finally by the Visitor at his nation's embassy for the President. The guest list with minor variations was the same for all; so was the food, drink, and incidental music; so were the speeches. Not merely for all three of a series, but for all such dinners.

I determined to vary the monotony of my evening in two ways, neither of which proved much of a success with Pandit Nehru. The first was in my after-dinner speech. Liturgically these speeches were supposed to deal with "the close and fruitful relations between our two countries" throughout history. One dinner would clearly exhaust this subject, and I did not feel equal to exploring the influence of the Code of Hammurabi upon Anglo-American-Indian jurisprudence. So I tried a novel gambit, improvising imaginary conversations between the legendary great of America and our Visitor to bring out his many-faceted quality. He would, as a father of his country, talk with the father of ours, General George Washington; as a great political ideologist of democracy, with Thomas Jefferson; as a tough political organizer and strategist, with Old Hickory; and as a spiritual leader who had suffered amid fratricidal strife, with the Great Emancipator. The result was very definitely a change from the routine and caught our distinguished Visitor unprepared, like a student who had not done his homework for what should have been a "gut-course." He was not pleased.

The other innovation also failed in its purpose. After the post-dinner reception he and I left for my house to have a purely private talk, leaving my wife and his daughter, Mme. Indira Gandhi, later Prime Minister of India, in charge at Anderson House. I had hoped that, uninhibited by a cloud of witnesses, we might establish a personal relationship. But he would not relax. He talked to me, as Queen Victoria said of Mr. Gladstone, as though I were a public meeting. Beginning with his desire to establish a stockpile of a million tons of wheat, he told me of his plan to reduce the price of wheat in relation to other prices in India. He hoped for help from us in selling them wheat at less than world prices. We were already at work on the problem, which I told him would require legislation, and hoped to have favorable action shortly.

Nehru on the Faults of Others • He had had a telegram, he said, from Hatta, the Indonesian leader, complaining that the Dutch wished them to assume too large a part of the Dutch Indies governmental debt largely incurred in fighting the independence movement. The Dutch should not "drag their feet until concessions lost all their grace." In agreeing, I cited Edmund Burke that "not the least of the arts of diplomacy is to grant graciously what one no longer has the power to withhold." We had already gotten the Dutch back up by our Ambassador Merle Cochran's sound and well-meant advice, but we would try again.

Pandit Nehru also found the French experiment in Indochina with Bao Dai hopeless and doomed to failure as the "Emperor" lacked the character, ability, and prestige necessary to succeed and was not given adequate scope by the French. I was inclined to agree but expressed doubt about any visible alternative. Nehru saw it in the nationalist movement, although he was convinced that Ho Chi Minh was a Communist. However, to believe that the Communists would use a popular-front government to liquidate their opponents was, he thought, to misapply Eastern European experience to Asian countries. In India and Burma, Communists had begun as the left wing of the nationalist movement, then attempted to take over the movement and failed. This, he hoped, would be repeated in Indochina. To me this was a clearly specious idea, since, as the experience of both France and Italy showed, the attempt to take over would be inevitable and the outcome would depend on the strength of the other side. With the leadership of the nationalist movement already in Ho's hands, the outcome in Indochina would seem pretty clear.

Thus far Nehru had kept the talk on the failings of the Dutch and French. I wanted, as innocently as possible, to get him to talk about one of his own. First of all, however, he went off on recognition of the Communist regime in China, where his views were of some interest because they obviously stimulated Bevin's. Bevin was not likely to let India take the lead in setting a recognition policy for the Commonwealth. Nehru's views, which he also expressed the next day in his meeting with the President, were that there was now no alternative to the Communists in China, since the Kuomintang had completely failed to handle the agricultural revolution. But communism as a doctrine was alien to the Chinese mind, and the foreign domination inherent in Moscow's role among Communist states would be deeply resented in China. India's proximity to China "indicated a leaning toward early recognition." The President hoped, as I had, that countries deeply concerned in Asian affairs would consult before recognizing. Although the Prime Minister agreed, I felt that we had had our consultation.

Nehru on Kashmir • When, finally, I urged Pandit Nehru to help me by a frank discussion of a practicable solution of the trouble over Kashmir, I got a curious combination of a public speech and flashes of anger and deep dislike of his opponents. The first part of it was a legalistic exposition that the first hostile act, and hence the aggression, was Pakistan's. From this it followed that India could not, and the United Nations should not, proceed with the merits of the problem until the aggression had been purged by the complete withdrawal of all Pakistani and tribesmen from Kashmir. This was interspersed with bitter denunciation of Pakistan deception and intrigue. Both Nehru's ideas of procedure, which seemed to preclude negotiation, and his notions on the dispute itself made any possibility of settlement dim indeed. A profound ideological issue, he said, was presented. Pakistan conceived of the foundation of its state as religious and claimed Kashmir because its inhabitants were largely Moslems. Such ideas, Nehru insisted, struck at the very basis of stability in the Indian subcontinent. In India the state was wholly secular. Religion was neither a qualification nor disqualification for citizenship; it was irrelevant. There were some thirty-five million Moslems in India, many in high office. To accept a religious basis for the adherence of provinces to either state would be profoundly unsettling everywhere, and a plebiscite campaign on such a basis would be most inflammatory and disastrous.

The conclusion of the matter, as the Prime Minister saw it, was that Pakistan as a state had no claim to Kashmir or any part of it, and its troops (but not India's) must be forced to withdraw. If the people of Kashmir wished to question the decision of the Maharajah and Sheikh Abdullah, the de facto Prime Minister, to adhere to India—which Nehru doubted—the preferable way to ascertain their will would be through a "constituent assembly of the natural leaders of the people elected to meet and discuss their future." This might lead to a countrywide decision or to a division.

By this time, having talked from ten-thirty to past one o'clock in the morning after a strenuous day, my guest had clearly earned a rest. For my part, I was becoming a bit confused. We therefore adjourned this interesting talk. It made a deep impression on me. I was convinced that Nehru and I were not destined to have a pleasant personal relationship. He was so important to India and India's survival so important to all of us, that if he did not exist—as Voltaire said of God—he would have to be invented. Nevertheless, he was one of the most difficult men with whom I have ever had to deal.

THE PARIS CONFERENCE

Bevin and I joined our colleague, Robert Schuman, in Paris on November 9. Again the President came to see us off. On this journey John Sherman Cooper of Kentucky went along as my Republican adviser. John had a long struggle to get established as Senator from Kentucky. Elected in 1946 and again in 1952 (both Republican years) to fill unexpired terms, in each case he met defeat two years later. Finally in 1956, elected for the third time to fill an unexpired term (this time Alben Barkley's), he was able to hang on to the seat. John was and is wise and delightful. No one could wish for a sounder adviser, better companion, or more loyal friend. His relaxed manner and gentle humor are authentically Kentuckian. He tells on himself of being stopped by a traffic policeman for some unrealized infraction while driving through Atlanta. The officer came over to the car.

"Stranger, aren't you?" he asked.

"Yes," replied John, adding in hope of currying favor and leniency, "Senator John Sherman Cooper of Kentucky."

"What's the middle name?" the officer shot back.

"Herman," John answered blandly.

Making a landing in Stevensville, Canada, to refuel and dine, we ran into a thunderstorm during which a ball of fire seemed to pass through the President's cabin across the table where my wife and John sat facing me. John asked us casually whether this often happened. My wife, usually more truthful, answered, "Quite." Colonel Williams, the skipper and pilot, told us that it required some later work on the sheathing of the plane but nothing to interfere with our journey.† In Paris the hospitable Bruces again took us in.

Our meetings began on the morning of November 9, with a thunderstorm of their own. With me were John J. McCloy, our High Commissioner in Germany; George Perkins, Assistant Secretary of State for European Affairs; Colonel Henry Byroade, Chief of the Office of German Affairs; and Paul Nitze of the Policy Planning Staff. McCloy has for thirty years been as useful and devoted a public servant, in and out of office, as this country has had. He is blunt and frank, often so with the press. On arriving in Paris from Bonn he replied to inquiries about the purpose of our meeting with candor and exactitude that it was to bring some relief in the program of dismantling German war plants and why. Since, as I have already pointed out, the French were reluctant and the British embarrassed to face the problem, this statement in advance of the meeting ruffled the dovecotes, especially Bevin's rather easily ruffled temper.

When the meeting opened, Bevin unleashed a violent diatribe, which worried us because of his bad heart. Fortunately, he soon ran out of breath without harmful consequences and Schuman turned to me for help. The problem was to make forgiveness possible before asking for it. The key lay in Ernie's sense of humor. Then it was that my youth in a rectory and a church school came to my rescue. *"M. le Président,"* I said to Schuman, "all that I can reply to Mr. Bevin is written in an English book, *The Book of Common Prayer:* 'The remembrance of our sins is grievous unto us; the burden of them is intolerable.' "

Waving aside translation, Schuman eagerly interjected, "It is the same in the Catholic book."

Ernie burst into laughter and threw up his arms in mock despair. "I wouldn't know," he said. "I'm only a bush Baptist."

"What in the world," I asked, "is a *bush* Baptist?"

"I don't know," he answered. "That's what they called us. Why don't you ask your President? 'E's probably one, too."

I said that I would, and later did. I have found this postscript to a letter I wrote Bevin on November 21 after returning home: "The authority on Baptists, Mr. H.S.T., says that in the early days the mountain people went for the principles of the Baptists in a big way, as they were regarded as a protest against the decadence of the cities. A 'bush Baptist' was a Baptist from the hills."

German Policy Issues • When the fracas subsided, Schuman asked, how should the allies treat Germany while the occupation still continued—as an enemy on parole, as a security problem, or in some other way? In Britain, said Bevin, Germany was regarded with bitter hostility.

To me, one conclusion seemed plain beyond doubt. Western Europe and the United States could not contain the Soviet Union and suppress Germany and Japan at the same time. Our best hope was to make these former enemies willing and strong supporters of a free-world structure. Germany should be welcomed into Western Europe, not kept in limbo outside, as had been the case after the war of 1914–18, relegated to maneuvering between the Soviet Union and the allies. If the former was to be done, "Western Europe" must become more than a phrase. American policy had been strongly directed to this end through the European Recovery Program, the North Atlantic Treaty, and military assistance. Both Bevin and Schuman had done the same in the Council of Europe, the Western Union, and their response to General Marshall's proposal.

To begin the task, I continued, the High Commissioners should speak with one voice in dealing with the German Government. Accordingly, when we had hammered out both what we wanted it to do and the concessions we were willing to make, we should leave to the High Commissioners the use of concessions on dismantling and on limited and prohibited industries in order to obtain German agreement to join the International Ruhr Authority, cooperate with the Military Security Board, and carry out the denazification and decartelization programs. The others agreed and we turned to specific problems.

With a brief rest the first night, we remained in practically continuous session until ending at two o'clock in the morning of November 11. Our session in many ways resembled those which often precede the deadline for a strike in industry. Couches were set up in anterooms on which the exhausted might rest —a facility found most helpful by Ernest Bevin. Tables at the side of the large meeting room were continuously provided with tea, coffee, and sandwiches.

Little groups of assistants charged with special problems would retire to work them out. At one time our meeting was interrupted so that the French Cabinet could give Schuman new instructions; at another to consult on matters of importance to them with the foreign ministers of the Benelux countries, who had come to Paris for the purpose. Issues moved from broad questions of policy to disposition of particular plants or products, to the weight to be given to competitive as against purely security considerations, and so on. The success of the sessions lay in their reaching a great many specific and clear decisions. It was a process in which time, immense good will, and tolerance were indispensable.

Bevin helped greatly by his frank, common-sense view. Dismantling needed immediate review. Plants useful only for war materials should be quickly dismantled and the rest kept, if only in reserve for future trade expansion and for negotiations with the Germans. He was already thinking of allowing an increase of steel capacity from eleven million to sixteen or seventeen million tons a year, even though this would cause "heartburn" in some countries (already one could see Schuman begin to suffer). Bevin was tired of the issue of German steel capacity, which had already dragged on far longer than had been contemplated at Potsdam.

Schuman's approach uncovered a novel gambit. Dismantling, he said, was less interesting as an end in itself than it had been as a means for providing reparations, but involved considerations of security in a new sense. Excess steel capacity in Germany would jeopardize the success of integration in Europe. Steel capacity must be looked at from the point of view of Europe as a whole, reconciling security interests, trade positions, and respect for international agreements, as well as our common interest in not subjecting the new German Government to undue strain. This seemed to me both too obscure and too smooth. I rather bluntly said that beyond purely war-use plants, some fifteen or twenty of which we were all agreed on, the choice was between destroying or leaving the rest. Leaving them seemed to me more sensible and less dangerous. The United States, I added, would not provide facilities to replace dismantled plants. The level of permitted steel production need not be presently raised because of a theoretical, but not actually operable, increased capacity. General Sir Brian Robertson, in command of the British zone, foresaw riots there if dismantling continued at Hamborn and Salzgitter. After many hours of talk the High Commissioners were asked to bring us back specific recommendations on each of the various plants. During our last meeting, the French Cabinet authorized limiting the dismantling as Bevin and I had suggested, provided that there should be no present increase in authorized steel production and that the Germans should accept the positions we had authorized the High Commissioners to take. Agreement on this most difficult subject marked a considerable step forward.

Another matter of some significance was settled before we adjourned, an authorized beginning of a German foreign office through a Bureau of Consular Affairs under the Chancellor and a consular service to care for a reviving German foreign trade.

Finally, a brief discussion of recognition of the Communist regime in

China brought us no closer to agreement. Schuman saw grave complications for France if the Chinese Communists established relations with Ho Chi Minh. He wished that we and the British could show support of the Emperor Bao Dai and the current French policy in Indochina. My view was that the treatment of Angus Ward, our Consul General in Mukden, by the Chinese Communists and their attitude toward our rights and Chinese obligations were precluding recognition. Before we could support French policy in Indochina, it was necessary for the French to act rather than merely make statements. Bevin agreed with this and went on to say that the British would probably not recognize the Communist regime before mid-December. To ward off protest, he ended with a dig at me. The Nationalists, he said, had a lot of arms on Formosa, which the British regarded not as potential strength against the Communists but as potential danger to Britain and France when, after Nationalist surrender, they might be used against Hong Kong and Indochina.

Too weary to rise to this fly, we approved the communiqué and adjourned.

FIRST MEETING WITH ADENAUER

From Paris the American group flew to Frankfurt on November 11 to stay with High Commissioner and Mrs. McCloy in Bad Homburg, around which security precautions were still extensive and severe. Germany was an only recently defeated enemy. Impressions of the scenes about me remain vivid—from the people, the troops, the bomb damage, to the high personalities, both German and allied. During our first day we motored to Heidelberg, the headquarters of General Thomas T. Handy, our Commander in Chief in Europe, to lunch with him and his staff and learn his views. The old university town was much as it had been forty years before when I had been there with my father. In the evening André François-Poncet and Sir Ivone Kirkpatrick, the French and British High Commissioners, dined with us at the McCloys' house, and later the senior members of the High Commission staff came in for a reception. Then on Sunday, McCloy's diesel train took us down the Rhine to Bonn to pay my respects to the President of the new republic, Theodor Heuss, and to have the first of many talks with the Bundeskanzler, Dr. Konrad Adenauer, the beginning of a warm friendship.

At this time Adenauer was not at all the well-known, patriarchal figure he later became. Seventy-three years of age, he had spent most of his mature years in the almost civil service position of a Bürgermeister in Cologne, becoming chief Bürgermeister, sometimes translated "lord mayor," of that city in 1917. There he continued, directing municipal affairs until the Nazis dismissed him in 1933 and imprisoned him twice in the next ten years. After the fall of Hitler, he became one of the founders of the Christian Democratic Union and, as political activity was permitted to Germans in the British zone, took an active part in Laender (state) and zonal affairs. The British, however, were suspicious of Adenauer's conservative and strongly Catholic orientation, and it was not until he became active in interzonal affairs that Americans began to recognize his very considerable abilities.

One's first impression of the Chancellor was as the human embodiment of the doctrine of the conservation of energy. He moved and spoke slowly, gestured sparingly, smiled briefly, chuckled rather than laughed, was given to irony. Sir Ivone Kirkpatrick recalls his observing that God made a great mistake to limit the intelligence of man but not his stupidity. Adenauer's inscrutability was enhanced by wide-set eyes and a flatness of the bridge of his nose that gave him an oriental look, caused—so wags insisted—by having been kicked by a horse in childhood.

Members of his Cabinet and the President of the Bundestag joined us for luncheon, at which the Chancellor talked learnedly and lovingly of the distinguished German white wines he had provided. Then he and Dr. Blankenhorn, his assistant, took McCloy, Perkins, and me to his office. Beginning slowly and pausing every few minutes for translation, he talked about his broad hopes and policies for Germany, saying that he had been told that the results of our recent meetings in Paris would be taken up with him by the High Commissioners.

I was struck by the imagination and wisdom of his approach. His great concern was to integrate Germany completely into Western Europe. Indeed, he gave this end priority over the reunification of unhappily divided Germany, and could see why her neighbors might look upon it as almost a precondition to reunification. All peoples to some extent, but Germans more than most, he thought, took on the color of their environment. Germans undiluted were different from Germans diluted; Germans in St. Louis, for instance, were different from Germans in Berlin, particularly prewar Berlin. He wanted Germans to be citizens of Europe, to cooperate, with France especially, in developing common interests and outlook and in burying the rivalries of the past few centuries. Their common heritage had come to them down the Rhine, as the successors of Charlemagne, who guarded European civilization when human sacrifice was still practiced in eastern Germany. They must lead in the rebirth of Europe. He had no interest, Adenauer concluded, in the rearmament of Germany. Too much blood had been shed; it was too dangerous at this stage to provide Germany with arms, menacing as was the recent appointment of Marshal Rokossovsky to command the reorganized Polish army. Even McCloy's high praise of Adenauer had not prepared me for views from the head of the German Government which raised such hope for a new day in Europe. His words took on added authority from the patriarchal impression he gave. Although some years younger than I am now, he was even then called *"Der Alte"* ("the Old Man"), perhaps because, as I suggested earlier, of his conservation and prudent use of energy.

I was soon to learn that not all Germans shared his views or his calm. His chief opponent, Kurt Schumacher, leader of the Social Democratic Party, combined a harsh and violent nature with nationalistic and aggressive ideas. Shortly after talking with Adenauer I met his adversary with two far more attractive lieutenants, Erich Ollenhauer and Dr. Carlo Schmid. Schumacher had lost the use of an arm and a leg, due, it was said, to Nazi torture. He walked supported by a husky blonde woman. Hardly had we exchanged greetings before Schumacher violently attacked Adenauer for collaboration with the occupation. His idea of sound policy for Germany was neutrality between East and West and evacuation of all foreign troops from German soil, thus winning Soviet agreement to the reunification of Germany. When I pointed out that Russian attitudes at the May foreign ministers' meeting in Paris left little ground for belief that such a policy would produce such a result, he turned his attack on me. I told him frankly that an attempt by the Social Democratic Party to curry favor with the voters or the Russians by baiting the occupation would be given short shrift. We had all made great sacrifices to remove Hitler and nazism from Germany and bring about her admission to the community of Europe. If he believed that the occupation would tolerate an attempt to play the Western allies and the Russians off against one another, he would find himself mistaken. Not long after this meeting Schumacher accused Adenauer in the Bundestag of being not the Chancellor of Germany but the Chancellor of the Occupation, for which he was suspended for three weeks. When death relieved the Social Democrats of Schumacher's leadership, the party rapidly assumed a constructive role in German political life.

After a large public reception the Chancellor drove us to our train at the Bonn railway station for the return journey. It was dark as we drove through the station square, packed with people, through the station itself and onto the platform beside our train. To the people waiting outside this must have been disappointing. It seemed to be unwise, too. Adenauer was not then the well-known figure he later became; he needed building up. To the horror of his security guards I persuaded him to walk out to the middle of the square with me alone, and there shake hands. The result was an instantaneous population explosion through the police lines and triumphal escort to our train by the cheering mob. What both Adenauer and the German people needed in 1949 was some good-natured disorder.

FIRST VISIT TO BERLIN

From Bad Homburg we flew the next day to Berlin. From first to last our visit there was a thrilling experience. The spirit of that exposed outpost was tremendous, from General Maxwell Taylor, Commandant of the American Sector, and the honor guard that awaited me, to Mayor Ernst Reuter and the Berliners themselves. In those days West Berlin was not the resplendent city it became later, but still the scene of grim destruction, with heaps of rubble and burned-out, roofless buildings. The moment one passed through the entrance to East Berlin at the Brandenburg Gate (this was more than ten years before the Wall), one passed from bustle and energy to a sort of furtiveness, a stillness without silence.

Almost the first subject of discussion during luncheon at the High Commissioner's Berlin residence was whether I should go to East Berlin. Some thought that it might be provocative and lead to an incident, even a dangerous one, in the Soviet sector. General Taylor became impatient with this talk.

"Come on," he said. "You have a right to be there. Let's exercise it." He and I went off in his car with a small national standard flying on the right mud-guard and a red one with the three stars of his rank on the left. These did not make it inconspicuous. At the Brandenburg Gate our military-police escort pulled off to the side and we passed through, I feeling very much alone. At the first intersection we were stopped by a red light and traffic closed in around us. The General turned to me cheerfully. "If it doesn't happen now," he said, "I think we're all right."

And we were. However, no one, I noticed, stopped to watch the car go by, despite its flags. To do so, explained the General, would attract undesirable attention to whoever did so. After a short drive along the Stalinallée, with its presentable shop fronts, we explored the streets on either side a block back. This disclosed the avenue to be a Potemkin façade for a drab wreck of a city.

Back in the western sectors, Mayor Reuter received us at the City Hall and presented his council. He was a truly impressive man of immense courage, representing the very essence of the Berlin spirit. Any idea, he told us, that the Soviet Union could be persuaded to withdraw its troops from East Germany was utterly absurd. The moment they were withdrawn, the local Communist collaborators would be swept aside in a bloody purge. The reception that the crowd gave us when the Mayor and I came out on the steps was tumultuous and moving. The Russian occupation of the city, the blockade, and the airlift were recent experiences. The Siberian soldiery had given them a demonstration of the nature of Soviet power more vivid than the analyses of more remote press pundits and the Schumacher school of disengagement. Their welcome to me carried the conviction that to the Berliners hope resided in the United States.

After a reception given by General Taylor for me to meet the British, French, and Soviet commandants and their staffs, our memorable visit to Berlin ended, but not before the arrival of General Chuikov, Military Governor of the Soviet Zone and Commandant of the Soviet Sector of Berlin, won a bet for me. Taylor told me that no Russian had attended a social function since the blockade had begun more than a year before. However, General Chuikov and I had enlivened a rather dull dinner party at the Soviet Embassy in Paris six months before, and I had bet that he would come.[3]

We left that evening at nine-thirty from Berlin for Washington, arriving early the next afternoon. At the bottom of the ramp stood the President with friends gathered around him. "An excellent job," he said. "Come back with me and talk it over.".

Ten days later on November 24 the Petersburg Protocol was released. This was a broad and highly satisfactory agreement worked out with the Chancellor by the High Commissioners (and named after their headquarters on a hilltop outside Bonn). It covered and largely put to rest most of the troublesome matters we had so exhaustively discussed in Paris. In 1949 we had advanced far along the road toward the rehabilitation of Germany.

38. A REAPPRAISAL OF POLICIES

WHILE OUR EFFORTS had helped Europe make great strides toward recovery, this had not been so in the Far East. Nor had political unity in foreign policy been maintained at home. The Nationalist Government of General Li had collapsed on the mainland before the victorious Communists, now supreme in every part of China. Their attitude was one of declared hostility to the United States, including the arrest and detention for over a year of Consul General Angus Ward and his staff at Mukden in Manchuria. Congress, still agitated over the publication of the White Paper on China, had been frightened in September by the announcement of the Soviet nuclear explosion.

Several days after my return from Europe in November the President met with our consultants on China, Philip C. Jessup, Raymond Fosdick, and Everett Case, for a long analysis of the reasons for the Communist success in China, looking toward some new policy conclusions when Ambassador Jessup returned from his approaching mission to China's neighbors. Reviewing the discussion with him later, neither of the principal alternatives open to us seemed inviting. A policy of harassment of the regime and seizure of every opportunity to weaken and if possible overthrow it offered little hope of success, short of massive military intervention—and not much even if that extreme measure were to be included. To encourage the influences that, over time, might detach China from subservience to Moscow, by a cautious application of our attitude toward Tito, would require first that the Chinese Communists follow Tito in stopping active abuse of us.

The President wished to be kept informed of our thought as it developed. Immediately, however, he put me to work on two even more pressing matters: the issue of whether or not to attempt development of a hydrogen bomb and a review of our foreign and military policy in the light of Moscow's atomic explosion. On the first of these he wanted recommendations from Secretary of Defense Louis Johnson, David E. Lilienthal, and me, and he wanted them quickly; on the second, as it ultimately transpired, Secretary Johnson and I were to report.

The international situation we were about to review not only resulted in intensified policies on the part of the Administration, but also led to intensified action by the opposition. The bipartisan foreign policy of the 1947–49 period gave way, from 1950 to 1952, to partisan in-fighting as bloody as any in our history. The essential difference in the two periods was that during most of the first the Republicans had looked forward confidently to a return to power, while in the second they looked back with bitter frustration to a fifth straight failure to retain or regain it. The success of the Chinese Communists and of Russian nuclear scientists at home and their subversive agents abroad, combined with the Administration's advocacy of political and military involvement in Europe and economic aid in undeveloped countries, produced in the pressure cooker of this frustration a veritable witches' brew. Sometimes it seethed; sometimes, under the influence of international crises, it simmered down. At the hands of one of the most unlovely characters in our political history since Aaron Burr, it was about to seethe.

The Soviet explosion and Communist successes in the Far East led the Administration directly to the United Command in Europe and the strengthening of our own and allied forces there. The Taft-Hoover neo-isolationist opposition drew the opposite lesson that we should rely on atomic weapons (later known as "massive retaliation") and move toward withdrawal of ground forces from abroad. Increased tensions in Europe and Asia led the Administration to turn to the State Department as never before for new policies to meet the new dangers. They led the opposition to conclude that State Department fumbling or worse was their cause, a conclusion confirmed for them by the trials of the leaders of the Communist Party and of Judith Coplon in New York, the conviction of Alger Hiss for perjury in early 1950, and the arrest of Klaus Fuchs in London for passing secret information to the Soviet Union. These and other accusations were used to fuse in the public mind criticisms of American foreign policy toward Europe and Asia with fears of disloyalty. All this occurred just as the Department was serving as the President's chief instrument for developing the foreign policy, to be followed by the United States for the next twenty years.

The Hydrogen Bomb Decision · While the immediate cause of the review of our military and foreign policies was the Russian atomic explosion, we had been unhappy in the Department since, in the summer of 1949, the President had fixed the limit of the military budget at thirteen and a half billion dollars. In fairness to Secretary Louis Johnson, the zeal with which he undertook to impose this decision upon the uniformed services came more from loyalty to the President and the zest of battle than from belief in it on the merits. However, he soon convinced himself on that score so completely that when reversal of the decision became necessary later on, he presented a major obstacle. Collapse of the Nationalist regime in China and the Soviet explosion made it clear that changes in power relationships were imminent. By October the Policy Planning Staff had started to work on a reappraisal of our position, inquiring initially whether the situation did not require a renewed attempt on our part to get international control of atomic energy. October also saw ferment in another agency. Commissioner Lewis Strauss of the Atomic Energy Commission had filed a memorandum proposing intensive work on the possibility of cracking the hydrogen atom and producing a hydrogen bomb. This led to a strong difference of opinion within the commission. On November 1 Senator Edwin

Johnson of Colorado announced over television what he called the "top-secret" fact that the United States was at work upon a "super-bomb" that might develop "1,000 times" the power of the Nagasaki bomb.[1]

In this situation Atomic Energy Commission Chairman Lilienthal came to see me on November 1. My education in nuclear physics had ended in 1946 with the impression gained from Dr. Robert Oppenheimer and other colleagues in the Acheson-Lilienthal group that the hydrogen atom could not be cracked. Lilienthal now told me that the chances seemed about even for doing it and that the commission's General Advisory Committee unanimously opposed Commissioner Strauss's proposal, while a majority of the commissioners tended in that direction. The reasons for this view varied: some believed the use of limited materials for experimentation would dangerously delay the production of atomic weapons, others that the chances of success were not so good as represented and that valuable time, effort, and material might be wasted.

A broader issue also evoked a great deal of moral fervor. This was that research should not be undertaken at all—the position Lilienthal has described as "forswearing development along this line." Enough evil had been brought into human life, it was argued by men of the highest standing in science, education, and government, through development of atomic weapons without adding the superhorror of thermonuclear ones. If the United States with its vast resources proved that such an explosion was possible, others would be bound to press on to find the way for themselves. If no one knew that a way existed, research would be less stimulated. Those who shared this view were, I believed, not so much moved by the power of its logic (which I was never able to perceive—neither the maintenance of ignorance nor the reliance on perpetual good will seemed to me a tenable policy) as by an immense distaste for what one of them, the purity of whose motive could not be doubted, described as "the whole rotten business."

The Pentagon was strongly pushing a crash program. Lilienthal believed that the decisions involved were essentially foreign policy decisions, and, indeed, required a thorough review of our whole foreign policy. He left with me the memorandum of the General Advisory Committee and a list of persons whose views I might find helpful. By letter of November 10, 1949, the President designated Louis Johnson, David Lilienthal, and myself, acting as the Special Committee of the National Security Council, to advise him regarding "whether and in what manner the United States should undertake the development and possible production of 'super' atomic weapons [and] . . . whether and when any publicity should be given this matter."[2]

Meanwhile, the Policy Planning Staff, and George Kennan in particular, had been at work on an approach to international control of the atomic race, a study which George completed after he left the Planning Staff to devote himself to the duties of Counselor to the Department on the first of the year. Immediately after my talk with David Lilienthal, I met with the whole Policy Planning Staff, all of whom recognized the far-reaching consequences of the even broader decision that now faced the President. The National Security Council also considered the need of a broad appraisal of the nation's foreign commitments, capabilities, and the existing strategic situation, and on January 5, 1950, began one. While Paul Nitze, Atomic Energy Adviser Gordon Arneson, and Legal Adviser Adrian Fisher were to work with me on the immediate problem of the H-bomb decision, Nitze, who succeeded to the post of head of the Planning Staff, would prepare for the broader inquiry being gestated by the National Security Council, supported in this effort by the whole Planning Staff.

Nitze was doubtful of the line of argument George Kennan had taken in his paper—a thesis he summarizes in his memoirs[3]—that if we wished to secure nuclear disarmament we should renounce first use of atomic weapons; rely on other weaponry for deterrence and defense against all threats short of atomic attack—threats he regarded as unlikely and probably even impractical; and make every effort to reach international agreement on control, even at a certain risk. I could only join Nitze in measuring the risks on a different scale, the one on which NSC-68 was to be based.

From the outset, in trying to outline with these groups the field of inquiry relevant to the decisions, I became aware, without full comprehension, that our colleagues Kennan and Bohlen approached the problem of policy definition with a very different attitude and from a different angle from the rest of us. At the time, impatient with obscure argument, I had to push through it to do what the President had asked of me. Now, understanding better what they were driving at and why, it seems to me rather more important and interesting than its application to the particular issues involved. Their viewpoint, clearly and sympathetically put by Professor Paul Y. Hammond,[4] deserves reading in full. It may be summarized, with some damage, in two points:

1. The attempt to compress into a manageable paper, "cleared" by superiors, the vast and infinitely complex considerations upon which such decisions as those involved here should rest, would so distort the issues presented as to affect the decisions.

2. The creation of such a document not only affects the immediate decision but also introduces into policy making a new rigidity that limits flexible response to unexpected developments and thus affects future decisions as well.

In short, concluded Professor Hammond, "at the extreme, the foreign service officer would . . . rely emphatically upon the personal skills and noncommunicable wisdom of the experienced career official and would view the requirements of large-scale organizations (such as the armed forces with their demands for forward planning) as a direct threat to the practice of this diplomatic art." On the other hand, the rest of us accepted "the necessity in the administration of large-scale operations of forward planning with all its rigidities, simplifications, and artificialities."[5] At the time I recognized and highly appreciated the personal and esoteric skill of our Foreign Service officers, but believed that insofar as their wisdom was "noncommunicable," its value, though great in operations abroad, was limited in Washington. There major foreign policies must be made by the man charged with that responsibility in the Constitution, the President. He rarely came to his task trained in foreign affairs, nor did his personal entourage. What he needed was communicable wisdom, not mere conclusions, however soundly based in experience or intuition, what the man in the street called "educated hunches." I saw my duty as gathering all the wisdom available and communicating it amid considerable competition. The alternative we have seen in doubtful operation in the Roosevelt, Kennedy, and Johnson administrations, when the President has used the White House staff as the agency for collection and evaluation of wisdom.

Due to the acerbity of Louis Johnson's nature, the Special Committee held only two meetings: one on December 22, the other on January 31. The first meeting turned into a head-on confrontation between Louis Johnson and David Lilienthal on the basic issue referred to us and produced nothing either new or helpful to the President. The issue as to whether the use of fissionable material in the experimentation on the H-bomb would be detrimental to A-bomb production would, it seemed to me, yield to further analysis; the "moral argument" appeared less persuasive as one examined it critically. Perseverance was necessary but not through meetings, so we examined one another's views and narrowed our differences by my shuttling among my colleagues.

As December wore on, Lilienthal and I seemed close to a recommendation to investigate the H-bomb, defer decision on production pending investigation, and immediately inaugurate a review of foreign and military policies, including the possibility of reopening discussion of international control of atomic energy. (Indeed, such a review was already under discussion in the National Security Council, which approved it on January 5, 1950.) The Defense Department's Scientific Adviser, Robert LeBaron, did not rule out such a program.

At this point Louis Johnson, becoming impatient with us, sent a memorandum from General Bradley directly to the President. Admiral Souers told me on January 19 of this unilateral approach, adding that communication could be held within the orderly Special Committee procedure if the committee would move soon. The President wished to do this, since he was being pushed by growing press and congressional speculation on conflicting views within the committee and on post-H-bomb policies. I too was very aware of this pressure, having recently engaged in a vigorous exchange of views with a group of senators which drew from me the remark that if their views should develop into governmental policies I would not want to remain Secretary of State—perhaps not the best argument to induce a change in their views. Reporting the committee close to—I hoped—unanimous agreement, I enlisted the Admiral's sympathetic interest in Lilienthal's desire for a thorough review of our foreign and military policies.

After Lilienthal and I had had another talk, the Special Committee met on January 31 in Admiral Souers' office, my former room in the old State Department. Having proposed that our report be restricted to recommendations and a statement to be made by the President, I had given my colleagues drafts based on the recommendations previously discussed with Lilienthal. He thought they did not go far enough and was further depressed when Louis Johnson objected to any statement that a decision on production should be postponed until after research was completed. Both Lilienthal and I foresaw correctly that the purpose was to open the way for renewed pressure for a decision on production.† However, nothing we recommended could prevent this, and I agreed.

Lilienthal then stated eloquently and forcefully his objection to authorizing investigation and research while a review of our policies was going on,
since this, he believed, would extinguish whatever faint hope there might be of
finding a way to prevent development of the weapon.† Equally or even more
important, to launch out on the path toward the H-bomb with so much haste
would tend to prejudge defense budgets and strategy and their relation to foreign policy. He believed other weapon systems were needed more. Much that he
said was appealing, and in our later review we were strongly persuaded toward
increased conventional capability. But I could not overcome two stubborn
facts: that our delaying research would not delay Soviet research, contrary to
an initial hope I had briefly entertained; and that the American people simply
would not tolerate a policy of delaying nuclear research in so vital a matter
while we sought for further ways of reaching accommodation with the Russians
after the experiences of the years since the war.

The paper was retyped after editorial changes agreed on by Johnson and
me. To my considerable surprise Lilienthal signed it, although insisting that he
wished to express his views to the President. The three of us with Admiral
Souers crossed the street to the White House to present it. After the President
had read the short recommendation and proposed statement, I asked him to
hear some additional views from Lilienthal. David began an outline similar to
the one he had given us but was soon interrupted by the President, who signed
the recommendations and the statement, saying that he felt further delay would
be unwise. Later the same day, acting on our recommendation, he instructed
the Secretaries of State and Defense "to undertake a re-examination of our objectives in peace and war and of the effect of these objectives on our strategic
plans, in the light of the probable fission bomb capability and possible thermonuclear bomb capability of the Soviet Union."[6]

CHINA TO THE FORE AGAIN

In early December 1949 Acting President Li Tsung-jen withdrew from
leadership, and Chiang Kai-shek gradually resumed control of the Nationalist
Government. The capital was moved to the island of Formosa on December 8,
thus reuniting in exile the government of China and its monetary reserves. On
December 16 Ambassador Franks told me, on Bevin's instructions, that the
British Government would soon withdraw recognition from Chiang's regime
and extend it to Mao's (which they did on January 5 and 6, 1950, respectively).
I replied that we would not,[7] and on December 29 Senator Connally stated his
own views to the same effect.[8] Meanwhile, United States policy regarding the
defense of Formosa had been raised again by the Secretary of Defense.

From October 1948 to the outbreak of the Korean war on June 25, 1950,
this policy—that United States forces would not be used to defend Formosa—
never wavered. The State Department had been directed to use its best efforts
by diplomatic and economic means to keep the island from falling into hands
hostile to the United States. Frequently reviewed and unanimously supported
by the State and Defense departments, including the Joint Chiefs of Staff, these

principles continued to receive the President's approval. In August 1949 I reported to the National Security Council that diplomatic and economic measures could no longer be counted on to keep Formosa out of hostile hands and asked for another review. Again refusal to involve military forces was affirmed.

In November Senator H. Alexander Smith, Republican of New Jersey, suggested in a letter to me that, pending a peace treaty with Japan, if we would take the view that Formosa remained Japanese territory the United States as the occupying power could assume a sort of protectorate over it.[9] Later he hinted that General MacArthur supported this view.[10] Then Secretary of Defense Johnson asked the Joint Chiefs of Staff for still another review and recommendation, this time from a purely military point of view without regard to political considerations—whatever these phrases meant. The Chiefs again objected to the involvement of American forces but proposed some funds for military material and a fact-finding mission. I objected to this toying with the mousetrap; the National Security Council supported my view; and the President endorsed it. A few days later Senators Knowland and Taft and former President Hoover publicly advocated U.S. naval protection for Formosa. One can see reason in the advice the Chinese Minister in Washington was said to have given to Chiang Kai-shek a few months earlier—that "if our procedure strictly follows the laws of the United States" former Ambassador Hu Shih was "off the beam" in opposing keeping in close touch with the legislative branch.[11]

Although it may seem impossible, still further confusion was to be introduced into the discussion of Formosa policy. During the summer General Wedemeyer had suggested the preparation of a guidance paper for press and public-affairs officers intended to minimize the significance and damage resulting from a quite possible fall of Formosa to the Chinese Communists. On December 23 such a paper was sent out to (among a great many other recipients) General MacArthur's headquarters in Tokyo. There someone—never discovered—put it in an outgoing box of press releases. Received with delighted unbelief, copious quotations from it were soon speeding around the world. Congress burst into uproar. Senator Knowland and others demanded release of the full text and the names of all who had worked on it. I refused both requests, assumed full responsibility for the paper, and waited for the storm to pass, which it did. One is left wondering whether this windfall for Messrs. Knowland and Smith flowed from a mere lucky combination of coincidence and stupidity.

Perhaps my own frivolity with the press had brought its penalty. Before Christmas I had wished for them "that Saint Nicholas will put in the sock of each of you a scoop and that it will have these qualities; first, that it will bring each of you a large raise in pay and, second, that it will not embarrass me." At least they got their part of the wish.

While I was wasting too much of Christmas week trying to arrange a meeting with the absent Senate Committee on Foreign Relations to straighten out our intentions toward Formosa, the Chinese Communists were charging, and citing the Taft-Knowland-Smith-Hoover proposals, that the United States was about to occupy the island. The President decided that he must speak at once, and speak in so crisp and brutally frank a manner as to end further propaganda and speculation. On January 5, the day following his State of the Union message to Congress, he put out a four-paragraph release in which, after declaring that the United States Government regarded Formosa as Chinese territory without qualification, he went on:

The United States has no predatory designs on Formosa or on any other Chinese territory. The United States has no desire to obtain special rights or privileges or to establish military bases on Formosa at this time. Nor does it have any intention of utilizing its armed forces to interfere in the present situation. The United States Government will not pursue a course which will lead to involvement in the civil conflict in China.

Similarly, the United States Government will not provide military aid or advice to Chinese forces on Formosa. In the view of the United States Government, the resources on Formosa are adequate to enable them to obtain the items which they might consider necessary for the defense of the Island. The United States Government proposes to continue under existing legislative authority the present ECA program of economic assistance.[12]

The afternoon of that same day I met with the press at the President's direction to make the policy clear to the most perverse intelligence. In my role of frustrated schoolteacher, I said that the United States speaks to the world not only through the State Department, or even through the President and the Congress, but through the sum total of the acts and words of the whole American people. For the better part of two weeks we had been speaking in this way to the world about Formosa. The ordinary processes of Washington life had played their familiar role. Leak had been followed by counterleak, gossip by countergossip. Distinguished statesmen had made their contributions. Rumor had been transmuted into report of fact. In other words, I continued, the American democracy was operating normally, with the result that the minds of both our own people and foreigners had become thoroughly confused. The President had wished to clarify them, not to state anything new.

First of all, the President had pointed out, our Government regarded Formosa as Chinese territory. Four years earlier we had captured it and, in accordance with promises publicly made, had turned it over to the Government of China, which had administered it since. Whatever political or legal quibbles others might wish to raise, as far as the United States Government was concerned, Formosa was Chinese.

Secondly, he had said that the United States Government would not use its military forces in the controversy within China over Formosa. It would not seize the island; it would not get involved militarily in any way. No responsible man in the Government, military or civilian, believed that we should involve our forces on the island.

Thirdly, the President had gone on to say, the United States Government would not give military supplies or military advice to the Chinese forces on the island. Those on the island had resources in plenty to buy whatever they might need. Vast quantities of supplies had been given them in the past. Whatever difficulty might confront them in maintaining the island would not lie in lack of supplies. The difficulty would lie elsewhere, "and it is not the function of the

United States nor will it or can it attempt to furnish a will to resist and a purpose for resistance to those who must provide for themselves."

My statement ended with an explanation of the President's phrase "at this time" as used in the sentence, "The United States has no desire to obtain special rights or privileges or to establish military bases on Formosa at this time":

That phrase does not qualify or modify or weaken the fundamental policies stated in this declaration by the President in any respect. It is a recognition of the fact that, in the unlikely and unhappy event that our forces might be attacked in the Far East, the United States must be completely free to take whatever action in whatever area is necessary for its own security.[13]

These two statements brought to an end, for some time at least, the public debate on Formosa.

THE "STRATEGIC CONCEPT"

One constructive achievement marked the end of the year. It will be recalled that Senator Vandenberg had inserted into the Mutual Defense Assistance Act of 1949 a provision which held up the funds authorized beyond one hundred million dollars until "the President of the United States approves recommendations for an integrated defense of the North Atlantic area which may be made by the Council and the Defense Committee to be established under the North Atlantic Treaty." As was pointed out in Chapter 34, it was impossible at that time for any treaty organization to devise any meaningful recommendations for an integrated defense. No treaty staff, military or civilian, existed to plan, and in the state of European recovery in 1949–50 adequate recommendations could not have been carried out. In short, the Vandenberg-Dulles amendment made sense only in that it was essential to get congressional approval; and, to get funds released to start upon defense forces, some "recommendations" had to be produced for the President's approval.

At a meeting on December 1 the defense ministers of the treaty states agreed on an ingenious recommendation, called a strategic concept, and passed it on to be considered by the NATO Council. The concept was not a plan but a collection of principles for devising an integrated defense. No European nation was to attempt a complete military establishment, but rather each was to make its most effective contribution in the light of its geographic position, economic capability, and population. The United States would be responsible primarily for naval and air forces with a supporting role on the ground; the British would concentrate on sea and air control of the western approaches, the Channel and the North Sea, with an Army of the Rhine; the French, largely on ground and air defenses in Europe and naval forces in the Mediterranean; and so on.

The paper went on to inventory what was presently available and included in defense budgets, what was most urgently needed over and beyond that for the assigned role of each. The "strategic concept" was admittedly a sketchy recommendation. It could hardly have been otherwise. A meeting of the council, convened in Washington on January 6, 1950, and attended by the signatories' diplomatic representatives in Washington, approved the "strategic concept." The President approved it on January 27, after I had signed agreements, as required by the Act, with each of the signatory states asking defense aid, and by executive order set the administration of the act in motion. It had been a long, hard struggle. I felt that the Norwegian Ambassador, Wilhelm Morgenstierne, was quite justified in paying on behalf of his treaty colleagues "a warm tribute to the initiative, the vision, and the constructive statesmanship of America ever since the inception of the idea of an integrated defense of the North Atlantic Area."[14] No one deserved it more than Senator Tom Connally of Texas.

Section B. Problems Came Faster in 1950

39. THE ATTACK OF THE PRIMITIVES BEGINS†

THE EARLY WINTER OF 1950 was a time of work and troubles, a somber time. The hydrogen bomb was not an exhilarating subject. Neither were the other themes that composed the counterpoint of that winter—China, internal Communist subversion, and appraisal of its external dangers. At home we had our own private worries about our daughter's health. She had found it necessary to return to Saranac, leaving her small son with us.

The last chapter has already recounted the President's statement of January 5 and my supporting one. On its eve I had written our daughter:

DA to MAB   *January 4, 1950*

The ball will then [i.e., after HST's statement] pass to me, and in the press, in the Congress and in a public speech I shall do my best to carry some sense of the problem in the Far East, the limitation of our power, the direction of our purpose. So much that is foolish, disloyal, and generally contemptible has been going on that it is good that we are—as I hope—free to go ahead on a clear and sensible course. The President has been superb through this whole affair. One could not ask for a commander with more directness, understanding and courage. As you see, I am, as I have been, for him. There are some others that we could, in a pinch, spare.

The public speech was to come within a week at the National Press Club, preceded by appearances before House and Senate committees. These public performances did not bother me; in fact, they were rather enjoyable if not too protracted. "The really rough task," I wrote at the time, "is to make the decisions which come up in all this confusion. They have been particularly rough this week and one knows that one's chances of being right are amazingly small. On the whole, I like it better when it is rough, tough, and full of fleas than when I have the problem staring at me in the undisturbed silence of an empty room." A thick folder full of marked-up drafts bears witness to efforts of devoted assistants to help me with the Press Club speech, and, indeed, they did by stimulating thought. But, in the end, I put the drafts aside and made the speech from a page or two of notes.

THE THEME OF CHINA LOST

The speech of January 12, 1950, "Crisis in China—An Examination of United States Policy," has been called "one of the most brilliant as well as the most controversial speeches ever made by Secretary Acheson."[1] Both adjectives are interesting: the first, because how complimentary it was meant to be obviously depends upon the author's unknown opinion of my other speeches; the second, because, although there was an immediate outburst, the principal controversy arose later and involved not what was said about China, but inferences drawn about a wholly different subject, Korea. The speech was another effort to get the self-styled formulators of public opinion to think before they wrote, and do more than report as news the emotional or political utterances of political gladiators. On the preceding day, one of these, Senator Taft, had been widely quoted charging in the Senate that the State Department had "been guided by a left-wing group who obviously have wanted to get rid of Chiang and were willing at least to turn China over to the Communists for that purpose."[2] Senator Vandenberg had rebuked him for saying this. At the time, Mao Tse-tung was in Moscow negotiating with Stalin what proved to be the Sino-Soviet Treaty of February 14, 1950. It was a supercharged moment to be speaking on Asian matters.

I began with an explanation of how it seemed to me that good and effective policies develop. Relations between people, I said, depend upon the fundamental attitudes, interests, and purposes of those peoples. Day-to-day actions grow out of those attitudes, interests, and purposes and are developed into policies. To be good policies they must come about on both sides in this manner. To be effective, they must become articulate through all the institutions and groupings of national life—press, radio, churches, labor unions, business organizations. In Asia, population, differences in race, ideas, languages, religion, culture, and development are vast. But, throughout, run two deep common attitudes—revulsion against the poverty and misery of centuries and against more recent foreign domination. Blended, they had evoked throughout Asia the revolutionary forces of nationalism. Resignation had given way to hope and anger.

Many, I continued, bewildered by events in China, failed to understand this background, looked for esoteric causes, and charged American bungling. No one in his right mind could believe that the Nationalist regime had been overthrown by superior military force. Chiang Kai-shek had emerged from the war as the leader of the Chinese people, opposed by only one faction, the ragged, ill-equipped, small Communist force in the hills. Chiang controlled the greatest military power of any ruler in Chinese history, supported and given economic backing by the United States. Four years later his armies and his support both within the country and outside it had melted away. He was a refugee on a small island off the coast.

To attribute this to inadequate foreign support, I said, was to miscalculate entirely what had been going on in China and the nature of the forces involved. The almost inexhaustible patience of the Chinese people had ended. They had not overthrown the Government. There was nothing to overthrow. They had simply ignored it. The Communists were not the creators of this situation, this revolutionary spirit, but had mounted it and ridden to victory and power.

This, I suggested, was a realistic explanation of what had been going on in Asia and of the attitudes of its people. Throughout our history the attitude of Americans toward the peoples of Asia had been an interest in them not as pawns in the strategy of power or as subjects for economic exploitation, but simply as people. For a hundred years some Americans had gone to Asia to offer what they thought was the most valuable thing they had—their faith. They wanted to tell the Asians what they thought about the nature and relationship of man to God. Others had gone to offer what they knew of learning; others to offer healing for Asian bodies. Others, perhaps fewer, had gone to learn the depth and beauty of Asian cultures, and some to trade. This trade was a very small part of American interest in the Far East, and it was a very small part of American interest in trade.

The outstanding factor in the interest of the American people in Asia— the people in towns, villages, churches, and societies—was that over the years it had been parallel and not contrary to the interest of the peoples of Asia. In China, the Philippines, India, Pakistan, Indonesia, and Korea it had strongly, even emotionally, supported people working out their own destinies free of foreign control. To say that our principal interest was to stop the spread of communism was to get the cart completely before the horse. Of course we opposed the spread of communism; it was the subtle, powerful instrument of Russian imperialism, designed and used to defeat the very interests we shared with the Asian peoples, the interest in their own autonomous development uncontrolled from abroad.

For generations, long before communism, I pointed out, Russia had aimed to dominate Asian peoples, and none more persistently than those in north China. The Soviet Union had gone on with this policy, attempting to spread its influence even to the extent of detaching Outer Mongolia, Inner Mongolia, Sinkiang, and Manchuria. This most significant, most important, fact should not be obscured. We should not deflect from the Russians to ourselves the righteous anger and hatred of the Chinese people. Now, as in the past, we shared their view that whoever violated the integrity of China was their enemy. Those who proclaimed their loyalty to Moscow proclaimed loyalty to an enemy of China.

From the political theme, the speech turned to "the questions of military security." Its purpose was to bring home what the United States Government had done to defend vital interests in the Pacific, not to speculate on what it might do in the event of various exigencies in Asia. Our defense stations beyond the western hemisphere and our island possessions were the Philippines and defeated, disarmed, and occupied Japan. These were our inescapable responsibilities. We had moved our line of defense, a line fortified and manned by our own ground, sea, and air forces, to the very edges of the western Pacific. Less than a year before, on March 1, 1949, General MacArthur had discussed the same subject in an interview in Tokyo:

> Our defensive dispositions against Asiatic aggression used to be based on the west coast of the American continent.
> The Pacific was looked upon as the avenue of possible enemy approach. Now the Pacific has become an Anglo-Saxon lake and our line of defense runs through the chain of islands fringing the coast of Asia.
> It starts from the Philippines and continues through the Ryukyu Archipelago, which includes its main bastion, Okinawa. Then it bends back through Japan and the Aleutian Island chain to Alaska.[3]

My defense line, called our defensive perimeter, followed General Mac-Arthur's, but was described from northeast to southwest: "This defensive perimeter runs along the Aleutians to Japan and then goes to the Ryukyus. We hold important defense positions in the Ryukyu Islands, and these we will continue to hold. . . . The defensive perimeter runs from the Ryukyus to the Philippine Islands."[4]

With the authority of the Joint Chiefs of Staff and General MacArthur behind me, it did not occur to me that I should be charged with innovating policy or political heresy. But to make sure that I would not be misunderstood or distorted, I added two more paragraphs to care for interests outside of our own defense line:

> So far as the military security of other areas in the Pacific is concerned, it must be clear that no person can guarantee these areas against military attack. . . .
> Should such an attack occur . . . the initial reliance must be on the people attacked to resist it and then upon the commitments of the entire civilized world under the Charter of the United Nations, which so far has not proved a weak reed to lean on by any people who are determined to protect their independence against outside aggression.

After a brief look at particular areas, I concluded that old relationships between East and West in Asia were ended. If new and useful ones were to succeed them, they must be based on mutual respect and helpfulness. We were ready to be helpful but could be so only where we were wanted and where the conditions of help were sensible and possible. So the new day just dawning could go on to a glorious noon or darken and drizzle out. Which would come about would depend on decisions of the Asian peoples, which no friend or enemy from the outside could make for them.

The press comment on the speech, moderate to favorable, was muffled by an event of far greater importance. On January 13, Jacob A. Malik, Soviet Representative on the UN Security Council, walked out of the chamber after announcing that the Soviet Union would not attend or recognize the legality of the council's actions until the Chinese Nationalist representative had been removed. This critical Russian error opened the way five months later to uniting the United Nations against the attack on South Korea.

However, the China bloc in Congress opened fire on me at once. Senator

Styles Bridges demanded a vote of censure against the Administration and a withholding of funds until it changed its policy. The next day a new uproar followed announcement that the Chinese Communists had seized our consular premises and property in Peking, thus repudiating the treaties of 1901 and 1943. Senator Knowland demanded my resignation. Mr. Vishinsky attacked me from Moscow. However, the Democratic senators voted to support our Far Eastern policy.

On January 19 came a bitter and unexpected blow. "This has been a tough day," I wrote our daughter, "not so much by way of work, but by way of troubles. We took a defeat in the House on Korea, which seems to me to have been our own fault. One should not lose by one vote. [The vote was 193 to 192.] We were complaisant and inactive. We have now a long road back."

The vehicle of this trouble was not an important or controversial bill, but a comparatively small supplemental appropriation for aid to Korea in 1950. In accordance with resolutions of the United Nations sponsored by us at the request of the Pentagon to get our remaining divisions out of Korea, all foreign troops (that is, Soviet and American) were to leave Korea and did so by mid-1949. For our part, only an advisory group of about five hundred officers and men remained to complete equipping South Korean forces. We wished to boost South Korean morale by some economic action. Hence the bill. It seemed so small and harmless that we neglected our usual precautions and were caught off guard by a combination of China-bloc Republicans and economy-minded southern Democrats and defeated on a snap vote.

The President and I expressed our "concern and dismay" over what had occurred and called for its early remedy. An extension of the China Aid Act for a few months was joined with the Korean appropriation and a little sweetening added for congressional adherents of Chiang Kai-shek. The new bill became law on February 14, 1950. But the damage had been done. Later it was argued that my speech "gave the green light" to the attack on South Korea by not including it within the "defensive perimeter." This was specious, for Australia and New Zealand were not included either, and the first of all our mutual defense agreements was made with Korea. If the Russians were watching the United States for signs of our intentions in the Far East, they would have been more impressed by the two years' agitation for withdrawal of combat forces from Korea, the defeat in Congress of a minor aid bill for it, and the increasing discussion of a peace treaty with Japan.

THE THEME OF COMMUNIST INFLUENCE

After both the First and Second World Wars waves of fear of communism spread over the country, reaching hysterical proportions. They were assiduously stirred by persons in authority. In 1919 Attorney General A. Mitchell Palmer told a congressional committee: "There is a condition of revolutionary intent in the country of sufficiently wide spread a character . . . to destroy or overthrow the government of the United States by physical force or violence." Judge Kenesaw Mountain Landis said to the American Legion on January 21,

1920: "What we need is a new definition of treason. Then we could use the side of a barn for those who would destroy our government." The ranks of those who stood out for sanity and a sense of proportion were small, indeed: Charles Evans Hughes, defending the Socialist members of the New York legislature against efforts to expel them; Federal Judge George W. Anderson of Massachusetts, pointing out that "the heresy hunter has throughout history been one of the meanest of men"; Frank I. Cobb, asking what old Sam Adams would say to the American Government's protecting the people against revolutionary propaganda; a group of Protestant clergymen rallying the churches of America to the "old faith in the fundamental principles of our civil liberty."[5]

After the Second World War a stronger case could be made for fear of Russian penetration in America. The Soviet Union was now a superpower, unabashedly hostile to us, operating all over the world through fifth columns of national communist parties. During the period of the Depression at the beginning of the 1930s many students had been attracted by communist doctrines, and some of these had found their way into Government. Perhaps more alarming was the possibility of betrayal of atomic secrets. Many scientists had a sense of guilt from having participated in the development of nuclear weapons. Many genuine idealists of the Henry Wallace type were misled into belief in Russian peace propaganda and proposals.

Russian agents were doubtless numerous and active in attempting to pick up what they could. Probably our internal security system was as good as an open, democratic society can have and unequaled anywhere. The most difficult people to guard against are amateurs, but fortunately few of them possess really vital information, and their ability to influence decisions in favor of a foreign power would be small indeed. Against this background it is understandable that the discovery of persons in Government with a history of past or present sympathy with communist doctrine or the Soviet state would cause a terrific uproar. The uproar would be unlikely to reflect danger to the interest of the United States.

The Conviction of Alger Hiss • Great as was the hubbub of the first part of January, it paled before that of the final week. While Washington had been torn by issues of China, Formosa, Korea, and the hydrogen bomb, Alger Hiss, a former State Department officer and later President of the Carnegie Endowment for International Peace, had been on trial in New York for perjury. His testimony during investigation of charges that he passed Government papers to the Soviet Union was claimed to have been false. The origin of this *cause célèbre* and my connection with Alger Hiss have been described in Chapter 28.

DA to MAB   *January 25, 1950*
   This has been one of those days easy in the intrinsic tasks, but hard and exhausting emotionally because of what was added. Today Alger Hiss was convicted and today I had my press conference. Alger's case has been on my mind incessantly. As I have written you, here is stark tragedy—whatever the reasonably probable facts may be. I knew that I would be asked about it and the answer was a hard one —not in the ordinary sense of do I run or do I stand. That presented no problem.

But to say what one really meant—forgetting the yelping pack at one's heels—saying no more and no less than one truly believed. This was not easy. I felt that advisers were of no use and so consulted none. I understood that I had responsibilities above and beyond my own desires. And all this one had to handle dependent upon the fall of some fool's question at a press conference.

At the end of the day I am tired, but I have no idea that there was any better way, though one could have wished for better words and thoughts in that crowded and slightly hot and sweaty room.

Excerpt from the transcript of press and radio news conference of January 25, 1950:

Q: Mr. Secretary, have you any comment on the Alger Hiss Case?
A: Mr. Hiss's case is before the courts and I think that it would be highly improper for me to discuss the legal aspects of the case or the evidence or anything to do with the case.

I take it the purpose of your question was to bring something other than that out of me. I should like to make it clear to you that whatever the outcome of any appeal which Mr. Hiss or his lawyers may take in this case I do not intend to turn my back on Alger Hiss. I think every person who has known Alger Hiss or has served with him at any time has upon his conscience the very serious task of deciding what his attitude is and what his conduct should be. That must be done by each person in the light of his own standards and his own principles. For me, there is very little doubt about those standards or those principles. I think they were stated for us a very long time ago. They were stated on the Mount of Olives and if you are interested in seeing them you will find them in the 25th Chapter of the Gospel according to St. Matthew beginning with verse 34.

Have you any other questions?[6]

After the press conference was over, Mike McDermott, Special Assistant for Press, who had served secretaries since Mr. Hull, walked with me in silence to my door. "I am going to ask a favor of the Secretary of State," he said, "which I have asked only once before in my service. May I shake your hand?" We shook hands and parted. Sending word ahead asking the President to receive me, I drove to the White House and told him the story, adding that, of course, my resignation was at his disposal. The news-ticker report was already on his desk. Two days later I reported his attitude in a letter to my daughter.

DA to MAB   *January 27, 1950*
My goodness, what a controversial figure I have become. The Congress flies into a tantrum. The press gets all excited. The only paper which seems to have no trouble with a simple statement seems to be the *Herald Tribune* in its editorial to-day.† And a great number of citizens write and telegraph me. Most are understanding, but some want me impeached or fired by the President.

He has been, as usual, wonderful about it and said that one who had gone to the funeral of a friendless old man just out of the penitentiary had no trouble in knowing what I meant and in approving it.†

So there we are, and as the Persian King had carved on his ring, "This, too, will pass." However, Congressman Walter Judd of Minnesota thought it ought not to be allowed. On the contrary, he said, the President should turn his back on me.[7]

DA to MAB *January 31, 1950*

I have been sitting up late for two nights signing answers to the flood of letters which I have been getting. They are very touching. I feel quite objective about them as it seems wholly improbable that the person they are addressed to has anything like a resemblance to me. They do give a faith that Walt Whitman knew more about America than some of his successors.

However, he did not know about Senator McCarthy and the Congress. That worthy, as we shall see in the next chapter, kept the pot boiling to the extent that prior to my appearance a month later before a Senate subcommittee, chaired by Senator McCarran of Nevada on the State Department appropriation for the fiscal year 1951, I was asked to come prepared to "clarify" my earlier statement. This, of course, was only a thin excuse to agitate the controversy over again, but could not be evaded and offered a chance to strike a blow for common sense. I made four points:[8]

First, the refusal to discuss the merits of the case *sub judice* did not seem to me debatable.

Second, why did I not let the matter rest there? Because, as the hubbub had shown, some regarded my attitude toward Alger Hiss as relevant to my fitness to hold office, and these people were entitled to know it. In expanding this point, I said: "There were also personal reasons for stating my attitude. One must be true to the things by which one lives. The counsels of discretion and cowardice are appealing. The safe course is to avoid situations which are disagreeable and dangerous. Such a course might get one by the issue of the moment, but it has bitter and evil consequences. In the long days and years which stretch beyond that moment of decision, one must live with one's self; and the consequences of living with a decision which one knows has sprung from timidity and cowardice go to the roots of one's life. It is not merely a question of peace of mind, although that is vital; it is a matter of integrity of character."

Third, regarding the substance of my attitude, Mr. Hiss was in the greatest trouble in which a man could be. The outcome of his appeal could have little bearing on his personal tragedy. It was toward a man in this situation that I found applicable the principle of compassion stated in the Gospel. It represented a tradition in which I had been bred going back beyond the limits of memory.

Fourth, I could not believe that what I had said carried the slightest implication of condoning the offenses that Mr. Hiss had been charged with or of which he had been convicted: "But for the benefit of those who would create doubt where none existed, I will accept the humiliation of stating what should be obvious—that I did not and do not condone in any way the offenses charged, whether committed by a friend or by a total stranger, and that I would never knowingly tolerate any disloyal person in the Department of State."

40. THE ATTACK MOUNTS

SENATOR MC CARTHY MERGES THE THEMES

JOSEPH R. MC CARTHY, REPUBLICAN, thirty-seven years old, was elected to the United States Senate from Wisconsin in the Republican upsurge of 1946. He was not heard from until he made his debut in Wheeling, West Virginia, on February 9, 1950, as a crusader against "Communists in government." From then until December 2, 1954, when he was "condemned" by the Senate for contempt of a subcommittee, abuse of its members, and insults to the Senate, he filled the newspapers of the nation and did incalculable harm to its governance. Then he disappeared from notice as rapidly as he had attained it and died in May 1957. When asked for a comment about him, I quoted the Latin maxim, *"De mortuis nil nisi bonum."* One could have said that his name, like those of Judge Lynch and Captain Boycott, had enlarged the vocabulary.

As I have mentioned earlier, Soviet attempts to penetrate American Government and other institutions through Communist agents had been known, discussed, and feared—sometimes to the point of hysteria—long before McCarthy appeared on the political scene. The situation in 1949 was similar to that following World War I.[1] Our concern with it here is as a means of attack on the Administration, how McCarthy came to be the instrument of attack, and the extent to which the attack affected the conduct of our foreign policy.

McCarthy's Wheeling speech was not a brilliant maiden effort in the traditional parliamentary or senatorial style. It was the rambling, ill-prepared result of his slovenly, lazy, and undisciplined habits with which we were soon to become familiar. No copy of the speech existed and newspaper reports varied. It was not until February 20, having created an interest in generalized charges of disloyalty against unnamed State Department employess, that he read in the Senate what he said was a recording of the earlier speech. In it and other speeches and interviews he charged that he had the names and records of eighty-one persons with communist leanings who were or had been in the Department; that the President's Loyalty Board had certified to me as disloyal some two hundred employees, of whom I had discharged eighty; that there were presently fifty-seven card-carrying Communists in the Department. Interspersed with these were charges against me, Assistant Secretary of State John E. Peurifoy (in charge of administration), and the Department's Security and Loyalty Board. All of these precipitated such an uproarious exchange of denials, countercharges, speeches, and further denials that on February 20 the Committee on Foreign Relations, by direction of the Senate, set up a subcommittee under the chairmanship of Senator Millard Tydings of Maryland to investigate McCarthy's charges. The Tydings committee began its hearings on March 8. On that day I opened my press conference[2] in this way:

> With all these charges flying around I want to tell you about the meeting which was being broken up by communists so that the chairman had to send for the police. When they entered the hall they started wielding their clubs pretty vigorously. The unfortunate chairman got a crack over the head and, when he protested, the cop shouted, "You're under arrest!"
>
> "I can't be," pleaded the chairman, "I'm an anti-communist."
>
> "I don't give a damn," hollered the cop, "whether you're a communist, or an anti-communist, or what kind of a communist you are. You're under arrest!"

At the same press conference I was asked:

Q: Are you aware, Mr. Secretary, that Senator McCarthy saw fit to inject Mrs. Acheson's name into the proceedings?
A: I understand that he made that contribution to the gaiety of the situation.
Q: Do you have anything to say in that particular situation?
A: Well, like any husband who finds his wife injected into a controversy the first thing is to go to headquarters and find out about it. So I telephoned my wife and said, "What's this you've been up to?" And she hadn't the faintest conception nor had she ever heard of the organization which Senator McCarthy accused her of belonging to. It was something like the Women's National Congress or something of that sort. So we looked up this organization and found that it was a merger of many others, among them one called the Washington League of Women Shoppers. That rang a bell. She said that ten years or so ago she had paid two dollars (she thinks, perhaps, she paid two dollars twice which she regards as rather extravagant under the circumstances) and she was given a list of stores in Washington classified as fair or unfair to their employees. That was the extent of her recollection of the matter.

I told her that it was charged that she was a sponsor of it. She said that was interesting and asked who were the other sponsors. So I read them to her and she said that sounded rather like the Social Register and she thought her position was going up, but she couldn't recall whether she had been a sponsor or not. I think that is the extent of the information I got from her over the telephone before coming down here.

The subcommittee furnished McCarthy with a platform, loudspeaker, and full press coverage for his campaign of vilification. He made a shambles of the hearings. Far quicker than Tydings, who was a man of character but unfortunately had a short temper and a pompous manner, McCarthy maneuvered the chairman into insisting on open and public hearings and bringing out the names of alleged Communists, thus providing a feast of privileged slander. More important, however, in the course of the hearings McCarthy stumbled on the combination of themes that made him a welcome tool for the conservative Taft-led Republicans. As already pointed out, five years earlier General Patrick Hurley had charged that conspiracy in the State Department had frustrated his efforts in China. Two years after that Congressman Walter Judd had voiced the same suspicions. McCarthy now took this line. China had been lost through the machination of Soviet sympathizers and agents in the State Department. In this category he placed John Carter Vincent, John Service, Philip C. Jessup, and Dr. Owen Lattimore of The Johns Hopkins University. The last named, he charged, was "the architect of our Far Eastern policy," though Dr. Lattimore had never been connected with the Department and I did not know him.

TAFT SUPPORTS MC CARTHY

Senator Taft, who had first regarded McCarthy as reckless, now decided to give him Republican backing and help. McCarthy, he was quoted as saying, "should keep talking and if one case doesn't work out, he should proceed with another."[3] Senator Knowland opened up with a series of speeches during the spring linking Lattimore's views—apparently on the theory that he was an adviser of mine—with current Communist pronouncements. At the end of March, Senator Bridges announced that a group of Republicans would "go after" me in public attacks, which he inaugurated on March 27;† and my old enemy, Senator Kenneth Wherry, the Nebraska undertaker, declared that I "must go" as a "bad security risk."[4] Taft, again returning to the battle, attacked "the pro-Communist group in the State Department who surrendered to every demand of Russia at Yalta and Potsdam, and promoted at every opportunity the Communist cause in China."[5] As William S. White, Taft's biographer, put it in discussing this "sad, worst period" in his life: "All this—the debacle of 1948 and the Eastern challenge to him again in early 1949—stirred him in most unfortunate ways. It seemed even to some of his friends and admirers that he began, if unconsciously, to adopt the notion that almost *any* way to defeat or discredit the Truman plans was acceptable. There was, in the intellectual sense, a blood-in-the-nostrils approach, and no mistake about it."[6]

For two or three weeks after the June 25 attack on South Korea the attack of the primitives quieted down, only to burst into full fury again on July 20, when the Tydings subcommittee filed its reports. (Its membership, besides the chairman, was Brien McMahon of Connecticut and Theodore Francis Green of Rhode Island, Democrats, and Henry Cabot Lodge, Jr., of Massachusetts and Bourke B. Hickenlooper of Iowa, Republicans.) All agreed that the charges had not been substantiated. The majority report criticized McCarthy bitterly as having tried to "inflame the American people with a wave of hysteria and fear on an unbelievable scale in this free nation" and added that "fraught with falsehood from beginning to end, its reprehensible and contemptible character defies adequate condemnation."[7] After a wild fight on the floor, the Senate adopted the report by a strictly party vote of 45 to 37. For a long time the only other articulate support in the Congress for decency came from Maine's Republican Senator, Margaret Chase Smith, and the honorable half dozen who joined her† in her "Declaration of Conscience" on June 2, 1950. She criticized her own party for allowing the Senate to have been "too often . . . debased to the level of a forum of hate and character assassination sheltered by the shield of congressional immunity." The statement continued: "The nation sorely needs a Republican victory. But I do not want to see the Republican Party ride to political victory on the Four Horsemen of Calumny—fear, ignorance, bigotry and smear."

On August 7 Wherry demanded my dismissal; on the fourteenth, my resignation; and on the sixteenth he declared that "the blood of our boys in Korea is on [Acheson's] shoulders, and no one else."[8] On the thirteenth, four of the five Republican members of the Foreign Relations Committee, followed by Senator Taft, accused President Truman and me of having invited the attack on Korea. The nadir of this shameful performance came in September during consideration of a bill to permit President Truman to appoint General Marshall, while still remaining a five-star general, as Secretary of Defense to succeed Louis Johnson, who had resigned. Senator William E. Jenner, Republican of Indiana, said of the man who, in the words of President Conant of Harvard, brooked only one comparison in our nation's history:

> General Marshall is not only willing, he is eager to play the role of a front man, for traitors.
>
> The truth is this is no new role for him, for Gen. George C. Marshall is a living lie....
>
> ... [As a result,] this Government of ours [has been turned] into a military dictatorship, run by Communist-appeasing, Communist-protecting betrayer of America, Secretary of State Dean Acheson....
>
> Unless he, himself [General Marshall], were desperate, he could not possibly agree to continue as an errand boy, a front man, a stooge, or a co-conspirator for this administration's crazy assortment of collectivist cutthroat crackpots and Communist fellow-traveling appeasers....
>
> ... How can the Senate confirm the appointment of General Marshall, and thus turn Dean Acheson into a Siamese twin, in control of two of the most important Cabinet posts in the executive branch of the Government? That is what we are asked to do.
>
> It is tragic, Mr. President, that General Marshall is not enough of a patriot to tell the American people the truth of what has happened, and the terrifying story of what lies in store for us, instead of joining hands once more with this criminal crowd of traitors and Communist appeasers who, under the continuing influence and direction of Mr. Truman and Mr. Acheson, are still selling America down the river.[9]

Immediately, an honorable gentleman from Massachusetts, Senator Saltonstall, followed by Senator Lucas, rose to rebuke such words as being as contemptible as any ever uttered in that place of easy standards.

THE ATTACK REACHES ITS CLIMAX

The height of the attack on me came in December. On the fifteenth the President proclaimed a national emergency arising out of the war in Korea; on the seventeenth I left Washington for Brussels to attend the North Atlantic Treaty Council meeting, which was to create the integrated force and the

united command and appoint General Eisenhower as Supreme Commander
Allied Forces Europe. As I left, the Republicans in the House and Senate
caucused and asked President Truman to remove me from office. At this he
blew up in typical fashion:

> There have been new attacks within the past week against Secretary of State
> Acheson. I have been asked to remove him from office. The authors of this sugges-
> tion claim that this would be good for the country.
>
> How our position in the world would be improved by the retirement of Dean
> Acheson from public life is beyond me. Mr. Acheson has helped shape and carry
> out our policy of resistance to communist imperialism. From the time of our sharing
> of arms with Greece and Turkey nearly four years ago, and coming down to the
> recent moment when he advised me to resist the Communist invasion of South
> Korea, no official in our government has been more alive to Communism's threat to
> freedom or more forceful in resisting it.
>
> At this moment, he is in Brussels representing the United States in setting up
> mutual defenses against aggression. This has made it possible for me to designate
> General Eisenhower as Supreme Allied Commander in Europe.
>
> If Communism were to prevail in the world today—as it shall not prevail—
> Dean Acheson would be one of the first, if not the first, to be shot by the enemies of
> liberty and Christianity. . . .
>
> It is the same sort of thing that happened to Seward. President Lincoln was
> asked by a group of Republicans to dismiss Secretary of State Seward. He refused.
> So do I refuse to dismiss Secretary Acheson.[10]

The foregoing summary of 1950's shameful and nihilistic orgy exag-
gerates its effect upon us. Our minds were occupied with great problems and
our time with equally great efforts to meet them, with which subsequent chapters will deal. The fight with the footpads brought its own zest and evoked some
generous responses from political opponents. Humor and "contempt for the
contemptible," in Douglas Freeman's phrase, proved, as always, a shield and
buckler against "the fiery darts of the wicked." At one of my press conferences
at the height of the mid-1950 attacks on me, I replied to a question about how
they affected me with the story of the poor fellow found on the prairie during
the days of Indian fighting in the West and brought into a fort hospital. He was
in bad shape, scalped, wounded with an arrow sticking into his back, and left
for dead. As the surgeon prepared to extract the arrow, he asked, "Does it
hurt very much?"

To which the wounded man gasped out, "Only when I laugh."

One of the pleasanter memories of this period concerns my extemporaneous remarks made at the end of a speech to the American Society of Newspaper Editors on April 22, 1950,[11] which led the late Joseph Pulitzer to utter a
rebel yell and shout, "Pour it on 'em, Mr. Secretary!" Some of these gentlemen,
I said, reminded me of Mr. Gladstone's explanation of his efforts to reform the
unfortunate "fallen women" who accosted him and of counsel's esthetic defense of pornographic art and literature. It was not the activity, but the sprinkling of holy water that one found tiresome.

In a few concluding minutes I tried to make my audience think of the Foreign Service and the State Department not as stereotypes but as people giving their whole lives to the United States, competent, courageous, devoted. Only the last week, I said, two of our missions had been bombed—bombs had been tossed in the window and had exploded. No one, fortunately, had been killed, but a lot of people had been hurt. Had any of my audience ever experienced this sort of thing? Would they stick to a job where it was an occupational hazard? It was quite likely that some of these men and women would be killed. But there was no squeak out of them. We had an officer just back from Asia who had been held prisoner by the Chinese for a year, jailed, tortured. He had applied again for foreign duty.

Scores of people, I continued, were serving in areas of hot war where bombs were dropping and bullets were flying, and others were serving where dangers to health were as great as bullets, doctors few, and mothers were nurses as well as schoolteachers. They knew their duty and did it. Some were behind the Iron Curtain, where they were treated as criminals and denied all association with the people of the countries.

Why, I asked, did the editors not try the experiment of writing an open letter in their papers to these Foreign Service officers, our first line of defense in dangerous and difficult parts of the world, explaining to them the attacks being made upon them and upon the service of which they were as proud as these editors were of their profession? "Explain that to them if you can. You will find it difficult to do."

It was not strange that efforts should be made to penetrate the Department, I continued. They had been made throughout its history. There was a right way and a wrong way to solve that problem. The right way met the evil and preserved the institution; the wrong way did not meet the evil and destroyed the institution. More than that, it destroyed the faith of the country in its Government, and of our allies in us. I explained to the editors what we were doing to protect the Department; it did not include irresponsible character assassination. What had been going on reminded me of a recent horrible episode in Camden, New Jersey. A madman had appeared on the street and begun shooting people whom he met—a woman coming out of a store, a couple in a car stopped by a traffic light, another passing motorist—no plan, no purpose. It recalled the whimsical, mad brutality of Browning's Caliban, comparing his god, Setebos, to himself watching a procession of crabs on the sand. He lets twenty go by, picks up the twenty-first, tears off a flipper and throws it down. Three more go by, a fourth he crushes with his heel to watch it wriggle.

I don't ask you for sympathy. I don't ask you for help. You are in a worse situation than I am. I and my associates are only the intended victims of this mad and vicious operation. But you, unhappily, you by reason of your calling, are participants. You are unwilling participants, disgusted participants, but, nevertheless, participants, and your position is far more serious than mine.

As I leave this filthy business, and I hope never to speak of it again, I should like to leave in your minds the words of John Donne . . .

> Any man's death diminishes me, because I am
>   involved in mankind.
> And, therefore, never send to know for whom
>   the bell tolls;
> It tolls for thee.

As I sat down, it was with a hope that here and there among those rows of white, and possibly stuffed, shirt-fronts a conscience pricked.

A FEW BRIGHT SPOTS

Another episode I remember with gratitude and pleasure occurred at the Governors' Conference at White Sulphur Springs on June 20, 1950. I had gone there at the governors' invitation to discuss with them the State Department and the charges being made against it. This was five days before the attack from the north on Korea. Standing for four hours before them, for the most part answering a barrage of questions, I had begun to think that I had no friends—for enemies are more articulate than friends—when two men began to intervene on my behalf. They objected to loaded questions, getting them rephrased; protested against sneers and insults stated as questions, insisting that the chairman rule them out of order; and corrected misstatements of fact embedded in long-winded questions. These two governors had been the Republican candidates for President and Vice President of the United States in the election of 1948—Thomas E. Dewey of New York and Earl Warren of California. Tom Dewey and I had been friends for a good many years; I had never before had the pleasure of meeting Governor Warren. As both of these gentlemen could wield a shillelagh right lustily, my assailants grew more cautious and began to lose zest for the fray. When it ended in time for lunch, the two governors carried me off for a reviving drink and then to lunch with them in the center of the dining room, where everyone, they said, including the press, could see us and draw the obvious conclusion. My gratitude to and affection for these two great gentlemen has never wavered throughout what is now nearly twenty years.

The last episode occurred in December 1950. While his colleagues were caucusing to ask the President to remove me from office, my friend Congressman James Fulton, Republican of Pennsylvania, came to the airport with other friends, including the President, to see me off to Brussels. He brought me two presents: a pair of cuff links to help me keep my shirt on if foreigners started treating me as my fellow countrymen did, and a beautifully printed and bound edition of the Koran. Since my enemies had not taken kindly to a certain reference to Christian principles, I might find the same ideas expressed more acceptably in the Koran.

Two other acts of public support touched me in those days of harsh attack. In the early summer Harvard University conferred on me the honorary degree of Doctor of Laws. I found it an intimidating experience to appear and speak from the same platform on the same occasion upon which my illustrious predecessor three years before had made his memorable speech proposing the Marshall Plan. In the autumn of the same year Freedom House in New York gave me its award for 1950. "This evening," I said, "spent with friends who have come together to do me honor and give me heart, is a cool spring to a thirsty wayfarer."[12]

I met McCarthy only once, when leaving the Senate office building, after one of the hearings on the removal of General MacArthur, accompanied by my guard and a pack of reporters and photographers. As we approached the elevators, the guard, a pleasant but stupid former football player, ran ahead to hold the elevator for me. As I entered, a man was already there. "Hello, Mr. Secretary," he said, and stuck out his hand. Instinctively I took it, simultaneously recognizing his much-cartooned, black-jowled face. Flashbulbs exploded as the doors slid shut. Neither of us spoke during our few seconds' ride. "What happened in the elevator?" the press asked him. "Neither of us," he replied, "turned his back on the other." It was a smart trick and, of course, got him on front pages across the country.

CONCLUDING THOUGHTS

A good deal of nonsense has been written about the effect of the attack of the primitives, before and during McCarthy's reign, on the China policy of the Truman Administration. Whatever effect it had on our successors, it had little on us. The fact was that, caught between the bungling incompetence of Chiang Kai-shek's Kuomintang and the intransigence of Mao Tse-tung's Communists, our choices for policy decisions were small indeed. The Chinese clearly found the United States far more useful as an enemy than in any other relationship, and went out of their way to insure that an enemy we remained. Those who tried to establish diplomatic and friendly relations with Peking found it a useless formality. The most deluded of them all, Nehru's India, received a military attack for her pains. Our European friends found their missions contemptuously isolated and neglected.

Relations with Formosa underwent a change on June 25, 1950, with the attack on Korea. Then the President announced a policy intended to seal off Formosa from the conflict. He interposed the Seventh Fleet to prevent any attack from either Chinese side upon the other, the purpose being to quarantine the fighting within Korea, not to encourage its extension. When General MacArthur toyed with undercutting this policy by suggesting, as some Republican senators had, using Chiang's refugee army in the Korean fighting, he was sharply rapped over the knuckles. Koreans were being trained and armed to defend their own country.

McCarthy's name has been given, as I have said, to a phenomenon broader than his own participation in it, the hysteria growing out of fear of Communist subversion that followed both world wars. His influence was purely domestic as gauleiter and leader of the mob in the last, mad massacre. The result was deplorable. The Government's foreign and civil services, universities, and China-studies programs in them took a decade to recover from this sadistic pogrom; congressional assaults on the executive branch under the leadership of McCarran and Bridges approximated those in 1919 to 1922 under Attorney

General A. Mitchell Palmer. The slaughter occurred in the night of the long knives from 1950 through 1953.

McCarthy was often and erroneously compared to Hitler, but he lacked the ambition, the toughness, the demonic drive to become a villain on a grand scale. He read Hitler. My wife insisted that this must be so because of his methods; I doubted. One evening, sitting beside President Nathan M. Pusey of Harvard, who had lived in Appleton, Wisconsin, when McCarthy lived there, she put the question to him. He confirmed her views, telling her that fellow boarders in the boardinghouse McCarthy lived in and patrons of the same barber shop he used had reported that McCarthy would produce *Mein Kampf* and read from it, chuckling and saying, "That's the way to do it." But he was essentially a lazy, small-town bully, without sustaining purpose, who on his own would soon have petered out. Flattered, built up and sustained by Taft, the Republican right, and their accomplice, the press, printing what was not news and not fit to print, he served their various purposes. After the election of 1952 they no longer had any use for him, but, encouraged by the fear of the timorous in high places, he was not shrewd enough to see that his day was over. For a year his own momentum carried him on. He became a nuisance; those who had used him dropped him. Finally a peppery little man from Vermont, Senator Ralph Flanders, tired of the antics of this boor in a supposed gentlemen's club, called upon the members to censure him for—of all things!—being rude in the clubhouse. This they did by just over a two-thirds majority. The very contemptuousness of his rejection broke him.

For my fifty-eighth birthday some of my friends with curious prescience had engraved, adding my name and the date April 11, 1951, an extract from a letter written by Thomas Jefferson to Judge James Sullivan on May 21, 1805. I say "curious prescience" because on that April 11 General Douglas MacArthur was relieved by President Truman of all his commands and a new torrent of abuse broke over the President and myself, chosen as chief villain by the Republican right. Mr. Jefferson had written:

You have indeed received the federal unction of lying and slandering. But who has not? Who will ever come again into eminent office, unanointed by this chrism? It seems to be fixed that falsehood and calumny are to be their ordinary engines of opposition; engines which will not be entirely without effect. The circle of characters equal to the first stations is not too large, and will be lessened by the voluntary retreat of those whose sensibilities are stronger than their confidence in the justice of public opinion. . . . Yet this effect of sensibility must not be yielded to. If we suffer ourselves to be frightened from our post by mere lying, surely the enemy will use that weapon; for what one so cheap to those of whose system of politics morality makes no part.[13]

41. A NEW DEFINITION OF
FOREIGN POLICY

EVEN BEFORE THE President on January 31, 1950, had ordered Defense and State to review our objectives in peace and war (see Chapter 38), Paul Nitze and the Policy Planning Staff had arranged a working relationship with the Liaison Committee of the Atomic Energy Commission and the Joint Strategic Survey Committee at the Pentagon. This connection had the blessing of Major General James H. Burns, who had returned to active duty as the Secretary of Defense's liaison officer with the State Department. To be sure, Louis Johnson had directed that Burns should consult solely with Freeman Matthews, Deputy Under Secretary, State's liaison officer with Defense, but this had seemed to mean that consultative arrangements must be authorized by these two officers, not conducted by them alone. I left the groups to get on with their work, for, as the last two chapters have perhaps suggested, January and February were full months. Moreover, a new nongovernmental duty had crowded into my schedule.

ACADEMIC INTERLUDE

In 1936 I had been elected a "life" fellow of the Yale Corporation. "Life" ended at sixty-eight, the compulsory retiring age that the corporation had fixed for the faculty and wisely applied to itself. Service on it for twenty-five years was one of the most rewarding experiences of a lifetime. Special zest was added by the fact that for most of this period Senator Robert A. Taft was one of my colleagues.[1]

Perhaps the corporation's most important duty is the election of a president of the university, a duty which engaged us in the academic year 1949–50, at the end of which President Charles Seymour would retire. Yale desperately needed young, vigorous, and imaginative leadership, and to some of us the man to provide it was at hand on our own faculty. However, in the eyes of most of our colleagues he had handicaps. They were serious—youth, little reputation (he was not in *Who's Who*), gaiety and the gift of mimicry, fierce intolerance of the shoddy and second-rate. His virtues were unfashionable and not so well known: excellent historical writing and teaching and a passion for education. This was a time of the public figure as university president—Dwight Eisenhower at Columbia, Harold Stassen at Pennsylvania.

Only four of us, then among the youngest fellows, believed Alfred Whitney Griswold was the man. To attain a majority in a group of seventeen required more than doubling our number, a task calling for discretion, some managerial skill, and, on occasion, guile. It would not, for instance, gain Bob Taft's vote for a candidate to know that I favored him. A committee narrowed the list of all those put forward. Our candidate remained on it; so did an able non-Yale man who was president of an eminent smaller college. We concentrated on him, talked of the need for new blood, the danger of inbreeding, the great contributions of President James Rowland Angell, Yale's only non-Yale president. Support for the outsider grew to two short of a majority. Two or three others split the true-blues. They became alarmed (so, incidentally, did we, since the ballots were secret). In the interval between the January and February meetings our manager, a classmate of Griswold's, former football captain, New York lawyer, and a sound Yale man, was approached to wean away some of those who had fallen for a foreign importation. He thought he might have some chance if he could report growing sentiment for Griswold. He was told that he could. The new president was elected on February 11.

Whitney Griswold, wholly unsuspecting, was amazed. He proved to be a superb president, bringing fresh vigor and innovation to the intellectual and educational life of the university. Although he hated the idea of raising money, it came to him because of the passion and purity of his interest. For just over a decade, until he was stricken with cancer, he grew until he stood with the three great figures of American university education—Charles W. Eliot of Harvard, Daniel Coit Gilman of The Johns Hopkins University, and William Rainey Harper of the University of Chicago. During those years I worked with him closely and loved him. On the afternoon he died I sat beside his bedside and, when talk tired him, held his hand.

Senator Taft Makes a Point · In the autumn of 1950 I went to New Haven to attend Whitney Griswold's inauguration. On arriving at Woodbridge Hall, the administration building, an old friend, Carl Lohmann, Secretary of Yale, told me bluntly that Senator Taft, my immediate senior on the corporation, beside whom I had sat and walked in processions for fifteen years, had said that he would be embarrassed to be photographed walking with me in the then state of political tension. Would I, Lohmann asked, help resolve the embarassment by dropping back, allowing another friend, Lucius Robinson, President of the Alumni Association, to be injected into the august ranks of the corporation? This would leave me in the company of an even older friend, and colleague, W. S. (Lefty) Lewis. I readily agreed.

When we had robed and formed up immediately behind the Senator and Lou Robinson, I remarked to Lewis in audible *sotto voce* that it was pretty hard after years of devoted service to Yale to have snatched from me the public recognition of walking beside Senator Taft. Lewis agreed, but pointed out that it was only one more sacrifice for Yale. The Senator froze, but Robinson turned around and suggested that we look at it from the point of view of a young man to whom had come this unhoped-for bonanza. We examined this aspect of the situation as the Senator's rising blood pressure turned his neck and ears pink but brought no other recognition of the contretemps. Then the procession moved off to Woolsey Hall, where the corporation mounted the platform to sit like the Supreme Court flanking the President and President-elect. Lou Robinson had been properly eliminated from the Sanhedrin.

The ceremony over, we filed out behind the new President and President-emeritus. Inevitably Bob Taft and I came together. All danger appearing over, the Senator was all affability, which I warmly reciprocated. As we came to the door of the back courtyard, on our way to our starting point, I bade the Senator farewell, saying that we were unlikely to meet again soon and held out my hand. He took it as we passed into the sunlight and a hundred flashbulbs caught us in this act of fraternal recognition.

NSC-68

A Difficult Pregnancy · After nearly three months of work by the State and Defense planners, with which I had kept in close touch—and kept the President in close touch—Nitze, General Burns, and I thought that the two groups should meet with Secretary Johnson and me to go over a preliminary draft report for such guidance as we might give before it was put into form for departmental review in both places. I was not sure to what extent General Burns had kept Johnson abreast of his own department's work. Because in our building at that time the Secretary did not have adequate conference facilities, Johnson and his people were invited to meet us on March 22, 1950, in Nitze's Planning Staff room, next door to my own. Copies of the draft paper had been given to him a week before.

After apparently friendly greetings all around, I asked Nitze to outline the paper and its conclusions. Nitze, who was a joy to work with because of his clear, incisive mind, began to do so. Johnson listened, chair tilted back, gazing at the ceiling, seemingly calm and attentive. Suddenly he lunged forward with a crash of chair legs on the floor and fist on the table, scaring me out of my shoes. No one, he shouted, was going to make arrangements for him to meet with another Cabinet officer and a roomful of people and be told what he was going to report to the President. Who authorized these meetings contrary to his orders? What was this paper, which he had never seen? Trying to calm him down, I told him that we were working under the President's orders to him and me and through his designated channel, General Burns. As for the paper, he had had it for a week. But he would have none of it and, gathering General Bradley and other Defense people, stalked out of the room. The rest of us were left in shocked disbelief. General Burns, who had stayed behind, put his head in his hands and wept in shame. I was then summoned into my own office, where Louis Johnson began again to storm at me that he had been insulted. This was too much. I told him since he had started to leave, to get on with it and the State Department would complete the report alone and explain why.

Rejoining the still shell-shocked group, I reported the latest episode to Admiral Souers and James Lay, who left, in turn, to inform the President. Within the hour the President telephoned me, expressing his outrage and telling me to carry on exactly as we had been doing. At the slightest sign of obstruction or foot-dragging in the Pentagon I was to report to him. From this time on until the President felt it necessary in September to ask for Johnson's resignation, evidence accumulated to convince me that Louis Johnson was mentally ill. His conduct became too outrageous to be explained by mere cussedness. It did not surprise me when some years later he underwent a brain operation.

Nitze and his group pressed on with their work, getting complete cooperation from their Pentagon associates. We had no more meetings with the Secretary of Defense. When the paper was completed early in April, I had it submitted to him so that he might sign it, if he chose to do so. To my surprise he did, and it went to the President on April 7, 1950, as a Joint Report. Johnson's signature, I learned later, did not surprise my colleagues as much as it did me, for they had submitted it to him bearing not only my signature but the concurrences of the Chiefs of Staff, the Joint Strategic Survey Committee, the Liaison Committee, and the secretaries of the three services. Johnson was not left in a strong offensive position.

NSC-68 lacked, as submitted, any section discussing costs. This was not an oversight. To have attempted one would have made impossible all those concurrences and prevented any recommendation to the President. It would have raised at once the extent and tempo of the program deemed necessary to carry out the conclusions and recommendations. Each department, each service, and each individual would have become a special pleader or an assistant President weighing all the needs of the nation and the political problems presented by each need. Our function was to get the international situation analyzed, the problems it presented stated, and recommendations made. After preliminary study, the President on the twelfth asked the Joint Chiefs to have cost estimates made. While this was being done with due deliberation, the paper was discussed with the President in the National Security Council on April 25 and became national policy, known as NSC-68.

The Threat Stated · Discussing the paper some years later with a group of veterans of this campaign, one who had entered it toward its end remarked that when he first read NSC-68 he thought that it was "the most ponderous expression of elementary ideas" he had ever come across. Allowing for the natural exaggeration and tartness of a bon mot, this was so. As Oliver Wendell Holmes, Jr., has wisely said, there are times when "we need education in the obvious more than investigation of the obscure." The purpose of NSC-68 was to so bludgeon the mass mind of "top government" that not only could the President make a decision but that the decision could be carried out. Even so, it is doubtful whether anything like what happened in the next few years could have been done had not the Russians been stupid enough to have instigated the attack against South Korea and opened the "hate America" campaign.[2]

NSC-68, a formidable document, presents more than a clinic in political science's latest, most fashionable, and most boring study, the "decision-making process," for it carries us beyond decisions to what should be their fruits, action. If it is helpful to think of societies as entities, it is equally so to consider their direction centers as groups of cells, thinking cells, action cells, emotion cells, and so on. The society operates best, improves its chances of survival most, in which the thinking cells work out a fairly long-range course of conduct before the others take over—provided it has also a little bit better than average luck. We had an excellent group of thought cells. They supported the facts of the paper by tables and tables of figures. Less than one per cent of these figures drew upon classified sources, but they put these "facts" beyond argument— facts about ourselves, our allies, and the Soviet Union. Conclusions on un- measurable matters were painstakingly checked against past performance. Upon the resulting analysis rested judgment, answers to the question: What should be done about it?

NSC-68 has not been declassified and may not be quoted, but its contents have been widely discussed in print.[3] Many of my own public statements were properly based upon the fundamental conclusions stated in this leading em- bodiment of Government policy.

The paper began with a statement of the conflicting aims and purposes of the two superpowers: the priority given by the Soviet rulers to the Kremlin design, world domination,† contrasted with the American aim, an environment in which free societies could exist and flourish. Throughout 1950, the year my immolation in the Senate began, I went about the country preaching this premise of NSC-68.

The task of a public officer seeking to explain and gain support for a major policy is not that of the writer of a doctoral thesis. Qualification must give way to simplicity of statement, nicety and nuance to bluntness, almost brutality, in carrying home a point. It is better to carry the hearer or reader into the quadrant of one's thought than merely to make a noise or to mislead him utterly. In the State Department we used to discuss how much time that myth- ical "average American citizen" put in each day listening, reading, and arguing about the world outside his own country. Assuming a man or woman with a fair education, a family, and a job in or out of the house, it seemed to us that ten minutes a day would be a high average. If this were anywhere near right, points to be understandable had to be clear. If we made our points clearer than truth, we did not differ from most other educators and could hardly do other- wise.

So our analysis of the threat combined the ideology of communist doc- trine and the power of the Russian state into an aggressive expansionist drive, which found its chief opponent and, therefore, target in the antithetic ideas and power of our own country. It was true and understandable to describe the Russian motivating concept as being that "no state is friendly which is not subservient," and ours that "no state is unfriendly which, in return for respect for its rights, respects the rights of other states."[4] While our own society felt no compulsion to bring all societies into conformity with it, the Kremlin hier- archy was not content merely to entrench its regime but wished to expand its control directly and indirectly over other people within its reach. "It takes more," I said, "than bare hands and a desire for peace to turn back this threat."[5]

Such an analysis was decried by some liberals and some Kremlinologists. The real threat, they said, lay in the weakness of the Western European social, economic, and political structure. Correct that and the Russian danger would disappear. This I did not believe. The threat to Western Europe seemed to me singularly like that which Islam had posed centuries before, with its combination of ideological zeal and fighting power. Then it had taken the same combination to meet it: Germanic power in the east and Frankish in Spain, both energized by a great outburst of military power and social organization in Europe. This time it would need the added power and energy of America, for the drama was now played on a world stage.

If these were the intentions of the Kremlin, what were its capabilities for realizing and ours for frustrating them? Ours was demonstrably the potentially stronger society, but did it have the strength now, and would it have it in the future, to frustrate the Kremlin design? At the end of the war we were the most powerful nation on earth, with the greatest army, navy, and air force, a monopoly of the most destructive weapon, and all supported by the most productive industry and agriculture. But now our army had been demobilized, our navy put in mothballs, and our air force no longer had a monopoly of atomic weapons. In three or four years at the most we could be threatened with devastating damage, against which no sure protection appeared. Surely we produced far more aluminum, for instance, than the Soviet Union; but while we splashed it over the front of automobiles, in Russia more went into military aircraft than here. On the other hand, our almost minute army cost many times what theirs did. A brief comparison of the pay, care, and equipment of private soldiers showed why. Half the total effort of their rival society went into creating military power, which in a short time at present rates could top ours. What relation did these facts have to foreign policy, national security, the existence of a spacious environment for free societies? How much of our national product would we need to divert, as sensible insurance, to an arms effort we loathed? The paper recommended specific measures for a large and immediate improvement of military forces and weapons, and of the economic and morale factors which underlay our own and our allies' ability to influence the conduct of other societies.

The Response Recommended · In explaining to the nation the course it recommended, I made clear, also—in an address in Dallas on June 13, 1950—those it would not recommend.[6] We should not pull down the blinds, I said, and sit in the parlor with a loaded shotgun, waiting. Isolation was not a realistic course of action. It did not work and it had not been cheap. Appeasement of Soviet ambitions was, in fact, only an alternative form of isolation. It would lead to a final struggle for survival with both our moral and military positions weakened. A third course, euphemistically called preventive war, adopted with disastrous results in other times by other types of people and governments than ours, would take the form of nuclear attack on the Soviet Union. It would not solve problems; it would multiply them. Then as now nothing seemed to me more depressing in the history of our own country than the speeches of the

1850s about "the irrepressible conflict." War is not inevitable. But talk of war's inevitability had, in the past, helped to make it occur.

While NSC-68 did not contain cost estimates, that did not mean we had not discussed them. To carry through the sort of rearmament and rehabilita-tion-of-forces program that we recommended, at the rate we thought necessary, for ourselves and with help for our allies, would require, our group estimated, a military budget of the magnitude of about fifty billion dollars per annum. This was a very rough guess, but, as the existing ceiling was thirteen and a half billion, the proposal—or rather the situation out of which it grew—required considerable readjustment of thinking. It seemed better to begin this process by facing the broad facts, trends, and probabilities before getting lost in budgetary intricacies. If that begins before an administration has decided what it *wants* to do, or made what diplomats used to call a decision "in principle"—in es-sence—the mice in the Budget Bureau will nibble to death the will to decide.

Furthermore, whatever the cost might be, some such program was essen-tial and well within national economic capacity. It obviously would raise some difficult choices between this and other uses of production, but the national product was not static and might be increased—as, indeed, it was. Our duty was not to make these decisions but to press for decisions, combining per-suasion with the most powerful statement of the case. Nor did our duty, as I saw it, stop there. It was not enough to give the President wise, though tough, advice and expect him to create acceptance in Congress and the country for the resulting action. We also had a duty to explain and persuade. An incident about this time illustrates my point. The Marquis of Salisbury, who had had long experience in the Foreign Office, coming into the main entrance of the State Department with me, saw posters announcing meetings with various groups then in session. When he asked about them, I suggested that we make a brief tour. In one room an officer was discussing with a group of schoolteachers our participation in the UN Educational, Scientific, and Cultural Organization; in another a foreign policy association was learning about a current crisis in the Middle East; in a third a Hispano-American group was talking about Latin American affairs. Lord Salisbury could not, he said, conceive of similar groups in the Foreign Office. "This is truly," he added, "democracy in action."

We Explain to the Country · The need to tell the country how we saw the situation created by the Soviet Union and the necessary response to it came soon after the President's announcement of his hydrogen bomb decision. Two friendly Democratic senators, Brien McMahon and Millard Tydings, made dramatic speeches in the Senate during February 1950.[7] They reflected liberal criticism of Administration policy and a sort of guilt complex common among atomic scientists about the atomic bomb. McMahon urged the end of atomic armaments and an era of "world-wide atomic peace" and "atomic-created abundance for all men." This was to be achieved by a "moral crusade for peace" and a fifty-billion-dollar "global Marshall Plan" financed by the United States and augmented by an undertaking by all nations to put two-thirds of their armament expenditures to "constructive ends." Tydings, Chairman of the

Armed Services Committee, proposed that the President convoke a world-disarmament committee to deal with all weapons. In one day's mail, I wrote our daughter, I had a letter from an old friend and leading liberal "which says that if I don't get up and lead, move, advance, radiate peace, etc., I shall be left watching an embattled country march by—where to, he says not. It is an interesting letter to one who is not inactive on a busy stage; but it is all meant well. I had the same from Mr. Trygve Lie, who is also more eager than aware."

At this time the Secretary General, preaching a ten-point program of negotiation with Moscow, was about to start off on a tour of United Nations capitals. This, he insisted, was not appeasement but "negotiation," which requires "honest give-and-take by both sides." "What we need," he said, "what the world needs, is a twenty year program to win peace through the United Nations."[8] It was to start off with something that, despite Mr. Lie's protestations, sounded very much like appeasement to me, luring the Soviet Union back to the United Nations, from which Malik and his cohorts had withdrawn, by the majority's reversing itself and seating the Communists as the representatives of China. To me all this made little sense. I said that on Chinese representation we held to our expressed views but would "accept the decision of any organ of the United Nations made by the necessary majority, and we [would] not walk out." So far as negotiations were concerned we would consider anything put forward in the United Nations, but, meanwhile, "we can't afford to wait and merely hope that [Soviet] policies will change. We must carry forward in our own determination to create situations of strength in the free world, because this is the only basis on which lasting agreement with the Soviet Government is possible."

My long press conference on February 8, 1950, immediately after the two Senate speeches, began a continued discussion of our response to the Soviet threat.[9] Four themes ran through it, beginning with the different conception in Soviet and Western thought of the purpose and role of negotiation in international relations and the consequences of this difference. In Western tradition negotiation was bargaining to achieve a mutually desired agreement. In communist doctrine it was war by political means to achieve an end unacceptable to the other side. In both cases it was a means to an end, but in the latter case the ends were, if understood, mutually exclusive. The second, related theme was that in dealing with the Soviet Union the most useful negotiation was by acts rather than words, and stability was better and more reliable than verbal agreement. From all this came insistence upon repairing weaknesses and creating "situations of strength" and, as a means to them, the NSC-68 program. Third came the transformation of our two former enemies into allies and their attachment by firm bonds of security and economic interest to the free nations in Europe and Asia. The fourth point was doubtless a futile one to make in view of existing political passions, but it had the small merit of being true. It was that continued quarreling within our own country regarding the proper mix of negotiation and strength in dealing with the Soviet threat created a major source of both weakness and the appearance of weakness.

I pointed out to the press that the speeches of the two senators dealt more with the goal toward which we were striving than with the way to get there; more with ends than means. If we could reach the ends on which we all agreed —peace, stability, and progress—by agreement on the means, that would be the simplest, easiest, and most desirable way to do it. Four years of trial had convinced us that agreement with the Kremlin was not then possible. Certain obstacles stood in the way that had to be removed. Among them was the existence in the non-Communist world of large areas of weakness, which by its very nature the Soviet system had to exploit. They presented irresistible invitations to fish in troubled waters. To urge them not to fish, to try to agree not to fish, was as futile as talking to a force of nature. One cannot argue with a river; it is going to flow. One can dam it or deflect it, but not argue with it. Therefore, we had been at work to create strength where there had been weakness, to turn our former enemies into allies, to replace the dams that once contained Russia to the east and to the west, to aid growth and progress in the undeveloped areas in the world.

The Need for National Unity · The next week I was talking to a group in the White House about the impediments to national unity that came from those who insisted upon the rightness and righteousness of their own paths to peace.[10] There were those, I said, who believed that good will and negotiation would solve all problems, that if only the President and Stalin would "get their feet under the same table" they could iron out any and all international difficulties. The problem lay not in where the leaders' feet were but where their minds were. We had tried most earnestly to get Kremlin minds running toward cooperation and failed. Then there were those who frightened themselves and their fellow citizens into paralysis by apocalyptic warnings of the end to come through nuclear weapons. The dangers were great enough in all conscience, but the fact that war could be even more terrible in the future than in the past should increase rather than diminish action to eliminate situations that might lead to it.

Other fomenters of disunity declared that the time had come to "call the bluff" of our opponents and "have a showdown" with them. These resorts to the language of poker showed the recklessness of the gamble inherent in them. Finally, I said in concluding my talk, there were purists who would have no dealings with any but the fairest of democratic states, going from state to state with political litmus paper testing them for true-blue democracy. They were repelled by some of the practices reported in Greece, Turkey, and North and South Africa, among other places, but curiously hopeful about the Russian future. All these points of view represented escapism in dealing with the world as it was and escape from building with the materials at hand a strong, safer, and more stable position for free communities of which we were one.

My constant appeal to American liberals was to face the long, hard years and not to distract us with the offer of short cuts and easy solutions begotten by good will out of the angels of man's better nature. "Until the Soviet leaders do genuinely accept a 'live and let live' philosophy . . . no approach from the free world . . . and no Trojan dove from the Communist movement will help to resolve our mutual problems," I said on one occasion;[11] on another: "The road to freedom and to peace which I have pictured is a hard one. The times in which we live must be painted in the sombre values of Rembrandt. The background is dark, the shadows deep. Outlines are obscure. The central point, however, glows with light; and, though it often brings out the glint of steel, it touches colors of unimaginable beauty. For us, that central point is the growing unity of free men the world over. This is our shaft of light, our hope, and our promise."[12]

These themes I repeated and elaborated from Massachusetts to Texas, on the Berkeley campus in California and at the United Nations in New York. What we expected to achieve by the creation of strength throughout the free world—military, economic, and political—to replace the inviting weak spots offered to Soviet probing was to diminish further the possibility of war, to prevent "settlements by default" to Soviet pressures, to show the Soviet leaders by successful containment that they could not hope to expand their influence throughout the world and must modify their policies. Then, and only then, could meaningful negotiation be possible on the larger issues that divided us. In the meantime the search for miracle cures for the earth's ills was a dangerous form of self-delusion, which only diverted us from the hard duties of our times.

In my speech at Berkeley in March 1950[13] I told my audience that even though important settlements through negotiation would be impossible for long years to come, there were some quite simple things the Soviet leaders could do to make coexistence a great deal more tolerable to everyone, while leaving much yet to do. For instance, for five years the Soviet Union had blocked all efforts to move toward ending the state of war and occupation in Germany, Austria, and Japan. Granted that peace treaties presented difficulties, some progress toward relaxation of tensions, return of prisoners, a peaceful settlement of Korea's problems would not seem impossible. Similarly, some relaxation of rule by Soviet force in Eastern Europe and lessening of Soviet obstruction in the United Nations or in continued discussion of atomic energy problems would be welcome. Perhaps on the most primitive level of international intercourse— the treatment of diplomatic representatives and the language of international communication—some improvement in debased Communist standards might be possible. "I must warn you not to raise your hopes," I told my listeners. "I see no evidence that the Soviet leaders will change their conduct until the progress of the free world convinces them that they cannot profit from a continuation of these tensions."

This visit to San Francisco, a most strenuous one requiring two major speeches and two lesser ones, holds poignant memories. One was of speaking after dinner at the Press Club. It was to be a private and confidential speech, what in other press circles is called "off the record." In San Francisco it is called "speaking behind the cat"—a large carved ebony cat carried in with ceremony and put before the speaker after the tables are cleared. The custom, I was told, began after the great earthquake and fire had destroyed the city in 1906. When the first daring spirits reached the ruins of the old clubhouse, all that remained to identify it amid the general devastation was the large fireplace in the lounge.

Curled up beside it was a half-starved and badly singed cat, which was promptly adopted and lived out its remaining eight lives near the hearth of the new club. The cat was famous for its discretion, for although it listened carefully to all that was said, it was never known to have repeated a word. When in time it went to its multiple rewards, it was reproduced, larger than life size, with eyes and mouth tight shut, looking altogether inscrutable, an outward and visible sign of the security pledged to one who spoke behind it.

The other memory is wholly personal. Throughout our daughter's illness the President and Mrs. Truman could not have been more thoughtful and solicitous. My absence on the Coast came at a time of a difficult, extensive, and worrisome operation. The President telephoned each morning to my wife at Saranac, and then relayed to me cheerful bulletins.

42. EUROPE AND THE SCHUMAN PLAN

ON MAY 6, after participating in a three-day state visit to Washington by Prime Minister of Pakistan Liaquat Ali Khan and Begum Sahiba, we climbed wearily aboard the presidential plane, *Independence*, for Paris en route to London and a ministerial meeting of the North Atlantic Treaty Council. Again the President came to the plane to see me off. We had been through a long, strenuous, wearying winter and spring. Colleagues in the State Department thought I might get a few days' rest and please Schuman by starting early and going via Paris for some friendly talks with the French before plunging into the series of meetings that always clustered about the North Atlantic Council. It turned out quite otherwise. The days in Paris, from the moment of my arrival on Sunday morning, May 7, were far from restful; and my presence there, in view of what occurred, convinced Bevin of a Franco-American conspiracy against him.

SCENE 1: PARIS

In the formal reception room in the American Embassy residence on the day of my arrival, Schuman, through an interpreter, disclosed to Ambassador Bruce and me his Coal and Steel Plan for Western Europe, which he and Jean Monnet had been developing in such secrecy that they had not yet discussed it with the French Cabinet. It was, indeed, as Bruce called it in a cable a week later, "the most imaginative and far-reaching approach that has been made for generations to the settlement of fundamental differences between France and Germany." The whole French-German production of coal and steel would be placed under a joint high authority, with an organization open to the participation of other European nations.

Schuman urged the utmost secrecy upon us. A leak before the Cabinet was aligned could wreck both the plan and the Government, so we were asked not to inform our colleagues in Paris or to send cables or to have memoranda transcribed for two days. Since the President was in the Far West, the matter of informing him did not arise for at least a day. Meanwhile, we agreed that Jean Monnet and John McCloy should be brought in to discuss the plan further with Bruce and me. This was a great help to us, especially to me. Training in the common law concentrates one's attention on the specific. The civil lawyer thinks in terms of principles. Those who have really great constructive ideas are often vague about what they mean specifically. To pin them down tends to frustrate them. Added to this handicap, Schuman and I were talking through an interpreter who was not familiar with the subject matter of our talk. Ideas had a hard time getting through in either direction.

Jean Monnet was soon revealed as the plan's originator. In him fanatical zeal for supranational points of view and organization was combined with shrewd business judgment and experience. During the First World War he had been impressed, through the work of the Allied Maritime Transport Council, by the degree to which an international staff could transcend national consider- ations, and even pressures, in administering the use of the merchant fleets of all the allies to achieve an agreed common purpose through agreed procedures. He firmly believed that the thinking of groups, even those as tightly indoctri- nated as business communities, was conditioned and confined by the frame within which it takes place. Once the small, restricting frame is broken, thought rapidly expands and accommodates itself to a wider setting. After that the effect is most unlikely to be undone. This belief, which I share, helped us both to survive General de Gaulle.

The Coal and Steel Plan was Monnet's reaction to a rather grandiose idea of Prime Minister Georges Bidault's put forth in a speech at Lyons on April 16 calling for an "Atlantic High Council for Peace." This appeared to combine propaganda, in the use of the word "peace," with the urge to pile machinery on machinery in an effort to form a holding company to "coordinate" the North Atlantic Treaty, the Western Union, the Organization for European Economic Cooperation, and the Council of Europe. Whatever idea may have lurked within this proposal was stillborn. Monnet's apparently more limited and modest plan was, in reality, more imaginative and far-reaching, because it picked out the basic materials of Europe's industrial economy, coal and steel, to put under the supranational control of an organization of the participating European states, with governmental powers and clearly defined purposes. The High Authority's immediate powers and effects would be great; its potential ones, still greater. Only by the patient coaching of Monnet and McCloy and their answers to our questions did this come home to us.

All sorts of questions at once arose. To begin with, was the plan cover for a gigantic European cartel? We became convinced that this was not the inten- tion of its founders and that provisions to guard against this result would be incorporated in the charter. The more we studied the plan, the more we were impressed by it. Nothing better expresses the purpose and method of the pro- posal than the first two paragraphs of the French Government's announcement on May 9, as it appeared the next morning in *The Times* of London:

World peace cannot be safeguarded without the making of efforts proportion- ate to the dangers which threaten it. The contribution which an organized and living Europe can bring to civilization is indispensable to the maintenance of peaceful relations. In taking upon herself for more than 20 years the role of champion of a united Europe, France has always had as her essential aim the service of peace. A united Europe was not achieved; and we had war. Europe will not be made all at once, or according to a single, general plan. It will be built through concrete achieve- ments, which first create a *de facto* solidarity. The gathering together of the nations of Europe requires the elimination of the age-old opposition of France and Ger- many. The first concern in any action undertaken must be these two countries.

With this aim in view, the French Government proposes to take action immediately on one limited but decisive point; the French Government proposes to place Franco-German production of coal and steel as a whole under a common higher authority, within the framework of an organization open to the participation of the other countries of Europe. The pooling of coal and steel production should immediately provide for the setting-up of common foundations for economic development as a first step in the federation of Europe, and will change the destinies of those regions which have long been devoted to the manufacture of munitions of war, of which they have been the most constant victims.

The genius of the Schuman-Monnet plan lay in its practical, common-sense approach, its avoidance of the appearance of limitations upon sovereignty and touchy political problems. What could be more earthy than coal and steel, or more desirable than a pooling and common direction of France and Germany's coal and steel industries? This would end age-old conflicts. It was not exclusive but open to all European nations who wished to participate in a coal and steel authority designed for specific purposes and with powers adequate to accomplish its purposes.

The Times—and, indeed, it was not alone—was perplexed by M. Schuman's method of announcement before official soundings in other capitals. When it reported him as saying that "the subject had not been broached in his talks with Mr. Acheson yesterday [May 8], even in 'the personal' conversation with which the day opened," both *The Times* and M. Schuman were correct. It had been broached on Sunday, May 7, when all good people, including reporters, should have been in church.

When the President had returned to Washington, I sent him a brief for his "eyes only" message, asking that, should rumors come from Europe of an impending important development, he withhold comment until I could inform him further. He agreed. The next day, the French Cabinet having approved the submission of the Schuman Plan to the Chamber of Deputies, an outline of the plan, to be kept secret until Schuman's speech, was sent to him with a request that after the speech I be authorized to express sympathetic interest pending further elaboration from Paris. Again the President approved. This set at rest my apprehension that upon receiving partial information the Antitrust Division in the Department of Justice might stimulate some critical comments, which would have been damaging at that stage.

SCENE 2: LONDON

On reaching London on Tuesday, May 9, the day Schuman was to make his statement presenting the plan, I found Ernest Bevin in distressing shape when we met him and his staff in midmorning. He had recently undergone a painful operation and was taking sedative drugs that made him doze off, sometimes quite soundly, during the discussion. His staff seemed accustomed to it, though I found it disconcerting. At any rate, our talk got nowhere, and not knowing what, if anything, had yet occurred in Paris, I did not feel able to inform our British friends of what Schuman might be doing at the moment. During luncheon with Bevin and Attlee word came to Bevin and me separately that early in the afternoon René Massigli, the French Ambassador, wanted an appointment with Bevin to convey an important message, and another with me an hour later. My embarrassment grew as the company speculated about this mystery. Again ignorance of what had happened or, perhaps, would be happening as Massigli talked still kept me silent. When he did call at midafternoon, it was to announce the proposal of the Schuman Plan to the Chamber, which had gone according to schedule and about which I quite obviously knew far more than Massigli did.

Waiting for us at the Foreign Office, Bevin was in a highly emotional state, very angry with me and, what was much worse, rapidly working himself into bitter opposition to Schuman and the Schuman Plan. He at once charged that Schuman and I had cooked up the whole plan, purposely keeping him in the dark, and that I had gone to Paris to put the finishing touches on it and get it publicly announced before he ever heard of it. The circumstantial evidence in support of this reconstruction of the crime was strong indeed. Clearly we had managed things badly. Schuman, understandably absorbed in the problems of piloting his plan through his own government and parliament, saw my presence as a windfall of encouragement before, and help after, it was accepted. But I had been stupid in not foreseeing both Bevin's rage at his apparent exclusion from the circle of consultation and the old socialist's difficulty with the problem the Schuman Plan presented to a socialist government of Britain. If it joined a freely competitive system in the basic commodities of coal and steel, how could it isolate and manage the rest of Britain's economy as a welfare state? If it did not join, how could Britain retain her basic markets on the Continent?

This was Bevin's dilemma. After the first flush of anger had passed, I think he did accept the innocence of my motives in going to Paris. But damage had been done. Despite my most earnest arguments, in the next few days Britain made her great mistake of the postwar period by refusing to join in negotiating the Schuman Plan. From the bitter fruits of this mistake both Britain and Europe are still suffering. If I had not gone to Paris, Schuman would have had a tricky problem of acting unilaterally or of coming to London to consult us both before going to his own parliament. But the better course would have been for him to have authorized me to run what risks there were in trying to persuade Bevin and Attlee to give the plan their support. That course might not have worked, but, as it was, anger was added to bad judgment to insure the triumph of the latter.

The next day both Bevin and I put out short statements. His was noncommittal, but not so hostile as it had threatened to be. I welcomed "a most important development" prompted by the desire to further "a rapprochement between Germany and France and progress toward the economic integration of Western Europe," objectives favored by the United States Government. Specific comment must await development of the proposals; meanwhile we "recognize[d] with sympathy and approval the significant and far-reaching intent of the French initiative."[1] A week later the President called the proposal "an act of constructive statesmanship" and a "demonstration of French leadership in the solution of the problems of Europe . . . in the great French tradition." He was "gratified at the emphasis the proposal places upon equal access to coal and steel products to all Western European countries . . . [and] the full benefits of the competitive process."[2]

In this way we both did our best to back the launching with a fair breeze. But Bevin was still growling.

SCENE 3: LANCASTER HOUSE

On May 11 Schuman arrived in London for tripartite meetings to precede the North Atlantic Council, both being held at Lancaster House. We both got word from Bevin asking to see us a half hour before the full meeting at a private session in my office. This was a pleasant room in a southern corner of Lancaster House looking out on a charming lawn with a flowered border and golden-chain trees in bloom. But my office seemed to me a strange place for Bevin to hold a meeting and might seem even stranger to Schuman. Bevin might be thinking of giving him some of his own back. This suspicion grew when Bevin launched into a strong attack upon the announcement of the Coal and Steel Plan without prior agreement, or even consultation, among the powers occupying West Germany. He spoke slowly and forcefully, Schuman's interpreter translating as Bevin spoke. He had a good case, but rather overdid it. I knew that Schuman could take care of himself, but did not want him to get the impression from the meeting's being in my office that it was so by reason of collusion between Bevin and me. There had been enough misunderstanding among us without creating more.

When Bevin finished, I asked to be permitted to say a word to make my own position clear since Mr. Bevin was not speaking for me. I had not, I said, told Mr. Bevin or anyone about the plan, in accordance with M. Schuman's request, until Massigli's message released me. Then I had explained our talks in Paris. These had annoyed Mr. Bevin, which was understandable. But Mr. Bevin was exaggerating their significance. We all understood our duty to one another as allies. Sometimes domestic and international matters became pretty much intertwined and occasions arose when each of us had to take his own line without consultation because of the exigencies of domestic politics. On this occasion M. Schuman had done this. I happened to think he had taken a brilliant line and was in favor of it. But quite apart from that I understood why M. Schuman had thought that secrecy was more important than consultation. "Similarly," I said, "last autumn at the time of the Bank and Fund meeting in Washington, Mr. Bevin and the British Government found it advisable to devalue the pound. That was a serious problem in which secrecy was also important. It affected France. M. Schuman and Maurice Petsche, the French Finance Minister, were in Washington. The impending devaluation had been discussed with Secretary of the Treasury Snyder and me but not with M. Schuman and M. Petsche. They had not complained, since they understood the need for secrecy." Bevin had had enough. "Let's join the others," he said, getting up. As we left the room, Schuman took my arm. "You have a large deposit in my bank," he said.†

On May 25 the French Government invited six governments to join in negotiating the Coal and Steel Plan, and in doing so asked that participating governments accept the main principles of the plan including the binding effect of the High Authority's decisions. Five nations accepted the invitation on these terms—the Benelux nations, Germany, and Italy. The British Government did not "feel able to accept in advance, nor do they reject in advance, the principles underlying the French proposal." They wanted a detailed discussion first to "throw light on the nature of the scheme and its full political and economic consequences."[3] If the French would change their attitude, they would be glad to join in negotiations on procedures. The French were not willing to do so and a conference among the six nations began on June 20 without Britain.

Some decisions are critical. This decision of May 1950 was one. It was not the last clear chance for Britain to enter Europe, but it was the first wrong choice—as wrong as General de Gaulle's tragic rejection of the penitent in 1963.

In mid-June the national executive of the Labour Party made clear that the reasons for the Government's decision were not procedural. In a party pamphlet entitled *European Unity,* the trouble for doctrinaire socialists with the plan was shown to lie just where Schuman had suspected it would: in the binding effect of the high authority's decisions. The issue was the sovereign right of a Labour Government to pursue democratic socialism. Important but secondary was the national policy of special ties with the Commonwealth and the United States.

The latter of these special relationships had created a problem for me almost on the moment of my arrival in London. It took the form of a paper on the special nature of Anglo-American relations that had come out of staff talks between some of my colleagues and Foreign Office officials while I had been in Paris. My immediate and intense displeasure with this document caused its origin to become obscure. It was not the origin that bothered me, but the fact that the wretched paper existed. In the hands of troublemakers it could stir up no end of hullabaloo, both domestic and international, within the alliance. Of course a unique relation existed between Britain and America—our common language and history insured that. But unique did not mean affectionate. We had fought England as an enemy as often as we had fought by her side as an ally. The very ease of communication caused as many quarrels as understandings. Mayor Thompson of Chicago had found the key to success at the polls in his proclaimed eagerness to "hit King George on the snout." Before Pearl Harbor, Communists and "America Firsters" had joined in condemning Britain's "imperialist" war. Sentiment was reserved for our "oldest ally," France.

My own attitude had long been, and was known to have been, pro-British. At the beginning of the Roosevelt administrations, I had urged FDR to relieve Britain of the intolerable and impossible burden of repaying the war debts of 1914–18. In 1939–40 I had preached that the renewal of the European Civil

War involved us, and I played a part in the destroyers-for-bases deal that followed Dunkirk. My annoyance with the staff paper produced in London was not caused by doubt about the genuineness of the special relationship, or about the real identity of British and American interests in Europe and elsewhere, however diverse they might appear to particular individuals or governments at the moment. This had been true since Canning had supported the Monroe Doctrine against the Holy Alliance, and Britain after wavering swung to the northern side in our Civil War, while Napoleon III occupied Mexico. My annoyance came from the stupidity of writing about a special relationship, which could only increase suspicion among our allies of secret plans and purposes, which they did not share and would not approve, and would give the Mayor Thompsons, McCarthys, McCarrans, and Jenners proof that the State Department was the tool of a foreign power. So all copies of the paper that could be found were collected and burned, and my colleagues, after a thorough dressing-down for their naïveté, were urged to channel their sentimental impulses into a forthcoming speech of mine before the Society of Pilgrims, which by tradition was granted dispensation for expressions of this sort.

BEHIND THE SCENES

The split between our principal allies over the Schuman Plan made it more important than ever that the forthcoming conference on the plan should be a purely European one without interference from the United States. Accordingly, a joint, circular instruction was sent out on June 2 by State and the Economic Cooperation Administration to our missions in Britain and the six countries concerned that there were to be "no further public statements except to reaffirm our general position. . . . The U.S. is not to be a party to negotiations and is to have no official association or observers. . . . We are to take no position concerning UK-French issues on the Plan." Immediately we put the instruction into effect by turning down a proposal from Bruce in Paris to put out a statement comforting to Paris after the British refusal to join the conference. Later on, the instruction continued, occasion might call for discreet aid to Schuman to avoid watering down his proposal or to retain "favorable economic elements . . . emphasized in HST May 18 statement," but State and ECA would instruct specifically on these occasions.

The Department kept in intimate touch with the negotiations, chiefly through McCloy and Bruce and their missions. This was most discreetly and skillfully done by those two masters of the diplomatic art. On July 25 Schuman announced that agreement had been reached on all major aspects of the plan. This perhaps contributed more to confidence in the negotiation than to dissemination of fact. Many hurdles remained and on these the quiet exercise of our influence was helpful. During the summer these issues were chiefly "watering-down" issues. One concerned broadening appeals from decisions of the Authority to those "affected" as against those "directly concerned." We supported the narrower right. Another raised the period during which subsidy payments would cushion marginal producers against the shock of a single European market. Again, we favored the shorter period. Perhaps the most important issue came in the autumn when, to anticipate, American proposals for German participation in the defense of Europe gave Bonn a stronger bargaining position than it had as an occupied country. Sensing this, the Germans began dragging their feet in Schuman Plan negotiations, trying to obtain two important objectives: a lifting of the ceiling on German steel production and a rescue of the German selling cartel for the Ruhr, Deutscher Kohlen Verkauf, from the operation of provisions of the occupation statute of 1949. Here the United States was directly concerned and acted clearly in support of the French position, which Monnet had been appointed to work out. They had taken the stand that the first German position was not only consistent with but required by the Schuman Plan, but that the second was totally at odds with it. In our view it was at odds also with the occupation statute and sound economic policy. The dispute was settled on this basis. The European Coal and Steel Community treaty was signed by the Six on April 18, 1951.

43. BALANCED COLLECTIVE FORCES

FOR EUROPE

ONCE BEVIN'S ANNOYANCE over the Schuman Plan had eased, our talks at the Foreign Office performed the useful task of identifying subjects for discussion with Schuman, and also the North Atlantic Council afterward, and an attitude of approach to them. Bevin quite frankly confessed doubts of his wisdom in recognizing the Chinese Communists. He foresaw little profit in it and urged that we prevent our different lines from causing a breach between us. I saw no reason why they should. Three matters seemed to me of the greatest importance: defense and economics in Europe; a peace treaty with Japan; and, of secondary but still great importance, the troubled situation in Southeast Asia.

The need for deterrent defense in Europe exceeded the strength of European economies and, therefore, they needed basic strengthening. Here we approached dangerous ground, but Bevin agreed. The then treaty structure was hopelessly deficient in producing drive for improvement. Work fell between committees; difficulties and weaknesses were accepted as insuperable. The French attitude that Germany could never contribute to the common defense was all wrong. The German economy and German participation in trade, aid to undeveloped countries, and—short of rearmament—common defensive arrangements were all essential. This was quite a program for our friends across the table, but Bevin did not dissent.

SOCIAL INTERLUDES

Not all our ten days in London were spent on official duties. Social engagements, some with a tinge of duty, too, intervened to bring pleasurable and more relaxing moments. The evening of our arrival in London I had the honor and pleasure of sitting beside the Queen at a dinner at the Middle Temple, one of the Inns of Court, of which the Queen was the Honorary Treasurer. The Inns of Court eschew the republican title of president for their chief officer and vest it where in British experience power has been found, in the Treasurer's office. Aside from the Queen, it was a men's dinner of lawyers in celebration of the reopening of the lofty and beautiful dining hall, one end of which with its rose window had been bombed out during the war. The Queen presided at the high table, sitting on the very edge of a massive state chair. This uncomfortable position, she told me, enabled her feet to touch the floor. A footstool would complicate her rising at moments of ceremony. We had met at the British

Embassy in Washington before the war and had much to talk about. As the dinner drew to a close, she explained to me a ceremony in which I was to participate and which, she forecast, I would muddle. When I protested at this slur on my ceremonial ability, she disclaimed any personal criticism. The fact was that everyone failed at the critical moment. A gorgeously robed official, a page carrying his train and he himself carrying a great silver goblet, would walk the length of the hall, mount the platform, and offer me the goblet. I was to take it and offer it to the Queen. She would sip from it and return it to me. Then, and only then, I was to sip and return it to the bearer. What, I asked, was the problem? Some psychological compulsion apparently drove every recipient to sip before the Queen. This was clearly an absurd superstition. Yet this is just what I did, to my intense annoyance and a gentle murmur of "Naughty, naughty" from my left. My defense was that the idea had been put into my mind, with malice aforethought.

The next day between meetings at the Foreign Office we were invited to Buckingham Palace, I to be received by the King, following which my wife and I would lunch with the King and Queen and the princesses. The King and I talked alone and most informally in a small, comfortable sitting room on the second floor of the palace. He questioned me keenly about persons and policies in Europe and my own impressions of both, but not much about the United States. I threw in a good many favorable remarks about Ernest Bevin, who, I gathered, rather baffled the monarch. As we talked, I ceased to notice his slight stammer and found our conversation easy and pleasant. His views about public questions, including British domestic matters, were clear, firmly held, and quite readily expressed. This seemed to indicate a degree of confidence in my discretion, which I was careful afterward to justify.

Within the hour the Queen and my wife joined us. Though we had a glass of sherry and some talk, the princesses did not appear, to the annoyance of their father. The Queen explained that Princess Elizabeth was returning from a visit to Malta and was being met by her sister. Some delay had held them up. The King's irritation grew. As an experienced father of daughters, I recognized the familiar blend of concern that something might have gone wrong and irritation at the greater likelihood that two girls had dallied to gossip. The King rang for the butler, ordered two places taken away, and directed that lunch be served. When we went into the adjoining dining room, the butler had wisely removed one place, thus enabling himself to move swiftly in either direction. When we were seated and the vacant place was about to go, in came Princess Margaret full of gaiety, explanations, and apologies. Her sister had been late in starting and, hence, in arriving, and begged to be excused from lunch to go home to see her family. The King was relieved and mollified, but only barely. He made clear his view that such conduct was discourteous and irresponsible. My wife pronounced such absolution as she could and steered the talk into happier channels.

In time it got around to a trouble Mr. Bevin and I had stumbled into that morning by believing that we had both been speaking a common language when, in fact, the same common English word—in this case, "executive"—had a different meaning on each side of the table. On the British side executive action connoted arbitrary, unauthorized, authoritarian action. On the American side, an executive body was a body authorized to act—the executive branch of our government, an executive committee of a larger body, the executive head of a corporation. Perhaps, I said, we should start in the State Department and the Foreign Office bureaus on the proper and improper use of the same word in the two countries. The Princess thought it a great idea and announced her intention to apply to us for a job. The King disparaged her qualifications for serious work. To head off controversy, the Queen demurred. As an authority, she observed, on the improper use of words or on the use of improper words, however one might express it, her daughter was not without qualifications. A luncheon that began with some tension ended as a most delightful and memorable one.

As we awaited Schuman's arrival on the morrow, I performed the duty of every Secretary of State by addressing a gala and distinguished company gathered at a dinner of the London branch of the Society of Pilgrims. Pleasant words were said about me in a message from Bevin, who had been put to bed to conserve his strength, and in person by the Prime Minister, Clement Attlee, and the Canadian Minister for External Affairs, Lester B. Pearson. Mike Pearson's speeches are always gay and witty, and this was no exception. He spoke of the grave threats that had once hung over his career but had been dispelled under the guiding hand of Divine Providence and the helpful cooperation of their guest of honor and of an equally distinguished guest present in spirit. In the last decade of the last century, Ernest Bevin had felt the lure of Mr. Pearson's great country and had gone so far as to buy a ticket to Canada with a view to emigrating. Then Providence intervened in form of a measles virus and laid Mr. Bevin low. By the time he was well again the mood, the ship, and perhaps the money were gone. Mr. Bevin remained in Britain to become its Foreign Minister. What a close call that had been!

Again, in the same decade of the same century, a young Canadian couple were married in Toronto. Instead of staying there, the young clergyman was called to Connecticut, where in 1893 he and his wife produced a citizen of the United States and its present Secretary of State. When, in due course, Mr. Pearson opened his eyes, he looked upon a fair and unblemished prospect which led only a little deviously to the unoccupied Ministry of External Affairs.

My own short speech[1] attempted to broaden traditional Anglo-American interest. In the past, I began, the dinners of this hospitable society had produced discussion largely of the relationship between our two countries. Philosophic and witty observations dealt with the asperities of our family relationship, often incomprehensible to others. Now our relationship had matured and broadened to include the concerns and fortunes of a wider community, to which we both belonged. It was healthy and good for us both to ameliorate the introspection of the past by looking outward to the common purposes and problems we shared with European friends, not the least of which were those shared with our late and bitter enemy, Germany. The tragic circumstances of the past half century, which had torn Germany so violently from the context of

European society, so nearly destroyed both Germany and Europe, and now threatened the peace of the world, posed problems that no nation or a divided Europe could solve. No harder enterprise or one more heavily encumbered with fears, sensitivities, and divergencies of outlook had ever been undertaken jointly by a group of nations. But it was an enterprise dictated to us by the demands of our times.

In a few days, I continued, leaders from twelve nations would meet in London to begin work in earnest on this task. Germany could not stand as a passive spectator of its own fate. The German people must accept a full measure of responsibility and risk. Victors and vanquished alike must approach one another in a spirit of national humility before the great catastrophes we had passed through and the even greater ones threatening a failure of our common enterprise. Its magnitude called for nothing less.

This was my principal theme. I ended with a reference to the "strange and confusing dissonance [that] has crowded the trans-Atlantic frequencies from America" in the past months. This, too, I said, flowed from the difficulty of present-day decisions and was a part of the method of making them. By the Mayflower Compact the Pilgrims had combined themselves into a "civill body politick" in which all the men would constitute a General Court, the source of all local political power and judicial decision. Our New England town meeting derived from it. Today the entire nation was engaged in such a meeting. Quantity and size had their effect. The klieg lights, the newsreel cameras, the radio, and the press had sometimes obscured, sometimes distorted, the original pattern, but the tradition was there. Noisy, often disorderly, this town meeting of the nation was open to all views—wise, foolish, and in between. It was nerve-racking to our friends (and often to the participants as well), and dangerously confusing to our enemies. But it had adapted itself over a hundred and seventy-five years to political upheaval, social change, scientific revolution, the challenge of size, the test of war—and all without the loss of our liberties. I had no doubt whatever that in our own way we should meet the test again.

THE TRIPARTITE MEETINGS

Bevin, Schuman, and I met six times in the next three days. These talks, as I have already suggested, proved a growing source of annoyance to our NATO allies, who suspected that we planned the meetings of the council. Not much emerged from all this talk. We were still digesting large bites taken during the past year into postwar problems. The shadow of the Schuman Plan hung over us. Obviously we must soon bite again and happily did not know how tough the chewing would be. Schuman started off our *tour d'horizon* by stressing the great yearning in Europe for peace, the anxiety over current tensions between West and East, and the effectiveness of the Soviet's initiative in peace propaganda. I confess to a certain irritation over foreign ministers acting as public relations officers for more than a sensible portion of their time. No one, I believe, devoted more energy and effort than I to explaining and urging support for policies designed to lay enduring foundations for peace. I understood as well as anyone that we were engaged in a struggle "for the minds of men" and accepted all the clichés about words being weapons, and so on. But I have always thought policies devised for propaganda purposes—foolish proposals designed to portray a greater passion for peace than that of an opponent rejecting them—were unworthy and dangerous maneuvers in American diplomacy. Schuman basically agreed, but he worried more about Russian propaganda. I always tried to keep my worry list to essentials, and took comfort from Mark Twain's advice: "Always do right. This will gratify some people, and astonish the rest."

After discussing propaganda, I suggested a list of priorities for our common efforts: (1) to recognize fully the dangers and threats to peace of the present situation and present them effectively to the public; (2) to proceed immediately to increase military strength; (3) to create the economic foundation for a European military program and to maintain a European standard of living; (4) to bring the productive capacity of Germany into this effort; (5) to prevent further erosion by Communists in the Far East; and (6) to evolve institutions to aid in attaining these objectives.

To these Bevin added that we must "win over the middle areas," and advanced the idea that the Chinese Communists "had a moral and legal case for UN membership." We agreed to his first suggestion, though how to do it was not so clear. Regarding his second, I argued that the question was not whether a case could be made out for the seating of the Chinese Communists but what the effect of doing so would be on situations of great importance to us. I submitted that it would be to increase greatly the capacity for Communist troublemaking in Indochina, Malaya, the Philippine Islands, and Indonesia. Furthermore, the vote in the Security Council was not likely to change unless the United States changed its position, which we saw no reason for doing. It seemed unlikely that the French would change theirs in view of Mao's recognition and support of Ho Chi Minh in Indochina, a view in which Schuman concurred. If one compared the evils resulting from the two courses, the harm to the United States of the Soviet walkout because of the presence of Nationalist representatives seemed clearly less than the dangers I had listed of Communist presence. Furthermore, it was not at all certain that expulsion of the Nationalists would result in the Communists taking their place in the United Nations unless that body took hostile action against the Nationalist regime on Formosa. We could end up, if we followed Bevin's suggestion, with no Chinese representatives in the United Nations and an extension of the Chinese war to Formosa and greater trouble throughout Southeast Asia. Bevin did not press the point. When we returned to European matters, I put forward a program of work in accordance with the priority list.

The great progress already made under the Marshall Plan, I said, gave real hope that after 1952 Western Europe, except possibly Austria, would not need grants in aid of economic development. But in the subsequent period, equal or perhaps greater cooperation within Europe and between Europe and North America would continue to be necessary. The remaining goals would be increased production and productivity, convertibility of currencies, reduction of tariffs, increasing supplies of raw materials and markets for manufactured goods, freer movement of peoples, equality of treatment for Germany, and opening fields for investment. All this required new ideas and methods as well as more activity. Mentioning the unmentionable, I said that Washington was in favor of the Schuman Plan and of the association of the United States and Canada with the Organization for European Economic Cooperation.

Turning to Germany, I urged my colleagues to remember that time was running out in which the occupation could exercise a useful and beneficial effect in reshaping Germany. The relation of victors to vanquished was basically an unpleasant one and no matter how wisely administered was gathering resentment as Germany recovered from the war, developed a generation free of guilt, and lost some of the present fear of Russian threat. A democratic and economically sound Germany should move quickly to take its own place in the European community. The Allied High Commission's influence in Germany could not be expected to be great beyond a couple of years more. The real interest of Germany lay in Western Europe. We must begin at once to lead Germany to "entangle and integrate" herself there. We could not begin too soon to transform the occupying forces into a new concept and new organization, a force for the protection of Western Europe.

Because of this situation, the High Commission was entering a new phase in which speed, restraint in method, and wisdom in substance would be necessary in striking a balance between maintaining the respect and confidence of the Germans and moving ahead of events. Here the implications of the French Coal and Steel Plan were particularly relevant and important. These were somber thoughts.

In the ensuing discussion it soon became evident that even Schuman had not fully appreciated that as the plan went into effect it would have far-reaching effects on the status of the occupation and the Ruhr Authority. Although my exhortations produced no immediate results in agreement, they acted as a useful spur to action that was soon to begin in earnest. Ratification of the Schuman Plan took rather more time than I had expected, but my estimate of the effective life of the occupation and the High Commission was accurate. Just two years later we concluded in Bonn and signed in Paris the agreements that began their end. Similarly, though not strangely, the occupation of Japan ended by the ratification of the Japanese peace treaty in the same summer.

Our talks on Germany produced two other useful results. In response to a formal inquiry from Chancellor Adenauer, we agreed and replied to him that an attack on our forces in Germany would constitute an armed attack within the meaning of Article 5 of the North Atlantic Treaty. To be sure, this was clear enough from a reading of the treaty, but few people read it and a statement from the three ministers gave reassurance in Germany. Our communiqué[2] also inspired hope and confidence there. It outlined the impressive record of German progress in the past twelve months and asserted our hope of maintaining the pace of free development while holding open offers made to the Soviet Union a year before to join in a treaty establishing a government for all Germany.

Declaration on the Middle East • In the course of these tripartite meetings we turned to the mounting troubles in the Middle East. In Palestine fighting between the Arab states and Israel had quieted down, but no solutions appeared for the problems left in its wake, of which the Arab refugees presented the most pressing and bitter. Each side armed against the other. The United Nations Conciliation Commission, without power, ideas, or hope, had returned its mandate to the General Assembly. In Iran and Egypt revolutionary unrest found anti-British expression, which continued to mount toward the explosions of 1951, the subject of Chapters 52 and 58. In May 1950 a brooding lull hung over the area.

In the hope of introducing a restraining and stabilizing influence the three ministers in London issued a declaration on the Arab-Israeli confrontation that is not easy to explain. The available records do not help. The declaration announced that the Arab states and Israel all needed to maintain "a certain level" of armed forces to protect their own security; that those of them to whom the three governments sold arms had all given assurances that they did not intend any act of aggression against any other state; and that should the three governments find that "any of these states was preparing to violate frontiers or armistice lines, [they] would immediately take action, both within and outside the United Nations, to prevent" it.[3] This was bold talk. President Truman endorsed the declaration, expressing the belief that it would "stimulate in the Arab states and Israel increased confidence in future security."[4]

Unfortunately, this belief was ill founded. Indeed, rarely has so large an undertaking been so unlucky in its timing or had so short-lived an effect. Soon all three declaring states were fully preoccupied elsewhere. Within a month the United States was locked in the desperate Korean battle; in a few months more all three governments were both deeply concerned and divided over the defense of Europe. By the year's end the Soviet Union was vigorously exploiting the divisive possibilities open to its propaganda in Europe, the Middle East, and the Far East. In the autumn of 1956, when one of the states mentioned in the Declaration of May 1950 did violate frontiers and armistice lines, the three governments were even more deeply divided. Britain and France took military action outside the United Nations, calling on Israel and Egypt to stop all hostilities; the United States and the Soviet Union within the United Nations, and the Soviet Union thundering threats of military intervention outside it, took action to stop the only military intervention then proceeding—that by Britain and France. Again, when two years later Lebanon complained ineffectively to the United Nations for protection against threats of foreign (Egyptian) intervention and then to the United States, American forces landed alone in July 1958. The Tripartite Declaration of May 1950 was dead, if it had ever lived.

THE FOURTH MEETING OF THE COUNCIL

A Sunday gave needed rest between one strenuous week and another. Prime Minister and Mrs. Attlee had invited us to lunch with them at the Prime

Minister's official country place, Chequers, about an hour west of London in Buckinghamshire. Through the imaginative generosity of Lord and Lady Lee of Fareham, this twelfth-century house and estate had been given and endowed as a haven of escape from Downing Street for the Prime Minister. Tradition has it that the name came from an early owner, a clerk in the exchequer. Of special interest to us were the portraits of Oliver Cromwell, "warts and all," which had come there through another owner, a descendant of the Lord Protector.

We drove out from London on a cold, "moist," allegedly spring day, through a countryside full of apple blossoms, bluebells, and hardy picnickers. Arriving thoroughly chilled, we found the house noticeably colder than the outdoors, so much so that Ernie Bevin had retreated with a stool inside an immense fireplace, where he was unsuccessfully attempting to warm his hands over a small coal grate. I resorted to the far more reliable device of straight gin.

The party was a pleasant, family one, relaxed and friendly, but warm only in gracious hospitality. As we entered the dining room, Mrs. Attlee thought it stuffy and had the "Wrens" who were serving lunch open the windows. As they did so, the curtains stood out. The American female guests, made of more fragile stuff, had wisely kept their fur coats. My inner glow was still glowing.

Basic Problems Emerge · As the council meeting, the last at which I was to preside, got under way, the basic problems, which NATO has never been able to solve, began to emerge. Both our third meeting and the Mutual Defense Assistance Program had recognized two goals—economic recovery and military defense—the first of which had been given priority. Meanwhile our studies in Washington earlier in the year, leading to the hydrogen bomb decision and NSC-68, had convinced us that a far greater defense effort on both sides of the Atlantic than either side had previously contemplated would be necessary. How could this be done in Europe without jeopardizing economic recovery, or leading Europeans to believe that it would be jeopardized? One thing was clear. Congress would not bear the cost of both economic recovery and rearmament in Europe as well as our own, and should not be asked to do so. And yet the obvious threat that had led the Europeans to want the North Atlantic Treaty was the threat of Soviet military power already greatly superior to anything Western Europe alone could produce.

Nor was this the only problem becoming daily more clear and destined to be equally recalcitrant. The North Atlantic Alliance was a body—or more accurately twelve bodies—without a head. The congressional requirement of an "integrated defense" had produced a system of committees. They met, but failed to produce continuing or authoritative direction. American military supplies were already moving across the Atlantic, but the council was experiencing the frustrations of the Continental Congress in 1776 before the appointment of General Washington. It recognized the need of forces in being and in position, but saw little possibility of getting either without organization, a command, and a strategy. The first, most pressing need seemed to be to replace the intermittent attention of committees with the continuing preoccupation of a permanent body.

When the meeting was called to order around a large circular table in the great hall of Lancaster House, the members tended to fly off to headlined international problems of the moment—the Soviet boycott of the United Nations and the increasing troubles in Southeast Asia. In time, they became persuaded that we could do little or nothing about these and might better concentrate on the closer but no less perplexing problems of our own area. We had before us reports of our Defense and Economic committees. Both pointed out distressing gaps: the former, between the defense forces we had and those we needed; the latter, between the needs and the ability to meet them. The Defense Committee urged a progressive increase in defense forces, based on the creation of balanced collective forces rather than balanced national forces. By this was meant a force for the defense of Europe, complete and balanced in its components when viewed as a collectivity, rather than a collection of national forces each complete with all the necessary component arms. The latter was beyond the economic means of Europe, even when supplemented by large grants of military aid from the United States.

This proposal produced a lively debate. Lange of Norway raised the point, later to become the center of General de Gaulle's creed, that the committee's recommendation would leave a nation imperiled if the collective force should not come to its aid. This was, of course, true but incomplete. Such a nation would be imperiled, however its individual defense force was constructed, if the aggressor should be the only likely one, the Communist bloc. In that case, both deterrence and effective defense could be provided only through the collective force, which would include all the power of the United States. Schuman was inclined to gloss over this point, saying that the two conceptions were complementary and not incompatible. To take this view seemed to be unwise. The issue was real and should be faced—how real became clear a few years later when the mistaken Eisenhower-Dulles doctrine of "massive retaliation" gave vogue to the idea that security in Europe lay in the threat to use nuclear arms and that conventional arms were obsolete. Then France broke away from NATO in favor of developing her own balanced national forces, including the *"force de frappe,"* independent of the collective force.

Intervening in the debate, I urged that this most important issue should not be masked, but it must be understood. Exposed portions of the area would need forces in position adequate to the danger. Nations with responsibilities outside the area would need forces for these purposes. All would need to meet the requirements for peacetime security and order, none of which were in question. The sole point at issue was that in raising the forces for the defense of the area, economic necessity required that all duplication of effort be eliminated. Neither considerations of prestige nor of attempting to achieve a stronger defense position than a neighbor should be permitted to impair the common plan, the common effort, the common strategy. Any such attempt would prove self-defeating both to the nation engaging in it and to the whole effort.

Concluding, I agreed that there was incompatibility between a balanced collective force and a collection of balanced national forces. It sprang from the limitation of our means. I would rather see a clear division in the council and find myself in the minority supporting the recommendation until my colleagues could be won over to it than go home with some ambiguous words masking a disagreement. By the end of May 17 the recommendation to governments for balanced collective forces, still a rather vague concept, was unanimously voted.

The council passed on to set up a continuing body of deputy members of the council to remain in continuous session in London in the attempt to push forward the development of the collective defense. Our representative was Charles M. Spofford of New York. The deputies were instructed to examine as one problem the adequacy of forces and the availability of means to provide them. Each member was to "make its full contribution through mutual assistance in all practicable forms."[5]

ACCOMPLISHMENTS AT LONDON

The fourth meeting of the council was a useful one. It took the most important steps yet taken to move from mere agreement to do something in case of trouble toward the creation of a new factor in international relations to prevent trouble. The meeting first brought moments of truth which pierced illusions and revealed the gap between ideas and reality. In this candid light the "strategic concept" was seen to be little more than a division of functions, which, beyond what could be done by our strategic bombing and naval capabilities, had little prospect of being performed. The requirements as calculated by the soldiers "from a strictly military point of view" were so great as to discourage our allies, particularly the French, already engaged beyond their strength in Southeast Asia. While we Americans talked of balanced collective forces, our own military planning and budgeting were undertaken aloof and apart from Europe. Neither we nor the British had undertaken any force commitments to Europe. Finally, Germany, central politically and militarily to any defense of Europe, both as the place where our troops were stationed and where trouble might be expected, was unmentionable in this context.

All these unmentionables were mentioned in London. Taboos were lifted. Where we were naked we began to admit it. It was at London that Schuman burst out with the remark that considered as a treaty contemplating the "liberation of Europe" the North Atlantic Treaty was of no use. None of the Europeans there present would live for that event. Discussing the London meeting some years later, Averell Harriman remarked that it laid the foundation for NATO; in fact, it put the "O" in NATO.

What Harriman meant was that London began the creation of an organization and the outlines of a charter to guide it. Perhaps what we all felt at London was something even more basic—an act of will, a decision to do something. We had planned and adopted resolutions long enough. Even though the most modest plans seemed hopeless of achievement, the time had come to start trying. At London we fashioned the first crude tools.

The council in permanent session was always something of a disappointment. Unlike the high authorities of the European communities, it lacked powers. But it did not lack persistence. While the principles laid down to guide it also lacked the clarity and authority of those given the communities, they had the same germinal seed. They contemplated a common effort, jointly managed and directed toward a common end. When the next step toward integration was to come—and it was to come much sooner than any of us suspected—the London meeting had provided the basic organization and ideas. These were worth a good many divisions and made those we soon got a good deal more impressive as evidence of a common will made flesh.

A REPORT TO CONGRESS

On Friday morning, May 19, a weary but happy company boarded the boat train for Liverpool, looking forward to a relaxed week on the *Britannic* en route to New York. No meetings, no speeches, no crises for a week—or so we thought. But hardly were we at sea when the President, always solicitous for me, was making plans. He had been much pleased by the course events had taken, by our communications with him, and by the role we had played. When Secretary Cordell Hull had returned from his journey to Moscow in 1943, the Congress had invited him to appear before a joint session of the two houses. President Truman was, he informed us, suggesting to the Speaker of the House and the President of the Senate that a similar invitation be issued to me. However, Mr. Hull had at different times in his career been a member of each house and had attained a state of beatification above and beyond partisanship. I was what the most friendly would have described as "a controversial figure." The opposition was engaged not in building me up—which they clearly discerned to be the President's purpose—but in tearing me down. The joint session was vetoed. The Vice President and the Speaker, however, reached a compromise with the Republican leadership, by which those two should invite me to speak in the auditorium of the Library of Congress to such members of the House and Senate as might choose to attend. Such a meeting would carry no congressional endorsement. Critics would be free to criticize. The "honor" attached to the occasion would be minimized. Lazy peace on the *Britannic* ended, as each morning the sun deck was deserted for a speech-writing session.

Even with this daily stint of work, the week at sea was a lifesaver for all of us, especially in view of what was to break over us within the month. On Saturday afternoon, eight days after we set out, the President met our plane in Washington and carried me off with him to the wharf at the naval gun factory, where the *Williamsburg* was waiting to take him down the bay for the weekend. We had a short talk and planned to continue it later.

My chief recollection of the speech to Congress is of heat approaching that traditionally reserved for the punishment of the damned.

DA to MAB   *May 31, 1950*
This was the day of my gala performance. It was a day of sweat. The small, crowded hall was well steamed up with animal heat. Then the television lights went on and it passed 100 degrees. As I spoke I sweated out of me all the sin of a mis-

spent life. My collar went, my shirt became a washrag, even my coat hung in loose, wet folds. But I was determined not to wipe my brow. That might mean to viewers of the airwaves that I was suffering—which I was. But I must always appear gay, cool and confident!

I was none of these; but damned glad when the questions were over and I could go home to bathe and change all. What this innovation may mean in our political life I don't know. But if it means more of this, then they ought to have two Secretaries of State, one who makes the appearances and one who is a member of the Politburo. I would choose the latter role.

However, the spies say that it went well. So who am I to complain?

The questions from the floor after the speech vividly illustrated a congressional characteristic that I have frequently noticed. With one exception, they had no relation whatever to the subject matter of the speech, to my negotiations about the future of Europe, to the development of a common defense force. Illustrating from a few of the opening questions: Senator Harry P. Cain asked why Greece and Turkey were not members of NATO; Congressman Robert Sikes wanted to know whether the State Department backed the Schuman Plan; Senator William Knowland, whether in London we agreed to admit Communist China to the United Nations; Congressman Robert Rich, why we had not had a conference on disarmament instead of rearmament; and so on. Judge John Kee, Chairman of the House Committee on Foreign Affairs, said at the time that every question was asked to gain publicity for the asker's pet notion.

All this added to rapidly accumulating evidence that turned me against a view strongly held by a much-respected senior, Colonel Stimson. This was that Cabinet officers should have the privilege of the floor of the houses of Congress for periodic question periods, following the practice in the British Parliament. Despite the fact that in the past this idea has had considerable vogue, even at one time gaining the favor of President William H. Taft,† I am convinced that it would add heavily to the burdens of the Secretary of State and increase friction, rather than cooperation, between him and the chairmen of the relevant committees of Congress.

British practice is no guide for American, since British parliamentary conceptions are post-Cromwellian, based on supremacy of Parliament, with the executive a committee of Parliament; American conceptions, based on the separation of powers, stem on the English side from Tudor and Stuart practice and, on the French, from eighteenth-century thought. One will get more insight into the relations between the American Congress and executive today from Sir John Neale's *Elizabeth and Her Parliaments* than from American political biography of the nineteenth century, when for the most part, except during wars, the Congress was supreme and the powers of the President awaited their rediscovery by the first Roosevelt.

However, in June 1950 I had no time for such historical speculation.

44. WAR IN KOREA: THE OUTBREAK

AFTER THE Governors' Conference on Tuesday, June 20, 1950, a Harvard commencement speech on Thursday, a Cabinet meeting, press conference, and preparation for a military assistance appearance on the Hill on Friday, we escaped Washington the next day, June 24, for a quiet weekend at Harewood Farm. As quiet, that is, as that haven could then be. The white telephone tied into the White House switchboard was used sparingly by considerate associates, but it was used. Even when evening came and the busy world was hushed and the fever of day was over, the movements of the security officers changing guard during the night echoed through that small house. The crank mail, which Senator McCarthy's attentions had increased, led to the undesired innovation of night as well as day shifts of guards around me, a regimen not conducive to relaxation. However, the weekend began well. After some hours of gardening and a good dinner I had turned in to read myself to sleep.

Saturday, June 24 • About ten o'clock the White House telephone had me up again. John Hickerson, Assistant Secretary for United Nations Affairs, Dean Rusk, Assistant Secretary for Far Eastern Affairs, and Philip C. Jessup, Ambassador at Large, had been called to the Department by a cable from our Ambassador in Seoul, Korea, John Muccio, an experienced and level-headed officer, reporting an attack from the north across the 38th parallel on South Korean forces. It described a heavy attack, different from patrol forays that had occurred in the past, and in Muccio's opinion was an all-out offensive against the Republic of Korea.

This cable had crossed an inquiry from the Department stimulated by disturbing press rumors out of Seoul. Hickerson and the others were in touch with Frank Pace, Secretary of the Army. Louis Johnson, Secretary of Defense, and General Bradley, Chairman of the Joint Chiefs of Staff, were in Tokyo. Other Chiefs of Staff had not yet been located, and former Senator Warren Austin, our Ambassador at the United Nations, was at his home in Burlington, Vermont. Asked for a recommendation, Hickerson suggested a meeting of the UN Security Council the next morning (Sunday) to call for a cease-fire, and urgent requests to our civilian and military missions in Korea for continuing information.

I approved, and authorized Ernest Gross, Ambassador Austin's deputy, to ask Secretary General Trygve Lie to call the Security Council. Overnight

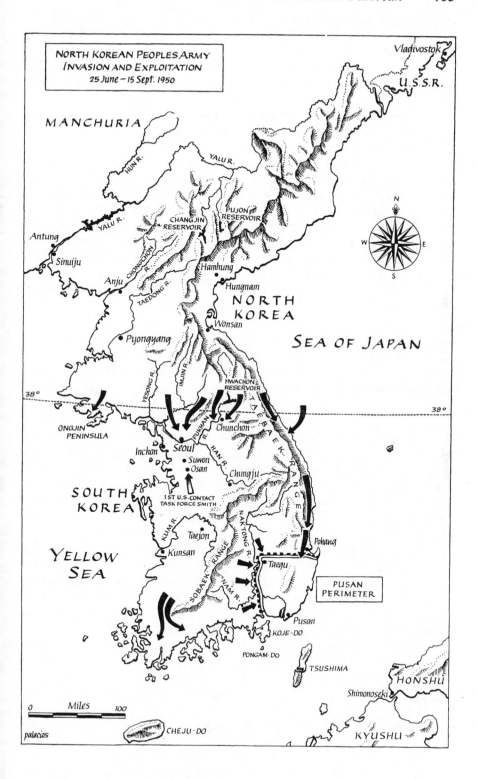

NORTH KOREAN PEOPLES ARMY
INVASION AND EXPLOITATION
25 June – 15 Sept. 1950

Hickerson, Rusk, and Jessup were to work with the Pentagon through Frank Pace to get up such orders as the President might wish to issue should he decide to take further action, military or otherwise. Meanwhile I would telephone the President, who was spending the weekend at his home in Independence, Missouri. Any changes he wished to make in my instructions could easily overtake them.

Independence time was two hours earlier than ours. The President had just finished a family dinner when he came to the telephone and learned the situation and the instructions given. He approved and suggested his immediate return to Washington. I dissuaded him from adding the unnecessary risk of a hurriedly arranged night flight and urged instead a further report from me next morning, when our information should be more complete, and his return to Washington later in the day. He agreed and asked whether he could do anything to help us overnight. Remembering the absurd restrictions that Louis Johnson had imposed on communication between the two departments in the spring, I asked the President to let Frank Pace know that he wanted the fullest cooperation between the departments. No difficulty of any sort developed in work between them. A call of confirmation to Hickerson completed my night's work, but not his.

Sunday, June 25 • The next morning at the Department the news was bad. A full-scale attack centering around a tank column was driving toward Seoul and Kimpo airport. South Korean arms were clearly outclassed. Recommendations had been prepared by the two departments for action in the light of present knowledge and a resolution drafted for presentation to the UN Security Council. A talk with the President gave him the facts, secured his approval of the resolution, and instructed me to have the available people from State and Defense meet with him at Blair House that evening. Later a message from the plane added that the group should come to Blair House for dinner at seven-thirty. I left word at Defense for the Secretary and General Bradley, due back that afternoon, the service secretaries, and the Chiefs of Staff, and took with me Under Secretary Webb, Assistant Secretaries Hickerson and Rusk, and Ambassador Jessup.

An early draft of our resolution determined that the "armed attack on the Republic of Korea by forces from North Korea" constituted "an unprovoked act of aggression." When this draft was shown to some members of the Security Council, they expressed doubt whether the information yet available established the conclusion. They were, however, prepared to say that it "constituted a breach of the peace." Their preference for this statement was strengthened upon learning that our representative had not yet been instructed what our course would be should the North Koreans disregard the call for an immediate cessation of hostilities and a withdrawal of their forces to the 38th parallel as provided in the resolution. To meet these views the change was made.

When the Security Council convened on Sunday afternoon, it was not known whether Malik, the Soviet Representative, who was boycotting the council because of the presence of a Nationalist Chinese and had returned to Moscow, would appear. He did not. There was no negative vote, and the resolution was declared adopted by a vote of 9–0, with Yugoslavia abstaining. I met the President with the news at the airport and drove with him to Blair House.

During the afternoon I had everyone and all messages kept out of my room for an hour or two while I ruminated about the situation. "Thought" would suggest too orderly and purposeful a process. It was rather to let various possibilities, like glass fragments in a kaleidoscope, form a series of patterns of action and then draw conclusions from them. Our recommendations for the President dealt with the next twenty-four hours or so, which was as far as we could see at the time. But what must we contemplate beyond that? One possibility was that the attack would be called off; the other, that it would not be. For some months, as tensions had mounted again after the Berlin blockade, we had run exercises on danger spots for renewed Soviet probing of our determination. Korea was on the list but not among the favorites. Berlin, Turkey, Greece, Iran—all seemed spots where the balance of convenient operation dipped in favor of the Soviets. Korea was too near major forces and bases of ours in Japan and too far from any of theirs to offer a tempting target, though they could have judged our interest in it less than in the other places. But now the attack had come there. What was likely to happen next and how should we determine our response? It seemed close to certain that the attack had been mounted, supplied, and instigated by the Soviet Union and that it would not be stopped by anything short of force. If Korean force proved unequal to the job, as seemed probable, only American military intervention could do it. Troops from other sources would be helpful politically and psychologically but unimportant militarily. My two weeks in Europe left little doubt of that.

Plainly, this attack did not amount to a *casus belli* against the Soviet Union. Equally plainly, it was an open, undisguised challenge to our internationally accepted position as the protector of South Korea, an area of great importance to the security of American-occupied Japan. To back away from this challenge, in view of our capacity for meeting it, would be highly destructive of the power and prestige of the United States. By prestige I mean the shadow cast by power, which is of great deterrent importance. Therefore, we could not accept the conquest of this important area by a Soviet puppet under the very guns of our defensive perimeter with no more resistance than words and gestures in the Security Council. It looked as though we must steel ourselves for the use of force. That did not mean, in words used later by General Mark Clark, that we must be prepared "to shoot the works for victory," but rather to see that the attack failed.

When I set off to meet the President, I had no plan, but my mind was pretty clear on where the course we were about to recommend would lead and why it was necessary that we follow that course.

The full group invited was assembled at Blair House. While waiting for dinner to be announced, Secretary Johnson asked General Bradley to read a memorandum that he had brought from General MacArthur on the strategic importance of Formosa. I recognized this as an opening gun in a diversionary argument that Johnson wished to start with me. Evidently another did also, for when General Bradley had finished, the President announced that discussion of the Far Eastern situation had better be postponed until after dinner when we would be alone. The subject was thereupon dropped and conversation, during an excellent dinner in the Blair-Lee House gotten up by the staff on a Sunday afternoon with the shortest notice, was kept to general topics. After dinner we remained at the table while the White House staff cleared it and retired.

The President then asked me to report the latest developments and any recommendations the two departments had prepared for him. I gave a darkening report of great confusion and read three recommendations:

1. General MacArthur should be authorized and directed to supply Korea with arms and other equipment over and above that already allocated under the Military Assistance Program.

2. The U.S. Air Force should be ordered to protect Kimpo airport during the evacuation of United States dependents by attacking any North Korean ground or air forces approaching it.

3. The Seventh Fleet should be ordered to proceed from the Philippines north and to prevent any attack from China on Formosa or vice versa.

I also urged that military assistance to Indochina be stepped up.

Each person around the room was then asked for his views. The recommendations were supported with varying degrees of detail. There was quite general uniformity of view that the occasion called for prompt and vigorous action as it became clearer. The President discussed with the soldiers the likelihood of the Soviet Union's pushing the crisis to general war. The consensus was to the contrary, since the military balance was more favorable to the United States and unfavorable to the Soviet Union than it was likely to continue in the longer run. They were not in favor of using ground forces under conditions then existing. General Joseph L. Collins pressed for and obtained the President's authority to have General MacArthur send a survey team to Korea to make a firsthand appraisal and report.

At the end, about eleven o'clock, the President accepted my recommendations, although reserving decision on what orders to issue to the Seventh Fleet until it should reach the Formosa Straits about thirty-six hours later and be able to carry them out. He also added two instructions of his own to me—to make a survey of other likely spots for Soviet strikes and to prepare a statement for him to make on Tuesday (perhaps to Congress) reporting what had been done. He said that he wanted the Department's best brains put to work on these tasks and added that "there are plenty of them there." These were the most cheering words from a President to or about the State Department in years. Before we broke up, he emphasized that no statement whatever was to be made by anyone until he spoke on Tuesday. There must be no leaks, not even background statements to the press. I reminded him that Louis Johnson and I had to appear before the appropriations committee on Monday. Nevertheless, he said, no statements on Korea were to be made by either of us.

At the end of the meeting I showed the President a message from Foster Dulles in Tokyo, to which he had just returned from a visit to Korea. "It is possible," the message said, "that South Koreans may themselves contain and repulse attack, and, if so, this is the best way. If, however, it appears that they cannot do so then we believe that US force should be used even though this risks Russian countermoves. To sit by while Korea is overrun by unprovoked armed attack would start disastrous chain of events leading most probably to world war. We suggest that Security Council might call for action."[1]

Monday, June 26 • A day of steadily worsening reports from Korea, but work went on. Assignments were made to carry out the President's instructions of the preceding evening. I went over my testimony for the Appropriations Committee, and then spent half an hour telephoning Senators Tom Connally and Alexander Wiley and Judge Kee of the House committee, repeating what was in the press; reporting our support for the United Nations, whose representatives were busy in Korea; and asking that any meeting with congressional committees be held off for a day, "until we had some hard information to report." The appropriations hearing went off without too much trouble.

On my return the news was much worse. More calls from and to the Capitol; finally Assistant Secretary Jack McFall went up to prepare the chairmen for what appeared a growing rout. After lunch the Korean Ambassador, distraught and weeping, called on the President with me to present President Rhee's plea for help. The President soothed him, and I gave him a statement to read as he went out which assured him that we were solidly backing the United Nations.

Returning to the Department, I conferred with those who had been working on the President's assignments. What followed is recorded in a minute by one of those present: "The Secretary broke off the discussions we had been having with him and said that he wanted to be alone and to dictate. We were called in about 6:30 P.M. and he read to us a paper he had produced, which was a first draft of the statement finally issued by the President, and which was not significantly changed by the time it appeared the following day."

After dinner downtown and further conferences with State and Defense officers, I telephoned the President that the situation in Korea was becoming so desperate that he would wish to hear about it firsthand and instruct us further. He summoned the same group to Blair House which had met there on Sunday.

It met there at nine o'clock, Deputy Under Secretary H. Freeman Matthews taking Webb's place. General Vandenberg reported that a Russian plane had been shot down by our forces and that the South Koreans were breaking all along the front under a formidable attack. In response to the President's request for suggestions, I recommended that:

1. The Air Force and Navy should give all-out support to the Korean forces, for the time being confining their efforts to south of the 38th parallel.

2. The Seventh Fleet should be ordered to prevent an attack on Formosa, the Nationalists told not to attack the mainland, and the Fleet told to prevent their doing so, if necessary.

3. U.S. forces in the Philippines should be strengthened and aid to Philippine forces accelerated.

4. Aid to Indochina should be increased and we should propose to the French that we send a strong military mission.

5. If the President approved the foregoing, he should issue the statement I had prepared as directed and which included actions recommended.

6. At the Security Council meeting called for the next morning we should propose a new resolution (which Hickerson read) calling on UN members to give Korea such help as might be needed to repel the armed attack and restore peace in the area. If Malik returned to the Security Council and vetoed the resolution, we would have to carry on under the existing one. If he did not return, it would pass without opposition.

We had speculated a great deal about the probable Soviet move. The uncertainty about it added one more element of chance to the puzzle before us. Charles Bohlen and George Kennan, who spoke with most experience on the subject, believed that the cumbersome Soviet bureaucracy was simply not equipped to make quick decisions. It would take some time, they thought, for Moscow to figure out the correlation of forces involved. The betting was against the presence of a Russian at the meeting on the morrow.

The recommendations met with general favor, including Louis Johnson's, and were approved by the President. The Army officers present doubted whether naval and air support could save the Korean forces, though the Navy and Air Force view was more optimistic. If it became necessary to commit ground forces in Korea, they thought some degree of mobilization might become necessary. The President asked that this be given immediate study.

He then raised the question of consultation with congressional leaders. After some discussion Secretary Johnson and I were directed to meet with him at the White House the next morning to talk with the Speaker—the Vice President would be away—the majority leaders, Senator Scott Lucas and Representative John McCormack; Senators Tom Connally, Walter George, and Elbert Thomas, Democrats, and Alexander Wiley and Alexander Smith, Republicans, from the Foreign Relations Committee, and Millard Tydings and Styles Bridges from the Armed Services Committee; Congressmen John Kee, Mike Mansfield, and Charles Eaton of Foreign Affairs and Carl Vinson and Dewey Short of Armed Services.

Orders to carry out the decisions of Monday evening issued at once and were immediately obeyed. The UN Security Council meeting set for Tuesday morning was postponed until the afternoon to enable the Indian representative to receive instruction. Thus some American action, said to be in support of the resolution of June 27, was in fact ordered, and possibly taken, prior to the resolution. Later on, Russian propaganda attempted to play this up, but the effort received the attention it deserved.

Tuesday, June 27 • At the President's meeting with the congressional leaders, Assistant Secretaries Matthews, Rusk, and Hickerson and Ambassador Jessup accompanied me. The Chiefs of Staff and service secretaries came with Secretary Johnson. The meeting was held in the Cabinet Room, Johnson and I flanking the President, with the legislators around the table and the others behind them. The President asked me to summarize the situation, and then stressed the prompt action of the Security Council, read the statement, later published,[2] of the orders he had already issued, and reported our efforts to communicate with the Soviet Government. He then asked for views. Various questions about military dispositions were asked and answered by the Chiefs, including the fact that no ground forces had yet been committed. Senator Wiley seemed to express the consensus by saying that it was enough for him to know that we were in there with force and that the President thought the force adequate. Senator Tydings reported that his committee had that morning recommended an extension of the draft act and presidential authority to call out the National Guard.

Questions having turned to the political field, the President stated that our actions were taken in support of the United Nations efforts to restore peace in the area. In regard to Formosa, however, his orders were ancillary, aimed at preventing any new outbreak of fighting. I discussed the proposed Security Council resolution, ventured the opinion that Malik would not attend the meeting, and pointed out that since the USSR had not yet publicly committed itself we were careful not to engage Soviet prestige at this time. Congressman Eaton inquired whether the United States was now committed to defend South Korea. The President answered yes, as a member of the United Nations and in response to the Security Council's resolutions. Asked about help from other nations, I replied that not much could be expected since others either had their hands full, like the French, or had little to spare. After assurance that Congress would be kept currently informed of developments and general agreement that release of the President's statement would make separate comments unnecessary, the meeting broke up.

While we were talking the Security Council met, without Malik, and adopted the United States resolution, with Yugoslavia dissenting and Egypt and India abstaining.

President Truman's statement[3] referring to the continuance of the North Korean attack despite the UN call for its cessation said: "In these circumstances, I have ordered United States air and sea forces to give the Korean Government troops cover and support." It added that an attack on Formosa under these circumstances would be a direct threat to the security of the Pacific area and to United States forces performing their lawful and necessary functions there. "Accordingly," the President's statement continued, "I have ordered the Seventh Fleet to prevent any attack on Formosa. As a corollary of this action, I am calling upon the Chinese Government on Formosa to cease all air and sea operations against the mainland. The Seventh Fleet will see that this is done."

The statement also recited the other actions that had been taken.

Later the same day we told the press of our note to the Soviet Union. In view of their Representative's refusal to attend the Security Council's meeting and of their close relations with the North Korean authorities, we were approaching them directly, we said, to ask their disavowal of responsibility for the attack and the use of their influence with the North Koreans "for withdrawal of the invading forces and cessation of hostilities." On the twenty-ninth they replied that the attack had been made by the South Koreans and responsibility for its consequences rested upon them "and upon those who stand behind their back."[4]

On Tuesday Governor Dewey of New York read to me over the telephone a statement giving his support to the Administration's action on Korea and asked for suggestions. I welcomed it with warmest appreciation and gratitude. He released it at once.

Wednesday, June 28 · Immediately following Governor Dewey's support, Senator Taft opened up in the Senate. His speech was typical—bitterly partisan and ungracious, but basically honest. The Administration was responsible, he said, for the trouble that had overtaken it. The division of Korea, failure to arm the South sufficiently, the "loss of China" to the Communists, my "invitation to attack" in the January 12 speech, had all made attack inevitable. Even now the President had done the right thing in the wrong way. The Senator would have approved a congressional resolution authorizing intervention but doubted the constitutionality of the President's executive action. The ground Senator Taft chose was typical senatorial legalistic ground for differing with the President, as we have seen earlier in the case of Senator Vandenberg. As a result, discussion in Congress of these differences is singularly lacking in understanding of substantive issues. When it escapes the shackles of the separation of powers, it is apt to bog down in the moral shortcomings of those foreign governments with whom the United States is cooperating. They are usually said to be lacking either in energetic action for the common cause or in moral fervor for democratic doctrines.

Of much greater importance to me than Senator Taft's opposition was Averell Harriman's return to Washington. For some time he had wished to return, as he believed that his work in Paris for the Marshall Plan had largely been accomplished. Washington was the center of the world; he felt isolated in Europe. I had been working with and on the President to bring Averell back. To find a place for him was not an easy task. Averell had immense prestige and was aware of it. Many were jealous of him. No one would wish to stand aside. Washington is like a self-sealing tank on military aircraft: when a bullet passes through, it closes up. Averell, the President agreed, could be immensely useful in smoothing out Cabinet relations on foreign affairs, especially with Defense, where they had not eased appreciably since the spring eruption. However, he warned me that should Harriman return to do this the press would have it that he was slated to succeed me and that long knives would be whetted to speed fulfillment of the prophecy. The fact that there would be gossip, I agreed, was of course true, but the President, Averell, and I would know that there was no truth in it. My forty-five years of confidence in Averell's integrity and honor would not be undermined by those whom Lincoln called "the scribblers."

Therefore, at a press conference on June 16 I had "warmly welcomed" word from the White House of Averell's impending appointment as Special Assistant to the President. The need for it had long been felt. So far as I was concerned there could not have been a happier choice. The President had worked it out after consultation with Mr. Harriman and me. Since 1905, I said, "which, perhaps, some of you don't remember, . . . we have been close friends and worked together at all sorts of things."

On Tuesday morning, June 27, Averell had telephoned me from Paris, carried away with enthusiasm about the President's action about Korea. He could not stand delaying his return another hour while Washington was electrifying the world. He would leave at once, counting on me to "square it with the boss." From that time on, through all the period we were in the Government together, he attended our nine-thirty meeting in the Department almost every day, and any other meeting he wished, read all the important cables, and had access to all information. The direst predictions of trouble to come and the greatest efforts to sow it were made without the slightest effect. Averell's loyal help and wise advice were invaluable to the President, to me, and to the whole Administration.

At the National Security Council meeting on the afternoon of the twenty-eighth I pointed out that we could not count on the continuance of the enthusiastic support that our staunch attitude in Korea had evoked in the country and in the world. Firm leadership would be less popular if it should involve casualties and taxes. The President, mistaking my purpose, which was to prepare for criticism and hard sledding, insisted that we could not back out of the course upon which we had started. The reply was typical of one of his most admirable traits. He was unmoved by, indeed unmindful of, the effect upon his or his party's political fortunes of action that he thought was right and in the best interest of the country, broadly conceived. A doctrine that later became fashionable with presidents, called "keeping all options open" (apparently by avoiding decision), did not appeal to Harry S. Truman.

Thursday, June 29 · Wednesday had been a day of pause in the rush of decisions. On Thursday it picked up again. Brigadier General John Church, who had been sent to Korea by General MacArthur to report the situation, had signaled that the *status quo ante* could not be restored without the commitment of United States troops, and by Thursday morning the news was much worse. All attempts to halt the South Korean retreat at the Han River south of Seoul failed. By noon the gloom deepened. The President called a meeting of the "Blair House Group" for five o'clock.

Decisions at this meeting increased the involvement of our air and naval forces to include military targets in North Korea, but not beyond, and authorized the use of ground forces to secure the port, airfield, and communications facilities at Pusan, considerably south of the combat zone. Meanwhile General MacArthur had gone by plane from Tokyo to make his own reconnaisance at the scene of the fighting. He was told that should Soviet forces intervene he was to provide for the security of his own troops and report at once to Washington. However, as I have already suggested, it was State's view that while the Chinese might intervene, the Russians would not.

Shortly after this meeting I returned to the White House with an offer by Generalissimo Chiang Kai-shek to contribute thirty-three thousand troops to the Korean action, to be transported and supplied by the United States. The President seemed to look with favor on this idea, which I argued against on the ground that these troops would be more useful defending Formosa than Korea. He directed me to bring it up the next day before the full group, when he could hear all views.

Friday, June 30 · General MacArthur, back in Tokyo after a hazardous expedition to the front in Korea, telegraphed General Collins, Chief of Staff of the Army, that the Korean retreat was a rout and that American combat troops were necessary to stop it. He asked for authority to send from Japan at once a regimental combat team as the spearhead of a two-division buildup as soon as possible afterward. This message came to Collins at three o'clock Friday morning and was immediately followed by a telecon discussion by General Collins, Secretary of the Army Pace, and Assistant Secretary of State Rusk at the Pentagon with General MacArthur in Tokyo. (A telecon is a secure device by which a typewriter operated at one end records both there and through a similar machine at the other end.) General MacArthur elaborated his telegraphed report, underlining the urgent need for American military help at the front.

Secretary Pace telephoned the President at five o'clock, finding him up and dressing for his morning walk. The President immediately granted authority to move the augmented regiment, promised a further reply in a few hours, and ordered a meeting of the Blair House Group at the White House at eight-thirty that morning. Rusk filled me in on the way to the meeting. The request from the front and the President's response came as no surprise to me.

At the White House the President informed us of what he had already done and asked for advice regarding the next step. He spoke favorably of Chiang's offer of troops immediately available. I opposed the latter on the ground that the net result might well be the reverse of helpful by bringing Chinese Communist intervention, either in Korea or Formosa or both. The Chiefs of Staff sided with me, saying that the transport could better be used for our own troops and supplies, since Chiang's best troops were not likely to be of much help against the North Korean armor. The unanimous advice of the group was to follow the force already authorized with the two divisions from Japan. The President so decided and approved the necessary orders.

The decision not to accept the Generalissimo's offer brought from General MacArthur the suggestion that he go to Formosa to explain it. Instinct told us what experience later proved—to fear General MacArthur bearing explanations. Furthermore, better uses for the theater commander at this juncture came to mind, so a State Department officer was sent from Tokyo to Formosa with the explanation.

At eleven o'clock I returned to the White House for a meeting with congressional leaders, taking Foster Dulles, just back from Tokyo, with me. The congressional group was perhaps twice as large as the one at the Tuesday meeting. The President reported the situation in Korea, reviewed the actions previously taken by the United Nations Security Council and the United States Government, and the orders he had issued that morning. A general chorus of approval was interrupted by, I think, Senator Kenneth Wherry questioning the legal authority of the executive to take this action. Senator Alexander Smith suggested a congressional resolution approving the President's action. The President said that he would consider Smith's suggestion and asked me to prepare a recommendation. The meeting ended with Representative Dewey Short stating that Congress was practically unanimous in its appreciation of the President's leadership. Short was a Republican from the President's home state of Missouri and ranking minority member of the Armed Services Committee.

Friday's decisions were the culminating ones of a momentous week. We were then fully committed in Korea.

45. WAR IN KOREA: THE FIRST CRISIS

THOUGHTS ON AN AUTHORIZING RESOLUTION

IN THE DAYS THAT followed I considered Senator Alexander Smith's suggestion, and on July 3 the President assembled a group at Blair House to hear and discuss my recommendation. Jessup and Rusk went with me. Secretary Johnson brought the service secretaries and General Bradley. The President had with him Secretaries John Snyder of the Treasury and Charles Brannan of Agriculture; Postmaster General Jesse Donaldson; Senate Majority Leader Scott Lucas; and Averell Harriman.

My recommendation was that the President make a full report on the Korean situation to a joint session of Congress. This would, of course, be largely formal but would bring the whole story together in one official narrative and meet the objection of some members that information had come to them only through the leaders and the press. I also recommended that the President should not ask for a resolution of approval, but rest on his constitutional authority as Commander in Chief of the armed forces. However, we had drafted a resolution commending the action taken by the United States that would be acceptable if proposed by members of Congress.

In the ensuing discussion it appeared that the two houses of Congress had just recessed for a week and the President was unwilling to call them back. Senator Lucas, General Bradley, and Secretary Johnson were opposed to both recommendations: to the report because it would come too long after the events to stand by itself and had better accompany a request for money and necessary powers; and to the resolution because the vast majority in Congress were satisfied and the irreconcilable minority could not be won over. They could, however, keep debating and delaying a resolution so as to dilute much of its public effect. The others were divided. My sympathies lay with the Lucas-Bradley view. So apparently did the President's, for he put off a decision until the "Big Four" (the presiding officers and majority leaders of both houses) would be back after the recess. By then we were pretty well won over to Senator Lucas' view.

There has never, I believe, been any serious doubt—in the sense of non-politically inspired doubt—of the President's constitutional authority to do what he did. The basis for this conclusion in legal theory and historical precedent was fully set out in the State Department's memorandum of July 3, 1950, extensively published.[1] But the wisdom of the decision not to ask for congressional approval has been doubted. To have obtained congressional approval,

August 1941. The "phony war" in Europe was no longer phony, and our entry lay just ahead. President Roosevelt's Cabinet organized the Economic Defense Council. *Seated, left to right:* Secretary of the Treasury Henry Morgenthau, Jr.; Secretary of the Navy Frank Knox; Vice President Henry A. Wallace; Secretary of War Henry L. Stimson. *Standing, left to right:* Acting Attorney General Francis Biddle; Secretary of Commerce Jesse Jones; the author, then Assistant Secretary of State; Secretary of Agriculture Claude R. Wickard.

International News

Secretary of State Cordell Hull *(left)* and his Under Secretary, Sumner Welles.

At left: Two of the most powerful voices of the Roosevelt years — Secretary of the Interior Harold Ickes (left) and Harry Hopkins, adviser, administrator, and friend of the President.

At right: A friend and counselor, Justice Felix Frankfurter, with the author on one of their many walks to work.

Below left: The author testifying before the Senate Foreign Relations Committee, December 1945. He was under attack from former Ambassador Patrick J. Hurley, who charged that he had wrecked American policy in Iran.

Below right: James F. Byrnes, Secretary of State from July 1945 to January 1947; the author served as his Under Secretary.

Wide World

The last day in office of the "Old Curmudgeon" — and good friend — Harold L. Ickes.

Wide World photos

Right: "Diplomatic action without the backing of military strength in the present world can lead only to appeasement." Secretary of State George C. Marshall before the Senate Armed Services Committee, March 1948.

January 8, 1949. The day after the author was nominated to succeed General Marshall as Secretary of State, he was thrown into the company of his long-time political opponent, Senator Robert A. Taft, at a meeting of the Corporation of Yale University. With them is Yale President Charles Seymour. The press-service caption claims that "Acheson declined to comment on any subject whatsoever." *Wide World*

The Senate Foreign Relations Committee hearings held to ascertain the author's qualifications to serve as Secretary of State, January 1949. *Above:* Edward Stettinius, former Secretary of State under whom the author had served, testifies.

Below: Two who truly mattered and were to have powerful voices in the years of bipartisan foreign policy to come — Senators Arthur H. Vandenberg, Republican *(left),* and Tom Connally, Democrat.

The "Years of Responsibility" begin — January 21, 1949. Chief Justice Fred M. Vinson swears in the author as Secretary of State.

Below: Reorganization of the Department formally begins with the swearing in of new assistants, some of whom are being congratulated by the Secretary. *Left to right:* George McGhee, Assistant Secretary for Near Eastern and African Affairs; Adrian Fisher, the new Legal Adviser; the author; Edward G. Miller, Jr., Assistant Secretary for Inter-American Affairs.   *Acme*

April 4, 1949. The Atlantic Pact is signed. *Left to right:* Vice President Alben W. Barkley, the President, the author.

Wide World photos

Off to Paris in May 1949. *Left to right:* Mrs. Acheson, daughter Mary (Mrs. William P. Bundy), the President, daughter-in-law Mrs. David Acheson, daughter Jane (Mrs. Dudley Brown).

The scene of the Big Four conference in May 1949 — the Palais Rose, owned by Anna Gould, Duchess of Talleyrand.

Acme photos

With Mrs. Acheson on a quiet day on the farm at Sandy Spring, Maryland.

Washington Warpath

After a year in office, the press seemed to feel that Congress was not totally approving.
The Newark News

Bipartisan foreign policy under strain. A meeting with a staunch supporter, Senator Tom Connally, Chairman of the Senate Foreign Relations Committee.
Acme

May 1950. Departure for the tripartite ministerial meeting in London. The President usually saw the Achesons off to foreign meetings and was there to greet them on their return. *Wide World*

At Lancaster House, London, in May 1950 with two the author liked and respected — Ernest Bevin of Great Britain and Robert Schuman of France.

Keystone photos

Prime Minister Clement Attlee in a jovial mood during a speech before the Society of Pilgrims in London, May 10, 1950.

A change of pace. In Dallas for a foreign policy speech, June 1950. *James S. Wright*

On the facing page, top to bottom:

A study in viewpoints, June 1950. The President had just rushed back from Missouri to Washington as the Korean crisis deepened. On his right is Secretary of Defense Louis Johnson; on his left, the author. *International News*

In late June, John Foster Dulles reported to the White House on his return from Korea and Japan. On his right, General J. Lawton Collins, Army Chief of Staff; on his left, the author and General Omar Bradley. *Wide World*

Leaving the White House conference at which it was decided to go all out to defend South Korea. *Left to right:* The author, Ambassador Philip Jessup, Assistant Secretary of State Dean Rusk. *Wide World*

July 1950. The Korean crisis enveloped the Government. Surrounding President Truman, whose back is eloquent of the man, are *(from the left)* Secretary of Agriculture Brannan, Postmaster General Donaldson, the author, Secretary of the Interior Chapman, and Secretary of Defense Johnson. *The New York Times*

The opening of the North Atlantic Treaty Council session in New York, September 15, 1950.

Clockwise from the head of the table: Dean Acheson and Charles M. Spofford of the United States; Paul van Zeeland and Fernand van Langenhove of Belgium; Lester B. Pearson and L. D. Wilgress of Canada; Henrik de Kauffmann and M. A. Vestbirk of Denmark; Robert Schuman Joseph Bech and André Clasen of Luxembourg; Dirk V. Stikker and Jonkheer A. W. L. Tjarda van Starkenborgh-Stachouwer of the Netherlands; Halvard Lange and Dag Bryn of Norway; Paulo A. V. da Cunha and Henrique Queiroz of Portugal; Ernest Bevin and Sir Frederick Hoyer

Time out for a most important matter — the installation of A. Whitney Griswold as the sixteenth President of Yale University on October 6, 1950.

October 18, 1950. General Marshall (*left*), at that time Secretary of Defense, and the author greet the President on his return from a deceptively congenial meeting with General MacArthur on Wake Island.

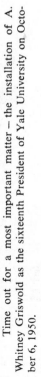

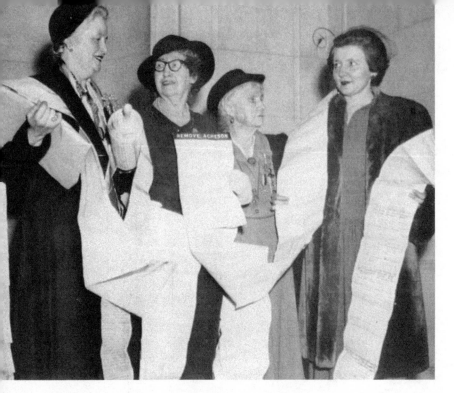

A petition calling for Secretary Acheson's removal from office, said to be a block long, was delivered to Senator Joseph McCarthy's office by ladies of the Anti-Communist League in December 1950. *Wide World*

Below: A November 1950 speech on the "re-examinist" — a new species discovered by Senator Taft — brought unexpected results. *Washington, D.C., Star*

Hazards of Holiday Hunting!

Jean Monnet, the intellect behind the Schuman Plan for European economic cooperation, which began with the pooling of coal and steel resources. *Wide World*

January 1951. General Eisenhower and the author confer (in the "presence" of General Marshall) before Eisenhower left to assume command of the NATO forces in Europe. *Acme*

General MacArthur had been relieved of his duties. He returned as though he were a conquering hero. *Above:* On parade in New York City, April 20, 1951.

    Below: A speech in Cleveland — "Our leaders can no longer be trusted.... There has been a steady drift toward totalitarian rule."

June 1, 1951 — a special sort of limelight. The author at the Senate investigations into the dismissal of General MacArthur. Seated at left are Republican Senators William Knowland and Harry Cain.

Acme photos

September 1951. The Japanese peace treaty conference in San Francisco. The author presided over a brisk opening session during which, as shown, the Polish delegate, Stefan Wierblowski, refused to yield the platform to the British delegate, Kenneth Younger, who had been recognized.

September 8, 1951. Prime Minister Shigeru Yoshida signs the Japanese peace treaty.
Below: A toast to the treaty; Ambassador Joseph Dodge is at left.   *Wide World*

Right: A respite — furniture making at Harewood Farm.   *Wide World*

Below: British Foreign Minister Anthony Eden with the author at the United Nations General Assembly session in Paris, November 1951.

Examining pictures of the Potsdam Conference.

The guest log of the presidential yacht, USS *Williamsburg*, for January 5, 1952.

Two men of character.

EARL MARSHAL'S OFFICE
ST. JAMES'S PALACE

Funeral of His late Majesty King George VI

on Friday, 15th February, 1952

The Earl Marshal has it in command from THE QUEEN

to invite

The Honourable

Dean Acheson

to take part in the procession

NORFOLK, E.M.

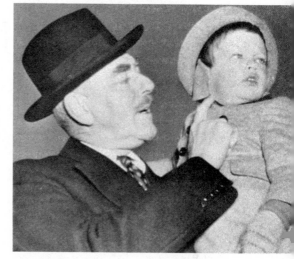

Michael Bundy, the author's grandson, sees him off to London on February 12, 1952.   *United Press*

February 15, 1952. The funeral cortege of King George VI of England.   *Wide World*

Salazar of Portugal, whose ancestors were fishermen, and the remarkable likeness to a possible ancestor in the *"painel dos pescadores"* painted by Nuno Gonçalves in 1465.

London, June 23, 1952. The author with Ambassador Walter Gifford *(right)* and Anthony Eden.

Bonn, May 26, 1952. Anthony Eden, Konrad Adenauer, the author, and Robert Schuman on hand for the signing of the Contractual Agreements between the allies and West Germany.

Honolulu, August 1952. Arriving for the ANZUS Council meeting — "An official reception at Honolulu airport is an ordeal difficult to surmount with an appearance of pleasure. . . . The leis that are hung around one's neck, as once around a sacrificial bull's, invariably conceal small crawling creatures . . ." *U.S. Marine Corps*

January 16, 1953. Farewell to the people of the State Department — "They may feel in their hearts that it was nobly done." The Secretary was presented with the chair he occupied as a member of the Cabinet. *Wide World*

Endurance under fire at the United Nations on October 29, 1952. Andrei Vishinsky *(right)* spoke for three and a half hours on the problem of a Korean settlement without advancing a new proposal. *At left, in front:* Secretary Acheson and Selwyn Lloyd; *in the second row:* Warren R. Austin and Sir Gladwyn Jebb. *The New York Times*

To Hon. Dean Acheson, with kindest regards and best wishes from Harry Truman

Harry S. Truman. "Free of the greatest vice in a leader, his ego never came between him and his job. . . . Among the thirty-five men who have held the presidential office, Mr. Truman will stand with the few who in the midst of great difficulties managed their offices with eminent benefit to the public interest."

it has been argued, would have obviated later criticism of "Truman's war." In my opinion, it would have changed pejorative phrases, but little else. Congressional approval did not soften or divert the antiwar critics of Presidents Lincoln, Wilson, and Roosevelt. What inspired the later criticism of the Korean war was the long, hard struggle, casualties, cost, frustration of a limited and apparently inconclusive war, and—most of all—the determination of the opposition to end seemingly interminable Democratic rule.

Nevertheless, it is said, congressional approval would have done no harm. True, approval would have done none, but the process of gaining it might well have done a great deal. July—and especially the first part of it—was a time of anguishing anxiety. As American troops were committed to battle, they and their Korean allies under brutal punishment staggered back down the peninsula until they maintained only a precarious hold on the coastal perimeter around Pusan. An incredulous country and world held its breath and read the mounting casualties suffered by these gallant troops, most of them without combat experience. In the confusion of the retreat even their divisional commander, Major General William F. Dean, was captured. Congressional hearings on a resolution of approval at such a time, opening the possibility of endless criticism, would hardly be calculated to support the shaken morale of the troops or the unity that, for the moment, prevailed at home. The harm it could do seemed to me far to outweigh the little good that might ultimately accrue.

The President agreed, moved also, I think, by another passionately held conviction. His great office was to him a sacred and temporary trust, which he was determined to pass on unimpaired by the slightest loss of power or prestige. This attitude would incline him strongly against any attempt to divert criticism from himself by action that might establish a precedent in derogation of presidential power to send our forces into battle. The memorandum that we prepared listed eighty-seven instances in the past century in which his predecessors had done this. And thus yet another decision was made.

Shortly after the seven days of June just described a paper came to me from the White House. I end this account with it, partly and unquestionably from pride, but also because it illustrates so well a quality of the President's that bound his lieutenants to him with unbreakable devotion. The paper was a longhand note:

Memo to Dean Acheson
Regarding June 24 and 25—   7/19/50
Your initiative in immediately calling the Security Council of the U.N. on Saturday night and notifying me was the key to what followed afterwards. Had you not acted promptly in that direction we would have had to go into Korea alone.

The meeting Sunday night at the Blair House was the result of your action Saturday night and the results afterward show that you are a great Secretary of State and a diplomat.

Your handling of the situation since has been superb.

I'm sending you this for your record.

Harry S. Truman

AN ANXIOUS SUMMER

After the seven days of decision my work was less heavily concentrated on Korean matters though still continuously involved with them. The attack helped to activate other problems that crowded anxious days—the battle with the Republican "irreconcilables," to use a phrase common just thirty years earlier, and the concern and fear of our European allies that our absorption in the desperate battle going on in Korea might dilute our attention to their security.

From the very start of hostilities in Korea, President Truman intended to fight a limited engagement there. In this determination he had the staunch and unwavering support of the State and Defense departments and the Joint Chiefs of Staff. Such a war policy requires quite as much determination as any other kind. It also calls for restraint and fine judgment, a sure sense of how far is far enough; it may involve, as it did in Korea, a great deal of frustration. In its execution, this policy invites dissent and criticism both from those who are afraid that the balance is being tipped against the possibility of keeping the war limited and from those who fear that keeping it limited precludes the possibility of victory and who believe that "there is no substitute for victory." The former, now called "doves," reduce the national objective with every reversal and soon wish to scrap the whole effort. The "hawks" would raise the sights with every success and call for unconditional surrender. Prominent, even in this early period, among the former were the British and the Indians, joined later on by the Canadians, and among the latter General MacArthur and the "hard China policy" men, especially the irreconcilable Republicans.

Anglo-Indian Peace Initiatives · The British Foreign Office had long believed, more than evidence seemed to warrant, that it understood the Russians and could negotiate with them compromise solutions of difficult situations. To others, the proposed compromises often resembled surrenders. In July, while our troops were fighting against heavy odds to keep a toehold in Korea, we found ourselves engaged in a month of discussion of their unsolicited initiative to bring about a "peaceful settlement" there. Independently, and unknown to the British, the Indians had started an effort of their own. My comment about British diplomacy vis-à-vis the Soviet Union would be quite inadequate to describe the Indian variety.

Immediately after the June 27 resolution of the Security Council, the British Government helpfully and loyally put British warships in Japanese waters at General MacArthur's disposal as the quickest method of furnishing help to Korea. Later they sent the heroic brigade of "The Glosters," which fought and suffered so gallantly. Almost at once His Majesty's Government also began its search for a peaceful settlement. In early July Sir David Kelly, British Ambassador to the Soviet Union, was trying to get in touch with Deputy Foreign Minister Gromyko, and Prime Minister Attlee proposed to the President talks in Washington between presidential nominees and Air Marshal Lord

Arthur Tedder and Ambassador Oliver Franks. I suggested that Ambassador Philip Jessup join General Omar Bradley, the President's choice from the services.

At the same time, Ambassador Alan G. Kirk reported from Moscow that Gromyko had asked Kelly whether he had any specific proposal for a peaceful settlement, and that Kelly had replied, "The *status quo ante."* Ambassador Kirk urged that we make clear to the British—who had meanwhile told us that further talks in Moscow would come only after full discussion with us—that a prerequisite for peaceful settlement was complete compliance by North Korea with the Security Council's call for a cease-fire and withdrawal of the invading forces north of the 38th parallel.

Before going into the month of Anglo-Indian maneuvers, a word about Ambassador Kirk. By 1950 both of our families—men, women, and children—had been close friends for thirty years. When we first met, Alan Kirk, then a Lieutenant Commander, was the Executive Officer of the presidential yacht, the *Mayflower,* and I was Justice Brandeis' law clerk. During the late war Kirk, by then a vice admiral, had brilliantly commanded the naval forces that put the American troops ashore in Sicily in 1943 and on the Normandy beaches in 1944. After the war he had been, I thought, shabbily treated by the Pacific-oriented Chief of Naval Operations, crusty old Admiral of the Fleet Ernest J. King, by being assigned to the Navy's moribund General Board. The post of Ambassador to Belgium became vacant. The Belgian Foreign Minister, Paul-Henri Spaak, was one of the distinguished and able European six, the others being Bevin, Schuman, Count Sforza in Rome, Dirk Stikker in the Netherlands, and Joseph Bech in Luxembourg. We needed an ambassador of perception, cultivation, and distinction to keep us in close touch with Spaak's always interesting and sometimes unpredictable ideas. Alan Kirk seemed to me well suited. He was also admirably supplemented by his wife, Lydia Chapin Kirk, very much a person in her own right, a Navy daughter as well as wife, able, gifted in languages and social grace, and possessing a sense of responsibility for the members of their mission.

The President thought well of the proposal and even better of it when he met Alan and watched his performance. When General Walter Bedell Smith resigned as Ambassador to Moscow in 1949, I asked Kirk to come to Washington for consultation and, over a long lunch, to hear me out before replying to a difficult request. I had the President's permission—without commitment yet on either side—to put up to Alan moving him from Brussels to Moscow. It would not be a pleasant move, but more important duty. He would tell me that he knew nothing about Russia or communist doctrine and operation. Many on his staff did know a good deal about both, including the Naval Attaché, Vice Admiral Leslie Stevens. At this particular turn in events, his lack of Russian was not an important drawback. Stalin was not a gossipy type; Vishinsky did not count; and Gromyko was walking on eggs. What we would expect of the Ambassador would not be brilliant suggestions on how to solve the Russian enigma but immediate and firm execution of his instructions, full reporting, and careful, solicitous attention to the condition and morale of the mission, beleaguered as it was and subject to traps and pressures. He and Lydia were just the people for this tough assignment.

He agreed; the President agreed; the Senate agreed; and the Kirks went to Moscow.

Returning to the British-Indian maneuvers, we were soon on the verge of severe disagreements with both London and New Delhi. On July 6 while dining with Sir Oliver Franks, I explained our unhappiness over Bevin's urging us to make concessions for a cease-fire, and the next day instructed Ambassador Lewis Douglas in London to say that we would not do this. The Kelly-Gromyko talks, he could add, might be useful if restricted solely to finding out what, if anything, Moscow had in mind. The Ambassador's visit garnered the information that a group in the Foreign Office, described as "influential," were eager to get the Communist Chinese into the United Nations as soon as possible to frustrate a supposed Russian desire to isolate China from the West.

It also produced a letter from Bevin. He wrote that the Kremlin really wished to restore the *status quo ante,* but he believed they would link a change in our position on Formosa with it. That position, he said, did not have the backing of the states that supported the UN Korean resolutions. We should avoid risking Western solidarity by playing down those parts of the President's statement of June 27 that did not bear directly on Korea.

One can easily imagine that this message did not please either the President or me. I therefore drafted and he approved a frank reply, dated July 10, 1950, which, indicating its joint authorship, made four points:

1. We would not agree to a forced trade of Formosa to the Communists for their withdrawal from Korea.

2. Our policy aimed at as early and complete a liquidation of the Korean aggression as was militarily possible, without concessions that would whet Communist appetites and bring on other aggressions elsewhere.

3. It also aimed at the peaceful disposition of the Formosan question, either in a peace treaty with Japan or through the United Nations.

4. If questions regarding Formosa or the representation of China in the United Nations were to be considered there, we regarded it essential that they be considered on their merits and not under the duress and blackmail then being employed.

Our Ambassador was also instructed to stress orally the undesirability of agitating in the present situation that China be represented on the Security Council by the Communist regime or that Malik return to it. He was to say, also, that both the President and I took a serious view of Mr. Bevin's note and the portent that its contents carried for future Anglo-American cooperation.

The Ambassador, who delivered this letter to Bevin in the hospital on July 11, found him taken aback by its vigor and defensive in explaining his own position. Bevin's written reply warned that we must not drive China into Soviet hands, and stated that although aggression must be repelled and he would not yield to blackmail, he wanted the Soviet Union and the Communist Chinese in the Security Council. The correspondence clearly had no future, so we dropped it.

The Tedder-Bradley talks also added nothing. General Bradley explained that some weeks would be needed to build our strength to a point where it would tell decisively. The Russians, he thought, would not intervene overtly, for that would mean war, and such a war would not be fought in Korea.

Meanwhile, the Indian initiative for peaceful settlement was gathering momentum in multisplendored confusion. In Moscow Indian Ambassador Radhakrishnan approached Deputy Foreign Minister Zorin; in Washington Mme. Pandit, Indian Ambassador and Nehru's sister, talked to me; in India Sir Girja Bajpai, Secretary General of the Foreign Office, spoke to U.S. Ambassador Loy Henderson; and in the United Nations Krishna Menon took on our people. Each presented the scheme a little differently and insisted that the effort must be kept secret from the British, which, of course, was not done. The general idea was that we were to support seating the Communist Chinese on the Security Council, which would then, with the Russians and Chinese Communists both on it, support a cease-fire, withdrawal of North Korean troops to the 38th parallel, and the re-creation of a unified and independent Korea.

On the eleventh Kirk learned via Radhakrishnan that Gromyko had rejected the second part of the proposal out of hand. With the President's approval, Kirk was authorized to tell his Indian colleague that we would agree to nothing that rewarded an aggressor, diluted the requirements of the June 25 and 27 resolutions of the Security Council, or left Korea after hostilities in an exposed and defenseless situation.

Then, on the thirteenth, Prime Minister Nehru sent personal letters to Stalin and to me making a proposal even less satisfactory to us than the one rejected in Moscow.[2] India's purpose, he wrote, was to localize the conflict and to facilitate an early peaceful settlement by breaking the present deadlock in the Security Council so that Communist Chinese representatives could take a seat there, the Russians could return to it, and, either within or outside the council, the United States, the Soviet Union, and China, with the help and cooperation of other peace-loving nations, could find a basis for terminating the conflict and for a permanent solution of the Korean problem. In this endeavor the Prime Minister wished to enlist my great authority and influence.

Although the logic of this proposal was obscure—to seat the Communists in the Security Council in order to permit informal contacts outside it—the effect was abundantly clear. It would transfer the center of attention and discussion from the aggression in Korea to who should represent China on the Security Council. The ousting of the Nationalists from the council—for that was the essence of the matter—was to be the price for the privilege of opening discussion about North Korean troop withdrawal. The next installment, clearly forecast by Bajpai to Henderson, would be the ousting of the Nationalists from Formosa. Meanwhile our troops would be fighting a rear-guard action down the peninsula of Korea as the Communists tried to drive them out of it. I felt no need for advice in making up my mind on such a proposal. However, I was to receive spiritual exhortation.

Mme. Pandit—a most charming lady—called on me on the seventeenth with an appeal from her brother. Apprehension that Peking's entry and Moscow's return to the Security Council might possibly lead to obstruction should not delay restoration of the council's full representative character. Insistence upon prior conditions—such as the return of North Koreans to the 38th parallel—would be used as evidence of a lack of desire on our part for peaceful settlement (sic!). If after taking their seats the Chinese should be unreasonable, world opinion would hold them responsible. Moscow, her brother thought, was seeking a way out; here was the real path to peaceful settlement. "It may be an act of faith, but the gravity of the alternatives seems to justify it," she said. I have never been able to escape wholly from a childhood illusion that, if the world is round, the Indians must be standing on their heads—or, perhaps, vice versa.

With the President's approval, I replied on July 18, trying to put first things first. The key paragraph stated: "A breach of the peace or an act of aggression is the most serious matter with which the United Nations can be confronted. We do not believe that the termination of the aggression from northern Korea can be contingent in any way upon the determination of other questions which are currently before the United Nations."[3]

This letter was said to have annoyed Mr. Nehru. The correspondence, however, continued through one more repetitious exchange, which led Bajpai, a pleasant little man, to report severely to Henderson of Nehru's hope that the United States did not prefer a United Nations without the Soviet bloc. Two days later Moscow announced Malik's return to the Security Council, which happily ended India's initiative, for it would have been hard to argue that the Russians would not return to the council without the Chinese Communists after they had, in fact, returned.

Other nations responded to the UN resolutions with contributions more helpful than fanciful peace proposals. By the end of the year fifteen members had armed forces in Korea or on the way and thirty had contributed to civilian relief and reconstruction. By the middle of the month, with the battle still going against us as we fell back on Pusan, the Administration resumed with new urgency the examination begun in the winter and spring of our own and our allies' military posture.

Arms and the Men • The dispatch of the two divisions to Korea removed the recommendations of NSC-68 from the realm of theory and made them immediate budget issues. In the State Department, therefore, we were distressed by the relaxed view of affairs taken by the Council of Economic Advisers in their midyear report, which assumed that fighting would be kept localized and concluded that no stand-by economic control powers were necessary. In our discussion we were unanimous in agreeing that not only what the country did but what it was obviously preparing itself to do, if necessary, would greatly affect what it might be called upon to do. We believed that the recommendations were totally inadequate and that opinion in the country was prepared for vigorous action. Willard Thorp was directed to express these views at White House meetings on economic matters and arrange for my attendance at them.

A report at a Cabinet meeting on July 14, which the President had asked from State and Defense on possible future Soviet action, gave an opportunity to raise the matter. We had concluded that the Soviet Union had the military capability of taking action, directly or through satellites, at one or more points along its periphery or of engaging in more general war. After suggesting places and causes for trouble, I reported that unanimity did not exist on the most probable spot or spots that might be chosen, but it did exist on the extreme danger of some such action flowing from either Soviet desire or the momentum of events. Any one or more of these outbreaks would call for the use of more military power than we could then deploy. I urged that the President ask for an immediate increase in authorized forces of all services, for substantial appropriations—too much rather than too little—for increased military production and powers to allocate and limit uses of raw materials, and state that this was to increase the capabilities not only of our own forces but of allied forces as well. Increase in military production seemed to me of special importance, since here lay our greatest effectiveness once it got started.

The President agreed with all of this. Five days later he delivered a report to Congress, which included all of it:

> Under all the circumstances, it is apparent that the United States is required to increase its military strength and preparedness not only to deal with the aggression in Korea but also to increase our common defense, with other free nations, against further aggression.
> The increased strength which is needed falls into three categories.
> In the first place, to meet the situation in Korea, we shall need to send additional men, equipment and supplies to General MacArthur's command as rapidly as possible.
> In the second place, the world situation requires that we increase substantially the size and materiel support of our armed forces, over and above the increases which are needed in Korea.
> In the third place, we must assist the free nations associated with us in common defense to augment their military strength.[4]

Appropriations and powers tumbled over one another, sometimes in such haste that supplemental appropriations virtually accompanied the regular fiscal-year bill they were supplementing. Thus in July the President signed fiscal year 1950–51 appropriations for mutual defense assistance of one billion two hundred million dollars and another four-billion-dollar supplemental appropriation in September. In August measures were taken to double the size of the armed forces. On September 6 the pre-existing Defense appropriation of fourteen billion six hundred million dollars was signed and on the twenty-seventh another twelve billion six hundred million added. Export controls and some powers over the economic life of the country were added. But the economic control side of the program had been weakened between the Cabinet meeting and the report under the powerful influence of Speaker Rayburn. This proved later to have been a mistake. Nevertheless, the country moved swiftly if in a somewhat disorderly way into a more formidable military posture.

It was often said that the Truman Administration and, particularly, the Secretary of State were "unpopular" and had trouble with Congress. It is true that many uncomplimentary things were said, but in Washington it is better to get what one wants than to be loved.

MacArthur Drops Some Bricks • Before 1950 General MacArthur had neither shown nor expressed interest in Formosa. It will be recalled that in discussing "our line of defense . . . against Asiatic aggression" with the press on March 1, 1949, he did not include that island. But the General was not deaf to political reports coming to him from the United States, particularly those emanating from the Republican right wing, which found our Far Eastern policy repulsive and occasionally mentioned the General as the charismatic leader who might end the obnoxious Democratic hold on the White House. When this group transferred its attention, as Chiang did his residence, to Formosa, Senator Alexander Smith hinted that General MacArthur had revised upward his estimate of Formosa's military importance, a view confirmed by the memorandum that General Bradley had brought from MacArthur and read to the first Blair House meeting. The curious disclosure, earlier in the year, from the General's headquarters of our propaganda paper on the line to be taken should Formosa fall to the Chinese Communists suggested more than clumsy blundering. And, finally, General MacArthur's eagerness to explain in person to the Generalissimo why his troop offer was not accepted should have, but did not, put us on our guard.

At the end of July the Joint Chiefs, interpreting President Truman's order not to permit an attack on or from Formosa as a change in view regarding its strategic importance (which was not the idea at all), recommended a military survey team to report on the state of its defenses.

Strange as it may seem in the light of these facts, official Washington was startled to read in the press on August 1 that General MacArthur had arrived in Formosa, kissed Mme. Chiang's hand, and gone into conference with her husband. To find out what was going on, I cabled William Sebald, Political Adviser in Tokyo, who had been appointed by the State Department. President Truman's comments evoked the admiration and envy of us all. General MacArthur's were, "To my astonishment, the visit to Formosa and my meeting with Chiang Kai-shek was greeted by a furor."[5] The Generalissimo crowed happily from Formosa that "now that we can again work closely together with our old comrade in arms" victory was assured. MacArthur reciprocated with praise of Chiang and assurances of the "effective military coordination between the Chinese and American Forces." He ordered three squadrons of jet fighters to Formosa without the knowledge of the Pentagon. Explicit orders then went to him emphasizing the limits of our policy regarding Formosa, and Harriman followed to reinforce them. A week later, on August 10, the General issued a statement that his Formosa trip had been "formally arranged and coordinated beforehand with all branches of the American and Chinese Governments." "This visit," he concluded, "has been maliciously misrepresented to the public by those who invariably in the past have propagandized a policy of defeatism and appeasement in the Pacific."

Harriman returned with an ambivalent report. On the one hand, he told the President and me that MacArthur, while disagreeing with our China and Formosa policy, had said that he was a good soldier and knew how to obey orders. Yet doubts persisted in Harriman's mind that he and MacArthur had come "to a full agreement on the way we believed things should be handled on Formosa and with the Generalissimo."[6] They certainly had not.

During the evening of August 25, Mike McDermott called me at Sandy Spring and read an Associated Press ticker report of a message that Mac-Arthur had sent to the annual convention of the Veterans of Foreign Wars. Although the dispatch had gone out to member newspapers, the publication date was to be two days later. The message consisted of a long description of the strategic importance of Formosa to the United States, including the following:

> Formosa in the hands of such a hostile power could be compared to an unsink-able aircraft carrier and submarine tender ideally located to accomplish offensive strategy and at the same time checkmate defensive or counter-offensive operations by friendly forces based on Okinawa and the Philippines. . . .
>
> Nothing could be more fallacious than the threadbare argument by those who advocate appeasement and defeatism in the Pacific that if we defend Formosa we alienate continental Asia. Those who speak thus do not understand the Orient. They do not grant that it is in the pattern of Oriental psychology to respect and follow aggressive, resolute and dynamic leadership—to quickly turn on a leadership characterized by timidity or vacillation—and they underestimate the Oriental mentality.[7]

Saying that I would come to the Department early the next morning, I asked to have Rusk, Jessup, Matthews, Webb, and Harriman meet me there. All of us were outraged at the effrontery and damaging effect at home and abroad of MacArthur's message. On July 19 the President had stressed to Congress and only the day before Ambassador Austin had restated to Trygve Lie, Secretary General of the United Nations, the limited purposes of our action regarding Formosa. General MacArthur had on July 8 been designated as United Nations Commander in Korea. We agreed that this insubordination could not be tolerated. MacArthur had to be forced publicly to retract his statement. Averell took the ticker dispatch to the White House.

For some time the President had had a meeting scheduled with the Secretaries of State, Treasury, and Defense, Harriman, and the Joint Chiefs of Staff for nine-thirty on that morning. When we filed into the oval office, the President, with lips white and compressed, dispensed with the usual greetings. He read the message and then asked each person around the room whether he had had any prior intimation or knowledge of it. No one had. Louis Johnson was directed to order MacArthur from the President to withdraw the message and report that he (MacArthur) had done so. The President himself would send directly to MacArthur a copy of Ambassador Austin's letter to Trygve Lie, from which he would understand why the withdrawal order was necessary. The business for which the meeting was called was hastily dispatched.

When we left the White House, nothing could have been clearer to me than that the President had issued an order to General MacArthur to withdraw the message, but Secretary Johnson soon telephoned to say that this could cause embarrassment and that he (Johnson) thought it better to inform MacArthur that if he issued the statement "we" would reply that it was "only one man's opinion and not the official policy of the Government." I said that the issue seemed to be who was President of the United States. Johnson then asked me an amazing question—whether "we dare send [MacArthur] a message that the President directs him to withdraw his statement?" I saw nothing else to do in view of the President's order.

At Johnson's request, I asked Averell Harriman whether he was clear that the President had issued an order. This shortly resulted in another call from Johnson saying that the President had dictated to him this message to go to MacArthur: "The President of the United States directs that you withdraw your message for National Encampment of Veterans of Foreign Wars, because various features with regard to Formosa are in conflict with the policy of the United States and its position in the United Nations."[8]

Still Johnson doubted the wisdom of sending the order and put forward his prior alternative. Stephen Early, his deputy, came on the telephone to support him, raised the question of General MacArthur's right of free speech, and proposed that the President talk to General MacArthur. At this point I excused myself and ended the conversation, duly reporting it to Harriman, saying that if Johnson wished to reopen the President's decision, he should apply to the President to do so. The President instructed Harriman that he had dictated what he wanted to go and he wanted it to go. It went. MacArthur's message was both withdrawn and unofficially published.

The President has written that at this time he considered relieving General MacArthur of the Korean command while leaving him with his responsibility in Japan, but decided against it. He has been quoted later as regretting that he did not then relieve him altogether. To do so did not occur to me at the time as appropriate to the offense, although if the future had been revealed, I should have advised it even at considerable cost. General MacArthur's weakness was his incredible arrogance and vanity, which led him to surround himself with sycophants, even though some able ones. General Marshall told me of a conference he had with General MacArthur during the war, at which the latter began a sentence with the phrase, "My staff tells me . . ." General Marshall interrupted him, saying, "General, you don't have a staff; you have a court."

The Crisis Eases • As American military power poured into Pusan, the long retreat down the peninsula halted and a tenuous stability was established by the Eighth Army within the Pusan perimeter. By July 20 General MacArthur, always optimistic, could cable the President that the enemy "has had his great chance and failed to exploit it." It took some weeks more of stubborn defensive fighting before we in Washington could be as convinced of this as the commanding general appeared to be.

An opportunity offered to escape from Washington for a few days to be with our daughter, whom I had not seen for nearly a year. We had taken a camp at Upper St. Regis Lake, near Saranac, where my wife and grandson could be with her daughter and his mother. Thither I flew for a happy week, keeping in sketchy touch with the Department through some complicated electronic devices the Navy had supplied. Fortunately, they never worked as well for me as they were supposed to. As a result I was only peripherally involved in the dispute between State and Defense over our bombing of Rashin, a prototype of similar disputes arising over the bombing in North Vietnam seventeen years later.

Situated seventeen miles from the Soviet border with northeastern Korea, Rashin was held to have military importance because of a chemical plant and railway switching yards, in which Soviet-furnished military supplies for North Korea were said to be marshaled. On August 12, the day after I left, the Department learned that Rashin had been bombed in bad weather, with undetermined results. State protested that this bombing violated the President's orders directing U.S. military aircraft "to stay well clear" of the border, and demanded prior consultation on further sorties of this dubious nature. Secretary Johnson denied that the border had been violated, which was not the point, and refused prior consultation. On my return, I let the issue drop, but in all future cases the President himself brought us into consultation.

Coming back full of Adirondack air and happy memories, I found the Department humming with discussion of policies for both sides of the world. Events in Korea had broken inertia of thought on many critical matters—a peace treaty with Japan, German participation in her own and European defense, and what to do in Korea when the aggression had been thrown back. All were pressing for and receiving simultaneous attention. At that time the Government could and did deal with more than one crisis at a time.

46. SEPTEMBER DECISIONS

IN THE FIRST WEEK OF September 1950 the President with his advisers came to three far-reaching decisions on issues arising on opposite sides of the globe. The first was to begin negotiation of a Japanese peace treaty and of an end to our military control of that country; the second, to propose the enlistment of our other former enemy, Germany, in a plan for the integrated defense of Europe; the third, to reach conclusions on what to do in Korea when the invader had been pushed back to the 38th parallel, and lay them before the General Assembly of the United Nations. Only the first of these produced the results hoped for from it.

A PEACE TREATY FOR JAPAN

The Situation in Japan · The situation with respect to Japan at the end of the Pacific war was very different from that of post-surrender Germany. Japan had been defeated primarily by American arms, while Britain and Russia had borne the brunt of the war in Europe before the United States entered it and both had enormous armies in the field at its end. In Europe and Asia the defeated armies surrendered to an American general who was also Supreme Commander for the Allied Powers, but the alliance that General Eisenhower symbolized was a very different one from General MacArthur's. General Eisenhower's supremacy dissolved almost at the moment of surrender. General MacArthur's position increased in power and prestige until doubt arose regarding the extent to which even the government whose commission he carried controlled him.

Moreover, in Germany the state itself, the Third Reich, was abolished and the land divided into four parts, in each of which government and law flowed from the will of the occupying conqueror. Agreements providing for cooperation among them soon broke down. We have already recounted the slow growth of two governments within the occupied area of Germany. In Japan the Emperor and the Government remained, subject to the orders of the conquering nation through its proconsul, the Supreme Commander. These orders were purely American in their conception and execution.

The "U.S. Initial Post-Surrender Policy for Japan,"[1] a wise and remarkable document worked out by the State, War, and Navy departments under the guiding influence of Secretary of War Stimson, Assistant Secretary of War McCloy, and Under Secretary of State Grew, was approved by the President on September 6, 1945, and set forth for General MacArthur his basic instruction.

Its fundamental provisions were sound and, equally important, clear. The occupation forces would be under "a Supreme Commander designated by the United States." On one thing we were determined: there would be no zones of occupation. Allied troops would be welcome to the Supreme Commander so long as they were unequivocally under his command and obeyed his orders. British Commonwealth troops from Australia, New Zealand, and India accepted this provision in due course and participated. The Soviet Union refused it and had no force in Japan. Our attitude was equally plain on control policies for Japan. While every effort would be made to establish policies satisfactory to "the principal Allied powers, in the event of any differences of opinion among them, the policies of the United States will govern."

As for American purposes in Japan, as outlined in the policy statement, these included the disarmament and demilitarization of Japan, the punishment of war criminals, encouragement of individual liberties and democratic processes, the direction of industry toward a peaceful economy, and the payment of agreed reparations in kind.

The form for an allied role in policy making for Japan was not resolved until Secretary Byrnes went to the Moscow Conference in December 1945. We had no intention of denying the participation that our allies, especially the Commonwealth allies who had fought the Far Eastern battles from the beginning, were entitled to. But we were determined that it should be advisory. Shortly before the Japanese surrender the United States had proposed to the allied governments that a Far Eastern Advisory Commission be established in Washington. The Soviets agreed to join, but added a desire, which they soon turned into a precondition, for the establishment of a Control Council consisting of the United States, the Soviet Union, the United Kingdom, and China. While unwilling to delay the formation of the Far Eastern Advisory Commission, we were willing to agree to a Military Control Council if it, too, were essentially advisory. While negotiations were never easy, references of Foreign Secretary Molotov to adoption of the Rumanian rather than the German Control Council as a model led us to hope for agreement. Ambassador Harriman discussed the idea of an Allied Military Council of the occupation commanders under the Supreme Commander with Premier Stalin at the famous meeting at Sochi (October 24–26, 1945), but was prevented from presenting it formally by last-minute objections from MacArthur.

On the eve of the Harriman-Stalin talks, I attempted in a telecon with Jack McCloy in Tokyo to get to the root of the dissent. Difficulties of physical transmission were compounded by those of human communication. The General, it appeared, thought his position would be jeopardized if he sat on a council that was advisory to him. We, on the other hand, felt that a political council subservient to the Supreme Commander—the suggestion from Tokyo —would give a great deal more opening for obstruction and parallel the job of the Far Eastern Advisory Commission. A new proposal was sent to MacArthur on October 25 and a few days later to Ambassador Harriman to be presented to Mr. Molotov. It provided for an Allied Military Council under the chairmanship of the Supreme Commander or his deputy with representatives of the four

countries including the Supreme Commander for consultation with and advice
to him on implementation of his directives. There was a great deal more back-
and-forth negotiation on the matter, but this was roughly the solution that
Secretary Byrnes got approved in Moscow. The General remained unreconciled
and managed to make his view felt by turning over his seat on the Allied Council to his deputy. Ambassador Sebald, who was the deputy in charge for much
of the occupation, thought the agreement a "masterpiece of diplomatic drafting." The eleven- (later thirteen-) nation Far Eastern Commission and four-
power Allied Council for Japan were instituted under complicated provisions,
which left the ultimate policy-making power in the United States and the
executive power in the Supreme Commander. As Professor (later Ambassador) Edwin O. Reischauer put it, the commission "settled down to a genteel
position of pompous futility," while the Allied Council became, first, a place
for "acrimonious argument" and then "lapsed into a moribund state."[2]

Territorial matters were settled in a preliminary way at Cairo, Yalta, and
Potsdam, prior to the occupation arrangements; neither the commission nor
the council was empowered to discuss them. Japan was limited, in these agreements, to four main islands and such minor islands as should be determined.
China took back Manchuria, Formosa, and the Pescadores; Korea was to be
free and independent; the Soviet Union occupied the Kuriles and southern Sakhalin. In addition to these specific dispositions, the United States occupied the
Ryukyu and Bonin Islands as well as Japan proper and took over Japan's former mandates, the Marshalls, Carolines, and Marianas, as trusteeship territory,
confirmed in 1947 by the United Nations.

The Nature of the Problem · What remained to be settled about a peace treaty
when I became Secretary of State was: What kind of treaty, harsh or conciliatory? By whom made? How? And when? In planning content and method,
four groups had to be reckoned with: the Communists, the Pentagon, our
allies, and the former enemy. Of these, the Communists gave the least trouble.
Their opposition to any tenable ideas was predictable and irreconcilable. It
could only be ignored. The most stubborn and protracted opposition to a peace
treaty came from the Pentagon. Until a way was found around that, we were
inhibited from discussion with both our allies and our late enemy, the Japanese
Government. It took until September 1950 to find the detour.

The military dug in on the line that a peace treaty was "premature." The
situation was too unsettled, they argued, to exchange the "secure" status
of military occupation for the uncertain results of a "peace conference." For
a time civilians argued among themselves the merits of a punitive and a conciliatory treaty, until a truth emerged that convinced us, but not the military,
that both our alternatives and theirs were unreal and nonexistent. This truth,
constantly asserted by the Supreme Commander, was that the occupation was a
wasting asset. Over the long run it rested upon the consent of the Japanese.
Force can overcome force, but a free society cannot long steel itself to dominate
another people by sheer force. The British and French governments learned
this and, perhaps as much from the pressure of domestic opinion as from

weakness, accepted the disintegration of their empires. Even the utterly ruthless Soviet occupations have to work through local communist parties, who manage some degree of local consent, if only by exterminating the most vocal dissent, or exiling it. Castro has done both. By the end of 1949 most of us in the Department shared the prognosis of John Allison, Director of the Office of Northeast Asian Affairs, that under the best circumstances and management the chances were not better than even that after the occupation the Japanese people would continue the liberal, democratic, and peaceful society we had sought to establish.

This view clearly ruled out a punitive treaty, loading Japan with reparations and controls. It underscored the extreme hazard of delay. Our Pacific allies, including the British, had joined the Japanese in pressing for a treaty. But two central puzzles still remained: How could we care for the vital security needs of ourselves, our allies, and the Japanese, and by what method could we accomplish a treaty of conciliation? Any kind of consultative or deliberative peace-conference procedure would end in stalemate or disaster. Russian intransigence in the Council of Foreign Ministers would tie up a Japanese treaty as hopelessly as it had the effort for a German treaty. In any larger body the same might still occur, with the added disadvantage that the United States might find itself outvoted by victims of Japan seeking reparations and, at the same time, punitive restrictions on Japanese industry and trade. Furthermore, while our Government was willing to sign a peace treaty without the Soviet Union, the Government of Japan was apprehensive. Finally, there loomed the question of through whom China, Japan's principal victim, should participate. Around the central questions of security and treaty procedure, discussion revolved in 1950.

Subsequent commentators have put forward two further views about a peace settlement with Japan than those already mentioned. While there seems to be an element of inconsistency between them, George Kennan has supported them both. The first was that instead of the security treaty that later was negotiated to accompany the peace treaty with Japan, the islands could safely have been left demilitarized and neutralized by international agreement based on an understanding with Russia. This, however, required—in the proponent's view —that the Japanese be given adequate police forces and that they achieve sufficient domestic stability and economic security to enable them to cope successfully with the efforts of their own Communists. The same view was put forward in regard to Germany by the critics of NATO—including Mr. Kennan —who favored American disengagement from Europe. It should be added that this view was put forward before the Soviet occupation of Czechoslovakia in 1968.

The other theory is that the Soviet Union precipitated the North Korean attack on South Korea in June 1950 in anticipation of United States decisions taken almost three months later (described in this chapter) to proceed, despite Soviet opposition, with a peace treaty designed to win Japan as an ally. Mr. Kennan has written that he has seen no evidence that such a causal connection "ever entered the mind of anyone in Washington except [him]self." I believe this to be true. In the Far East almost from the end of the war, and in Europe before it, Soviet breaches of interallied agreements had begun. By 1948 the Soviet blockade of Berlin was in effect and the Soviet armament of North Korea for offensive warfare far advanced. I must confess that there never entered our minds the idea that unilateral concessions—to avoid pejorative terms—would change, by ameliorating, Soviet policy.

To return to our narrative, a letter to Secretary Johnson of October 3, 1949, asking for the Defense Department's requirements in the peace treaty brought a reply by December 23, deprecating the psychological effect in Japan of even discussing a treaty and enclosing a Joint Chiefs of Staff view that a treaty was still premature. The Chiefs also opposed carrying on any negotiations without assurance that, in effect, the Soviet Union and Communist China would sign a treaty that assured the continuation of United States bases. This proviso later led me to remark at a meeting with Secretary Johnson and the Chiefs on April 24, 1950, that in view of the Chiefs' conditions for negotiation, their conclusion that discussion of a treaty was premature amounted to a "masterpiece of understatement."

The Defense decision of December brought an immediate difficulty to the Department of State. Ernest Bevin had been after me directly and through Ambassador Franks to give him an outline of our thoughts about a Japanese peace treaty prior to his January 1950 Commonwealth Conference in Colombo, Ceylon. He did not want the conference, which would be most interested in a peace treaty, and probably a highly punitive one, to get itself committed to positions we would not accept. Embarrassing as it was not to make a helpful reply to so sensible and well-meaning a request, we had to explain the situation quite frankly and content ourselves with cautionary warnings against demands that the Japanese would be in no position to meet.

The chief spokesman for Defense in our discussion of a treaty, Under Secretary of the Army Tracy Voorhees, was infinitely resourceful in discovering obstacles, legal and military, to what the State Department regarded as a just and practical course. He quoted General MacArthur. This led to a succession of pilgrimages to Tokyo by Messrs. Jessup and Butterworth and the Chiefs of Staff, following in Mr. Voorhees' footsteps to hear the word direct. The oracle gave his military colleagues small comfort. He agreed with the State Department that a treaty, and a conciliatory one, was urgent, believed that the Chiefs, having only "lightly considered" the matter, expected to be overruled, and believed that I should urge the President to do so. Secretary Johnson regarded our approach as an offside play and demanded that we cease to discuss military matters with General MacArthur directly or through William Sebald, his Political Adviser, and do so only through Mr. Voorhees. This repetition of earlier attempts to limit our relations with Defense to an official and censored channel was quietly ignored.

The President had been kept fully informed of our troubles and I had little doubt of his full support if and when a confrontation with the Pentagon became necessary. The problem, it seemed to me, was only a part of the larger problem of Louis Johnson. The Chiefs' recorded position was obviously untenable and their necessary security requirements could be met. They would, I believed, cheerfully accept being overruled, as General MacArthur had suggested to us. But a public battle with Louis Johnson over a wholly false claim that the projected settlement neglected essential defense requirements, while appeasing the Japanese aggressors and perpetrators of the Bataan Death March, would be fatal to the treaty. It would be difficult enough to muster two-thirds of the Senate to ratify a good treaty with Japan without starting off with a row within the Administration. On February 20, 1950, the President, after reviewing with me the various ideas we had discussed in the Department, requested that a National Security Council paper be prepared for his consideration. This had the highly desirable effect of suggesting that time limits were being set to the Pentagon filibuster, though the end was still months away.

In March Walton Butterworth was assigned to work directly with me on the Japanese peace treaty for the next two months before he left to be Ambassador to Sweden. He had served loyally and ably in highly exposed posts that I had asked him to take on as General Marshall's chief assistant in China during the Marshall mission and later as Assistant Secretary for Far Eastern Affairs. He was attracting increasing attack from the opponents of our China policy. As a career officer whose future could be seriously damaged, he was entitled to a change of duty, and both he and I believed that the success of the treaty required a new cast of characters for its negotiation. One of his last tasks in the Department was to arrange and brief me for the meeting with Secretary Johnson and the Chiefs of Staff on April 24.

This meeting, already mentioned, was not entirely a failure, although most of it was taken up by dreary repetition of the Chiefs' reasons why discussion of a treaty was premature. Tiring of this, I told them that this attitude did not meet the needs of the time or of the country. The President wanted a National Security Council paper. If they would give us their military requirements, we would do our best to have them met and did not doubt that we could do so. But the situation was deteriorating. The Japanese wanted a treaty; our allies wanted a treaty. Even the Sino-Soviet treaty had recited the need for a peace treaty with Japan. If we did not move swiftly to control and direct pressures at play, either our opponents would or the situation would get out of control. This shook the Chiefs up and resulted in agreement that they would take a fresh look at the situation. Frank Pace, newly appointed Secretary of the Army, shortly took over from Mr. Voorhees the task of doing so and of dealing with us on treaty affairs.

A New Cast of Characters · Another important step was taken soon afterward. When Butterworth's transfer to Sweden was decided upon, Dean Rusk came to me with an offer that won my high respect and gratitude. He said that he was applying for demotion from his then post of Deputy Under Secretary for substantive matters. He would, if I wished, take on Butterworth's responsibilities for Far Eastern Affairs. The area and its problems were not unfamiliar to him, as he had served on General Stilwell's staff in the China-Burma-India theater during the war and had, as part of his present duties, been in close touch with them. The President would, I told him, be as happy and grateful as I was for this offer "above and beyond the call of duty"—as, indeed, it was—and I accepted it at once. He served faithfully and successfully in this most difficult of posts. Years later, when President-elect Kennedy in December 1960 asked me to make recommendations for the Secretaryship of State in his Cabinet, I told him this story and placed Dean Rusk's name very high on the list.

In the spring of 1950 the three of us—Rusk, Butterworth, and I—discussed who should be given responsibility for writing a paper asking for presidential authority to prepare a Japanese peace treaty and, if it was given, to negotiate it. We all agreed that John Foster Dulles was the man. He had returned to the Department, as I have told, in April. He had had no prior contaminating contact with the subject matter of his new duties. As already indicated, views within the State Department on broad policy questions were pretty well agreed, and had the President's support. The task remaining was essentially one of negotiation both within and without the Government. For this Foster Dulles was well qualified. He was competent, ambitious—particularly to succeed me—close to Vandenberg, and in good standing with both the Dewey and Taft wings of the Republican Party. These qualities would lead him to do a good job and to get the treaty through the Senate, if this was possible at all, with the necessary bipartisan support.

The President saw the situation as we did. In later years he used to charge me with responsibility for having made Foster Dulles Secretary of State, to which I would reply with the countercharge that it was he who resuscitated former President Hoover and gave him a new career and reputation. Senator Lehman was reconciled to the assignment of Dulles to this task by my assurance that absorption in it would take him out of the senatorial race in the autumn. On May 18, the day Butterworth was nominated as Ambassador to Sweden, Foster Dulles took over this work with me on the treaty, the knowledgeable John Allison being detailed as his assistant. On the same day the President most helpfully told his press conference that responsibility for a Japanese peace treaty lay with the Secretary of State and that he hoped the treaty was not too far off. This announcement and the assignment of Dulles to work on the treaty were not lost on Secretary Johnson, who had just announced that he and General Bradley were to go in June on a thirteen-day inspection of our Pacific bases. It seemed to us that Dulles and Allison should make a similar trip of their own to serve warning that discussion of a peace treaty was no longer "premature."

The Filibuster Ends • General MacArthur had prepared a memorandum in advance of the arrival of the Washington teams. Its thoughts were congenial and helpful to the State side. The military side, which had hoped to persuade MacArthur that delay was the order of the day, found arguments that ran the other way. One of MacArthur's points paralleled an earlier British suggestion that while a peace treaty that imposed on Japan continued occupation by American troops would not be acceptable either to the Japanese Government or to many of our allies, a bilateral defense treaty between Japan and the United States would be quite a different matter. He further suggested that the defense treaty might provide for the presence of U.S. forces at "points" in Japan "until irresponsible militarism is driven from the world." The words were borrowed from the Potsdam Declaration, but in 1950 the "irresponsible militarism" meant the Sino-Soviet threat to Japan. The virtue of this idea was that it avoided having to negotiate over a direct mention of the requirements for bases or other contemplated arrangements in the security treaty and left them to be quietly worked out on a bilateral basis after the settlement as a whole had been completed.

The conception of one comprehensive treaty reconciling the interests and desires of all who had been engaged in war with Japan became the more impossible the more one analyzed it. The interests and desires were too varied and incompatible to be imposed upon Japan in a treaty intended to be conciliatory. The concern of the Philippines, New Zealand, and Australia over their own security was of this nature. Moreover, it could not be satisfied nearly so well by restrictions on Japan as by treaties with the United States, especially if Japan could be brought into the defensive equation as well. Similarly, while some of the Far Eastern allies wanted reparations from Japan, Britain pressed restrictions on her foreign trade. Here again the purpose of a conciliatory treaty was to avoid reparations and trade restrictions. It gradually became clear that the road to solution lay in separate agreements between Japan and those seeking compensation for injury. In the final treaty, clauses provided that under such agreements the services of the Japanese would be made available for manufacture and repairing damage with raw materials supplied by claimants.

Thus the idea grew of several treaties and agreements, all contributing to a settlement with Japan. If all, or nearly all, including the Japanese and excepting the Russians, could be satisfied to the point of accepting a settlement devised in this way, Russian and Chinese Communist opposition might be ignored without dangerous risk. Moreover, it was appropriate that a number of treaties should be the final result of our efforts, for American purposes went beyond a settlement of the issues raised by Japan's challenge and defeat. They had to do as well with interests and desires brought forth in the intervening years.

With such ideas germinating in our minds we set about formulating an agreement with Defense on ends to be achieved with the hope of then getting the President's approval for the designation of a working group or task force under Foster Dulles to devise the ways and means of achieving them by exploratory talks within the government and separately with most of our allies.

Agreement and Decision to Go Ahead · As already recounted, when the North Korean attack occurred, Mr. Dulles was in Tokyo. He returned to Washington with the conviction that the negotiation of a treaty with Japan had become more rather than less important. War at the doorstep had awakened Japan and stirred apprehension among its people, Dulles reported. Delaying the treaty might lose us more than successful resistance of the attack might gain. He noted that American policy often suffered from the tendency to abandon political aims for purely military ones when war broke out. We must not do that here. With this advice I wholly agreed. Indeed, earlier in June I had told a congressional group that an attack on Korea would be regarded by the Japanese as aimed at them, and stressed the importance of a conciliatory peace treaty in maintaining a Japan independent of Soviet influence. After the attack I had reported to the Cabinet the fear aroused in Japan of increased Soviet pressure in the Far East and the possibility of agitation for a neutralized and undefended Japan, a proposition already espoused by the Japanese Socialist Party.

While the attack had put new problems in the way of a treaty, particularly for our soldiers, it had also produced new urgency. As early as mid-July General Bradley told Ambassador Jessup that State and Defense could work out their differences sufficiently to begin consultation with key allies and preparation of a broad plan for a peace settlement. Shortly thereafter the President encouraged me to press on with a plan to lay before him.

Throughout August successive treaty drafts marked our progress. Louis Johnson made ominous dissenting noises in the beginning, but Mr. Dulles argued, convincingly it seemed, that the current requirements of both MacArthur and the Joint Chiefs of Staff were being carefully incorporated in the treaty drafts. I canvassed with Dulles steps for forwarding the treaty process once Administration agreement was reached, and he got together a list of successive consultations. Toward the end of the month Louis Johnson suggested, and I agreed, that General Carter B. Magruder and John Allison should discuss the treaty and the few remaining outstanding points at issue in detail. I suggested, and Johnson did not object, that a list of governing principles for the negotiators such as the Joint Chiefs had at one point provided should be developed for National Security Council consideration rather than presenting the treaty draft itself. Allison met with Magruder, quickly ironed out difficulties with the draft treaty, and on September 4 had ready to lay before me a joint memorandum to be presented by both secretaries to the President. This memo combined a list of governing principles, which spelled out the security requirements of the Defense Department, with the outline of next steps prepared by Dulles. On September 7 Louis Johnson and I signed the agreed memorandum and on the next day the President approved it. Exactly one year later, on September 8, 1951, the peace and defense treaties with Japan were signed in San Francisco.

The vast importance of the agreement and decision lay in getting the negotiating process started and determining the method by which the settlement with Japan should be reached, rather than in the security principles that it laid down. In order to obtain the former, the State Department had to accept many Defense Department positions that proved to be utterly unworkable and more than half of which had to be abandoned or drastically altered over the next year. What made this possible was the replacement of Secretary Johnson by General Marshall and the President's unwavering support of Mr. Dulles and myself throughout the negotiations. But in September 1950 it was no small achievement to reach without casualties or bitterness a government decision that a peace treaty was no longer "premature." To this was added a crucial decision that agreement should be sought in a series of negotiations through diplomatic channels rather than by the more conventional procedures of multilateral peace conferences. The tenor and pace of negotiations would thus respond to a constructive American lead. These discussions were to be extended to the Supreme Commander and the Japanese Government to insure Japanese participation in the treaty-making process and genuine acceptance of the result. The State Department was charged also with continuing throughout the negotiations informal discussions with members of the Senate Foreign Relations and Armed Services committees. The diplomatic agent for all these discussions, staffed by the Department and guided throughout by the Secretary and the President, was to be Foster Dulles.

As already mentioned, the section on "security requirements . . . [to] be regarded as vital" was less helpful and fortunately less enduring. It would be of little interest today to go through it in detail; one illustration will suffice. The first principle in this section sought to preserve the essence of the Fabian principle so stubbornly adhered to by the Pentagon. It provided that a treaty should not become effective until after favorable resolution of the military situation in Korea. The first skirmish over this principle came in December 1950, when I wrote General Marshall asking for agreement on a number of proposals, including "seeking an early conclusion of a peace settlement with Japan without awaiting a favorable outcome of the situation in Korea" and sending Mr. Dulles and a representative of the Defense Department to Japan under presidential authority to begin discussions. The Chiefs opposed this request on the ground that Chinese intervention in Korea had made proceeding with the treaty inopportune. General Marshall agreed to my request after Mr. Dulles had discussed it with the Chiefs of Staff and the President then approved it.

Again in June 1951 the Chiefs opposed a draft of Article 23 of the treaty that in effect gave the United States a veto over the coming into force of the treaty between Japan and any other signatory for nine months after Japanese ratification, wishing instead to have power retained by the United States to postpone the treaty's coming into effect indefinitely in case hostilities in Korea continued. An appeal was taken to the President, to whom General Bradley and I stated the opposing views. The President asked Robert Lovett, Deputy Secretary of Defense, for General Marshall's opinion, since the General was testifying and could not be at the meeting. The General's view, said Mr. Lovett, was that the State Department's advice should be pretty nearly controlling; its negotiator had already obtained a great deal to meet the military needs growing out of the exigencies in Korea, and to send the treaty back now for renegotiation might do harm. The President decided in favor of the treaty as it stood. This episode is not untypical of differences over specific policies and provisions, which continued even after the treaties were signed and the administrative agreement was being negotiated. However, we were on our way.

GERMANY AND THE DEFENSE OF EUROPE

The Need for German Participation · For some years the Defense Department had held that Europe could not be defended without the willing and active participation of Western Germany, but the State Department had not yet gotten that far. Indeed, as late as June 5, 1950, after returning from London, I had said, in asking for Mutual Defense Assistance funds, that the United States would continue the policy of German demilitarization. "There is no discussion of doing anything else," I said. "That is our policy and we have not raised it or revalued it."[3] Some doubt should have been cast on my familiarity with the subject, however, when the next day General Bradley said: "From a strictly military point of view, I do believe the defense of western Europe would be strengthened by the inclusion of Germany, . . . because we do know that they have great production facilities that we could use and we know that they are very capable soldiers and airmen and sailors."[4] He added that there were political considerations on which he did not feel qualified to pronounce. A few, very few, voices had been raised in Europe to express the same thought. Field Marshal Viscount Montgomery, General Lucius Clay, and Konrad Adenauer early in 1950 had all seen a place for a German contribution toward a general European defense effort.† During the summer a steady stream of cables came from our missions in London, Paris, and Bonn, urging a greater participation by Germany in European defense. In mid-July McCloy put it most dramatically. The probability was that we would lose Germany, politically as well as militarily, without hope of getting it back, if we did not find means for that country to fight in event of an emergency. If there should be a real war, we would have lost a most valuable reserve of manpower—a reserve the Russians could certainly use against us. Even though planning for German participation would require radical changes, it was time to consider our plans for European defense in the light of Korea. His thoughts, McCloy added, were preliminary ones only.

The need for increased military strength was in the air, given a renewed fillip by the Korean attack. In July General Bradley noted that "communism is willing to use arms to gain its ends. This is a fundamental change, and it has forced a change in our estimate of the military needs of the United States."[5] During the same month both the Germans and the French, looking with apprehension at the sixty thousand East German military police and twenty-seven Russian divisions also in East Germany, with more behind them, found little comfort in NATO's twelve ill-equipped and uncoordinated divisions with little air support. Both Adenauer and the French Cabinet inquired about additional American help. Our missions kept up a steady drumfire of recommendations for more American and new German additions to European defense. At the end of the month we asked through the NATO deputies what our allies were prepared to do to strengthen their own defense. When the replies were tabulated, even including substantial British and French efforts, the total available on the central front in Europe fell far short of any candid military view of an adequate defense.

French Desire for U.S.-European Integration · The French circulated with their reply a memorandum that gave us pause. They proposed to apply the principles of integration to the political, military, economic, and financial institutions supporting a NATO defense system. Integrated organs for foreign policy decisions, military command, military budget, and munitions and economic supply should be established, binding together all the member states. I paled at the thought of bringing so vague, unexplored, and enormous an idea before the Congress. The proposal, I told Ambassador Henri Bonnet, raised issues of such fundamental character, requiring consideration and decision at the highest level of government, that it would not be possible for the United States to reply during the present crisis on both sides of the world. We must have time for study.

My conversion to German participation in European defense was quick. The idea that Germany's place in the defense of Europe would be worked out by a process of evolution was outmoded. Korea had speeded up evolution. If there was to be any defense at all, it had to be based on a forward strategy. Germany's role must be not secondary, but primary—not only through military formations, but through emotional and political involvement. On the last day of July in a long talk with the President I reported that some were urging that we first ask him for a decision on whether Germany should be rearmed and then, if he approved, go into methods. This seemed to me the wrong way to go at the problem. The real question was not whether Germany should be brought into a general European defense system but whether this could be done without disrupting everything else we were doing and giving Germany the key position in the balancing of power in Europe. To create a German military system, complete from general staff to Ruhr munitions industry, would weaken rather than strengthen European defense and repeat past errors. The President agreed and illustrated the point from European history in the last century. We went on to discuss some way of merging Germany's military contribution into a European Army or North Atlantic Army with an integrated command and, perhaps, supply. The latter could move German industry further into a European system already started by the Schuman Plan. The President was enthusiastic about this approach and wished to have the matter brought back to him through the regular channel of the National Security Council when further work had been done on it.

The "One Package" Proposal · First, however, the United States Government must come to grips with the basic problem involved in the defense of Europe— what were we prepared to do? So far we had made no commitments of ground and air forces for which we were being pressed by our allies. So far, also, we had done nothing to give reality to the strategic concept of an "integrated defense." When in August we turned to serious discussion with our colleagues in the Pentagon, we found ourselves confronted by an ugly dilemma. The Defense Department required no persuasion that the defense of Europe needed, in their phrase, "beefing up," nor did its officers doubt that the beef would have to be provided by increased allied forces, increased American troops and military aid, the inclusion of armed German units, and—to integrate and direct the whole effort—a unified command. But—and here came the rub—they wanted all of these elements in (their phrase again) "one package." They would not recommend any more American forces in Europe, or the responsibility of this country's assuming the unified command, unless the whole scheme should be made a viable one. To do this required wholehearted German cooperation. I knew that this was the stiffest fence on the course. To make it the first and the *sine qua non* of the rest seemed to me to be going about the project the hard way with a vengeance.

Two weeks or so of debate across the Potomac ensued. The Pentagon stood united and immovable. I agreed with their strategic purpose and objective but thought their tactics murderous. Once we established the united command and had a planning center, the inevitable logic of mathematics would convince everyone that any plan without Germany was untenable. To insist on requiring the inclusion of Germany at the outset would delay and complicate the whole enterprise. I was right, but I was nearly alone. McCloy had won over Byroade and the German office early in August. The creation of a European defense was moving too slowly, he cabled; there was a real chance to solve the problem of a genuine European Army with Germany in it; we should start immediately to work it out; there must be no delay in German participation. Douglas and Spofford joined in the bombardment from London. On August 11 the Consultative Assembly of the Council of Europe, with West Germany participating for the first time, called for the immediate creation of a unified European Army under a European Minister of Defense.

The President called a meeting for August 26—the same meeting that began with the fracas about MacArthur's message to the Veterans of Foreign Wars—to discuss the differences between State and Defense. On the eve of this meeting a new factor entered the situation, already complicated enough. Sir Oliver Franks reported Prime Minister Attlee's wish to come to the United States to talk with President Truman. Although the Ambassador was vague about subjects to be discussed, it was not hard to see that NATO pressure for rearmament in Europe and the United States, as well as the possibilities of the war in Korea, was raising serious questions for the British exchequer and the British economy. On the one hand, increased military expenses would add to already high British taxes; on the other, general rearmament would raise the price of the raw materials that Britain must buy. However, the President, with the best will in the world, would be in no position to consult with Attlee helpfully until the necessary preparatory work was done and the general extent of rearmament was clearer. I explained enough of this discreetly and confidentially so that Ambassador Franks could keep the matter on an informal and personal basis for a few days more.

The next day the President pointed out that at the ministerial meeting of the NATO Council, due within a month, the most urgent problem would be how to strengthen the defense of Europe and the nature of the German contribution to it. He gave Secretary Johnson and me a list of questions upon which he wanted our joint recommendation by September 1, later extended to September 5.

I was clearly outflanked and, in the euphemism of wartime communiqués, again found it necessary to "fall back and regroup." Moreover, this hazardous maneuver had to be executed under some harassment from friend and foe alike. First Louis Johnson and I appeared together at an executive hearing of the

Senate Committee on Appropriations, a tricky performance, since an ill-disposed senator could easily engineer a conflict of views. In the course of such an endeavor my faithful enemy, Senator Wherry, began badgering me from directly across a narrow table, finally leaning over it and shaking a menacing finger in my face. I have a reputation for "not suffering fools gladly." However—the adverb aside—until that moment I had suffered as many fools patiently as any man. But quite suddenly I had had enough of Kenneth Wherry and was on my feet admonishing him in tones and language far from diplomatic not to shake his "dirty finger in my face." He bellowed that he would, and he did. My answering haymaker was interrupted by my friend and colleague, Adrian Fisher, Legal Adviser to the Department and a former Princeton football player. "Take it easy, boss," he said soothingly, as he pushed me down in my chair while Senator McKellar, presiding, restored order.

The next day I called on the Chairman to express regret. "Not at all, my boy, not at all," he said. "Funniest thing I've seen in thirty years on this hill. After you left I called Harry Truman and told him he could pay off the national debt by putting you two on vaudeville."

More serious was the task of keeping the discussion within the Administration out of the press until we had reached some measure of agreement. Our allies were disturbed enough without a daily crop of rumors out of Washington. On August 31 the President said that he had no intention at present of increasing the number of American troops in Europe. A few days later the irrepressible McCloy, after seeing him, said on the steps of the White House, "In some manner, in some form, the Germans should be enabled, if they want to, to defend their own country,"[6] adding that he favored strengthening U.S. forces in Germany. All these public comments and congressional hearings, which whether or not in secret session appeared in the press, slowed up agreement with Defense on the answers to the President's questions. These were finally agreed and presented on September 5.

The position outlined in the answers consisted of additional U.S. ground forces for Europe in the neighborhood of from four to six divisions on the assumption of substantial increases in French forces and in British troops on the continent. All forces of European members, if possible, and the British and U.S. forces in Europe should be combined into a European defense force with an international staff and a Supreme Commander. A German contingent should be added at the divisional level without a German general staff. An executive group should be established in the NATO Military Production and Supply Board to coordinate and increase European military production and supply. The United States would accept the responsibility of supreme command only if (1) our allies requested it, (2) they undertook the obligations of the plans as outlined, and (3) only long enough to discover whether they could and would perform them. We hoped, also, that in time the Standing Group could work out a combined-chiefs-of-staff function.

After three days of study and further discussion, the President, on September 8, approved the plan as set out in a rewritten document. The next day he issued a public statement to dispel some of the uncertainty about our governmental position: "On the basis of recommendations of the Joint Chiefs of Staff, concurred in by the Secretaries of State and Defense, I have today approved substantial increases in the strength of United States forces to be stationed in Western Europe in the interest of the defense of that area. . . . Our plans are based on the sincere expectation that our efforts will be met with similar action on their part."[7]

Due to these maneuverings, we were running out of time. Although I kept Sir Oliver Franks informed of developments, Schuman and Bevin were to come to New York by sea, arriving on September 12. It was essential that they should know as soon as possible the position the President would approve. On September 2 our embassies were instructed to tell them of the "tentative" conclusions we had in mind. Sir Oliver was also told that the President thought it better for me to talk these over with Bevin before the Prime Minister and the President met. Schuman replied urging us not to put our plan on the NATO agenda because discussion of it might reveal such differences, especially on German rearmament, as we might not wish to disclose to our other colleagues. This ominous message boded ill for our meeting in New York. Moreover, it boded correctly.

The "one package" decision—to lump together the united command, increased American military forces, and an armed German element—has been called a mistake. I am inclined to agree, and held out against it until convinced that it was the necessary price for Pentagon acceptance of a united command. Even that conclusion was proved to be unsound when General Marshall succeeded Louis Johnson. Indeed, the united command was approved by NATO in December with German participation accepted only "in principle." Six years were to pass before principle matured into fact. During that period the European Army was conceived and miscarried. At the time, however, the danger to Europe seemed to us great and immediate, and these decisions were not being made in the unhurried calm of an academic study. In the first three weeks of September not only was the enlistment of Germany in European defense put forward, but General MacArthur landed at Inchon and began the rout of the North Korean Army, the "Uniting for Peace" proposal was made in the General Assembly in New York, the President authorized us to proceed with a peace treaty with Japan, Louis Johnson was removed as Secretary of Defense, and the primitives in the Senate reached a crescendo of vituperation over General Marshall's nomination to succeed him. Those were noisy and active days.

47. SEPTEMBER SURPRISES

GENERAL MARSHALL RETURNS TO THE PENTAGON

NEVER have talks been so dominated by offstage action as were ours in New York. No sooner had we arrived at the Waldorf Towers, where the Secretary of State lives during sessions of the United Nations, than a half dozen telephone calls—Averell Harriman's among them—informed me that Louis Johnson had resigned as Secretary of Defense and that the President had obtained General Marshall's agreement to succeed him.

Johnson's behavior had passed beyond the peculiar to the impossible. I have already stated my belief that this was the result of a brain malady, which ultimately proved fatal. It had caused acute problems at the Pentagon, which had to be brought to the President's attention. Moreover, Averell Harriman had learned that Johnson had discussed with the opposition my removal from office and had felt obligated to report it over my dissent. At the time the President did not mention the matter to me, nor I to him. Later he told me of the unhappiness the dismissal caused him. He recalled also that a telephone call to General Marshall was long delayed in reaching him and that the General was unusually abrupt in giving his assent. Later he discovered that the General had had to be brought some distance to an open telephone in a country store, where a group of customers had assembled to hear the distinguished general talk with the President of the United States.

No change could have been more welcome to me. It brought only one embarrassment. The General insisted, overruling every protest of mine, in meticulously observing the protocol involved in my being the senior Cabinet officer. Never would he go through a door before me, or walk anywhere but on my left; he would go around an automobile to enter it after me and sit on the left; in meetings he would insist on my speaking before him. To be treated so by a revered and beloved former chief was a harrowing experience. But the result in government was, I think, unique in the history of the Republic. For the first time and, perhaps, though I am not sure, the last, the Secretaries of State and Defense, with their top advisers, met with the Chiefs of Staff in their map room and discussed common problems together. At one of these meetings General Bradley and I made a treaty, thereafter scrupulously observed. The phrases "from a military point of view" and "from a political point of view" were excluded from our talks. No such dichotomy existed. Each of us had our tactical and strategic problems, but they were interconnected, not separate.

Before coming to New York I had met in executive session with the Senate and House foreign committees to outline for them what we were going to propose. This had been a gerat success; everyone had approved, wished me well, and expressed full confidence in me. The meetings in New York did not accomplish their purpose. Only three months later, when I was starting off for another meeting in Europe on the same subject, the congressional opposition voted that I had lost the confidence of the country, could not regain it, and should be dismissed. That meeting turned out to be a complete success. Thus one learned that congressional approval is pleasant but largely irrelevant to the outcome of international enterprises, unless they call in one way or another for congressional votes.

THE "ONE PACKAGE" PROPOSAL STALLS

With us on our mission to New York went Rear Admiral Thomas H. Robbins, Jr., known as "One Package" Robbins, to keep watch over me to see that I never wandered from the straight-and-narrow "one package" path. It was said that he neither slumbered nor slept.

From the outset Schuman took the indivisible proposal very hard. He embraced every part of it enthusiastically except German military participation, wishing to go even further toward allied integration along the lines of his midsummer memorandum. For days his opposition to the central German provision was skillfully obscured by a kind of filibuster in which various elements of the plan were elaborated and wholly unacceptable roles for the Germans proposed in contributions, material and financial, and in service of supply functions, indicating an all too obvious second-class status. Finally, his opposition became flat and absolute. The French Government would be willing to discuss the formation of German military units only when the NATO allies had first been rearmed and an integrated defense force had been created into which the German units could be merged.

Bevin, on the other hand, though cautious at first for lack of a Cabinet decision, found himself in the position in which I had been earlier. His own Chiefs of Staff, I learned from him, were like ours ahead of the Foreign Office. They too had concluded that no defense of Europe was feasible without German military participation. But Bevin had foreseen French opposition, the danger of Soviet reaction, and anti-German resistance in Britain. He favored following up Adenauer's request to the High Commission to form a gendarmerie, or Bereitschaften, to counter the forces already created in East Germany and which he very much feared. This, he thought, avoided most of the difficulties. "You've got the right idea, me lad," he said to me, "but you're goin' about it the hard way." But to us a Bereitschaften could too easily develop into a separate German army.

Since the three of us could not stay locked in secret stalemate while our other NATO allies fretted on the leaking edges of discussion, we alternated meetings. On September 12, 13, and 14 the three ministers met without agreement. Both Schuman and Bevin then asked their governments for instructions. NATO meetings began on Friday, the fifteenth (D Day plus one at Inchon), and, skipping Sunday, continued through the eighteenth. The three ministers met again on the eighteenth and nineteenth. At this point all meetings recessed to permit me to make the "Uniting for Peace" speech at the General Assembly on the twentieth. The three agreed to resume on the twenty-second, this time with the help of the defense ministers. Jules Moch, Emanuel Shinwell, and General Marshall joined us on Friday and Saturday. All Monday I spent privately with the Benelux ministers, and on Tuesday, the twenty-sixth, the NATO Council met again and put the "one package" proposal in suspense with comforting phrases until we could make arrangements with the French in which both of us would yield something.

The notable fact about these ten days of discussion was that, frustrating and inconclusive as they seemed at the time, they comprised the first real debate NATO had had about the twin subjects of Germany and European defense and greatly advanced the thinking in all allied countries on both subjects. In May we had talked long and earnestly but about abstractions and phrases. In September we closed with facts and brutal comparison of aims and capabilities. Discussion in the two groups followed the same course, the smaller group preparing the way for the larger one. To begin with, I laid out the subject of debate in a series of propositions, each of which received careful examination:

1. The Korean attack had shown that the USSR was prepared to use force (initially, at least, through satellites) to achieve political ends, and had also shown the vital importance of strength in being and in position and of a plan of campaign.

2. The significance of the President's announced willingness to increase American forces stationed in Europe was its acceptance of the European aim of a defense of Europe as against a liberation of Europe.

3. A defense of Europe required more forces than any proposed plans provided for and a united command, with staff, commander, and agreed strategy.

4. The United States would join in such a defense if—and only if—it was to be a viable defense capable of achieving its purpose.

5. To achieve its purpose the defense would require not only increased forces from its members in being and in position, but also the enthusiastic participation of Germany and armed German units.

6. The United States was opposed to a separate German army and a German general staff.

7. The United States would agree to any plan the allies wanted to give their forces a lead—say of two years—in rearmament over the German formations, but the plan called for them to begin rearmament at once and at the same time to agree definitively to the creation of German units.

8. Finally, the plan was a single entity, to be considered as such; it was not a series of proposals, any one or more of which could be accepted apart from the others.

As the debate progressed, and with it opportunity for the foreign ministers to communicate with their governments, it appeared that five shared our views —Britain, Canada, Italy, the Netherlands, and Norway. The rest hung back, watching the French. With the arrival of the defense ministers each of the foreign ministers was strengthened in his position. Moch, whose son had been captured by the Germans while working for the French Underground and garrotted, passionate in his hatred of the Germans, strongly backed Schuman. Shinwell brought solid Cabinet backing for Bevin to urge acceptance of the unprecedented offer of the United States to become permanently integrated into the defense of Europe.

To me General Marshall brought immense help in two ways. His great prestige and calm, compelling exposition left no doubt in any mind, including the French minds, that without Germany the defense of Europe was not possible. He also became convinced himself, and was able to persuade the Pentagon, that the tactic of the rigid and brusque "one package" proposal would not work. "Don't press so hard," said Hervé Alphand, Schuman's assistant; "we will find a solution." And wise old Joseph Bech, Foreign Minister of Luxembourg, drew me aside during a recess in one of the meetings, urged me to be more relaxed, and told me that Paris was working on a European military system based on the Schuman Coal and Steel Plan. (It later emerged as the Pleven Plan.) When I asked why Schuman did not tell me so, he answered, "He doesn't know it yet." Bech had gotten word from an associate of Jean Monnet in Paris. General Marshall also did useful work in private talks with Moch by getting him off generalities and onto specifics, the matching of needs and resources.

Adjournment with Progress • To General Marshall and me it had become clear that to press further at the time would only harden differences and that the better course was to record the progress made and put over further discussion until the meeting of the NATO defense ministers in October. The President, who had been kept in intimate touch with each day's discussion and by periodic appraisals of the situation, agreed with our view. Despite the rhetoric over German participation, a good deal of progress had been made both by the council and by the ministers. The former announced on September 26[1] agreement upon the establishment as soon as possible of "an integrated force under centralized command . . . to deter aggression and to ensure the defense of Western Europe." The force would be organized by NATO and under its political and strategic guidance. It would have a Supreme Commander with power to organize and train it in time of peace as an integrated force for the event of war. The commander would be supported by an international staff and subject to the strategic direction of the Standing Group. The "finalization" by the council of these arrangements would await recommendations by the Defense Committee regarding the force's organization, command, and strategic direction. Decisions regarding allocation of forces would be sought from member governments at an early date, and recommendations made by the Defense Committee of methods by which Germany could most usefully make its contribution. This meeting ended my chairmanship of the council, which passed to Paul van Zeeland, Foreign Minister of Belgium.

The fact of progress had become evident even earlier. When Bevin, Schuman, and I had prepared our tripartite communiqué of the nineteenth[2] we had been surprised at how much had been hammered out in the rough-and-tumble of frank and honest talk. A series of measures was being inaugurated to move Germany further from the position of defeated and occupied enemy to that of ally. In the field of foreign relations the Federal Republic was recognized as the only German government freely and legitimately constituted and hence entitled to speak for the German people. To that end a Ministry of Foreign Affairs and the authority to enter into diplomatic relations with foreign nations would be authorized. Furthermore, the necessary steps would be taken to terminate the state of war with Germany. In internal affairs far-reaching reduction in economic and political controls was announced and limitations were relaxed on steel production and shipbuilding. Regarding security, the ministers noted the creation of outright military units in the Soviet zone of occupation, pledged an increase of their governments' forces in the Federal Republic to protect and defend it and Berlin, declared that any attack on the Federal Republic or Berlin would be treated as an attack on their own nations, and authorized the establishment of mobile police formations on a Laender basis capable of being called into federal service to meet exigencies. Recently expressed German sentiments in favor of participation in an integrated force for the defense of European freedom were at the time the subject of study and exchange of views. Altogether this amounted to no small record of achievement.

The day after these communiqués were completed the President summoned me to Washington to go over with him and General Marshall definitive orders to General MacArthur (see pages 452–54).

NEXT PHASE IN KOREA

To pick up the thread of events in Korea and of thought about policy there, we must go back to the time of my return to Washington on August 21 after a week's holiday. In the Department two views were then locked in what seemed to me wholly unnecessary conflict. One was that under no circumstances should General MacArthur's forces cross the 38th parallel. The other denied this and advocated (or some proponents did) going wherever necessary to destroy the invader's force and restore security in the area. The latter view seemed the right one if properly restricted. Troops could not be expected, as I put it, to march up to a surveyor's line and stop. Until the actual military situation developed further, no one could say where the necessity for flexibility in tactics ended and embarkation upon a new strategic purpose began. One conclusion was clear: no arbitrary prohibition against crossing the parallel should be imposed. As a boundary it had no political validity. The next important conclusion was not clear. After knocking out the invasion and as much of the invasion force as seemed practical, what then? The official United Nations purpose was to create a unified, independent, and democratic Korea. But how and by whom? These were words and empty words; they were not policy. One of our greatest problems lay in ever getting beyond them.

In a memorandum awaiting my return, George Kennan, who was lecturing at the National War College, left me his advice on this and some other problems, a memorandum typical of its gifted author, beautifully expressed, sometimes contradictory, in which were mingled flashes of prophetic insight and suggestions, as the document itself conceded, of total impracticality. Our action in Korea, it said, was right, the aggression must be defeated and discredited, but disturbing emotional and moralistic conclusions were being drawn from this fact. It was not essential to us or within our capabilities to establish an anti-Soviet regime in all of Korea.

The Koreans could not maintain their independence against both Russian and Japanese pressures, Kennan maintained, and while Japanese influence might be preferable from our point of view to Russian, the power to exert it did not now exist. Hence it would be unrealistic to exclude the possibility of a period of Russian domination. Curiously, the memorandum did not mention what within a few months was to be a far more likely possibility—Chinese domination. Such was national interest in the abstract. In view of public opinion and political pressures in the concrete, ideas such as these could only be kept in mind as warnings not to be drawn into quicksands.

All this was good, even if purely negative, advice. It was well to be cautious. If we had been able to peer into General MacArthur's mind, we should have been infinitely more cautious than we were a few weeks later in giving him instructions and in formulating policy at the United Nations.

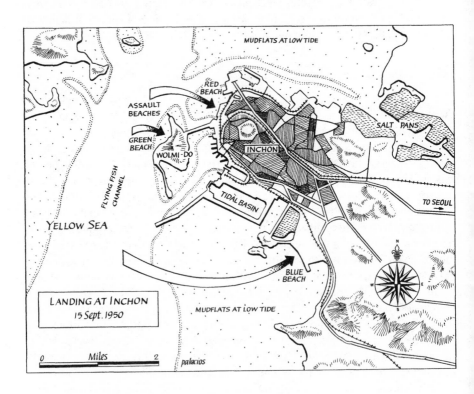

Inchon: "Operation Common Knowledge" · Three days after we arrived in New York, the First Marine Division began, on September 15, its landing at Inchon on the west coast of Korea about thirty-five miles south of the 38th parallel, and approximately the same distance west of Seoul, the occupied capital of South Korea. By September 27 Seoul was recaptured and pretty well shattered in the process. General Walker's Eighth Army, attacking simultaneously in the south, broke out of the Pusan perimeter and drove the retreating North Koreans before them until, intercepted by MacArthur's forces west of Seoul, their army was utterly destroyed by the two American forces. Perhaps thirty thousand stragglers out of an army of approximately four hundred thousand men made their escape without equipment across the parallel. By the end of the month General MacArthur's command approached the parallel, virtually without opposition.

"Perilous Gamble or Exemplary Boldness?"[3] · The Inchon counteroffensive succeeded brilliantly. It would be regarded today as one of the classic military victories of history had it not been the prelude to the greatest defeat suffered by American arms since the Battle of Manassas and an international disaster of the first water. To understand why this is so, it is necessary to look further into the nature of the Inchon operation. In doing so it would be untrue and unfair to intimate that General MacArthur should be charged with sole responsibility for disaster in Korea, though he certainly must bear the lion's share. Other mistakes were made, as will appear, to which I made a contribution.

Until August 23, General MacArthur was almost alone in favoring the risky Inchon operation. This was no mere outflanking operation but a strike deep in the enemy's rear to cut his line of communications and destroy him between the two jaws of a massive pincers. The Joint Chiefs of Staff opposed it, especially the Army and Navy chiefs, who were present in Tokyo; so did the Army, Navy, and Marine commanders who would have to carry it out. So did General Walker, commanding the Eighth Army at Pusan, for his force was to be weakened to augment the northern landing corps. If anything went wrong at Inchon, he saw himself overwhelmed by the North Koreans. And a lot could go wrong. General MacArthur himself assessed Inchon as a 5,000-to-1 risk, and saw in the very improbability of its being attempted a guarantee of an essential element in success—surprise.

The approach to Inchon harbor was narrow and rendered hazardous by rocks, shoals, and enormous tides, from an average of twenty-three to a maximum of thirty-three feet. Only a maximum tide would float the landing craft to the sea wall, which even then rose fourteen feet above the water. Maximum tides could be expected only on September 15 and October 11. At ebb tide the harbor became a mud flat, where stranded landing craft could be pounded to pieces by artillery. One does not wonder at the remark of a naval staff officer that they had drawn up a list of every conceivable natural handicap and Inchon had them all. They were all stated at the meeting on August 23 in General

MacArthur's Tokyo headquarters, but he brushed them aside in a brilliant defense of his plan, ending in a dramatic hush, "I can almost hear the ticking of the second hand of destiny. . . . We shall land at Inchon and I shall crush them."[4]

Such was the prestige of General MacArthur—"I wish I had that man's confidence," as Admiral Forrest Sherman put it—that ultimately and reluctantly the Joint Chiefs of Staff and the President concurred in the Inchon operation. MacArthur's tide of luck was in, and taken at flood led on to success. So great was his luck that Typhoon "Kezia" with winds of a hundred and twenty-five miles an hour, heading for the invasion fleet, veered off to the east, and Communist spies, who had learned of the plan due to faulty security, were unable to get word through to the North Koreans. The nickname of Inchon in Japan was "Operation Common Knowledge."

One must understand the tremendous risks assumed by General MacArthur at Inchon, and the equally great luck that saw him through, to understand the hubris that led him to assume even more impossible chances in his march to the Yalu at a time when his luck—and, unhappily, the luck of the United States also—ran out.

Uniting for Peace • On July 29 the Soviet Foreign Office had announced the end of the long, helpful Russian boycott of the United Nations Security Council. Its representative, Jacob Malik, would return to preside over it during August. His performance there following his return exceeded even lively expectations. Hickerson's bureau in the Department was put to work on the obvious problem of how to provide United Nations guidance for policy after the attack had been repelled. To repel it was the first goal set by the resolution of June 27, and it had been achieved by the end of September. The second goal was to "restore international peace and security in the area." The words were not pregnant with significance in themselves. They had been taken from Article 42 of the United Nations Charter, which empowered the Security Council, if it found "the existence of . . . any breach of the peace or act of aggression"—as it had here—to "take such action by air, sea, or land forces as may be necessary to maintain or restore international peace and security." A sensible interpretation of the resolution would have been that after repelling the armed attack the Security Council wanted to make reasonably sure that it would not be renewed as soon as the guardians of peace withdrew. Malik, wielding the Soviet veto in the Security Council, would obviously prevent the adoption there of any plan to assure peace unpalatable to the North Koreans.

However, in the light of history, the second clause in the resolution might be construed to mean something more than the prevention of a new attack. It might include a goal of the UN resolution of 1947, "an independent, united Korean government," then thought a foundation, if not a prerequisite, to peace and security in the area. Behind the slogan lay a reality. The division of Korea at the 38th parallel, with the northern half in the Soviet sphere of influence and the southern half in the American, was, indeed, the chief obstacle to peace and security in the area. On the other hand, the American Government was not willing to commit its forces to the task of creating an independent and united Korea against any and all opposition.

American occupation of South Korea came about as an incident of the surrender of Japan. Prior to Japan's annexation of the country in 1910, control of it had been the subject of intense rivalry with China and Russia. During the war with Japan the four principal powers engaged in it had vaguely agreed on a free and independent Korea with a preliminary, and hopefully brief, four-power trusteeship. Japan's sudden collapse precipitated arrangements for the surrender of her considerable forces there. The Joint Chiefs proposed that the United States accept surrender in the south, nearest Japan, and the Russians, in the north, nearest Siberia. A young officer recently returned to the Pentagon from the Chinese theater, Colonel Dean Rusk, found a convenient administrative dividing line along the 38th parallel. This would give the United States a northern port of embarkation at Inchon and a southern one at Pusan to facilitate repatriation of the surrendered troops. The plan, accepted by the President and Marshal Stalin, was promulgated by General MacArthur in General Order No. 1 on September 2, 1945. But almost at once, as General John R. Hodge, in command in Korea, reported, "dissatisfaction with the division of the country" began. We soon found that the Soviet Union considered the 38th parallel not as a line of military administrative convenience but as a wall around their preserve. This was a lesson we were learning painfully in Germany, Berlin, and Iran, and we were determined not to permit the same situation in Japan and Austria.

Secretary Byrnes and Molotov took up the problem in Moscow in December 1945, working out an agreement for a joint commission for the unity and independence of Korea. For nearly two years every effort to work through the commission was frustrated. Just before I retired as Under Secretary, Secretary of War Patterson recommended the withdrawal of our troops from Korea to meet greater needs for our limited military resources elsewhere. The other needs and the limited resources were plain enough and there seemed ground for hope —in those days of hope—that the success in uniting Iran through the United Nations might be duplicated in Korea. The President having approved, the United States laid the question of Korean independence and the withdrawal of foreign troops before the United Nations General Assembly in a resolution calling for both withdrawal of troops and elections of local representatives of North and South to work out unification. Interpreting this as what it was, an attempt to terminate our responsibilities in Korea, the Russians accepted withdrawal and opposed United Nations-supervised elections. They proposed leaving it to North and South Koreans to agree on unification without interference after foreign withdrawal. This plain invitation to civil war was rejected and the American resolution adopted. The UN election commission, barred from the North, held elections in the South and a government for the Republic of Korea was recognized by the General Assembly as the only legitimate government in Korea. The Russians promptly responded by creating a People's Republic of Korea in the North, which also claimed jurisdiction over the entire country.

When this regime attacked the South and in the process lost most of its military force, the tempting possibility of achieving an independent and united Korea without more military effort or risk beckoned the United Nations. But to make this effort, or even the more modest one of preventing renewal of the attack, required a UN decision that could not be blocked by a Soviet veto in the Security Council. The purpose of my "Uniting for Peace" speech on September 20 was to make further UN decisions possible by action in the General Assembly. Some time earlier we had asked the British Foreign Office its views on a proposal to turn to the General Assembly in cases of aggression should the Security Council be paralyzed by a veto. The response was a cool one. The Foreign Office wisely forecast the dangers of the idea in the future if the then majority in the United Nations should give way to one holding contrary views. But present difficulties outweighed possible future ones, and we pressed on.

My speech[5] proposed strengthening the system of collective security within the existing Charter. Article 1 ascribed to the United Nations as a whole and to its members the purpose of maintaining peace and opposing aggression. The Security Council was the principal instrument for carrying out this purpose, but if it should be paralyzed by a veto the duty remained and powers given by Articles 10, 11, and 14 gave the General Assembly responsibility and authority in maintaining international peace. We would offer a plan to increase Assembly effectiveness by: (1) providing for an emergency session of the General Assembly upon twenty-four hours' notice if the Security Council should be prevented from acting; (2) establishment by the Assembly of a security patrol—a peace patrol—to provide immediate and independent observation wherever international conflict might threaten; (3) designation by each member within its armed forces of United Nations units to be available continuously for United Nations service; and (4) establishment of a special committee to develop further means of collective action.

This plan, in a resolution sponsored by Canada, France, the Philippines, Turkey, the United Kingdom, the United States, and Uruguay, was adopted by the General Assembly on November 3, 1950, by a vote of 52 to 5, with India and Argentina abstaining. Its immediate purpose was to lay a foundation for a policy declaration by the General Assembly on the Korean situation, the final adoption of which actually preceded that of the "Uniting for Peace" resolution by nearly a month.

Within the United States Government discussion of this vital policy question had been going on since the beginning of the attack. On June 29, before commitment of ground forces, I had said to the Newspaper Guild that our action in response to the UN resolutions was "solely to be for the purpose of restoring the Republic of Korea to its status prior to the invasion from the north and of reestablishing the peace broken by that aggression,"[6] and on July 10 had written to Paul Nitze that in the immediate future "we have got to put in the force necessary to reoccupy to the 38th," subject to new problems that Russian or Chinese intervention would raise. In the longer run, if we should succeed in reoccupying the South, the question of garrisoning and supporting it would arise. This would be a hard task for us to take on, and yet it hardly seemed sensible to repel the attack and then abandon the country. I could not "see the end of it. In other words, as the Virginians say, we have bought a colt." Nowhere in my memorandum appears any thought of an independent and united Korea as the U.S. or UN war aim. Similarly, a series of discussions going on within the Government—between the President and the Secretary of State, within State, within Defense, and within the Central Intelligence Agency— seemed to approach the longer-run question through an even more immediate tactical problem: what to do about crossing the 38th parallel.

Long-Range Policy and Crossing the Parallel · The President agreed that nothing should be said about postaggression policy until the course of the fighting was much clearer than it was in mid-July, but on the seventeenth he asked the National Security Council to prepare substantive recommendations for him.

Within the Department a difference of opinion developed, which inhibited clear-cut thinking and led to a wait-and-see attitude. The Far Eastern Division, under Dean Rusk and John Allison, strongly urged that a crossing of the 38th parallel should not be precluded. Only events could clarify whether it should be crossed, but in their view peace and stability would not exist in Korea while the country was divided. Paul Nitze's Policy Planning Staff, influenced by George Kennan's views, took the opposite position and argued that General MacArthur should be directed to announce, as UN Commander, that his troops would not cross the parallel in pursuit if the North Korean forces withdrew to the north of it. On July 13 the problem was further complicated by President Syngman Rhee's announcement that Korean forces would not stop at the parallel and the reply of a U.S. Army spokesman that U.S. forces would stop there and would compel South Korean troops to do likewise. I hastily cabled Ambassador Muccio to do all he could to stop such public statements and discussion, which prejudiced the position of the United States. This cable also resolved the internal dispute within the Department.

Then, on July 31, planners across the river in the Pentagon made proposals of a far-reaching nature. I have long noticed that military recommendations are usually premised upon the meticulous statement of assumptions that as often as not are quite contrary to the facts and yet control the conclusions. So it was here. The recommendation was that the UN Supreme Commander should be directed to cross the parallel, defeat the enemy's forces, and occupy the country, provided the following assumptions held:

1. That the United States would mobilize sufficient resources to attain the objective and strengthen its military position in all other areas of strategic importance.

2. That the Soviet Union would not intervene in Korea or elsewhere.

3. That the President would proclaim, the Congress endorse, and the United Nations adopt as our war aim a united, free, and independent Korea, and that the United States and other nations would maintain their troops in Korea under the UN Command as occupying forces as long as needed.

Not the least interesting aspect of this remarkable intellectual exercise is that, without orders and without the existence of anything approaching these assumptions, General MacArthur would later act along the lines suggested.

On September 1 the departments had agreed through the National Security Council upon a policy recommendation dealing solely with military operations to carry out the narrow interpretation of the June 27 resolution. This concluded that the resolution was sufficient to authorize military operations north as well as south of the parallel to repel the invasion and defeat the invaders and that General MacArthur should be authorized to conduct them, provided that neither the Russians nor the Communists entered the conflict or announced their intention of doing so. The President approving, the Joint Chiefs went to work on instructions for General MacArthur—a meticulous process, which sought his comments at midmonth on an analysis of the problem.

During September, through the Indian Government, we continued to seek evidence of Chinese intentions toward Korea. Earlier Chinese troop movements into Manchuria had established a means of intervention. At first, however, Ambassador K. M. Panikkar reported Chou En-lai as emphasizing China's peaceable intentions, in which the Indian agreed. However, after Inchon, others in Peking took a different tack and early in the morning on October 3, Chou summoned Panikkar to the ministry to inform him that if American troops crossed the parallel China would enter the war. Since on the same day Vishinsky was calling on the United Nations for a cease-fire, the withdrawal of all foreign troops, and a coalition government to rule all Korea until national elections could take place, it was obvious that a combined Sino-Soviet effort was being made to save the North Korean regime. Chou's words were a warning, not to be disregarded, but, on the other hand, not an authoritative statement of policy.

Instructions to General MacArthur · The Joint Chiefs' instructions to General MacArthur for operation north of the 38th parallel, completed toward the end of September, approved by the State Department, and authorized by the President, were dispatched to him on the twenty-seventh. They contained an instruction: "You will also submit your plan for future operations north of the 38th parallel to the JCS for approval." General MacArthur, while protesting this order by which the Chiefs sought to retain final approval of operations, nevertheless filed a plan of operations on the twenty-eighth.

During these days I was in New York, presenting both our "Uniting for Peace" proposal to the General Assembly and our "one package" plan to the North Atlantic ministers. On September 28 the President called me to Washington to discuss the developing Korean situation with him and General Marshall. After lunch in Blair House on the twenty-ninth an officer, with the aid of a large map of Korea showing the position of all American, South Korean, and North Korean units, described the movements proposed by the General.

First, the Joint Chiefs of Staff instructions of September 27:

Your military objective is the destruction of the North Korean Armed Forces. In attaining this objective you are authorized to conduct military operations, including amphibious and airborne landings or ground operations north of the 38th parallel in Korea, provided that at the time of such operations there has been no entry into North Korea by major Soviet or Chinese Communist Forces, no announcement of intended entry, nor a threat to counter our operations militarily in North Korea. Under no circumstances, however, will your forces cross the Manchurian or USSR borders of Korea and, as a matter of policy, no non-Korean Ground Forces will be used in the northeast provinces bordering the Soviet Union or in the area along the Manchurian border. Furthermore support of your operations north or south of the 38th parallel will not include Air or Naval action against Manchuria or against USSR territory.

In the event of the open or covert employment of major Soviet units south of the 38th parallel, you will assume the defense, make no move to aggravate the situation and report to Washington. You should take the same action in the event your forces are operating north of the 38th parallel, and major Soviet units are openly employed. You will not discontinue Air and Naval operations north of the 38th parallel merely because the presence of Soviet or Chinese Communist troops is detected in a target area, but if the Soviet Union or Chinese Communists should announce in advance their intention to reoccupy North Korea and give warning, either explicitly or implicitly, that their forces should not be attacked you should refer the matter to Washington.[7]

The General proposed to send the Eighth Army across the parallel on the west coast through Kaesong and Sariwon to take the northern capital, Pyongyang, while the X Corps would be water-lifted to Wonsan on the east coast. It would link up with the western troops along the Wonsan-Pyongyang road. (Unfortunately, mine-clearing in Wonsan harbor delayed the landing until October 26, enabling the North Korean Army to escape through the gap. Korean troops sent overland arrived at Wonsan on October 11.) Mindful of the warning in the directive, the General proposed to use only South Korean troops north of the line Chungjo-Yongwon-Hungnam, about fifty miles north of Pyongyang-Wonsan and sixty miles southeast of the Yalu at its mouth. He would provide detailed plans later and ended by saying that there was no indication of "present entry into North Korea by major Soviet or Chinese communist forces."

The plan seemed excellently contrived to create a strong military position from which to exploit the possibilities of the North Korean defeat—either to insure the South by a strong defensive line against a renewal of the attack or, if the South Koreans were strong enough and the Chinese did not intervene, to move toward the UN goal of a united, free, and independent Korea. With these thoughts in mind General Marshall and I recommended, and the President approved, the plan of operation.

The same day General Marshall sent General MacArthur a for his "eyes only" telegram saying, "We want you to feel unhampered tactically and strategically to proceed north of the 38th parallel," to which MacArthur replied, "Unless and until the enemy capitulates, I regard all Korea as open for our military operations." Later this exchange was to cause trouble, MacArthur citing it along with other implausible evidence as release from the inhibition against using other than Korean troops in the northern-border provinces. Although I had no knowledge of the messages at the time, it is inconceivable that

General Marshall should have arrogated to himself authority to give General MacArthur dispensation to violate instructions from the Joint Chiefs of Staff approved by the President and MacArthur's own plan of operations also approved by the President and himself that very day. To me, the message seems directed toward soothing MacArthur's irritation at being required to submit his plan of operations. He was assured that Washington wanted him to feel unhampered in proceeding north, except as his orders confined him. His plan showed that he understood this perfectly.

"A United, Independent, and Democratic Korea" • A resolution to restate UN policy for Korea had been drafted with our participation and on September 30 was introduced by Kenneth Younger, British Minister of State, co-sponsored by Australia, Brazil, Cuba, the Netherlands, Norway, Pakistan, and the Philippines. It represented a view that had been growing in the Far Eastern and United Nations divisions of the Department during August and was given a strong push by the success at Inchon. Ambassador Gross had discussed the idea during August with India's Sir Benegal Rau, and Ambassador Austin put up a trial balloon by a speech in the Security Council on August 17. Both seemed to win a favorable reception. The trouble inherent in the resolution itself and in the encouragement it gave to General MacArthur's adventurism lay in the fact that it was not thought through and it masked in ambivalent language the difficulties and dangers against which Kennan had warned in the memorandum discussed earlier.

In effect, the resolution revived the dormant United Nations plan of 1947 for what it called "a unified, independent and democratic government" of Korea. This long-term aim was to be achieved by (1) insuring conditions of stability throughout the country, (2) holding elections under UN auspices and taking other constituent acts necessary to establish the government, (3) inviting all sections and representative bodies in the country to cooperate with the United Nations in this effort, (4) maintaining UN forces in the country only as long as necessary to achieve these objectives, and (5) providing for the economic rehabilitation of Korea. The resolution was passed October 7.

Behind this proposal lay the belief that effort to carry out the 1947 resolution had been blocked by Soviet military power. Soviet forces, however, had been withdrawn and the substituted North Korean troops defeated and scattered. No opposing military force remained in the North to frustrate UN efforts, and the chances were believed good that neither Russian nor Chinese troops would intervene if only Korean soldiery attempted to establish whatever degree of order was possible in the rugged country of the extreme north, where even the Japanese had had only nominal sovereignty. If the Koreans encountered too heavy resistance, they could fall back to the strong position across the neck. In the light of retrospect, this seems a naïve view of the probabilities, but retrospect is to some degree colored by MacArthur's subsequent conduct. If, for instance, General Matthew B. Ridgway had been given the task of carrying out the instruction of September 30 and such orders as would have come to him from Washington to assist the UN Commission in charge of operations under the October 7 resolution, the results would most certainly have been different. With the cast of characters as it was, however, the resolution of October 7 increased the hazards, for which I must bear a measure of responsibility.

General MacArthur at once stripped from the resolution of October 7 its husk of ambivalence and gave it an interpretation that the enacting majority in the General Assembly would not have accepted. Nowhere did the resolution declare that the Eighth Army would impose a unified and democratic government on all Korea. Its task was to "ensure conditions of stability throughout Korea." On October 9 General MacArthur broadcast a second surrender demand, quoting the resolution of the seventh and declaring: "In order that the decisions of the United Nations may be carried out . . . I . . . for the last time, call upon you and the forces under your command . . . forthwith to lay down your arms and cease hostilities. . . . Unless immediate response is made by you . . . I shall at once proceed to take such military action as may be necessary to enforce the decrees of the United Nations."[8] If there had been doubt before that "the unified, independent and democratic government of Korea" would, so far as the Supreme Commander was concerned, be established by his "terrible, swift sword," it was now removed.

Early in October President Truman conceived the idea of meeting General MacArthur on Wake Island in the mid-Pacific for a heart-to-heart talk that would establish a thorough understanding between them. Each man was to think that an understanding had been established, but each would have a different idea of what it was.

48. OCTOBER ODYSSEYS

OCTOBER 1950 was a month of journeyings in which none of the wayfarers found what each sought, nor did serendipity put in their way anything else useful. President Truman flew to Wake Island in search of understanding with General MacArthur; the NATO foreign ministers came to Washington to find a role for Germany in the defense of Europe; the unlucky United Nations Command trudged toward the Yalu in pursuit of General MacArthur's mirage of victory. It was a frustrating month.

PILGRIMAGE TO WAKE

When the President told me of his intended pilgrimage and invited me to join him, I begged to be excused. While General MacArthur had many of the attributes of a foreign sovereign, I said, and was quite as difficult as any, it did not seem wise to recognize him as one. It was agreed between us that what the President might need from the State Department could be furnished by Ambassador Muccio, Dean Rusk, Philip Jessup, and Averell Harriman, all of whom would be there. I had not been consulted in arriving at the decision to hold the meeting and offered no suggestions after it had been made. The whole idea was distasteful to me. I wanted no part in it, and saw no good coming from it. I could not then or now explain this strong presentiment, beyond the conviction that talk should precede, not follow, the issuance of orders. The latter only befogs them. So I contented myself with seeing the President off on October 11 and welcoming him back on the eighteenth.

The President and General MacArthur spent between two and a half and three hours together, from approximately six-thirty in the morning to a little after nine. For half of that time they were alone. The President has written his recollection of the talk.[1] We were soon to get an intimation of the General's; it bore out my worst forebodings. The discussion that followed with colleagues present was more immediately and fully reported—more fully, due to a circumstance that was later to cause the proverbial tempest in a teapot. Miss Vernice Anderson, Ambassador Jessup's secretary, was waiting next door to the conference room to help with the communiqué. The door was open and the conversation audible. Having nothing to do and knowing that a memorandum of conversation would be worked out on the way home, she took stenographic notes. When this became known at the hearings on General MacArthur's relief, charges were made that it was akin to "bugging" the conference. This was utter nonsense.

In the large meeting the General expressed optimistic views that the end of the fighting was close (he had told the President probably by Thanksgiving and that our troops, except for two divisions, could begin withdrawal from Korea by Christmas) and that the Chinese would not intervene. If, however, they should do so, not more than fifty to sixty thousand could cross the Yalu, and they would be slaughtered if they attempted to go south. The party returned full of optimism and confidence in the General. The President's speech two days later in the San Francisco Opera House exuded both. In explaining his journey to Wake, he concluded: "I also felt that there was pressing need to make it perfectly clear—by my talk with General MacArthur—that there is complete unity in the aims and conduct of our foreign policy." That perfect clarity did not outlast the month.

ANOTHER ROUND IN NATO

While the President and the General were meeting in the Pacific, Secretaries Marshall and Snyder of Treasury and I stayed home for discussion with two French ministers, Jules Moch of Defense and Maurice Petsche of Finance. After that General Marshall was scheduled to meet with the assembled defense ministers of the Atlantic Treaty countries. Before the French arrived on October 12, preliminary plans were worked out with Robert A. Lovett, who had been recently appointed Deputy Secretary of Defense. (When we were in New York together shortly after his appointment, General Marshall had talked about filling the post. He very much wanted Lovett but felt that to ask this of him would be unfair, since he had been back in his banking business only a year and a half after long and faithful service in Washington. I told the General that nothing would please Lovett more than to work again with his former chief and I bet that if he called Lovett that evening at home Lovett would be so close to the telephone he would answer it himself. He was and did.) Lovett and I agreed that if the French still opposed our "interim plan" for getting on with the defense of Europe we would not accept the burden of thinking up a new one, but leave the ball in their court. Unfortunately, they had thought of this too, and put forward a proposal designed for infinite delay on German participation.

Our financial talks proved not only a failure but a future source of misunderstanding. This happened all too frequently with Franco-American discussion on finance, partly due to language difficulties and partly because even when our language was clear our governmental position was not. Four departments and the Congress were all involved—State, Defense, Treasury, and the European Recovery Administration were all putting forward ideas. To increase confusion in this case the French wanted a commitment for aid beyond the period for which funds had been appropriated, which we could not legally give. Due to their war in Vietnam, they would run into a budget deficit for the calendar year (also their fiscal year) 1951 of about a billion dollars, a sizable portion of which was in foreign exchange deficits. In addition to aid in the form of military hardware, they wanted dollar aid to help on these deficits and on manufacture in France of military items necessary, they said, both to speed up rearmament and to furnish employment there.

At best it was a complicated puzzle. When four departments had explained in two languages what could and could not be done under existing law, with the French choosing to believe what pleased them most, a deep, serious, and lasting misunderstanding had been created. So far as the written word went, we made commitments for the period January to July 1951, the first half of the French fiscal year 1951 and the last half of the U.S. fiscal year 1951. We could make no commitment of funds beyond that time but would review the situation with them before July 1, 1951. To the French our talk of the need for congressional appropriations appeared to be pure legal formalism. They believed, and later insisted, that for the months July through December 1951 we had promised them *at least* as much dollar aid as in the preceding six months, and more if we could get it out of Congress. Attempts to explain our true and only possible position struck them as a rather shabby descent into sharp practice. This long-dead and unimportant quarrel is worth mentioning only to warn that all diplomacy does not deal with great principles and broad policies and that our constitutional separation of powers is not a pure boon to the State Department. As we parted, Maurice Petsche made a remark that I cherished and passed on to our daughter at Saranac.

DA to MAB   *October 17, 1950*
We have been having the devil's own time with the French over the last five days. . . .

But this is ungrateful, I suppose, since old Petsche said after our meetings: "I like to make with you the business. You have the outside of the Englishman, but you think like a Frenchman." It was meant for the best.

We had hardly finished these financial talks and heard the reports from Wake when the French announced in Paris a counterproposal for German participation in defense, which caused us consternation and dismay. It came to be known as the Pleven Plan, after its alleged originator, Prime Minister René Pleven. In essence it proposed that, in addition to the elements of their national forces that the European allies would pledge to the defense of Europe under the command of a Supreme Commander in time of war (but which would remain under national control in peacetime), a special European force would be created under a European Minister of Defense and its own command and staff structure, in turn under the Supreme Commander. Into this army would go contributions from the allies and German contingents at the battalion level, the whole army amounting to some one hundred thousand men. To the French the Pleven Plan had the attraction of a German contribution to the defense of Europe, though a small one, without "the rearmament of Germany"—that is, without the creation of a German Ministry of Defense, armament industry, or general staff. Aside from the minimal accretion to European defense that the plan offered, the second-class status accorded Germany was all too plain. There the Social Democratic opposition through Schumacher denounced the plan, while Adenauer for the Government more moderately pointed out the subordinate position into which it sought to place the German contingents.

Announcement of the plan in Paris was followed by ringing endorsement of it by the Council of Ministers and by the National Assembly with a vote of 349 to 235, remarkable in the Fourth Republic. We issued phrases of "welcoming the initiative" and "sympathetic examination," and I received copious explanations from M. Bonnet, the French Ambassador; but to me the plan was hopeless, a view confirmed by General Marshall and concurred in by the President, and protracted discussion of it dangerous. The French were united and dug in. While our Paris embassy believed that discussion in NATO might bring modification of the plan by threatening the French with isolation, that seemed to me too blind and dangerous an alley to enter. Better, I thought, to modify our own position—the "one package" proposal, which I had never liked —and proceed as I had originally wanted to do in August, by accepting the Supreme Commander in return for a unanimous agreement "in principle" for German participation, and to try to get it with united allied military support on our side.

Here General Marshall, in complete agreement, was of immense help in the Pentagon, and the President had always thought the State Department's plan the better course if not undercut by military opposition. The soldiers, too, were ready for a change of strategy. We had loyally supported the "one package" plan through a hard-fought and bloody campaign. It had not worked. They were now in a mood, led by General Marshall and General Bradley, to try it our way. Since the Pleven Plan had made obsolete our ideas of compromise through the defense ministers' meeting of October 28–31, it was decided to relax tensions by more easy discussion, reference of the problem to the NATO Council deputies for further study and preparation of our change of attitude at a meeting of all NATO ministers in December. This was done. It was a relief to get myself unstuck, if only briefly, from the cloying problem of German participation in defense.

A BAD FRIGHT

At this time all of us in Washington had a bad scare. It occurred on November 1, 1950. The Cabinet had assembled in midafternoon in the National Cemetery at Arlington, where the President was to unveil a monument to Field Marshal Sir John Dill, a great British soldier who had died in Washington during the war while serving as the British resident member of the Combined Chiefs of Staff. My wife and I were sitting with General and Mrs. Marshall. John Snyder, Secretary of the Treasury, joined us.

"An attempt has been made," he said, "to assassinate the President. I don't know what has happened. Shooting has been reported in front of Blair House [where the President was living]. I think the President is all right, but I don't know." A buzz of conversation broke out around us as those who had overheard passed the word to those behind them. Just then the Marine Band broke into "Hail to the Chief" as the President stepped out of his car and walked to the rostrum looking as though he had not a care in the world. The small and now relieved group burst into applause. He went through his speech without a hitch, adding from time to time little bits about Sir John that he had learned from General Marshall, a close and devoted friend.

Afterward he told us of the attempt of two demented Puerto Rican nationalists to break into Blair House to assassinate him. One of the men and one of the guards had been killed and others wounded. Mr. Truman, who had been awakened from his nap by the shooting, went to the open window and saw a man lying on the steps of Blair House. A policeman shouted to him to get back. He hastily dressed, reassured Mrs. Truman, and joined Charles Ross, his Press Secretary, who was waiting to accompany him to Arlington. "I never saw a calmer man," reported Ross.

I CRITICIZE MY CRITICS

During the pause in hostilities in the first three weeks in November, two speeches of mine stirred up the animals, to use a favorite phrase of President Truman. They were a form of self-indulgence, which in one case annoyed our opponents and in the other puzzled the well-meaning. One exposed a pompous fraud, the other suggested that international affairs were more complicated than some of the simplistic solutions, especially moral ones, often advanced.

Senator Taft had argued that the recent November election—which had resulted in the usual off-year loss of seats by the party in power—constituted a mandate to "re-examine" our foreign policy. At the beginning of a scheduled speech before the National Council of Negro Women on November 17, as much to amuse myself as to answer the Senator, I improvised a bit about a new species recently discovered by research in the natural history of public life.[2]

This new discovery had occurred, interestingly enough, just as another species of *Homo sapiens* had been reported to have become extinct. The latter was the isolationist. Here research was difficult since no one would so identify himself, as the word itself had become a pejorative term and inquiry was regarded as insulting. ("Only an idiot would be an isolationist today," Senator Taft had only recently remarked.) The isolationist was reported, therefore, as dead as the dodo or the saber-toothed tiger.

Just at this juncture the new species had emerged and was named the re-examinist because its distinctive call was "Let's re-examine all our policies and programs." Now, we had been doing this for years. Indeed, Congress forced us to do so. I myself appeared four times a year before different committees to re-examine every policy and program and justify every dollar appropriated for every one of them. So a species that merely called for something as old as the nation could hardly be called new.

Perhaps, however, I continued, the new species was one without memory or constancy. Perhaps it was distinctive for pulling up its crops every morning to see what had been planted or from doubt as to whether they should have been. Perhaps this species was noted for re-examining its spouse each morning over the breakfast table and reappraising the relationship, or for the habit of its members in showing up at their offices wondering why they ever got into such a business or associated with such people. A wise navigator re-examined his course every day or night by checking his relation to the sun or the stars, but doubtless re-examinists continually asked themselves whether it had been a good idea to have started or would be wise to continue on that particular voyage.

We might, I suggested, get a clue to the nature of this species by noting that it obviously did not think of itself as part of a great moving stream of life. Rather it sat alone at the center of its little universe, at the point from which all routes emerged and were to be chosen according to changing whim or ancient tradition. Sitting alone was often called isolation. Could it be that the new species was not new at all, I asked in conclusion. Were re-examinists only isolationists with a change of name? The possibility was worth thinking over. These banderillas drew satisfying bellowing and earth-pawing from enraged bulls.

The other speech, before the World Organization for Brotherhood of the National Conference of Christians and Jews,[3] sprang less from a desire *pour épater le bourgeois* than to indulge a favorite theme—that in foreign affairs nothing was more dangerous than to base action upon moral or ideal conceptions unconnected with hardheaded practicality. Matthew Arnold, I recalled, had praised Sophocles because "he saw life steadily and saw it whole." This steadiness and wholeness of view applied with special force to that part of life we called foreign affairs and, especially, in achieving a union between moral purpose and physical power. Intellectuals were quick and correct in pointing out that ultimate reality in foreign affairs was not found in terms of power alone. They were not always so quick to see that neither was it to be found in moral or political principle alone. Many leaders in "the battle for the minds of men" were looking for a one-page statement of the democratic faith with all the impact of the Gettysburg Address and the Lord's Prayer combined. It seemed to me possible that democratic faith might be imparted better by contagion than by argument.

This wholeness of view was part of our American tradition, I said. Out of our past came the admonition to "put your faith in God and keep your powder dry." Today we phrased it, "Praise the Lord and pass the ammunition!" Even beyond this recognition of compatibility between moral purpose and physical power lay a deeper truth. As Reinhold Niebuhr had said, "There is always an element of moral ambiguity in historic responsibilities," and as he had added, "Our survival as a civilization depends upon our ability to do what seems right from day to day without . . . alternate moments of illusion and despair."

In the rugged Roman militancy of St. Paul's words to the Ephesians one found stirring inspiration: "Wherefore take unto you the whole armor of God, that ye may be able to stand in the evil day, and having done all, to stand." The "wholeness" we sought included not only the shield of faith but also dry powder and the will to pass it.

MAC ARTHUR MOVES NORTH

By mid-October General MacArthur's forces had reached the line established in accordance with his plan of operations approved September 29. North of this line the plan permitted the use of Korean troops only.

On the twenty-fourth General MacArthur without warning or notice to Washington ordered his commanders to "drive forward with all speed and full utilization of their forces."[4] The restraining line in the north was thus abolished and with it the inhibition against other than South Korean troops in the border provinces. The Army moved swiftly. One element of the Eighth Army, the 7th Regiment of the South Korean 6th Division, reached the Yalu near Chosen on October 26 without opposition and turned back. Then things began to happen. So stunned was the Pentagon that the Joint Chiefs of Staff sent out a timorous inquiry to MacArthur saying that although he undoubtedly had sound reasons for issuing this order they would like to be informed of them "as your action is a matter of some concern here," a magnificent understatement. Back came one of the purple telegrams with which we were to become familiar during November as the drive north ran its ill-fated course. General MacArthur had lifted the restriction "as a matter of military necessity," since the South Korean troops were neither sufficiently strong nor well-enough led to handle the situation. (In which case, it had been supposed that they would be withdrawn to the supporting line.) The directive of September 27 was not, he said, a "final directive," since it stated that it might later be amended (a proposition true also of the Constitution of the United States). Furthermore, he said, the Chiefs of Staff had not banned the use of other than South Korean forces in the extreme north, but had merely stated that "it should not be done as a matter of policy." In any event, he continued, General Marshall's cable of September 29 had modified prior instruction of the Chiefs. General MacArthur understood "the basic purpose and intent of your directive, and every possible precaution is being taken in the premises. The very reverse, however, would be fostered and tactical hazards might even result from other action than that which I have directed." Then the final clincher: "This entire subject was covered in my conference at Wake Island." President Truman stated on October 26 that it was his understanding that only Korean troops would approach the northern border. However, General MacArthur replied through the press on the twenty-seventh that "the mission of the UN force is to clear Korea."

"Tactical hazards" immediately encountered were somewhat different in nature from those of which the General had warned. On October 26 the 7th Regiment of the South Korean 6th Division, returning as reported from the Yalu, blundered into a large concentration of Chinese troops, which had already crossed the river, and was destroyed. The next day the South Korean II Corps to the north of Unsan in northwest Korea and the 5th and 8th U.S. Cavalry to the west of it were attacked by overwhelming force. At the end of four days and nights of incessant and often hand-to-hand fighting the II Corps was no longer an organized force and the 8th Cavalry had lost half its strength and most of its equipment. The enemy broke contact and General Walton Walker regrouped II Corps back at the Chongchon River, reporting to General MacArthur that he had been ambushed by "well organized and well trained units."

SCHIZOPHRENIA AT GHQ

It took time for report of the events of October 25–November 1 to percolate from North Korea through Tokyo to Washington, if, indeed, it ever did percolate in recognizable form. For instance, in a press conference on November 1,[5] I reported that the UN Command was investigating the reported presence of Chinese Communist troops in Korea. The survivors of the 8th Cavalry regiment might have thought the fact established. Meanwhile Russian MIG-15 jets made their first appearance over Korea on October 31. MacArthur's reports were schizophrenic. On November 4, responding to the President's request for fuller information, he sent a calming evaluation warning against "hasty conclusions which might be premature" and urging patience during "a more complete accumulation of military facts."[6]

However, within twenty-four hours he was rejecting his own advice. By October 25, the restrictions on the U.S. Fifth Air Force had been eased to allow close support missions "under control of a tactical air control party or a Mosquito observer, as near the border as necessary." However, there was to be no bombing within five miles of the border. In spite of all instructions on October 9, U.S. planes as the result of acknowledged "navigation error and bad judgment" had fired on an airfield a hundred kilometers inside Soviet territory, for which we expressed regret and offered to pay damages. Now, on November 5, General MacArthur ordered General George E. Stratemeyer to use his full air power to knock the North Koreans and their allies out of the war.[7] "Combat crews are to be flown to exhaustion if necessary," the Korean ends of all Yalu bridges were to be taken out, and, excepting Rashin, Suiho Dam, and other hydroelectric plants, every means of communication, installation, factory, city and village in North Korea, destroyed. He also informed the UN Security Council that the UN forces "are presently in hostile contact with Chinese Communist military units," listing twelve encounters.[8]

General Stratemeyer informed the Pentagon of his orders three hours before his planes were due to take off on their mission against the bridges from Sinuiju to Antung. Shortly after ten o'clock that morning Robert Lovett brought the order to me in the State Department, saying that he doubted whether the bombing would importantly interrupt traffic across the river and that the danger of bombing the Manchurian city of Antung was great. Mr. Rusk, who was with us, contributed that we were committed not to attack Manchurian points without consultation with the British and that their Cabinet was meeting that morning to reconsider their attitude toward the Chinese Communist Government. We had also asked the UN Security Council for an urgent meeting to consider General MacArthur's report of Chinese intervention in Korea. Ill-considered action at this moment could be unfortunate. We agreed and telephoned General Marshall, who thought that the Joint Chiefs of Staff should be asked to postpone MacArthur's action until the President's instructions could be obtained. This was done.

Fortunately, the President was reached by telephone in Kansas City on his way home to vote. I explained the situation, adding that MacArthur's reports as late as the day before had contained no hint of movements across the river. The President said that he would authorize anything necessary for the security of the troops. Could I, he asked, call MacArthur and ascertain the facts? I replied, and he agreed, that communications with MacArthur on military matters should be through military channels. The President told me to handle the matter as Lovett and I thought best, adding that he would be available by telephone if needed and that the security of the troops should not be jeopardized. Subject to that, he agreed on the importance of postponing the action until we had a statement of the justifying facts.

Lovett left with a summary of the President's views for the meeting of the Joint Chiefs at eleven-fifteen that morning, just one and three-quarters hours before Stratemeyer's planes were due to take off unless already stopped. The Chiefs reaffirmed their order against bombing within five miles of the border, stated that the Government was committed not to take action affecting Manchuria without consulting the British, and asked for MacArthur's reasons for bombing the bridges. Back came another purple paragraph:

Men and material in large force are pouring across all bridges over the Yalu from Manchuria. This movement not only jeopardizes but threatens the ultimate destruction of the forces under my command. . . . The only way to stop this reinforcement of the enemy is the destruction of these bridges and the subjection of all installations in the north area supporting the enemy advance to the maximum of our air destruction. . . . Under the gravest protest that I can make, I am suspending this strike [at Sinuiju] and carrying out your instructions. . . . I trust that the matter be immediately brought to the attention of the President as I believe your instructions may well result in a calamity of major proportion.[9]

Since MacArthur was in responsible command and represented the emergency as so urgent, the President—as he expressed it—"told Bradley to give him the 'go-ahead.' " The skepticism of the Chiefs shows through the correct language of their reply:

The situation depicted in your message [of November 6] is considerably changed from that reported in last sentence your message [of November 4] which was our last report from you. We agree that the destruction of the Yalu bridges would contribute materially to the security of the forces under your command unless this action resulted in increased Chinese Communist effort and even Soviet contribution in response to what they might well construe as an attack on Manchuria.

However, in view of first sentence your message [of November 6] you are authorized to go ahead with your planned bombing in Korea near the frontier including targets at Sinuiju and Korean end of Yalu bridges provided that at time of receipt of this message you still find such action essential to safety of your forces. The above does not authorize the bombing of any dams or power plants on the Yalu River.[10]

MacArthur's messages of November 6 and 7 confused the situation for those of us in Washington even more than it had been before.

The first one, a public communiqué,[11] depicted the "practical end" of the war with the North Koreans by his capture of their capital and destruction of their army. Then had begun a wholly new war by a new enemy, the Communist Chinese, through "one of the most offensive acts of international lawlessness of historic record"—i.e., crossing the Yalu. The new enemy had also massed reinforcing divisions behind the river in a "privileged sanctuary." "A possible trap" was avoided with minimum losses only by "timely detection and skillful maneuvering"—a euphemistic phrase for running into an ambush. His mission he saw as defeating the forces arrayed against him in North Korea (presumably the new enemy) and achieving the United Nations objective of bringing unity and peace to the Korean people.

The next day, November 7, MacArthur added to his public message, with its implied criticism of the Government's policy, two private judgments.[12] In one he concluded that his estimate of November 4 that the Chinese had not made a full-scale intervention had been right, although they might be able to force on him a "movement in retrograde." However, he was planning to move forward to take "accurate measure . . . of enemy strength." The second message of November 7 contained a strong protest against the "present restrictions"— that is, against planes flying over Manchuria—which "provide a complete sanctuary for hostile air immediately upon their crossing the Manchuria-North Korean border." This was to lead to the "hot pursuit" argument, which broke out some days later. On November 9 he cabled his opinion that with his "air power, now unrestricted so far as Korea is concerned, . . . I can deny reinforcements coming across the Yalu in sufficient strength to prevent the destruction [sic] of those forces now arrayed against me in North Korea."[13]

The five days from November 4 to 9 give an excellent example of General MacArthur's mercurial temperament. In this period he went from calm confidence, warning against hasty judgment until all the facts were in, through ringing the tocsin on the sixth to proclaim that hordes of men were pouring into Korea and threatening to overwhelm his command, to confidence again on the ninth that he could deny the enemy reinforcement and destroy him. In fact, his troops were being secretly surrounded by overpowering numbers of Chinese.

Washington could not follow his moods. During the depressive period of November 6–8 the Chiefs of Staff informed him that his "objective" (the destruction of the North Korean Army) stated in the September 27 directive might have to be re-examined as the eventuality mentioned in it—the entry of Communist China into the war—seemed to have occurred. This suggestion drove MacArthur to manic reaction and deep into the realm of United Nations political policy. It would be fatal to weaken the UN policy of destroying resisting forces and bringing unity and freedom to Korea, he said. Anything less would destroy the "morale of my forces and its psychological consequences would be inestimable." To give up any portion of Korea to aggression would be immoral, bankrupt our leadership, and make our position untenable, politically and militarily. He deprecated the "Munich attitude" of the British. He meant to launch his attack about November 15 and to keep on going until he got to the border.[14]

The Joint Chiefs were intimidated but not convinced by this blast. They believed, as they always had, that Chinese power, if the Chinese chose to exert it, could be defeated militarily in North Korea only by a greatly augmented and determined American effort and that we had other and more pressing needs for our forces elsewhere. The goal of a free and united Korea belonged, if it were achievable at all, in the field of diplomatic effort. Therefore, they recommended —with presidential approval through the National Security Council—that the mission assigned to General MacArthur should be kept under review but not changed at that time.

THE LAST CLEAR CHANCE

Here, I believe, the Government missed its last chance to halt the march to disaster in Korea. All the President's advisers in this matter, civilian and military, knew that something was badly wrong, though what it was, how to find out, and what to do about it they muffed. That they were deeply disturbed and felt the need for common counsel is shown by the unprecedented fact that in the three weeks and three days from November 10 until December 4, when disaster was full upon us, the Secretaries of State and Defense and their chief assistants met three times with the Chiefs of Staff in their war room to tussle with the problem, the two secretaries met five times with the President, and I consulted with him on five other occasions. I have an unhappy conviction that none of us, myself prominently included, served him as he was entitled to be served.

Our bafflement centered about the two principal enigmas of this situation: What were the facts about Chinese military presence in North Korea and what were their intentions? (The first would throw light on the second.) And what was General MacArthur up to in the amazing military maneuver that was unfolding before unbelieving eyes? Regarding the first, the forces that had struck the Eighth Army during the last days of October and the opening days of November had been powerful, fully equipped, and competent—and yet they seemed to have vanished from the earth. The most elementary caution would seem to warn that they might, indeed probably would, reappear as suddenly and harmfully as they had before.

However, General MacArthur was taking no precautions. As at Inchon, he had divided his forces in the presence of the enemy. The Eighth Army under General Walker in the west and the X Corps under General Edward M. Almond in the east were widely separated, leaving both their flanks exposed. Their only coordination came through Tokyo on the basis of intelligence thirty hours old when received. Moreover, division of forces had been carried further. The X Corps moved north in three separate columns through rugged country without capacity of mutual support. The Eighth Army was likewise divided into four or more separate columns covering a broad front with little or no lateral connection. Winter was coming on fast, when the frozen Yalu would furnish easy crossing without regard to bridges. Here surely was a soldier's nightmare, equally ill adapted to taking "accurate measure . . . of enemy strength" (the November 7 declared purpose) and to reaching and holding the border in the face of winter.

At our first meeting with General Marshall and the Chiefs of Staff on November 21, after General Ridgway had pointed out the startling dispositions, I stated our concerns. General MacArthur seemed to have confused his military directive (to follow and destroy the remnant of the North Korean Army unless Chinese intervention in force made it evident that he could not succeed in this task) with his civil affairs directive intended to follow military success (helping the UN Commission establish a government for a united Korea). At this point our object was not "real estate" but an army. An attempt to establish a united Korea by force of arms against a determined Chinese resistance could easily lead into general hostilities, since both the Chinese and the Russians, as well as the Japanese, had all regarded Korea as a road to somewhere else rather than an end in itself. Very definitely the policy of our Government was to avoid general war in Asia. Apparently General MacArthur could not determine the degree of Chinese intervention without some sort of a "probe" along his line; therefore we did not oppose that. When I privately expressed a layman's concern to Generals Marshall and Bradley over MacArthur's scattering of his forces, they pointed out that the Chiefs of Staff, seven thousand miles from the front, could not direct the theater commander's dispositions. But under this obvious truth lay, I felt, uneasy respect for the MacArthur mystique. Strange as these maneuverings appeared, they could be another 5,000-to-1 shot by the sorcerer of Inchon. Though no one could explain them, and General MacArthur would not, no one would restrain them.

Going on to diplomatic methods of easing the dangerous showdown that might be coming by such a method as Bevin favored—a cease-fire and a demilitarized zone along the border—or as others had urged by falling back to the neck of Korea, concentrating our forces, and doing our probing with Korean forces, as was thought to be Government policy at the end of September, I was sure that General MacArthur would frustrate any such efforts until he had felt out Chinese strength. Accordingly, I had persuaded the British to hold up any initiative in the United Nations. Finally, I said that clearly no troops would be released from the Far East by Christmas, or for a long time afterward, and that, as NSC-68 had pointed out, military strength was badly needed elsewhere. Hence our establishment must be increased to provide it. From this conclusion and from the one that General MacArthur had to have his try no one dissented. The rest of the discussion went over old ground but presented no new ideas.

When we met again in the National Security Council a week later, the whole face of things had changed. On November 17 MacArthur had informed the Chiefs that on the twenty-fourth he would start a general offensive to attain the line of the Yalu.[15] His air attacks had isolated the battlefield from enemy reinforcements. While the supply situation was unsatisfactory, he nevertheless proposed to clear the country of enemy forces before the Yalu froze and furnished a crossing for overwhelming numbers. Such was the reasoning. A cautionary cable from the Chiefs of Staff urging him to stop on the high ground commanding the Yalu valley was brushed aside as "utterly impossible." In the full optimism of the manic tide he flew to Eighth Army headquarters on the Chongchon River and proclaimed the general offensive in the northwest, declaring, "If successful this should for all practical purposes end the war, restore peace and unity to Korea, enable the prompt withdrawal of United Nations military forces, and permit the complete assumption by the Korean people and nation of full sovereignty and international equality."[16]

As I look back, the critical period stands out as the three weeks from October 26 to November 17. Then all the dangers from dispersal of our own forces and intervention by the Chinese were manifest. We were all deeply apprehensive. We were frank with one another, but not quite frank enough. I was unwilling to urge on the President a military course that his military advisers would not propose.† They would not propose it because it ran counter to American military tradition of the proper powers of the theater commander since 1864. President Lincoln had stopped meddling by Washington in military operations, had appointed Grant a lieutenant general, and had put him in full command of the armies of the United States. If General Marshall and the Chiefs had proposed withdrawal to the Pyongyang-Wonsan line and a continuous defensive position under united command across it—and if the President had backed them, as he undoubtedly would have—disaster would probably have been averted. But it would have meant a fight with MacArthur, charges by him that they had denied him victory—which they, perhaps, would have uneasily felt might have been true—and his relief under arguable circumstances. So they hesitated, wavered, and the chance was lost. While everyone acted correctly, no one, I suspect, was ever quite satisfied with himself afterward. Undoubtedly the same might have been true had we all played it the other way. It is a good bet that had we done so MacArthur's reputation would be higher today.

THE ARMY, against the deepest forebodings of General Walker, moved forward into the ominously silent and apparently deserted mountain area of northwest Korea. Four days later massive Chinese counterattacks exploded all around its many columns, in their front, on their flanks, and in their rear. A series of fiercely fought and largely separate battles developed. General MacArthur plunged from the height of optimism to the bottom of his depressive cycle. "We face an entirely new war," he reported on November 28. "This has shattered the high hopes we entertained . . . that . . . the war in Korea could be brought to a rapid close by our movement to the international boundary and the prompt withdrawal thereafter of United Nations forces."[1] All hope of localizing the Korean conflict, he cabled the Joint Chiefs of Staff, was gone. The Chinese wanted nothing less than the "complete destruction" of his army. What had been shattered was MacArthur's dream, the product of his own hubris. Unfortunately the Eighth Army was to be pretty well shattered also.

In this atmosphere the National Security Council met on the same day. General Bradley led off with a summary of the military situation so far as known. General MacArthur under heavy attack had turned to the defensive. The offensive had been to find out the dimension of Chinese intervention; now we knew. The extent of our predicament and the nature of new directives must await clarifications. The three hundred aircraft, including two hundred bombers, on Manchurian airfields constituted a serious threat to our forces and our planes crowded on Korean fields. To bomb them invited retaliation from Chinese and Russian aircraft. So far they were quiescent. General Vandenberg concurred in not initiating the bombing, certainly not until some of our own planes had been removed to Japan.

General Marshall produced a report by three service secretaries, with which he and the Joint Chiefs agreed, recommending that we should continue to act as the executive agent of the United Nations and with its support, not be drawn into a separate conflict with Communist China. Hence we should use all means to keep the war limited, not strike Chinese territory, not use Chinese Nationalist forces (which, the Chiefs noted, might cause withdrawal of the much more effective British forces). They also urged a rapid increase in U.S. military power to meet increasing needs for it.

In Korea, Generals Marshall, Bradley, and Collins pointed out, General MacArthur would have to get along with the forces he had. Troops for replacement of losses would not be ready until the new year, nor new divisions until after March 1, 1951. Then competing demands for the latter would be heavy.

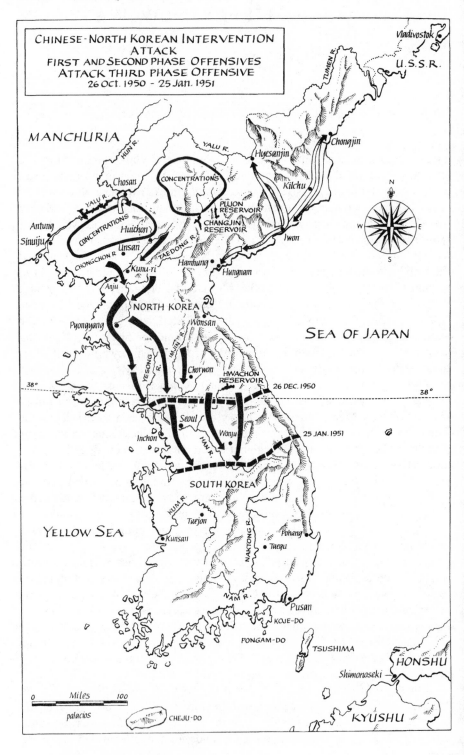

All the soldiers were distressed at General MacArthur's exposed and scattered tactical position. They would call his attention to it, but it was for him to solve; it would not help to interfere with operations on the spot.

The Vice President, in obviously sincere puzzlement, caused some embarrassment by wondering what General MacArthur had in mind in making his statement about getting the troops out of Korea by Christmas. Could it have been a hoax for the Chinese? Unhelpfully the President said that he would have to draw his own conclusions. In General Bradley's view General MacArthur had full confidence in the success of his attack and no inkling of the strong concentration in the high mountains on his right. It certainly was no hoax. To General Marshall it was an embarrassment that we must get around in some manner.

My own views were that we were closer than we had yet been to a wider war. There had always been a Chinese involvement in Korea. It had been progressively uncloaked until now we faced a full-scale attack. Behind this was the somber possibility of Soviet support in any one of many forms. We should consider Korea not in isolation but in its worldwide setting of our confrontation with our Soviet antagonist. We had objectives to reach and dangers to avoid. The State Department would take on the task of uniting the United Nations against the Chinese Communist aggression and branding it as such, regardless of a Soviet veto in the Security Council. The memorandum of the three secretaries and the comments were very wise. General MacArthur faced a new situation. This time we should see that he understood his instructions. He seemed to have been under the misapprehension that he was supposed to occupy the north and northeastern parts of Korea. We should tell him plainly that that was not his mission. We wanted to terminate that involvement. We could not defeat the Chinese in Korea because they could put in more men than we could afford to commit there.

The imperative step was to find a line that we could hold and hold it. Such proposals as a cease-fire or demilitarized zone in the North could be considered, but there was no indication that any such arrangements could be made. To pull out of Korea at this stage would be disastrous for us. Outside of Korea we should speed building our own military strength and that of our European allies.

The meeting ended without recommendations for decisions by the President.

DISASTER RATTLES THE GENERAL

The next few days were a time of anxiety and confusion as the debacle in Korea deepened and General MacArthur's depression grew to near panic. When, on November 29, the Chiefs of Staff urged him to coordinate the Eighth Army and X Corps "to prevent any enemy forces from passing between them or outflanking either of them," he rejected the advice and called for reinforcements and new directives.[2] On the twenty-eighth he sent a message to Ray Henle of the *Three-Star Extra* news broadcast explaining his position;[3] on the thirtieth, another to Arthur Krock of *The New York Times* justifying his march north; and on December 1 gave an interview to *U.S. News and World Report* in which he said that orders forbidding him to strike at Communist forces across the Manchurian border had put UN forces under "an enormous handicap, without precedent in military history." Others followed to the United Press, International News Service, the *London Daily Mail,* and the Tokyo press corps.

At length (December 5), his patience exhausted, the President ordered a moratorium on governmental speeches concerning foreign or military affairs and had Secretary Marshall and me direct, on presidential authority, that military commanders and diplomatic representatives abroad must cease "direct communication on military or foreign policy with newspapers, magazines or other publicity media in the United States."[4] This was aimed at MacArthur. "I should have relieved [him] then and there," the President wrote later.[5]

He himself had added to the confusion on November 30 by an unfortunate answer to a loaded press question about the use of atomic weapons in Korea, which brought Prime Minister Attlee scurrying across the ocean. We shall come to that visit shortly.

On December 1 a State-Defense meeting was again convened at the Pentagon. I pointed out that the contingency mentioned but not discussed at our last meeting—the failure of General MacArthur's attack—was hard upon us. A state of panic seemed to exist at the United Nations; complaints were being made that U.S. leadership had failed; and disunity was observable in Asia and Europe. We must act to restore confidence and unity among our friends, which entailed coordinating military and political measures. There was no use in my going to the General Assembly until the United States had an agreed plan. The first questions were whether and where it was possible to hold a line, what political measures would help to stabilize the situation, and whether or not they should be started at this stage. If it was not possible to hold a line, a whole new set of questions arose that we should begin to examine, such as either extending the conflict or seeking for a way to end it. Here again, military and political measures must march together.

The upshot of a very full and frank discussion was that it was not possible to answer my questions yet. Indeed, so confused and confusing were the reports from headquarters that General Marshall asked General Collins to go at once himself and find out what was going on. Reinforcements were apparently coming to the Chinese from Manchuria; our troops were still too widely dispersed. We might have to fall much farther back and, unless the Eighth Army and X Corps could be united and regrouped, we might not be able to hold a line at all, but be forced into beachheads at Inchon, Wonsan, and Pusan. In such an eventuality, the possibility of holding the beachheads against possible Chinese and Russian bombing was doubtful. The use of nuclear weapons by us could lead to incalculable consequences. For the present, and unless the preservation of our troops required it, the balancing of the pros and cons of bombing Manchurian territory, including air and other bases, was against doing so. On this the Chiefs of Staff and civilian secretaries were unanimous.

General MacArthur's other nostrums—blockading the China coast and using Nationalist troops from Formosa—were examined again and ruled out for both a tactical and strategic reason. At best they could be of only peripheral value. Furthermore, until we knew whether our forces would have to be evacuated from Korea or moved about by water, the Navy's fighting ships and transports should not be sent off on secondary missions. But even more basically the peripheral gain from these measures would put us on our own and lose us the great advantage of our UN position, leadership, and support.

Of the various political aids to battle—cease-fire, demilitarized zones, and so on—the only practicable and useful one seemed to be holding the United Nations to a condemnation of the Chinese, useful in itself and as a counteroffensive to Russian resolutions attacking our position regarding Formosa. The concluding discussion on Europe brought the only bright note into this dismal morning. I had urged that we must do something in Europe to break the defense stalemate and the growing neutralism in Germany. The military men all agreed that it would be futile to call another meeting of the Military Committee or of the defense ministers unless agreement was assured in advance. Our position ("one package") not only held up appointment of a Supreme Commander but of a North Atlantic commander of "the ocean sea" as well. General Bedell Smith, head of the Central Intelligence Agency, wisely observed that in any event no commanders could be agreed upon until "El Supremo" was selected. This General Marshall capped by his abrupt, authoritative statement that it was no use talking about divisions, integrated forces, or commanders until we faced and solved the problem whether we wished to moderate our present determined ("one package") stand. That I left to sink in without gilding.

WASHINGTON PLANS NEXT MOVES

The next day, Saturday, was a busy one, working out among ourselves, then going over with General Marshall and together with the President, plans for our course at the United Nations. Ambassadors Warren Austin and Ernest Gross came down from New York to work with us. Suggestions of approaching the Chinese or the Russians with proposals for a cease-fire, either through Sir Benegal Rau or Sir Girja Bajpai of India or the Russians directly through our embassy, were vetoed. By the end of the afternoon the group had provided a memorandum for me to discuss with the President. I myself had to leave them to work on the forthcoming visit of Prime Minister Attlee.

Toward the end of the day, armed with satisfactory briefing notes and intelligence material on Chinese and Russian intentions, I set off for Secretary Marshall's apartment to concert recommendations with him. Then with General Bradley we went to the President about eight o'clock, received his instructions, with which I returned to a group awaiting me in the Department. When the long day closed at ten o'clock, I went wearily home to a famished wife for sustenance, spirituous and solid.

The intelligence paper made these points: Chinese deployment and action in Manchuria and Korea were aimed to make the U.S.-UN position in Korea untenable. The attitude of the regime and the magnitude of military preparations in China itself indicated an appreciation of the risk of general war with the United States that this effort entailed. It was unlikely that the Chinese would have run this risk without some assurances of support from the Soviet Union. Support would probably include, in ascending order: continued provision of materiel, technicians, and perhaps, if necessary, "volunteers"; air units and anti-aircraft batteries for defense of targets in Manchuria should U.S.-UN air attack them; appropriate military support under the Sino-Soviet treaty in the event of U.S.-UN operations against other Chinese territory. Furthermore, the Soviet Union must have appreciated and decided to risk the increased danger of both general U.S.-Chinese war and global war, which Chinese intervention on the then existing scale might cause.

Finally, the Kremlin probably saw advantages to it in the U.S.-Chinese war flowing from the diversion, attrition, and containment of U.S. forces in an indecisive theater; the creation of conflict between the United States and her European allies and the obstruction of NATO plans; the disruption of UN unity against the original aggression in Korea, thus also aiding Communist objectives in Southeast Asia. If, however, the United States should decline the gamble of war with China and withdraw from Korea, the USSR might be counting on collecting the stakes in Korea and Indochina. In any event, the United States Government should expect aggressive Soviet pursuit of its attack on the world position of the United States. Other aggressions in Asia and Europe were not to be counted out.

Doubtless present-day "revisionist" writers would conclude that this paper and the agreement of the three of us with its conclusions as a guide to action represented "overreaction" to Communist action. Even with such help as hindsight gives—which I do not regard as much—I do not agree and am glad that we did not consider the conclusions overdrawn.

After discussing our recommendations for UN action in response to Chinese intervention, the President accepted some and rejected others. We were directed to put immediately on the agenda of the General Assembly an item with an accompanying memorandum raising the Chinese Communist intervention in Korea. It should leave open the action that we would urge after consultation with Attlee, who was arriving in thirty-six hours. We should, however, propose to him to renew in the General Assembly under the "Uniting for Peace" doctrine the resolution that the Soviet Union had vetoed in the Security Council and which combined assurance to China concerning its "legitimate interests" with an urgent appeal to desist from interference in Korea. Its provisions were not wholly appropriate to the changed fortunes of war, but it had the advantage of keeping our own position steady and calm and holding our UN allies together for a while, at least. The President wished us to meet with the Chiefs of Staff first thing the next morning to consider latest developments and report to him again immediately afterward. When all this was reported to my waiting colleagues, I designated Jessup, Rusk, Matthews, and Nitze to go with me and had a message sent to Harriman requesting his attendance.

Reports the next morning depicted MacArthur in a blue funk, sorry for himself, complaining of the restrictions against expanding the war, and sending to press and Pentagon what Lovett called "posterity papers." He cabled the Pentagon on December 3 that "this small command" was now facing an entire

Chinese nation in battle and called for reinforcements. Three days later he spelled out his predicament statistically: "It is estimated that the Chinese Communist forces [opposed to us in North Korea] now total 268,000. . . . In their rear, stretching back to and across the Yalu River is . . . a minimum of 550,000 men. . . . The remainder of Communist China constitutes another . . . reserve . . . about 4 million men under arms."† The Chiefs of Staff at once replied: "We consider that the preservation of your forces is now the primary consideration. Consolidation of forces into beachheads is concurred in."

The meetings of December 3 at the Pentagon and reported at the White House took place amid deepening gloom. The generals told us that in two to three days the situation would reach its crisis and, perhaps, a crash state. X Corps could and should be evacuated, perhaps with heavy losses unless a cease-fire could be arranged. It would rejoin the Eighth Army unless that, too, had to be withdrawn. I opposed efforts to obtain a cease-fire until Mr. Attlee had arrived and been consulted, and until the need for it had become unmistakably clear. The Communist price for a cease-fire could be very high indeed—perhaps too high for any *quid pro quo* other than that of saving our forces. The least they would ask would be withdrawal to the 38th parallel, but more probably from all Korea, to which they might add abandonment of Formosa, and a demand that the Conference of Foreign Ministers with Communist China added take over negotiation of a Japanese peace treaty to diminish our influence in Japan.

General Marshall had raised the night before the dilemma that evacuation of Korea would pose between saving our troops and our national honor. We all agreed again that we could not in good conscience abandon the South Koreans to their Chinese-North Korean enemies. This made evacuation a last-ditch resort. Even a Dunkirk type of operation, General Marshall observed, would be hard if Sino-Soviet air entered the battle. I urged that the bombing of Manchurian airfields and territory also be considered as a last-ditch operation to be undertaken only if necessary to save our forces, and that the decision should not be left to General MacArthur but retained by the President and General Marshall with General Collins remaining at the front to report the facts. I had lost all faith in MacArthur's judgment.

At our meeting in the Pentagon General Ridgway, after pointing out on the map the course of the battle and listening to the usual discussion of the propriety of interference by Washington with the theater, asked to be allowed to state his own opinion. As he has written in his book, "I blurted out . . . that I felt we had already spent too damn much time on debate and that immediate action was needed. We owed it, I insisted, to the men in the field and to the God to whom we must answer for those men's lives to stop talking and to act."[6] This was the first time that someone had expressed what everyone thought— that the Emperor had no clothes on.

Finally turning to the domestic situation, I urged the President to declare the existence of a national emergency. Only in this way could the public be made aware of the seriousness of the situation and that the Government was fully alive to it. Furthermore, the President might soon need the powers the proclamation would bring him to control prices and wages and to establish far-reaching production controls. He indicated agreement.

STEADY AS YOU GO

Early the next morning I met Mr. Attlee's plane on the President's behalf, returning immediately to a small senior-staff meeting at the Department. There I found a short note from George Kennan, so wise and inspiriting that I must quote it in full:

Dear Mr. Secretary:
There is one thing I would like to say in continuation of our discussion of yesterday evening. In international, as in private, life what counts most is not really what happens to someone but how he bears what happens to him. For this reason almost everything depends from here on out on the manner in which we Americans bear what is unquestionably a major failure and disaster to our national fortunes. If we accept it with candor, with dignity, with a resolve to absorb its lessons and to make it good by redoubled and determined effort—starting all over again, if necessary, along the pattern of Pearl Harbor—we need lose neither our self confidence nor our allies nor our power for bargaining, eventually, with the Russians. But if we try to conceal from our own people or from our allies the full measure of our misfortune, or permit ourselves to seek relief in any reactions of bluster or petulance or hysteria, we can easily find this crisis resolving itself into an irreparable deterioration of our world position—and of our confidence in ourselves.   George Kennan

I agreed enthusiastically and read it to the group, which included George himself. We were being infected, I said, by a spirit of defeatism emanating from headquarters in Tokyo. How should we begin to inspire a spirit of candor and redoubled and determined effort? They all had good suggestions. Rusk said that the military men were too dejected. They needed some of the do-or-die spirit that had led the British in two world wars to hang on against overwhelming odds and with no visible hope of success. We had the men, putting the divided forces together again, to take a terrible toll from the Chinese, which was the best way to save both our forces (by stopping the enemy or forcing a tolerable cease-fire) and our position in Asia and Europe. He ended with a radical suggestion, the first foreshadowing of the future. Perhaps the President, he threw out, would wish to think of placing General Collins in supreme command in Korea and letting General MacArthur concentrate on his duties in Japan, including the peace treaty.

Kennan added that the worst possible time to negotiate with the Communists was from a position of defeat. They would correctly interpret it as weakness; threats would only make them refuse altogether to negotiate. Webb contributed that the best way to start on a campaign to revive spirit in the Pentagon was for me to talk with General Marshall.

I called him at once to ask him to discuss with Rusk and Kennan an idea we had been talking over. The Korean campaign had been cursed, I said, by violent swings between exuberant optimism and the deepest depression and despair. Both seemed to me unwarranted. We had had enough logic and analysis; what we needed was dogged determination to find a place to hold and fight the Chinese to a standstill. This was a far better stance for the United States than to talk about withdrawing from Korea or going off on a policy of our own of bombing and blockading China. The General replied that he agreed, with two provisos: first, he must see with what success MacArthur got X Corps out of the east coast; second, we must not dig ourselves into a hole without an exit. I accepted the amendments and sent Rusk and Kennan to see him.

General Marshall repeated to them the conditions to making a stand he had stated to me, but Kennan pushed him. The State Department was not, he said, trying to determine military policy. If it was really true that an attempt to hold a beachhead would mean the loss of our entire forces or any other exorbitant consequence, that was that, and we had to accept it. But we must point out the political implications of this decision and make sure that they were borne in mind in whatever decision might be taken by the military authorities. Lovett, on joining the group, said that he had just come from Capitol Hill, where he and Admiral Sherman had been briefing the House Armed Services Committee. The prevailing feeling there seemed to him to have been that our entire entry into Korea had been a mistake and that we ought to pull out as rapidly as possible. General Marshall was not impressed. This sort of fluctuation in congressional opinion was not new to him. The present mood might not last for long.

Morale in the Pentagon was not improved by General Collins' first report from Tokyo of MacArthur's view that without either a cease-fire or a new policy of air attacks against and blockade of China, reinforcements from the United States and Formosa, and the possibility of using atomic weapons in North Korea, he would have to evacuate his forces.

My own plea to the country for steadiness in adversity had been made in a broadcast on the evening of November 29.[7] In it I described the full violence of the blows we were receiving in the field, as heavy as in the worst days of the desperate, last-ditch struggle about Pusan. No one could guarantee that a wider war would not come. The crisis was extremely serious. Whether reason would prevail was only partly for us to decide. We should hope and strive for the best while we prepared for the worst. The responsibility for doing this, for showing ourselves as a nation possessed of steadiness, moderation, restraint, constancy of purpose, and inflexibility in action, rested not only on members of the Government and the Congress but on every single American citizen. The nation was merely the sum total of these. It would show itself to the world bearing its ill fortunes and bettering them as its citizens showed themselves. Every individual must understand the forces we were dealing with and the role required of us. No one could dodge that responsibility.

The moment I finished speaking the President was on the telephone to cheer and thank me.

50. DECEMBER DESPONDENCY

THE ATTLEE VISIT

DECEMBER OPENED by bringing us a Job's comforter in Clement Attlee, the British Labour Prime Minister. He was a far abler man than Winston Churchill's description of him as "a sheep in sheep's clothing" would imply, but persistently depressing. He spoke, as John Jay Chapman said of President Charles W. Eliot of Harvard, with "all the passion of a woodchuck chewing a carrot." His thought impressed me as a long withdrawing, melancholy sigh. The fright created in London when the British press misconstrued and exaggerated the unfortunate answers President Truman gave to questions at his press conference on November 30, 1950, propelled him across the ocean. This episode followed two earlier ones. In August Secretary of the Navy Francis P. Matthews in a speech in Boston called for preventive war. He was made Ambassador to Ireland. Then General Orville Anderson, Commandant of the Air War College, announced that the Air Force, equipped and ready, only awaited orders to drop its bombs on Moscow. He was retired.

In the course of the press conference mentioned above, the President had stated that "the forces of the United Nations have no intention of abandoning their mission in Korea." Then the questions began, illustrating vividly the dangers that lurk in the American press conference, with its stress on candid answers to questions that seem to be without guile. To one such the President answered that we would "take whatever steps are necessary to meet the military situation, just as we always have." Did that "include the atomic bomb?" It included "every weapon that we have." Had there been "active consideration of [its] use?" "There has always been active consideration of its use." Other questions, unconnected with the bomb, led to obviously correct answers that the application of appropriate weapons to appropriate targets lay within the province of the theater commander.[1] In London the House of Commons, engaged in a two-day foreign policy debate, received an erroneous report that General MacArthur might be given discretion to use the atomic weapon. Cries of alarm came from every quarter of the House, coupled with demands that before the die was cast the British must participate in deciding their fate. At the end of the debate the Prime Minister announced to cheers that he had cabled to the President his desire to fly to Washington for "a wide survey of the problems which face us today."

Meanwhile a damage-control party had gathered at the White House to prepare a "clarifying statement," issued within the hour:

The President wants to make it certain that there is no misinterpretation of his answers to questions at his press conference today about the use of the atom bomb. Naturally, there has been consideration of this subject since the outbreak of the hostilities in Korea, just as there is consideration of the use of all military weapons whenever our forces are in combat. Consideration of the use of any weapon is always implicit in the very possession of that weapon.

However, it should be emphasized, that, by law, only the President can authorize the use of the atom bomb, and no such authorization has been given. If and when such authorization should be given, the military commander in the field would have charge of the tactical delivery of the weapon.

In brief, the replies to the questions at today's press conference do not represent any change in this situation.[2]

Before the morning was much older, Sir Oliver Franks, the British Ambassador, received reassuring words and returned at the end of the afternoon with a telegram from Attlee. The Prime Minister wanted as soon as convenient to discuss with the President three items: the possible extension of the war in the Far East; raw-material supplies and their effect upon our joint ability to play our respective parts; and Western European defense. Asked whether the Prime Minister was seeking greater understanding of the situation and of our intentions or some form of agreements, which would need much more careful staff work here, Sir Oliver replied that the principal pressure was from the British domestic political situation and increasing public anxiety over present developments. He promised a clearer answer to my question and some suggested dates.

By coming to America the Prime Minister had not done with alarums and excursions. On the third morning of his visit, December 6, soon after my arrival at the Department, Deputy Secretary of Defense Lovett telephoned a report and an instruction from the President. Our early-warning radar system in Canada had picked up formations of unidentified objects, presumably aircraft, headed southeast on a course that could bring them over Washington in two or three hours. All interception and defense forces were alerted. I was to inform but not advise the Prime Minister. The Pentagon telephones would be closed for all but emergency defense purposes and he could not talk again. Before he hung up, I asked whether he believed that the objects picked up were Russian bombers. He said that he did not.

Getting Oliver Franks on the telephone, I repeated the message. He asked whether the President had canceled the eleven-thirty meeting with Attlee, and was told that he had not. We agreed to meet there. Before ending the talk, he wondered about the purpose of my message. I suggested fair warning and the opportunity for prayer. As we finished, one of our senior officials burst into the room. How he had picked up the rumor I do not know, perhaps from the Pentagon. He wanted to telephone his wife to get out of town, and to have important files moved to the basement. I refused to permit him to do either and gave him the choice of a word-of-honor commitment not to mention the matter to anyone or being put under security detention. He wisely cooled off and chose the former. When we reached the White House, Lovett told us that the unidentified objects had disappeared. His guess was that they had been geese.

In the State Department one never lacks helpful suggestions. Two days before Prime Minister Attlee arrived, one of these came from Bernard M. Baruch via Mr. Lovett as agent for his apparently reluctant chief, General Marshall. In Mr. Baruch's view the American people increasingly favored use of atomic weapons in Korea, though he and they were imprecise about where and against whom. In Mr. Baruch's opinion the President should convey the fact of this popular attitude to Mr. Attlee, regretfully, but not minimizing its strength. The stated purpose of doing so was to lead an alarmed Prime Minister to return to Europe to work out and insist upon some workable plan of appeasement in Korea, thus relieving the President, General Marshall, and me of the burden of doing so. Mr. Lovett declared that his only responsibility for this message was to deliver it; I wished him to note that my only response or responsibility was to listen to him do so.

Our five days of talks are not worth a day-by-day, play-by-play account. The chief impression they left with me was a deep dislike and distrust of the "summit conference" as a diplomatic instrument. Contrary to popular belief, Sir Winston Churchill and President Roosevelt did not invent it and, with perhaps two notable exceptions—the meetings of Münster and Osnabrück, which produced the Peace of Westphalia after the Thirty Years War (1648) and the Congress of Vienna (1814), and possibly the Congress of Berlin in 1878—it has not been successful. Although the summit may be high and therefore glamorous, some of its participants have often been ill prepared and others unreliable —or both, as in the case of the meeting of Francis I and Henry VIII at the Field of Cloth of Gold in 1520. The result has all too often been a gamble, the experience nerve-racking, and the results unsatisfactory. Philippe de Comines, a competent diplomatist, expressed the views of many of his latter-day colleagues that "two great Princes who wish to establish good personal relations should never meet each other face-to-face, but ought to communicate through good and wise ambassadors."[3] Frank I. Cobb counseled Colonel House in a memorandum of November 4, 1918, that "the moment President Wilson sits at the council table with these Prime Ministers and Foreign Secretaries he has lost all the power that comes from distance and detachment. . . . He becomes merely a negotiator dealing with other negotiators."[4]

When a chief of state or head of government makes a fumble, the goal line is open behind him. This I was to learn in my first experience with this dangerous diplomatic method, which has such attraction for American presidents.

The first purpose of the British group was to find out what was going on and why in North Korea. The explanation was entrusted to General Bradley, cross-examined by Field Marshal Sir William Slim, and took up most of our first day. The truth was hard to state and harder to believe. But Omar Bradley's patent integrity was equal to the first task, which he did not attempt to gloss. Before the meetings ended, General Collins had returned from the front and reported to the joint group. The long retreat had almost reached the 38th parallel. The prospect of extracting X Corps from the east coast appeared good.

Generals Walker, MacArthur, and Collins all believed that a line south of Seoul could be held. The hysteria about evacuation had, temporarily at least, subsided.

As the Prime Minister became reassured that alarm over the safety of our troops would not drive us to some ill-considered use of atomic weapons, his purposes in coming emerged more clearly. He wished us to end our conflict with the Chinese in order to resume active participation in security for Europe; to resume also, as in the Second World War, a joint control with Britain of the allocation and pricing of raw materials, since the inevitable growth of rearmament would make them scarce and dear; and, finally, he wished Britain to be admitted to some participation with us in any future decision to use nuclear weapons. The Congress was not far behind us in sensing that Mr. Attlee had not come here for a lecture on current events. Indeed, while the conference was going on, twenty-four Republican senators introduced and debated vigorously, but failed to pass, a resolution requiring ratification by the Senate, as of a treaty, of any agreement made by the President and Prime Minister. At the same time in New York and through the American press our public was regaled by attacks upon the United States from Soviet Ambassador Malik and special Chinese Communist envoy General Wu Hsiu-chuan. The General's presence resulted from an invitation of the Security Council to discuss what it politely termed the "new turn of events" in Korea. He chose instead to join in support of Malik's resolutions condemning American "aggression" in Formosa and Korea. While our allies voted these resolutions down, their high enthusiasm of the autumn had evaporated, and none of them, including the British, would join in a counteroffensive in the United Nations against Chinese intervention. The proceedings in both Washington and New York were not helpful in rallying the country to meet major military reverses and to bear the vagaries of a recalcitrant general. I wished then, as often before and since, that the headquarters of the United Nations were anywhere except in our own country.

Mr. Attlee's method of discussion was that of the suave rather than the bellicose cross-examiner. He early noticed a tendency of the President to show concurrence or the reverse in each statement of his interlocutor as he went along. Framing his statements to draw presidential agreement with his exposition, he soon led the President well onto the flypaper. At the second meeting, as the procedure started again, I stepped on the President's foot and suggested that it might be helpful to the Prime Minister to let him complete his whole statement without interruption. It was far from helpful to the Prime Minister, as his glance at me indicated, but we fared better.

The line of Mr. Attlee's argument was that the position of our forces in Korea was so weak and precarious that we must pay for a cease-fire to extricate them. He believed that withdrawal from Korea and Formosa and the Chinese seat in the United Nations for the Communists would not be too high a price. There was nothing, he warned us, more important than retaining the good opinion of Asia. I remarked acidly that the security of the United States was more important. President Truman and General Marshall added that the preservation of our defenses in the western Pacific and the belief of the Asian peoples in our fighting power were a path to securing their good opinion.

Intervening at the President's request, I gave the British comfort where they seemed entitled to it. The central opponent, I said, was not China but the Soviet Union. There had been foolish and irresponsible talk, repudiated by the Administration, for all-out war against China. Not many of the President's advisers would urge him to follow that course with the involvement it implied. On the other hand, the moment seemed to me the worst one for negotiation with the Russians since 1917. They saw themselves holding the cards and would concede nothing.

At the next meeting I suggested that Mr. Attlee would be making a serious mistake to believe that the American people would follow a leadership that proposed a vigorous policy of action against aggression on one ocean front while accepting defeat on the other. The public mind was not subtle enough to understand so ambivalent a policy, which was fortunate because it would be a wrong policy. Discussion of priorities was one thing; wholly different attitudes on the same issue on two sides of the world was another. We had with the almost unanimous approval of our allies gone after a small aggressor in Korea. Now a big one had come along and given us a licking. To cut, run, and abandon the whole enterprise was not acceptable conduct. The Chinese might be able to force it on us, but I doubted it. There was a great difference between being forced out and getting out. Upon this issue the President, General Marshall, and General Bradley moved up their big guns. After some exchanges on whether the Chinese were Soviet satellites or not and whether the Cairo declaration led logically to Formosa's going to the Chinese Communists, the engagement ended without any meeting of minds.

Since the talks were not going well, Sir Oliver Franks with the two senior Foreign Office officials, Roger Makins and R. H. Scott, and I with Matthews, Jessup, Nitze, and Rusk tried meeting informally each day to agree on how the agenda for the next should be handled. But the experiment did not work. The same records were played over again to less receptive ears.

When we came to the raw-material situation, we agreed entirely with the British on the problem and the need for allocation and price control but could not get them to understand that 1950 was not 1941–45. Then we two were the only allies able to impose worldwide controls. In 1950 neither producers nor consumers would tolerate Anglo-American control, nor did any alternative method come to mind. We set up study groups to devise, if possible, some methods for voluntary arrangements open to others, but not much came of it.

Attlee not only did not want to discuss European defense but positively eluded attempts to draw him into it, leaving discussion to his field and air marshals, Slim and Tedder. Yet the subject called urgently for an agreed approach by us both. Since the defense ministers' talks in October, the Soviet Union had put on a major campaign to scare the Germans and Western Europeans out of including Germany in defense arrangements. First of all, notes were sent to the British, French, and ourselves informing us that the Soviet Government would "not tolerate such measures [as we had discussed together in September] . . . aimed at reviving the German regular army in Western Germany," denouncing us for asserting that East German police units were in reality military ones, and turning the argument back on us. Then a conference of Eastern European foreign ministers, meeting at Prague with Molotov presiding, demanded a four-power agreement to prevent German rearmament, a treaty of peace with Germany, and its unification through an all-German council with equal representation of East and West Germany. This was followed by another Soviet note of November 3, 1950, to the three Western occupying powers requesting without delay a meeting of the Council of Foreign Ministers to carry out the Potsdam pledge to demilitarize Germany. Deputy Premier Nicolai Bulganin at the celebration of the October (Old Style) Revolution made a stump speech calling upon the Soviet people to stand up for their rights "with arms in hand."

To impress the British and French again with the intensity of Russian objection to associating Germany with defense measures, notes were sent to them insisting that this association advocated by the United States ran directly counter to both the Franco-Soviet and the British-Soviet treaties. Thus by December our proposals had produced not only division within the alliance but a massive attack from the opposition. At Brussels we would need help both to persuade the French and to instill courage into all our allies.

At the British Embassy after dinner on December 6, Field Marshal Slim and Marshal of the Air Force Lord Tedder said to me sorrowfully that their chief had muffed the ball I had passed to him during the European defense talks. They wished to have another try that evening and rounded up a group that included the President, the Prime Minister, Generals Marshall and Bradley, our host, and themselves. We talked from nine-thirty till after midnight. Asked for an agenda, I saw two main points. First, the President and General Marshall must be convinced that the British were doing or would do all they could toward European defense. Rightly or wrongly, the country and the Congress were not convinced of this, which made strengthening the American contribution very difficult. Second, the only way to make progress with NATO was for our two countries to go ahead and through a judicious combination of bullying and cajolery get the others to follow. We could not do it alone and most of our talk that day had been off the point.

Attlee, who apparently liked to operate behind a smoke screen, proceeded to get further off the point. He raised the "difficult and delicate question" of General MacArthur's conduct of the Korean war and absence of any allied say in what was done. Our two generals defended MacArthur and said that a war could not be run by a committee. The British had been consulted on matters tending to extend the war, such as the "hot pursuit" of enemy planes into Manchuria and the bombing of airfields there, and their views had been reflected in the action taken. The President added that since all involved had confided the unified command to the United States we would have to run it as long as that situation continued and we continued to supply so preponderantly the means and men to carry on the war. Supporting the President, I pleaded incompetence to discuss General MacArthur's military ability or judgment, but pointed out that so far as the strategic conduct of the war was concerned the

Prime Minister and his advisers had been discussing that question for three days with our highest advisers, including the Commander in Chief himself. As I recalled, aside from the political purpose of ending the war as soon as possible, the Prime Minister had no criticism of the plan of campaign outlined to him. The President capped this rather bluntly by stating that we would stay in Korea and fight. If we had support from others, fine; if not, we would stay on anyway. On this note the Slim-Tedder second try sputtered out. However, they did noble work on the communiqué.

On the last day of the talks we had one of those close calls that lurk in summit meetings. General Collins had given his report from Korea. We were waiting in the Cabinet Room of the White House for a draft from the communiqué writers. The President had taken the Prime Minister to the privacy of his study. When secretaries distributed copies of the draft, our chiefs came back. They had, said the President cheerfully, been discussing the atomic weapon and agreed that neither of us would use these weapons without prior consultation with the other. No one spoke. The President asked the chief drafter to begin reading the communiqué for amendments. As he started, Lovett leaned over my shoulder to say that we were teetering on the edge of great trouble and that I must carry the ball. A whispered conversation with the President and a note passed across the table to Oliver Franks brought the three of us and the Prime Minister together in the President's office, while others continued revision of the draft.

I pointed out that over and over again the President had insisted that no commitment of any sort to anyone limited his duty and power under the law to authorize use of the atomic weapon if he believed it necessary in the defense of the country, and that he had gone far in declaring that he would not change that position. If he should attempt to change it, he would not be successful, since Congress would not permit it. The resolution of the twenty-four Republican senators gave fair warning of the temper of Congress. The suggestion he had made in the Cabinet Room would open a most vicious offensive against him and the British, whereas a program of keeping in close touch with the Prime Minister in all world situations that might threaten to move toward violence and hostilities of any kind would be widely approved.

All agreed with this, albeit Mr. Attlee a little sadly, and we began drafting a suitable paragraph, Oliver Franks acting as scribe. The President pulled out the slide at the left of his desk. Oliver left his chair and knelt between mine and Attlee's to write on it. "I think that this is the first time," said the President, "that a British Ambassador has knelt before an American President." Sir Oliver went right on drafting and produced a solution, which was inserted without comment in the communiqué when we returned to the Cabinet Room: "The President stated that it was his hope that world conditions would never call for the use of the atomic bomb. The President told the Prime Minister that it was also his desire to keep the Prime Minister at all times informed of developments which might bring about a change in the situation."[5]

The communiqué ended my first summit conference, accompanied by an ungranted prayer that I might be spared another, and by the grateful recognition of the gap between Mr. Attlee's brief and the consent decree—to use lawyers' terms—that he had signed.

Congressional and public response to the communiqué was, on the whole, good. In the Senate committee the two senior members, Connally and Wiley, stalwart soldiers and sensible men, carried the others along in a statement, after my meeting with them, that pretty well concluded the fuss. There was little to add, they said, to so complete a communiqué. One thing was clear to them— that the British and American positions were "substantially closer than would have appeared a week ago." If ever a true word was spoken this was it. Senator Knowland was, of course, "shocked"; he saw "the making of a Far Eastern Munich contained in its language." President Syngman Rhee strangely thought that "it would have been better if the United Nations had not helped us at all if we are to be abandoned now." However, the furor that the announcement of the Attlee visit had kicked up fizzled out and was soon forgotten.

A NATIONAL EMERGENCY PROCLAIMED

As noted earlier, the President had been considering for some time the suggestion that a national emergency be proclaimed, more funds be obtained, production of military equipment enhanced, and controls on the economy imposed. On December 13 he invited leaders of both parties to the White House to discuss it.

The meeting gave rise to a curious episode, revealing the bitterness of the time. The Republicans, among whom were Senators Taft, Wherry, and Alexander Smith, remained unusually silent and noncommittal during the meeting. After it ended and the Cabinet table was being tidied up, a paper on stationery of the Republican Policy Committee but not otherwise identifiable was found where Senator Wherry had been sitting. It advised against Republican involvement in the proclamation of a national emergency, which was described as designed to gain additional powers for the President, in order to preserve the party's position in case of possible impeachment proceedings. It was later reported to me that one of the White House staff telephoned Wherry to report that a sealed envelope had been found where he had been sitting and to ask whether he had lost anything. He was said to have replied, "So that's where I left it!" The envelope was returned—sealed.

The attack, however, was not on the President but on me. I have already recounted in Chapter 40 the resolutions of House and Senate Republican members asking the President to remove me from office and his indignant rejection of them.

THE BRUSSELS CONFERENCE

In the middle of December, Administration attention, freed from its crisis preoccupation with Korea, turned to the development of European defense, which had been quietly maturing since October. General Marshall, as I have related, had mitigated the rigidity of the military view sufficiently to permit the appointment of an American as Supreme Commander with command of an integrated force, provided the principle of German participation in it was accepted and steps inaugurated to bring it to pass. The French had also accepted "the Spofford Plan"—a proposal that the unit for incorporation of German troops into the unified command should be the regimental combat team, a self-contained unit of approximately six thousand men, on condition that this be combined with approval of the longer-term goal of a European Army, a refinement and improvement of the Pleven Plan. We had obtained Attlee's grudging acquiescence in this compromise during the Washington visit.

While a Supreme Allied Commander had precedents in both world wars, including Marshal Foch in France and Field Marshal Sir Henry Maitland Wilson in Italy, we now had to face a critical and censorious opposition, which would be looking for constitutional flaws in any scheme. This prospect made attention necessary to niceties in the chain of command from our constitutional Commander in Chief, the President, through the Supreme Allied Commander in Europe to our forces in the field. The prevalent supposition that the Supreme Commander would be General Eisenhower did not assure acquiescence in the scheme of command, as his Republicanism was not then a matter of public knowledge, or even known to the President. As Mr. Truman has told us, he regarded the General in 1948 as a potential candidate of Democratic liberals for the nomination for the Presidency, an aspiration which the General assured him he did not have, but for other than party reasons.[6] Each of our allies also had its own technical political problem.

Our difficulties were solved by the "two hat" theory. General Eisenhower as Supreme Commander Allied Forces Europe would also be appointed Commander U.S. Forces Europe, receiving the latter authority directly from the President. With our allies we arranged that the NATO Council should ask the President to make available a United States officer to be Supreme Commander, adding that due to its great respect for and confidence in General Eisenhower, the council would be happy if the President's choice should fall on him. The President would acquiesce. The council would appoint General Eisenhower as Supreme Commander of the integrated force and each government would put under his command its troops assigned to the integrated force.

With Frank Pace, Secretary of the Army, as my companion and colleague, we took off in the President's plane, *Independence,* for Europe and the beginning of five strenuous days. The brisk tempo began on our arrival in Brussels at twelve-thirty, with a drive to the Foreign Ministry to call on Mr. van Zeeland, the Minister, then to the embassy for a change of clothes and lunch, and on to a meeting of the NATO Council. Frank Pace was amused at the smoothness with which proceedings moved through the preliminary stages toward final action the next day. It was, he said, reminiscent of the Arkansas legislature, where the machine began with a simple majority and went on to attain unanimity. Our aim was acceptance of the communications from the council to the President and back without amendments, which would surely cause confusion at both ends. Appropriately enough, the code name for the proposed message from the council was "Courage," and for the President's reply it was "Unity."

The atmosphere of the meeting was tinged with fear, for the Russian gambit had worked. George Perkins, Assistant Secretary for European Affairs, reported that Hervé Alphand, Schuman's assistant, took him aside to ask, "Do you really think we are going to be in war in three months?" Perkins gathered further that the President's answer to the Republican senators had put to rest doubts about my position and future, but that the assembled company was puzzled and worried about our country's state of mind. The meeting adjourned in time for the ministers to dress for van Zeeland's dinner and reception after it. Then back we went to the embassy for a midnight meeting.

The nineteenth started with a review by me for the American civilian and military officers in Brussels of the crowding events of the past two or three weeks. The NATO meeting began at ten o'clock and went so smoothly that we were able to send cable "Courage" shortly after noon and make our way to the palace to be received by young Prince Royal Baudouin, to whom King Leopold had recently transferred his royal powers. I found him very touching. Barely twenty years of age, his father a storm center in Belgium, his mother killed in a motor accident, he bore great responsibilities looking solemn and vulnerable in heavy spectacles. I thought of my own son, ten years older, as the Prince drew me aside to ask me shyly Alphand's question to Perkins—did I think war was coming? I did not, but assured him with even more conviction than I had that this cup would not come to him.

At one-fifteen the council met again to receive the President's reply, "Unity." By four o'clock we had established the integrated force, assigned troops to give it substance, and appointed General Eisenhower to command it. We also set up a Military Production and Supply Board, which subsequently proved to be a failure. At five, refreshed by a hasty lunch, I met with Schuman, Bevin, and our three High Commissioners in Bonn for a four-hour discussion of German participation. Here, too, results of the Russian blitzkrieg were apparent. Bevin wanted to go slowly on defense arrangements with the Germans. (God knows we had done so and would continue to do so without need of exhortation!) Schuman kept finding difficulties in the four-power agreements. I lost patience with this attitude and argued that we must beware of being mesmerized into accepting the Russian position that we were bound by these agreements but they were not. We must get on with the rest of our program and not be tied up by Yalta or Potsdam—documents outmoded and dead. On the other side, we must make no further concessions to the Germans until they carried out the New York decisions, acknowledged their debts, and shouldered their proper burdens, but then be ready to move ahead toward equality and modification of the occupation.

We authorized two simultaneous approaches to German participation: one, by the High Commissioners to Adenauer on the Spofford Plan for the raising of German forces (these discussions began on December 21); the other, to provide the institutional framework of the European Defense Community, of great promise and ill fate. Thence we took ourselves back to Bob Murphy's embassy residence for a sorely needed cocktail and an excellent ten o'clock dinner. On the way I called his attention to, and besought his intercession with the Belgian army to correct, a peculiarity of our escort. Not only had we the usual motorcycle police but an army weapons carrier forward and another aft, each—unless my eye was off—with its swivel-mounted machine gun pointed directly at me. Bob raised the possibility that I might be the safest man in the car.

Of all the takeoffs of the beloved *Independence,* the one I least enjoy recalling took place the next morning, December 20. Heavy overcast and freezing fog blotted out even the side lights of the runway more than two lights ahead; frozen rutted slush promised a real shaking-up if we could start. An hour or more passed while we waited near the plane for a momentary lifting of the fog, while crews sprayed the *Independence* with glycerine to prevent ice coating. At last we got the signal and, heavily strapped in our seats, went on a veritable buckboard ride down the runway. The liftoff brought blessed smoothness and, in minutes, bright sunshine above a five-hundred-foot fog. The plane headed for the Azores, as all Western Europe and Iceland were closed in. As we crossed the coast of France, the fog bank formed a perfect map of the Europe coast line below us. A hospitable layover in the Azores, which I had visited forty years before with my father, refreshed us, while the winds and weather became more favorable over eastern Canada. Then we resumed our journey via Stephensville, arriving in Washington at three o'clock in the morning on December 21, and so to bed. The next morning the President received me, my mission accomplished; I was full of gratitude for his magnificent support of me. He told me of Mr. Hoover's speech of thirty-six hours before, a follow-up of the Taft re-examinist one.

THE GREAT DEBATE OPENS

On December 22 the two foreign affairs committees on Capitol Hill awaited my appearance to tell them about Brussels, a matter of pure protocol and formality. There all was affability. Nothing sweetens relations between the Secretary and his guardian committees like a little success. The late unpleasantness about my dismissal was forgotten, a political charade born of MacArthur's willful folly in Korea and our own troubles with our allies. Congressional displays of emotion are stage properties wherein indignation and anger are as false as bonhommie.

The Great Debate, however, was more serious—although, as it turned out, more critical than serious. On December 12 our somewhat less than reliable former Ambassador in London, Joseph P. Kennedy, as yet undistinguished through his progeny, described American policy as "suicidal" and "politically and morally bankrupt," denounced a weak United Nations and ungrateful allies, and demanded withdrawal from Korea, Berlin, and the defense of Western Europe, a refrain not unfamiliar seventeen years later. The main statement of the charges, however, was made by former President Herbert Hoover. Briefly put, Mr. Hoover laid down certain postulates, from which he derived governing principles.[7] The postulates:

1. A land war by sparse non-Communist forces against the Communist land mass would be a war without victory—we could never reach Moscow.

2. The United States alone by air and sea power could prevent Communist invasion of the western hemisphere.

3. Atomic weapons were far less dominant than once thought.

4. The United Nations had been defeated in Korea by Communist China.

Based on these postulates, Mr. Hoover proposed "certain principles and action":

First and fundamental, "preserve this Western Hemisphere Gibraltar of Western Civilization."

Second, with air and sea forces hold the oceans, with one frontier on Britain and the other on Japan, Formosa, and the Philippines.

Third, arm our air and sea forces to the teeth.

Fourth, after this initial outlay, reduce expenditures, balance the budget, avoid inflation.

Fifth, aid the hungry of the world.

Sixth, no appeasement, and no more Teherans and Yaltas.

Seventh, the prime obligation to defend Europe should rest with the nations of Europe—America could not create or buy spiritual force for them.

Europe, as seen on my recent visit, had been worried and frightened, but had responded to leadership and action. The stench of spiritless defeat, of death of high hopes and broad purposes, given off by these statements deeply shocked me. It took a day of talking with my associates for the situation to sink in. That afternoon would usher in the Christmas weekend, leaving no time for speech writing; so, with a few notes, I went to a December 22 press conference.[8] How could one make that audience see that "no man, having put his hand to the plow, and looking back is fit for the kingdom of God"—or for confidence in this world. To invoke the compulsion of national decision would be useless, for a nation is no more than a constantly changing stream of persons who, having experienced and decided, give way to strangers to both the experience and the decision. Constancy is the result of continued relearning and faith.

The best way of explaining what was done at Brussels, I said at the press conference, was to describe it as the conclusion of a chapter in a book in which the previous chapters were history and chapters to come would be written by future action. The book dealt with our search with others for means and methods to bring about peace and security. Each chapter recorded a struggle between those who believed in the search and the effort and those who thought it futile, who urged retirement to our own continent, there to isolate ourselves from world problems and secure ourselves from world dangers. The decision was never unanimous and the debate would doubtless go on, as it was going on at that very moment. These debates had brought our government and, so far, a majority of our people to a number of conclusions, which had seemed controlling:

First, American withdrawal to this hemisphere would give to the Soviet Union such a dominating position over so vast an area, population, and military and economic resources as would make our problems unmanageable.

Second, placed in such a position, the Soviet Union would have the capability and desire to nullify such power to impede Soviet plans as we might possess.

Third, such developments would minimize the possibility through evolution or negotiation, or both, of a peaceful adjustment of interests on any basis other than Soviet desires.

Fourth, the alternative to acceptance of Soviet will would appear to be an appeal to the ultimate violence of nuclear weapons.

Fifth, in the meantime, however, it appeared likely that isolation in Fortress America or the "Gibraltar of the Western Hemisphere" would so change the spacious freedom of American life as to undermine its cultural, moral, political, and constitutional bases.

These conclusions had led Government and people to reject "any policy of sitting quivering in a storm cellar waiting for whatever fate others may wish to prepare for us." We were resolved to build our strength side by side with our allies, calling upon the entire free world to maintain its freedom, also.

In other words, having put our hands to the plow, we would not look back but remember that "he that ploweth should plow in hope." Thus the pleadings were filed and the case was ready for argument at the next term of court.

Section C. 1951: Year of Troubles and Progress

51. CALMING WORRIES AT HOME
AND TO THE SOUTH

THE GREAT DEBATE FLARES AND FIZZLES

EVEN BEFORE THE debate on the stationing of American troops in Europe opened, there were hints that it would not be a purely party battle, but rather an assault by the bipartisan right upon the Administration's postwar foreign policy. As 1950 closed, Mr. Dulles in a nationwide broadcast pointed out flaws in the thesis that the undoubted Soviet threat called for abandonment of the whole idea of collective security and concentration upon building western hemisphere defenses. Later, when the debate was well launched, Governor Dewey took a more forthright position that more troops should be sent to Europe and the home front mobilized more quickly. Governor Harold Stassen and General Lucius Clay also supported sending the troops.

The leader of the opponents, as might have been expected, was Senator Robert Taft. He it was who opened their argument by a long speech in the Senate on January 5, 1951. The Senator's attack was no narrow argument against the deployment of troops abroad, but a smashing attack against the whole internationalist position. It suffered from a defect of Taft's otherwise excellent mind, which Justice Holmes found also in that of Justice John Marshall Harlan the elder. "Harlan's mind," he said, "was like a vise, the jaws of which did not meet. It only held the larger objects." Taft asked and gave answers to three questions: Could the United Nations maintain or restore peace? How should we prepare militarily for a Russian attack against us and our allies? Could a proposed policy be maintained without inflation and a loss of liberty at home? A fourth—how to win the battle for men's minds against communism —seemed to disappear in the delivery.

His answer to the first question, a flat no, was and is hard to quarrel with; the proposed remedy was not so clear. The United States should "formulate . . . an ideal organization, insist upon a full discussion . . . and if . . . finally blocked by Soviet Russia, bring about the dissolution of the United Nations and the formation of a new organization which could be an effective weapon for peace."[1] What this ideal organization was to be, how it was to be brought into existence, and how this proposal squared with his next were matters not disclosed; presumably they were details to be worked out.

The Senator's military policy, like Mr. Hoover's, was based primarily on air and sea forces. Superiority in these arms throughout the world, he argued, could achieve other purposes than defense of America: assistance to free nations in preserving their freedom and maintenance of a balance of power under which more peaceful relations could be developed. He did not argue for a complete abandonment of the rest of the world, but rather that we interest ourselves in areas from which Communist influence could be excluded by means of effective control of air and sea. This, he believed, had been done for the past five years in Europe.

On the immediate question the Senator took the position that the Pentagon had just abandoned and added his own notion that the President had no power to send troops abroad without congressional authority. If, he argued, we assumed responsibility for leadership and command in NATO, we would be constantly called on to increase our commitment. Furthermore, we would add to the likelihood of war by provoking the Russians to anticipate suspected aggression. The better policy would be to encourage the Europeans to develop their own forces and to let our air and sea forces cooperate with them in the defense of Europe. Later on, if and when our allies showed the capacity to develop a defense with a good chance of success, he would "not object to committing some limited number of American divisions to work with them in the general spirit of the Atlantic Pact."[2]

President Truman used to say that budget figures revealed far more of proposed policy than speeches. The Senator gave his own figures in the January speech: twenty billion dollars for a Navy and Air Force of seven hundred thousand men each, the money equally divided between current operations and new equipment; twenty billion dollars for an army of one and a half million men; and twenty-five billion dollars for all other expenditures, including foreign assistance, a total national budget of sixty-five billion dollars. The President's budget for fiscal 1952 (July 1, 1951–June 30, 1952) went to Congress on January 15. In it he asked for appropriations of seventy-two billion dollars and new contract authority (under which payments and hence appropriations would be required in later years) of ninety-four billion dollars. The appropriation request was divided forty-one billion four hundred million dollars for the military services, seven and a half billion for foreign assistance, and twenty-three billion for domestic purposes. Of the ninety-four billion dollars for contract authority, seventy-one billion was for military and foreign procurement, as was a good deal of the increase of ninety per cent of the appropriations requested for these items over the prior year. Whereas the Senator posited his figures upon a military establishment of two million nine hundred thousand men, the President's were based upon one of three and a half million. The difference between these conceptions of our need for rearmament was as great as the change recommended by the National Security Council paper of the preceding spring, NSC-68, discussed in Chapter 41.

Senator Taft, on the day of the President's budget message, called on Congress to assert itself and its right to determine fundamental principles of foreign policy, adding that he was "quite prepared to sit down with the President . . . or anyone on the majority side, and try to work out a program which could command the unanimous and consistent support of the people of the United States."[3] Seeing the danger of crossing up communication with our friends on the Foreign Relations Committee, I commented that the usual channel for communication with the Senate was through that committee.

While these exchanges were going on, a newcomer to this controversy with an important stake in it entered the arena, the new Supreme Commander, General of the Army Dwight D. Eisenhower. Coming to call on me on January 4 with General Alfred Gruenther, who one day was to occupy the same post, he spent several hours going over past history and present and future problems. Until the election campaign of 1952 our relations were cordial and he professed to find them, as I did, helpful. I was not, however, drawn to him as were so many who were exposed to his personality. Since it had been some time since he had turned over his duties in Germany to General Clay, we went over the political background of the treaty and something of the psychological purposes and problems of military integration. What I said survives and, as it gives an inside and contemporaneous view of the Government's case in the Great Debate, it may be worthwhile to summarize it.

Briefing the Supreme Commander · The exposition went as follows: At the end of the war, despite warnings of some far-sighted persons in the West, hope spread that the Soviet Union would cooperate with its former allies in an era of peaceful reconstruction. This soon proved to be an illusion, as was demonstrated by ruthless action of the Soviet Government and the various communist parties toward a dominating position in Europe and Asia. In this they were aided by the fact that the complex societies of Europe recovered more slowly from the war's social, political, and economic dislocation than did the simpler organism of Russia driven through brutal hardships by a totalitarian state.

Assuming leadership, since to do otherwise was impossible, the United States tackled the economic problem first, as the basic one, and obtained immediate results to a point. However, economic measures alone were insufficient to create the strength necessary to allay the fear of Communist takeover through internal subversion aided by foreign force, already demonstrated in Greece and Iran and possible anywhere in Europe. This apprehension negatived the return of native capital, upon which real recovery must depend. To meet this need, the North Atlantic Treaty sought to add the power of the United States to create a true balance of power in Europe as a stabilizing and preventive force. The treaty was more than a purely military treaty. It was a means and a vehicle for closer political, economic, and security cooperation with Western Europe. Together with the Inter-American Treaty, its purpose was to provide not only physical protection but the sense of security necessary to keep these two areas, which were essential to a viable free world and more susceptible than others to our influence, free from Communist penetration, physical or political. Hence these two treaties were fundamental to our foreign policies.

The first fifteen months of the treaty had been spent in determining its function and building a structure for its development. The search for the former had passed through the conception of a purely political engagement to aid a victim of aggression after the trouble had started and had come to rest on the notion of deterrence, not liberation. This had found expression in organization with the decision to create a force in being and in place, integrated in strategy and command. The task now was to develop the strategy and the force. The latter raised the difficult question of German participation, which I described.

The role of the Supreme Commander would be to become the embodiment of NATO. Europe had no confidence in committees or councils; it looked to men. The Supreme Commander's greatest handicap was being created at this very moment here at home by the current debate, carrying to Europe with every new broadcast doubts of American constancy toward its defense. This we must terminate as soon as possible. I described the attitudes of the European countries toward the Commander's efforts, dividing them into the more solid and steady northern countries with the smallest communist parties—the United Kingdom, Norway, Denmark, and the Netherlands; the more volatile southern group swinging from optimism to despair—Belgium, France, Italy, and Portugal; and vitally important Germany, beginning to realize her importance and inclined to bargain. All of us in Europe and America must be brought to see that none of us had any alternative but to provide adequate defensive strength and unity. The Supreme Commander would be the embodiment, the constant and visible leader, of that aspiration.

The Debate Reaches Its Apogee · All through January the debate continued with mounting intensity, the Government gaining encouragement from a manifesto of eight hundred seventy-five social scientists supporting me and from speeches by two important Republicans, Senators Lodge and Knowland, in favor of troops for Europe. The opposition was aided by the argument of two Democrats, Senators George and Douglas, that the President should obtain congressional approval, by the panic in the United Nations caused by the Eighth Army's loss of Seoul and continued retreat to the Han River line, and by "A Declaration of Policy," signed by a hundred and eighteen Republicans in the House, which called upon the Administration to revise its "tragic" and "costly" foreign programs, to adopt in essence the Hoover policy, and (their own idea) to "conclude peace treaties with Germany, Japan, and Austria," though with whom and how they did not reveal. On January 22 Senator Wherry called for hearings on the troop question. There the issue rested until General Eisenhower's report on his tour of NATO capitals. This he gave to an informal joint session of the House and Senate on February 1,[4] followed up by a private session with the Armed Services and Foreign Relations committees. These committees had already received a resolution from Senator Wherry on January 8 which provided that "no ground forces of the United States should be assigned to duty in the European area for the purposes of the North Atlantic Treaty pending the formation of a policy with respect thereto by the Congress."[5]

The General reported favorably on the spirit of determination and will to resist in Europe, recommended that in the absence of any other acceptable leader the United States should take the leadership, that American troops in

Europe should be increased but that no rigid formula or limit should be laid down, and that "the great crying need today . . . is equipment." Within the limits of solvency we should "go to the production of equipment exactly as if we were preparing for an emergency and war." This support of the Administration's proposals and budget Senator Taft branded as only making the matter "more hazy and indefinite and uncertain in outline"—a reaction to the General's attitudes that the Senator was perhaps to experience more often in later years. At the moment, however, it caused him to waver; he "would not object," he said, "to a few more divisions, simply to show the Europeans that we are interested and will participate in the more difficult job of land warfare while we carry out also our larger obligations."

General Marshall Damps the Fire • Into this gap in the line General Marshall, testifying before the joint committees on Feburary 15,[6] drove his counterattack with devastating effect. How many was "a few more"? With the President's consent, General Marshall revealed in public testimony what the Administration had in mind. It was four more divisions, making a total of six. Neither he nor General Bradley would be led into making that number a ceiling. It was, at the time, the meeting point of need and convenience; that point could in the future move up or down. They refused to speculate. Senator Taft was neatly caught. "A few" was more than two, three anyway, which reduced the great strategic issue, as had been stated by President Hoover—of holding the oceans by air and sea power versus involvement on land—to an argument over one division to Europe.

Realizing his predicament, Senator Taft tried to shift his front under attack, a difficult maneuver at best, to the issue of constitutional policy. He did not object, he said after General Marshall had finished his testimony, to the four divisions, which was "about what [he] expected." But "no divisions should be committed to an international army until an agreement is reached with the other countries of the Atlantic Pact . . . and approved by Congress. Then we can thresh out the question of limiting the number of troops we provide."[7] This new position amounted to an invitation to a protracted filibuster that could last years and insure the death of the integrated force and command. General Bradley and I hammered it[8] when we followed General Marshall.

We both attacked the problem from the same point of view: the principal goal was deterrence of aggression in whatever form; the pressing need, immediacy of action to correct the invitation to our opponents offered by continued weakness. General Bradley, one of the best colleagues in a fight I have ever known, took the military side, I the political. The object of our plan, I said, was "to prevent an attack; to prevent Europe from being conquered by other means; and to prevent Europe from being taken by force. . . . Our allies are building their forces *now;* the time for our own contribution is *now.* If each [of us] should wait to appraise its partners' efforts before determining its own, the result would be as disastrous as it would be obvious." The talk went on until April, but the steam in the opposition's effort—that is, the possibility of winning votes—sank below the danger point.

In the end the Republicans dropped all thought of legislation in favor of a Senate resolution merely expressing the sense of the Senate without force of law. The resolution had in it a present for everybody, which gave it the comforting majority of 69 to 21, though one provision unpalatable to the Administration was adopted by the close vote of 49 to 43.† The main provisions of the resolution voiced Senate (not legislative) approval of General Eisenhower's appointment, of sending abroad such armed forces as might be needed to contribute to European defense, but not more than four divisions "without further Congressional approval," desire that the President should consult with the Joint Chiefs of Staff and that they should certify that the other allies were making a "full and realistic" effort toward collective defense before our troops were sent, and a request for semiannual progress reports and consideration of using the military resources of West Germany and Spain.

REASSURANCE FOR THE GOOD NEIGHBORHOOD

On December 16, 1950, before setting out for Brussels, I had announced that we would ask the Council of the Organization of American States to call a Meeting of Consultation of Ministers of Foreign Affairs for the purpose of enabling the American states to consider mutual problems confronting the nations of the western hemisphere in the emergency resulting from international Communist aggression, particularly the aggression in Korea. The Latin Americans had been particularly loyal in the Korean crisis. Cuba and Ecuador cast crucial votes for the Security Council resolutions of June 25 and 27, 1950, and the Council of the Organization of American States, on June 28, 1950, pledged support of UN decisions and continental solidarity. In February 1951 the American republics would support the resolution condemning the Communist Chinese and, shortly after the Fourth Meeting of Consultation, would also support the embargo on strategic materials.

For some time the Assistant Secretary of State for Inter-American Affairs, Edward G. Miller, Jr., had reported growing unhappiness in the hemisphere as its economic situation grew more precarious and our attention seemed to Latin America more and more engrossed in European and Far Eastern affairs to the neglect of the Good Neighborhood. In 1948 the Ninth International Conference of American States had recommended that a special inter-American economic conference be convened, but the U.S. Government, doubtful of what practical results could be obtained in the existing circumstances, had been unenthusiastic at the prospect. Unfavorable comparisons were drawn with the days when Cordell Hull and Sumner Welles were so preoccupied with Latin America's problems. Complaints were also leveled at the treatment Latin America had received in the war and early postwar years. During the Second World War the Anglo-American combined purchasing commissions and supply boards held prices of raw materials down and made scant allocations for Latin American civilian needs. After the war, when Latin America entered the U.S. market as a purchaser, price controls were off and supplies largely allocated to European recovery. More recently, although rearmament for the Korean war and Western European defense put up raw-material prices in 1950, the needs of rearmament were also creating scarcities and high prices among many of the manufactured goods that South America needed for industrial development.

Running through all of this, in part caused by it, was a strong current of anti-Yankee hostility, nurtured and led by President Juan Perón in Argentina. It was time, thought Miller, to take the initiative in calling a Meeting of Consultation and in anticipating complaints, at least insofar as these complaints sprang from our common efforts to meet the Communist belligerencies.

The Fourth Meeting of Consultation of the Ministers of Foreign Affairs of the American States was opened at Washington by President Truman on March 26, 1951, and closed by me on April 7. Experts in these matters judged it a success, though little if anything concrete happened as a result of it. However, pent-up resentments were released, thus reducing emotional pressures; innumerable resolutions were passed after hot debate and saving compromise through the adroit rearrangement of a few words; and a great many intimate interviews were arranged for private talk. I had one or more of these with nearly all the foreign ministers. The one who impressed me most was Manuel Tello, the Acting Secretary of Foreign Affairs of Mexico, a career diplomat who was able, amused, and completely forthright with me. We got on together from the start.

Toward the end of the conference I tried to get some practical help from him in fulfilling the sentiments expressed in documents being prepared under the first item of our agenda, the defense of the American republics. Under this item, the conferees would state, in the Declaration of Washington, the intention of the American republics to remain united in the face of threats present and future, and to uphold the OAS and UN systems. They would also recommend that "each of the American Republics should immediately examine its resources and determine what steps it can take to contribute to the defense of the Western Hemisphere and to United Nations collective security efforts" in order to achieve "the aims and purposes of the 'Uniting for Peace' resolution of the General Assembly."[9] I was trying to go beyond words and get some troop contributions for the United Nations Command in Korea, hoping that Mexico and Brazil, whose soldiers were tough fighters—as the Brazilians had shown in Italy—would give a lead. Tello listened to my plea, complimented us on our far-sighted action in Korea, and expressed pain to have to say what he was about to say. Mexican opinion, he said, was not yet prepared to send troops outside Mexico. It was still in the state of the United States opinion during the campaigns of 1916 and 1940. The present period, too, he stressed, was a pre-election time in Mexico, hardly the ideal occasion, as I would understand, to educate public opinion. This was good; I recognized the master's hand.

João Neves da Fontoura, Brazil's Minister of State for Foreign Affairs, was more circuitous and Fabian in his tactics. Although the former administration of President Eurico Gaspar Dutra had decided against troop contribution, the Minister would take the question up with President Getúlio Vargas immediately upon his return. Meanwhile we arranged that General Paulo de Figueiredo would confer with General Charles L. Bolté of the United States

Army on what was desired and how a contribution from Brazil could best be made. Nothing came of this effort. In fact, all that came from Item One on defense was a bevy of resolutions,[10] the eventual arrival in Korea of a battalion of Colombian volunteers.

Item Two—strengthening the internal security of the American republics —received the same exclusively verbal support. Here again Manuel Tello was helpful in drawing my attention to a proposal of our own to set up a group to study means for identifying subversive elements in our countries. He was doubtful that it could be done. As we were already having the greatest difficulty with this sort of thing in our own security program and causing injustice and hardship along the line, I agreed with him heartily and suggested the need for help in revising the plan. The Final Act shows substantial modifications, which stress the need to preserve "political and civil rights and liberties."

The economic item on cooperation in production for military and civil supply and in economic development brought, as might be expected, the most discussion and greatest welter of resolutions. We were lucky that the conference came so early in the year, for the market for raw materials held up until midsummer, when the slump began. Inflation accompanied the boom and continued after it. By the end of the year Latin American terms of trade and balance-of-payments situations were unfavorable once again.

Nevertheless, the Fourth Meeting of Consultation went into inter-American annals as a moderate success. The extent to which personal elements entered into this judgment is shown by Neves da Fontoura's comments to our Ambassador on his return to Brazil. He had gone as a friend and returned more impressed than ever by the worldwide political and military importance of the United States, more determined than ever to strengthen American-Brazilian relations. He had been deeply gratified by his reception and talk with the President and by the letter that had been entrusted to him for delivery to President Vargas. He spoke warmly of the Secretary of State's affording him opportunities for personal talks and his understanding attitude toward him and toward Brazil. All this had strengthened and clarified his own position in Rio. Such relationships and impressions play an important part in weaving the fabric of the Good Neighborhood.

52. DOUBLE TROUBLE IN IRAN

THE FIRST HALF OF 1951 was particularly notable for tasks that distracted us from the main constructive work of rebuilding, out of the ruins of the nineteenth-century European imperial system, a free world to deal with local troubles real enough in their indigenous origins but magnified by efforts of our Communist opponents to increase our difficulties.

Events all over the world moved swiftly to bring us new troubles and make some old ones harder to manage. The new ones sprang up chiefly in those areas variously called underprivileged, undeveloped, colonial, or emerging. They ranged in extent from the western hemisphere to the East, Near and Far, and in intensity from protest to revolt against things as they were, the established order, and former colonial powers. Since the United States represented by far the most opulent of the established societies and was allied with many former and existing colonial powers, it was not hard for skillful Soviet and Chinese propaganda to turn this unrest and protest into anti-Americanism. Despite American s⸳ ..pathy, helpful political intervention, and large material aid for these areas, the advantage in the propaganda battle was heavily on the side of the big lie, for, as Thomas Jefferson pointed out, no weapon is so effective and so cheap to those in whose systems of politics morality plays no part.

CRISIS IN IRAN

The Near East—thus distinguished from the Far East—was the name given by Europeans to that large stretch of country from the eastern Mediterranean to and including the Indian subcontinent. It had always held a special lure for them. There, when Islam had succeeded the eastern Roman Empire, the Crusaders spent themselves in the vain effort to redeem the holy places from pagan profanation. There Venice

> Once did . . . hold the gorgeous east in fee;
> And was the safeguard of the west.[1]

More recently Napoleon had lost there his dream of oriental empire, and a century later Kaiser Wilhelm II, after entering Jerusalem in shining armor, did the same. There the British and French established spheres of influence supported by arms and Russia pushed against the northern borders of Iran, always "Persia" to Sir Winston Churchill. However, in the long history of this region, once thought to be the cradle of the human race, perhaps the most prolific causes of conflict, controversy, and unrest were the discovery and development in the Persian Gulf area of immense oil deposits and "the establishment in

Palestine of a national home for the Jewish People," to use the historic words of the Balfour Declaration. The British early in this century were largely instrumental in bringing about both of these situations. The decision of Winston Churchill, as First Lord of the Admiralty, and Lord Fisher, as First Sea Lord, to make the British Navy oil-burning led to that government's buying into the Anglo-Persian Oil Company and the rapid development both of the fields and the refinery at Abadan and of British interest in Persia. Oil development in other Persian Gulf countries followed rapidly with French, Dutch, and American interests participating. The Balfour Declaration issued by the British Government during their 1914–18 war with the Ottoman Empire has been called "the product as much of political calculation as of generous idealism."[2] The British as the mandatory state for Palestine were enabled to carry it out.

Throughout the Near East lay rare tinder for anti-Western propaganda: a Moslem culture and history, bitter Arab nationalism galled by Jewish immigration under British protection and with massive American financial support, the remnants of a colonial status, and a sense of grievance that a vast natural resource was being extracted by foreigners under arrangements thought unfair to those living on the surface. This tinder could be, and was, lighted everywhere; it flared up first in Iran.

Early in the nineteenth century the efforts of American missionary groups to save souls in Persia were neither troublesome nor successful enough to arouse local opposition or the ready suspicion of the British or Russians. This was not true of the more official interest shown early in the next century, when in 1911 Morgan Shuster was employed by the Persian Government as Treasurer-General to reorganize and purify its fiscal system. The distaste of all was so manifest that the next year he was forced to retire after armed Russian intervention. An economic mission organized by Arthur C. Millspaugh after the First World War lasted a little longer, from 1922 to 1927. Twenty years later I was involved in a much larger operation in Iran, briefly referred to in Chapter 22. A route was opened through Iran for supplies moving to the Soviet Union, our Government sent a mission under Colonel H. Norman Schwarzkopf to train an Iranian gendarmerie and police force and dispatched a Persian Gulf Supply Command under Major General D. H. Connolly with thirty thousand troops to move lend-lease supplies to Russia and distribute some in Iran. Arthur Millspaugh returned as Administrator of Finance, but was hardly more successful on his second try than on his first. These last two missions withdrew at the end of the war.

Then Iran felt the heavy hand of the Soviet Union in the north, refusing to withdraw forces, but rather using them to support local communist party leaders in their attempt to detach the northern province of Azerbaijan. The United States, as told in Chapter 22, played a helpful part in resisting this attempt. After Russian withdrawal, our attention was drawn westward as Soviet pressure moved to Greece, Turkey, and then to Western Europe, but in 1949 it moved back to Iran. Foreign interference during the war had intensified xenophobia among the landowners, mullahs, and politicians, who wished to drive foreign interests from the country and opposed bitterly the internal reforms favored by the Shah. Growing passion centered about a dispute between the Majlis (parliament), represented by its special Oil Commission under Mohammed Mosadeq, a demagogue of considerable shrewdness and ability, and the Anglo-Iranian Oil Company. Mosadeq was aided by the unusual and persistent stupidity of the company and the British Government in their management of the affair. Hope for stability and progress in Iran lay in the young Shah, although American liberals clung to the illusion that some other moderate leadership existed between the Tudeh Party Communists and the feudal reactionaries and mullahs. In the ensuing struggle between the extremists of the Majlis and the company-government complex, which the United States Government vainly tried to ameliorate, the Prime Minister was murdered, the King fled, the country was bankrupted, and the British lost their Iranian oil concession and properties for four years and very nearly forever.

The story of my involvement in this tragic affair runs through several phases, four of which will be dealt with here and two in Section D (1952).

PHASE ONE: THE SHAH'S ATTEMPT

The Shah's program was an ambitious one, in all of which he enlisted American help. This in turn intensified Soviet propaganda and Tudeh Party activity against him. The American police and military advisory missions who remained after the war continued on and did good work. The army was reorganized and started on re-equipment with American arms. Millspaugh returned on a mission of governmental reform but acted unwisely, soon found himself in grave difficulties with Iranians of all groups, and withdrew amid mutual recriminations and ill will. The Seven Year Plan of internal development worked out by a group of American advisers headed by Max Thornburg, formerly Petroleum Adviser to the State Department, a grandiose plan beyond the capacity of the Iranian Government, began to run into trouble. In February 1949 an attempt was made on the life of the Shah, which drove him to ban the Tudeh Party and seek to limit the obstructive power of the Majlis by constitutional amendments. As the year wore on, his difficulties and frustrations increased and pushed his conceptions of need for American aid to unrealistic proportions.

In this state of affairs the Near Eastern and African Bureau of the Department prevailed upon me, and I, in turn, upon the President, to invite the Shah for a state visit to Washington. This seemed a good way to help the prestige of the young ruler at home and let him learn at first hand the realities and limitation of American aid. I have already expressed intense dislike of "meetings at the summit"; the same emotion extends to "state visits." All presidents, I believe, have shared this view of them, but not the geographic divisions, which prize them highly, doggedly refusing to learn from experience. Moreover, the pressure from potential guests to be invited grows as invitations go out. What I say has no invidious application to the Shah's visit, but springs from such disparate visits as those of Prime Minister de Gasperi of Italy and Presidents Elpidio Quirino of the Philippines, Galo Plaza of Ecuador, and Gonsález

Videla of Chile. Shortly after if not before his arrival, a guest would tell us that "to send him home empty-handed" would destroy him politically. He must have a loan or a treaty or something else particularly hard for the State Department to provide. We would end up with an offering that the Department could ill afford to give, that our guest believed he could barely afford to accept, and that usually led both parties into trouble. The only successful visit that comes to mind is one by Robert Menzies, Prime Minister of Australia, who slipped into town hardly noticed and in a day and a half was gone again with a loan of two hundred fifty million dollars from the World Bank for Australia's great water and power development. But Bob Menzies knew the ropes as well as or better than we did ourselves.

Twenty years ago the Shah was not as experienced or wise as he is today. My wife and I gave one of the gayer state dinners for him at Anderson House. The plans, military and economic, that the Shah unfolded were too ambitious for the means available, both financial and in his government's capability. He thought of an army half the size of the Turkish on a much narrower national base and of its function like that of Venice, as "the safeguard of the west." The plans of Overseas Consultants, Inc., for industrial development were far larger than could either be supported by the neglected agriculture of Iran and that portion of its population capable of industrial employment or entrusted to the dubious integrity of its bureaucracy.

The visit turned out to be a disappointment to all. However, the next spring we tried again, moving Henry Grady, our successful Ambassador in Athens, to Teheran and reinforcing him with a sizable and competent economic mission. General Ali Razmara, an energetic soldier and national hero for his part in suppressing separatism in Azerbaijan, was appointed Prime Minister. We failed again; for a year the State Department and the field fumbled the financial ball between them. We lacked decisiveness and vigor; they suffered from the habit learned in Athens of thinking in terms of large financial resources, with the result that both the mission and the Shah disdained the funds available, nothing got done, and confidence suffered all around. By the autumn of 1950 tempers became badly frayed. The Iranian Government indignantly rejected a proposal by a World Bank mission for a four-million-dollar loan. An American Export-Import Bank offer of a twenty-five-million-dollar loan was never accepted by the Majlis. Point Four funds bogged down. Both Ambassador Grady and the Shah were critical of the State Department (the Ambassador calling for a loan of a hundred million dollars for its psychological effect); the Department, which had no funds, nagged at the lending agencies but could hardly fault their judgment that Iran in the absence of some agreement with the Anglo-Iranian Oil Company did not look like a good risk. On November 4 an Iranian-Soviet barter-trade agreement was announced, and on the fourteenth the Iranian Government ended its Persian-language broadcasts of Voice of America and other foreign programs. On January 8, 1951, it canceled the contract with Overseas Consultants, Inc. Storm signals were already flying when Razmara was shot by a religious fanatic on March 7 as he entered a mosque.

PHASE TWO: THE MOSADEQ REVOLUTION

The controversy with Anglo-Iranian began in an anti-Russian action of the Majlis in 1947, widely hailed in the West at the time. Tucked away in its act rejecting the Soviet-Iranian oil contract for a concession in the north, negotiated as part of the settlement by which Russian troops evacuated Azerbaijan, was a provision requiring the Government to review the Anglo-Iranian concession of 1933 with a view toward safeguarding the rights of the people in the economic wealth of the country. This was done and on July 17, 1949, a Supplemental Oil Agreement was initialed providing Iran with a more favorable arrangement than then enjoyed by any other oil-producing country in the area. A year later the Oil Commission of the Majlis recommended its rejection.

General Razmara appealed to the oil company to sweeten the supplemental agreement by concessions on certain points that the Oil Commission had criticized and that would cost nothing, such as a right to look at the books of the company, of which the Iranian Government was twenty per cent owner, an increase in Iranian personnel, pricing oil sold in Iran on cost in Iran rather than on world prices, a right to know where exported oil was sold. Despite a plea by George McGhee, Assistant Secretary for Near Eastern Affairs, to the British Foreign Office and the Anglo-Iranian Oil Company, it refused to budge. In January 1951 the Majlis directed the Oil Commission to recommend new legislation, which could hardly be anything but nationalization. At this point the Arabian-American Oil Company (Aramco) announced a new contract with Saudi Arabia providing for a fifty per cent profit division with the Government. This made obsolete both the supplemental agreement and Razmara's proposal. Only at the end of February 1951 did Anglo-Iranian indicate willingness to reopen discussion along the Aramco terms. Razmara kept this information to himself, appealing to the Majlis and the Oil Commission to support him in a negotiated settlement on the most favorable terms, arguing that in the absence of Iranian technical and marketing competence nationalization would be futile.

Three days later he was dead. On March 15, 1951, the Majlis and on the twentieth the Senate unanimously passed Mosadeq's recommended nationalization bill. He became Prime Minister on April 28 and nationalization was proclaimed as law on May 2. Never had so few lost so much so stupidly and so fast.

Mosadeq: A Sketch from Life • From the first moment I saw him a few months later Mosadeq became for me the character Lob in James Barrie's play *Dear Brutus*. He was small and frail with not a shred of hair on his billiard-ball head; a thin face protruded into a long beak of a nose flanked by two bright, shoe-button eyes. His whole manner and appearance was birdlike, marked by quick, nervous movements as he seemed to jump about on a perch. His pixie quality showed in instantaneous transformations. Waiting at Union Station in Washington, I watched a bent old man hobble down the platform supporting himself with a stick and an arm through his son's. Spotting me at the gate, he dropped the stick, broke away from his party, and came skipping along ahead of the others to greet us.

He had, I discovered later, a delightfully childlike way of sitting in a chair with his legs tucked under him, making him more of a Lob character than ever, with many and changing moods. I remember him sitting with the President and me after lunch in Blair House, his legs under him, when he dropped a mood of gay animation and, suddenly looking old and pathetic, leaned toward the President.

"Mr. President," he said, "I am speaking for a very poor country—a country all desert—just sand, a few camels, a few sheep . . ."

"Yes," I interrupted, "and with your oil, rather like Texas!" He burst into a delighted laugh, and the whole act broke up, finished. It was a gambit that had not worked. No one was more amused than he. He then went to work on the President for financial aid to fight the British imperialists. But the President was having none of it. Our aid, he said, was not for that purpose. Iran had resources aplenty and we were ready to help them with sensible accommodation in their development.

Another of Mosadeq's marked characteristics was his distrust of his own countrymen; he would never talk with any of them present. At this same luncheon there were many guests, including the Iranian Ambassador. Mosadeq waited until they had gone and the doors were closed, leaving the three of us and Colonel Walters, our interpreter, for our private talk. Seeing that the Ambassador had been shut out, I intervened to retrieve this mistake, only to find it was no mistake at all. Averell Harriman discovered in Iran that Mosadeq would talk freely only alone and with an American interpreter—never an Iranian. Nitze and McGhee learned it in New York. When they wanted to get the whole Oil Commission into a meeting, Mosadeq demurred. "It's no use," he said. "You can't convince *them*." In a service often trying I found compensation, indeed joy, in the qualities of friendly colleagues, of hostile combatants, and sometimes of neutral freebooters like Mosadeq. Only bores were insufferable.

Mosadeq's self-defeating quality was that he never paused to see that the passions he excited to support him restricted his freedom of choice and left only extreme solutions possible. We were, perhaps, slow in realizing that he was essentially a rich, reactionary, feudal-minded Persian inspired by a fanatical hatred of the British and a desire to expel them and all their works from the country regardless of the cost. He was a great actor and a great gambler. Speaking in the Majlis, he would rant, weep real tears, and fall in a faint at his climactic moment. He told us once that nationalization would cost Iran nothing, since any damages which Anglo-Iranian could prove would be exceeded by Iranian counterclaims. This unique character truly sowed the wind and reaped the whirlwind.

A Critical Spring • As Mosadeq made his entrance upon the stage, my trusted and admired friend, Ernest Bevin, left it. He resigned as Foreign Minister on

March 9, 1951, and died on April 14, being succeeded by Herbert Morrison. Mr. Morrison was a long-time House of Commons man and a great expert on the government of London, the London County Council, of which he had been an early architect. He knew nothing of foreign affairs and had no feel for situations beyond the sound of Bow bells. Perhaps to compensate for a sense of insecurity, he accentuated a natural abrasiveness of temperament. The change was not a fortunate one at this tense period.

Before March—and certainly April—was over, a distinct cleavage appeared between the British and American governmental approach to the Iranian threat of nationalizing the oil industry. To understand it, we must understand what the Anglo-Iranian Oil Company had, what Iran proposed to take, and the difference between legal rights and claims and the power to enforce them. The British Government owned only a stock interest in Anglo-Iranian. The company owned its refinery at Abadan but did not own the oil fields, which the Iranian Government claimed to own. Anglo-Iranian had a contract with the Government, made in 1933 and running until 1993, to extract the oil, pipe it to Abadan, and there refine and export it for sale abroad—all for certain payments to be made to Iran. It was to amend this contract that the parties to it had been negotiating up until Razmara's death. Nationalization meant that Iran proposed to expropriate the refinery, pipelines, and other physical property and to terminate the concession contract. Iran recognized the obligation to make some payment for what it proposed to take, but how much or even upon what basis it should be computed remained vague.

In simpler times and places armed intervention, known as "gunboat diplomacy," would have resolved this problem in favor of the stronger power, but the United Nations Charter put obstacles, to say the least, in the way of that. Our approach to the problem, growing out of the expropriation of American oil interests in Mexico, was that the sovereign power of a state to take such property could not be denied, but raised the obligation to pay prompt and just compensation equivalent to the fair market value of the property taken. As our own experience showed, these comfortable words were only an introduction to a long negotiation, since there was no international sheriff or court into which the defendant could be haled. Furthermore, the defendant was usually without cash or transferable property on which to levy. If he paid at all, it would have to be out of earnings from the oil fields and properties.

The British denied the right to nationalize the oil fields and properties on the ground that Iran had given it up by contract, but conceded a willingness to negotiate a modification of the contract within its major terms, such as duration and British control. Since both approaches led ultimately to negotiation, the difference would have been a mere matter of semantics were it not, as we shall see, that the semantics proved to be the heart of the matter on which neither side would yield. The Iranians insisted that mutually agreeable terms must be based upon recognition of Iran's sovereign right to nationalize; the British adamantly refused this, regardless of the terms, because of their asserted belief that otherwise all their foreign investments, their very lifeblood, would be jeopardized.

Our view was that their own folly had brought them to their present fix, which Aramco had avoided by (in Burke's phrase) graciously granting what it no longer had the power to withhold. Having lost their chance to negotiate the desirable way, they now had to use the Iranian vocabulary; the longer they delayed, the more difficult the Iranians would be. Our interest lay in the threat that this controversy held for everyone's interest in the Near East: it upset relations with the oil-producing states and opened rare opportunities for Communist propaganda; Britain might drive Iran to a Communist *coup d'état,* or Iran might drive Britain out of the country. Either would be a major disaster. We were deeply concerned.

Violence Impends • During the spring a constant flow of telegrams and many meetings in Washington and London only developed this divergence of approach. Both General Bradley and I before congressional committees and press conferences made clear that action by us would be limited to good offices. I put out a series of statements urging moderation, which have been described as recalling "the helpless solicitude of a Greek chorus."[3] In Iran possibilities open to us shrank as loans became less and less bankable and more and more open to the charge of merely "financing nationalization." Strikes and periodic interruption of communication with the oil fields impeded operation of the refinery. British troops moved to bases in the Near East and warships appeared off Abadan. On the basis of a National Security Council decision, I warned British Ambassador Franks on May 17 that a substantial difference was developing between our views on the permissible use of force in Iran and those to which some elements in London appeared to be adhering. Only on invitation of the Iranian Government, or Soviet military intervention, or a Communist *coup d'état* in Teheran, or to evacuate British nationals in danger of attack could we support the use of military force.

In June tension increased. Mosadeq's contribution had been a typical one. Responding to an announcement of extremist leader Naveb Safavi that he had ordered the execution of Razmara and would order others, Mosadeq told the Majlis that his life was in danger and asked to be allowed to live in the parliament building until nationalization had been accomplished. Then, apparently, he would be willing, though not eager, to give his life for his country. On June 1, 1951, the President in letters to Mosadeq and Attlee urged renewed negotiation. By the twentieth an Anglo-Iranian Oil Company delegation had gone to Teheran with a reasonable proposal (on the basis of its concepts), but had failed. The mounting threats were followed by counterthreats. Morrison asked the International Court of Justice for an injunction and said that Britain would not stand by idle if lives of British nationals were in jeopardy. Iran denied the jurisdiction of the court and gave Manager A. E. C. Drake at Abadan and British employees of Anglo-Iranian a week to decide either to work for the new National Iranian Oil Company or leave. Anglo-Iranian threatened to shut down operations, which, I cabled London, would be a disaster. It would face us with the possibility of an economic collapse in Iran, a Communist coup and loss of

Iranian oil to the West, and the probability that once British personnel were withdrawn they would never be permitted to return.

At this point the British escalated their pressure a notch. Drake was withdrawn from Iran to Basra and notice given that other personnel would follow because of a new antisabotage law before the Majlis. The Majlis passed the law. All tankers at Abadan awaiting permission to load oil from storage tanks were withdrawn. (The refinery would have to close down when the storage tanks were full.) HMS *Mauritius* proceeded to the vicinity of Abadan. Mosadeq's National Front Party replied that the first shot fired would "signal the start of World War III." I urged both parties to pause on the brink and consider an interim operating agreement without prejudice to the position of either, but Morrison, thinking that Mosadeq was weakening, wanted to wait a while longer. Convinced that both sides were pressing their luck to the point of suicide in this game of Russian roulette, I asked Averell Harriman to arrange a meeting on his hilltop veranda looking down the Potomac with Ambassador Franks, just back from London.

PHASE THREE: THE HARRIMAN MISSION

In the group meeting on Averell Harriman's veranda that afternoon of July 4 to consider what appeared to be a British declaration of independence were Ambassador Franks, Paul Nitze, Doc Matthews, George McGhee, our host, and myself. For two hours we examined the consequences of the course threatened by the Government in London, not arguing about them but analyzing them with candor. Sir Oliver left no doubt how seriously and angrily both the British Government and public viewed what they regarded as the insolent defiance of decency, legality, and reason by a group of wild men in Iran who proposed to despoil Britain. He did doubt whether the Government should or could attempt to withstand the widespread demand in the country that Mosadeq's spoliation by *force majeure* should be met with greater force.

The afternoon's sober discussion brought us to some unanimous conclusions. Armed intervention by Britain at Abadan in the south would, in all probability, lead to armed intervention by the Soviet Union in Azerbaijan in support of their oil concession, which the Iranian Government had negotiated and the Majlis had rejected. Even though some in London might not be shocked at a partition of Iran into spheres of influence, it would both fail to gain control of the oil fields for Britain—a more difficult assignment than seizing the refinery—and create an uproar in the United Nations. In this battle it seemed inevitable that Washington, in view of its leadership of the 1946 fight to get Russian troops out of Iran, would end up at loggerheads with London. Finally, if Mosadeq or an even more extreme government invited Russian intervention in the hope of forcing withdrawal of both foreign forces, we might end up with the British out and the Russians in. In short, armed intervention offered nothing except great trouble.

Before the meeting broke up I proposed that to stop the drift toward intervention and likely disaster Averell should go to Teheran to have a try at getting negotiations started again. The others—with the exception of Averell, who appeared a most reluctant bride—thought this a good idea. The next day, when we reported our meeting to the President, he warmly welcomed it and immediately sent a cable to Mosadeq, from whom he had an unanswered letter reciting grievances against the British and asking help from us. Mr. Harriman, the President said, would go to Iran not as a mediator but, in the interest of peace and stability, to urge the resumption of direct talks between the Iranians and the British in a mutual search for a solution. In the meantime, Sir Oliver cabled a report of our meeting to the Foreign Office and I asked Ambassador Walter Gifford to repeat our analysis of the effect of intervention to Prime Minister Attlee. To the great credit of the Labour Government, it stood against jingo pressures. This, with the calming effect of Harriman's visit to Teheran, stopped the drift toward intervention.

The initial response of both London and Teheran to Harriman's proposed visit was cool, the British Ambassador in Teheran publicly stating, and then withdrawing, the view that there "was not much point" to his coming; but on second thought Mosadeq welcomed it and Morrison found it less distasteful. The President, General Marshall, and I were all photographed and recorded wishing Averell well as he departed on July 14. He arrived the next day in time for a large Tudeh-sponsored demonstration in which several hundred people were injured and twenty were killed. Thus this able and devoted servant of the Republic set out on another of the many journeys, often exhausting and danger-ous, that he has undertaken on its behalf and performed with fidelity and dis-cipline. Temperament has never gotten between him and his duty.

This mission succeeded in its immediate purpose of turning back Britain and Iran from the brink of hostilities. It failed in its more ambitious purpose of finding a solution to the oil dispute, though often seeming close to a break-through. It failed, I believe, for the same reason that the Marshall mission to China in 1946 failed, because neither party to the dispute wanted a solution; each wanted to defeat the other on a central nonnegotiable issue. However, on August 2 Sir Oliver Franks, who earnestly wanted a settlement, told me that I might pass on his personal view to Averell that his going had been a "godsend" and that only his "very able handling of the situation both in Teheran and in London" had brought about a resumption of negotiations.

Sir Oliver referred to Harriman's accomplishments in two weeks of work, first in Teheran and later in London. He persuaded the Shah to overcome his reluctance to involvement in the nationalization controversy and enlisted his help in pressing Mosadeq to settle it while Harriman was available. Mosadeq and his colleagues on the Oil Commission were in turn persuaded to resume discussion with the British Government "on behalf of the former Anglo-Iranian Oil Company" on the basis of recognition of "the principle of nationalization of the oil industry in Iran." To get Mosadeq's agreement to diplomatic negotiation was a major achievement, since he was arguing in the World Court that the British Government had no standing as a mere stockholder in Anglo-Iranian to raise the nationalization issue. Harriman wisely refrained from writing out these agreements, having observed that in Teheran anything written immediately leaked and was repudiated.

To get British agreement to negotiate on these terms he decided to go to London himself and to take British Ambassador Francis M. Shephard along with him, so that he could keep an eye and ear on this unimaginative disciple of the "whiff of grapeshot" school of diplomacy. In London he found an arbitrary and unyielding attitude based on what he thought an erroneous appraisal of the situation in Iran, doubtless Ambassador Shephard's. I ran into the same attitude and appraisal in my talks with Herbert Morrison and his party during September in Washington. When I suggested to Morrison a joint intelligence appraisal in an effort to get together on the facts—my information being that the British military took a different view from the civilians—he refused.

Nevertheless, Harriman brought the British Government to agreement on resumption of negotiations through a minister of Cabinet rank and under the as yet secret "Harriman formula." He had hoped that Hugh Gaitskell, the Chancellor of the Exchequer, might be able to undertake the negotiations, believing that once on the scene he would grasp the situation and the peculiar problem presented by Mosadeq's personality. But Gaitskell could not be spared from London, where events were rapidly moving toward a general election, and the choice fell on the Right Honorable Richard Rapier Stokes, Lord Privy Seal and Minister of Materials. Sir Oliver described him to me as a "bluff, genial, and hearty man," without experience in dealing with the Near Eastern mentality. This proved to be sheer flattery. On the day his appointment was announced—July 30, 1951—Harriman headed back to Teheran and Anglo-Iranian shut down the refinery at Abadan.

Almost at once the negotiations ran into trouble. Stokes put forward some proposals, which Harriman thought reasonable and within the formula, but contrary to his advice Stokes made them public. They became the subject of general debate and in accordance with customary practice were rejected by Mosadeq on August 15. Stokes clumsily alienated Hussein Ala, a former Ambassador to Washington and at that time Minister of the Court and the Shah's chief confidant. It seemed to Harriman—and Stokes too—that the talks were doomed and that they should be recessed for a cooling-off period, hoping for more propitious times and, perhaps, negotiators. The missions to Teheran came home at the end of August.

PHASE FOUR: HOPE FADES

Back in Washington we believed that Harriman's noble try for settlement had failed because of the bad luck of the Stokes appointment and that the strong national interest of both parties in settlement would overcome their obduracy. However, they did their best to dispel that belief. On September 5 Mosadeq announced that if the British did not arrange in two weeks for the resumption of negotiations, the residence permits of British technicians would be canceled. The British promptly broke off negotiations altogether, sent four destroyers to join the ten warships in the Persian Gulf, withdrew conversion privileges of

Iranian deposits in the Bank of England, and filed a condemnatory resolution in the Security Council. The technicians were duly expelled and peacefully evacuated.

During some of this period Morrison in Washington was giving me the now familiar hard-nosed line on how to deal with Iran, in the course of which he informed me of what seemed oddly heterodox socialist doctrine—that Iran by setting the terrible precedent of taking over property without justification was making strong action necessary. To this my notes record me as replying that keeping cool might do more to solve the problem. We also advised against the resolution in the Security Council, since not only would the Soviets veto it, but it would probably fail of a majority anyway, which would not strengthen Britain's position. Mosadeq himself came to New York to argue Iran's case in the Security Council, which he did with great skill and all the drama he had made familiar in the Majlis. Overnight he became a television star, quite outshining the British representative, Gladwyn Jebb, who had made a reputation the year before in his debates with Malik over Korea. Mosadeq, aware of his opportunity, used it to the full in building up his prestige at home.

While Mosadeq was in New York, George McGhee, who was thoroughly familiar with the oil business, spent a great deal of time in discussion with him, drawing in Paul Nitze and Harold Linder, Deputy Assistant Secretary for Economic Affairs, both of whom had had extensive business experience. In these talks Mosadeq made the surprising statement that the refinery at Abadan had not been nationalized. If this was true, it still belonged to Anglo-Iranian on any theory. Mosadeq also appeared willing to have it operated by a "neutral" company—for instance, a Dutch company. Sometimes he would seem agreeable to the presence of a few Englishmen, sometimes not. Working from these premises the three devised an ingenious scheme by which Anglo-Iranian would get Iranian oil for export on a basis that represented the same fifty-fifty profit division between government and company in effect elsewhere in the Persian Gulf.

After the British resolution had been defeated in the Security Council, Mosadeq came to Washington for medical diagnosis and possible treatment and, while there, to see the President. He entered the Army's medical center, Walter Reed Hospital, delightedly occupying the President's suite. Everyone petted and took care of him. He held court in pajamas and bathrobe, receiving me and my three negotiators in a large, sunny sitting room. For four hours we went over their talks with him. It was like walking in a maze and every so often finding oneself at the beginning again. On price, particularly, he pretended to be very vague and stupid, though in fact we were only a few cents per barrel apart. I remember that McGhee and I explained oil economics to him in terms of the wide spread between the price we got for beef cattle on the hoof on our farms and the price we paid for a prime roast of beef in the butcher's shop. He explained to us that peasants were always exploited.

Thinking that we had the makings of a deal, I set out for a series of foreign ministers', NATO, and General Assembly meetings in Europe, taking Linder with me to report to the British. The British elections had returned the Conservatives, replacing Herbert Morrison at the Foreign Office with Anthony Eden, a great and signal improvement, except on Iran. In that area Eden continued to take advice from the same sources which had, I thought, poisoned the judgment of the Labour Party—the bureaucracy of the Anglo-Iranian Oil Company, the Ministry of Fuel and Power, and the Treasury, where Sir Leslie Rowan played the part of St. Michael, the avenging angel. Rowan decreed that Mosadeq, leading the attack on British foreign investments, had to fail, to be crushed and punished. This adamant British attitude ruled out further discussion or search for face-saving formulas of retreat for Mosadeq. So Linder went home to break off the operation.

Nitze and McGhee ended the negotiations on the ground that Mosadeq had never been definite enough on price to give the British a proposal capable of development, but they told me that Mosadeq never believed them. He knew that the British wanted a fight to the finish and he took the declaration of a fight to the finish with dignity.

"You have never understood," he said to them, "that this is basically a political issue." On November 13 the United States Government "regretfully concluded that, while progress has been made [in discussion of the Iranian oil controversy], no new basis has emerged on which a practicable solution could be reached."[4] Mosadeq packed up and went home.

It would be far too optimistic to say that a deal could have been made at this time if the British had been more forthcoming. Perhaps Mosadeq would have danced away again, but I have always regretted that we were not given the opportunity to press him.

53. ATTEMPTS TO STABILIZE
THE KOREAN WAR

To STABILIZE THE Korean war involved nearly simultaneous efforts on three separate fronts: the front in Korea, the front in the United Nations, and the front in Tokyo. The most intractable was the last.

ON THE KOREAN FRONT

An event of incalculable importance occurred on December 23, 1950, though we in Washington—that is, we civilians—did not recognize it as such. General Walker, commanding the Eighth Army, was killed when his jeep crashed on an icy Korean road and Major General Matthew B. Ridgway was appointed to succeed him. Two days later—measured by Korean time—General Ridgway reported to General MacArthur and took over command of the Eighth Army, soon to be joined by X Corps. General MacArthur concluded their meeting, as General Ridgway has told us, by saying, "The Eighth Army is yours, Matt. Do what you think best."

He never uttered wiser words. Within a month the longest retreat in American history ended and the Army, its fighting spirit restored, "started rolling forward," to use its commander's words.[1] Temporarily checked by a heavy Chinese counterattack in mid-February, the advance continued with Operation Killer on March 7, designed primarily—as its name indicates—to inflict heavy losses on the Chinese, which it did. On March 15 Seoul was retaken, not to be lost again, and by April 9 the Army was established on the Kansas line north of the 38th parallel, where General Ridgway held it concentrated, coordinated, and urgently preparing to meet another Chinese offensive that appeared to be in the making. Both he and Washington were confident that the Army could absorb all the Chinese could throw at us and were clear that there was to be no more talk of withdrawal from Korea unless the Soviet Union should intervene in strength, which we deemed unlikely.

ON THE UNITED NATIONS FRONT

Our last glimpse of the scene in New York was one of some confusion. Malik and General Wu were attacking the United States for its stand on Korea and Formosa, we were trying to rally our friends to vote a condemnation of Chinese aggression in Korea, and the Indians and others were striving for a cease-fire resolution. Since the United Nations was one of the belligerents, a cease-fire resolution was obviously an appeal by the weaker to the stronger side. For this reason the United States Government in the current military situation would neither participate in the effort nor block it. The Chinese, however, did the latter. General Wu declared illegal a resolution asking Nasrollah Entezam of Iran, President of the Assembly, and two associates to determine the basis on which a cease-fire could be arranged, and Chou En-lai announced that as "the only acceptable basis for negotiation" of a peaceful settlement in Korea all foreign troops must be withdrawn and the domestic affairs of Korea left to Koreans; that American forces must be "withdrawn" from Formosa; and that the Chinese Communist Government must be seated in the United Nations.[2] Mr. Entezam reported failure on January 2.

Not content with this rebuff, the British, Canadians, Indians, and others produced another bid to the Chinese, a resolution proposing five principles for peaceful settlement in Korea: (1) a cease-fire; (2) a political meeting for restoring peace; (3) a withdrawal by stages of all foreign forces; (4) arrangements for an immediate administration of all Korea; (5) a conference, after a cease-fire, of the United Kingdom, the United States, the Soviet Union, and the Chinese Communists to discuss Far Eastern problems, including the future of Formosa and the representation of China in the United Nations.

The choice whether to support or oppose this plan was a murderous one, threatening, on one side, the loss of the Koreans and the fury of Congress and press and, on the other, the loss of our majority and support in the United Nations. We chose, after painful deliberation in the Department—and after I recommended to the President what may well have been, even without hindsight, the wrong alternative—to support the resolution. We did so in the fervent hope and belief that the Chinese would reject it (as they did) and that our allies would then return (as they did) to comparative sanity and follow us in censuring the Chinese as aggressors. The President—bless him—supported me in even this anguishing decision. At once the political roof fell in, and the Senate, already deep in the Great Debate, added a new facet to it as Senator Taft attacked us with great violence. Fortunately the storm soon blew itself out. The resolution proposed on January 11 and adopted on the thirteenth was rejected four days later by the Chinese. Our allies—rather grudgingly, as they believed that the United States was getting the best of both worlds when the State Department supported the five principles and the country rejected them—joined us on February 1 in passing a condemnation of Chinese aggression but dragged their feet until May in taking any action to punish the aggressor.

Thus the United Nations front fell into restless stability, disturbed by echoes of the irrepressible conflict in progress between Washington and Tokyo.

ON THE TOKYO FRONT

When the Chinese attacks exploded all around his forces in North Korea late in November, General MacArthur cabled to the Chiefs of Staff that all hope of localizing the Korean conflict had gone. The Chinese wanted, he said, the complete destruction of his forces; they could be saved only by carrying the war to China. To General Collins in Tokyo he characterized as essentially a policy of surrender a refusal to authorize air attacks on China, a naval blockade of the China coast, reinforcements from Formosa, or a consideration of atomic bombing in North Korea. At the same time, as already noted, he complained to the press of "an enormous handicap without precedent in military history," in which he included the ban on "hot pursuit" of enemy aircraft into Manchuria and the "privileged sanctuary" provided the Chinese by refusal to permit bombing of Manchurian airfields and military targets. He did not, however, note our own counterbalancing sanctuaries in South Korea.

On the day after Christmas the President summoned Secretary of the Treasury Snyder, Generals Marshall and Bradley, and myself to a strategy meeting at Blair House. It was a long one. I proposed a rewriting and clarification of General MacArthur's directives. The stakes in Korea were so high that the United Nations should not withdraw until we had tested Chinese strength fully and found that dire military necessity required it. General MacArthur should not be required to defend any particular line but to inflict the maximum losses on the enemy by the use of air, sea, and land power, including Korean forces (the strategy later adopted by General Ridgway). He should not risk the destruction of his troops, since on them lay the ultimate responsibility for the defense of Japan. The generals saw an increased threat of general war and were clear that it should not be fought in Korea. They agreed to the rewriting of the directive, and the President authorized it.

The next day a draft was discussed by the Generals with the President and me and sent off on December 29. In brief it stated: †

1. If, with present UN strength, we could resist at some point in Korea without our incurring serious losses, and if the apparent military and political prestige of Chinese Communists could be deflated, it would be of great importance to our national interests.

2. "In the face of increased threat of general war" the Joint Chiefs of Staff would not commit additional U.S. ground forces in Korea. Major war should not be fought in Korea.

3. "Therefore . . . your directive now is to defend in successive positions, subject to safety of your troops as your primary consideration, inflicting as much damage to hostile forces in Korea as is possible."

4. Decision was to be made ahead of time by the Joint Chiefs on the last reasonable opportunity for orderly evacuation. General MacArthur's views were requested on the conditions which should determine evacuation.[3]

General MacArthur has recorded his views on receiving this message: it seemed to him "to indicate a loss of 'will to win' in Korea"; it was "unrealistic" because it offered no reinforcements, and it was "especially fantastic" in expecting the Eighth Army to be responsible for the defense of Japan.[4] On the same day (December 30) he put forward four recommendations: to blockade the coast of China; to destroy China's industrial capacity by bombing; to use Nationalist Chinese troops in Korea; to encourage action by Formosa against the Chinese mainland. Barring these actions and without reinforcement, withdrawal to Pusan was the only way evacuation of Korea could be effected—a course that he attributed to the Chiefs of Staff.[5] On January 9, 1951, the Chiefs repeated their order to defend in successive positions, inflicting maximum losses on the enemy, and that MacArthur's primary consideration should be the safety of his troops and the defense of Japan.[6] In case of necessity to achieve either of these, he was authorized to withdraw to Japan. His suggestions, they said, were under consideration but they pointed out the major objections to adopting them. This portion of the reply was to be used later by General MacArthur and his apologists as evidence that the Chiefs agreed with the recommendations (which they did not), but that I and others torpedoed them.

At this point MacArthur attempted to put a squeeze on the Chiefs. He "shot a query right back"—in his own phrase.[7] It was self-evident, he cabled, that his command was incapable of holding a position in Korea and at the same time protecting Japan against external attack. He referred to the bad morale of his troops. (When General Marshall read this, he remarked to Dean Rusk that when a general complains of the morale of his troops, the time has come to look into his own.) The Government must decide on grounds of high policy which it was to do. "Under the extraordinary limitations and conditions imposed upon the command in Korea, as I have pointed out, its military position is untenable, but it can hold, if overriding political considerations so dictate, for any length of time up to its complete destruction. Your clarification requested."[8]

Here was a posterity paper if there ever was one, with the purpose not only of clearing MacArthur of blame if things went wrong but also of putting the maximum pressure on Washington to reverse itself and adopt his proposals for widening the war against China. Nothing further was needed to convince me that the General was incurably recalcitrant and basically disloyal to the purposes of his Commander in Chief. Deeply disturbed, I was not then aware that General Ridgway was to save the situation from disaster. After a hasty series of meetings, including one of the National Security Council, the President with infinite patience decided on another attempt by three messages to get through to the Supreme Commander the purposes and problems of the United States Government. He also dispatched Generals Joseph Collins and Hoyt S. Vandenberg to Korea to report back on what the actual situation was, stripped of MacArthur's colorful rhetoric. For purposes of clarity each of the messages dealt with a separate facet of the Korean problem in the hope that MacArthur, too, would keep them separate—a vain hope.

In the first of the messages, the Chiefs repeated their current operating directive (for the third time).[9] "Based upon all the factors known to us, including particularly those presented by you in your present message," it appeared to the Chiefs "infeasible under existing conditions" to hold the position in Korea for a protracted period. However, it would be to the interest of the United States and the United Nations to gain some further time for military and diplomatic consultation before beginning evacuation. Therefore, the Chiefs stressed the importance of inflicting "maximum practicable punishment" on the enemy and of not evacuating Korea "unless actually forced by military considerations."

In their second message, of January 12, 1951, delivered personally by General Collins (and read by him to General MacArthur to insure his getting it direct and not through some staff interpretation), the Chiefs discussed what might be done should the situation worsen *and the UN Command be forced to evacuate Korea.*[10] Sixteen possible actions, including General MacArthur's four, all or some of which might be taken after evacuation, were put forward for study in preparation for military and diplomatic consultations. The Chiefs had "tentatively" approved them for this purpose. General Marshall had not; neither had I. We were to discuss them in the National Security Council with the President on January 17. By that date, however, Generals Vandenberg and Collins had returned from Korea and reported a wholly changed situation. The morale of the Army was good, and Ridgway was preparing to take the initiative. He did not feel hampered by the restrictions against operations outside of Korea. It was his and their opinion, in which—*mirabile dictu!*—MacArthur now concurred ("No one is going to drive us into the sea," he announced[11]), that short of active Soviet intervention the Army could continue operations in Korea without endangering its security as long as the national interest required. The Chinese were now having their own difficulties.

The sixteen possible actions for study never went farther. Nevertheless, General MacArthur was "gratified," his Chief of Staff has reported, "to learn that ... the Joint Chiefs of Staff had finally overcome their illusion that fighting back against China would bring on global war" and had advised the carrying out of his recommendations.[12]

Generals Marshall and Bradley joined me in urging the President that he, rather than the Chiefs of Staff—with whom General MacArthur would argue—should send him a third message setting out authoritatively "our basic national and international purposes" in Korea. It was an imaginatively kind and thoughtful letter for the Chief of State to write his theater commander, admitting him to his private mind.[13] The President worked hard and long over a rough draft we had prepared for him. He began by assuring the General that the situation in Korea was receiving his "utmost attention," and then listed ten specific purposes to which continued resistance to aggression would contribute; stressed the necessity of consolidating and holding our support in the United Nations as a strong deterrent to Soviet intervention and, for the same reason, of avoiding widening the war; referred to the adverse possibilities against which he was urgently increasing our military strength; and ended with generous praise of General MacArthur's "splendid leadership" and the "superb performance" of his forces. If ever a message should have stirred the loyalty of a commander, this one should have done so.

Within a month, however, exculpations and complaints began again. The future in Korea, the General complained on February 13, depended on "international considerations and decisions not yet known here." His own field strategy upon Chinese intervention, consisting of a rapid withdrawal, lengthening the enemy's supply lines, and "pyramiding of his logistical difficulties" by "an almost astronomical increase" of air bombardment, had worked well. But he still suffered from the enemy's "unprecedented military advantage of sanctuary protection for his military potential against our counterattack upon Chinese soil."[14] Generals Vandenberg and Collins had reported that this was not the case. Once again MacArthur was refused authority to attack Chinese territory.

THE PARALLEL ONCE MORE

While General MacArthur was fighting the Pentagon, General Ridgway was fighting the enemy. The Eighth Army, joined by X Corps, its fighting spirit restored, its fire power concentrated and greatly increased, took the offensive. General Ridgway held it, to use a term of horsemanship, tightly collected. Its mission was not to recover territory but to destroy enemy forces. This it did with terrible efficiency, even falling back before enemy offensives to lead him into prepared fields of fire. Relentlessly the Army moved north and, once again, approach to the parallel brought new policy discussions between the Department and Ambassador Muccio and across the Potomac between State and Defense.

Two memoranda and meetings between high officers of both departments reveal a situation that was the exact reverse of criticisms made at the time and later by partisan political sources as well as by academicians. It has been charged both that the State Department dominated or tried to dominate the military conduct of the war and that the Chiefs of Staff did the same in the diplomatic and political field. In fact, both charges were wrong and the truth was quite the opposite. Memoranda from State, dated February 13 and 23, 1951, and meetings of the same dates make plain the position of each department that it could not make definitive recommendations in its own field without conclusions of the other. Indeed, so insistent was each upon having guidance from the other that it gave rise to some sharp expressions suggesting avoidance of responsibilities. The later paper, a tentative approach of my own for General Marshall, was rather tartly described by the Chiefs as "an unsound approach," since State should first formulate the political objectives before the Chiefs could devise the military means to achieve them. This is worth noting in connection with a commonly held view that the two departments were in a constant struggle for domination. Conflict was not unknown, as these pages amply show; but when the going was tough each showed great deference to the other in the assumption of responsibility.

In the end we found ourselves agreed on some fairly simple and sensible conclusions. To begin with, and despite some illusions to the contrary, United Nations and United States war aims had not included the unification of Korea by armed force against all comers, and Chinese intervention had now removed this as a practical possibility. The aim was to repulse the aggression and to bring about such a condition of stability that the large UN army could be withdrawn by stages and a line held against the North Koreans by a rearmed and competent Korean Army. The ultimate political aim—a Korea united by peaceful means—though clearly remote, should be retained. The line to be sought and held should be north of the parallel and chosen for its tactical defensive possibilities and practicality of attainment. As April opened, General Ridgway entered the area over which he was to fight for two years, continually weakening and bleeding the enemy without risking his Army, a mission regarding which he and his Government were in complete accord. In this area he found and held the line which became that of the ultimate cease-fire.

THE FINAL SHOWDOWN

"Whom the gods destroy they first make mad," wrote Euripides.

Early in March 1951 General MacArthur's communications revealed surprise and pique over General Ridgway's success in executing the Government's purposes and strategy with the forces available to him. This MacArthur contemptuously called an "accordion" war. Chinese aggression, he believed, according to his Chief of Staff, "could not be stopped by killing Chinese"[15]— although in fact it was. Unless the enemy's war potential was opened to counterattack, he stated publicly on March 7, 1951, the battle lines would in time "reach a point of theoretical military stalemate."[16] He seemed both unable and unwilling to understand that General Ridgway was seeking to establish such a battle line at an advantageous and defensible point as the first step in ending the aggression and the war. He called for decision at the "highest international levels" to provide "an answer to the obscurities which now becloud the unsolved problems raised by Red China's undeclared war in Korea."

On March 15 the General took a step beyond private harassment of the Government. Openly defying the President's order of December 6 to military commanders forbidding unauthorized statements to the press, he gave one to Hugh Baillie, President of the United Press.[17] It criticized stopping the Eighth Army's advance at the 38th parallel or short of "accomplishment of our mission in the unification of Korea." He had been told over and over again that this was not his mission.

Nine days later he perpetrated a major act of sabotage of a Government operation. For some time we had been discussing within the Government and with our allies an idea strongly held in the General Assembly that further diplomatic efforts toward settlement should be made before major forces moved north of the parallel. The idea crystallized in favor of a statement to be made by the President on behalf of the unified command stating that there was a basis for peace in Korea and that the UN Command was prepared to enter into arrangement for a cease-fire to open the way for a broader settlement. On March 21 a draft approved by the President was submitted to the governments participating with troops in Korea. Their responses were favorable. On March 20 the Chiefs of Staff informed General MacArthur of what was in the wind and asked whether he had "sufficient freedom of action for next few weeks" to provide for the security of his forces and keeping contact with the enemy.[18] He replied that he had.

At eleven o'clock in the evening of March 23, Deputy Secretary of Defense Robert Lovett, with Alexis Johnson, Dean Rusk, and Lucius Battle of the State Department, came to me with a pronunciamento that General MacArthur had issued that morning (March 24 in Tokyo). Bob, usually imperturbable and given to ironic humor under pressure, was angrier than I had ever seen him. The General, he said, must be removed and removed at once. After reading the statement I shared his sense of outrage. It can be described only as defiance of the Chiefs of Staff, sabotage of an operation of which he had been informed, and insubordination of the grossest sort to his Commander in Chief. We discussed it and its consequences until one o'clock.

MacArthur's statement† began with a paragraph of bombastic self-praise of his brilliance in defeat, followed by one of denigration of the enemy. China's "exaggerated and vaunted military power" lacked the necessary industrial base for modern war. Its military weakness had been revealed even against a force under the inhibitions from which he suffered. The Chinese would never conquer Korea, he wrote, and if his inhibitions were lifted and their coastal areas and interior bases struck, they would be doomed to military collapse. Once these basic facts were recognized, the Korean problem no longer "burdened by extraneous matters . . . such as Formosa and China's seat in the United Nations" would not be difficult to solve. MacArthur, as the UN commander, would be willing to confer in the field with the enemy commander to find military means whereby the political objectives of the United Nations could be realized.

When, the next morning, the President called Lovett, Rusk, and myself to the White House, Lovett had simmered down. The President, although perfectly calm, appeared to be in a state of mind that combined disbelief with controlled fury. Asking first whether his order of December 6 was clear to us and being assured that it was, he dictated a message to MacArthur which laid so plainly the foundation for a court-martial as to give pause even to General MacArthur:

> The President has directed that your attention be called to his order as transmitted 6 December, 1950. In view of the information given you 20 March 1951 any further statements by you must be coordinated as prescribed in the order of 6 December.
>
> The President has also directed that in the event Communist military leaders request an armistice in the field, you immediately report that fact to the JCS for instructions.[19]

MacArthur's career as an independent spokesman to the public or the enemy was obviously coming to an end. In his memoirs President Truman has written that this act of MacArthur's left him no choice; that he could no longer tolerate his insubordination; and that he had already made up his mind before the last straw was laid on his patience.[20] I have no doubt of it, but can add that he said no word of his decision to me nor, so far as I know, to anyone else. When the next incident occurred on April 5, it took the form of the revelation of a statement made before the order of March 24 and falling outside flat disobedience of a direct order of a superior officer.

To Joseph W. Martin of Massachusetts, Minority Leader of the House of

Representatives, General MacArthur had written on March 20 agreeing with
Mr. Martin's view that, contrary to his superiors' decision, the UN Command
should use Nationalist Chinese forces in the Korean war.[21]

The General then proceeded, addressing the leader of the opposition, to a
direct attack on the President's policies as he had explained them in his personal
message a week earlier: "It seems strangely difficult for some to realize that
here in Asia is where the Communist conspirators have elected to make their
play for global conquest, and that we have joined the issue thus raised on the
battlefield; that here we fight Europe's war with arms, while the diplomats
there still fight it with words; that if we lose this war to Communism in Asia
the fall of Europe is inevitable; win it and Europe most probably would avoid
war and yet preserve freedom. As you pointed out, we must win. There is no
substitute for victory."

On April 5 Mr. Martin released this letter, an open declaration of war on
the Administration's policy, and read it in the House. Also on April 5 the *London
Daily Telegraph* published a dispatch from Hong Kong relating an interview allegedly given by General MacArthur to Lieutenant General H. G.
Martin of the British Army. General MacArthur was quoted as saying that
"United Nations forces were circumscribed by a web of artificial conditions.
. . . He found himself in a war without a definite objective. . . . It was not the
soldier who had encroached upon the realm of the politician [but the other way
around]. . . . The true object of a commander in war was to destroy the forces
opposed to him. But this was not the case in Korea. The situation would be
ludicrous if men's lives were not involved."

Senator Homer Ferguson, Republican of Michigan, proposed that a congressional committee should go to Tokyo and ascertain directly from the General his views on how the war should be run. When a request came from the
President to meet with him and General Marshall immediately after the Cabinet
the next morning, April 6, I was in little doubt what the subject of our discussion would be.

54. THE RELIEF OF
GENERAL MAC ARTHUR

THE DAYS OF DECISION

AFTER THE Cabinet meeting on Friday morning, April 6, General Bradley and Averell Harriman, who had attended to report on the war, with General Marshall and me, followed the President into his office. The President asked and we discussed for about an hour what should be done about General MacArthur's open defiance of him. From the moment of reading the telegram to Congressman Martin my mind was clear on the nature of the problem. It was not so much what should be done as how it should be done. The situation could be resolved only by relieving the General of all his commands and removing him from the Far East. Grave trouble would result, but it could be surmounted if the President acted upon the carefully considered advice and unshakable support of all his civilian and military advisers. If he should get ahead of them or appear to take them for granted or be impetuous, the harm could be incalculable.

As we talked the matter over, it became very clear to me that Generals Marshall and Bradley would need time for unhurried discussion with the Chiefs of Staff, free from any pressure from prior conclusions, even tentative ones, expressed by the Commander in Chief. The Chiefs were out of town and could not be reassembled for deliberation and recommendation until the weekend. My whole effort, therefore, was to keep discussion going and conclusions at bay until all views could be in and all persons committed. There was no doubt what General MacArthur deserved; the sole issue was the wisest way to administer it.

In the afternoon of the same day General Marshall, Averell Harriman, and General Bradley met in my office for further discussion. Either then or in the morning General Marshall asked our opinion on the merits of calling General MacArthur home for consultation and reaching final decision after that. We were all strongly opposed. To me this seemed a road to disaster. The behavior of the extreme Republican right (with some Democratic support), as evidenced by their use of McCarthy and the Policy Committee staff's suggestion of impeachment of the President, convinced me that their attachment to constitutional procedures was a veneer at best. Furthermore, the effect of MacArthur's histrionic abilities on civilians and of his prestige upon the military had been often enough demonstrated. To get him back in Washington in the full panoply of his commands and with his future the issue of the day would not only gravely impair the President's freedom of decision but might well imperil his own future. General Marshall, who had not pressed the idea, was convinced.

We four met again briefly with the President on Saturday morning, when General Bradley reported that the Chiefs were returning to town and would be ready for continuous sessions over Sunday. We were dismissed to meet again on Monday morning, with our matured and final recommendation. However, I was summoned again, and this time alone, on Sunday morning. The President told me that he had drawn John Snyder, Secretary of the Treasury, into the circle of his advisers on this matter, but not what his advice had been. I urged him to continue his very wise course of not disclosing the trend of his thoughts until all recommendations were in and he was ready to decide and act. Whatever his action, all of us would be examined and questioned. On one matter we should all be clear and under no necessity to plead privilege: the President had never intimated to any of us his opinion and intended action until, having heard the recommendations of all the responsible civilian and military officers, he announced his decision.

It may be interesting to recall, as an illustration of the speed with which we in the Department had to turn from one matter to another wholly unrelated one, that on Saturday morning after leaving the President's office I went to the Pan American Union, presided over the closing session of the Fourth Meeting of Consultation of the Ministers of Foreign Affairs of American States, and made the valedictory address. That evening my wife and I attended a large dinner that the foreign ministers gave for President and Mrs. Truman and then went on to a reception at the Pan American Union given for us, which with true Hispanic gaiety and color continued far into the night.

To the group assembled once more in the President's study on Monday morning, April 9, General Marshall announced that the Chiefs of Staff, meeting under the chairmanship of General Bradley, unanimously recommended that General MacArthur be relieved of all his commands and that both he and General Bradley concurred in the recommendation. Averell and I, asked for our views, concurred also. The President said that he was of the same opinion and asked whether the generals had a recommendation for a successor to General MacArthur. They proposed and the President accepted Lieutenant General Matthew B. Ridgway, which delighted both Harriman and me. We were all asked to return the next day with the draft orders to put these decisions into effect.

THE COMMUNICATIONS MIX-UP

The orders and other necessary papers were given to me by the President on Tuesday afternoon to be sent through our code to Ambassador Muccio in Pusan for delivery to Secretary of the Army Pace, who was at the front. Pace was instructed to fly at once to Tokyo and present them to General MacArthur. We had discussed the method of delivery and concluded that the one just described would save the General the embarrassment of direct transmission through Army communications, with the inevitable leaks of such interesting news. The trouble was that something went wrong with the commercial cable line through which the Department had to transmit. By midnight, although the cable company insisted that delivery had been made in Pusan, we had heard nothing from Muccio, who had been instructed to reply in clear "cable received" upon receipt. Thereupon the President and General Bradley, having heard rumors of press inquiries, dispatched the orders direct through the Army's own system. In Tokyo this was believed, quite mistakenly, to have been an unnecessary affront.

Meanwhile our message was received in Pusan, decoded, and telephoned to Pace, who was with Ridgway in his headquarters tent. Pace later told me that he received the message during a hailstorm, when the noise in the tent was like that inside a drum when vigorously beaten. He and Ridgway took the instrument outside to pick up enough of the amazing message to send them scurrying off to Pusan to get it straight and then on to Tokyo, from which the General returned immediately to await his relief, General James A. Van Fleet.

In Washington my day was not notably more relaxed. On Tuesday afternoon after the orders had been sent to the code room, I kept a strange appointment on Capitol Hill with Senators McCarran and Bridges. This was a product of quite a diplomatic negotiation. Our relations had been so strained that they were not sure that I would receive them if they asked for an appointment, so they asked Deputy Under Secretary Carlisle Humelsine to sound me out. To their surprise I said I would be delighted to call on them, which I did. After wholly insincere cordiality on both sides, they disclosed their purpose. The President, they feared, was headed for an ill-considered row with General MacArthur, which he was sure to lose. The General's view would have great support in Congress and the President's would not. They pressed me to get the President to reconsider his attitude and come to an accommodation with the General. I told them that the President would be deeply interested in the views of such distinguished and influential senators, which I would faithfully report— as I did. Of course, when the next day's news of the relief broke, they accused me of misleading them by silence—a charge not without some justification, though no other course was possible—and our relations deteriorated further.

With the change in the communications channels, a busy night opened before us. Shortly after midnight my two secretaries, Luke Battle and Barbara Evans, arrived at my house and telephoning began. I spoke to Senators Tom Connally of Texas and Robert Kerr of Oklahoma, who had great influence, and to Leslie Biffle, Secretary of the Senate, and Boyd Crawford, Clerk of the House Committee on Foreign Affairs, asking them to speak on my behalf to such members of the Senate and House, respectively, as they thought wise, leaving old Judge Kee, Chairman of the House committee, who had a bad heart, until morning. We then went through the ambassadors of states that had troops in Korea under MacArthur's command.

I also got Foster Dulles out of bed and over to see me. He was dismayed by the news and even more dismayed to learn that the President wanted him to go at once to Tokyo to reassure Prime Minister Shigeru Yoshida that no change in policy toward Japan or the treaty would result. He must have time, he said, to consult with Senator Taft and others. I told him to get on with it, to be ready to start within a day or so, and to go with me the next day to the White House, where the President would give him a message for Mr. Yoshida. (He was airborne in thirty-six hours.) By four o'clock our day was over; less than five hours later the next began. It was my fifty-eighth birthday, marked by a luncheon in my honor given by the Secretary of the Senate in his dining room in the Capitol. Most of my staunch friends—and other senators—were there.

A day or two later at the next Cabinet meeting the President asked me to give my impression of the events of the last few days. It was summed up, I said, by the story of the family with the beautiful young daughter who lived on the edge of a large army camp. The wife worried continually, and harassed her husband, over the dangers to which this exposed their daughter. One afternoon the husband found his wife red-eyed and weeping on the doorstep. The worst had happened, she informed him; their daughter was pregnant! Wiping his brow, he said, "Thank God that's over!"

We settled down to endure the heavy shelling from press and Congress that the relief was bound to and did produce. The General returned to the United States and a hero's welcome, made a demagogic speech to Congress and—via television—to the country, and appeared on May 3, 1951, before the Senate Committees on Armed Services and Foreign Relations as the first witness in their "Inquiry into the Military Situation in the Far East and the Facts Surrounding the Relief of General of the Army Douglas MacArthur from his Assignments in that Area." This inquiry, conducted with great skill for eight weeks by Senator Richard Russell, Chairman, exhausted both committees, bored the press and the public, publicized a considerable amount of classified material, and successfully defused the explosive "MacArthur issue." Such detached opinion as there was concluded that the hero had been a troublesome one and that the harassed President had done about what he had to do. We shall skip ahead a bit, recount my part in the hearings and let General MacArthur fade away.

THE SENATE HEARINGS

The manner, form, and rules of the hearings set a record for Senate ambivalence. They were conducted in secret, but the stenographic transcript was made public every evening. However, before its release Admiral Arthur C. Davis, acting for the Pentagon, censored those parts whose publication he considered prejudicial to national defense. His censoring was not severe.

The combined committees had a membership of twenty-six senators, each of whom in order of seniority had an equal right to question each witness. In order to give themselves equal access to publicity the senators voted to restrict questioning to a short period at bat with as many turns as necessary to satisfy the members. This gave a witness with some adroitness the opportunity to deprive the questioning of much continuity and penetration, since he could talk as long as he wanted in answering each question, thus putting off searching follow-up until the next time around, which the senator might miss.

My testimony before the committees may conservatively be described as extensive. It began on Friday morning, June 1, 1951, at 10:06 and continued all day every day except Sunday until Saturday afternoon, June 9 at 5:05. Before recessing, Senator Russell observed dryly:

> Mr. Secretary, I do not know whether it would be the source of pride or consolation to you, but your examination here has been the most extensive of any witness who has been before a hearing that has become somewhat noted for the thoroughness not to mention the repetition of the examination.
>
> You have far exceeded in the number of questions, the number of words and the number of hours that you have been upon the stand the record of any previous witness.[1]

Then with some kind words of appreciation he released me.

Early in the questioning the senators began touching on our postwar relations with China. It was clear to me that a hash would be made of this complex matter if it was covered only by hit-or-miss questions and answers in the interstices of examinations that wandered from my qualifications to discuss military operations with the Chiefs of Staff to the admission of German scientists into the United States to the problems of oil companies in Iran and on to the loyalty program in the Department of State. I asked and obtained permission to postpone questions on China until Monday, when I would make a complete statement on the subject, after which I would be happy to be cross-examined. Adrian Fisher alerted the Far Eastern Bureau to collect for me the principal documents, arranged in chronological order, which I would take to the country for study through Saturday night and Sunday, unbothered by people or suggestions.

For weary hours, aided by coffee and a farmhouse policed into silence by my wife, with a security officer at the gate, I culled out the most telling documents and made a pile of rough notes. On Monday morning, June 4, at 10:03, tired but loaded, I heard Senator Russell launch my effort:

> The committees will be in order.
>
> Under motion made and passed at the last sitting of the committees, the Secretary of State was to make a statement to the committees this morning on China policy.
>
> Mr. Secretary, you may proceed in your own way.

The statement[2] occupied most of the morning. It covered largely the history familiar to the reader in the later part of the introduction to this work and in Chapters 16 and 23 on the Marshall mission to China, and went off surprisingly well. For the first time it put together in colloquial, popular form an account of the century-long disintegration of China's ancient institutions and ways of life from collision with the Western world. To this I added as frankly as I could the reasons for the failure of our effort to aid in reconciling the two Chinese attempts at creating a modern and united China—the Nationalist effort and the Communist effort—a reconciliation they both professed to want. Most of this was new and perplexing to the senators; they never quite regained the initiative in dealing with it or me. Senator Alexander Wiley, the first to question me after the statement, voiced this perplexity: "I think you should be complimented on a pretty clear-cut statement as to the facts that heretofore were not brought to our attention in relation to this Chinese situation, and a very clear-cut statement of the complex position that we occupied in seeking to find the way to combat the Communist influence."[3] Perhaps the most plaintive, if somewhat naïve, cry of "Foul!" came from Senator Owen D. Brewster, Republican of Maine, who complained that I had an "unfair advantage" over the senators through greater knowledge of the subject matter. The Senator had what Senator Wiley might have called a "clear-cut" point.

Senator Russell piloted the two committees into safe haven with great skill and wise judgment. Aware that any reference to the committees' terms of reference would only open partisan rifts and bickering, he treated those terms with intelligent neglect. Instead of a majority report, which would have invited a minority report, he dealt with those gloriously broad generalities to which the wise and just could repair, thus turning the committees from unhappy differences to universal agreement. "The issues which might divide our people," he told our friends and enemies alike, "are far transcended by the things which unite them. If threatened danger becomes war, the aggressor would find at one stroke arrayed against him the united energies, the united resources, and the united devotion of all the American people."[4] This is the sort of political management at which "leaders" in the Senate become past masters. If it does not heal old wounds, it does not inflict new ones. It records that the virulent period of a political virus has passed.

REFLECTIONS

As one looks back in calmness, it seems impossible to overestimate the damage that General MacArthur's willful insubordination and incredibly bad judgment did to the United States in the world and to the Truman Administration in the United States. During the Senate hearings a good deal of discussion revolved about whether the General had disobeyed orders in a court-martial sense of the phrase. I believe that he probably did not and that the debate is beside the point. The General was surely bright enough to understand what his Government wanted him to do. General Ridgway, who succeeded him, understood perfectly and achieved the desired ends. MacArthur disagreed with the desired ends, and wished instead to unify Korea by force of arms even though this plan would involve general war with China and, quite possibly, with the Soviet Union as well. Indeed, far from being dismayed by this prospect, he seemed, as his letter to Congressman Martin strongly suggests, to welcome the wider war, for it was in Asia, as he saw it, that "the Communist conspirators [i.e., the Soviet Union and China] have elected to make their play for global conquest, and that we [i.e., he] have joined the issue thus raised on the battlefield."[5] Having joined the issue thus raised on the Asian battlefield, he was willing, not to say eager, to fight it out there. This was exactly what his Government had told him, beginning with the directive of September 27 and continuing until his relief, that it would not do, even if to avoid it involved withdrawal from Korea. Nevertheless he pressed his will and his luck to a shattering defeat.

In appraising its consequences, two conclusions stand out: the defeat with its losses of men and national prestige was quite avoidable had he followed the agreed plan of campaign; the defeat and MacArthur's conduct in defeat profoundly changed both the national attitude toward the war and our allies' confidence in the judgment and leadership of the United States Government and, especially, in its control over General MacArthur. Regarding the first conclusion, we have already noted that when General Ridgway took over command of the Eighth Army and later the supreme command, he was able, starting much farther south, after a defeat and opposed by a strong enemy, to stabilize the front as MacArthur had been told to do and to hold it. Had General MacArthur, who faced no opposition after Inchon and the defeat of the North Koreans, occupied one of the strong positions in mid-Korea, fortified it, and kept his forces collected, he could have shattered a Chinese assault just as Ridgway did.

The effect of defeat and the General's ill-concealed disaffection upon domestic and foreign confidence were equally plain. The enthusiasm with which our people and allies received President Truman's bold leadership of the United Nations in military resistance to aggression survived even the hard fighting of the retreat to the Pusan perimeter and the surprising discovery of North Korean military competence and toughness. It was heightened by the September victories and the complete collapse of the invasion of South Korea. Opinion at home and abroad would have remained steady and united had the Army under the September 27 plan and directive sealed off the South from further attack until the war should peter out, as it eventually did, even though this would require, as it also did, some hard fighting to prove the strength of the line.

What lost the confidence of our allies were MacArthur's costly defeat, his open advocacy of widening the war at what they rightly regarded as unacceptable risks, and the hesitance of the Administration in asserting firm control over him. What disturbed and divided our own people was the stream of propaganda flowing out of Tokyo that the cause of MacArthur's disasters was not his own stubborn folly, but conspiracy in Washington, probably inspired by concern for national interests other than our own. The method and source of propaganda are well illustrated by a later effusion of MacArthur's Chief of Staff, General Courtney Whitney: "Who it was who won over President Truman's confidence and corrupted his logic to the extent of defying the experienced advice of his best military experts, has always been a well-kept Washington secret. Certainly the Secretary of Defense, Louis Johnson, did not favor this kind of appeasement. So the likely person to bear the enormous blame for this incalculable mistake would seem to be the then Secretary of State Dean Acheson, possibly acting under pressure from the British Foreign Office."[6]

Nor does this apt pupil of McCarthy spare the President. Whitney states that MacArthur's "qualified guess" given the President at Wake Island, which deprecated the possibility of Chinese intervention, was based on the assumption that intervention would result in forceful retaliation, not continued sanctuary. Someone must have told the Chinese that they could intervene with impunity.

The Wake Island conference, he concludes, was "a sly political ambush" set by the President for the General.

That General Whitney included all persons in high office in the plot against his hero is clear in his exculpation of the General for his sabotage of the President's intended statement before our forces crossed the 38th parallel for the second time: "What had happened was that by sheer accident, in his statement [of March 24, 1951] and in its reference to settling the war without reference to Formosa or the United Nations seat, MacArthur had cut right across one of the most disgraceful plots in American history. Or was it not accident, but intuition? This I do know: had MacArthur fully realized the hornets' nest he would stir up, he still would not have been deterred."[7] The last sentence I am inclined to believe. The continued seepage of this poison, like that administered by McCarthy, had a highly toxic effect on the American public. Like McCarthy's, it was skillfully used by the Republican right and had an effect in undermining confidence in the very institution of government in areas far wider than those where such slanderous nonsense was believed. Like air pollution, one did not have to believe in it to be poisoned by it.

This loss of confidence at home and abroad in the conduct of our foreign affairs was not the proximate cause of any change in our foreign policy, but it added to our difficulties and by so doing diminished our effectiveness. The loss of support in the United Nations and the increased energy spent on countering unwise proposals we shall see as one manifestation of this. Another was to be growing opposition in other parts of the world to the policies and interests of the United States. This flame of opposition was skillfully and strongly fanned by the Soviet Union in 1951.

55. THE MOVE FOR AN ARMISTICE
IN KOREA

AT THE TIME OF General MacArthur's relief and General Ridgway's succession to Supreme Command, the UN forces were dug in on the Kansas line with a Chinese offensive ominously building up. To prepare for this, General Ridgway pushed a salient forward in the center of his line toward first the Utah and then the Wyoming line. The offensive burst with great fury ten days after General MacArthur's relief and continued for a month, checked in midcourse by General Van Fleet's counterattack.

For two weeks the Eighth Army gave ground as successive collapses of South Korean units under pressure opened gaps in the line. None of these, however, was permitted to develop into a breakthrough. As it fell back across the 38th parallel the Army traded ground for terrific losses inflicted on the enemy. When the first Chinese effort was spent, General Ridgway resumed the offensive, straightened his line on ground that he had strongly prepared, and sternly forbade his forces to be separated or strung out in pursuit. The Chinese resumed their attack in mid-May, but by the end of the month, after heavy losses, were in flight north of the parallel. The Eighth Army followed collectedly, soon had South Korea cleared of the enemy, and, resuming its position on the Kansas line, felt out the enemy's forces dug into strong positions farther north.

During early June, the White House, the State Department, the Pentagon, and the Supreme Command in Tokyo found themselves united on political objectives, strategy, and tactics for the first time since the war had started. The political purpose was to stop the aggression and to leave the unification of Korea to time and political measures. The strategy was to fight it out on the Kansas-Wyoming line and the Punch Bowl just north of it if it took all summer, or more than two summers; our tactics were to lure the enemy into assaults on strongly fortified lines through prepared and calibrated fields of fire. Experience had taught a costly lesson: to push the Chinese back upon their border—their source of reinforcement and supply—only increased their strength, as Hercules increased that of Antaeus when he threw him upon his Mother Earth, while decreasing our own as our forces attenuated their lines of supply, became separated, and lost touch with their air support as they moved north. The generals, among them Van Fleet and Mark Clark, who later declared that they had been deprived of their chance for total victory were antedating thoughts conceived in tranquillity.[1]

While General Ridgway was pushing the Communists north, I had an

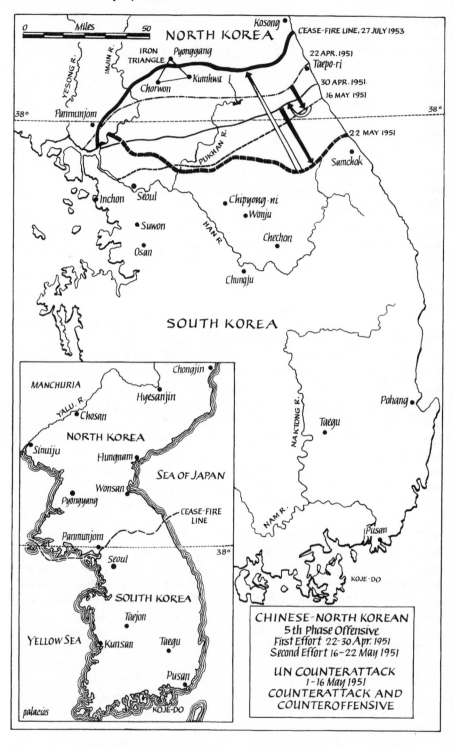

0 Miles 50
NORTH KOREA
CEASE-FIRE LINE, 27 JULY 1953
Kosong
YESONG R.
IMJIN R.
IRON TRIANGLE
Pyonggang
Kumhwa
Chorwon
22 APR. 1951
Taepo-ri
30 APR. 1951
16 MAY 1951
38°
Panmunjom
PUKHAN R.
38°
22 MAY 1951
Samchok
Inchon
Seoul
Chipyong-ni
Wonju
Suwon
HAN R.
Chechon
Osan
Chungju
SOUTH KOREA
NAKTONG R.
Pohang
Taegu
NAM R.
Pusan
KOJE-DO

Chongjin
MANCHURIA
Hyesanjin
YALU R.
Chosan
NORTH KOREA
Sinuiju
Hungnam
SEA OF JAPAN
Wonsan
Pyongyang
CEASE-FIRE LINE
Panmunjom
38°
Seoul
SOUTH KOREA
Taejon
YELLOW SEA
Kunsan
Taegu
Pusan
palacios
KOJE-DO

CHINESE-NORTH KOREAN
5th Phase Offensive
First Effort 22-30 Apr. 1951
Second Effort 16-22 May 1951

UN COUNTERATTACK
1-16 May 1951
COUNTERATTACK AND
COUNTEROFFENSIVE

opportunity to drive home before the Congress and the public the difference between the war aims of the United Nations Command and the long-range United Nations political purposes first stated in 1947 and since reiterated in the resolutions of October 7, 1950, and May 18, 1951. They had become confused by General MacArthur's oratory during the period from October 1950 to April 1951, when the General was repeatedly speaking and acting in disregard of President Truman's orders. Twice during the MacArthur hearings on June 1 and 2, 1951, I took the opportunity to make this distinction clear beyond doubt.[2]

Secretary Acheson: Our objective is to stop the attack, end the aggression on that [Korean] Government, restore peace, providing against the renewal of the aggression. Those are the military purposes for which, as we understand it, the United Nations troops are fighting.

The United Nations has since 1947 and the United States has since 1943 or 1944 [the Cairo Declaration of December 1, 1943] stood for a unified, free, and democratic Korea. That is still our purpose, and is still the purpose of the United Nations.

I do not understand it to be a war aim. In other words, that is not sought to be achieved by fighting, but it is sought to be achieved by peaceful means, just as was being attempted before this aggression.

Chairman Connally: After the fight—by peaceful means after the fighting is over.

Secretary Acheson: Yes, sir.

The next morning Senator Smith of New Jersey took me over the same ground and asked specifically whether my answers suggested "the possibility of a cease-fire at or near the thirty-eighth parallel?" I replied: "If you could have a real settlement, that would accomplish the military purposes in Korea. That is if the aggression would end and you had reliable assurances that it would not be resumed, then you could return to a peacetime status, and we would hope gradually to remove the troops from Korea, both Chinese troops and United Nations troops."

While the diplomatic front in the United Nations and among our allies was relatively calm, we could not count on its remaining so. On May 18 months of effort had resulted in a UN vote for an embargo against sending strategically important items to China and North Korea. But a vote and an actual embargo were not the same thing; plenty of opportunity remained for congressional sanctions against nations that continued to export. We remembered, too, the anguish caused by the UN First Committee's Five Principles for Discussion which we in the State Department thought it best to accept and which our fellow citizens rejected in no uncertain manner. Not being eager for further UN initiatives, it was incumbent upon us to devise our own. The only hopeful path pointed toward an armistice which might harden into an end to belligerency. An agreed settlement seemed both impossible and unreliable if achieved. One conclusion we shared unanimously: that exploration through the public procedures of the United Nations or through leaky foreign offices like the Indian would be fatal.

We therefore cast about like a pack of hounds searching for a scent. First Charles Bohlen, who was then in Paris at the Palais Rose, sounded out Vladimir Semyonov, Political Adviser to the Chairman of the Soviet Control Commission in Germany, without result. Then Ernest Gross and Thomas Cory at the United Nations got a faint scent from some informal words spoken by either Malik or Semen K. Tsarapkin, the alternate Soviet UN Representative, or both. The prompt appearance of a similar rumor in *The New York Times* drew protests and denials from the Russians, during which the scent died away. That channel proved to be too amateur. A suggestion with some credentials of reliability came to us that an approach to Peking might be more productive. We tried it secretly through both American and Swedish channels to Moscow without result. Charles Burton Marshall of the Policy Planning Staff went to Hong Kong and made himself available for contacts, but with no success. A last effort, however, initiated with the President's approval, produced results, not all of them foreseen.

THE KENNAN-MALIK TALKS

Our colleague George Kennan was on leave of absence from the Department working at the Institute for Advanced Study in Princeton. Remembering Jessup's success with Malik over the Berlin blockade in 1949, Doc Matthews asked Kennan to Washington in mid-May 1951 to talk with him and me. We wanted him to see Malik. Kennan was not a part of but was close to the official establishment and deeply interested in U.S.-Soviet relations (on which, in fact, he was then writing a history). They could talk seriously but without commitment. Our two countries seemed to be headed for what could be a most dangerous collison over Korea. This was definitely not the purpose of American actions or policy. It was hard for us to believe that it was desired by the Soviet Union. Whether or not it was desired by Peking, it seemed the inevitable result of the course the Chinese were steering. If the drift to serious trouble was to be stopped, the method would seem to be an armistice and cease-fire in Korea at about where the forces were. We would like to know how Moscow viewed the situation, and what, if any, suggestions it might have. We also wished to be sure that it understood our desires and intentions. If hostilities were to end, it was a good time to set about ending them.

We did not want George to negotiate anything, but to make sure that our purposes and intentions were absolutely clear to the Russians and that they were realistically aware of the course on which all were adrift and of its more than likely terminus. He agreed to take on the mission in his own way and alone. Through the Chiefs of Staff we let Ridgway know that an operation was on and that he should be prepared to advise on all relevant military matters and to conduct proceedings in the field as needed. He welcomed the development.

George, in a longhand note delivered by a young assistant in our UN delegation to Malik at his apartment in New York, asked to see him and for a reply by phone to Princeton. A prompt reply invited him to Malik's summer house on Long Island. Kennan drove from Princeton. They met quite alone on May 31 and spoke in Russian. Overcoming an initial embarrassment when Malik upset a tray of fruit and wine on himself, they circuitously approached the question, which, predictably, Malik was unable to answer, and as circuitously retreated from it, agreeing to meet again when he had had a chance to consider the matter, a euphemism for consulting Moscow. The next week, when they met again on June 5, Malik was able to tell him that the Soviet Government wanted peace and a peaceful solution in Korea and as rapidly as possible. It could not appropriately take part in discussions of a cease-fire. Malik's personal advice was to approach the North Koreans and Chinese. No doubt existed in any of our minds that the message was authentic. It had, however, a sibylline quality which left us wondering what portended and what we should do next.

Clarification began soon afterward, when on June 23 Malik delivered a speech on the UN radio program. The Soviet peoples believed, he said, that the conflict in Korea could be settled: "[A]s a first step discussions should be started between the belligerents for a cease-fire and an armistice providing for the mutual withdrawal of forces from the 38th parallel."[3] Could such a step be taken? he asked, and answered that it could if both sides really wished to stop the fighting. This sounded as official as it was possible to be, but doubts were expressed at home and abroad, publicly and privately. Inquiry made through Ambassador Kirk in Moscow confirmed that the views expressed were those of the Soviet Government and that Gromyko was uninformed about those of the Chinese.

THE DECISION TO NEGOTIATE THROUGH RIDGWAY

The ambassadors of the nations with forces in the UN Command met and approved the opening of negotiations. The question was how. The case for military talks through commanders in the field was strong, for the following reasons:

First, because neither the Chinese nor the North Korean authorities were official entities recognized by the United States.

Second, because it was highly desirable to exclude from the talks political questions such as Formosa, the recognition of Communist China and its membership in the United Nations, and Indochina, which the Communists had tried to introduce earlier.

Third, because General Wu Hsiu-chuan's visit to the United Nations in New York to represent China there left no doubt that the UN was the worst of all places to conduct discussions.

Fourth, because the very fact that negotiations were in prospect was dictated by the relation of forces on the battlefield.

Fifth, because neither the Chinese Communists nor the Soviet Government accepted any responsibility for Chinese forces in Korea. They were supposed to be "volunteers," acting on their own responsibility. However, their commander could speak for them, as Gromyko pointed out to Ambassador Kirk.

Strong, however, as were the arguments for military conduct of discussions at the front, the military did not grasp for this responsibility; on the contrary, they were most reluctant to be tagged with it. When the President decided they should handle it, however, they loyally accepted the assignment.†
Two basic papers were prepared in accordance with President Truman's orderly procedures: a small State-Defense group at Assistant Secretary-flag rank drafted a message covering Ridgway's opening of contact with the enemy and instructions, to be supplemented later, regarding the purposes, content, and conduct of the talks. These were gone over and revised by the Chiefs of Staff, General Marshall, General Ridgway, and me; submitted to the President; and, after incorporation of his changes, signed and dispatched. We also kept Ambassador Muccio informed and later, through him, President Syngman Rhee. I myself saw that Senators Connally and Wiley and Representatives Richards and Eaton were abreast of developments. Muccio soon warned us that we were in for trouble with Rhee, as indeed we were. What Muccio called "his mania for reunification" would and did lead him to regard as "unacceptable" (a word of the old diplomatic vocabulary denoting a cause for restrained fury) any cessation of our fighting for the reunification of Korea. Some rather plain telegrams restored better behavior but did not gain real acceptance of the policy.

On June 30, Tokyo time, General Ridgway broadcast to the Commander in Chief, Communist Forces in Korea, that if, as reported, the Communist commander was prepared to negotiate a cease-fire and armistice, Ridgway was prepared to send a representative to begin discussions. How different this simple, soldierly, and disciplined announcement was from the unauthorized bombast by which General MacArthur frustrated President Truman's proposed announcement of a similar sort three months before—not that an earlier one, if it had been made, would have produced a useful response. General Ridgway's six months of hard fighting and the terrible punishment he had inflicted upon the enemy had drastically changed the situation. Furthermore, his conduct had restored respect for the governmental integrity of the United States.

FOUL-UP AS NEGOTIATIONS START

On July 2 the Communist commanders replied favorably to General Ridgway's message. Whereas he had suggested meeting on a Danish hospital ship in Wonsan harbor, they proposed Kaesong, a town at that time between the two lines. General Ridgway accepted the change and the delegations met on July 10. Almost at once we learned the truth of Bret Harte's observation a century before:

> That for ways that are dark
> And for tricks that are vain,
> The heathen Chinee is peculiar.[4]

Whereas Kaesong had been between the lines when General Ridgway agreed to it as the seat of discussions, by the time discussions began the Communists had surrounded it and proceeded to make an arrogant and offensive propaganda demonstration, excluding the allied press and behaving in their customary ill-mannered and boorish way. Whereupon we broke off contact until they restored the neutral aspect of the meeting place.

Then we ran into the now familiar trouble of agreement on the agenda items. The first two substantive items on the Chinese agenda caused the trouble. The first of these was "establishment of the 38th Parallel as the military demarcation line between the two sides and establishment of a demilitarized zone, as basic conditions for the cessation of hostilities in Korea"; the second was "withdrawal of all armed forces of foreign countries from Korea."[5] We could not accept either. The 38th parallel had been amply proved to be indefensible and to us had no political or historic significance. We had no intention of giving up the strong positions of the Kansas line; indeed, we hoped to improve them. The second item had been familiar Communist propaganda for months in regard to both Asia and Europe. Their aim, of course, was to push American forces back to North America.

Expecting months of verbal quibbling on these items, as there had been at the Palais Rose, General Marshall and I both made public statements. President Rhee, as I have said, was most disturbed by the armistice discussions. We doubted whether his morale could withstand a long propaganda battle at Kaesong directed at leaving the South Korean Army without allies after an armistice on an indefensible line. I spoke on July 19 and General Marshall on the twenty-fourth, strongly affirming that the removal of foreign troops was a political matter inappropriate for discussion by commanders arranging an armistice. A United Nations force must and would, we said, remain in Korea until peace was firmly established. This greatly comforted President Rhee, who thought, according to Muccio, that the "message was fine, very reassuring, just what we wanted." The Korean National Assembly also approved a message of gratitude. President Truman directed us to stick to this line, keeping in close touch with him.

To our great surprise, however, the Communists dropped the battle over the wording of the agenda. They rephrased the item on a military demarcation line and a demilitarized zone so as not to refer to any particular line, and dropped the withdrawal-of-forces item. But, as the talks moved to take up agenda topics, they made it plain that on the 38th parallel, at least, they had not at all changed their substantive position. The line of demarcation must still be the 38th parallel. With the agenda agreed in two weeks—a phenomenal feat—we settled down to discuss it, happily unaware that final agreement would not be reached until two years later and that even agreement on the first item would take the next six months.

How and why did this happen? Were we deceived and led into an endless propaganda morass? To some degree. Was it due to a relaxation of military pressure on the enemy? Certainly not in 1951. Was it due to a change of mind by the Russians or a difference of view between them and the Chinese? To some extent, the latter. The reasons, I believe, were far more complex than many simplistic explanations given over the years. One, I think, unsuspected by me at the time, was of our own making and occurred at the very beginning.

Three years after these events some of us who had been deeply involved in their direction met from time to time to discuss old campaigns, as soldiers will, and analyze, with more time and detachment than the press of events had permitted, the reasons why we and others acted as we did. At one of these meetings several of my colleagues suggested that the Russians and Chinese could well have been surprised, chagrined, and given cause to feel tricked when at Kaesong we revealed a firm determination as a matter of major principle not to accept the 38th parallel as the armistice line. There were several reasons why they might have felt so. In the first place, when Kennan spoke to Malik, the Eighth Army had only recently crossed the 38th parallel; indeed, its western flank was south of it. While Kennan spoke only vaguely of a truce line, Malik in his radio address was very precise in referring to a "mutual withdrawal of forces from the 38th parallel." Furthermore, our initial agenda provided for "limitation of discussion to purely military matters related to Korea only,"[6] and since the Japanese surrender we had insisted that the parallel was wholly a military line without political significance. To change it, therefore, might well have, in the Communists' minds, political significance. Even more important, and unknown to us either in 1945 when the parallel was chosen or in 1951, the 38th parallel had been a most important line to both Imperial Russia and Imperial Japan prior to the Russo-Japanese war and the annexation of Korea by Japan, for it was the line proposed by Japan but rejected by Russia as too restrictive as the demarcation of their spheres of influence in Korea.

So it seems to me highly probable that the Russians and the Chinese, for whom they were acting, received a considerable shock when at the start of a negotiation to restore, as they thought, the *status quo ante* they found us demanding a new line for our sphere of influence, not only more militarily significant but involving considerable loss of prestige for them. They would never imagine that what appeared to be trickery was wholly inadvertent on our part. It was exactly the sort of maneuver in which they would have delighted.

Toward the end of July 1951 in response to a thoughtful letter from Herbert Morrison, I speculated on what might come out of these talks and their possible aftermath, allowing my mind to roam ahead. Chinese purposes, I thought, might be narrower and more immediate than Russian, with the former more concentrated on gaining control of the peninsula and the latter looking toward the longer-range purpose of slowing down or stopping the military defense of the West. But this difference would hardly benefit us. I thought that the prospects of "a general settlement in Korea" were not good, which was Morrison's view also. The Communists wished to eliminate our influence from Korea altogether; the MacArthur aim of unifying Korea by force entailed costs greater than we were prepared to pay. I would regard an armistice, therefore, as something that we must live with for a considerable time and that must be adapted to that end. On this issue we must expect trouble from Rhee, with his "mania for reunification"; he would oppose anything less and might try to prevent it. So I saw the best hope as not searching for an illusory general solution, but in aiming persistently toward an armistice that would stop the fighting in a posture favorable to the defense and, given the presence of UN troops over a considerable time, might harden into a maintainable peace. Morrison was gratified that we were thinking along the same lines. We must now wait and see what would develop, he said. And wait we did.

NEGOTIATIONS OFF AND FIGHTING ON

At Kaesong the discussion wore on repetitively about the demarcation line, interrupted from August 4 to 10 when armed Chinese forces violated the neutrality of the conference zone. Our negotiators, understandably frustrated by the endless and circuitous path they trod, urged that we give the Communists a limited time to choose between alternatives, and if they did not, that we break off negotiations. But we in Washington felt that being ahead so far we must put the onus for a break squarely on the other side. On August 20 brief hope dawned when the Communists seemed willing to consider the "line of contact" on the crucial date rather than "the general area of the battle line"— our phrase—as the armistice demarcation line. But before the significance of this phrase could be explored, the other side broke off negotiations, charging that an American plane had bombed and strafed Kaesong. The United Nations Command investigated and denied the charges. On September 6 General Ridgway proposed that talks be resumed at a new site, but four days later one of our planes did strafe the Kaesong conference site. Proper disciplinary action was taken, and the Communists, their *amour propre* satisfied, proposed resumption of negotiations but at Kaesong, not at a new site. This started a new procedural controversy.

Since the beginning of the second year of the war, negotiating and fighting had been going on together, the latter more successfully from our point of view. After a review of strategy by the commanders in the field, they rejected ideas of advancing to the neck of Korea along the Pyongyang-Wonsan line in favor of strengthening and shortening the Kansas line by taking over the enemy positions ringing the Punch Bowl. These were strong positions that enabled the Communists to enfilade the Kansas line. When, in early autumn after heavy fighting and severe casualties on both sides, Bloody Ridge had been taken, the Eighth Army made another assault to add a further strong point from which the enemy menaced its right flank. Appropriately named Heartbreak Ridge, it was in our hands by mid-October.

NEGOTIATIONS RESUMED AT PANMUNJOM

A week or so later—possibly motivated by these successes of our arms— the Chinese accepted General Ridgway's proposal to resume negotiations at Panmunjom in a neutral and unoccupied zone. During the summer I put the Department to work devising courses to follow should the negotiations succeed and the fighting end, or should they fail and the enemy intensify his efforts. It seemed to me that inevitably and soon we should face one or the other of these contingencies; yet although we remained in office for another year and a half, we faced neither. The war neither stopped nor blazed up again in that time. It slumbered like an ominous and infinitely dangerous dragon, with no St. George at hand to slay it.

After the event both professional and armchair warriors have criticized the Government for not maintaining heavy offensive pressure on the enemy to speed up conclusion of the armistice. I am happy to say that the Supreme Commander took no such callous attitude toward the lives of his men, but, as General Ridgway himself has told us, did his best to keep our losses at a minimum and undertook no major offensives after perfecting his line.[7]

The Department's studies produced two works, known as the "optimistic paper" and the "pessimistic paper," the chief value of which was to assure us that no new ideas had been spawned since the days of the MacArthur crisis. They confirmed the views of all of us, soldiers and civilians alike, that we were on the only sound course and that we had to pull together to make it work. If still further confirmation were needed, we got it in September from the visits of Morrison and Schuman and our talks with them.

Their enthusiasm for the Korean war had reached an irreducible minimum. The "optimistic paper," which looked forward to conferences for a settlement in Korea, seemed to them, as it did to us, beyond the realm of possibility. The "pessimistic paper" terrified them. Possible bombing of Chinese bases, blockades of China, trade embargoes, with the chances of Russian intervention in the Far or Middle East, proposals of expediting Japanese rearmament—all seemed as dangerous and undesirable to them as they did to us. We, however, were closer to the need for new fields of action. From the British side came the familiar exegesis on the perils to Hong Kong and the dangers of driving the Chinese into the arms of the Russians or vice versa. I often regretted that no embracing arms seemed ready to receive the United States if pushed too far.

Before turning to the hardly more tractable troubles of NATO, we may take a refreshing look at the great diplomatic success of 1951, the conclusion of a treaty of peace with Japan.

56. PEACE WITH JAPAN

As RELATED IN Chapter 46, the President's decision of September 8, 1950, gave the State Department an operator's license and an operator but not an automobile. We had been told to go out and make one ourselves. "However," as we concluded the earlier account, "we were on our way."

The Defense Department's roadblock, built of the conception that a peace treaty with Japan was "premature," had been demolished, although the soldiers were not yet purged of all obstruction. The peace treaty itself would be a short and simple document re-establishing peace without punitive provisions or burdening Japan with reparation payments, foreign occupation, or arms limitations. A bilateral United States-Japanese defense treaty would provide for such U.S. military protection and facilities in Japan as might be agreed. Separate security arrangements between the United States and Far Eastern nations fearing Japanese aggression would be used if necessary. The treaties should all be negotiated by the United States diplomatically. When agreed, a conference of the cooperating states should meet to sign but not further negotiate the treaties.

Furthermore, in John Foster Dulles we had a negotiator domestically acceptable to both Administration and opposition. He was closely meshed into the working of the Department, was staffed by leading figures in the Far Eastern Division, and was kept in close touch with both the President and me, who carried him through battles within the Administration. He was on his own in dealing with his Republican colleagues in the Congress, particularly the Senate, and in his many negotiations around the world. From time to time the heavy artillery of the Department and the White House was moved up to help him in these.

Once the Administration was agreed within itself on the course to be followed, which it had been since the beginning of 1951, the work of preparing the complex of treaties and negotiating the solvable problems of those who really wished to join in signing them was accomplished in the short space of eight months. And what an eight months! It covered the Great Debate, the removal of General MacArthur and the Senate's inquisition into it, the stabilization of the Korean battlefront, and the opening of armistice discussions. To accomplish the treaty negotiations in so short a time required the continuous application of intense and concentrated energy guided by good sense. This Mr. Dulles and his able assistants provided. It also required a determination mounting at times to ruthlessness in dealing with opposition. Whatever the purpose of

Soviet and Indian opposition to our plans, the effect would have been delay and division if we had been drawn into it. We therefore kept both governments informed and extended ample opportunities for consultation. But we also quite early reconciled ourselves to the realization that neither government intended to sign any treaty and hence we indicated our willingness to go forward without them (and ultimately Burma and Yugoslavia as well), and made no concessions. Nor did we shrink from the Soviets' continued invitation to public debate, but on the contrary accepted it with verve. Our note to Moscow of May 19, 1951,[1] came back from submission to the White House with the postscript: "Dean: This document is a jewel. HST." Similarly, to those who demanded reparations as a condition to agreeing to a treaty we made clear that Japan could not pay monetary reparations and that we would not. The Japanese were willing to negotiate with them within the realm of the possible.

Mr. Dulles' first formal negotiating expedition in January-February 1951 got us into pretty solid agreement with Prime Minister Yoshida's Government and broad sections of Japanese opinion on the main lines and forms of the treaties, left the Filipinos simmering in their dream of eight billion dollars in reparations, and brought the Australians and New Zealanders to the realistic views that reparations were not possible and that security relations with us were superior to punitive or restrictive provisions in the Japanese treaty. It became clear, as competing considerations were put forward on security arrangements, at this time and later, that a set of interlocking agreements focusing on U.S. relations in the area would be most acceptable. The British were reluctantly willing to accept this solution as not incompatible with their interests in general nor with their positions in Malaya and Hong Kong in particular. They were also doing some treaty drafting on their own. By the end of March we had put on paper, distributed to the principal parties concerned, and outlined to the public a tentative draft for discussion and suggestions. Then came the MacArthur removal and the Dulles trip to Japan to keep the Japanese steady.

When he returned, the treaty tournament moved into the semifinals. Since most of the applicants for security treaties wanted one with us but no one else, we agreed on separate treaties with Japan, with the Philippines, and with Australia and New Zealand, whose mutual toleration went that far. The British advanced from obscurity to cooperation with the arrival in Washington of their own draft treaty at the beginning of April and, at the end of the month, of a drafting party to share the task of merging the two texts into a joint Anglo-American proposal. While preferring our own short form, we did not let pride of authorship stand in the way of accepting some prolixity if accompanied by agreement on substance. Two important unresolved issues were settled by a process of elimination during the London part of a European trip by Mr. Dulles. A disagreement over the recipients to whom the Japanese should transfer sovereignty over Formosa, the Kuriles, and southern Sakhalin was settled by having none and providing for a simple renunciation of Japanese sovereignty. A question whether the Nationalist Chinese or the Communist Chinese—or both or neither—should be invited was settled by inviting neither and providing that Japan, during the first three years after the peace treaty came into effect, enter into a similar bilateral peace treaty with any state that had been at war with Japan and had adhered to the Declaration of the United Nations of January 1, 1942. Japan's future attitude toward China, they agreed, "must necessarily be for determination by Japan itself in the sovereign and independent status contemplated by the Treaty."

When Mr. Dulles went to Paris, he was faced with three demands: the first for two billion dollars in reparations from Japan; the second for a Japanese commercial agreement protecting French interests in Indochina; the third for participation by the three associated states in Indochina in the signing of the treaty. The first was dropped, the second left for bilateral negotiations, and the third eventually accepted. A number of states—the Netherlands, the Philippines, and Indonesia among them—remained unhappy over the failure to obtain reparations and were reluctant about signing the treaty. This, we believed, was a self-liquidating problem.

We now moved into the final stage of treaty preparation. In it the final text was prepared, invitations to a conference were issued, and two controversies settled or were thought to be settled. One of these was the Pentagon's Last Stand; the other, a tussle between the Australians and the Chiefs of Staff. The first, already mentioned in Chapter 46, brought up for the last time, if in an oblique or flanking attack, the Chiefs' hard-fought attempt to postpone the coming into effect of the treaty until after the end of hostilities in Korea. Since State refused to yield, we took the matter to the President. There Lovett, with the approval of General Marshall, defected, and the Chiefs—abandoned and overruled—were ready to agree to make peace effective at once. We gave them a consolation prize, however, by agreeing with them against the Australians in a dispute over the Australia-New Zealand-United States (ANZUS) security treaty, in which Australia had sought some joint planning relationship with our Chiefs. Fear of proliferation of such a relationship throughout the treaties led to its elimination, but in agreeing, Percy (later Sir Percy) Spender, the Australian Foreign Minister, received the impression from Mr. Dulles that some informal relationship would exist, which had not been intended. This rose to cause trouble at our first meeting a year later in Hawaii.

On July 20 a semifinal Anglo-American draft treaty, an earlier version of which had already been seen by all states at war with Japan, was formally circulated among them, asking for comments. With it went an invitation from the United States Government to a Conference for Conclusion and Signature of a Treaty of Peace with Japan on the terms of a text that Great Britain and the United States proposed to circulate on August 13. The conference would open in San Francisco on September 4, 1951. Never was so good a peace treaty so little loved by so many of its participants in the weeks preceding its signing as was this one. Its co-sponsor, His Majesty's Government through its Minister of State, Kenneth Younger, thought it necessary, "little as one feels enthusiasm for it."[2] The Australian Government offered reluctant support, but the opposition expressed extreme objection. The Foreign Affairs Committee of the French National Assembly voiced regret at the lack of French participation in the drafting of the treaty. The Netherlands Government accepted the invitation but reserved freedom of action on signature. Burma, India, and Yugoslavia declined to attend. Neutralist elements in Japan were critical. The big surprise was the Soviet Union's acceptance of the invitation to attend, with Andrei Gromyko, Deputy Foreign Affairs Minister, leading the delegation to "present the proposals of the Soviet Government." This evoked a somewhat panicky statement from Foster Dulles that "responsible nations" would not let the Russians become a "wrecking crew," while the Department more sedately observed that the "invitation was 'to a conference for conclusion and signature of a treaty' " on the terms of a specific text, not "to reopen negotiations on the terms of peace." We immediately set to work to assure that this would, indeed, be its nature.

THE RULES OF PROCEDURE

When the Russians informed us that they would attend the conference and present their own proposals for peace with Japan, I had no doubt that it would fall to me to prevent a "wrecking" operation. For one who had spent as long an apprenticeship as I had under Speaker Sam Rayburn of the House of Representatives and its Rules Committee, this did not present a perplexing problem. It did require, however, experience and a degree of managerial skill that I believed I had to supply myself. Foster Dulles contributed to my doing so. He had consulted me about our respective roles at the coming conference, suggesting that in view of his greater familiarity with the negotiations he should serve as floor leader and pilot the treaty through the conference, while I should take the honorific position of its presiding officer. The procedure I had in mind would require neither floor leader nor pilot, but it seemed best to accept his proposal.

Under the procedures of the House of Representatives a bill comes up on report from the Rules Committee accompanied by a rule governing its consideration. An "open rule" may permit amendments to the bill and set the time for debate on each amendment and for debate on the amended bill. A "closed rule" usually permits no amendments and fixes the time for debate, after which "without amendment or further dilatory procedure" the bill is put to a vote. With rules drafted on such a model and a majority of the conference supporting me, I felt confident that we could prevent a wrecking operation. I set out to provide both.

The Rules of Procedure were simplicity itself. They provided that the conference would be conducted in accordance with the invitation extended by the Government of the United States. The Temporary President would be the chairman of the U.S. delegation—i.e., myself; the permanent President and other officers would be elected by a majority vote of participating states. The other usual provisions regarding languages, order of seating, and credentials were provided. Then came the crucial article, which is best given in its own words:

Art. 17. Having regard to the special and limited Terms of Reference of this Conference, its business, after adoption of the Rules of Procedure, shall be confined to:

1. Election of Officers.

2. Report on Credentials.

3. Statements on behalf of the two governments jointly sponsoring the Treaty text.

4. Statements by participating Delegations.

5. Report of Secretary General on conformity of the different language texts of the Treaty.

6. Ceremony of signing the Treaty of Peace with Japan.[3]

The rules also provided that the statement of each delegation should not exceed one hour. After all had been heard, the conference should decide what, if any, further statements might be heard and under what circumstances. No one might speak without previous recognition by the presiding officer, who might call a speaker to order and terminate his recognition. Points of order might also be made by any delegate. Exceptions to rulings of the presiding officer should be put to a vote without debate. Motions to suspend or adjourn a meeting or to close a debate were to have precedence over all other motions and should not be debated.

These were severe rules. The Canadians and Australians thought them alien to their own parliamentary practices and to those of the UN General Assembly; they might find it difficult to give them public support. I remained unmoved, and insisted that we were determined to obtain a result and that the only rules the Russians would approve would be of a type that might prevent our doing so. The permissive "second round" of statements under majority approval was a concession to the parliamentary purists.

The critical moments of the conference under my plan would be the first few before the rules were adopted, when an adroit opposition might get the floor and go off on a frolic hard to control. Once, however, the rules were voted and I remained in the chair controlling a majority of the delegations, the Russians would be under complete control. Thus the first order of business would have to be a motion to adopt the rules. For this the Temporary President needed, like Horatius, two stout and reliable comrades, one to make the motion, the other to second it. The first we found in Sir Carl Berendsen, the Ambassador of New Zealand in Washington, the second in Oscar Gans, Minister of State of Cuba.

While preparing our campaign in San Francisco, I did not neglect our rear. On August 30 with the President's approval I submitted to the National Security Council for formal approval a memorandum prepared by Dean Rusk. It pointed out that the conference might bring on increased international tensions. The USSR, finding itself unable to prevent the signing of the treaty by parliamentary means, might resort to "shock tactics" to reduce the number of signatories, reduce the effect of the treaty in Asia, delay it, amend it, or arouse Japanese fears. The USSR might produce a competing treaty, attack our security arrangement, start a major offensive in Korea, or submit an ultimatum of some sort. The delegation must be prepared to respond instantly to a variety of moves and asked authority to do so within the lines of existing instructions— that is, to proceed with the treaty for as early signing and execution as possible, to reject attempts at renegotiation, and to refuse to compromise issues else-where as well as in the Far East. We would be in constant touch with Washing-ton, but in case of necessity I wanted authority to decide and act. With Vice President Barkley staunchly supporting and the others concurring, the President at once approved and had the memorandum and his approval entered on the minutes.

A suggestion from Bernard M. Baruch that General MacArthur should be invited to the conference was answered by Mr. Dulles, to whom the General had already indicated that he would appear only on invitation by the whole conference rather than by the United States alone. I had not provided for this in the rules and was not inclined to do so.

THE CONFERENCE

Before leaving Washington, Secretary of Foreign Affairs Carlos Romulo and I signed the Philippine-United States Mutual Defense Treaty in the presence of Presidents Truman and Quirino on August 30, after which we went to Blair House for an official luncheon and speeches, which left no echo. Similarly, after arriving in San Francisco, Sir Carl Berendsen and Percy Spender, the Ambassadors to the United States from New Zealand and Australia, joined me on Saturday, September 1, at the beautiful Presidio, the old fort at the Golden Gate, to sign the Australian-New Zealand-United States treaty, followed by a reception and a tripartite dinner at the Fairmont.

The next day started a strenuous round of dealing with dissidents and solidifying our majority. Prime Minister Yoshida of Japan came to see me with his delegation, which included an old friend, Ryuji Takeuchi, who was then Chief of the Japanese Government Overseas Agency at Washington and was destined to be its Ambassador in Washington ten years later. With the Prime Minister there began a warm friendship which continued until his death. His quick intelligence, delightful humor, and complete integrity made him an un-equaled colleague in our joint absorbing interest, Japanese-American friend-ship and collaboration. There, too, my wife and I met his charming and culti-vated daughter, Mme. Tabakichi Aso, who remains a cherished friend. The Prime Minister caught at once the design and purpose of the conference rules and the importance of indicating at the outset a tone of constructive effort and the avoidance of bickering. He agreed to overlook protocol and to make the approaches to other delegations, especially those who had a sense of grievance at the way we had handled the reparations issue.

Foster Dulles expanded on this matter, stressing the necessity of con-vincing them that Japan would negotiate in good faith as soon as possible after the conference, and urging on Yoshida the great utility of the reparations clause in creating employment in Japan through processing foreign materials. He wisely urged avoiding, for the present, all discussion of amounts. I underlined the necessity for complete secrecy during the conference regarding the security treaty, because otherwise the Russians would seize the opportunity to deflect discussions from the peace treaty to the security treaty, to the possible serious damage of both. Responding to a question about Japan's future relations with China, I urged that the Prime Minister relegate a matter of such importance to Japan to deliberate study and careful decision after the conference and conclusion of the treaty, with which he agreed. In general we urged on the Prime Minister an attitude of friendly calm and confidence. Some delegations were not at present prepared to sign the treaty and perhaps some would not do so. While careful and tactful discussion would undoubtedly reduce the number, it would not be disastrous if a few persevered. They could always sign a similar treaty later on. Obstinacy should not lead us into either ill will or panic. With this advice, our wise and good friend went off to create an excellent impression and good results among the delegations.

With Yoshida in a forthcoming mood, I talked on Monday, September 3, with Dirk Stikker of the Netherlands and Ahmad Subardjo and Ali Sastroamidjojo of Indonesia, and on the following day with Zafrullah Khan and the foreign ministers of Cambodia, Laos, and Vietnam. On Monday I also met President Truman at the airport.

After a preliminary meeting late on Monday evening with the Brazilian, Chilean, Cuban, and Mexican delegates, I conferred on Tuesday with all the Good Neighbors, going over the strategy and tactics of the conference, the Rules of Procedure, and the moments when their cooperation would be invaluable. We had done the same with the non-Communist members of the Far Eastern Commission. Having now done all, I was content, like Oliver Cromwell, to leave the issue in the hands of the Lord of Battles, particularly as only the devoted and skilled ministrations of the President's physician, Major General Wallace Graham, so dealt with an acute attack of ptomaine poisoning as to permit me to open the conference that evening. If I have ever felt worse, the memory of it mercifully escapes me. The Mayor of San Francisco, Governor Warren, and the President welcomed the delegates. Since the conference inaugurated nationwide television in the United States and continued to be televised throughout the sessions, the whole country followed our sometimes dramatic proceedings with absorbed interest. After escorting the President to a reception given by the American delegation, I left him in the tender care of my wife and slipped away to bed.

The work and fireworks accompanying the first test of wills began promptly the next morning. I opened the first plenary session in San Francisco's Opera House by reminding the delegates that the purpose of the conference was the conclusion and signing of a treaty already negotiated by diplomatic means, and then recognized Sir Carl Berendsen, who moved the adoption of the rules. When Oscar Gans had seconded the motion and the floor had been opened for discussion of it, Mr. Gromyko took the floor to observe the absence of any delegates from the Chinese People's Republic and to move that they be invited. I ruled the motion out of order and on appeal from the ruling allowed five minutes for a speech in support of the appeal and the same for one against it.

A Polish delegate, Stefan Wierblowski, supported his Russian friend, but declined to stop at the end of five minutes, when the gavel fell. I recognized

Kenneth Younger, who found himself blocked from the lectern by the vociferous Pole. Repeatedly I told the latter to take his seat, without result, for although he was wearing earphones for the instantaneous translation they were not plugged in. The situation was rapidly moving from the amusing to the critical, as the Pole quite openly defied me. Having neglected to provide the conference with a sergeant at arms, it became obvious that I had to assume that post; so, rising, I announced that I would escort our Polish friend to his seat and approached the speaker's rostrum.

Three thousand miles away my Cabinet colleague Bob Lovett was driving through the Long Island village of Locust Valley when he was flagged down by the local garageman. "Come in, Mr. Lovett," he said, "and look at the television. Your friend Acheson is going to take a swing at a Pole!" Bob joined the circle to watch the scene in San Francisco, as Wierblowski backed away from the rostrum, his voice fading from the air. Younger darted into the vacant place, while I stood guard to prevent a counterattack. The Locust Valley audience, Lovett reported, broke into a cheer and for the first time in village history a Secretary of State became a local hero. Mr. Wierblowski, wrote James Reston in *The New York Times* on September 6, "outshouted, outcharged, outchallenged and outraged" every other delegation.

With my ruling sustained, the debate returned to the motion to adopt the Rules of Procedure. The indomitable Pole returned to urge the conference to write its own rules and not docilely accept those sought to be imposed upon it. A series of amendments was proposed by the Soviet Union, Poland, and Czechoslovakia, and then debated. We had intended to let this go on for some time so that the Soviet group and others might blow off some of their steam, but had not allowed for the enthusiasm of our Latin American friends to get on with the conference. I headed off an incipient motion by Oscar Gans to terminate the debate on the rules, but only temporarily. He stimulated Luis Francisco Thomén of the Dominican Republic to make the motion, which Gans himself seconded. I pointed out that it was a privileged motion to be put without debate. It was adopted by a vote of 25 to 8 with a good many abstentions. The amendments were then voted down and the rules were adopted by a majority of 48 to 3.

After this the fight seemed to go out of the Soviet bloc. Before going to San Francisco, we anticipated disruptive moves that they might make. To our surprise they used only about a third of them. In a later discussion of their surprising behavior, the Turkish Ambassador suggested that they never fully appreciated the devastating consequences of the Rules of Procedure—once they were adopted the parliamentary battle was over.

With the rules adopted, only an extraparliamentary crisis could deflect the conference from its course. Each step on the agenda brought us closer to the signing. The next was the election of officers. Again Gromyko attempted a diversion by reverting to his proposal to invite delegates from the Chinese People's Republic; again I ruled him out of order, and again my ruling was appealed and sustained. The elections took only a few minutes—my own as permanent President, Percy Spender's as Vice President. In the afternoon, almost two days ahead of schedule, the statements would begin. After lunch Spender took over the chair, letting me sit with the delegation to hear Dulles and Younger present the treaty.

That first day we had sessions in the morning, afternoon, and evening. When the Soviet turn to speak came, Gromyko launched into a tirade against the treaty and began to propose amendments, contrary to the rules. When Percy Spender broke in to query Gromyko's intention, he switched to justifying them as a "declaration." I gave a delighted President, who had been watching the high moments, a report that we were leading by a comfortable margin. Even the treaty was becoming popular.

As the evening session on Friday, September 7, opened, I announced that, each delegation having spoken, the order of business under the rules would be a statement by the Japanese delegation. Mr. Yoshida's speech was simple, honest, and brief. According to the rules it could be followed by such statements from other delegations as the conference might permit. J. R. Jayewardene of Ceylon moved that statements, none longer than thirty minutes, might continue until eleven o'clock, after which no more statements should be heard. Mr. Gromyko rose to inquire when the Soviet amendments to the treaty would be debated. Here was his last chance. I replied blandly that under the rules the treaty was not open to amendment. He appealed from the ruling and lost again. Remarks by Gromyko, Younger, and Dulles closed this phase of the proceedings.

During Younger's speech Gromyko had risen, looked about him as though collecting his flock, and slowly walked out up the center aisle of the auditorium, followed, after some hesitation, by one after another of the Communist delegations, including the lady delegate from Czechoslovakia. Here, the press decided, was the great walkout. Photographers rushed, pushing and shouting, to the back of the auditorium as the television cameras in the balconies lost the disappearing parade. The delegates stood up to watch it. Poor Kenneth Younger went bravely ahead with his speech, completely inaudible. Gromyko reached the end of the aisle, turned left, and disappeared into the gentlemen's retiring rooms, followed by his henchmen, but leaving his henchwoman, the lady from Czechoslovakia, in puzzled isolation. The din increased; reporters raced for telephones; even Younger took time out. In the fullness of time, out came Gromyko followed by his procession; they marched back down the aisle to their seats, with the lady embarrassed but loyal, blushing at the applause from the galleries, which Spender did not attempt to check. Younger resumed his speech. Warren Kelchner, the Secretary General, reported the translations of the treaty to be in order, and, fixing the hour for signing at ten o'clock the next morning, I adjourned the session.

The whole group of American delegates and advisers came to my suite for mutual congratulations and gossip, the main topic, of course, being the curious conduct of the Russians throughout. (The next morning none of the Communist bloc appeared; they just vanished away.) We concluded that doubtless the Turkish explanation was the right one: they must have failed completely to grasp the significance of the rules, though these were published in *The New York Times* well before the conference opened. Gromyko must have been very nervous on the flight home.

So esteemed had the conference become, as television during the past week had turned it into a sort of modern miracle play, that Herbert Morrison, who had thought of meeting Schuman and me in Washington, confirmed his decision to fly out for the closing session. As co-sponsor of the treaty, he opened the session; as President, I was to close it. Both Dean Rusk and my wife had strong views about how I should do this, by different routes arriving at the same conclusion. This was no occasion, they said, for a staff-written speech; my wife went further and said I should have no text at all. Both agreed that I should say what was in my mind as I watched perhaps the most terrible war in history brought to its formal end. So, sitting there while group after group came to the stage to sign, I jotted down a few notes.

When the Japanese delegation ended the signing, I thanked my colleagues of the conference for the trust they had placed in me and our hosts in San Francisco and California for their quite endless kindness and generosity to us all, and then continued:

I know that as you sat here this morning and watched this very moving cere-mony, a great crowd of memories came into your minds—not only into the minds of the delegates in this hall and the audience in this hall, but in the vast audience which was looking on at this ceremony throughout the length and breadth of the United States—a great flood of memories of past days, days which were anxious, days which were full of sorrow, days which were full of grim determination. And I know that many families today were conscious of absences. Many were conscious that those who were absent had given their lives to bring about this day.

It is fitting, it is very fitting, that all of those memories of all of these people here, throughout this country, throughout the world, should culminate today in this act of reconciliation; because what you have seen this morning is something unique in history. You have seen an act of greatness of spirit, a true act of reconciliation. And because it was that, it was an act which, as Mr. Jayewardene pointed out, and Mr. Zafrullah Khan pointed out, as Mr. Dulles pointed out, is in accordance with the fundamental moral principles of the great spiritual teachers and leaders of all nations and of all religions. And it was for this reason, I think, again as Mr. Dulles suggested to us last night, that we were able to accomplish here what we have ac-complished, because all of us, in the words of Benjamin Franklin, "doubted some-thing of our infallibility," and all of us worked together, giving up much that was close to our hearts, much that was close to our economic interests, for the purpose of bringing about this peace of reconciliation. And we were able to do that because we were doing something which lifted our spirits, something of which we were proud.

There was nothing mean, there was nothing sordid, left in any corner of this treaty. There was nothing hidden, nothing that could not bear the broad light of day; and we were able to join in that sort of an effort, and we were able to settle our differences, because we were going forward in a great effort, making a great new step in history, and hoping from this day forward that a new chapter is opening in the history of the world.

As Mr. Morrison said to you this morning, this is not an ending, this is a be-ginning. We signed this great treaty this morning and we must live this treaty from this day onward. And it devolves upon each nation represented here, each individual of each nation, to make this treaty be what it is in words.

And by no means least of all, it rests with our Japanese friends to see that this treaty reaps its true fruits. And I say to them: A great broad highway to a position of equality, of honor, of friendship in the world lies open to you. All the obstacles on that highway have been cleared away so far as governments can clear them away. The obstacles that remain, only you can remove, and you can remove those if you act with other peoples with understanding and with generosity and with kindness. All those qualities are inherent in the nature of your people; and what we urge you to do is to make those qualities, which are so inherent in the Japanese people, the policy of the Japanese Government.

We regret that there are some who were unable or unwilling to join our meeting; and others, we regret, who came here but were unable or unwilling to join in this great constructive effort. But what we have done here we have done both for ourselves and for those who did not come here, because we have made a great peace for all peoples—not merely those here, but for all peoples throughout the world. And those who were unwilling to work with us, those who criticized our efforts, for those people we feel no bitterness; but we urge them now to join in the great effort which lies before all of us.

And may I close this Conference with words which in many languages, in many forms, in many religions have brought comfort and strength: "May the peace of God which passeth all understanding be amongst us and remain with us always."

The Conference for the conclusion and signature of the treaty of peace with Japan is concluded.[4]

When the last word was spoken to a hushed audience, Senator Alexander Wiley jumped to his feet shouting, "Everybody up!" and led a tumultuous ovation. While it was going on, a television man on the floor near my wife called to a cameraman in the gallery, "Get Acheson!" My wife, amused, said to the wife of one of our Republican delegates beside her, "Even at a time like this they still want to 'get' him." To which she got the comforting reply, "I don't think they meant it that way, my dear."

With the peace treaty signed, our delegation for the Japanese security treaty gave a luncheon for the Japanese and went on in the afternoon to sign it. We released the text an hour or so before. The memorable week closed with a visit to the Veterans' Hospital, where I talked with our men wounded in Korea, a moving experience and one which increased my eagerness for progress at Panmunjom, and with a dinner given by the Citizens' Committee for all the delegates. Here I had the first of many delightful opportunities to talk with Mrs. Earl Warren.

In the diplomatist's life no provision is made for a "triumph" on the Roman model or on any other. Already attention, our own and other peoples', was shifting from the notable successes of the treaties that made up the Japanese peace settlement to a blast, as from Roland's horn, calling for help from the other side of the world. The diplomatist had best regard his tasks as donkey's work and get on with them. He only deceives himself when, like G. K. Chesterton's donkey, he muses:

I also had my hour;
One far fierce hour and sweet:
There was a shout about my ears,
And palms before my feet.

The shout and palms are not for him.

Early Sunday morning we had already turned a page to a new chapter as we flew east, taking with us Morrison and Schuman and their ambassadors, Oliver Franks and Henri Bonnet.

57. NATO IN STAGNATION

HAVING TRACED the pleasant and successful story of the peace treaty with Japan from September 1950 to September 1951 we must turn back almost as far to pick up the far less happy account of our dealings with our European allies—and especially France—about Germany. After the December 1950 NATO meeting at Brussels had dressed the wounds suffered by Franco-American relations over German participation in Western defense, both governments had made strenuous efforts to reach better understanding. Early in the new year the most eminent French statesmen had come to consult with President Truman—René Pleven, the Prime Minister, Robert Schuman, the Foreign Minister, and Vincent Auriol, the President of the Republic. High on the agenda for these and other discussions were three subjects to which the French had been giving a great deal of thought. One was the conference they had called on January 26, 1951, to consider the formation of a European Defense Community, which I had warmly welcomed in accepting their invitation to send an observer along with Canada's; another was France's deepening trouble in Indochina; and the third, the Soviet notes of the previous autumn protesting against allied policy toward Germany and proposing a four-power conference on "the German question." As matters stood at the end of January 1951, a tripartite reply had declared a conference to discuss only this one subject "inadequate and unreal."

Each Franco-American meeting evoked a variety of French viewpoints, varying from deep suspicion of Germany to great hopefulness of Soviet tractability. President Auriol held both. M. Schuman, however, looking to the future, saw European unity in Franco-German rapprochement and in unity a reduction of tension with the Soviet Union. Two of these subjects held contradictions, which the French were quite able to see but not so able to resolve. The Russian pressure for a four-power meeting on "the German question" was, without doubt, for the purpose of defeating German participation in defense. Each of our French visitors wished—or said he wished—to discuss European defense with the Germans and the German question with the Russians. The phrase was "to close no doors," yet each visitor had different sympathy for each discussion. The President, General Marshall, and I had no sympathy for four-power discussion on Germany, which we regarded as purely a spoiling operation. Recognizing it as meant to cause trouble between us and our European friends and, more generally, to depict us to the world as warmongers, we had to tread warily. Mere opposition would have aided Russian propaganda.

Since talks with the French, into which the British were drawn, and negotiations between the three and Moscow went on through the late winter and spring, the results gave a basis for appraisal. In Germany, the Soviet notes and demand for discussion of the German question had the expected effect. Chancellor Adenauer on February 10 rejected any "neutralization" of Germany as "a disaster for Europe . . . and the German people." He pressed for ten to fifteen divisions as the German contribution to defense. At once I denied that "neutralization" was under consideration and in our talks pressed the French hard to expedite agreement between the High Commission and Adenauer on liberalization of the occupation. Important agreement was announced on March 6, 1951—the formation of a German Ministry of Foreign Affairs and a diplomatic and consular corps, the abolition or reduction of many reserved powers, and negotiations for a German international debt settlement.[1]

Under the "Spofford Plan" a regimental combat team had been adopted as the "national unit" for the German contribution to the NATO united command. While Auriol and Schuman were with us, from March 25 through 30, Colonel Henry Byroade, whom we had seconded from the Army to handle our German office, told me that such a six-thousand-man regimental team was unworkable and should be increased. I urged Schuman to get military advice, and found him wholly receptive to a militarily workable unit rather than a politically palatable one. The French in June agreed with the Germans on a divisional unit of ten thousand men. While Schuman and I were working toward this solution, Auriol was telling Harriman that the Germans were revengeful, nationalistic, and could not be trusted, a view he pressed with passion on me a year later. France was not of one mind on policy toward Germany, as the defeat of the European Defense Community three years later was to make unmistakably clear.

Pleven in his turn raised on two occasions a signal of future trouble, which I was not acute enough to recognize. It was a proposal for a three-power consultative body (with Britain) to coordinate policy on a worldwide basis. This was later, when not accepted, to be one of General de Gaulle's aims and chief grievances against "les Anglo-Saxons." In 1951 my difficulty was in getting from Pleven what he wanted the new body to do. What specifically did he want to coordinate? In Europe our tripartite responsibility for Germany and constant meetings to discharge it, as well as our tripartite position in the Standing Group of NATO, already gave the three such pre-eminence in the alliance as to cause painful jealousy. In the Far East, France refused to (and could not) assume responsibility beyond Indochina and was deeply suspicious of any intrusion by others there. The impression left with me was that the appearance of France on a worldwide tripartite body, rather than the functioning of the body, was what interested our guests. However, all in all, our discussions on German and defense matters had useful results.

The same cannot be said about our talks on France's predicament in Indochina. Here the trouble seemed to spring from the lack of any practicable French policy and their refusal to face that fact squarely and devise one. They were engaged in the most dangerous of all activities—deceiving themselves.

General Alphonse Pierre Juin explained that the drain in Indochina was so great as to threaten France's European and African positions. He spoke of the possible need of help should an emergency evacuation be necessary, a panic theme with which General MacArthur had familiarized us. Their immediate needs were for military material, especially planes, the loan of another aircraft carrier, and monetary assistance to pay local forces. The last we could not do and what we could do fell a good deal short of their needs.

At this time we began an effort—a frustrating and unsuccessful one—to get our friends to see and face the facts in Indochina. France was engaged in a task beyond her strength, indeed, beyond the strength of any external power unless it was acting in support of a dominant local will and purpose. To us this meant a much more rapid transfer of responsibility and authority to indigenous institutions than the French had in mind, and this, in turn, required administrative and military training applicable to local needs and capacities rather than adapted from French methods. We urged them to observe and use methods we had found effective in Korea. Although talks of this sort went on for three years, they had no effect and the drain on France continued until the effort failed in 1954.

As already pointed out, all through the first half of 1951 Moscow pressed for a four-power conference on "the German question." When the French came to think about this, their two main preoccupations emerged. The first concerned the French political situation. The public must be convinced, said Pleven, that we had met the Russians halfway in an effort to resolve our differences with them over Germany. Only if convinced that the Soviet Union remained obdurate, would the French public support a movement into the dangerous waters of German rearmament. The second preoccupation lay in the persistent hope in France that Russian policy, faced with this alternative, would so change as to make possible re-examination of German rearmament. Such an idea was exactly what the Soviet maneuver was designed to plant in European minds. I pointed this out and added another one to it. If, by what would seem almost divine intervention, Russian policy did so change as to make rearmament unnecessary, this would affect the situation of others as well as Germany. Indeed, it might renew a fast-fading wartime hope of the practicality of disarmament. It seemed highly unlikely, but the possibility could not be ruled out. General Marshall was inclined to believe that it could be ruled out and strongly supported steadiness and continuity of policy rather than a start-and-stop approach attuned to Russian moods and propaganda.

When, however, we all turned our minds specifically to what an agenda of a four-power conference should contain, real difficulties began to appear. I have already referred to the importance that the Russians attached to the agenda of a meeting and the tendentious purposes for which they would use it. They would refuse to discuss matters not specifically included, argue that language used in describing items limited the discussion in various ways, or use the language in propaganda before the conference to cause concern. They would attach great importance to the order of items, sometimes refusing to go from one to another item until the preceding one was completed and then refusing to return to it.

We discussed this agenda problem with the French and the British for a whole month through Phil Jessup and Ambassadors Bonnet and Franks until a bright idea occurred to them. Why not precede the four-power ministerial conference by a four-power meeting of deputies to try to work out what their principals should later meet to discuss? In this way the Western allies would not be put in the position of refusing to meet and would have an excellent opportunity to find out whether the Russians had serious proposals in mind or only propaganda.

PROPAGANDA AT THE PALAIS ROSE

The meeting of deputies opened at the Palais Rose in Paris on March 5, 1951. Ambassador at Large Philip C. Jessup represented us; Alexandre Parodi, Secretary General of the Foreign Office, France; Ernest Davies, Under Secretary of State for Foreign Affairs, the United Kingdom; and Andrei Gromyko, Deputy Minister of Foreign Affairs, the Soviet Union. The conference held seventy-four sessions and adjourned on June 21 without accomplishing its purpose—preparation of an agenda for a conference of foreign ministers.

During that time Phil Jessup with great skill and tenacity won two concurrent campaigns: one a propaganda battle with the Soviet Union; the other, a more difficult one—to stiffen the backbones of our allies. The complicated moves of these simultaneous games of diplomatic chess need not be detailed, but a few highlights may be interesting to suggest the purposes, the skills, and the achievements of the players. The Russians were trying to block execution of NATO's Brussels decisions and divide us from our allies and both of us from Germany; the French, who had an election at midyear, and the British, who expected one not much later, were anxious not to alienate the left-wing voters susceptible to Russian peace propaganda; we wished to aid our friends, including Adenauer, and to make clear generally that, while we would discuss any serious Russian proposals, we would not undermine the confidence of the German people in the constancy of our European policy.

An Agenda As a Weapon of War · As the conference opened, each side squared off by presenting its agenda. Ours was neutral and uncolored; theirs strongly slanted.

THE ALLIED AGENDA

1. Examination of the causes of present international tensions in Europe and the means to secure a real and lasting improvement in relations.
2. Completion of the Austrian treaty.
3. Problems relating to the re-establishment of German unity and the preparation of the peace treaty.

THE SOVIET AGENDA

1. Fulfillment of Potsdam Agreement on the demilitarization of Germany and the prohibition of its remilitarization.
2. Acceleration of conclusion of peace treaty with Germany and the withdrawal of occupation forces.

3. Improvement of the situation in Europe and the immediate passing over to the reduction of the armed forces of the four powers.

Then began the dreary weeks of repetitious argument, duly leaked to the press. Gromyko aggressively strengthened the slant of his agenda by adding another item: "Atlantic Pact and the creation of United States military bases in England, Norway, Iceland, and other countries of Europe and the Near East." Parodi and Davies grew progressively weaker and wanted to compromise by accepting some of Gromyko's items, or parts of them, their eager aim being to convene a conference of foreign ministers at seemingly any cost. Jessup began to despair of holding the line. At the end of March he got help from an unexpected quarter. Herbert Morrison, who had come to Paris in March, invited David Bruce, Chip Bohlen, and Jessup to meet with him, his assistant, Bob Dixon, and Davies at the British Embassy to review the situation. Bohlen and Jessup strongly and eloquently presented their case for allied firmness and unity, arguing that if the Russians really wanted a meeting they would accept a fair and unslanted agenda. Davies wanted to accept an item on "demilitarization of Germany." Morrison overruled him.

In April, Bohlen and Jessup worked out an ingenious move, which became known as "the triple play," and incorporated some of Parodi's and Davies' ideas. During the month successive modification of our agenda containing some approaches to Soviet demands had been offered at the strong urging of Parodi and Davies. Gromyko rejected them all out of hand. The triple play was sprung on May 2, after eight weeks of futile talk. It gave the Russians their choice of three agendas. All contained five items, all of which in some form the two sides wanted included. The Russian item on American bases was omitted from all three. One made an important concession to the Soviet Union in return for a compensating concession to us. The second left these two points for decision or disagreement by the ministers at the conference. The third merely enumerated the broad items without description or color. Gromyko rejected them all.

For the benefit of those who like to believe that American diplomacy is all oratory at the United Nations, I venture to stress the brilliance of this maneuver. In the eyes of the world it left Gromyko an unreasonable bumpkin who had nothing to offer, wanted no meeting, and sought only to stave off all allied action until the Kremlin could think of some new way of delaying European defense. To prove the point the deputies offered a conference of foreign ministers without an agenda, which Gromyko also rejected. After the French election took place on June 17, Jessup's French and British colleagues were induced to move and carry adjournment of the Palais Rose meeting *sine die*. The meeting remains a puzzling example of maladroit Soviet diplomacy.

THREE MINISTERS IN SEARCH OF SOLUTIONS

During the second and third weeks of September 1951 we returned from the high achievements of the first week in San Francisco to that mixture of frustration and progress that is the daily grind of foreign affairs. During these

weeks, first in Washington and then in Ottawa, Morrison, Schuman, and I with
our ministerial and official colleagues tackled problems so intractable that they
still bedevil our successors. The futile weeks at the Palais Rose had convinced
even the reluctant French that agreement with the Soviet Union on Germany
was not possible. This threw us back on the immensely difficult problems of
bringing Germany into the European community and its defense and of finding
a fair and workable division of the economic and financial burdens of European
defense. The Middle East also was presenting its own insistent problems. The
very toughness of these problems acted as an abrasive upon our personal relations, a process exacerbated by attitudes of mind in all three of our countries,
long-suppressed—among the British and French these attitudes were the result
of their humiliating retreat from empire; among us, of an unsought war in the
Far East and a frustrating attempt to rally our harassed allies to an effort in
Europe beyond their strength and will. In retrospect I wonder that the frustrations did not seem to be greater at that time than they did; perhaps it was because some matters, such as the European Defense Community, then appeared
to offer hope, which would be dashed in the clouded future.

For German and Defense Problems · There was nothing buoyant about Mor-
rison. He could be counted on to deepen the gloom that surrounded our talks.
European integration was all very well, he told us, provided it was done right.
But was it? The United Kingdom was impatient with the irresponsibility of the
Council of Europe, and could not accept the Schuman Plan. So far, the political
containment of the Soviet Union had been a success. He would not deny that.
But it could go too far and precipitate world war. So far as Germany was concerned, he discerned a tendency to exploit the allies, to squeeze them into paying
occupation expenses that the Germans should carry. He had said flatly, he told
us, to the German and Austrian chancellors that the occupation forces were
providing their defense and that the beneficiaries must pay for it.

Here was something with which Schuman could agree. The Germans were
always harping on equality of treatment, he added; let them learn that it should
include equality of burdens. The national incomes of Germany and France, he
went on, were about the same; hence the Germans should spend the same
amount as the French for defense, including the French overseas expenditures.
However, the Germans should not be allowed to have a greater contingent in
the European Army that he was devising; the difference should go to pay allied
occupation costs in Germany. This neat theory would go far to kill any prospect
of an adequate German contribution to defense. Sometimes Schuman's ingenuity in devising original solutions to problems seemed exceeded only by his
cleverness in circumventing them.

My colleagues set about driving another nail in the coffin of the European
Army by their concern for the preservation of democracy in Germany. As they
saw it, the threat came not only from the East but from resurgent fascism within
Germany. The constitutional order in Bonn might be overthrown as it had been
in Weimar; therefore, the occupation must retain power to intervene whenever
constitutional or public order might be in danger—in other words, the Germans

must be persuaded to pay not only for an allied occupation to protect them against the Russians and themselves, but for a German contingent as great as the French, but no greater.

As Chief Justice White used to say, to state this proposition was to answer it. My colleagues did not really believe it. They were partly blowing off steam and partly countering what they thought was my too favorable view of Adenauer. But form at least required that I respond to this dialectical departure from reality before trying to get from the British more understanding support for Schuman's European Army and for a further easing of the occupation. This we were able to do despite the inauspicious start.

During the summer of 1951 I had come to the conclusion that the best way to an adequate German contribution to defense lay in strong support of the French proposal for a European Defense Community. The negotiations in Paris about this had become so involved that the only two Americans who claimed to understand them were Ambassador David Bruce and a Treasury attaché named Tomlinson who had forsaken foreign exchange problems to become a passionate supporter of and expert on the Community. Neither of them could impart understanding of the negotiations to the rest of us; indeed, Bruce would not try. The Europeans, he said, liked to do things in a way that seemed to us like beating up a soufflé of generalizations. It would come out all right, if we would leave it alone and worry about something else. I accepted the first but not the last part of his advice and, therefore, worried alone and in the clarity of ignorance. Two ideas helped me to my conclusion.

The adoption of our Constitution, I reflected, was aided by the delusion of innocuousness created by its simplicity. The Congress, said the Founding Fathers at Philadelphia, should have power to regulate commerce with foreign nations, among the several states, and with the Indian tribes. They either did not foresee or were not telling what complexities these few words concealed and what powers the Supreme Court would produce from them as a magician the unexpected from his hat. And the vast authority contained in the war power was even more modestly clothed. If the states had been able to foresee all this, the Constitution would never have been adopted. It might be that, intentionally or not, Schuman was cloaking incursions upon sovereignty by complexity instead of simplicity and, it might be, with equal success. But what was he up to? And was it sensible? Studying General Eisenhower's chart of the integrated command of NATO, I got a glimpse of what he might have in mind and reassurance that it might be sensible.

Under General Eisenhower's supreme authority were to be a Northern Command, a Southern Command, and a Central European Command under General Juin. Into this last would fall the Benelux, French, and British forces and most of the American with responsibility for dealing with any military thrust across the Eastern European plain toward Germany. Here was the nucleus of the European Army with a European commander, in which European troops could be incorporated in times of both war and peace, for training and operations, and with American troops attached as at present. Add to this a civilian organization for supply and finance and some cooperative recruiting functions in Germany, and one had a European Army with Germany divisions but no German defense department or general staff. The civilian politico-economic additions should not be allowed to become too complicated or specific or they would create alarm and concern about infringements of sovereignty; they should be developed as need and experience required. The main stress should be on the military aspects of the problem.

These ruminations I incorporated in a memorandum which suggested that only by prompt and vigorous action along these lines could we make progress with the interconnected problems of bringing Germany into European defense, ending the occupation of Germany, and moving into a constructive phase of the integration of Western Europe, all of which were now stalemated. After some discussion in the Department my memorandum on July 16 became the agenda for a meeting at the Pentagon with General Marshall, Bob Lovett, General Bradley, Frank Nash, and Colonel Beebe, their German expert, to which Phil Jessup and Doc Matthews accompanied me. Unanimous agreement and a State-Defense paper signed by Lovett and me was taken to the White House at the end of the month and received the all-important endorsement, "Approved, July 30, 1951, Harry S. Truman."

In many respects this was an epoch-making series of decisions, removing many important matters from the realm of discussion to that of execution and enabling the Administration with clear instructions to carry out policy. In later years the prevailing doctrine of "preserving options" precluded this continuity of decisive action so typical of the Truman years. My memorandum and the interdepartmental one based on it concluded that an effective defense of Europe, ending the occupation in Germany, and integration in Western Europe were all interrelated and all waited upon a solution of the allied military problem acceptable to France and Germany. The only one in sight seemed to be the European Army. We proposed, therefore, that the United States go all out for it as I had deduced it to be, without stirring up trouble by asking for clarifications from Paris.

With the President's decision in hand we went into the Washington talks united on pressing hard for progress with the European Army and for the inauguration of another even larger plan, which became known as the "contractual relation" with Germany. Since the Russians were blocking a treaty of peace with Germany such as we had just made with Japan, our plan was to enter into a "contract" with West Germany which would end the occupation and clothe that government with as many of the attributes of sovereignty as we safely could in view of the situation in East Germany. The Germans should be given full power to run themselves. Our mission there should cease to be that of occupation of a defeated enemy's territory and become that of an ally contributing by agreement to mutual defense. We should retain authority in four fields only: the protection of our troops, Berlin, the unification of Germany, and subsequent peace settlement and territorial questions.

To work out this agreement would be a colossal job, for the United States Government did not have in Germany, as it had had in Japan, the last decisive word. Many vested interests in the occupation had grown up beyond our control. Fortunately our High Commissioner, John J. McCloy, possessed the tireless persistence, persuasiveness, and force that the task demanded. He was to find a vigorous coadjutor in Adenauer.

The correctness of this analysis and strategy seemed borne out by the Washington meeting. Assured of strong American support for the European Army, Schuman grew more flexible and forthcoming on the "contractual program" and together we moved the British ahead, if not to enthusiasm, at least to an attitude of friendly cooperation with the European movement, as exemplified by the Schuman Plan and the European Defense Community. All this appeared in our communiqué and declaration, both of September 14.[2]

For Economic and Rearmament Problems • For some time in 1951 it had been dawning on us that we were trying to move our allies and ourselves faster toward the rearmament for defense than economic realities would permit. The gap between goals and performance, both on the part of the separate nations and of the group, was daily more apparent and more painful. In Britain Mr. Churchill, of all people, was criticizing Mr. Attlee for overstressing the military program; and in April, Aneurin Bevan resigned as Minister of Health in the Labour Government, protesting against cuts in his programs to find funds for rearmament. In France the press and elections of June 17 reflected similar sentiments, and in Washington on June 21 a major meeting took place to discuss a paper revealing a shortfall in European defense programed through June 30, 1952, by all the allies and Germany of about twenty-five billion dollars. With Generals Marshall and Bradley concurring, we anticipated Mr. Churchill by several months with a stretch-out of the program to achieve by mid-1954 what we had hoped to accomplish by mid-1952. In this discussion that least militant of soldiers, General Marshall, pointed out how much closer the people of Europe were to personal sacrifice than we were. A cut of five per cent, he said, in the European standard of living meant the difference between white bread and black on the table, while in similar American homes such a cut would mean forgoing a radio or television.

Secretary of the Treasury Snyder hoped that we need not go into lagging European performance with Congress until after it had passed the tax bill. This, however, involved another danger, and I opposed his suggestion. Congress was moving toward a course that would cause us more harm than increased hesitation in raising taxes. This was to cut off aid funds to any of our allies whose restrictions against exports to Communist countries were less stringent than our own. As usual, Congress saw this issue in moralistic terms of black and white; but it was not as simple as that, just as trade by European neutrals with Germany during the war, while undesirable, was not as simple an issue as the War Department had seen it in 1942–43. Our exports to Communist countries were of negligible importance to our businessmen and Government, but this was not so in Europe, as the most extreme examples—British trade through Hong Kong and Portuguese through Macao—were cited to show. To interrupt this, except in the case of strategic materials, could have grave political and military, as well as economic, results. Then, too, views regarding what materials were strategic differed; and, finally, as in the case of neutral trade with Germany, the State Department believed that persuasion and bargaining was a more effective and less damaging method of reducing it than blunt coercion.

To steer Congress away from petty squabbling with our allies when increased help to them was more than ever necessary, we should not avoid mentioning the gap but explain it fully. Since the beginning of the Korean war, European military budgets had doubled (though ours had trebled); their industrial production, including military, was up twenty per cent, necessitating a sharp rise in high-cost imports, prices, and the cost of living. Their trade deficit had widened, and their reserves had fallen. Congress should be educated, I believed, not appeased like a testy old lady continually revising her will as some of her nephews and nieces met her standards of good conduct and others fell from grace. The Kem Amendment, punishing recalcitrant allies by withholding aid—and thus slowing defense—was already in the offing and gaining strength. Our legislators' exasperation with foreigners (whose weaknesses are very much like their own) has a strong influence on their views of foreign policy.

As a result of this work and talk at home we were prepared and sympathetic when Hugh Gaitskell and René Mayer joined us with their tale of woe in mid-September. Even our own Treasury head, who had glumly said to us a few weeks before that while we were willing to put a ceiling on what Europe should be asked to do we never took the same lenient view toward our own country, had softened a bit. Gaitskell, Chancellor of the Exchequer, reported an estimated deficit between Britain's foreign receipts and payments of a billion dollars, half of which came from the increased cost of raw materials brought on by our purchases for rearmament. A substantial part of the balance would come from diverting manufacture of exports into manufacture of arms. The British were already behind in their own program for 1951; the increased requests of General Eisenhower were out of the question. Not only was it impossible for them to do more, but they could not long continue the present rate of rearmament.

Mayer, Minister of Finance, corroborated from French experience. Industry was working a forty-five-hour week, in some cases up to fifty-two hours; already shortages were developing in power and coke. The nation faced a deficit in foreign payments of six hundred million dollars and rising inflation. He enlarged upon Schuman's complaint that defense requirements were being fixed by military men without knowledge of economic and financial realities. France would press at Ottawa for a full review of the economic capacity of the NATO countries. It made no sense to destroy them in the name of defending them; new ideas must emerge.

Thoroughly convinced, I drew Harriman, Nitze, and the Pentagon into talk with our allies about methods and means and with the President for his authority to follow up the French suggestion. This he readily gave. Thus the week of talks ended with a surprising degree of agreement on the general line of action we should seek in the economic and rearmament field.

SCHUMAN ON MOROCCO

On another matter, however, which would continue to plague us for the rest of our tenure—French resentment over what was thought to be our uncooperative attitude toward French policy in North Africa—we made no progress. The French Cabinet, Schuman said, had been gravely concerned when earlier in the year we had told them that, should the Moroccan situation come up in the UN General Assembly, we could not support the French position that it should not even be put on the agenda for discussion. This attitude they found impossible to understand. France was granting us vital air bases in Morocco. She was trying to make a modern democratic state in Morocco through the reforms of General Juin, opposed by a reactionary Sultan and the medieval attitude of the Berbers. He pleaded for our support in discouraging the Arab states from using the General Assembly as a propaganda forum to stir up disaffection and disorder in Morocco, and urged us to join in consultation to devise a common policy. France recognized her duty to lead Morocco to independence in the French Union as she was doing in Indochina, where her success had been recently demonstrated, so Schuman thought, by the attitude of the Associated States at San Francisco.

It was all so reasonable and so utterly hopeless. Opinion in the Department was united on the continued need for French influence and guidance in Morocco and in nearby Tunisia and on the ineffectiveness of current French policy in accomplishing that result. The European and Near Eastern divisions differed on the practicality and wisdom of pressing the French Government to the extent necessary to adoption of the extreme measures the situation demanded. The European Division believed—probably correctly—that the Government would see such a decision as its own death warrant; the Near Eastern Division believed—less demonstrably—that anything short of it would mean the end of French influence in Morocco. I made an understandable, but possibly the worst, decision—to push Schuman hard enough to annoy but not hard enough to succeed. To both our short- and long-term interest there did not seem to be much difference between success and failure.

58. EGYPT AND THE
MIDDLE EAST COMMAND

ANOTHER MATTER we gave a push along in our Washington tripartite talks was the Middle East Command.

At the end of January 1951, in a letter to General Marshall, I asked the cooperation of the Defense Department in a review of American interests and policies in the whole area extending from the eastern Mediterranean to India. Over the past four years in an unplanned, undesired, and haphazard way American influence had largely succeeded French and British in that part of the world. As ours had waxed and theirs waned, our popularity there had declined, no power had been substituted for theirs to maintain peace and order, and major conflicts were growing apace between the Arabs and the Israelis, between the nationalist movements in both Egypt and Iran and British interests and government, and between Pakistan and India. As the situation was developing, increasing opportunities were offered for the historic movement of Russia southward to warm water, to oil, and to mischief-making.

My letter assured the General that we did not propose to involve the United States in a Middle East security treaty or to commit our combat forces to the area. Our idea was that the primary responsibility of the British and the Commonwealth to supply armed forces for the defense of the area and the considerable assistance that we were furnishing to individual countries there could be made more effective if all of this could be coordinated under a plan for the defense of the area as a whole. The general plan upon which we wanted the Pentagon's help was, after making our purpose clear to all the countries involved, to make available to the Arab states and Israel small military training missions, an increased number of places for their officers in U.S. military schools, and token amounts of arms and ammunition for training purposes. Strange as it may seem nearly twenty years later, we were still innocent enough in 1950–51 to see promise in such a plan.

In addition, the letter went on to propose discussion with the British Government of a combined U.S.-U.K. military agency to stimulate and coordinate the efforts of all the countries of the area and of the United Kingdom and the United States for the defense of the area as a whole and to create stability in depth in the Arab states and Israel so that Greece, Turkey, and Iran could make effective use of the fighting power we were developing there. In referring to the "defense of the areas as a whole against aggression," the letter meant, and was understood to mean, Soviet military aggression, direct or through satellites or "volunteers." As we were to be reminded very soon, to the Middle Eastern states the controversies within the area were much more vivid and menacing than any threat from the north. The Soviet Foreign Office, aware of this, did its best to keep the impression alive.

General Marshall and the Chiefs of Staff approved the idea, provided—and we agreed to this—that the coordination of Greek and Turkish military effort should be through NATO, which they were clamoring to join. In this form the President approved the exploration, so that when Morrison in September 1951 proposed to us what he called a "new approach" to Middle Eastern problems, he talked about ideas thrown out by his predecessor a year before and worked over by us for almost as long. However, he was badly in need of a "new approach."

The British position in Iran, as we have seen, and in Egypt had deteriorated badly in 1951. A Wafdist government pledged to get the British out of Suez and the Anglo-Egyptian Sudan had been re-elected. Britain's proposals of April 11, 1951, for revision of their 1936 treaty with Egypt and for joint defense arrangements had been rejected by Nahas Pasha, Egypt's Prime Minister. After further exchanges between the two governments, he announced on August 6, 1951, that Mr. Morrison had "closed the door" to further discussions and that the Egyptian Government would abrogate the British treaty before the autumn. At this point Morrison sent him a remarkable letter. He was going away on a short holiday, he wrote, and would give the defense matter further thought while he was away. He was confident that "Your Excellency meanwhile would not wish that . . . anything should be done at this juncture which might prejudice the possibility of reaching a settlement."[1] Mr. Morrison's confidence was misplaced; furthermore, his sense of the time available was off.

Arrangements for defense in the Mediterranean and the Middle East were getting a bit complicated. The British were resisting the appointment of an American as NATO commander in the Mediterranean. On the other hand, the Chiefs of Staff—we thought rightly—saw Admiral Robert B. Carney's Sixth Fleet as the chief support in the south for the six U.S. divisions, then the nucleus of European defense. Greece and Turkey insisted upon being associated in the common defense through NATO and not indirectly through some regional organization. Furthermore, Turkey would not cooperate with a Middle East organization until her admission to NATO had been assured. Finally, if the British were to have a command of equal rank with General Eisenhower's, the French wanted one, too, in recognition of their Mediterranean naval power. Complicating it all was Mr. Churchill's intense annoyance over the provisional Anglo-American decision to appoint U.S. Admiral William M. Fechteler Supreme Allied Commander Atlantic. The prestige of the "former Naval Person" and the possibility of an imminent election in Britain resulted in shelving the decision for the moment.

On September 8, the day we signed the Japanese peace treaty in San Francisco, George McGhee in Washington brought a British working group and the Pentagon into agreement on a Middle East Command, consisting of a Supreme Allied Commander Middle East and his headquarters, which would be in Cairo and include Egyptian officers and be directed by a Middle East Chiefs of Staff Committee. The British base in Egypt would be given to Egypt, which would put it under the Supreme Commander with Egyptian participation in its operation. British troops not allocated to the Supreme Commander should be at once withdrawn from Egypt; the number remaining would be determined by the Commander in agreement with the Egyptian Government. The Pentagon agreed to the plan because it wanted Britain to remain responsible for the defense of the Suez Canal and the Middle East, while noting her declining capability to perform the mission; we agreed because there seemed to be no practicable alternative and carried the President on the same basis; and Morrison agreed because, as he naïvely put it, British troops would remain in Egypt without incurring any charge of British "occupation." My own view was that what the Pentagon and Morrison could see as advantages in the proposal the Egyptians could and would see as disadvantages; the sweeteners in the form of military training and arms could hardly overcome this.

In the Washington talks we could go no further than a tentative approval of the Command, since Turkish cooperation could not be obtained until NATO invited her to join its membership, and the French withheld final approval until the status of their Mediterranean fleet was satisfactorily adjusted. When later at Ottawa NATO solved the Turkish problem by admitting her, Turkey agreed to support the Command along with Australia and New Zealand in a new approach to Egypt. French naval sensitivities were salved by a plan worked out by our naval adviser, Admiral Jerauld Wright, by which the French Mediterranean fleet reporting directly to General Eisenhower was given the task of keeping western Mediterranean communications between France and North Africa open and safe. We were now ready for a new approach to Egypt by the four states.

For the rest of September and the first week in October the Labour Government diddled, perhaps conferring with Commonwealth countries and the political opposition. General Bradley with the British and French Chiefs of Staff went to Ankara to confer and was going on to Cairo. When on October 6 Morrison told the Egyptian Government that within a few days he hoped to put forward new defense proposals, they responded the next day by sending to King Farouk, and the day after to Parliament, legislation abrogating the treaty of 1936 and the Sudan condominium agreement of 1899. Nevertheless, the Middle East Command proposal was presented on October 13, 1951.[2] Prime Minister Nahas Pasha rejected it without reading it. Two days later the Egyptian Parliament abrogated the two treaties.

If ever there was a political stillbirth, this was it. But the Foreign Office could not believe it. In November the four governments published the principles by which they were guided in proposing the command.[3] It brought no response from the Middle East but a sharp one from the Soviet Union. The Western proposal, the Kremlin wrote, was "directed toward assuring the presence of foreign armed forces in the mentioned countries . . . [and] the possibility of continuous interference in the internal affairs of the Near and Middle East countries and the deprivation of their national independence." The Soviet

Union could not "pass by these new aggressive plans . . . in an area situated not far from" its borders.[4] While the four of us replied to this "completely erroneous interpretation" of the Middle East Command, I doubt whether in Egypt and Iran it was regarded as so far from the mark.

THE NEW CRISIS OF "BLACK SATURDAY"

We jump ahead a few months to the crisis of late January 1952, which relegated the Middle East Command to its inevitable disappearance. In Britain the October general election, which resulted in the narrow defeat of the Labour Party, had replaced Herbert Morrison by Anthony Eden at the Foreign Office and in January brought a visit to Washington, as we shall see, from the Prime Minister and Foreign Secretary. A preparatory memorandum from the Department to me carried a note of foreboding and a warning of the different appraisal by the British and our own missions in Egypt of the probable course of events there and their danger. Ours saw no relaxation in the Egyptian demand for the evacuation of British troops, the hazard in letting matters drift, and the urgency of getting Anglo-Egyptian talks started, in which we, the French, and perhaps the Turks might join, if invited. The Prime Minister, however, saw no need of urgency, was determined to show no signs of weakness, and was unwise enough to repeat in his address to Congress a suggestion, to which we had given a cold reception when made privately to us, that "token" U.S. forces might join the British in the canal area.

This brought me an agitated visit from the Egyptian Ambassador for clarification. Mr. Churchill, I said, had made the statement, not we; our Government's attitude on Anglo-Egyptian problems had been made very clear. Both nations were bound by treaties that neither had the right to denounce unilaterally. A proposal had been made by the four powers that Egypt had contemptuously rejected. This was no way to solve difficult problems that required statesmanlike discussions with those whose interests were involved. This I earnestly urged on the Ambassador.

Events moved rapidly. Mr. Churchill's speech had been made on January 17. My talk with the Ambassador occurred on January 21. Within a day or two fighting broke out around Ismailia between General George Erskine's forces and Egyptian troops. On the twenty-fifth Eden informed me that Erskine's action had been necessary for the security of British forces in the canal zone and might be forced on them in the delta area to protect civilian lives, including American. He asked for full support from us. I replied that we would participate only to protect and evacuate American nationals, if necessary, and that naval action at Alexandria involving even limited military occupation and control would be incompatible with our policy. While these cables were being exchanged, on Black Saturday mobs swept through the streets of Cairo, burning Shepheard's Hotel and looting and killing throughout the city. On January 27 King Farouk dismissed Nahas Pasha and his Government. The British extended their military measures.

We immediately threw ourselves into a major effort to damp down these fires, which threatened to involve North Africa in bloody conflict. Ambassador Jefferson Caffery in Cairo was in personal touch with King Farouk through a two-way radio circuit, over which they talked in an effort to separate British and Egyptian forces engaged in restoring order so as not to revive mutual combat. Through Ambassadors Walter Gifford in London and Sir Oliver Franks in Washington I pressed Eden to swap conciliatory statements for Egyptian restraint. Everyone cooperated in a withdrawal from the edge of the abyss. Eden sent me a copy of a most helpful instruction to the British Ambassador, Sir Ralph C. S. Stevenson, outlining a resumption of talks with the Egyptians. We warmly praised it and offered help, adding that we had had a close shave and that the present opportunity might not last. The new Egyptian Prime Minister, Maher, might be our last chance, and Eden's initiative was all the more pleasing to us. Caffery was instructed to support Stevenson in pursuing Eden's move. He was to point out that the four-power proposals had been in no sense a "ganging up" on Egypt but a sincere attempt to harmonize Egypt's interests with those of the free world in the security of the Middle East.

On February 5 Eden made an admirable and calm statement in the House of Commons, which in a personal message I said was exactly right in tone and would help us in realizing our common aim. I told the Ambassador that I was anxious to know Eden's thinking concerning the Sudan, for the thorny problem of King Farouk's title as King of the Sudan had in the past shattered hopes of broad constructive settlement with Egypt and it could do so again, with consequences one would hate to contemplate.

Later in the month when I was in London (see Chapter 64) the Department kept me well supplied with suggestions to take up with Eden and with their messages to Caffery in Egypt for blending into a constructive policy our four main concerns in the area—Egyptian aspirations, the security of the Suez Canal, the British position in the Middle East, and the need for stability where the old order was passing and new xenophobic ferment, fanned from Moscow, grew daily. While we did aid in damping the crisis of January, our efforts brought no result in the long-term relations between Egypt and Britain. By March 1952 these had reached a new low.

DRIFT TO STALEMATE

Long and futile discussions between Washington and London on the use of our only apparent lever, King Farouk's great interest in his claim to the title of King of the Sudan, came to an end through the coup of July 22–23, 1952, which removed Farouk and set up General Nagib as the front for the colonels led by Nasser behind the scenes. This change appeared to us as mildly encouraging, somewhat as did the February 1917 Russian revolution to President Wilson; but we soon discovered that, between the colossal ignorance and inexperience of the military junta and the deep skepticism of the British Foreign Office, progress with Nagib was as difficult as it had been with Maher and Farouk. Finally, in September, a representative of General Nagib secretly approached our embassy with a proposal to cooperate with the United States and to undertake certain commitments, including participation in the Middle East Command, in return for military and economic aid. We agreed to explore the proposal, asking General Nagib to define more clearly the help for which he proposed to ask and the extent to which he was prepared to plan with the United States and the United Kingdom for the defense of the area and to settle the canal zone problem in a way that would assure effective maintenance of strategic facilities there. We also asked for London's views and specifically for a base settlement plan that would be strategically sound and, at the same time, could realistically be accepted by Egypt.

By November preliminary replies came in, welcoming our efforts, but on the British side evidencing trouble, understandably enough, in preparing a practicable base settlement plan and, on the Egyptian, not being as forthcoming as we had wished. We in our turn had familiar internal problems. The Department of Defense told us that it could not prepare a specific program of assistance to Egypt in the absence of an approved strategic plan and force requirements for the area. This was the sort of attitude that made one want to shake the Joint Chiefs of Staff until their ribbons fell off. Instead, I wrote Lovett a polite letter urging the Joint Chiefs to prepare their idea of a practicable base settlement, strategic plan, force requirements, and assistance program. They would also need to get on with it.

January and our last weeks in office came with no one in satisfactory shape for the secret talks to begin. Harriman and I called on the President to recommend that we begin economic aid to Egypt at once, to keep doors open, and leave the matter of military aid, as indeed we must, to the next administration. The President agreed. There was no more progress in 1952 in breaking the Anglo-Egyptian impasse than there had been in 1951, the Conservatives being no improvement over Labour. Our successors were to prove no more productive than we had been.

REFLECTIONS

Leaving aside the colossal blunders by everyone involved with the Egyptian-Suez crisis of 1956, of which I have written elsewhere,[5] it is difficult even now to see how the United States in the earlier years could have done more than it did to ameliorate Anglo-Egyptian problems. Nasser's attempt at the role of a male Cleopatra playing off the two superpowers and British stubbornness in clinging to the remnants of empire were bound to bring a clash, and a bad one, though not one in which we lost, as we did, the confidence of everyone. However, it has seemed to me that in the last half of the present decade more alert American and British governments might have brought science and technology to their aid in mitigating some of the problems presented to them by Egypt, the Suez Canal, and the dependence of Western Europe on the oil of the Middle East. A fraction of our investment in the space program put into the development of a practicable electric automobile and of nuclear power plants here and, with European cooperation, in Europe could do much to solve our air pollution problems and free Europe from dependence upon the Middle East and the Soviet Union from much of its motive in penetrating it. It would also deprive Nasser of the blackmail potentialities of closing the Suez Canal. The investment still seems to me a profitable one for Europe and the United States for their own welfare and security and for world peace.

59. OTTAWA AND EXCURSIONS
WITHOUT ALARUMS

A FUTILE COUNCIL MEETING

My memory of the NATO Council meeting in Ottawa from Saturday, September 15, through Thursday, September 20, is of the most tiring, perhaps, of our sessions. I came to its six days of long meetings, speeches, and boring formal social engagements weary from two strenuous and exhausting weeks. Behind the scenes a good deal was done to clear obstacles from our path, but we hardly advanced toward our goal. Morrison's unfortunate manner constantly rasped our patience. This was his last appearance, for the Conservatives came to office in the October election. Our first day in Ottawa, as it appears in my engagement book, gives a fair sample of the grind:

> Left Washington 8:30 A.M.
> Arrived Ottawa 11:00 A.M.
> Delegation Meeting 11:30 A.M.
> First Council 12:30 P.M.
> Luncheon at Embassy Residence.
> Second Council 3:30 P.M.
> Governor's Reception 7:00 P.M.
> Dinner at Embassy Residence.
> Third Council Meeting 9:00 P.M.

The succeeding days were much the same, with a speech over the Canadian radio or a press conference thrown in for good measure. When we got back to Washington on Thursday evening, I was thoroughly tired out.

Invitations to Greece and Turkey · At Ottawa the NATO Council appointed a Temporary Council Committee to correlate ends (defense) to means (resources) and issued invitations to Greece and Turkey to join the alliance. In both efforts we ran into sulky resistance from our smaller associates, caused by a belief that the three larger allies arrogated too much to themselves, that the U.S. Congress was trying to control their trade with the Communist bloc, and that their economic troubles flowed from U.S. pressures for rearmament. The bloom was off NATO, the fears of a year before had faded as music wafted westward from the World Festival of Youth and Students for Peace in East Berlin. All this led politicians and writers in Western Europe to question the danger from the East and the need for rearmament upon which the Americans so continually harped.

A press leak in May that Britain, France, and the United States were consulting together about invitations to Greece and Turkey alarmed and annoyed the other allies. The "North Atlantic" had been stretched in 1949 to include Italy; now we were trying to take in the eastern Mediterranean, a snake pit of troubles. How could Northern European statesmen convince their people that attacks in the Levant should be regarded as attacks on Scandinavia or the Low Countries? In carrying the debate for the invitations, I pointed out the absence of any feasible alternative. A year before, recognizing the importance of Greece and Turkey as an eastern flank of European defense, the NATO Council had decided to associate the two countries through a defense planning agency, but it had not worked. They wanted full membership, which from our point of view had the advantage of mutuality of obligations. The idea of a Mediterranean defense treaty including Greece and Turkey and some but not all of the NATO allies (which some had advocated) really made no sense, because if some of us got to fighting, the other NATO allies could not escape danger of involvement but would have no voice in the initial decision, surely a poor position for them. Finally, if Greece and Turkey became allies and were attacked, not every ally would be called upon to fight in the eastern Mediterranean. Action there would have to be geared into a strategic plan for European defense as a whole. All these decisions would affect their security and require their participation. Frank Pace, Secretary of the Army, supported me with military arguments. On the last day of the Ottawa sessions, after much private exhortation, the NATO Council unanimously voted to extend the invitations.

The Temporary Council Committee · The idea of a small committee (the "Three Wise Men") to bring rearmament more in line with capabilities was a French one, broached in Washington by Schuman and René Mayer. Morrison and I, while approving, left it to them to make the running, a wise decision as our French friends ran into solid resentment against Anglo-French-American "guided democracy." Our allies approved the end but were determined to broaden the means. They wished a committee of the whole to undertake the survey. The highlight in the discussion of the economic problem was Dirk Stikker's speech. "Any further lowering of the present standard of living in Europe," said the Netherlands Foreign Minister, "without the prospect of a rise in the near future, will endanger the social peace on the home front which is so essential to our defense effort." Others eagerly caught up this theme.

John Snyder, Secretary of the Treasury, believing that he saw where the discussion was likely to end, intervened with more bluntness than tact to tell our allies not to expect the United States "to foot the bill" for their defense. During this week he was chiefly concerned with the possible effect of Ottawa decisions upon pending Treasury refunding operations. At last the unruly flock entered the fold, a twelve-man Temporary Council Committee was created with authority to set up a three-man working group and with instructions to report by December 1 in time for another discussion at a meeting to be held that month in Rome. So the idea of the "Three Wise Men" survived and became incarnate in the persons of Averell Harriman, Jean Monnet, and Sir Edwin Plowden, men of outstanding ability and common sense.

Since Canada had been pressing for action authorized by Article 2 of the treaty in the social, economic, and cultural fields, originally proposed by Canada, we created a ministerial committee to recommend what could be done. With fitting justice, Lester B. Pearson of Canada was made its chairman and the ministers of Belgium, the Netherlands, Norway, and Italy were added. Their labors were prodigious but barren.

Just as we reached the end of our official tasks, two announcements from Europe fluttered our dovecote: on September 19 it became known that the British Government would call a general election for October 25; and on September 20 General Eisenhower at Rocquencourt called for an increase of thirty-three per cent in European arms production in 1952. We could only be thankful that neither had come earlier.

When we got back to Washington that evening, President Truman met our plane, told me I had done a "magnificent job," a generous exaggeration, and sent me off to the country.

DE GASPERI'S VISIT

On Monday, September 24, Alcide de Gasperi, at the time Prime Minister and Foreign Minister of Italy, arrived in Washington. We had been together at Ottawa, and I had met him earlier, in January 1947, when he had come to this country seeking and getting a substantial loan for Italy. He was one of those foreign office colleagues for whom I acquired great respect and affection. Honest, straightforward, deeply devoted to Italy and, beyond that, to a broad and humane conception of Europe, he was a brave and gallant gentleman and an enlightened statesman of the same liberal stamp as Robert Schuman. Like him a border man—coming from Trentino, territory disputed for years between Italy and Austria—he too looked for peace in Europe to broader conceptions than nationalism. During Mussolini's time he had taken refuge in the Vatican, where he had worked as librarian.

Before becoming Secretary I had had little to do with Italian affairs. Mr. Byrnes had handled these matters himself, since they were all drawn together in the Italian peace treaty, which absorbed his attention in 1946. The Italian election of 1948, which established de Gasperi's Christian Democratic Party so firmly in power, occurred after I had returned to private life. I picked up responsibility in 1949 with the negotiations over Italy's entrance into NATO. It did not take long for me to learn that the Italians believed firmly in the remission of sins. They saw their desertion of Il Duce and of his and their Nazi ally as absolving them from all consequences of losing the war, as, indeed, putting them at the head of the queue asking favors. In their eyes, however, favors had been transmuted into simple justice, which, if denied, might undermine

Italy's firm identification of her interests with those of the NATO allies. Only de Gasperi's transparent honesty prevented such statements from carrying a suggestion of blackmail.

After I had met the Prime Minister's train and the President had received him at luncheon, we plunged into three days of talks, separated by one evening reception held by my wife and me at Anderson House and a dinner given by Ambassador Alberto Tarchiani and his wife. By the end of the week some of my ailments acquired at San Francisco and Ottawa returned and I was packed off for another ten days at our farm.

High on de Gasperi's agenda of requests were Italian claims in Trieste, revision of the Italian peace treaty, Italy's admission to the United Nations, economic and military aid, and an outlet for Italy's burgeoning population. Among these items, the one most passionately held, and as passionately resisted by Yugoslavia, was the Italian claim to Trieste. In 1946 the Italian peace conference nearly broke up over Trieste, which threatened a resumption of hostilities. The outcome was a patched-up, temporary compromise. The city and and its environs were made a Free Territory with two zones: Zone A, the city, predominantly Italian, was administered by the United States and Britain with purely municipal functions turned over by them to a local authority; Zone B, the environs, largely inhabited by Yugoslavs, was administered by Yugoslavia. On March 20, 1948, before the Soviet-Yugoslav break, Western relations with Tito were tense, and when Italy was entering the critical election of that year, France, Britain, and the United States issued a declaration favoring the transfer of the entire Free Territory to Italy. De Gasperi called for the redemption of the expectation raised by this declaration. Nothing could have done more to heal the breach in Communist ranks.

De Gasperi argued his position wherever he found an audience, to us in the Department, to the President, to the Congress. When I told him that the March 20, 1948, declaration could not possibly be the basis of a settlement because of the intensity of Yugoslav opposition to it and the immense harm that would result to all Western interests, especially Italian, should Tito be driven to make his peace with Stalin, he replied that he would rather give up his post than the declaration. Furthermore, he doubted whether any Italian political figure would take his post if it meant renouncing the declaration. To the President he said that without a satisfactory settlement of the Trieste question no democratic government in Italy could get parliamentary support for a joint defense effort. If Italians should think that their allies could not save Trieste for Italy, the result would be a dangerous trend toward neutralism. His coalition would lose votes to the left and right. It was clear that no agreement on this point was possible between us. Although we reverted to the question several times in the next year, agreement was not reached until after we both left office.† In between my talks with de Gasperi the Yugoslav Ambassador called on me to urge the opposite point of view. Attempting to play fairly and openly with both, I said the same thing to each—that the declaration of March 20, 1948, had been overtaken by events and that the basis of settlement had to be founded on the ethnic principle, helped if necessary by exchanges of population in stubborn situations.

On one other question, too, I found myself out of sympathy with de Gasperi—his belief that Italy's overpopulation was a common problem, which we should help solve by easing our immigration laws. Here the President and I were in close agreement, though I never probed the reasons for his similar conclusions. It seemed to me that if Italy wished to regard birth control from the medieval point of view of what was then Vatican policy, she had only herself to blame. To ask others to mitigate her own blindness seemed to me wholly unwarranted. So we refused to make any commitments in advance of the international conference on the subject called for January 1952.

On the other subjects we were able to reach accord and helpful statements,[1] though they were no more than agreement on the nature of the economic problem, as had been the case with the British and French a few weeks before, or hopeful views of the future. The important result of the meeting was its effect upon Italian morale and self-respect. They had been received on the same basis of respect and cordiality as those states with whom they so desperately hoped to equate themselves.

Even as I went away for relaxation and rest, two new problems plucked at my ear.

THE ATTACK ON JESSUP

On September 10 President Truman had sent to the Senate the names of ten persons for its advice and consent to their appointment as representatives of the United States at the sixth General Assembly of the United Nations. Among them was included Philip C. Jessup, Ambassador at Large, who had on three prior occasions been nominated and confirmed for this same position. A subcommittee of the Foreign Relations Committee held hearings on charges made against Ambassador Jessup by Senator Joseph McCarthy and Harold E. Stassen, then President of the University of Pennsylvania.[2] The charges were false and reckless, as might have been expected of McCarthy, but were, at the time, surprising coming from Stassen, who still retained some of the aura of his early promise and only then disclosed the exceptionally bad judgment and passion for notice and office that characterized his later career. "The record of the hearings," President Truman wrote later in October, "shows that charges to the effect that he [Jessup] was sympathetic to Communist causes were utterly without foundation, and some of the so-called documentation introduced in support of those charges bordered on fraud. And even two of the three members of the subcommittee who voted against his confirmation went to great pains to make it clear that they had no doubt of his loyalty and integrity. Then Ambassador Jessup was attacked for being at a meeting which he did not attend and for policy recommendations which he never made."[3]

The subcommittee reported favorably to the full committee on the other nine nominations, but the full committee took no action at all in the hope—a vain hope—of getting the President to withdraw Jessup's nomination, thus saving the committee what was then considered the embarrassment of overriding a smear on the loyalty of one of the ablest and most upright servants the Republic has ever had. Instead of this, however, we evolved a different strategy.

On October 19, by motion made on the Senate floor, the committee was discharged from further consideration of nine of the nominations and these were confirmed. By unanimous consent Ambassador Jessup's nomination was left "without prejudice" before the Committee on Foreign Relations, thus opening the way for a recess appointment when the Senate should adjourn, which it promptly did. While I was at the Capitol, working out this operation, it was almost sunk by collision with another initiative of the President's of which I was not fully informed.

Ambassador to the Vatican • While the echoes of "Rum, Romanism, and Rebellion" were still reverberating in the country, Congress had enacted in a rider on an appropriation act that no appropriated funds might be used to maintain a diplomatic mission at the Vatican. During the war President Roosevelt sent Myron C. Taylor to Vatican City as his "personal representative" in the belief that in this way he would get information from within German-held Europe. If he did so, I could find no evidence of anything substantial after I had access to secret information or from many talks with Mr. Taylor. In any event, the Pope quite understandably became dissatisfied with this morganatic relationship and let it be known tactfully that if we could not establish a diplomatic mission, as thirty-seven other states had done, it would be better to have no representative at the Vatican. Within the first few days of my tenure as Secretary, I received from the White House a letter, drafted by Mr. Taylor, from the President to the Pope suggesting that the "personal representative" be discontinued and that in the future he be superseded by an ambassador. After consulting within the Department, I discussed the letter with the President, telling him that the Department favored the proposed step, but that I earnestly begged him not to take it for the present. To do so would surely start a religious controversy all over the country just when we never had greater need for national unity to meet the growing Russian menace. Already the long period of Democratic rule and the bitterness of the Republican right promised division enough. The President conceded that I had a good point and, although he insisted on sending the letter, promised that he would do nothing to execute the plan until we had conferred again regarding an appropriate time for doing so.

It was not difficult, amid the crowding events and crises of the ensuing years, to convince him that the appropriate time eluded us. Just as I was concluding that this trouble, at least, had passed, it was upon me. At one of our meetings early in October the President observed that I was an even greater practitioner of the delaying tactic than Fabius Maximus Cunctator himself and that, if left to me, no appropriate time would come. While waiting for it, he was drifting into a breach of his promise to the Pope and this he would not do. I was tempted to point out that the Pope could give him absolution from that promise, if anyone could, but the President was in no mood to argue. He asked whether I would think it fair for him, after nearly three years, to recover his freedom to act without further consultation with me. Of course I agreed. He knew my views thoroughly; he was the boss and carried the responsibility. What he had in mind seemed to me unwise, as he knew, but it was certainly not unfair. I accepted notice that he was a free agent and wished him a happy landing, which I doubted he would have.

The Collision • Friday, October 19, was not one of my better days. It began with various requests that I "comment" (obnoxious and lazy word!) on the prior day's performance of the American Legion convention in Miami. There former defenders of the nation, after a stormy session, sought to protect it from me by urging the President to remove me from office. All that was needed, apparently, to produce this request from some group was the announcement that I was going to Europe to represent the country.

Having survived these inquiries, a Cabinet meeting, and a haircut, I faced—although I did not know it—the moment of real hazard. At four I met Senator Tom Connally at the Capitol to put the finishing touches on the plan for Ambassador Jessup's recess appointment. The Senator's agreement and collaboration were essential to success, even though Senator John Sparkman of Alabama, chairman of the subcommittee, would handle the operation on the floor. All had been cleared with the President, who knew of my date, but the Senator moved slowly. At length he agreed and by five o'clock I was back in the State Department, where my secretaries were in a state of shock. The President had been trying to reach me with the news that he had informed Senator Connally that the next day he would nominate General Mark W. Clark to be Ambassador to the Vatican. I gathered from later talks that the President had hoped the General's eminence in Masonic circles would reconcile Protestants to his mission to the Papacy. Poor Luke Battle and Barbara Evans saw the Capitol dome collapsing on top of me.

A telephone call to Tom Connally found him incoherent with rage. Minutes passed before he would listen to my protestation that I had known no more about the nomination than he. Within the limits of loyalty I deflected his rage where it could be more justly vented. Not only was he angry because he had not been consulted on a matter that greatly affected his position in the Senate, but outraged at the selection of Mark Clark, who had been in command of the landing at Salerno in Italy where a Texas division, due to alleged miscalculations, had run into heavy casualties. Texan hostility to him would threaten Connally's position at home. In the resulting hubbub the President found himself without defenders in Congress; General Clark, aghast at the commotion he had contributed to, asked to have his name withdrawn from nomination; and the whole proposal collapsed. To use an unfortunate expression of mine, when the dust settled—indeed, in it—the maneuver to appoint Phil Jessup went through unnoticed. It was, as the Iron Duke said of Waterloo, "a damned near thing," but it came off. Years later, visiting the battlefield of Salerno, the President was reported to have remarked that the Salerno and Anzio landings were the work of "some squirrel-headed general."

PREPARATION FOR PARIS

Aside from these rather more than normal alarms, the main business of October, after my return from the country and before our departure on October 25 aboard the SS *America* for more restful days en route to Le Havre, was preparation for the sixth regular session of the UN General Assembly in Paris. This has been called the "disarmament session" and was to open on November 6, 1951. The year 1951 had seen a continuous and vigorous propaganda war between the principal powers with many battles fought in various settings: the long-drawn-out battle of the Palais Rose, our attack at the United Nations on Communist China as an aggressor, and the Communist counter-offensive at the same place and with the same charge against us regarding Formosa. In July the President transmitted to President Nicolai M. Shvernik the McMahon-Ribicoff Resolution containing a "Declaration of Friendship from the American People to All the Peoples of the World, Including the Peoples of the Soviet Union" and an attack on the "artificial barriers" that kept the Russian people ignorant of our desire for friendship. Moscow replied with a proposal for a five-power peace pact and prohibition of atomic weapons and the World Youth Festival in East Berlin. Marshal Voroshilov attacked the United States, and on September 17 President Truman replied that Soviet agreements were not worth the paper they were written on. The Kremlin called a meeting of the World Peace Council at Vienna to coincide with the General Assembly.

After a summer of exchanges, which diminished in effectiveness as they increased in invective, Assistant Secretary of State John Hickerson proposed that at the coming session of the General Assembly we put forward, with the British and French if possible, a sober and workable plan for the limitation and control of armaments. He recognized that the chance of Russian acceptance of such a plan was small, since their conduct clearly disclosed a desire to catch wishful thinkers everywhere rather than to undertake a practicable plan for reducing the immense dangers that faced us all. However, it seemed to him and to all of us that to put forward a plan that by its provisions rather than by oratory proclaimed its sincerity would restore confidence in American intentions and leadership. If by any chance the Soviet Union should be willing to explore its possibilities, we might veer around to a sane international venture upon which all shades of opinion in the United States could unite.

With ready agreement and encouragement of the President and General Marshall, the Department began to develop a plan. For a year or more we had been discussing the subject in London and Paris without much progress. Jessup, Parodi, and Davies had talked about it together at the Palais Rose. From mid-September on we worked in earnest, telling our allies that we were doing so, and that as yet we had no fixed ideas or formulated proposals. Aside from a few exchanges with the British Embassy people in Washington and the familiar complaint from the French Minister Counselor, Jean-Henri Daridan, that the French were not being kept informed, we got nothing from either.

Not until October 23 did we have the outlines of a plan for presentation to the President. Having obtained his approval, it went the next day to Morrison and Schuman. Before sailing for Europe, word came to me from the former, sent on the eve of the British election, that he could not commit His Majesty's Government and complaining of the shortness of time for study, tripartite discussion, and joint drafting of a proposal to be made at the coming session of the General Assembly. I sent word back that "on balance the advantages of submitting a program of this nature to the General Assembly outweigh the disadvantages." By the time the message arrived, Mr. Morrison had ceased to be Foreign Minister. Both Mr. Eden, who succeeded him, and Prime Minister Churchill were in favor of going full speed ahead.

60. THE "DISARMAMENT ASSEMBLY"

SINCE THE SIXTH General Assembly was to be held in Paris, we could not rely on the large staff of the United States UN Mission in New York. So eighty-one persons—representatives, alternates, advisers, congressional staff advisers, assistants, and information officers—moved in waves to Paris. We took over the old Hotel Astoria, overlooking the Arc de Triomphe, to provide office space. The list seems appalling now, but at the time I went over it carefully and pared it down to the minimum necessary for the work of the Assembly and liaison with fifty-nine other delegations. The hospitable Bruces took my wife, Luke Battle, and me into the embassy residence at the end of the Avenue d'Iéna and across a small park from the Palais de Chaillot, where the Assembly would be held.

Indeed, its proximity threatened to banish sleep from my side of the embassy. In preparation for the opening, the Palais staff each night tested the car-calling electronic equipment, choosing hours well after midnight. A voice as loud as St. Peter's calling up the saints on the Day of Judgment counted, *"Un! deux! trois! quatre! cinq!"* and so on and on. I complained bitterly but ineffectively, until Philip Jessup's wife presented me with a box of pills which she said would induce sweet slumber. Late that night, really tired, I remembered them, was surprised to find them rather large, and decided to chew one up before washing it down. In a moment, to my horror I seemed to have lockjaw and appealed to my wife for aid through clenched teeth. A glance at the box reassured her that I had bitten into a large wax earplug. An hour or so later I was cured of lockjaw, after which the prescribed use of the plugs brought sleep.

At this assembly Anthony Eden and I became close friends. We had known and liked one another for fifteen years or more but had never been thrown closely together. Now we were, working with Schuman and Lester Pearson of Canada on the chief matters before the Assembly. Added to this my wife and I met his recent bride, née Clarissa Churchill, a niece of the Prime Minister and a lady of rare charm and intelligence, who came to Paris for a few days. She has shown since, not surprisingly, equally rare steadfastness and courage in the face of deep anxiety. Their friendship has been a joy to us over nearly twenty years. Eden and I worked easily together, agreed on basic matters, where he was a resourceful and strong ally. In some cases, however, as in Iran and in approaching European integration, he was more cautious than I in departing from traditional policies, quite understandably, as he had been far more deeply involved in making them.

THE MOROCCAN QUESTION

In the days before the opening of the session on November 6 we met constantly to align French, British, and American positions on the major issues. In this we were pretty successful, although starting with difficulties. Initial problems arose between us and the French, in which Eden proved an admirable conciliator. We were all agreed in supporting the French "on the merits" of the Moroccan issue, which meant on opposing any UN action critical of French policy regarding Morocco. But Schuman wanted us to go further, and to vote against inscribing the item on the agenda. To do this ran counter to the "town meeting of the world" principle of the Vandenberg days shared by many of our delegation who had attended these sessions from the beginning of the United Nations. The Senator had believed that nothing should be excluded from the agenda and discussion, but that action must be strictly confined within the limited powers prescribed in the Charter.

This typically senatorial attitude toward the purgative quality of talk seemed to me harmfully misapplied here. The purpose of raising the issue was to create pressure against France and unrest in Morocco on a matter that the French claimed was a purely internal one from which the Charter specifically excluded the United Nations. If the item once got on the agenda, it would automatically be referred to a standing committee, where the merits of French policy and the issue of UN competence to consider it would be debated in a hopeless jumble and some kind of compromise resolution reported to the General Assembly. To one with legal training it seemed preposterous that the issue of jurisdiction should not be discussed and decided first and apart from the propriety of French policy. If there was no jurisdiction, as the French claimed, they should be protected against busybody and disruptive inquiries into their internal affairs. If there was jurisdiction, they should answer on the merits. They were entitled to a clear-cut decision of the jurisdictional issue.

To meet the problem, I urged that instead of opposing the inscription of the item, which carried an aura of cloture, we propose postponing it until the General Committee could consider and decide the issue of jurisdiction, on which we could support France. If decided favorably to France, this would dispose of the matter. Eden warmly supported this view, arguing effectively that it would attract more votes, as indeed it did, than a straight vote on inscribing, from which the United States would abstain. Schuman agreed to the attempt. Fortunately, with a good deal of hard work and some luck the plan worked, the vote in the General Committee being six for (U.S., U.K., Canada, Dominican Republic, Norway, France), four against (USSR, Iraq, Poland, Yugoslavia), and four abstaining (Thailand, Chile, China, Mexico).

By persistence and mutual accommodation we reached agreement on a surprising number of points: to propose and support postponing a vote on the question of Chinese representation until the end of the session; to support Padilla Nervo of Mexico for President of the General Assembly; to issue the statement of principles on the Middle East Command on November 10; to meet with Adenauer for the first time in a group before going to Rome; and to go through with the Rome meeting of NATO on November 24 despite doubts as to its usefulness. I strongly urged sticking to regular dates for the semiannual council meetings rather than moving them about because of supposed convenience.

REDUCTION AND CONTROL OF ARMS

Most important of all, we agreed on the text of the arms limitation proposal and the dates and manner of presenting it. A short release would be issued in the three capitals at ten o'clock Paris time on Monday, November 7. That evening President Truman would speak about the purpose and nature of the plan in a "fireside chat."[1] I would develop it further to the General Assembly the next morning; Eden and Schuman would follow with supporting speeches. Finally, after the general debate concluded, I would present the plan before the First Committee in detailed exposition. This took place on November 19, so that for nearly two weeks continuous and serious attention was paid to the development of the plan.

My speech on November 8[2] was made to a crowded session and packed galleries, and against a background of calls for a "summit meeting" by President Auriol of France in formally opening the sixth General Assembly and by Prime Minister Churchill on the same day in the House of Commons. Summit meetings of heads of government, except to ratify agreements already reached, were anathema to me. However, the Auriol and Churchill speeches heightened the sense of crisis in which to launch a serious proposal to limit and control the arms race. Ours captured world attention as well as that of the General Assembly. That afternoon Vishinsky made a mistake of major proportions. From the rostrum he told the General Assembly[3] (and the world) in a diatribe of an hour and three-quarters that "I could hardly sleep all night last night having read that speech [President Truman's]. I could not sleep because I kept laughing."[4] The sheer bad taste of this boorish remark shocked both Assembly and press. Speaker after speaker rose to rebuke Vishinsky and to welcome the proposal. We wisely decided to leave that expression of outrage to others.

So wide was this attitude, however, that it affected the responses to Soviet moves. The General Committee had adopted a Thai resolution to postpone consideration of the Chinese Communist claim to represent China until the end of the session. Dissatisfied, Vishinsky moved in a plenary meeting to overrule this action and place the issue on the agenda. He was defeated 37 to 11 with four abstentions. I strenuously objected to the idea of even debating the seating of the Peking regime "at the very time when its international conduct [was] so low that it would take considerable improvement to raise it to the general level of barbarism." Obviously realizing that some constructive gesture toward arms control was necessary to salvage a bit of the USSR's peace image from the wreck, Vishinsky made one on November 16 as the general debate was nearing its end.

Coming to the General Assembly with a captive dove—a bit of gaucherie that Khrushchev later could have carried off but which made Vishinsky appear as foolish as he clearly felt—he presented a hastily pasted-together disarmament collage made up of sections from past propaganda. Atomic weapons would be unconditionally prohibited (without inspection); reduction within one year of the arms and armed forces of the Big Five by one-third; presentation by all nations of "complete official data" on arms and armed forces; an international control organ within the framework of the Security Council (i.e., with a Soviet veto). To the obvious satisfaction of the Assembly, I made a short statement to the effect that analysis of the not unfamiliar Soviet proposals had best await committee consideration and that the accompaniment of dialectics had best be ignored.

The next day the First Committee—Political and Security—made up of members from all delegations, adopted its agenda, placing the tripartite plan as the first item upon it and the Soviet proposal as the last.

The Tripartite Plan • My purpose in a long speech[5]—eighty minutes—in the informal attitude around the large committee table was not only to explain the proposal but to make clear to the delegates and to the public by press and television the complex and multifarious problems with which it dealt. Soviet propaganda and proposals were designed to ensnare minds unacquainted with the problems and ready to believe that the statement of ideal goals provided the means of achieving them.

Our proposals, I said, were for an international approach to the four main problems of the control and reduction of all armaments of all nations having any of significant size, rather than being patented solutions for them. The problems were, first, the provision of full, accurate, public, and continuously current information on all armaments of all nations, thus removing them from their present jealously guarded secret status, which could be done through disclosure and verification; second, the limitation and reduction of armaments; third, the abolition of atomic weapons; and, fourth, the creation of safeguards.

Obviously, I pointed out, a conference of sixty or more nations could not draft an international agreement on this subject. We proposed, therefore, a Disarmament Commission with the same membership as the Atomic Energy Commission and the Commission for Conventional Armaments and replacing these two. This commission should be charged with the duty of drafting the treaty or treaties necessary in accordance with the broad guidance of the resolution introduced by the three nations. To administer the treaties and carry on the various inspections required, there should be one continuing international body—perhaps more, or one with separate divisions—with defined powers to review operations and recommend amendments as needed.

The proposing states believed that work on the treaties could and should begin at once. The treaties could not go into effect until the fighting in Korea was ended, but that was not likely to cause a real delay. This was our only condition. There was, as any sensible person could see, a relation between world affairs and the successful operation of such a plan as that outlined. Nations would not be likely to agree on a system of arms limitation and reduction in a period of mounting international tensions and frictions. On the other hand, if we should enter seriously upon the negotiation of this proposal, that in itself would help to reduce tensions and increase the possibility of solutions for them.

A great opportunity lay before us, I concluded, to turn from the dark and noisome alleys of propaganda to a broad, clear road to hope and peace. My country and our colleagues in France and Britain were ready to seize it; scores of delegates were ready, I believed, to join us. Were all or enough of us ready to do so? That was what the debate then opening would disclose.

A DINNER AT THE ELYSÉE PALACE

That evening President and Mme. Auriol gave a dinner for the delegates and their ladies with all the pomp and style the French employ so tastefully and effectively. After dinner Secretary General Trygve Lie urged me to speak to Vishinsky, who was standing nearby with a group of Russians and Eastern Europeans. As I did so, accompanied by our interpreter, the whole room turned to watch. After greeting the group, I said to Vishinsky that I hoped he had noticed that contrary to his practice I had avoided in my speech any offensive remarks about him or his Government. I hoped that he would feel free to discuss any matter with me without risking embarrassing dialectics. Jacob Malik interrupted to say that I had charged the Soviet Union with maintaining slave-labor camps. Turning to Vishinsky, I said that I was addressing him and had no wish to argue with Malik. As Vishinsky well knew, I had said nothing of the sort or anything else offensive and did not intend to.

We were both lawyers, I went on, and not sensitive to the cut and thrust of hard argument. In private we could relax and joke with one another. But I got no amusement from, indeed I deeply resented, heavy-handed and tasteless humor in public and on most serious issues. Malik interrupted again to say that I was not sincere or constructive, which I ignored. Concluding the discussion, I said that I had done my best to conduct the debate in a useful manner and it was now up to him. Indeed, if he wanted to stop fooling around with doves and get on a twig himself, I would get on a twig beside him and try to work something out. He mumbled a few words, which the interpreter did not get. So I said good night and left him.

The only result of the interview I could discern was to raise his style of debate to the barely tolerable.

THE PROPOSAL STRAGGLES TO ITS END

When we flew to Rome a few days later for the NATO Council meeting, Ambassador Jessup took charge of the disarmament proposal and other political matters at the General Assembly. On November 24, the day after we left Paris, Vishinsky attacked the tripartite proposals. On November 30 the Political

Committee constituted representatives of the four powers and the President, Padilla Nervo, a subcommittee to work out a disarmament plan by December 10, thus beginning the familiar search for compromise in the Assembly in which substance perishes and only formulas remain.

The British representative on the subcommittee, Selwyn Lloyd, Minister of State and later Minister of Foreign Affairs, had a weakness, which reappeared a year later, for bridging gaps by abolishing them—that is, by abandoning the essence of one's own position and adopting the opposing one. At various times he proposed separating out atomic weapons, abandoning limitation and reduction of armaments, abandoning levels of armaments adequate for defense as a criterion of limitation, and so on. Our Government and delegation wisely rejected all these suggestions, unwilling to becloud the real problems surrounding disarmament or the real issues between us and the Soviet Union.

The subcommittee reported, on the date set, the divergent and unbridged proposals of the three and of the USSR, Ambassador Jessup reviewing with force and clarity the reasons for Soviet dissent. These centered on the very provisions that were essential for the security of all; that is, the knowledge by all that each had performed his obligations. A month later Moscow attempted to befog the issues with a new set of proposals of the same deceptive sort, which I analyzed in a press conference on January 16, 1952.

Our joint proposals of 1951 had failed of their principal purpose—to ease the dangers and burdens of the arms race. But they had succeeded in the other purpose. No doubt existed any longer about who stood where or for what.

WE MEET WITH ADENAUER

After the presentation of the disarmament proposal to the Assembly, Chancellor Konrad Adenauer came to Paris in response to tripartite invitation to meet with Schuman, Eden, and me. On the first day of his visit, November 21, he paid separate calls on each of us; the next day he met with us together. Since this was his first visit to Paris since the war and the first joint meeting of the four foreign ministers, it proved to be a landmark in German-allied relations. In a report from the three allied High Commissioners we had already learned that their negotiations with the Chancellor, authorized in September at our Washington meeting, had made satisfactory progress. These involved granting to the Federal Republic as much sovereignty as the divided state of Germany and our responsibility in Berlin seemed to permit and advancing association of the Republic with the defense of Europe. Some problems remained, due, as might be expected, to the American desire to move farther and faster than the French were willing to go, with the British in between us. We did our best to keep these differences to discussion among the three of us and not expose them to the Germans.

Adenauer seemed to me to have grown in assurance over two years and to have become an impressive figure. He and I met for our first discussion at lunch at the embassy with Ambassador Bruce, High Commissioner McCloy, and Assistant Secretary of State George Perkins. The Chancellor had with him State

Secretary Walter Hallstein, operating officer of the Foreign Office, which Adenauer himself headed. After lunch, while we talked in the living room, the Chancellor bluntly stated what was clearly his principal concern. Would the occupying powers, he asked, use Germany as a pawn in attempting to reach a settlement with the Russians? He had the gravest worries about our British and French associates. Both public and governmental opinion in those countries, shown in press and parliaments, was deeply suspicious and hostile toward Germany, and understandably so. What attitude could he expect from the United States? Not merely from President Truman, who had made his position and his Government's very plain, but over time from the country? He was aware, he said, that we would have an election within a year and of the speculation regarding it that our press carried.

The question seemed a fair and honest one, deserving a forthright and honest answer. Due to our different position and experience, I said, the American people did not share the suspicion and hostility toward Germany that existed in France and Britain. However, this attitude existed among us toward the Soviet Union and Communist China to a far greater extent than in either of the other countries. He could be sure that neither the present U.S. Government nor any now-discernible successor from either party, in asking Western Europe and Germany to join with us in common defense arrangements against Soviet aggression, would countenance the sacrifice of one of our allies in an attempt to appease the Communist powers—an effort as futile as it was immoral. McCloy and Perkins, I pointed out, were members of the Republican Party and I asked them to express their own views, which they did to the same effect. We all analyzed the winter debate on "troops for Europe" to point out the weakness of the isolationist position in America at the time.

We went on to argue that the attitude of not only the occupying powers but of all Western Europe toward Germany would depend upon German conduct. If Germany pressed on, as it had been doing, to be a good European neighbor and to carry its weight of the cooperative defense burden, it could and would be received as an equal partner with an equal voice in policies and decisions. In rebuilding mutual confidence in the West after the experiences of the past two and a half decades, suspicion was natural on both sides, but Adenauer should remember that ground for suspicion was far more plentiful to the British and French than to the Germans. We proposed to deal openly and honorably and insist that others do the same. If that sort of relationship should break down, the principal sufferer would be all of Europe.

Afterward McCloy told us that Adenauer was much impressed by the frankness of this talk. He was also impressed, McCloy said, by the relations he observed in the meeting the next day between Eden, Schuman, and me—the informality, the friendliness, and the mutual understanding that existed among us. It was, McCloy added, a completely new idea to Adenauer—whose experience in international affairs had been very limited—that representatives of important powers could conduct themselves as understandingly, indeed warmly, as we did. He gained a sense that he was dealing with people among whom everything was frank, friendly, and aboveboard. After that, discussion between Adenauer and the High Commissioners went better than ever.

Before our meeting with the Chancellor on the afternoon of November 22 at the Quai d'Orsay, the three of us had conferred with the High Commissioners to get a common view of several matters to propose to the Chancellor. The High Commissioners had gone far in working out with him the contractual relationship, consisting of a general agreement and four or more subsidiary agreements, which would supersede the Occupation Statute, the Allied High Commission, and the various Land Commissions with their powers of intervention in German affairs. Some questions remained for discussion by the Chancellor and ourselves. In general, these were either theoretical, impossible to be settled without Russian agreement, or not yet ripe for solution. They were dealt with in different ways.

In the first category, for instance, was Adenauer's worry that the allied reserve power to resume authority in Germany in the event of danger to the state from foreign invasion or civil disorder might be unduly prolonged. He wanted some arrangement for appeal. This, I pointed out, was wholly unrealistic since a danger from invasion could not be foreseen in advance and dealt with judicially, and one from domestic disorder would either be clearly terminated or not. In one case we would be only too eager to return authority; in the other we could not. But to resolve any doubts of our good faith, I suggested a review on request by the NATO Council, which all were ready to accept.

Of the same nature was Schuman's desire to have in the agreements a list of armaments that Germany should be prohibited from producing. Here it seemed to me that we must make up our minds whether we regarded Germany as an ally or an enemy; to take an ambivalent attitude would be fatal. With the President's support, I suggested to Eden and Schuman that we either leave to the European Defense Community the matter of allocating weapons manufacture among its members or work out with Adenauer a unilateral declaration of what weapons Germany would not produce. Important steps along these lines were taken a few months later in London at our second quadripartite meeting.

In the second category was the Chancellor's desire for some statement on Germany's eastern boundary. Here the solution was found not in an unwise attempt to draw or define it but in agreement "that an essential aim of the common policy of their [four] Governments is a peace settlement for the whole of Germany freely negotiated between Germany and her former enemies, which should lay the foundation for a lasting peace. They further agree that the final settlement of the boundaries of Germany await such a settlement."[6] This met one of Adenauer's principal worries, already mentioned, of a dictated peace treaty on the Versailles Treaty model, worked out among the three of us and the Russians and forced upon him.

Questions of German contribution to defense both in the support of allied troops in Germany and through German military formations were just as difficult for the Germans at this stage as for the French. With the latter we went again, as we had done in 1950, through the anguish of probing their budgetary position to discover whether the six hundred million dollars they asked of us was to meet a foreign exchange deficit or a budget deficit or both. Insofar as it was the former, we could not spend dollars in France until the French had provided the land and facilities to house our ground and air forces, which for internal political reasons they were agonizingly slow in doing. We had our own troubles, too. Our funds were all expendable through three men who, although good friends, were also good poker players and not eager to assume one another's just obligations—Harriman of Mutual Aid, Lovett of the Defense Department, and Snyder of the Treasury. Added to this was the infuriating American practice of reviewing every decision to death. One never knew when a commitment could be regarded as final and not subject to review by some group not conversant with the facts. In the end, however, we gave the French assurances which, although unsatisfactory and productive of future misunderstandings, enabled them to strengthen their forces.

The problem of the German contribution to defense was complicated by a difference in approach by the French and British on one side and the Germans on the other. At the moment it was clear that amounts paid by Germany for the support of occupation forces were too high to be continued as aid to allied defense garrisons. But a reasonable figure was not yet ascertainable. Nor was it possible at that time to determine the cost of German forces still not agreed upon. The French and British proposed agreeing on a total figure of thirteen billion deutsche marks, a reasonable total figure for German defense costs, and working back from that to an appropriate division. The Bundestag, like any parliament, would have great trouble with authorizing so large an amount with so little knowledge of its precise uses. Our discussions, *à trois* and *à quatre,* brought out these difficulties but not solutions for them. It would take another meeting of the three at Lisbon and of the four at Bonn in 1952 before sufficient precision could be provided to make agreement possible.

The tone of the meeting with Adenauer rapidly became informal and friendly. One amusing barometer of this appeared in the matter of translation. At the outset everything said in French or English was translated into German for Adenauer and his remarks were put into French and English. Most of the discussion soon became an exchange between Adenauer and Schuman, who had spoken German before he had spoken French. Before long he began replying to Adenauer in German without waiting for any translation. This did not bother Eden or me, as we counted on learning sooner or later what they were talking about, but it greatly upset Schuman's Foreign Office aides, who were great sticklers for the use of French. They would pull at his coattails to make him wait until what he had understood perfectly was repeated in French and English.

I summed up my impressions in a cable to the President: Our meeting had been held in a good atmosphere. I thought the specific agreements we had reached were of less importance than the fact that we had met on a basis of equality. We had satisfactorily reassured Adenauer as to his main fear, which was that the allies might, at German expense, conclude a deal on German unification with the Soviets. On his concern about eastern borders, he had been assured that Mr. Byrnes's position still held. I added, however, that we had not been able to move beyond bare fundamentals when it came to the problem of Germany's defense contribution and that the High Commissioners had been authorized to start negotiations on a total figure of thirteen billion deutsche marks for the fiscal year beginning April 1, 1952. We had also repeated the security declaration for Germany of September 1950, which should tide us over until Germany could be formally linked to the North Atlantic Treaty.

61. NATO MEETS IN ROME

CHANGES IN THE DEPARTMENT

THE BRUCES ACCOMPANIED US to Rome, as the Ambassador was our only and indispensable expert, as I have noted earlier, on the negotiations for the European Defense Community. For another reason also it was fortunate. In Rome I got word from Under Secretary James Webb that an increase in the severe migraines from which he suffered required his immediate resignation for diagnosis and treatment. In Rome, also, were two of the three men who would be most affected by Webb's retirement—David Bruce, who would come to Washington as Under Secretary, and James Dunn, who would move to the embassy in Paris. The third, Ellsworth Bunker, who would come to Rome, was in Buenos Aires. I pondered a long time and spent many hours of discussion with Carlisle Humelsine, our solid Pennsylvania Dutch Deputy Under Secretary for Administration, who came over from Washington, before making these recommendations to the President. Most considerations argued against moving these men, who were doing outstanding work in critical and difficult posts. The current presidential term had only a year more to run, beyond which the future was unforeseeable. The President had given no indication of an intention to seek another term. Mrs. Truman, who had great influence with him, was frankly apprehensive of four years more of such strain as he had been through. A change of Presidents might well bring a change of ambassadors early in 1953 before new appointees in 1952 had settled in.

One powerful argument moved us the other way. David Bruce would bring immense help and strength to the Department, to me, and to the President. He was well regarded by Congress—in part because of the charm that distance had lent during his years in Europe—and by influential people throughout the country. One important obstacle was his own strong distaste for some aspects of the Under Secretary's usual work, principally public speeches and appearances before congressional committees. To get him to consider the appointment, I pointed out that Dean Rusk and I had been doing a large part of the general testimony and speechmaking and would continue it. We had able men in the Department who would have taken over admirably—Dean Rusk, Paul Nitze, and Freeman Matthews, to name three outstanding men—but moving them within the Department would not have added to it.

On balance we judged that we would most help the whole effort by bringing David Bruce to the Washington front and sending Ellsworth Bunker to the European. Having come to that conclusion, Dunn's transfer to Paris seemed unanswerable. He knew the postwar situation in Europe from the beginning, first as head of the European Office in the Department and for the past five years from the vantage point of Rome. The critical spots in Europe during 1952 would be Bonn and Paris. Dunn could pick up the situation in Paris faster than anyone else and we would do our best to hang onto McCloy's coattails in Bonn until the contractual relation was worked out and the occupation largely liquidated. Personal obligations called insistently for his return to private life.

Ellsworth Bunker's work and conduct in Argentina had so impressed the President and all of us in the Department that I was eager to try him in a different and even more difficult setting. In a remarkably short time Bunker had shown the qualities of that *rara avis,* a natural professional in diplomacy. Edward Miller and I had known him for many years—I from university days—and admired his coolness and judgment. On Miller's suggestion, we had appealed to him to abandon a successful business career to try a diplomatic course in Argentina that, of late, we had not been able to achieve. Successive ambassadors had approached Perón either with a challenge to combat, which they lost, or bearing gifts, which they lost also. We had proposed that our Ambassador treat him with aloof correctness, initiating nothing, giving nothing without a *quid pro quo* in hand, debating nothing, and seeing to it that any harm to our interests was met by one to his. In no time Bunker, icily cold, meticulously correct, hard as a rock in negotiation, had won the respect of Perón and Argentine officialdom. He could not have cared less about the public's attitude toward him. With Italy in the mood suggested in Chapter 59, it seemed to me a little of this treatment would not be amiss. I learned later that it was even more effective than I had hoped.

ANOTHER COUNCIL MEETING STALLS

The Rome meeting of the NATO Council like that in Ottawa continued to stall through lack of progress outside NATO circles on the two fundamental obstacles to European defense: an arrangement for enlisting a strong German contribution to it and a reconciliation of the military needs of defense with the capabilities of the European economies and political structures. The arrangement for a German contribution had made more headway in the negotiations between Adenauer and the High Commission at Bonn than in Schuman's negotiation of the European Defense Community, which seemed stuck in subministerial technical bickering under Hervé Alphand. The Three Wise Men of the Temporary Council Committee were hard at work on the second—reconciling needs and capabilities—but were not yet ready to report and would not be for two or three months. So the meetings were destined to frustration. "The big problems remained unsolved," I cabled the President in a personal appraisal of the session,† "and will need most energetic work for the next sixty days if we are to solve them. In the international field we are experiencing what the production people call 'slippages.' " Both Eden and I, the report added, believed, and had impressed on Schuman, that he must aim for some conclusion of his efforts by the end of the year. Otherwise we would be threatened by a permanent deadlock and would have to drop the European Defense Community. Eden was a most stalwart ally, despite ambivalent attitudes expressed by Mr. Churchill in London.

The depressing attitude of the meetings themselves was heightened by a revolt of the Benelux ministers and my getting what a Roman doctor regarded as ambulatory pleurisy with occasional relapses into bed. General Gruenther, General Eisenhower's Chief of Staff, opened the meetings with a hair-raising description of how devastating a Soviet attack on Western Europe would be if the Russians brought their full power into play. Whether or not the accuracy of the figures Gruenther used was borne out by later intelligence, this sort of exegesis tended to discourage rather than encourage the European defense effort, since failure to speak frankly of the deterrent factor of American nuclear weapons made the task of defense seem impossible. While the ministers were digesting this somber report, General Eisenhower gave an inspirational address on the pressing necessity of the political unification of Europe. After this speech the council took a coffee break, during which the American group mingled with the others to gather impressions created by the addresses. These were almost uniformly critical of the effect created by the military command apparently trying to bring pressure for a political result, European integration. Unknown to the General, the political lecture was delivered to a group already heatedly divided on this very issue.

My wise, shrewd, and humorous friend, Joseph Bech, Foreign Minister of Luxembourg, added another comment. "Before long," he said, "I think we shall lose our Supreme Commander." I was puzzled. "Yes," he went on, "the signs are unmistakable. Our commander will soon leave us to run for President of your country." And so he did, less than four months later.

In the Paris discussions of the Defense Community a considerable fissure had opened between the Benelux countries, led by Paul van Zeeland of Belgium, and France, Italy, and Germany regarding the degree and scope of integration to be sought in the Community. The issue was framed in terms of Benelux reluctance and constitutional difficulty in placing all their military forces in peacetime as well as war under supranational command. The problem, however, ran deeper. They believed that in the economic field their Benelux integration was working well in a tidy, small area with largely similar conditions. If sucked into the larger, more confused, and disparate economic affairs of France, Italy, and Germany, they would be submerged and powerless. Furthermore, they were being drawn into these problems not primarily for economic reasons but because of military problems, where their part must necessarily be small.

These were very valid objections. For the time being they were postponed by provisions for approaching integration in nonmilitary fields by stages. Later when the Defense Community idea collapsed in 1954 and was followed by the Messina negotiation of the European Economic Community (Common Market), these same problems required a great deal of patient discussion and adjustment. At the moment, however, they were in the phase of generating heat.

Some of the annoyance of the Benelux group over the Eisenhower speech rubbed off on me through suspicion that I had encouraged it. This was quite untrue but understandable, since under European practice a soldier would not have discussed political matters unless directed to do so. After de Gasperi's official dinner for his NATO visitors at the Villa Madama, Dirk Stikker and I, walking in the garden, came upon a group of Benelux colleagues, who began attributing their troubles to me. As their comments sharpened, Stikker intervened.

"Come, come," he said. "We must make a Treaty of Villa Madama with our American colleague. Whatever they call you, Dean, it will never be a louse. Remember the watchword, 'N.A.L.'—never a louse!" Afterward he always signed his personal cables and letters to me, "N.A.L. Stikker," which puzzled the Department. It was thought to be a code; in a way, it was.

The Villa Madama, one of the most delicate and beautiful examples of early Renaissance architecture, was designed and decorated by Raphael, whose frescoes still grace the T-shaped hall where we dined, and was built by a Medici pope for a lady; hence its name. On one side of me at dinner was the Italian Minister of Public Works. In order to stay away from the inevitable subject of Italy's claim to Trieste, I asked him to consider three questions and give me his answers when he had pondered them. They were: Would he like to have been the cardinal charged with building the Villa Madama? Did he wish that it had not been built? Did he think that Raphael would enjoy the dinner party?

His time for thought gave us an opportunity to enjoy a course of the delicious dinner. Then he answered all my questions in the negative. Beautiful as the Villa Madama was, it was the product of exactions and forced labor for which he was glad not to have been responsible. On the other hand, he did not wish that it had never been built. Its beauty lived and continued to give delight, while ancient sorrows were easy to bear. We regretted them, but did not weep. Finally, he could not picture Raphael enjoying our dinner. For one thing, the absence of ladies would have seemed deplorable, as would the absence of artists of any and every kind. He would have been lost and perhaps bored in the midst of a group so purposefully concentrated on thoughts of war and politics. I gave my partner high marks on his answers and thanks for a delightful conversation.

We were returning to America by sea on the SS *Independence,* sailing from Naples on December 4 for New York. In the days following the adjournment of the NATO Council I completed arrangements for the personnel changes in the Department and embassies, performed some chores, such as addressing the embassy staff and the UN Food and Agriculture staff, visited the Villa d'Este, Hadrian's Villa, and the ruins of Rome's ancient port of Ostia, and indulged my maladies. But most interesting was the luncheon my wife and I had with the de Gasperis at their place in the country near the Pope's Castel Gandolfo. It was a small house in a small village, built by the Christian Democratic Party as a retreat for de Gasperi, who had no money of his own. He, his wife, and daughter received us alone for a simple meal, which they and a maid prepared and served.

After lunch we drove to an ancient spot, Monte Cavo, which had been over the ages Sybil's cave, Christian refuge, Christian shrine, and now public park looking over the campagna. It was a lovely mild late-autumn afternoon. As we walked about the little park at the top of the mountain, a group of Italian customs or border guards from north Italy recognized the Prime Minister and introduced themselves as from his own countryside. After greeting them, we walked down the old Roman road, with its stone paving rutted by chariot wheels, to be picked up by our car lower down. The guards sat on the park walk and sang for de Gasperi songs of his own country, their voices growing fainter as we wound down the mountain. Against this setting I remember him affectionately.

On November 29 Anthony Eden asked me to a farewell lunch at the British Embassy, where he told me of Mr. Churchill's desire to pay the President a visit in Washington before Christmas. He also wanted to address a joint session of Congress. It was a poor time to have picked. The President would be deep in his State of the Union and Budget messages. The new session of Congress would not have convened and could not be addressed by anyone until after it had met on January 8. Official visits were never relaxing and always time-consuming affairs. On both counts, Mr. Churchill's usually topped the list. A compromise was finally reached. He would divide his visit, meeting with the President from January 5 to 10, then on to Canada, returning on the seventeenth to address the Congress and conclude his business.

YEAR-END SUMMARIES

A sea voyage, even across the December Atlantic, brought welcome rest after a strenuous month in Europe, during which I had conferred individually with between thirty-five and forty foreign ministers, with some of them many times, and had taken an active part in many large and often public meetings. The weeks waiting for me promised no relaxation of the pressure. December always brings with it year-end reviews for press and public. These I provided in a long press conference on December 19[1] and in an address to the Jewish War Veterans at New York.[2] As I read them now, I am impressed by their buoyancy of spirit in reviewing what seems in retrospect a discouraging year. For instance in speaking about Europe, I began with winter thoughts: "In the weeks before spring comes there is intense activity in the earth. Life in every form has cracked the shell that holds it, and is pushing up through the half-frozen earth. Some hardy forms are already through. Over all hangs the threat of a late frost. So, I believe, it is here."

A year before, I continued, the defense of Europe had lain largely in the realm of hope engendered by the appointment of General Eisenhower as Supreme Commander and the adoption of the plan for an integrated defense. Now the Supreme Headquarters was a reality. American troops had reinforced Europe and Europe itself was moving ahead on three fronts. Mr. Harriman's Temporary Council Committee was hard at work bringing zeal and practicality together to produce concrete results. Our discussions with Chancellor Adenauer looked toward restoring substantial sovereignty to Germany and enlisting her in the effort for collective security. M. Schuman's efforts toward a European Defense Community were moving forward and promised, with the Coal and Steel Plan—already ratified by an impressive majority of the French parliament—two great strides toward European unity and strength.

Our spring meeting with the hemisphere's foreign ministers had prepared us to meet the economic troubles then afflicting Latin America, I said. In the Middle East, however, we had lost ground. The bright spots, Greece and Turkey, both building economic, social, political, and military strength as they entered the NATO association, were overshadowed by the trouble threatening in Iran and Egypt. In the Far East great progress toward stability and peace had been made in Korea and the Philippines, and conditions seemed better in Southeast Asia. The great step forward in this area had been the bold and successful negotiation of peace with Japan and the treaties for security that accompanied it.

To end the year we and our British and French allies had returned to a hope and goal that had been growing faint of late because of bitter opposition from Moscow—that of lifting from the hearts and shoulders of mankind the fear of war and the burden of armaments. Mr. Vishinsky had laughed at us, but when the rest of the world had convinced him that it was no laughing matter, he turned to more subtle opposition. Other critics found our proposal pedestrian because it did not soar above the difficulties to facile conclusions. But the difficulties concerned the vital security of all the peoples of the world. The General Assembly thought so and appointed a commission to work from proposals to agreements. We would do our best with hope, whether or not with belief, that in time it might be possible.

I left my hearers with Lincoln's words: "With firmness in the right, as God gives us to see the right, let us strive on to finish the work we are in."

I wish that I felt as buoyant today.

Section D. 1952: Success and Failure at the End

62. THE CHURCHILL VISIT

THE NEW YEAR brought word that the British were coming, this time causing as much consternation in Britain as in America. Legislators in both countries fretted that each group would knuckle under to the other—the Commons, that the Prime Minister would be led astray by Washington, while the House of Representatives demanded again, as it had at the time of Prime Minister Attlee's visit a year before, "full and complete information" on any "agreements, commitments or understandings" reached during the discussions. Curiously enough, while among our allies the French consistently caused us trouble and made considerable demands upon us, the more forthright British were suspected of dominating us.

President Truman approved some general conclusions we had reached about the visit. Of first importance would be the tone and atmosphere of the meetings. Mr. Churchill should return home in a good mood. This did not require material concessions or changes in U.S. policy, but long, intimate, and frank discussions conducted with respect and good will. The impression we hoped he would leave behind was that Britain was doing and would do its share. In this he was brilliantly successful.

It was important that he and Mr. Eden should get the President's views, and the reasons behind them, on some matters on which our governments had diverged during the period of Labour Party control, such as our attitude toward the Soviet Union and the likelihood of détente; our attitude toward the cold war and China; our attitude toward European integration, including the European Defense Community, on which we needed British support at Brussels and The Hague; and our hope for greater flexibility on the part of the Conservative Government in dealing with growing nationalism in the Middle East, with special reference to Iran and Egypt.

A WORD ABOUT MR. CHURCHILL

Mr. Churchill did not come to Washington as a stranger to the President or to me. The President had met both him and Stalin at the Potsdam Conference on July 16, 1945, for the first time. On July 25 both Mr. Churchill and Mr. Attlee, then Deputy Prime Minister in the War Cabinet, went to England to learn the results of the general election. Only Mr. Attlee returned. I had met

Mr. Churchill during the war, when Harry Hopkins had summoned me to the White House with some information he and Mr. Churchill needed. I found them about ten o'clock in the morning in the Lincoln bedroom, where Harry was propped up in the big four-poster, with Mr. Churchill in his pajamas and bathrobe sitting on the foot of the bed smoking a cigar. They examined me for a half hour or so.

Later, in 1946, after Mr. Churchill's Iron Curtain speech in Fulton, Missouri, to which the President had escorted him, my wife and I lunched with him and his daughter Sarah and Ambassador and Lady Franks at the British Embassy. My wife, who idolized Mr. Churchill, anointed him with ample flattery, which he obviously enjoyed. When the talk turned to painting and he discovered that she had seen reproductions of his work and was herself a painter, he asked for a criticism of his. In doing so he passed from a field in which he was a world master to one in which she accorded him no superiority whatever. While she liked his work, she pointed out areas where improvement was possible. This was not what he expected or wanted; she did not yield an inch. He puffed harder on his cigar and fought back. Our hostess broke up the criticism by rising. He chuckled as we walked out of the dining room, and remarked to me that the critic had plenty of spirit—a quality of which we were already aware. When we were in London in 1950 (and Mr. Churchill was in opposition), the Churchills entertained us at luncheon and my wife was shown the originals of the works she had criticized.

The bulk of my association with Mr. Churchill came during 1952. Eminent authorities differ as to when the weight of age and physical infirmity noticeably affected Mr. Churchill's grasp of affairs and his influence upon them. Lord Moran, Mr. Churchill's physician, saw the beginning of a decline toward the end of the war.[1] Lord Normanbrook, Secretary to the Cabinet, would place it as late as 1953. To me in 1952 the old lion seemed to be weakening, though still formidable and quite magnificent. We shall see him more intimately later on; here a word or two on his larger significance may not be amiss.

President Truman often spoke of Mr. Churchill as the greatest public figure of our age. This, I believe, is an understatement. One must go back four centuries to find his equal, for one cannot find it merely in a soldier, a statesman, or an orator, or in a combination of all three. There must be added that "romantic attachment" which, as Sir John Neale has pointed out, existed between the English people and the great Queen, and for which, he added, "the closest parallel in our history is that between Englishmen and Winston Churchill in our own time."[2] In both cases this flowed not only from great qualities of heart and brain, indomitable courage, energy, magnanimity, and good sense, but from supreme art and deliberate policy. These fused the other elements into the leadership that alone can call forth from a free people what cannot be commanded and enabled the English people to face and fight alone the greatest military powers of two ages.

Art, great art, transformed courage, right decisions, magnificent oratory into something different and superlative. What Churchill did was great; how he did it was equally so. Neither action nor style could have accomplished the result alone. Everything felt the touch of his art—his appearance and gestures, the siren suit, the indomitable V sign for victory, the cigar for imperturbability. He used all the artifices to get his way, from wooing and cajolery through powerful advocacy to bluff bullying; yet he never overruled the Chiefs of Staff. Lord Alanbrooke has ventured the opinion that if Hitler had acted in the same way the outcome of the war might have been different. What we are discussing here is not merely the direction of great affairs, but the creation and development of personality. Napoleon understood it. So did Franklin Roosevelt. General Washington did not.

Churchill mastered it. His speeches were not only wise and right in content but were prepared with that infinite capacity for taking pains that is said to be genius. He used it to clothe the bedrock of sense and necessity with romanticism, which even in the dark hour of the fall of France brought hope and spirit to French and British hearts:

Good night then. Sleep to gather strength for the morning. For the morning will come. Brightly will it shine on the brave and true, kindly upon all who suffer for the cause, glorious upon the tombs of heroes. Thus will shine the dawn. Vive la France![3]

And Elizabeth, at a no less critical moment, with the Armada at sea, clothed resolution in romance:

I know I have the body of a weak and feeble woman, but I have the heart and stomach of a king, and of a king of England, too.[4]

Here is romantic emotion, not for its own sake, but as a vital element of action directed toward result.[5]

FIRST STAGE OF THE VISIT

The days of this visit were strenuous ones. For nine days we had Mr. Churchill or Mr. Eden or both in town and I met with either one or both sixteen times. Each meeting, including six formal ones with the President in the Cabinet Room, took from one hour to five. During the days of our guests' absence in Ottawa other duties pressed upon me—two appearances before congressional committees, a speech, and a press conference. Little was accomplished by way of final agreement beyond ending our differences over the Atlantic Command. The British were nudged closer to positions toward Germany that made possible the contractual arrangements of the following May. For the most part, the time was spent in feeling out one another's minds. The new Government viewed the Far Eastern questions much more as we did than had their predecessors, and discussion in all respects but one brought us closer together. Regarding the Middle East, a remark of Mr. Churchill's struck me as profoundly revealing both of the British view of their predicament and of the nature, and perhaps hopelessness, of their search for a solution. The situation in that area, he said, had been deeply altered over the past decade by the disappearance of the Indian army—an idea echoed in his speech to Congress. Indeed, it had been, and by the greater phenomenon to which that was related. The decay of European power had opened wide the doors to nationalism. The British effort to substitute for what had been lost an American, Australian, British, and Turkish military presence, through the Middle East Command, seemed to me a forlorn hope.

On Saturday, January 5, after welcoming ceremonies at the airport and an official luncheon at Blair House, we reassembled on the presidential yacht for a cruise down the Potomac. The "former Naval Person" was piped aboard arrayed in the blue jacket and brass buttons of the Brethren of Trinity House, the corporation chartered in Tudor times as the Mariners of England and charged with providing aids to navigation. With him were Lord Cherwell, known as the Prof, Lord (Pug) Ismay, Minister of Commonwealth Relations, Anthony Eden, and Sir Oliver Franks. Snyder, Lovett, Bradley, Ambassador Gifford, Harriman, and I made up the American contingent. The Prime Minister loved every minute of the evening. At its end he said to the President that he had never felt relations between our countries to be more close and cordial. And of me he asked more sententiously, "Did you feel that around the table this evening there was gathered the governance of the world—not to dominate it, mind you, but to save it?" Frankly, I had been more conscious of omnibrooding problems than of overshadowing salvation.

In the aft saloon before dinner the President and the Prime Minister found themselves before a large engraving of an American ship of the line bombarding with apparently satisfactory results an opponent flying the white ensign. "That's not the way my history book reported it," growled the Prime Minister, whereupon Eden and I drifted out of range for private talk. Despite, he warned me, some rhetoric from Mr. Churchill expressing personal distaste for Mr. Schuman's European Defense Community, the Prime Minister was prepared to play a helpful part. I responded with a report of the latest discussions about it in Paris by the six ministers and of the division between the large and small countries. He spoke optimistically of developments in Egypt, and he found both surprising and distressing my view that the World Bank's efforts in Iran had collapsed in complete failure. We then moved below for dinner.

There, with apparent spontaneity and the aid of the Prof and his slide rule, Mr. Churchill put on what I was told was a favorite act. He first established from the President the dimensions of the dining saloon of the *Williamsburg,* and then that over a period of sixty years he had consumed on the average a quart of vinous and spirituous liquors a day, some days more, some less, some not at all, as when he had been a prisoner of war in South Africa or hiding after his escape. If, he asked the Prof, all this liquid were poured into the dining saloon, how high would it rise? His vast disappointment when, instead of drowning us all in champagne and brandy, the flood came only up to our knees provided the high point of the performance.

For the rest of dinner general conversation ceased and Sir Oliver and I plunged into a matter within Lord Ismay's province that was causing us acute distress. All too often when we discussed something with His Majesty's Government in supposed confidence, they talked with Commonwealth countries. The more responsible ones—Canada, Australia, South Africa—were annoyed that we should appear to deal with them, independent states with their own diplomatic missions, as though they were still British colonies; the less responsible ones would promptly leak to the press. This had become intolerable. The choice before the British Government was clear: to let us choose our own confidants or themselves forgo confidences. Lord Ismay seemed utterly dumbfounded. It seemed to him wholly normal that we should deal with the Commonwealth through London. Sir Oliver supported me in saying that once anything got into Lord Ismay's department it was on its way to the press and that the attitudes of Commonwealth countries were as I had stated them. All evening Lord Ismay kept muttering about this vast new problem. It remained a perennial headache.

After dinner the President and Prime Minister withdrew to the aft saloon while the table was being cleared, in a few minutes sending for Mr. Eden and me. The President opened by a complaint that I instantly recognized as coming from a persistent and infuriating practice of the Navy. Through his naval aide the President would be given what was known in the trade as "raw intelligence," reports not analyzed and appraised in accordance with required procedure—in this case a list of British ships, with the gross (not cargo) tonnages, said to have called at Chinese ports over the past year. The practice, as in this case, resulted in extreme and unsupportable conclusions being drawn and caused considerable trouble until the ounce or two of truth had been extracted from the blubber. Our guests were understandably disturbed by possible conclusions. I pointed out that the matter had not been brought to my attention, as it should have been, and asked that it be left to Mr. Eden and me to investigate. When fully analyzed and put together with other data, including known trade between Hong Kong and the mainland, this Navy bombshell amounted to very little.

I then raised a question over which our governments were at odds. The Japanese Government wished to make arrangements with the Nationalist Government of China to establish peaceful and political relations with it so far as Nationalist-controlled areas were concerned. Mr. Eden opposed this as prejudicing Japanese future relations with China contrary to the Dulles-Morrison agreement. When, after discussion, differences persisted, the problem was referred back to Mr. Eden and me. Our efforts to solve it resulted in a contretemps, as we shall see.

Mr. Churchill, taking over, gave his unfavorable view of Schuman's European Defense Community, which was to be repeated often. He pictured a bewildered French drill sergeant sweating over a platoon made up of a few Greeks, Italians, Germans, Turks, and Dutchmen, all in utter confusion over the simplest orders. What he hoped to see were spirited and strong national armies marching together to the defense of freedom singing their national anthems. No one could get up enthusiasm singing, "March, NATO, march on!" Eden patiently explained, as he had doubtless done before, that the proposal did not contemplate any such heterogeneous mixing of nationalities, but a creation of national units in the form of divisions, or groupments, of approximately twelve thousand men. They might, where numbers permitted, be further combined into army corps of perhaps three or four groupments. A strong and spirited German army was what bothered the French. I added that General Eisenhower approved the proposal and found no language or other difficulty not already present in his united command and in the army that NATO would hope to put into the field in case of trouble.

These arguments seemed to win Mr. Churchill's acquiescence. But each time the subject came up, we went back to the baffled drill sergeant. The fact was that, although on occasion he could be brought to say a good word for the Defense Community, at heart he did not approve of it.

He then moved to the Middle East, where the British were carrying heavy burdens. In some cases we could be of positive help; in others we might refrain from hindering. For instance, if we would put only a brigade into Suez, the British could withdraw a division for service in other troubled spots, yet the net effect on the Egyptians of this demonstration of solidarity would lead to a solution of many troubles. On the other hand, the oil controversy would never be solved in Iran so long as we gave the Iranians financial support. Stop it, and they would come to terms in short order. The President suggested that we continue the discussion with the others below in larger quarters.

Settled at the cleared dining table and suitably provided, the Prime Minister resumed, beginning with a delightfully paradoxical analysis of Soviet policy. Its central factor was fear, but not of the usual sort. The Russians feared our friendship more than our enmity. He hoped that the growing strength of the West might reverse this, for when the Kremlin began to fear our enmity, it might be led to seek our friendship. He moved on to praise American nuclear power as the main guarantee of peace, augmented by NATO and by the close relation of the United States and the United Kingdom. He was warm in admiration of President Truman's firm stand in Korea. From the springboard of general agreement and pleasant appreciation, he plunged into the proposals already recounted about the Middle East, adding to his regret over our financial aid to Iran criticism of his predecessors in office who had scuttled and run from Abadan when a splutter of musketry would have ended the matter. Indeed, he was prepared to generalize. He would follow the President's lead in the Far East, if the President would follow his in the Middle East.

No wonder foreign ministers dislike meetings at the summit, where their chiefs are likely to take the bit in their teeth and have a gay canter across country! To slow the tempo, I wondered aloud whether we could get the Congress and the country to follow along the path suggested for us, taking Palestine as a test case.

In the pause that followed I was asked what I saw immediately facing the two governments. The Soviet Union did not, I thought, appear to be threatening direct trouble to Western Europe at the moment so much as exhaustion through inspired peripheral combat, as in Korea and Indochina. Three European problems, practical and clear, called for action within sixty days: the new contractual relationship with Germany; the European Army; and agreement in NATO on Harriman's economic and rearmament report. The first required a realization by Britain and France that Germany could not join as a dependable ally in the defense of Europe unless demands for German support of foreign troops and for the prohibition of German production of armaments were moderated. Germany could not successfully be dealt with as both ally and enemy. The second required action while both Schuman and Adenauer were powers in their own countries. Time was running out for both of them. In six months our own country would be plunged into a presidential election. Mr. Harriman's report must be acted on at the next NATO Council meeting. Two meetings had already been failures.

The Middle East presented a picture that might have been drawn by Karl Marx himself—with the masses a disinherited and poverty-stricken proletariat, no middle class, a small and corrupt ruling class pushed about by foreigners who sought to exploit priceless resources, whether oil or canal. Was there ever such an opportunity to invoke inherent xenophobia to destroy the foreigner and his system and substitute the Communist solution? Anglo-American solidarity on a policy of sitting tight offered no solution, but was like a couple locked in warm embrace in a rowboat about to go over Niagara Falls. It was high time to break the embrace and take to the oars. This brought a chuckle from the Prime Minister, who kept muttering, "Take to the oars!"

Eden was more optimistic than I, seeing hope in recent appointment of advisers to the King of Egypt and in the mission of the World Bank, which had just returned from Iran (as I saw it, after complete failure). Lord Cherwell painted a dark picture of Britain's economic and financial state due to the thinness of her reserves, a view amply supported over the years that followed. The rest of the evening was taken up by more detailed exposition from my colleagues, Secretaries Snyder and Lovett, General Bradley, and Mr. Harriman, on the three immediate tasks awaiting us in Europe before the end of winter.

The next evening talk continued in a smaller group at the British Embassy, Lovett, Bradley, and I dining with the Ambassador, Mr. Churchill, Mr. Eden, and Lord Cherwell and talking until after one o'clock. The talk centered on Far Eastern and Middle Eastern problems. I was struck, as this second evening's discussion went on, with evidences of six years in opposition and the absence of familiarity with frustrating detail and of intuition instilled by the daily pain of decision and action. In appraising alternatives, our visitors were drawn, as Congress often is, to courses high in debating appeal whose impracticalities are revealed only through considerable factual knowledge. In discussing the conflict with Mosadeq, I argued that the policy of sitting tight in solidarity offered little promise for British interests in Iran and considerable danger for ours elsewhere in the Middle East; indeed, I pressed this point on Mr. Eden with such asperity and impatience as to require subsequent amends, which were good-naturedly accepted.

The formal meetings at the White House did little more, with one exception, than to review in more detail the subjects already covered informally for the benefit of a larger group, including the Chiefs of Staff and high Foreign Office and State Department officials. In some instances where time pressed—as in the case of the German contractual arrangements—working groups were set up to solve specific problems. In the case of the Korean armistice negotiations we explored the future, including the chances of success, possibilities of a more lasting situation, and alternatives in the event of failure.

After the first day of these meetings the President asked Lovett, the Chiefs of Staff, and me to stay behind with the Prime Minister, Eden, and the British Chiefs. He wished, he said, to open the subject of the Atlantic Command. This had been set up by NATO and unanimous agreement reached that the commander should be an American officer. No action, however, had been taken to carry out the decisions because of the imminent election in Britain, its results, and Mr. Churchill's strong opposition voiced in the House of Commons. In a brief, courteous, but firm reply the Prime Minister made clear that his objection continued. Both we and he knew that this objection was individual and not shared. When our Chief of Naval Operations, Admiral William Fechteler, intervened more heartily than tactfully, he plainly touched an exposed nerve. After one more exchange between the two heads of government, it was left that the Prime Minister would think the matter over during his trip to Ottawa. When we learned from Ottawa that he had been talking of a complicated two-command solution, it was clear that reflection was reinforcing resolution. He had also pressed on the Canadians the restoration of "Rule Britannia" as the official anthem of the Canadian Navy in the place of the more nationalistic "Vive la Canadienne." His hosts had compromised by agreeing to play it when a British admiral should board a Canadian ship. For good measure its strains accompanied Mr. Churchill to his place at the state dinner. Trouble lay ahead.

THE ATLANTIC COMMAND

On January 17, Mr. Churchill for the third time addressed a joint and crowded session of the Congress, an experience that, as he said, was "unique for one who is not an American citizen." That honor, too, would be conferred on him by an admiring Congress. On the evening of his address my wife and I gave a dinner and reception for him at Anderson House with all the pomp and glitter we could muster. The next day we held our last meeting of the visit and faced the issue of the Atlantic Command.

The meeting was to take place in the afternoon. The British group spent the morning at the Pentagon, where Lovett briefed them on our nuclear armament and provided luncheon. While Mr. Churchill went back to the British Embassy for a nap, the soldiers and sailors, including the jaunty Scottish First Sea Lord, Admiral Sir Roderick Robert McGrigor, drafted a joint communiqué in effect ratifying the earlier NATO decisions. Without Mr. Eden, who had returned to London, or Mr. Churchill, who was with the President, a shaken British group joined us in the Cabinet Room. Mr. Churchill had read their draft communiqué in the President's anteroom, torn it up, and tossed the pieces into the air. "Hurricane warnings along the Potomac," said Admiral McGrigor.

Our two chiefs entered and the President brusquely announced the business of the meeting as the uncompleted subject of the Atlantic Command. Then followed one of Mr. Churchill's greatest speeches, unfortunately unrecorded and lost. Only phrases remain with me. For centuries England had held the seas against every tyrant, wresting command of them from Spain and then from France, protecting our hemisphere from penetration by European systems in the days of our weakness. Now, in the plenitude of our power, bearing as we did the awful burden of atomic command and responsibility for the final word of peace or war, surely we could make room for Britain to play her historic role "upon that western sea whose floor is white with the bones of Englishmen."

As the majestic speech rolled to its conclusion, a note came from Sir Oliver Franks across the table, warning me to be "very, very careful." The best course seemed a preclusive one, to get the floor and hold it until some opening appeared. A whispered request to the President gave me what no one else wanted. I praised the Prime Minister's matchless statement and sympathized with his unwillingness to accept what he had publicly opposed and still thought wrong. He nodded vigorously. All of us on occasion, I went on, had had to weigh continuing opposition against a distasteful course to the point of impeding a broader purpose of which we approved. He nodded even more vigorously. I asked the President to let some of us—mentioning Ambassador Franks and Secretary Lovett, the two admirals, Air Chief Marshal Sir William Elliot, and General Bradley—retire to bring in a suggestion. Mr. Churchill agreed.

When we reached the President's office, Admiral Fechteler burst into protest against this endless talk, until suppressed by his military colleagues. We had nearly botched the operation, I pointed out, by trying to get the Prime Minister to endorse Attlee's approval, for the British Government, of the command and commander. If allowed to continue his disagreement with it, there was a good chance that he would no longer block its execution. It was worth trying. A draft communiqué along these lines was quickly drafted and typed. I was to read it and no one would say more. Handing one copy to the President and one to the Prime Minister, I read it with what my children in their early school days called "expression," bearing down on the words italicized and sliding over the others.

The statement referred to discussion by the President and Prime Minister of "the arrangements about the Atlantic Command recommended by NATO and accepted by the late Government of the United Kingdom. As a result of their discussions they agreed . . . [to] recommend to NATO *certain alterations in the arrangements designed to extend the United Kingdom home command* to the 100 fathom line. They also agreed on the *desirability of certain changes which would provide greater flexibility* for the control of operations in the *Eastern Atlantic. These changes however do not go the full way to meet the Prime Minister's objections to the original arrangements.* Nevertheless, the Prime Minister, *while not withdrawing his objections,* expressed his readiness to allow the appointment of a Supreme Commander to go forward in order that a command structure may be created and enabled to proceed with the necessary planning in the Atlantic area. *He reserved the right to bring forward modifications* for the consideration of NATO, if he so desired, at a later stage."[6]

For an interminable minute the Prime Minister studied the paper; then, looking across at the President, he said, "I accept every word of it."

So did the President. He also declined the suggestion of one of his secretaries that it be reviewed for style before release to the press. He and Mr. Churchill, he said, had both been over it, and one of them, at least, used fair English.

THE YOSHIDA LETTER

As already recounted in Chapter 56, Mr. Dulles had agreed with Foreign Secretary Morrison in June 1951 that neither claimant government of China would be invited to sign the peace treaty with Japan, adding that under international law, "Japan's future attitude toward China must necessarily be for determination by Japan itself in the exercise of the sovereignty and independent status contemplated by the Treaty."[7] The Foreign Office, not unreasonably, believed that this sovereign and independent status could exist only when the treaty created it by becoming effective upon ratification. Prime Minister Yoshida knew of the agreement and the British interpretation of it.

In mid-September fifty-six senators signed and sent to the President an ominous warning: "Prior to the submission of the Japanese Treaty to the Senate, we desire to make it clear that we would consider the recognition of Communist China by Japan or the negotiating of a bilateral treaty with the Communist Chinese regime to be adverse to the best interests of the people of both Japan and the United States."[8]

By statements in the Diet which appeared to be facing both ways, Mr. Yoshida had caused perplexity about his future attitude toward China, particularly in the minds of two important senators, H. Alexander Smith and John J. Sparkman, both members of the Far Eastern subcommittee of the Committee on Foreign Relations, who traveled to Tokyo with Mr. Dulles in mid-December. Mr. Dulles urged Mr. Yoshida to clear up the ambivalent position in which he had put himself.

At the end of December, Mr. Dulles and the senators having returned to Washington, Prime Minister Yoshida handed our Ambassador the famous letter of December 24.† In brief, it referred to statements, made in the Diet during the debates on ratification of the treaties, that had given rise to misapprehension, which he wished to clear up. On November 17, 1951, Japan had established a Government Overseas Agency in Formosa, the highest form of relationship with other countries then permitted to Japan. When the peace treaty had been ratified and was in effect, Japan would be prepared to conclude a treaty with the Nationalist Government to re-establish normal relations in respect of all territories under that Government's control. Also, for reasons stated in the letter, the Japanese Government had "no intention to conclude a bilateral Treaty with the Communist regime of China." It might have been expected that before use was made of the letter an effort would be made at the Truman-Churchill talks to get British acquiescence. The remarkable fact, however, is that no real effort was made to do so. This resulted not from sharp practice, as some (but not Mr. Eden) have charged, but from clumsy action based on what seemed to be a true reading of one another's minds.

After the short discussion on the *Williamsburg,* Mr. Eden, Sir Oliver

Franks, and I talked again on January 10 about the need for a public statement by the Japanese on the China policy. The Yoshida letter was not, so far as I can remember, mentioned. It had, however, been shown to Ambassador Franks. Mr. Dulles' view of his agreement with Mr. Morrison, familiar to the Foreign Office, was that Japan's "sovereign and independent status contemplated by the Treaty" would, as a practical matter, exist when the Supreme Allied Commander's control over Japanese relations with other states was withdrawn. This, he claimed, had already occurred and been recognized by many signatories of the treaty, as shown by their acceptance of negotiations with the Japanese. Moreover, the direction of Japanese intentions had already been made clear by the establishment of the Japanese Government Overseas Agency in Formosa. The argument was not unanswerable, but respectable. At any rate, the area of discussion did not after January 5 touch upon amendment or interpretation of the Morrison agreement but rather stressed that what the Japanese might do about their relations with China should be done on their decision in the existing circumstances, and required not Anglo-American agreement but mutual tolerance.

To us it appeared that we and Mr. Eden were tacitly recognizing two political realities: first, that neither of us wished to risk failure of American ratification of the peace treaty because of Senate misapprehension of Yoshida's intentions; second, that neither of us wished Mr. Eden to face opposition criticism in a suspicious House of Commons for rescinding an agreement obtained by his predecessor. Leaving the matter to the Japanese seemed a skillful solution. This is where we thought it was left on January 10 when, after a farewell call on my wife and me, Anthony Eden left us to return to London after a few days in New York. He left New York on the late afternoon of January 15, arriving in London the next morning to be met by the Yoshida letter, which had been released in Washington and Tokyo on the morning of the sixteenth. This was an inexcusable bungle, which understandably embarrassed and annoyed Mr. Eden. As I wrote Lester B. Pearson a few days later: "The talks with Eden were very useful and I think established a good relationship between him and me. The incident of the Yoshida letter has perhaps cast a shadow over this. To some degree I think we were at fault in not being more explicit about the whole matter and not informing him specifically about the publication, but I think in some degree also there was some fumbling and error on the British side. I have made my regret very clear to Eden and I do not think that he believes we intentionally misled him."

On January 30 Mr. Eden, in reply to questions in the Commons, said that His Majesty's Government had repeatedly made clear to the U.S. Government its position that the matter should be left for the Japanese to decide when the peace treaty had entered into force; that His Majesty's Government had not taken part in drafting or publishing the letter; and that the British liaison mission in Tokyo was told of the letter on the morning of the sixteenth. A month later in the Commons Mr. Morrison said that, contrary to his agreement with Mr. Dulles, the Americans had brought pressure on the Japanese Government to state before the treaty came into effect its intention to recognize Nationalist

China. In my next press conference I said that in my opinion Mr. Dulles had not violated his agreement with Mr. Morrison and that I had supported Mr. Dulles throughout in what he had said to Mr. Yoshida. At that point, believing that there was enough justification for everyone, I was happy to let the matter rest.

HANDS ACROSS THE SEA

Gossip about the Churchill visit and the aftermath of the Yoshida letter gave rise to a series of rumors of a strain between Eden and me, culminating in an article in *Newsweek* about a "clash of personalities," full of falsity and mischief. This could not be permitted to pass unnoticed. On my fifty-ninth birthday I wrote him a longhand letter. (On the preceding birthday I had had sent the less agreeable message conveying the orders relieving General MacArthur.)

Dear Anthony: *April 11, 1952*
    I have just seen in the latest edition of *Newsweek* a most mischievous and false account of an alleged "clash of personalities" between you and me. I have been subjected to so much of this press sniping that I would pass it by with indifference and contempt were it not for the thought that, in your generous way, you might be concerned because I might be concerned. For yourself you need not and would not give it a thought.
    My own "personality," as my wife and daughters frequently point out, is a most defective one. But it would take a worse one than mine to clash with you from whom I have always received kindness and friendship. The opinion attributed to me, I do not hold; the facts stated are false; and the attempted psychoanalysis was done by a plumber.
    What is really vicious about the article is its reference to your call on Mr. Hull. As I told you at the time, nothing pleased me more than that you could see him because of the pleasure that it would bring him. Nothing would hurt him more than the suggestion that I would feel otherwise. Well, I suppose this sort of thing is part of the lives we lead. I shall not be sorry to be free of it after the first of the year. Among the few regrets that time will bring will be the end of the—to me—very happy comradeship we have had in some great constructive work together.
    I am deeply sorry that our work together has subjected you to this sort of cheap gossip. The only outlet to my feelings is to send you once again my affectionate regards and gratitude for all your kindnesses.   As ever,
                                                                                       Dean

Back came an answer in Anthony's own hand:

My dear Dean,   *April 18, 1952*
    I was sincerely touched by your letter and still more by the thought that prompted you to write it.
    I had not seen the *Newsweek* article until Walter Gifford told me about it. Certainly it was about as mischievous as it could be, though I should have thought too silly to be effective except with the most naive. I laughed a good deal at my knowledge of Latin quotations. They couldn't be weaker! Few but faithful, as Winston once said of his own.
    I agree that the remark about Cordell Hull is particularly pernicious. Actually we spent much of our time in a duet in your praise. A pity the writer couldn't hear.

I well remember how pleased you were when I said I was going to visit him, as I was when you told me you were going to see Mrs. Bevin. You also told me the moving story of how Cordell gallantly came down to the State Dept to support you publicly when the mean attacks upon you were at their height.

In some ways, however, I am grateful to the writer of that article for having been the cause of your writing to me a letter I shall always value. I am indeed happy that you feel, as I do, how very pleasant and intimate has been our work together. I could not possibly have asked for a kinder and more understanding colleague to hold my hand when I came back to the ruthless jungle of public life.

Yours ever,
Anthony

63. DEATH OF A KING

AFTER SEEING Mr. Churchill off on January 19—not at all perturbed about the Yoshida letter—we plunged into three weeks of frantic and multifarious work before, unexpectedly early, I was away again on my travels. Many problems clamored for attention. On Monday morning, January 21, the Senate Committee on Foreign Relations heard me as the first witness in support of the President's request for its advice and consent to the ratification of the Japanese peace treaty. The same day I took up with Messrs. Dulles and Lovett a draft of administrative agreement with Japan, and with others a proposed loan to Iran (with memories of Mr. Churchill), and then lunched at the White House and dined at the Netherlands Embassy with Prime Minister Willem Drees. What was left of the afternoon went to welcoming an incoming foreign ambassador, saying farewell to a departing one, and giving a reception at home for a bevy of new ones.

In the following days the Department press corps, which felt neglected, claimed me for a dinner off the record and then a press conference; the Americans for Democratic Action had to be appeased by a speech at their dinner in New York, Senators Connally and Wiley and Congressman Richards by luncheon meetings, and the House Appropriations subcommittee by an appearance on the Department's budget and a *tour d'horizon*. Details of the changes of ambassadors agreed at Rome had to be worked out, and arrangements perfected for the appointment of Supreme Allied Commander Atlantic. Underlying all the daily chores, our two pressing preoccupations with the outside world—the war and armistice negotiations in the Far East and the crisis in the grand alliance in Europe—made their unrelenting claims. The latter would come to a head at the NATO Council meeting to take place in Lisbon, for which we were trying to arrange a February date.

In the midst of such a welter of involvement with life, death intruded. At noon on February 6, 1952, the British Ambassador accompanied by representatives of all other Commonwealth countries called on me to inform our Government of the death of that devoted and kindly man, His Majesty King George VI, and the accession of Her Majesty Queen Elizabeth II. Of the late King I said: "The courage with which he bore his own suffering in the last years was a symbol of his indomitable spirit. It is a characteristic English spirit and the King possessed it in abundance." And for his daughter, I asked that "God bless the young Queen and grant her the strength and wisdom to fulfill her high responsibilities as her father did before her. May her reign be long and her peoples prosper throughout it." This ceremony completed, I left the Department for the funeral of my own old and close friend, Harold L. Ickes, formerly Secretary of the Interior.

When it was decided that the King's funeral would be on February 15, followed a week later in Lisbon by the NATO Council meetings, the President concluded that I should attend the funeral as his representative and use the following week for a supreme effort to remove the obstacles blocking the establishment of a defense for Europe. The situation there, particularly between France and Germany, had worsened materially since the turn of the year. The Bundestag, sensing Germany's rising importance in Europe, sought to raise German conditions for contributing to defense, and the French Chamber amid increasing fears pushed harder to impose discriminatory restrictions on German rearmament and arms production. French ambivalence between treating Germany as potential ally or enemy was paralyzing action.

Issuance from the impasse depended entirely upon the United States. In February the French Cabinet was once again in trouble, and within it Schuman in deeper trouble. Adenauer could control the Bundestag but not lead in Europe, though both McCloy and Bruce reported to me in January that he was the most stalwart supporter of the European Defense Community in Europe. Italy and the Northern European allies were deeply worried, fearing Franco-German domination if the Community succeeded and German adventurism if it failed. British opinion, hostile toward Germany and apathetic toward Europe, received no lead from the Prime Minister. A lead—and perhaps a push, too—had to come from the United States. Ever since the past midyear our Government had brought pressure on the French and British to get on with the German program theoretically agreed at Brussels in December 1950. General Eisenhower had hammered away at European governments through Chiefs of Staff and defense ministers, especially for the European Army; John McCloy had put all his great energy into pressure on the Chancellor and the High Commissioners to move the contractual arrangements; Harriman had done the same to bring all military programs, including the German, within the limits of economic and financial feasibility; and I had harried the foreign ministers, sometimes to the point of revolt. The crisis had only increased, to reach its peak in this period of prelude to Lisbon.

At the end of January I had had a disturbing letter from Schuman in which French fear of Germany was discernibly destroying French hope for the Defense Community. The French Government, he wrote, could see no possibility of a German defense contribution except through the Community, but Bonn insisted that the Community not discriminate against Germany. Therefore, the restrictions and prohibitions upon German rearmament could not be written into the document, but must be accomplished by the contractual arrangement between the three occupying powers and Germany. Moreover, the German military force in the Community must be limited to one-fifth of the whole, so that it should not exceed that of France (which, of course, would not include her forces outside Europe). Germany must agree to an economic union between France and the Saar and must be precluded from seceding from the Defense Community and from joining NATO.

The idea that Adenauer could accept such a position was, of course, absurd. Plainly Schuman's excellent judgment had been overborn in the Cabinet and Foreign Office. David Bruce, a wise adviser, urged me not to answer the letter but to hold it for discussion in London. An earlier answer, he feared, might solidify French politicians and bureaucracy behind the Schuman letter. However, I decided upon an opposite course in the effort to strengthen Schuman against instructions that would destroy any possibility of success at London or Lisbon. My reply went off on February 2.

NATO, I wrote, could not survive another failure, another postponement of hope for a defense of Europe. I saw no point in holding a conference unless our friends were determined to join us in making it a success. Surely Germany must contribute to the support of allied troops stationed there for her and Europe's defense, and would do so if her position was made consistent with her self-respect. What armaments she produced should not be determined by imposed prohibitions but by her own unilateral renunciations and by allocations of production by the European Defense Communty among its members. The Saar bid fair to upset great and far-reaching plans. That issue must be removed from current discussions by an initiative from Schuman and Adenauer; Britain and the United States would support it. Germany should not be precluded from future membership in NATO, a dangerous and destructive idea. Adenauer would accept an intermediate and temporary association. "If I may indulge in the vanity of quoting myself," I added, " 'I do not believe that the way to solve a difficult question is to inject one which is presently insoluable.' "

The letter ended with praise for Schuman's great work toward unity in Europe, which the United States had supported from the start and in which all of us had an enormous stake. I pleaded with him not to risk it all with irritations and unnecessary problems. Let us "reach agreement before and in London so that the contractual arrangements and EDC can be concluded; and that Lisbon can achieve marked accomplishments by approving the reorganization of NATO, admitting Greece and Turkey, considering and accepting the TCC recommendations, approving the establishment of EDC and its relationship to NATO, and noting with approval the contractual relationship with Germany."

"Either we must guide the events we have set in motion to the goal we have chosen," the letter concluded, "or they will move themselves, we cannot tell where." Lisbon was to be the supreme gamble upon which we would stake our whole prestige, skill, and power.

Even as we prepared to fly to London the Bundestag and the French Assembly further exacerbated the situation. The more fully Schuman and Adenauer fashioned the principal features of Defense Community, the more parliamentary interest quickened in each country. Soon each body sought to instruct its negotiator on conditions, qualifications, and desiderata—all reducing maneuverability, hardening positions, and making compromise more difficult. On February 8 the Bundestag set forth in a resolution German conditions to membership in the Community. The French National Assembly began debate on February 11 and on the sixteenth voted on its own "recommendations" regarding the restrictions and limitations to be imposed on Germany, and demands for a guarantee by the United States and United Kingdom against German secession from the European Defense Community and of continued maintenance of their forces on "the continent for as long as seems necessary." With these unhelpful contributions overhanging us, we took off for London in the *Independence* on February 12, to be met at noon the next day by Mr. Eden and another old friend from the Foreign Office, Derrick Hoyer Millar, who was to guide me through the coming ceremonies.

THE KING'S FUNERAL

For three days the ceremonial of the royal funeral was mixed with work. My wife and I stayed with the kind Giffords at the embassy residence, 14 Prince's Gate, facing on Hyde Park. Since the house had once belonged to J. P. Morgan, it was clearly not a cottage; neither did it approach the mansion already given by Barbara Hutton to the Government for the Ambassador's residence, but not yet occupied. The more modest situation seemed to me more fitting, but unfortunately the old house was disintegrating.

In the afternoon we joined the throng in Westminster Hall filing by the King's bier surmounted by orb and scepter resting on a purple-covered catafalque, and guarded by men from the services and colorful ceremonial figures recalling English history since the Middle Ages. From there we went on to "sign the book" at Buckingham Palace, Clarence House (the Queen's residence), and Marlborough House (Queen Mary's residence). Later in the afternoon Harriman and Spofford, our resident representative on the NATO Council, reviewed with me the remaining issues to be resolved in Harriman's Temporary Council Committee report for Lisbon. Then Spofford accompanied me to see Mike Pearson of Canada, the current chairman of the council.

That evening and the next day, Thursday, February 14, made possible two long meetings with Eden, at the second of which Schuman was present, one with the Prime Minister and Eden, and another with King Paul of Greece. The last was unimportant but took time. The King had asked me to call upon him to tell me of his and Queen Frederika's desire to pay a state visit to the United States in the spring. This was not possible, since Queen Juliana of the Netherlands and Prince Bernhard had already pre-empted the spring visiting season.

On both evenings we dined at the Foreign Minister's official residence at 1 Carlton Gardens. The Permanent Under Secretary, Sir William Strang, was with Eden; Harriman, William Draper, head of our European aid mission, Ambassador Gifford, and Bruce were with me. The talk was friendly but blunt. When our host raised the issue of the NATO Council location and the selection of a Secretary General, I said that to separate him and his staff from supreme headquarters seemed wholly without justification, a view in which a telephone call to General Eisenhower found him in full concurrence. A British Secretary General would have our backing. If they had no candidate, Mike Pearson seemed to us highly eligible. We would state our position but not argue; the Europeans seemed pretty clear on the first point, at least.

As long ago as December we had told the French that if they did not make marked progress toward the European defense treaty by midwinter, we would reconsider our support of it. This was the time, I urged on Eden, for both of us to push Schuman; Adenauer would not be a problem. If the present drift continued, the whole plan would disintegrate. The key to success lay in the contractual arrangements and specifically in decisions now on the German defense contribution and in ending French and British attempts to keep Germany hedged about by restrictions and limitations on rearmament wholly inconsistent with the position of a self-respecting ally. My colleagues pitched into the debate, supporting me nobly. It was apparent that we were making an impression.

In the morning Ambassador Gifford, Mr. Eden, and I called on the Prime Minister, hearing from him again his now familiar views on the Defense Community as reported in the last chapter. Eden again took on the also familiar straightening-out process, I contenting myself by asserting that it was now or never if we were to have any sort of European defense. The choice was between the European Defense Community and a national German army, general staff, and all the rest. He said that the United States would have to guarantee Europe against German secession from the Community, which I pointed out contemplated another civil war in Europe—an impossible way to build a defense alliance. He thought rightly that the French had been acting badly about the Saar, and then made a plea for the NATO Council to remain in London. A pretty vigorous presentation of the arguments on the other side surprised him and left him hard up for answers.

The afternoon returned me to ceremonial duties. The Queen and Prince Philip received the special ambassadors and their ladies at Buckingham Palace. We were arranged in a large room in a long crescent and, when double doors were thrown open into a smaller room where the Queen and Prince were standing, entered, a couple at a time, to be presented and exchanged a few words before returning to our places. It happened that the day we left Washington my wife had lunched with Prince Philip's mother, Princess Alice. When I had murmured the conventional words, my wife reported this fact and that Princess Alice, knowing of our forthcoming mission, had enjoined her to testify from personal observation to her health and well-being. This led to a lively conversation with both Queen and Prince, continued after the individual presentations when they both walked down our line and spoke with us again.

In the evening Schuman, who had come to London for the King's funeral, and I met with Eden at Carlton Gardens for a working dinner. Sir William Strang, Ambassador Gifford, and Schuman's interpreter completed the company. At Eden's request, I led off by repeating the items that seemed to me essential to be agreed between us before or at Lisbon. When we had run over them, Schuman agreed to including them all on the agenda of the London meetings. He also agreed to invite Adenauer to attend the final two days and to bilateral discussions between them in a real effort to find a solution to the Saar question within the framework of growing European unity. When he suggested to me an American guarantee against secession from the Defense Community, I was very firm that we must keep our commitments within existing congressional authorization and treaties and would not enter into any new ones.

From there we turned to security controls to be imposed on Germany. Here Schuman and Eden had moved, but still not enough. They were willing to accept a unilateral declaration by Germany on what would not be produced there and would not press for prohibitions to be included in the contractual agreement, but the French pressed for inclusion of "heavy military equipment" in the self-denying declaration, and Eden for civil aircraft. I objected strongly. The former could be controlled through the Defense Community without raising an issue of discrimination, and the latter was no more reasonable than to prohibit making automobiles because the same facilities could be converted— as they were during the late war—to the production of military aircraft. But they pressed their points vigorously, causing me to note that we should prepare for trouble later. When Schuman left after dinner I stayed behind to urge on Eden the great importance of settling these points before Lisbon.

The Pilgrimage to Windsor • A cold, foggy Friday morning, with patches of drizzle following one another across the Thames, found me at eight-thirty, on February 15, standing on the sidewalk outside Westminster Hall's cobbled yard, beneath a large sign bearing the letter K under the watchful eye of a Guards officer. He clearly expected little sense and less cooperation from his wards, the special ambassadors. We had an hour to wait due to a deplorable subserviency to official time schedules and punctuality drilled into me at school. My ever-solicitous secretary had purchased for me long woolen underwear, rubbers, a thin black raincoat to go under a more respectable top coat, and a small container of alcoholic restorative.

An acquaintance, Foreign Minister Moshe Sharett of Israel, another early arrival, chatted with me as we watched the military contingents take their places. To my casual observation that doubtless he had never been caught up in the military machine, he said that I could not be more wrong. As a loyal soldier of the Imperial Ottoman Army he had repulsed allied aggressors at Salonika and in northern Greece, then pursued in the Hejas a notorious bandit named Lawrence, as elusive as the mist coming off the Thames. The Turkish bureaucracy, in its wisdom, then transferred a hardened infantry officer to the operation of the Turkish railways, which did not operate because of the aforementioned bandit. It was a frustrating experience but invaluable in the training of a foreign minister. By the time a few colleagues had suggested the possibility of development loans or tariff reductions the Queen arrived and the procession got under way. The King's coffin on a caisson drawn by sailors of the Royal Navy and escorted by the Household Cavalry was followed by the royal ladies in carriages and ambulatory chiefs of state on foot. Then came the special ambassadors, formed up by the Guards officer about eight abreast in no apparent order. I walked behind Jacob Malik, who, bundled up as I was, moved to the slow march with the inevitability of a Sherman tank. More dignitaries, the band of the Coldstream, and the pipers of the Scots Guards, with detachments of both, followed us.

The march from Westminster to Paddington Station, about three miles, at slow time took three thoroughly exhausting hours. So slow was the step that one's arms ached from inability to swing them. The route, however, furnished plenty of interest. The Household Cavalry and royal coaches ahead provided hazards to navigation that kept us alert—all but Malik, who took what came in his stride. An ambassador ahead of us in full diplomatic uniform began shedding decorations, which a colleague and I collected and restored to him during a pause. His wife's unfamiliarity with the safety catch, he explained. The entire route was lined with troops and behind them great crowds of people; both were interesting.

First the Royal Navy lined the streets, looking smart and capable; then several blocks of Guards and Royal Air Force, also smart. After that two miles of conscripts in battle dress looked anything but smart. As the coffin and the Queen passed, the troops presented arms, then reversed them and leaned over the rifle butts with bowed heads. Each group executed the maneuver differently —the Navy quickly and with snap, the Guards slowly as a solemn ritual. The Air Force after reversing the rifle extended the right arm horizontally to the right, then swung it around till the hand was on the rifle butt, following with the same movement with the left, then bowed the head. The effect was unhappily comic, like a good yawn and stretch before dropping off.

The crowds interested me, too, first of all for their complete silence—no movement, no talk, almost no expression on hundreds of thousands of faces, unless a suggestion of permanent sadness. One gathered the impression of people slightly under middle size, with few ruddy complexions or distinctive types of features, mostly pale and neither dark nor blond. They looked like a tired people.

Along Whitehall we marched and the Mall, past St. James's Palace, turned left into Picadilly at the Ritz Hotel to Park Lane at Hyde Park Corner. A minute gun fired in Hyde Park as we marched along it, past the Marble Arch and into Edgware Road, eventually turning off to Paddington Station. There a fair amount of the sawdust put on the ramp to deaden the sound of the caisson's wheels entered our shoes. Our train stood across the platform from the royal one. As I searched for a seat in the car assigned to us, a voice called my name; it was General Harry Crerar, the wartime commander of the Canadian Army. He was in a compartment with the British Chiefs of Staff, all of whom I knew and who shared sandwiches and other refreshments with me on the short journey to Windsor.

There we formed ranks again but with some confusion. The Chiefs of Staff adopted me, as I seemed hopelessly separated from my colleagues, and if our Guard's officer ever saw me, he did not claim me from such exalted military patrons. Avoiding the short, steep road from the station to St. George's Chapel, we took a longer and easier one to the castle's main gate. The supply of adult military manpower to line the route having run out, school cadets and

Boy Scouts took over at Windsor Station. At length we entered the main court-yard of the castle, a barren and ugly place of gray stone ascribed, an inscription told us, to "George IV, 1827." Another archway marked "E.R. 1583" led us downhill and through still another arch to an earlier Tudor courtyard sur-rounded by half-timbered brick and plaster buildings upon which St. George's Chapel fronted.

The coffin was carried into the choir. We followed and stood in the nave. My wife and Ambassador Gifford were seated to our left. I stood by the royal heralds in their fantastic costumes looking like the animated playing cards in *Alice in Wonderland*—black tights and short, loose coats made up of all the coats of arms of the royal family with big flaps of the same material covering their arms. On our other side were assembled all the field marshals of Britain, active and retired. As the service began one old soldier fainted; immediately from nowhere a nurse and stretcher bearers appeared and carried him igno-miniously off into the shadows. After a short and almost inaudible service, I joined the Ambassador, Alice, and Sir Derrick Hoyer Millar in the short down-hill walk to the returning train.

Sir Derrick, making his only *faux pas,* ushered us into an elegant coach arranged for tea. From this we were promptly ejected by a steward who ex-plained that it was reserved for royal personages. Hardly were we comfortably installed in an adjoining car when Prince Bernhard of the Netherlands took me back again to discuss with Queen Juliana details of her forthcoming visit to the United States. She was sitting with King Haakon of Norway and Crown Prince Olaf. The former had received us in Oslo, then Christiania, thirty years before when our firm represented his Government in a litigation with the United States at The Hague. He was kind enough to say that he remembered me—perhaps, even more, the large judgment we won. Prince Olaf had lived in Washington for periods during the war, where we had met at his embassy. On rejoining our own party, Miss Evans' restorative seemed more effective than tea as sustenance during the ride back to London, where a long, hot bath would soothe aching muscles.

64. FOUR MINISTERS MEET

IN LONDON

SATURDAY, FEBRUARY 16, began the most important discussions the ministers had had since September 1950, when we first proposed bringing Germany into the grand alliance for defense. Eden and I opened it with a duet. The next day Schuman's return from a debate in the National Assembly raised it to a trio. On Monday morning Adenauer's arrival completed the quartet, which continued until three of us left for Lisbon on Tuesday afternoon. These were formal conferences, held in the Foreign Office with advisers and busy notetakers present in considerable numbers. Gone were the informality and easy exchange of after-dinner conversation.

My admiration for Adenauer continued to grow during the London meetings. He was quick in understanding issues through the welter of interpretations, wise in judgment, and decisive. Often I found myself agreeing with him contrary to the views of the other two. When working groups brought in drafts of proposals, he would accept, reject, or propose a specific change at once. My impression, too, was that his judgment was based on long-range views of purposes and consequences and not on immediate political convenience. Schuman disclosed—it became much clearer three months later—a consciousness of diminished authority with the Cabinet and Assembly and a hesitance to move from authorized positions. Eden then, and even more at Lisbon and later in Bonn, could be counted on to end up on the side of the angels, which I tended to identify with my own. If sometimes it took him a little while to get there, he was well worth waiting for.

TWO BEGIN THE SESSION

Since Schuman was detained in Paris, Eden and I used the time to find common ground on troublesome problems. We must do our best to get Schuman over his neurotic obsession with a guarantee against possible future secession of Germany from the European Defense Community. It was an impossible idea; neither of us proposed to be members; I would not ask Congress for any further extension of the already great commitments we had undertaken to Europe. Eden would reassure Schuman of Britain's solid support in case of such a drastic change in the European situation, should it occur. We also agreed that together we must bring great pressure upon both Schuman and Adenauer to stop pushing each other about the Saar and remove this issue for the present from active agitation. France wanted economic union with the Saar and feared its *Anschluss* with Germany. Germany wanted political freedom for the Saar to decide its own fate and feared that economic unity with France was a method of foreclosing it. Schuman and Adenauer by solemn agreement endorsed by us should postpone a Saar decision for the present and stop actions which prejudiced it. Again Eden would take the active role.

Another matter that called for decision before the contractual arrangements moved the occupation toward its end was a review of sentences for war crimes imposed by occupying authorities in their zones and which would have to be carried out by German authorities. Here we agreed to recommend a review board composed of three allied and three German members—with a neutral if Adenauer wanted one. Unanimous decisions should be binding upon all; less than unanimity should be recommendatory only to the German authorities. On the troublesome problem of civil aircraft production in Germany, Eden had a political problem at home, while we had no direct interest. The happy thought occurred to us of putting the problem up to Adenauer, who might decide that with military aircraft production not permitted it would be more economical to buy than to build planes for civil use.

Finally we decided to push the relationship between the European Defense Community and NATO which we had discussed with Schuman two days before —joint meetings of their councils at any time by mutual agreement or on the call of any member of either claiming the existence of a threat to its security.

SCHUMAN JOINS US

Our first task when Schuman joined us was to simplify and make orderly for discussion with Adenauer the complex and tangled question of German contribution for the support of allied troops to be stationed in Germany for the common defense. Three decisions helped greatly to do this: first, to consider only the next two German fiscal years beginning in April, in the first of which we would assume that the Defense Community would not yet be in effect and in the second that it would be; second, to appoint a work group under the High Commissioners to review the charges and practices which the victorious forces had imposed on occupied Germany and reduce them to what a host ally might properly contribute to guest forces come to aid in the joint defense; and, third, to assume for discussion that the total German budget item for defense (including provision of its own forces and support of allied) should be the amount recommended by the Temporary Council Committee report, ten billion deutsche marks. For the first year the issues for ultimate decision would be to fix a total sum for support that would be less than Germany was now paying and that would fall well within the budget figure, since German military forces would not yet have been organized. For the second year the issues would be in one respect simpler and in another more difficult. French forces in the Defense Community would be chargeable to the Community budget, as would those of other members, and contributions to the budget would be worked out by its own procedures. German contribution to support of British and American forces would have to be determined by a negotiation among the United Kingdom, the United States, Germany, and the Defense Community. Difficult as some of these issues were, they were now understandable.

Turning to security controls over German production of certain war materials, the French had now adopted the British idea of what they called a binding unilateral declaration not to produce certain items. We preferred the less discriminatory method of having the Defense Community establish "forward zones" in which these items would not be produced by anyone. More important to us, however, was striking "gun barrels" and "propellants"— i.e., explosives—from the list. Twenty per cent of the military aid asked of us by our European allies was for ammunition, a substantial amount for artillery. To exclude Germany from production of both continued the burden, wholly unnecessarily, on us. Schuman's plea not to rebuild Krupp was not persuasive if Germany was to rearm herself for the common defense.

We easily agreed that Adenauer must stop procrastinating over the decartelization program and complete it by spring. High on the list for dissolution was Deutscher Kohlen Verkauf, sales agency for the Ruhr's coke and coal. Schuman promised that during this visit he would work out with Adenauer a plan to remove the Saar from the field of controversy.

ADENAUER COMPLETES THE GROUP

When Adenauer joined us on Monday, February 18, both the tempo and the size of the meetings increased. I had with me Ambassadors Gifford and Bruce; High Commissioner McCloy, with Samuel Reber, Perry Laukhuff, and Jacques Reinstein of his staff; Assistant Secretary for European Affairs George Perkins and Colonel Henry Byroade of the German Office; Paul Nitze of the Policy Planning Staff; and Assistant Secretary of Defense Frank Nash. Other ministers were similarly supported. Quick agreement was reached on the review of war crimes sentences, as the three of us had proposed. Discussion of German contribution to allied troop support was put off a day to permit Adenauer to consult Finance Minister Fritz Schäfer on the Temporary Council Committee's revised report, available only the day before. At lunch time my wife met me to go across the street to Number 10 for lunch with the Prime Minister and Mrs. Churchill.

The family was still living on the top floor in what had been servants' quarters, as the residential and state rooms had been closed since the war. The Prime Minister used the Cabinet Room on the ground floor, almost completely filled by a huge circular table, as his office. We were received in a small, bright sitting room on the top floor overlooking the Horse Guards Parade. During lunch, recalling a talk with the late King two years before and his deep appreciation of Mr. Churchill's tireless courtesy in keeping him fully abreast of everything during the war, I spoke of it and asked whether the same relation would be possible with a young woman, whose interests must clearly be different. He seemed surprised at the question. She was the monarch; he, her first minister. Their relationship was a matter of duty on both sides. He would conduct it as he had before and would hope to hold her interest. She had a good head. Might, I ventured, a husband complicate the relationship? How the monarch wished to conduct their interviews was for her to decide; his duty was to keep her informed. This he would do. Very good, I thought, unaware that his persuasiveness would soon lead me astray.

Back in the Foreign Office, Adenauer accepted readily the proposal for joint sessions of the NATO and European Defense Community councils and for a declaration by him that Germany would not produce certain war materials if we could agree on the list. He went further and stated his willingness to accept a Defense Community decision not to have the materials produced in a forward zone, which would include Germany and all or parts of other countries. Schuman began a rambling speech on the adverse psychological effects of the rebuilding of German war factories. This seemed pointless unless directed to newcomers to the discussions from the French Foreign Office. To avoid creating troubles for ourselves I suggested putting a group to work on a memorandum combining these ideas for the ministers to consider in the morning.

A large company of us dined that evening with Mr. Eden at Carlton Gardens. I found myself between Schuman and André François-Poncet, the French High Commissioner, with Adenauer across the table beside Eden. The talk got onto the writing of memoirs. "I will be kind to you in my memoirs," said Adenauer to François-Poncet, "if you will be kind to me in yours." François-Poncet agreed. Schuman whispered to me, "Adenauer will lose; he will die first." After dinner Eden put Adenauer and Schuman in a room by themselves to agree on a method of getting the issue of the Saar quieted down and removed from discussion while we made progress with more pressing matters. While they talked, he and I gave some guidance to the working group on security controls and sent them off to draft. Later the two conferees emerged from their room tired but smiling and told us that they were agreed.

A BUSY NIGHT

Returning to Prince's Gate near midnight, I found the household asleep—all but that Admirable Crichton of butlers, Epps, who had waited to hand me a bulky envelope from 10 Downing Street. Should I open it and spoil slumber or keep it for a fresh mind at breakfast? Duty prevailed. The envelope contained a note from Mr. Churchill and a speech he proposed to deliver in Parliament unless he had word from me in the morning objecting to anything in it. We were leaving London in the afternoon. A glance through the speech disclosed the reason for this midnight message. It was a reply to a Labour motion critical of Mr. Churchill's support of the U.S. position in Korea, and an admirable speech in every way but one. To stress how seriously the situation might develop, Mr. Churchill had referred to top-secret contingency orders given to General Ridgway of which the British Chiefs had been informed because of the British brigade serving in Korea. Public reference to these orders would be impermissible.

Wearily I awoke Luke Battle, whose room was on the floor with ours. He told Epps to expect a busy night involving callers and the need for coffee, telephoned my secretary, Barbara Evans, and Paul Nitze of the Planning Staff, asking them to come to the residence at once, and informed the Marine guard at the chancery that they would be returning there in an hour or two. In due course Barbara typed a letter to Mr. Churchill informing him that I could not consent to any reference to General Ridgway's orders. Only President Truman could do that and I was convinced that he would not. If the Prime Minister wished to see me, I would be at his service. Luke was instructed to present the letter to Number 10 at nine o'clock and to sit there until he put it in the Prime Minister's own hand. Paul Nitze and I then struck through the objectionable part of the speech and interlined in red pencil a different, but passably Churchillian, passage depicting the serious times which might lie ahead and the need for the fighting allies to stick together in meeting them. This act of mayhem on the speech was not to be then disclosed to the Prime Minister but held in reserve. Paul took the speech to be photostated. Not many hours remained before breakfast on our last busy day in London.

AN EQUALLY BUSY MORNING

After an early breakfast, Nitze, Battle, and I had a last look at the Churchill papers. The letter was signed and sent to Number 10; the speech I put in my pocket. After that our considerable staff briefed me for a tripartite meeting followed by a quadripartite one. The first was partially but not wholly successful in an attempt to re-establish unity for our last discussion of the series with Adenauer. We had hardly begun this when an urgent request came from Mr. Churchill asking me to come to him at once. That was unfortunately not possible and I had to ask him to let me come when our meeting ended. By the time his answer arrived that meeting, too, was precluded by a message from the Queen asking the visiting ministers' attendance on her at two-fifteen that afternoon, which would require our staying in session until then. Again Mr. Churchill had to be put off. During a coffee recess Eden, curious about this flurry of messages, told me that the Tories somewhat maliciously were letting the Prime Minister fret about the Labour motion, mainly aimed at him and which would be easily defeated.

Quadripartite Meeting Resumed · Eden read a new draft about security controls, which would deal with the problem by an added provision in the European Defense Community treaty giving that organization authority to decide what should be produced in various areas. Adenauer would write two letters: one to Defense Community countries saying that provided that the equipment of German troops was the same as all other contingents, Germany would not regard as discriminatory a decision not to allocate to forward areas the production of weapons stated in an annex to the treaty; the other was to the United States and Britain saying that the Defense Community treaty would become domestic law in Germany.

When it came to the contents of the list, I again vigorously opposed the inclusion of gun barrels and propellants. Schuman defended it. After dreary repetition of arguments, Eden proposed suspension of these items from the list for a limited time pending reconsideration by experts and a report to the ministers by spring. This was agreed.

Civil aircraft came next. True to our hope, Adenauer disposed of the matter by saying that Germany had no intention of producing planes. It would be far too expensive; he would purchase them. Schuman observed that this decision could be revoked at will, to which Adenauer replied by gently urging him to have a little faith that Adenauer's successors would not be wholly mad. Schuman would have to consult his Government, but it was clear to us that this issue was for practical purposes decided.

Turning to the most critical of all our issues, the financial ones, Adenauer said that Bonn agreed to publication of the Temporary Council Committee's report and saw no difficulty to agreement on the total German contribution before ministers concluded the Lisbon meeting. He thought our plan for negotiations excellent. On this cheerful note we adjourned and took our separate ways to Clarence House and the royal presence.

Audience with the Queen • Her Majesty, said the equerry—Sir Alan Lascelles —as he ushered me into a small drawing room in Clarence House, would receive each of the foreign ministers separately, indicating herself when the audience was to be terminated. Present with Her Majesty would be Prince Philip and Mr. Eden. After a cordial greeting, the Queen motioned me to a seat beside her and regretted that London had offered us its usual February weather. This being undeniable we passed on to the current meetings, which she hoped had been satisfactory. Remembering Mr. Churchill's views about keeping the monarch informed, I decided to follow them.

The meetings had gone only fairly well, I answered, failing to reach full agreement. I could not blame the Germans for this since in the disagreements I had found myself siding with the German positions. Illustrations were asked for and given with the result of enlivening the proceedings rather more than I had intended to. The Prince, evidently believing that a hare had been started, cried me on; Mr. Eden looked pained. The equerry kept reminding us that Mr. Schuman was waiting. Finally Her Majesty rose, releasing me to call on Mr. Churchill. Mr. Eden was to dine with us that evening in Ambassador Mac-Veagh's Lisbon embassy, where I knew that my irresponsible conduct would bring me a good wigging. Under the beneficent influence, however, of a good dinner and excellent wine a repentant sinner received absolution.

Confronting the Old Lion • Shown at last into the Cabinet Room at Number 10, I found Mr. Churchill in a carefully arranged and dramatic setting. Alone, huddled at the great green-covered table, he barely greeted me, muttering instead, "naked among mine enemies" and "the sword stricken from my hand." When I remained cheerful amid this dolor and asked him how I could be of service to him, he in turn put a question. Having vetoed the heart of his speech (an exaggeration), had I an alternative to it? To suggest one, I said, would involve the great impertinence of editing a Churchill speech. He waved that aside, listened carefully while I read Paul Nitze's substitute, and asked to have it read again. His whole mood changed to one of buoyancy. "I can win with that," he said, and took the speech and read it over himself. When he offered to give me a copy with the change, I declined it. His acceptance of the change was enough.

On my way to the door he asked in a sly sort of way when I had found time to do so much after receiving his note. By adopting his practice, I answered, of working at night and sleeping by day, which I would now do on the flight to Lisbon.

Although the President had been kept informed day by day of our talks in London, they had been too kaleidoscopic to permit a personal appraisal until they ended. This I gave him from Lisbon. At first, I cabled, it had been doubtful whether Schuman could meet with Adenauer at all since his Government might fall at any moment. But with Adenauer in town for the King's funeral, arrangements were made. Another hazard lay in discussing, as we had to do, matters just debated and voted on by the Bundestag and which the French Assembly was debating and did vote on while we talked. Adenauer felt that he had preserved enough latitude for maneuver, while Schuman, though fatigued and worried, gallantly took a chance on the leaks and went further toward compromise than I had thought possible. This delicate situation explained why our communiqués were so restrained. Some important, indeed critical, matters—such as German support for allied troops in Germany and the prohibited list for German war production—must await decisions during the current week in Lisbon, but we were in much better shape to make a good showing than we had been a week earlier. Much had been decided; much had been advanced toward decision; irrelevant obstacles like the Saar and the war crimes sentences had been removed from the stage.

The message was one of hope.

65. LISBON

LOOKING BACK ON the Lisbon conference two years later, I said of it, "The heart of that operation was to solve the French financial and the German arms production problems, both of which grew out of French difficulties. If that could be done all the other pieces would fall into place."

In Lisbon we stayed at our embassy residence in the old town, which had survived the disastrous earthquake and fire of 1755, when twenty thousand people perished. Our Ambassador, Lincoln MacVeagh, and a younger brother had been my friends from school days. At President Roosevelt's request, MacVeagh had come from publishing to diplomacy before the war to negotiate our base arrangement with Iceland and then toward the war's end moved to Greece, where he gave invaluable help in the rescue of Greece from internal subversion and external attack. Coming to Portugal, he negotiated Portuguese entry into NATO and the Azores base. Arrangements had already been made to move him to Madrid to discuss bases in Spain. He was both close friend and wise adviser.

The problem of the daily walk from residence to chancery proved more difficult in Lisbon than elsewhere. The police were agreeable enough until on the second day we ran into trouble. At the bottom of our hill, where we crossed the Largo do Rato—the Square of the Mouse—hundreds of children suddenly surrounded us demanding autographs. There we stayed until I paid the ransom and reinforcements arrived to extricate us. From then on, we played a game that Lisbon made into a betting pool. Preceded and followed by police cars, the Ambassador would take us to a spot from which we would walk to another spot, both chosen only as we started off. We still got our walk and Lisbon enjoyed the game.

Of all the council meetings I attended, the one at Lisbon was the busiest and most productive. The real work, however, was done not at its formal sessions but in almost continuous negotiations held privately on German and French problems and on some lesser, but serious, ones that had blocked agreement. At the opening formalities in the hall of the Portuguese National Assembly, Portuguese Foreign Minister Paulo A. V. da Cunha welcomed us, adding the unpopular suggestion that Spain should be asked to join the alliance. He then turned the meeting over to me to make the "keynote address." The note was one of crisis. We had come a long way in the short time since 1949, but "the hardest part of the journey still lies ahead. What we have done will be of little value unless we finish the job. We must make decisions that will not be easy to make, and we must take actions that will strain all of us to the utmost.

... We will succeed because we *must* succeed."[1]

Moving after this session to the Superior Technical Institute, the council heard three formal reports, one from the Military Committee on progress made since Rome, another from General Gruenther on the financial needs of the infrastructure program—i.e., lines of communication, supply depots, and air-fields—and a third from Mr. Harriman, who submitted the voluminous and thorough report of the Temporary Committee. After the meeting Mr. Schuman came back to the embassy with me for a relaxed, friendly tea. There we heard the encouraging news from Bonn that the Chancellor was already carrying out his part of the London agreements. Germany, he had announced, would not engage in production of nuclear energy, missiles, or heavy warships. The Government would ask for legislation to carry out the antitrust program. This helped the general atmosphere at once.

Almost at the beginning of the Lisbon week a heated disagreement in our own delegation between Harriman and General Bradley showed me how thin was the ice we had to cross. Harriman pressed the General to endorse the view that the military forces which the Temporary Committee report recommended as being within the economic capability of the European countries would provide an adequate defense for Europe. Bradley refused to do so. I listened to the discussion until it seemed to be getting out of hand and then adjourned the delegation meeting, asking the disputants to meet alone with me. Pointing out that General Bradley was being asked to lend his great reputation to the support of a proposition that one could see was, at least, open to doubt, I asked whether he thought the forces recommended were better than what we had, were the best we could get, and, taken together with our nuclear capacity, would have a strong deterrent effect upon any desire to test their adequacy. The General said that he most certainly did think so. Harriman, I urged, ought to be able to find language that Bradley could accept and would carry the desired meaning. This was done.

FRENCH AND GERMAN MILITARY FINANCES

We began at once to wrestle with our most baffling as well as our central problem—French and German military finances and their interrelation. We continued to wrestle with it all through the conference and the night that followed its adjournment. For a while, but fortunately only a short while, the French Minister of Defense, Georges Bidault, was present. He was one of the most rattlebrained men I have ever tried to work with. A cold that rapidly grew worse caused his unlamented return to Paris. The new Prime Minister, Edgar Faure, who seemed to me more informed and competent, took over and soon brought order into the discussion. He proposed a military budget that would raise French military expenditures from ten to twelve per cent of French gross national product, the highest ratio in Europe. Because of the war in Indochina, however, French divisions in the European Defense Community would be cut from fourteen to twelve and its air-power contribution would be cut also. The cost of his proposal would be higher than the Temporary Council Committee recommendation and higher than the current budget. France would need American help. Reports of his plan, which promptly leaked, brought predictions in the Paris press that Faure would fall and a charge by General de Gaulle of a "sellout" and a policy of "bankruptcy and debasement" on the part of French leaders.

On the last scheduled day of the conference (Monday, February 25, 1952) continuous meetings by ministers and technical assistants charged with special aspects of the problem brought us within sight of solutions. Faure's budget, with its twelve divisions and twenty-seven air squadrons for service with NATO-EDC could be financed with approximately six hundred million dollars of U.S. aid and the German contributions to allied troop support under discussion with the High Commissioners in Bonn. We were prepared to furnish the aid provided all other questions could be worked out.

In Bonn, however, discussion had stalled over two questions: first, whether, as Adenauer claimed, such expenses as frontier police, veterans' care, and defense of Berlin already in the West German budget should be included in the eleven-billion-deutsche-mark military budget to which he had agreed on February 21; second, whether a definite figure for allied troop support could be settled before the four governments had agreed what items of support were allowable. Adenauer was ready to pay half a billion deutsche marks a month until agreements were made from which calculations could follow. This seemed sensible to me. It also seemed to me highly probable that—as proved to be the case—the allowance for existing expenses to be allocated against the agreed defense budget could be liquidated at a reasonable round sum.

Since these unsettled questions would undoubtedly be appealed to the three ministers in Lisbon, we would do well to get all other matters agreed before this occurred.

OTHER PIECES FALL INTO PLACE

While the talks with the French delegation went on day after day and the wires were busy between Lisbon and Bonn, we worked at putting together other segments of our puzzle. Starting on February 21 with a meeting between the Benelux ministers and those of the occupying powers, we reported on the great progress of the London visit, the relations being worked out between the European Defense Community and NATO, and the continuing interest of the United States in the movement toward European integration. This cheered Stikker. I met with Halvard M. Lange of Norway and Ole Björn Kraft of Denmark to bring them relief from pressure by our Air Force to station units on the NATO-built airfields in their countries. This publicized demand had brought countervailing pressure from the Soviet Government. A solution was found in Air Force visits and a system for quick occupation upon alert.

Most important of all, however, was the adoption on the twenty-second by the council of a resolution approving the establishment of the European Army[2] —which we had been unable to get at Rome—followed by a buoyant press conference by Lester Pearson, Chairman of the NATO Council, supported by

Eden, Schuman, and me, pointing out how far NATO had come in its three years of life.

On the same day, the Temporary Committee's report on the economic and military goals for NATO and its individual members during the next three years was adopted and an annual review procedure established to call attention to successes and failures. The military goals, as experience proved, were not achieved, although in my view they were achievable. The cause was the receding tide of political will that became discernible in 1952 and unmistakably obvious in later French repudiation of the European Defense Community after Schuman left the scene and Pierre Mendès-France took over leadership in 1953.

Eden reported on the progress of the arrangements being made with Germany to bring the occupation to an end, obtaining council endorsement. The difficult matter of infrastructure financing, patiently and ably guided by Lovett, was agreed, reducing the U.S. share of the cost from forty-eight to forty-two per cent. Finally, after a great deal of private discussion the troublesome problem of the headquarters of the council and the selection of a Secretary General was resolved. After dinner at our embassy on Sunday evening, February 24, Eden told me that if the consensus was in favor of Paris for the council headquarters, he would not object. I agreed with him that Sir Oliver Franks would be an ideal Secretary General. We both knew that Mike Pearson was an undeclared candidate, which might create another problem. Mr. Eden undertook to ascertain Sir Oliver's position.

Apparently by the next morning he had not done so, for then the council voted to establish the headquarters in Paris and authorized Pearson to invite Sir Oliver to become its Secretary General. Sir Oliver needed time to reflect and consult his Government. After our meeting had adjourned, he declined the appointment and Lord Ismay was chosen.

THE GRAND SLAM

The ninth meeting of the NATO Council adjourned at seven o'clock on Monday evening, February 25, but a long night's work remained for the three ministers and their assistants, who had been hard at it all day, for on that morning Adenauer's memorandum of appeal from the High Commissioners on the two unsettled questions and a group from the High Commission arrived in Lisbon. We met at the British Embassy residence at ten in the evening. Long reports were made by the High Commission group on ways to pull together Adenauer's figures, Faure's budget, and our aid proposals. With everyone tired and nerves on edge, quibbling arguments broke out, which confused an exhausted Schuman and bored Eden, who was catching cold. I was relying on midnight weariness to solve them. This it did, whereupon a working group instructed by the three of us retired to the dining room to draft a closing proposal, and Schuman went to bed.

While Eden and I were waiting for the message, the group returned to us, deadlocked over a matter on which the French had understood the instructions differently than their colleagues. We could not move them; they would not wake

Schuman and proposed to call the night session off. Then Anthony Eden exploded in a most spectacular and satisfying pyrotechnical display, accompanied by animadversions upon French national deficiencies. In one telling sentence, he observed that no sooner did a crisis occur than some damned Frenchman went to bed. If the staff did not straighten this out, he would go to the embassy himself and set it straight. That did it. A puzzled Schuman confirmed our understanding and told his people in case of further doubts to accept our word. When, soon afterward, Eden himself decided to go to bed, I reminded him of his observation about Frenchmen in a crisis and demanded and received supreme power by right of survivorship. Fortunately, it was not necessary to test it. By four o'clock the message was completed and dispatched, accompanied by a private one from me to Adenauer, urging him to accept the comparatively minor adjustments and complete our remarkably successful work at London and Lisbon.

The next morning word came back that he had done so. To the President I sent an exultant final report on the conference, ending, "We have something pretty close to a grand slam." The four ministers immediately issued a statement confirming our agreement.[3] To a press conference that afternoon I added, "This clinches it." We seemed to have broken through a long series of obstacles and to be fairly started toward a more united and stronger Europe and an integrated Atlantic defense system. The world that lay before us shone with hope. The momentum of the past month would carry on to midsummer before it slackened, as some, wearied by the pace, fell behind and the shadows of a change of governments fell across France and the United States.

However, that lay ahead. Our last day in Lisbon passed in busy meetings of farewell and of preparation for the future. Of the first sort was a speech to the whole Lisbon staff to thank them for the great pains they had taken to respond to the extra demands that the council session had made upon them; of the second, were two long tripartite meetings to review the preparation for our next effort at Bonn in May. We also went over with the Benelux ministers the agreements of the past two days with Germany and the plans for spring achievement. Then came a meeting with de Gasperi and his group to discuss Italian matters. After a gay farewell dinner with our host, who had been kindness itself, the time had come to leave his hospitable roof and the city to which we had become so attached.

At the airport a great throng had come to wish us Godspeed—Portuguese and American friends and departing colleagues. In the throng shaking hands Frank Nash of Defense said he had instructed an aide to put aboard the plane a basket of Portuguese "wine"—"Porco do Lisboa," he said it was. Slowly while saying good-bye to others, the significance of what he had said dawned on me. Horrified at the threat to the President's plane, I asked whether the basket contained a pig. It did, and a great idea it was, Frank insisted, sure of press coverage—"bringing home the bacon." More likely, I insisted, "a pig in a poke." Luke Battle dashed off to join Colonel Williams in saving the plane from this profanation. From a popular point of view Frank may have had a point. At the end of my report to the House Committee on Foreign Affairs, Chairman

Richards said that at Lisbon we "took time by the forelock and brought home the bacon," but he added, perfecting the metaphor, "We're not at the end of the road yet."[4]

Four days after adjournment at Lisbon a cold wind came across the Atlantic from Paris. Faure's government had fallen. But the Lisbon decisions still stood.

DR. SALAZAR

Not all our time in Lisbon was given over to work. We were entertained most hospitably and given opportunities to see the city and the surrounding countryside. I found both country and people sympathetic; later that year I was to feel the same warm response to Portugal's former colony, Brazil. Dr. Salazar's dinner for the visiting ministers, their wives, and a goodly number of Portuguese ladies and gentlemen could not have been more delightful. The setting alone insured that—the eighteenth-century Palace of Queluz, which means "what light," on the outskirts of Lisbon, silver-pink under the moon. The drive approaching this miniature Versailles, with all its fountains playing, was lighted by a double row of flares held by soldiers in eighteenth-century uniforms. The palace itself was ablaze with light from gleaming chandeliers and decked with flowers. The dinner was saved from the danger of shoptalk by the presence of ladies—in my case by delightful Portuguese ladies—who kept us far from the problems that had been harassing us all day.

The next morning Dr. Salazar kindly invited the Ambassador and me to call on him. We took with us a truly great interpreter, Ted Xanthaky of our embassy staff. Ted kept within a few words of the speaker so that his translation was instantaneous. Seemingly effortless, it caught the emotions of the speaker —humor, irony, solemnity, all came through. The office, a small affair, was in a government building approached by a private entrance, guarded only by an old uniformed doorman. There an aide took us up one floor in a sedate, paneled lift. The anteroom contained two desks, another young man, and no sign of the paraphernalia of an office. Without waiting or announcement, our guide ushered us into Dr. Salazar's study, a room of medium size furnished with an unencumbered desk, no telephone, comfortable leather chairs, and bookshelves with paintings above them.

A tall, slight man received us at the door. Below graying hair an oval face with long, straight nose and equally straight mouth was given a tinge of melancholy by large, dark eyes and a quizzical cast by mobile eyebrows arched in the center. Ted Xanthaky gave me a startling likeness of that face. It was in a reproduction of an altarpiece painted about 1465 by Nuno Gonçalves for the Mosteiro do Saõ Vicente. In the *"painel dos pescadores"* there is Salazar—a portrait no doubt of one of his ancestors, who were fisherfolk. His manner, easy and relaxed, carried no trace of authority or pomposity. As we sat down, he sank back in his chair, elbows on its arms and fingers steepled together before him. When he talked, one was struck by the beauty of the hands, moving expressively with his words. They were as sensitive as the face. I felt drawn to him as rarely on first meeting.

When I remarked on the quiet of his office compared to the bustle of the White House west wing, he pointed out that he did not administer, but directed. The captain of a ship often seemed the least busy person on it. The Department of the Presidency carried out his orders as an executive officer would do on a ship. The metaphor caught his fancy. What the captain required was knowledge of how to keep to his course and to deal with the vagaries of the sea. When he lost sight of Europe, bound for Rio, his compass, sextant, and seamanship enabled him to keep headed for his goal and handle the buffetings of weather and currents until one day there, before him, lay the great harbor of Rio. I recalled an old epigram which had often comforted me, that the future comes one day at a time. This so delighted him that he asked for the Portuguese rights to it.

Under the Ambassador's guidance, Dr. Salazar was led to talk of the economic and political theories of his policies. This he did with relaxed objectivity, spicing his talk as all good teachers do with illustrations and humor, for he had been for a while a professor of economics at Coimbra University. General Carmona lured him away from the classroom to run a country that for twenty years had been sinking into economic chaos and political anarchy, involving the assassination of a monarch and his heir, the abolition of the monarchy, the collapse of the currency, and a coup by the Army. Dr. Salazar was not a dictator in his own right as Stalin was, but a dictator-manager employed and maintained by the power of the Army—not under his control—to run the country in the interest of the middle class, from which for the most part the officers and noncommissioned officers came. Indisputably, political liberty, in the modern British and American sense, does not exist in Portugal and, judging from past experience, would probably be incompatible with the economic stability and growth that over forty years Dr. Salazar created. The Salazar regime had widespread acceptance and did not depend, as did Stalin's in Russia, on harsh suppression of individual liberties. A convinced libertarian—particularly a foreign one—could understandably disapprove of Salazar. But I doubt that Plato would have done so.

66. ONCE MORE UNTO THE BREACH

THE THREE MONTHS between the Lisbon and Bonn meetings were a time of growing weaknesses in the alliance and greater efforts by us as we girded ourselves and rallied our allies for a supreme effort to achieve the European Defense Community and end the occupation in Germany before ebb tide in Europe and America lowered the level of will too far. In Germany Adenauer was having trouble with the opposition parties, Schumacher in his bitterness declaring that anyone who would sign the contractual arrangement was not a German. In France the shaky government of Antoine Pinay, which followed Edgar Faure's, staggered through increasing troubles in Indochina, North Africa, the United Nations and with the value of the franc—all of which increased French resentment against the United States. Curiously, Arab-Asian hostility to us also increased, because of our asserted support of French policies. Eden was calm and helpful throughout.

Hardly had we returned from Lisbon when a clap of thunder on the left warned that Moscow had been disturbed by the results achieved at London and Lisbon and was determined to prevent the further integration of Germany into the West and into a unified Western Europe. Already the wholly false charges of our use of chemical and biological weapons in Korea were being recklessly issued from Peking and Moscow when on March 10 Vishinsky handed identical notes to the British, French, and United States ambassadors.

THUNDER ON THE LEFT

The notes called for four-power talks on steps to be taken for a peace treaty with a new all-German government along lines different from those already put forward by the Western powers and, indeed, from some earlier Soviet positions. The proposal called, on the political side, for a unified Germany, the withdrawal of all foreign troops and bases from German soil not later than a year after the treaty went into effect, for a guarantee of "democratic rights" and the banning of organizations "inimical to democracy," equal civil and political rights to all former German soldiers and Nazis, and no German coalition or military alliance against any power whose armed forces had fought against Germany. The territorial boundaries of Germany were to be "as agreed at Potsdam." No economic restrictions were to be imposed there on peaceful production, but the national armed forces would be established in the peace treaty and the production of war materials and equipment would be limited in "quantity and type" to the requirements of the treaty forces.

To the foreign ministers this was a familiar Russian gambit. We—with Ernie Bevin instead of Anthony Eden—had been through this same maneuver just three years before when, after the failure of the Berlin blockade, Stalin had used it in an unsuccessful attempt to block the formation of the West German Government. The weeks of sterile debate at the Palais Rose in the summer of 1951 ran through the same plays to preclude the inclusion of Germany in the defense of Europe, for equal representation of East and West Germans in an all-German government, for inclusion of Communist and Communist-front parties and the exclusion of organizations "inimical to democracy"—i.e., the formation of a people's democracy—for a neutralized Germany, a small, ineffective German army, and the existing boundaries in the East. Here again was a spoiling operation intended to check and dissipate the momentum toward solutions in the West brought about by three years of colossal effort.

Old and obvious as this gambit was, it had strong appeal to timid and wishful thinkers—in France, those who feared a reunited and strong Germany and hoped for a "matured" and "satisfied" Soviet Union; in Germany, those who grasped at a chance of reunification, however slim, and hoped for security without the cost and risk of alliance with Western Europe and America. The same hopes and fears were preached elsewhere in Europe and found echoes in the western hemisphere.

When the note was received, the President was in Key West, Florida, trying to shake off a bronchial infection. I wrote him that we had not yet had time to give it careful study, but that at first glance it had the usual hooks in it, though shrewdly disguised to appeal to the Germans and to impressionable opinion everywhere. We had been expecting some move of this sort as a last-ditch effort to prevent German integration with the West along the lines worked out at Lisbon. To turn it down out of hand would be ill advised. The President would be getting more from us on this matter later.

Schuman also saw the note as aimed at the Germans. It provided something for all elements in Germany—for the Socialists, unity; for the industrialists, markets; for the soldiers, an army; and for the Nazis, reinstatement. This amounted to an attack on Adenauer and his policies. A second objective was to break up the unity of Western Europe. The French public, he believed, had seen the danger in the military provisions, which had caused embarrassment even to the French Communists. Schuman hoped to meet with the British and ourselves at an early date to coordinate our replies.

Adenauer took two attitudes toward the Soviet note. To disarm the opposition in Germany he favored four-power talks; to reassure his allies and his own right, he rejected a number of expected Russian demands.

Eden made the largest contribution to analysis and policy. He agreed that the Soviet note was their counter to our meetings in London and Lisbon, and believed that if handled adroitly it might be turned to our advantage. The heart of the matter lay in the extent to which the Soviet Union was prepared to depart from prior positions regarding the creation of an all-German government. If it was not prepared to move from them, we need not even reach divisive discussion of the substance of a German peace treaty. The propaganda battle could be fought as before on the preliminary issue. If, however, the Soviet Government was prepared to pay the price of an honestly non-Communist government for all Germany in order to block German association with the West, we must tread very warily, as we could arrive at the same stalemate as in Austria, with a government for the whole country but no progress toward a peace treaty or the end of the occupation or stability of any sort in Europe.

He suggested, therefore, that to find out how the land lay, our reply concentrate on the vague proposal for the creation of an all-German government, stressing that the allies and the Federal Republic had already put forward in the United Nations and elsewhere specific proposals on this subject. A draft reply from London along these lines became the foundation of our common consultations thereafter. Arrangements were made to consult among the three very shortly and then with Adenauer. I suggested identical notes to avoid any possibility of Soviet exploitation of any divergence even if inadvertent. On March 21 a draft note agreed *ad referendum* in Paris went to the President, still in Florida. I drew his attention to some innovations from earlier drafts and asked his expeditious approval. Identical notes were delivered to Vishinsky on March 26,[1] a little over two weeks after the delivery of his notes to our ambassadors. Ambassador Dunn, backed up by High Commissioner McCloy, had ably represented us.

The notes made a few brisk points. First they pointed out that, as the Soviet Government itself asserted, an all-German government was a prerequisite to a peace treaty, free elections were prerequisite to an all-German government, and free conditions prerequisite to free elections. In order to ascertain whether these conditions existed, the United Nations had appointed a commission to carry out a simultaneous examination of the Federal Republic, Berlin, and the Soviet zone. Necessary facilities had been assured in the Federal Republic and West Berlin. Would they be assured in the Soviet zone and East Berlin? Second, the Soviet note did not state the international position of the all-German government. The allies considered that it should be free before and after the conclusion of a treaty to enter into associations compatible with the United Nations Charter. Third, it did not seem possible to enter into discussion of a German peace treaty until an all-German government existed capable of joining in those discussions. Fourth, the Soviet note stated that Germany's frontiers were established by the Potsdam Conference. However, that conference provided that the final boundaries of Germany must await the peace settlement. Finally, the notes observed that the Soviet proposal for the formation of German national land, air, and sea forces was a step backward and inconsistent with the achievement of German participation in a purely defensive European community designed to prevent aggression and preclude the revival of national militarism. (Adenauer had worried over the implications of this statement, should the European Defense Community fail to come to fruition.)

Although what Eden called "the battle of the notes" continued for two months—indeed, the last Soviet note burst among us when we were meeting in Bonn at the end of May—it was plain from the first response that Moscow was not prepared to wager high stakes in order to stop the Lisbon program.

The notes caused some nervousness and apprehension but did not impede progress. In a speech to the American Society of Newspaper Editors I described the Soviet moves of this period as the "golden apple" of discord tactic. Several golden apples had been tossed over the Iron Curtain in the hope of causing discord among the allies, but the tactic had failed.

In looking over this speech I see that my good friend, Senator Alexander Wiley of Wisconsin, ranking Republican member of the Foreign Relations Committee, spoke from the same platform. Possibly with the idea of causing a little discord myself, I paid the Senator a warm tribute, ending: "He knows also that things cannot always go according to our hopes. And so to him, as one of our novelists has said, 'A trouble is a trouble and to be taken as such; he feels no obligation to snatch the knotted cord from the hand of God and deal out murderous blows.' I salute him with affectionate esteem."[2] The warmhearted Senator replied in kind. This unseemly fraternization with the enemy raised a fine brouhaha in the press and among his partisan colleagues in the Senate.

THE PRESIDENT WITHDRAWS

The President came back from Key West sunburned and healthy to throw a most disconcerting bombshell of his own into the domestic and international situation. It burst in the Washington armory during the Jefferson-Jackson Day Democratic Party Dinner on the evening of March 29. On our way to the dinner my wife asked whether I thought the President might disclose his political future in his after-dinner speech. "Not at all," I said, in, as she subsequently told me, an offensively superior manner. It would be too early to announce an intention to run again for the Presidency, and to the large party gathering too disappointing to state the contrary. That evening she sat beside him. As the time for speechmaking approached, he opened the binder that held his speech and showed her the last page written in his own hand and terse style containing the fateful announcement that he would not seek the Presidency again. "You, Bess, and I," he said, "are the only ones here who know that."

My wife protested and wanted to get me, a few places away at the table, to argue with him. He refused to let her do so. It would have been quite futile in any event. A little later we were stunned by the announcement. The party was quite unprepared to find a new leader and the material from which to choose seemed thin. Only slowly did it become clear what the process of changing governments would do to our nation's effectiveness in the international community. That slowly declined as the administration's tenure ran out and only slowly picked up again as its successor gained the experience and confidence necessary to effectiveness. Some work in process we were able to carry through at home and abroad; other mattters, such as the Korean armistice negotiations, languished while "the great external realm" waited to see what manner of men would follow us.

Though greatly regretting it at the time, I am sure in retrospect that the President's decision was wise. It would have been better all around if the constitutional calendar had called for an election a year later rather than at that peculiarly critical moment. With a longer life-span the existing government would have had a good chance of helping Schuman get the European Defense Community through the French National Assembly and convincing the Chinese and North Koreans to bring the Korean war to a close. The virtual interregnum of more than a year was costly. Otherwise, both personally and nationally it was time for a change. The President, nine years older than I, was when we left office in January 1953 tired out and run down, as was I. If he had won again, neither of us could have gone on with the same energy and zest. Probably our judgment would have reflected the decline. To leave positions of great responsibility and authority is to die a little, but the time comes when that must be faced.

From the national point of view, also, the Democratic Party had been in office for twenty years to the great detriment of the opposition. It seems both illogical and dangerous that a party that had shown ineptitude in politics and recklessness in destroying popular faith in government itself should be reclaimed to a sense of responsibility by a recall to power. This, however, seems necessary to the working of a democratic system, which Sir Winston Churchill has observed is the worst form of government, except for the alternatives. The process of changing horses in the middle of a stream now began with its incidental private pains and public penalties.

SPRING IN WASHINGTON

The witch hunt for supposed subversives involving both pains and penalties warmed up as politics stoked the fires. The House Un-American Activities Committee, Senator McCarran's Internal Security Subcommittee, and Senator McCarthy of Wisconsin in his own right found new issues to exploit in charges against Professor Owen Lattimore of The Johns Hopkins University, Senator William Benton of Connecticut, the motion picture industry, and the State Department. When I reversed a departmental recommendation that a Foreign Service officer, Oliver Edmund Clubb, be found to be a security risk, my action raised so much controversy and misrepresentation that I explained the case at some length in a press conference.† An article in the April *American Mercury,* "Freedom's Case Against Dean Acheson," used—so a Department statement said—the technique of the "Big Lie."[3]

On April 10 General Eisenhower asked to be relieved from his duties as Supreme Commander in Europe and pledged his full efforts if nominated for the Presidency by the Republican Party. Meanwhile Taft and Eisenhower Republicans girded for the preliminary bout. John Foster Dulles, having resigned from the Department, toured the country denouncing a passive policy of "containment," which he attributed to us, and called for a new and activist policy against the "Reds," later known as a policy of "rollback." In early April the President aroused new controversy, and litigation as well, by attempting to seize and operate the steel plants in order to prevent a nationwide strike and interruption of essential war production.†

The mood of Congress in this spring and summer of political turmoil was a curious and unpredictable one. The Japanese peace and security treaties were overwhelmingly ratified by the Senate, as were those with the Philippines and with Australia and New Zealand. Later on, the same quick and impressive approval was given to the agreements I brought back from Bonn. This had a reassuring effect abroad. On the other hand, the McCarran-Walter bill restricting immigration was passed over the President's veto, and the Bricker Amendment restricting the scope of the treaty-making power was strongly pushed by members of Congress and the American Bar Association. The Mutual Security Appropriation Act, carrying the President's request for seven billion nine hundred million dollars and strongly supported by General Eisenhower and by two appearances of mine, was cut in the vital Western European section by one and a half billion dollars. Even with cuts, however, the appropriation exceeded that made in any subsequent year.

Hardest hit by the political revolt in Congress was the whole program to increase international trade by removing national restrictions upon it. In the preceding autumn an amendment had been attached to the Defense Production Act of 1951 restricting agricultural imports by quotas and other devices forbidden by most of our trade agreements. Half of Western Europe as well as Canada, New Zealand, and Australia were up in arms and threatening retaliatory tariffs against our agriculture. In January the Senate rejected an attempt to repeal this short-sighted challenge to a tariff war. In March I wrote to Senator Burnet R. Maybank of South Carolina, chairman of the committee considering an extension of the life of this obnoxious legislation, but without effect. Meanwhile the "escape clause" legislation of the preceding year permitting increased duties in derogation of trade agreements, where the Tariff Commission found that increased imports imperiled domestic interest, further increased apprehension abroad.

The Administration stood staunchly for a liberal trade policy, but the old protectionist Adam was strong in Congress, which slyly and without comprehension of the responsibility of our new creditor position went about reducing imports. Its economics were those of most of its members, country lawyers and big-city politicians. I battled for two-way trade in press conferences, speeches during World Trade Week, in public correspondence with the Italian and British governments, and in Congress against the Battle Act and the Kem Amendment aimed at trade with Eastern Europe and countries trading with that area. However, the spirit of the brave new world that had inspired our Government from the days of wartime lend-lease agreements was on the wane.

During the spring we also made a new attempt to break the ice pack around the Austrian peace treaty.[4] The British and French foreign offices simultaneously with the Department made public a new short version, which we hoped could establish peace and end the occupation, leaving some less important issues for later discussion. For five months the Soviet Union did not deign to notice our proposal, and then merely refused to discuss it. I have often wondered who convinced the foreign offices of Communist countries that bad manners were a basic requirement for the conduct of international relations, Marx or Engels? Whoever did so, it was a great pity.

THE APRIL PILGRIMAGE

Nowhere are Chaucer's words so true as in Washington:

> Whan that Aprille with his shoures sote
> The droghte of Marche hath perced to the rote
>
> * * *
>
> Whan Zephirus eek with his swete breeth
> Inspired hath in every holt and heeth
> The tendre croppes . . .
> Then longen folk to goon on pilgrimages
>
> * * *
>
> And specially from every shires ende
> Of [America], to [Washington] they wende

Not only do school children, in their uncounted busloads, but chiefs of state and heads of government invade the White House itself,

> The holy blisful martir for to seke
> That hem hath holpen, whan that they were seke.

Our exalted visitors in April of 1952 began with Queen Juliana of the Netherlands and Prince Bernhard. That forthright lady addressed a joint session of Congress on April 3, talking to its members like a Dutch aunt. She reminded them that their responsibilities extended beyond their own constituents and country to the whole world—responsibilities, she added, that nobody envied them because of the enormous repercussions of their decisions. "We have never before been so keenly aware," she continued, "that in this world of ours we need cooperation as intimate as that among the cells of one body."[5] This was good doctrine and no one had earned a better right to preach it than the Dutch, who had marched in the forefront of the European and Atlantic movements. But her words did not soften opposition to imports of Dutch cheese. Here fear of constituents exceeded fear of world repercussions.

When the time came in the conventional progression of dinners—the President's, the Queen's, and the Secretary of State's—and it fell to my wife and me to entertain the royal couple at Anderson House, I tried desperately to find something that had not already been said, in the course of the search reading a good many of the Queen's speeches. One of them especially caught my fancy, a speech thanking the Canadian people for their hospitality in receiving her and her children in their exile after Hitler's invasion of 1940. In a moving passage she commended her children to the kindness of her hosts. They would like them, she said; they smiled easily. After dinner in proposing the Queen's health, I said that among her other attainments was one for which in a queen we had to go back four hundred years to the great Elizabeth. This was her command of English prose style, requiring as that did simplicity and directness. I would read a passage and let our guests judge. Our large dinner party applauded heartily.

After we had drunk the toast and while we waited for quiet for the Queen to reply, she seemed distressed and told me that honesty required her to say that she had not written the speech. I pointed out that honesty would be quite out of place in an exchange of courtesies and that at the present time no one supposed that high personages wrote their own speeches. The moment of danger passed without the need of my threatening the return of New York to the Dutch, a penalty out of proportion to the offense.

While in Washington the Queen presented to the American people as a token of gratitude from her own people a carillon, which now stands in the National Cemetery at Arlington near the Marine Corps Memorial. The visit also gave an opportunity for two long talks with my close friend Dirk Stikker, the Dutch Foreign Minister, on a host of matters of common concern to us both in Europe, the Caribbean, the Far East, and the United Nations. No minister was ever so meticulously informed on all matters that fell within the purview of his department as this most able public servant. At this time, too, began the privilege of a friendship with Prince Bernhard, which has continued since and been refreshed by the meetings of the Bilderberg group, inspired and so skillfully chaired by him.

During May we had visits from two other heads of government, Dr. Leopold Figl, the Chancellor of Austria, with Frau Figl, and Prime Minister Robert G. Menzies of Australia. Dr. Figl, the first Austrian Chancellor to visit the United States, insisted that I should be the first American Secretary of State to visit Austria. He pressed this fancy during his visit with such gay persistence that I fell in with it, accepting his kind invitation for the end of June, if business in Bonn, Paris, and Washington could be dispatched in time. My wife and I became much attached to the Figls, Austria, and the Austrians. As head of the Peasant Party, Figl had since 1945 governed through a coalition with the Socialists led by Vice Chancellor Adolf Schaerf, whom I met in March.

The Chancellor, a small, red-headed man with sharp foxlike features and a red mustache, handled the Russian occupation with irrepressible Austrian raillery and stubbornness, which baffled the more phlegmatic Slavs. What could not be prevented Figl did not oppose; but what could be frustrated he and his compatriots proceeded to confuse and bewilder until in many instances the Russians gave up in baffled disgust. For instance, though Austria was occupied by Russian troops in the east, allied in the west, and by all four in Vienna, the Austrian Government's writ ran throughout the country. Only Austrian foreign affairs were controlled by the High Commissioners. When Figl wished to visit his parents' farm in the Soviet zone, the Russians insisted that he have a Russian pass. He refused to recognize any restriction upon the right of the Chancellor of Austria to travel anywhere within the country and tore up their passes. Each time he was stopped, he waited patiently while an officer went to headquarters to obtain permission to let him through. These waits often resulted in impromptu political meetings with a friendly crowd. If the officer returned with a new pass, that would be torn up amid cheers.

The Chancellor's visit was to give our country a chance to show its admiration of the gallant stand he and his fellow citizens were making against stubborn Soviet refusal to end the occupation by a peace treaty, and, conversely, to give him a glimpse of the immensity and power of the United States.

Our friend Bob Menzies, with his Foreign Minister, Percy Spender, later to be Ambassador to the United States and a Judge (and President) of the International Court of Justice at The Hague, stopped off on their way to London for—as much as anything—a long heart-to-heart talk with the President and me. In Australia they felt very far from developments in Europe and North America that were of immense importance to them and very conscious of the hundreds of millions of oriental people to the north of them. Their twelve million people seemed a small drop in that vast ocean of humanity. Menzies wanted to discuss some way in which Australia could participate in discussions of what he referred to as "global strategy," chiefly on the military side. As he saw it, discussions of this sort occurred either in NATO or in the meetings of our own Joint Chiefs of Staff. The first was incorrect. Furthermore, the idea of enlarging the North Atlantic to include the South Atlantic and Pacific and to involve our European partners in Asian problems when European ones seemed too much for them was not a beckoning prospect. The Australians' most cherished idea, to have a direct and permanent relationship between their Chiefs of Staff and ours, was already developing into a serious and embarrassing problem.

During discussion of the Australian-New Zealand-United States security treaty in 1951 this idea had been strongly pressed by our friends. It had been as strongly resisted by our Chiefs of Staff, who found their domestic duties difficult enough. The idea of combining the duties of three general staffs and the command functions of three services in a committee of five men was not, to begin with, a master stroke of organizing genius. Our Joint Chiefs of Staff Committee, which also had to represent the uniformed services in dealing with the Secretary of Defense, the President (the Commander in Chief), and the Congress (the Provider in Chief), had been placed by the NATO Council, with the British and French, on the Standing Group, an executive body established to direct the Supreme Commander Allied Forces Europe. When, therefore, Mr. Dulles informed the Chiefs of the Australian-New Zealand proposal, they broke into such a sustained tantrum of negation that I took it upon myself to withdraw the suggestion. So tactfully, however, did Mr. Dulles communicate its fate to our friends that they received the impression that it was happily on its way through the bureaucracy. With Mr. Dulles hot on the campaign trail against us, I was left to face the moment of truth alone. At the time, the best solution of Australian troubles was to put them off until we had our European ducks in a row. This we did by arranging a full-dress meeting of the Australian-New Zealand-United States (ANZUS) Council in Hawaii in August, when the whole accumulation of woes would be aired.

DISTRACTIONS CROWD IN

While we were struggling with desperate haste to complete preparations for the Bonn meeting, troubles proliferated around us.

Trieste · Trieste made its spring appearance by a de Gasperi speech in London adopting as Italian demands the allied tripartite statement of 1950 wholly unacceptable to Belgrade. A municipal election in the Free Territory increased the agitation. Yugoslavia's Foreign Minister, Edward Kardelj, protested against irresponsible Italian negotiation through "public polemics" and offered to talk with the Italians on the basis either of a division of Trieste or maintaining the Trieste Free Territory. He did not propose to continue making proposals that Rome merely rejected without discussion. I had a good deal of sympathy with his point of view. However, on May 9 the allied negotiations in London granted Italy new authority in the area and later in the month the local elections went in favor of pro-Italian candidates.

Tunisia · In April Tunisia came to an acute international boil, with our poor friend Schuman getting into a progressively more difficult situation. In January Dr. Habib Bourguiba, by far the most moderate of the North African Arab leaders, had announced the breakdown of negotiations with the French and that Tunisia would appeal to the United Nations Security Council. He and other leaders were promptly arrested, whereupon rioting broke out. Again I saw us faced with the same question that had arisen the preceding autumn in the General Assembly over Morocco. Once again French policy would not deal with the problem, but only with trying to prevent discussion of it in the Security Council. We might succeed in keeping the item off the agenda since in the Security Council seven affirmative votes were necessary to inscribe it. Nevertheless, the merits of the issue would be discussed while debating whether to inscribe it.

The real difficulty with the French position was that France had no policy in North Africa except repression and hanging on, as appeared very clearly from a talk with former Prime Minister Paul Reynaud. Her allies, therefore, had a hard time defending her. On March 19, 1952, I called in Henri Bonnet, the French Ambassador, in an attempt to fend off the trouble before it arose, but he would have none of it. He would only repeat that the Tunisian question was a purely French domestic one. In him Gallic logic consisted in stubbornly asserting an erroneous conclusion deduced from an erroneous premise. My plea to the French Government was to release the arrested leaders, and, whether or not they did this, to announce a policy of continued negotiation and devise a negotiable policy. Then their allies could give them effective help. Mere solidarity in denying the Security Council's right to discuss a matter that it would discuss anyway seemed a pretty sterile policy. During Dirk Stikker's visit in Washington in early April I learned that he agreed with this view and had been similarly unsuccessful in attempting to move Schuman to a more positive policy.

Meanwhile, Mrs. Franklin Roosevelt was urging me from our mission at the United Nations not to side with the French attempt to exclude the item from the agenda. She had loyally supported me in Paris in our stand with France on excluding the Moroccan question, but believed that to do the same thing regarding Tunisia in view of no effort by France to advance a solution in either case would do us harm with the Arab-Asian states and increase instability in the area.

In Paris the French Government dug in its heels and resisted. In April the Security Council, after nearly two weeks of discussing all sides of the Tunisian issue, voted on putting it on the agenda. We abstained and the motion failed, with only five affirmative votes. At a press conference on April 16 I pointed out that the mere proposal by anyone at any time of a resolution on any subject could not require the United States to consider and vote upon it. Especially was this true when, as here, we believed that to do so would hinder a solution much better sought by continuance of bilateral negotiations. This won us no acclaim from the French, the Arabs, or our domestic critics, who seemed to believe that a fight was always desirable and always had a right side—theirs. Vice President Barkley used to tell of a constituent who, when asked whom he supported for sheriff, said, "I haven't made up my mind yet; but when I do, I'll be bitter as hell."

Berlin · May also brought us Berlin trouble, a warning to the Germans. Soviet authorities refused allied military patrols access to the Helmstedt-Berlin autobahn, while the East Germans closed many crossing points to East Berlin and interrupted telecommunications. East German Premier Walter Ulbricht took an even more bellicose position, calling for a general strike in West Germany to end rearmament plans and threatening a fratricidal civil war in Germany should Germans in the West be led by the allies to participate in aggressive war. All this led to a final attempt by the Russians at intimidation by a note to Bonn delivered just as we arrived there.

The St. Lawrence Seaway · One of our spring troubles was of our own making. Every American administration since President Wilson's had endorsed the development of the St. Lawrence Seaway and electric power as a joint project with Canada, but American legislative approval had been blocked by a combination of interests—railroads, eastern seaboard ports, coal, eastern grain elevators. Canada, finally wearying of the delay, wished to build the seaway on the Canadian side. We were not unsympathetic with this idea as a method of blasting some of our own obstruction out of the way. Foreign Minister Pearson came from Ottawa to discuss the matter, ending with a long conference with the President, who spoke most appreciatively of Canadian patience and forbearance. He asked for another month of grace to permit the Foreign Relations Committee and the Senate to act on a bill before the committee. My own connection with the legislation dated from my days as Assistant Secretary and Under Secretary, when our chief advocate had been Senator Vandenberg of Michigan. His death had sadly weakened us.

The result of our talks was agreement that the seaway and power development would be a joint Canadian-United States undertaking. Both countries would file applications with the International Joint Commission to permit the power development, while the Canadians would proceed with the seaway at once on their own side of the river. The Senate still remained recalcitrant. The committee reported the bill without recommendation to the Senate, which in mid-June recommitted it by a narrow margin. At once the two governments filed with the International Joint Commission requests for power development in the international-rapids section of the river, the seaway to be built by Canada alone. The application was granted in October. The opponents of the seaway had maneuvered themselves and their compatriots into a thoroughly untenable position from which later on, after we had left office, they had to extricate themselves. Some of us were uncharitable enough to find pleasure in their unhappiness.

SPRING THAW IN BONN

The central theme of our thought and work in the spring of 1952 was the negotiation in Bonn, conducted through and among the High Commissioners and Adenauer, to bring to fruition the contractual arrangement with Germany and the group-of-six discussion in Paris to conclude the European Defense Community. All the rest was obbligato. In the three months between the London and Bonn meetings a vast amount of work was done; issues were debated and agreements reached. It was a period not only of settling differences but of growth of understanding. In his final report High Commissioner McCloy put it this way: "The final conventions bear little resemblance to those which were initially proposed, and the differences are primarily due to Allied concessions to the German negotiators and to Allied recognition that in the new relationship the Federal Republic was justified in demanding full equality."[6] McCloy with great energy pushed the discussions in Bonn. He and the old Chancellor were inexhaustible, often wearing down argumentative colleagues and staff members to agreement as dawn broke over the Rhine. Ambassador Dunn followed the European Defense Community discussions in Paris, keeping us informed and putting forward our suggestions for breaking deadlocks.

The major problems that remained after Lisbon were of two general types —those of high policy and those that, while involving policy, also involved vast and complicated detail. Of the first type, so far as the contractual arrangement was concerned, were the extent of allied reserved power to declare an emergency and resume authority in Germany and the extent to which a future all-German government should or could be bound by the present government; of the latter type, the division of the German defense budget between German military effort and allied troop support, and the review of items that might properly be charged to German support of allied troops stationed there. Lesser but still troublesome questions concerned an amnesty policy for war crimes and the period of preferential tax treatment for allied businesses in Germany.

In the European Defense Community discussions the insistent French demand for guarantees against German secession remained a major problem for the ministers. It represented the accumulation of all the French Government's neuroses—fear of inflation, of German economic recovery and domination of the Community, of the outcome in Indochina and North Africa, of French Communists on the left and General de Gaulle on the right, and of Moscow's "golden apple" policy, which appealed to both left and right. All these fears produced hesitation, suspicion, second thoughts, and, almost inevitably, irritation with the United States. We were the main force, as they saw it, behind their troubles, or most of them—behind the drive for European defense and the emancipation of Germany, behind impatience with stand-patism in North Africa and Indochina, behind their own ideas, which they were beginning to re-examine, of integration and supranationalism in Europe.

Two matters in particular stimulated French annoyance. It will be recalled that Faure resigned when his cabinet refused to support the taxes necessary to finance his ambitious military budget. Pinay, who succeeded him, retained the budget but not the tax program. In looking for funds for military needs, he found increased American aid an alluring solution, and proposed another half billion dollars over the next three years in addition to the six hundred million for 1950. Since in addition to that we had also assumed about a quarter of the cost of the French war in Indochina, we were able to find only a third of the new request. The French, arguing that they had taken on more than Harriman's Temporary Council Committee had recommended, believed that unwillingness to give all the help they asked amounted to "a raw deal." They also freely stated that our "meddling in Tunisia," already mentioned, was unhelpful. Nevertheless, the European Defense Community treaty was initialed in May, although the French Cabinet on May 22 voted to require a guarantee against German secession from the Community as a condition to French signature of the contractual arrangement with Germany.

In this negotiation, as in its Paris counterpart, progress while substantial had not been smooth. Adenauer characteristically had provoked trouble, then overridden it. At the end of April he informed the coalition parties of the state of the negotiations, hailing the progress made in securing equality of treatment for Germany, and proposed to conclude the discussions and sign the document in time for consideration by the United States Senate before its final adjournment, scheduled for July. This produced a storm of protest from the Bundestag, which claimed that its members were being asked to approve complicated and far-reaching measures "at five minutes before twelve." Two leading supporters of the Chancellor, Dr. Heinrich von Brentano, later Foreign Minister, and Dr. Franz Blücher, made public a letter demanding postponement of the signature to allow for careful re-examination by the Bundestag. This would have thrown United States legislative consideration into a new Congress and a new administration. Moreover, the Bundestag voted against the principle of a German defense contribution.

The Chancellor, however, only intensified his drive toward signature, skillfully using the opposition of the Bundestag to extract a few more concessions from the High Commissioners. After a week of night sessions the High Commissioners started redrafting in mid-May. Then work was begun on the vexed question of the amount of the defense contribution to be allocated to allied troop support. This had been exacerbated by unusually high occupation costs for March in a drive to clean up past accounts. A three-man team was sent over from Washington with power to act and the issue was prepared for ministerial action. Finally, a Social Democratic attempt to stage a long debate was beaten and opposition in the Bundestag subsided as quickly as it had arisen.

At last, the nightmarish weeks of being held immovable by difficulties as the clock ticked away the time for action came to an end. When on the afternoon of May 22 the President saw us off on the *Independence* for Cologne and Bonn—in those days via a refueling stop in Canada—the bulk of our delegation had gone ahead. My wife, Ambassador and Mrs. Philip C. Jessup, Assistant Secretary George Perkins, and my assistants, Luke Battle and Barbara Evans, went with me. This mission, the culmination of the effort launched at London and Paris, was to be the most critical one of my tenure of office.

67. BONN AND PARIS

ON FRIDAY AFTERNOON, May 23, 1952, the ministers met at Bad Godesberg, a suburb of Bonn. Schuman and Eden had come directly from a meeting of the Council of Europe at Strasbourg. A briefing session that evening with McCloy's staff instructed me on the issues that remained for the ministers to resolve before the contractual agreements could be agreed and signed.† Our meetings would be held in the conference rooms of the American chancery as the most adequate allied quarters, and I would act as chairman. This arrangement made available as staff McCloy's group, which had by far the best organization and knowledge of the material to be discussed.

Promptly the next morning the ministers met in tripartite session, joined by the High Commissioners, and, with interludes for lunch and dinner together and for a four-power meeting in the afternoon, they remained in session until the early hours of Sunday. The atmosphere of these meetings is best given in a personal cable to the President sent on May 26:

Since I had said good-bye to him on Thursday, we had gone through greater emotions than any mystery story could provide. The unusual thing about this thriller was that the villain changed his identity. Prior to my departure from Washington the complications had stemmed principally from the Dutch. As he knew, they were practical and traditionally turned toward the sea and the world rather than the continent at their back. They were forever afraid that membership in the European Defense Community would reduce the aid which they expected to receive from us. Their hesitations had been an unending series, the last one of which was their demand that they be able to withdraw from the Community if NATO were dissolved before the fifty-year term of the EDC. While this sounded reasonable, it reflected a fundamental cleavage, as the French, Germans, and Italians were going into this undertaking with the idea that it was permanent and felt that any doubt about permanence would prevent treaty provisions leading to permanence.

Two days before at Strasbourg agreement (it was not perfect, but it was agreed to by all) had been reached by the foreign ministers of the EDC countries on this point: if, before the end of the fifty-year term of the Community, NATO should be dissolved or Britain or we should withdraw from it, the EDC countries would consult as to what to do. I believed that all this was largely theoretical, because seventeen years hence either the European Defense Community would be strong and vital, and no component would wish to withdraw, or else long before then it would have received the kiss of death.

When I got to Bonn, I told the President, French problems took the place of Dutch. The French could not quite believe that Germany's perspective had fundamentally changed, and the present government of Pinay was definitely more traditionally minded than its immediate predecessors.

We had heard, I continued, just before my departure that the French would not sign unless satisfied about many points. Most of these could be reduced to their fear of being outdistanced by their German neighbors and by such things as their burden in Indochina and maintaining their position in North Africa. These fears crystallized into: What could the United States and Britain do to guarantee France against German secession from the EDC? It was only because of the President's personal approval of our counterproposal the evening before that they had gone along.

In conclusion, I stressed that Eden had been most cooperative and had helped much in overcoming both Schuman's and French difficulties. Adenauer, although a good and patriotic bargainer, had revealed himself again as a European statesman, knowing when it was essential to compromise to save a possibly great future from the threat of present difficulties of detail.

The visible presence of French disquiet lay in Schuman's changed mien. In London and Lisbon he had obviously not been in assured command of French foreign policy. In Bonn he seemed not even to be in control of his own ministry and was obviously tired, nervous, and depressed. On Sunday Adenauer said to me, "Can't you give some confidence to our poor friend?" Adenauer himself needed no such help.

Major Prerequisites to Final Agreement • A good many questions in the numerous and complicated documents that ended the occupation and brought Germany into the defense of Europe required the final decision of the ministers. In most of these the various national staffs (and to some extent the High Commissioners) had acquired such vested interest and pride in divergent positions that compromise was difficult for them. Here the need was for decision. The ministers listened to statements of the issues and summaries of the arguments. As chairman I would propose a decision; my colleagues would amend or agree, or sometimes one would withdraw his staff's objection. In this way we covered a great deal of ground. However, four matters required national negotiation at the top. It was by no means a foregone conclusion that agreement could be successfully accomplished on at least two of them—those relating to guarantees to the European Defense Community by Britain and the United States; the third related to the division of the German defense budget and the last to the binding effect of the agreements on a future all-German government.

The matter of the guarantees was reached Saturday night and continued far into the early hours of Sunday morning. We had already worked out with the Germans an exchange of treaty agreements among the signatories of the North Atlantic and the European defense treaties (who were the same except for Germany in the latter) by which each extended to the others the obligations of Article 5 of the North Atlantic Treaty (to treat an attack on one as an attack on all). This bound Germany into the common defense bond. But, as we have seen, the French wanted more, a guarantee by Britain and the United States against German withdrawal. Eden was ready to negotiate a treaty with France on the matter, but in discussions with the President before leaving for Europe, we had concluded that such negotiation was impossible for his dying administration and to attempt it might throw the whole effort we had worked on so long into the uncertainties of a new administration in 1953. We determined that on this matter we could go no further than the existing legislation permitted.

A suggestion by Philip Jessup, which the President approved, offered an escape from a dangerous impasse. Article 4 of the North Atlantic Treaty bound its members to consult together should one or more believe its security to be threatened in order to find means to remove the threat. The Jessup suggestion was for a tripartite declaration by Britain, France, and the United States reciting the reasons why the three governments had "an abiding interest in the effectiveness of the [EDC] treaty and in the strength and integrity of that community." Then came the operative sentences: "Accordingly, if any action from whatever quarter threatens the integrity or unity of the Community, the two governments will regard this as a threat to their own security. They will act in accordance with Article 4 of the North Atlantic Treaty." It ended with a reference to our expressed resolve to station forces in Europe, including Germany, as might be appropriate to the defense of the area having regard to our obligations under the North Atlantic Treaty and our interest in the Defense Community.

This proposal we held in reserve, knowing that whatever we offered the French would want more. When I put it forward, Eden picked it up with great enthusiasm, telling Schuman what a great success he had had. If he would make the most of it instead of picking flaws in it, his own position and French morale would both have a lift. The proposal was cabled to Paris. While we waited, we took up other points. The evening wore on. Paris at last replied, wishing to leave out the reference to Article 4, calling for consultation, and saying merely that in event of any threat to the integrity or unity of the Community the two governments would act in accordance with the treaty. This change, I pointed out, would give (as it was intended to do) the impression that they would regard any threat to the integrity of the Community as an attack on themselves and would cause infinite trouble when the Senate came to ratify the exchange of guarantees between the two treaty groups. As the debate continued, with Hervé Alphand leading for the French, Robert Schuman kept going to sleep. Messages flew back and forth to Paris. Finally, with minor changes, our proposal was accepted and the largest obstacle overcome.

The next morning an early meeting with von Brentano and some of his colleagues from the foreign relations committee of the Bundestag found an escape from the theoretical problem that bothered them. They thought that an attempt to bind a future and as yet nonexistent all-German government was both impossible and wrong. I suggested avoiding the problem by having the present Federal Republic Government agree that it would not join in creating and transferring its power to any new government that did not agree to assume and abide by the international obligations of the Federal Republic. This happily resolved another source of difficulty.

At this point the Soviet Union, with a clumsiness to which it was more prone then than now, aided us greatly with German opinion. In West Germany, and especially among the Social Democrats, opposition to the contractual agreements, passionately voiced by Schumacher, grew out of the powers reserved by the allies because of the division of Germany, the Soviet occupation of the eastern zone, and the precarious position of Berlin. When, on May 25, Moscow delivered to Bonn a bullying, threatening note aimed at frightening the Germans away from completing any of the agreeements under negotiation, it had quite the opposite effect. Almost before our eyes we saw German opinion solidified behind Adenauer, the reservation of allied powers abundantly justified, and the contractual agreements acclaimed. We were fortunate in our opponent.

The final meeting of the four was scheduled for Sunday morning, but weariness had adjourned the night session of the three before they had come to agreement among themselves. Our meeting with Adenauer was put off first until after lunch, then until four o'clock. Meanwhile time was running out. When we did meet, Adenauer made final agreements possible. He silenced his advisers and took over the discussion himself, making decisions without further consultation. The German defense contribution and its division were agreed, and he and I worked out the problem of the future all-German government's obligations, which the others accepted. A dozen or more difficult but unimportant problems were decided on the spot without further argument. The spur of the Soviet note was having a most beneficial effect. Our meeting adjourned in time to dress for a large and gala dinner given by the Chancellor in the Palais Schaumburg, the former residence of the Archbishop of Cologne, and later of the Kaiser's sister, situated on the bluff overlooking the Rhine.

After dinner the scene took on the gay and somewhat bizarre aspect of one from a Viennese comic opera. The company had come out from dinner upon a large stone terrace from which semicircular steps gave upon the lawn. The river reflected moonlight through openings in the border of trees. A German choral society sang at the bottom of the steps, its leader conducting from the top. My wife nudged me.

"Watch!" she said. "A scene from *The Student Prince at Bonn*. A conspirator approaches the old and faithful minister. Soon he will come bearing messages. A naïve novice from America must beware of him." Hervé Alphand was talking into Schuman's ear, received an instruction, and after a look around started in Anthony Eden's direction. We decided to play hide-and-seek with him among the guests and waiters. A moment with Eden, then he made for me as we wandered into more populous areas. At last he ran us to earth and delivered a message I have long since forgotten. The choral group sang on unaware that high diplomatic exchanges were taking place before their upturned faces.

Monday morning, May 26, was the time set to sign the considerable number of documents that made up the contractual agreements. The Social Demo-

crats in the Bundestag had planned to boycott the signing ceremonies, but overnight the Russian note had turned German opinion strongly in favor of the new
step toward closer ties with the West, and the bulk of them attended. We were
not certain that some last-minute hitch would not occur in Paris. It was a relief
to see Schuman appear smiling and relaxed. The signing took place in the room
where the Bundesrat, the German senate, met, the glass side of which opened
upon stands filled with spectators. Each minister in turn took his place at a
small table covered with gray velvet and signed several master copies of the
documents as attendants produced them.[1]

When we had finished, each of us spoke briefly. By our acts, I said, the
Federal Republic attained "the independence in foreign affairs and authority
in domestic matters which befit a free state." The other free nations were now
joined by "a new partner in their great effort to establish peace and security in
the world. . . . On behalf of the President of the United States and the American
people, I welcome the Federal Republic on its return to the community of nations."[2] Then I sent a cable to the President, already mentioned, telling him that
the agreement between Germans and the three allies had been signed. As of yesterday this agreement had seemed hardly possible. I thought we had reason to
be pleased for we had now completed successfully another phase in our policy,
which was containment of the new threat with the cooperation of our former
enemy. While the EDC was not yet signed, that was pure formality.

After lunching with the Chancellor, we all took off for Paris to complete
that formality.

APPREHENSION IN PARIS

All the problems attendant upon the negotiation of the European Defense
Community had now been worked out. Unfortunately, though we did not
realize it at the time, those which ultimately blocked French ratification of it
had not. All that remained for the present was to sign it and the appurtenant
documents—nineteen altogether. This ceremony took place in the Clock Room
at the Quai d'Orsay. Eden and I sat at either end of a long table with representatives of the other NATO nations along one side and a horde of photographers
and newsreel men behind ropes on the other. After the signing, full of hope and
elation, I expressed ". . . my profound conviction that what we have witnessed
today may well prove to be one of the most important and most far reaching
events of our lifetime. . . . We have seen the beginning of the realization of an
ancient dream—the unity of the free peoples of Western Europe."[3]

Brave words! And, in part, true, but spoken without reckoning on the ebb
tide in France and the future roles of M. Mendès-France and General Charles
de Gaulle. The apprehension in Paris began to appear as soon as the signing
was over. The next day it was manifest first in a long morning meeting with
Eden and Schuman devoted to the last Russian note and the French position in
Indochina. The meeting was attended by the Premier, Antoine Pinay, and three
former premiers of France—Henri Queuille, René Pleven, and Robert Schuman—as well as the Minister of France Overseas, Jean Letourneau, and a

number of important figures in the Quai d'Orsay. The first subject was soon disposed of as a weak effort, on which we concerted our reply to be coordinated with Adenauer through the High Commissioners, soon to become ambassadors. The French then made a long and rather disheartened statement on their troubles in Indochina, with undertones suggesting that their efforts were unappreciated. Eden and I stressed our belief that they were as fully in the general interest as the British stand in Suez and Malaya and ours in Korea. I added that we had already given very considerable aid to the creation of the Vietnamese National Army and would discuss increasing this aid when Letourneau paid his expected visit to Washington.

Should we not, I asked, all consider together, in advance of the event, our course should the Chinese Communists take a more active role in Indochina? It would be better, if possible, to prevent this rather than to wait to resist it. Also, we should each be clear on what each would do, both politically and militarily. The United States, for instance, would not contribute ground forces to a war in Indochina, but we would consider with our allies air and naval participation if it was considered necessary to interrupt communication between China and Indochina. The prerequisite to planning was a French political and military policy that her allies could help toward success. None was ever provided.

In the afternoon we met again at French request to hear the complaints regarding the attitude of the Administration, the Congress, and the press in the United States toward French policy and conduct in North Africa. Pinay pronounced the indictment with passion and clarity. In a word, our failure as a government to stand firmly and staunchly beside France in denouncing United Nations discussion of her internal affairs encouraged its continuance, while the sympathetic attitude toward Arab complaints voiced in press and congressional discussion—all this despite everything France had done to grant us air bases in North Africa—inflamed them. Wishing to get the whole subject fully exposed before replying, I encouraged all our French friends to speak at length, holding nothing back. They fully enjoyed complying and disclosed—while also easing —a good deal of pent-up resentment in the process.

Although the chance was small that reason could reach the heart of this highly emotional problem, I was determined to have a try at it. To begin with, I said, we should raise frankly and dispose of an unspoken suspicion, which one did not need to dig deeply to find, that the United States did not wish to strengthen but on the contrary would like to replace French influence in Africa. This was totally untrue. I wished to make this unmistakably clear. We believed that France had contributed vastly to North Africa and had more to contribute. While many Americans criticized French policy, no one wished to supersede France in Africa or to eliminate her influence. I insisted upon this point fully and frankly and, whether or not my hearers were convinced, they accepted it.

Even such intelligent Frenchmen as my present hearers, I continued, seemed to believe that criticism of French policy in North Africa by American and congressional opinion was inspired and even guided by the American Government. This showed vast ignorance of our society. Even when the Government desperately wished to guide opinion, as in the case of the Marshall Plan and the North Atlantic Treaty, it required colossal effort and large privately organized participation to do so. On one subject, however, private American opinion needed no guidance and had been historically consistent and vigorous —its tradition of sympathy for any people who alleged that they were oppressed by any other people. This was the heart of our anticolonialism and it made little difference whether or not the allegedly oppressed were, in fact, oppressed. A prima facie case was made out if they were of a different race or color from those complained against.

My foreign friends protested that this was irresponsible opinion, to which I agreed, adding that most opinion was both irresponsible and ignorant, although, on the whole, the American public was better informed by their press and radio than most. For instance, I asked, how many French ministers present knew that in Puerto Rico we had the problem of moving from a colonial relationship to something else and in what direction we were moving? No one knew.

Another attitude of Americans that entered into the problem we were discussing was that they believed nothing should be regarded as immune from discussion. They had no reticences and suspected that those who had were covering up something that would not bear examination. This included the private lives of public people. As a result, the prime defense of the French in the United Nations—that French North African problems were internal matters and could not be discussed—was to most Americans a confession of guilt. To them talk was not interference; everyone at home and abroad talked about our problems—divorce, crime waves, race relations.

Perhaps, I concluded, the Americans, as pictured, appeared as interfering, nosy people whom the French would do well to regard with distaste. However, before reaching this conclusion, we might examine another characteristic, which —aside from our usefulness in repeatedly coming to the rescue of our friends— might commend us. Almost as deep-seated as our sympathy for the underdog had been our sympathy for the constructive as opposed to a destructive approach to any problem. To be "constructive" was one of our highest accolades. I urged my hearers to ponder the implications of this attitude. The French policy of silence on the issues in North Africa, of negative acts like the arrest of the Tunisian leaders, could never bring a sympathetic response in America. But if the French side were the proposer of solutions and others assumed the negative role of objecting, picking flaws, dragging feet, the French would have seized the constructive position with its strong claim to sympathy.

Pinay was quick to pick me up. We would issue a joint communiqué, he said, in which the United States would support the role of France in North Africa and a plan for the settlement of outstanding issues there, which the French Government was even then devising. I escaped the formal statement by pleading the greater wisdom of seeing the plan before endorsing it, but the substance of the idea was promptly leaked to the always-eager French press. My intentions were good but French official understanding of the American mind continued as remote as the development of a practicable French policy for

North Africa. Only René Pleven seemed impressed. When we adjourned for tea, he observed that if he ever ran into trouble with law and was guilty as charged, he would wish to retain me as his advocate.

The note of pain and strain was echoed from the Elysée, where I called at President Auriol's request. He and Mme. Auriol had been very kind and friendly to my wife and me during our many visits to Paris. On this occasion I found him passionately and dramatically disturbed as he received me in his private study, alone save for his private interpreter. What had I done, he asked tragically, mistaking the real danger in Europe and leading Schuman into the dreadful error of rearming Germany? For an hour he reviewed the unchanging menace of Germany. I was argued-out for the day. After suggesting the absence of any helpful alternative to an attempt to reform and change our former enemy into an ally and being told that to revive the triple entente and add the United States to it would suffice, I went wearily back to the embassy residence for dinner with the Dunns.

The last day in Paris was devoted to a final go-around with the French on their budgetary and financial trouble, which the miracle drug of "off-shore procurement" (the official jargon for American purchase in France of military items for them and other allies) was supposed to cure. As usual it was confusing, but, I hoped, did not add to the existing confusion, or not much. Then, really exhausted, we took off for Washington. There our elation lasted a little longer. I presented for ratification by the Senate the documents signed in Europe. The hearings and debate went easily, though the political conventions to nominate candidates for the Presidency impended. The Senate came through magnificently, ratifying on July 1 the Bonn convention by a vote of 77 to 5 and the protocol to the North Atlantic Treaty by 72 to 5. The past six months had been for us a successful period, most happily complementing the preceding autumn's triumph of the Japanese peace treaty.

We still fought on in Korea.

68. KOREA: FRUSTRATION, RIOT, AND REVOLT

WHILE WE IN Washington were concentrating on the crisis in NATO, another first-class crisis had built up in Korea and burst upon General Ridgway just as he had been ordered to turn over the Far Eastern Command to General Mark Clark and take over General Eisenhower's command in Europe. As we have seen, in the last quarter of 1951 military action in Korea tapered off, reducing casualties progressively and drastically. General Ridgway took advantage of the lull to clean up the troublesome jetsam of the Communist retreat which had been left in the rear of the Eighth Army. By January 1952 nineteen thousand stragglers and guerrillas were killed or rounded up and the problem pretty well solved.

As the year began, General Ridgway was dug in on the Kansas line largely north of the parallel, the enemy facing him in an equally strong position. The armistice talks had stalled after agreement on the battle line of November 27, 1951, as the armistice line should an armistice be concluded within a month, which did not occur. The fallback arrangement then came into effect, which provided that the battle line on the date of the armistice, whatever and whenever that might be, would be the demarcation line. General Ridgway quotes with approval General Clark's summary of the military situation: " 'We never had enough men [to clear the Chinese out of Korea], whereas the enemy had sufficient manpower not only to block our offensives, but to make and hold small gains of his own. To have pushed it to a successful conclusion would have required more trained divisions and more supporting air and naval forces, would have incurred heavy casualties, and would have necessitated lifting our self-imposed ban on attacks on the enemy sanctuary north of the Yalu.' "

To this statement General Ridgway has added that "lifting that ban would have laid Japan open to attack and, if that had happened, would have greatly and immediately widened the war. No responsible leader in the United States at that time could have sold such a course to the American public."[1] Or, I might add, desired to do so. Furthermore, statements made in the press in recent years that commanders in the field (Van Fleet has been mentioned) urged heavy offensives only to be turned down in Washington are not true. The field and home commands were united on political and military policy.

The charge has been made that the military strategy carried out by Generals Ridgway and Clark of maintaining a strong defensive position by active tactical operations prolonged the war and greatly increased the casualties over the prior offensive period. That it prolonged the war is a purely argumentative assertion unsupported by any responsible military opinion of the period. There was no sensible alternative. Regarding casualties, however, the charge is provably erroneous. The Korean war was fought for a month and two days over three years. Armistice discussions began at the end of the first year—the year of the longest continued heavy fighting—and continued, off and on, for two years. United States casualty figures—which are the only accurate ones—were as follows:

	June 1950–June 1951 (*inclusive*)	*July 1951–July 1953* (*inclusive*)
Killed	21,300	12,300
Wounded	53,100	50,200
Missing or captured	4,400	700
TOTAL	78,800	63,200

Thus the total figures for the next two years were less than for the first year alone. More than one-quarter of the casualties occurred during the last two months of the war, when the Communists put on two heavy offensives to try to get better terms from President Eisenhower than President Truman would give them. Their own losses for these two months have been calculated at 108,458. In the end the terms were exactly the same.[2]

VOLUNTARY REPATRIATION OF PRISONERS

The prisoners of war whom our forces had captured in Korea presented two problems of which we were aware and one that took us by surprise. The first was where to put so many prisoners—as many as 170,000 at one point—in a country where it was not possible to get very far from the battlefront. The second was determining the composition of the mass. How many of the prisoners were Chinese and what kind of Chinese—Communists or captured and impressed Nationalists? How many were North Koreans and collaborating South Koreans or captured and impressed southerners, soldiers and civilians? The third problem was a plot, early put into preparation by the enemy, to stir up revolt among this, to them, expendable mass to the propaganda disadvantage of the United States.

The first problem was thought solved by putting the prisoners in cantonments on the small and wholly inadequate island of Koje-do, where they soon became greatly overcrowded and got out of the control of the small and largely incompetent personnel detailed for the unpromising and disagreeable duty. The enemy resolved their problem by reducing their prisoner list from 65,000 to 11,559 by means of prisoners allegedly "released at the front" and re-enlisted in the North Korean forces, like the mass conversions practiced by the knights of the Teutonic Order in the fourteenth century. The task of classification began in deceptive calmness. Thirty-seven thousand were found to be South Koreans and were later released. In the process of screening, however, both sides became aware of broader problems. On our side, we saw ourselves confronted again with the horrors encountered in Europe in 1945 when large numbers of Soviet civilians and Soviet soldiers who had deserted to the Germans and been recaptured by the allies committed suicide as they were being forcibly repatriated. The Communists on their side were determined never to open wide the invitation to desertion and escape that voluntary repatriation presented.

Not only did the matter precipitate a deep issue between the two sides, but also one between the State and Defense departments. The military were, understandably enough, primarily concerned with getting back their own men (a much smaller number) at the end of the fighting. They had been properly interested in separating out of the prisoner pens those of our own Korean allies who had been swept up in the confusion of war. But to insure the return of our enemy-held prisoners, the Pentagon favored the return of North Korean and Chinese prisoners and civilian internees regardless of their wishes. While no final position was taken within our government for several months, Admiral Ruthven E. Libby was instructed to put forward a proposal at Panmunjom on January 2, 1952, by which all prisoners should be released under equitable terms providing for voluntary repatriation as determined by an impartial organ such as the International Committee of the Red Cross. South Korean soldiers and civilians captured, whether or not incorporated in the North Korean armies, should be released and allowed to return home.

The proposal was immediately rejected and a violent propaganda war launched, enhanced by lurid Communist charges of germ warfare practices employed by the Americans against North Korea and China. The debate in Washington went through several stages. My colleagues and I were moved by humanitarian reasons and by the effect upon our own and Asian peoples of the forcible repatriation of prisoners whose lives would be jeopardized. We were also aware of the deterrent effect upon the Communists of the escape offered to their soldiers by falling into our hands.

When our military colleagues argued that the Communists would never agree to voluntary repatriation, thus blocking an armistice, which we both believed to be in our interest, we suggested following the example of our enemies. This would mean finding out which prisoners would forcibly resist repatriation, releasing them at some appropriate time and then offering to exchange the rest. Even then a serious problem would remain—what to do with the non-Koreans who refused repatriation. In the meantime our proposal lent another argument to the urgent need for a screening and classification of the prisoners. At this point Senator Jenner of Indiana, who had been contemplating a Senate resolution on this complex subject, was dissuaded by the invaluable efforts of Secretary of Defense Lovett and a group of senators from hopelessly prejudicing General Ridgway's negotiations.

At the end of February a series of meetings with the President, in which the top civilian officers of Defense did not oppose State, resulted in his decision that the United States would not and could not agree to forcible repatriation. Thus we took our basic position, from which we never afterward wavered. The execution of the decision did not proceed as planned. Circumstances unforeseen and embarrassing intruded.

At this stage in the negotiations at Panmunjom we were hopeful that only three major obstacles stood in the way of concluding an armistice. The fighting had died down; it was agreed that the armistice line should be drawn at about that held by the forces when the armistice was signed; and a good many other arrangements had been worked out. The prisoner-of-war issue, our insistence that airfields in North Korea not be repaired or new ones constructed, and the composition of the armistice-supervising commission remained. Our plan, developed by mid-March, was to screen the prisoners and to trade off the first two issues—voluntary repatriation to be accepted by them and repair of airfields by us. The two sides were theoretically agreed on an impartial commission, but by impartial they meant noncombatant—specifically, they wanted the Soviet Union a member—while we meant neutral. One solution for this was to have a really neutral commission or, if they chose, a really bipartisan one with both the United States and the USSR and some real neutral like the Swiss. General Ridgway, fearing retaliation against our captive men, preferred to continue the effort for agreed screening. In the course of this our negotiators made an unfortunate guess, communicated to the other side, that 116,000 of the 130,000 or more prisoners held by the UN Command would be repatriated. Early in April the Communists agreed to screening by both sides. We seemed to be making progress.

By mid-April a disconcerting report came in from General Ridgway. At the time of the movement to Koje-do, prisoners of South Korean origin were separated from North Koreans. This produced camps predominantly and violently (but not unanimously) anti-Communist and pro-Communist. In February trouble between South Korean guards and internees in a civilian compound had begun over screening, resulting in seventy-seven prisoner fatalities. Again in March twelve prisoners were killed. General Ridgway now reported that 37,000 prisoners in seven of the seventeen compounds could not be screened without the use of force. The Communists reported 12,000 prisoners—7,900 Korean, 4,100 non-Korean—willing to return. It was a rough estimate, then, that the UN Command gave: 70,000 could be repatriated without force—5,100 Chinese and 64,900 Koreans. The rest could not be.

REVOLT IN THE COMPOUNDS

When our figures were reported to the Communists, they were greeted by violent and angry outbursts, charges of bad faith, refusal of neutral screening, and increased disorder in the compounds. It had become clear that this disorder was directly controlled from Panmunjom by messengers surrendering to our forces for the purpose of bringing orders and by concerted action arranged through conferences in the prisoners' hospitals and by other means. On May 7, the day before open plenary sessions were resumed at Panmunjom with the prisoner issue now the outstanding one left, Brigadier General Francis T. Dodd, inadequately attended, entered POW Camp No. 1 to negotiate with the prisoners and was himself taken prisoner and held as hostage for the satisfaction of their demands. After the earlier riots and again on May 5, General Ridgway had ordered, without results, that discipline be restored in the camps. He was due to leave within the week for his NATO command, where I was to meet him in three weeks' time.

Faced with this new insurgency, Ridgway ordered that the camps be entered immediately and discipline restored. Although forces were assembled, no action was taken. General Dodd was released on the eleventh after his successor, Brigadier General Charles F. Colson, had accepted the humiliating terms negotiated by Dodd. General Mark Clark promptly repudiated the agreement, relieved both Dodd and Colson with recommendation that they be demoted, and renewed General Ridgway's orders. On June 10 our troops entered the camps and, after a pitched battle in which thirty-one prisoners and one American soldier were killed, began the re-establishment of control. The prisoners were redivided, separating the pro-Communist and anti-Communist and ending the overcrowding by sending many to new camps elsewhere. With the exception of an attempted break-out in one camp in December, in which eighty-five were killed and a hundred hospitalized, trouble within the prisoner-of-war camps ended.

This bungled military operation in the field, like General MacArthur's disastrous advance to the Yalu, shook our allies' faith in the good judgment and competence of our command, creating doubt of our ability to furnish leadership in the great affairs where it had been entrusted to us. I felt this dubiety in May when I reached Europe. We had not yet restored order in the prisoners' camps and the fury of the propaganda campaign against us, to which we had so generously contributed, continued unabated. I was to feel it again in the autumn, when the return of the prisoners would become the principal question before the General Assembly.

Senator Russell of Georgia, Chairman of the Armed Services Committee, suggested to the President that to reassure foreign opinion of the good faith of our conduct toward the prisoners a military commission from neutral nations—he mentioned India, Indonesia, and Pakistan—be asked to observe our treatment of the prisoners. The President approved, added Sweden and Switzerland to the list, and asked Secretary Lovett to invite the inquiry. This was one of the very few instances when the President did not consult me on a matter of foreign policy. I heard of it over the radio and immediately warned him that the invitation would be declined. India and Indonesia backed away from the idea, and after a week or two it was permitted to fade out.

Before I went to Europe at the end of May, my colleagues in the Department, in discussions with their British associates, had come to believe that Chinese intentions about the prisoner issue might be profitably probed by the Indian Government through Ambassador Panikkar in Peking. To my mind the operation would be more likely to produce confusion from misinformation and imprecise ideas, but I agreed to speak to Eden about it. He favored it and our offices cooperated in the effort. As it came to nothing, no purpose would be served in following the labyrinthine course beyond noting an idea evolved by the Indians, which was to cause us trouble later in the autumn of 1952 during the maneuvering and negotiations at the General Assembly. This was to conclude an armistice on the basis of exchanging all the prisoners who would not forcibly resist repatriation and merely hold the rest for further negotiation. Both Defense and State rejected this nonsolution. It would, we believed, put a great strain on a fragile armistice and unconscionable pressure on the prisoners held in limbo.

When at the end of the summer private and public discussion of the prisoner issue had involved it in confusion and obscurity, the United Nations Command restated its proposal to cut through semantics and propaganda to reality. Three alternative proposals were put forward. Under the first, as soon as an armistice agreement went into effect all prisoners of war on either side would be entitled to release and repatriation. To give effect to this right they were to be brought in an orderly and manageable manner to an exchange point in the demilitarized zone and there identified and checked off against a list. Those not resisting repatriation were to be expeditiously exchanged. The others would be taken from the zone and released. Under the second, those who had indicated to the United Nations Command that they would forcibly resist repatriation would be entirely freed from military control of either side and interviewed by representatives of countries not participating in the Korean hostilities and freed to go to the side of their choice as then indicated. Under the third, nonrepatriates would be freed in the demilitarized zones to go where they chose.

Such was our position as we entered the session of the United Nations General Assembly beginning in mid-October 1952.

BOMBING BOTHERS BRITAIN

As already mentioned, fighting on the ground died down in 1952, with an occasional flare-up. Old Baldy was won in the summer and lost and won again in September. The Communist attack on White Horse Hill failed in October, as did ours at Snipers' Ridge and Triangle Hill. At year's end the stalemate continued. But an enemy buildup was continuing, which Operation Strangle, an air campaign, had not at midyear been able to check. It was decided, therefore, within the Government to step up Operation Strangle.

At just this time Lord Alexander, Minister of Defense, and Selwyn Lloyd, Eden's deputy, were returning via Washington from a scouting mission to Korea. They had asked for a senior British officer on General Clark's staff to keep them better informed, to which we would agree, and a representative at Panmunjom, which we would refuse. While they were conferring with Secretary Lovett and General Bradley, the United Nations air and naval forces, in the largest combined air operations of the war, bombed power installations in North Korea on June 23 and 24, 1952. The largest plant hit was at Suiho on the Yalu, supplying both North Korea and Manchuria. Although this plant had been spared in prior bombing of power plants because it had been dismantled, it had been put back into operation and was supplying the Manchurian airfields. The attack on it, asked for by General Clark, had been widely cleared, including with me, and no objections had been interposed. A storm broke at once, and nowhere more violently than in London and in the Commons on June 24. Mr. Churchill and Mr. Eden, conceding that Britain had not been consulted, manfully defended the operation: power plants were legitimate military targets; there was good reason to attack them; they regretted that Her Majesty's Government had not been consulted but there was no obligation to do so. No one could ask more, but the House of Commons did.

I was in London at the time. Moreover, through the kindness of Mr. Eden I had been invited to address a group of members of all parties and both Houses of Parliament on June 26 in a large assembly room in Westminister Hall. Need I add that I had not planned it this way? At any rate, there was no need to worry about attendance, especially as I had agreed to respond to questions. The meeting was off the record, which gave me more latitude than would otherwise have been proper in a matter about which the Government and the opposition differed. Reports of what I said leaked out in garbled form and began to arouse some of my easily agitated critics in the Senate. To calm them the Department released the transcript on this subject:

If I may digress for a moment, I shall make some remarks about a matter which is one of controversy and which I would not speak about in England were it not for the fact that this is off-the-record. I shall restrict my remarks to what I think it is my duty to say to you at this time. This is about the matter that you have been debating in the last 2 or 3 days.

You would ask me, I am sure, if I did not say this, two questions, and I should like to reply very frankly to both of them. One question you would ask is: Shouldn't the British Government have been informed or consulted about this? To that, my answer would be "yes." It should have been; indeed, it was our intention to do it. It is only as the result of what in the United States is known as a "snafu" that you were not consulted about it.

I am sure that you are wholly inexperienced in England with government errors. We, unfortunately, have had more familiarity with them, and, due to the fact that one person was supposed to do something and thought another person was supposed to do [it], you were not consulted. . . . You should have been. We have no question about that.

If you ask me whether you had an absolute right to be consulted, I should say "no," but I don't want to argue about absolute right.

What I want to say is that you are a partner of ours in this operation, and we wanted to consult you; we should have, and we recognize an error.

Now you ask me whether this was a proper action. To that I say: Yes, a very proper action, an essential action. It was taken on military grounds. It was to bomb five plants, four of which were far removed from the frontier, one of which was on the frontier. We had not bombed these plants before because they had been dismantled, and we wished to preserve them in the event of unification of Korea. They had been put into operation once more; they were supplying most of the energy which was used not only by airfields which were operating against us but by radar which was directing fighters against our planes.[3]

My hearers seemed to approve. They applauded heartily when in reply to a question I said that the attack had been highly successful. Nevertheless, when I met privately with Eden, he pleaded for "no more surprises."

69. A SENTIMENTAL JOURNEY

IN A BUSY LIFE no convenient time ever comes to go visiting in cold blood. Some pragmatic stimulant is necessary. Boswell noticed this in his hero, Dr. Johnson: "on clean-shirt-day he went abroad and paid visits." Invitations had been accumulating that should be accepted "sometime"—Mayor Reuter's to lay the cornerstone of the American Memorial Library in Berlin, Chancellor Figl's to visit Vienna, Foreign Minister Neves da Fontoura's to visit Brazil. Clean-shirt-day for me—the coincidence of occasion and desire—came when Eden brought me a message in Portugal from Oxford University inviting me to Encaenia (the conferring of degrees) on June 25, 1952, to receive the honorary degree of Doctor in Civil Law. I have not been a collector of honorary degrees. Harvard touched me deeply during the attack of the primitives in 1950 by conferring on me, as she had on my great predecessor, the doctorate of law. I was similarly moved by this action of the oldest university in the English-speaking world as my public career neared its end. The President strongly favored my accepting these invitations and making the visits to Austria and Brazil state occasions. To emphasize this aspect he insisted that I should fly in the presidential plane, the *Independence,* and underlined it again by seeing us off himself. My wife and I, Ambassador and Mrs. Jessup, Assistant Secretary and Mrs. George Perkins, Luke Battle, and Barbara Evans took off for London at eight o'clock on Sunday evening, June 22. Even in that magnificent aircraft the transatlantic flight was not then what it is today. We stopped in northeastern Canada to refuel and arrived in London the next afternoon after a fourteen-hour flight.

ENGLAND

Secretaries of State can find no hiding place from meetings. We spent five days in England, one of which was in Oxford. The remaining four were given over to almost continuous meetings, one with a parliamentary group, four with Eden and his Foreign Office associates, still others with Eden and Schuman and their assistants. They were long and tiring; their usefulness—and they were useful—was in the joint and comradely exploration of problems, largely insoluble or, at any rate, unsolved. If, like Omar Khayyam, we evermore came out by the same door where in we went, we each had his day in court within. We shall come back to these meetings after going to Oxford.

Oxford Encaenia · On a lovely June afternoon Ambassador and Mrs. Gifford motored us into Oxfordshire countryside. The old university town, Charles I's headquarters in the civil war, had been engulfed, since Alice and I had known it thirty years before, punting on the Isis, by the new city created by Lord Nuffield's Morris Motor Works. But from the Warden's garden at Wadham College, where we stayed, one was aware only of the distant rumble of traffic. Our delightful host, Sir Maurice Bowra, the Warden of Wadham and Vice Chancellor of Oxford, gave us a gay evening and a welcome rest. (The eastward Atlantic flight with its abrupt collapse of time always calls for some days of adjustment.) One of the most charming and wise members of our party, Miss Helen Kirkpatrick (later Mrs. Robin Milbank) of the Western European Office, had warned Luke Battle, in a memorandum entitled "Ice in Oxford," of possible dangers to be encountered:

Our most up-to-date reports, many of them unofficial, indicate that British policy on ice, although considerably modified in the West End of London, is still based in Oxford on the 1689 concept. It therefore follows that any form of refreshment likely to be offered the Secretary in Oxford will range in temperature from 59 to 90 degrees, depending on where the bottles are kept. Lack of sunshine, however, makes the higher reading improbable. The 1689 concept is reinforced by a number of Scottish purists who believe that ice destroys the quality of good whiskey.

You will perhaps wish to brief the Secretary on Martinis. Owing to the influx of Italians into England, a carry-over of Francophobia due to the Napoleonic wars, and the semantic precision of the British, it is very likely that when he is offered a "Martini," he will receive just that:—a glassful of Italian (Martini) vermouth with a light sprinkling of warm gin on top. This, of course, is not true of the West End of London or of other areas where American imperialism has introduced the American version of Martinis.

Luke, as usual, took all precautions, but they were not needed.

The next day the honorands and their escorts met with the Chancellor, Lord Halifax, to robe, partake of the Creweian Benefaction in the hall of Wadham College, which meant sherry and biscuits, and to form in procession. The Chancellor cut a noble figure in his black satin knee-length britches and gold-trimmed coat with white ruffles at throat and wrists, patent leather shoes with great golden buckles, long cape from the shoulders carried like a train by two pages in black, and an admiral's black-plumed hat. Awed, we followed him to the Sheldonian Theatre. A few signs scrawled on walls commented adversely on the Korean bombing and my presence in Oxford, but the crowd called to me good-naturedly from the sidewalk. The Chancellor and his attendants entered the Sheldonian to ceremonial music while we, to be honored, were held back by our guards. At length we were admitted to march down a long aisle until the crossed lances of two academic uhlans on either side of it stopped us before the Chancellor seated upon his raised throne. There the Public Orator and I remained standing while the others took seats.

The Public Orator then presented me for my degree, after which I advanced to stand at the foot of the throne to receive it from the Chancellor. The Public Orator's presentations were spoken in Latin and contained witticisms about the person or his exploits, which amused the learned. Happily we had been given, in advance, English translations of his remarks so that we could smile knowingly at approximately the right places.† As each degree was conferred, the recipient mounted some steps to sit beside the throne. After various dissertations, mostly in Latin or Greek, the procession re-formed behind the Chancellor to march to All Souls College for lunch. In the process of negotiating the very narrow stairs, our fellow honorand, Somerset Maugham, started to plunge to the marble floor but was fortunately intercepted.

A garden party in the Warden's garden occupied the afternoon until time for the dinner, a "Gaudy," or full-dress affair, at Christ Church, the college established by Cardinal Wolsey. Around the walls hung innumerable portraits of the college's sons who, over more than four centuries, had been among England's great. A neighbor at the table remarked that only one had been painted in arms or armor and that the odds would be heavily against a guess who it was. William Penn, the Quaker, appeared in breastplate of steel; he looked as incongruous as would Benjamin Franklin in an admiral's frock coat and epaulettes.

Sir Oliver Franks and I had been told that we would be called upon to speak, and sternly admonished that all remarks that evening must be limited to four minutes, not a second more. We strictly complied but noticed that the toastmaster, Hugh Trevor-Roper, later to become Regius Professor of History, rambled on for forty-five. In my remarks I recalled that a son of Oxford, John Davenport, had traveled far to become a founder of New Haven, the site of my own university. Something of his stern training descended to his great-grandson, Colonel Abraham Davenport. May 19, 1780, has remained in Connecticut a day of awful memory as a portent of the day of judgment. By noon in Hartford on that day the sky had turned from blue to gray to deepest black. By midafternoon it was midnight. Many prayed for salvation before the end came.

The Connecticut House of Representatives adjourned, unable to transact business. In the Council of Safety—the upper house—the motion to adjourn was put. Colonel Davenport obtained recognition. He said, "The Day of Judgment is either approaching, or it is not. If it is not, there is no cause for adjournment. If it is, I choose to be found doing my duty. I wish, therefore, that candles may be brought."

After dinner at a reception in the Master's garden we were sharply reminded that Oxford's latitude is about the same as that of Goose Bay in Labrador. Ladies in fur coats stood shivering about great braziers.

Ministerial Meetings • The day before and after Oxford were given over to Mr. Eden. On the first of these my wife and I lunched with the Prime Minister and Mrs. Churchill in the cozy top-floor apartment at 10 Downing Street. The meetings at the Foreign Office were anything but cozy. Since their subjects included Far Eastern, Middle Eastern, Mediterranean, and European questions, Eden had present from ten to twenty-two associates; I, from four to ten. When Schuman and the French were added later, the numbers became imposing indeed. The added expertise hardly compensated for the loss of intimacy and candor.

Since the meetings decided little, details are unnecessary. Both then, and now in retrospect, there seemed great difficulty in getting at and dealing with the substance of a problem because lesser attendant problems got in the way. For instance, we were agreed that the latest Russian note demanding four-power talks on Germany was solely for the purpose of delaying ratification of the Bonn agreements (which the Senate Committee on Foreign Relations had approved the day we arrived in England) and the Defense Community. Hence the proper response was to keep pounding away for the UN investigation of conditions necessary for free elections in all parts of Germany, to which Moscow would never agree. But whenever we approached this fence Schuman balked for fear of giving the impression that we did not want the talks, a lesser danger than having them. In time, however, he jumped it. Again, he wanted more help in Indochina; we offered materiel and training for Vietnamese forces, but he would accept only the former, fearing our motives in offering the latter. In doing so, he decreased the usefulness of the military aid.

The British, too, spent hours discussing whether we should go ahead with the Turks and the Commonwealth countries to set up the Middle East Defense Organization in the hope of attracting adherence to a going concern, or delay organization until the Arabs had been persuaded to join in it. The eventual outcome was the ineffectual one adopted by my successor, called the Baghdad Pact until the collapse of the Baghdad Government. These talks merged into those on the state of affairs in Anglo-Egyptian relations, which seemed to be nebulous and confused in the extreme. Pending the establishment of a Middle East defense system of some sort, British troops in Egypt were not welcome guests, if they could be called guests at all. Their use in a local emergency might produce the most far-reaching consequences. The agreements under which they had come had been canceled, and the possibility of negotiating new ones involved finding a new relationship between Egypt, the Sudan, and Britain.

But of what sort? The Sudanese were said not to know, or be agreed, and no one seemed to know how to bring about either condition. Three states had recognized Farouk's title as King of the Sudan and three more were on the verge of doing so. The King did not like to discuss his title. Between the King's title, a role for Egypt in the Sudan acceptable to the Sudanese, and the flying of the Egyptian and British flags side by side there, the situation was said to be delicate. I ventured the brash opinion that it was impossible and that a likely result seemed to be that Egypt would lose the Sudan and Britain her Suez Canal base. Sir Ralph Stevenson, the British Ambassador, thought me unduly pessimistic. As things turned out, I was not.

The British excitement over the Korean bombing had been eased by Lord Alexander's report and by U.S. agreement, which I reported to Eden on June 27, to the appointment of a British deputy to General Mark Clark. This also made it easier to turn down another British suggestion of international political guidance to the Supreme Commander. He had a good deal of this, I pointed out, through our own government and through the General Assembly's Ad Hoc Committee, which itself could do with some guidance. The trouble over the Yalu bombing was not due to lack of guidance but lack of consultation with the British. I also discouraged a British feeler about an observer at the coming meeting of the ANZUS Council, knowing that Australia would resent this chaperonage. A final talk about Iran I found disquieting. The idea seemed to be abroad that Mosadeq's fall was imminent and might "need a push." We should coordinate our policies in such an event. Indeed, we should. Our policies had suffered for a year or more for lack of coordination and would continue to do so for our remaining tenure. After we left office, a push was administered, with surprising and nearly disastrous results.

Before we finished our talks, the Prime Minister asked Schuman, Eden, and me to lunch with him in his small apartment at Number 10. Before lunch, while having sherry in the sunny sitting room overlooking the Horse Guards Parade at the back of the house, he took me to a window and ostentatiously began describing an improvement he had in mind. The manner of his remarks and several pokes warned me that ribbing was in progress. "Yes," said the Prime Minister, "all those trees"—pointing to a line of poplars along the garden wall—"they're all coming out. Every last one. Spoil the view. Can't see a thing when they're trooping the color."

Outraged, Eden left his conversation with Schuman to join ours.

"You can't do that, Winston," he protested.

"Why not?" demanded the Prime Minister. "I live here, don't I?"

Eden agreed, but added reasonably enough that living there did not mean owning the place. Then the trap was sprung.

"Ah!" Churchill said sadly. "I see what you mean. I'm only the life tenant. You're the remainderman." To my relief Schuman got the point without translation or explanation.

ON TO BERLIN

The next afternoon we flew to Berlin. The Russians had continued their harassment of communications begun in May—telephone service was interrupted, Russian fighter planes maneuvered in the air corridors, and ground communications were delayed. We took retaliatory measures. Our own fighter planes were alerted to our flight plan. As we entered the corridor, members of the crew took up observation posts along either side of the cabin, but nothing occurred to interfere with our landing at Templehof on schedule. There I took the nineteen-gun salute of a formation of tanks and inspected an honor guard. From this ceremony we went on to a reception by Major General Lemuel Mathewson, Commandant of the United States Sector of Berlin, and later a dinner given by Mayor Reuter, where it was my happy duty to present to the Mayor as a gift from the people of the United States to the new library the original correspondence between President Abraham Lincoln and our devoted and distinguished German-born adopted son, Carl Schurz.

The next morning before the cornerstone laying, the inevitable work meeting intervened. The Chancellor's chief aide in the Foreign Office, Dr. Walter Hallstein, breakfasted with McCloy, Jessup, Perkins, and me to go over our draft reply to the Soviet note and German suggestions regarding it. Knowing that Hallstein was apt to press harder than his chief for Foreign Office points and aware of the difficulties of four-power drafting, we reduced changes to the minimum.

The site of the new library, a block from the Soviet sector, overflowed with a great crowd of East and West Berliners (this was nine years before the wall), all German and allied officialdom, and the workmen building the library, wearing the ceremonial dress of their guilds. The cornerstone, containing a box of historical documents, was put in place. With the master mason's hammer I tapped it and spoke a wish for the building's future. A host of sponsors followed, each with a tap and wish. Then from a nearby platform I made my speech, standing in the sun. It would have been even shorter had I known then that soon afterward under the spot where I had stood some workmen would unearth an unexploded bomb dropped there during the war.

At one o'clock, after laying a wreath at the memorial to the gallant men who gave their lives during the airlift, we were airborne in the corridor toward Munich to pick up the eastward corridor to Vienna. Three hours later we touched down at Tulln Airport, the U.S. Air Force Vienna field in the Soviet zone of Austria twenty miles from the city.

VIENNA, CITY OF DREAMS

Geographical necessity placed Tulln Airport in the Soviet zone. There Austrian Foreign Minister Karl Gruber and American Ambassador Walter Donnelly with their attractive ladies met us. The ceremonies of reviewing the Air Force Guard of Honor and greeting the press over, we boarded a two-car train for the hour's journey to Vienna and more ceremony. On the way the Austrian people gave us a glimpse of their spirit. A beautiful June Sunday afternoon had brought many to the country. Everywhere there were picnickers who waved as we passed. In the towns and villages the track was lined with people. Gruber, Donnelly, and I on the back platform were saluted with flowers and cheers. Behind the Austrians, lines of Soviet troops turned their backs, obviously on order, as we passed. But the people paid no attention to them.

At the Vienna station Chancellor Figl and Vice Chancellor Adolf Schaerf welcomed and escorted us to the plaza to review Austrian gendarmerie and receive the thunderous welcome of a great crowd of Viennese. I thought of how much my beloved friend, Felix Frankfurter, born in Vienna and always imbued with what he called a Blue Danube spirit, would have enjoyed this visit. On the way to the Ambassador's residence, Brigadier General William T. Fitts, Commander of the U.S. troops in Vienna, took us to the Stiftskaserne barracks, the headquarters of the 796th Military Police Battalion of the United States occupation force, for retreat and then a "march past" of the battalion. The morale of our forces in these beleaguered posts, Berlin and Vienna, was reflected in their smartness—white cap tops and chin straps, white gloves, rifle slings, and laces in their high boots. With our appearance in the courtyard, the battalion came to attention and, on the first note of retreat, presented arms as the flag came down. Then the band crashed into the national anthem with verve and fire equal to the "Marseillaise" at its best. Finally the battalion passed in review and the great courtyard was left in silence.

A few experiences stand out in our short visit. Our first evening was among the most memorable. Our gay and imaginative host, Chancellor Figl, undaunted by the fact that the Vienna Opera season had ended, had persuaded the orchestra and a group of artists to return from their summer activities for a performance of Mozart's *The Marriage of Figaro* in that eighteenth-century gem, the Redoutensaal, built for the composer in the Hofburg Palace. The hall is a rectangular room, seating about one hundred and fifty on either side of an aisle on a slope to the orchestra pit, behind which is the stage with no proscenium arch and a curtain on a wire drawn open by two pages. The flawless and intimate performance was worthy of Hilde Gueden and Maria Reining, as we gratefully told them when the cast joined the Chancellor and his guests in the Emperor's retiring room for a glass of champagne between the acts.

In the morning I paid an official call on a grand old gentleman, General Theodor Koerner, President of Austria. He received us in an apartment almost lost in the vast complex of the Hofburg Palace, where he had once served the Emperor Franz Josef. An erect, small man with a white square beard, pink cheeks, and very blue eyes, he had served his country through two disastrous wars, Hitler's *Anschluss,* and the present occupation. "Vienna," he said, "is an imperial city without an empire." He led us through vast and elaborate rooms where emperors—and the Empress Maria Theresa—had once affected Europe's destiny, to the balcony from which the Emperor on his birthday had taken the salute of his troops and the cheers of his subjects. Beyond it lay the Ring, a spacious open circle around which rose grandiose government buildings, the Opera, and famous churches. Beyond them lay the city.

"Once," he said sadly, "the lives of fifty million people centered here. Now our poor seven million cannot afford such grandeur." Another abode of shadows was the Schönbrunn, the beautiful summer palace on the outskirts of Vienna, beyond whose garden a long vista rises to be crowned on the hilltop against the sky by the triumphal arches of the Gloriette. In a small room in the palace Maria Theresa's children had done their schoolwork. Some of their drawings had been framed and hung, of which a few stood out. Closer inspection showed the promising artist to have been Marie Antoinette. In that sunny room what endless happiness must have seemed to stretch ahead for her!

Even on such a pleasant visit, meetings intervened and the inevitable subject was how to get the Russians to sign a treaty of peace and end the occupation. But several hundred meetings by the deputies of the four foreign ministers had been unable to bring it about, and it was plain that we in Vienna could not do so. Our movements about the city—to the reconstruction work on St. Stephan's Cathedral, the Opera House, and other places of interest—had been announced. What interested me as we drove about were not crowds, which are easily attainable and usually meaningless, but the friendly greetings shouted by people on the streets and in passing buses. Perhaps the most touching personal note occurred after a press conference. A correspondent came to me with an excellent bronze figure of a bear standing erect, which now decorates my office. He was acting, he told me, for his landlady, who had given it to him and had said, "Please give this to Mr. Acheson from an old woman as a thank offering for having kept the Bear from her door."

On our second and final evening in Vienna the Chancellor gave the state dinner in that beautiful room in the Ballhausplatz where the Congress of Vienna met. The table excellently appointed, flowers everywhere, a symphony orchestra playing, and the historic crystal chandeliers ablaze with candles—one could well imagine the handsome Lord Castlereagh and his beautiful lady, the lame and cynical Talleyrand, the wise old fox Count Metternich, and the dashing Czar Alexander I about to join us. After dinner and appropriate toasts, the table rose and the Chancellor offered my wife his arm. Most of the guests, like myself, missed the ensuing drama; in fact, I knew nothing of it for almost a year. Alice's evening gown had a wide skirt held out by a crinoline petticoat. As she rose something gave way. With Napoleonic decisiveness, she saw that ameliorative measures would be embarrassing and futile. So she let the petticoat drop and gave it a kick under the table, instantly becoming transformed from the crinoline to the directoire, more appropriate to the setting. If the Chancellor noticed, his English was inadequate to the occasion. However, the Chef de Protocol did notice. Later as he put us into the car, I heard him murmur, "Madam's article is in the trunk." "Thank you," she replied, adding, "My fur. The room was so warm."

After dinner the Chancellor gave further evidence of his imagination. Vienna had artists of every sort, but those he chose to entertain us were the little girls of the Vienna ballet school, children from six to their early teens tremendously serious about their dancing. The older ones were already acquiring professional competence, while the youngest were delightfully wobbly, avoiding spills by the narrowest of margins. At the end of the last dance of an enchanting evening each child with a deep curtsy presented each lady with a small bouquet.

Early the next morning the two of us accompanied by Barbara Evans and Luke Battle, with many farewells, flowers, and presents, boarded the *Independence* and were soon on our way to Dakar to pause overnight before a flight across the South Atlantic.

DAKAR

The first leg of our flight took us over the Alps twice, flying into and out of northern Italy. Continuous mountain ranges ran along on our left, becoming more formidable as we flew west. One could easily understand why the ragged migrations, pushed westward from Asia and Eastern Europe, shied away from these rugged barriers toward the Northern European plain. Not until one was directly over the Alps and looking straight down could one see the traitorous winding passes that opened to the more adventurous invaders the gates of Italy and the heart of empire.

Along the Riviera and the Costa Brava we flew; over the Pillars of Hercules into the unknown sea edging the world where Ulysses ventured and Vasco da Gama followed the coast around the Cape of Good Hope to India. At Port Lyautey refueling gave us a chance to stretch our legs. A ten o'clock touchdown at Dakar brought us out of an air-conditioned cabin into a night of heat and humidity unprecedented even for Washingtonians. The French High Commissioner, Bernard Cornut-Gentille, and his wife took us, after reviewing a guard of immense Senegalese in heavy woolen scarlet cloaks and armed with wicked-looking sabres, to the Governor General's palace, a sumptuous penthouse atop a new office building.

The night was not made for sleeping. The wind carried and deposited so heavy a cargo of moisture that sheets became sodden with it. Even the wind was shut out when the ladies drew curtains as the sentries marched around the gallery of our penthouse. Luke saved the situation by negotiating with the officer of the guard the immobilization of the sentries. In the morning a weary and limp group looked forward to Rio, where it would be winter.

At breakfast two overgrown and clumsy puppies led Barbara Evans to remark how my son's children would delight in them. M. Cornut-Gentille with alacrity said that we should have them; however, they were not puppies but lion and cheetah cubs. Politely, but very firmly, we declined his generous gift. Soon the *Independence* was airborne on her two-thousand-mile course across the South Atlantic to Recife, easternmost point on the bulge of Brazil.

An hour or two out of South America Colonel Williams announced to us gathered in the President's cabin that we were approaching the equator. Suddenly he lifted the great ship in a surprising jump over the barrier and brought her safely over. Afterward we each received from the crew a memento of our equator crossing.

A luncheon date with the Governor of Pernambuco we kept on the dot. As Brazilians do not impair digestion by rushing meals or toasts and as the Governor was determined that we should greet gay crowds and see the principal sights, our take-off was delayed until late afternoon, and our arrival in Rio until ten o'clock. Here again were salutes, national anthems, a guard inspection, speeches, and replies, which prolonged a day already lengthened by the doubled hours of the western flight. All of us were thoroughly tired when the cavalcade arrived at the lovely house where we were to stay.

RIO DE JANEIRO

A charming and generous friend, Walther Moreira Salles, then Brazilian Ambassador to the United States, had lent us his beautiful modern house on the outskirts of Rio, moving out of it himself. All four of us and Assistant Secretary Edward G. Miller, who had flown in from Washington to meet us in Recife, were to stay there. Eddie had been in Brazil during the war helping Brazilian authorities in the seizure of enemy property and knew Brazil, Brazilians, and Portuguese like a native. He was also one of Ambassador Moreira Salles's closest friends. The house was built around a glass-covered patio where orchids bloomed and fountains played; few of the rooms were rectangular and some of the walls were definitely not perpendicular but furnished no less satisfactory backgrounds for frescoes by Portinari and other distinguished painters.

Visits by Secretaries of State were not the rarity in Rio that mine had been in Vienna. Secretaries Root, Hughes, Hull, Stettinius, and Marshall had all preceded me. However, the Brazilians outdid themselves in enthusiasm and hospitality. Their warmth and spontaneity came through both in individual meetings and in large groups. Upon one of the men who interested me particularly, President Vargas, I promptly paid an official call, bearing a present from President Truman.

At this time Vargas was going through a brief period of almost dazed euphoria at the unexpected change in his fortunes. In 1945 after a long period of dictatorial rule he had been ousted from the Presidency by a military coup. His successor, General Eurico Gaspar Dutra, during a visit to Washington, had told me that his principal remaining purpose in office was to give Brazil an honest election and to turn over his office to the winner. In 1951 that winner proved to be Getúlio Darnellas Vargas, and the old General punctiliously carried out his promise. Vargas started out with a good administration—Neves da Fontoura at the Foreign Office; Horácio Lafer (to whom I shall return) at the Ministry of Finance; Ricardo Jafet, one of several able sons of a Syrian peddler, President of the Bank of Brazil; and Roberto Campos, one of the ablest economists in the hemisphere, Brazilian Joint Chairman of the Brazilian-American Joint Economic Commission.

In our talk Vargas kept dwelling on his return to office as the genuinely popular choice of the Brazilian people and comparing his election to that of President Truman in 1948. He seemed to be convincing himself that he had always been better than, perhaps, he had realized. The very naïveté of his talk was appealing. Poor man, it was not to last. Some of his family and others around him had not adjusted themselves to the reformed style. Two years after our visit charges of corruption brought an attempted *coup d'état,* in the course of which President Vargas committed suicide. Far away to the north, I felt a pang of sorrow that it should have ended so.

After the official calls Miller and I went to see the old General living in simple retirement on the edge of Rio. This pleased him mightily, quite destroying the taciturnity for which he had been famous during the Washington visit. At the dinner my wife and I had then given for him we sat on either side of him, each with an interpreter, quite wearing ourselves out with sprightly conversation, to which he replied monosyllabically. During a pause I asked my wife in an untranslated aside to identify a beautiful blonde lady sitting down the table. Without a second's pause President Dutra said, "A good question. I confess that it had occurred to me, too." This visit to an old friend pleased the Brazilian press.

The third and fourth of July were busy days, during which I must have spoken more than a dozen times. A lunch given by Finance Minister Lafer and a large and gala dinner by the Foreign Minister at Itamaratí Palace, where afterward we walked in its beautiful garden, both called for speeches. The next day included addresses to both the Senate and Chamber of Deputies, three separate Fourth of July celebrations, and another large dinner by the Mayor of Rio and two receptions afterward. Apparently we were the only weaklings in Rio who went to bed during our visit. I used to meet Eddie Miller as I was dressing in the morning and he was coming home in his evening clothes to change into battle dress.

My first speeches in Brazil came from a portfolio prepared in Washington for all the occasions of a carefully arranged schedule, but I soon joined my audiences in being bored by them. Walking to the Chamber of Deputies from the Senate, where I had read a Washington product, I told Miller that I was forsaking the Department's stately cadences for my own less inhibited style. The tumultuous reception given me by the Chamber, which continued from our entrance until I had been seated on the right of the President of the Chamber, spurred me on. When the introduction had been made, I laid my typed speech on the President's desk, suggested that it be printed in the record, and asked permission to speak to friends from my heart. The Chamber stood and cheered, as it did continuously through the speech, which dwelt on the greatness of Brazil, our firm friendship evidenced by her gallant troops who fought beside ours up the length of Italy, and by our Joint Commission, which was planning future cooperation in the development of Brazil and the hemisphere.

This theme I enlarged upon often both in Rio and later in São Paulo, which impressed me even more as the embodiment of the restless energy and potential power of Brazil. That country, I am convinced, will be one of the great nations of the future. It has much in common with our own country in size, population, resources, and legal development just after the civil war. It needs, as we did, capital and Western European immigrants to aid in its development. If Brazil lacks some of our resources, it has a compensating lack of some of our problems. As countries to bet on for the future both Edward Miller and I looked to Brazil and Mexico. We were more impressed by the "key country approach" to the development of the hemisphere than is now fashionable among advocates of the Alliance for Progress.

After three strenuous days in Rio we paid a farewell call on President Vargas, spent a secluded and restful Sunday in our temporary home, and on Monday morning, July 7, made the hour's flight to São Paulo, where we were to be the guests of Horácio Lafer and his charming wife. Lafer and I had taken to each other at first meeting. The son of an immigrant Bessarabian rabbi, Lafer had himself studied for the rabbinate, but finding it uncongenial turned to business. Marrying into one of Brazil's leading families, he and his brothers-in-law improved its ample resources. He told me, as evidence of Brazil's amazing resources, of their venture into newsprint production. During the war Brazil's dependence on imported newsprint had rendered her press painfully vulnerable to foreign control, a situation with which I had had some familiarity. The family acquired a large and remote wooded tract in the State of Paraná. When communications had been established and operations begun, a hotel was needed in the small town growing about the mill. Lafer picked out a site to windward of the fumes and put a stake in the ground. There steam shovels digging a cellar uncovered one of the world's great phosphate deposits.

Installed luxuriously in Lafer's residence, I greeted the press, then started out with the Mayor, Dr. Armando de Arruda de Pereira, for a nonstop tour of the magnificent industrial city, which he told me was growing so fast that he had to get aerial photographs every week to keep track of its boundaries. São Paulo, a couple of hundred miles inland on a high plateau southwest of Rio, is the industrial capital of Brazil, well laid out, booming, proud of its cultural life as well as its business eminence. Alice and I each unveiled a new acquisition of the art gallery—she a Toulouse-Lautrec, I a Renoir. By a pleasant Brazilian custom we became, respectively, godmother and godfather of the paintings we unveiled and made brief speeches in praise of the painters.

Then I went on to a huge luncheon in my honor given by the Chamber of Commerce at which the Mayor made me an honorary citizen of São Paulo and presented a symbolic key to the city. In expressing my appreciation of the honor, by happy chance I recalled St. Paul's claim of Roman citizenship before Caesar Augustus and said that henceforth, when called upon to declare myself, I could proudly say in the manner of the great saint whose name the city bore, "I, too, am a Paulista!"

Our visit ended with Governor Garcez's dinner at the Campos Elyseos Palace, followed by a gala ball given by the gracious Jorge Silva Prados, which for some lasted all night. Our host and hostess had for the occasion added a pavilion to their mansion, complete with beautiful crystal chandeliers, and had orchestras that spelled one another and staffs who served endless champagne and suppers. Our stamina proving unequal to the challenge of so great an event before so early a take-off the following day, we faded well before daylight.

The next morning the *Independence* had collected a fair complement of passengers for the long flight north, but they were not a companionable lot. My wife had developed a wretched cold, which, with what she had taken for it, had her in a long deep sleep before we were decently airborne. As I walked through the plane in search of a conscious traveling companion, it looked like a stricken field of battle with comatose forms strewn everywhere. At last Burke Knapp, the American Chairman of the Joint Economic Commission, gave unmistakable signs of wakefulness. I settled down beside him to listen to his most informative views on the path and problems of Brazilian development.

By afternoon, when we put down to refuel at Belém at the mouth of the Amazon, almost on the equator, some of our company were stirring, but not Alice. Rain was falling heavily and, the tower informed us, the Governor and a guard of honor awaited us. Coated, in equatorial temperature, with umbrellas which gave some protection from the water coming down but none against it bouncing up, I followed the path of duty into the downpour. During the national anthems the tuba players gave up when their horns filled. The Governor and I, having given the guard of honor the briefest of inspections, sought the doubtful sanctuary of the airport's lunchroom and drank fruit juice. When I commented that obviously we had called during the rainy season, the Governor reported that Belém had two seasons, both rainy. In one it rained every day; in the other, all day. Refueling completed, we departed Belém, without regret, for Trinidad.

A late arrival at Port-of-Spain brought us another Governor, this time a British one, another honor guard, and a comfortable night in an airport hotel to permit an early start in the morning. Alice barely woke up long enough to go to bed, but was much restored in the morning. One more all-day flight brought us home again to find our ever-considerate President at the bottom of the ramp to welcome us back from our travels, tired but happy.

70. INDOCHINA

SINCE MENTION OF our decisions and actions regarding Indochina is scattered through this book and in view of the importance that Vietnam assumed in American life two decades later, my connection with policy making in that area is briefly pulled together in this chapter. It began in an important way only after I had become Secretary of State and falls roughly into three periods: the first, before the outbreak of the Korean war in mid-1950; the second, until the end of 1951, covering the first year and a half of that war and the beginning of rearmament in Europe; and the third, 1952, a year of increasing involvement and frustration.

THE PRE KOREAN WAR PHASE

At the beginning of 1949 the French were still trying to re-establish their authority in Cambodia, Laos, and Vietnam, called collectively Indochina. President Roosevelt had been unsympathetic to the effort, and during the war the United States Government had furnished aid to indigenous leaders, notably Ho Chi Minh, in the hope that they would make difficulties for the Japanese. By 1949 Ho's Viet Minh regime was exercising authority over a large part of the country and was in revolt against the French. Another leader, Prince Bao Dai, was prepared to cooperate with the French in establishing something called "self-government within the French Union," which, as time revealed, meant different things to the Vietnamese and the French. Bao Dai had ability and claims to stature and leadership, as the legitimate claimant to the throne, which could have been an important asset in Vietnam. His handicap was long residence on the French Riviera and the suspicion of being a captive king.

After intricate maneuvering, President Auriol of France and Bao Dai exchanged letters in March 1949 at the Elysée Palace on the future of Vietnam. These very general Elysée Agreements promised Vietnam its own army for internal security, membership in the Frencn Union, a role in foreign and defense policies, and a bank of issue. Further details were to be worked out in subsequent meetings. In general these agreements moved in the direction of United States aims in Asia, though the Department doubted whether they moved far enough or would be carried out fast enough.

As we saw our role in Southeast Asia, it was to help toward solving the colonial-nationalist conflict in a way that would satisfy nationalist aims and minimize the strain on our Western European allies. This meant supporting the French "presence" in the area as a guide and help to the three states in moving toward genuine independence within (for the present, at least) the French Union. It was not an easy or a popular role. The French balked, with all the stubbornness that I was later to know so well, at moving swiftly where they could move, in transferring authority over internal affairs; and the Vietnamese pushed for control where they were least able to exercise it, in the conduct of their foreign relations. The Southeast Asian Office of the State Department doubted whether the Elysée Agreements would work as written; the Western European Office doubted that there was any chance that pressure would induce the French leaders to move further, and thought that it would only stiffen and antagonize them. The result was a decision to work with the British in getting Indian and Philippine help to push both French and Vietnamese toward further realistic steps.

In June 1949 Bao Dai became chief of state of Vietnam and, later, head of government. However, 1949 was to straggle to an end before the French did anything further. Meetings aplenty took place: between Schuman and me and tripartite ones with Bevin present. The French representatives, Schuman and High Commissioner Léon Pignon, would be "personally" in favor of further immediate steps, but reported that the domestic political situation in Paris was the obstacle. Bevin and I argued in April and September 1949 that France's allies could not help her until the National Assembly ratified the Elysée Agreements, made supplementary agreements transferring administration functions, shifted relations between the three Indochinese governments and the French Republic from the Ministry of Overseas Affairs to that of Foreign Affairs, and issued an official statement that the Elysée Agreements were only a first step toward a treaty to be made with a duly elected Vietnamese government.

Finally, on December 30, 1949, the French announced transfer of internal authority to the Vietnam Republic and Prince Bao Dai took over, and a month later the French National Assembly ratified the Elysée Agreements accepting Vietnam, Cambodia, and Laos as independent states within the French Union. We and the British had tried to get some Asian states to take the lead in recognizing the three new states, but, while they hung back, the Soviet Union recognized Ho Chi Minh's Viet Minh regime in Vietnam. On February 7 Washington and London thereupon recognized the three states, we stressing "our fundamental policy of giving support to the peaceful and democratic evolution of dependent peoples toward self-government and independence."[1]

During the spring of 1950, after some hesitation, we in the Department recommended aid to France and the Associated States in combating Ho's insurgency, which was backed by the Chinese and Russians. The aid was to be limited to economic and military supplies, stopping short of our own military intervention. If Chinese or Soviet forces should intervene directly, the situation would be reconsidered. The hesitation came from the belief of some of my colleagues that, even with our material and financial help, the French-Bao Dai regime would be defeated in the field by the Soviet- and Chinese-supported Viet Minh. All of us recognized the high probability of this result unless France swiftly transferred authority to the Associated States and organized, trained, and equipped, with our aid, substantial indigenous forces to take over the main burden of the fight.

By May the President had approved economic support and military supplies for Indochina. This policy was agreed after discussions with Schuman and Bevin and with groups and committees of the Congress. French opposition to direct dealings by us with the three states seemed weakened somewhat, and a Special Technical and Economic Mission was set up and dispatched to work with them on economic (as distinguished from military) aid but very little was agreed and moved in 1950. Military aid was to be arranged through Paris.

Both during this period and after it our conduct was criticized as being a muddled hodgepodge, directed neither toward edging the French out of an effort to re-establish their colonial role, which was beyond their power, nor helping them hard enough to accomplish it or, even better, to defeat Ho and gracefully withdraw. The description is accurate enough. The criticism, however, fails to recognize the limits on the extent to which one may successfully coerce an ally. Withholding help and exhorting the ally or its opponent can be effective only when the ally can do nothing without help, as was the case in Indonesia. Furthermore, the result of withholding help to France would, at most, have removed the colonial power. It could not have made the resulting situation a beneficial one either for Indochina or for Southeast Asia, or in the more important effort of furthering the stability and defense of Europe. So while we may have tried to muddle through and were certainly not successful, I could not think then or later of a better course. One can suggest, perhaps, doing nothing. That might have had merit, but as an attitude for the leader of a great alliance toward an important ally, indeed one essential to a critical endeavor, it had its demerits, too.

THE EFFECT OF THE KOREAN WAR

One of the first decisions announced by President Truman after the attack on South Korea was that military aid to the Philippines and Indochina would have to be intensified.[2] Congress responded by adding four billion dollars to funds for military assistance, of which three hundred and three million was for Korea, the Philippines, and "the general area of China." By mid-September, when the foreign ministers met in New York, both the French Government and ours had concluded that the creation of indigenous armies in Indochina was the only way to save the situation there and preserve the French army in Europe. Schuman and Defense Minister Moch insisted that to raise these armies France must have our help in finance and military equipment. Meanwhile, Ambassador Donald R. Heath from Saigon reaffirmed the need, adding, however, that the desired political and psychological effect could be obtained only if the Associated States were given a real role in the arrangements.

Throughout the autumn action dragged while the military situation in Vietnam deteriorated. The French, virtually besieged in their bases, called for still more aid when the ministers, this time including Finance Minister Maurice

Petsche, again came to Washington to discuss the whole French military budget for the coming calendar year. These talks have already been recalled in Chapter 48; it is enough to mention here that French ministers proposed to add ten divisions to the French army in Europe and to increase the Vietnamese battalions from twelve to thirty. Livingston Merchant, who had been working on French military problems, sent to me through Dean Rusk an urgent memorandum stressing that the military situation in Vietnam was extremely serious; that military aid should receive highest priority; that Prince Bao Dai should be pushed to assume maximum effective leadership; that although Indochina was an area of French responsibility, in view of French ineffectiveness it would be better for France to pull out if she could not provide sufficient force to hold; that we should strengthen a second line of defense in Thailand, Malaya, Laos, Cambodia, the Philippines, and Indonesia; and that the military problem was essentially one of men and the sinews of war. We could supply the second; the first must come from national forces in Vietnam.

We agreed to a large increase in military aid. Although the French complained that our aid was not enough, it was more than Indochina was able to absorb. The French complained, too, that their allies did not appreciate their efforts in Indochina and that the Vietnamese did not cooperate. Bao Dai answered that Paris was hesitant and niggardly in letting him create the essentials of an independent state. While this bickering was going on, General MacArthur had begun his ill-fated march to the Yalu and by early November had captured his first Chinese prisoners. At Thanksgiving disaster burst upon him. Until General Ridgway had stabilized the Korean battle, our concern over Indochina was of necessity relegated to second place. Even before the disaster, however, a perceptive warning came from an able colleague in the Department, John Ohly, urging that the appearance of the Chinese in Korea required us to take a second look at where we were going in Indochina. Not only was there real danger that our efforts would fail in their immediate purpose and waste valuable resources in the process, but we were moving into a position in Indochina in which "our responsibilities tend to supplant rather than complement those of the French." We could, he added, become a scapegoat for the French and be sucked into direct intervention. "These situations have a way of snowballing," he concluded. The dangers to which he pointed took more than a decade to materialize in full, but materialize they did.

I decided, however, that having put our hand to the plow, we would not look back. Moreover, the immediate situation appeared to take a turn for the better. In November the National Assembly voted a strengthening of French national forces and creation of national forces in the Associated States. Local internal administration was to be turned over early in 1951, though the transfer date kept being postponed. General de Lattre de Tassigny, one of France's best soldiers but unhappily doomed to die soon of cancer, was appointed as both High Commissioner and Commander in Chief in Indochina. Meetings and statements continued.

Our military aid mounted in the year 1951 to over half a billion dollars. General de Lattre came twice to Washington to demand more aid and faster delivery and to urge us to declare that loss of Indochina would be a catastrophic blow to the free world; yet he resented inquiries about his military plans and his intentions regarding transfer of authority to the three states. Too little seemed to be happening in Vietnam in developing military power and local government responsibility and popular support. While in 1951 the Vietnamese forces rose to four divisions, they had only seven hundred Vietnamese officers out of the two thousand required, and their military academy at Dalat was graduating only two hundred a year. Our offer of instructors from our military mission in Korea, which was mass-educating officers for twelve Korean divisions, was refused.

As the year wore on without much progress and we ourselves became bogged down in the negotiations at Panmunjom, our sense of frustration grew. A review of the situation in late August, before I left for a series of meetings in the autumn of 1951, brought warning from the Joint Chiefs of Staff against any statement that would commit—or seem to the French under future eventualities to commit—United States armed forces to Indochina. We did not waver from this policy.

INCREASING AID AND FRUSTRATION

In January 1952 the French at a meeting in Washington of the British, French, and American Chiefs of Staff returned to the question of the action to be taken in the event of direct Chinese intervention in Indochina. Our Chiefs, however, would go no further than to agree that such an intervention would be a matter of concern to the United Nations. Two weeks later our delegate to the General Assembly, then meeting in Paris, was instructed to state, as were British and French delegates, the same thing. This still left undetermined what, if anything, any or all of us would do about such an intervention, though fear of it was prevalent throughout that spring.

At Lisbon in February we agreed to an increase in our military aid to France, including the forces being raised in Indochina. Before setting out for Bonn in May to conclude the contractual agreements ending the occupation of Germany and instituting the European Defense Community bringing Germany into the common defense arrangements, I was called to the White House on May 19, 1952, with Secretary Lovett and General Bradley to discuss Indochina. The upshot of this meeting was an instruction to discuss four points with Eden and Schuman: further development of indigenous forces and our willingness to give additional help to the effort; a possible tripartite warning to Peking against aggression in Indochina, including preparatory diplomatic and military discussions; the anticipated reaction of Peking; and the courses of action open and acceptable to the three powers should the warning be ignored. I was to avoid mentioning any specific amount of further aid and of internal changes in Indochina beyond the development of the forces. It was thought that such an agenda would keep the French to the points of immediate practical importance and avoid irritation on secondary and peripheral matters.

The talks in Paris, conducted, as indicated in Chapter 67, in a wider setting, resulted in a decision to pursue this matter further with Jean Letourneau, French Minister for the Associated States, after he should return from a reconnaissance in Indochina. Meanwhile, cables from Paris and Saigon show the quandary in which we found ourselves. Paris told us that the French connected Indochina with the Tunisian-Moroccan problem and resented what they considered "United States intervention." Both Paris and Saigon agreed that Indochina needed to be "revitalized" or the drain on French resources might cause a decision to cut losses and withdraw. Bao Dai was not the man to pull Vietnam together, yet the French must go further to speed the evolution of the Associated States, just when de Lattre's death had removed effective French leadership. Saigon, while recognizing French sensitivities, believed that we should insist on information and action at the same time that the French asked us for aid. This, of course, is what we had been doing for two years.

Dutifully, in mid-June when Letourneau, who had succeeded de Lattre as High Commissioner, asked for more aid, I insisted, as my colleagues had suggested, that at a time when we were contributing more than a third of the cost of the campaign in Indochina it did not seem unreasonable to expect that we should be given the information to explain to our people why we were doing so and what progress was being made. Furthermore, friendly suggestions on the conduct of affairs from an ally so actively supporting them would not seem to be officious meddling. While Letourneau did not dissent, not much happened as a result. No one, however, seriously advised that, with the Bonn agreements awaiting ratification by the Senate and the French National Assembly and the situation in Indochina in its usual critical state, it would be wise to end, or threaten to end, aid to Indochina unless an American plan of military and political reform was carried out. Instead we recognized in a communiqué[3] that the struggle in Indochina was a part of the worldwide resistance to "Communist attempts at conquest and subversion," that France had a "primary role in Indochina," such as we had assumed in Korea, and stated that within the authority given by Congress we would increase our aid to building the national armies. Letourneau went home issuing optimistic statements of military and political progress in Indochina and the prediction that during the next six months American aid would increase to forty per cent of total French expenditures in Indochina.

When Schuman, Eden, and I met in London at the end of June, we discussed whether we should warn Peking against direct military intervention in Vietnam. Pointing out that to issue a warning and then take no action if it was disregarded would be calamitous, I urged that we first come to some conclusion on the steps each of us could and would take to meet an intervention. It should be understood at the outset that with our commitments in Korea and Europe, further effort in Indochina by us could not go beyond air and naval participation. In the past, action of this sort against China had, when suggested, met with opposition in many quarters. The idea of a warning was not pursued further.

In mid-December the Department noted the rising uneasiness in France about Indochina and a large gap in our government's information about the situation there and about French military plans, and it recognized as no longer valid an earlier French intention to so weaken the enemy before reducing French forces in Indochina that indigenous forces could handle the situation. It seemed clear to our observers that Vietnamese forces alone could not even maintain the existing stalemate. At the council Schuman pleaded for relief from France's "solitude" in Indochina and for volunteers to share the burden. He did not ask for troops, but for financial help (we were already carrying forty per cent of it) and for recognition of the equal importance of the struggle in Indochina and Korea. Letourneau also spoke to the council, which responded with a resolution of support for the struggle against communism in Indochina but with no pledges of financial aid.

After the council had adjourned on December 18, Schuman asked Eden and me to come to the Quai d'Orsay at seven o'clock in the evening, three hours before my scheduled departure for Washington. Letourneau spoke for an hour of imminent enemy offensives in Laos and Vietnam and of the need to raise more troops, and for aid; he began to outline plans. At this point, tired, hungry, and exasperated, I ran out of patience. I asked Schuman for permission to make a brief statement and leave for my plane. We would be glad to send a working party to Paris after Christmas to get from the French full and detailed information about all aspects of the situation in Indochina. We were thoroughly dissatisfied with the information we had been given. This had to be remedied. We must know exactly what the situation was and what we were doing if, as, and when we were to take any further step.

Letourneau and Schuman agreed and suggested that the group go to Saigon, where the information was. I said it would go where Letourneau was; if he wanted to work with it in Saigon, that was satisfactory, but we would not struggle any longer to extract information from inferior officials who never seemed to have the authority to give it. He wanted aid; we wanted information. The next move was up to him.

With those parting thoughts I left and was soon airborne for Washington. A month later I was a private citizen, free of the responsibilities of office. Here my story of Indochina should appropriately end. To cut it off would leave the reader dangling, however, so a brief epilogue seems indicated.

A military mission did go to Indochina in the early summer of 1953 under Lieutenant General J. W. O'Daniel. It recommended that, in addition to the four hundred million dollars in aid set aside for Indochina, three hundred eighty-five million more should be made available before the end of 1954. On September 30, 1953, the United States pledged this aid and France promised to do (but did not do) all that we had been asking of her over the past two years. During the last quarter of 1953 the situation in Indochina deteriorated, the French became more eager to disengage, and the British more inclined to induce the Soviet Union to help in making this possible. On February 19, 1954, the foreign ministers of Britain, France, the Soviet Union, and the United States agreed in Berlin to a conference to bring about a peaceful settlement in Korea and Indochina. A month later President Eisenhower declared Southeast Asia to be "of the most transcendent importance" to the United States, and during April 1954 consideration was given to getting united tripartite military action there with the British and French. Dienbienphu fell on May 7, 1954, and on July 20 the Convention of Geneva ended the hostilities and French Indochina, and divided Vietnam.

The United States did not sign the final agreement of Geneva. Another mission recommended the continuance of aid to South Vietnam, and the Southeast Asia Treaty was signed in Manila, under which South Vietnam was entitled to ask the signatories for protection. Before us lay the road against which John Ohly had warned, where our responsibilities might supplant those of France. As he had so presciently observed, "these situations have a way of snowballing."

71. A SECOND TRY IN IRAN

WHEN OUR FIRST SERIES of efforts to settle the Anglo-Iranian oil dispute failed after my talks with Mr. Eden in November 1951, as told in Chapter 52, the dispute relapsed into static trench warfare with only a few spectacular raids which did not involve us. We cut off military aid to Iran in January 1952 and maintained the merest trickle of economic help, encouraging the World Bank through its Vice President, John Garner, and Mosadeq through his adviser, Camille Gutt, former Finance Minister of Belgium and former head of the International Monetary Fund, to try their hands at a settlement. They failed as completely as we had.

Next a gambit of the British Government's went down to ignominious defeat. An action brought in the International Court of Justice was dismissed for want of jurisdiction in June 1952 on the ground that the agreement sued on —the concession contract of 1933 with Anglo-Iranian Oil Company—was not a treaty or convention. This left the British Government worse off than ever. In the same month an end run by Iran was broken up by the British. An oil tanker, the *Rose Mary*—owned by a Panamanian company, flying the Honduran flag, chartered to a Swiss company, commanded by an Italian, carrying oil loaded by the National Oil Company of Iran at Bandar Mashur, and consigned to an Italian company in Italy—was "persuaded" by an RAF plane to put into Aden. There the Anglo-Iranian Oil Company libeled the ship, claiming title to the cargo. Even by any other name the *Rose Mary's* venture would have smelled as sour to the British court that upheld Anglo-Iranian's claim.

Meanwhile Mosadeq, after returning in triumph from his victory at The Hague to tumultuous arguments with the Shah in Teheran, resigned on July 16. For five riot-packed days Qavam attempted to rule; then the Shah acceded to all Mosadeq's demands and returned him to office. At first blush the convulsion looked like the end of trench warfare and a new period of perhaps decisive movement. We sprang to action, urging the British to prepare a practicable plan of settlement that a new government following Mosadeq could seize as a source of immediate funds. We also urged an immediate and joint survey by our new Ambassador, Loy Henderson, and their Chargé d'Affaires, George Middleton, of possible alternative governments in this fluid situation and of what might bring them to power or facilitate the process.

Mosadeq, too, was whirling like a dervish. One day he would appear to offer arbitration or compensation; the next, to withdraw his offer. The situation, I thought, called for simple, temporary, and easily understood proposals to get oil flowing to the British and funds flowing to Iran without prejudice to the bargaining positions of either side, leaving more enduring arrangements to grow out of actual operations under more relaxed relations. Here Eden's general attitude toward the situation was directly opposed to mine. He saw in it no great crisis or need for haste. Iran's economy, he said at the time and wrote later,[1] was too primitive and flexible to crash, and Communist rule was not the only alternative to Mosadeq. On the first point he was probably right, although I doubted it at the time; on the second I believed that further temporizing in the hope of a change of government for the better would run unwarranted risks for all of us in the Middle East when a feasible alternative seemed possible.

At the end of July the situation in Teheran as reported to us by Henderson appeared to me to be disintegrating so fast that I sought and obtained the President's permission to try for a joint Anglo-American approach to Mosadeq without going through the time-consuming process of obtaining all the usual departmental clearances and agreements. The approach would be of the simple, temporary, and nonprejudicial character already mentioned, based on three points. The United States would make an immediate grant of ten million dollars to Iran. The British would take over the oil presently stored in Iran, paying the then-quoted Persian Gulf prices less a suitable discount. Mosadeq would agree to the establishment of an international commission to determine the compensation due to the British. These points were put in an *aide mémoire* and explained to Sir Oliver Franks, who sent them to London.

Back came a reply about two weeks later, related and relevant to our proposal, as I said to Sir Oliver among the mildest of my comments, only by being expressed on paper by means of a typewriter. The Ambassador did an excellent job of calming me down and cooling me off in his incomparable quiet and humorous way. The British counterproposal was indeed a formidable one and hardly drafted to enhance its appeal to Mr. Mosadeq. With all due deference to me, he saw in the draftsmanship the hand of the lawyers rather than the Foreign Secretary. Perhaps if we considered it further we might find the seeds of a common approach. Unlikely as it seemed, we agreed to try and to cover our meeting with the cloak of silence.

Our answer the next day, friendly and well reasoned, made no impression. The whole tone of the correspondence on the British side suggested that it was edited by the Anglo-Iranian Oil Company. Indeed, the substance of the British note was that company officials should meet with Iranian officials to see whether a basis existed for formal negotiations to settle British claims and Iranian counterclaims. Past history made abundantly clear the unsuitability of the company to the role of diplomatic agent.

NEW CHARACTERS ENTER

At this time two new characters entered the act, one in London, one in Teheran. "During Anthony's absence," as he put it, Mr. Churchill took over the Foreign Office management of the Iranian problem. He proposed to President Truman that they make a joint approach to Mosadeq. This was worked out during August and presented at the end of the month.[2] Mosadeq not only rejected it but asserted that before any discussion of financial settlement could begin, Anglo-Iranian must pay the forty-nine million dollars claimed by Iran for back taxes and royalties. Our plan was substantially based on the one I had proposed to Eden a month before, thus making clear that my ideas about a settlement were no more productive than Eden's.

The other new character on stage complicated matters considerably. W. Alton Jones, President of Cities Service Oil Company of New York—a sales company, not a producer—appeared in Teheran and opened discussion with Mosadeq about a part for his company in the distribution and sale abroad of nationalized Iranian oil. Despite the Department of State's reiteration that Mr. Jones was privately pursuing his company's private interests, his presence in Iran and his known friendship with General Eisenhower disturbed Anglo-Iranian officials and aroused British suspicions. It also encouraged Mosadeq's principal purpose, even obsession, throughout the dispute: to eliminate the British company, its employees, and its influence from Iran. Mr. Jones and his discussions got nowhere, but did enhance Mosadeq's obduracy. In October he broke diplomatic relations with Britain.

Another period of uneasy quiet and stalemate spread over the deadlocked scene, marked only by propaganda on both sides. It was at this time in the autumn that the idea came from London that not only could no settlement be made while Mosadeq was in control but that he was not so strong as he might appear. His struggle with Qavam, Kashani, Speaker of the Majlis, and the Shah had been won by the Teheran mobs and the help of the Tudeh (Communist) Party. However, other groups as yet inadequately organized were threatened by him and, in time, might be able to supersede him. We responded that time was the one element we did not have available, and hence that the discussion was one that must await the imminent assumption of office by our successors.

LAST TRY

We had one more big effort left in us. President Truman stimulated it by wishing aloud to David Bruce in October that the Anglo-Iranian dispute could be settled before his term expired, adding in his kindly, disarming way that he had no criticism of the way we had handled the matter and no suggestions. My thoughts went back to some I had had before Mr. Churchill intervened. Mosadeq would not make a new concession contract with Anglo-Iranian even on very favorable terms, and the British insisted on "compensation" for terminating the old one. The trouble with arbitrating the terms and counterclaims was that the parties could not agree on the elements of value—such as future profits—to be considered without arousing domestic political trouble for either including or excluding them. Here lay the great value of a lump-sum net settlement. It need not be spelled out, and if it could be stated in terms of a number of barrels of oil to Anglo-Iranian over a good many years, the monetary amount and reasoning could be vague enough to allow each side to make a good case for itself at home. We could then get on with means for producing the oil and marketing what did not go to Anglo-Iranian, presumably about half.

Within our government my own colleagues in the State Department and in Treasury and Defense had come to the conclusion that the British were so obstructive and determined on a rule-or-ruin policy in Iran that we must strike out on an independent policy or run the gravest risk of having Iran disappear behind the Iron Curtain and the whole military and political situation in the Middle East change adversely to us. Their sense of exasperation and alarm was easily understandable, but an independent American solution over British opposition was also more easily said than done. Aside from the damaging ill will it would create between our two countries, it would require the cooperation of the major American oil companies, who alone, aside from Anglo-Iranian, had the tankers to move oil in the volume necessary. Moreover, these tankers were engaged in their own businesses. The degree of coordinated management required would be considerable. Would the oil companies be willing to enter such an effort? And would the Department of Justice, which was already proceeding against them for alleged violation of the antitrust laws in their Middle East operations, allow them to even if they wished to?

This field must be explored, for even if a wholly independent policy would in all likelihood be undesirable, some degree of independent capability might be a powerful persuader in London. So we began with the Department of Justice, having two long meetings with Attorney General James McGranery and his aides from the Antitrust Division along with Secretary of Defense Lovett, General Omar Bradley, and our own Middle Eastern people. McGranery, courteous and patient, listened and reserved judgment on what might be possible. Not so the police dogs from the Antitrust Division; they wanted no truck with the mammon of unrighteousness, were a good deal more certain of what would be permissible under the law than the Supreme Court up to that time had shown itself to be, and had no hesitation in disagreeing with me on foreign policy aims and with Lovett and Bradley on the military risks and consequences of an absorption of Iran in the Soviet system. When they went off to confer, I had little hope of help from that quarter. Although the Attorney General had the power of decision, his aides had the power to leak information with insinuations for which he would have no stomach.

About this time we had an opportunity to turn a liability into an asset. After the oil dispute arose, we had quietly discouraged American private purchases of oil in Iran. They could achieve nothing of importance in solving the problem unless, as pointed out, the major oil companies engaged in them and the inevitable litigation could cause irritation. This attitude could not continue without some burst of publicity, so why not precipitate it by a statement that might have some effect in softening the Foreign Office? Accordingly, I wrote Eden a note on November 4 pointing out the increasing attempts to purchase and the necessity on short notice of our making a statement. The draft enclosed was described as minimizing implications of discord between us and stressing our continuing common efforts, which it did by reviewing our efforts to find a solution and saying that whether individuals should purchase oil in Iran must be left to the individual judgment and appraisal of the legal risks involved. The statement was released on December 6.[3]

THE PRESIDENT APPROVES A VARIANT

On November 7 I laid a tough question before the President: Would he, if it proved necessary to save Iran—and subject to his approval of a final plan—be willing to use his authority under the Defense Materials Procurement Act to advance up to a hundred million dollars to Iran against the future delivery of Iranian oil and approve a voluntary program under the Act in which one or more U.S. companies (including major oil companies), alone or in conjunction with Anglo-Iranian, would purchase and market Iranian oil? On the same day he answered my question: "Approved Harry S. Truman."

When, through Gifford and Franks, we told the Foreign Office how our minds were running, we got a reaction that seemed to show some, even though small, movement. Stage one still remained an agreement to arbitrate compensation. After an agreement to arbitrate, stage two would begin. Iran would then be free to sell oil to anyone, but Anglo-Iranian would not enter into other negotiations until the arbitral award was made. Paul Nitze, in London, tried without much success to move things along. On November 20 Eden and I met for a talk on this inexhaustible subject in New York where we were both wrestling with Korean armistice problems at the General Assembly. I again pressed the point that Iran was on the verge of an explosion in which Mosadeq would break relations with the United States, after which nothing could save the country from the Tudeh Party and disappearance behind the Iron Curtain. Large numbers of civilian and military personnel were already being purged.

Nitze, I said, had been over British plans for stage two, which contained the carrot designed to make acceptable stage one, the agreement to arbitrate compensation. This was wholly inadequate, as it contemplated lifting from Abadan only from seven to ten million tons per annum. Considering the amount needed to pay the British compensation and to repay American advances, nothing short of twenty million tons would leave adequate funds to keep the Iranian economy moving. I also pressed the idea of lump-sum compensation and some methods taken from our expeditious wartime legislation. We believed that some new move should be made, preferably by the British or by us jointly, by the time Loy Henderson returned to Teheran in two or three weeks. Failing that, however, we could not remain idle while the Middle East drifted toward chaos. If Anglo-Iranian could not itself move oil in sufficient quantity, we had ideas, approved in the highest quarters, by which the United States Government and American companies would help temporarily. Mr. Nitze would return to London at once to discuss these. We would make every effort to act with the British, but time was short and soon we might have no alternative to acting in the best manner to save Iran. This stirred up turgid waters in London.

The next item on the agenda was to consult with the major American oil companies, no easy task. In the face of the Department of Justice's suit against them and its expressed attitude that they should not even meet with me, I went to our common superior. As usual he proved an ever-ready help in time of trouble. On November 26 the President sent me written authority under the Defense Production Act of 1950, referring to a proposal to allow American companies to act with Anglo-Iranian in the oil dispute and authorizing me "to discuss with US oil companies and AIOC to determine what type of action by me would produce the desired result. . . . Consult with the UK and others as necessary. Inform the Attorney General."

This letter, copies of which were given to the companies invited to meet with me, was designed to protect them from attacks by the Antitrust Division and gave them heart to attend meetings with me in the Department on December 4 and 9. Time was indeed running out. The first meeting was like approaching the shyest of wild creatures. Some time elapsed before they could be induced to talk at all. Then their worries began to come out. They had little doubt of the advanced stage of decay in Iranian economic and political, even social and military, affairs; doubted, with Eden, the ability to correct it with Mosadeq in control; realized the instantaneous effect on their own arrangements in other countries if Mosadeq by his intransigence secured better terms than they had arranged; and disliked even the appearance of hovering like vultures over the carcass of Anglo-Iranian. "There but for the grace of God"—and a little more common sense—"go I" was the predominant note. The meeting reinforced my belief in the vast importance of joint action with the British—even if reluctant and a bit coerced. No agreement was reached but the "sense of the meeting" was that Nitze should go to London and if Anglo-Iranian would move along the line suggested they would under our protecting arm try to work out a way to help.

I had little doubt that this attitude would seep through to Anglo-Iranian. Our position was not as strong as we had hoped, but it was better than it had been. When Eden and I talked again a week later, he still did not like the idea of a lump-sum settlement. Accordingly, I agreed that Henderson would not raise it at the start of his talks with Mosadeq nor until he had cleared it with me. I would bear in mind that Eden wished to try again to dissuade me from raising it, but reserved the right to go ahead without further discussion if a crisis seemed to demand it.

Henderson saw Mosadeq on Christmas Day, speaking in the broadest terms and stressing the great pains being taken by the President and Secretary of State to find a solution. The talk went on for hours. Mosadeq seemed agreeable to an arbitration of compensation, interposed no conditions precedent, even appeared willing to consider the loss of future profits. Once arbitration could be agreed to, said Henderson, the United States could make large and immediate payments against future delivery of oil; Anglo-Iranian could, with the help of American companies if necessary, lift in the neighborhood of twenty million tons of oil; Defense was prepared to supply picket boats for the Persian Gulf and the Export-Import Bank to revive a twenty-five-million-dollar loan agreement. It would all take flexibility in arranging. Henderson was hopeful, but after another talk on December 31 he was less so. We tried to add some spice to the proposals before submitting them in writing, as we did on January 15. They contained, as he put it, "no disagreeable departures from our previous plan." Eden, however, refused to go further. As he wrote later, he "thought we should be better occupied looking for alternatives to Mussadig rather than trying to buy him off."[4]

In Washington, however, our time ran out over the weekend. On Tuesday, January 20, the new Administration took over.

EDEN'S VINDICATION

Although the end of the story lies beyond the limits of this book, it would be unfair to the reader to hold back the cliff-hanging finish.

On January 29 Mosadeq went back on his intimation that future profits might be considered in the arbitration of compensation to the Anglo-Iranian Oil Company and insisted that the only element to be valued was the company's physical property in Iran. In February he opened a propaganda attack on the Shah, with demands that he leave Iran. A royalist-led mob attacked Mosadeq's house at night, from which he had to escape in his pajamas over the garden wall to be rescued by the gendarmerie. In March he rejected the joint offer in toto, and in April ousted Kashani as speaker of the Majlis and dissolved the Senate.

From then on Iran moved rapidly toward civil war. In July Mosadeq won a referendum demanding a choice between him and the hostile Majlis and then moved to dissolve it. An attempted royalist *coup d'état* went askew, with the Shah fleeing first to Baghdad, then to Switzerland. Mosadeq dissolved the Majlis. Pressed now from the left by the Communists, he had to call on the police for help. The Army first withheld its help, then cast its decisive strength on the side of the still-sputtering royalist coup. With Mosadeq in jail, the Shah returned from his wanderings to preside over an Army-dominated government.

The alternative to Mosadeq for which the British had been looking had been found. But, as the Iron Duke had said of Waterloo, it was "a damned near thing." In the end a new concession agreement was worked out with the Iranian Government by a consortium of oil companies, American and European, in which Anglo-Iranian had less than a half interest—a far less favorable result than it could have obtained from Razmara in 1950 if it had acted expeditiously. (See Chapter 52.) It also drew upon our proposals of 1952. Once again one reflects on Oxenstierne's question: "Dost thou not know, my son, with how little wisdom the world is governed?"

72. ELECTION SUMMER

THREE WEEKS after we had come home from our travels to Europe and South America we were off again to Hawaii. The first anniversary of the signing of the treaty with Australia and New Zealand would soon be upon us; we all agreed that an ANZUS Council meeting should be held before that. No important questions awaited decision but, as mentioned before, our friends in the antipodes felt a long way from their allies and far too close to war in Indochina and Korea and civil unrest in Indonesia and the Philippines. More than anything else they wished to exchange views on probable developments and what they portended for all of us.

The time of the meeting was set for early August and the place at a fair point between us, the Marine Corps Air Station at Kaneohe, across the island of Oahu from Honolulu. The intervening weeks were full of action. At home the Republican convention had nominated General Eisenhower. The President had received from Governor Adlai Stevenson of Illinois the impression that he did not want the Democratic nomination. Vice President Barkley had ambitions but no support. After the Governor's welcoming speech to the convention in Chicago, it nominated him on July 25. I had known and worked with Stevenson during the war, when he served as an assistant to Secretary of the Navy Knox, a newspaper publisher from Chicago; my wife had known the Stevenson family since childhood. My impression of the Governor was summed up for me some years later by Harold Macmillan—a good staff officer but without the stuff of command.

Abroad, the situation in Egypt had deteriorated rapidly. Almost a month to the day from the date of my gloomy predictions in London to Mr. Eden and Ambassador Sir Ralph Stevenson (see Chapter 69), General Nagib proclaimed himself commander in chief of the Egyptian Army and surrounded the Royal Palace with tanks and troops. On July 26 King Farouk abdicated. Reports from Iran were also disturbing.

The dependable *Independence* being engaged elsewhere, our party was given another Air Force plane for the flight to Hawaii. It soon developed engine trouble and limped into Lowry Air Force Base at Denver, where we were all comfortably housed at the base hospital, thereby alarming President Truman, who telephoned me at once to find out what had happened. As General Eisenhower was staying a few miles away at his western campaign headquarters, I reported that we had defected to the enemy but were otherwise well. Another day spent waiting for a substitute aircraft put us into San Francisco for a second night before flying on. However, the company was a pleasant one—Admiral Arthur W. Radford, Commander in Chief Pacific, who was to be our most helpful military adviser, and Ambassador Philip Jessup, Assistant Secretary George Perkins, and Deputy Assistant Secretary John Allison.

For the first time Lucius Battle was left behind. Looking toward the day my enemies might be in a position to wreak vengeance on anyone who had long been associated with me, Luke's friends had concluded, with my sad concurrence, that he would be less conspicuous if he were assigned to a foreign post. In time, however, his loyal service to me became an all too apparent handicap, which led him to spend a few years in private life until the McCarthy-Cohn-Schine influence on the Department had run its course and a new administration taken over. He was then recalled to a brilliant diplomatic career. Luke chose as his successor a worthy one, Jeffrey Kitchen, to whom we soon became devoted. Both of these men and their charming wives are today among our most cherished friends.

An official reception at Honolulu airport is an ordeal difficult to surmount with an appearance of pleasure, to say nothing of dignity. The leis that are hung around one's neck, as once around sacrificial bulls, invariably conceal small crawling creatures that find their way down a shirt collar and induce an urgent desire to tear off one's shirt. Instead one stands in the hot sun and watches hula dancers shuffle about on a lauhala mat designed to preserve them from incineration on the cement. The thought occurs that such might be too kind a fate. In due course, however, it ended and after an opportunity for delousing and suitable refreshment we went on to a reception by Governor Oren Long and then to the Old Royal Iolani Palace, now a museum, to see portraits of the King of the Hawaiian Islands, Kamehameha III, and his consort, Queen Kalama, painted in 1849 by Alice's grandfather, John Mix Stanley.

The site and arrangements of our meeting could not have been improved. The officers' quarters of the base—houses, club, and swimming pool on the shore overlooking the Pacific—had been turned over to the delegates and their staffs, the visitors being headed by Richard Casey of Australia and T. Clifton Webb of New Zealand. Casey, whom we had known well since his visit to Washington more than a decade before as Australian Minister, is, as I write, Lord Casey and Governor General of Australia. He called at once to talk over plans for the meeting. This provided a much-desired opportunity to dispose of two embarrassing issues which had a long history and, despite much discussion —or perhaps because of it—had not been put to rest: the relation of the United Kingdom Government to our ANZUS Council and of the Australian and New Zealand military to our own Joint Chiefs of Staff.

Both issues grew out of Foster Dulles' negotiation of the Japanese peace treaty, as had the treaty with the two island states. It will be remembered that in his discussions with the Australian and New Zealand governments both had been unwilling to forgo severe treaty restrictions on Japanese rearmament unless they should receive direct security commitments from the United States. In exploring this idea with them, we had canvassed all the possible alliance combinations. The British Government had strongly objected to any arrangement that excluded them, while the Australians had leaned toward wide-reaching arrangements that might ultimately include European states having "interests" in the Pacific as well as interconnections with other security arrangements of which any of the three states might be members.

Neither State nor Defense had been able to accept those broad proposals. To us in the State Department they implied a guarantee of European colonial possessions in or on the Pacific, and to the Chiefs of Staff such an entanglement of the work of the NATO military staff and of the Inter-American Defense Board with Western Pacific matters that planning, to say nothing of action, would be well-nigh impossible in those fields. The three governments had then fallen back on the idea of the United States as the connecting security link in the Pacific through three separate treaties: one with Australia and New Zealand, another with the Philippines, and a third with Japan. Reference to interconnections with other security systems had been eliminated, and the possibility for broader arrangements left to the future. This had left unsatisfied the British desire not to be "excluded" and the Australian desire for a direct planning arrangement between their Chiefs of Staff and ours. These matters, which were still unsolved in August 1952, had first to be settled within our own government.

Admiral Radford's presence on our plane as my military adviser was intimately connected with the conclusions reached in Washington on these problems. Military planning and liaison with our treaty allies was to center with the Commander in Chief Pacific at Pearl Harbor. There adequate time and attention could be given to this important task; it would be lost amid the multifarious activities of the Pentagon and the far too many claims upon the attention of Chiefs of Staff. Admiral Radford was of immense help in having this arrangement happily accepted by our allies. So far as a British observer was concerned, our instruction was to stand firm against opening the postern gate to enlargement of the treaty.

Therefore when the Australian Foreign Minister asked my thoughts about the agenda, I suggested first what we should avoid. Chief on the list was not to get bogged down with these two matters. I told him very frankly what my instructions were, that Eden had raised the observer question with me, as he had doubtless done with him, and that I had discouraged him while deferring any decision to this meeting. If the Australians wanted close relations with us, they would not be furthered by the introduction of observers, a process unlikely to stop with a British group. Dick Casey did not press the point. Regarding military liaison, I suggested that in private session we let Admiral Radford explain his plan in detail before engaging in any discussion. To this he agreed.

The next morning a plenary session of the council was welcomed by the Governor and the Commander in Chief, after which I was elected chairman for the meeting and added my word. We then recessed for coffee, reassembling in private session, where an agenda was adopted beginning with a review of world affairs and ending with adoption of working arrangements under the treaty.

"It seemed to me," I cabled the President at the end of the council meeting, "that both countries suffered from a paucity of knowledge of what was going on and faulty appreciation of current situations. They felt remote, uninformed, and worried by the unknown. So Admiral Radford—who has been the greatest possible help to us and contributed in an outstanding way to the success of this conference—and I decided that instead of starving the Australians and New Zealanders we would give them indigestion." For two days we went over every situation in the world, political and military, with the utmost frankness and fullness. At the end they were very happy with political liaison through the council and military planning through the Commander in Chief Pacific.

"I hope to see you next Monday," I concluded, "and report fully. The newspapers tell me that you look rested and in top form. Your word for it, they say, is chipper. That is good news."

Work did not absorb all our time and energies. One evening Casey, Webb, and I spoke at a World Brotherhood meeting being held in Honolulu; on another, we dined with Admiral and Mrs. Radford and the officers of his staff and their ladies. Then the three ministers entertained our kind civilian and military hosts at dinner in Honolulu. On another memorable afternoon Admiral Radford took us on a tour of Pearl Harbor with its sad relics of the Japanese attack and then flew us to the "Big Island"—Hawaii—where the volcano Kilauea was in eruption. From the Volcano House veranda we watched the sky turn a deep rose as evening came on. The Greek proprietor, a colorful character himself, entertained us by his tale of how he brought on the eruption, which he pointed out was the foundation of business for his hotel. Convinced that Pele, the Hawaiian goddess of volcanoes, had been introduced to gin by riotous whaling seamen of an earlier day, he undertook to bring a long period of volcanic quiet (and poor business) to an end by offerings to the goddess. Every day, with appropriate invocation of her aid, he tossed a bottle of Beefeater into the crater with no result. Then it occurred to him that he had underrated her capacity, so to make up for this slight he tossed in a whole case. The result was instantaneous. With a roar the whole place blew up. To keep the lady's favor he continued contributions of a case a week.

After dinner a government volcanologist went with us some miles to a park on the edge of the crater, where a most inadequate pipe fence held back the too adventurous. A mile in diameter, the crater held crimson molten lava to a level of about five hundred feet below us, most active toward its center. Every few minutes a muffled explosion would throw a great spout of scarlet lava a hundred feet or more above our heads. As it spread out and fell back, Alice pointed out that the spout separated into darker forms that took on shapes and postures from the ballet. This rhymthic leap and fall back had its hypnotic fascination, which held us against the fragile fence until the Admiral called for the return flight. Years have not dimmed the images of that evening.

SPEECHES POLITICAL AND OTHERWISE

A Secretary of State is always a political figure. Even General Marshall became such, perhaps to his surprise. But he does well to avoid purely partisan involvement and flights of partisan oratory. His office depends upon his party's success, but the success of his office will depend upon bipartisan support. Accordingly, as the autumn of 1952 approached, I made some speeches, not in direct support of Governor Stevenson's candidacy, but of the type known as "keeping the troops happy." The American trade unions had been very loyal to the President and helpful in supporting his foreign policies. Two of my speeches took the form of reports at union conventions on our handling of foreign affairs. A third corrected for the press some of General Eisenhower's misapprehensions. A fourth was nonpolitical.

When Al Hayes, President of the powerful Machinists Union, asked me to speak at their national convention in Kansas City in early September,[1] I was glad to go. Republican orators, led by Foster Dulles, were criticizing some of our actions, which, when taken, had received solid bipartisan support. For the benefit of our loyal friends the record should be kept clear and straight. I reviewed our efforts since the war to develop institutions for the maintenance of peace, the international control and reduction of armaments of all kinds, and the increase of production, trade, and standards of living everywhere. I spoke of Soviet obstruction all along the line, its hate campaign and our development of a military shield for free nations with its salutary results. This would require continued effort. We could not, I said, "walk through the dangers of the present on a bridge of glittering adjectives." Discussion of policy required grappling with real issues and concrete situations. It was fine to advocate being dynamic, positive, and affirmative, but what did this mean in terms of economic help for developing countries, military aid for our allies, freeing trade, spreading truth, and the blood, sweat, and tears of Korea?

It was a new experience, I continued, to be urged to be dynamic, positive, and bold by those who had hitherto had their hands on the horn and their feet on the brakes. Our coattails were ragged from being held back by those who thought we had shown too much of these admirable qualities in Greece and Turkey in 1947, Berlin in 1948, the Marshall Plan in the same years, in NATO in 1949, and Korea in 1950. We heard harsh words (from Foster Dulles) about the "negative, immoral, and futile" policy of "containment." Whether that word was a good short description of "what we have been doing and propose that we continue"—and I personally did not think it was—was not the issue. The issue was whether there were "better concrete, specific acts with which to meet concrete specific problems." Words would not solve our problem, which was the problem of leadership among free peoples, I concluded: "The pattern of leadership is a pattern of responsibility."

As the political campaign warmed up, our opponents directed some of their fire on me. In the Senate the Republican right, as I left for the General Assembly in New York, gave me their usual support in a renewed demand for my dismissal from office. Before that, however, General Eisenhower began discussing foreign policy in terms surprising for him. The great chain of events begun under his benefactor, General Marshall, he called a "purgatory of improvisation."[2] In the same speech, relating what he termed some "plain facts" about the period leading up to the attack on South Korea, the General grossly distorted my Press Club speech (referred to in Chapter 39), and, when I publicly set the record straight, severed all relations with me. It appears to be true that one who unjustly injures another must in justification become his enemy. During the eight years of his Presidency I was never invited into the White House or to the State Department or consulted in any way. However, this involved no invidious discrimination, since my chief, President Truman, was treated the same way.

To return to General Eisenhower's Cincinnati speech, he revived the Taft charge that I had, in effect, invited the attack on Korea, starting with a highly expurgated quotation of my speech: "In January of 1950 our Secretary of State declared that America's so-called 'defensive perimeter' excluded areas on the Asiatic mainland such as Korea. He said in part: 'No person can guarantee these areas against military attack. It must be clear that such a guarantee is hardly sensible or necessary. . . . It is a mistake . . . in considering Pacific and Far Eastern problems to become obsessed with military considerations.' "[3]

That statement, I said,

purports to be a quotation and an accurate paraphrase of a speech I made before the National Press Club in Washington on January 12, 1950.

As stated it tortures the facts. It says things I didn't say and omits a significant and relevant part of what I did say. The General could have discovered this by reading my speech.

In my Press Club speech I spoke of the Aleutian Islands, Japan and the Ryukyus, and the Philippines being our "defensive perimeter" in the Pacific area. The Aleutians are part of our own nation, we had occupation forces in Japan and the Ryukyus, and we have special military arrangements as well as unusually close bonds of friendship with the Philippines. My point was that if this line were attacked we would defend it alone if necessary—just as we would our continental area.

The General's speech says [that] I "excluded areas on the Asiatic mainland such as Korea." Now, "areas on the Asiatic mainland" also include Indo-China, Malaya, Thailand, Burma, Pakistan, India and Afghanistan—so presumably he meant I excluded them also. The fact is, however, that I used no language whatever "excluding" Korea or any other area in the Asiatic mainland or suggesting any lack of interest by the United States in the event of an attack on any area of the Asian mainland in general or Korea in particular. The General's statement represents me as saying what I did not say.

On the contrary, I referred specifically to these "other areas in the Pacific."

The General or those upon whom he relied dealt with my specific statement on these other areas by cutting it out from between two other sentences they quoted to make their point.[4]

Since interest in this old canard has long ceased—except, curiously, among college students—I shall not rehash the argument. Anyone interested may find the remainder of the statement in the Notes.

Before the Electrical, Radio, and Machine Workers convention, of which my friend Jim Carey was President, I dealt with the dual nature of the struggle against communism, its economic and political side and its military side.[5] It was no accident, I pointed out, that the man who had done most to stiffen the back of the free world against communism—President Truman—had also cared most about, and had done most about, human needs at home and abroad. He had held to a steady and consistent course, which I reviewed, unmoved by the fainthearted who tired when the going began to get tough, the optimistic who found no need for further effort at the first mention by Soviet leaders of "peaceful coexistence," and the impatient and reckless who wished to throw off all restraint, draw lines, and have a showdown. Man's desire to be free was our cause and our greatest source of strength.

"Think this over," I said, "and remember that we have always had patriots who had no heart for the long pull. They were vocal in 1787, and 1863, and they're still vocal. Is freedom worth one or two years of high taxes and meeting force with force, but not four years, or ten, or twenty? Is there a new American principle that after a good try at defending our freedom, and all that one word means, we give up, sell America short, and get taxes down? Think it over. It's worth a lot of thought."

The fourth speech was of a wholly different nature, before a great concourse at the Armory in Washington, convened by the National Council of Churches to inaugurate a new translation of the Bible.[6] I had been deputized to represent the President and spoke on "The Role of the Bible in Our National Life." Acknowledging an unconquerable attachment for the King James version because the origins of my life lay in it and in the Connecticut Valley, I spoke of the merging of the two in the almost theocratic community of early New England. There the Book was all. People had come there to live their own interpretation of it. It was spiritual guide, moral and legal code, political system, and sustenance of life, whether to endure hardship, struggle with nature, battle with enemies, or face one's journey through life to death. To those who cast the mold of this country it instilled specific and clear rules of thought and conduct. It taught sternly that the omnipresent battle in every life every day was the struggle between good and evil. The test of what was good and what evil lay not in one's own will or desire, not in dictate of government or the opinion of the day, but in the will of God as revealed by the Book and to be found in the last analysis by individual conscience—guided, instructed, chastened, but in the end, alone.

Out of the travail of these lives the idea of God-fearing was given powerful content and effect. It meant a voluntary and militant submission to a moral order overriding the wills of the lowly and the great and of the state itself, carrying with it the notion of areas blocked off into which none might enter because here the duty of the individual conscience must be performed.

In that community the idea of God-fearing was balanced by the idea of God-loving, which embraced the love and service of man. What was written in the Book was taught by life. Never had self-reliance been so linked with mutual help. The words "neighbor" and "neighborliness" took on meanings in the New World that they had never had in the old. No characteristic so marked Americans to this day as the quick and helping hand offered not only to neighbors, but to fellowmen everywhere.

It therefore shocked and surprised us, I said, to learn from a Soviet encyclopedia that "Soviet patriotism is indissolubly connected with hatred toward the enemies of the Socialist Fatherland. . . . The teaching of hatred toward the enemies of the toilers enriches the conception of Socialistic humanism by distinguishing it from sugary and hypocritical 'philanthropy.' "

It was sad that people who once read the same books as we should be taught to hate. One did not have to hate in order to love one's country. Certainly here there was enough to inspire love: the country itself, simpler than notions of national entity, institutions, history, and power, "some piece of earth with the sky over it." This love of a specific place gave "great strength and comfort to the human heart."

These reflections . . . are made vivid for me as I go home these autumn evenings. With me as I leave are the worries, the exasperations, the frustrations of the day. Then the rush of the city traffic falls away. Instead there are fields and lines of cattle facing the same way, with heads down. Lights spring up in the thinning houses. In time, the road becomes a dirt lane, which leads through a grove of oaks around a Quaker Meeting House, hidden in its ivy, beside it the graveyard, with its rows of little headstones. I know that as I breast the hill there will be lights at the end of the lane.

And there is peace. . . .

In the times in which we live there is no safe lodging and no rest. But all that we do and shall do is that there may be peace among men. So striving, we may find peace within ourselves.

WE LOSE THE ELECTION

The evening of election day—Tuesday, November 4, 1952,—we were at the house of friends, watching and listening to the returns come in. The company was made up of close friends all deeply involved in what was happening. Aside from Justice Frankfurter and ourselves most of those present were young —our children and their and our associates in various activities of the Government. As the news came in a feeling of despair, almost of panic, came over the group as though they were suddenly learning of a stunning natural disaster, which they could not believe or bear. How were they to face it? They asked me, what were they to do? Later, at Felix Frankfurter's urging, they pieced together what I had said to them:

Most of you are so used to a Democratic Administration and recollect so little of anything else that you think of this state of affairs as normal. But it was not normal. What has just happened was bound to happen. It is not only wrong to feel angry about it, it is unrealistic. Tonight you, especially the younger ones, feel angry and bitter and gypped. You exaggerate the campaign and call the election a "steal" and claim that it was won by demagogues and vilifiers.

You must realize that we Democrats have been in power for a long time and it is natural and normal for there to be a change. That fact, you might as well accept, and also that it is not necessarily a bad thing. You must accept it the way that some day you accept growing old.

From this moment you should not go on fighting battles that have been lost. Don't, above all, go on fighting them the way the League of Nations battle was fought over thirty years. Do what nature requires, that is to have a fallow period. Just let the field of your emotions stay barren, let new seeds germinate, until May, or next year, or until 1954; that is what happens in nature. Have different activities, think of something else. Don't read *The New York Times* from cover to cover every day.

Then when you come back into the scene, you will come back fresh. And you should think of the problems that exist then, and not of the problems that existed a year before. Say, "These are new problems. I am going to attack the new problems in a creative way."

This gets us to the point of how you should act now. The people who come in will have a responsibility which they haven't had for twenty years. Actually the problems will remain the same. They are very difficult problems, in some cases just about insoluble. The new people will find this out, and the chances are that they are not going to be able to find miraculous solutions any more than we have done. But now they will have the responsibility. They will have fresh minds and a fresh approach, and it is possible that they will be able to think of some things that we haven't thought of and to do some things that we haven't done. If so, that is all to the good. And we should give them a chance to do their best.

One thing that we shouldn't do is reduce their chances of getting somewhere. We probably could if we tried. Because the new people won't understand the great complexities and the ramifications of the things they have to deal with. But that's all right, because they will soon, and we should try to help them as much as we can. Whatever we may have thought of some of the men who will come into the new administration when they have been so critical of us, there's no sense in continuing to voice these past opinions of the new men. We must give them a chance. Their purposes are the best interests of this country, just as ours are. So that's the second thing to keep in mind: Don't undermine the whole foundation by hammering at mistakes the Administration will make from the beginning and by discrediting the new Administration as rapidly as its problems arise. This is not only tempting, but extremely easy. Quite a few of us know enough to make life intolerable for the new Administration. We should not by our actions make it impossible or more difficult for them to accomplish what all of us have been trying to accomplish over the last seven years.

Above all, we shouldn't organize ourselves into factions that are anti-this or anti-that. We shouldn't form anti-Dulles clubs, if he is the next Secretary of State, or anti-anybody clubs. That doesn't get you anywhere.

After things have settled down a bit and the new people have taken over and are doing what they can, we will have ideas about how to solve some of the difficult questions that will come up. We will have a chance to be constructive by throwing out those ideas. If they are wise ideas, they will be picked up and will be helpful. We probably won't be able ever to put our ideas into operation ourselves. But if we can think of them, and advocate them, the new people in the Democratic Party, people whom we don't even know yet because they haven't appeared, will have something to go on. There is no sense in having our ideas simply ideas of how badly the Republicans are doing things. What we need to have and what the country will need to have are ideas that are constructive and helpful in solving new problems that it will face.

The next morning I got a typically warm note from Felix: "Would that all our people had had the good fortune to hear your words to the young last night. ... Those words of yours could have been spoken only by one who had lived them in the fiery furnace that burns out all that is petty and personal, and sees the contingencies of life in the perspective of the enduring."

With these thoughts and the demands in the Senate for my dismissal I went off to the United Nations Assembly to try to stop a war on the other side of the globe.

73. AN OPEN COVENANT OPENLY
CONNIVED AGAINST

FOR TWO MONTHS in the autumn of 1952 the General Assembly, meeting for the first time in its new headquarters in New York, sought a solution to the prisoner-of-war problem in Korea, which its members thought, quite erroneously, was holding up an armistice. The armistice was not to come until eight months later, after our election and bitter battles and heavy casualties in Korea had convinced the Communists that they could get no better terms than had already been proposed to them. From mid-October to early December I plunged more deeply than ever before into politics and diplomacy as practiced in the General Assembly, spending more time and playing a larger part in the new modernistic palace at Turtle Bay than I ever had done in the refurbished World's Fair building at Flushing Meadows or the sham and shoddy Palais de Chaillot.

The General Assembly, like all large international gatherings from Vienna to Versailles, had a public and a private side. In public, arguments were addressed to delegates only as they furnished a setting for broadcasts to world audiences, including, in this case, an American electorate engaged in a presidential campaign. So tricky did this last factor make the situation that both Eden and Schuman put off their arrival in New York until after the election of November 4. In private, leaders of various groups persuaded, exhorted, and intrigued to hold major allies together, to gain adherents for positions thought to affect negotiations at Panmunjom, or the will of belligerents, or—in some cases—merely to manipulate a large, unwieldy, and confused body to some conclusion.

My own purpose was to support armistice terms that our Government, carrying the main responsibility for conducting the war, believed would end the fighting with the greatest hope of keeping it ended and of stability thereafter. To do this required holding the British steadily on course with us, keeping the support of the Latin American and European states, a group that could defeat any harmful proposal and was essential to any useful one, and, finally, guarding against proposals of two adroit operators, Krishna Menon of India, leader of the Arab-Asian states, and Lester B. Pearson of Canada, President of the Assembly. These would give the appearance, without having the effect, of achieving our purpose, thus gaining support among delegates from "uncommitted" nations.

Before leaving Washington for New York, we did our best to calm the fracas set off by our Ambassador to the Soviet Union, George F. Kennan. On arriving in Berlin en route to an ambassadorial conference, he replied to press questions about life in Moscow by comparing it to his internment by Hitler during the war. This unusual statement by an experienced diplomat brought a protest from the Soviet Government, a declaration that he was *persona non grata,* and a demand for his recall, all of which produced some commotion in the press and a counterdemand upon me by choleric Senator William Knowland of California to break relations with the Soviet Union and send its Ambassador home. I pointed out to him the seriousness of the step he proposed, the need for wise and calm judgment in the national interest, and our intention to examine all aspects of the problem including his recommendation; then I sent Charles E. Bohlen† to accompany Ambassador Kennan to Switzerland, there to await the arrival of Mrs. Kennan and their children with such patience and taciturnity as he could summon. Believing that the best defense was a strong offense, we informed the Soviet Government that our Ambassador accurately and in moderate language had described the position of foreign diplomats in Russia. It was this treatment "systematically applied over a period of years by the Soviet Government, which grossly violates the traditions and customs in international intercourse developed over generations."[1] Neither Vishinsky nor I mentioned the matter during the next two months.

THE CENTRAL ISSUE AND ITS AMBIANCE

The central issue to occupy the seventh General Assembly was how to bring about an armistice in Korea, which by the time the Assembly met had centered upon the question of the return of prisoners of war. The account of negotiations at Panmunjom (in Chapter 68) ended with our attempt to focus attention upon the real issue by rephrasing our proposals for granting the right to repatriation without compulsion upon captor or prisoner to force an unwilling prisoner to submit to return. In their new form these proposals were submitted to the other side on September 28 and categorically rejected by them. Lieutenant General William K. Harrison, our chief negotiator, suspended further meetings until the other side had something to propose. At my press conference on October 8 I supported this position, stressing our willingness to resume discussion of old or new proposals but not to compromise the humane principles we had enunciated. To continue to put forward proposals in the face of adamant rejection could soon amount to negotiating with oneself.

Among other matters pressed upon the General Assembly's attention two were causing bitter controversy in our own Congress. While our effort was to get priority for the armistice issue, in which we were successful, brief notice of other issues will set the stage for the principal debate and connected maneuvers. Both Assembly and Congress were deeply interested in the proportion of UN budget expenses to be assessed against the United States, but for opposite reasons—the Assembly to keep it up, the Congress to get it down. Of the expenses for 1951, 38.92 per cent had been assessed against the United States; for 1952, 36.9 per cent, despite congressional demands that the amount not exceed one-third. In the final outcome a compromise resolved acrimonious debate; for 1953 we would accept an assessment of 35.12 per cent of the budget, and thereafter not more than one-third.

Another matter that agitated the Congress was the charge that the United Nations Secretariat had in its employ United States citizens with Communist affiliations. Under the stimulus of Senators Joseph McCarthy of Wisconsin and Patrick McCarran of Nevada, then at the height of their power, the charge kicked up quite a row and soon had both the State Department and the Secretary General taking embarrassing positions inconsistent with those they had previously maintained. From the outset we had urged that the United Nations should build a staff truly international in outlook, responsible and loyal to the organization and not nominated or directed by any national states. Secretary General Trygve Lie took the same view. Both he and we knew that citizens of Communist member states, some of whom would have to be included in the Secretariat, would be selected and directed by their respective governments, but neither of us wished United States citizens chosen by him to be in that category. I did not want to claim a right to police his appointments and appointees, and, while he refused to appoint anyone suspected of subversive action against any government, he could hardly require appointments to turn upon a candidate's views in a field where the orthodoxy of one superpower became heterodoxy, or even criminality, as seen by another. Practical men could have solved the problem easily, but not so long as the two senators and the press saw it as a source of news and publicity. The day before the General Assembly opened, the Internal Security Committee (a subcommittee of Senator McCarran's Judiciary Committee), meeting in New York, opened a highly publicized hearing into the loyalty of Americans employed by the United Nations. Soon a federal grand jury opened a competing show on the same topic in the same city. Both called UN employees as witnesses, some of whom asserted their constitutional protection against self-incrimination. The result was highly unfavorable opinion of the United Nations in the United States and of the United States in the United Nations. If I needed confirmation of my opposition to having the UN headquarters in New York—which I did not—we had plenty of it during the autumn of 1952.

Other matters calling for attention and ultimately finding their way onto the agenda included complaints against France regarding Morocco and Tunisia, against South Africa over her treatment of persons of Indian origin, by Greece that Greek children kidnaped during hostilities were still held by her neighbors, questions of the Austrian peace treaty, Kashmir and Palestine, and the perennial debate over Chinese representation. All of these matters required talk among our own delegation and with others. Furthermore, so large a congregation of foreign ministers produced many requests for appointments, sometimes for no reason at all, often for reasons unconnected with the Assembly.

More wearing than the constant jumping from topic to topic was the heavily guarded, claustrophobic life both in the Waldorf Towers and while being transported four times a day to and from the apartment and the United States

UN Mission, hemmed in by a group bulging with artillery. One felt like a prisoner going from the Tombs to the courthouse. One morning brought me the joy of finding myself in the opposite position. We were waiting for an elevator in the Towers. With me were a New York plainclothes officer, a uniformed policeman, two State Department security men, and Jeff Kitchen. The elevator stopped and out stepped an unmistakable member of the "oldest profession." Faced with a formidable array of her traditional enemies, she lost all color not externally affixed, but not her spirit. With fists on hips she demanded, "So, it's a pinch. So what?"

The genial police officer eased her mind. "Run along, sister," he said. "We aren't interested in you." She scuttled off down the hall.

Usually "general debate" at the opening of General Assembly annual meetings bored everyone and wasted time. However, in 1952, the time wasted in October was well spent, for although the opening date had been delayed a month, the American election was still three weeks off. General statements fairly innocuously disposed of half this time. My own contribution to them, sober but bland, is not worth recalling. By the last week in October even the most ebullient orators at Turtle Bay had run dry and the beginning of committee discussion could be put off no longer. The Korean armistice was the first item on the agenda of the First Committee and I was the first speaker. Debate opened on October 24. At the time I gave the President my key impression. "The outstanding fact of the Assembly so far," I wrote, "is its dominance by the Arab-Asian bloc."

We had not, however, wasted the first two weeks. In order to highlight the issue of the debate we prepared, and twenty nations† joined us in sponsoring, a resolution that called upon the Chinese and North Koreans to "agree to an armistice which recognizes the rights of all prisoners of war to an unrestricted opportunity to be repatriated and avoids the use of force in their repatriation." Leading off in support of the resolution, I made a long speech.[2] There was no hurry, and to give the whole history of the Korean issue from its beginning in the Cairo Declaration of December 1, 1943, that Korea should be free and independent—a proposition accepted by the Soviet Union later—seemed to me the best way to answer all the falsehoods of Communist propaganda. Carefully documented and, to hold attention, made from notes rather than read, it took four hours to deliver. Afterward Sir Muhammad Zafrulla Khan, Foreign Minister of Pakistan and later Judge of the International Court of Justice, said to me, "I had no idea our case was so powerful."

We had hoped for quick action on the twenty-one-nation resolution, but it was not to be. The U.S. election was only eleven days away; my authenticity as a spokesman for the United States was at low ebb, for General Eisenhower's announcement that if elected he would go to Korea indicated that he was committing himself to nothing. My report to the President the day after the speech† shows me unduly optimistic.

About this time Mrs. India Edwards of the Democratic National Committee sent me a message through one of my colleagues, who should have had more sense than to deliver it. It was a request to announce that in the event of Democratic victory I would not continue in public office. This message I thought best to treat with intelligent neglect.

THE MENON CABAL

On October 28 Selwyn Lloyd, British Minister of State, who was substituting for Eden, told me of a plan Krishna Menon was hatching. Lloyd purported to regard it as dubious, though I soon discovered that he was deep in it too. The idea—Menon refused to reduce anything to writing—was to turn the prisoners over to a commission under vague instructions looking toward repatriation. Menon was said to argue that this would produce an armistice and any arguments about its administration would be between the Communists and the "protecting powers"—that is, the commission—rather than with the United Nations Command. I strongly opposed this nebulous idea, which had every vice, since the Eighth Army would have to control the prisoners and bear all of the risks of a breakdown in the armistice without any control over the administration of the vital prisoner-release part of it. On October 31 a talk with Mike Pearson revealed that he had joined the cabal too. I told him, as my minute recalls, "that his interest in these proposals bothered me a great deal and implored him to keep in very close touch with me." I noted to my assistants that "this is a dangerous situation which we should watch very closely."

A return to Maryland to vote made possible a talk with the President and a report that in view of General Eisenhower's imminent trip to Korea it was very doubtful whether the General Assembly would support our twenty-one-nation resolution. It seemed impossible to get any expression of the General's views until he had made up his mind what, if any, liaison he would establish with us. The President told me of his efforts to establish one. For the present, we concluded, I should play a blocking, defensive game in New York. Also, he insisted, I should accept Prime Minister Louis Stephen St. Laurent's invitation to pay an official visit to Ottawa later in the month.

A week later, Schuman and Eden having arrived in New York, the kettle came to its first boil. Ernest Gross, Acting Ambassador to the United Nations, and I probed Menon, Lloyd, and Pearson to the point where it seemed to us that Menon, using his fuzziness of expression and unwillingness to furnish any written text as handmaidens of deception, had enmeshed the other two in a proposal that was an about-face. It was, I wrote the President, "as they say in strike settlement lingo, [giving] us the words and the other side the decision." Though none of the three would be candid, the result of their proposal seemed to be that those prisoners who agreed would be repatriated, and those who did not would be held prisoners until they did agree. In this way the principle of repatriation and of the negation of force both appeared to be observed. An earlier Mexican proposal that UN countries should each take some of the non-repatriable prisoners as temporary working visitors would have met the difficulty more responsibly.

The addition of Eden to the discussions only confused them further. He had not had the education I had in the sophistries of Menon, Lloyd, and Pearson and, while agreeing with me that the prisoners should not be coerced into repatriation, was persuaded by Lloyd that Menon's ideas were not inconsistent with this. As fast as I would explain, Lloyd would confuse. In my letter to the President, already mentioned, I said that while all I needed for the moment was sympathy, a firm instruction would soon be necessary, since a definite break might be impending. Menon was proceeding on the pragmatic maxim that if you can't lick 'em, join 'em, while, following General Grant, I was prepared to fight it out on our line. Vishinsky's speech on November 10 had given us the kind of help prayed for by the preacher pursued by the bear: if it did not help us, neither did it help the bear. The Soviet Government, he said, would "not budge" on the prisoner issue. The Canadians thought the speech was not as bad as it might have been; the Australians, that the Chinese wanted an armistice but the Soviets did not; most of the Latins, Burma, Thailand, and the Philippines, that it closed the door. I added that it "slammed the door" but would be helpful in dispelling illusions. However, those of Menon, the Canadians, and the British were proof against it.

A series of futile meetings followed with the three and with the group of twenty-one—in which we pleaded for action and the British for delay, while Menon fiddled. I asked for instructions and got them from the President: " . . . inform the Secretary that the United States Government will strongly oppose any resolution which does not clearly affirm and support the principle of non-forcible repatriation." We were now almost ready for a showdown, first with the conspirators, and then in the General Assembly.

As I saw the situation, it was that the armistice terms had been almost completed at Panmunjom. Only the prisoner exchange, airfields, and armistice supervisory commission articles remained to be agreed. I was fully persuaded that the Communists would not reach final agreement with our dying administration, especially since General Eisenhower, who was highly critical of our management of the war, was going to Korea to form his own views. The twenty-one-nation resolution was intended to get Assembly support for the terms submitted at Panmunjom on September 28 and rejected, thus leaving our position with strong international support for our successors in office when they took over on January 20, 1953. Menon's attempt was to transfer the writing of the armistice terms from Panmunjom and the United Nations Command to New York and the General Assembly under the leadership of India and the Arab-Asian bloc with British and Canadian support. We were determined to prevent this.

Not yet despairing of persuasion, I made one more attempt to win the British and Pearson. At my request Secretary Lovett and General Bradley came to New York on November 16 for a meeting with them. My purpose was to get away from talk about what would influence the Chinese Communists toward an armistice and to have those responsible for the Eighth Army state clearly the dangers in the field that Menon's loose plan for dealing with the prisoners would present. My colleagues did their best but the meeting was too large; the talk wandered and did not have the effect I had hoped for.

The next day, November 17, Menon circulated his resolution, which had the defects I have already mentioned. At a meeting of the twenty-one delegations I spoke against Menon's resolution but offered to amend ours to incorporate a repatriation commission, provided it had a neutral chairman with powers of effective executive action. Eden and Pearson argued for taking Menon's resolution as a basis and carried a majority with them. However, a small group was set up to draft a revision of the Menon proposal. The United States was a member and asked to prepare a draft to work from. Long experience had taught me the advantage that lies in preparing the paper for discussion: the burden of making changes is on dissenters.

Other action seemed necessary to protect the interests committed to me. I met with the American press to discuss with them—not for attribution to me—those parts of Menon's proposal that were quite unacceptable to us. All of this appeared in the press at once and at considerable length. One of my hopes, as I returned to Washington at the President's call to meet with him and General Eisenhower about matters requiring action before January 20, was that the General might make some helpful statement on Korea. A full account of this meeting on November 18 will come later; it is enough now to mention that part of it that bore on the controversy at the General Assembly.

A serious situation was developing in New York, I said at the meeting in the Cabinet Room. The debate so far had brought general acceptance of the idea that force should not be used to repatriate prisoners when an armistice took effect. However, some neutral nations led by India and supported by Britain, Canada, France, and some others sought to circumvent this principle in the mistaken belief that to do so would produce an armistice. They proposed that the prisoners be turned over to a commission, which should repatriate those willing to return and hold the others captive. The only escape from captivity would be repatriation. Certain results would flow from this: we would be justly viewed as having repudiated our own principle; we would have to use force to turn over the prisoners to the commission or hold them for its disposition; and we would have a precarious armistice, which would deprive us of observation behind the enemy's line and ability to break up concentrations and supply lines and would carry the constant threat of riots in the rear of our army.

The situation in New York called for energetic action on our part. A showdown was coming; debate would begin the next day and voting by the end of the week or early the next week. The President and his Cabinet advisers were firm. I had explained to our European friends that division among us on this essential matter would bring grave disillusionment in the United States regarding collective security, which would not be confined to Korea but would extend to NATO and other arrangements of the same sort. In this crisis a statement by General Eisenhower supporting the view held by the Government would be of the greatest possible assistance. I had prepared a suggestion for consideration, which I handed to Senator Lodge. The General made no commitment, but the next day Senator Alexander Wiley, senior Republican on the Senate Foreign Relations Committee and a member of our delegation in New York, announced the General's support for the principle of no forcible repatriation.

A SHOWDOWN IMPENDS

Back in New York on November 19, Eden and I met three times, twice with Lloyd, and then—at my request—alone. At the last meeting I proposed that he take over the management of the amendment for both of us, provided he would accept two minimum conditions below which we would not go: first, a neutral chairman with executive powers (we would refuse to turn over prisoners resisting repatriation to a commission paralyzed by the requirement of unanimity); second, an alternative to repatriation other than indefinite imprisonment. There had to be an end to their detention, though where they would go would obviously have to be worked out later, probably by some United Nations agency. Eden refused to commit himself. This, I pointed out, could only mean that he had already decided, or wanted to be free to decide, to infringe these conditions in concessions to Menon. There was another explanation, he insisted; if he made an agreement with me, he must inform Menon of it, which would destroy his influence with him. To me it amounted to the fact that we were not acting together, but at arm's length.

The struggle with the British and Canadians went on in and out of the group of twenty-one, and took the form of a debate not only as to how far amendments should go but also whether the Menon resolution should be given priority and whether this should be done before or after amendment. Eden and Pearson feared that Menon might withdraw his resolution—which had become the accepted vehicle of action—if it was treated severely. At this point I was unwilling to trust anyone, an attitude in which I found an ally in Sir Percy Spender, who had been made chairman of the subcommittee of the twenty-one. Sir Percy had been left as chairman of the Australian delegation when Richard Casey went home, instructed, however, to support the Menon resolution, with which Spender did not agree. He decided to construe his instruction broadly, agreeing with me to try to get Menon amended before we supported him— what might be called a "cash and carry" proposition. The amendments were worked out; the British wanted to negotiate with Menon; Spender would put them to the subcommittee on Friday, November 21.

This was the day on which I was making an early-morning flight to Ottawa for my state visit. Pearson was supposed to go with me but at the last moment sent word that his duties as President of the Assembly precluded it. By separating, each left his rear exposed to hostile action, but I left an energetic and able lieutenant, Ambassador Ernest Gross, in charge in New York, while both Pearson and his aide were there, leaving Ottawa exposed. This was a mistake. The struggle in the subcommittee produced a draw; no action was taken.

CANADIAN INTERLUDE AND FINALE

Prime Minister St. Laurent, a charming and courteous gentleman, gave us a warm welcome and a delightful visit in Ottawa. At a luncheon given by the Canadian Club—which was also the name of a whiskey competing with one once made by my mother's family—I raised a cheer by referring to this happy occasion as the blending of these two famous Canadian products. A call on the Governor General, Vincent Massey, who had been the first Canadian Minister in Washington, was followed by the Prime Minister's dinner and another speech. On Saturday morning the Prime Minister invited me to attend a meeting of the Canadian Cabinet, the first time, he said, that any member of another government not a member of the Commonwealth had done so. As we walked to the Cabinet Room in the east block of the Parliament buildings, I recalled to him that William Herridge, another Canadian Minister in Washington and a much-loved friend, had said of it, "Here is where the rude forefathers of the hamlet sleep."

The Prime Minister made a graceful speech of introduction. Other members echoed his welcome. Many of them knew some of my mother's family and the older ones knew my father. Mr. St. Laurent suggested that my hosts would be interested in any reflections I might share with them out of a long and varied service in government. Not without some purpose, I spoke about the problems that the new mass diplomacy posed in conducting international discussion through assemblies and public debate. The model—legislative procedure in democratic countries—was very ill adapted to the wholly different facts of international meetings, as I had just been observing in New York. The basic anomaly that struck one was the vast separation that existed between the few with the responsibility and capability for taking whatever action might be necessary and the many not only willing but eager to prescribe what that action should be and how it should be managed. I gave as an illustration the prisoner-of-war issue in New York and the opinion of our military on the dangers of an armistice unaccompanied by a prompt and complete disposition of the prisoners, of whom tens of thousands would fight repatriation or indefinite captivity.

At this point my good friend Brooke Claxton, Minister of Defense, interjected that he and many people thought our generals were wrong about this. I replied that his report brought out my point. Our generals were on the spot and in command—at the request of the United Nations—of six American divisions and twelve Korean divisions, equipped, trained, and supported by us, who with welcome but token assistance from others were fighting this war. It seemed to me that the military opinion that should be listened to was that which bore the responsibility of command. The Prime Minister agreed; so far as he was concerned, he said, there was no answer to that observation. The point had been made where it counted, and no more talk seemed necessary. Our visit ended with a luncheon at Government House given by the Governor General and a dinner given by the American Ambassador, Stanley Woodward, for the Prime Minister. On Sunday morning we returned to New York with pleasant memories.

There high agitation reigned. Gross had reported to me in Ottawa the unproductive results of his talks with Eden and Pearson and theirs with Menon. We agreed that their position was unacceptable and that he should tell them we would oppose it in the First Committee and put forth our own amendments. This he did, and apparently enough of his fighting spirit carried through to a press conference so that *The New York Times* of November 23 carried a story of a major break between the British and ourselves. Gross was upset about this, as were the British, but it seemed to me time to shed some light on the intrigue. Everyone would think that his was a calculated indiscretion, so we might as well act as though it were. When Pearson called me on the telephone and later saw me, he seemed much more cooperative.

Before the group of twenty-one met that evening, Menon had circulated amendments that met some but not all of our objections. At the meeting I urged that we stop negotiating with Menon, adopt the additional amendments necessary, and report out the amended resolution. What was needed were clear provisions both for terminating the repatriation procedure at a definite time after the signature of the armistice and for some other disposition of those prisoners unwilling to accept repatriation. While Lloyd asked and was given another chance to move Menon, two events occurred the next day, the twenty-fourth, that resolved the crisis: the President authorized me to go forward with our own proposal despite the British, and Vishinsky publicly and harshly rejected Menon's initiative. Here was another illustration of the Russians uniting us after we had gotten ourselves thoroughly divided. It quite destroyed the impression, assiduously cultivated by Menon, that he was in touch with the Communist side and that they were in sympathy with his efforts.

I followed Vishinsky before the First Committee, expressing sorrow at his disruptive attitude toward agreement on an armistice and praising the statesmanship of Eden and Menon. A few minor amendments would bring the resolution in accord with the admirable purposes stated in their speeches. I urged that these be made. A week of some confusion followed, during which Eden went home and I wanted to. Upon learning that the Chinese had endorsed Vishinsky's views, Menon wanted to withdraw his resolution but was induced not to. The final form of the resolution began to crystallize. The Latin American states lined up with us. "Events in the past twenty-four hours," I telegraphed the President, "have moved swiftly here and with all the elements of an old-fashioned melodrama." On December 1, the First Committee amended the resolution to provide a workable commission and assure that three months after the armistice was signed the repatriation procedure would end. Provisions for remaining prisoners, if any, would be determined by either a political conference or the United Nations itself. The General Assembly on December 3 adopted the resolution by a vote of 54 to 5, and Mr. Pearson sent it to Peking with a conciliatory note.

Ten days later the Chinese flatly rejected it and the North Koreans followed suit. At the same time the Communist prisoners in our compounds at Pongam-do refused to obey orders to cease military drilling, hurling missiles at troops who tried to enforce the order. In the resulting battle eighty-five prisoners were killed. Gromyko introduced a resolution in the General Assembly to condemn the "mass murder" of prisoners of war. It was defeated by 45 to 5 with ten abstentions. I had already returned to Washington on December 2 to prepare for my last NATO Council meeting in Paris ten days later, leaving other Assembly items to my colleagues on the delegation.

74. CHANGING THE GUARD

THE RELUCTANT CONQUEROR

IN THE SUMMER OF 1952 President Truman in his orderly and conscientious way gave a great deal of thought to familiarizing our successors, before they took office, with the matters with which they would soon be dealing. He himself had suffered greatly from President Roosevelt's failure to keep him adequately informed. The country was entitled to as smooth a transfer as possible, which meant a transfer to men familiar with the state of affairs. The President would work out with the President-elect the method by which this would be done; each of us would then execute it with his successor. We should each assume that whatever the result of the election we would be replaced. It would be understood that the President and his department heads would retain responsibility until noon on January 20; the new administration should not be asked to share this, but would be kept fully informed. The plan would work only if the incoming administration wished to be informed. To a large extent, as was true of President-elect Roosevelt in early 1933, it shied away from involvement of any sort.

Plans were made and papers written, but our meeting on November 18 with General Eisenhower and two aides convinced me that little could come of them. The General's companions, Senator Henry Cabot Lodge of Massachusetts and Joseph Dodge of Detroit, who had previously advised us on our financial relations with Japan after the peace treaty, were both good men. I have already mentioned returning to Washington from the United Nations for this meeting and my report to it of the Korean armistice debate in the General Assembly. General Eisenhower's attitude perplexed me. The good nature and easy manner tending toward loquacity were gone. He seemed embarrassed and reluctant to be with us—wary, withdrawn, and taciturn to the point of surliness. Sunk back in a chair facing the President across the Cabinet table, he chewed the earpiece of his spectacles and occasionally asked for a memorandum on a matter that caught his attention. His attitude seemed to reflect a continuance of that disclosed in his letter of August 16, 1952, to President Truman declining the latter's invitation to meet with him and members of his Cabinet during the campaign to receive reports on the state of public affairs. The President's phrase for it, "frozen grimness," pictures it exactly.[1]

In addition to the review of the Korean situation already referred to, I went over the renewed discussion of settlement in the Anglo-Iranian oil dispute, which might be approaching a crisis as the new administration took over. Prob-

lems precipitated by French weakness in European defense and in their war in
Southeast Asia might well reach the same state at the same time. Finally, I
mentioned our grave concern that the whole economic underpinning of the
Western alliance was too flimsy for safety. All of this discussion is well told in
President Truman's account of this meeting.[2]

The meeting left me with the conviction that the President's hope for an
orderly and efficient changing of the guard was doomed to failure. During it I
urged that the incoming administration should attach to the various departments
an increasing number of persons who would exercise responsibility after January 20. I was therefore dismayed to hear General Eisenhower say that his liaison
with the outgoing administration would be entrusted to two men: Mr. Dodge
would keep in touch with the Bureau of the Budget in its preparation of the
budget for the fiscal year July 1, 1953–June 30, 1954, which President Truman
would have to present to Congress shortly before the inauguration; and Senator
Lodge would be responsible for all other liaison. This was so fantastic a mis-
conception of the problem as to be ludicrous. In fact, so far as the State Department was concerned, we had no further contact with anyone, except for two
calls from Mr. Dulles. On December 3 he dropped in for a thirty-minute chat,
during which he told me that he would devote himself almost entirely to policy
matters and not spend as much time as I had done on personnel and administrative concerns. Nice work, I thought, if one could get it. On December 24 he
called again, at my request, to go over some matters that he should know about.
I shall return to this meeting later.

FAREWELL TO NATO

Ten days after my return from the General Assembly and a change in my
course of study from Korean armistice to European defense I was off again in
the *Independence* to Paris for my last NATO Council meeting. There we found
a very different atmosphere from that existing at Lisbon ten months before.
Soon after our arrival Jean Monnet, the brilliant originator of the Schuman
Coal and Steel Plan and the European Defense Community, called on me.
Adenauer, he said, would push ahead with ratification of the Defense Community when he had extricated himself from domestic troubles. The principal
troubles affecting European political unification, however, in his opinion came
from Belgium and Britain, with secondary ones raised by the French Socialists.
Britain, he continued, must awake to the need of supporting, and not impeding,
the unity of the Continent.

Sometimes it seemed to me that Monnet forgot—as do the rest of us—
Justice Holmes's admonition that certainty is not the test of certitude. The
trouble seemed to me to run far deeper and to lie at the very root of popular
acceptance of European unity. I pointed out to him the amazing distance the
United States had gone, often in cooperation with European initiatives as
brilliant as they were novel, in the Marshall Plan, the Organization for European Economic Cooperation, the North Atlantic Treaty with its concomitants
of the unified command, the stationing of American troops abroad, the restora-

tion of German sovereignty and participation in defense through the European Defense Community. Now momentum in Europe was being lost and retrogression had set in to the point of threatening disaster. A continuance of American interest and effort in Europe on the scale of the past six years depended upon the continuance in Europe of policies designed to create a community united politically and strong economically and militarily. Such a community we could and would support as a central point in our foreign policy.

However, if the European effort should fall apart, the whole basis of our supporting effort would disintegrate. That effort was worthwhile and necessary if it helped Europeans build a new and strong Europe. It would be quixotic to continue it if Europeans were giving up the struggle. If the European Defense Community went to pieces, I foresaw great difficulties for the new administration. What was hard for me to understand was how the Germans and French, who had seen us go to great lengths to respond to statesmanlike efforts on their part, could risk their own defense and future, as they were now doing, in petty political squabbling. At any rate, my personal responsibility would soon end. Monnet went off to talk with von Brentano and Schuman.

The immediate troubles in France and Germany came from the handling in both countries of the Bonn treaties and the Saar. In Germany Adenauer pushed the treaties in the Bundestag, while in France Schuman delayed their consideration in the National Assembly. Both tactics proved to be mistaken. Adenauer's view that ratification by a simple majority of the Bundestag would satisfy constitutional requirements was disputed by the Bundesrat, where the German states were represented and which claimed ratifying jurisdiction. Others regarded the treaties as making a constitutional change and requiring a new election or two-thirds majority in the Bundestag. President Heuss asked for an advisory opinion from the Federal Constitutional Court. When the Bundestag moved ratification to its final stage by a mere majority, 218 to 164, less than two-thirds, Adenauer, fearing an adverse decision from the court, persuaded President Heuss to withdraw his request and delayed the final vote, awaiting developments in France.

There they were far from reassuring. In October Edouard Herriot, President of the National Assembly and one of the most respected of French leaders, who only three years before led the formation of the Council of Europe and the movement for European unity, made a stirring speech to his party Congress denouncing the European Defense Community treaty as contrary to the French Constitution and inimical to French interests. Other French leaders joined him. Even Prime Minister Pinay was lukewarm. Meanwhile a new Saar crisis burst upon Europe as the result of a pro-French victory in the Saar election on November 30. Recriminations bounced back and forth between Bonn and Paris.

In such an atmosphere we met in Paris. Our colleagues treated us with the gentle and affectionate solicitude that one might show to the dying, but asked neither help nor advice nor commitment for a future we would not share with them. For this they were waiting for our successors. Since Lisbon, also, the new organization of the council secretariat under Lord Ismay and his international staff had taken over, so that our permanent representative played a less prominent part than before in making arrangements for the meeting. However, we—that is, Secretary of the Treasury John Snyder, Secretary of Defense Robert Lovett, and Averell Harriman, since 1951 Administrator of Mutual Security—carried out the agenda authorized by the President.

In one respect we failed. Despite our offer to pay forty per cent of the four hundred million dollars requested by General Ridgway for construction of airfields and fuel storage and distribution facilities over the years 1953 and 1954, the other countries cut the amount nearly in half. The General was properly upset by this action in view of the Russian preparations in Poland and East Germany. At the next council meeting in May 1953, our successors were able to get approval of the full amount requested. It was plain to us that a reaction was under way in NATO from the high moment of renewed energy and hope at Lisbon. The 1952 force goals had been pretty well achieved—in numbers, if not in combat effectiveness—but it was clear that those planned for 1953 and 1954 would not be met. The effect of the war in Indochina and disappointments in the amount of our aid—caused by a billion-dollar congressional cut in the appropriation and slowness in deliveries—had already led the French Government to cancel its planned increase in the number of French divisions in Europe.

Other factors were also having a chilling effect upon the will of our European colleagues. In addition to the growing belief that military plans were outgrowing the economic means to execute them, they were distracted from defense effort by developments in the West and East. The campaign and election in the United States convinced them that a new wind was blowing from the west and that they had better wait and see how much of a change it portended. It might mean—and, indeed, did—more than a change in faces in places of authority; it could forecast—and, indeed, did—a change of important degree in direction and in intensity of purpose. For a substantial time this led to a cessation of pressure from the west.

Moreover, at the very time the NATO Council was having its somewhat sterile meeting in Paris, a competing attraction was mounted in Vienna. The Congress of the Peoples for Peace, with delegates from eighty-five countries, met there with the usual Communist demands for a five-power peace pact, a disarmament treaty, withdrawal of foreign forces and bases, and the outlawing of nuclear, biological, and chemical warfare, race discrimination, and colonialism. Was this a new bid from the East to a new administration in the West for the long-sought "relaxation of tensions" between them? The hopes of many in Western Europe led them to believe that it might be. Here was another reason to wait and see.

In a farewell speech to the council I did my best to assure the ministers that the change of administration would bring no change in the American attitude toward NATO, but stressed that the need for reassurance was mutual. The coming months in which European parliaments would be considering the European Defense Community treaty would disclose an unmistakable decision on an essential step toward the European unity that I had outlined to them.

It was impossible to exaggerate the importance that their ally across the Atlantic would attach to this decision. A continued development of European unity and strength would be a centripetal force bringing Britain across the Channel and Canada and the United States across the ocean into ever-closer association with Europe. If Europe turned to disunity and weakness, instead of unity at the center, it would inevitably spread disunity throughout the Atlantic community. This momentous decision in Europe might well determine whether the twentieth century would be known for the work that we had done together since the war rather than for the disasters that had preceded it.

At the next meeting of the council others would represent the United States. They were well known to us. We gave assurance that they would continue loyal and devoted work for the great association that our country had so freely and unanimously joined, and urged our colleagues to give them their confidence and friendship. We received in response affectionate farewells.

Among the few actions of the council, two brought satisfaction to their proponents but little else. One declared that the French struggle in Indochina was of deep concern to NATO; the other approved a compromise with Prime Minister Churchill over a Mediterranean Command. There would be two commands. The NATO Southern European Command, under Admiral Carney at Naples with authority over land and air forces in Italy, Greece, and Turkey, would retain command over the United States Sixth Fleet. Admiral Lord Mountbatten at Malta, designated as Commander in Chief Mediterranean, would in wartime be responsible for sea communications. The shadowy nature of his line of command and his forces appeared from his theoretical responsibility to Supreme Commander Allied Forces Europe, and the provision that his British, French, and Italian naval contingents would remain under national command for national tasks. How these two commands would be coordinated— if at all—remained vague. The Prime Minister in his statement to the House of Commons supposed that they would "help each other." The struggle recalled the one over the Atlantic Command, with which the year opened. The "former Naval Person" still lived in that time of glorious memory when Britannia ruled the waves. Within a little over a decade three of Britain's strongholds in the Mediterranean (Suez, Cyprus, and Malta) would be independent and the guardian of the Atlantic entrance, Gibraltar, would be hard-pressed.

LOYALTY PROBLEMS ONCE MORE

In mid-December, while I was in Europe, the President's Loyalty Review Board reached, by a vote of 3 to 2, a conclusion of "reasonable doubt" regarding the loyalty of John Carter Vincent, with whom I had worked closely on China matters (see Chapters 16 and 23). Charges against him arising during Senator Joseph McCarthy's campaign against the Department had been investigated and dismissed in the preceding February by the departmental Loyalty and Security Board. Upon the presidential board's decision, he was suspended from active duty in his post as Minister to Morocco and Diplomatic

Agent at Tangier, pending my return and action. I knew John Carter and the charges against him well enough to know the imputation of disloyalty was unfounded and that the charges were in reality based upon the policies that he had recommended and the valuations of situations he had made and that largely I had accepted. I also had high regard for the Department's board and its chairman and none for the President's board and its chairman, Senator Hiram Bingham of Connecticut. At one time I had thought the latter's decisions were binding upon me, a view corrected by our Legal Adviser, Adrian Fisher, who reported them as purely advisory.

Thus I could disregard its advice and restore Vincent to active duty. This, however, would do him little good since Senator McCarthy would delight in renewing charges against him and demand that my successor act upon the presidential Review Board's decision. After consulting with the President, we decided that the better course would be to appoint a group of unimpeachable authority and reputation to review the record and the two conflicting recommendations.† Its advice, if it came while we were still in office, would give my decision added authority and permit Mr. Dulles to let it stand; if it came later, it would fortify him. I had no doubt what a fair and judicial decision would be. On January 3 we announced the appointment of the following committee to review the record and advise me: Judge Learned B. Hand, until his retirement senior Judge of the United States Circuit Court of Appeals for the Second Circuit, Chairman; John J. McCloy, former High Commissioner for Germany; James Grafton Rogers, former Assistant Secretary of State under Secretary Stimson; G. Howland Shaw, retired Foreign Service officer and Assistant Secretary of State under Secretary Hull; and Edmund Wilson, retired Foreign Service officer and former Ambassador.

Before taking this action, however, I thought it proper to inform Secretary-designate Dulles of what I was about to do. As already mentioned, he called on me at my request on the afternoon of Christmas Eve.

In our telephone conversation making the appointment for that meeting he had asked my opinion of Robert Murphy for the vacant position of High Commissioner to Germany. Though sharing his high opinion of Mr. Murphy, I doubted the wisdom of moving him from Japan, where he had just been appointed as our first ambassador since the war. At the time of our meeting on the twenty-fourth Dulles was considering President James B. Conant of Harvard. I told him of having tried and failed to get Mr. Conant a year before, when Mr. McCloy first asked for relief, but I agreed with Dulles' judgment and knew of Chancellor Adenauer's eagerness to have the post filled by a strong man as quickly as possible.

We talked also of the Chancellor's and Schuman's problems in getting the European Defense Community ratified and the help that General Eisenhower could lend, perhaps in a New Year's message to General Ridgway and his former comrades at Supreme Headquarters Allied Powers Europe, referring to the importance of the European Defense Community in the larger context of the movement toward European unity. It might meet the General's belief that his support of the Defense Community was too well known to need repetition to remind him that repetition was the essence of education. I also brought the Secretary-designate abreast of the discussion with the Iranians over the oil dispute with Britain, which would soon be in his hands.

Then I raised the Vincent matter. It seemed to me that the opinion of the Loyalty Review Board had passed judgment not on Mr. Vincent's loyalty but on the soundness of the policy recommendations he had made. If disagreements on policy were to be equated with disloyalty, the Foreign Service would be destroyed. I was considering, therefore, asking an eminent judge and some others familiar with the service to look at the record and advise me on this aspect of the case. Some of those approached had asked whether they must conclude their work in the month of time that remained to me. Anything that Mr. Dulles could authorize me to say would be welcome. After some discussion, in which Mr. Dulles showed an appreciation of the dangers to the Foreign Service that I had suggested, he said that he would regard the work of the board as helpful and would be glad to talk with any members who might wish to talk with him. He stressed the fact that the appointment of the board and the whole procedure should be wholly my responsibility, and not a joint responsibility. I said that I fully appreciated this.

I reported this conversation to Judge Hand and urged him to get on with the review without further discussion outside his group, reporting when they had finished to the Secretary of State at that time. On January 20, even before Mr. Dulles had been appointed to or taken office, the Judge wrote to him asking whether he would like the board to continue and report to him. Mr. Dulles replied on January 29 that the regular procedures had already been followed in this case, that theirs was "a special mandate received from [his] predecessor." According to established procedure the responsibility for decision was his. "Therefore," he said, "I do not think that it will be necessary for you and your associates to act as a special review group to consider this particular case,"[3] whereupon they dropped the matter.

On March 4 Secretary Dulles rendered his decision:

1. I do not believe the record shows that Mr. Vincent is a "security" risk. . . .

2. I do not find that "on all the evidence, there is reasonable doubt as to the loyalty" of Mr. Vincent. . . .

3. I have, however, concluded that Mr. Vincent's reporting of the facts, evaluation of the facts, and policy advice during the period under review show a failure to meet the standard which is demanded of a Foreign Service officer of his experience and responsibility at this critical time. I do not believe that he can usefully continue to serve the United States as a Foreign Service officer.

Public Law 495 recognizes the special responsibilities which, at this time of dangerous international tensions, devolve on the Secretary of State and reflects an intent that he should act to safeguard what he, in his discretion, deems the interests of the United States. I believe that that legislative purpose is sound and I am responding to it according to my best judgment.

Mr. Dulles' conclusion was:

While this memorandum was in course of preparation, I talked with Mr. Vincent and told him generally of my views. Subsequently Mr. Vincent submitted his resignation as Minister to Morocco and Diplomatic Agent at Tangier and placed in my hands his application for retirement. I am granting his application for retirement effective March 31, 1953.[4]

This action rejected the advice of the President's Review Board and, in effect, dismissed the charges against Mr. Vincent. However, it terminated his career because Mr. Dulles "concluded" that Vincent's professional judgment in a most difficult and controversial matter fell below a standard, which Mr. Dulles "demanded" but did not define. Mr. Dulles' six predecessors, under all of whom Mr. Vincent had served in the China field, did not find his judgment or services defective or substandard. On the contrary, they relied upon him and promoted him. Mr. Dulles' administration was later to find the morale of the State Department personnel in need of improvement.

United States Citizens Employed by the United Nations • In the closing days of 1952 the Senate Internal Security Subcommittee called Assistant Secretary of State for United Nations Affairs John D. Hickerson before it to testify regarding the current investigations into the loyalty of Americans employed by the United Nations. Asked to give the subcommittee a list of officers in the Department who had participated in evaluating information regarding American UN employees, he replied that he could not do so under existing instructions, even in executive session.

A similar request was made of a Department officer called to testify before a subcommittee of the House Judiciary Committee investigating the Department of Justice. In a letter to the Chairman on December 30, by direction of the President, I declined to furnish the names.[5] The work of the Department was conducted, I wrote, under the direction of the Secretary of State and his assistant secretaries. They were responsible and answerable for it. Subordinates had to perform the tasks to which they were assigned whether they liked them or not. To make public the names of those assigned to controversial tasks would inevitably put pressure on them to seek to avoid these tasks or to perform them with an eye to popular emotions and to their own defense. This would not be in the interest of the United States. Our subordinates had our confidence or they would not be where they were. We senior officers were responsible for them and their work.

The next day, December 31, I was summoned before the subcommittee and through an hour and a half of cut and thrust maintained our position. Even the Chairman's appeal to me to be more cooperative on the ground that he had opposed attempts in Congress to cut my salary left me unmoved. Nor would I concede that the security of the United States was involved in the type of citizen employed by the United Nations. Asked whether I was disturbed that information, on occasion, had not been furnished the United Nations as quickly as possible, I replied that if so it was too bad "but it would not lead me to snatch the knotted cord from the hand of God and deal out murderous blows to my associates." Finally, when a member put a question and added, "I am interested in your hindsight, Mr. Secretary," I pleaded that my hindsight was pretty "sore at this point."[6]

We parted in good temper. Ten days later the President tightened up the procedures.[7]

A FINAL MEMORANDUM

In December the President, at length convinced that his hopes and plans for a model transition from the old to the new administration would not bear fruit, instructed Lovett, Harriman, and me to re-examine our current plans for national security in the light of the latest appraisal of the dangers to the country. We put an able staff to work mobilizing our agencies on the task: Paul Nitze from State, Frank Nash from Defense, and Richard Bissell from Mutual Security. Their memorandum was submitted to us on January 7, approved and forwarded to the President with our own note on the sixteenth, and approved by him.

The memorandum was not a general restatement, we told the President, of our world position and security needs in relation to it, but rather a statement of additional needs due to developments in the two months or so since the last basic survey. We were particularly conscious of the diminished prospects of an armistice in Korea, as disclosed by the last General Assembly, the diminished prospects of early ratification of the European Defense Community, advances in the development of a thermonuclear device, and the latest intelligence estimates of Soviet intentions to press cold war offensives as derived from the recent Communist Party Congress. In brief, our conclusion was that there was a need —which was spelled out—for additional continental defense, civil and otherwise, and deterrent defense through a more secure striking force. A continuation of the Korean conflict might require additional production for military aid to free-world forces. Since the action taken by our successors was to cut rather than increase the military budget, further discussion of this memorandum is unnecessary.

75. LAST FAREWELLS

ASIDE FROM THE memorandum for our successors on national security needs and a last effort to mediate the Anglo-Iranian oil dispute, already recounted, the three weeks of January were given over to farewells. On the eighth, Prime Minister Churchill paid us a visit. His principal purpose in coming was to have a talk with General Eisenhower in New York and then a vacation in the sun of Jamaica. I met him at the airport, presenting the President's greetings, and again in the afternoon at the White House when, accompanied by my old friend Roger Makins, the newly arrived British Ambassador, he paid a courtesy call on the President. John Snyder, Bob Lovett, and I were with the President.

Mr. Churchill was in holiday mood. He was touched by the President's thoughtfulness in having the *Independence* fly him from New York and in making it available to fly him on to Jamaica. He hoped that the President and Mrs. Truman would in the not too distant future visit England, where they would be assured of a very warm welcome. The President rather wistfully spoke of how much they would enjoy a visit to England but how careful he must be not to do anything that would be misconstrued. The Prime Minister, chuckling, observed that he himself had been misconstrued for fifty years and that no one had really found him out yet. He hoped his stopping off in the United States en route to Jamaica had not been inappropriate. Not at all, the President said; it was important that he and General Eisenhower—for whom the President had a high regard—should keep in close touch.

For each of us he had a pleasant word: to Lovett, about the advances made since the last war in precision bombing as demonstrated in Korea; to John Snyder, about Britain's progress in overcoming her balance-of-payments difficulties, in which our Treasury had been most helpful; to me, about our current efforts to resolve Britain's troubles with Iran, about which Anthony Eden had spoken to him in a hopeful vein. He warmly praised the President for his courageous action in Korea and accompanying rearmament program, which he believed had saved the free nations of the world.

That evening the President dined at the embassy in a company including General Marshall, Robert Lovett, Averell Harriman, Omar Bradley, myself, and some members of Mr. Churchill's personal staff. The Prime Minister got the dinner off to an unpromising start by asking the President whether he would have his answer ready when they both stood before St. Peter to account for their part in dropping the atomic bombs on Japan. Before the President could answer, Bob Lovett, with admirable presence of mind, provided a diversion from this lugubrious subject. Was the Prime Minister sure that he and the President would undergo that interrogation in the same place? The Prime Minister took the switch, insisting that God would not condemn him without a hearing. True, agreed Lovett, but not in the Supreme Court to begin with; and, possibly, in quite a different jurisdiction. By this time everyone had relaxed and the Prime Minister, with the aid of his champagne, was enjoying the game. He admitted the possibility suggested, but insisted that wherever the hearing might take place it would be conducted in accordance with the principles of the English common law.

Coming to Bob's aid, I suggested that it seemed hardly flattering to the Creator's imagination to limit him to procedures evolved on a tiny island on a small star in one of His lesser universes. Mr. Churchill was willing to give some ground here but stuck on trial by a jury of his peers. So Lovett and I began to empanel it, calling and having Mr. Churchill accept Alexander, Caesar, Socrates, and Aristotle. He caviled, however, at Voltaire and Cromwell. When we announced Washington, he decided to waive a jury, "but not *habeas corpus.* You'll not put me in any black hole." At this point the President intervened. We had taken liberties enough. The evening had, however, been saved. It went on gaily with many anecdotes and selections on the piano from the President.

The next morning at the Cabinet meeting, on behalf of my colleagues, I presented the President with his Cabinet chair, which we had purchased from the Government. That evening the chief officers of the Department dined with me and presented me with a remembrance of our service together.

THE LAST PRESS CONFERENCE

My relations with the press—in reality relations with a fair number of distinct individualists—had been varied, but for the most part conducted pleasantly and courteously in face-to-face meetings. Most of those who treated me abusively and discourteously—and there were some—I had never seen. Our last formal meeting I opened with a word of leavetaking:

My Friends and Colleagues of many years: This is our last meeting. Ours has been a long and often tumultuous life together. But rarely dull! We have known one another too well to expect sentimentality or grandiloquence at this changing of the guard.

So we can say at noon what one said by moonlight, that "parting is such sweet sorrow." And we can agree with another poet that "the one who goes is happier than those he leaves behind," without overdoing the happiness or the sweetness of the sorrow.

This is an end and to be taken as such.

The President has told what we have aspired to do and [have] done, and why, in one of the great state papers of our Republic—the message on the State of the Union. He will speak again tomorrow. And he should speak, and speak alone, for his has been the great task and burden of leadership simply and bravely carried.

My testament is much shorter and easier. It is a final word to fellow craftsmen, a word out of long striving. It is not a word for popular consumption, no "message," no inspirational paragraph.

I don't need to tell you that the Secretary and the Department of State are only and, in their field, the chief servants and advisers of the President and that only by mutual loyalty in those roles can the Republic be best served. I need not say, I think, that in my experience this loyalty has been mutual and complete. I am deeply grateful for that.

But now the roles of command and advice and the travail of alien knowledge which goes with it pass to other hands. And our thoughts are with them. I ask for them something beyond good will and a fair chance.

"Efficiency," says Conrad, "of a practically flawless kind may be reached naturally in the struggle for bread. But there is something beyond—a higher point, a subtle and unmistakable touch of love and pride beyond mere skill."

This place cannot live without that, nor prosper without your recognition of it. So do not keep your eyes too close to your pencil points. And do not think too ill of my successor if occasionally there is a reminiscent note. For continuity of tradition is strong even in this new building.

Think, rather, of Prester John:

> Then he walks us to his garden where
> we sees a feathered demon
> Very splendid and important on a sort
> of spicy tree!
> "That's the Phoenix," whispers Prester,
> "which all eddicated seamen
> Knows the only one existent, and *he's*
> waiting for to flee!
> When his hundred years expire
> Then he'll set hisself afire
> And another from his ashes rise most
> beautiful to see!
> With wings of rose and emerald most
> beautiful to see!"

Perhaps "wings of rose and emerald" are too much to expect of the foreign policy of the United States. But wings there have been and will be, strong and buoyant; and in their fashioning will continue to be that "subtle and unmistakable touch of love and pride beyond mere skill."[1]

When the meeting was opened to questions, one relating to the new French Government action in seeking amendments to the already signed European Defense Treaty gave me an opportunity to review the state of Europe and leave the press with something to work on during what was bound to be an interregnum. It followed the line of my speech to the foreign ministers in Paris.

That evening the President and a group of friends, including Chief Justice Fred Vinson and Clark Clifford, came to dine with me at home. It was a gay and relaxed evening, during which the Chief Justice was presented for the crime of *lèse majesté* because of words alleged to have been addressed to the President in the intensity of a poker game. The Chief Justice did not deny the use of the expression charged but defended on the ground that it was ejaculatory only and not addressed to the President. The latter, who was presiding, delivered a Scotch verdict of "not proven."

FAREWELL TO THE DEPARTMENT

Friday, January 16, our last day of business, will ever live in my memory. The Cabinet met at eleven o'clock and adjourned *sine die*. Then followed a convocation of Department employees in the open space behind the building on 21st Street—Foggy Bottom—to which we moved in General Marshall's day. That open space is now covered by the huge and hideous building that today houses a good part of the State Department. Several thousand employees had gathered there to give me my Cabinet chair and to hear my farewell to them.

Few experiences have so moved me. They had been through three years of bitter persecution and vilification, largely at the hands of fools and self-seeking blackguards, touted by the press. The worst, I feared, was still ahead of them, when what protection the President and I had been able to interpose against abuse would be withdrawn. They, without doubt the best foreign office and service in the world, had served loyally and well. I tried to put into my farewell what encouragement and comfort I could.

Robert J. Ryan, Assistant Chief of the Division of Foreign Service Personnel, on their behalf presented the chair:

Mr. Secretary and Mrs. Acheson. The employees of the Department and the Foreign Service are very proud of your many and outstanding achievements.

Your high sense of duty, your statesmanship, your courage, your patience, and your fortitude have been an inspiration to all of us.

You, sir, are a true public servant.

As you take your leave of the Office of the Secretary of State, may we express to you our thanks and sincere appreciation for your leadership and support. Our most sincere wish, sir, is that the years ahead will bring every happiness to you and your family.

Mr. Secretary, this chair is the chair which you occupied during your tenure as a member of President Truman's Cabinet. It is a great privilege and honor, on behalf of the employees of the Department and the Foreign Service, to present it to you as a small token of our esteem and affection.[2]

In thanking and taking leave of my colleagues, I said:

Mr. Ryan, and my very dear friends: I am more deeply touched than I will be able to tell you this morning at what Mr. Ryan has said, and the fact that you should have wished to make me the gift of this chair, and that so many of you should have come here this morning to say good-bye to me.

I hope that I can see many of you again this afternoon. My door will be open, and I should be delighted to shake hands with any and all of my friends from the Department who find it possible to come in to see me.

This chair will be a gift which I shall treasure through my life. I think I can say of my Cabinet chair what the Supreme Court of the United States said of something quite different. The Supreme Court in one of its cases, referring to this quite dissimilar object said: "It is not a place of rest or final destination."

I have simply not found in this chair a place of rest.

There were occasions when it seemed likely that it might be my place of final destination.

I shall treasure it because it will bring to my mind every time I look at it two memories which are very dear to me. It was in this chair that I have sat for four crucial, tumultuous, and strenuous years at the right hand of my Chief.

It was in this chair that I have sought to bring him all the help and support and loyalty of which I am capable. And it is sitting there that I have received from him that unswerving support and loyalty without which no one in my position can ever hope truly to serve his country. So it will bring him very close to my mind when I see it.

But it is also in this chair that I have attempted to lay before him the distillation of all your work and all your wisdom and all your experience because no Secretary of State by himself can possibly be of such help to the President of the United States as he can be if he acts as the agent through whom your help goes to the President. That is what I have tried to do.

Through the long years in which we have been friends and companions, I have grown every day to know more and more that you are a part of a great and goodly company which stretches back through the years to the very beginning of our Nation, and that, today, as always, there is here that devotion to country, that loyalty to your work, that wisdom which is so necessary for our country.

Yours is not an easy task nor one which is much appreciated. You don't ask much of your fellow citizens, and if any of you are so inexperienced that you ever do, you receive very little. Certainly not much in the way of material recompense; certainly not very much in the form of appreciation of your work, because you are dealing with matters which, though they affect the life of every citizen of this country intimately, do it in ways which it is not easy for every citizen to understand.

And so you are dealing in a field which I called the other day a field of "alien knowledge," which seems strange to many of your fellow citizens.

One thing I think you are entitled to ask—that you should not be vilified; that your loyalty should not be brought in doubt; that slanders and libel should not be made against you.

You know, and I know, that in the times in which we live there is a security problem before our country. We know that that is a problem which must be dealt with wisely and justly and quietly by people who are expert in dealing with it. And I believe that the difficulties through which you have been will be temporary difficulties because they are not in tune with the great traditions of American life.

We have traditions here in the United States about the Government. One which grows out of our early history sometimes makes our life a little uncomfortable. In the early days of our country, government was conceived as something alien and something which threatened the liberties of the citizen. Therefore, we have a tradition in this country of skepticism about government, of looking at it very carefully, of seeing whether our public servants can take it.

That isn't always comfortable, but, on the whole, it is good. Any time when there are governments in the world which are crushing the liberties of their citizens, it is good that in this great country people look with some skepticism upon government as such. That is one of our traditions.

But we have another, and I think far deeper, tradition and that is the tradition of public service. I should like to mention two compatriots of ours, who worked in the field in which you and I have worked. One of them, before our country was a nation, worked in the field of foreign affairs: Benjamin Franklin—one of the first ambassadors this Nation ever had and who served it abroad before it was a nation. The other, a very great and illustrious predecessor of mine, to whom I feel often very close indeed, is John Quincy Adams, a peppery old fellow, to be sure. But he, like Benjamin Franklin, never for one moment believed that the holding of office was a source of power—it was an obligation of service.

Both of these men, and other men who have served in important positions, and thousands of people who have served less prominently, have been moved by the same deep tradition of public service. It is only by that that a democracy, a republic such as ours, can live. And it will live, and this Department will continue, as it has throughout its history, to be honored by those whose honoring is really worth while, and probably abused by those whose abuse is unimportant.

In saying one last word to you, I should like to put it in the words of farewell which appeared almost as our language began to appear. You will find it in Bunyan's *Pilgrim's Progress.* There another met with his friends to say good-bye, and he said to them. "My sword I give to him who shall succeed me in my pilgrimage, and my courage and skill to him that can get it. My marks and scars I carry with me to be a witness for me that I have fought his battles who now will be my rewarder."

Thank you from the bottom of my heart.[3]

All that afternoon my office door stood open and a steady line of well-wishers passed through to shake my hand and say a word of farewell.

Two more official acts remained. Wishing my term of office to expire at the same instant as the President's, I wrote and submitted my resignation, asking him to accept it.[4]

Dear Mr. President:

I hereby present my resignation as Secretary of State effective at the end of your Presidential term and request your acceptance of it.

In presenting my resignation, Mr. President, may I express my gratitude to you for the confidence you have placed in me, for your unwavering support and for the great kindness which you have always shown me. You have given me the honor of serving my country under a leader who has had and has my full devotion and respect.

May rest and happiness and peace be yours for years to come.

Most respectfully,
Dean Acheson

Dear Dean:

I have your letter of resignation effective at the end of my term, January 20, 1953, and I accept it with warm thanks for a job well done. I am glad I've had you with me all the way.

You have been my good right hand. There is no need for me to go into detail about all that you have accomplished. Certainly no man is more responsible than you for pulling together the people of the free world, and strengthening their will and their determination to be strong and free.

I would place you among the very greatest of the Secretaries of State this country has had. Neither Jefferson nor Seward showed more cool courage and steadfast judgment.

Our association has been a grand experience from start to finish. I hope Mrs. Acheson prevails on you to take a good long rest. You deserve it.

Sincerely yours,
Harry S. Truman

There remained my last call on the Senate Committee on Foreign Relations. The newly organized committee, with its Republican majority and my friend Alexander Wiley of Wisconsin as Chairman, received me on Monday morning, January 19. The Chairman welcomed me by saying that our meeting was my fiftieth with the committee since I had become Secretary of State. After a brief New Year's look at the world, I said good-bye to each member of the committee with which I had had so long and, on the whole, so profitable a relationship.

JANUARY 20, 1953

On Tuesday, the twentieth, we members of the President's Cabinet made our way to the Capitol, meeting him in the rotunda and following him down a ramp to a platform on the east front while the Marine Corps band greeted him for the last time with "Hail to the Chief." Chief Justice Vinson administered the oath of office to General Eisenhower and we were all private citizens once more.

My colleagues had asked Alice and me to arrange on their behalf at our house a final luncheon for the President and Mrs. Truman and Margaret and the members of the President's staff and Cabinet with their ladies. We were delighted to do so. The group came to thirty-eight persons. On finally getting through the inauguration crowd and back to our house, I was amazed to see P Street for the length of our block jammed with friends while the police diverted traffic and had a time getting guests to our door. Each arrival was familiarly hailed and vociferously cheered. Even after we were all present and accounted for the cheering and chants of "We want Harry!" continued until I produced Mr. Truman on the little terrace in front of the house to thank them. Georgetown was having its own farewell party for a special favorite.

While we were having cocktails, Alice presented to Mrs. Truman from the Cabinet ladies a fine Lowestoft platter that she had selected. After an informal and most pleasant buffet luncheon, which overflowed most of the first floor of our house, the Truman family went incognito to an aide's house for a rest before their late-afternoon train to Kansas City.

At dusk Union Station was packed with a vast crowd. The seemingly impossible task of getting through it to the presidential car at the end of the train was aided by friendly and good-natured folk, who recognized Alice and me and our need for a last greeting. At length we were admitted to the line passing through the car. Then admonitory toots from the engine hastened departing guests as doors and gates were shut and red lanterns swung. The car moved away, three figures waving from the rear platform as the crowd roared its farewell. Soon it passed beyond the lighted platform and disappeared into the darkness of the winter night.

IV

EPILOGUE

Retrospection in Tranquillity

76. SUMMING UP

ON THE EVE OF his fifty-ninth birthday—my own age at the time this story ends—Chief Justice Oliver Wendell Holmes, speaking at a dinner tendered him by the bar, summed up his years upon the Supreme Judicial Court of Massachusetts:

> I ask myself, what is there to show for this half lifetime that has passed? I look into my book in which I keep a docket of the decisions of the full court which fall to me to write, and find about a thousand cases, a thousand cases, many of them upon trifling or transitory matters, to represent nearly half a lifetime. . . .
>
> Alas, gentlemen, that is life. . . . We cannot live our dreams. We are lucky enough if we can give a sample of our best, and if in our hearts we can feel that it has been nobly done.[1]

This must be the honest epilogue to any pilgrim's progress.

Of the years covered in this book the first five were for me preparation for the last seven. Those seven, the period of Mr. Truman's Presidency and of the immediate postwar years, saw the entry of our nation, already one of the superpowers, into the near chaos of a war-torn and disintegrating world society. To the responsibilities and needs of that time the nation summoned an imaginative effort unique in history and even greater than that made in the preceding period of fighting. All who served in those years had an opportunity to give more than a sample of their best. Yet an account of the experience, despite its successes, inevitably leaves a sense of disappointment and frustration, for the achievements fell short of both hope and need. How often what seemed almost within grasp slipped away. Alas, that is life. We cannot live our dreams.

This, however, is the mood of retrospect; it was not the mood of action. I have already quoted C. V. Wedgwood that in writing history "we know the end before we consider the beginning, and we can never wholly recapture what it was to know the beginning only." The mood of the beginning, of the early postwar period of action, grew out of a trinity that marked a prior burst of human energy—which we call the Elizabethan Age—ignorance of the true situation, daring, and buoyant determination.

THE STRUGGLE THROUGH ILLUSION TO POLICY

Many times in the course of this book I have remarked upon our misconceptions of the state of the world around us, both in anticipating postwar conditions and in recognizing what they actually were when we came face to face with them. This was true not only of the extent of physical destruction, damage, and loss caused by the war, but even more of social, economic, and political dislocations undermining the very continuance of great states and empires. Only slowly did it dawn upon us that the whole world structure and order that we had inherited from the nineteenth century was gone and that the struggle to replace it would be directed from two bitterly opposed and ideologically irreconcilable power centers.

The first and perhaps most glaring example of our unawareness has appeared in the account of our slow realization of the extent of postwar relief and rehabilitation needs. At first we saw them almost as capable of being met by semiprivate charity, as in Belgium during the earlier phase of the European Civil War; gradually our conception enlarged to the international program of UNRRA, and then, three years after the end of the war, to the massive effort of the Marshall Plan and the associated foreign aid plans.

Again, as we looked further into political and economic problems, and particularly as we began to meet them, our preliminary ideas appeared more and more irrelevant to the developing facts and the attitudes, purposes, and capabilities of other actors on the scene. Mr. Hull's establishment had drawn its blueprints from Wilsonian liberalism and a utopian dream. They were founded on a refurbished and strengthened League of Nations, which assumed continued cooperation of the wartime alliance in banishing war and the use of force. Economic arrangements—even the new ideas of Maynard Keynes—were to be brought into conformity with the classical economic goals of removing obstructions from the free movement of goods, people, and funds as means of expanding trade and development. And economic development was to take on an evangelistic character in support of social justice and democratic institutions.

Furthermore, within months, even weeks, of the surrender of Germany and Japan, unilateral disarmament was under way in the Western nations. In some cases military defeat, in others approaching-bankruptcy and the end of lend-lease, in the United States the conviction that militarism had gone forever and a new day had dawned led to wholesale demobilization of armed forces. While from the viewpoint of Europe and Asia future prospects looked grim enough, twelve million Americans in uniform and as many others, like myself, serving the government in other ways, wanted to get back to accustomed work and life in a world redeemed and remade.

My own attempted escape, as I have told, was frustrated before it got under way and I was brought back to learn how false were our postulates. Both friends and enemies had been sorely stricken and were *in extremis*. One powerful ally of the war years had become an enemy in and of the hoped-for new order, which itself was proving an illusion. The first three years after the war —the time of my Under Secretaryship and brief return to private life—brought painful enlightenment to me and prepared my fellow citizens to meet the call for action soon to come. It was in that period that we awakened fully to the facts of the surrounding world and to the scope and kind of action required by the interests of the United States; the second period, that of President Truman's second administration, became the time for full action upon these conclusions and for meeting the whole gamut of reactions—favorable, hostile, and merely recalcitrant, foreign and domestic—that they produced. In the first period, the main lines of policy were set and begun; in the second, they were put into full effect amid the smoke and confusion of battle.

These lines of policy, which have guided the actions of our country for nearly two decades, were not sonorous abstractions—much less what President Lincoln called "pernicious abstractions"—written down in a sort of official book of proverbs. Nor were they rules or doctrines. Rather they were precedents and grew by the method of the Common Law into a *corpus diplomaticum* to aid the judgment of those who must make decisions. Its central aim and purpose was to safeguard the highest interest of our nation, which was to maintain as spacious an environment as possible in which free states might exist and flourish. Its method was common action with like-minded states to secure and enrich the environment and to protect one another from predators through mutual aid and joint effort.

The *corpus* differed from Mr. Hull's preconceptions by relegating to the future the attempt at universality in a sharply divided world. Like our own Constitution, the *corpus* in its order of priorities rated ahead of promotion of the general welfare the insurance of domestic tranquillity and provision for the common defense. It placed the strategic approach to practicable objectives, concretely and realistically conceived, ahead of generalizations, even those wearing the garb of idealism. It developed institutions and means to aid in achieving these more limited and, it was hoped, transitory ends.

In later years, the conceptions of this *corpus diplomaticum* have been criticized because its very success in meeting the urgent problems and dangers it was designed to meet in Europe and Korea has led our allies to relax their efforts, partly in the hope that they are no longer necessary and partly in the lurking belief that they were never quite so necessary as represented. Hardly had American leadership in collective political and military measures brought an end to Soviet aggressive activism initiated by the blockade of Berlin and the attack on South Korea than the successful measures were doubted by advocates of détente with the Soviet Union and disengagement abroad. Again illusions obscured reality, although the Soviet Union in Hungary in 1956 and in Czechoslovakia in 1968 showed with the most blatant brutality the nature of its fears, its intentions, and its capabilities. It is a mistake to interpret too literally and sweepingly the poet's admonition that things are not what they seem. Sometimes they are, and it is often essential to survival to know when they are and when they are not.

Another source of instability in foreign affairs is the popular conception that, as in women's fashions and automobile design, novelty and change are essential to validity and value. A combination of illusion and fashion leads to a demand for yearly models in diplomatic design. The pursuit of unity and strength in the face of Soviet aggressive hostility can almost overnight give way to popular demand for a détente style, then for an Asian motif recognizing Asia's hundreds of millions, that motif soon to be displaced by a new primacy accorded to the southern hemisphere. The simple truth is that perseverance in good policies is the only avenue to success, and that even perseverance in poor ones often gives the appearance of being so, as General de Gaulle has so continuously demonstrated.

The great exponent of perseverance, William the Silent, Prince of Orange, never wavered in the face of every hardship and disaster from striving for the unity and independence of the Netherlands. The immortal sentence in which he epitomized his life cannot be repeated too often: "It is not necessary to hope in order to act, or to succeed in order to persevere."

STRIKING THE BALANCE IN ACTION

Important as it is to know the truth and to respond relevantly and steadfastly to it, the test of action is in its results. How should we sum up the results of our actions during these postwar years?

The balance sheet of our relations with "the vast external realm" for this time is well in the black. Our efforts for the most part left conditions better than we found them. This was plainly true in Western Europe. At the beginning of the period that half continent, shattered by its years of civil war, was disintegrating politically, economically, socially, and psychologically. Every effort to bestir itself was paralyzed by two devastating winters and the overshadowing fear of the Soviet Union no longer contained by the stoppers on the east, west, and south—Japan, Germany, and British India.

Eight years later the economic life of Western Europe had largely recovered its prewar vigor and was moving on to new heights of productivity undreamed of before. Brilliant leaders had inspired their peoples with a new will and new vision of a political, social, and economic integration so that the economic help and military security we offered was used with full invigorating effect. To be sure, achievement of their highest hopes eluded them, but hopes still beckon, awaiting new leaders and new will to bring achievement.

In Asia, except for Japan, both leaders and popular will and capacity to make full use of help were lacking. Only some of the missing components of order, economic growth, and social and political development can be furnished to any society from without. The rest must be indigenous. So results have been spotty. Japan has repeated the spectacular achievements of Western Europe. In the past ten years South Korea has made considerable progress. The Philippines remain handicapped by their own weakness. Malaysia with British assistance has done well. Indonesia, only recently free of Sukarno's baneful squandering of great human and material resources, has started to move ahead.

Chiang Kai-shek was given a great chance in China and threw it away. The United States defeated the Japanese enemy and removed over two million Japanese soldiers and civilians from China. Nationalist troops were lifted from the extreme southwestern corner of the country, were rearmed and equipped, and put in possession of areas that the Japanese had held. But we could not keep them there. Chiang's failure to rally his fellow countrymen to his support, the administrative incompetence of his lieutenants, and their political and military folly lost him the position to which he had been returned. His armies and what support he had in the country faded away. General Marshall returned frustrated from his mission to aid the warring factions in their professed desire to re-create a united Chinese state and government. Soon Chiang with his gold bullion and some of his troops sought refuge on the island of Formosa, a hundred miles off the Chinese coast. China had been unified and was started on the road to power, but not by us or in our interest.

The dissolution of the European empires by their civil war had left various former colonial areas, large and small, facing the difficulties of independent existence and economic development with human and material resources for the tasks varying from none at all to too little. Again, attacking a multiplicity of problems with large appropriations of our resources and almost missionary fervor, we threw ourselves into providing, directly and through international organizations, capital, education, and technological instruction. Again we learned the immensity of the task and the strength of the four horsemen of the enemy—human fecundity, human ignorance, human pugnacity, and human stubbornness. Foreign aid remains both a noble aim and a dirty word. Here we must be content with hoping that we gave a lead and a sample of what the best might be. My own conclusion is that the criterion for giving foreign aid should not be the extent of the need alone, but even more importantly the capacity of the recipient to make productive use of the aid given. Charity—except to meet an emergency—is more likely than not to increase dependency and despair.

Finally, these eight years engraved on my mind a conviction which I have often heard Winston Churchill express, that the hope of the world lies in the strength and will of the United States. He would not object to my adding—and in its good judgment as well.

THE PRESIDENT'S CONTRIBUTION

It is usually a waste of time to discuss whether any of our contemporaries should be called great. The word means too many different things to different people. To some it carries implications of immense impact upon one's times or future development, as in the case of Alexander, Augustus, Charlemagne, Galileo, or Einstein; to others, it is a moral or spiritual leader, as was Confucius, Buddha, or Jesus; to some, a political leader with spiritual overtones like Lincoln, or an artistic genius like Raphael, Leonardo da Vinci, or Beethoven. Always the term involves some larger dimension than is possessed by even outstanding mortals. For my purposes it is enough to say of Mr. Truman, as was remarked at the beginning of the startled reappraisal of him that came soon after the political hubbub he loved to create had quieted down, that if he was not a great man, he was the greatest little man the author of the statement knew anything about.

Among the thirty-five men who have held the presidential office, Mr. Truman will stand with the few who in the midst of great difficulties managed their offices with eminent benefit to the public interest. On assuming responsibility in 1945, he followed the second most controversial President in a century, who was, when living, perhaps also the most popular in our history. The world outside of the United States had just gone through greater disruptive change than at any time during the life of our nation. As suggested in the Apologia, the President's task was reminiscent of that in the first chapter of Genesis—to help the free world emerge from chaos without blowing the whole world apart in the process. To this task, Mr. Truman brought unusual qualities.

The first of these was one for which he can claim no credit. Some remote ancestor, like the undistinguished squire-ancestor of the Villiers family in England, bequeathed him the priceless gift of vitality, the lifeforce itself that within certain strains bubbles up through the generations, endowing selected persons with tireless energy. Mr. Truman could work, reading and absorbing endless papers, and at times play, until well past midnight and be up at six o'clock walking deserted streets with hardy Secret Service men and reporters. He slept, so he told us, as soon as his head touched the pillow, never worrying, because he could not stay awake long enough to do so.

Energy brought bounce and cheerfulness. Not long after we left office, one of our colleagues revisited the White House offices. Seeing a well-known and more genial than informed character heading for the President's office, he cocked an inquiring eyebrow. "Oh," he was told, "he's going in to cheer up the President."

"That's funny," said my friend, "in our day the President used to cheer us up." A namesake gave the same cheer the night before Agincourt:

> . . . every wretch, pining and pale before,
> Beholding him, plucks comfort from his looks. . . .
> His liberal eye doth give to every one . . .
> A little touch of Harry in the night.[2]

The "little touch of Harry," which kept all of us going, came from an inexhaustible supply of vitality and good spirits. He could, and did, outwork us all, with no need for papers predigested into one-page pellets of pablum. When things went wrong, he took the blame. One "little touch of Harry" appeared in a motto framed on his desk—"The buck stops here." When things went wrong, he took the blame; when things went right, he followed his hero, "Marse Robert," General Robert E. Lee, by giving one of his lieutenants the credit. None of his aides had a trouble in his public or private life that the President was not quick to know and quick to ease.

These are qualities of a leader who builds esprit de corps. He expected, and received, the loyalty he gave. As only those close to him knew, Harry S. Truman was two men. One was the public figure—peppery, sometimes belligerent, often didactic, the "give-'em-hell" Harry. The other was the patient, modest, considerate, and appreciative boss, helpful and understanding in all official matters, affectionate and sympathetic in any private worry or sorrow. This was the "Mr. President" we knew and loved.

Today no one can come to the Presidency of the United States really qualified for it. But he can do his best to become so. Mr. Truman was always doing his level best. He aspired to the epitaph reputed to be on an Arizona tombstone—"Here lies Bill Jones. He done his damnedest." His judgment developed with the exercise of it. At first it was inclined to be hasty as though pushed out by the pressure of responsibility, and—perhaps also—by concern that deliberateness might seem indecisiveness. But he learned fast and soon would ask, "How long have we got to work this out?" He would take what time was available for study and then decide. General Marshall has called this capacity the rarest gift given to man and often said that President Truman had it to a high degree.

No one can decide and act who is beset by second thoughts, self-doubt, and that most enfeebling of emotions, regret. With the President a decision made was done with and he went on to another. He learned from mistakes (though he seldom admitted them), and did not waste time bemoaning them. That is, he learned from all mistakes but one—the fast answer in that nightmare of presidents, the press conference. We kept on hand, as a sort of first-aid kit, a boxful of "clarifications" for these events.

The capacity for decision, however, does not produce, of itself, wise decisions. For that a President needs a better eye and more intuition and coordination than the best batters in the major leagues. If his score is not far better than theirs, he will be rated a failure. But the metaphor is inadequate; it leaves out the necessary creativity. A President is not merely coping with the deliveries of others. He is called upon to influence and move to some degree his own country and the world around it to a purpose that he envisions. The metaphor I have often used and find most enlightening is that of the gardener who must use the forces of life, growth and nature, to his purpose—suppressing some, selecting, encouraging, developing others. The central role of directing so great an effort of imagination, planning, and action cannot come, as some seem to imagine, from such spontaneous intuition among the hired hands as guides a flock of shorebirds in flight. It must come from the head gardener. If he tries to do it all himself—to "be his own Secretary of State" or Defense, as the phrase goes—he will soon became too exhausted and immersed in manure and weed-killer to direct anything wisely.

When the Truman government found its footing in foreign affairs, its policies showed a sweep, a breadth of conception and boldness of action both new in this country's history and obviously centrally planned and directed. We had seen it in the early domestic policies of the New Deal and in our vast military effort in the 1941–45 war, but not before in foreign policy. The 1947 assumption of responsibility in the eastern Mediterranean, the 1948 grandeur of the Marshall Plan, the response to the blockade of Berlin, the NATO defense of Europe in 1949, and the intervention in Korea in 1950—all those constituted expanding action in truly heroic mold. All of them were dangerous. All of them required rare capacity to decide and act. All of them were decided rightly, and vigorously followed through.

Furthermore, to have restored the health and strength of our allies and sought their help in this effort would have been novel enough in American history, if one remembers the aftermath of the First World War. But the new conception went beyond that, persevering, over considerable opposition from our allies, in restoring and enlisting the help of our former enemies as well. Earlier enticing mistakes were put aside in favor of a peace of reconciliation and a policy of transforming liabilities into assets, enemies into allies. As in the case of Castlereagh and Metternich, a distinction was made between a nation and its leaders. As France was restored to an honored and responsible place in the earlier period, the same was done with Germany and Japan in the later one.

What sort of mind and methods had the man who directed American leadership in this constructive period? To answer this question, we must go beyond the nature of the individual and of his relations with fellow workers to some idea of his postulates and his habits in decision and action. These are easier to describe than to explain. No one was more attached to the democratic bases of American life and institutions than Mr. Truman and no one was less bemused by the prophets of the Enlightenment about how these came about and what moved peoples. He did not overestimate, as they did, the influence of wisdom, virtue, and understanding of experience and even "enlightened self-interest." Deeply trained in the moral values of Graeco-Judaic-English thought, he was also aware of the power of suspicion and fear when aroused against domestic opponents or against foreigners by a Hitler, a Perón, a Nasser, a Sukarno, or a McCarthy.

Similarly, he did not share the indiscriminate condemnation of power in politics, domestic or foreign, that American liberals had learned from Lord Acton. Military power he had experienced in use. He knew its nature, its importance, and its limitations. He knew that its primary effectiveness was in overcoming opposing military power or deterring another's use of it, or in overawing an opponent and gaining acceptance of one's own will. He knew that its limitations in administering subject or conquered peoples sprang from the cultures of both its potential users and victims. Only utterly ruthless possessors of power could use it to crush resistance in those not wholly under the restraint of caution or fear of physical suffering. The less ruthless were soon reduced to the process of persuasion in gaining consent, even to the extent of giving up dominion, whether in Ireland, India, North Africa, or occupied Germany and Japan.

He learned also, and learned quickly, the limits of international organization and agreement as means of decision and security in a deeply divided world. Released from acceptance of a dogma that builders and wreckers of a new world order could and should work happily and successfully together, he was free to combine our power and coordinate our action with those who did have a common purpose.

These postulates were held by a truly hospitable and generous mind, that is, a mind warm and welcoming in its reception of other people's ideas. Not in any sense self-deprecating, his approach was sturdy and confident, but without any trace of pretentiousness. He held his own ideas in abeyance until he had heard and weighed the ideas of others, alert and eager to gain additional knowledge and new insights. He was not afraid of the competition of others' ideas; he welcomed it. Free of the greatest vice in a leader, his ego never came between him and his job. He saw his job and its needs without distortion from that astigmatism.

Mr. Truman brought another major asset to decision. He had a passion for orderly procedure and a deep, if simple, idea of how to attain it. Although many presidents had been lawyers, none of them—notably his immediate predecessor—utilized in administration the law's most fundamental procedure. For centuries courts have required all parties in interest to be present before the court at the same time with the right to be heard and to hear one another. President Truman introduced this procedure into executive administration. To it he added an equally ancient, and in administration equally novel, practice of law: the decision was immediately reduced to writing.

The vehicle for these innovations was the National Security Council. This was created in the Truman years and reached its highest usefulness during them. It was kept small; aides and brief-carriers were excluded, a practice—unfortunately not continued—that made free and frank debate possible. Those present came prepared to present their views themselves, and had previously filed memoranda. Matters brought before the council were of importance worthy of the personal attention of the highest officers and decision by the President. In succeeding administrations practice deteriorated in two ways. The first was toward a desire by the President for "agreed recommendations." This was a deathblow. Agreement can always be reached by increasing the generality of the conclusion. When this is done, the form is preserved but only the illusion of policy is created. The President gives his hierarchical blessing to platitudes. To perform his real duty must involve the anguish of decision, and to decide one must know the real issues. These have to be found and flushed like birds from a field. The adversary process is the best bird dog.

Another way in which a President's role can become diluted and weakened is through yielding to the temptation to take over and run all operations. This not only wastes a vast amount of time and effort by a committee system for executing every important task and making all minor decisions, but limits, by narrowing, the President's attention to a few subjects that he allows to absorb him. The administrative tasks of the great departments of government are beyond the capacity of even the President's large personal staff to assume. To attempt to do so impairs both the broad direction of national affairs and the specific administration of particular parts of the whole. President Truman's strength lay not only in knowing that he was the President and that the buck stopped with him, but that neither he nor the White House staff was the Secretary of State, or Defense, or Treasury, or any other. To him the heads of departments were secretaries of state and members of his staff, as Lord Burghley was to the first Elizabeth. He made the ultimate decisions upon full and detailed knowledge, leaving to lieutenants the execution. This conception of the supreme role runs the risk that a lieutenant may fail as Longstreet did at Gettysburg or MacArthur in North Korea. The other conception runs the greater and more hazardous risk that the chief will fail in his infinitely more important role. It was such a failure, I fear, that blighted the high promise of President Johnson's administration.

The decision made in writing was also an innovation of the Truman administration in this country, though Mr. Truman was not the first head of government to employ it. On July 19, 1940, Prime Minister Churchill sent a note to the Secretary of the Cabinet: "Let it be very clearly understood that all directions emanating from me are made in writing, or should be immediately afterwards confirmed in writing, and that I do not accept any responsibility for matters relating to national defence on which I am alleged to have given decisions, unless they are recorded in writing."[3] His Military Assistant Secretary, Sir Ian Jacob, adds his comment: "Much of the conduct of the war was determined by the personal habits of the Prime Minister. Everything had to be done in writing, and he made it clear at the outset that nobody who said that the Prime Minister had ordered this or that was to be heeded unless the Prime Minister had written so in black on white."[4]

In Washington the Secretary of the National Security Council, first Admiral Souers and later James S. Lay, Jr., issued the President's orders to all members.

Justice Holmes has said that "legal progress is often secreted in the interstices of legal procedure." No small part of Mr. Truman's distinction in the presidential role derives from the fact that he instituted procedures that contributed to the statesmanship of his decisions and the quality of their execution. They insured that a flow of ideas would be encouraged, that his colleagues in the Administration would be welded together in loyalty to one another and to him by considerate, fair, and orderly consultation, and that decisions should be precise and known to all on equal terms. President Roosevelt has been praised for a supposedly deliberate secrecy in consultation and vagueness in decision that left policy fluid, relationships uncertain, and great freedom of maneuver for the President. In the currently fashionable phrase, his constant purpose was "to keep his options open." Flexibility in maneuver may be highly desirable in certain circumstances, but when it leaves one's own and friendly forces and commanders uncertain of the nature and purpose of the operation or of who has responsibility for what, it can be a handicap. Machiavelli was writing advice for weak princes.

In the last analysis Mr. Truman's methods reflected the basic integrity of his own character. He could have said of them what Mr. Lincoln said of his: "I desire to so conduct the affairs of this administration that if, at the end . . . I have lost every other friend on earth, I shall have at least one friend left, and that friend shall be down inside of me."

THE DEPARTMENT'S CONTRIBUTION

President Truman looked principally to the Department of State in determining foreign policy and—except where force was necessary—exclusively in executing it; he communicated with the Department and with the foreign nations through the Secretary. After one experience, when Chief Justice Vinson was almost dispatched on a diplomatic mission, experimentation with amateur virtuosity ceased. The Secretary saw his own role as Chief of Staff to the President in foreign affairs, directing and controlling the Department, keeping the President abreast of incipient situations that might call for decisions or action, acting as principal assistant in making the decisions and assuring action upon them. To do so meant avoiding too intimate involvement either in the work of the White House, tempting and flattering as that might be, or in the work of the Department.

General Marshall was an ideal instructor on the line that should be drawn between directing lieutenants and interfering with them. He bequeathed to his successor the invaluable legacy of respect from above for jurisdictional privacy. An anecdote of his gave courage in a not dissimilar situation. During the war, when a news magazine of national circulation had made a bitter attack on President Roosevelt, a White House aide came to the Chief of Staff of the Army reporting a presidential wish that the pocket edition of this issue printed for distribution to the troops be withheld. General Marshall replied that immediately upon his receipt of such an order in writing, it would be obeyed and his own resignation as Chief of Staff would go to the White House. The matter was never mentioned again.

Like General Marshall, his successor never forgot who was President, and the President most punctiliously remembered who was Secretary of State. This mutual restraint is basic to a sound working relation between the two.

What has just been written runs the risk of oversimplification. Foreign policy cannot be so neatly isolated and pigeonholed. For instance, one often reads that President Eisenhower left foreign affairs entirely to John Foster Dulles. However, at the beginning of his administration, at least, it might have been more accurate to conclude that President Eisenhower left foreign affairs to the decisions of Secretary of the Treasury George Humphrey. It was the Humphrey policy of retrenchment for fiscal and economic reasons that led to drastic cuts in Army and Navy expenditures in the early Eisenhower years. These, in turn, rather than considerations of foreign policy or military strategy, led to the Dulles rationalization of necessity—the policy of massive nuclear retaliation to acts of Soviet aggression. As a policy it was unworkable, outmoded when uttered, and profoundly disturbing to our allies and to our relations with them.

Similarly, Mr. Truman's period of retrenchment in 1948 and 1949, so vigorously applied to the Army and Navy by Secretary of Defense Louis Johnson, put means out of relation with ends. However, the recrudescence of Soviet aggressive actions, our own policy decisions in NSC-68, and the supersession of Secretary Johnson by General Marshall made harmonious policy possible. With ends and means in reasonable adjustment, the further requirements of an active and capable department were that lines of command should be kept clear, that lieutenants be given freedom and prestige commensurate with their responsibilities, that avenues be held open for the occasional brilliant suggestion caught in the bureaucracy to circumvent it and reach the top. The Secretary was aware that final decisions must be held open for the President.

With the President he met alone two times a week, and on two other occasions, once with the National Security Council, and once with the Cabinet.

In critical times other meetings would be added. Memoranda were prepared in advance of private meetings on matters to be discussed and the President's wishes or instructions passed back to action officers in the Department. The meetings of the National Security Council have already been described.

Each President conducts Cabinet meetings in his own way. They have come a long way from their function in the early days of the Republic as a closely knit consultative body, as has the Privy Council in England. Observation under four presidents justifies the belief that they can become an unorganized and discursive waste of time. President Truman soon organized his Cabinet meetings into useful weekly instruction of its members in the outstanding issues of the week, about which most of them had been informed, on matters outside their departments, only by the press. The meetings became an important means of keeping the leaders of the executive branch a united and knowledgeable group and putting an end to such gaffs as Navy Secretary Matthews' speech, already mentioned, approving preventive war with the Soviet Union. In such a meeting, for instance, I got my first knowledge of the "Brannan (Farm) Plan," for a time discussed by everyone and understood by few. Since during the Truman years foreign affairs were much to the fore and Cabinet officers sorely tempted to discuss the subject in public speeches or respond to questions involving it, the Secretary of State, at the President's invitation, opened the meeting with a review of the current situation and a recommendation of the public line to be taken. He rarely disclosed classified— that is, secret—information. A hearer cannot long remember what is secret and what is not.

Each member in order of seniority of his department would then inform his colleagues of what they should know of what his department was doing. No wise man asked the President's instruction in Cabinet meetings; he would surely find a number of articulate and uninformed colleagues intervening with confused and confusing suggestions. The Cabinet, despite its glamour, is not a major instrument of Government; the National Security Council, properly run, can and should be.

A hasty study of my engagement books warrants a guess that consultation with my constitutional superior, the President, and my constitutional critic, the Congress, occupied about a third of my working time.† If one adds the time spent away from Washington on conferences and speeches, these three activities would consume half of the Secretary's time. Since the days were not long enough for all other demands, they had to be sternly, even harshly, organized and disciplined.

To do this required devolving responsibility for energizing and directing work upon the assistant secretaries and their equivalents; to make these lieutenants acceptable to foreign governments required making plain how great was their influence on decisions. One vast benefit of achieving this result—to the Secretary but not to his indispensable aides—was to make them sought-after substitutes for diplomatic dinners and national-day receptions. Participation in these General Marshall and I probably cut below the acceptable limits.

The organization for assigning responsibility for tasks—the nine-thirty meeting—and for seeing that work on them was vigorously pressed—the Executive Secretariat—has already been described. During the last six years of the Truman Administration the Secretary usually stayed his hand until work upon any matter reached the point where guidance and decisions were necessary. General Marshall's military experience led him as a rule to put this point rather later than I did, and not to intervene until the Under Secretary asked him to do so. I, more aware of the deep-seated differences of view originating between different lieutenants' fields of responsibility—say, between Far Eastern affairs and European, or American Republic affairs and economic affairs—would meet with the groups as soon as an issue appeared, to hear and decide upon it. Furthermore, the group would more happily accept as final a decision from the top.

Since it was not possible, due to the great volume of the work, to have every interested officer brought into every decision, arbitrary inclusions and exclusions had to be made to get the work done. This was undesirable and was avoided as much as possible, but even so led to wounded feelings and sometimes to enduring criticism. We escaped, however, from what can be, and often has been, the alternative, endless discussion and inability to decide. General Marshall's often-quoted ejaculation—"Don't fight the problem. Decide it!"—put an end to this tendency in his day.

In short, the State Department of the Truman period became an effective organization for the imaginative and original formulation and proposal of foreign policy. It was tough and energetic. It took a lot of punishment and got through a prodigious amount of work. It may not have "gotten along well" with Congress, but Congress respected and, for the most part, supported the Department.

In 1941 Kaiser Wilhelm II referred to "Britain's contemptible little army." When it had taught him to revise that opinion, its survivors often referred to themselves as "the old contemptibles." I am happy to greet my comrades of President Truman's State Department with this affectionate appellation and assure them, as they look back upon their service under his leadership during those puzzling and perilous times, that they played a vital role in setting the main lines of American foreign policy for many years to come and that they may feel in their hearts that it was nobly done.

Appendices

NOTES

3

I have already described my feelings about President Roosevelt as follows:
The impression given me by President Roosevelt carried much of this attitude of European—not British—royalty. The latter is comfortably respectable, dignified, and bourgeois. The President could relax over his poker parties and enjoy Tom Corcoran's accordion, he could and did call everyone from his valet to the Secretary of State by his first name and often made up Damon Runyon nicknames for them, too—"Tommy, the Cork," "Henry, the Morgue," and similar names; he could charm an individual or a nation. But he condescended. Many reveled in apparent admission to an inner circle. I did not; and General Marshall did not, the General for more worthy reasons than I. He objected, as he said, because it gave a false impression of his intimacy with the President. To me it was patronizing and humiliating. To accord the President the greatest deference and respect should be a gratification to any citizen. It is not gratifying to receive the easy greeting which milord might give a promising stable boy and pull one's forelock in return.

This, of course, was a small part of the man and the impression he made. The essence of that was force. He exuded a relish of power and command. His responses seemed too quick; his reasons too facile for considered judgment; one could not tell what lay beneath them. He remained a formidable man, a leader who won admiration and respect. In others he inspired far more, affection and devotion. For me, that was reserved for a man of whom at that time I had never heard, his successor. [Dean Acheson, *Morning and Noon* (Boston: Houghton Mifflin Company, 1965), p. 165.]

4

The decision to intervene did not flow from a general principle of foreign policy, but as a specific distrust and fear of German intentions and ruthlessness. German miscalculation and stupidity fanned the fear. Barbara Tuchman, in The Proud Tower: A Portrait of the World Before the War, 1890–1914 *(New York: The Macmillan Company, 1965), gives us the mood of Nietzschean madness corrupted by bombast which Anglo-Saxons profoundly mistrust; and in* The Zimmerman Telegram *(New York: Viking Press, 1958) she describes the unveiling of Machiavellian maneuver that confirmed mistrust. It would seem difficult for any potential enemy to paint himself as a more depraved villain than the Germans did from 1914 to 1917, but both the Germans and the Japanese succeeded in doing so two decades later. The last push to intervention was added in 1917 by the announcement of unrestricted submarine warfare and the fact of ships being sunk within sight of our coast. The ocean, which for a century and a half had been our protection, then appeared as an avenue for an enemy's stealthy approach.*

5

John K. Fairbank, in an article entitled "On America and China" in Harvard Today *(Autumn 1968, p. 13), observed: "Through the treaty we set our diplomatic frontier way out into Manchuria. But we did not put our military frontier out there; in fact, in the 1920's we disarmed west of Hawaii. That meant we had an imbalance between what we*

PAGE

5 *(continued)*

were promising to achieve and what we were capable of achieving. When the Japanese moved back into China in the 1930's we were unable to do anything about it."

7 *(first note)*

When the British took the not unreasonable view that the colonies should contribute more substantially to their own defense, an attitude that we today take toward our European allies, the Americans switched sides, and with the indispensable help of Rochambeau's troops and de Grasse's ships at Yorktown became an independent state. The Americans stayed switched in the ultimate phase of the European struggle. While there was little to choose from between the interference of the combatants with our trade, the French menace had been removed from Canada by British arms and from Louisiana by Jefferson's purchase, but the British still held the old French forts along the Monongahela River as collateral for compensation to the Loyalist exiles.

7 *(second note)*

The relevant portion of Tennyson's "Locksley Hall" is:

> Till the war drum throbbed no longer,
>   and the battle flags were furled
> In the Parliament of Man, the Federation
>   of the World.
> There the common sense of most shall hold
>   a fretful realm in awe
> And the kindly earth shall slumber,
> Lapt in universal law.

The American attitude of missionary evangelicism in foreign policy was emotionally stated in President Lyndon B. Johnson's Inaugural Address on January 20, 1965:

Our destiny in the midst of change will rest on the unchanged character of our people and on their faith. They came here—the exile and the stranger, brave but frightened—to find a place where a man could be his own man. They made a covenant with this land. Conceived in justice, written in liberty, bound in union, it was meant one day to inspire the hopes of all mankind, and it binds us still. If we keep its terms, we shall flourish. . . .

The American covenant called on us to help show the way for the liberation of man, and that is our goal. Thus, if as a nation there is much outside our control, as a people no stranger is outside our hope.

. . . Terrific dangers and troubles that we once called "foreign" now constantly live among us. If American lives must end, and American treasure be spilled, in countries that we barely know, that is the price that change has demanded of conviction and of our enduring covenant. . . .

For we are a nation of believers . . . in justice and liberty and union. . . . We believe that every man must some day be free. [111 *Congressional Record*, 89th Congress, 1st Session, pp. 985–86.]

19

I have described these Sunday-morning meetings as follows:

Candor, I believe, requires us to go further and to concede that sometimes training and experience in the dialectics of legal or political controversy—a most useful aid in persuading others to accept a conclusion already chosen or imposed—can be handicaps in making a choice in the first instance. Lawyers, who are habituated to having their main choices made for them by the necessities of their clients, are often at a loss when, as in government, for instance, they have wide latitude in a choice of policy.

Secretary of State Cordell Hull, for years a lawyer and judge, then Congressman and

19 *(continued)*

Senator before heading the State Department, was, at first, a puzzle and then a source of delight in this matter of making a choice. For many years he would summon his principal assistants to a Sunday-morning conference in his office, a practice which should have been forbidden by the constitutional prohibition against "cruel and unusual punishment." During the winter the office was kept so warm that one had a half-fainting sensation of being detached from one's own body. He was sure at some point to ring for his assistant, an excellent Foreign Service officer, Cecil Gray, known as "Joe."

When he appeared, Mr. Hull would say, "Joe, look at that thermometer."

Joe would do so, and report, "Eighty, Mr. Secretary."

"I thought so," Mr. Hull would say. "Let's have some heat."

The main business of the morning was to review events and attempt to reach some decisions on future courses. For the first few weeks I thought that the heat was affecting my mind or Mr. Hull's, since he seemed to be taking contradictory positions on the same question. I soon discovered that this was his process of decision. He was trying out various views of the matter under discussion to find out how they went both with us and to himself. He would more likely than not settle on one which sounded the most convincing. This method of aural thinking and analysis is a long way from the working of the more sophisticated legal minds I have been discussing. It is not uncommon, however, as witness the apocryphal old lady who said, "How can I know what I think till I hear what I say?" [*Morning and Noon,* cited, pp. 147–48.]

58 *(first note)*

Stanton Griffis was a shrewd bargainer. He had been Chief of the Motion Picture Bureau of OWI, and later, from 1949 to 1952, would be our Ambassador, in turn, to Poland, Egypt, Argentina, and Spain.

58 *(second note)*

"Molliter et molle manu"—*"gently and with a gentle hand." From an old Norman pleading in which a man so described beating his wife.*

66

Article 4 of the Atlantic Charter states: "Fourth, they will endeavor, with due respect for their existing obligations, to further the enjoyment by all States, great or small, victor or vanquished, of access, on equal terms, to the trade and to the raw materials of the world which are needed for their economic prosperity."

82

The U.S. delegation to the International Monetary Conference held at Bretton Woods in July 1944 consisted of Henry Morgenthau, Jr., Chairman; Fred M. Vinson, Director of the Office of Economic Stabilization, Vice Chairman; Dean Acheson, Assistant Secretary of State; Edward E. Brown, President of the First National Bank of Chicago; Leo T. Crowley, Administrator of the Foreign Economic Administration; Marriner S. Eccles, Chairman of the Board of Governors of the Federal Reserve System; Mabel Newcomer, Professor of Economics at Vassar College; Brent Spence, Chairman of the House Committee on Banking and Currency; Charles W. Tobey, member of the Senate Committee on Banking and Currency; Robert F. Wagner, Chairman of the Senate Committee on Banking and Currency; Harry D. White, Assistant to the Secretary of the Treasury; and Jesse P. Wolcott, member of the House Committee on Banking and Currency.

103

This is about what Roosevelt did, ending up with three votes in the General Assembly for the USSR (including the Byelorussian and the Ukranian Soviet Socialist Republics) and three for the United States. The United States waived its extra votes at the San Francisco conference; the USSR did not.

PAGE

112

Dag Hammarskjold, in the Introduction to the Annual Report of the Secretary General of the United Nations, made public September 4, 1957, wrote:
The events of the past year have, I believe, cast a clearer light upon the role of the United Nations in these times. The Charter, read as a whole, does not endow the United Nations with any of the attributes of a super-state or of a body active outside the framework of decisions of member governments. The United Nations is, rather, an instrument for negotiation among, and to some extent for, governments. It is also an instrument added to the time-honored means of diplomacy for concerting action by governments in support of the goals of the Charter. This is the role the organization has played, sometimes successfully, sometimes with disappointing setbacks, throughout its life. [*The New York Times,* September 5, 1957.]

In closing the 1968 session of the General Assembly, its President, Emillo Arenales of Guatemala, observed:
I believe that the most striking feature which I have repeatedly observed during this Assembly and which is a defect of the United Nations is the unrealistic, emotional and I might even say demagogic approach of a majority of the delegates.

I use the word unrealistic because it is inevitable and sad to note so often that delegations or delegates use all their talents and all their diplomatic efforts to produce a number of resolutions for each item, forgetting that the evils of this world are not cured simply by negotiated resolutions but by the actions of governments.

I use the word emotional because often emotion is placed before reason, regardless of the consequences for the organization or for the world. [From an editorial in the *Washington Post,* December 23, 1968.]

125

Following is the international portion of the Special Message to Congress on Atomic Energy, October 3, 1945:
The other phase of the problem is the question of the international control and development of this newly discovered energy.

In international relations as in domestic affairs, the release of atomic energy constitutes a new force too revolutionary to consider in the framework of old ideas. We can no longer rely on the slow progress of time to develop a program of control among nations. Civilization demands that we shall reach at the earliest possible date a satisfactory arrangement for the control of this discovery in order that it may become a powerful and forceful influence towards the maintenance of world peace instead of an instrument of destruction.

Scientific opinion appears to be practically unanimous that the essential theoretical knowledge upon which the discovery is based is already widely known. There is also substantial agreement that foreign research can come abreast of our present theoretical knowledge in time.

The hope of civilization lies in international arrangements looking, if possible, to the renunciation of the use and development of the atomic bomb, and directing and encouraging the use of atomic energy and all future scientific information toward peaceful and humanitarian ends. The difficulties in working out such arrangements are great. The alternative to overcoming these difficulties, however, may be a desperate armament race which might well end in disaster. Discussion of the international problem cannot be safely delayed until the United Nations Organization is functioning and in a position adequately to deal with it.

I therefore propose to initiate discussions, first with our associates in this discovery, Great Britain and Canada, and then with other nations, in an effort to effect agreement on the conditions under which cooperation might replace rivalry in the field of atomic power.

I desire to emphasize that these discussions will not be concerned with disclosures relating to the manufacturing processes leading to the production of the atomic bomb itself. They will constitute an effort to work out arrangements covering the terms under

125 *(continued)*

which international collaboration and exchange of scientific information might safely proceed.

The outcome of the discussions will be reported to the Congress as soon as possible, and any resulting agreements requiring Congressional action will be submitted to the Congress.

But regardless of the course of discussions in the international field, I believe it is essential that legislation along the lines I have indicated be adopted as promptly as possible to insure the necessary research in, and development and control of, the production and use of atomic energy. [*Public Papers of the Presidents of the United States: Harry S. Truman*, 1945 (Washington, D.C.: U.S. Government Printing Office, 1961), pp. 365–66.]

126

The eleven senators, all Republicans, were: Brooks (Ill.), Butler (Nebr.), Capehart (Ind.), Capper (Kans.), Moore (Okla.), Reed (Kans.), Revercomb (W. Va.), Robertson (Wyo.), Shipstead (Minn.), Wilson (Ia.), and Young (N.D.).

143

Letter from President Harry S. Truman to General George C. Marshall, December 15, 1945:

My dear General Marshall:

On the eve of your departure for China I want to repeat to you my appreciation of your willingness to undertake this difficult mission.

I have the utmost confidence in your ability to handle the task before you but, to guide you in so far as you may find it helpful, I will give you some of the thoughts, ideas and objectives which Secretary Byrnes and I have in mind with regard to your mission.

I attach several documents which I desire should be considered as part of this letter. One is a statement of U.S. policy toward China which was, I understand, prepared after consultation with you and with officials of the Department. The second is a memorandum from the Secretary of State to the War Department in regard to China. And the third is a copy of my press release on policy in China. I understand that these documents have been shown to you and received your approval.

The fact that I have asked you to go to China is the clearest evidence of my very real concern with regard to the situation there. Secretary Byrnes and I are both anxious that the unification of China by peaceful, democratic methods be achieved as soon as possible. It is my desire that you, as my Special Representative, bring to bear in an appropriate and practicable manner the influence of the United States to this end.

Specifically, I desire that you endeavor to persuade the Chinese Government to call a national conference of representatives of the major political elements to bring about the unification of China and, concurrently, to effect a cessation of hostilities, particularly in North China.

It is my understanding that there is now in session in Chungking a People's Consultative Council made up of representatives of the various political elements, including the Chinese Communists. The meeting of this Council should furnish you with a convenient opportunity for discussions with the various political leaders.

Upon the success of your efforts, as outlined above, will depend largely, of course, the success of our plans for evacuating Japanese troops from China, particularly North China, and for the subsequent withdrawal of our own armed forces from China. I am particularly desirous that both be accomplished as soon as possible.

In your conversations with Chiang Kai-shek and other Chinese leaders you are authorized to speak with the utmost frankness. Particularly, you may state, in connection with the Chinese desire for credits, technical assistance in the economic field, and military assistance (I have in mind the proposed U.S. military advisory group which I have ap-

143 *(continued)*

proved in principle), that a China disunited and torn by civil strife could not be considered realistically as a proper place for American assistance along the lines enumerated.

I am anxious that you keep Secretary Byrnes and me currently informed of the progress of your negotiations and of obstacles you may encounter. You will have our full support and we shall endeavor at all times to be as helpful to you as possible.

Sincerely yours, Harry Truman

149

Not only a social faux pas, *but a regrettable lapse of memory. Too late to change the placement of the episode, I find it occurred in the fall of 1946, not January of that year. But the episode, I assure the reader, did occur, and the details are vivid in my recollection.*

156

What Mr. Baruch heard, if anything, no one could identify. He was very deaf and very suspicious.

158 *(first note)*

The Joint Intelligence Committee included representatives of the Office of Naval Intelligence, Military Intelligence Service (Army), Assistant Chief of Air Staff (Intelligence), Department of State, Office of Strategic Services, and the Foreign Economic Administration. Much of the work of coordination was carried on by specialized subcommittees: Technical Industrial Intelligence Committee, Joint Subcommittee on Technical Information, Joint Topographical Subcommittee, Joint Intelligence Study Publishing Board, Intelligence Archives Section, Weekly Summary Editorial Board, Publications Review Subcommittee. See Unification of the War and Navy Departments and Post-War Organization for National Security, *Report to the Secretary of the Navy, by Ferdinand Eberstadt (Senate Committee Report, Committee on Naval Affairs, October 22, 1945), pp. 161–62.*

Much of the growth in the intelligence operation was probably due to Donovan's energetic personality. "Wild Bill" Donovan, once described as a man who could "visualize an oak when he saw an acorn," would have surprised no one if in effect he "left one morning and returned the previous afternoon." [Henry A. Murray et al., Assessment of Men *(New York: Rinehart, 1947, 1950), p. 10.] He had led the Fighting 69th in World War I, won a Congressional Medal of Honor, and then returned to his law practice in New York and to New York politics. In 1940 and 1941 FDR had sent him on two confidential missions to Europe and the Middle East, on which trips he had been shown what the British were doing in espionage, resistance movements, and commando operations. See Roger Hilsman,* Strategic Intelligence and National Decisions *(Glencoe, Ill.: The Free Press, 1956), pp. 28–29, and Harry Howe Ransom,* Central Intelligence and National Security *(Cambridge: Harvard University Press, 1958), pp. 64–65.*

158 *(second note)*

President Truman has written: "On becoming President, I found that the needed intelligence information was not co-ordinated at any one place. Reports came across my desk on the same subject at different times from the various departments, and these reports often conflicted." [Harry S. Truman, Years of Trial and Hope, *Vol. II, Memoirs (New York: Doubleday & Company, 1956), p. 56.] For the text of Executive Order 9621, "Termination of O.S.S. and Disposition of Its Functions," see* Department of State Bulletin, *Vol. XIII, September 23, 1945, p. 449.*

On August 31, 1945, President Truman had abolished the Office of War Information and transferred its functions to State and to Inter-American Affairs. For the text of this Executive Order (9608), see Department of State Bulletin, *Vol. XIII, September 2, 1945, p. 307.*

PAGE
163

Under Secretary Dean Acheson's letter of resignation to Secretary of State James F. Byrnes, April 17, 1946:

My dear Mr. Secretary:

In our talk a few days ago I explained that my long-neglected personal affairs unhappily but pressingly call for attention, and asked for your understanding help in returning to them. I agreed, of course, in view of your imminent departure for Paris and the uncertain length of your stay there that I would remain with the Department until the first of July, 1946. It seems to me, after a great deal of careful thought, that I will not be able to put off longer than this date my return to private practice, and I should be very grateful to you if you could find it possible before your departure to hand the President my letter of resignation and obtain from him his acceptance of it.

It is with a very great deal of regret that I have come to this decision. We have been through a good deal together. You have given me a rare opportunity to make such contribution as I could to matters of great moment. But most of all this year has enabled me to add to what was always a high regard for you a deep personal affection. I know that you understand and sympathize with the compelling reasons which have determined the course I have to follow.   Sincerely yours, Dean Acheson

Under Secretary Dean Acheson's letter of resignation to President Harry S. Truman, April 17, 1946:

My dear Mr. President:

As the Secretary of State will tell you, I have spoken to him of the compelling necessity which confronts me of returning to private practice as soon as it is possible for me to do so. He has been most sympathetic with my problem and has consented to bring it to your attention before he leaves for Paris at the end of this week. In view of his departure, I have, of course, agreed to stay in the Department until his return and, since that date is necessarily uncertain, have thought that to fix July 1, 1946 as the effective date of my resignation would care for all contingencies.

This has not been an easy decision for me to make. I shall always be deeply grateful to you for the opportunity you afforded me of serving under your leadership and that of Secretary Byrnes during the past year, and I am particularly happy that there have been so many opportunities of working closely with you during the periods I have been Acting Secretary. It has been a great privilege and a source of much happiness for me. It is only with reluctance and in the face of the most pressing demands that I have decided to ask you to let me return to private life not later than the first of the coming July.

You have my sincerest and deepest wishes for your continued success in carrying the immense burdens that are upon you.   Respectfully yours, Dean Acheson

188

In the early part of this century, chaotic conditions in some of the Latin American countries had brought and were threatening to bring further European intervention in this hemisphere. In his annual message to Congress on December 6, 1904, President Theodore Roosevelt set forth the essence of what is known as the Roosevelt Corollary: "Chronic wrongdoing or an impotence which results in a general loosening of the ties of civilized society, may in America, as elsewhere, ultimately require intervention by some civilized nation, and in the Western Hemisphere the adherence of the United States to the Monroe Doctrine may force the United States, however reluctantly, in flagrant cases of such wrongdoing or impotence, to the exercise of an international police power." [39 Congressional Record, 58th Congress, 3rd Session, p. 19.]

193

Following is President Truman's account:

When General Eisenhower, whom I had appointed Chief of Staff of the Army to

PAGE

193 *(continued)*

succeed General Marshall, went on an inspection trip to the Far East later that year, I told him that I had a message I wanted him to give to Marshall when he saw him in China. I said that I wanted him to tell Marshall that my Secretary of State had stomach trouble and wanted to retire from office and that I wanted to know if Marshall would take the job when it became vacant.

When Eisenhower returned, he reported that he had delivered the message and that Marshall's answer had been "Yes." When Marshall's mission to China came to an end, I announced his appointment without asking him again." [Harry S. Truman, *Year of Decisions,* Vol. I, *Memoirs* (New York: Doubleday & Company, 1955), p. 553.]

200

Bob Hannegan, although a tough politician brought up in a tough school whose effect on the Truman Administration was not altogether benign, was a most attractive and amusing man. Two of his stories particularly delighted me. One was about his beginnings at the law in St. Louis, when he appeared before a justice of the peace, a retired policeman and a friend of his father's. The hearing was held in the justice's parlor. As Bob came in, the old man motioned him into a corner. "Move for a change of venue, kid," he whispered hoarsely, "I've been reached!"

The other concerned Bob's first day as judge of the Police Court in St. Louis, before which came traffic violations. Before he mounted the bench, the clerk had given him the docket of cases for the day, explaining that the traffic cases would come first and that those with a dot after the defendant's name had been fixed with the City Council and should not be called. He took his seat, opened the docket, and saw on page one four cases— City of St. Louis versus So and So, defendant—each with a dot after the defendant's name. The same on page two. He turned the page; again, a dot after each name, until he came to the last. As Bob reported it: "Poor friendless sonofabitch," he thought—and put a dot after his name.

207

James A. Forrestal's account of the report at the Cabinet meeting on August 2, 1946, is as follows:

Dean Acheson, at the President's invitation, gave a report on the present situation in China. He forecast that there would be attacks on our policy with a view to determining us by the force of public opinion to withdraw the Marines. He said the Marines had been necessary in China to provide for the orderly evacuation of a million-odd Japanese soldiers and of many hundreds of thousands of civilians. This had been accomplished, and the reason for the Marines being in China now was to support policy and efforts of General Marshall to bring about order, a constitutional government and a unified National Army. He said it was true that the existing Nationalist government of Nanking was not all that could be desired and that Marshall was not getting any great help in his endeavors to secure peace. But he felt that we should back Marshall up to the limit until he himself has said that there is no longer any hope of gaining his objective and that it is time to come out and reconsider our position in China and our general policy in the Far East. [Walter Millis, ed., *The Forrestal Diaries* (New York: Viking Press, 1951), pp. 189–90.]

211

Final agreement upon their terms was reached at the New York meeting of the Council of Foreign Ministers; they were signed in Paris on February 10, 1947.

276

Secretary Acheson's press conference, January 26, 1949:

First of all, I hope that you all understand the setting of "Point 4" in the President's inaugural address. It was one of four major courses of action which the President said

PAGE
276 *(continued)*

would be carried out by his administration over the next four years for the purpose of achieving the great objective which he talked about mainly in that address. That objective was to make clear in our own country and to all the world the purpose of American life and the purpose of the American system. That purpose is to enable the individual to attain the freedom and dignity, the fullness of life, which should be the purpose of all government and of all life on this earth except in so far as it may be a preparation for some other life.

The President went on to point out that the other theory—of the place of the individual in society—was not a modern theory, was not a radical or a new view, but was reactionary in the extreme. It is a view which goes back to the period before the Renaissance. It is a view which is founded on the basic idea that status is the governing factor in life, that every person is born into the world in a position, and that that person becomes a mere cog in a machine. That is a basically reactionary attitude and philosophy. It is not, as I say, modern. It is an attempt to crawl back into the cocoon of history. The American view of life is one which flows directly from the Renaissance and is one which says that the worth and dignity and freedom of the individual are the objectives of government.

Then the President went on to point out courses of action which we were going to take over the next four years to try to bring about that purpose of life, not only in this country, but in any other country which wished our help and association in that effort. To me the essential thing about it is that it is the use of material means to a non-material end. It is not that we believe that other people need or wish things for their own purpose merely to have these material objects. It is not that material objects in and of themselves make a better or fuller life; but they are the means by which people can obtain freedom, not only freedom from the pressure of those other human beings who would restrict their freedom, but help in the ancient struggle of man to earn his living and get his bread from the soil. That is the purpose; that is the objective of this program.

Now, the President was not announcing a project to be completed within a few weeks or months. He was announcing in this, as in the other three respects, a long program for his administration. It was a program on which much has been done in the past and on which more can be done in the future. The President pointed out that the United States has no monopoly of skills or techniques. Other countries have vast reservoirs of skill. In almost every country there is some nucleus of skill, some group of people whose technical abilities can be expanded with help from the outside. With all of those people, the President stated, we wish to work. He particularly stated that we wished to work through the United Nations and all those affiliated organizations which are associated with it. He pointed out that in so far as his program is successful and in so far as peoples in less developed areas acquire skills, they may also create the conditions under which capital may flow into those countries. He did not say this was to be governmental capital; and, indeed, if the proper conditions are created, the reservoirs of private capital are very great indeed. He pointed out that these must be two-way operations. There is abroad in the world an idea that there is a magic in investment. There is an idea that if every country can only have a steel mill, then all is well. There is a failure to understand that it is a long and difficult process to develop the skills which are necessary to operate many of these plants. There is sometimes failure to understand that plants should be located where the natural resources exist and not on purely nationalistic bases. There is also in many places a failure to understand that unless the conditions are created by which investors may fairly put their money into that country, then there is a great impediment to development. It is no solution to say: "Well, the private investors won't do it. Therefore governments must." So he pointed out that it must be a two-way street.

Now, as I say, much has been done in the past to try to make technological skill and advice available from the United States and from other countries, through the United Nations and through many of its organizations. All of those efforts can be brought together and intensified. The President pointed out that we are willing and anxious to work with

PAGE
276 (continued)
every country that wishes to really enter into a cooperative system with the rest of the world to this end and with every country that wishes to help other countries to develop.

Now, that is the broad background of the inaugural address. I have talked at some length about this because it seems to me important that it be put in its setting of American foreign policy. [*Department of State Bulletin*, Vol. XX, February 6, 1949, pp. 155–56.]

280
I believe it to be true that Congress has never "declared war." Beginning with the Declaration of Independence, it has found that some foreign power has made war on the United States and that a state of war exists with that power.

304 (first note)
In 1949 I had met to discuss China policy in February with thirty members of the House; in June with the House Foreign Affairs Committee and Senate Foreign Relations Committee; in July with House committee and, when the Senate committee could not find time because of a crowded legislative calendar, individually with Senators Tom Connally, Arthur Vandenberg, and Alexander Smith; and in October with the Senate committee. Messrs. Philip Jessup, Raymond B. Fosdick, and Everett Case, the consultants on China, also conferred with members of the Senate committee.

304 (second note)
On May 12, 1949, I proposed to the President that the Wedemeyer report be published in the White Paper. Clark M. Clifford, Counsel to the President, replied, "The President has carefully read your memo to him with reference to the Wedemeyer Report on China. I am returning herewith your memo containing the President's approval of your recommendation that the Wedemeyer Report on China be released as a part of the State Department's White Paper on United States policy to China. You are also authorized to inform the Senate Subcommittee on Appropriations of the reasons why the Report was not previously published, and to inform the Subcommittee that the State Department expects to release the Report as a part of the White Paper."

306
Memorandum from Secretary Acheson to Senator Tom Connally, March 15, 1949:

The following comments on S. 1063 are offered in response to your request as conveyed by Mr. O'Day, Clerk of the Committee on Foreign Relations, in his letter of February 28, 1949. It is the Department's view that the Bill proposes aid of a magnitude and character unwarranted by present circumstances in China.

Despite the present aid program authorized by the last Congress, together with the very substantial other aid extended by the United States to China since V-J Day, aggregating over $2 billion, the economic and military position of the Chinese Government has deteriorated to the point where the Chinese Communists hold almost all important areas of China from Manchuria to the Yangtze River and have the military capability of expanding their control to the populous areas of the Yangtze Valley and of eventually dominating south China. The National Government does not have the military capability of maintaining a foothold in south China against a determined Communist advance. The Chinese Government forces have lost no battles during the past year because of lack of ammunition and equipment, while the Chinese Communists have captured the major portion of military supplies, exclusive of ammunition, furnished the Chinese Government by the United States since V-J Day. There is no evidence that the furnishing of additional military material would alter the pattern of current developments in China. There is, however, ample evidence that the Chinese people are weary of hostilities and that there is an overwhelming desire for peace at any price. To furnish solely military material and advice would only prolong hostilities and the suffering of the Chinese people and would arouse in them deep

306 *(continued)*

resentment against the United States. Yet, to furnish the military means for bringing about a reversal of the present deterioration and for providing some prospect of successful military resistance would require the use of an unpredictably large American armed force in actual combat, a course of action which would represent direct United States involvement in China's fratricidal warfare and would be contrary to our traditional policy toward China and the interests of this country.

In these circumstances, the extension of as much as $1.5 billion of credits to the Chinese Government, as proposed by the Bill, would embark this Government on an undertaking the eventual cost of which would be unpredictable but of great magnitude, and the outcome of which would almost surely be catastrophic. The field supervision of United States military aid, the pledging of revenue of major Chinese ports in payment of United States aid, United States administration and collection of Chinese customs in such ports, and United States participation in Chinese tax administration, all of which are called for by the Bill, would without question be deeply resented by the Chinese people as an extreme infringement of China's sovereignty and would arouse distrust in the minds of the Chinese people with respect to the motives of the United States in extending aid. While the use of up to $500 million in support of the Chinese currency, as proposed in the Bill, would undoubtedly ease temporarily the fiscal problem of the Chinese Government, stabilization of the Chinese currency cannot be considered feasible so long as the Government's monetary outlays exceed its income by a large margin. After the first $500 million had been expended, the United States would find it necessary to continue provision of funds to cover the Chinese Government's budgetary deficit if the inflationary spiral were not to be resumed. That China could be expected to repay United States financial, economic and military aid of the magnitude proposed, which the Bill indicates should all be on a credit basis, cannot be supported by realistic estimates of China's future ability to service foreign debts even under conditions of peace and economic stability.

The United States has in the past sought to encourage the Chinese Government to initiate those vital measures necessary to provide a basis for economic improvement and political stability. It has recognized that, in the absence of a Chinese Government capable of initiating such measures and winning popular support, United States aid of great magnitude would be dissipated and United States attempts to guide the operations of the Chinese Government would be ineffective and probably lead to direct involvement in China's fratricidal warfare. General Marshall reflected these considerations when he stated in February 1948 that an attempt to underwrite the Chinese economy and the Chinese Government's military effort represented a burden on the United States economy and a military responsibility which he could not recommend as a course of action for this Government.

Despite the above observations, it would be undesirable for the United States precipitously to cease aid to areas under the control of the Chinese Government which it continues to recognize. Future developments in China, including the outcome of political negotiations now being undertaken, are uncertain. Consideration is being given, therefore, to a request for Congressional action to extend the authority of the China Aid Act of 1948 to permit commitment of unobligated appropriations for a limited period beyond April 2, 1949, the present expiration date of the Act. If during such a period, the situation in China clarifies itself sufficiently, further recommendations might be made. [*United States Relations with China* (Washington: U.S. Government Printing Office, 1949), pp. 1053–54.]

337

Senator Cooper's troubles were not confined to the political sphere but followed him on his air travels. Actually, it was on a later trip on the Independence *that lightning hit our plane. On this, the November trip to Paris and Bonn, one of the two trips we did not make on the* Independence, *a Stratocruiser chartered for our trip had broken down on its way from New York to pick us up, and our party became notorious as the press reported that*

337 *(continued)*

European-bound passengers at Idlewild were dislodged, bag and baggage, from their Strato-cruiser when it was diverted to Washington to take the Secretary of State and his party to Paris. On a third flight with the Senator we were all asleep in our bunks—a luxury afforded by the Independence—*when complete silence from the four motors awakened us to an uneasy few seconds before our four engines came back to life. By this time the Senator could be forgiven if he had some qualms about flying with the Secretary of State, and perhaps vice versa. The reader will forgive me if once again unchecked memory has confused one amusing recollection with another.*

348

Thus on February 24, 1950, the Secretary of Defense and the Joint Chiefs of Staff recommended that our program be stepped up by "immediate implementation of all-out development of hydrogen bombs and means for their production and delivery." The Special Committee of the National Security Council, to which this recommendation was referred, reported on March 9, 1950, that "there are no known additional steps which might be taken for further acceleration of the test program." President Truman decided to assume that the test would be successful and on March 10 directed the Atomic Energy Commission to begin planning at once for production in quantity so that there should be no delay in getting under way if the bomb proved feasible. See Truman, Years of Trial and Hope, *cited, pp. 309–11.*

349

David E. Lilienthal's own account of the H-bomb controversy, the work of the National Security Council Special Committee, and the meeting with the President is well worth reading. It is found, interlarded with other reflections, in The Atomic Energy Years, 1945–1950, Vol.II, The Journals of David E. Lilienthal *(New York: Harper & Row, 1964), pp. 580–636.*

354

The title of this chapter is derived from a phrase of John Duncan Miller of The Times *of London: a "revolt of the primitives against intelligence." Quoted in Norman A. Graebner,* The Secretary of State: An Uncertain Tradition *(New York: McGraw-Hill Book Company, 1961), p. 284.*

360 *(first note)*

The editorial in the New York Herald Tribune, *January 27, 1950:*

The moving statement by Secretary Acheson concerning his attitude toward Alger Hiss was phrased with straightforward simplicity. The Secretary made three points. First of all, he would not discuss the law or the evidence or anything to do with the case itself. It would be "highly improper" for him to do so while it was "before the courts." Second, regardless of the ultimate fate of the case, he did not intend "to turn his back on Alger Hiss." Third, this decision was a matter of individual conscience, to be reached by "each person in the light of his own standards and his own principles." For a definition of his own standards and principles he referred the listeners to the Gospel of St. Matthew.

The verses in question are among the noblest in the New Testament. They include the words: "I was in prison and ye came unto me," and "inasmuch as ye have done it unto one of the least of these my brethren, ye have done it unto me." Perhaps the voice of the late Bishop of Connecticut, Mr. Acheson's father, sounded in the citation.

The Secretary might have used more words to state his point of view and might have defined it in more detail and with more precision. But we do not see how anyone desiring to be fair could take these words to be a defense of Alger Hiss. To suggest that he was giving the slightest opinion as to guilt or innocence is to ignore an express declaration. To

360 *(continued)*

argue that he was in any possible sense defending Communism, in or out of the State Department, seems to us equally untenable.

This newspaper has felt it necessary at times to criticize and oppose Mr. Acheson in his policies. We may well be compelled to do so again. But of this statement made on Wednesday in a difficult hour, we are glad to declare that in our judgment it was as courageous as it was Christian.

360 *(second note)*

In early 1945 Mr. Truman, then Vice President, had paid compassionate tribute to his friend Thomas J. Pendergast by flying, accompanied by Mrs. Truman, to his funeral in Kansas City. He was much criticized for his loyalty to an old friend.

364 *(first note)*

On April 5, 1950, I wrote to President Truman (who was in Key West) as follows: "Bridges is, I believe, coming around, although he may feel it necessary to have one last fling in response to your press conference. I am hoping that he will not do this. He has a date to spend some time with me on Friday afternoon at my house. We are going over the various grievances which he has against me. I do not know yet what they are, but hope that a good talk, eased with some bourbon, may result in eliminating what I am sure are misunderstandings." On April 7 Senator Bridges and I did meet and did make our peace.

This meeting came about on my initiative, instigated by Assistant Secretary John Peurifoy. The Senator believed that I had insulted him in private conversation. The reconciliation was fragile but made relations more pleasant for about a year. It broke down after an interview we had on April 11, 1951, regarding General MacArthur, who was, unknown to the Senator, being relieved from duty that day. The Senator believed that my silence regarding this (for a few hours) highly secret order misled him. He was correct. It was intended to.

The press conference referred to above was the one the President held at Key West on March 30, 1959, during which he was asked, "Do you think Senator McCarthy is getting anywhere in his attempt to win the case against the State Department?" The President replied, "I think the greatest asset that the Kremlin has is Senator McCarthy."

After further questions and answers relating to the purpose and effect of the effort of McCarthy and other Republican senators to find an issue that would destroy the bipartisan foreign policy and "make a bid for the control of Congress" in 1951, the President was asked whether he would "name any others besides Senator McCarthy who have participated in this attempt to sabotage our foreign policy." The President named Senators Wherry and Bridges.

When he was then asked if his original remark could be given in direct quotation marks, the President rephrased it as follows: "The greatest asset that the Kremlin has is the partisan attempt in the Senate to sabotage the bipartisan foreign policy of the United States." See Public Papers of the Presidents of the United States: Harry S. Truman, 1950, cited, pp. 234–36.

364 *(second note)*

The co-sponsors of Senator Margaret Chase Smith's resolution were Republican Senators Tobey of New Hampshire, Aiken of Vermont, Morse of Oregon, Ives of New York, Thye of Minnesota, and Hendrickson of New Jersey. Supporting it were Democratic Senators Lehman of New York and Humphrey of Minnesota.

375

In the State Department itself we ran into a stultifying and, so I thought, sterile argument between the Planning Staff and the Soviet experts. The latter challenged the belief which

PAGE
375 *(continued)*

I shared with the planners that the Kremlin gave top priority to world domination in their scheme of things. They contended that we attributed more of a Trotskyite than Leninist view to Stalin and that he placed the survival of the regime and "communism in one country" far ahead of world revolution. We did not dissent from this, but pointed out that, assuming the proper semantic adjustment, the effect of their point bore on the degree of risk of all-out war which the Soviet Government would run in probing a weak spot for concessions. Granted that they might not go as recklessly far as the Japanese had gone at Pearl Harbor—where they really did give the East Asia co-prosperity sphere priority over the certainty of war and the gravest risk to the regime—the difference seemed to me more theoretical than real in devising courses necessary to eliminate the weak spots which so tempted Moscow to probe our resolution and that of our allies. Khrushchev's conduct in the 1962 missile crisis seems to have borne us out. When the argument reached the point which President George Vincent of the University of Minnesota has described as the "you hold the sieve while I milk the barren heifer" stage, the way to peace and action required separating the chief contestants for a cooling-off period. Accordingly, one stayed in Washington, one went to South America, and the third to Europe.

A decade and a half later a school of academic criticism has concluded that we overreacted to Stalin, which in turn caused him to overreact to policies of the United States. This may be true. Fortunately, perhaps, these authors were not called upon to analyze a situation in which the United States had not taken the action which it did take. See Marshall D. Shulman, Beyond the Cold War *(New Haven: Yale University Press, 1966), and Louis J. Halle,* The Cold War As History *(New York: Harper & Row, 1967). The literature of this period is listed and analyzed by Hans J. Morgenthau in "Arguing About the Cold War,"* Encounter, *May 1967, p. 37 ff.*

387

In an earlier book I continued the anecdote:

But Bevin had his revenge. Some days later at the end of a day I got a message to stop in his room at Lancaster House before going home.

"I know you like a Martini," said Ernie, "and it's hard to get a good one in London." Something was definitely afoot. I expressed guarded anticipation. At Bevin's signal, an ancient butler began operations at a sideboard. With growing disbelief I watched him pour into a tumbler one-third gin, one-third Italian Vermouth, and one-third water without ice, then bring the tumbler to me on a tray.

Ernie was observing all this with what he thought was a Mona Lisa smile—but was more like the grin of a schoolboy up to deviltry.

It was clear that I could never drink this horror if I tasted it. The only course was to take it in one gulp, or call "uncle." I chose the former, and down it went.

"Have another," Ernie almost commanded.

"No, thank you," I said. "No one could make another just like that one."

[Dean Acheson, *Sketches from Life* (New York: Harper & Row, 1961), pp. 40–41.]

401

See my A Citizen Looks at Congress *(New York: Harper & Brothers), 1956, pp. 77–80. The practice of the President and Secretaries appearing before Congress for questioning was tried at the beginning of our constitutional government, and followed for a relatively brief time. Washington in 1789 submitted to the procedure, but his displeasure at his reception was such that he did not return. In the same year Jefferson as Secretary for Foreign Affairs and Secretary of War Knox appeared before one or both houses of Congress.*

After the practice had lapsed, various efforts were made to establish the right and duty of Cabinet officers to appear on the floor. Two select committees, one of the House in 1864 and another of the Senate in 1881 (the Pendleton Committee), urged that the pro-

401 *(continued)*

cedure be adopted. *The Pendleton Committee set forth its view that "the system will re-quire the selection of the strongest men to be heads of Departments, and will require them to be well equipped with the knowledge of their offices. . . . It will bring these strong men in contact, perhaps into conflict, to advance the public weal, and thus stimulate their abilities and their efforts and will thus assuredly result to the good of the country."* [U.S. Senate Reports, *46th Congress, 3rd Session, Vol. 1, No. 837, February 4, 1881, p. 8.*]

President Taft's views were set forth in a message to Congress on December 19, 1912 [49 Congressional Record, *62nd Congress, 3rd Session, p. 895*], *when he recommended legislation which would make it the duty of Cabinet members "at convenient times to attend the session of the House and Senate, which shall provide seats for them in each House and give them the opportunity to participate in all discussions and to answer questions of which they have had due notice." He was "sure that the necessity . . . of rendering upon their feet an account of what they have done . . . will spur each member of the Cabinet to closer attention to the details of his Department, to closer familiarity with its needs, and to greater care to avoid the just criticism which the answers brought out in questions put and discussions arising between the members of either House and the members of the Cabinet may properly evoke."*

436

In November 1949, on a visit to the United States, Field Marshal Viscount Montgomery said that the only plausible solution to the inadequacy of forces planned at the moment was the use of German manpower [The New York Times, *November 29 and 30, 1949, and December 6, 1949*]. *On November 20, 1949, General Lucius D. Clay spoke up in favor of a limited German contribution to a composite European force* [The New York Times, *November 21, 1949*]. *On December 9, 1949, Konrad Adenauer said that if German troops were to be raised, it must be on equal terms and in a European army* [The New York Times, *December 10, 1949*].

468

Martin Lichterman, in his study "To the Yalu and Back" in American Civil Military Decisions, *edited by Harold Stein (University of Alabama Press, 1963, p. 602), attributes to me a statement that goes much farther than this one. Quite incorrectly, he quotes me as telling him that Secretary Marshall and the Joint Chiefs of Staff asked me to recommend to the President that he issue an order to General MacArthur to halt his advance and consolidate his position, adding that they would not make such a recommendation themselves. He cites as authority a letter from me of January 30, 1957, and an interview of March 27, 1957. The letter contains no such statement but contains a criticism of a wholly different point in his study. I have no memorandum or recollection of the interview.*

I have discussed this alleged statement of mine with General J. Lawton Collins and reaffirm what I said to him, that no such request was made to me. A footnote on this matter in Chapter 8 of General Collins' book, War in Peacetime *(to be published in late 1969 by the Houghton Mifflin Company) is entirely correct.*

475

On November 17 Ambassador Muccio reported General MacArthur's view of his operations in November. Not more than twenty-five thousand to thirty thousand Chinese could get across the river without detection, if they continued the secrecy of movement they were obviously practicing. The General would blow up the Korean end of the Yalu bridges, leaving the surrounding area a desert. North Korea would be cleared of hostile forces within ten days. He would then release all North Korean prisoners and take all Chinese prisoners to the border, sending them back to Manchuria. The Eighth Army would return to Japan, leaving the X Corps, other national contingents, and the South Korean forces to stabilize the situation.

496

The provision was that "no ground troops in addition to . . . four divisions should be sent to Western Europe in implementation of article 3 of the North Atlantic Treaty without further congressional approval" [97 Congressional Record, 82nd Congress, 1st Session, p. 3095].

514

Following is a paraphrase of the summary of the message sent by the Joint Chiefs of Staff to General Douglas MacArthur on December 29, 1950:

Chinese Communists now appear, from estimates available, capable of forcing evacuation by forces of UN. By committing substantial United States forces which would place other commitments, including safety of Japan, in serious jeopardy, or by inflicting serious losses on him, enemy might be forced to abandon exercise of his capability. If with present UN strength successful resistance at some position in Korea without our incurring serious losses could be accomplished and apparent military and political prestige of Chinese Communists could be deflated, it would be of great importance to our national interests. In the face of increased threat of general war JCS believe commitment of additional United States ground forces in Korea should not be made, since our view is that major war should not be fought in Korea.

Not considered practicable to obtain at this time significant additional forces from other United Nations. Therefore in light of present situation your basic directive, of furnish to ROK assistance as necessary to repel armed attack and restore to the area security and peace, is modified. Your directive now is to defend in successive positions, subject to safety of your troops as your primary consideration, inflicting as much damage to hostile forces in Korea as is possible.

In view of continued threat to safety of Japan and possibility of forced withdrawal from Korea it is important to make advance determination of last reasonable opportunity for orderly evacuation. It appears here that if Chinese Communists retain force capability of forcing evacuation after having driven UN forces to rear it would be necessary to direct commencement of your withdrawal. Request your views on these conditions which should determine evacuation. You should consider your mission of defending Japan and limitation on troops available to you. Definite directive on conditions for initiation of evacuation will be provided when your views are received.

For the present—this message which has been handled with ultimate security should be known only to your chief of staff and to Ridgway and his chief of staff. [Senate Committees on Armed Services and Foreign Relations, 82nd Congress, 1st Session, *Hearings to Conduct an Inquiry into the Military Situation in the Far East and the Facts Surrounding the Relief of General of the Army Douglas MacArthur from His Assignments in That Area*, pp. 2179–80.]

519

Statement issued by General Douglas MacArthur on March 24, 1951:

Operations continue according to schedule and plan. We have now substantially cleared South Korea of organized Communist forces. It is becoming increasingly evident that the heavy destruction along the enemy's lines of supply caused by our 'round-the-clock massive air and naval bombardment, has left his troops in the forward battle area deficient in requirements to sustain his operations.

This weakness is being brilliantly exploited by our ground forces. The enemy's human wave tactics definitely failed him as our own forces become seasoned to this form of warfare; his tactics of infiltration are but contributing to his piecemeal losses, and he is showing less stamina than our own troops under rigors of climate, terrain, and battle.

Of even greater significance than our tactical success has been the clear revelation that this new enemy, Red China, of such exaggerated and vaunted military power, lacks

PAGE

519 *(continued)*

the industrial capacity to provide adequately many critical items essential to the conduct of modern war.

He lacks manufacturing bases and those raw materials needed to produce, maintain and operate even moderate air and naval power, and he cannot provide the essentials for successful ground operations, such as tanks, heavy artillery and other refinements science has introduced into the conduct of military campaigns.

Formerly his great numerical potential might well have filled this gap, but with the development of existing methods of mass destruction, numbers alone do not offset vulnerability inherent in such deficiencies. Control of the sea and air, which in turn means control over supplies, communications and transportation, are no less essential and decisive now than in the past.

When this control exists, as in our case, and is coupled with the inferiority of ground firepower, as in the enemy's case, the resulting disparity is such that it cannot be overcome by bravery, however fanatical, or the most gross indifference to human loss.

These military weaknesses have been clearly and definitely revealed since Red China entered upon its undeclared war in Korea. Even under inhibitions which now restrict activity of the United Nations forces and the corresponding military advantages which accrue to Red China, it has been shown its complete inability to accomplish by force of arms the conquest of Korea.

The enemy therefore must now be painfully aware that a decision of the United Nations to depart from its tolerant effort to contain the war to the area of Korea through expansion of our military operations to his coastal areas and interior bases would doom Red China to the risk of imminent military collapse.

These basic facts being established, there should be no insuperable difficulty arriving at decisions on the Korean problem if the issues are resolved on their own merits without being burdened by extraneous matters not directly related to Korea, such as Formosa and China's seat in the United Nations.

The Korean nation and people which have been so cruelly ravaged must not be sacrificed. That is the paramount concern. Apart from the military area of the problem where the issues are resolved in the course of combat, the fundamental questions continue to be political in nature and must find their answer in the diplomatic sphere.

Within the area of my authority as military commander, however, it should be needless to say I stand ready at any time to confer in the field with the commander in chief of the enemy forces in an earnest effort to find any military means whereby the realization of the political objectives of the United Nations in Korea, to which no nation may justly take exceptions, might be accomplished without further bloodshed. [*Hearings on the Military Situation in the Far East*, cited, pp. 3541–42].

534

All the services shared in the task. The negotiating team consisted of Vice Admiral C. Turner Joy, U.S. Navy, chief delegate; Major General Paik Sun Yup, Republic of Korea Army; Major General Laurence C. Craigie, U.S. Air Force; Major General Henry I. Hodes, U.S. Eighth Army; and Rear Admiral Arleigh A. Burke, U.S. Navy.

572

It was not until October 5, 1954, that Italy and Yugoslavia, with active United States and United Kingdom diplomatic participation, were able to sign an agreement providing for Italian civil administration in Zone A and similar Yugoslav administration in Zone B. In addition, Italy promised to maintain the Free Port of Trieste according to the peace treaty and both bound themselves to respect the rights of ethnic minorities as well as past political attitudes.

PAGE
589

Cable from Secretary Acheson to President Truman, December 1, 1951:

I am most grateful for your kind note of encouragement. It may be helpful to you to have some impressions from me at the end of the NATO meeting at Rome.

The first is that the big problems remain unsolved and will need most energetic work for the next sixty days, if we are to solve them.

In the international field we are experiencing what the production people call slippages. Three months ago we hoped that the Ottawa meeting would start the wheels moving for decisions at this Rome meeting on a defense program geared to economic capacity and upon the integration of Germany, both in the community of free nations and into the Western defensive organization. But as you know, it became clear before this meeting that the complexity of the German problem and the current stage of Harriman's work in the Temporary Council Committee meant that the Rome meeting would have to be a spur to get decisions by the end of January.

The realization that the session could not reach important decisions affected the atmosphere in which the meeting was held. There was definitely less of enthusiasm and interest.

Another depressing factor was the knowledge that after Harriman's report, the governments will have to decide definitely on the precise degree of military, economic, and financial effort to be made in the next year. In Europe, this decision is hard because of low standards of living and, in many cases, minute parliamentary majorities. In France, the slender majority consists of a weak coalition of parties which do not see eye-to-eye on many key issues. The Communist parties remain strong in France and Italy and proclaim daily that the defense effort is leading to runaway inflation and economic chaos.

In this situation, our goals for this meeting were:

1. Convince the various nations to take the necessary steps to achieve complete battle worthiness by the summer of 1952 for the military forces which now exist on paper.

2. Lay the ground-work for government decisions concerning the findings of the Temporary Council Committee which should be expressed at the next Council meeting.

3. Ascertain the chances of success of the EDC and establish a deadline by which the Paris conference, which has been drafting the treaty since March 15, will have to report either success or failure.

I think all the countries now appreciate the urgency of making our existing forces fully combat-effective by next summer and of continuing to do so gradually as strength develops instead of placing our primary reliance on the development by 1954 of forces which at that theoretical date could, insofar as can be predicted now, insure the protection of the West against Soviet attack. Here the US plays a key role. The combat effectiveness of the forces which flank our own in Germany today, depends upon our giving priority to equipping them instead of the reserve formations at home.

As to future action on Harriman's final report, our friends now know that it is quite impossible to expect an adequate defense without paying the corresponding price. They know that we cannot and will not pick up the check. I think that they will come through, but it will take them longer than we had hoped. On our part, I think that we can and should demand greater efforts and greater efficiency in Europe, but we should not urge a degree of economic effort which is quite impossible for them to adhere to and which, if attained, would have internal and economic results which would set back the whole re-armament program.

We were able to accomplish very little in the Council on the European defense force and the related question of the German contribution to defense. . . .

The formal discussion in the Council on this subject did not reflect the confusion and strain presently in Europe over the establishment of a European Defense Force. There is a general feeling among the Foreign Ministers that the project is not going well, that the French chairmanship of the discussions is weak and confused, and that the people making

P A G E
589 *(continued)*

plans for the establishment of the Force are approaching the problem without regard to the political and parliamentary realities in Europe.

Although Adenauer did not raise the question, his key advisors indicated to us in Paris their concern that present plans of the French led to a half-way solution which would not work without a complete federation in Europe. They indicated on their part that they were ready to go all the way to federation. In this situation the French, deeply divided at home and unsure of the Parliamentary approach, seem uncertain as to which way to move. The problem is further complicated for Schuman in that there are two completely opposite views held in French circles as to the proper approach to Germany. In general the Foreign Office clings to its view that Germany is a major threat of the future and must continue to be bound by restrictions of an occupational nature, while those Frenchmen working on the creation of a common force in Europe are convinced that there must be real equality given to Germany or the whole effort will fail.

I spoke to Schuman privately about this range of problems, making it very clear that in our judgment these negotiations must be completed by the end of the year and success or failure registered by that time. I assured Schuman that we consider the European Defense Community formula to be the best method of obtaining Germany's participation but that I had serious doubts that agreement could be reached unless negotiations were taken up by the Ministers themselves, particularly such matters as the establishment of a common budget and common production procedures. This has been arranged. I am asking Bruce to furnish me without delay with actual texts now under negotiation at Paris and for all other information that may allow us to take a still more active role than we have heretofore in an effort to guide this complex project to early realization.

Eden shares my view that we must move quickly or face a possible complete stalemate on the creation of a European defense force. He asked my view as to whether we thought it would help if they took a more active role and was considering, I believe, the possibility that British forces on the Continent could be placed inside a common force through some arrangement. I said that injecting this new element now would complicate negotiations and make impossible meeting the deadline of December 31. He should therefore hold off now. But in the end it might be the catalyst that can pull the whole matter together. If it later becomes obvious that the French Parliament will turn down the French initiative for the creation of this Force or if the Benelux countries, with their close ties to Britain, appear about to bolt the effort, a move by Britain along the above lines could be extremely beneficial. In view of the traditional British position towards developments on the Continent, I consider Eden's statement to be significant and extremely encouraging.

In separate meetings here with Schuman and Eden on tripartite matters left over from Paris, (1) we reached sufficient agreement on a short-term solution to the question of Germany's financial contribution to defense to allow McCloy and his colleagues to start negotiations with the Germans. With a reduction of expenditures by Allied forces in Germany to the minimum consistent with military effectiveness, and with a real appreciation of the cost of raising German forces during their fiscal year which starts in April, we expect the Germans could meet expenditures without any serious gap during that period.

However, there had been no agreement concerning the nature and extent of prohibitions on the manufacture of military items in Germany.

While the visible effects of the Rome meeting are not impressive, I believe that the meeting served to impress everyone with the urgency of moving forward. The frictions and anxieties mentioned above are bound to accompany decision of matters affecting Germany and the establishment of a common force in Europe. It is useful that the Ministers here had a chance in private to express their feelings on these problems. . . . There is no doubt, however, that to reach a solution we will have to take a very active part, particularly with the French to help them make their own plan and initiative a success. . . .

Letter from Prime Minister Shigeru Yoshida to John Foster Dulles, consultant to the Secretary of State, December 24, 1951; released to the press on January 16, 1952:

Dear Ambassador Dulles:

While the Japanese Peace Treaty and the U.S.–Japan Security Treaty were being debated in the House of Representatives and the House of Councillors of the Diet, a number of questions were put and statements made relative to Japan's future policy toward China. Some of the statements, separated from their context and background, gave rise to misapprehensions which I should like to clear up.

The Japanese Government desires ultimately to have a full measure of political peace and commercial intercourse with China which is Japan's close neighbor.

At the present time it is, we hope, possible to develop that kind of relationship with the National Government of the Republic of China, which has the seat, voice and vote of China in the United Nations, which exercises actual governmental authority over certain territory, and which maintains diplomatic relations with most of the members of the United Nations. To that end my Government on November 17, 1951, established a Japanese Government Overseas Agency in Formosa, with the consent of the National Government of China. This is the highest form of relationship with other countries which is now permitted to Japan, pending the coming into force of the multilateral Treaty of Peace. The Japanese Government Overseas Agency in Formosa is important in its personnel, reflecting the importance which my government attaches to relations with the National Government of the Republic of China. My government is prepared as soon as legally possible to conclude with the National Government of China, if that government so desires, a Treaty which will reestablish normal relations between the two Governments in conformity with the principles set out in the multilateral Treaty of Peace. The terms of such bilateral treaty shall, in respect of the Republic of China, be applicable to all territories which are now, or which may hereafter be, under the control of the National Government of the Republic of China. We will promptly explore this subject with the National Government of China.

As regards the Chinese Communist regime, that regime stands actually condemned by the United Nations of being an aggressor and in consequence, the United Nations has recommended certain measures against that regime, in which Japan is now concurring and expects to continue to concur when the multilateral Treaty of Peace comes into force pursuant to the provisions of Article 5 (a) (iii), whereby Japan has undertaken "to give the United Nations every assistance in any action it takes in accordance with the Charter and to refrain from giving assistance to any State against which the United Nations may take preventive or enforcement action." Furthermore, the Sino-Soviet Treaty of Friendship, Alliance and Mutual Assistance concluded in Moscow in 1950 is virtually a military alliance aimed against Japan. In fact there are many reasons to believe that the Communist regime in China is backing the Japan Communist Party in its program of seeking violently to overthrow the constitutional system and the present Government of Japan. In view of these considerations, I can assure you that the Japanese Government has no intention to conclude a bilateral Treaty with the Communist regime of China.

Yours sincerely, Shigeru Yoshida

Letter from Mr. Dulles to Prime Minister Yoshida, January 16, 1952; released to the press on January 17, 1952:

My dear Mr. Prime Minister:

I acknowledge the receipt . . . of your letter of December 24, 1951 in which you express the intentions of your Government with reference to China. This clear statement should dispel any misapprehensions which, as you suggest, may have arisen from statements, separated from their context and background, made during the course of debate in

P A G E
603 *(continued)*

Japan on the ratification of the Japanese Peace Treaty and the U.S.–Japan Security Treaty.

I am grateful to you for your letter and I respect the courageous and forthright manner in which you face up to this difficult and controversial matter.

Sincerely yours, John Foster Dulles

[*Department of State Bulletin,* Vol. XXVI, January 28, 1952, p. 120.]

633 *(first note)*

Extemporaneous remarks by Secretary Acheson at his press conference of March 5, 1952, concerning the case of Oliver Edmund Clubb:

Now, I should like to talk with you this morning about a matter which has been much agitated in the press recently, and that is the Clubb case. Various questions have been put to me about it. I have not answered any of those until this morning, and I shall now discuss the whole matter fully with all of you here.

First of all, I should like to remind you that the loyalty and security program of the Department was put into effect in 1947 under a Presidential order, which required such action, and it has been carried out in accordance with general rules laid down by the President and his Loyalty Review Board ever since.

The purpose of this whole program is to accomplish several things: First of all, it is to protect the Government against employing any persons whose loyalty may be doubtful, or whose security may be doubtful, so that the Government may be assured that its employees are loyal and devoted to its interests. A second great purpose of the program is to be completely fair and just to all employees of the Department, and, particularly, to an employee who may be under investigation. It is only in that way that the Government can be assured not only of the negative fact that it does not have disloyal employees, but of the positive fact that it has enthusiastic, trusted, and competent employees.

This program has resulted in the investigation of all people employed in the Department at the time the program went into effect, and with all those who have come into the Department since.

When these investigations, or information brought to the attention of the Department, require more formal proceedings, we go into a different stage of the program.

There is a Loyalty and Security Board in the Department of State. Information which comes to us, either through our own investigation or other investigations, is laid before that Board. If the Board believes that this requires a hearing—response from the person involved—a notice is sent to him setting forth the information to which he is required to respond.

The Board then holds hearings. The Board then comes to conclusions. Those conclusions are reported to the Assistant Secretary in charge of these matters. If he approves of them, they are then transmitted by him to the individual concerned. If the individual concerned is dissatisfied with the finding, that individual has the right, under the regulations, to appeal to me. I can, if I choose, hear that appeal and read that record myself, or I can have that procedure followed under my direction by some officer who is deputized by me to represent me.

I should like to stress that all steps which are taken under this program are taken under my responsibility. The Secretary of State must remain responsible for the conduct of this whole procedure.

At this point I should like to bring in something somewhat more complicated. There are two general types of matters which come up in these investigations: One has to do with loyalty—if there is a reasonable doubt of the loyalty of the individual he may be separated from the service. The other question which comes up is whether the person involved is a security risk. Both of these matters are defined with certain criteria in the regulations which are available to you.

The reason I mention this is because if the finding is that a person is, or is not, disloyal, or there is reasonable doubt as to his loyalty, that matter may be reviewed by the

633 *(first note, continued)*
President's Loyalty Review Board. However, in security questions, that is, if the man is found to be a security risk or not a security risk, that determination is final with me. It is not subject to review by the President's Board.

It has been our practice in the past not to discuss the procedural steps in any case, not to say what the result of each of these steps was. I am going to depart from that practice this morning because somewhat of a mystery has been made of this case. I regret that I have to do that, and I think that, on the whole, it is not in the best interests of the program. The reason I think that is that the purpose of this whole program, and of all these investigations, is for me ultimately to determine whether or not an employee should be separated from the service for one or the other of these two reasons.

It is important that at the conclusion of this whole procedure an employee is either clearly separated or clearly reinstated; that is, cleared of the action of the charge made against him or that he is separated. There should not be twilight zones. There is a twilight zone if you report that in a particular case a certain group of my associates came to one conclusion under the procedure that was reviewed, and another person or group of my associates came to another conclusion, and that, finally, I, who have the ultimate responsibility, came to either one or the other of those conclusions, or, possibly, a third one. That does not leave the employee either completely cleared or clearly separated. In other words, we do not want to run box scores by innings on these investigations. However, in this case I think the interests of both the individual concerned, and the Government, and the public will be served by my going into the various steps in Mr. Clubb's case.

The hearing before the Loyalty and Security Board of the Department of State in Mr. Clubb's case involved two questions: One was—Was there reasonable doubt of his loyalty to the United States? The other was: Was he a security risk?

On the first question the Board found that there was not any doubt about his loyalty to the United States. That was reviewed and confirmed, so that that whole question of Mr. Clubb's loyalty was resolved in his favor throughout the procedure.

We now come to the question of security—security risk. On that matter the Board found that Mr. Clubb was, in their judgment, a security risk. That finding was sent to the Assistant Secretary who reviewed it, and approved it for forwarding to Mr. Clubb, and it was forwarded to him with the statement that under the procedure he had a period of time within which to appeal to the Secretary of State if he chose to do so. Mr. Clubb chose to appeal and within the appropriate time he appealed to me.

I have never, as I said before, been able to read these records and hear the arguments myself. I, therefore, designated one of our most experienced and trusted Foreign Service Officers to act for me, which he did. He very faithfully, very patiently, and very thoroughly reviewed the entire record. He listened to the arguments of Mr. Clubb's counsel, and he reached a conclusion, and wrote an opinion on it. That conclusion and opinion was that Mr. Clubb was not a security risk. That opinion was sent to me. I read it very carefully. I did not study the record because, as I have said, I do not have time to do that. It seemed to me that this trusted officer, who was my deputy, had reached the right conclusion—I adopted his conclusion; I am responsible for the ultimate judgment which was that Mr. Clubb was not a security risk.

That decision was communicated to Mr. Clubb. Mr. Clubb applied for retirement. That application was considered in the Department and granted. There have been suggestions made, which I dislike very much to refer to but must, that there was some connection between my conclusion and his retirement. That is utterly and absolutely untrue. The final decision that he was not a security risk was reached on the basis of the record by my deputy, approved by me, and had nothing whatever to do with Mr. Clubb's retirement. His decision to retire was made when he had the decision of the Secretary of State before him.

That is the statement which I wish to make to you this morning, and I wish to end, as I began, by saying that I am doing this to remove any element of obscurity or mystery

633 *(first note, continued)*

from this matter, in the interests of the Government, in the interest of Mr. Clubb, and in the interest of public information. But I shall not make this a practice, and in the future I hope I will not again be called upon to go into the various steps, and I hope you will understand that always the responsibility for these decisions must rest on me. It is mine under the law; it is mine under any proper administration; I must shoulder it. If there is any criticism for any result, that criticism must be directed at me and not at the various people who take part in the procedure, because each of them acts as my agent for me, as part of a procedure which is meant to give the greatest protection to the Government and the greatest protection to the individual. [*Department of State Bulletin,* Vol. XXVI, March 17, 1952, pp. 437–38.]

633 *(second note)*

In June the Supreme Court affirmed decisions enjoining this action of the President (Youngstown Sheet and Tube Co. et al. v. Sawyer, 343 US 579, June 2, 1952). A seven-week strike resulted.

643

The following explanation of the meaning of the contractual agreements was released by the Allied High Commission in Bonn on May 26, 1952:

The effect of the Contractual Agreements is to include the Federal Republic in the community of free nations as an equal partner.

The convention on relations and the related conventions aim to liquidate a situation which arose out of the war and the Occupation. In addition, they regulate the stationing in the Federal Republic of substantial foreign forces to assist in the common defense. It has consequently been necessary not only to establish broad principles, but to make provisions of a detailed character, such as normally appear in peace treaties and military conventions.

In considering the Contractual Agreements as a whole, it should be borne in mind that they have had to take into account an unprecedented situation.

In the first place, as long as there is no agreement between the Three Powers and the Soviet Union, the unity of Germany cannot be realized nor can all-German problems be settled. Hence the problem has posed itself of according to the Federal Republic full authority over its external and internal affairs while preserving the means of negotiating German unity and of maintaining rights of the Three Powers in Berlin. Subject to the realization of these aims, the Three Powers have no desire to infringe German sovereignty or German equality of rights.

Secondly, an unusual situation has been created by the need to station in time of peace a very large number of troops for defense purposes in a foreign country. The presence of troops of the Three Powers in Germany is vital to the defense of Germany. This naturally imposes a burden on Germany, although already it is bringing an important economic advantage in the shape of the expenditure of foreign currency, a factor which with the passage of time will play an increasingly important role. On the other hand, it must not be forgotten that the despatch of these troops abroad imposes a severe military and financial burden on the other Western Powers, who have committed very important military and air forces to this theatre. In order to fulfill their role, these troops and air forces must be operational. They must have facilities for training, they must be provided with lines of communication, and their essential military requirements must be met; furthermore, they must have the assurance of the requisite liberty of action if need arises. Otherwise Germany cannot be defended and these troops will be exposed to unnecessary hazards unacceptable to their Governments. The problem has been to reconcile the preservation of the rights of the Federal Republic and its citizens with the legitimate operational requirements of the foreign defense forces.

Thirdly, in view of the fact that a general peace treaty cannot now be concluded, the agreements take the unprecedented step of liquidating the war and the controls of the

PAGE
643 *(continued)*
Occupation regime before conclusion of a final peace settlement. Hence the appearance of a number of provisions which would normally have been included in a peace treaty. The liquidation of a long and bitterly contested war is not a simple matter, but the provisions have been designed to meet to the minimum acceptable extent the principal aims of the Allies while at the same time imposing the least possible burden on the structure and economic stability of the Federal Republic.

Because of the special status of the city, the Contractual Agreements do not apply to Berlin. However, in consonance with their new relationship to the Federal Republic, the Three Powers have published a declaration that they will grant the Berlin authorities the maximum liberty compatible with the citys' special situation. [*Department of State Bulletin,* Vol. XXVI, June 9, 1952, p. 888.]

660
Translation of the Public Orator's presentation of Dean Acheson to the Chancellor of Oxford University for admission to the honorary degree of Doctor of Civil Law, June 25, 1952:
PRESENTATION BY THE PUBLIC DEFENDER

Our American guest is not likely to feel any nervousness in the presence of a crowd so well-disposed towards him; indeed it is said that even when encircled by opponents he can always keep cool and tone down any over-seriousness on their part by raising a laugh. If, however, the slightest diffidence does happen to assail him, let him know that his friend Felix Frankfurter had no trouble in surviving this Oxford fashion of applauding merit; nor did those two mainstays of the world's economy Edward Stettinius and George Marshall, under both of whom he served as an assistant and one of whom he succeeded as Secretary of State. Let him know, too, that for him also generous applause is in store —and this on two grounds: he is whole-hearted in carrying through the world-saving Plan taken over from his predecessor; and he has himself been the author of many salutary measures. How difficult and how complex are the problems he handles. Is there no intermediate state between peace and war, as Cicero once said? Is the modern saying true, that no distinction any longer exists between home and foreign affairs? This alone I know, that in most difficult times our guest has proved himself a man of great vision, equal to any task, and a true friend to his friends. His deep sense of human brotherhood was apparent at the close of a conference of delegates from enemy-occupied countries, when he quoted from John Donne the following passage, far more effective than any speech: "No man is an *Iland,* intire of it selfe; every man is a peece of the *Continent,* . . . If a *Clod* bee washed away by the *Sea, Europe* is the lesse, as well as if a *Promontorie* were. . . . Any man's *death* diminishes *me,* because I am involved in *Mankinde;* And therefore never send to know for whom the *bell* tolls; It tolls for *thee."*

I present to you for admission to the honorary degree of D.C.L. our staunch ally, Mr. Dean Acheson.
ADMISSION BY THE CHANCELLOR

My valued friend, whose care is for all mankind, with what courage you have proceeded—setting foot upon a dangerous crust of ashes which fires underlie! I admit you by my own authority and that of the whole University to the honorary degree of Doctor in Civil Law.

691
Following is the remainder of the statement about General Eisenhower's remarks, made at my press conference on September 26, 1952:
In an address in Cincinnati on September 22, 1952, General Eisenhower related what he termed some "plain facts" about the period before the Communist attack in Korea. He said: "In January of 1950 our Secretary of State declared that America's so-called 'de-

PAGE
691 *(continued)*

fensive perimeter' excluded areas on the Asiatic mainland such as Korea. He said in part: 'No person can guarantee these areas against military attack. It must also be clear that such a guarantee is hardly sensible or necessary. . . . It is a mistake . . . in considering Pacific and Far Eastern problems to become obsessed with military considerations.' "

That statement purports to be a quotation and an accurate paraphrase of a speech I made before the National Press Club in Washington on January 12, 1950.

As stated it tortures the facts. It says things I didn't say and omits a significant and relevant part of what I did say. The General could have discovered this by reading my speech.

In my Press Club speech I spoke of the Aleutian Islands, Japan and the Ryukyus, and the Philippines being our "defensive perimeter" in the Pacific area. The Aleutians are part of our own nation, we had occupation forces in Japan and the Ryukyus, and we have special military arrangements as well as unusually close bonds of friendship with the Philippines. My point was that if this line were attacked we would defend it alone if necessary—just as we would our continental area.

The General's speech says I "excluded areas on the Asiatic mainland such as Korea." Now, "areas on the Asiatic mainland" also include Indo-China, Malaya, Thailand, Burma, Pakistan, India and Afghanistan—so presumbly he meant I excluded them also. The fact is, however, that I used no language whatever "excluding" Korea or any other area in the Asiatic mainland or suggesting any lack of interest by the United States in the event of an attack on any area of the Asian mainland in general or Korea in particular. The General's statement represents me as saying what I did not say.

On the contrary, I referred specifically to these "other areas in the Pacific."

The General or those upon whom he relied dealt with my specific statement on these other areas by cutting it out from between two other sentences they quoted to make their point.

Here is what I said about the other areas of Asia: "Should such an attack occur— one hesitates to say where such an armed attack could come from—the initial reliance must be on the people attacked to resist it and then upon the commitments of the entire civilized world under the Charter of the United Nations which so far has not proved a weak reed to lean on by any people who are determined to protect their independence against outside aggression."

That was the warning which I gave in January, 1950.

That was the warning which the aggressor disregarded.

That was the warning which the United States and its allies of the United Nations backed up with deeds.

General Eisenower's combination of paraphrase and quotation left out that warning and thus enabled him to go ahead and discuss the Korean situation just as if no such utterance had occurred and as if his own Government rather than the aggressor bore the guilt for Korea's tragedy.

Now all those innocent little dots in the General's quotation permitted another misrepresentation by omission. By this omission, General Eisenhower gives the impression that I was minimizing the importance of military considerations in these matters. My actual words, however, pointed out that the danger in these areas was not only a military one, but also one of penetration and subversion. I said: "But it is a mistake, I think, in considering Pacific and Far Eastern problems to become obsessed with military considerations. Important as they are, there are other problems that press, and these other problems are not capable of solution through military means. These other problems arise out of the susceptibility of many areas, and many countries in the Pacific area, to subversion and penetration. That cannot be stopped by military means."

Now I raise this matter not just because I share the common dislike of being misquoted on a matter of real importance, but in order to make two points, which are essential to an understanding of our foreign policy, absolutely clear.

691 *(continued)*

The first has to do with the defensive perimeter of the United States in the Pacific. This is the line which the U.S. had to defend alone if necessary and to man with its own troops. The defensive perimeter as I described it was the line developed by our military authorities at that time. I cannot believe General Eisenhower now means to imply that Korea should have been included by me within the defensive perimeter and that it should have been manned by American troops. Certainly, as Chief of Staff of the Army, his opinion was quite to the contrary and wholly in accordance with the statement I made.

The second point has to do with the fact that the United States had then as it has now great interest in the security and well-being of other nations in the Pacific area. Therefore, in my speech, I dwelt on the necessity of working with them to guard against subversion, penetration, political disintegration and economic disorders. I also made it clear that the defense of all these areas was not a responsibility which it was just or wise or possible for the United States to bear alone. Instead, I stated that the defense of these nations of Asia against aggression lay properly first with themselves and then with the commitments of the entire civilized world under the Charter of the United Nations. I cannot believe this vital point of foreign policy is meant to be challenged any more than the first. [Department of State Press Release No. 761, September 26, 1952.]

697

There was no successor to Kennan until March 27, 1953, when Charles E. Bohlen was confirmed as Ambassador to the Soviet Union.

699 *(first note)*

The twenty nations joining the United States in sponsoring the resolution were Australia, Belgium, Canada, Colombia, Denmark, Ethiopia, France, Greece, Honduras, Iceland, Luxembourg, the Netherlands, New Zealand, Nicaragua, Norway, the Philippines, Thailand, Turkey, the United Kingdom, and Uruguay.

699 *(second note)*

Letter from Secretary Acheson to President Truman, October 25, 1952:

Dear Mr. President:

After the first ten days of this session of the General Assembly, I think it is fair to report that things are moving for us perhaps better than we might have expected. This is, as you know, a tough session for us, because we are caught in the middle on most of the colonial issues, but we have done our best to make a virtue out of our predicament.

The organizational phase of this session has gone off more quietly and smoothly than usual. Partly, this reflects a gingerly feeling about our elections. And partly, this may be because the Russians have so far been operating under wraps. They have gone through a restrained rehash of their charges from previous years, but they have acted either with hesitancy or restraint. They have clearly not yet shown their full hand.

As we anticipated from our analysis of the Communist Party Congress in Moscow and related actions, the Russians are doing their best to isolate us from our allies, and to play upon all the differences in the non-Communist world. We have been interested to see how they would meet the dilemma of trying to woo the British and French away from us, and at the same time appeal to the people of the colonial areas. It looks as if they have decided to stress the latter, and let the former go for another time. They have lumped the British and French together with us as the Atlantic warmongers, and have made strenuous appeals, both on the floor and in the lobbies, to the Arab-Asian bloc.

It appears to me that the outstanding political fact of the Assembly thus far has been the domination of the proceedings by the Arab-Asian group, which has been successful in every major effort up to this point. The Arab-Asian bloc has been exceptionally skillful in allying themselves with both Latin American and Soviets on particular issues, obtaining majorities which could not be countered by votes of Western European and Common-

699 *(second note, continued)*

wealth members. The solidity of this Arab-Asian bloc, which is based on high-keyed nationalist and racial issues, is going to give us much more difficulty this year than ever before.

As a consequence, the mood of the British, French and other Western European delegations is bitter. These delegations are determined to fight against attacks on their colonial policies, but it is a retreating, holding operation in which their prospects for success are small. If the Arab-Asian bloc pushes the GA too hard, the reaction of the Western European and Commonwealth states may be violent. In the case of South Africa, whose segregation policies are for the first time under direct attack, there is serious danger that the Delegation may actually withdraw from active participation in the Organization. If this should initiate a general trend on the part of the French and other colonial powers, the result may be the most serious internal threat the UN has yet had to face.

For a while, the French had their backs up over an affirmative vote by us that the Political Committee take up the Tunisia and Morocco items immediately following the debate on Korea. This vote was cast in a situation in which, according to our estimate, the outcome would have been the same however we voted. By so voting, we were able to pick up a little leverage with the Arab-Asian group which may enable us to moderate the debate when the items are discussed. We have talked to the French both here and in Paris, and while their reaction is still acute, I think their initial sharp reaction is subsiding. They are faced with such an unstable and inflamed political situation at home that they are having a very difficult time here, and are difficult for us to deal with as a consequence. However, they have joined with us in sponsoring the resolution on Korea, thus indicating that we do not have a serious division on our hands, at least so far.

The Political Committee began its work on the Korean item Thursday. During the first day of debate, we had a majority against issuing an invitation to the North Koreans but the voting indicated that many of our Asian friends were still inclined to sit on the fence. Therefore, in my opening statement yesterday, I felt it necessary to lay it on the line pretty heavily, to show who started this business, and to remind the members how earnestly we have tried to restore peace in Korea, without any cooperation from the Communists. Reactions afterward indicated that we picked up considerable support as a result of this approach. We have introduced a resolution which would vote confidence in the way the United States has conducted the negotiations in Korea, and explicitly in our position on prisoners of war; the resolution would also call on the Communists to agree to an armistice on a basis consistent with the principle of non-forceable repatriation. Twenty other governments have joined with us in sponsoring this resolution. This includes virtually all the governments with troops in Korea. I believe we stand a good chance of presenting a good firm majority on Korea, which may have an effect on the Communist expectations.

By putting heavy stress on the Soviet responsibility for the Korean affair in my presentation yesterday, I feel that we may have helped to increase the liability to the Russians of a continuation of the Korean episode, and particularly to make them feel the contradiction between this running sore in Asia and their pretensions of peace. I hope this speech will have met at least some of the requirements of the speech you spoke to David Bruce about having me do here.

I felt it necessary to dispel the impression Vishinsky was trying to create, that the Communists had really offered some new concession in their note to General Harrison of October 8th. So far, there has been no indication that the Russians are ready to make any genuine move on Korea, but we are watching the situation closely.

In summing up the situation here, it appears to me that our principal job is to hold our friends and allies together in the face of a determined Soviet effort to drive wedges between us. Although we are still in the very early stages of this session, I think it looks reasonably promising so far. By starting out with a tone of moderation and letting the

699 *(second note, continued)*
Soviets hang themselves with their own invective, we have picked up support from some of our friends with neutralist tendencies.

I have been endeavoring to do as much in the way of informal contacts here as possible, particularly with Latin American and Middle Eastern representatives. This kind of personal spade-work is extremely useful, not only here, but in terms of our work on many other problems.

According to present indications, the Soviet reply to my statement in the Political Committee on Korea may come early next week. Because of the importance of the Korean issue, I believe I should remain here at least through the first rebuttal to Vishinsky's presentation, and then take a new reading on how much longer it would be useful for me to remain.   Most respectfully, Dean Acheson

711
Memorandum from Secretary Acheson to President Truman regarding the case of John Carter Vincent, contained in the White House press release of January 3, 1953:
I have recently been advised by Chairman Bingham of the Loyalty Review Board that a panel of the Loyalty Review Board has considered the case of Mr. John Carter Vincent, a Foreign Service Officer with class of Career Minister. Chairman Bingham also advises me that while the panel did not find Mr. Vincent guilty of disloyalty, it has reluctantly concluded that there is reasonable doubt as to his loyalty to the Government of the United States. Chairman Bingham further advises me that it is therefore the recommendation of the Board that the services of Mr. Vincent be terminated.

Such a recommendation by so distinguished a Board is indeed serious and impressive and must be given great weight. The final responsibility, however, for making a decision as to whether Mr. Vincent should be dismissed is that of the Secretary of State. I am advised that any doubt which might have previously existed on this point has been removed by the recent decision of the United States Circuit Court of Appeals for the District of Columbia in *James Kutcher, Appellant,* v. *Carl Gray, Jr., Veterans Administration, Appellee.* That case establishes that the action of the Board is a recommendation "just that— nothing more" and that in the last analysis upon the Head of the Department is imposed "the duty to impartially determine on all the evidence" the proper disposition of the case.

A most important item on which I must rely in exercising this responsibility, is the communication from Chairman Bingham in which he advised me of the conclusion reached by his panel. This communication contains elements which raise serious problems.

In the first place, I note a statement that the panel has not accepted or rejected the testimony of Mr. Budenz that he recalls being informed by others that Mr. Vincent was a Communist and under Communist discipline. The panel also states that it does not accept or reject the findings of the Committee on the Judiciary of the Senate with respect to Mr. Vincent and the Institute of Pacific Relations or the findings of the Committee with respect to the participation of Mr. Vincent in the development of United States policy towards China in 1945. The panel, however, proceeds to state that, although it has not accepted or rejected these factors, it has taken them into account. I am unable to interpret what this means. If the panel did take these factors into account, this means that it must have relied upon them in making its final determination. Yet I am unable to understand how these factors could have played a part in the final determination of the panel if these factors were neither accepted nor rejected by the Board.

This is not merely a point of language. It is a point of real substance. It is difficult for me to exercise the responsibility which is mine under the law with the confusion which has been cast as to the weight which the panel gave to the charges of Mr. Budenz or the findings of the Senate Committee.

The communication from the panel raises another issue which goes to the heart of operation of the Department of State and the Foreign Service. It is the issue of accurate

711 *(continued)*

reporting. The communication contains the following statement: "The panel notes Mr. Vincent's studied praise of Chinese Communists and equally studied criticism of the Chiang Kai-shek Government throughout a period when it was the declared and established policy of the Government of the United States to support Chiang Kai-shek's Government."

Mr. Vincent's duty was to report the facts as he saw them. It was not merely to report successes of existing policy but also to report on the aspects in which it was failing and the reasons therefor. If this involved reporting that situations existed in the administration of the Chinese Nationalists which had to be corrected if the Nationalist Government was to survive, it was his duty to report this. If this involved a warning not to underestimate the combat potential of the Chinese Communists, or their contribution to the war against Japan, it was his duty to report this. In the hearings which followed the relief of General MacArthur, General Wedemeyer has testified that he has made reports equally as critical of the administration of the Chinese Nationalists.

The great majority of reports which Mr. Vincent drafted were reviewed and signed by Ambassador Gauss, an outstanding expert in the Far East. Ambassador Gauss has made it crystal clear that in his mind the reports drafted by Mr. Vincent were both accurate and objective.

I do not exclude the possibility that in this or in any other case a board might find that the reports of an officer might or might not disclose a bias which might have a bearing on the issue of his loyalty. But in so delicate a matter, affecting so deeply the integrity of the Foreign Service, I should wish to be advised by persons thoroughly familiar with the problems and procedures of the Department of State and the Foreign Service. This involves an issue far greater in importance than the disposition of a loyalty case involving one man. Important as it is to do full justice to the individual concerned, it is essential that we should not by inadvertence take any step which might lower the high traditions of our own Foreign Service to the level established by governments which will permit their diplomats to report to them only what they want to hear.

The memorandum from Mr. Bingham indicates that the Board also took into account "Mr. Vincent's failure properly to discharge his responsibilities as Chairman of the Far Eastern Subcommittee of State, War and Navy to supervise the accuracy or security of State Department documents emanating from that Subcommittee." The statement which refers to the security of the files seems to me to be inadvertent. Presumably it is a reference to the fact that State Department documents were involved in the *Amerasia* case. However, in the many Congressional investigations which have followed that case it has not been suggested that Mr. Vincent had any responsibility for those documents. I have not discovered any such evidence in the file in this case. The reference to the accuracy of the State Department documents emanating from that Committee is obscure. In any case, while it might be relative to Mr. Vincent's competence in performing his duties, it does not seem to me to have any bearing on the question of loyalty.

The report finally refers to Mr. Vincent's association with numerous persons "who, he had reason to believe," were either Communists or Communist sympathizers. This is indeed a matter which, if unexplained, is of importance and clearly relevant. It involves inquiry as to whether this association arose in the performance of his duties or otherwise. It further involves an inquiry as to the pattern of Mr. Vincent's close personal friends and whether he knew or should have known that any of these might be Communists or Communist sympathizers.

All these matters raised in my mind the necessity for further inquiry. This further inquiry was made possible by the documents in this proceeding which you provided me upon my request. I find upon examining the documents that the recommendation made by the panel of the Loyalty Review Board was made by a majority of one, two of the members believing that no evidence had been produced which led them to have a doubt as to Mr. Vincent's loyalty. In this situation, I believe that I cannot in good conscience and in

711 *(continued)*

the exercise of my own judgment, which is my duty under the law, carry out this recommendation of the Board. I do not believe, however, that in the exercise of my responsibility to the Government, I can or should let the matter rest here. I believe that I must ask for further guidance.

I, therefore, ask your permission to seek the advice of some persons who will combine the highest judicial qualifications of weighing the evidence with the greatest possible familiarity of the works and standards of the Department of State and the Foreign Service, both in reporting from the field and making decisions in the Department. If you approve, I should propose to ask [these] persons to examine the record in this case and to advise me as to what disposition in their judgment should be made in this case. . . . [*Department of State Bulletin*, Vol. XXVIII, January 19, 1953, pp. 122–23.]

Following is President Truman's reply to the above memorandum, January 3, 1953:

I have read your memorandum of today concerning the case of John Carter Vincent. I think the suggestions which you make are well taken and I authorize and direct you to proceed in the manner which you have outlined. [*Department of State Bulletin*, Vol. XXVIII, January 19, 1953, p. 122.]

736

I have discussed this in an earlier book, as follows:

As nearly as I can reconstruct it from my appointment books, I met during four years as Secretary on 214 occasions with these groups. One hundred twenty-five of these were formal committee meetings, usually stenographically reported. The remainder were informal meetings. Many committee meetings occupied half a day, measured from the Secretary's portal-to-portal (if more, each half-day is counted as a meeting). Informal meetings were usually shorter, running from an hour to two or three. In my experience preparation for meetings required at least as much time as the meetings themselves, usually more, since the ground which would be covered was never precisely predictable. I will not be far wrong, then, in estimating that each formal meeting took half a day and preparation half a day, or a total of 125 days; that each informal meeting took about one-quarter of a day. This is in the neighborhood of one-sixth of my working days in Washington. Periods of absence on international conferences are excluded. There were, of course, additional and more relaxed opportunities for exchange of views on social occasions after working hours.

General figures cannot reflect the peaks of pressure which the work with Congress involves. There are occasions when not a sixth of the Secretary's time but all of it is occupied on the Hill. For instance, from June 1 to June 9, 1951, inclusive, I testified every day (except Sunday) and nearly all day before joint Senate committees investigating the relief of General MacArthur. Preparation began on May 8, with work, at the outset, chiefly at night, and continued every day until it filled pretty much the whole day. With these hearings concluded, I began preparation on June 22 for hearings before the House Committee on Foreign Affairs on the $8.5 billion foreign aid bill. The actual hearings occupied June 26, 27, and 28. So for this seven-week period, from May 11 to the end of June, fully half of the Secretary's time and energy was spent on work with congressional committees. [Dean Acheson, *Private Thoughts on Public Affairs* (New York: Harcourt, Brace & World, 1967), pp. 41–44.]

REFERENCES

APOLOGIA PRO LIBRE HOC

1. Page Smith, *John Adams* (New York: Doubleday & Company, 1962), Vol. I, pp. 128, 216–26.

2. C. V. Wedgwood, *William the Silent* (London: Jonathan Cape, 1967), pp. 35, 212–14.

1. ENLISTMENT FOR THE WAR TO COME

1. See Dean Acheson, *Morning and Noon* (Boston: Houghton Mifflin Company, 1965).
2. Same, pp. 213–14.
3. Desmond Donnelly, *Struggle for the World— The Cold War: 1917–1965* (New York: St. Martin's Press, 1965), p. 10.

4. Maurice Collis, *Foreign Mud* (New York: Alfred A. Knopf, 1947).
5. A. K. Cairncross, *Home and Foreign Investment, 1870–1913* (Cambridge: Cambridge University Press, 1953), p. 3.

2. THE "OLD" STATE DEPARTMENT

1. Cordell Hull, *Memoirs* (New York: The Macmillan Company, 1948), Vol. I, p. 161.
2. Same, Vol. II, pp. 1230–31.
3. Fred L. Israel, ed., *The War Diary of Breckinridge Long* (Lincoln: University of Nebraska Press, 1966), pp. 175–76.
4. Quoted in Lord Kinross, *Ataturk, a Biography of Mustafa Kemal, Father of Modern Turkey* (New York: William Morrow & Company, 1965), p. 458.
5. Albert T. Volwiler, ed., *Memoirs of the American Philosophical Society: The Correspondence Between Benjamin Harrison and James G. Blaine, 1882–1893* (Philadelphia: The American Philosophical Society, 1940).
6. Townsend Hoopes, "The Persistence of Illusion: The Soviet Economic Drive and Amer-

ican National Interest," *Yale Review*, Spring 1960, p. 325.
7. *Department of State Bulletin*, Vol. IV, March 8, 1941, p. 271.
8. *Foreign Relations of the United States, 1941* (Washington, D.C.: U.S. Government Printing Office), Vol. III, p. 201.
9. Israel, cited, p. 169. Henry F. Grady of California was Assistant Secretary of State from 1939 to 1941.
10. *Department of State Bulletin*, Vol. III, July 6, 1940, pp. 11–12.
11. Quotations in this and the next four paragraphs may be found in *Foreign Relations of the United States: Japan, 1931–1941* (Washington, D.C.: U.S. Government Printing Office), Vol. II, pp. 219–25, 237.

3. THE YEAR WE HELD OUR BREATH

1. Arthur M. Schlesinger, Jr., *The Coming of the New Deal*, Vol. II, *The Age of Roosevelt* (Boston: Houghton Mifflin Company, 1959), p. 529.
2. Henry L. Stimson and McGeorge Bundy, *On Active Service in Peace and War* (New York: Harper & Brothers, 1948), p. 369.
3. William L. Langer and S. Everett Gleason, *The Undeclared War, 1940–1941* (New York: Harper & Brothers, 1953), p. 442.
4. John Morton Blum, *Years of Urgency, 1938–1941*, Vol. II, *From the Morgenthau Diaries* (Boston: Houghton Mifflin Company, 1965), p. 339.
5. Same, p. 332.
6. *Foreign Relations of the United States: Japan, 1931–1941*, cited (Ch. 2), Vol. II, pp. 266–67.
7. *Foreign Relations of the United States, 1941*, cited (Ch. 2), Vol. IV, pp. 841–42.

8. *Foreign Relations of the United States: Japan, 1931–1941*, cited (Ch. 2), pp. 264–65.
9. *Foreign Relations of the United States, 1941*, cited (Ch. 2), Vol. IV, pp. 881–87.
10. Same, pp. 903–4.
11. *Foreign Relations of the United States, 1941*, cited (Ch. 2), Vol. III, p. 12.
12. Same, p. 15.
13. Same, p. 12.
14. Same, pp. 16–17.
15. Same, pp. 15, 41–42.
16. Same, pp. 43–45.
17. *Foreign Relations of the United States, 1942* (Washington, D.C.: U.S. Government Printing Office), Vol. I, p. 530.
18. Same, pp. 535–36.
19. *Department of State Bulletin*, Vol. V, November 8, 1941, pp. 365–66.

4. RETROSPECT

1. *Foreign Relations of the United States: Japan, 1931–1941*, cited (Ch. 2), Vol. II, p. 780.
2. Langer and Gleason, *The Undeclared War, 1940–1941*, cited (Ch. 3), pp. 909–10.

3. Roberta Wohlstetter, *Pearl Harbor: Warning and Decision* (Stanford: Stanford University Press, 1962).

5. ECONOMIC WARFARE AT HOME

1. *Department of State Bulletin*, Vol. VI, April 13, 1942, p. 337.
2. *The New York Times*, April 28, 1942.
3. *Department of State Bulletin*, Vol. VI, May 23, 1942, pp. 475–76.
4. Same, Vol. VII, November 21, 1942, p. 948.
5. Israel, *The War Diary of Breckinridge Long*, cited (Ch. 2), p. 289.
6. Same, pp. 289–90.
7. *Department of State Bulletin*, Vol. VII, November 28, 1942, p. 971.
8. Israel, *The War Diary of Breckinridge Long*, cited (Ch. 2), pp. 291, 299.

9. *Department of State Bulletin*, Vol. VIII, March 27, 1943, p. 256.
10. Same, April 3, 1943, p. 279.
11. Same, June 26, 1943, pp. 575–79.
12. Hull, *Memoirs*, cited (Ch. 2), Vol. II, p. 1230.
13. James F. Byrnes, *All in One Lifetime* (New York: Harper & Brothers, 1958), p. 197.
14. *Department of State Bulletin*, Vol. IX, September 25, 1943, p. 205.
15. Robert E. Sherwood, *Roosevelt and Hopkins: An Intimate History* (New York: Harper & Brothers, 1948), p. 757.

6. ECONOMIC WARFARE ABROAD: DEADLOCK

1. William N. Medlicott, *The Economic Blockade*, 2 vols. (London: Her Majesty's Stationery

Office and Longmans, Green and Company, 1959).

2. See Acheson, *Morning and Noon*, cited (Ch. 1), p. 151.
3. Erik Boheman, *På Vakt* (Stockholm: P. A. Norstedt & Sonners, 1964), pp. 203 ff.
4. *Foreign Relations of the United States, 1943* (Washington, D.C.: U.S. Government Printing Office), Vol. II, p. 866.
5. Same, pp. 888–92.
6. *Foreign Relations of the United States, 1944* (Washington, D.C.: U.S. Government Printing Office), Vol. IV, pp. 708–9.
7. Herbert Feis, *The Spanish Story: Franco and*

the Nations at War (New York: Alfred A. Knopf, 1948), p. 123.
8. David L. Gordon and Royden Dangerfield, *The Hidden Weapon* (New York: Harper & Brothers, 1947), p. 99.
9. *Foreign Relations of the United States, 1944,* cited, Vol. IV, p. 375.
10. *Department of State Bulletin*, Vol. X, April 15, 1944, pp. 335–42.
11. *Foreign Relations of the United States, 1944,* cited, Vol. IV, p. 717.
12. Same, pp. 498, 500.

7. ECONOMIC WARFARE ABROAD: DEADLOCK ENDS

1. *Foreign Relations of the United States, 1944,* cited (Ch. 6), Vol. IV, p. 564.
2. Same, p. 748.
3. Same, pp. 762–63.
4. For quotations from here through page 60, see *Foreign Relations of the United States, 1944,*

cited (Ch. 6), Vol. IV, pp. 383–409.
5. Same, p. 527.
6. Same, p. 538.
7. Same, pp. 706–7.
8. Same, pp. 679–81.

8. PREPARATION FOR AN UNKNOWN WORLD

1. Many of the documents and quotations cited on pages 65 through 68 are included in the section titled "Establishment of UNRRA" to be found in *Foreign Relations of the United States, 1942*, cited (Ch. 3), Vol. I, pp. 89–162.
2. Harley A. Notter, *Postwar Foreign Policy Preparation, 1939–1945* (Washington, D.C.: U.S. Government Printing Office, 1949).
3. See Acheson, *Morning and Noon*, cited (Ch. 1), pp. 183–84.
4. *Foreign Relations of the United States, 1943*, cited (Ch. 6), Vol. I, pp. 890–91.

5. Same, pp. 853, 856.
6. Same, p. 867.
7. Same, p. 903.
8. Arthur H. Vandenberg, Jr., ed., *The Private Papers of Senator Vandenberg* (Boston: Houghton Mifflin Company, 1952), pp. 67–68.
9. 89 *Congressional Record*, 78th Congress, 1st Session, p. 7237.
10. Vandenberg, *The Private Papers of Senator Vandenberg*, cited, pp. 70–71.
11. Same, p. 68.
12. Same, p. 72.

9. THE INTERNATIONAL CONFERENCE STAGE

1. *Department of State Bulletin*, Vol. VIII, April 10, 1943, p. 298.
2. *The New York Times*, April 21, 1943.
3. Same, May 19, 1943.
4. *Foreign Relations of the United States, 1943*, cited (Ch. 6), Vol. 1. p. 944.
5. Same, pp. 980–81; *Department of State Bulletin*, Vol. IX, September 25, 1943, p. 213.
6. *Department of State Bulletin*, Vol. IX, October 9, 1943, p. 245.
7. Same, November 13, 1943, p. 319.
8. *Foreign Relations of the United States, 1943,*

cited (Ch. 6), Vol. I, pp. 929–31.
9. Same, pp. 954–57.
10. For Senator Vandenberg's statement, see Senate Committee on Foreign Relations, 78th Congress, 2nd Session, *Hearings on H.J. Res. 192 to Enable the United States to Participate in the Work of the United Nations Relief and Rehabilitation Administration*, p. 13; for that of Representative Vorys, see House Committee on Foreign Affairs, 78th Congress, 1st and 2nd Sessions, *Hearings on H.J. Res. 192*, p. 25.

10. THE BRETTON WOODS AGREEMENTS

1. *Department of State Bulletin*, Vol. X, May 27, 1944, p. 498.
2. Roy F. Harrod, *The Life of John Maynard Keynes* (New York: Harcourt, Brace & Company, 1951), p. 583.
3. For a "bare bones" account, see *Foreign Re-*

lations of the United States, 1944, cited (Ch. 6), Vol. IV, pp. 1108–53.
4. William Hayter, *The Diplomacy of the Great Powers* (London: Hamish Hamilton, 1960), p. 24.

11. A CHANGE OF SECRETARIES AND OF JOBS

1. Israel, *The War Diary of Breckinridge Long,* cited (Ch. 2), pp. 386, 387–88.
2. Hull, *Memoirs*, cited (Ch. 2), Vol. II, pp. 1714–20.

3. *Department of State Bulletin*, Vol. XI, December 10, 1944, p. 687.
4. Same, p. 689.

12. CHIEF LOBBYIST FOR STATE

1. Vandenberg, *The Private Papers of Senator Vandenberg*, cited (Ch. 8), p. 451.
2. Same.
3. *Myers* v. *United States*, 272 U.S. 52, 293 (1926).
4. Those who wish a more thoroughgoing study will find it in Dean Acheson, *A Citizen Looks at Congress*, republished in *Private Thoughts*

on Public Affairs (New York: Harcourt, Brace & World, 1967, by arrangement with Harper & Row).
5. Woodrow Wilson, *Congressional Government* (Boston: Houghton Mifflin Company—15th edition; first published 1885), p. 271.
6. 91 *Congressional Record*, 79th Congress, 1st Session, p. 1618.

13. SUCCESS, DISENCHANTMENT, AND RESIGNATION

1. George E. Allen, *Presidents Who Have Known Me* (New York: Simon & Schuster, 1950).

2. *Department of State Bulletin*, Vol. XIII, July 29, 1945, pp. 137–38.

14. A NEW JOB AND WIDENING RESPONSIBILITIES

1. *Department of State Bulletin*, Vol. XIII, August 26, 1945, p. 284.
2. Harry S. Truman, *Year of Decisions*, Vol. I, *Memoirs* (New York: Doubleday & Company, 1955), p. 476.
3. Same.
4. Stimson and Bundy, *On Active Service in Peace and War*, cited (Ch. 3), p. 642.
5. Same, pp. 644–45.
6. *Public Papers of the Presidents of the United States: Harry S. Truman, 1945* (Washington,

D.C.: U.S. Government Printing Office, 1961), p. 366.
7. Same, p. 326.
8. *Department of State Bulletin*, Vol. XIII, September 23, 1945, p. 427.
9. Senator Taft's views will be found in 91 *Congressional Record*, 79th Congress, 1st Session, pp. 8908, 8888.
10. *Department of State Bulletin*, Vol. XIII, September 30, 1945, pp. 481–83.

15. TROUBLE IN HIGH PLACES

1. *Department of State Bulletin*, Vol. XIII, November 18, 1945, pp. 787–88.
2. Same, pp. 781–82.
3. Same, p. 812.
4. Same, December 23, 1945, pp. 985–86.
5. Same, December 16, 1945, p. 945.
6. Truman, *Year of Decisions*, cited (Ch. 14), pp. 551–52.
7. Same, pp. 190–93.

16. WASHINGTON AGENT FOR THE MARSHALL MISSION: PHASE ONE

1. *United States Relations with China, with Special Reference to the Period 1944–1949* (Washington, D.C.: U.S. Government Printing Office, 1949), pp. 144, 148.
2. Harry S. Truman, *Years of Trial and Hope*, Vol. II, *Memoirs* (New York: Doubleday & Company, 1956), p. 68.

17. THE ACHESON-LILIENTHAL REPORT

1. For text, see *The New York Times*, February 10, 1946.
2. George F. Kennan, *Memoirs: 1925–1950* (Boston: Little, Brown and Company, 1967), pp. 547–59.
3. Department of State Press Release No. 274, April 23, 1946.
4. James F. Byrnes, *Speaking Frankly* (New York: Harper & Brothers, 1947), p. 269; for Lilienthal's views, see David E. Lilienthal, *The Atomic Energy Years, 1945–1950*, Vol. II, *The Journals of David E. Lilienthal* (New York: Harper & Row, 1964), pp. 30–31.
5. Bernard M. Baruch, *My Own Story* (New York: Henry Holt & Company, 1957).
6. Byrnes, *Speaking Frankly*, cited, p. 271.

18. THE DEPARTMENT MUFFS ITS INTELLIGENCE ROLE

1. Commission on Organization of the Executive Branch of the Government (Second Hoover Commission), *Report to the Congress:* "Intelligence Activities" (Washington, D.C.: U.S. Government Printing Office, 1955), p. 26.
2. *Dictionary of United States Military Terms for Joint Usage* (Washington, D.C.: Departments of Army, Navy, and Air Force, May 1955), p. 53, as quoted in Harry Howe Ransom, *Central Intelligence and National Security* (Cambridge: Harvard University Press, 1958), p. 7.
3. Sherman Kent, *Strategic Intelligence* (Princeton: Princeton University Press, 1949), p. viii.
4. For quotation of Secretary Acheson, see *The New York Times*, November 27, 1945; of General Eisenhower, see Dwight D. Eisenhower, *Crusade in Europe* (New York: Doubleday & Company, 1948), p. 32; of General Marshall, see Senate Committee on Military Affairs, 79th Congress, 1st Session, *Hearings on the Department of Armed Forces*, p. 61.
5. Wohlstetter, *Pearl Harbor*, cited (Ch. 4).
6. Ransom, *Central Intelligence and National Security*, cited, pp. 52–53.
7. Senate Committee on Naval Affairs, 79th Congress, 1st Session, Ferdinand Eberstadt, *Report to the Secretary of the Navy:* "Unification of the War and Navy Departments and Postwar Organization for National Security," p. 163. Admiral Souers had done much of the work on this report.
8. Senate Committee on Appropriations, Subcommittee, 79th Congress, 1st Session, *Hearings on First Supplemental Surplus Appropriations Rescission Bill, 1946*, pp. 227–35.
9. Kent, *Strategic Intelligence*, cited, p. 113.
10. Senate Committee on the Judiciary, Subcommittee to Investigate the Administration of the Internal Security Laws, 83rd Congress, 1st Session, *Hearings on Interlocking Subversion in Government Departments*, p. 862. Other citations to this document are: second paragraph on page 160—pp. 1372–74; Russell Plan, referred to on page 161—pp. 865–69; quotation of J. Anthony Panuch on page 162—pp. 905–6.
11. Sherman Kent, "Prospects for the National Intelligence Service," *Yale Review*, Autumn 1946, p. 125.
12. Congressman May's charge, Secretary Byrnes's reply, and Colonel McCormack's letter can be found in *The New York Times* of March 15, March 16, and March 22, 1946, respectively.
13. *Department of State Bulletin*, Vol. XIV, May 12, 1946, pp. 826–28, 928.

19. THE QUEBEC AGREEMENT

1. Leslie R. Groves, *Now It Can Be Told* (New York: Harper & Brothers, 1962), p. 130.
2. *The New York Times*, April 6, 1954.
3. Richard G. Hewlett and Oscar E. Anderson, Jr., *The New World, 1939–1946*, Vol. I, *A History of the United States Atomic Energy Commission* (University Park: Pennsylvania State University Press, 1962), p. 327.
4. Truman, *Year of Decisions*, cited (Ch. 14), p. 544.
5. Walter Millis, ed., *The Forrestal Diaries* (New York: Viking Press, 1951), p. 338.
6. Vandenberg, *The Private Papers of Senator Vandenberg*, cited (Ch. 8), p. 361.

20. THE PUZZLE OF PALESTINE

1. Truman, *Years of Trial and Hope*, cited (Ch. 16), pp. 132–33.
2. Francis Williams, *A Prime Minister Remembers* (London: Heinemann, 1961), pp. 185–86.
3. Truman, *Years of Trial and Hope*, cited (Ch. 16), p. 135.
4. Same, p. 140.
5. *Public Papers of the Presidents of the United States: Harry S. Truman, 1946* (Washington, D.C.: U.S. Government Printing Office, 1962), pp. 218–19.
6. *House of Commons Debates*, 5th Series, Vol. 422, Column 195–97.
7. *The New York Times*, June 13, 1946.
8. *Public Papers of the Presidents, 1946*, cited, pp. 442–44.

21. TROUBLE BREWS IN WASHINGTON

1. *The New York Times*, October 5, 1945.
2. *Department of State Bulletin*, Vol. XIII, October 7, 1945, p. 552.
3. For Larreta's proposal, see *Department of State Bulletin*, Vol. XIII, November 25, 1945, pp. 864–66; for Secretary Byrnes's reply, see same, December 2, 1945, p. 892.
4. See excerpts from "Consultation Among the American Republics with Respect to the Argentine Situation," *Department of State Bulletin*, Vol. XIV, February 24, 1946, pp. 285–89.
5. The Inter-American Military Cooperation Act; for President Truman's letter of transmittal, May 6, 1946, see *Department of State Bulletin*, Vol. XIV, May 19, 1946, pp. 859–60.
6. Same, June 30, 1946, p. 1129.
7. Same, April 21, 1946, p. 666.
8. Truman, *Year of Decisions*, cited (Ch. 14), p. 552.
9. *Department of State Bulletin*, Vol. XV, September 15, 1946, pp. 496–501.
10. *The Fight for Peace* (New York: Reynall & Hitchcock—A Pamphlet Press Book, October 1946), pp. 17–22.
11. *Public Papers of the Presidents, 1946*, cited (Ch. 20), pp. 426–28.
12. *The New York Times*, September 13, 1946.
13. Byrnes, *Speaking Frankly*, cited (Ch. 17), p. 240.
14. *The New York Times*, September 19, 1967.
15. Byrnes, *Speaking Frankly*, cited (Ch. 17), pp. 240–42.

22. TROUBLE BREAKS IN EUROPE

1. *The New York Times*, January 12, 1946.
2. *Department of State Bulletin*, Vol. XV, September 1, 1946, pp. 421–22.
3. Same, Vol. XIV, June 16, 1946, p. 1047.
4. Same, March 24, 1946, p. 483.
5. Winston Churchill, *Triumph and Tragedy*, Vol. VI, *The War Years* (Boston: Houghton Mifflin Company, 1953), p. 227.

23. WASHINGTON AGENT FOR THE MARSHALL MISSION: PHASE TWO

1. Byrnes, *All in One Lifetime*, cited (Ch. 5), p. 387.
2. *Department of State Bulletin*, Vol. XVI, January 19, 1947, pp. 86–87.

24. GENERAL MARSHALL TAKES OVER

1. *Department of State Bulletin*, Vol. XVI, February 23, 1947, p. 366.
2. Public Law 253, July 27, 1947 (61 Stat. 495).

25. THE TRUMAN DOCTRINE

1. *Public Papers of the Presidents of the United States: Harry S. Truman, 1947* (Washington, D.C.: U.S. Government Printing Office, 1963), pp. 178–79.
2. *New York Herald Tribune*, March 18, 1947.
3. Vandenberg, *The Private Papers of Senator Vandenberg*, cited (Ch. 8), p. 345.
4. These hearings have been described most interestingly in Joseph M. Jones, *The Fifteen Weeks: February 21–June 5, 1947* (New York: Viking Press, 1955), pp. 189–98.
5. Senate Committee on Foreign Relations, 80th Congress, 1st Session, *Hearings on S. 938 to Provide for Assistance to Greece and Turkey*, p. 13.

26. BIRTH OF THE MARSHALL PLAN

1. *Department of State Bulletin*, Vol. XVI, May 11, 1947, pp. 920, 924.
2. Same, May 18, 1947, pp. 991–94.
3. Jones, *The Fifteen Weeks*, cited (Ch. 25), pp. 239–56.
4. Ellen Clayton Garwood, *Will Clayton, A Short Biography* (Austin: University of Texas Press, pp. 119–21.
5. *Department of State Bulletin*, Vol. XVI, June 15, 1947, p. 1160.
6. Same.
7. Harry B. Price, *The Marshall Plan and Its Meaning*, published under the auspices of the Governmental Affairs Institute (Ithaca: Cornell University Press, 1955), p. 28.

27. MUSTERED OUT

1. Henry W. Nevinson, *Changes and Chances* (New York: Harcourt, Brace & Company, 1923), p. vi.
2. Commission on Organization of the Executive Branch of the Government (First Hoover Commission), *Report to Congress: "The National Security Organization"* (Washington, D.C.: U.S. Government Printing Office, 1949), p. 8.
3. For Recommendation 20, Secretary Forrestal's remark, and the Hoover Commission's statement, see *Report to Congress: "Foreign Affairs,"* cited, pp. 61–64.
4. Secretary's Advisory Committee on Personnel, *A Report to the Secretary of State: "An Improved Personnel System for the Conduct of Foreign Affairs"* (Washington, D.C.: U.S. Government Printing Office, 1951), pp. 15–40; see *Department of State Bulletin*, Vol. XXIV, April 30, 1951, pp. 715–16.
5. See same, p. 715, and May 14, 1951, p. 799.
6. Secretary of State's Public Committee on Personnel, *Report: "Toward a Stronger Foreign Service"* (Washington, D.C.: U.S. Government Printing Office, 1954), p. iv.
7. Same, pp. 3–5.
8. McGeorge Bundy, ed., *The Pattern of Responsibility* (Boston: Houghton Mifflin Company, 1952), p. xx.

28. RECALLED TO ACTIVE DUTY

1. Senate Committee on Foreign Relations, 81st Congress, 1st Session, *Hearings on the Nomination of Dean G. Acheson to Be Secretary of State*, January 13, 1949.
2. *The New York Times*, January 15, 1949.
3. Vandenberg, *The Private Papers of Senator Vandenberg*, cited (Ch. 8), p. 469.

29. THE WORLD THAT LAY BEFORE US

1. *Department of State Bulletin*, Vol. XV, September 15, 1946, p. 499.
2. Same, Vol. XVI, May 8, 1947, p. 994.
3. For a first-hand account of the crisis in Germany in 1948, see Lucius D. Clay, *Decision in Germany* (New York: Doubleday & Company, 1950), Chapters 18–20.
4. For sources of quotations in this paragraph, see Clay, *Decision in Germany*, cited, pp. 374, 359; Robert D. Murphy, *Diplomat Among Warriors* (New York: Doubleday & Company, 1964), p. 317; Truman, *Years of Trial and Hope*, cited, (Ch. 16), p. 125.
5. Murphy, *Diplomat Among Warriors*, cited, p. 321.

30. AN EVENTFUL SPRING

1. 94 *Congressional Record*, 80th Congress, 2nd Session, p. 7801.
2. Peter F. Drucker, "A Warning to the Rich White World," *Harper's*, December 1968, p. 71.
3. *Department of State Bulletin*, Vol. XX, February 13, 1949, pp. 192–94.
4. Same, May 15, 1949, p. 631.
5. *London Observer*, October 2, 1960.

31. THE NORTH ATLANTIC TREATY

1. For remarks of Senators Donnell, Vandenberg, Lodge, and Connally, see 95 *Congressional Record*, 81st Congress, 1st Session, pp. 1163–67.
2. *The New York Times*, February 16, 1949.
3. *Department of State Bulletin*, Vol. XX, February 27, 1949, p. 263.
4. *The New York Times*, March 19, 1949; *Department of State Bulletin*, Vol. XX, March 27, 1949, pp. 384–88.
5. Same, p. 388.

32. ALLIED POLICY TOWARD GERMANY

1. Senate Committee on Foreign Relations, 81st Congress, 1st Session, *Hearings on the North Atlantic Treaty*, p. 26; Senator Hickenlooper's question and the reply are found on page 47 of same.
2. *The New York Times*, March 23, 1949.
3. See 95 *Congressional Record*, 81st Congress, 1st Session, for the speeches of the senators: Connally, pp. 8812 ff; Vandenberg, 8891 ff; Donnell, pp. 9023 ff; Taft, pp. 9205 ff; Flanders, pp. 9011 ff; Dulles, pp. 8275 ff; Jenner, pp. 9552 ff.
4. *Department of State Bulletin*, Vol. XX, May 8, 1949, p. 588.

33. THE FOREIGN MINISTERS MEET IN PARIS

1. *Department of State Bulletin*, Vol. XX, May 29, 1949, pp. 675–76.
2. Dean Acheson, *Sketches from Life* (New York: Harper & Brothers, 1961), pp. 15–16.
3. *Department of State Bulletin*, Vol. XXI, July 4, 1949, pp. 860–61.

34. SUMMER BRINGS DIFFICULT DECISIONS

1. *Department of State Bulletin*, Vol. XXI, August 15, 1949, p. 237.
2. *United States Relations with China*, cited (Ch. 16), p. xvi.
3. *95 Congressional Record*, 81st Congress, 1st Session, p. 8294.
4. Tang Tsou, *America's Failure in China, 1941–50* (Chicago: University of Chicago Press, 1963), pp. 363–64.
5. *United States Relations with China*, cited, p. 970.
6. Same, p. 774.
7. Same, pp. 314, 354.
8. Same, pp. 325–38.
9. Same, pp. 358–59.
10. Same, p. 305.
11. Same, p. 409.
12. Millis, *The Forrestal Diaries*, cited (Ch. 19), p. 459.
13. *The New York Times*, September 29, 1949.
14. Vandenberg, *The Private Papers of Senator Vandenberg*, cited (Ch. 8), pp. 503–4.
15. House Committee on Foreign Affairs, 81st Congress, 1st Session, *Hearings on a Bill to Promote the Foreign Policy and Provide for the Defense and General Welfare of the United States by Furnishing Military Assistance to Foreign Nations*, pp. 9–43.
16. For this quotation and the one in the next paragraph, see Vandenberg, *The Private Papers of Senator Vandenberg*, cited (Ch. 8), p. 508.
17. Senate Committees on Foreign Relations and Armed Services, 81st Congress, 1st Session, *Joint Hearings on a Bill to Promote the Foreign Policy and Provide for the Defense and General Welfare of the United States by Furnishing Military Assistance to Foreign Nations*, p. 5.
18. Same, pp. 5–15.
19. *Department of State Bulletin*, Vol. XXI, October 3, 1949, p. 487.

35. ANGLO-AMERICAN ATOMIC COOPERATION REVIEWED

1. *The New York Times*, May 23, 1949.
2. *Department of State Bulletin*, Vol. XXI, August 8, 1949, p. 185.
3. *The New York Times*, September 29, 1949.

36. DEVALUATION OF THE POUND

1. For the tripartite communiqué of September 12, 1949, see *Department of State Bulletin*, Vol. XXI, September 26, 1949, pp. 473–75.

37. MORE MEETINGS AT HOME AND ABROAD

1. *Department of State Bulletin*, Vol. XXI, September 26, 1949, pp. 462–66.
2. Same, October 3, 1949, pp. 489–92.
3. For more about General Chuikov, see Acheson, *Sketches from Life*, cited (Ch. 33), pp. 88–90.

38. A REAPPRAISAL OF POLICIES

1. *Current Developments in United States Foreign Policy* (Washington, D.C.: Brookings Institution), Vol. II, No. 4, November 1949, pp. 4–5.
2. Truman, *Years of Trial and Hope*, cited (Ch. 16), p. 309.
3. Kennan, *Memoirs: 1925–1950*, cited (Ch. 17), pp. 471–76.
4. Warner R. Schilling, Paul Y. Hammond, and Glenn H. Snyder, *Strategy, Politics, and Defense Budgets* (New York: Columbia University Press, 1962), pp. 307–18.
5. Same, pp. 317–18.
6. David E. Lilienthal, *The Atomic Energy Years, 1945–1950*, cited (Ch. 17), p. 624.
7. Senate Committee on Foreign Relations, Subcommittee, 82nd Congress, 1st Session, *Hearings on the Nomination of Philip C. Jessup*, p. 625.
8. *The New York Times*, December 30, 1949.
9. *96 Congressional Record*, 81st Congress, 2nd Session, pp. 150–51.
10. *The New York Times*, December 2, 1949; Tang Tsou makes this point very clearly in *America's Failure in China, 1941–50*, cited (Ch. 34), p. 528.
11. *98 Congressional Record*, 82nd Congress, 2nd Session, p. 3970.
12. *Department of State Bulletin*, Vol. XXII, January 16, 1950, p. 79.
13. Same, p. 81.
14. Same, February 6, 1950, p. 199.

39. THE ATTACK OF THE PRIMITIVES BEGINS

1. Tang Tsou, *America's Failure in China, 1941–50*, cited (Ch. 34), p. 34. The text of the speech may be found in the *Department of State Bulletin*, Vol. XXII, January 23, 1950, pp. 111–18.
2. *96 Congressional Record*, 81st Congress, 2nd Session, p. 298.
3. *The New York Times*, March 2, 1949.
4. *Department of State Bulletin*, Vol. XXII, January 23, 1950, p. 116.
5. Sources for quotations and references in this paragraph are: A. Mitchell Palmer and Kenesaw Mountain Landis, a pamphlet entitled "Tory England and Democratic America," the National Popular Government League, Washington, D.C.; George W. Anderson, an unpublished speech before the Harvard Liberal Club, January 12, 1920; Frank I. Cobb, an address before the Women's City Club of New York, December 11, 1919, printed and circulated by George Foster Peabody; a group of Protestant clergymen, *The Churchman*, January 24, 1920.
6. *The New York Times*, January 26, 1950.
7. Same, January 27, 1950.
8. Senate Committee on Appropriations, Subcommittee, 81st Congress, 2nd Session, *Hearings on Departments of State, Justice, Commerce and the Judiciary Appropriations for 1951*, pp. 636–38.

40. THE ATTACK MOUNTS

1. See, for instance, Acheson, *Private Thoughts on Public Affairs*, cited (Ch. 12), pp. 70–73, 158 ff., and Earl Latham, *The Communist Controversy in Washington* (Cambridge: Harvard University Press, 1966).
2. *The New York Times*, March 9, 1950, summary.
3. William S. White, *The Taft Story* (New York: Harper & Brothers, 1954), p. 85.
4. *The New York Times*, March 22, 1950.
5. Richard P. Stebbins, *The United States in World Affairs, 1950* (New York: Harper & Brothers, 1951), p. 57.
6. White, *The Taft Story*, cited, pp. 84–85.
7. Senate Committee on Foreign Relations, 81st Congress, 2nd Session, *Report Pursuant to S. Res. 321:* "A Resolution to Investigate Whether There Are Employees in the State Department Disloyal to the United States," p. 152.
8. *The New York Times*, August 17, 1950.
9. *96 Congressional Record*, 81st Congress, 2nd Session, pp. 14914–17.
10. Truman, *Years of Trial and Hope*, cited (Ch. 16), pp. 428–29.
11. *Department of State Bulletin*, Vol. XXII, May 8, 1950, pp. 711–16.
12. For texts of these two addresses, see *Department of State Bulletin*, Vol. XXIII, July 3, 1945, pp. 14–17 (Harvard) and October 16, 1950, pp. 613–16 (Freedom House).
13. Andrew A. Lipscomb, ed., *The Writings of Thomas Jefferson* (Washington, D.C.: Thomas Jefferson Memorial Association of the United States, 1903), Vol. XI, pp. 72–73.

41. A NEW DEFINITION OF FOREIGN POLICY

1. See Acheson, *Sketches from Life*, cited (Ch. 33), p. 133.
2. See Schilling, Hammond, and Snyder, *Strategy, Politics, and Defense Budgets*, cited (Ch. 38), for Paul Y. Hammond's discussion, entitled "NSC-68: Prologue for Rearmament," pp. 271–378.
3. See Samuel P. Huntington, *The Common Defense* (New York: Columbia University Press, 1961), pp. 50–51.
4. *Department of State Bulletin*, Vol. XXII, March 13, 1950, p. 403.
5. Same, Vol. XXIII, October 16, 1950, p. 613.
6. Same, Vol. XXII, June 26, 1950, pp. 1037–41.
7. 96 *Congressional Record*, 81st Congress, 2nd Session, pp. 1338–40 (McMahon), and pp. 1473–78 (Tydings).
8. *The New York Times*, March 22, 1950.
9. *Department of State Bulletin*, Vol. XXII, February 20, 1950, pp. 272–74.
10. Same, March 20, 1950, pp. 427–30.
11. Same, Vol. XXIII, July 3, 1950, p. 16.
12. Same, October 16, 1950, pp. 615–16.
13. Same, Vol. XXII, March 27, 1950, pp. 473–78.

42. EUROPE AND THE SCHUMAN PLAN

1. *The New York Times*, May 11, 1950.
2. *Department of State Bulletin*, Vol. XXII, May 29, 1950, p. 828.
3. Raymond Dennett and Robert K. Turner, eds., *Documents on American Foreign Relations* (Princeton: Princeton University Press, 1951), Vol. XII, January 1–December 31, 1950, p. 88.

43. BALANCED COLLECTIVE FORCES FOR EUROPE

1. *Department of State Bulletin*, Vol. XXII, May 22, 1950, pp. 789–91.
2. Same, pp. 787–88.
3. Same, June 5, 1950, p. 886.
4. Same.
5. Same, May 29, 1950, p. 830.

44. WAR IN KOREA: THE OUTBREAK

1. Truman, *Years of Trial and Hope*, cited (Ch. 16), p. 336.
2. *Department of State Bulletin*, Vol. XXIII, July 3, 1950, p. 5.
3. Same.
4. Same, p. 5, and July 10, 1950, pp. 47–48.

45. WAR IN KOREA: THE FIRST CRISIS

1. *Department of State Bulletin*, Vol. XXIII, July 31, 1950, pp. 173–78.
2. Same, p. 170.
3. Same, pp. 170–71.
4. *Public Papers of the Presidents of the United States: Harry S. Truman, 1950* (Washington, D.C.: U.S. Government Printing Office, 1965), p. 532.
5. For sources of quotations of General MacArthur in this paragraph, see Douglas MacArthur, *Reminiscences* (New York: McGraw-Hill, 1964), p. 340, and Courtney Whitney, *MacArthur: His Rendezvous with Destiny* (New York: Alfred A. Knopf, 1956), pp. 372–73; for quotation of Chiang Kai-shek, see *The New York Times*, August 2, 1950.
6. Truman, *Years of Trial and Hope*, cited (Ch. 16), p. 351.
7. Senate Committees on Armed Services and Foreign Relations, 82nd Congress, 1st Session, *Hearings to Conduct an Inquiry into the Military Situation in the Far East and the Facts Surrounding the Relief of General of the Army Douglas MacArthur from His Assignments in That Area* (hereinafter cited as *Hearings on the Military Situation in the Far East*), pp. 3479–80.
8. Truman, *Years of Trial and Hope*, cited (Ch. 16), p. 356.

46. SEPTEMBER DECISIONS

1. *Department of State Bulletin*, Vol. XIII, September 23, 1945, pp. 423–27.
2. Edwin O. Reischauer, *The United States and Japan* (Cambridge: Harvard University Press, 1957), p. 48.
3. House Committee on Foreign Affairs, 81st Congress, 2nd Session, *Hearings on Proposals to Amend the Mutual Defense Assistance Act of 1949*, p. 22.
4. Same, p. 54.
5. House Committee on Appropriations, 81st Congress, 2nd Session, Subcommittee, *Hearings on Supplemental Appropriation Bill for 1951, Department of Defense and Mutual Defense Assistance Program*, p. 20.
6. *The New York Times*, September 6, 1950.
7. *Department of State Bulletin*, Vol. XXIII. September 18, 1950, p. 468.

47. SEPTEMBER SURPRISES

1. *Department of State Bulletin*, Vol. XXIII, October 9, 1950, p. 588.
2. Same, October 2, 1950, p. 530.
3. The title of the official Army history of the landing; see David Rees, *Korea: The Limited War* (New York: St. Martin's Press, 1964), p. 95.
4. For a splendid account of the Inchon planning, landing, and a marshaling of the authorities, see Chapter 5 of Rees, *Korea: The Limited War*, cited; the quotation from General MacArthur appears on p. 83.
5. *Department of State Bulletin*, Vol. XXIII, October 2, 1950, pp. 523–29.
6. Same, July 10, 1950, p. 46.
7. RAD JCS 92801, JCS Personal to MacArthur, 27 Sept. 50, as seen in James F. Schnabel, *Policy and Direction: The First Year*, draft manuscript (Washington, D.C.: Department of Army, Office of Chief of Military History, 1967).
8. *Hearings on the Military Situation in the Far East*, cited (Ch. 45), p. 3483.

48. OCTOBER ODYSSEYS

1. Truman, *Years of Trial and Hope*, cited (Ch. 16), pp. 365–70.
2. *Department of State Bulletin*, Vol. XXIII, November 27, 1950, pp. 839–41.
3. Same, November 20, 1950, pp. 799–801.
4. The message of October 24, RAD CX 67291, CINCUNC to All Commanders 24 Oct. 50, and the JCS inquiry, RAD JCS 94933, JCS Personal to MacArthur, 24 Oct. 50, all seen in Schnabel, *Policy and Direction*, cited (Ch. 47). General MacArthur's reply to JCS inquiry has been put together from texts in *Hearings on the Military Situation in the Far East*, cited (Ch. 45), p. 1241; Truman, *Years of Trial and Hope*, cited (Ch. 16), p. 372; and Schnabel, *Policy and Direction*, cited (Ch. 47).
5. *The New York Times*, November 2, 1950.
6. Truman, *Years of Trial and Hope*, cited (Ch. 16), p. 373, and RAD C68285, CINCFE to DA for CSUSA for JCS, 4 Nov. 50, as seen in Schnabel, *Policy and Direction*, cited (Ch. 47).
7. USAF Historical Study No. 72, *United States Air Force Operations in the Korean Conflict, 1 Nov. 1950–30 June 1953* (Washington, D.C.: Air Force, Historical Division, 1955 and 1956), p. 22.
8. *Department of State Bulletin*, Vol. XXIII, November 27, 1950, p. 858.
9. Truman, *Years of Trial and Hope*, cited (Ch. 16), p. 375.
10. Same, p. 376.
11. *Department of State Bulletin*, Vol. XXIII, November 13, 1950, p. 763.
12. Truman, *Years of Trial and Hope*, cited (Ch.

16), p. 377, and JCS C68445, 7 Nov. 50, as seen in Schnabel, *Policy and Direction*, cited (Ch. 47).
13. CINCFE to DA for JCS C68572, 9 Nov. 50, as seen in Roy E. Appleman, *South to the Naktong, North to the Yalu* (Washington, D.C.: Department of the Army, Office of the Chief of Military History, 1956), p. 765.
14. Summary from Schnabel, *Policy and Direction*,

cited (Ch. 47), RAD C68572, CINCFE to DA for JCS, 9 Nov. 50.
15. MSG C69211, CINCUNC to DA, 18 Nov. 50, Schnabel, *Policy and Direction*, cited in Appleman, *South to the Naktong, North to the Yalu*, cited, p. 774.
16. *Hearings on the Military Situation in the Far East*, cited (Ch. 45), p. 3492.

49. "AN ENTIRELY NEW WAR"

1. *Hearings on the Military Situation in the Far East*, cited (Ch. 45), p. 3495.
2. RAD JCS 97592, JCS to CINCFE, 29 Nov. 50; TEL CINCFE to JCS C50095, 30 Nov. 50; also RAD C50332 CINCUNC to DA for JSC, 3 Dec. 50, as seen in Schnabel, *Policy and Direction*, cited (Ch. 47).
3. *Hearings on the Military Situation in the Far East*, cited (Ch. 45), p. 3492; for message to Arthur Krock, see same, p. 3496; for *U.S. News and World Report* interview, see same,

pp. 3532–33; for messages to United Press, see same, pp. 3534–35.
4. *Hearings on the Military Situation in the Far East*, cited (Ch. 45), p. 3536.
5. Truman, *Years of Trial and Hope*, cited (Ch. 16), p. 384.
6. Matthew B. Ridgway, *The Korean War* (New York: Doubleday & Company, 1967), p. 62.
7. *Department of State Bulletin*, Vol. XXIII, December 18, 1950, pp. 962–67.

50. DECEMBER DESPONDENCY

1. *Public Papers of the Presidents, 1950*, cited (Ch. 45), pp. 724–28.
2. *Department of State Bulletin*, Vol. XXIII, December 11, 1950, p. 925.
3. Quoted in Harold Nicolson, *The Evolution of Diplomatic Method* (London: Constable & Company, 1953), p. 43.
4. Herbert Hoover, *The Ordeal of Woodrow Wilson* (New York: McGraw-Hill, 1958), p. 62.

5. *Department of State Bulletin*, Vol. XXIII, December 18, 1950, p. 961.
6. Truman, *Years of Trial and Hope*, cited (Ch. 16), pp. 185–87.
7. Herbert Hoover, *Addresses Upon the American Road* (Stanford: Stanford University Press, 1955), pp. 3–10.
8. *Department of State Bulletin*, Vol. XXIV, January 1, 1951, pp. 3–6.

51. CALMING WORRIES AT HOME AND TO THE SOUTH

1. *97 Congressional Record*, 82nd Congress, 1st Session, pp. 54–61.
2. Same, p. 60.
3. *The New York Times*, January 16, 1951.
4. *Department of State Bulletin*, Vol. XXIV, February 12, 1951, pp. 245–51.
5. *97 Congressional Record*, 82nd Congress, 1st Session, p. 94.
6. *Department of State Bulletin*, Vol. XXIV, Feb-

ruary 26, 1951, pp. 328–30.
7. *The New York Times*, February 16, 1951.
8. *Department of State Bulletin*, Vol. XXIV, February 26, 1951, pp. 323–28 (Acheson), pp. 330–32 (Bradley).
9. Same, April 16, 1951, p. 606.
10. For Final Act, see *Department of State Bulletin*, Vol. XXIV, April 16, 1951, pp. 606–13.

52. DOUBLE TROUBLE IN IRAN

1. William Wordsworth, "On the Extinction of the Venetian Republic."
2. Michael Howard and Robert Hunter, *Israel and the Arab World: The Crisis of 1967* (London: Institute of Strategic Studies, 1967), p. 1.

3. Richard P. Stebbins, *The United States in World Affairs, 1951* (New York: Harper & Brothers, 1952), p. 273.
4. *Department of State Bulletin*, Vol. XXV, November 26, 1951, p. 864.

53. ATTEMPTS TO STABILIZE THE KOREAN WAR

1. Ridgway, *The Korean War*, cited (Ch. 49), pp. 83, 106.
2. *The New York Times*, December 23, 1950.
3. RAD JCS 99935 JCS Personal to MacArthur, 30 Dec. 50, seen in Schnabel, *Policy and Direction*, cited (Ch. 47).
4. MacArthur, *Reminiscences*, cited (Ch. 45), p. 378.
5. *Hearings on the Military Situation in the Far East*, cited (Ch. 45), pp. 2180–81; also, MacArthur, *Reminiscences*, cited (Ch. 45), p. 378–80.
6. Truman, *Years of Trial and Hope*, cited (Ch. 16), pp. 433–34, and JCS 80680 JCS Personal to MacArthur, 9 Jan. 51, as seen in Schnabel, *Policy and Direction*, cited (Ch. 47).
7. MacArthur, *Reminiscences*, cited (Ch. 45), p. 380.
8. *Hearings on the Military Situation in the Far East*, cited (Ch. 45), p. 906.
9. JCS 80902, 12 Jan. 51, in same, p. 907.
10. For text with deletions, see same, pp. 333–34.

11. *Washington Post*, January 21, 1951.
12. *Hearings on the Military Situation in the Far East*, cited (Ch. 45), p. 13; Whitney, *MacArthur: His Rendezvous with History*, cited (Ch. 45), p. 462.
13. Truman, *Years of Trial and Hope*, cited (Ch. 16), pp. 435–36.
14. *Hearings on the Military Situation in the Far East*, cited (Ch. 45), p. 3539.
15. Whitney, *MacArthur: His Rendezvous with History*, cited (Ch. 45), p. 462.
16. *Hearings on the Military Situation in the Far East*, cited (Ch. 45), pp. 3540–41.
17. *New York Herald Tribune*, March 16, 1951.
18. *Hearings on the Military Situation in the Far East*, cited (Ch. 45), p. 411.
19. Truman, *Years of Trial and Hope*, cited (Ch. 16), p. 443.
20. Same, pp. 441–45.
21. *Hearings on the Military Situation in the Far East*, cited (Ch. 45), p. 3544.

54. THE RELIEF OF GENERAL MAC ARTHUR

1. *Hearings on the Military Situation in the Far East*, cited (Ch. 45), p. 2290.
2. Same, pp. 1837–57.
3. Same, p. 1858.
4. Same, p. 3125.

5. Same, p. 3544.
6. Whitney, *MacArthur: His Rendezvous with History*, cited (Ch. 45), pp. 370–71.
7. Same, p. 468.

55. THE MOVE FOR AN ARMISTICE IN KOREA

1. See, for example, Ridgway, *The Korean War*, cited (Ch. 49), p. 181.
2. *Hearings on the Military Situation in the Far East*, cited (Ch. 45), pp. 1729–30, 1782.

3. *Department of State Bulletin*, Vol. XXV, July 9, 1951, p. 45, footnote 1.
4. Francis Bret Harte, "Plain Language from Truthful James."

5. Walter G. Hermes, *Truce Tent and Fighting Front,* second volume published in the *United States Army in the Korean War* (Washington, D.C.: Office of the Chief of Military History,

U.S. Army, 1966), p. 24.
6. Same, p. 23.
7. Ridgway, *The Korean War,* cited (Ch. 49), pp. 182–83.

56. PEACE WITH JAPAN

1. *Department of State Bulletin,* Vol. XXIV, May 28, 1951, pp. 852–56.
2. *House of Commons Debates,* 5th Series, Vol. 494, Column 896.
3. *Conference for the Conclusion and Signature*

of the Treaty of Peace with Japan, Record of Proceedings (Washington, D.C.: U.S. Government Printing Office, 1951), p. 25.
4. Same, pp. 308–9.

57. NATO IN STAGNATION

1. *Department of State Bulletin,* Vol. XXIV, March 19, 1951, pp. 443–49.
2. Same, Vol. XXV, September 24, 1951, pp. 485–86.

58. EGYPT AND THE MIDDLE EAST COMMAND

1. *Records of Conversations, Notes and Papers Exchanged Between the Royal Egyptian Government and the United Kingdom Government, March 1950–November 1951* (Cairo: Egyptian Ministry of Foreign Affairs, 1951), p. 155.
2. *Department of State Bulletin,* Vol. XXV, Octo-

ber 22, 1951, pp. 647–48.
3. Same, November 19, 1951, pp. 817–18.
4. Same, October 31, 1951, pp. 1054–55.
5. See Dean Acheson, *Power and Diplomacy* (Cambridge: Harvard University Press, 1958), pp. 109–16.

59. OTTAWA AND EXCURSIONS WITHOUT ALARUMS

1. For text of the joint communiqué, see *Department of State Bulletin,* Vol. XXV, October 8, 1951, pp. 563–64.
2. Senate Committee on Foreign Relations, Sub-

committee, 82nd Congress, 1st Session, *Hearings on the Nomination of Philip C. Jessup.*
3. *Department of State Bulletin,* Vol. XXV, November 5, 1951, p. 737.

60. THE "DISARMAMENT ASSEMBLY"

1. For text of radio address by President Truman on November 7, 1951, see *Department of State Bulletin,* Vol. XXV, November 19, 1951, pp. 799–803.
2. Same, pp. 803–8.
3. *General Assembly Official Record,* 336th Plenary Meeting, November 8, 1951, pp. 19–28.
4. *The New York Times,* November 9, 1951.

5. *Department of State Bulletin,* Vol. XXV, December 3, 1951, pp. 879–89.
6. For text of Joint United States, United Kingdom, French, and West German Statement on Germany, issued at Paris on November 22, 1951, see *Department of State Bulletin,* Vol. XXV, December 3, 1951, p. 891.

61. NATO MEETS IN ROME

1. *Department of State Bulletin,* Vol. XXV, December 31, 1951, pp. 1047–50.
2. Same, Vol. XXVI, January 7, 1952, pp. 3–7.

62. THE CHURCHILL VISIT

1. Lord Moran, *Churchill—Taken from the Diaries of Lord Moran* (Boston: Houghton Mifflin Company, 1966), pp. ix, xi; for Lord Normanbrook's appraisal, see *Action This Day: Working with Churchill* (London: Macmillan, 1968), p. 30.
2. John E. Neale, *England's Elizabeth* (Washington, D.C.: The Folger Shakespeare Library, 1958), p. 8.
3. Winston Churchill, *Their Finest Hour,* Vol. II, *The War Years* (Boston: Houghton Mifflin Company, 1949), p. 512.
4. From the speech to troops at Tilbury on the

approach of the Armada, 1588.
5. The preceding five paragraphs were taken from Dean Acheson, "A Word About Mr. Churchill" in *Churchill by His Contemporaries* (London: Hedder & Stoughton, 1965), pp. 36–40.
6. *Department of State Bulletin,* Vol. XXVI, January 28, 1952, p. 116.
7. Herbert Morrison's statement in *House of Commons Debates,* 5th Series, Vol. 496, Column 949.
8. 98 *Congressional Record,* 82nd Congress, 2nd Session, p. 2331.

65. LISBON

1. *Department of State Bulletin,* Vol. XXVI, March 10, 1952, pp. 370–71.
2. For text of communiqué, see same, pp. 367–68.

3. Same, March 17, 1952, p. 423.
4. *The New York Times,* February 29, 1952.

66. ONCE MORE UNTO THE BREACH

1. *Department of State Bulletin,* Vol. XXVI, April 7, 1952, pp. 530–32.
2. Same, April 28, 1952, p. 647. The reference slightly misquoted from memory is to William McFee, *Casuals of the Sea* (New York: Doubleday, Page & Company, 1916), p. 22.
3. *The New York Times,* May 20, 1952, in connection with an article by Felix Wittmer, "Freedom's Case Against Dean Acheson," *American*

Mercury, April 1952.
4. *Department of State Bulletin,* Vol. XVI, March 24, 1952, pp. 448–50.
5. Same, April 14, 1952, p. 580.
6. Office of the High Commissioner for Germany, *Report on Germany (Final),* September 21, 1949–July 31, 1952 (Cologne: Greven & Bechtold, 1952), p. 14.

67. BONN AND PARIS

1. For summary, see *Department of State Bulletin,* Vol. XXVI, June 9, 1952, pp. 888–94.
2. Same, pp. 887–88.
3. Same, p. 895.

68. KOREA: FRUSTRATION, RIOT, AND REVOLT

1. Ridgway, *The Korean War,* cited (Ch. 49), pp. 203–4.
2. Casualty figures supplied by Walter G. Hermes, Office of Military History, U.S. Army; see

Hermes, *Truce Tent and Fighting Front,* cited (Ch. 55), p. 477.
3. *Department of State Bulletin,* Vol. XXVII, July 14, 1952, p. 60.

70. INDOCHINA

1. *Department of State Bulletin,* Vol. XXII, February 20, 1950, pp. 291–92.

2. Same, Vol. XXIII, July 3, 1950, p. 5.
3. Same, Vol. XXVI, June 30, 1952, p. 1010.

71. A SECOND TRY IN KOREA

1. Anthony Eden, *Full Circle* (Boston: Houghton Mifflin Company, 1960), p. 222.
2. *Department of State Bulletin,* Vol. XXVII,
September 8, 1952, p. 360.
3. Same, December 15, 1952, p. 946.
4. Eden, *Full Circle,* cited, pp. 232, 236.

72. ELECTION SUMMER

1. *Department of State Bulletin,* Vol. XXVII, September 22, 1952, pp. 423–27.
2. *The New York Times,* September 23, 1952, reporting a speech in Cincinnati, the home of Senator Robert A. Taft.
3. Same.
4. Department of State Press Release No. 761, September 26, 1952.
5. *Department of State Bulletin,* Vol. XXVII, October 20, 1952, pp. 595–99.
6. Same, October 13, 1952, pp. 555–57.

73. AN OPEN COVENANT OPENLY CONNIVED AGAINST

1. *Department of State Bulletin,* Vol. XXVII, October 20, 1952, p. 603.
2. For texts of the proposed Resolution and ex-
cerpts from the speech, see same, November 3, 1952, pp. 679–92, and November 10, 1952, pp. 744–51.

74. CHANGING THE GUARD

1. Truman, *Years of Trial and Hope,* cited (Ch. 16), p. 521.
2. Same, pp. 517–20.
3. *Department of State Bulletin,* Vol. XXVIII, February 9, 1953, p. 241.
4. Same, March 23, 1953, pp. 454–55.
5. Same, January 12, 1953, pp. 57–58.
6. House Special Committee to Investigate the Department of Justice, 82nd Congress, 2nd Ses-
sion, *Hearings on H. Res. 95,* pp. 1730–54; Hickerson's statement can be found in Senate Committee on the Judiciary, Subcommittee to Investigate the Administration of the Internal Security Act, 82nd Congress, 2nd Session, *Hearings,* p. 291.
7. *Department of State Bulletin,* Vol. XXVIII, January 12, 1953, pp. 62–63.

75. LAST FAREWELLS

1. *Department of State Bulletin,* Vol. XXVIII, January 26, 1953, pp. 129–30.
2. Same, p. 161.
3. Same, pp. 161–62.
4. Same, p. 162.

76. SUMMING UP

1. Oliver Wendell Holmes, Jr., *Collected Legal Papers* (New York: Harcourt, Brace & Howe, 1920), pp. 245–46.
2. William Shakespeare, *King Henry V,* Act IV.
3. Churchill, *Their Finest Hour,* cited (Ch. 62), pp. 17–18.
4. Ian Jacob, "Churchill As a War Leader" in *Churchill by His Contemporaries,* cited (Ch. 62), p. 82.

INDEX